1994 Novel & Short Story
Writer's Market

1994

Novel & Short Story Writer's Market

Editor: Robin Gee

**WRITER'S
DIGEST
BOOKS**

Cincinnati, Ohio

Distributed in Canada by McGraw-Hill Ryerson, 300 Water St., Whitby, Ontario L1N 9B6. Distributed in Australia by Kirby Books, Private Bag No. 19, P.O. Alexandria NSW 2015.

Managing Editor, Market Books Department: Constance J. Achabal; Supervisory Editor: Mark Garvey; Production Editor: Jamie Harding

1994 Novel & Short Story Writer's Market.
International Standard Serial Number
ISSN 0897-9812
International Standard Book Number
0-89879-613-X

Cover illustration © Josie Yee

Contents

The Markets

Resources

From the Editor

Each year I write this message as one of my last duties before turning *Novel & Short Story Writer's Market* over to the printers and the powers that be. It comes last because by that time the book has taken shape and it's easier for me to step back and look at the edition as a whole. I find it amazing that, like a short story collection, the whole is always much more than the sum of its parts. Each edition takes on its own character or theme and this year's edition is no exception.

Welcome to what I call our "editors-speak edition." Through my contacts with a number of you at conferences and through the mail in the last year, you told me you wanted to hear more from editors — how to approach them, what they really want and what they think about the industry. This year I asked a number of editors to answer these questions and so you will find this edition chock full of answers from all types of editors — from literary journals and large publishers, major magazines and the small press.

From the editors

In our Writing Techniques section we include an article by Ronald Spatz, the editor of *Alaska Quarterly Review*. In addition to overseeing a staff of student editors who work on the journal at the University of Alaska, he teaches a class on editing. As part of the class Spatz's students study literary magazines to better understand the editorial slant of individual periodicals. He shares what his class has learned in On Target: Zeroing in on the Right Market for Your Fiction.

In our Small Press Roundtable, we invited four editors from successful small presses to answer questions about the small press field and what small press publication can mean to writers. Included in our discussion are editors from Coffee House Press, Four Walls Eight Windows, Milkweed Editions and Zoland Books.

You will notice we've changed the format of our interviews scattered throughout the markets sections of the book. Although we've included writer interviews in the past, this year's selection of "Insider Viewpoints" is devoted to a diverse group of editors including Kim Mohan from *Amazing Stories*, Barbara Dicks from Fawcett Books and Hannah Wilson from the *Northwest Review*. C.W. Truesdale of New Rivers Press tells why editing is a labor of love and George Witte from *Turnstile* explains how editing his magazine is very much a group effort.

We've expanded our own editorial comments in this edition and continue to include the Commercial Fiction Report, where we compile what we've learned about the various categories of fiction publishing from editors, publishers and trade experts. Romance author Nora Roberts and novelist Ann Hood both discuss with us the importance of their own editors and why building a good relationship with your editor can make all the difference in your career.

Giving you more

We've refined our Business of Fiction Writing article this year to include more information for writers who have been published, such as material on giving readings and self promotion tactics.

As the number of our readers in Canada continues to grow, we decided it was a good time to add more information of special interest to them. Canadian readers will find a special sidebar for them in the Business of Fiction Writing and will notice we now use a maple leaf symbol to clearly identify Canadian markets.

An invitation

Approaching editors is sometimes the hardest part for new writers. In fact, one of the most frequently asked questions at writers' conferences is "What goes into a good cover letter?" Here's where you come in. Do you have a successful cover letter, one that helped lead to the acceptance of your short story? Was your story selected by one of the publications listed in *Novel & Short Story Writer's Market*? If the answers are "yes," we'd like to invite you to enter our first-ever Short Story Cover Letter Contest.

Here are the rules: We're looking for a letter that helped lead to the *acceptance* of a short story between June 1993 and June 1994. Keep in mind the letter must include the elements of a good cover letter as outlined in our Business of Fiction Writing article. The deadline is June 15, 1994. Send the letter with your address and phone number and proof of acceptance (a copy of the letter of acceptance will do) to me at 1507 Dana Ave., Cincinnati OH 45207. Include SASE, if you'd like your letter returned.

The winning letter will be printed in the 1995 edition of *Novel & Short Story Writer's Market* along with commentary from the writer and the editor who accepted the story. In addition, the writer will receive a small cash payment for publication of the letter, a copy of the book and the opportunity to select two additional titles from our Writer's Digest Books catalog.

I'll close with another invitation: Feel free to write us at anytime with questions and comments about our book and how we can help you. While we are always looking for ways to improve the information contained within these pages, our goal remains the same: to help you find the best market for your fiction and to aid in getting your work into that editor's hands.

Robin L. Gee

Editor

How to Get the Most Out of This Book

Like most of the people who use *Novel & Short Story Writer's Market*, chances are you've already put a great deal of time and effort into your writing. Many of you write regularly and are well-read, especially in the area in which you write. Some of you are studying writing formally, while some are receiving feedback on your work by sharing it with a writer's group. You've been spending lots of time on writing and rewriting your work, honing it until it sings and now you feel it's time to share your work with others.

If we could open this book with just one piece of advice it would be this: Take as much care searching for potential markets for your work as you have in crafting it. With this in mind, this book is designed as a tool to help you in your search and we hope you will use it as a starting place, a component, if you will, of your overall marketing plan. The temptation with using any book like this is to go straight to the listings and start sending out your work. Perhaps this is the fastest, but it's not the most efficient route to publication.

While we do offer listings of about 1,900 markets and other opportunities for fiction writers, the listings contain only a portion of the information available to you in *Novel & Short Story Writer's Market*. In addition to the listings, we offer interviews with published authors and editors and a wide range of articles and introductory material on the craft of writing and all aspects of marketing and publishing your work. Reading the material covered here, as well as other books on writing and publishing, will help you make informed decisions that will further your writing career.

What you'll find here

Novel & Short Story Writer's Market is divided into three parts, each presenting a different type of information. The first part is Writing Techniques. Here we provide in-depth interviews with established authors, articles on the craft of writing and informational pieces on the business of publishing. This is where you will find the Business of Fiction Writing and the Commercial Fiction Trend Report, in addition to other articles on writing and publishing fiction.

Following Writing Techniques is The Markets, the heart of our book. This part is divided into five sections. The largest is the Literary and Small Circulation Magazine section, which includes literary journals of all sizes and smaller magazines whose circulations are under 10,000. Next comes the Commercial Periodicals section, featuring magazines with commercial appeal and circulations of more than 10,000. After this section is the Small Press section, which includes small presses and some larger independents. The Commercial Publishers section comes next and features listings of major publishers of commercial hardcover, trade paperback and mass market books. Finally, the Contests and Awards section offers listings for contests, awards and grants available to fiction writers.

Within the two magazine and two book publisher sections, you will find a main section of markets from North America [Canadian markets are noted with a maple leaf symbol (✸)] followed by international markets. Many of these markets are open to English-writing authors from all over the world. The contest section also includes international markets, but these are not listed separately.

Throughout The Markets, you'll find interviews called Insider Viewpoints. These are short interviews with editors, publishers and writers designed to give you an inside look at specific writing areas and a behind-the-scenes look at particular publications or publishers. In these pieces you'll find out more about what certain editors are looking for, including their immediate needs, how to approach them and sell to them.

The last part of the book is Resources. We like to refer to this as our "community" part, because it offers listings of places and outlets where writers can make contact with other writers. This part includes the Conference and Workshops, Retreats and Colonies, Organizations and Resources, and Publications of Interest to Fiction Writers sections.

Developing your marketing plan

After reading the articles and interviews that interest you, the next step in developing your marketing plan is to use the book to come up with a preliminary list of potential markets. If you are not sure in what categories your work fits or if you just want to explore the possibilities, start by reading the introductions and browsing through the sections to find markets that interest you. The browsing method also helps you to become familiar with the many different types of markets and may lead you to a market you haven't thought of before.

To help you with your search, we include a Category Index at the back of the book, just before the Markets Index. The Category Index is divided into sections corresponding to the two magazine and two book publisher sections in The Markets. Under each of the sections in the index, you'll find a list of fiction subjects such as romance, mystery, religious, regional, etc. The subject headings are then followed by the names and page numbers of listings expressing an interest in that subject.

You may notice that not all the listings in the magazine and book publisher sections appear in the Category Index. Some magazines and publishers indicated they were open to all types of fiction. Others said they were only interested in very specific topics such as fiction about hiking or caving or about the Civil War. If your writing subjects are varied, we recommend a combination of the browsing method and the Category Index method.

To further help you narrow your list, we include ranking codes to help you determine the level of openness of each listing. These codes are Roman numerals (I through IV) and they appear just after the listing's name. In the magazine and book publisher sections, by openness we mean the level of work considered by the listing. While some are open to work from writers on all levels, some are only open to work by established writers. Others limit their field to work by writers from a certain region or who write on a specific subject. Ranking codes are also used in the contest section, but these refer to the work that can be submitted—published or unpublished or work from certain groups of writers or certain regions. The ranking codes and explanations for each are outlined after each section introduction.

We use a few symbols at the start of some listings. Listings new to our book this year are indicated by a double dagger symbol (‡). Many are newly established markets, and often these are most open to the work of new writers. Some are not new, but have recently decided to list with us because they have increased their fiction needs. In the book publisher sections, we also use other symbols to indicate different types of publishers. Check the introductions to these sections for more information.

Reading the listings

Once you've come up with a list of potential markets, read each listing carefully. You will find you can further streamline your list based on the market's editorial statement, advice, specific needs, terms, payment and reputation.

While different sections contain slightly different listings, there are some things all listings have in common.

After the name and contact information for each listing, you'll find a brief description of the market's publishing philosophy and intended audience. Following this is often a physical description of the magazine or books published. Physical descriptions can tell you a lot about the market's budget and give you hints about its quality and prestige. Check also the establishment date, circulation or number of books published.

In some listings, following the profile, we've added our own comment, set off by a bullet. This added feature notes information about the market's honors or awards, its treatment of writers and related listings in the book. This is our place to pass on additional information we've learned about the listing.

Next comes the Needs section of the listing. In addition to a list or description of the type of work the market is seeking, you'll also find how much work the market receives from writers in a given time and how much it publishes. This will help you determine your competition. Also included here are specifics on length and other requirements.

After the Needs section come the Terms and Payment sections. When possible, we've provided a range of payment, but note that many publications in the Literary and Small Circulation section pay only in copies or subscriptions. We also indicate when you will be paid and for what rights. For more on rights and what to look for concerning terms, see the Business of Fiction Writing.

Remember your marketing research should begin with a careful study of the listings, but it should not end there. Whenever possible obtain a sample copy or catalog. As Ronald Spatz says in his Writing Techniques article, "On Target," there is no substitution for reading copies of magazines that interest you and we would add, you should also familiarize yourself with the books of publishers to whom you'd like to submit.

To find out more about potential markets, send a self-addressed, stamped envelope for guidelines. Most magazines have sample copies available for a modest price. For book publishers, check *Books in Print* at the library to find the publishers of books you admire or feel are similar to the one you are writing. The library also has publishing industry magazines such as *Publishers Weekly* as well as magazines for writers. Some of these magazines are listed in the Publications of Interest to Fiction Writers section located later in this book. These can help you keep informed of new publishers and changes in the field.

The follow through

After careful study and narrowing your list of potential markets to those who represent the most suitable places for your work, the next step, of course, is to mail out your work. If you have any questions on how to present your work, see the Business of Fiction Writing. When in doubt, remember to make it as easy as possible for editors to read and respond to your work. They're a busy lot and will not waste time with submissions that are messy and difficult to read. It may be good writing, but the editor may never read it to find that out. If you show you care about your work, the editor will too.

Also keep careful records. We've asked our listings to indicate how long it will take them to report on a submission, but at times throughout the year the market may get behind. Keeping track of when you sent your manuscript will help you decide when it is time to check on the status of your submission.

About our policies

We occasionally receive letters asking why a certain magazine, publisher or contest is not in the book. Sometimes when we contact a listing, the editor does not want to be listed because they: do not use very much fiction; are overwhelmed with submissions; are having financial difficulty or have been recently sold; use only solicited material; accept work from a select group of writers only; do not have the staff or time for the many unsolicited submissions a listing may bring.

Some of the listings do not appear because we have chosen not to list them. We investigate complaints of unprofessional conduct in editors' dealings with writers and misrepresentation of information provided to us by editors and publishers. If we find these reports to be true, after a thorough investigation, we will delete the listing from future editions. See Important Listing Information for more about our listing policies.

If a listing appeared in our book the previous year but is no longer listed, we list it at the end of each section with an explanation, if provided. Sometimes the listing does not appear because the editor did not respond in time for our press deadline or it may not appear for any of the reasons mentioned above.

If you feel you have not been treated fairly by a market listed in our book, we advise you to take the following steps:

● First, try to contact the listing. Sometimes a phone call or letter can quickly clear up the matter.

● Be sure to document all your correspondence with the listing. When you write to us with a complaint, we will ask for the name of your manuscript, the date of your submission and the dates and nature of your subsequent correspondence.

● We will write to the publisher or editor and ask him to resolve the problem. We will enter your letter into our files.

● The number, frequency and severity of unresolved complaints will be considered in our decision whether to delete a listing from the book.

Listings appearing in *Novel & Short Story Writer's Market* are compiled from detailed questionnaires, phone interviews and information provided by editors, publishers and awards directors. The publishing industry is volatile and changes of address, editor, policies and needs happen frequently. To keep up with the changes between editions of the book, we suggest you check the monthly Markets column in *Writer's Digest* magazine.

Club newsletters and small magazines devoted to helping writers also list market information. For those writers with access to online services, several offer writers' bulletin boards, message centers and chat lines with up-to-the-minute changes and happenings in the writing community.

We rely on our readers as well, for new markets and information about market conditions. Write us if you have any new information or if you have suggestions on how to improve our listings to better suit your writing needs.

Writing Techniques

Nora Roberts Discusses Crossing Over (and Back Again)

by Anne M. Bowling

"It's so hard. It's so frustrating. It's so demoralizing when the words just won't come. So why in the hell did we get into this business in the first place? What does a writer do? I'll tell you what this writer does. She sits in this little disaster of an office . . . and she prays a lot. Please, God, just let me fill the page. Just let me get this one chapter down, and I swear I'll see to it that the kids have clean underwear. At the end of the day . . . I turn off the machine and wonder why I've just spent the last eight hours writing what must be garbage." — Nora Roberts, from her keynote address at the Romance Writers of America 1986 national conference in Minneapolis, Minnesota.

If any writer is blessed with the peace of mind that comes with knowing her writing is publishable — although it's a rare condition in the field — it should be Nora Roberts.

Roberts began committing her stories to paper "just to keep myself sane," she says, when a blizzard kept her housebound with two children in her rural Keedysville, Maryland, home during the winter of 1979. Although her first book will never see print ("there's nothing that can be done to save that," she says), she's gotten more than a few novels published since that serendipitous snowstorm. In fact, Roberts is a novelist for whom the adjective prolific won't do the job. She has had no fewer than 94 — yes, 94 — books published, primarily category romance novels with a handful of later mainstream fiction titles.

Lest readers cock a cynical eyebrow and ask 'yes, but how good are they?', stand notified: Roberts is the first author from a field of hundreds inducted into the Romance Writers of America Hall of Fame (1986). In what has become an enormously competitive industry for genre writers, Roberts has more than 27 million books in print. She has won widespread acclaim in the romance genre — her list of awards is longer than many writers' list of published titles. Roberts's writing has been recognized with awards from both Waldenbooks and B.Dalton Books, and her mainstream novels *Genuine Lies* and *Carnal Innocence* made *The New York Times* bestseller list.

The long, hard road to success

Roberts says despite the countless hours she has spent tapping away at her PC, writing hasn't gotten any easier for her since she first sat down to write during that blizzard, or since she recounted praying for divine intervention as the keynote speaker at the Romance Writers of America 1986 conference.

"Every book I write is harder than the last book. You would think that it would get easier in time, but it doesn't," Roberts says, "because the challenges are bigger, and your own ego pushes you to do better . . . you want your writing to be cleaner, and I don't want to repeat myself — and that gets hard after so many books — but you don't want the same

---

Anne Bowling *is a freelance writer, newspaper stringer and editor.*

© Russell Kirk

plot line, and the same characters, you want to keep it fresh. That's one of the hardest things, but it's just absolutely necessary."

Most aspiring writers would be happy to have such problems, and there was a time Roberts was included in that category. Her first novel, which she says included "every stock element that I had ever read in any romance novel," was turned down. So was her second, and her third, and her fourth, and so on. Her seventh novel, *Irish Thoroughbred*, was the one that broke through, and led to publication of five of the first six that were previously rejected. "My agent called it my magic drawer," Roberts recalls. "I was pulling them out of my drawer, sprucing them up and shipping them off like little cannonballs."

Serendipity played a second role in Roberts's career with the acceptance of *Irish Thoroughbred*. Roberts had been submitting her manuscripts to Harlequin, which at the time published primarily British authors, with the exception of American writer Janet Dailey. "That was what one of my rejection letters said: The book showed promise, but they already had their American author," she says. But in 1981, Simon & Schuster opened Silhouette, which was actively seeking authors for category romance novels with an American flavor. "I really lucked out as far as the timing went," Roberts says. "It was perfect."

Irish Thoroughbred, the story of an Irish immigrant who came to live with her horse-trainer uncle on a thoroughbred farm in Maryland and became involved in a romance with the farm's owner, was the first of Roberts's novels to attract the following of readers which now numbers in the millions.

Discipline, pure and simple

Although before 1979 Roberts said she had "always assumed everybody made up stories . . . I never really thought about writing them down," the publication of *Irish Thoroughbred* catapulted her into a fulltime writing career. A homemaker and mother of two, Roberts wrote whenever the children were at school or sleeping, she says, sometimes logging 14 hours per day at the PC.

Since publication of her first novel, Roberts has cut back to an average eight-hour work day, but that first novel—which was "really, really bad"—had lessons in perseverance to teach, she says. "It taught me that I could do it—beginning, middle and end, and plot, character and setting," she says. "Even though it wasn't a good plot, and they weren't particularly good characters, it was all there."

She credits discipline, pure and simple, for her ability to produce at the volume and quality level she has achieved and maintained. "I work a lot," Roberts says. "I don't think you can write successfully without drive, discipline and desire. Talent isn't enough on its own. You have to have those other things . . . paranoia is a big help; guilt is a big help; and the Catholic education which teaches you guilt and discipline walk hand in hand is an enormous help to me. They might drive other people crazy . . . but they just work for me."

That discipline led Roberts to publish roughly 10 novels per year from 1983 to 1986. Basic mathematics would lead anyone to the conclusion that Roberts—who does not work on novels simultaneously—averaged about a novel per month during that peak period. But she maintains, "I couldn't tell you if you put me on the rack how long it takes me to write any book. I never keep track—that's a paranoia game I play with myself. Because if the next book takes less time, well, I must have rushed; it must not be good. And if it takes more time, well, I must be slipping. I must be losing my touch. You have enough to sweat over without timing it like a cake."

Caring about your characters

And there are plenty of elements of a good novel to sweat over, as Roberts can attest. First there's the big picture: The plot must be compelling; the characters must be worthy of empathy; and the story must ring true. And then there's the detail work, no less important to the success of the entire structure. But good characters, above all, are required to grab and hold readers, Roberts says.

"I would pin the success of my books on characters," she says. "Certainly that's the feedback [from readers] that I get. . . . If you don't care about the people who things are happening to in the book, why read on?

"I think the writer has to care," Roberts adds. "If you don't love these people, or if they're villains and you don't hate them, if you don't feel strongly about them, the reader is never going to feel strongly about them. It has to come from you first."

So how does a writer make sympathetic characters out of a pack of thieves? Just such a cast was featured in Roberts' mainstream *Honest Illusions* published in 1992 by G.B. Putnam's Sons, and since released in paperback by Jove. Called "spell-binding" by *Publishers Weekly* and "good escape reading" by *Kirkus Reviews*, the novel features Roxanne Nouvelle, daughter of master magician and traveling-carnival owner Maxmillian Nouvelle, and her brother-by-circumstance Luke Callahan. Jewel thieves by trade, the three and their accomplices relieve the exhorbitantly well-to-do of their excess. It's artful and it's exciting, but it's theft. These guys should be the bad guys.

"If my character's not entertaining, right there, I've lost it," Roberts says. "I think you have to have a fun story. You may do some very serious work within it — Luke had a very abusive background, there were some hard things in *Honest Illusions* as well — but you have to add humor to it, and the characters have to have fun, and the readers should have fun reading the book."

Taking time for research

All levity aside, the detail work can be very serious business, Roberts says. Authenticity in setting is critical if the plot hinges on the location. Eagle-eyed readers happily pick up mistakes — misplaced streets in major cities, inaccurate depictions of flora and fauna, airline flights which could never connect. "I once had a heroine pump gas in Oregon, because as far as I knew — and obviously the copy editor, too — self-service gas stations were everywhere," she says. "Well, it's against the law to pump your own gas in Oregon. I never thought to check that out, and I got three letters on it."

While writing *Honest Illusions*, in which stage magic was a prominent part of the plot, Roberts estimates she referred to between 20 and 30 books on the subject. She studied the performance of card tricks and the history of magic, and the specifics of other stage magic acts to describe her characters' life-work accurately. While Roberts says she rarely makes special trips to research her locations, she does her homework, referring to area chambers of commerce, libraries and maps to keep specifics accurate — which side of town is affluent, which side struggling, the names and stops of local mass transit systems, and other details, details, details.

"People live there," Roberts says. "And hopefully some of the people who live there are going to read this book. And if you don't get it right, they're going to let you know."

Creating authentic dialogue is another skill at which Roberts excels, and she uses conversations liberally both to propel the plot and reveal information about her characters. While Roberts says she knows of people who have recorded conversations to study their flow and train themselves in creating dialogue, that skill was a natural for her. "Even from the beginning, when I didn't know what I was doing, I could write dialogue," she says. "I think you have to have an ear for the way people talk, the rhythms and the accents and the syntax, and the whole thing . . . people talk in half-sentences and they talk in contractions, and they flow from one idea to another. But you can't always put that dialogue in a book, because it would be confusing.

"You have to look at your character, and ask 'what kind of person is this?', and 'how do they express themselves?,'" Roberts says. "I don't even think about dialogue when I'm writing it. It comes straight from the characters I've created. It just sort of springs out of them."

Working without a net

Roberts' ideas for her novels and the plot lines come about in much the same way. Most often, "they just sort of come," she says. And come they do. Her lengthy list of novels features tales of time travel, television talk show hosts, witches, telephone mistresses, concert violinists—Roberts's goal of keeping it fresh requires almost boundless imagination to have published so many novels without repeating characters or plot lines.

"You never know where your ideas are going to come from," Roberts says. "Sometimes an idea is just floating around in space, and it snags you. Other times it's a definite thing, but that's much more rare for me." An issue of a popular magazine which featured a rock star and his grown daughter triggered her 1993 novel *Private Scandals*, but that's one of the few specific sources she will cite for her ideas. Usually, the premises for her books come together in much the way *Honest Illusions* went from initial idea to full story: "You start playing that game of What If?," Roberts says. "What if I did a book on magicians? But that's just not enough. So what if they were [also] thieves? And if they were really charming thieves who didn't really harm anyone—they didn't rob convenience stores and they didn't carry guns—they're sophisticated, and artists on stage. And what if you had a boy and a girl grow up together, almost as brother and sister, what would the dynamic be then when they got older and fell in love? And then you start."

Like probably half the world of published authors, Roberts chooses to write without an outline. It's not because she craves the thrill of working without a safety net, or dislikes being confined by that format. It's because "I've never been able to," she says. "When my agent said 'well, you can sell on outline now,' years ago, I was afraid to tell her I didn't use one, because I was still intimidated at that time. So I would write the whole book and write the outline from the book. When [my agent] found out, she said 'never mind, never mind.' "

Roberts, who has taught writing seminars for Romance Writers of America and Silhouette, says writers should choose their own method—to outline or not to outline—depending on their individual work style. While she admits that often when working on her novels "I have no idea what's going to happen . . . it has to come through the characters while I'm writing," outlines can provide writers with a useful tool to keep them on the trail. She says: "I do think you can deviate as much as you want from an outline. It's your map and you can take detours. I don't think you have to be confined by them . . . you can say 'I've decided not to take that route, I'll take this one.' And you still end up in pretty much the same place, but it's a more interesting road."

One peril writers all too frequently encounter when they stray from the path is the abyss of writer's block. It makes sense that a writer as prolific as Roberts says she refuses to believe in that particular malady, and calls discipline its remedy. "I think as long as I refuse to believe in it, I won't get it," she says. "I really have tremendous sympathy for someone who runs into a wall. But I find if I keep up the habit of writing, and even if it's not very good, you can fix it. It's like exercise. You haven't let those muscles go lax. And eventually you'll break through the wall, and come through on the other side. And you fix or toss out whatever you've done."

A love for the love story

While Roberts' plot and character ideas come from a range of sources and vary so widely, all share one common theme — a love story. Whether it's category romance or mainstream fiction, with suspense or a murder mystery as a backdrop, there's a heroine and her man at the center of each of Roberts's novels. But those heroines have come a long way, baby, from the days when fluttering lashes and helplessness were prerequisites to a happy (read passionate) ending.

There are still guidelines category romance writers must follow: rules regarding character, plot and content that govern what a writer can do within the parameters of the publisher's specific line, such as Silhouette's Intimate Moments or Harlequin's historical romances. Aspiring romance novelists should contact their targeted publisher for those guidelines before writing and submitting a novel which would be unsuitable for that category. But the heroines have changed to better reflect today's women — they can be assertive, smart and tough in their own right, without depending on the man for identity.

And the market for new novelists is healthy, Roberts says. "The category romance industry now is enormous. More than 40 percent of books bought in paperback are romance, whether it's category romance, single title romance, historical, contemporary, romantic suspense, what have you. It's very healthy. Five years ago, the genre was a little slack, except for the brand-name authors — but now it's booming all over again. You have a loyal following, and then you have new generations coming in."

The widespread readership for Roberts's mainstream romance novels, *Carnal Innocence* and *Genuine Lies* indicates writer are definitely returning to romance! Perhaps Serendipity's third role in Roberts's career was to bring romance novels back into widespread popularity at a time when she was ready to break out of her "roots" in category romance and move into single-title fiction writing.

Writing category romance novels — which Roberts once compared to dancing the ballet "Swan Lake" in a telephone booth — is often harder than it looks for aspiring writers, Roberts says. "They're so short. People look at them and think they must be a snap to write. But they're even more difficult a lot of the time than a bigger book, because you have to come up with something fresh and new within that framework every time. And it really takes a steady hand to tell a story simply."

While Roberts says she enjoys writing mainstream romance novels, which allows her to develop sub-plots and full casts of characters, she plans to continue writing category romance novels. "I really like the change of gears," she says, "going back and doing a category, maybe two, and then doing a couple of different types with the [romantic] suspense single." The forms are similar enough, she says, to permit writers with the discipline and talent that flexibility. "You still have to be able to tell a good story," Roberts says. "You can never lose sight of that. It has to be a good, entertaining story."

Other than the ability to create that good, entertaining story, aspiring writers have to do more writing than aspiring, Roberts says. "I think one of the most important things is you don't send your first manuscript out and have it rejected — as 99 percent of the time it's going to be — and give up. You have to be persistent, keep at it. And you don't want to only write when you feel the creative fairy has landed on your shoulder. Because she's a liar. It's very important to develop your own discipline. There really are no muses."

Ann Hood Urges Writers: Be Your Own Critic

by Lauri Miller

A year after her graduation from the University of Rhode Island, Ann Hood embarked on a career as an international flight attendant and continued to keep private her literary ambition. "I was probably the biggest closet writer on the planet," she says. During her three years as an attendant, she submitted "a really bad story to *Cosmopolitan*" and following that one rejection, stopped sending her work out.

Hood may have gone on as an unpublished writer had it not been for the professional misfortune and personal tragedy that befell her in 1982—a layoff from Trans World Airways and the death of her brother. She went into an "emotional tailspin," from which she emerged realizing life was too short not to do what she really wanted—to pursue her writing more seriously. She enrolled in graduate school at New York University and set into motion her life as an-out-of-the-closet writer.

Before even finishing the program, she sold to Bantam Books a series of stories that would become the critically acclaimed novel *Somewhere Off the Coast of Maine*. She has since gone on to write four more novels, most recently *Places to Stay the Night*, called her "big book, her breakthrough" by one reviewer. Although Hood considers New York City her home, where she writes, teaches (at NYU), and maintains an apartment, she has opted "to step out of the loop for awhile" and live in Rhode Island—to tend to her newborn son and to "slowly" begin work on her next novel. As her mother babysits, she speaks lovingly, thoughtfully, and humorously of her life as a writer and of her craft.

Lauri Miller: What graduate program did you enter at NYU and why?

Ann Hood: It was an interdisciplinary master's in English. I wasn't that far along with my writing, or so I thought. As it turns out, I was more along than I thought I was. I had only a few scattered stories, nothing in shape to apply to a writing program, and so I enrolled in a program that focused on American literature. I believed then and believe now that you really have to be a reader to be a writer—a critical reader. I thought that through this program I might be able to take some writing workshops and get some guidance on my writing. In the course of being there my writing so dominated, and that's really the direction I took off in.

LM: Were there any instructors that had a particularly strong influence on you?

AH: I took several writing workshops with a man named William Decker, who had been an editor at Viking and had retired and was teaching at NYU. And he's the one who gave me the good advice to go to the Bread Loaf Writers' Conference. There I worked with Nicholas Delbanco, and he also was very encouraging, so I think it was the combination of those two people in that short span of time, within a year really, that set me on the right path.

LM: Would you recommend writing programs to those desiring to make a career of writing? And what is your feeling on writing groups?

AH: I definitely would because if you're not around other writers, you kind of write in a vacuum. I think you keep making the same beginning writer mistakes over and over, no

Lauri Miller is a freelance writer and book editor based in San Francisco.

matter how much you read and try to teach yourself. Once you get into a community of other writers, you're forced to look at work critically, you're forced to be challenged, and you're forced to write better. Once you have that as a stepping stone, you can then impose those workshop comments and criticisms on yourself. They're in your mind forever more. Although I have not been in a writing group, I have as a teacher been involved with them and have seen from the other side how beneficial they are.

LM: While you were at NYU you began writing the stories that evolved into *Somewhere off the Coast of Maine*. How long had you been carrying the seeds of this novel around in your mind?

AH: That's a hard one to answer. The novel began with a short story and that came to me fresh. I hadn't tried to write it before or even tried to deal with the issues, although they were themes that had always been in my mind. They were the themes of what happened to the people of the sixties. My cousins and my brother, who were a few years older than me, were living it. I kept wanting to hurry up and get older so I could get involved in it too. But I saw what happened with their lives and where they sort of spun out. I thought about that a lot. In fact, I remember going to someone's house and being surprised that he was living just a regular suburban life. In 1969 he had seemed to me the coolest possible living person, and I expected great and strange and wonderful things to happen to him, but he just worked in an office and drove a Volvo and lived in the suburbs. I was floored and disappointed, and it forced me to step back and think about whether this was so bad and what it all meant. That is one of the themes I had been living with for my whole life. And the other is the relationship children have to their parents and how we're alike and how we're different.

LM: How did you end up at Bantam?

AH: One of the greatest things about taking my first workshop with this man Bill Decker was that he took me aside and said, "You have what it takes." And that gave me the incentive to just pursue it very strongly, and when I went to Bread Loaf, Nicholas Delbanco said the same thing. It was also through Bread Loaf that I was hooked up with an agent, who wanted to represent me on the basis of 50 pages of *Somewhere Off the Coast of Maine* — four short stories. She said, "Write some more; 50 pages isn't very much," and I got up to about 90 before I said I really didn't know how to turn it into a novel. I was so bent on writing it as short stories. She said, "Well, let me see if I can sell it this way," and Bantam bought it like that.

LM: Have you had the same editor with Bantam throughout the publication of all of your books?

AH: I have, all five novels have had the same editor. That is a rarity these days.

LM: How would you describe your relationship with your editor?

AH: It's wonderful, absolutely wonderful. When *Somewhere off the Coast of Maine* was submitted, those 90 pages of it, someone at another publisher was interested; we had a telephone conversation. I hung up the phone and thought, "Well, I don't know much about publishing, in fact, I know nothing. But she doesn't seem to understand what I'm doing. Now is that my fault?" I mean what did I know; I was such a novice. That was on a Friday. I had my meeting with Deb Futter, my [future] editor at Bantam, on that Monday, and within ten minutes of meeting her, it was like love at first sight. She knew exactly what I wanted to say and what I was trying to do. I realized it was so worth not jumping the gun that [previous] Friday just to be published. Your relationship with your editor is like a marriage, hopefully a long lasting marriage; it has to work. But it's just wonderful because she understands my perspective, my mission, and my way of writing, which is really impor-tant because everyone writes differently and comes to the finished product differently. If you tamper with that in a bad way, it can really be destructive.

LM: How would you describe your "mission?"

AH: To tell a story and to tell it well. I believe in traditional story telling, and being honest, and getting out an emotional truth, and I just try to figure out different ways of doing this each time. I'm very character driven, and so I guess my goal is to create characters that relate to each other and the world in a way that reveals some bigger truth.

LM: How would you say the publishing environment is different now from when your agent submitted *Somewhere off the Coast of Maine*?

AH: Although I haven't experienced this personally because I've had several novels published, I think it's harder now for first novelists to get published, and because editors are changing houses so much, it's very hard to have the continuity that I have. I've seen so many writers really suffering because the person that was really behind them is gone. Either these editors have left publishing altogether, or they have changed houses. From personal experience I feel it's so important to have that continuity. It keeps you confident and constantly encouraged. I think it's harder and harder to get that.

LM: Do you feel that it's really important to have an agent?

AH: I feel that it's crucial—for a lot of reasons. For example, my editor, after my fourth novel, changed from Bantam to Doubleday, and I went with her. Although they're owned by the same umbrella company, they are different companies with different publishing philosophies, and I was under a contract with Bantam. If I didn't have an agent, I don't know how I would have switched over to Doubleday and dealt with all the little negotiating. That can happen just as well to a first novelist, and if you don't have an agent, what do you do? I believe that a good novel could be bought without an agent, that you could send something into a publishing house and that some lucky editor would find it and be very happy to publish it, but there are so many small details of publishing that I don't think we're equipped as writers to handle.

LM: Could you describe the feeling of first publication? What was that like?

AH: I don't think I can because it was so wonderful. I think it was probably one of the best experiences of my life. And happily, every book has a bit of that. It's great to see your book in a bookstore window. (I still go around taking pictures of this.) But it's the private moment of receiving the first copy that is the most exciting. Because, really, as a writer, it's just you and your work. It's not a public thing. I thought my impulse would be to run wildly through the streets with it, or at least to my mother's house, but instead it's a really private moment, and there's just no duplicating it. And each time that is the part that is incredible and hard to describe, because you've worked for however long it takes and there it is.

LM: How long is that?

AH: About two years. My system is first just to get it out on paper. Then I have this big hunk of words that I have to figure out. It's almost like sculpting; you have a big chunk of something and have to keep honing away at it. I think revising is the least talked about part of the process and probably the most important.

LM: When you are starting a new novel, do you submit an outline or your preliminary ideas to Ms. Futter?

AH: I never do an outline. I've never even tried to do one. I also never write chronologically. In fact, at the end of each novel, I need to sit down and make a time line and shuffle the chapters so they make chronological sense. I always start with either a visual image or with a character in a visual sense—a picture almost. I walk around sometimes for months, trying to figure out what that image means to a bigger work. So I would say I know my theme right off, my beginning, and my ending, but getting to those places is always an adventure. I feel that were I to make an outline, it would keep me from the free process that I have. On the other hand, as I get ideas, I write them on Post-its and stick them on the wall near where I write. Surprisingly, few of those are used. I end up going in a different direction or getting to my ending in a different way.

LM: How many times do you go through and revise your manuscripts?

AH: I can't even begin to guess. I do the daily revision on the computer when I sit down to write, reading out loud the last thing I've written. I find that you really become aware of clunky sentences, of cliches, of tired writing, when you hear it. Also you'll find that if you're embarrassed to read it out loud to yourself, it definitely needs work. Then as I print out that chapter, I revise on the paper, and then I revise my big chunk when I have it all together, and then I send it to my agent, and she has revision suggestions, which I do, and then it goes to my editor. And then the real revising begins. So before it even gets to her, I've done three or four revisions. And I would say it goes through at least that many again.

LM: After receiving such praise for your first novel, was it then difficult to begin on the second?

AH: I think had I waited, it might have been. That's another piece of advice I can't stress enough. Never wait and see what happens—even when it's a short story coming out. Every day you start from zero—that's the way you have to look at it. When I was waiting for publication on the first one, I had started on my second, and I've done that throughout. It can be damaging if a book isn't well received. It can stop you from beginning something new, and if it's very well received, it can also stop you. I think if you can just send it out there and let the writing gods do what they will with it, and just start from zero, you're better off.

LM: And how do you structure your writing? Do you write during the day? At night?

AH: I was going somewhere recently, and I asked what the attire was. They said, "Dress as a writer." I said, "You mean, you want me to wear my bathrobe?" I have to preface this by saying that I don't write every day. I write when I feel my head's going to explode if I don't. Otherwise I feel I write really badly. Now there are writers who do write every day, and that's part of their system. I'm just not one of them. But when I do write, I don't usually write till the afternoon, and I will write at night, too. I'm not a morning person, and so as a result, if I'm on deadline or really struggling with a revision, I'll force myself to do it all day; otherwise, I don't usually sit down till about 2 o'clock.

LM: How often do you feel like "your head's going to explode"—perhaps every second or third day?

AH: It isn't that structured. I might go a couple of months without writing at all, but I think when we talk about writing we mean sitting down at the computer or typewriter and writing. I feel that I "write" every day because I'm carrying my writing problem or that image that I talked about with me. I feel like I do work on stuff every day, but then when I do sit down and write, I might write a chapter in a week or two weeks, writing ferociously every day. I might be struggling through a chapter and write a little bit every day for a month or two, or I may not be writing at all. To me there's a method to my madness, but it isn't something that I can really pinpoint.

LM: So do you spend a fair amount of time just out and about observing people?

AH: Absolutely, that is what I mean when I say I feel like I write all the time. When I'm sort of stuck, and I don't mean writer's block, because I never really have that, but stuck with a thematic question or a point-of-view problem, my days are spent—especially when I was in New York, but also here [in Rhode Island]—walking, sitting in cafes, going shopping. I love to cook, and I will tackle very difficult recipes. That puts me out into the world to find strange ingredients. It gets me out there. Talking on the phone is my favorite pastime when I'm stuck. Writing letters, reading letters from friends. All of that really sort of jogs things.

LM: Do you keep a journal?

AH: I don't and I never have. Back when I was in fifth or sixth grade, I kept a diary. I wanted to be a writer then, too. And I wrote every day. I found it recently and was very disappointed. I led the most boring life and had no insights on anything. The most exciting thing I wrote was, "Dear Diary, I just heard Paul McCartney got married. Oh God, don't let it be true." That's the only emotion I showed. So I learned my lesson, that I'm not a very good journal keeper, although I admire writers who are. I just spent a weekend with a writer friend of mine. We were out in the Berkshires, and I would see her out there writing in the woods and I thought, "Oh, that's what writers should be doing."

LM: Do you need to be in the location you're writing about? For *Places to Stay the Night*, for example, did you spend a fair amount of time in Massachusetts to get the location down?

AH: Quite the opposite. I need to be away from the spot to write about it. With my ex-husband in our early years of marriage, we spent a great deal of time in Massachusetts; it's where we went for weekends, the winter, and part of the summer. I hadn't been there in a couple of years when I wrote *Places*. Just as I think you need to be away from an emotional landscape to write about it objectively, I feel it's the same with an exterior landscape.

LM: What is your work space like, and how has having a child influenced your writing?

AH: My work space changes so much because I move so much. Right now it's a small room off of my bedroom, very far from the baby's room. Having a child has really thrown everything into more chaos than it was. I find that I've been writing more at night, when he's asleep. And I find that it's best if I can get him out of the house and safe into grandma's hands. Then I can go back and write.

LM: Do you read while you write? What are you reading now?

AH: Yes. Some people say that it's bad to read because you can be influenced by others. I don't find that. I'm usually so on my own mission that reading frees me or relaxes me in a way. So I've always got two or three books that I'm reading at a time. My current books are *The Virgin Suicides*, which I just started and a book about how writers use their dreams in their writing. And then I'm reading a short story collection—I always keep one in my diaper bag—*The Tomcat's Wife*, by Carol Bly.

LM: Who are the writers who have most influenced you?

AH: Well, for different reasons, not style-wise, I always point to Jayne Anne Phillips and Bobbie Ann Mason as the two writers who made me realize that there were contemporary women writers right then, back in the early eighties, when I first started to pursue my writing. I came across the book *Black Tickets*, by Jayne Anne Phillips and *Shiloh and Other Stories*, by Bobbie Anne Mason, both short story collections. Although this seems like an obvious thing, it was almost like a lightning bolt for me. I thought, "Hey, there are women writing right now who are your age or a little bit older. It's happening now, so get to work." They influenced me in that they were very inspirational.

LM: What about in terms of style?

AH: That's hard for me to say. Often in reviews I'm compared to other people but, although I'm flattered, I can't say that I necessarily see it. These are people like Anne Tyler and Alice Hoffman and Ann Beatty, all people I admire, but I can't say that I really see the influence.

LM: What would you say is the part of novel writing that comes easiest to you? And what is the hardest part?

AH: The easiest part is the first part of just spilling it out. Although you're aware of structure on some level and theme and character, you don't let these things dominate you. In revision you need to rein those things in so that you have a narrative tension, a narrative focus, and a narrative thread. But I love the part where it's okay if a character looks slightly different in different chapters and it's okay if a theme gets out of hand, or that a character is in that later will be cut out, and you're sort of becoming aware that she's less important than you thought. It's that real pure form of writing that I love.

LM: Do you get feedback on your writing before sending it to your agent?

AH: Not really. I still am in a way, I guess, a closet writer. When I first sold *Somewhere off the Coast of Maine*, and I told former roommates of mine that I had sold a novel, they said, "You write books?" I mean, they were floored. I still sort of keep that privacy. It's almost as though by showing it, something is taken from it. Now if I wasn't getting feedback from an agent and an editor, I think I would be showing it because in some part of the process you need criticism.

LM: When did you feel you had really found your voice?

AH: I think it was when I wrote the first chapter of *Somewhere off the Coast of Maine*. I always wanted to write, which is a funny phrase, because I did write. But I was my own worst critic, and I think this is where beginning writers go wrong. They fall in love with their ability to manipulate language, and that's just not enough. I would write a story and think, "This is really good," and then read it again and know it wasn't as good as stories I was reading that were being published. And I was really harsh on myself, which is why I didn't send things out. Yet, I think people who suffer a lot of rejection oftentimes jump the gun and send work out when it's not ready. I mean you're going to get rejected even with really good stuff, but I think if we could only be more critical readers — and that's the benefit of being in writing groups and around other new writers — you see what they're doing that's right and wrong and learn from that, and then you have some sort of barometer of your own progress.

LM: The despair of loss is a theme that runs throughout your books. Why do you think this is so?

AH: When we talk about "write what you know" or truth in fiction, what we should be talking about or meaning is an emotional truth. All writers have an emotional truth that identifies them. With me I think it is loss and dealing with loss. What you do as a writer is get that emotional truth out, so that people can understand it and feel it and look at it in a new and different way. You just keep writing about it, and change the props each time, so that in one story or book it's about a divorce or an unhappy marriage and in another, it's about death, and in another it's about the possibility of death, and in another, it's about a broken heart. But really the truth of it is about dealing with loss.

LM: What is it about the human condition that most interests you?

AH: That there's hope, so that by looking at loss, I can show that no matter what, there's always hope at the end. How people come to that is what fascinates me. The dynamic within relationships is something else that appeals to me. I just read a Raymond Carver essay in which he says that he likes writing in which there are people that we know in situations that we understand. I guess I would have to say the same thing. I like to read about people that seem real, whose problems seem real. I think when writers are dealing with that, you can't help but relate to what they're saying.

LM: Are your characters ever based in part on people that you know and if so, do you ever feel inhibited by this?

AH: No, they're composite people. Fiction is not life to me; it's representational, so that to make the truest person, you need a little of a lot of people.

LM: In both *Something Blue* and *Places to Stay the Night* New York City seems to represent for several characters the possibility of attaining one's dreams, reaching one's potential. They often feel pulled between the allure of the city and the comfort of life in the small towns they come from. Is there some of you in these characters?

AH: I would say there are two answers. The first is that I think there's a little bit of me in all the characters, even males and children. You take a part of you that perhaps hasn't developed or that you're afraid to develop or that you only develop in a fantasy, and you give it to a character and then you can run with it safely. The city and small town conflict is one I've had my whole life, something that I struggle with all the time.

LM: Are you conscious of the reader as you write? And how do you hope the reader feels as a result of having read one of your novels?

AH: No. I'm only conscious of telling the truth. I think readers respond to that. I want them to be able to point to one character and say, "That's me" or "I have felt that" and to gain something from the experience, so that perhaps when they read my books, they're in a circumstance that I'm illustrating and they see a way out or understand something about themselves or the world around them that they didn't understand before.

LM: *Places to Stay the Night* has been called your "big book," your "breakthrough." Do you agree?

AH: I don't know. It's sort of like being compared to other writers. It's very difficult to see that about yourself or your own work. I just feel each book has accomplished something different, even though it's hard for me to pinpoint what that is. Each time I finish a novel, I feel that I've done something different, that I've challenged myself, and that I've found a new way to convey my truth. It's hard for me to gauge my work any other way.

LM: What are you working on now?

AH: I'm working very slowly on a book about two sisters. I haven't played with that relationship before. Their parents are selling their family home; it's about how each one deals with the past.

LM: What do you think is required of a novelist in terms of temperament, approach to life. What sacrifices do you think he or she must be willing to make.

AH: I always get frustrated with somebody who says, "I'd like to write a book, but I don't have time." Because know what? Nobody has time. You have to want to do it, be dedicated, and just sit down and do it. It takes a lot of time, and you have to be able to put your ego aside and say, "This doesn't work. I didn't write this as well as I should have." And perseverance, because it takes a long time.

LM: Is there any other advice you have for emerging or mid-career fiction writers?

AH: To read everything and write every day, even if it doesn't mean sitting down at your computer. You have to be in your "writing head" for part of every day. And you have to learn to be your own critic, to establish rules of good writing—to follow them and to apply them to your own work.

How to Handle Description

by Madge Harrah

When I wrote my first novel I thought that "good writing" meant "beautiful writing"— long descriptive passages filled with adjectives, adverbs, metaphors and similes.

"Reads like poetry," I told myself with satisfaction.

Then I got my first rejection letter in which the editor said, "This book is over-written and pretentious."

A second editor said, "Too much description, not enough action and dialogue."

At first I sulked. Then I rebelled. Obviously those editors did not recognize good writing when they saw it. I gave the novel to a friend to read, expecting her to praise my talent and soothe my damaged ego. Instead, she said, "This is a good idea for a novel, but I got lost in all that description. I ended up skipping those pages so I could get to the action."

Shock. Dismay. I'd spent hours on those descriptive passages yet she hadn't even read them.

The next time I read a novel I caught myself doing the same thing my friend had done. I either skimmed or skipped altogether the lengthy descriptions of landscape, architecture, cars, clothing, furniture. I looked ahead for dialogue, because dialogue meant that people had reentered the story, which filled me with anticipation: Would the characters come into conflict? Would there be a crisis?

That's when it hit me: Readers care more about the people in the story than they care about the trees and rocks. I began to wonder if I should go back to my own novel and take out all the description. Obviously, that was not the answer. Without some description my story would lack mood, color, a sense of time and place. But how could I include descriptive passages and still hold the reader's interest?

Thus began my search for ways to enliven description.

Although I never did sell that first novel, I have since published a number of other novels for adults and young readers, as well as short stories, nonfiction articles and plays. During these years, as I've worked to improve my writing skills, I've continued to ask: What are the ways a writer can create vivid descriptive images that will capture the reader's attention? How can one describe a situation, set a mood or define a character while using an economy of words?

It's been a long quest filled with trial and error, but here are some of the things I've learned.

Bring in the five senses

We see, touch, taste, smell and hear the world around us. That's why sensuous description enhances a scene. I used to concentrate on two of the senses, sight and hearing, and I've since noticed that many other authors do the same thing. But taste and touch are important, too, and scientists recently announced that smell seems to be the sense most likely to evoke nostalgia. Therefore, when writing I now try to keep all five senses in mind. This harkens back to the old axiom, "Show, don't tell."

Madge Harrah, *who studied under the late Rod Serling, is the winner of 11 national and international writing awards for plays, stories and novels. Her latest children's novel,* No Escape, *is a mystery from Avon.*

"Telling" means that the author provides information to the reader in a nondescriptive way, i.e.:

> When John opened the door and stepped outside, he found that it was sleeting and the wind was blowing.

There is nothing grammatically wrong with the above sentence. It moves John from one place to another and tells us what the weather is like. But that's the problem: It *tells* us; it doesn't *show* us.

The scene becomes much more vivid when the reader is allowed to discover for himself what is happening by bringing in the sense of touch:

> When John opened the door and stepped outside, a sudden gust of wind drove needles of ice into his face.

Here is another scene that tells but does not show:

> The apple pie smelled good. When Mary took a bite she found that it tasted good, too.

Again, the information is there, but the scene is flat. Bring in the senses and the scene takes on life:

> Steam wafted upward from the slice of apple pie to fill Mary's nostrils with the scent of summer orchards. When she put a bite in her mouth, the warm syrup caressed her tongue with a gift of flavors: sugar, cinnamon, butter and just a hint of nutmeg.

Notice that the above examples use specific verbs and nouns. Saying the wind "*drove needles* of ice into his face" evokes a shudder that "*blew bits* of ice into his face" does not. Having the syrup *caress* the tongue creates a more sensuous image than having the syrup *flow* over the tongue. *Cinnamon* and *nutmeg* trigger specific olfactory memories, while *spices* does not.

Is it possible to overdo sensuous description? Yes. Bringing in all five senses in every scene would begin to sound contrived. When the reader notices a particular writing device that the author is using and stops to think about it, that breaks the flow of the story. The goal is to make the reader shudder or salivate without pausing to figure out why. Therefore, keep sensuous description in mind at all times, but develop an awareness, which comes through practice, of the subtle balance that lies between too little and too much.

Combine description with action

Imagine a scene from a television show: A girl, stalked by a killer, flees into a room and slams the door. The killer kicks the door open and lifts his gun. The camera moves away from the two people to focus on the objects in the room, one by one: the couch, the chair, the coffee table, the magazines, the vase of roses, the carpet. Finally the camera pulls back to show the girl cowering against the wall, the killer with gun still aimed.

What happens to the tension in that scene? It falls to zero while the camera "describes" the room. You'll probably never see that happen in a film, but unfortunately you will come across it in novels. All action stops while the author describes the room or landscape in detail, object by object.

Let's take the previous scene again. What if the girl flees into the room and falls over the couch, striking her head against the coffee table? The magazines slide to the floor, the vase tips over. Roses slither across the table and shower down around the girl. Dazed, she scuttles backwards over the carpet and presses against the wall. The killer kicks the door open and lifts the gun . . .

The viewer/reader moves right into the middle of the action and discovers the objects in the room as the action takes place.

This business of working the description into the action has been a hard lesson for me to learn, particularly when it comes to historical fiction. I enjoy research and I'm often tempted to freeze my characters on the page while I take time out to explain how a musket works or how a stagecoach is constructed. In fact, I've done so much research on steamboats for three of my historical novels that I think I could design one, and sometimes I'm tempted to show off that knowledge.

Fortunately, I belong to a critique group made up of experienced writers who say, "Wait a minute, don't just *tell* us about that steamboat. Show us that steamboat through your character's senses and actions."

Therefore, in my historical gothic novel, *Shadow of the Cat*, I let the heroine—and the reader—experience a steamboat in the following way:

A creaking noise, rhythmic and insistent, brought me upright on the bench while my eyes flew open to see a stevedore turning a handle on a winch. Already the stageplank was lifting into the air, drawn by an arrangement of pulleys and ropes. Even as I half rose from the bench, still debating whether or not to disembark, the stageplank folded up against the side of the boat where another stevedore secured it with a heavy hook. The whistle split the air once more with its piercing cry, the engines coughed, the paddle wheel turned, the boat shuddered, and we moved slowly out into the current, heading eastward up the river toward the retreating clouds. Behind us to the west the descending sun cast a ruddy glow over the water and gilded the buildings of the town.

Note again how specific nouns and verbs enliven the action in that scene: stageplank, stevedore, coughed, shuddered. Yes, I've sprinkled in a few adjectives and adverbs to brighten the color, but only a few. Too many modifiers weaken the action. Watch what happens when we burden one of the above sentences with additional adjectives and adverbs:

The whistle rendingly split the air once more with its high-pitched, piercing cry; the engines coughed asthmatically; the tall, groaning paddle wheel turned round and round; the whole boat shuddered violently; and we moved slowly out into the dark, swirling current, heading eastward up the winding river toward the retreating clouds.

Again, there is nothing structurally wrong with that sentence, but it lacks the power of the original.

Include an emotion or attitude

One factor that unites all people on earth, no matter what their background, is emotion: fear, joy, rage, love.

When I watch a television newscast of an earthquake in Turkey and I see a woman weeping over her dead child, I immediately empathize with her distress. It doesn't matter that her clothes are not the same as mine, I know that woman and her grief in a way that reaches beyond cultural differences.

The same goes for other emotions, such as happiness. When I watch two people who are strangers to me run toward each other in an airport, arms out, eyes shining with love, my heart lifts at their joy.

Therefore, when writing description, I try to include the emotional reaction of my character to the situation or person described. This helps the reader identify more strongly with the character and also defines the mood of the scene. If the character reacts with fear to the stealthy footstep on the stairs, then the reader, too, feels apprehension. If the character reacts with eagerness to the footstep, because it signals the approach of a lover, then the reader feels anticipation.

Here is how the protagonist in my novel, *Call of the Dove*, reacts when she finds herself alone with a strange man on a lookout platform that encircles the top of a tall building:

> Reaching the corner, Bethany glanced back to see if the man was still in the same place. With fear burning her throat, she saw that he was moving toward her and that he was staring at her again. For one split second she looked directly into his black eyes, deep set beneath thick, dark brows. A mistake, she told herself angrily. She should never have allowed herself to make eye contact with him. Now he would think she was inviting his approach. She hurried around the corner, hoping that someone else might be there, after all. Instead, the walkway stretched before her, bleak and empty, like the battlement of a deserted castle.

Notice how this scene combines emotion, action and a few strong descriptive words. First, fear burns Bethany's throat when a stanger moves toward her and stares at her from eyes that are deep set beneath thick, dark brows—an ominous image. She becomes angry with herself for having made eye contact with the stranger and flees, hoping to find safety in the company of another sightseer. That hope is dashed when she realizes she is indeed alone on a walkway that is bleak, empty, deserted—three loaded adjectives that emphasize her danger.

Focus on unique details

Back at the beginning I posed the question: How can one create description, using an "economy of words," that will capture the reader's attention?

One way is to choose details so unusual that a scene or character comes alive in an instant, as if illuminated by the sudden flash of a camera. In Suzi MaKee Charnas's young adult novel, *The Bronze King*, here is how 14-year-old Tina describes her new-found friend:

> His name was Joel Wechsler. I liked his sort of cranky hawk looks and his bright scarf and his nervous, long-fingered hands that kept torturing the rim of his wax-coated paper Coke cup all the time we talked.

Charnas might have taken a whole page to describe Joel's nervousness. Instead, she uses one unique detail—hands torturing the rim of the cup—to give us the essence of Joel's personality while maintaining the scene's momentum.

In Paula Paul's novel, *Lady of the Shadows*, she sets a mood of mystery inside a church by combining sensuous description with an unusual simile:

> Light filtered through the stained-glass windows and left mottled patterns on the backs of parishioners like the mark of the Beast of Revelations. But the beast, if he existed, would have been calmed by the rose and blue hue of the light as well as the droning stains of the organ.

Comparing the mottled patterns from the stained-glass windows to the mark of Beast is indeed unique. Sometimes authors get lazy, however, and rely upon clichés: "quiet as a mouse," "strong as an ox," "nervous as a cat." Clichés and colloquialisms are acceptable when used in dialogue, but should not be used in the narrative.

In her novel, *Dark Heart*, Betsy James avoids the pitfall of cliché when she finds this simile to describe a hillside:

> There had been a burn there once, and now the whole mountainside was thatched and interwoven with second growth: blackberry and barberry, hawthorn and scrub oak, dense as a dog's coat.

That bit of description occurs in a paragraph that is preceded and followed by dialogue between two people in conflict. Consequently, the reader sweeps into that paragraph and reads it without skipping.

Metaphors, too, can be useful in illuminating a scene with that sudden flash. In my children's novel, *Honey Girl*, 12-year-old Dorothy reacts impulsively to situations and does not like being told by her parents that she should be patient. After several failed attempts, I finally came up with the right metaphor to describe her feelings:

> Patience, to Dorothy, was an old woman sitting in a rocking chair and knitting a scarf ten miles long.

Again, the paragraph containing that metaphor is short and is immediately preceded by strong emotion and dialogue. I know that children read and remember that metaphor because they mention it when I appear as guest author in schools.

I often revise the descriptive passages in my novels and short stories a number of times before I'm satisfied. Then I bounce those passages off the members of my critique group to see if they shuffle in their chairs and yawn. If so, that tells me I must enliven the description through the use of the action, emotion, unusual details and the five senses. Yes, it's difficult. But when a reader says to me, "I love your description," I then know the hard work has been worth the challenge.

Tools for Creating Emotionally Powerful Fiction

by Colleen Mariah Rae

Writing itself is not hard; it's shaping the product into a well-crafted form that creates panic in most of us. Through analyzing my own approach to fiction writing and through studying the methods of other authors, I've developed techniques that help turn creative expressions into polished and publishable forms. One that's particularly useful because it focuses on the main character's dilemma is what I call a Continuum Trait, a single, identifying, trait from which grows the character's need. At the base of this technique are five questions to ask of the character.

Finding your character's Continuum Trait

The first question to ask characters is this: "What do you want?" It's a simple question, but within the answer often lies the story. For instance, let's say my main character, a college professor, says he wants to climb a mountain. He looks in good enough shape; why not? Sure, this will be a story about climbing a mountain. But in fiction, just as in real life, there's usually someone or something that'll make it hard. So the second question is: "So what's stopping you?" In my mind's eye, I get an image of a woman dressed in climbing gear and hear a name, "Sarah." This in itself is enough to begin a story: We've got the main ingredients—a character who wants something and someone who'll stand in his way.

The third and fourth questions should be asked of all characters who want to make an appearance in our stories. They are: "What's your greatest strength?" and "What gets you into the most trouble?" Frequently, a character will answer one, but not the other. For instance, I have a con man in one of my stories, and when I asked what got him into the most trouble, he laughed and said, "Nothing. Nothing gets me in trouble." When I asked his greatest strength, he answered, "I can talk anybody into anything." Easy to guess what also gets him into the most trouble.

The answer to these two questions will usually be the same because just as in real life, what gets a character in trouble is often that character's strength. Think of the reports your grade-school teachers sent home. The teachers who admired tenacity would often comment positively on how "determined" Suzy was; the teachers who weren't such fans of tenacity might call her "bullheaded." I call Suzy's tenacity a Continuum Trait because it has both its good and bad sides, as Sophocles illustrated well in *Oedipus Rex*.

In Sophocles's telling of this old tale, an oracle foretold that Oedipus would murder his father and marry his mother. As a baby, he was given to a shepherd who was to leave him on a mountaintop to die. This shepherd, however, took pity on the boy, and gave him instead to a shepherd from the other side of the mountain, who took him to be reared by the king and queen of Corinth who were childless.

As a man, Oedipus learned of the prophecy, and he determined to thwart the fates by leaving his home. On the road, he met, argued with and murdered a man. Once he arrived

Colleen Mariah Rae *teaches creative writing privately and is the founding editor and publisher of the* Sante Fe Literary Review. *She is the author of the novel* Perchance to Dream *(Haven Hill) and is working on an instructional writing book,* Secrets: Writing Fiction from the Inside Out.

in Thebes, he solved the Sphinx's riddle which lifted the plague, and, thus, he was given the widowed queen as his wife. It was only many years later that he learned that the old man on the road was his birth-father, and the queen, his birth-mother. In trying to beat the fates at their own game, he'd fallen right into their hands. But it's out of his Continuum Trait that his tragic error comes.

In his notes to his translation of Aristotle's *Poetics*, published by W.W. Norton & Co., James Hutton points to Oedipus's Continuum Trait: "Oedipus's *harmartia* or mistake is the slaying of a man who might be his father but whose relationship to himself he does not know, and this after warning from the oracle that he was destined to slay his father. This mistake might seem incredible had not Sophocles provided Oedipus with the hasty and irascible temper that makes it probable that he would act thus in circumstances of extreme provocation" (W.W. Norton & Co., 1982).

But it isn't his temper that got Oedipus into trouble: it's the Continuum Trait out of which that temper grew, a Continuum Trait Oedipus exhibited when he thumbed his nose at the fates and left his "hometown." Oedipus would bow to none: not to the fates, and certainly not to a contentious old man on the road.

It should be easy to see, however, that what brings about his downfall also brought him his successes. And that's why I call it a Continuum Trait; it has its positive side as well. It is strength unless pushed to an extreme. Think of a Continuum Trait as a number line:

$$-1 \underline{\hspace{9cm}} 0 \underline{\hspace{9cm}} +1$$

On the positive side of the number line, we'd write what Oedipus's friends might have said of him: "He knows his worth" or "He bows to no man." On the negative side, write what his enemies might have said: "He heeds none" or "He thinks himself greater than the gods." At zero on the number line, we'd write a word or phrase that describes Oedipus but that lacks any emotional connotation: "confident." Confident is "value neutral": It isn't "good" or "bad"; it just is.

This then is Oedipus's Continuum Trait. And as in all good stories, this trait leads him to make each of the several choices that brings him to the story's conclusion. Because that conclusion grows out of his action, it satisfies the reader.

Creating dilemma from the Continuum Trait

But knowing our main character's Continuum Trait alone does not a story make. We need our readers to *care* about our characters. This does not require them to like the protagonist or even respect him or her, but the reader has to feel enough to continue the story to the end. Here the key is dilemma—but not any dilemma: It must grow out of the character's Continuum Trait, which it will do automatically if we let our characters tell us their stories.

Take for example Mabel. Mabel is a woman in her sixties, a woman who collects things. She collects newspapers, magazines, string. Imagine her sitting in her chair in her living room, surrounded by stacks of newspapers. Why does she do this? Many reasons may come to mind, but in writing fiction, the source is always the character: We ask Mabel. The page in a writer's notebook might look something like this:

Mabel, What's your greatest strength?
I don't know, really. I'm not sure I have any, really.
Well, what gets you into the most trouble?
[She laughs.] Collecting things, I guess.
Why do you collect things?

Oh, just to be safe. You never know when you'll need a bit of string.

Although she hasn't said much, she's given a wealth of information. What does she want? She's told us: to be safe. A need for security of some sort motivates her. And what's her Continuum Trait? It's easy to imagine her friends calling her things like "provident" and "thrifty," but those who didn't like her would probably call her a "pack rat" or worse. But what's a "value neutral" word for her Continuum Trait? "Frugal" seems a good one. So our number line would look like this:

pack rat   frugal   thrifty

-1 _____ 0 _____ +1

So, now we know Mabel's Continuum Trait. She's frugal and we know what she wants: to be safe and secure.

Art resembles life. Anytime we want something, there's always someone or something ready to stand in our way.

Enter Sam, Mabel's husband. He stops by the door, not even attempting to navigate the maze of newspapers stacked floor to ceiling. Sam sees Mabel sitting with her arm on a stack of magazines, rolling string around the huge ball in her lap. What does Sam say? He says, "Mabel, I can't take it anymore. Either these things go or I go."

When I use this example in classes or workshops, I have the participants experience it in their mind's eye as though they were reading it in a book. When I say Sam's words, their faces express emotion. Mabel's cluttered room might have sparked curiosity in them; evidence of her "frugality" might have made them interested. But when Sam delivers his ultimatum, they become engaged. It's a good illustration of the power of a dilemma that grows out of a Continuum Trait: It makes the reader care.

And Mabel's got a dilemma. Not the watered-down "dilemma" of the weakening of this word's meaning. No, this is no mere quandary. This is a "damned if you do/damned if you don't," right "on the horns of the bull" dilemma. If she gives up either her collection or her husband, she gives up something she *needs*.

But consider June: June loves to travel. All her 40 years of adult life, she's been on the move, and as she went from country to country, she collected curios and knickknacks. Now, imagine June in her living room, surrounded by her collection. June's husband Harvey comes into the room and says, "Look, June, either these go or I go." What does June say? She just might say, "What's stopping you?"

Because June's collecting doesn't tie to her Continuum Trait, no dilemma's created when she's asked to choose. (Ask her, however, to choose between a travel-averse husband whom she loves and a continuing life of travel, and we may have another story.)

Once you know your character's dilemma, you can follow a fifth question to the story's end: "What's this character going to do?" And that's the question that leads to not only a well-crafted story, but to one that holds a reader's attention. As the fiction author and teacher John Gardner said in *On Becoming a Novelist* (Harper Colophon Books, 1983), "In the final analysis, real suspense comes with moral dilemma and the courage to make and act upon choices. False suspense comes from the accidental and meaningless occurrence of one damned thing after another."

Mabel's story will grow out of the choices she makes that propel her to the win or the lose or the draw of the story's conclusion. Her dilemma forces those choices, but they are hers because they will be made from her Continuum Trait and, concomitantly, from her need.

Using the Writing Wheel

The use of dilemma for shaping a story doesn't stop here. After the story is written, there are a few more questions, such as: Is your character's dilemma clear from the beginning? Does every scene have an action that grows out of this "damned if you do/damned if you don't" situation? Does the conclusion resolve the dilemma?

To answer those questions, I use a technique I developed to help my college students organize their essays. I've found it so helpful that I use it for all my own writing, including my fiction. Because it's meant to look like a bicycle wheel, I call the technique The Writing Wheel, see below.

The Writing Wheel works best with a story that's done but in need of crafting. Take a story that you've finished, and on each of the spokes write one of your story's scenes, adding more spokes if it has more than five scenes. Just a few words to capture the scene will do. For instance, the spokes for my story "God's Will" read "wakes and knows," "barn," "courting/rape," "father coming today," "wedding," and "baby born in June."

After you've listed all of your scenes, ask yourself, "What is each of these scenes about?" Next to the spoke, on the edge of the wheel, write a word or phrase that sums up that scene's objective. Next to each spoke on my "God's Will" Wheel happen to be the same words "doing God's will."

Then ask, "What's this *story* about?" With "God's Will," it's easy to answer because it's a crafted story. But the Wheel is a tool for revision, so it may be that only some of your spokes will be about the same thing. That word or phrase that sums up what most of your spokes are about *suggests* the story's premise.

What drives a story is meaning. A story's premise reflects this. Take for example Lynna

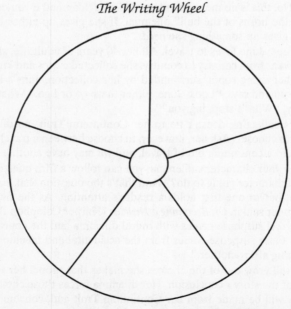

The Writing Wheel

© 1986, 1990 by Colleen Rae

Williams's "Things Not Seen" (*The Atlantic Monthly*, May 1990). Her story's premise appears in the third paragraph: "Love doesn't make people safe or keep them safe."

Often, even though your story is done, you won't consciously know its premise. This isn't bad. To write from a premise gives us something akin to an Aesop's fable. If we're doing what most writers do—writing to discover our story—we can't know what it's about until the end. Interestingly, the premise often shows up in some form in the story—often quite near the end.

Here's a good example: In Louise Erdrich's "A Wedge of Shade" (*The New Yorker*, March 6, 1989), the last two lines of the story read, "And so, in the dark, I hold hands with Gerry as he settles down between my mother and me. He is huge as a hill between the two of us, solid in the beating wind." These two lines carry the meaning of the story, which is about a young woman who wants "a wedge of shade" between her mother and herself. And it's sitting right there at the end of the story, as it often is.

So look through your story and see if you can find a sentence or two that holds the story's meaning. Unless it's expressed as clearly as is Williams's, you'll have to turn it into a premise statement. Once you do, write it around the rim of the Wheel.

You've got your spokes, and you've got your rim. Now look at your premise statement: Is there one word or phrase you absolutely cannot remove without completely changing the statement's meaning? To answer this, you look to your character's dilemma.

Williams shows her character's dilemma in the first paragraph of the story:

> Several times, when David comes home from the hospital to eat with his family, or calls Jenny to come quick and listen to Zanny pick out words in her bedtime book, or looks up at the bathroom mirror and sees Jenny behind him, in the bedroom, pulling on jeans and a sweater, he sees a difference in his wife's face, some subtle but fundamental alteration, and he knows that she is remembering what has been done to her. At first, each time it happens, he goes to her. He stops the night she tells him to please wait, that she will come to him.

With only a few words, Williams gives us enough information to see David caught tight between the horns. And the reason he's *damned if he does and damned if he doesn't* we sense already and know in the next paragraphs of the story: David's Continuum Trait is "protector." And his need? It's suggested in the story's premise: to make and keep people safe. And that's his dilemma: In the very act of being himself, he becomes something his Continuum Trait cannot allow him to be—someone who violates another. Can you see how this would be untenable? He must act to resolve the values conflict the situation produces.

In the hub, then, goes the word or phrase from the premise that ties to our character's need, Continuum Trait, and, thus, dilemma. It's a word that suggests the character's action through the story. For "Things Not Seen," that word is *safe*.

Find your own hub word and write it in the center of your Wheel. Now look at each of the scenes you've written on the spokes. Does each tie to the hub word? If not, you'll need to revise that scene until it does—or you'll need to remove it. Even if it's your best part of the story, if it isn't tied to the hub, it doesn't belong. Save it for some other story.

So, those are the questions. Other questions might lead to a well-crafted story, but these that focus on a character's need, Continuum Trait, and dilemma bring the story into its most emotionally powerful form.

Writing the Big Scene

by Sara Orwig

Have you ever put down a book with a regret to see it end, and a decision to find other books by the same author? Chances are, along with a satisfying story, appealing characters, and an intriguing plot, there is a final big scene that held you captivated and lingers in your memory long after the last page is turned.

A grabber beginning will hook a reader into a story, but it is a great climax and ending that will send the reader hunting for another book by the same author.

If you think back over the books and movies you felt were outstanding, certain scenes probably come to mind. This is what you as a writer want to achieve, the big scene that is the gripping climax of the book that will stay in your reader's memory long after the book has been placed on the shelf.

A novel opens with a dilemma that raises a question, or gives an overriding goal for your character. All through the plot twists and turns there is rising tension as you move toward the big moment, the final dramatic climax that packs the wallop that dazzles your reader and either achieves the goal for your character or loses the goal. This is the most dramatic moment of the novel.

If this moment falls flat, the reader will feel cheated. Climax is defined as the point of highest dramatic tension or a major turning point. If it comes out with a tiny pop instead of a big bang, the reader will be let down. The reader expects to see the protagonist triumph against all odds, and the villain get his comeuppance. Or if the protagonist is going to lose, he loses in a catastrophic, emotional disaster that shatters him.

What makes your big scene vivid and memorable? Through my writing experience I've found careful pacing, plotting and well-drawn characters are essential to developing a blockbuster scene.

Everything in the story should build toward the big scene

Throw your character into the most suspenseful situation you can conjure up to fit your story. Remember as you write your novel, you are building to this moment. So if you have an earthquake and fire with devastating consequences on page 50, you should have something even more dramatic on the last pages of the book. You will have to top the earthquake and fire or your reader will feel a letdown as the story progresses.

When you start your plotting, know where you are going. Have an idea what the big scene will be, what you're working up to. It's like building a dog house or making a dress — you have an idea what you want the finished product to look like and everything you do along the way is to achieve that final effect.

You have opened with a question or a goal, now in the climax this goal is resolved for better or worse for your character — and it is resolved in the *most gripping way possible*. This is a moment by moment acting out, the reader mentally seeing the character grapple with the dilemma in a situation where it looks as if the outcome can be only disaster.

This scene should not be told in narrative. It must have action, emotion, and dialogue.

With six million copies in print, **Sara Orwig***'s 40 published novels include a historical trilogy,* New Orleans, Memphis *and* Atlanta, *NAL/Onyx. She lectures often on writing the novel.*

To use an example, let's say we have a story opening with a man named Jake Colter as the protagonist. Jake is attacked and almost killed by a renegade, Wiley Wicked, leaving Jake on the brink of death and vowing revenge. So now Jake's goal for the story is revenge, and all the rising complications along the way should lead to this goal.

The final dramatic scene should be the ultimate moment when that goal, revenge, is achieved or lost. Here Jake should have a confrontation with Wiley Wicked. In this dramatic clash, Jake should fight and achieve his goal of revenge, or lose his goal and fail.

This big scene is essential to your story. The story cannot wind up without it and you will lead up to this moment from the beginning of the novel. Your reader will be primed and ready for the scene.

This is your protagonist's darkest moment

For this scene to be gripping, you must box your protagonist in so that the problems are enormous, the outcome looks dreadful, the odds are against success. The more threatening the obstacles that confront your protagonist, the more riveting the climax will be for the reader. The more you box in your protagonist, the more heroic and courageous the protagonist will be when he or she overcomes the obstacles.

At this point everything works against the protagonist. And at this moment everything is at stake. Often this is a life and death struggle. Occasionally it is a nation versus nation, involving many lives, but even when the stakes are national or international, the struggle should come down to your protagonist versus the villain or versus the evil.

The object the protagonist has to battle can be a great white shark, a typhoon, a flood, or a crazed killer. The villain can be man, nature, the supernatural—but whatever it is, your protagonist has to come to grips with the villain and ultimately act alone against whatever the evil is.

The more the character stands to lose—his love, his life, his country—the more important the scene becomes. For instance, Jake can risk his reputation, his life, the woman he loves, or all three, in facing Wiley. Or he can risk all three while at the same time trying to defend a town. If he loses, the entire town loses.

This final big scene is dominated by conflict. When conflict becomes part of any scene, the scene immediately becomes more interesting—and also easier to write. If you have built up your story with an appealing sympathetic character who won the reader in the beginning, then by the climax, the reader will be identifying with and pulling for your character. As your protagonist suffers and triumphs, the reader will suffer and triumph vicariously, giving the reader an intense sense of satisfaction when the protagonist overcomes seemingly impossible odds.

Add dilemma

Going back to Jake and Wiley—we can box Jake in, have him singlehandedly defending the town of Fern Valley against Wiley and Wiley's 20 men who not only will destroy Jake, but also Fern Valley. Make the situation worse by having the townspeople afraid to help Jake.

Now add another complication: Make the heroine, Priscilla, whom Jake loves, the daughter of Wiley. The stakes become even bigger because now Jake is thrown into a dilemma—to achieve his goal of revenge by killing Wiley and saving the town, thereby losing the woman he loves, or give up revenge, lose the town, perhaps his life, yet keep Priscilla's love.

Add to this climax scene something even more dramatic. Wiley sets the town ablaze and Jake has to fight not only Wiley and the 20 men, but worry about the town burning down at the same time.

Put Jake in one of the burning buildings with Wiley and the chance of drama is heightened. Now Jake is boxed in by fire, by being outnumbered 20 to one, by being torn emotionally between his hatred of Wiley and his love for Priscilla. So you see how it goes and as you write, you can work toward the complications that will make obstacles look insurmountable for your protagonist and cause the greatest emotional upheaval in his life.

And, if you can add a surprise twist, it will make the climax of the story far more interesting.

One caution—you have to make a choice about how much trouble to heap on your character. You want enough problems at the onset of the scene that the outcome looks hopeless, but don't place so many barriers in the character's way that the scene becomes a melodrama. Don't strain the story's credibility.

You can have many dreadful obstacles if you've given the right buildup and a believable background and made clear your protagonist's emotional state, but there comes a point where the fine line between high drama and melodrama vanishes. If we place Jake in the burning building against 100 men and a tornado hits while there is a mad dog running amok, instead of gripping the book and turning pages, the reader may break into chuckles, and your big scene will have lost its punch.

Include vivid and memorable imagery

Here's where your style and choice of words will make a difference between memorable and forgettable. Everything in the story builds toward this moment. As the moment draws closer, the buildup gets even more detailed. Get the setting in ahead of time because once the action starts, you can't go into a description of surroundings.

Take enough space to set the scene fully with all the sensory perceptions working. Make the reader aware of the colors in the background, the smell of the water or fire or diesel engines, the noise of wheels grinding or dynamite exploding or the sheer quiet of an empty building where a killer stalks.

If the street is lined with tall green oaks or the courtroom has a musty odor as the late afternoon sun comes through the high windows, get all this in because these are the facts with which the reader can identify.

These sensual details of how the background looks and smells and sounds are what ground the story in reality and give a sense of something actually happening.

And, the more clearly you can draw a vivid mental image of the setting, the easier it will be for the reader to see the scene as it is acted out. If you succeed fully, it will stamp the scene in the reader's mind clearly enough to become unforgettable. The sensory details are the bedrock of a memorable scene. If you haven't set the background in a clear manner so that the reader has a good sensual image of it, then the dramatic action of your character will be forgotten.

Your protagonist has to make a choice between at least two courses of action

Will the hero kill the villain or run from him? Will the heroine accept the hero's proposal of marriage or refuse? Will the hero risk his life to save a ship filled with people or escape to save himself?

At this point at least two courses of action should confront the protagonist and the protagonist has to make a choice. If there is a possibility of a third course of action, it could make the plot more suspenseful to the reader.

This climax scene is a test of character. Your protagonist is forced to choose between several courses of action and in choosing reveals his/her true character and courage.

This final act has to be irreversible. It is the ultimate commitment, the shoot-out, the life or death decision, the self-sacrifice, the confession that cannot be reversed.

In our example, this is the moment Jake is poised in town to face Wiley, knowing that if he fights Wiley, he may lose the love of Wiley's daughter, Priscilla. If he doesn't fight him, Wiley will destroy the town and try to destroy Jake. Suppose our hero decides to save the town and risk his love, so he fights Wiley—once he has made a commitment, there is no turning back and he will fight until either he or Wiley is dead.

Remember, too, a ticking clock always heightens suspense. If Jake has a year before Wiley will attack the little town, all sense of desperation is lost. In a year, Jake could get help from a U.S. Marshal, get help from the army, convince the townspeople to fight; in that amount of time he could do innumerable things to protect the town. Also, in a year he could win Priscilla and ride off into the sunset with the town secured. But if Jake learns 24 hours before Wiley is supposed to appear that Wiley is riding into town with his men to destroy Fern Valley, then Jake has limits on what he can do and the suspense grows for the reader. This time limitation is another powerful way of boxing in your protagonist.

Make room for emotions

Look back to the opening when your character faced a dilemma, and a goal or problem was established. Your tale will show how your protagonist handles the problem, achieves the goal, and grows or changes as he/she does. And this growth or change is in your character's emotions. Your protagonist's emotions are a vital part of the story and essential to a successful big scene. The climax should be the most emotional moment in the story.

Emotion is what makes a story live; this is the heart of your novel, so give enough space to your protagonist's emotions in this big scene. Make clear your protagonist's inner feelings and suffering or anger.

Your reader has probably never been in a submarine about to explode, but your reader can understand the emotions of a man or woman caught in such a situation. The reader can understand the emotional reactions of a man striving to save the life of a child from a killer. The reader can understand Jake's anger at Wiley, who has tried to kill him and who will destroy a town.

Whatever is at stake, there must be an emotional effect on the reader for the scene to be satisfactory. Your reader is in the fight with the protagonist and when the protagonist finally wins, the reader wins, but in the dark moments, the reader should be wrapped up in the story.

Create an emotional stake

Anticipation creates suspense. Build up the coming crisis with the emotional involvement of the character. Then, when the big scene comes, it should be a major upheaval in the character's life, a turning point. And this change will stir the character's emotions because people react emotionally to change.

It is essential that your protagonist has an emotional stake in this final big scene. If the character isn't tied up emotionally at this climax, then you lose all the effect of the drama of the story. When the character feels strongly about something, cares about something, the reader will have the same reaction.

Make certain your character's actions are in keeping with your character. If our character Jake has been easy-going, slow to anger, patient, then in this crisis and shoot-out, he will still be deliberate in his actions, pushed to a limit before he reacts. And his emotional state should always be made clear to the reader.

The emotional reaction comes first, and then the action. To try to change anything in his life or avoid change, your protagonist has to be in the grip of emotion. If he feels no emotion over an event, he won't react to it, but will shove it aside and forget it.

Action and timing are crucial

Courage is what the character will show when he faces challenges and rises to meet them. Your reader will get a vicarious pleasure and will admire the character for this courage. And this courage is what makes the character fight on, even when the battle appears hopeless.

Your protagonist has to take this decision and this action, this moment on alone. If you have a hero and heroine sharing the climax, each must have his or her own part, his own commitment, her own act and outcome. The cavalry may arrive later to save the day, but the hero has already done so and eliminated the biggest threat or the villain.

At this point action is crucial. The character is moved by pure emotion, going on feelings instead of stopping to ponder the consequences of action or debate the possibilities. Blind reaction in the heat of emotion is true character. The reader will believe the character in action.

The big scene checklist

Here is a final checklist to use in going over your big scene:

1. Have you given your character seemingly insurmountable obstacles?
2. Does your character have a strong emotional reaction to these obstacles?
3. Does the protagonist stand to lose anything important in this scene?
4. Does the protagonist act in a courageous manner?
5. Is the goal raised at the beginning of the book achieved or irrevocably lost?
6. Do you have a vivid, sensory description of the background of the scene? How many senses are involved?
7. Is this scene the most dramatic moment in the novel?
8. Does the character have a choice between two courses of action?
9. If the character wins or loses, is there enough emotional reaction given to the results?
10. Is there enough space given to a buildup for this scene?
11. Is there a time element where something has to be done within a certain amount of time?
12. Does the villain get what he deserves? Has the villain been a big enough threat to make the hero look heroic?

If you have covered these essentials and gone over your climax with the checklist, you should have all the ingredients for a powerful big scene. If it still doesn't seem to work, check again on the emotional impact and the odds against your protagonist. Your character must have a deep emotional commitment that is plausible to the reader and your character must have terrifying obstacles to overcome.

When faced with a life-or-death choice and impossible odds, your protagonist must act decisively and courageously in the most dramatic scene you can write and must *win* (or lose) through his own efforts. Do all this and you will have a blockbuster climax that should hold your reader enthralled.

Weaving the Novel Tapestry: What Makes a Subplot Work

by Donna Levin

Henry James once called the novel "a loose, baggy monster," but if you've written a novel, or tried to write one, you know that Mr. James was being overly kind.

A well-plotted novel reads as if it's all of one piece, as seamless as a crystal vase. Funny thing—when you try to construct one of those novels yourself, you feel as though you are the sole engineer responsible for threading together all of the freeways of Los Angeles.

That's one reason writers find novels so intimidating, and it's also a reason that sometimes writers who have mastered the short story have a tough time making the transition to novels. Some short story writers think all they have to do is keep the short story going for 300 pages, instead of stopping after 20, and they'll have a novel. Not so.

A novel is not only longer than a short story, it's wider. It has a main plot, but even a relatively short, slight novel has at least one subplot, and most novels have several. You can't avoid being devoured by the baggy monster that is a novel by keeping your story simple. No, because then you end up with a novel that will be thin and uninvolving. But neither can the subplots you do put in place be just arbitrary, other-things-that-happen. They are part of the composition of a novel which, once complete, seems so effortless and whole. So how do you come up with one of these perfectly fitting subplots?

Well, you create a subplot that exists for a reason: It either highlights the theme of the book, drives the main plot forward or, at the very least, provides us with a context for that main plot. It might even accomplish all three.

The thematic subplot

It's always satisfying for us as readers to see subplots that intersect with main plots; it appeals to our wish to see life itself makes sense. By "intersect," I mean that the same characters appear in both the plot and subplots. It's sort of like the way Mr. Drucker was in both "Green Acres" and "Petticoat Junction."

But for a subplot to function, it is not absolutely necessary for it to intersect with the main plot. A classic example of this is *Anna Karenina*. *Anna Karenina* is the story of a beautiful Russian aristocrat, Anna, who's married to the upright but uptight Alexei Karenin. She's a virtuous woman, but also a lively, emotional one. Meanwhile, her husband is the kind of guy whose idea of a good time is to clip his fingernails. So when the fatally charming and handsome Count Vronsky falls in love with her, although she tries to resist his advances, it isn't long before she succumbs and embarks on an affair with him.

Anna finally leaves her husband and child for Count Vronsky, but her own conscience, in part, won't let her live with this choice, and eventually, she commits suicide by throwing herself under the wheels of a train.

The premise, or the point, of Anna's story is that *adultery leads to death*. (Not always the case in real life, of course, but the point of Anna's story nonetheless.) In the same book,

Donna Levin *is the author of the novels,* Extraordinary Means *(Arbor House) and* California Street *(Simon & Schuster), and* Get That Novel Started *nonfiction from Writer's Digest Books. She teaches a novel-writing workshop at the University of California at Berkeley extension.*

however, Tolstoy included a subplot, the story of Konstantin Levin, a noble landowner who woos and finally wins the lovely Kitty Shcherbatsky. They marry and have a child, and suffer some rather typical trials and tribulations of the first year of marriage, a sort of Russian *Barefoot in the Park*. They fight over little things, and reconcile over big things. The love of his wife and child make Levin a stronger yet gentler man, and towards the end of the book, Levin, who has been an agnostic up until now, experiences a religious conversion. The premise, or point, of Levin's story is that *fidelity (or a happy family life) leads to salvation*.

The characters in Anna's story and the characters in Levin's story overlap, but only incidentally. For the most part, the purpose of the subplot, and thus the unity of the novel, arises because the two stories make two sides of the same argument. They are thematically linked.

When the plot and subplots of the novel do not intersect, then it is crucial that they all prove a single theme, otherwise the subplots *will* seem arbitrary, like stories that belong in other books.

For example, let's say that you want to write a searingly insightful young-people-adrift-in-the-big-city book. You assemble a group of various types—an artist, a shrewd entrepreneur and a lawyer who wants to help the poor among them—and tell their stories in episodic fashion. The entrepreneur starts selling the hats she designs on the street; the promising artist is seduced by drugs; the lawyer tries to find ways to compromise with the system without losing her ideals. Meanwhile, these characters don't interact much with each other except that they're sharing the same loft space so they have to wait in line for the others to get out of the shower.

When you get to the end of the stories about these young people in New York, whatever happens to all of them will have to be consistent with a single point that you, as the author, have proven. Perhaps the point will be, *only the strong survive in the big city*. In that case, we'll have to see how, indeed, the strong characters overcome the obstacles they face while the weak characters wind up broke and alone, or worse, become discouraged and go back home to Peoria.

The thematic link in a book such as this can be the difference between an amateurish, rambling novel about nothing in particular and one that possesses that seamless, crystal-vase quality.

An even better way

The thematic link of plot and subplot has worked well in many books, and anything that's good enough for Tolstoy is good enough for me.

However, it doesn't hurt to devise subplots that also drive the action of the main plot forward. As an example, let's look at one of the emblematic books of the 1980s, Tom Wolfe's *The Bonfire of the Vanities*. *Bonfire* tells the story of Sherman McCoy, an arrogant bond trader whose life unravels after he and his mistress get lost in the Bronx and run over a young black man. The hit-and-run accident becomes a *cause célèbre* for the entire city of New York, a symbol of racial oppression; ironically, in the end, Sherman's punishment isn't to go to jail but to get stuck in a kind of criminal justice system limbo in which he must defend himself forever.

Although Sherman himself does not really have the stature of a hero, his downfall results from forces outside of his control and his tragic dimensions. Also, while Sherman is a bit of a pompous snob and occasionally a buffoon, he isn't the most evil character in the novel (there's lots of competition for that honor), nor is he responsible for all the social injustice that is visited upon him personally.

The two main subplots of *Bonfire* (there are several, more incidental subplots as well) concern, first of all, Larry Kramer, an assistant district attorney who is looking for a Great White Defendent to bolster his career, and secondly, Peter Fallow, an alcoholic British journalist who similarly must find a good story to cover. Wolfe creates complex lives for both Larry Kramer and Peter Fallow, but for each of them, the central goal becomes to nail Sherman, the perpetrator of the hit-and-run. Therefore, as each character either comes closer to or is pushed farther away from his goal, Sherman is affected and thus Sherman's story moves forward even when he's off-scene.

This makes for an admirably dense novel, because the same phenomenon works in reverse. When we read about Sherman, we are also reading about Larry Kramer and Peter Fallow, because the outcome of Sherman's story—whether or not he achieves *his* goal of escaping the consequences of his involvement in the hit-and-run accident—affects them as well.

This is a fairly tricky concept, so once again, let's take an invented example to illustrate further. Say that you're writing a novel in which the main character is a mailman. One day he witnesses a murder through the window of one of the houses on his route. The killer sees him. Now Mailman knows that he has to flee or the killer will have to kill him, as well, in order to eliminate the only witness to his crime.

Now cut to the Mailman's home where we learn that Mrs. Mailman has been unhappy in her marriage to Mailman for years and has finally taken a lover. She and her lover would like nothing better than to get rid of Mailman and move in together. But the house is in Mailman's name and Lover has recently been fired from his bank teller's job, so they have no money. (Mrs. Mailman is a former socialite who is morally opposed to working because it might damage her manicure.)

Mrs. Mailman hears Mailman's key in the door. What's he doing home in the middle of the day? Lover escapes through the bathroom window just before Mailman bursts in, declaring that she must hide him. Ah ha! says the reader (though perhaps not aloud)— because the reader knows that Mrs. Mailman might *want* to see Killer find Mailman and do him in, because then she would get the house and the AT&T stock and be able to be with her lover. It would resolve her story.

What's crucial here, and what causes these two plots to drive each other forward, is the way in which both Mailman and Mrs. Mailman have different stakes in the outcome of the same problems. Will Mrs. Mailman actually *help* Killer find her husband? Or, seeing Mailman vulnerable, will she fall in love with him all over again and decide that she must protect him, so that Mr. & Mrs. Mailman now must flee Killer together? Or will Mailman learn of Mrs. Mailman's affair and go after Lover? Either way, the two stories—Mrs. Mailman wanting to be with her lover, Mailman running from Killer—affect each other.

The subplot as social context

The effect of plot and subplots doesn't have to be reciprocal, though. Take *Gone With the Wind*: History itself is a subplot throughout the book, but especially in the first part, in the form of the Civil War. We follow the victories and defeats of the two armies, and then, when Sherman's army comes upon Atlanta, it forces one of the more dramatic incidents of the book: Scarlett and Melanie must flee on the very day that Melanie gives birth.

By the way, this should be the case to a greater or lesser extent in any historical novel: that the true, historical incidents will affect the lives of the invented characters. Heck, if that didn't happen, why not just set your novel entirely in the Mall of America in 1994?

It is also in a historical novel that a subplot can provide a context for a main plot, that is, help us understand the characters and what their choices are. However, this is really a nice way of saying that the subplot of historical events impacts the main plot more subtly. In the case of *Gone With the Wind*, the sweeping economic changes that follow the Civil War force Scarlett to reveal sides of her personality we might not otherwise see: scrabbling for financial security, her dormant ruthlessness comes to the fore. More specifically, for example, the shift in power that occurs during the Reconstruction enables Tara's former overseer to levy taxes on Tara that Scarlett can't pay. This causes her to marry Frank Kennedy, a man at whom she otherwise wouldn't bother to wink, so that she can get the money.

The subplot that works as "context" isn't confined to the historical novel, however. Some of the more minor subplots of *The Bonfire of the Vanities* illustrate this principle as well. Early in the novel, Edward Fiske III, who represents a church group, goes to see a certain Reverend Bacon. Fiske is trying to ascertain what happened to the $350,000 that the church gave the Reverend for a day care center. The Reverend, in turn, subtly threatens Fiske, implying that he can, if he wants, create unrest and even violence in the black community, and that even if he can't account for the $350,000, it isn't much to pay for peaceful neighborhoods. The conflict between Fiske and Reverend Bacon forms a complete, if small, subplot. Fiske is worried about what will happen to his job if he can't recover the money, while the Reverend has every intention of keeping it. But the reason this subplot functions is that it provides a context for the main story line. The background it gives us about poverty in Harlem and the Bronx helps to explain, in part, how it is that when Sherman is inadvertently responsible for running over a young black man, he unleashes so much rage.

When theme meets plot and it all ends happily (or otherwise)

In the very best-plotted novels, not only do the main plot and the subplots affect each other, but they also form a thematic whole. For this, let's look at F. Scott Fitzgerald's *The Great Gatsby*. Like *The Bonfire of the Vanities*, *Gatsby* captures the spirit of an age, and like *Bonfire*, it embodies that spirit in some very specific people.

The main plot of *Gatsby* is the story of Jay Gatsby's unwavering love for Daisy Buchanan, a young woman who represents not only all his naive and intense ability to love but the insouciance of America in the 1920s. Gatsby pursues the elusive Daisy for years, refusing to abandon his image of her as an unspoiled angel who loves him equally in return, even though she's married another man and had a child.

A subplot involves Daisy's husband, Tom, who is having an affair with an auto mechanic's wife, Myrtle. From a thematic point of view, this subplot provides a contrast to Gatsby and Daisy's story: While Gatsby idolizes Daisy, Tom's affair is completely cynical.

The two stories drive each forward as well, in the way we've discussed, because Gatsby, Daisy and Tom have a stake in the outcome of each other's relationships. For example, when Daisy becomes involved with Gatsby, it's in part motivated by her anger at her husband's infidelity.

But the real joining of plot and subplot comes late in the book. Gatsby runs over Myrtle in his car, killing her. At least, that's what Myrtle's husband, the auto mechanic, believes (in fact, Daisy killed Myrtle), and it is in the wake of this outrage that Myrtle's husband kills Gatsby, whom he also believes was her lover. Thus the resolution of the subplot (Tom's affair with Myrtle, which is resolved with her death) provides a fairly thorough resolution to the main plot—Gatsby's relationship with Daisy obviously ends with *his* death. But yet another character is affected and yet another subplot indirectly resolved by this event: Nick Carraway, the narrator (although a secondary character) of the book, is so disgusted by the way that Gatsby's so-called friends, and Daisy herself, abandon him in death, that it drives him from this land of the Lifestyles of the Rich and Famous from Hell. Nick leaves the East and returns home.

When two or more plots simultaneously resolve each other this way, the reader has the sense of reading something inevitable, something plotted by Fate itself.

Yes, it's harder than it looks (but that doesn't mean you can't do it)

Sure, it's no sweat for us to take apart the great works of Western literature. Sort of makes you want to say "Okay, Leo, okay, Scott, now it's my turn!"—all the while knowing that when you sit down to weave your own perfect tapestry of plot or subplot, you may find your threads getting a little knotted up along the way.

Before you start your novel, spin out several versions of what happens. Brainstorm and experiment with various scenarios. Ask yourself what the characters need from each other. If there isn't anything, then make something up. Once you have a main character who is embroiled in a story, don't let your secondary characters sit on the sidelines to comment on the action. Ask yourself, what stake might each of them have in the outcome of that main character's story?

Or, ask yourself, what is the point of the main character's story? Then, how can you demonstrate some other aspect of that story through the secondary characters' lives? For example, if your main character is a surgeon wrestling with the ethics of his profession (i.e., cutting down on hospital stays under pressure from insurance companies), then logical subplots would deal with other doctors who in different areas either abuse their positions (perhaps doing makework surgery) or who continue to fight the good fight to maintain high standards (spending extra time with patients even when there's no extra money or glory in it).

Look, too, at how the setting of your novel might provide opportunities for subplots. No one is entirely independent of the culture in which she lives. Whether the novel is historical or contemporary, there are always social forces at work impacting the characters. So ask yourself: Does the Rotary Club approve of the new teacher's methods? Is there nuclear testing going on nearby? Is some revolutionary cell trying to recruit your protagonist?

But most of all, look to the characters themselves. Ultimately, the most stirring plots emerge from character, characters who are active and who create their own destinies. As you write about the characters and get to know them, their more subtle qualities will emerge, leading you to more plot ideas. This isn't the same as saying that a character "takes over the book," which is one of those quaint writing myths perpetuated by novelists who forget that characters aren't real people.

In the early stages of writing your novel, there will almost inevitably be gaps in your own plotting logic. But we novelists must put a lot of faith in our unconscious minds to provide us with the raw material; then we must use our conscious minds, and elbow grease, to shape that raw material into something fine. Something like a crystal vase, even.

On Target: Zeroing in on the Right Market for Your Fiction

by Ronald Spatz

No one knows better than a literary magazine editor how difficult it is to get fiction published these days. Editing a magazine is a humbling experience, even more so if the editor is also a fiction writer like me. Nowhere is this more apparent to me than when I teach "Contemporary Literature: Trends in Literary Magazine Publication," a graduate seminar at the University of Alaska Anchorage. The purpose of the seminar is to get a sense of the pulse of literary magazines, their marketing strategies, their philosophies and biases and, ultimately, their influences on contemporary art.

So picture this scene where the fiction editor of *Alaska Quarterly Review* (also the professor) and the graduate student associate editors sit around a conference table intensively studying a cross-section of the world of literary magazines. The students (and the professor) are a diverse group, coming to our program from every region in the United States. We range in age from 23 to 46. (The professor is *not* the oldest.) What we all have in common is that everyone in the room is a fiction editor and a fiction writer. Many have published fiction and/or received awards; all are serious about their writing.

By the end of the seminar, the graduate student editors have a much clearer context in which to evaluate their own philosophy and biases as editors. Moreover, with a comprehensive understanding of the literary marketplace, and the ability to see the marketing of a manuscript from an editor's perspective, the graduate student editors discover publications most likely to be interested in their fiction.

What we learned

Was there a useful "revelation" to emerge after all of this careful, academic literary study? Well, there was one simple truth that seemed to incite passionate denials: *Literary magazines are a business and publishing a story is a business transaction (for the editor as well as the writer even if the magazine only "pays" in copies).*

Why the debate on something so obvious? A group of the more idealistic members of the class simply wanted to believe that literary magazine publication is done solely for the sake of art and if it isn't, it *should* be! They argued that because most lit mags rarely break even on revenues for sales and subscriptions, let alone make big profits, they're not subject to the financial pressures of the marketplace. After all, they reasoned, the lit mags rely on unpaid staff, grant support, donations and institutional support to cover the balance, so the editors of lit mags can't possibly have the same concerns as the editors of mass market publications.

Ronald Spatz is Executive Editor of Alaska Quarterly Review *and Director of the MFA Writing Program at the University of Alaska Anchorage. A writer and filmmaker, his stories have appeared in magazines, anthologies, and won National Endowment for the Arts and Alaska State Council on the Arts awards. His most recent film,* For the Love of Ben *(The Cinema Guild), was broadcast nationally on public television.*

The idealists concluded that it is the special mission of literary magazines to ensure that new writers are on equal footing with the more established writers—the two assumptions being (1) that good work deserves a publisher without regard to the reputation or publishing credits of the writer and (2) that lit mags serve as the primary market for new writers where craft is valued and where originality and literary risk-taking (the "front line" of publishing) are welcomed and rewarded, where stories that cannot find a home in high-paying publications like *The New Yorker* or *The Atlantic Monthly* will certainly be assured their time in the sun (in print). Old myths die hard for the true believers.

That literary magazines have a business side may not seem like much of an insight to some writers, especially those working within the requirements of genre writing. Maybe there was a little wishful thinking in the ivory tower, but high ideals and talent (these folks have both) are pretty good qualities in any neighborhood.

So what are the basic facts of the lit mag marketplace? With an estimated market of more than 2,000 literary magazines and small presses, one would think there would be ample opportunities for writers to market their fiction and for editors to select fiction that will fit the needs of their journals. So much for theory. The market is flooded with many *good* stories (albeit not always ones sent to the magazines right for them), authored by new writers as well as by established writers—far more than can be published in the space available for them. In fact, on average only about one or two percent make it into print (substantially less than that in major literary magazines).

At *Alaska Quarterly Review* we receive between 1,400 and 1,700 unsolicited fiction submissions each year. Of these we have space to print up to 24. In certain newer or local magazines, the percentages are somewhat more encouraging. But no matter how you look at the situation, the odds of placing a story are, at first blush, quite daunting. Even more perplexing, some editors complain, privately and publicly, that they have trouble filling their magazines with the kind and quality of fiction they are seeking.

Quite a contradiction. But does it make any sense? It does *if* one recognizes that the purposes and goals—not to mention biases—of each literary magazine are not necessarily the same. Hence you have to target a market where your manuscript is *likely* to fit in.

How it applies to all writers

Does a writer have to take a graduate seminar to gain these insights? Absolutely not. (Remember, our seminar is primarily to enhance the skills of the *Alaska Quarterly Review* editors.) So what does a writer have to do to gain these insights about a magazine's purpose, goals and biases?

To begin, one needs to narrow the field of publications to find those suitable for their manuscript. To this end, the use of up-to-date directories like *The Novel & Short Story Writer's Market*, *The International Directory of Little Magazines & Small Presses*, *The CLMP Directory of Literary Magazines*, or any number of others is indispensable to your research.

Read these listings carefully, especially noting what the editors say they're looking for and what they do not want. With so many choices, why waste your postage and, more importantly, your time (and their time) targeting a market where your manuscript doesn't stand a chance. Another useful bit of information included in some directory listings is the ratio between the number of manuscripts published in a year and the number of manuscripts received. This gives some indication of the "odds" or competition for space in this market.

It should be emphasized, however, that although directories offer an appropriate place to start your search for the right markets for your work, to rely *exclusively* on them is a big mistake. As we found in the seminar, you can pretty much take on face value an editor's word about what type, length, content, or style is *not wanted* for the magazine. For example, if an editor says he does not publish genre writing, or novel excerpts, or stories for children, or experimental pieces, *believe it.* On the other hand, once you identify the publications that sound as though they would be receptive to the kind of work you're doing, then it's prudent to investigate further.

Check your local library or bookstore for the magazines you're interested in. If they don't carry the publication you want, you should consider buying a sample copy. Most magazines offer affordable rates for samples. If you can't spend the money, at least write for their writer's guidelines. But remember, *nothing* can replace the tried and true method of *reading* the magazine.

Some questions every writer should ask

Without question then, the way to maximize your chances of finding a market right for your work is to *read* the magazine before you submit your manuscript to its editorial staff. After you've carefully read the magazine, you might want to ask yourself a few of the questions that we used in the seminar to make sure this is a market you want to try:

Do I really want to be published in this magazine?

One often assumes that writers are so hungry for publication credits that they really don't care about the fine points of the magazine at all. If that notion is true at all, the seminar proved it is more true *before* one has read the magazine. After carefully reading the magazine, one might be surprised to find, as some of the graduate students did, that they did not want to have their work published by some of these folks, period.

With such intense competition, why would a writer exclude a potentially receptive market? It's an entirely personal decision, of course. Only you can decide the criteria that are right for you. As examples, here are the reasons why students in the seminar decided not to submit their fiction to what initially appeared (in the directories) to be "credentialed" and "credible" literary magazines:

● "This magazine is poorly edited. The quality of the stories is poor to mediocre, at best. The editors do not appear to copy edit their magazine either. Typos are everywhere. Unprofessional."

● "We found the anti-black, anti-semitic, egoistic remarks in the editor's notes abominable."

● "Examination of the fiction selections reveals a tendency toward stories that portray women negatively—as victims, as manipulators, as sexual objects and as being unable to cope and/or be successful while living life without a man. The editor also seems to favor stories that include references to skin magazines and which are almost exclusively told in a male, first-person point of view."

● "This magazine is skewed toward political correctness: Everything else is excluded. Quality is clearly secondary. All stories promote *cause* through subject matter."

You can see that with the range of these responses, selecting a magazine is a decision which must be based on both your professional and personal comfort level with the magazine.

How much fiction is published by this magazine in a year?

Many high quality fiction markets really do not publish much fiction each year—maybe only one or two stories per issue. Most of their content pages are usually devoted to nonfiction. So the "odds" at one of these publications do not favor the fiction writer. Moreover, given the few pieces that are published, space is often reserved for established writers (and sometimes the stories are solicited). It's worth seriously considering those magazines that devote a substantial portion of their pages, or all of them, to works of fiction.

Writers should also be aware that some magazines publish special issues. By definition *special* means the rules that apply to the regular issue may not apply to the special issues. The implication for new writers is that, although the special issues may contain only fiction (and lots of it), the stories are often not selected in an open process. The ripple effect is this: When a magazine commits to do a special issue, for example, on Native American writing, or Hispanic American writing, or Irish American writing, and so forth, there will necessarily be fewer opportunities for nonspecialized writing in the magazine. Space in the regular issues is also likely to be much more competitive simply because special issues and their fiction may take the place of regular issues with nonspecialized fiction. So, although in one sense the magazine can rightly claim they publish a great deal of fiction, this may not help you in marketing *your* stories to them.

Does this magazine pay its contributors?

Generally, when a publication has the resources to consistently pay its writers (a set fee, or an honorarium, in addition to copies of the magazine), the competition for space on its pages is going to be fiercer than in the nonpaying magazines.

Is the magazine open to new writers?

Whether or not a magazine devotes the lion's share of its pages to fiction, those pages may not really be open to new writers. To answer this question, it's helpful to scan several issues of the magazine—relying on just one issue can be quite misleading. Check the bio notes. This often provides a good deal of information. It will generally be pretty clear whether they publish a mix of established writers and new writers. Likewise, it will be obvious whether or not they reserve most of their space for the same writers over and over again.

Also notice whether they publish their own editorial staff, friends, faculty at their own (or nearby) institutions. If this is the case, it's a sure bet that it will be very difficult for new writers outside the clique to have much of a chance. However, some magazines actually bill themselves as serving a local or regional market, and, if you live in this area, you'll have an advantage (although local and regional publications are certainly not immune from publishing their buddies and associates).

Some editors feel that there is a direct correspondence between publishing writers with "name recognition" and enhanced prestige of their magazine—even if the works being published by these firmly established writers are far from the quality that made their reputations in the first place. Unfortunately, this practice is fueled, in part, by the readers themselves (and reviewers too), many of whom would rather read work by an author whose name they recognize, than by a writer who is unknown to them. By reading the magazine, you can tell if this is the *modus operandi* of the magazine. Although there's not much one can do about literary politics, it should motivate writers to do their homework and read the magazine before submitting a manuscript to it.

What kind of fiction do they publish? Traditional? Experimental? Both?

You could write the best story of its kind in years, utilizing six points of view to create a collage of settings and characters, an absolutely stunning, brilliant *tour de force*, and alas, have it rejected by a magazine that prints only traditional narratives. Some magazines make that very clear up front. But it's not unusual for a magazine editor to be quoted in the directories as saying something like "We're open to all forms; quality is what we're after." But when you read the magazine, you'll never find anything but a well-crafted, plotted short story, complete with plot complications, a climax, falling action, and a solid and satisfying resolution. Good stuff, for sure. But they won't touch even the tamest of postmodernist experiments.

After you've read the magazine, you'll have the proof: there just won't be any unconventional stories. You'll also discover that they'll never publish genre stories of science fiction, detective, gothic, fantasy, western adventure, or historical romance, even though they don't explicitly say so.

In general, traditional stories, with a strong sense of realism, have more markets. Very long stories and experiments in form are harder to market. A number of magazines favor inventive, experimental works exclusively. A few markets favor very long pieces. Many more will not even consider very long pieces. There are also literary magazines (*Alaska Quarterly Review*, for example) that have a strong commitment to publishing both traditional and experimental stories.

These magazines also consider both very short pieces and very long ones. But it is a fact that the very long stories or novel excerpts are still more difficult to market simply because they take up so much space. An editor has to feel *very* strongly about such a piece to commit so much space to it. That was the case two years ago at *Alaska Quarterly Review*. We accepted a long manuscript (about 60 pages, double-spaced) by a writer that had previously never published any fiction. We loved it, and it wound up winning a Pushcart Prize.

Do they have an overriding philosophy?

This is where a careful reading can really pay off. If you see example after example of intellectual, academic fiction in a magazine, chances are they feel this is their editorial bias and they are unlikely to risk "cluttering" their magazine with other kinds of work. On the other hand, one good read after another—popular choices all—might signal a magazine that values entertainment value over literary value.

Theme is important to some editors. Their magazines will evidence a strong sense of social and political investment in the fiction they choose—an agenda, if you will. Therefore those underlying philosophies can and *do* influence editorial choices. For example, a competent feminist story, or a story with a strong environmentalist theme may be selected or rejected on that basis.

Certain magazines have a very strong regional commitment, even though they do accept stories from outside of their region. These magazines focus on stories of their region (often ones that translate a sense of their cultural identity to the rest of the country).

Then there are the magazines that are not really committed to anything. A close reading of these publications will reveal that they aim to be part of the latest trend, and so what's "in" at the moment (or what they *think* is in) is what they're going to select.

Who are the readers?

Finally, there is one more question to explore. How would you characterize the audience for this magazine? In other words, who does the editor have in mind as the readers of the magazine? Once again, carefully reading a magazine will reveal important clues. For example, most of the stories accepted for a particular magazine may feature characters in their 20s or early 30s, reflecting the youthful emphasis in the demographics of the readership and marketing. This is indeed the business side of the house raising its horns and tail again, but an editor who does not know who his readers are (or indeed prints works that someone will want to read) is an editor not likely to have much luck keeping the magazine afloat. So this business side is not necessarily always crass or pandering. It's often good common sense (pun intended).

Despite all that's been said, thousands of new writers break into print each year. So take heart and take aim. Hard work, careful preparation—in this case, crafting your manuscript and finding a suitable market for it—along with persistence, have always been necessary ingredients for success in any field. Amy Hempel perhaps said it best about writing, when she observed that *will* counts as much as talent. So to those literary idealists out there: You can't relax. Not for a minute.

Small Press Roundtable

by Robin Gee

The changes that have occurred in the small press in the last 10 to 15 years have created no less than a revolution in the publishing world. Not only has the number of small presses grown significantly, but several have done quite well, expanding their businesses despite stiff competition from their larger counterparts.

While new technology—especially computers and desktop publishing—has made publishing much easier for small, independent presses, not all the growth in this sector can be attributed to cheaper production costs. Although most of these presses were started (and continue) as labors of love rather than money, many of these publishers have become quite savvy about the business side of their operations and are enjoying increased sales, better exposure and more prestige for their efforts.

For many writers, the growth of the small press has been a boon, offering more opportunities for publication at a time when the commercial market for fiction has been shrinking. This is especially true for those who are new or whose work is literary, experimental or in some way considered "not commercial enough" for the big houses.

To find out more about what this growth means to publishers and what small press publication can offer writers, we've asked a group of small, independent literary editors and publishers to answer our questions. Participating in the discussion are Allan Kornblum, fiction editor for Coffee House Press; John Oakes, publisher of Four Walls Eight Windows; Emilie Buchwald, editor for Milkweed Editions and Roland Pease, publisher of Zoland Books. They have all received awards and recognition for a number of the books they've published and, in the eyes of writers, readers, booksellers and other publishers—both large and small—each is considered a literary (and publishing) success. Below are our questions followed by the publishers' responses:

In your opinion, what are the advantages for writers working with the small press?

"In the small press writers have more say in how their book is marketed, how it is presented to the public. In short you have more influence on the end product," says John Oakes.

The reason for this is not just that smaller publishers have more time to spend with writers because they do less books, although it is certainly a factor, but also because "listening to writers" seems to be part of these publishers' basic philosophies. Adds Roland Pease, "I respect writers and believe they have good ideas that can help their books, from cover ideas to jacket copy to promotion and marketing strategies."

Emilie Buchwald agrees, "Small press books seem to get more personal attention and writers can express preferences, especially for things like their cover. We welcome their involvement in promotion and we promote every book we do."

Her comment brings us to another point: Small press publishers tend to treat all their books equally in terms of marketing and promotion. Allan Kornblum explains: "First of all the size of a small literary publisher's list is small. There's no midlist—each book has to carry its own weight. Large presses tend to allocate all their resources on a few books and dump the rest. They do a large number of books but they'll say 'we have these five or ten books likely to pull in lots of money so we should put most of our money into [marketing] them and allow the others to sink or swim.' So some books released by a large house have less money spent on them than those in the small press. The small press has less money to spend overall but they disburse it more evenly. Books published by a small press are less likely to be cast adrift."

Another advantage, says Buchwald, is "writers have the opportunity to work closely with the editor of their book." In contrast, Oakes says editors at larger presses "change like the weather."

"On the editorial side, there's a lot of job hopping in the large press," says Kornblum. "It's rare you'll find someone like Maxwell Perkins who started at Scribner's and retired there. It's more likely you'll find a young editor who will leave for a slightly better job at another company in one or two years. What happens then is manuscripts are dumped in the lap of a new editor, one who has no emotional stake in the books. In the small press there's more editorial continuity. In most instances the editor is the founder of the press, guiding it through the publishing process and being there when the book comes out."

What about disadvantages?

Kornblum says growth can actually cause problems for many small publishers. "When a small press begins to build a reputation they can become flooded with far more manuscripts than the editorial staff can handle. While a trade publisher might keep a manuscript too long, there's more chance of a small press that has recently undergone a growth period to be overwhelmed and to hold onto a manuscript 9, 12, even 18 months before it is processed, read, etc.

"Also the large press is better able to keep an adequate supply of books at all times, which helps if yours is a hot title. In the small press we have fewer resources and can't do a press run of 25,000 copies no matter how much we like a book. We're more likely to do around 5,000 copies, so we could get caught if a title becomes "hot" and we don't have enough books in the warehouse."

This is a problem Kornblum says Coffee House faced recently. The company had a very popular title, but had to wait until all of the initial printing of 5,500 copies were sold out before they could have the warehouse space available to be able to authorize a reprint. The problem with this, he says, is that it can take three weeks between restocks.

Budget constraints can be a real problem, too. Says Buchwald, "The initial advance is smaller, sometimes significantly so." Yet money problems typically affect more than just the advance.

"On the one hand," says Kornblum, "a small press offers a more equitable disbursement of resources, but if yours is a book the large press would have spent the money on, it would have been a lot more. The large press has more money to spend and more connections. Their books garner more review attention that can help sell second serial and foreign rights. They do have more advertising money and can spend more on tours and things like that. But again, if yours is a literary book or does not have a [commercial] focus on rape, murder, pillage, scandal . . . you have a better chance in the small press to have money spent on promoting your book."

Writers, therefore, need to know their books and be realistic about how much a small publisher can do. "Writers should realize we are working with small budgets, limited employee power and we don't have the same clout as the big publishers in getting reviews, readings, etc.," adds Pease.

How is the role of the writer any different in the small press than it is in "big press" publishing?

"I think the role can be the same in either a small or large publisher," says Kornblum. "Involvement depends on the author. It takes energy, aspiration and hutzpa to get out there and help promote your book. The big houses are as grateful as the small press, but it might be a little more important with the small press because we don't have the resources the larger publishers do. Still, it's pretty important no matter who you publish with."

"We give writers the opportunity to be involved," says Buchwald. "Since we do promote heavily, reading and signing books is a big factor in most of our promotions. We try to get the writer involved as much as possible in their geographic region and in the media. Sometimes we send our writers on tour, but in a much more limited way than a larger publisher. We research a niche market for every book we do and we try to take advantage of the fields in which the writer is involved."

Still, Kornblum says, the level of involvement a writer takes should be left up to the writer. Some people are not comfortable or are unable to take on heavy promotion duties. Writers should remain "true to their natures," he says.

Pease says, however, writers must be realistic about how much their publishers can do as well. "Authors can be a tremendous help promoting their books, but they must respect our position—we share a common goal and we will do all we can to help their books, but we are working on a number of books at once, and we are not the employees of the writer. There's a fine line. In general we are open to a close working relationship, and the large publishers can't quite offer that much."

Despite the downturn in the economy in the last 10 years or so, there seem to be more small presses than ever and many seem to have grown stronger over this time period. What factors do you feel have contributed to the continued resilience of small press publishing? What are the things that seem to make or break a press?

"I think a lot has to do with the zeal and endurance of the publishers," says Buchwald. "It depends on how small you are. In a one- or two-person operation, the burnout factor comes into play. For a press to make it, to evolve, it has to include three, four or more people. Under this, it's just too hard not to become discouraged. The amount of work it takes to keep a press running is tremendous. It's a seven-day-a-week kind of job.

"You must be able to attract readership," she says. "You have to find a niche. Presses are becoming very knowledgeable about getting books to the right audience."

Kornblum agrees, "It makes sense to go with your strengths. Booksellers have learned this. It's suicide to try to beat the chain stores with discounts, so to survive they have to have more knowledge, do more reaching out to the community—to the African-American, Hispanic, Asian communities. These stores offer diversity that a chain store does not and they offer a knowledgeable staff.

"By the same token an independent small literary press can't try to beat a New York publisher at their game. They can't do celebrity biographies, political scandals, novels about rape, murder, pillage and assorted nasties . . . Our strength comes from recognizing top literary talent offering thoughtful aspects of examined lives, especially writing about non-white, non-dominant cultures. Small presses have grown because they have stayed true to their strengths and to their constituencies. Whether it is feminist, multicultural or literary writing, we must stay true to our roots and what we know best."

While finding and maintaining a niche is a key factor in the success of many small presses, Buchwald says a low overhead and the ability to move quickly on trends in the market have also helped presses get ahead. "That's it—low overhead, the ability to move quickly when we see new opportunities, to recognize opportunities and to get a book out in a year (major presses take longer to go through the whole publishing process). If one person makes the final decision the whole process is going to go faster."

Pease says many small presses are doing well, simply because they fill a real need. "Most people in small press publishing are doing what they are doing because they care about literature. That's what keeps me going. Certainly the economics of a book are extremely challenging and successes—great reviews, strong sales—are essential, if not for every book, for enough of them. Small presses exist, though, because there is a great need for them. The large publishing companies focus more on 'commercial' books than ever, so more literary books are looking for a home."

Yet Oakes says he doesn't think the growth in the small press field is necessarily a good thing. "I disagree with the basic statement. I don't see it as resilience [in the market] but, rather, there has been a steady number of people who *think* they can make it. I think the democratization of the field can be a good thing, but there is a bad side in that some people feel anyone can be a publisher, editor or writer. Sure, there's a huge amount of people coming into the field, but at a lower level."

What are the challenges you face as a small press publisher and how have you coped with funding problems and other pressures?

"Two words: cash flow!," says Oakes. "What do we do to cope? Sometimes I wish we had a padded room in the back where people could just go and scream. Dan [Oakes' partner, Dan Simon] plays a regular game of tennis; I go to karate a lot . . . Actually, I don't know how we do it but we do."

"Cash flow is of tremendous importance to all publishers, because we must invest in something long before we see any return, so the ability to generate cash as you need it is a concern," explains Buchwald. "More foundations are setting up loan funds, though, and also funding for nonprofit presses. Yet, applying for loans," she says, "is a very time-consuming task in itself."

"Money *is* a problem," echoes Kornblum, "and it causes a number of symptoms. For example, if a press has grown in reputation it could go from receiving 300 manuscripts a year to 3,000, but it may not be able to afford to add another editorial position to handle the load. Money shortages crop up in day-to-day operations, too.

"Yet, there are other issues as well as money. In our attempt to stake out a claim for providing a venue for writers from different cultures, we must try not to cheapen it by grabbing at anything that comes in. In general I think the literary press can't be accused of that. It's done a wonderful job of presenting those writers with dignity and commitment, but there can be a danger . . . The biggest problem or challenge is to avoid getting away from what we do best."

Pease lists a number of other problems—keeping overhead costs down, increasing sales and maintaining a stable work force. "People come and go, so a three-person office is too often in turmoil when turnovers occur." Still, he sums up the feelings expressed by all the participants, "These challenges exist everyday in every way, but it is a worthwhile, meaningful struggle."

What would you say is the single-most important change that has occurred in the small press field in the last few years and why is it important?

"On the positive side: writers of talent who might ordinarily have sought out larger publishers are looking at smaller presses," says Pease. "On perhaps the not so positive side: The superstores are beginning to crowd out the independent bookstores, and they are not as receptive to small press books. That's a troubling trend."

Buchwald agrees. "The past few years have been a big challenge for bookstores, a real shakeout in bookselling. With the encroachment of the new large chains, independent bookstores are becoming severely challenged and because independent bookstores devote space to the small press, this could factor in the way things happen for us, too."

Yet one promising trend, she says, is that some of the really big stores are beginning to purchase small press books. "People are beginning to recognize that small, independent presses play a significant role in American literature. Both readers and funders are seeing that there is a field of literary publishers who really are making a significant contribution."

"In the small literary press I've noticed a growing professionalism and an increased awareness of how to serve our audiences as well as our writers," says Kornblum. "Many small press publishers came in with a commitment to writers and writing, but not much know-how about how to publish (and market) good books. We've grown in the marketing and administrative parts of our operations. Small presses are keeping better track of books, the money owed, sales. We've learned to take care of our houses and how to adequately serve our audiences. We're making really good use of the tools now available."

Tools—especially computers—have made a lot of things easier for small presses. Oakes sees this as just the beginning. "To me, your question is easy. The increasing use of the personal computer has been the most important change. The reason is it allows small presses to cut production costs all around—both design and typesetting. We're heading toward eliminating these outside costs and we're just starting to use the technology."

What do you see as the small press's future and how do you think it will affect writers?

"The future is very bright right now," says Kornblum. "As larger presses continue their trend toward consolidation, their books have to bear the burden of the rising costs of marketing and production and the servicing of their many departments. This has led to a more cautious editorial stance. Many top mid-list writers who used to have a home in the large press are looking to small press publication.

"Also as small presses are making a contribution to the literary community of writers and readers, more in the philanthropic community are starting to realize how important our role is and they are having a greater interest in helping us."

Oakes sees the "computer revolution" taking the small press in new directions. "It would be logical to assume that electronic publishing is going to expand, that composition and other production costs will become cheaper. The amount of people who have the technology is growing. Yet, I don't know how this will affect writers. Nonfiction publishers are starting to think about interactive material. Maybe there will be a new form of fiction as well. There's a lot of exciting possibilities. These are not necessarily good or bad, but they will happen."

Buchwald says she expects to see even more growth. "I see the urge to publish as one that will continue and I expect to see more small presses started. I expect to see more growth in those that have already become established. In 10 to 20 years these will stabilize and become landmarks in the field. The more of us and the more stable we become the better it will be for the future of American letters."

"Small independent presses will have a stronger role to play in the publishing world," predicts Pease. "As many of these presses 'grow up' and become recognized for their strong literary programs, they cannot be ignored or denied. And this can only be a good development for all writers."

Using Setting As a Key to Promoting Your Book

by Nancy Berland

After laboring nine months to write the first novel I sold, I learned a shocking fact of publishing life. Once in the stores, *Midnight Blue* would have a four-week shelf life. All copies not sold by the "pull date" would be stripped—their covers ripped off and returned to Harlequin for full credit. The stripped books would be destroyed. Neither the publisher nor I would earn a cent on the stripped copies.

Moreover, I learned mass market paperback publishers keep score. Those big guys in commercial publishing, like Harlequin Books, count how many copies go out their doors and how many covers come back. Using those figures, they compute what is known in the industry as an author's sell-through—the percentage of books sold versus books shipped to retail and wholesale accounts.

What makes an author of commercial novels jittery is that her sell-through is as important to her career as her storytelling ability. If, on two consecutive books, her sell-through falls below 50 percent, the figure most commercial paperback publishers consider a healthy performance, she may very well kiss her sweet publishing career good-bye. She's a non-seller, a loser, regardless of the fact that so-so covers or unavoidable botch-ups in distribution may have influenced her sales. Add in the fact that few commercial publishers devote promotion budgets to authors who aren't proven bestsellers, and the picture is clear. Other than writing a good book, the only thing a fledgling author can do to affect her sell-through is to invest her own time and money in sales-boosting promotions.

Develop a promotional plan

That's why six months before my first Harlequin Superromance hit the stores, I carved time from my writing schedule to develop a promotional plan for *Midnight Blue*. My first question was, what would be my promotional hook? From my public relations background, I knew people enjoyed reading books set in their communities. The familiar landmarks and sensory detail enable them to slip into the skin of the characters and lose themselves in the stories.

My editors had already told me they were enchanted with my novel's setting, the turn-of-the-century Texas town of Granbury, population 5,000. Although my plot revolved around a fictitious Granbury mayor who had schemed and murdered, I figured the book would appeal to local residents. I had researched the town meticulously, portrayed it favorably and set scenes in places familiar to them. As for other setting-based sales potential, *Midnight Blue* opened with a zany bed race around the restored town square, which my research revealed had actually taken place during one of Granbury's annual Fourth of July celebrations. That day-long event attracts more than 20,000 people with money in their pockets

Nancy Berland *is a member of Romance Writers of America and Novelists, Inc. She is the author of five published romance novels, with two more scheduled for release. Her current project is a romantic suspense series about a "L.A. Law"-type public relations agency in Phoenix, which she based on her experiences as public information director of a national trade association.*

to Granbury. What better souvenir of their visit than a $3.95 book set in Granbury with an opening reminiscent of the actual Fourth of July festivities?

Harlequin had designated the book as a June release. In a call to the public relations department I learned several thousand copies would be available for special shipment to Granbury for Fourth of July signings. I had found a promotional hook and determined availability of books. Next I needed a partner in promotions.

I mailed a copy of my line-edited manuscript to Dee Gormley, the independent bookseller on Granbury's town square. In my cover letter I offered to do a signing on the Fourth of July in her store, Books on the Square.

By the end of three weeks, though, Dee hadn't responded to my letter. I gathered up my courage and called for her verdict. She said she had only one problem with the book. My writer's insecurity kicked in. I thought, she hates it. She's going to call my editor and demand Harlequin cease plans to publish it. My career will be over before it begins. Then Dee explained the problem. She said I had portrayed Granbury so accurately, she feared Harlequin wouldn't print enough copies beyond their advance orders to fill her needs.

That phone call launched a friendship that endures to this day. Although I was a trained public relations professional, Dee Gormley taught me loads about book promotions. Working together, we sold 2,500 copies of *Midnight Blue* in that town of 5,000 people. Our promotions earned us extensive coverage in the local newspaper and numerous other publications, plus a dandy feature in the *Fort Worth Star-Telegram* that was picked up and distributed by the Associated Press. Fort Worth's NBC affiliate, KXAS-TV, caught the wire story and sent a crew to Granbury to film a news feature on *Midnight Blue* that they broadcast during the holiday weekend.

The success of our setting-based promotions earned the attention of Harlequin, articles in and a promotional award from *Romantic Times* magazine, and speaking engagements at writers' and book publishers' local, regional and national conferences. As my royalties later showed, the media coverage and this secondary round of attention generated sales across the country that favorably impacted my sell-through.

Be creative

While the specifics of my experiences concern promotion of a novel with a small-town setting hook, the principles can be applied to a book set in a city of any population.

To maximize media coverage, create a promotions tie-in that will benefit a local charity or nonprofit organization. *Midnight Blue*'s main theme, which I gleaned from my setting research, was historical preservation. In Granbury proud citizens of all ages pitch in to preserve the town's rich cultural heritage. (The older gentlemen there needlepointed the cushions in the Opera House, which was restored as a playhouse with its own resident company.) Dee tacked a buck on to the book's $2.95 cover price with a label explaining the extra dollar would go into a fund to restore Granbury's old electric power plant as a museum for the town's artifacts. Although she gave book buyers the option of refusing to pay the added dollar, all but a few customers cooperated. This nonprofit angle provided the media with a community interest news hook, which they covered extensively, mentioning dates, times and locations of book signings.

Be creative about locations of book signings, if possible utilizing places that play key roles in your novel's plot. At Dee's suggestion, I spent five days in Granbury surrounding the Fourth of July. During that time she staged several signings, including a "Meet the Author" riverboat cruise on the Brazos River that borders the town. (A key scene takes place on the riverboat.) A local restaurant owner catered the on-board wine and cheese party, donating ticket sale profits to restoration of that electric power plant. Dee was there with her money box, and I signed books until my hand hurt.

Generate excitement about the book in advance of the author's appearance. Because Dee was enthusiastic about how I had portrayed Granbury, she created local interest by passing my manuscript among town leaders, one chapter at a time. I had worked hard to end each chapter on a hook. Dee said those influential people who read the advance copy of my manuscript kept pestering her for the next chapter, and they talked about it with their friends.

Celebrity status sells books. Readers like to buy books from authors they think have stardust on their shoulders. Because local residents don't know an author from out-of-town, they're likely to believe she's a bigger celebrity than someone they see every day. If your book is complimentary to their city, these same people will be flattered you thought enough of their community to set a book there.

Dee talked a Granbury restauranteur into donating a free dinner at her restored Queen Anne Victorian mansion. To give me the aura of celebrity, Dee auctioned me off as "Dinner with a Famous Author" at that restaurant during the Optimists' Club local fundraiser a couple of weeks prior to the Fourth of July weekend. (By the way, a fictitious Queen Anne Victorian mansion played heavily in my novel's plot.)

For the parade, Dee put me in the back of a flashy Corvette convertible that a friend of hers drove in the parade. I enlarged the cover of my book and mounted it on a sturdy $2' \times 3'$ board, then affixed the poster to the back of the Corvette. On both sides of the car Dee stretched a banner which read, "Meet Nancy Landon" (my Harlequin pen name), with the time and location of the booksigning that followed the parade. A first-time author, I was uncomfortable with this sudden celebrity status, but I kept reminding myself of my goal: to impact my book's sell-through.

Work with the media and others

Increase the chances the media will run stories on your appearances by sending them tailored releases. Prior to the Fourth of July weekend, Dee mailed me a list of 50 media outlets in surrounding towns, from which Granbury traditionally draws visitors to its Fourth of July festivities. I wrote a basic release but tailored the lead paragraph to fit each newspaper. For example, the release I wrote for the Graham, Texas newspaper began, "Graham residents who take in Granbury's all-day Fourth of July festivities will find a celebrity guest who turned the holiday in this neighboring town into a successful novel."

Consider this critical timing factor when selecting booksigning dates: The news media are like other employers—short staffed around holidays, when people take vacations. Because retail stores advertise heavily at these times to encourage shoppers to drop in during their days off, the news media may find themselves short of staff and long on need for copy with a local tie-in.

Remember that editors are busy people. When contacting one in advance, say something like, "If you're looking for a Fourth of July feature with a local angle, I have a fresh idea for you." Then describe *in one sentence* your event and its uniqueness. Make your initial contact three to four weeks in advance of the event.

Generate advance sales. At the actual signing an author can autograph only so many books. Contact local organizations, such as women's clubs, in advance with order forms on which their members may affix their payments and specify to whom they wish their books autographed. As soon as you arrive in town, tackle the task of signing these books. Buyers can either pick up their orders in the book store at their leisure, or the bookseller can deliver the signed copies to the organization at its next meeting. For a promoted signing, books will sell in the store at least one week prior and one week after the event. If possible, generically autograph copies of your book to be sold during these periods.

Speaking engagements and other personal appearances prior to the booksigning provide excellent opportunities to promote your novel. Dee scheduled me to drop in on two groups that meet informally on the Granbury square, and I spoke to a civic group. If there's a local writers' group, by all means offer to speak. Other possibilities include gardening, book review and professional clubs, plus junior high, high school and college classes in English and professional writing.

Don't try to create a crowd for a booksigning; take advantage of an existing crowd. For Dee and me, that meant the 20,000 people who swamped Granbury's town square for the Fourth of July parade and craft fair. Dee set up tables and a cash register on the sidewalk outside her store. Buyers lined up to buy autographed copies. We sold 300 copies during that one signing.

Be prepared for rejection. Write your book from your heart. *If* the final story is complimentary to the setting community, *if* you can afford time away from your writing, *if* you're willing and able to invest time and money in book promotions, contact a bookseller in that community. Give her the opportunity to read your manuscript before asking her to cooperate with you on promotions. If her response is lukewarm, her reticence to cooperate may be because her vision of her community differs from yours.

Know your responsibilities

Prima donnas need not bother to promote. Neither Dee nor I complained about the blazing sun or the 95-degree heat during that booksigning on the sidewalk. We sat at those tables as long as anyone wanted to buy a book. That meant we worked beyond the originally scheduled closing of the three-hour signing. I wrote a personal dedication to each buyer on the title page, which required more effort but increased chances books wouldn't be returned (and stripped). Always we smiled—at the customers, at the fabulous store employees who talked up sales during the signing and the week before, and at the remote radio crew who interviewed us.

Don't expect the bookseller to pay for all the promotions. Dee and I discussed in advance our respective responsibilities, as well as who would pay for what. Because we secured considerable coverage in the news media with our restoration of the old electric power plant tie-in, the need for advertising was reduced, but Dee assumed this expense, as well as printing and postage for 400 invitations for the riverboat party and a myriad of miscellaneous items. The expenses I covered included postage for and long distance calls to the media; travel to and lodging in Granbury; press kits, media releases and one-color flyers promoting the Fourth of July booksigning that we posted in other stores in Granbury and used as bag stuffers the week prior to the big event. I provided attractive, two-color bookmarks promoting *Midnight Blue*, the giant book cover blow-up for the parade car and personal publicity photos.

Don't expect to earn, through book sales in the setting city, the money you invest in your promotions. The publicity you generate will prompt more book sales elsewhere, help build your career and earn publishers' respect for you as an effective promoter. Although that ability will not guarantee you'll sell a book to a publisher, it may, in the future, earn you a bigger advance on royalties or a higher slot on a publisher's list. Generally, the higher the slot on the list, the larger your print run, and the more money you'll earn in royalties.

Promptly after the promotions, write thank you notes to all those who helped. The Granbury newspaper printed my thank you letter to the editor, prompting even more book sales.

Some lessons learned

The *Midnight Blue* promotions, keyed to the book's setting, produced results beyond my wildest dreams and gave me a respectable sell-through. For that success and the attention it earned me in the publishing business, I credit that savvy bookseller, Dee Gormley. Our ability to work together, the fact that we began our promotions early, my public relations background and simple luck all combined to produce successful results.

My luck hasn't always been that stellar. Bolstered by the *Midnight Blue* successes, I developed a similar promotional plan for my second Harlequin Superromance. An October, 1990 release, *Sound Waves* focused on the hearing impaired and revolved around Tulsa, Oklahoma's Labor Day raft race down the Arkansas River. Tulsa's KRMG Radio, a major sponsor of the annual race, agreed to cooperate with me in the promotions. On the strength of the earlier book's sales, KRMG estimated they would need 6,000 copies of *Sound Waves* during the Labor Day weekend. I agreed to spend a few days in advance of the race in Tulsa, doing personal appearances and live interviews about the book and its local flavor. Since my book's heroine trained hearing ear dogs, the extra buck tacked on to the book's cover price would go to the organization that trained such dogs in Oklahoma.

Everything hinged on one factor—Harlequin's ability to ship to Tulsa from the Buffalo, N.Y. distribution center 6,000 books in time for the raft race, which was three days prior to the scheduled release. Harlequin was willing, but their corporate hands were tied. Federal regulations prohibit a publisher from giving one segment of its customer base an unfair advantage over others. Simply put, Harlequin couldn't ship *Sound Waves* early to the coordinating Tulsa bookseller without making copies available to all other segments in that marketing area. The implications for Harlequin were staggering. When my editor learned of the problem, she tried to move the release date forward a month but couldn't juggle the schedule.

Lesson learned: Before proceeding with elaborate plans to promote a book in the setting city, check first with your publisher for book availability. Usually the person to contact isn't your editor but your publisher's public relations department. If such a department doesn't exist at your publisher, ask who is responsible for making sure special orders arrive in time for author signings and contact her.

While some promotions may work and some may fail, one fact is clear. Writing and promoting a book set in an existing community can generate extra book sales, increase an author's sell-through and thus help earn publishers' respect. When an author moves from genre fiction to the mainstream arena, that respect may translate into a better spot on a publisher's list, a heftier advance, bigger print run and healthier royalty checks.

Commercial Fiction Trend Report

by Robin Gee

It looks like the cautious optimism demonstrated by publishers in recent years is starting to pay off. While sales were not up significantly, most publishers reported modest increases last year, putting the U.S. publishing industry sales figures at just over $16 billion. In an October 4, 1993, *Publishers Weekly* report, the nation's top 11 largest general trade publishers' sales rose an average of 6 percent last year—that's pretty good news after some fairly bad years.

It will be awhile, however, before any of this moderate good fortune will trickle down to most writers. Publishers are still exercising caution. A few have added new lines, but many are either holding steady or cutting back the number of titles published in each line. For writers, therefore, competition at larger publishers remains keen.

Although established-name authors still get the lion's share of advance money and promotion funds, publishers are continuing to look for promising new writers. While Michael Crichton and John Grisham continue to land big-money deals, so have newcomers like Allan R. Folsom whose first book, the thriller *The Day After Tomorrow*, garnered a record advance of more than $2 million from a deal with Little, Brown and Warner Books. Nancy Taylor Rosenberg's first book, the courtroom thriller *Mitigating Circumstances* published by Dutton, brought her a six-figure movie deal, and rights for her second book, *Interest of Justice*, have already been sold for a television mini-series.

Yet, as we mentioned in this report last year, publishers are beginning to realize that it is the less sensational, but steady-selling midlist authors who are the real strength behind a solid fiction list. Some of these authors have found a home at small literary and university presses in the last few years, and it is our prediction that large publishers will be working on ways to combat this trend. Some have come up with programs to support newer books and highlight literary authors. We expect more of this in the next few years.

Some trends and events

As for specific trends in publishing this year, perhaps the most interesting is the growth of the superstore bookstore. Barnes and Noble and Borders Books have opened enormous stores across the country and early reports are that these are doing quite well. These megastores offer the widest selection of books possible and many feature in-house coffee shops and cafes and special stages for book signings, readings and other community events.

For writers, this is a mixed blessing. Unlike the cramped mall-style chain stores, these stores have the capacity to include more backlist, and publishers are learning that a good fiction backlist is a definite plus. Publishers are finding this is especially true if the author's latest book has received recent attention and praise. These stores also have room for books from smaller presses and some are beginning to seek these out. On the downside, this may hurt small, independent stores, whose expertise and loyal customer bases have supported many a literary and small press writer.

For readers, the whole process seems like a win-win situation. Not only are the big stores offering more services and wider selection, the competition between superstores and independents has created a flurry of readings and other community-oriented events aimed at attracting or keeping customers.

Several stories in the trade press recently deal with the importance of the repeat book buyer, and publishers are looking for ways to help bookstores keep buyers coming back. Stores, with the help of publishers, are offering special discounts and little "perks" like bookmarks and samplers. Samplers are books created by the publisher that include opening chapters from one or several books. A few mass market publishers have also included excerpts of new books at the end of other books by the same author—just enough to whet the reader's appetite for more.

Interest in things literary seems to be growing and this can only be a good trend for writers. While the number of people who buy books remains small, it seems book-related events are becoming popular across the country. Once readings were relegated to a few literary bookstores and coffee houses mostly in college areas, but now it seems more and more restaurants and local taverns are holding reading nights. Book groups—groups of people who meet regularly to read and discuss specific books—are cropping up everywhere and publishers are supporting this by offering books on how to start and maintain a group. A few publishers have even created companion books for groups designed to supplement the books they are reading.

Although we wouldn't call it a trend yet, we've seen a few more electronic book publishers this year and the industry is beginning to discuss the possible impact of electronic books on the market. Electronic rights are the big issue right now and the agents' professional organization, the Association of Authors Representatives, recently released a paper on the subject. Writers' groups are watching matters closely to make sure writers' rights are protected.

About market-watching

The most important thing to remember about the market for fiction is that, while there are some definite trends, publishers buy books up to two years in advance. What is being published now may not necessarily reflect what publishers are currently interested in. On the other hand, the changes in book publishing tend to be gradual, so it may take several years for a so-called trend to peak. If you are a savvy market watcher, you can spot trends as they begin to take hold.

The commercial book publishing market appears to be cyclical. A particular type of book will catch on and publishers try frantically to duplicate the success by publishing more like it. New writers who happen to be writing books of that type are in demand and many break into publishing on the tails of a good trend. Over time, however, if the trend continues too long, too many books of that type—of both good and bad quality—flood the market and publishers cut back. At that time, no matter how well-written your book is, you'll have a tougher time selling it. Yet, that particular type of book may not be necessarily dead. Time goes by and, if another book of that type does well, it may signal a resurgence.

Watch out for saturation. Some trends that may be past their prime include serial killers, hard-boiled female private eyes and courtroom thrillers. This is *not* to say that if your book includes any of these subjects it won't sell. It means you may have an uphill battle. The best insurance, of course, is quality—and persistence.

Some specific growth areas

Overall, audience expansion continues to affect all areas of fiction. Right now you'll find picture books designed to appeal to adults and toddlers alike, mysteries with science fiction elements and high-tech thrillers with religious themes. As the audience expands for the various genres, the tendency for these books to crossover to mainstream and other areas increases.

Before looking at the various categories of popular fiction, we'd like to mention a few other areas of growth within the fiction publishing industry. We'll start with children's books as this is an area that has experienced tremendous growth in the last few years. Things are starting to slow down, however. The "boom" in children's book publishing in the 1980s was based on the large number of children whose parents were baby boomers. Now these children are middle-graders and young adults, an age group that tends to do less reading than their younger counterparts.

Where there once was a surge in pre-school and young reader books, now the emphasis is on books for older children, especially young adult. There's one word to remember in young adult fiction right now—horror! Zebra's new young adult imprint, Z-Fave, includes the series "Scream" and "Nightmare Club" and Scholastic has "Goosebumps" for middle readers. Some authors to watch in this area are Christopher Pike, John Peel and R.L. Stine, whose "Fear Street" series for Pocket/Archway is doing very well. Other publishers offering young adult horror include Bantam, Random House and Knopf Books for Young Readers.

Multiculturalism is still a key term in children's book publishing. For a discussion of writing that includes multicultural themes see the 1994 *Children's Writer's and Illustrator's Market*, a good source of markets for both children's writers and artists. The growth in the number of multicultural books for children is uneven, says Editor Christine Martin, because, while there are more books focusing on African-American characters and themes, readers are asking for books featuring other ethnic groups and cultures. Writers whose work is about Hispanic or Asian-American characters are in demand. One fairly new publisher, Lee and Low Books, is publishing books featuring American children with different backgrounds from Japanese to Guatemalan and their books are doing well. Another publisher to watch is Curbstone, known for its interest in multicultural books for adults. In line with the emphasis on multicultural themes, books that can be published in both Spanish and English simultaneously are also in demand.

Religious fiction is another area of growth. In fact, while fiction books are only a small portion of the religious publishing field, it is the fastest growing area. Recent reports indicate the number of religious fiction books published in the last five years has doubled.

The big news in religious fiction, however, is the changing nature of its subject matter. Publishers are not very interested in heavy-handed, preachy material any more. What they want are contemporary themes and hard-hitting subject matter. More and more religious writers, led by writers such as Frank Peretti, are making it onto mainstream book lists. Not only is religious fiction crossing over to the mainstream, more religious fiction publishers are venturing into category romance, mystery and even science fiction. Crossway has become a leader in this field of fiction, but other publishers including Zondervan, Harvest House and Bethany House are also doing their share of these books. Writers to watch in this area are Roy Maynard who writes a series of Christian detective novels and thriller author Dave Hunt.

According to *Publishers Weekly*, series books are doing well with religious publishers. Moody Books has several including the "Christian Epic" series featuring Christian heroes; "Daughters of Courage," a multigenerational family saga; and the "Jack Preston Mystery" series. Western and romance series are very popular, too.

There's an interesting trend starting to happen in the comic books field. Comics featuring African-American superheroes are in demand. Led by independents like Big City Comics who first introduced *Brother Man* comics in 1991, larger publishers are now trying to get in on the act. DC Comics recently signed a deal with the small publisher Milestone Media to publish an African-American comic and a group of independents, ANIA, has banded together to publish four such series. With names like *Hardware, Ebony Warrior* and *Heru, Son of Ausar*, these comics are becoming very popular. While right now much of this work is still self-published, watch for the big hitters—Marvel and DC—to express interest in acquiring similar comic series.

Graphic novels are still doing well and the number of adult comics is growing. Although for a long time this was a sort of underground venture and much of it still is, the growing popularity of this type of work will not keep it there much longer. For example, several big-name authors have granted permission to have their work featured in graphic form. HarperCollins and Eclipse comics recently signed a deal to put Dean Koontz's work in graphic format.

June 1993 marked the second year for National Gay and Lesbian Book Month, and growth in this market has been tremendous. As with other categories of fiction in growth periods, there is lots of crossover between the gay and mainstream markets. Books most likely to move into mainstream are written by gay authors but tend to have broad-based subject matters. Overall, there's a growing acceptance for work by gay and lesbian writers. For example, Dorothy Allison's book *Bastard Out of Carolina* has been met with critical acclaim from all sectors of the publishing community. At this time it appears male writers have the edge in mainstream publishing, however. You'll find more gay than lesbian writers at large publishing houses, but this may change soon.

Despite the recent success in the broader field, many gay and lesbian writers maintain close ties to their communities and keep a careful watch on how they are being treated by mainstream publishers. Gay and lesbian writers in PEN recently formed a special committee to combat censorship against writers in their community.

Fantasy

While most publishers continue to publish science fiction and fantasy together, fantasy has clearly become a large enough sector in the field to warrant separate examination. Elves are big this year—particularly elves who mingle with humans, often wreaking havoc. This area has actually been dubbed "elves in the real world" and a good example is Baen's "Serrated Edge" series by veteran fantasy author Mercedes Lackey. Magic also continues as an important topic as does work with medieval themes, dragon fantasy and humorous fantasy.

Most fantasy continues to be published in series, usually in trilogies. Fantasy epics are also gaining in popularity featuring sagas that continue for several books. Del Rey's David Eddings and Daw's Tad Williams are two writers whose books have become long series.

The market for young adult fantasy is growing in line with all sectors of the young adult fiction market. Walker and Company recently expanded its young adult fantasy line. Watch for a crossover in this part of the market from dark fantasy to horror.

Horror

A few years ago it appeared the market for horror was almost dead, but it seems to have come back strong in recent months. This can be directly attributed to two things: the young adult horror surge and the influx of talented women horror writers.

As mentioned earlier, publishers seem to be falling over each other trying to beef up their existing young adult lines to include horror or they are creating new lines to accommodate the growth in this area. Some say they are searching for more horror aimed at middle-grade readers in the eight-to-12-year-old age group. These readers are not quite ready for Stephen King, but they do like graphic horror. While in this age group girls are the big readers, publishers are striving to make these books appeal to boys and girls alike.

Thanks to Dell's Abyss line, the horror field is seeing a lot of good new female authors including Melanie Tem, Tanith Lee and Kathe Koja. Also watch new Dell author Poppy Z. Brite, whose first novel *Lost Souls* received several good reviews. Strong characters and literary horror appeal to women readers, and publishers are actively pursuing this audience. Look for more horror featuring subjects that play particularly on women's fears such as child abuse, spouse abuse, sexual harassment and rape.

Perhaps one of the strongest literary figures in horror is the vampire. Vampire books, such as Kim Newman's *Anno Dracula*, are doing so well they could become a subgenre in themselves. Vampires also lead the way in erotic-themed horror, another growth area. Anne Rice's books in particular blend sensuality and horror.

As with any genre going into its maturity stage, the number of crossover horror books is growing. You'll find romances and mysteries with clear horror elements from ghostly love stories to hard-boiled vampire detectives. P.N. Elrod's vampire detective series is a good example of this trend.

Markets open to short horror fiction continue to be mainly anthologies rather than magazines, although there are a number of small journals devoted to horror. Dell has continued its anthology series featuring both original work and reprints. The latest in this series are *The Ultimate Witch* and *The Ultimate Zombie*. Ellen Datlow and Terri Windling continue their much acclaimed anthology for St. Martin's Press, *The Year's Best Fantasy and Horror* and DAW books publishes *The Year's Best Horror Stories*. Carroll and Graf also publishes *Best New Horror*. The list of anthologies is endless and most include both original and reprinted work.

Mystery

The mystery field has long been the sales leader in category fiction and it remains so, perhaps because so many mysteries crossover into the mainstream market. The President gave the mystery field a little boost this year by making his mystery reading habits public. In fact, the Mystery Writers of America made him their "Reader of the Year."

Yet even without help from the White House, it's been a good year for mystery. Many books are being made into movies and this trend not only helps the book from which the film is made but it gives a boost to the author's entire backlist. Publishers are paying more attention to mystery backlist in general these days, as they've grown to realize mystery readers tend to read all the books by their favorite authors—a successful book can send readers back to the stores demanding books published years before. A good example of this is Lillian Jackson Braun. Her recent success with her "Cat Who" series sparked a revival of demand for books she wrote years ago.

Because of the importance of backlist in mystery, independent mystery bookstores have become an important factor in keeping mystery sales up. There are about 100 of these stores across the country with the space to keep most or all of an author's books in stock.

A few mystery events worth noting this year: It was the 100th birthday of Dorothy L. Sayers, one of the leading writers of British detective fiction. A Nancy Drew conference went well in Iowa and may signal an interest in young adult mystery. The founder of Mysterious Press, Otto Penzler, sold his company to Warner Books and opened a new company under his own name. His first books were published in Fall 1993, while the original press, now a Warner imprint, is also doing well. Berkley launched a new hardcover program which will include mysteries and Zebra started a new paperback imprint, Partners in Crime.

Medical and legal thrillers are still doing well. The emphasis on "different" detectives for the sake of difference is waning, however. Watch for continued crossover between science fiction, romance, horror and mystery.

Lastly, 1993 was a sad year in mystery as it marked the passing of television's best-known detective, Perry Mason, also known as Raymond Burr. The mystery world also mourns the loss of Leslie Charteris, author of "The Saint" series.

Romance

The market for romance continues to do well, as publishers seem to be getting farther and farther away from "formula" publishing. One subject very popular in romance seems to defy formula: the futuristic romance. These books feature romances set in future worlds, but they may also involve time travel. Another related area that is sometimes grouped with these are fantasy or supernatural romances involving vampires, ghosts or other "dark" heroes. Leisure Books leads the way in this area, but almost every publisher is making room for these types of romance on their lists.

This year Leisure introduced Lovespell, its new imprint devoted to time travel and future themes. Also NAL's new Topaz line features Topaz Dreamspun for ghost romances. Harlequin has added a time-travel subseries to its Intrigue line and Zebra has made its Pinnacle line open to this type of romance. In keeping with the trend toward supernatural and other horror elements, Silhouette started its "Shadows" line this year and the publisher describes it as "soft horror."

Other trends in subject matter include homey, pioneer themes, now called Americana, and several romances featuring older characters. Zebra's To Love Again line features characters in the "second half" of their lives. Fatherhood is also a popular theme. Zebra has discontinued its Lucky in Love line, but plans a line devoted to married couples as well as one featuring African-American characters.

Trilogies are also very big, especially in Americana and western romance lines. Short romance fiction still has few outlets, but romance publishers are putting together more holiday and summer-reading collections. Although it is actually a market for long fiction, the Starlog Group, a well-known magazine publisher, launched two romance magazines this year—*Moonlight* for contemporary romance and *Rhapsody* for historicals. These magazines are published in alternating months, and each issue features one complete novel.

A few other romance events: Cover-boy Fabio has penned his own romance, *The Pirate* for Avon. The Meteor Publishing Corporation's British owner decided to close up shop in the U.S., ending the well-respected Kismet line of romances. And romance writers report more interest in online networking with other romance authors. Most popular is RomEX on Genie.

Science fiction

There was a little shifting around in the science fiction field this year. Notably, John Silbersack left Warner Books to start a new science fiction line at HarperCollins and Betsy Mitchell joined Warner to help revitalize that line. TOR Books will continue using its name for their mass market line of books (where they publish most of their science fiction), but has developed two new imprints, Forge Books for mainstream novels and pyschological horror hardcover fiction and Orb trade paperbacks which will help keep older works in the market. *Expanse* is a new science fiction magazine and *Tomorrow*, originally a Pulphouse venture, is now published by Algis Budrys.

Lester del Rey, founder of Del Rey died last year, marking yet another passage of a science fiction publishing pioneer. Some publishers expressed concern that with the death and aging of many of those considered pioneers in the field, there seems to be a need for new, young writers.

Subjects doing well in science fiction these days include paramilitary science fiction and cyberpunk—yes, cyberpunk. Despite a death knell a few years ago, thanks to a new book by William Gibson (the father of cyberpunk) and writers like Pat Cadigan and Bruce Sterling, this subgenre is alive and kicking. For the uninitiated, cyberpunk involves computers, virtual reality and lead characters who must often stand alone against a corrupt system.

Hard science fiction is doing well, too. The movie *Jurassic Park* sparked an interest in genetic engineering, and books featuring all types of biological futures are becoming popular.

Science fiction readers and writers have led the way in using online services for networking. This year *Omni* magazine launched its magazine online via America Online, featuring interactive conferences with those featured in the magazine and, of special interest to writers, regular reports from Fiction Editor Ellen Datlow on the science fiction and fantasy fields.

Speaking of magazines, *Locus*, the news magazine of the science fiction world, had its 25th anniversary in 1993. The editors celebrated by inviting writers to send them photos and letters explaining where they were in 1968.

Westerns

Although it is a small market, westerns are holding their own. This year the Dell Magazine Group launched the *Louis L'Amour Western Magazine* and *Western Tales*, a smaller publication, made its debut. Both of these promise to fill a much-needed niche for short western fiction.

"Novels of the West" seem to be doing better than shorter, category westerns, as these tend to have more mainstream crossover potential. Also popular right now are books by and about Native Americans and frontier novels. Westerns have become a large segment of the audio market, although these are usually tapes of previously published works rather than originals.

The Western Writers of America's publication got a new look this year. *The Roundup Quarterly* became *The Roundup* magazine and it seems to be tackling more tough topics such as the tension between politically correct and historically accurate and the role of women writers in the western field.

Keeping an eye on the market

There are numerous ways to keep an eye on the publishing industry. The writer's best friend can be his or her local bookseller. These are the people on the front lines. Not only are they painfully aware of what is not selling well or what seems to be flooding the market, they are also keen observers of what is growing in popularity. It's their business to know what readers want.

Other writers can be great sources of "insider" information. In addition to your local writing group, there are hundreds of regional and national writers' organizations throughout the U.S. and Canada. Some are open to all writers, while others are open to those who write a particular genre or fiction category. No matter what the focus of these groups, however, almost all publish some form of market newsletter.

Another way to meet writers, editors, agents and publishers is to attend a writers' conference. Most include panel discussions on various concerns (and trends!) within the industry. You'll find listings of writers' organizations and conferences in the Resource section of this book.

Writers' magazines and trade journals also can help you keep up with the market for fiction. *Writer's Digest* features a monthly markets column and smaller publications such as *Gila Queen's Guide to the Markets* are devoted entirely to sharing market information. For the industry, *Publishers Weekly* takes the lead with up-to-date news on publishing and bookselling.

It's good business to know your market and your competition, but keep in mind trends only go so far. Writers, editors, agents, publishers and booksellers all agree: If you write the book you believe in and take time to carefully craft your prose, by all means send it out. There's always room for well-done fiction regardless of trends.

The Business of Fiction Writing

by Robin Gee

It's true there's no substitute for talent and hard work. A writer's first concern must always be attention to craft. No matter how well presented, a poorly written story or novel has little chance of being published. Yet, on the other hand, a well-written piece may be equally hard to sell in today's competitive publishing market. Talent alone is just not enough.

To be successful, writers need to study the field and pay careful attention to finding the right market. While the hours spent perfecting your writing are usually hours spent alone, you're not alone when it comes to developing your marketing plan. *Novel & Short Story Writer's Market* provides you with detailed listings containing the essential information you'll need to locate and contact the markets most suitable for your work.

Yet once you've determined where to send your work, you must turn your attention to presentation. We can help here, too. Over the years we've made our listings as concise as possible in order to leave more space for new listings. In this effort, however, we took out some of the very basics of manuscript preparation. We've included these basics below, along with a compilation of information on submission procedures, approaching markets and the basics of manuscript mechanics. This year we've expanded The Business of Fiction Writing to address some of the issues you may face once your work has been published. In particular we've added information on setting up and giving readings. We also include tips on promoting your work. Canadian writers will find a new section with information and sources specifically designed to help them. No matter where you are from or what level of experience you have, you'll find useful information here on everything from presentation to mailing to selling rights to promoting your work—the "business" of fiction.

Approaching magazine markets: While it is essential for nonfiction markets, a query letter by itself is usually not needed by most magazine fiction editors. If you are approaching a magazine to find out if fiction is accepted, a query is fine, but editors looking for short fiction want to see *how* you write. A cover letter, however, can be useful as a letter of introduction, but it must be accompanied by the actual piece. Include basic information in your cover letter—name, address, a brief list of previous publications—if you have any— and two or three sentences about the piece (why you are sending it to *this* magazine or how your experience influenced your story). Keep it to one page and remember to include a self-addressed, stamped envelope for reply. See "Short Story Cover Letter" on page 72.

Approaching book publishers: Some book publishers do ask for queries first, but most want a query plus sample chapters or an outline or, occasionally, the complete manuscript. Again, make your letter brief. Include the essentials about yourself—name, address, phone number and publishing experience. Include only the personal information related to your story. Show that you have researched the market with a few sentences about why you chose this publisher.

Book proposals: A book proposal is a package sent to a publisher that includes a cover letter and one or more of the following: sample chapters, outline, synopsis, author bio, publications list. When asked to send sample chapters, send up to three *consecutive* chapters. An outline covers the highlights of your book chapter by chapter. Be sure to include details on main characters, the plot and subplots. Outlines can run up to 30 pages, depending on the length of your novel. The object is to tell what happens in a concise, but clear, manner. A synopsis is a very brief description of what happens in the story. Keep it to two or three pages. The terms synopsis and outline are sometimes used interchangeably, so be sure to find out exactly what each publisher wants.

Agents: Agents are not usually needed for short fiction and most do not handle it unless they already have a working relationship with you. For novels, you may want to consider working with an agent, especially if marketing to publishers who do not look at unsolicited submissions. For more on approaching agents see *The Guide to Literary Agents & Art/Photo Reps* (Writer's Digest Books, 1507 Dana Ave., Cincinnati OH 45207).

Approaching markets outside your own country: When sending return postage to another country, do not send stamps. You must purchase International Reply Coupons (IRCs). The publisher can use the IRCs to buy stamps from his/her own country. In the U.S., IRCs cost 95 cents each and can be purchased at the main branch of your local post office.

Main branches of local banks will cash foreign checks, but keep in mind payment quoted in our listings by publishers in other countries, is usually payment in their currency. Also note reporting time is longer in most overseas markets. To save time and money, you may want to include a return postcard (and IRC) with your submission and forego asking for a manuscript to be returned.

Some mailing tips: Manuscripts under five pages long can be folded into thirds and sent in a business-size (#10) envelope. For submissions of five pages or more, however, mail it flat in a 9×12 or 10×13 envelope. Your manuscript will look best if it is mailed in an envelope only slightly larger. For the return envelope, fold it in half, address it to yourself and add a stamp (or clip IRCs to it with a paper clip).

Mark both of your envelopes in all caps, FIRST CLASS MAIL or SPECIAL FOURTH CLASS MANUSCRIPT RATE. The second method is cheaper, but it is handled the same as Parcel Post (Third Class). First Class mailing assures fastest delivery and better handling.

Book manuscripts should be mailed in a sturdy box (a ream-size typing paper box works well). Tape the box shut and tape corners to reinforce them. To ensure your manuscript's safe return, enclose a self-addressed and stamped insulated bag mailer. You may want to check with the United Parcel Service (UPS) or other mailing services for rates.

If you use an office or personal postage meter, do not date the return envelope—it could cause problems if the manuscript is held too long before being returned. First Class mail is forwarded or returned automatically. Mark Third or Fourth Class return envelopes with "Return Postage Guaranteed" to have them returned.

It is not necessary to insure or certify your submission. In fact, many publishers do not appreciate receiving unsolicited manuscripts in this manner. Your best insurance is to always keep a copy of all submissions and letters.

Manuscript mechanics: A professionally presented manuscript will not guarantee publication. Yet a sloppy, hard-to-read manuscript will not be read—publishers simply do not have the time. Here's a list of suggested submission techniques for polished manuscript presentation:

● Use white, 8½×11 bond paper, preferably 16 or 20 lb. weight. The paper should be heavy enough so that it will not show pages underneath it and strong enough to take handling by several people. Do not use onion skin or erasable paper.

● Type your manuscript on a typewriter with a dark ribbon. Make sure the letters are clean and crisp. You can also use a computer printer, but avoid hard-to-read dot matrix.

● Proofread carefully. An occasional white-out is okay, but don't send a marked up manuscript with many typos. Keep a dictionary, thesaurus and stylebook handy.

● Always double space and leave a 1¼ inch margin on all sides of the page. For a short story manuscript, your first page should include your name, address and phone number (single-spaced) in the upper left corner. In the upper right, indicate an approximate word count. Center the name of your story about one-third of the way down, skip two or three lines and center your byline (byline is optional). Skip three lines and begin your story.

● On subsequent pages, put last name and page number in the upper right hand corner.

● For book manuscripts, use a separate cover sheet. Put your name, address and phone number in the upper left corner and word count in the upper right. Some writers list their agent's name and address in the upper right (word count is then placed at the bottom of the page). Center your title and byline about halfway down the page. Start your first chapter on the next page. Center the chapter number and title (if there is one) one-third of the way down the page. Include your last name and page number in the upper right of this page and each page to follow. Start each chapter with a new page.

● If you work on a computer, chances are your word processing program can give you a word count. If you are using a typewriter, there are a number of ways to count the number of words in your piece. One way is to count the number of words in five lines and divide that number by five to find an average. Then count the number of lines and multiply to find the total words. For long pieces, you may want to count the words in the first three pages, divide by three and multiply by the number of pages you have.

● Always keep a copy. Manuscripts do get lost. To avoid expensive mailing costs, send only what is required. If you are including artwork or photos, but you are not positive they will be used, send photocopies. Artwork is hard to replace.

● Most publishers do not expect you to provide artwork and some insist on selecting their own illustrators, but if you have suggestions, please let them know. Magazine publishers work in a very visual field and are usually open to ideas.

● If you want a reply or if you want your manuscript returned, enclose a self-addressed, stamped envelope (SASE). For most letters, a business-size (#10) envelope will do. Avoid using any envelope too small for an 8½×11 sheet of paper. For manuscripts, be sure to include enough postage and an envelope large enough to contain it. If you are requesting a sample copy of a magazine or a book publisher's catalog, send an envelope big enough to fit.

● When sending electronic (disk or modem) submissions, contact the publisher first for specific information and follow the directions carefully. Always include a hard copy with any disk submission.

● Keep accurate records. This can be done in a number of ways, but be sure to keep track of where your stories are and how long they have been "out." Write down submission dates. If you do not hear about your submission for a long time—about three weeks to one month longer than the reporting time stated in the listing—you may want to contact the publisher. When you do, you will need an accurate record for reference.

Rights: Know what rights you are selling. The Copyright Law states that writers are selling one-time rights (in almost all cases) unless they and the publisher have agreed otherwise. Below is a list of various rights. Be sure you know exactly what rights you are selling before you agree to the sale.

● All Rights allow a publisher to use the manuscript anywhere and in any form, including movie and book club sales, without further payment to the writer.

● Copyright is the legal right to exclusive publication, sale or distribution of a literary work. This right is that of the writer or creator of the piece and you need simply to include your name, date and the copyright symbol © on your piece in order to copyright it. You can also register your copyright with the Copyright Office for additional protection. Request information and forms from the Copyright Office, Library of Congress, Washington DC 20559. To get specific answers to questions about copyright (but not legal advice) you can call the Copyright Public Information Office at (202)707-3000 weekdays between 8:30 a.m. and 5 p.m. EST. Publications listed in *Novel & Short Story Writer's Market* are copyrighted *unless* otherwise stated. In the case of magazines that are not copyrighted, be sure to keep a copy of your manuscript with your notice printed on it. For more information on copyrighting your work see *The Copyright Handbook: How to Protect and Use Written Works* by Stephen Fishman (Nolo Press, 1992).

- First Serial Rights mean that the publisher has the right to publish your work for the first time in any periodical.
- First North American Serial Rights are the same as First Serial, but they are only for publication on the North American continent.
- One-time Rights allow a publisher to publish a story one time.
- Reprint Rights are permission to print a piece that was first published somewhere else.
- Second Serial Rights allow a publisher to print a piece in another periodical after it appeared for the first time in book form or in a magazine.
- Subsidiary Rights are all rights other than book publishing rights included in a book contract such as book club rights, movie rights and paperback rights.
- Work-for-hire is work that does not belong to the creator. If you do work-for-hire, you do not own the copyright and cannot sell any rights. For example, if you write a pamphlet for your company as an employee, generally the rights to that material do not belong to you. Writers doing work-for-hire are usually paid a flat fee for the work and do not collect royalties or other payments.

Readings: Attending public readings of poetry and fiction has become very popular in many cities. The general public seems to be just now catching on to something writers and avid readers have known for years: Readings offer a unique opportunity for those who love literature to experience it together.

If you are comfortable in front of a crowd and you'd like to share your work with others, try giving a reading. Not only does a reading allow you the opportunity to gauge reaction to your unpublished work, it's also an invaluable tool for promoting published short story collections and novels.

While there are some very prestigious reading series such as the "Main Reading Series" sponsored by The Unterberg Poetry Center of the 92nd Street Y in New York City, many readings are local events sponsored by area writers' clubs. You can start small, if you like, with one of the open-mike readings held in most cities in neighborhood coffee houses and taverns or, if you are published, look for bookstores that offer readings by authors whose books they sell.

Other reading outlets include libraries, churches, hospitals, radio stations and public-access cable television stations. Some series are well-established, while in other cases, you may have to approach a location and suggest a reading. It all depends on the amount of time and effort you'd like to invest.

If you decide to create your own reading opportunity, you may have to supply publicity and refreshments as well as a location. Established authors sometimes charge fees to sponsoring organizations, but newer writers usually feel the exposure is enough. If you have published work, however, you may want to bring copies to sell or arrange with your local bookstore to set up a table to sell your books. If you want to join an established series, keep in mind it can be competitive. You may be asked to submit work for consideration and a formal application.

❦Canadian writers take note

While much of the information contained in this section applies to all writers, here are some specifics of interest to Canadian writers:

About postage: *At press time, the cost of one International Reply Coupon in Canada is $1.25 (Canadian). A 7 percent GST tax is required on postage in Canada. Since Canadian postage rates are voted on in January of each year (after we go to press), the Canadian Postage by the Page chart provided may change. Contact a Canada Post Corporation Customer Service Division, located in most cities in Canada, for the most current rates.*

About copyright: *For information on copyrighting your work and to obtain forms, write Copyright and Industrial Design, Phase One, Place du Portage, 5th Floor, 50 Victoria St., Hull, Quebec K1A 0C9.*

About the public lending right: *The Public Lending Right Commission has established that eligible Canadian authors are entitled to payments when a book is available through a library. Payments are determined by a sampling of the holdings of a representative number of libraries. To find out more about the program and to learn if you are eligible, write to the Public Lending Right Commission at P.O. Box 1047, Ottawa, Ontario K1P 5V8. The Commission, which is part of The Canada Council, produces a helpful pamphlet,* How the PLR System Works, *on the program.*

For information on grants available to Canadian writers: *Most province art councils or departments of culture provide grants to resident writers. Some of these, as well as contests for Canadian writers, are listed in our Contests and Awards section. For national programs, contact The Canada Council, P.O. Box 1047, Ottawa, Ontario K1P 5V8 or call (613)598-4334 for information. The Council publishes a program information and application kit,* Programs in Writing and Publishing.

For more information: *More details on much of the information listed above and additional information on writing and publishing in Canada are included in the* Writer's Essential Desk Reference, *edited by Glenda Tennant Neff and published by Writer's Digest Books. In addition to information on a wide range of topics useful to all writers, the book features a detailed chapter for Canadians, "Writing and Selling in Canada," by Fred Kerner.*

See the Organizations and Resources section of Novel & Short Story Writer's Market *for listings of writers' organizations in Canada. Also contact The Writer's Union of Canada, 24 Ryerson Ave., Toronto, Ontario M5T 2P3 or call them at (416)868-6914. This organization provides a wealth of information (as well as strong support) for Canadian writers, including specialized publications on publishing contracts; contract negotiations; the author/editor relationship; author awards, competitions and grants; agents; taxes for writers, libel issues and access to archives in Canada.*

A few tips for giving the reading:
- Practice reading aloud; work out the stumbling blocks beforehand.
- Time your reading. Plan to read for around 30 minutes, depending on the length of the program and the number of other writers on the bill.
- When selecting a short story to read, choose one that can be completed in the time allowed. If this is not possible you can paraphrase the opening to your story as long as you

are brief. Treat it as a lead-in to your story. When cutting a story to fit, pay careful attention to avoid cutting vital information.

● When reading from a novel, look for the chapter that is most inclusive—one that won't require too much lead-in or that would leave too much dangling—yet, you can leave the audience wanting to know more. Look for drama and action.

● Don't forget to invite family and friends (a little moral support never hurt anyone!). And don't be disappointed if the crowd is small. Most readings attract from 20 to 30 people.

For listings of sponsored readings, see *Author & Audience* and *Literary Bookstores* by Poets & Writers Inc., 72 Spring St., New York NY 10012. Poets & Writers publishes other publications on readings including "How to Create Readings and Workshops Series." Write to them for information. *The Writer's Book of Checklists* by Scott Edelstein (published by Writer's Digest Books) includes information about giving readings as well.

Promotion tips: Everyone agrees writing is hard work whether you are published or not. Yet, once you arrive at the published side of the equation the work changes. Most published authors will tell you the work is still hard but it is different. Now, not only do you continue working on your next project, you must also concern yourself with getting your book into the hands of readers. It becomes time to switch hats from artist to salesperson.

While even bestselling authors whose publishers have committed big bucks to promotion are asked to help in promoting their books, new authors may have to take it upon themselves to plan and initiate some of their own promotion, sometimes dipping into their own pockets. Yet, this does not mean that every author is expected to go on tour, sometimes at their own expense. It does mean authors should be prepared to offer suggestions for promoting their books.

Depending on the time, money and the personal preferences of the author and publisher, a promotional campaign could mean anything from mailing out press releases to setting up book signings to hitting the talk-show circuit. Most writers can contribute to their own promotion by providing contact names—reviewers, home-town newspapers, civic groups, organizations—that might have a special interest in the book or the writer.

Above all, when it comes to promotion, be creative. What is your book about? Try to capitalize on it. For example, if you've written a mystery whose protagonist is a wine connoisseur, you might give a reading at a local wine-tasting or try to set something up at one of the national wine events. See "Using Setting as a Key to Promoting Your Book," by Nancy Berland, earlier in this book, for tips on using locale in your promotional plans. And for more suggestions on promoting your work see *The Writer's Guide to Promotion & Publicity,* by Elane Feldman (published by Writer's Digest Books).

Samples

This year we've included a sample cover letter that would accompany a short story manuscript. Cover letters should be no more than one page, proofread carefully, neatly typed. Paragraphs should be single-spaced, separated by a space between paragraphs. You should notice the following about our sample letter:

● The letter is direct and to the point, giving the purpose of the letter and the title of the manuscript in the first line.

● The writer explains why she feels her story would fit in well with the magazine. It's almost as if she wrote the story specifically for that publication.

● In the second paragraph she displays familiarity with the magazine. (She's done her homework.)

● She mentions her work experience because it gives her credibility. Notice, she only

The Short Story Cover Letter

Address
Phone

February 3, 1994

Ms. Marcy O'Connor, Editor
Small Town Romance Monthly Magazine
Street address
City, State, Zip

Dear Ms. O'Connor:

Enclosed is my short story, "No Time Now for Romance," for your consideration. Set in Husfeld, Pennsylvania, I think it will fit in nicely with your small-town theme. In particular, since it is set in 1862, it is well-suited for your current Civil War story series.

I have been a reader of your magazine for a long time and was very pleased when you started to include historical romances earlier this year.

As a research librarian for the Holton County Historical Society, I am very familiar with the Civil War period, especially in Pennsylvania. I have had both children's stories and romances published in *Midwest Monthly* and *Pennsylvania Woman's Lifestyle Magazines* and am working on a romance novel set in ancient Rome.

I look forward to your reply. I've enclosed SASE for your convenience. Thanks for your consideration.

Sincerely,

Susan Writer

---

includes those personal details that relate directly to the story she has written.
- The writer gives a brief list of her publication credits.
- She has enclosed a self-addressed, stamped envelope for a reply.

For more on cover letters and formats see *The Writer's Digest Guide to Manuscript Formats*, by Dian Dincin Buchman and Seli Groves. The sample letter is followed by postal charge charts for the U.S. and Canada.

U.S. Postage by the Page
by Carolyn Hardesty

Mailing costs can be an appreciable part of writing expenditures. The chart below can help save money as well as time by allowing you to figure the fees for sending your manuscripts to prospective publishers.

Postage rates are listed by numbers of pages (using 20 lb. paper) according to the most commonly used envelopes and their self-addressed, stamped envelopes (SASEs). While most writers prefer to send their work First Class, Third Class is becoming a choice for some. Third Class moves more slowly, but it costs less than First Class after the first 4 ounces. Also, it is permissible in Third Class to include a letter pertaining to the material inside.

First Class mail weighing more than 11 ounces is assessed according to weight plus geographical zone so it needs to be priced at the Post Office.

Postcards can be a bargain for writers. If the postage costs are higher than another computer printout or photocopied version of a manuscript, a postcard can be used for the editor's reply. The cost is 19¢.

For short manuscripts or long queries, use a #10 (business-size) envelope with a 29¢ stamp. Four pages is the limit if you are including a SASE. Another option is the 6×9 envelope. For 1-3 pages, postage is 29¢ in the U.S. For 4-7 pages with SASE, cost is 52¢.

Computer diskettes may be sent in official mailers or mid-size envelopes with stiffening for 75¢.

Ounces	9×12 9×12 SASE number of pages	9×12 SASE (for return trips) number of pages	First Class Postage	Third Class Postage	Postage from U.S. to Canada
under 2	...	1 to 2	$ .39*	$ .39*	$ .63*
2	1 to 4	3 to 8	.52	.52	.73
3	5 to 10	9 to 12	.75	.75	.86
4	11 to 16	13 to 19	.98	.98	1.09
5	17 to 21	20 to 25	1.21	1.21	1.32
6	22 to 27	26 to 30	1.44	1.21	1.55
7	28 to 32	31 to 35	1.67	1.33	1.78
8	33 to 38	36 to 41	1.90	1.33	2.01
9	39 to 44	42 to 46	2.13	1.44	2.24
10	45 to 49	47 to 52	2.36	1.44	2.47
11	50 to 55	53 to 57	2.59	1.56	2.70
12	56 to 99	58 to 101	2.90	1.56	2.80

*This cost includes an assessment for oversized mail that is light in weight.

Carolyn Hardesty's *short fiction and essays have appeared in* Four Minute Fictions, The North American Review, Cream City, The Montana Review *and others.*

Canadian Postage by the Page

by Barbara Murrin

The following chart is for the convenience of Canadian writers sending domestic mail and American writers sending an envelope with International Reply Coupons (IRCs) or Canadian stamps for return of a manuscript from a Canadian publisher. Unfortunately these figures are approximate, because the Canadian Postal Service meets to determine new fees in January each year, after we go to press. Check your post office for changes.

Manuscripts returning from the U.S. to Canada will take a U.S. stamped envelope although the original manuscript was sent with Canadian postage. This applies to return envelopes sent by American writers to Canada, too, which must be accompanied with IRCs or Canadian postage.

In a #10 envelope, you can have up to five pages for 43¢ (on manuscripts within Canada) or 49¢ (on manuscripts going to the U.S.). If you enclose a SASE, four pages is the limit. If you use 10×13 envelopes, send one page less than indicated on the chart.

IRCs are worth 49¢ Canadian postage but cost 95¢ to buy in the U.S.

Canada Post designations for types of mail are:

Standard Letter Mail Minimum size: 9×14cm (3⅝×5½"); Maximum size: 15×24.5cm (5⅞×9⁹/₁₆"); Maximum thickness: 5mm (³/₁₆")

Oversize Letter Mail Exceeds any measurement for standard; Maximum size: 27×38cm (10⅞×15"); Maximum thickness: 2cm (¹³/₁₆")

International Letter Mail Minimum size: 9 × 14cm (3⅝×5½"); Maximum size: Length + width + depth 90cm (36"); Greatest dimension must not exceed 60cm (24")

Insurance: To U.S.—65¢ for each $100 coverage to a maximum coverage of $1,000. Within Canada $1 for first $100 coverage; 45¢ for each additional $100 coverage to a maximum allowed by country of destination.

Registered Mail: $2.95 plus postage (air or surface—Canadian destination). Legal proof of mailing provided. No indemnity coverage.

Weight up to	9×12 envelope, 9×12 SASE number of pages*	9×12 SASE (for return trips) number of pages	Canada Standard	Oversize	First Class to U.S. Standard	Oversize
30 g/1.07 oz.	...	1 to 3	$ .43	$ .86	$ .49	$ 1.10
50 g/1.78 oz.	1 to 4	4 to 7	.67	.86	.72	1.10
100 g/3.5 oz.	5 to 14	8 to 18	...	.86	...	1.10
200 g/7.1 oz.	15 to 46	19 to 49	...	1.35		2.10
300 g/10.7 oz.	47 to 57	50 to 61	...	1.95		3.60
400 g/14.2 oz.	58 to 79	62 to 82	...	1.95		3.60
500 g/17.8 oz.	80 to 101	83 to 104	...	1.95		3.60
1.0 kg/2.2 lbs.	102 to 208	105 to 212	**	**	(air pkt.)	9.75

*Based on 20 lb. paper and 2 adhesive labels per envelope.
**For Canadian residents mailing parcels 1 kg. and over within Canada (domestic mail), rates vary according to destination. Ask your Post Master for the chart for your area.

Barbara Murrin *teaches music and business subjects at a private school. One of her short stories has been included in* Insight's Most Unforgettable Stories, *a compilation of stories from 20 years of publication.*

The Markets

Important Listing Information

● *Listings are* not *advertisements. Although the information here is as accurate as possible, the listings are not endorsed or guaranteed by the editor of* Novel & Short Story Writer's Market.
● Novel & Short Story Writer's Market *reserves the right to exclude any listing that does not meet its requirements.*

Key to Symbols and Abbreviations

‡ *New listing in all sections*
* *Subsidy publisher in Small Press and Commercial Book Publishers sections*
■ *Book packager or producer*
● *Comment by editor of* Novel & Short Story Writer's Market
🍁 *Canadian listing*
ms — *manuscript;* mss-*manuscripts*
b&w — *black and white (photo)*
SASE — *self-addressed, stamped envelope*
SAE — *self-addressed envelope*
IRC — *International Reply Coupon, for use on reply mail from other countries.*

(See Glossary for definitions of words and expressions used in writing/publishing.)

The Markets

Literary and Small Circulation Magazines

Welcome to the largest and most diverse section in *Novel & Short Story Writer's Market*. Here you will find hundreds of markets for short fiction, including more than 120 markets new to the book this year. You'll find every type of publication—from tiny personal fanzines to mid-size regional magazines to prestigious literary journals—offering writers on all levels of experience a vast array of publishing opportunities.

Publication in a small journal or magazine can result in a stepping-stone effect. Many writers get their start in smaller publications and go on to publication in large-circulation magazines. Editors at major magazines and those who work in the front lines of fiction book publishing look to literary journals and small magazines for new talent.

While some of the well-established literary journals offer several hundred dollars for a short story, many of the magazines listed in this section offer little or no cash payment. Most pay in contributor's copies and/or a subscription to the magazine. Yet publication in literary and small circulation magazines offers writers a long list of less tangible (but no less real) benefits including experience, exposure and prestige.

An array of opportunities

You will find in this section literary journals of all sizes and small magazines with circulations of under 10,000. A number of markets in this section are very receptive to the work of new writers and to writers whose work is considered literary, experimental or written for a specialized audience.

There are, indeed, hundreds of opportunities for writers here. We include most of the well-known prestigious journals such as *The North American Review*, *The Southern Review* and *Story*, but you'll also find publications devoted to publishing the work of beginning writers such as *Square One* and *Writers' Open Forum*. Also found here are magazines devoted to particular subjects, such as *Random Realities* for fantasy writing and *Western Tales* for western stories. Regional publications, such as *Washington Review* from the DC area and *Hyphen Magazine* out of Chicago, make up a number of our listings.

One way to categorize the magazines in this section is by type. University and state-supported journals often feature the work of well-known writers along with that of talented newcomers. Fiction in these tends toward literary and traditional. Fanzines or micro-press magazines are usually one- or two-person operations, mostly featuring the work of new writers. Material included in these runs the gamut from traditional fiction to personal rants to highly experimental work. Highly specialized publications take very little fiction, but are always looking for stories treating their particular interests. *Llamas Magazine*, looking for fiction about llamas and *Dance Connection*, interested only in fiction featuring dance themes, are two examples of such highly-specialized markets.

If you write a particular type of fiction, the best way to zero in on those markets most likely to be interested in your work is to check the Category Index for the appropriate subject heading. For those whose work is more general or, in fact, very specialized, you may wish to just browse through the listings, perhaps looking up those published in your state or region. You're sure to find magazines devoted to almost every topic, every level of writing and every type of writer.

Selecting the right markets for your work

In addition to browsing through the listings and using the Category Index (which appears at the back of this book) just before the Markets Index, check the ranking codes at the beginning of listings to find those most likely to be receptive to your work. This is especially true for beginning writers, who should look for magazines that say they are especially open to new writers (I) and for those who say they give equal weight to both new and established writers (II). For more explanation about these codes, see the end of this introduction.

Once you have a list of magazines you might like to try, read their listings carefully. Much of the material within each listing carries clues that tell you more about the magazine. How to Get the Most Out of This Book, starting on page 3, describes in detail the listing information common to all the markets in our book, but there is some information in this section that pertains only to magazines and especially to literary and small publications.

First, you may notice that some university-affiliated publications rotate editors. Whenever possible, we've indicated this, the name of the current editor and the length of the editor's term. Most of these listings give specific instructions on how to address your submissions after the editor's stated term ends.

The physical description appearing near the beginning of the listing can give you clues about the size and funding commitment to the publication. This is not always an indication of quality, but chances are a publication with expensive paper and four-color artwork on the cover has more prestige than a photocopied publication featuring a clip art self-cover. If you're a new writer or your work is considered avant garde, however, you may be more interested in the photocopied publication.

This is the only section in which you will find magazines that do not read submissions all year long. Again, many of those with limited reading periods are tied to the university schedule, but some just limit their reading periods to accommodate the needs of a very small staff.

Furthering your search

It cannot be stressed enough that reading the listing is only the first part of developing your marketing plan. The second part, equally important, is to obtain fiction guidelines and read the actual magazine. In his article, On Target: Zeroing in on the Right Market for Your Fiction, beginning on page 42, Ronald Spatz gives a list of questions you should ask when reading copies of a magazine to determine the fine points of the magazine's publishing style and philosophy. There is no substitute for this type of hands-on research.

Unlike commercial periodicals available at most newsstands and bookstores, it requires a little more effort to obtain some of the magazines listed here. The new super chain stores are doing a better job these days of stocking literaries and you can find some in independent and college bookstores, especially those published in your area. You may, however, need to send for a sample copy. We include sample copy prices in the listings whenever possible.

Another way to find out more about literary magazines is to check out the various prize anthologies and take note of publications receiving special awards or honors. Studying prize anthologies not only lets you know which magazines are publishing award-winning work, but it also provides a valuable overview of what is considered to be the best fiction published today.

Last year we added our own editorial comments, set off by a bullet (•). This feature allows us the opportunity to note award-winning publications, as well as other information we feel will help you determine if a listing is the right market for you. We checked several sources including the magazines themselves for information on awards and honors. The comments section also allows us to explain more about the special interests or requirements of a publication and any information we've learned from our readers that we feel will help you choose potential markets wisely.

Among the awards and honors we note are inclusion of work in:

• *Pushcart Prize: Best of the Small Presses*, published by Pushcart Press, Box 380, Wainscott NY 11975.

• *Prize Stories: The O. Henry Awards*, published by Doubleday/Anchor, 1540 Broadway, New York NY 10036.

• *Best American Short Stories*, published by Houghton Mifflin, 222 Berkeley St., Boston MA 02116.

You may also want to take a look at the most recent *Writer's Digest* Fiction 50, mentioned in our comments. It's a list of magazines ranked best for writers by the editors of *Writer's Digest* and published every other year in June. We note the market's last ranking, but watch for the next Fiction 50 list, due out in June 1994.

The well-respected *Poet* magazine (published by Cooper House Publishing Inc., PO Box 54947, Oklahoma City OK 73154) created a new awards program in 1993 to honor the best literary magazines. The program is titled The American Literary Magazine Awards and all recipients of editorial content awards (winners and runners-up) have listings in this section. To find out more about the awards, see the *Poet*'s Fall issue.

For more information

See The Business of Fiction Writing for the specific mechanics of manuscript submission. Above all, editors appreciate a professional presentation. Include a brief cover letter and, if you want your manuscript returned, send a self-addressed envelope in a size large enough to accommodate it and stamps or International Reply Coupons (for replies from countries other than your own).

North American publications are listed in the following main section of listings, and this is followed by listings for other English-speaking markets around the world. To make it easier to find Canadian markets, this year we've added a maple leaf symbol (❋) at the start of those listings.

If you're interested in learning more about literary and small magazines, see *The International Directory of Little Magazines and Small Presses* (Dustbooks, Box 100, Paradise CA 95967) or you may want to contact the Council of Literary Magazines and Presses (3-C, 154 Christopher St., New York NY 10014-2839), a group that supports the small press and publishes a directory of their magazine members, the *Directory of Literary Magazines*.

If your tastes run toward fanzines and the micro-press, you may be interested in obtaining a catalog from the recent exhibit by the Hemingway Western Studies center titled "Some Zines: American Alternative & Underground Magazines, Newsletters & APAs." The exhibit featured several of the more unusual offerings from the 'zine world and an examination of the role of these publications in our culture. For information on ordering the catalog, write to The Bookstore, Boise State University, 1910 University Dr., Boise ID 83725. Also see the newly revamped periodical *Factsheet Five* (PO Box 170099, San Francisco CA 94117-0099).

The following is the ranking system we have used to categorize the listings in this section.

    I **Publication encourages beginning or unpublished writers to submit work for consideration and publishes new writers regularly.**

    II **Publication accepts work by established writers and by new writers of exceptional talent.**

    III **Publication does not encourage beginning writers; prints mostly writers with previous publication credits; publishes very few new writers.**

    IV **Special-interest or regional publication, open only to writers in certain genres or on certain subjects or from certain geographical areas.**

ABERATIONS, (I), Experiences Unlimited, 544 Ygnacio Valley Rd., #13, or (POB 8040), Walnut Creek CA 94596. (510)682-9662. Editor: Jon L. Herron. Fiction Editor: Rich Blair. Magazine: digest-sized, 5½ × 8½; 64 pages; 20 lb. bond; 80 lb. glossy cover; b&w illustrations and photographs. "Adult horror, science fiction and dark fantasy short stories and poems for an over-18 audience." Estab. 1992. Circ. 2,700 +.
    ● *Aberations* was rated #27 on the latest *Writer's Digest* Fiction 50 list. See also the listing for *Midnight Zoo* in this book.
Needs: Erotica, experimental, fantasy (dark), horror, humor/satire, prose poem, science fiction (hard science). No formula stories. Receives 200-300 unsolicited mss/month. Buys 10-12 mss/issue; 120 mss/year. Publishes ms "within 12 issues." Published work by Jeff Vandermeer, Kevin J. Anderson, Brad Boucher. Length: 4,000 words preferred; 500 words minimum; 9,000 words maximum. "Always" critiques rejected mss and recommends other markets.
How to Contact: Send complete ms with cover letter that includes Social Security number, telephone number and bio. Reports within 16 weeks. SASE. Simultaneous and electronic submissions (MicroSoft Word 5 or Word Perfect) OK. Sample copy for $4.50 postpaid. Fiction guidelines for #10 SAE and 1 first-class stamp (IRCs).
Payment: Pays ¼¢/word, plus contributor's copy; extra contributor's copies for reduced charge. Maximum payment: $7.
Terms: Pays on publication for first North American serial rights or one-time rights. Sends galleys to author on request.
Advice: "With the advent of the personal computer the small press magazine market has boomed. I expect the market to continue growing into the next decade. We don't want erotica just for erotica sake, but we want good stories where the sex, gore, profanity is instrumental to the story not just thrown in for the sake of blood, guts, sex etc. We will print stories that other magazines might reject just because of the usage of certain words etc."

‡ABOVE THE BRIDGE, (IV), Up North Publishing, 120 McLaughlin, Skandia MI 49885. (906)942-7486. Editor: Lynn DeLoughary St. Arnaud. Magazine: 8½ × 11; 48 pages; 80 lb. text paper; 80 lb. LOE cover stock; illustrations and photos. "For and about the Upper Peninsula of Michigan." Quarterly. Estab. 1985. Circ. 2,500.
Needs: Regional. "Any stories pertaining to the Upper Peninsula of Michigan." Upcoming themes: "Fishing in the UP" (March 1); "Shipping on the Great Lakes" (June 1); "Outdoor Winter Sports" (December 1). Receives 15-20 unsolicited mss/month. Accepts 2-3 mss/issue; 8-12 mss/year. Publishes ms up to 2 years after acceptance. Length: 800-1,000 words average; 300 words minimum; 2,000

● *A bullet introduces comments by the editor of* Novel & Short Story Writer's Market *indicating special information about the listing.*

words maximum. Publishes short shorts. Length: 300-400 words. Also publishes literary essays, literary criticism.

How to Contact: Send complete ms with a cover letter. Should include estimated word count, bio, name, address, phone number. Reports in 6-8 months. Send SASE (or IRC) for reply, return of ms or send a disposable copy of ms. Simultaneous and reprint submissions OK. Sample copy for $3.50. Fiction guidelines free.

Payment: Pays 2¢/word.

Terms: Pays on publication for one-time rights.

Advice: "Make certain that the manuscript pertains to the Upper Peninsula of Michigan. If you've never been there, don't fake it."

ABYSS MAGAZINE, "Games and the Imagination," (II, IV), Ragnarok Enterprises, P.O. Box 140333, Austin TX 78714-0333. (512)472-6535. Fax: (512)472-6220. Editor: David F. Nalle. Fiction Editor: Patricia Fitch. Magazine: 8×10; 48 pages; bond paper; glossy cover; illustrations; photos. "Heroic fantasy fiction: some fantasy, horror, SF and adventure fiction, for college-age game players." Bimonthly. Plans special fiction issue. Estab. 1979. Circ. 1,500.

● *Abyss Magazine* can be contacted through Internet online service as well as their own electronic bulletin board.

Needs: Adventure, fantasy, horror, psychic/supernatural/occult, cyberpunk, science fiction, heroic fantasy, sword and sorcery. "Game-based stories are not specifically desired." Upcoming themes: "Horror Issue" (spring); "Review Issue" (summer). Receives 20-30 unsolicited mss/month. Buys 1 ms/ issue; 7 mss/year. Publishes ms 1-12 months after acceptance. Published work by Antoine Sadel, Kevin Anderson, Alan Blount; published new writers within the last year. Length: 2,000 words average; 1,000 words minimum; 4,000 words maximum. Publishes short shorts occasionally. Also publishes literary essays and literary criticism. Sometimes critiques rejected mss or recommends other markets.

How to Contact: Send for sample copy first. Reports in 6 weeks on queries; 3 months on mss. "Do send a cover letter, preferably entertaining. Include some biographical info and a precis of lengthy stories." SASE. Simultaneous submissions OK. Prefers electronic submissions by modem or network. "Call our BBS at (512)472-6905 for ASCII info." Sample copy and fiction guidelines $5. Reviews novels and short story collections (especially fantasy novels).

Payment: Pays 1-3¢/word or by arrangement, plus contributor's copies.

Terms: Pays on publication for first North American serial rights.

Advice: "We are particularly interested in new writers with mature and original style. Don't send us fiction which everyone else has sent back to you unless you think it has qualities which make it too strange for everyone else but which don't ruin the significance of the story. Make sure what you submit is appropriate to the magazine you send it to. More than half of what we get is completely inappropriate. We plan to include more and longer stories."

ACM, (ANOTHER CHICAGO MAGAZINE), (II), Left Field Press, 3709 N. Kenmore, Chicago IL 60613. Editor: Barry Silesky. Fiction Editor: Sharon Solwitz. Magazine: 5½×8½; 150-200 pages; "art folio each issue." Estab. 1977.

● Work appearing in *ACM* was selected for inclusion in the 1991 *Pushcart Prize* anthology. *ACM* is best known for experimental work or work with political slants, clear narrative voices.

Needs: Contemporary, literary, experimental, feminist, gay/lesbian, ethnic, prose poem, translations and political/socio-historical. Receives 75-100 unsolicited fiction mss each month. Recently published work by David Michael Kaplan, Diane Wakoski, Wanda Coleman; published new writers in the last year. Also publishes literary essays.

How to Contact: Unsolicited mss acceptable with SASE (IRC). Publishes ms 6 months to 1 year after acceptance. Sample copies are available for $8 ppd. Reports in 3 months. Receives small press collections.

Payment: Small honorarium plus contributor's copy.

Terms: Acquires first North American serial rights.

Advice: "Get used to rejection slips, and don't get discouraged. Keep introductory letters short. Make sure ms has name and address on every page, and that it is clean, neat and proofread. We are looking for stories with freshness and originality in subject angle and style, and work that encounters the world and is not stuck in its own navel."

THE ACORN, (I,II), 1530 7th St., Rock Island IL 61201. (309)788-3980. Editor: Betty Mowery. Newsletter: 8½×11; 8-10 pages; illustrations. "Manuscripts of interest to K-12th grade audience or K-12th grade librarians and teachers." Bimonthly. Estab. 1989. Circ. 150.

Needs: Ethnic, juvenile, mainstream, mystery/suspense (young adult), prose poem, regional, religious/inspirational, romance (contemporary, historical, young adult), science fiction, young adult. "We use some adult manuscripts, if they are of interest to young people. No erotica or anything degrading to race or religion or background." Receives 50 unsolicited fiction mss/month. Accepts 10-12 mss/issue; 60-70 mss/year. Publishes ms within 2 months after acceptance. Length: 500 words preferred; 200 words minimum; 500 words maximum. Accepts short shorts. Length: 200 words. Sometimes critiques or comments on rejected mss and recommends other markets.
How to Contact: Send complete ms with cover letter. Reports in 1 week. SASE. Simultaneous submissions and reprints OK. Sample copy for $2. Fiction guidelines are contained in publication.
Payment: No payment.
Terms: Acquires first rights.
Advice: Looks for "tight writing and a manuscript that has something to say and isn't preachy, but still gets the point across. I am open to all manuscripts from both published and unpublished writers. I'm eager to help a beginning author get into print. "

ADRIFT, Writing: Irish, Irish American and . . . , (II), #4D, 239 E. 5th St., New York NY 10003. Editor: Thomas McGonigle. Magazine: 8 × 11; 32 pages; 60 lb. paper stock; 65 lb. cover stock; illustrations; photos. "Irish-Irish American as a basis — though we are interested in advanced writing from anywhere." Semiannually. Estab. 1983. Circ. 1,000 + .
Needs: Contemporary, erotica, ethnic, experimental, feminist, gay, lesbian, literary, translations. Receives 40 unsolicited mss/month. Buys 3 mss/issue. Published work by Francis Stuart; published new writers within the last year. Length: open. Also publishes literary criticism. Sometimes critiques rejected mss and recommends other markets.
How to Contact: Send complete ms. Reports as soon as possible. SASE for ms. Sample copy $5. Reviews novels or short story collections.
Payment: Pays $7.50-300.
Terms: Pays on publication for first rights.
Advice: "The writing should argue with, among others, James Joyce, Flann O'Brien, Juan Goytisolo, Ingeborg Bachmann, E.M. Cioran, Max Stirner, Patrick Kavanagh."

THE ADVOCATE, (I, II), PKA Publications, 301A Rolling Hills Park, Prattsville NY 12468. (518)299-3103. Editor: Remington Wright. Tabloid: 9⅜ × 12¼; 32 pages; newsprint paper; line drawings; b&w photographs. "Eclectic for a general audience." Bimonthly. Estab. 1987.
Needs: Adventure, contemporary, ethnic, experimental, fantasy, feminist, historical (general), humor/satire, juvenile (5-9 years), literary, mainstream, mystery/suspense, prose poem, regional, romance, science fiction, senior citizen/retirement, sports, western, young adult/teen (10-18 years). Nothing religious, pornographic, violent, erotic, pro-drug or anti-environment. Receives 24 unsolicited mss/month. Accepts 6-8 mss/issue; 36-48 mss/year. Publishes ms 4 months to 1 year after acceptance. Length: 1,000 words preferred; 2,500 words maximum. Sometimes critiques rejected mss and recommends other markets.
How to Contact: Send complete ms with cover letter. Reports in 2 weeks on queries; 2 months on mss. SASE. No simultaneous submissions. Sample copy for $3 (US currency for inside US; $5.25 US currency for Canada). Writers guidelines for SAE and 1 first-class stamp (IRC).
Payment: Pays contributor's copies.
Terms: Acquires first rights.
Advice: "The highest criterion in selecting a work is its entertainment value. It must first be enjoyable reading. It must, of course, be original. To stand out, it must be thought provoking or strongly emotive, or very cleverly plotted. Will consider only previously unpublished works by writers who do not earn their living principally through writing."

AETHLON, (I,II,IV), East Tennessee State University Press, Johnson City TN 37614-0683. Editor: Don Johnson. Fiction Editor: Fred Boe. Magazine: 6 × 9; 180-240 pages; illustrations and photographs. "Theme: Literary treatment of sport. We publish articles on that theme, critical studies of author's treatment of sport and original fiction and poetry with sport themes. Most of our audience are academics." Semiannually. Plans "possible" special fiction issue. Estab. 1983. Circ. 800.
Needs: Sport. "Stories must have a sport-related theme and subject; otherwise, we're wide open." No personal experience memoirs. Receives 10-15 fiction mss/month. Accepts 4-8 fiction mss/issue; 10-15 fiction mss/year. Publishes ms "about 6 months" after acceptance. Length: 2,500-5,000 words average; 500 words minumum; 7,500 words maximum. Also publishes literary essays, literary criticism, poetry. Sometimes critiques rejected mss.

How to Contact: Send complete ms with cover letter. Reports in 6 months. SASE. No simultaneous submissions. Reprint submissions OK. Sample copy $12.50. Reviews novels and short story collections. Send books to Professor Brooke Horvath, Dept. of English, Kent State University, 6000 Frank Ave., Canton OH 44720.
Payment: Pays 1 contributor's copy and 5 offprints.
Terms: Sends pre-publication galleys to author. Publication copyrighted.
Advice: "Too many people with no talent are writing. Too many people think a clever idea or an unusual experience is all it takes to make a story. We are looking for well-written, insightful stories. Don't be afraid to be experimental."

AGNI, (II), Creative Writing Program, Boston University, 236 Bay State Rd., Boston MA 02215. (617)353-5389. Editor-in-Chief: Askold Melnyczuk. Magazine: 5½×8½; 320 pages; 55 lb. booktext paper; recycled cover stock; occasional art portfolios. "Eclectic literary magazine publishing first-rate poems and stories." Semiannually. Estab. 1972.
  • Work from *Agni* has been selected regularly for inclusion in both *Pushcart Prize* and *Best American Short Stories* anthologies.
Needs: Stories, excerpted novels, prose poems and translations. Receives 200 unsolicited fiction mss/month. Buys 4-7 mss/issue, 8-12 mss/year. Reading period October 1 to April 30 only. Published work by Joyce Carol Oates, Stephen Dixon, Andra Neiburga, Ha Jin. Rarely critiques rejected mss or recommends other markets.
How to Contact: Send complete ms with SASE (IRC) and cover letter listing previous publications. Simultaneous submissions OK. Reports in 1-4 months. Sample copy $7.
Payment: Pays $10/page up to $150; 2 contributor's copies; one-year subscription.
Terms: Pays on publication for first North American serial rights. Sends galleys to author. Copyright reverts to author upon publication.
Advice: "Read *Agni* carefully to understand the kinds of stories we publish. Read—everything, classics, literary journals, bestsellers."

THE AGUILAR EXPRESSION, (II), P.O. Box 304, Webster PA 15087. Editor: Xavier F. Aguilar. Magazine: 8½×11; 10-16 pages; 20 lb. bond paper; illustrations. "We are open to all writers of a general theme—something that may appeal to everyone." Semiannually. Estab. 1989. Circ. 150.
Needs: Adventure, ethnic/multicultural, experimental, horror, mainstream/contemporary, mystery/suspense (romantic suspense), romance (contemporary). No religious or first-person stories. Will publish annual special fiction issue or anthology in the future. Receives 10 unsolicited mss/month. Acquires 1-2 mss/issue; 2-4 mss/year. Publishes ms 1 month to 1 year after acceptance. Published work by Aphrodite Mitsos, Linda Keegan, Loueva Smith. Length: 1,000 words average; 750 words minimum; 1,500 words maximum. Also publishes poetry.
How to Contact: Send complete ms with cover letter. Reports on queries in 1 week; mss in 1 month. SASE (or IRC) for a reply to a query or a disposable copy of the ms. No simultaneous submissions. Sample copy for $6. Fiction guidelines for #10 SAE and 52¢ postage.
Payment: Pays 1 contributor's copy. Additional copies at a reduced rate of $3.
Terms: Acquires one-time rights. Not copyrighted. Write to publication for details on contests, awards or grants.

‡ALABAMA FICTION REVIEW, (II), P.O. Box 210458, Montgomery AL 36121-0458. Editor: David Wimberley. Electronic publication available via computer modem. Data line: (205)244-7078. "*Alabama Fiction Review* publishes fiction for readers who because of time or distance might not often reach a well-stocked library, or who because of expense limit their bookstore purchases of short fiction. Readers pay for only the stories they want. The menu is arranged to minimize long-distance telephone time." Weekly. Estab. 1993. Circ. 500.
Needs: Experimental, literary, mainstream/contemporary, serialized novel, translations; also "interested in reprints; and translations from Russia and Latin America." Receives 50 unsolicited mss/month. Accepts up to 5 mss/issue; 250 mss/year. Publishes ms 1 week to 1 year after acceptance. Agented fiction 33%. Recently published work by Madison Jones. Length: open. Publishes short shorts.
How to Contact: Send complete ms with a cover letter. Should include estimated word count, brief bio and list of publications with submission. Reports in 5 months. SASE. Simultaneous, reprint and electronic submissions OK. "Anyone may log on and read samples free of charge." Fiction guidelines for #10 SAE and 1 first-class stamp (IRC).

Payment: Pays $10-1,000 and subscription.
Terms: Pays on publication for exclusive electronic publishing rights for a specified period of time, usually one year.

ALABAMA LITERARY REVIEW, (II), Smith 253, Troy State University, Troy AL 36082. (205)670-3286, ext. 3307. Editor: Theron Montgomery. Fiction Editor: Jim Davis. Magazine: $6 \times 11\frac{1}{2}$; 100+ pages; top paper quality; some illustrations; photos. "National magazine for a broad range of the best contemporary fiction, poetry, essays, photography and drama that we can find." Semiannually. Estab. 1987.
   ● The editors say they are "proud of finding new talent" . . . provided work is well-written. They've increased the number of fiction manuscripts accepted each issue from 2 to 5.
Needs: Contemporary, ethnic, experimental, fantasy, feminist, historical (general), humor/satire, literary, prose poem, regional, science fiction, serialized/excerpted novel, translations. "Serious writing." Receives 50 unsolicited fiction mss/month. Acquires 5 fiction mss/issue. Publishes ms 5-6 months after acceptance. Published work by Manette Ansay, Ed Peaco, Pete Fromm, John Holman and Mary Sue Weston; published new writers within the last year. Length: 2,000-3,500 words average. Publishes short shorts of 1,000 words. Also publishes literary essays, literary criticism, poetry. Sometimes comments on rejected mss and recommends other markets.
How to Contact: Send complete ms with cover letter or submit through agent. Reports on queries in 2 weeks; on mss in 2 months (except in summer). SASE. Simultaneous submissions OK. Sample copy for $4 plus 50¢ postage. Reviews novels or short story collections. Send to Steve Cooper.
Payment: Pays in contributor's copies.
Terms: First rights returned to author upon publication. Work published in *ALR* may be read on state-wide (nonprofit) public radio program.
Advice: "Read our publication first. Avoid negative qualities pertaining to gimmickry and a self-centered point of view. We are interested in any kind of writing if it is *serious* and *honest* in the sense of 'the human heart in conflict with itself.' "

ALASKA QUARTERLY REVIEW, (II), University of Alaska, Anchorage, 3211 Providence Dr., Anchorage AK 99508. (907)786-1327. Fiction Editor: Ronald Spatz. Magazine: 6×9; 146 pages; 60 lb. Glatfelter paper; 10 pt. C1S black ink varnish cover stock; photos on cover only. Magazine of "contemporary literary art and criticism for a general literary audience." Semiannually. Estab. 1982.
   ● Work appearing in the *Alaska Quarterly Review* has been selected for the *Pushcart Prize* and cited in *Best American Short Stories* anthologies. See "On Target," by Ronald Spatz in the Writing Techniques section of this edition.
Needs: Contemporary, traditional, experimental, literary, prose poem and translations. Receives 140 unsolicited fiction mss/month. Accepts 7-13 mss/issue, 15-24 mss/year. Does not read mss May 15-August 15. Published new writers within the last year. Publishes short shorts. Occasionally critiques rejected mss.
How to Contact: Send complete mss with SASE (IRC). Simultaneous submissions "undesirable, but will accept if indicated." Reports in 2-3 months. Publishes ms 6 months to 1 year after acceptance. Sample copy $4.
Payment: Pays 1 contributor's copy and a year's subscription. Pays honorarium when grant funding permits.
Terms: Acquires first rights.
Advice: "We have made a significant investment in fiction. The reason is quality; serious fiction *needs* a market. Try to have everything build to a singleness of effect."

ALPHA BEAT PRESS, (II, IV), (formerly *Alpha Beat Soup*), 31 A Waterloo St., New Hope PA 18938. Editor: Dave Christy. Magazine: $7\frac{1}{2} \times 9$; 95-125 pages; illustrations. "Beat and modern literature—prose, reviews and poetry." Semiannually. Estab. 1987. Circ. 600.
   ● Work from *Alpha Beat Press* appeared in the *Pushcart Prize* anthologies in 1988 and 1991. Alpha Beat Press also publishes poetry chapbooks and supplements.

✝ *The double dagger before a listing indicates that the listing is new in this edition. New markets are often the most receptive to submissions by new writers.*

Needs: Erotica, experimental, literary and prose poem. Plans another magazine, supplementing*Alpha Beat Press*, and an *ABS Anthology*. Recently published work by Charles Bukowski, Neeli Chevkovski and Joan Reid; published new writers within the last year. Length: 600 words minimum; 1,000 words maximum. Also publishes literary essays, literary criticism, poetry. Sometimes recommends other markets.

How to Contact: Query first. Reports on queries within 2 weeks. SASE (IRC). Simultaneous and reprint submissions OK. Sample copy for $10. Reviews novels and short story collections.

Payment: Pays in contributor's copies.

Terms: Rights remain with author.

Advice: "*ABP* is the finest journal of its kind available today, having, with 9 issues, published the widest range of published and unpublished writers you'll find in the small press scene."

‡ALTERNATE HILARITIES, The Magazine of Speculative Humor, (I, IV), P.O. Box 6732, Syracuse NY 13217-6732. (315)475-5925. Editor: Alexandra Zale. Fiction Editor: Devon Tavern. Magazine: 8½×11; 26 pages; 90 lb. white paper; 90 lb. white cover; illustrations. "Humor in the speculative genres of science fiction, fantasy and horror. We want laughs from out of this world, deep within the realm and under the bed." Quarterly. Estab. 1993. Circ. 300.

Needs: "Humorous sci-fi, fantasy and horror. Funny stories in the speculative fiction genre." Plans to publish annual special fiction issue or anthology. Receives 60-80 unsolicited mss/month. Accepts 6-10 mss/issue; 24-40 mss/year. Publishes ms 1-3 months after acceptance. Recently published work by Frank O. Dodge, Lorin Emery, Daveed Gartenstein-Ross. Length: 500 words minimum; 5,000 words maximum. Publishes short shorts. Also publishes poetry (if it is humorous and speculative). Often critiques or comments on rejected mss.

How to Contact: Send complete ms with a cover letter. Should include estimated word count, bio, Social Security number and list of publications. Reports in 1 week on queries; 3 weeks on mss. Send SASE (or IRC) for reply, return of mss or send a disposable of ms. Simultaneous and electronic submissions OK. E-mail by: Genie: TalesTwiceto or Internet: TalesTwiceTo@genie.geis.com. Sample copy $3. Fiction guidelines for #10 SAE and 1 first-class stamp. Reviews novels and short story collections. Send review copies to Devon Tavern.

Payment: Pays 2 contributor's copies; additional copies $1.50.

Terms: Acquires first rights on publication. Sends galleys to author.

Advice: "I accept fiction that makes me laugh, but humor is very subjective."

AMATEUR WRITERS JOURNAL, Four Seasons Poetry Club Magazine, (I), R.V. Gill Publishing Co., 3653 Harrison St., Bellaire OH 43906. (614)676-0881. Editor: Rosalind Gill. Magazine: 8½×11; 38 pages; 20 lb. paper; illustrations. "Stories, articles, essays and poetry on all subjects. No avant-garde or porno-type manuscripts of any kind accepted. Poetry, when seasonal, published only in the season for which it is appropriate. Same rule applies to stories. For a family audience." Quarterly. Estab. 1967. Circ. 700+.

Needs: Adventure, contemporary, fantasy, humor/satire, mainstream, mystery/suspense, religious/inspirational, romance (contemporary), science fiction, young adult/teen. Receives around 300 fiction mss/month. Accepts 8 fiction mss/issue; 48 mss/year. Publishes ms "within 3 months" after acceptance. Length: 1,200 words average; 1,500 words maximum. Also publishes literary essays, poetry. Sometimes critiques rejected mss and recommends other markets.

How to Contact: Send complete ms with cover letter. State whether you are offering first rights, or, if material has been published elsewhere, the name of the publication in which your work appeared. Reports on queries in 1 month; on mss in 1 week. SASE. No simultaneous submissions. Sample copy available for $2 and 3 first-class stamps. Fiction guidelines for #10 SAE and 2 first-class stamps (IRCs).

Payment: No payment.

Terms: Acquires one-time rights.

Advice: "I believe that all fiction writers should have a showplace for their work, and my magazine readers prefer fiction to nonfiction, although I accept both."

AMBERGRIS, (II), Dept. N, P.O. Box 29919, Cincinnati OH 45229. Editor: Mark Kissling. Magazine: 5×8; 120-180 pages; illustrations. "*Ambergris* is a non-profit magazine dedicated to quality literature, and to fostering the emerging author." Annual. Estab. 1987. Circ. 1,000.

• See the Contests and Awards section for the *Ambergris* Annual Fiction Contest.

Needs: "We are looking for literary short stories, experimental short fiction, and literary essays (particularly essays with fictional elements—essays that read like fiction)." Simultaneous submissions OK (if noted). No poetry, no genre fiction, nothing strictly for children or young adults, and no novel excerpts (unless the excerpt is unpublished and completely self-contained). Also no scholarly articles or academic essays. Receives more than 1,000 mss/year. Buys 8-12 mss/year. Does not read in May, June and July. Publishes most mss within a year of acceptance, but "writers are notified on offer of acceptance if a ms is not to be published for more than a year." Recently published work by Mona Simpson, William Allen and Randall Silvis. Length: 5,000 words maximum.

How to Contact: Send complete ms with cover letter which should include a three-line biographical sketch. One work of fiction per submission *only*. Please include computer disk specs and availability if applicable. Reports in 3 months, "longer if a ms is under serious consideration." Enclose sufficient SASE (IRC) for return of ms, "or at least a #10 SASE for reply. Submissions without either will not be considered or returned." Current issue $5.95; sample copy $3.95. Fiction guidelines for #10 SASE.

Payment: Pays $5/published page, $50 maximum. Writers also receive 2 contributor's copies, extras available at a discount.

Terms: Buys first North American serial rights and the right to reprint.

Advice: "*Our reading period is August through April.* Manuscripts received at other times will be returned unread, and then only if SASE is enclosed. We attempt to foster the emerging author, but we strongly encourage beginning writers and others not familiar with our format to invest in and *read a sample copy* before submitting work. There is simply no other way to determine what kind of fiction and essays this or any other literary magazine publishes without first reading an issue. We also give special consideration to works by Ohio authors and about the Midwest in general."

AMELIA, (II), 329 E St., Bakersfield CA 93304. (805)323-4064. Editor-in-Chief: Frederick A. Raborg, Jr. Magazine: 5½×8½; 124-136 pages; perfect-bound; 60 lb. high-quality moistrite matte paper; kromekote cover; four-color covers; original illustrations; b&w photos. "A general review using fine fiction, poetry, criticism, belles lettres, one-act plays, fine pen-and-ink sketches and line drawings, sophisticated cartoons, book reviews and translations of both fiction and poetry for general readers with eclectic tastes for quality writing." Quarterly. Plans special fiction issue each July. Estab. 1984. Circ. 1,250.

● The editor of this well-respected magazine also edits *Cicada* (devoted to Oriental-style writing) and *SPSM&H* (devoted to sonnets and sonnet-inspired work). The magazine also sponsors a long list of fiction awards. Listings for the other publications and for the *Amelia* Awards appear in this book. *Amelia* also ranks #28 on the latest *Writer's Digest* Fiction 50 list.

Needs: Adventure, contemporary, erotica, ethnic, experimental, fantasy, feminist, gay, historical (general), humor/satire, lesbian, literary, mainstream, mystery/suspense, prose poem, regional, science fiction, senior citizen/retirement, sports, translations, western. Nothing "obviously pornographic or patently religious." Receives 160-180 unsolicited mss/month. Buys up to 9 mss/issue; 25-36 mss/year. Recently published Michael Bugeja, Jack Curtis, Maxine Kumin, Eugene Dubnov and Merrill Joan Gerber; published new writers within the last year. Length: 3,000 words average; 1,000 words minimum; 5,000 words maximum. Usually critiques rejected ms. Sometimes recommends other markets.

How to Contact: Send complete manuscript with cover letter with previous credits if applicable to *Amelia* and perhaps a brief personal comment to show personality and experience. Reports in 1 week on queries; 2 weeks-3 months on mss. SASE. Sample copy for $7.95. Fiction guidelines for #10 SAE and 1 first-class stamp (IRC).

Payment: Pays $35-50 plus 2 contributor's copies; extras with 20% discount.

Terms: Pays on acceptance for first North American serial rights. Sends galleys to author "when deadline permits."

Advice: "Write carefully and well, but have a strong story to relate. I look for depth of plot and uniqueness, and strong characterization. Study manuscript mechanics and submission procedures. Neatness does count. There is a sameness—a cloning process—among most magazines today that tends to dull the senses. Magazines like *Amelia* will awaken those senses while offering stories and poems of lasting value."

AMERICAN DANE, (II, IV), The Danish Brotherhood in America, 3717 Harney, Omaha NE 68131-3844. (402)341-5049. Editor: Jennifer Denning-Kock. Magazine: 8¼×11; 20-28 pages; 40 lb. paper; slick cover; illustrations and photos. "*American Dane* is the official publication of the Danish Brotherhood. Corporate purpose of the Danish Brotherhood is to promote and perpetuate Danish culture and traditions and to provide fraternal benefits and family protection." Estab. 1916. Circ. 6,500.

Needs: Ethnic. "Danish!" Receives 4 unsolicited fiction mss/month. Buys 1 ms/issue; 12 mss/year. Reads mss during August and September only. Publishes ms up to one year after acceptance. Length: 1,000 words average; 3,000 words maximum. Also publishes literary essays, some literary criticism, poetry.
How to Contact: Query first. SASE. Simultaneous submissions OK. Sample copy for $1 and 9×12 SAE with first-class postage for 2.5 oz. Fiction guidelines for #10 SAE and 1 first-class stamp (IRC). Reviews novels and short story collections.
Payment: Pays $15-50.
Terms: Pays on publication for first rights. Publication not copyrighted.
Advice: "Think Danish!"

‡**AMERICAN FICTION, (II),** English Dept., Moorhead State University, P.O. Box 229, Moorhead MN 56563. Editor: Alan Davis. Magazine: 5¾×8¼; 200-300 pages; Annually. "No themes, just a yearly open national contest." For "serious readers of fiction." Circ. 5,000.
Needs: Contemporary, experimental, traditional literary. Receives 750-1,200 mss/year. Buys or accepts 20-25 mss/year. "We accept stories *only* from February 1-May 1. Write for further information." Publishes ms within 12 months of acceptance. *Charges $7.50 reading fee per story.* Published work by Ursula Hegi, Florri McMillan, Clint McCown, Perry Glasser, Antonya Nelson. Length: 5,000 words average; 10,000 words maximum. Publishes short shorts. Sometimes critiques rejected mss.
How to Contact: "Send ms, cover/bio, *after* reading our ads in *AWP* and *Poets & Writers* each spring" SASE for query. "We don't return mss." Simultaneous submissions OK. Fiction guidelines for #10 SAE and 1 first-class stamp. For sample copy (strongly encouraged) write Birch Lane Press, 600 Madison Ave., New York NY 10022.
Payment: Pays $50 maximum and contributor's copies. "$1,000, $500, $250 awards to top 3 stories based on guest judge's decision."
Terms: Pays on publication for first North American serial rights. "The *American Fiction* series is a contest. Top 20-25 stories published, with awards given to judge's top 3 stories. 1992 judge was Tobias Wolff; 1993 judge was Wallace Stegner."
Advice: Looks for "moving, interesting, engaging characters, action, language." The next edition will be published by New Rivers Press and nationally distributed through the Talman Company, New York City.

AMERICAN LITERARY REVIEW, A National Journal of Poems and Stories, (II), University of North Texas, P.O. Box 13615, Denton TX 76203. (817)565-2127. Editors: Scott Cairns and Barb Rodman. Magazine: 7×10; 128 pages; 70 lb. Mohawk paper; 67 lb. Wausau Vellum cover. "Publishes quality, contemporary poems and stories." Semiannually. Estab. 1990. Circ. 800.
Needs: Mainstream and literary only. No genre works. Receives 50-75 unsolicited fiction mss/month. Accepts 7-10 mss/issue; 14-20 mss/year. Publishes ms within 2 years after acceptance. Published work by Gordon Weaver, Gerald Haslam and William Miller. Length: 3,500 words preferred. Critiques or comments on rejected mss when possible. Also accepts poetry.
How to Contact: Send complete ms with cover letter. Reports in 8-12 weeks. SASE. Simultaneous submissions OK. Sample copy for $5. Fiction guidelines free.
Payment: Pays in contributor's copies.
Terms: Acquires one-time rights. Sends pre-publication galleys to author.
Advice: "Give us distinctive styles, original approaches, stories that are willing to take a chance. We respond to character first, those that have a past and future beyond the page." Looks for "literary quality and careful preparation."

AMERICAN SHORT FICTION, (II), University of Texas Press, English Dept., University of Texas at Austin, Austin TX 78712-1164. (512)471-1772. Contact: Editor. Magazine: 5¾×9 1/4; 128 pages; 60 lb. natural paper; 8015 karma white cover. "*American Short Fiction* publishes fiction *only*, of all lengths, from short short to novella." Quarterly. Estab. 1990. Circ. 1,200.
Needs: Literary. "No romance, science fiction, erotica, mystery/suspense and religious." Receives 500 unsolicited mss/month. Acquires 6 mss/month; 25-30 mss/year. Does not read mss April 30-September 30. Publishes ms up to 1 year after acceptance. Agented fiction 20%. Published work by Reynolds Price, Ursula K. Le Guin and Rick Bass. Length: open. Publishes short shorts. Length: under 500 words.
How to Contact: Send complete ms with cover letter. Reports in 3-4 months on mss. Send SASE (IRC) for reply, return of ms; or send disposable copy of the ms. Simultaneous submissions OK if informed. Sample copy for $7.95. Fiction guidelines for #10 SAE with 1 first-class stamp.

Payment: Pays "comparably to *Story*."

Terms: Acquires first rights. Sends galleys to author.

Advice: "We pick work for *American Short Fiction* along simple lines: Do we love it? Is this a story we will be happy reading four or five times? We comment only *rarely* on submissions because of the volume of work we receive."

THE AMERICAN VOICE, (II), 332 W. Broadway, #1215, Louisville KY 40202. (502)562-0045. Editor: Frederick Smock. Magazine: 6×9; 130 pages; photographs. "Avant-garde feminist literature." Triannually. Estab. 1985. Circ. 2,000.
- Work from *The American Voice* has appeared in the *Pushcart Prize* anthologies. The magazine is also a member of The Council of Literary Magazines and Small Presses.

Needs: Feminist, literary. Receives 200 unsolicited mss/month. Buys 5 mss/issue; 15/year. Publishes ms 6-12 months after acceptance. Agented fiction 5%. Recently published work by Susan Griffin, Michelle Cliff, Isabel Allende, Reynolds Price. Publishes short shorts. Also publishes literary essays, literary criticism, poetry.

How to Contact: Send complete ms with cover letter. Should include bio and list of publications. Reports in 2 weeks on queries; 1 month on mss. Send SASE (IRC) for reply, return of mss or send a disposable copy of the manuscript. Does not consider simultanous submissions, reprints or electronic submissions. Sample copy for $5.

Payment: Pays $400 maximum, free subscription to the magazine, 2 contributor's copies. Additional copies at a reduced rate, $2.50.

Terms: Pays on publication for first North American serial rights. Sends galleys to author.

THE AMERICAS REVIEW, A Review of Hispanic Literature and Art of the USA, (II, IV), Arte Publico Press, 4800 Calhoun, University of Houston, Houston TX 77204-2090. (713)743-2841. Editors: Dr. Julian Olivares and Evangelina Vigil-Pinon. Magazine: 5½×8½; 128+ pages; illustrations and photographs. "*The Americas Review* publishes contemporary fiction written by U.S. Hispanics—Mexican Americans, Puerto Ricans, Cuban Americans, etc." Triannually. Estab. 1972.

Needs: Contemporary, ethnic, literary, women's, hispanic literature. No novels. Receives 12-15 fiction mss/month. Buys 2-3 mss/issue; 8-12 mss/year. Publishes mss "6 months to 1 year" after acceptance. Length: 3,000-4,500 average number of words; 1,500 words minimum; 6,000 words maximum (30 pages maximum, double-spaced). Publishes short shorts. Sometimes critiques rejected mss and recommends other markets.

How to Contact: Send complete manuscript. Reports in 3-4 months. SASE (IRC). Accepts electronic submissions via IBM compatible disk. Sample copy $5; $10 double issue.

Payment: Pays $50-200; 5 contributor's copies.

Terms: Pays on acceptance for first rights, and rights to 40% of fees if story is reprinted. Sponsors award for fiction writers.

Advice: "There has been a noticeable increase in quality in U.S. Hispanic literature."

‡ANGST: An Intellectual Cesspool of Graphic Realism, Hostility, and Mental Masturbation, (I, II), P.O. Box 836141, Richardson TX 75083-6141. Editor: Stuart G. Babitch. Magazine: 8½×11; 75 pages; 20 lb. uncoated paper; coated cover stock; illustrations. "Intense, reality based stories, cynical and pessimistic in nature, which display the bleak, dismal aspects of life; incorporating elements of isolation, desperation, disappointment, dehumanization, and rejection, vividly, with depictions of excessive, graphic acts, of self-indulgent thought, social deviation, violence, and gratuitous gore." Quarterly. Estab. 1993. Circ. 650.

Needs: Adventure, experimental, horror, mystery/suspense (police procedural). Upcoming theme: a tribute to filmmakers Woody Allen, Martin Scorsese, Paul Schrader, Harvey Keitel, James Toback, Jack Nicholson, Mickey Rourke, and all films of the 70's (April issue). Upcoming themes available for SASE. Publishes special fiction issue or anthology. Receives 10 unsolicited mss/month. Accepts 4 mss/issue; 16 mss/year. Publishes ms 3-6 months after acceptance. Agented fiction 5%. Length: 10,000 words maximum. Publishes short shorts. Always critiques or comments on rejected mss.

How to Contact: Send complete ms with a cover letter. Should include estimated word count, brief bio, social security number and list of publications. Reports in 1 month on queries; 3 weeks on mss. Send SASE (IRC) for reply. Simultaneous and reprint submissions OK. Sample copy for $4, 9×12 SAE and 2 first-class stamps. Fiction guidelines for #10 SAE and 1 first-class stamp.

Payment: Pays 2 contributor's copies; additional copies for $3.
Terms: Pays on publication for first North American serial rights. Sends galleys to author.
Advice: "No formulated storylines, plot devices, high-concept gimmickry, political rhetoric about the injustices and corruption of the U.S. government and its economic system of capitalism, premises which incorporate the supernatural, or anything which suspends or fails to acknowledge reality."

‡**ANIMAL TRAILS, (II, IV),** Tellstar Productions, P.O. Box 1264, Huntington WV 25714. Editor: Shannon Bridget Murphy. Magazine: 8×11; black ink illustrations and photographs. "A magazine for people who like to read fiction and true stories about animals; animal issues. Reading suitable for all ages. Name/address of veterinarians included free of charge with subscription." Semiannually. Estab. 1993. Circ. 500.
Needs: Fiction about animals: adventure, childrens/juvenile (5-9 years, 10-12 years), young adult/teen (10-18 years). Publishes annual special fiction issue or anthology. Receives 2-5 unsolicited mss/month. Accepts 2-5 mss/issue; 4-10 mss/year. Publishes ms 6 months-1 year after acceptance. Length: 1,000 words minimum; 7,000 words maximum. Publishes short shorts. Also publishes literary essays, literary criticism and poetry. Always critiques or comments on rejected mss.
How to Contact: Send complete ms with a cover letter. Should include estimated word count, bio (150-200 words) and list of publications. Reports in 1 month. Send SASE (or IRC) for return of the ms or send a disposable copy of the ms. Simultaneous, reprint and electronic submissions OK. Sample copy for $7. Fiction guidelines for $1. Reviews novels and short story collections.
Payment: Payment depends on budget.
Terms: Pays on publication for first or one-time rights.
Advice: Looks for "good, thought-out plots with animals primary focus of interest. Stories that communicate animal/human relationship in format of adventure, historical, humorous, mystery and true story. Experiment with ideas and themes. Use imagination for plots and be creative." Would like to see more "stories and essays about personal pets, material that gives animals human abilities, stories written by young people and college students." Write to Animal Trails for details about contests, annual photograph contest.

ANSUDA MAGAZINE, (I, II), Ansuda Publications, Box 158J, Harris IA 51345. Editor/Publisher: Daniel R. Betz. Magazine: 5½×8½; 72 pages; mimeo paper; heavy stock cover; illustrations on cover. "We prefer stories to have some sort of social impact within them, no matter how slight, so our fiction is different from what's published in most magazines. We aren't afraid to be different or publish something that might be objectionable to current thought. *Ansuda* is directed toward those people, from all walks of life, who are themselves 'different' and unique, who are interested in new ideas and forms of reasoning. Our readers enjoy *Ansuda* and believe in what we are doing." Published 2 times/year. Estab. 1979. Circ. 300.
Needs: Literary, psychic/supernatural/occult, fantasy, horror, mystery, adventure. "We are looking for honest, straightforward stories. No love stories or stories that ramble on for pages about nothing in particular." Accepts reprints. Accepts 4-6 mss/issue. Receives approximately 35-40 unsolicited fiction mss each month. Published new writers within the last year. Length: 8,000 words maximum. Also publishes poetry. Sometimes recommends other markets.
How to Contact: Send complete ms with SASE (IRC). Simultaneous submissions OK, if noted. Reports in 1 month. Publishes ms an average of 6 months after acceptance. Sample copy $3.75.
Payment: Pays 2 contributor's copies. Cover price less special bulk discount for extras.
Terms: Acquires first North American serial rights and second serial rights on reprints.
Advice: "Read the magazine—that is *very* important. If you send a story close to what we're looking for, we'll try to help guide you to exactly what we want. We appreciate neat copy, and if photocopies are sent, we like to be able to read all of the story. Fiction seems to work for us—we are a literary magazine and have better luck with fiction than articles or poems."

ANTAEUS, (III), The Ecco Press, 100 West Broad St., Hopewell NJ 08525. (609)466-4748. Editor-in-Chief: Daniel Halpern. Managing Editor: William Craeger. Magazine: 6½×9; 275 pages; Warren old style paper; some illustrations and photographs. "Literary magazine of fiction and poetry, literary documents, and occasional essays for those seriously interested in contemporary writing." Quarterly. Estab. 1970. Circ. 5,000.
  ● This prestigious literary journal is published by The Ecco Press, also listed in this book. *Antaeus* has been a past winner and finalist in the National Magazine Award for fiction and has some of the most beautiful covers I've ever seen (unfortunately, they don't reproduce well in black and white).

Needs: Contemporary, literary, prose poem, excerpted novel, and translations. No romance, science fiction. Receives 600 unsolicited fiction mss/month. Published fiction by Richard Ford, Donald Hall, Joyce Carol Oates; published new writers within the last year. Rarely critiques rejected mss. Also publishes poetry.

How to Contact: Send complete ms with SASE. No multiple submissions. Reports in 6-8 weeks. Sample copy $10 plus $1.50 postage. Fiction guidelines for SASE.

Payment: Pays $10/page and 2 contributor's copies, 40% discount for extras.

Terms: Pays on publication for first North American serial rights and right to reprint in any anthology consisting of 75% or more material from *Antaeus*.

Advice: "Read the magazine before submitting. Most mss are solicited, but we do actively search the unsolicited mss for suitable material. Unless stories are extremely short (2-3 pages), send only one. Do not be angry if you get only a printed rejection note; we *have* read the manuscript. Always include an SASE. Keep cover letters short, cordial and to the point."

‡ANTERIOR FICTION QUARTERLY, (II), Anterior Bitewing Ltd.®, 7735 Brand Ave., St. Louis MO 63135-3212. (314)522-6166. Editor: Tom Bergeron. Newsletter: 8½×11; 20 pages; 20 lb. bond paper; 20 lb. bond cover; illustrations. "Good, easy-reading stories with a point or punch-line, general interest; audience tends to be over 50." Quarterly. Estab. 1993. Circ. 50.

Needs: Adventure, historical (general), humor/satire, literary, mainstream/contemporary, mystery/suspense, psychic/supernatural/occult, regional, romance, sports. No "protests, causes, bigotry, sickness, fanatacism, soap." Receives 10 unsolicited mss/month. Accepts 10 mss/issue; 40 mss/year. Publishes 3-15 months after acceptance. Recently published work by Thomas Lynn, Denise Martinson, J. Alvin Speers. Length: 1,000 words preferred; 500 words minimum; 2,500 words maximum. Publishes short shorts. Length: 100-500 words. Always critiques or comments on rejected mss.

How to Contact: *Charges $1 reading fee/story.* Reports in 1 week on queries; 2 weeks on mss. Send SASE (IRC) for reply, return of ms or send a disposable copy of ms. Simultaneous, reprint and electronic submissions OK. Sample copy for $2. Fiction guidelines for SAE and 1 first-class stamp.

Payment: Pays $0-25; "$25 prize for best story in each issue. No other payments."

Terms: Pays on publication for one-time rights.

Advice: Looks for "good gimmicks; twists; imagination; departures from the everyday. Read Bernard Malamud; James Thurber; Henry James."

ANTIETAM REVIEW, (II, IV), Washington County Arts Council, 7 W. Franklin St., Hagerstown MD 21740. (301)791-3132. Editor: Susanne Kass. Magazine: 8½×11; 60 pages; photos. A literary journal of short fiction, poetry and black-and-white photographs. Annually. Estab. 1982. Circ. 1,500.

●*Antietam Review* has received several awards including Baltimore Artscape 92 Award for fiction and an Honorable Mention for Editorial Content from the American Literary Magazine Awards. Work published in the magazine has been included in the *Pushcart Prize* anthology and *Best American Short Stories* 1992.

Needs: Contemporary, ethnic, experimental, feminist, literary and prose poem. "We read manuscripts from our region—Delaware, Maryland, Pennsylvania, Virginia, West Virginia and Washington D.C. only. We read from September 1 to February 1." Receives about 100 unsolicited mss/month. Buys 7-9 stories/year. Recently published work by Wayne Karlin, Elisavietta Ritchie, Maxine Clair; published new writers within the last year. Length: 3,000 words average.

How to Contact: "Send ms and SASE with a cover letter. Let us know if you have published before and where." Reports in 1 to 2 months. "If we hold a story, we let the writer know. Occasionally we critique returned ms or ask for rewrites." Sample copy $5.25. Back issue $3.15.

Payment: "We believe it is a matter of dignity that writers and poets be paid. We have been able to give $100 a story and $25 a poem, but this depends on funding. Also 2 copies." Prizes: "We offer a $100 annual literary award in addition to the $100, for the best story."

Terms: Buys first North American serial rights. Sends pre-publication galleys to author if requested.

Advice: "We look for well-crafted work that shows attention to clarity and precision of language. We like relevant detail but want to see significant emotional movement within the course of the story—something happening to the central character. This journal was started in response to the absence of fiction markets for emerging writers. Its purpose is to give exposure to fiction writers, poets and photographers of high artistic quality who might otherwise have difficulty placing their work."

"We chose this cover, 'Meditation, South India,' for its strong composition and haunting quality," says Antietam Review *Executive Editor Susanne Kass. "We make a determined effort not to match photographs with text, as we believe each should stand on its own merits." This photo, by Schuyler Fonaroff, is part of a permanent display at the international headquarters of the American Leprosy Missions, Inc.* Antietam Review *publishes 8-10 short stories per issue, all written by natives or residents of Maryland, Pennsylvania, Virginia, West Virginia, Delaware and Washington DC. Kass says, "We look for high quality literary fiction from both established and emerging writers."*

✿THE ANTIGONISH REVIEW, (II), St. Francis Xavier University, Antigonish, Nova Scotia B2G 1C0 Canada. (902)867-3962. Editor: George Sanderson. Literary magazine for educated and creative readers. Quarterly. Estab. 1970. Circ. 800.

Needs: Literary, contemporary, prose poem and translations. No erotic or political material. Accepts 6 mss/issue. Receives 25 unsolicited fiction mss each month. Published work by Arnold Bloch, Richard Butts and Helen Barolini; published new writers within the last year. Length: 3,000-5,000 words. Sometimes comments briefly on rejected mss.

How to Contact: Send complete ms with cover letter. SASE or IRC. No simultaneous submissions. Accepts disk submissions compatible with Apple, Macintosh, WordPerfect (IBM) and Windows. Prefers hard copy with disk submission. Reports in 6 months. Publishes ms 3 months to 1 year after acceptance.

Payment: Pays 2 contributor's copies.

Terms: Authors retain copyright.

Advice: "Learn the fundamentals and do not deluge an editor."

ANTIOCH REVIEW, (II), Box 148, Yellow Springs OH 45387. (513)767-6389. Editor: Robert S. Fogarty. Associate Editor: Nolan Miller. Magazine: 6×9; 160 pages; 60 lb. book offset paper; coated cover stock; illustrations "seldom." "Literary and cultural review of contemporary issues in politics, American and international studies, and literature for general readership." Quarterly. Published special fiction issue last year; plans another. Estab. 1941. Circ. 4,000.

Needs: Literary, contemporary, translations and experimental. No children's, science fiction or popular market. Buys 5-6 mss/issue, 20-24 mss/year. Receives approximately 275 unsolicited fiction mss each month. Approximately 1-2% of fiction agented. Length: any length the story justifies.

The maple leaf symbol before a listing indicates a Canadian publisher.

How to Contact: Send complete ms with SASE (IRC), preferably mailed flat. Reports in 2 months. Publishes ms 6-9 months after acceptance. Sample copy $6; Guidelines for SASE.
Payment: Pays $15/page; 2 contributor's copies. $3.30 for extras.
Terms: Pays on publication for first and one-time rights (rights returned to author on request).
Advice: "Our best advice, always, is to *read* the *Antioch Review* to see what type of material we publish. Quality fiction requires an engagement of the reader's intellectual interest supported by mature emotional relevance, written in a style that is rich and rewarding without being freaky. The great number of stories submitted to us indicates that fiction apparently still has great appeal. We assume that if so many are writing fiction, many must be reading it."

‡**APALACHEE QUARTERLY, (II),** P.O. Box 20106, Tallahassee FL 32316. Editor: Barbara Hamby. Fiction Editors: Pamela Ball, Bul McCall, Ann Turkle. Magazine: 6×9; 130-200 pages; 20 lb. paper; 80 lb. cover stock; illustrations and photos. "We are looking for the best fiction, poetry, essays and interviews. We are especially interested in work that takes risks." Quarterly. Estab. 1973. Circ. 600.
   • Work appearing in the *Apalachee Quarterly* has been selected for inclusion in the O. Henry Prize anthology.
Needs: Ethnic/multicultural, experimental, feminist, gay, lesbian, literary and translations. No genre fiction. Publishes annual special fiction issue or anthology. Receives 200 unsolicited mss/month. Buys 4-8 mss/issue; 8-16 mss/year. Does not read mss in the summer. Recently published work by Pamela Houston, Roberto Fernandez and Edward Liminov. Length: 2,500 words preferred; 250 words minimum; 5,000 words maximum. Publishes short shorts. Also publishes literary essays and poetry. Sometimes comments on rejected mss.
How to Contact: Send complete ms with a cover letter. Should include bio (25 words or less). Reports on mss in 3 months. Send SASE (IRCs) for reply, return of ms or send disposable copy of ms. Simultaneous submissions OK. Sample copy for $5. Fiction guidelines for #10 SAE and 1 first-class stamp. Reviews novels and short story collections (usually only reviews authors who have appeared in the magazine or who are published by small presses.)
Payment: Pays 2 contributor's copies. Additional copies ½ price.
Terms: Acquires one-time rights. Sends galleys to quthor.
Advice: "Voice, style, intoxication with language" make a manuscript stand out. Would like to see more "fresh looks at odd occupations, experiments with language, mixed-genres, translations of interesting foreign writers." Avoid "stories that begin with a character waking up. Kafka did it, but rarely does anyone match his surprise. We also see too many stories that are little more than the sexual fantasies of young men—we call them the 'sex in cubicle' stories. Subjects that are overdone—dead grandparents, dogs, birds; crazy mothers; sexual abuse."

APPALACHIAN HERITAGE, (I, II), Hutchins Library, Berea College, Berea KY 40404. (606)986-9341. Editor: Sidney Farr. Magazine: 6×9; 80 pages; 60 lb. stock; 10 pt. Warrenflo cover; drawings and b&w photos. "*Appalachian Heritage* is a southern Appalachian literary magazine. We try to keep a balance of fiction, poetry, essays, scholarly works, etc., for a general audience and/or those interested in the Appalachian mountains." Quarterly. Estab. 1973. Circ. 1,100.
Needs: Regional, literary, historical. Receives 20-25 unsolicited mss/month. Accepts 2 or 3 mss/issue; 10 or more mss/year. Recently published work by Robert Morgan, David Whisnant, Denise Giardina, Gurney Norman; published new writers within the last year. Length: 2,000-2,500 word average; 3,000 words maximum. Publishes short shorts. Length: 500 words. Occasionally critiques rejected mss and recommends other markets.
How to Contact: Send complete ms with cover letter. Reports in 3-4 weeks on queries; 4-6 weeks on mss. SASE (IRC) for ms. Simultaneous submissions OK. Sample copy for $5.
Payment: Pays 3 contributor's copies; $5 charge for extras.
Terms: Acquires one-time rights. No reading fee, but "would prefer a subscription first."
Advice: "Trends in fiction change frequently. Right now the trend is toward slick, modern pieces with very little regional or ethnic material appearing in print. The pendulum will swing the other way again, and there will be a space for that kind of fiction. It seems to me there is always a chance to have really good writing published, somewhere. Keep writing and keep trying the markets. Diligent writing and rewriting can perfect your art. Be sure to study the market. Do not send me a slick piece of writing set in New York City, for example, with no idea on your part of the kinds of things I am interested in seeing. It is a waste of your time and money. Get a sample copy, or subscribe to the publication, study it carefully, then send your material."

ARARAT QUARTERLY, (IV), Ararat Press, AGBU., 585 Saddle River Rd., Saddle Brook NJ 07662. (201)797-7600. Editor: Dr. Leo Hamalian. Magazine: 8½×11; 72 pages; illustrations and b&w photographs. *"Ararat* is a forum for the literary and historical works of Armenian intellectuals or non-Armenian writers writing about Armenian subjects."
Needs: Condensed/excerpted novel, contemporary, historical (general), humor/satire, literary, religious/inspirational, translations. Publishes special fiction issue. Receives 25 unsolicited mss/month. Buys 5 mss/issue; 20 mss/year. Length: 1,000 words average. Publishes short shorts. Length: 500 words. Also publishes literary essays, literary criticism, poetry. Sometimes critiques rejected mss and recommends other markets.
How to Contact: Send complete ms with cover letter. Reports in 1 month on queries; 3 weeks on mss. SASE (IRC). Simultaneous and reprint submissions OK. Sample copy $7 and $1 postage. Free fiction guidelines. Reviews novels and short story collections.
Payment: Pays $40-75 plus 2 contributor's copies.
Terms: Pays on publication for one-time rights. Sends galleys to author.

ARBA SICULA (II,IV), St John's University, Jamaica NY 11439. Editor: Gaetano Cipolla. Magazine: 5½×8½; 85 pages; top-grade paper; good quality cover stock; illustrations; photos. Bilingual ethnic literary review (Sicilian-English) dedicated to the dissemination of Sicilian culture. Published twice a year. Plans special fiction issue. Estab. 1979. Circ. 1,800.
Needs: Accepts ethnic literary material consisting of various forms of folklore, stories both contemporary and classical, regional, romance (contemporary, historical, young adult) and senior citizen. Material submitted must be in the Sicilian language, with English translation desirable. Published new writers within the last year. Critiques rejected mss when there is time. Sometimes recommends other markets.
How to Contact: Send complete ms with SASE (IRCs) and bio. Reports in 2 months. Publishes ms 1-3 years after acceptance. Simultaneous submissions and reprints OK. Sample copy $8 with 8½×11 SASE and 90¢ postage.
Payment: 5 free author's copies. $4 for extra copies.
Terms: Acquires all rights. Publication copyrighted.
Advice: "This review is a must for those who nurture a love of the Sicilian language."

ARCHAE, A Paleo-literary Review, (II), Cloud Mountain Press, 10 Troilus, Old Bridge NJ 08857-2724. (908)679-8373. Editor: Alan Davis Drake. Magazine: 7×8½; 50-70 pages; illustrations. "For a literary, anthropological, general audience." Semiannually. Estab. 1990. Circ. 425.
Needs: Contemporary, experimental, historical, humor/satire, literary, mainstream, prose poem, translations. "No confessional material." Receives 8-10 unsolicited fiction mss/week. Accepts 1-2 mss/issue; 2-4 mss/year. Publishes mss 2-3 months after acceptance. Length: 3,000-6,000 words preferred; 8,000 words maximum. Publishes short shorts. Length: 500 words. Also publishes literary essays, criticism, poetry. Occasionally critiques or comments on rejected mss and recommends other markets.
How to Contact: Query first. Reports in 1 week on queries; in 1-2 weeks on mss. SASE. Simultaneous submissions OK. Accepts electronic submissions. Sample copy for $7, 8×9 SAE and 4 first-class stamps. Fiction guidelines for #10 SAE and 1 first-class stamp (IRCs). Make checks payable to "Alan Drake." Reviews novels and short story collections.
Payment: Pays in contributor's copies.
Terms: Aquires first North American serial rights. Sends pre-publication galleys to author.

ARGONAUT, (II, IV), Box 4201, Austin TX 78765-4201. Editor: Michael Ambrose. Magazine: 5⅜×8½; 64 pages; 60 lb. paper; coated cover stock; illustrations. *"Argonaut* is primarily a science fiction magazine. Our readers want original, literate, unusual stories with a strong science fiction or weird element." Semi-annually. Estab. 1972. Circ. 500.
 ● The editor says he's now exclusively looking for science fiction — especially hard science fiction — as opposed to horror or fantasy. Argo Press (publisher of *Argonaut*) won the 1992 Austin Book Award with author Mark Smith for the fiction collection *Riddle.*
Needs: Science fiction (especially hard science) and some weird fantasy. Receives 40-50 unsolicited fiction mss each month. Acquires 5-8 mss/issue. Recently published work by Dan Persons, William John Watkins, Ken Wisman and Denis Tiani. Length: 2,500-7,500 words. Publishes short shorts. Length: 500-1,000 words. Also publishes poetry. Sometimes recommends other markets.
How to Contact: Send complete ms with SASE (IRC). "Cover letter OK but not necessary." Reports in 1-2 months. "We do not consider simultaneous submissions or reprints." Sample copy for $4.95. Guidelines available for #10 SASE.

Payment: Pays 3 or more copies. Extras at 50% discount.
Terms: Acquires first North American serial rights.
Advice: "We are not interested in heroic or 'high' fantasy, horror, or media-derived stories. Our main focus is upon science fiction, particularly of the 'hard' variety, although we also publish weird fantasy of a highly original, unusual nature. We are looking above all for a *good story* with credible characters. Too often, a writer will forget these basics in building up the idea."

‡**THE ARIZONA UNCONSERVATIVE, Arizona's Progressive Voice, (II),** Vida Productions, P.O. Box 23683, Tempe Az 85285. Editor: Aaron Heresi. Fiction Editor: C. Ehren Hay. Newsletter: 8½×11; 4 pages; recycled 20 lb. paper. "Be yourself, and avoid clichés. Be honest, and don't repress any thoughts that some may consider unacceptable." Monthly. Estab. 1991. Circ. 250.
Needs: Erotica, ethnic/multicultural, experimental, feminist, gay, lesbian, literary, mainstream/contemporary, psychic/supernatural/occult. Receives 20 unsolicited mss/month. Accepts 0-1 ms/issue; 6-12 mss/year. Publishes ms 2 months after acceptance. Agented fiction 10%. Recently published work by Lyn Lifshin, Terrance X. Olson. Publishes short shorts, up to 500 words. Also publishes literary essays, literary criticism and poetry. Often critiques or comments on rejected mss.
How to Contact: Send complete ms with a cover letter. Should include estimated word count, brief bio, and list of publications. Reports in 1 month on queries; 1-2 months on mss. Send SASE (IRC) for reply or return of ms. Simultaneous submissions OK. Sample copy for $1, #10 SAE and 1 first-class stamp. Fiction guidelines for #10 SAE and 1 first-class stamp.
Payment: Pays $1-5 and 1 contributor's copy.
Terms: Pays on publication for one-time rights. Not copyrighted.
Advice: "Be fresh. Surprise me."

ARNAZELLA, (II), English Department, Bellevue Community College, Bellevue WA 98007. (206)641-2373. Advisor: Laura Burns Lewis. Editors change each year; contact advisor. Magazine: 5×6; 104 pages; 70 lb. paper; heavy coated cover; illustrations and photos. "For those interested in quality fiction." Annually. Estab. 1976. Circ. 500.
 ● The advisor says *Arnazella* needs more fiction manuscripts! (They receive a great deal of poetry and not enough fiction.)
Needs: Adventure, contemporary, ethnic, experimental, fantasy, feminist, gay, historical, humor/satire, lesbian, literary, mainstream, mystery/suspense, prose poem, regional, translations. Submit in fall and winter for issue to be published in spring. Published new writers within the last year. Publishes short shorts. Also publishes literary essays and poetry. *Preference will be given to Northwest contributors.*
How to Contact: Send complete ms with cover letter. Reports on mss in spring. "The months of June through October are very hard for us to read mss because we have no staff at that time. The best times to submit are October through January." SASE. No simultaneous submissions. Sample copy for $5. Guidelines for SASE (IRCs).
Payment: Pays in contributor's copies.
Terms: Acquires first rights.
Advice: "Read this and similar magazines, reading critically and analytically."

‡**ARRAY, (II),** B.A. Holloway, #104, 3575 28th St., Boulder CO 80301. (303)440-4207. Editor: Bess Holloway. Fiction Editor: Hazel Hart. Magazine: 5½×8½; 22 pages; 20 lb. paper; 24 lb. cover. "We view *ARRAY* as an antidote to the harshness, violence and hopelessness of modern society; therefore, authors must generally show a glimmer of hope or personal victory. General audience. Poetry, personal essay, fiction." Triannually. Estab. 1992. Circ. 100.
Needs: Adventure, ethnic/multicultural, historical (general), humor/satire, literary, mainstream/contemporary, mystery/suspense (amateur sleuth, romantic suspense), regional (contemporary, historical), science fiction (soft/sociological). Receives 2 unsolicited mss/month. Accepts 2-3 mss/issue; 9 mss/year. Publishes ms 1-6 months after acceptance. Recently published work by Hazel Hart, Donald A. Put, Judith T. Graham. Length: 1,250 words preferred; 750 words minimum; 2,000 words maximum. Publishes short shorts. Length: 400-500 words preferred. Also publishes poetry. Sometimes critiques or comments on rejected mss.
How to Contact: Send complete ms with a cover letter. Should include estimated word count, very short bio, and list of publications. Reports in 1-2 months. SASE (or IRC) for return of ms. Simultaneous submissions OK. Sample copy for $4.35. Fiction guidelines for #10 SAE and 1 first-class stamp.

Payment: Pays contributor's copies (1 minimum; 2 for stories occupying 3-5 pages in *ARRAY*); additional copies for $3.35.
Terms: Buys one-time rights. Sends galleys to author.
Advice: Looks for "tight construction. Many stories would come within our word limit if writers eliminated small words throughout. Clear focus and good characterization is mandatory. Do not use obscenities to indicate anger or frustration in a character. Clearly indicate story setting within first two paragraphs." Would like to see "a full development of the relationship between characters who are of widely differing ages. Stories should end with main character resolving problems presented in the text, not by simply fleeing the scene." Avoid "dull dialogue! Avoid one and two-word exchanges; avoid having characters engage in long arguments. Give characters both first and surnames. Avoid overuse of personal pronouns, especially 'I.' "

ARTEMIS, An Art/Literary Publication from the Blue Ridge and Virginia, (IV), Box 8147, Roanoke VA 24014. (703)365-4326. Editor: Dan Gribbin. Magazine: 8×8; 85 pages; heavy/slick paper; colored cover stock; illustrations; photos. "We publish poetry, art and fiction of the highest quality and will consider any artist/writer who lives or has lived in the Blue Ridge or Virginia. General adult audience with literary interest." Annually. Estab. 1976. Circ. 2,000.
Needs: Literary. Wants to see "the best contemporary style." Receives 50 unsolicited fiction mss/year. Accepts 3-4 mss/issue. Does not read mss Jan.-Aug. Publishes ms 4-5 months after acceptance. Published works by Rosanne Coggeshall, Jeanne Larsen, Kurt Rheinheimer; published work by new writers within the last year. Length: 1,500 words average; 2,500 words maximum. Also publishes poetry.
How to Contact: Submit 2 copies of unpublished ms between Sept. 15-Nov. 15, name, address and phone on title page only. Reports in 2 months. SASE (IRCs) for ms. No simultaneous submissions. Sample copy $6.50.
Payment: Pays 1 complimentary copy.
Terms: Acquires first rights.
Advice: "We look for polished quality work that holds interest, has imagination, energy, voice."

ARTFUL DODGE, (II), Department of English, College of Wooster, Wooster OH 44691. (216)263-2000. Editor-in-Chief: Daniel Bourne. Magazine: 150-200 pages; illustrations; photos. "There is no theme in this magazine, except literary power. We also have an ongoing interest in translations from Eastern Europe and elsewhere." Annually. Estab. 1979. Circ. 1,000.
● *Artful Dodge* won an Ohioana Library Association Book Award for Editorial Excellence in 1992.
Needs: Experimental, literary, prose poem, translations. "We judge by literary quality, not by genre. We are especially interested in fine English translations of significant contemporary prose writers." Receives 40 unsolicited fiction mss/month. Accepts 5 mss/year. Published fiction by Edward Kleinschmidt, Sesshu Foster and Zbigniew Herbert; and interviews with Tim O'Brien, Lee Smith and Stuart Dybek; published 1 new writer within the last year. Length: 10,000 words maximum; 2,500 words average. Also publishes literary essays, literary criticism, poetry. Occasionally critiques rejected mss.
How to Contact: Send complete ms with SASE (IRC). Do not send more than 30 pages at a time. Reports in 5-6 months. Sample copies of older, single issues are $2.75 or five issues for $5; recent issues are double issues, available for $5.75. Fiction guidelines for #10 SAE and 1 first-class stamp.
Payment: Pays 2 contributor's copies and small honorarium.
Terms: Acquires first North American serial rights.
Advice: "If we take time to offer criticism, do not subsequently flood us with other stories no better than the first. If starting out, get as many readers, good ones, as possible. Above all, read contemporary fiction and the magazine you are trying to publish in."

ART:MAG, (II), P.O. Box 70896, Las Vegas NV 89170. (702)734-8121. Editor: Peter Magliocco. Magazine: 5½×8½; 60 pages; 20 lb. bond paper; b&w pen and ink illustrations and photographs. Publishes "irreverent, literary-minded work by committed writers," for "small press, 'quasi-art-oriented' " audience. Estab. 1984. Circ. under 500.
● *Art:Mag* plans a collaboration with *Vagabond's House* magazine "featuring several fictional works, from off-beat to formal-traditional; similar future projects possible." *Art:Mag* is interested in art-related themes.
Needs: Condensed/excerpted novel, confession, contemporary, erotica, ethnic, experimental, fantasy, feminist, gay, historical (general), horror, humor/satire, lesbian, literary, mainstream, mystery/suspense, prose poem, psychic/supernatural/occult, regional, science fiction, translations and arts. No "slick-oriented stuff published by major magazines." Receives 1 plus ms/month. Accepts 1-2 mss/issue;

4-5 mss/year. Will read only between July and October. Publishes ms within 3-6 months of acceptance. Recently published work by Stephen D. Gutierrez, Elizabeth Gunderson, L.E. McCullough and James Theobald. Length: 2,000 words preferred; 250 words minimum; 3,000 words maximum. Also publishes literary essays "if relevant to aesthetic preferences," literary criticism "occasionally," poetry. Sometimes critiques rejected mss and recommends other markets.

How to Contact: Send complete ms with cover letter. Reports in 3 months. SASE (IRC) for ms. Simultaneous submissions OK. Sample copy for $4.50, 6×9 SAE and 79¢ postage. Fiction guidelines for #10 SAE and first-class stamp.

Payment: Pays contributor's copies.

Terms: Acquires one-time rights.

Advice: "Seeking more novel and quality-oriented work, usually from solicited authors. Magazine fiction today needs to be concerned with the issues of fiction writing itself—not just with a desire to publish or please the largest audience. Think about things in the fine art world as well as the literary one and keep the hard core of life in between."

‡ART'S GARBAGE GAZZETTE, (I), 214 Dunning, Madison WI 53704. (608)249-0715. Editor: Art Paul Schlosser. Newsletter: 5½×8½; 8 or more pages; photocopied bond paper. "Media, funny, scary, artistical, with good moral, or complaining about life, some gossip. Our philosophy is: We try to make people think and question and ponder at what life is." Quarterly. Estab. 1990. Circ. 20-40.

• Currently this publication is a few, folded-over, photocopied sheets featuring the editor's work, but he plans to include fiction by others, if available.

Needs: Adventure, childrens/juvenile (5-9 years, 10-12 years), condensed novel (very), ethnic/multicultural, experimental, fantasy (children's fantasy, science fantasy), historical (general), horror, humor/satire, literary, mainstream/contemporary, mystery/suspense (amateur sleuth, romantic suspense, young adult mystery, humorous detective), religious/inspirational, romance (gothic, historical, young adult, humorous), science fiction (hard science, soft/sociological, humorous), serialized novel, sports, translations, westerns (frontier, traditional, young adult western), young adult/teen (10-18 years). List of upcoming themes available for SASE. Receives 1 unsolicited ms/month. Accepts 0-5 mss/year. Publishes ms several months after acceptance. Recently published work by Richard Steingesser. Length: 0-1,000 words. Publishes short shorts. Also publishes literary essays, literary criticism and poetry. Sometimes critiques or comments on rejected mss.

How to Contact: Send complete ms with a cover letter. Reports in 6 months to 1½ years. Send SASE (or IRC) for reply, return of ms or send a disposable copy of ms. Simultaneous and reprint submissions OK. Sample copy 50¢ (for 2 pages). Reviews novels and short story collections.

Payment: Pays 1 contributor's copy.

Terms: Buys one-time rights.

Advice: "What is it about? Is it boring? Is it funny? Does it make you think? Does it speak to me? Does it have good sentences? Does he use too many swear words? If you were talking would you say things like that? Short is better than long. Make sense, not long-winded nonsense. Write as if you were telling it to a friend. Happiness, peace, love, joy, Murphy's Law, problems and romance all have a funny side. Wisdom helps guide people to the truth. Write from your heart guided with your mind."

‡AS IF, (II), Box 3223, 1601 Harkrider, Conway AR 72032. (501)329-1970. Editor: Clint Catalyst. Magazine: 8½×11; 52+ pages; 20 lb. paper; 20 lb. 2-color cover stock; black and white illustrations and photographs. "*As If* is a collection of images, poetry, and interviews geared primarily to Gothic subculture. For those who live in the worlds of agony and ecstasy, attraction and repulsion, faith and disbelief, harmony and discord, emotional exuberance and decay, *As If* exists." Triannually. Estab. 1993.

Needs: Erotica, gay, psychic/supernatural/occult, romance (gothic). Plans to publish special fiction issue or anthology. Receives 30-50 unsolicited mss/month. Accepts 1-3 mss/issue; 4-6 mss/year. Publishes ms 1-3 months after acceptance. Length: 300-600 words preferred; 1,500 words maximum. Publishes short shorts. Sometimes critiques or comments on rejected mss.

How to Contact: Query or send complete ms with a cover letter. "The method of contact is irrelevant; it is the quality of work that is important." Include "whatever information the writer finds relevant." Reports in 1-3 months. Send SASE (IRC) for reply or send a disposable copy of ms. Simultaneous or reprint submissions OK. Sample copy for $4 plus $1 postage (payable to Clint Green).

Payment: Pays 1-3 contributor's copies; additional copies for $2.50.

Advice: "Emotion, not precision, is essential in a work. Surprise us!" Would like to see more "erotica that is actually *erotic*." Avoid sending "trite vampire themes, melodramatic 'misunderstood teen' nonsense."

ASYLUM ANNUAL, (II), (formerly *Asylum*), P.O. Box 6203, Santa Maria CA 93456. Editor: Greg Boyd. Magazine: 8½ × 11; 160 pages; 10 pt. C1S cover. "For a literary audience." Annually. Estab. 1985. Circ. 2,500.
Needs: Contemporary, erotica, experimental, literary, prose poem, translations. "We have published a 'best of' fiction collection entitled: *Unscheduled Departures: The Asylum Anthology of Short Fiction*." Receives 100 unsolicited mss/month. Accepts 80 mss/issue. Publishes ms 6-18 months after acceptance. Agented fiction 1%. Publishes short shorts. Also publishes literary criticism, poetry. Rarely critiques rejected mss or recommends other markets.
How to Contact: Send complete ms with cover letter. Reports in 1-4 weeks on queries; 1-6 months on mss. SASE (IRC). No simultaneous submissions. Sample copy for $8. Reviews a limited number of novels and short story collections each year.
Payment: Pays contributor's copies.
Terms: Acquires first rights. Sends galleys to author.
Advice: "Short, tightly written prose fiction and prose poems stand the best chance of gaining acceptance in *Asylum Annual*. Writers should read the magazine before submitting work."

ATALANTIK, (II, IV), 7630 Deer Creek Drive, Worthington OH 43085. (614)885-0550. Editor: Prabhat K. Dutta. Magazine: 8½ × 11; approx. 80 pages; paper quality and cover stock vary; illustrations and photos. "The publication is bilingual: Indian (Bengali) and English language. This was started to keep the Indian language alive to the Indian immigrants. This contains short stories, poems, essays, sketches, book reviews, cultural news, children's pages, etc." Quarterly. Estab. 1980. Circ. 400.
• In 1992 Editor Prabhat K. Dutta received an award for excellence in magazine editing from the West Bengal Journalist Association, "Dishari." Fiction appearing in *Atalantik* tends to be on themes which appeal to those interested in Indian culture, especially Bengali.
Needs: Adventure, condensed novel, contemporary, ethnic, experimental, historical (general), humor/satire, juvenile (5-9 years), literary, mainstream, mystery/suspense, psychic/supernatural/occult, romance (romantic suspense), science fiction (hard science), translations, travelogue, especially to India. No politics and religion. Plans special issues, upcoming themes: "Bengali Literature"; "India." Receives 25 unsolicited fiction mss/month. Publishes about 2-4 fiction mss/issue; about 20-50 mss/year. Publishes ms an average of at least 9 months after acceptance. Length: 1,000-3,000 words average. Publishes short shorts. Length: 1-2 pages. Also publishes literary essays, literary criticism, poetry. Sometimes comments on rejected mss and recommends other markets.
How to Contact: Query with clips of published work or send complete ms with cover letter; "author's bio data and a synopsis of the literary piece(s)." Reports on queries in 1 month; on mss in 4 months. SASE. Simultaneous submissions OK. Sample copy $7; fiction guidelines for #10 SASE (IRC). Reviews novels and short story collections.
Payment: Pays in contributor's copies; charge for extras.
Terms: Acquires all rights. Sponsors contests for fiction writers.
Advice: "A short story has to be short and should have a story too. A completely imaginative short story without any real life linkage is almost impossible. The language should be lucid and characters kept to a small number. A short story is not simply the description of an incident. It goes far beyond, far deeper. It should present the crisis of a single problem. Usually a successful short story contains a singular idea which is developed to its conclusion in a uniquely charted path. A smaller version of *Atalantik* is managed by Keshab K. Dutta (36B, Bakul Bagan Rd., Calcutta 700025, India), for distribution in India and other Asian countries."

ATHENA INCOGNITO MAGAZINE (II), 1442 Judah St., San Francisco CA 94122. (415)665-0219. Editor: Ronn Rosen. Magazine: 8½ × 11; approximately 30-40 pages; illustrations; Xeroxed photos. "Open-format magazine with emphasis on experimental and/or any type of quality writing. Emphasis on poetry and experimental artwork especially." Quarterly. Estab. 1980. Circ. 100.
Needs: Any subjects OK. Receives 15 unsolicited mss/month. Publishes ms usually 2-3 months after acceptance. Requires magazine subscription "to cover postage and expense of publication" of $4 (for 1 issue) before reading ms. Published new writers within the last year. Publishes short shorts. No long pieces over 2 pages. Sometimes critiques rejected mss.
How to Contact: Send complete ms with cover letter. Reports in 2 weeks to 1 month. SASE. Simultaneous and reprint submissions OK. Sample copy for $4; fiction guidelines for SAE and 1 first-class stamp (IRC).
Payment: Pays in contributor's copies.
Terms: Acquires all rights. Publication not copyrighted.
Advice: "Experiment and practice eclecticism of all kinds! Discover! Pioneer! Dada lives!"

THE ATLANTEAN PRESS REVIEW, (II), P.O. Box 361116, Milpitas CA 95036. (408)262-8478. Editor: P. LeChevalier. Magazine: 6×9; 80 pages; book stock paper; 10 pt C1S cover; black and white illustrations and photographs. "*The Atlantean Press Review* publishes work in the school of Romantic-Realism: stories that are carefully plotted and have strong, heroic characters whose values drive the story." Quarterly. Estab. 1992. Circ. 300.
  • Note this magazine has changed its format and has gone from an annual to quarterly publication.
Needs: Adventure, literary, mainstream/contemporary, mystery/suspense (private eye/hard boiled, amateur sleuth), science fiction (if realistic), sports, translations, westerns. "Not interested in ethnic stories—we look for *universal* values." Receives 20 mss/month. Buys 8-10 mss/year. Publishes ms 5 months after acceptance. Published work by Edward Cline, Andrew Bernstein, Bill Bucko. Length: 5,000 words average. "Length is open (longer stories will be published in installments)." Also publishes literary essays, literary criticism, poetry. Often critiques rejected mss.
How to Contact: Query first. Should include estimated word count and one-page bio with submission. "Tell us your purpose and ambitions in writing." Reports in 3 weeks on queries; 3·months on mss. Send SASE (IRC) for reply, return of ms or send a disposable copy of the ms. Simultaneous, reprint and electronic·submissions OK. Sample copy for $5. Guidelines for #10 SAE and 1 first-class stamp or IRC.
Payment: Pays $15-100, plus 3 contributor's copies.
Terms: Pays on publication for first North American serial rights or one-time rights. Sends galleys to author.
Advice: Looks for "clarity, originality, logic, strong plot, heroic characters. It should be clear that you spent much longer *planning* the story than drafting it. Read *Atlas Shrugged*, *Quo Vadis*, *Shane* and Victor Hugo. Study a sample copy. Digest Rand's *The Romantic Manifesto*."

ATROCITY, Publication of the Absurd Sig of Mensa, (I), 2419 Greensburg Pike, Pittsburgh PA 15221. Editor: Hank Roll. Newsletter: 8½×11; 8 pages; offset 20 lb. paper and cover; illustrations; photographs occasionally. Humor and satire for "high IQ-Mensa" members. Monthly. Estab. 1976. Circ. 250.
Needs: Humor/satire. Liar's Club, parody, jokes, funny stories, comments on the absurdity of today's world. Receives 20 unsolicited mss/month. Accepts 2 mss/issue. Publishes ms 3-6 months after acceptance. Published new writers within the last year. Length: 50-150 words preferred; 650 words maximum.
How to Contact: Send complete ms. "No cover letter necessary if ms states what rights (e.g. first North American serial/reprint, etc.) are offered." Reports in 1 month. SASE. Simultaneous and reprint submissions OK. Sample copy for 50¢, #10 SAE and 2 first-class stamps (IRCs).
Payment: Pays contributor's copies.
Terms: Acquires one-time rights.
Advice: Manuscript should be single-spaced, copy ready. Horizontal format to fit on one 8½×11 sheet. "Be funny."

THE AZOREAN EXPRESS, (I, IV), Seven Buffaloes Press, Box 249, Big Timber MT 59011. Editor: Art Cuelho. Magazine: 6¾×8¼; 32 pages; 60 lb. book paper; 3-6 illustrations/issue; photos rarely. "My overall theme is rural; I also focus on working people (the sweating professions); the American Indian and Hobo; the Dustbowl era; and I am also trying to expand with non-rural material. For rural and library and professor/student, blue collar workers, etc." Semiannually. Estab. 1985. Circ. 600.
  • *Azorean Express* is published by Art Cuelho of Seven Buffaloes. He also publishes *Black Jack Hill and Holler* and *Valley Grapevine* listed in this book. See also his listing for the press.
Needs: Contemporary, ethnic, experimental, humor/satire, literary, regional, western, rural, working people. Receives 10-20 unsolicited mss/month. Accepts 2-3 mss/issue; 4-6 mss/year. Publishes ms 1-6 months after acceptance. Length: 1,000-3,000 words. Also publishes short shorts, 500-1,000 words. "I take what I like; length sometimes does not matter, even when longer than usual. I'm flexible." Sometimes recommends other markets.
How to Contact: "Send cover letter with ms; general information, but it can be personal, more in line with the submitted story. Not long rambling letters." Reports in 1-4 weeks. SASE. Sample copy for $5.75. Fiction guidelines for SASE (IRC).

Payment: Pays in contributor's copies. "Depends on the amount of support author gives my press."
Terms: Acquires first North American serial rights. "If I decide to use material in anthology form later, I have that right." Sends pre-publication galleys to the author upon request.
Advice: "There would not be magazines like mine if I was not optimistic. But literary optimism is a two-way street. Without young fiction writers supporting fiction magazines the future is bleak, because the commercial magazines allow only formula or name writers within their pages. My own publications receive no grants. Sole support is from writers, libraries and individuals."

BABY SUE, (I), Box 1111, Decatur GA 30031-1111. (404)875-8951. Editor: Don W. Seven. Magazine: 8½×11; 20 pages; illustrations and photos. *"Baby Sue* is a collection of music reviews, poetry, short fiction and cartoons," for "anyone who can think and is not easily offended." Biannually. Plans special fiction issue. Estab. 1983. Circ. 1,500.
• Sometimes funny, very often perverse, this 'zine featuring mostly cartoons and "comix" definitely is not for the easily offended.
Needs: Erotica, experimental and humor/satire. Receives 5-10 mss/month. Accepts 3-4 mss/year. Publishes ms within 3 months of acceptance. Publishes short shorts. Length: 1-2 single-spaced pages.
How to Contact: Query with clips of published work. SASE (IRC). Simultaneous submissions OK.
Payment: Pays 1 contributor's copy.
Advice: "If no one will print your work, start your own publication—it's easy and cheap. It's also a great way to make contact with other people all over the world who are doing the same."

BAD HAIRCUT, (II), P.O. Box 2827, Olympia WA 98507. Editors: Ray Goforth, Kim Goforth. Magazine: 5½×8½; 30 pages; illustrations. Published irregularly. Estab. 1987. Circ. 1,000.
Needs: Experimental, humor/satire, prose poem, translations, political, world-conscious. Receives 20 fiction ms/month. Accepts 1-3 mss/issue; 4-12 mss/year. Publishes short shorts. Also publishes literary essays, poetry. Almost always critiques rejected mss and recommends other markets.
How to Contact: Query with or without clips of published work; send complete ms with cover letter; or "send by special messenger." Reports in 1 week on queries; 2 months on mss. SASE. Simultaneous and reprint submissions OK. Sample copy for $4. Fiction guidelines for #10 SAE and 1 first-class stamp (IRC).
Payment: Pays subscription to magazine or contributor's copies; charge for extras. Additional payment (token cash amount) "depends on our financial state."
Terms: Acquires first North American serial rights. Rights revert to author.
Advice: "We focus exclusively upon politics, human rights and environmental issues. Always include a nice cover letter describing who you are and why you're sending your stuff to us."

BAHLASTI PAPERS, The Newsletter of the Kali Lodge, O.T.O., (I), P.O. Box 15038, New Orleans LA 70115. (504)899-7439. Editor: Soror Chén. Newsletter: 8½×11; 12 pages; 20 lb. paper; 20 lb. cover; 2 illustrations; occasional photographs. "Occult, mythological, artistic, alternative and political material for the lunatic fringe." Monthly. Estab. 1986. Circ. 200.
Needs: Condensed/excerpted novel, erotica, ethnic, experimental, fantasy, feminist, gay, horror, humor/satire, lesbian, literary, psychic/supernatural/occult, science fiction, serialized novel, "however our emphasis is on the occult. We do not publish poetry." Plans special compilation issues. Receives 10 unsolicited mss/month. Accepts 2 mss/issue; 24 mss/year. Publishes mss approx. 6 months after acceptance. Published work by Nancy Collins, Steve Canon and Darius James. Publishes short shorts. Also publishes literary essays, literary criticism.
How to Contact: Send complete ms with cover letter telling "why author is interested in being published in *Bahlasti Papers.*" Reports in 2 weeks on queries and 1 month on mss. SASE. Simultaneous and reprint submissions OK. Sample copy for $2.25 with 6×9 envelope and 2 first-class stamps (IRCs). Occasionally reviews novels and short story collections.
Payment: Pays subscription to magazine.
Terms: Publication not copyrighted.
Advice: "We look for the odd point-of-view; the individual; independence of thought; work which breaks down established archetypes and so liberates us from social programming. We are noted for our occult and mystical slant, and our concern for fresh, insightful, and odd points-of-view, with an emphasis on healing."

BAKUNIN, P.O. Box 1853, Simi Valley CA 93062-1853. Editor: Jordan Jones. Magazine: 5½×8½; 120 pages; acid-free paper; b&w high contrast illustrations; half-tone photographs. "A magazine for the dead Russian anarchist in all of us. We are looking for well-written stories and do not pre-judge

themes or styles. For a literary, counter-culture audience." Semiannually. Estab. 1990. Circ. 750.
● For a look at this publication, you may want to check out their special June 1993 issue on the Los Angeles "uprising." *Bakunin* often includes works of social commentary.

Needs: Confession, erotica, ethnic, experimental, feminist, gay, lesbian, literary, prose poem, serialized novel, translations (translators must submit proof of their right to translate that author's work.) "No formula fiction." Receives 45 unsolicited mss/month. Accepts 6-8 mss/issue; 12-16 mss/year. Usually publishes ms within 6 months after acceptance. Published work of Harold Jaffe, Mark Wisniewski, Barbara Jamison, Stephen Dixon. Length: 2,000 words or less preferred; 4,000 words maximum. Publishes short shorts. Sometimes critiques rejected mss and recommends other markets.
How to Contact: Send complete ms with cover letter. Cover letter should include short biographical note. Reports in 2 weeks to 3 months on mss. SASE. Simultaneous submissions (if noted) OK. Accepts electronic submissions via disk (IBM-DOS high-density or Macintosh high-density format). Sample copy for $5. Fiction guidelines for #10 SAE and 1 first-class stamp (IRCs).
Payment: Pays 2 contributor's copies.
Terms: Acquires first North American serial rights.
Advice: "We are looking for well-written work. Much of the work we accept is humorous and/or anti-establishment."

‡BALL MAGAZINE, (II), Side 'O' Fries Press, P.O. Box 775, Northampton MA 01061. (413)584-3076. Editor: Douglas M. Kimball. Fiction Editor: Paull Goodchild. Magazine: 8½×11; 80 pages; newsprint paper; 80 lb. gloss cover; black and white illustrations and halftone photographs. "*Ball Magazine*'s content is dictated by the quality of the submissions. We publish all styles and genres." Semiannually. Estab. 1993. Circ. 2,000.
Needs: Erotica, ethnic/multicultural, experimental, fantasy (science fantasy), feminist, gay, humor/satire, lesbian, literary, mainstream/contemporary, science fiction (soft/sociological), serialized novel and translations. "No rim shot or punchline fiction." Plans to publish annual special fiction issue or anthology. Receives 60-100 mss/month. Accepts 6-10 mss/issue. Publishes ms 6-12 months after acceptance. Agented fiction 0-20%. Recently published work by Lenora Rogers, F.O. Dodge, D.F. Lewis. Length: 7,000 words maximum. Publishes short shorts. Also publishes poetry. Often critiques or comments on rejected mss.
How to Contact: Send complete ms with friendly note ("no publicity crap"). Should include bio (3 lines). Reports in 1 week on queries; 2 months on mss. Send SASE (or IRC) for reply, return of ms or send a disposable copy of ms. Simultaneous submissions OK. Sample copy for $4.95, 8½×11 SAE and $1.21 postage. Fiction guidelines free with #10 SAE and 1 first-class stamp. Reviews novels and short story collections.
Payment: Pays 2 contributor's copies; additional copies for $3.95.
Terms: Acquires first or one-time rights.
Advice: "We are more likely to give more time to a new idea than a boring old crone cliché. If you find yourself agonizing about how something might be perceived then you'd better get a day job. We rarely see guts or insight. We are interested in work from any genre that breaks new ground."

BAMBOO RIDGE, The Hawaii Writers' Quarterly, (II, IV), P.O. Box 61781, Honolulu HI 96839-1781. (808)599-4823. Editors: Darrell Lum and Eric Chock. "Writing that reflects the multicultural diversity of Hawaii." Published 2-4 times/year. Estab. 1978.
Needs: Ethnic, literary, Hawaii interest. "Writers need not be from Hawaii, but must reflect Hawaii's multicultural ethnic mix." Publishes annual special fiction and poetry issues (special collections by single authors). Publishes ms 6 months-1 year after acceptance. Length: up to 25 typed pages, double-spaced. Publishes short shorts.
How to Contact: Query first. Reports in 1 month on queries; 3-6 months on mss. SASE. Photocopied submissions OK. Fiction guidelines for #10 SAE and 1 first-class stamp (IRCs).
Payment: Pays 2 contributor's copies, small honorarium and 1 year subscription depending on grant money. Charges for extras (40% discount).
Terms: Pays on publication for first North American serial rights.

✹BARDIC RUNES, (IV), 424 Cambridge St, Ottawa, Ontario K1S 4H5 Canada. (613)231-4311. Editor: Michael McKenny. Magazine. Estab. 1990.
Needs: Fantasy. "Traditional or high fantasy. Story should be set in pre-industrial society either historical or of author's invention." Length: 3,500 words or less.
Payment: Pays ½¢/word.
Terms: Pays on acceptance. Reports in 2 weeks.

‡**BARE WIRE, (I, II)**, P.O. Box 825, Azusa CA 91702-0825. Editor: d. ray smith. Magazine: 7×8½; 60 pages; 20-24 lb. paper; 90 lb. cotton or linen cover. Semiannual. Estab. 1994. Circ. 150.
  • This publication's first issue is due Spring 1994.
Needs: Erotica, ethnic/multicultural, experimental, gay, humor/satire, lesbian, literary, mainstream/contemporary. Accepts 2-3 mss/issue; 4-6 mss/year. Publishes ms 6 months-1 year after acceptance. Length: 5,000 words maximum. Publishes short shorts. Also publishes literary essays and poetry. Sometimes critiques or comments on rejected mss.
How to Contact: Send complete ms with a cover letter. Should include estimated word count. Reports in 1 week on queries; 3-4 months on mss. Send SASE (or IRC) for reply, return of ms or send a disposable copy of ms. Simultaneous submissions and reprints OK. Fiction guidelines for #10 SAE and 1 first-class stamp or IRC.
Payment: Pays 1 contributor's copy.
Terms: Not copyrighted.
Advice: Looks for "works with an honest voice—ones that kick and scream and jump off the page—send work that you would put on your tombstone. Send your best—the stuff that gives you chills when you read it. Send work that is on the verge of being out of control. Find a voice that is your own. Don't drink cheap beer. Develop characters fully. Let them tell the story. Be honest or don't get caught lying. Don't rush to send out work, let it sit with you awhile."

BEING, A Celebration of Spirit, Mind & Body, (I, II, IV), PPRN (Publications of Peggy and Richard Navarro), P.O. Box 891510, Temecula CA 92589-1510. (909)676-0504. Editor: Marjorie (Peggy) Talarico-Navarro. Associate Editor: June Georg. Magazine: digest-sized; 50-75 pages; "desk-top published;" soft cover; black-and-white, pen-and-ink illustrations. "*Being* is a New-Age style quarterly featuring short stories, articles and poetry." Quarterly.
Needs: Themes issues only. Upcoming themes: "Angels, Angels Everywhere!" Short stories up to 6,500 words, featuring angels: their existence/purpose/gifts that influence/help in our daily lives. No dark angel/angel-from-hell material, please. Deadline: March 25, 1994; "Sex and Spirituality: The True Meaning/Celebration of Life." Same short story/article/poetry lengths as above. Subject matter for this issue may be erotic, but not pornographic. Deadline: July 25, 1994; "Channeling: The World of the Spirit." Short stories featuring channeling/the world of spirit. Same lengths as above. Deadline: September 25, 1994. Recently published work by Paul Truttman, Valerie von Weich, Anne M. Valley.
How to Contact: Charges reading fee to nonsubscribers; $2/story. Send complete ms with cover letter. "I like to know a little bit about the author, credits (if any; don't worry if you have none, we enjoy discovering new talent. That's one of the big reasons we're here.) and what prompted author to write this particular story." Reports in 16-18 weeks. SASE. Will look at simultaneous and reprint submissions, but rarely use. Sample copy for $7 (payable to Marjorie Talarico-Navarro). Fiction guidelines for #10 SAE and 1 first-class stamp (IRC).
Payment: No payment. Tearsheets available on request for SASE.
Advice: "Looking for fresh originality! Surprise me! Bend your imagination and keep me breathlessly turning the pages. (If there is artwork to go along with the story/article/poem, I would like to see it)."

THE BELLETRIST REVIEW, (I, II), Marmarc Publications, Suite 290, 17 Farmington Ave., Plainville CT 06062. Editor: Marlene Dube. Fiction Editor: Marc Saegaert. Magazine: 8½×11; 80 pages. "We are interested in compelling, well-crafted short fiction in a variety of genres. Our title *Belletrist*, means 'lover of literature.' This magazine will appeal to an educated, adult audience that appreciates quality fiction." Semiannually.
  • *The Belletrist Review* will offer a special fiction contest in September 1994. The award is $200—check with them for details.
Needs: Adventure, contemporary, erotica, horror (psychological), humor/satire, literary, mainstream, mystery/suspense, regional. "To give writers an idea of our eclectic tastes in fiction, we are inspired by the masters such as Poe, Chekhov, and O. Henry, and contemporary authors such as Richard Selzer, Ray Bradbury and Isaac Bashevis Singer." No poetry, fantasy, juvenile, westerns, or overblown horror or confessional pieces. Accepts 10-12 mss/issue; approximately 25 mss/year. Publishes ms within 1 year after acceptance. Length: 2,500-5,000 words preferred; 1,000 words minimum; 5,000 words maximum. Comments on or critiques rejected mss when time permits and recommends other markets on occasion.
How to Contact: Send complete ms with cover which should include brief biographical note and any previous publications. Reports in 1 month on queries; 2 months on mss. SASE (IRC). Simultaneous submissions OK. 1994 Fiction Contest Guidelines for SASE.

Payment: Pays contributor's copies.
Terms: Acquires one-time rights.
Advice: "In order to give your writing the consideration it deserves, please be sure your manuscript is neatly typed and professionally presented, and only submit one manuscript at a time. Don't tell us about the story or its merits in your cover letter; let us discover this for ourselves. Also, many submissions we receive tend to read more like a narration of an event than a story. Re-read your drafts aloud and cut, ruthlessly, anything that instead of furthering the plot, bogs it down with unnecessary detail."

‡**THE BELLINGHAM REVIEW, (II),** 1007 Queen St., Bellingham WA 98226. Editor: Knute Skinner. Magazine: 5½×8; 64 pages; 60 lb. white paper; varied cover stock; photos. "A literary magazine featuring original short stories, novel excerpts, short plays and poetry of palpable quality." Semiannually. Estab. 1977. Circ. 700.
Needs: All genres/subjects considered. Acquires 1-2 mss/issue. Publishes short shorts. Published new writers within the last year. Length: 5,000 words or less. Also publishes poetry. Critiques rejected mss when there is time.
How to Contact: Send complete ms. Reports in 2 weeks to 3 months. Publishes ms an average of 1 year after acceptance. Sample copy $2. Reviews novels and short story collections.
Payment: Pays 1 contributor's copy plus 2-issue subscription. Charges $2 for extras.
Terms: Acquires first North American serial and one-time rights.
Advice: Mss are rejected for various reasons, "but the most common problem is too much *telling* and not enough *showing* of crucial details and situations. We also look for something that is different or looks at life in a different way."

BELLOWING ARK, A Literary Tabloid, (II), Box 45637, Seattle WA 98145. (206)545-8302. Editor: R.R. Ward. Tabloid: 11½×16; 28 pages; electro-brite paper and cover stock; illustrations; photos. "We publish material which we feel addresses the human situation in an affirmative way. We do not publish academic fiction." Bimonthly. Estab. 1984. Circ. 500.
• Work from *Bellowing Ark* appeared in the *Pushcart Prize* anthology in 1991. The editor says he's using much more short fiction these days. Remember he likes a traditional, narrative approach and "abhors" minimalist and post-modern work.
Needs: Contemporary, literary, mainstream, serialized/excerpted novel. "Anything we publish will be true." Receives 450-500 unsolicited fiction mss/year. Accepts 2-3 mss/issue; 12-18 mss/year. Time varies, but publishes ms not longer than 6 months after acceptance. Recently published work by Kim Silviera Wolterbeek Shelly Uva, Dorothy Worfolk, Loren Sundlee and Robin Sterns; published new writers within the last year. Length: 3,000-5,000 words average ("but no length restriction"). Publishes short shorts. Also publishes literary essays, literary criticism, poetry. Sometimes critiques rejected mss and recommends other markets.
How to Contact: No queries. Send complete ms with cover letter and short bio. "Prefer cover letters that tell something about the writer. Listing credits doesn't help." No simultaneous submissions. Reports in 6 weeks on mss. SASE. Sample copy for $3, 9×12 SAE and $1.21 postage.
Payment: Pays in contributor's copies.
Terms: Acquires all rights, reverts on request.
Advice: "*Bellowing Ark* began as (and remains) an alternative to the despair and negativity of the Workshop/Academic literary scene; we believe that life has meaning and is worth living—the work we publish reflects that belief. Learn how to tell a story before submitting. Avoid 'trick' endings—they have all been done before and better. *Bellowing Ark* is interested in publishing writers who will develop with the magazine, as in an extended community. We find *good* writers and stick with them. This is why the magazine has grown from 12 to 28 pages (we are considering going to 32 pages soon!)."

BELOIT FICTION JOURNAL, (II), Box 11, Beloit College WI 53511. (608)363-2308. Editor: Clint McCown. Magazine: 6×9; 150 pages; 60 lb. paper; 10 pt. C1S cover stock; illustrations and photos on cover. "We are interested in publishing the best contemporary fiction and are open to all themes except those involving pornographic, religiously dogmatic or politically propagandistic representations. Our magazine is for general readership, though most of our readers will probably have a specific interest in literary magazines." Semiannually. Estab. 1985.
• Editor Clint McCown is featured in an interview in the 1993 edition of this book. Work first appearing in *Beloit Fiction Journal* has been reprinted in award-winning collections, including the *Flannery O'Connor* and the *Milkweed Fiction Prize* collections.

Needs: Contemporary, literary, mainstream, prose poem, spiritual and sports. No pornography, religious dogma, political propaganda. Receives 400 unsolicited fiction mss/month. Accepts 8-10 mss/issue; 16-20 mss/year. Replies take longer in summer. Publishes ms within 9 months after acceptance. Length: 5,000 words average; 250 words minimum; 10,000 words maximum. Sometimes critiques rejected mss and recommends other markets.

How to Contact: Send complete ms with cover letter. Reports in 1 week on queries; 1-6 weeks on mss. SASE (IRC) for ms. Simultaneous submissions OK, if identified as such. Sample copy $5. Fiction guidelines for #10 envelope and 1 first-class stamp.

Advice: "Many of our contributors are writers whose work we have previously rejected. Don't let one rejection slip turn you away from our—or any—magazine."

‡**BIG RAIN, (II),** P.O. Box 20764, Sedona AZ 86341. (602)284-1763. Editor: Clint Frakes. Magazine: 10½×17; 60 pages; 40 lb. bookstock; cardstock cover; b&w illustrations and photos. "New movements in American writing; we publish essays, stories and poetry; our audience probably rests in under 40 years old, but makes its way to universities and primarily western region." Annually. Estab. 1991. Circ. 750.

Needs: Erotica, feminist, gay, humor/satire, lesbian, literary and translations. No "sci-fi, romance, hyper-political, self-righteous" writing. Plans to publish special fiction issues or anthologies in the future. Receives 5 unsolicited mss/month. Acquires 3 mss/year. Publishes ms 6 months after acceptance. Recently published work by Andy Hoffmann, Nick Burns and Brenda Coultas. Length: open. Publishes short shorts. Also publishes literary essays, literary criticism and poetry. Sometimes critiques or comments on rejected mss.

How to Contact: Send complete ms with a cover letter. Should include bio (50 words). Reports in 2-4 weeks on queries; 2 months on mss. SASE (IRC). Simultaneous and reprint submissions OK. Sample copy for $6.

Payment: Pays 2 contributor's copies. Additional copies $2.

Terms: Acquires first North American serial rights. Sends galleys to author.

Advice: Looks for "something new, with interesting language, soul and guts."

BILINGUAL REVIEW, (II, IV), Hispanic Research Center, Arizona State University, Tempe AZ 85287-2702. (602)965-3867. Editor-in-Chief: Gary D. Keller. Scholarly/literary journal of US Hispanic life: poetry, short stories, other prose and short theater. Magazine: 7×10; 96 pages; 55 lb. acid-free paper; coated cover stock. Published 3 times/year. Estab. 1974. Circ. 2,000.

Needs: US Hispanic creative literature. "We accept material in English or Spanish. We publish original work only—no translations." US Hispanic themes only. Receives 50 unsolicited fiction mss/month. Accepts 3 mss/issue; 9 mss/year. Publishes ms an average of 1 year after acceptance. Recently published work by Judith Ortiz Cofer, Leo Romero, Connie Porter and Nash Candelaria; published work of new writers within the last year. Also publishes literary criticism on US Hispanic themes and poetry. Often critiques rejected mss.

How to Contact: Send 2 copies of complete ms with SAE and loose stamps (IRCs). Reports in 1-2 months. Simultaneous and high-quality photocopied submissions OK. Sample copy for $9. Reviews novels and short story collections.

Payment: Pays 2 contributor's copies. 30% discount for extras.

Terms: Acquires all rights (50% of reprint permission fee given to author as matter of policy).

Advice: "We do not publish literature about tourists in Latin America and their perceptions of the 'native culture.' We do not publish fiction about Latin America unless there is a clear tie to the United States (characters, theme, etc.)."

‡**BLACK FIRE, (I, IV),** BLK Publishing Co., Box 83912, Los Angeles CA 90083. (310)410-0808. Fax: (310)410-9250. Editor: Alan Bell. Magazine: 8½×11; 48 pages; book 60 lb. paper; color glossy cover; illustrations and photographs. Bimonthly. Estab. 1992.

● BLK also publishes *Black Lace*, a magazine featuring lesbian-oriented fiction, listed in this book. BLK is a member of COSMEP.

Needs: Ethnic/multicultural, gay. Accepts 4 mss/issue. Publishes short shorts. Also publishes poetry.

How to Contact: Query first, query with clips of published work or send complete ms with a cover letter. Should include bio (3 sentences). Send a disposable copy of the ms. No simultaneous submissions; electronic submissions OK. Sample copy for $5.95. Fiction guidelines free.

Payment: Pays free subscription, 5 contributor's copies.

Terms: Acquires first North American serial rights and right to anthologize.

THE BLACK HAMMOCK REVIEW, A Literary Quarterly, (I, II, IV), P.O. Box 1642, Oviedo FL 32765. (407)628-4014. Editor: Edward Anthony Nagel. Magazine: 8½×11; 40+ pages; 20 lb. paper; illustrations and photos. "*The Black Hammock Review* is published by Quantum Press, a Florida non-profit cooperative. It was established to publish works which reflect rural motifs, for example, such settings as Oviedo, Geneva, Chuluota and the Black Hammock area in east-central Florida." Quarterly. Estab. 1992.
- Note that *The Black Hammock Review* appears to be published co-operatively with memberships required and members share publishing costs.
Needs: Ethnic/multicultural, experimental, fantasy (artistic), humor/satire, literary, mainstream/contemporary, psychic/supernatural/occult, regional, romance (contemporary), science fiction (soft/sociological), serialized novel, translations, "bucolic themes." Receives 10 unsolicited mss/month. Buys 4 mss/issue; 16+ mss/year. Publishes ms 3 months after acceptance. Length: 2,500 words preferred; 1,500 words minimum; 3,500 words maximum. Publishes short shorts. Length: 500 words. Also publishes literary essays, literary criticism and poetry. Always critiques or comments on returned mss.
How to Contact: Send complete ms with a cover letter. Should include bio (short), list of publications and brief statement of writer's artistic "goals." Reports in 2 weeks. Send SASE (IRCs) for reply, return of mss or a disposable copy of the ms. No simultaneous submissions. Sample copy for $4 and 8½×11 SAE. Reviews novels and short story collections.
Payment: *Charges membership fee $25 for individual; $50 for 3 writers.* Each member of the cooperative is assured publication of at least one carefully edited piece each year, subject to approval by our editors. Expenses not covered by the fees and subscriptions will be shared by the members, pro rata, not to exceed an amount fixed by the members, prior to the publication each quarter. Pays $50-75 *for selected works of established authors.* Pays 6 contributor's copies. Additional copies at a reduced rate, $2.
Terms: Pays on publication for one-time rights.
Advice: Looks for "work that evokes in the reader's mind a vivid and continuous dream, vivid in that it has density, enough detail and the right detail, fresh with the author, and shows concern for the characters and the eternal verities. And continuous in that there are no distractions such as poor grammar, purple prose, diction shifts, or change in point of view. Short fiction that has a beginning, middle and end, organically speaking. Immerse yourself in the requested genre, format i.e., bucolic themes, work the piece over and over until it is 'right' for you, does what you want it to do; read the masters in your genre on a stylistic and technical level, begin to 'steal instead of borrow.' Transmute your emotions into the work and 'write short.' "

THE BLACK HOLE LITERARY REVIEW, (I), 1312 Stonemill Court, Cincinnati OH 45215. (513)821-6670 or (513)821-6671. Editor: Wm. E. Allendorf. Electronic Bulletin Board. "This is an attempt to revolutionize publishing—no paper, no rejection slips, no deadlines. For any person with access to a home computer and a modem." Estab. 1989. Circ. 8,000.
Needs: "Any or all fiction and nonfiction categories are acceptable. Any size, topic, or inherent bias is acceptable. The only limitation is that the writer will not mind having his piece read, and an honest critique given directly by his readership." Plans future hardcopy anthology. Publishes ms 1-2 days after acceptance. Length: 2,000-10,000 words. Publishes short shorts, poetry, essays. "Critique given if not by editor, then by readers through Email."
How to Contact: Upload as EMAIL to the editor. Cover letter should include "titles, description (abstract), copyright notice." Reports in 1-2 days. Simultaneous submissions OK.
Payment: Pays in royalties, but charges fee for initial inputting (see below).
Terms: Charges $5 minimum subscription. Submissions cost $.50+ (deducted from subscription). Royalties are accrued each time the piece is read. Contact editor for details. Buys one-time rights.
Advice: "If the concept of the electronic magazine goes over with the public, then the market for fiction is limitless. Any piece that an author has taken the trouble to set to print is worth publishing. However, *The Hole* is looking for writers that want to be read—not ones that just want to write. The electronic magazine is an interactive medium, and pieces are judged on their ability to inspire a person to read them." Writers interested in submitting should: "Do it. You would be the first to be rejected by *The Hole*, if we did not use your piece; to make matters easier for all concerned, submit your piece as a ASCII text file via the modem. If you do not have access to a home computer with a modem, buy one, borrow one, steal one. This is the wave of the future for writers."

BLACK ICE (IV), Campus Box 494, Boulder CO 80309-0494. (303)492-8947. Editor: Mark Amerika. Magazine: 5½ × 8½; 100 pages; glossy cover; photography on cover. "Publishes the most experimental innovative writing being written today for writers, critics, sophisticated readers." Published 3 times/year. Estab. 1984. Circ. 700.
Needs: Experimental, literary, translations. Does not want to see "anything that's not ground-breaking." Receives 50-75 unsolicited mss/month. Accepts approx. 12-15 mss/issue; approx. 40 mss/year. Publishes ms 2-4 months after acceptance. Published work by Raymond Federman, Eurudice, Ricardo Cruz, Diane Glancy. Sometimes critiques rejected mss and recommends other markets.
How to Contact: Send complete manuscript with cover letter. Reports in 3-6 months on queries; 3-6 months on mss. SASE. Simultaneous submissions OK. Sample copy $7. Fiction guidelines for #10 SAE and 1 first-class stamp (IRC).
Payment: Pays in contributor's copies.
Terms: Acquires first rights.
Advice: "Expand your 'institutionalized' sense of what a story should be so that you include (open yourself up to) language play, innovative spatial composition, plots that die trying, de-characterizations whipped up in the food processor, themes barely capable of maintaining equilibrium in the midst of end-of-the-century energy crisis/chaos, etc."

BLACK JACK, (I), Seven Buffaloes Press, Box 249, Big Timber MT 59011. Editor: Art Cuelho. "Main theme: Rural. Publishes material on the American Indian, farm and ranch, American hobo, the common working man, folklore, the Southwest, Okies, Montana, humor, Central California, etc. for people who make their living off the land. The writers write about their roots, experiences and values they receive from the American soil." Annually. Estab. 1973. Circ. 750.
• *Black Jack* is published by Art Cuelho of Seven Buffaloes Press. He also publishes *Valley Grapevine* and *Azorean Express* also listed in this book. See also his listing for the press.
Needs: Literary, contemporary, western, adventure, humor, American Indian, American hobo, and parts of novels and long short stories. "Anything that strikes me as being amateurish, without depth, without craft, I refuse. Actually, I'm not opposed to any kind of writing if the author is genuine and has spent his lifetime dedicated to the written word." Receives approximately 10-15 unsolicited fiction mss/month. Acquires 5-10 mss/year. Length: 3,500-5,000 words (there can be exceptions).
How to Contact: Query for current theme with SASE (IRC). Reports in 1 week on queries; 2 weeks on mss. Sample copy for $5.75.
Payment: Pays 1-2 contributor's copies.
Terms: Acquires first North American serial rights and reserves the right to reprint material in an anthology or future *Black Jack* publications. Rights revert to author after publication.
Advice: "Enthusiasm should be matched with skill as a craftsman. That's not saying that we don't continue to learn, but every writer must have enough command of the language to compete with other proven writers. Save postage by writing first to the editor to find out his needs. A small press magazine always has specific needs at any given time. I sometimes accept material from country writers that aren't all that good at punctuation and grammar but make up for it with life's experience. This is not a highbrow publication; it belongs to the salt-of-the-earth people."

‡BLACK LACE, (I, IV), BLK Publishing Co., Box 83912, Los Angeles CA 90083. (310)410-0808. Editor: Alycee Lane. Magazine: 8½ × 11; 48 pages; electrabrite paper; color glossy cover; illustrations and photographs. Quarterly. Estab. 1991.
• BLK also publishes a magazine of gay-oriented fiction, *Black Fire*, listed in this book. BLK is a member of COSMEP.
Needs: Ethnic/multicultural, lesbian. Accepts 4 mss/year. Publishes short shorts. Also publishes literary essays, literary criticism and poetry.
How to Contact: Query first, query with clips of published work or send complete ms with a cover letter. Should include bio (3 sentences). Send a disposable copy of the ms. No simultaneous submissions; electronic submissions OK. Sample copy for $5.95. Fiction guidelines free.

Market categories: (I) Open to new writers; (II) Open to both new and established writers; (III) Interested mostly in established writers; (IV) Open to writers whose work is specialized.

Payment: Pays free subscription, 5 contributor's copies.
Terms: Acquires first North American serial rights and right to anthologize.

‡BLACK LACE, Old Fashioned Tales of Ghosts and the Supernatural, (I, II), The Victorian Press, P.O. Box 172363, Tampa FL 33672. (813)251-0784. Editor: Patricia Gomez. Magazine: 8½×11; 36-40 pages; bond paper; cardstock cover; illustrations and photographs. "To bring back the style of the old 'horror' masters of the 18th century, like M.R. James, Sheridan Le Fanu, Poe, etc." Quarterly. Estab. 1993. Circ. 100.
Needs: Horror (also gay and lesbian with horror theme), psychic/supernatural/occult. No pornography, explicit violence or gore. Receives 30-40 unsolicited mss/month. Accepts 5-6 mss/issue; 25 mss/year. Publishes ms 1 year after acceptance. Recently published work by DF Lewis, James P. Roberts, Lorrie Beaver Levesque, Charles Hefflefinger. Length: 2,000-3,000 words preferred; 1,000 words minimum; 9,000 words maximum. Also publishes literary essays and poetry. Sometimes critiques or comments on rejected mss.
How to Contact: Query first or send complete ms with a cover letter. Should include estimated word count, bio (2 paragraphs or so), and list of publications. Reports in 1-2 weeks on queries; 2 months on mss. Send SASE (or IRC) for a reply or send a disposable copy of the ms. Simultaneous and reprint submissions OK. Sample copy for $4.50. Fiction guidelines for #10 SAE. Reviews novels or short story collections.
Payment: Pays 1 contributor copy; additional copies for $3.
Terms: Buys first North American serial rights.
Advice: Looks for "old fashioned way of scaring me. Am looking for stories in the style of M.R. James, Le Fanu, Poe, Lovecraft and others in the 18th century school of writers. Scare me with a good ghost story. Give me a tale that drips with atmosphere. Make me afraid to go into that dark room. Vampires, ghosts, haunted houses, etc., will do nicely. Follow the guidelines. Send for a sample copy. It's very difficult for modern, younger writers to understand what I'm looking for."

BLACK MOUNTAIN REVIEW, (IV), Lorien House, P.O. Box 1112, Black Mountain NC 28711-1112. (704)669-6211. Editor: David A. Wilson. Magazine: 5½×8½; 48 pages; 60 lb. offset paper; 65 lb. cover stock; occasionally illustrations and photographs. "Each issue covers an American writer and all material must fit the theme." Annually. Estab. 1987. Circ. 150.
Needs: Literary. "The category of fiction is not as important as meeting the requirements of the theme. Guidelines for SASE." Receives 5 unsolicited mss/month. Buys 1-2 mss/issue. Publishes ms 6 months to 1 year after acceptance. Published work by Maureen Williams. Length: 1,000 words preferred; 2,000 words maximum. Publishes short shorts.
How to Contact: Query first. Reports in 1 week. SASE. Sample copy for $6. Fiction guidelines for #10 SAE and 1 first-class stamp (IRC).
Payment: Pays $15.
Terms: Pays on publication for one-time rights.
Advice: "Wait! Hold it! Don't send that ms . . . until you have written for the guidelines. General material is not wanted. We are covering Carl Sandburg and O. Henry in the near future. Submitted material is read carefully for content and (aagh!) spelling, but not the name/fame of the writers. There must be evidence of research within the story, and details must be accurate. There is still room for creativity. Do a good story, and you are welcome here."

BLACK RIVER REVIEW, (II), 855 Mildred Ave., Lorain OH 44052. (216)244-9654. Editor: Deborah Glaefke Gilbert. Fiction Editor: Jack Smith. Magazine: 8½×11; 60 pages; recycled paper; mat card cover stock; b&w drawings. "Contemporary writing and contemporary American culture; poefry, book reviews, essays on contemporary literature, short stories." Annually. Estab. 1985. Circ. 400.
Needs: Contemporary, experimental, humor/satire and literary. No "erotica for its own sake, stories directed toward a juvenile audience." Accepts up to 5 mss/year. Does not read mss May 1-Dec. 31. Publishes ms no later than July of current year. Published work by David Shields, Jeanne M. Leiby, Louis Gallo. Length: up to 3,500 words but will consider up to 4,000 maximum. Publishes short shorts. Also publishes literary essays, literary criticism, poetry. Sometimes critiques rejected mss and recommends other markets.
How to Contact: Reports on mss no later than July. SASE. No simultaneous submissions. Sample copy for $3 back issue; $3.50 current. Fiction guidelines for #10 SAE and 1 first-class stamp (IRC). Reviews novels and short story collections.

Payment: Pays in contributor's copies.

Terms: Acquires one-time rights.

Advice: "Since it is so difficult to break in, much of the new writer's creative effort is spent trying to match trends in popular fiction, in the case of the slicks, or adapting to narrow themes ('Gay and Lesbian,' 'Vietnam War,' 'Women's Issues,' etc.) of little and literary journals. An unfortunate result, from the reader's standpoint, is that each story within a given category comes out sounding like all the rest. Among positive developments of the proliferation of small presses is the opportunity for writers to decide what to write and how to write it. My advice is support a little magazine that is both open to new writers and prints fiction you like. 'Support' doesn't necessarily mean 'buy all the back issues,' but, rather, direct involvement between contributor, magazine and reader needed to rebuild the sort of audience that was there for writers like Fitzgerald and Hemingway."

BLACK WARRIOR REVIEW, (II), Box 2936, Tuscaloosa AL 35487. (205)348-4518. Editor-in-Chief: Leigh Ann Sackrider. Fiction Editor: Ashley Gibson. Magazine: 6×9; approx. 144 pages; illustrations and photos sometimes. "We publish contemporary fiction, poetry, reviews, essays and interviews for a literary audience." Semiannually. Estab. 1974. Circ. 1,300-2,000.

• Work that appeared in the *Black Warrior Review* has been included in the *Pushcart Prize* anthology for 1991 and 1993, *Best American Short Stories* 1993, *Best American Poetry* 1993 and in *New Short Stories from the South*.

Needs: Contemporary, literary, mainstream and prose poem. No types that are clearly "types." Upcoming theme: Special essay section on Alabama women writers (Spring 1994). Receives 200 unsolicited fiction mss/month. Buys 5 mss/issue, 10 mss/year. Approximately 25% of fiction is agented. Published work by Dennis Johnson, Reneé Manfredi, Joy Williams; published new writers within the last year. Length: 7,500 words maximum; 3,000-5,000 words average. Also publishes literary criticism, poetry. Occasionally critiques rejected mss.

How to Contact: Send complete ms with SASE (1 story per submission). Simultaneous submissions OK. Reports in 2-3 months. Publishes ms 2-5 months after acceptance. Sample copy $6. Fiction guidelines for SASE (IRC). Reviews novels and short story collections.

Payment: Pays $5-10/page and 2 contributor's copies.

Terms: Pays on publication.

Advice: "Become familiar with the magazine(s) being submitted to; learn the editorial biases; accept rejection slips as part of the business; keep trying. We are not a good bet for 'commercial' fiction. Each year the *Black Warrior Review* will award $500 to a fiction writer whose work has been published in either the fall or spring issue, to be announced in the fall issue. Regular submission deadlines are August 1 for fall issue, January 1 for spring issue."

‡BLIS MAGAZINE, A collection of poetry and fiction for a new age, (II), Suite 289, 1096 Casitas Pass Rd., Carpinteria CA 93013. Editor: Meltem Persion. Magazine: 8½×11; 32 pages; coated stock paper; heavy coated cover stock; line drawing illustrations and black and white photographs. "The thread that connects all the science fiction, fantasy, literary, humor, and spiritual stories we publish is the New Age element in all of them, be it an underlying theme of love and kindness or something as physical as crystals or UFOs. New Age readers as well as science fiction and fantasy readers are the intended audience." Quarterly. Estab. 1993.

Needs: New Age: fantasy, humor/satire, literary, science fiction. No religious fiction. Receives 200 mss/month. Accepts 4-5 mss/issue; 16-20 mss/year. Publishes ms up to 6 months after acceptance. Recently published work by Diane Moomey, Judith B. Cohen, Jay Von Tobel, Juanita Nelson. Length: 3,000 words preferred; 500 words minimum; 5,000 words maximum. Publishes short shorts. Length: 500 words. Also publishes poetry.

How to Contact: Send SASE for guidelines first. Then send complete ms with SASE and with or without a cover letter. Should include estimated word count. Reports in 1 month on queries; up to 6 months on mss. Send SASE (or IRC) for reply, return of ms or send a disposable copy of ms. Simultaneous and reprint submissions OK. Sample copy for $5. Fiction guidelines for #10 SAE and 1 first-class stamp.

Payment: Pays $20 and 2 contributor's copies.

Terms: Pays on acceptance for first North American serial rights.

Advice: "Acceptance is based on original, skillful, and competent writing. Strong plots, unique and memorable characters, and dynamic, tight dialogue are of utmost importance." Would like to see more "stories that have a subtle level of higher spiritual ideas where awakenings, deeper understanding, and acceptance take place without being preachy. Character growth and change throughout the story are important. The novel *2150*, by Thea Alexander, is a good example. Humor is always welcome. Show, don't tell."

✷BLOOD & APHORISMS, A Journal of Literary Fiction, (II), Suite 711, 456 College St., Toronto, Ontario M6G 4A3 Canada. (416)972-0637. Publisher: Timothy Paleczny. Fiction Editor: Hilary G. Clark. Magazine: 8½×11; 50 pages; bond paper; illustrations on cover."We publish new and emerging writers whose work is fresh and revealing, and impacts on a literary readership." Quarterly. Estab. 1990. Circ. 900.
Needs: Ethnic/multicultural, experimental, humor/satire, literary. No gratuitous violence or exploitive fiction. Publishes anthology every 2 years. Receives 50 unsolicited mss/month. Acquires 12-15 mss/issue; 45-55 mss/year. Publishes ms 3-6 months after acceptance. Recently published work by Lawrence Hill, Oakland Ross, Michelle Alfano. Length: 2,500-4,000 words average; 150 words minimum; 4,500 words maximum. Publishes short shorts. Often critiques rejected mss.
How to Contact: Send complete ms with a cover letter. Should include estimated word count, short bio, list of publications (optional) with submission. Reports in 2 weeks on queries; 2 months on mss. SASE or IRC for a reply to a query or return of ms. Simultaneous (please advise), electronic (disk with hard copy) submissions OK. Sample copy for $5 (Canadian). Fiction guidelines for SAE and 1 IRC. Reviews novels and short story collections. Send books to Craig Proctor, 9 Haslett Ave., Toronto, Ontario M4L 3R1.
Payment: Pays subscription to the magazine and 1 contributor's copy. Additional copies $4.
Terms: Acquires first North American serial rights.
Advice: "Be honest; take chances; find the strength in your own voice; show us your best – we're ready for anything and keep an open mind. Know the magazine you're sending to."

BLOODREAMS, A Magazine of Vampires & Werewolves, (II, IV), 1312 W. 43rd St., North Little Rock AR 72118. (501)771-2047. Editor: Kelly Gunter Atlas. Magazine: 8½×11; 80-100 pages; 20 lb. paper; 60 lb. stock cover; b&w drawings. "*Bloodreams* is dedicated exclusively to the preservation, continuance, and enhancement of the vampire and the werewolf legends for adult fans of the genre." Biannually. Estab. 1991. Circ. 100.
● The publishers of *Bloodreams* hope to launch another publication, *Spectre*, later this year. It will deal with "ghosts, e.s.p., astral projection, etc." Watch the magazine for details.
Needs: Vampires and werewolves. "We do not want to see gore, unnecessary violence, or pornography." Receives 10-12 unsolicited mss/month. Acquires 10-12 mss/issue; 20-24 mss/year. Does not read mss in April, July, October, January. Publishes mss 6 months after acceptance. Recently published work by Gregory L. Norris and Jeffrey A. Stadt. Length: 1,500 words average; 250 words minimum; 2,500 words maximum. Publishes short shorts. Length: 250-500 words. Also publishes poetry. Sometimes critiques rejected mss and recommends other markets.
How to Contact: Send complete ms with cover letter. Include a brief introduction and past credits if any. Reports in 1 week on queries; 4-6 weeks on mss. SASE. Simultaneous submissions OK. Sample copy for $7.50 (payable to Kelly Atlas). Fiction guidelines for #10 SAE and 1 first-class stamp.
Payment: Pays in contributor's copies. Charges for extras.
Terms: Acquires one-time rights.
Advice: "We look for well-written, concise short stories which are complete within themselves. We like writers who have their own sense of style and imagination who write with their own 'voice' and do not try to copy others' work. We are open to a variety of interpretations of the vampire and werewolf legends. For example, we like anything ranging from Stephen King to Anne Rice to Robert R. McCammon to Brian Lumley."

‡BLUE RYDER, (II), Box 587, Olean NY 14760. Editor: Ken Wagner. Tabloid: 11×14; 16-24 pages; newsprint; color cover; many illustrations and photographs. "Publishes 'The Best of the Underground' reprinting from the underground press, the ultra-alternative press, the alternative press, the special interest and newsletter press, the small literary & poetry press, and the micropress for a general audience interested in comix, strangeness, music, fringe culture, arts, politics, news, reviews, and mail order." Bimonthly. Estab. 1989. Circ. 2,000.
Needs: Contemporary, experimental, fantasy, historical (general), horror, humor/satire, literary, prose poem, science fiction. "*Blue Ryder* usually reprints fiction after it has appeared in another magazine. Writers should submit clear photocopies or tearsheets of the piece the way it originally appeared." Receives 10-30 unsolicited fiction mss/month. Buys 1-2 mss/issue; 6-12 mss/year. Publishes mss 2-24 months after acceptance. Recently published or will be publishing reprints from the following

publications: *Baby Sue, Urbanus, Barrelhouse*. Length: 500-1,000 words preferred; 1,500 words maximum. Publishes short shorts.

How to Contact: Query with published clips of work or send complete ms with SASE (IRCs). Reports "immediately" on rejection and 3-6 months on acceptance. SASE. Sample copy for $2.

Payment: Pays in contributor's copies.

Terms: Acquires one-time or reprint rights. Not copyrighted.

Advice: "I seem to have no problem finding suitable articles, poetry, and comics, but it is extremely difficult to find the quality of fiction and humor/satire that I'm looking for. That's why I prefer to reprint work after it has proven itself elsewhere. *Blue Ryder* is internationally known, and nationally distributed over-the-counter as 'The Best of The Underground.' I don't want to see mediocre manuscripts with the writer thinking, 'well, it's worth a try,' because if it's not the best you've got, then it's not worth a try."

THE BLUE WATER REVIEW (II), 8045 S.W. 100 St., Miami FL 33156. (305)596-7113. Editor/Publisher: Dennis M. Ross. Magazine: 5½×7; 45 pages; 60 lb. paper; standard cover stock; illustrations and photos. "No theme. We want quality writing: fiction, interviews with well known writers and critics, poetry, and photos." Semiannually. Estab. 1989. Circ. 5,000.

 • The editor says they were hit hard by Hurricane Andrew last year, making response time a little slower than usual.

Needs: Adventure, contemporary, ethnic, experimental, humor/satire, literary, mainstream, mystery/ suspense (amateur sleuth, police procedurals, private eye), regional, science fiction (soft/sociological), sports. "No pornography, no handwritten or single-spaced submissions, no manuscripts without SASE." Receives 15 unsolicited mss/month. Accepts 3-4 mss/issue; 10 mss/year. Publishes ms 1-3 months after acceptance. Agented fiction 10%. Length: 3,000 words maximum. Publishes short shorts. Sometimes critiques rejected mss.

How to Contact: Send complete manuscript with cover letter. Reports in 4-5 months. SASE. Simultaneous submissions OK. Fiction guidelines for #10 SAE and 1 first-class stamp (IRC).

Payment: Pays 1 contributor's copy; charge for extras.

Terms: Acquires one-time rights.

Advice: "Manuscripts should have classic elements of short story, such as meaningful character change. Submit your best work no matter the publication. We want quality. Use standard form as illustrated in *Writer's Digest* (short stories)."

BLUELINE, (II, IV), English Dept., SUNY, Potsdam NY 13676. (315)267-2000. Editor: Tony Tyler. Magazine: 6×9; 112 pages; 70 lb. white stock paper; 65 lb. smooth cover stock; illustrations; photos. "*Blueline* is interested in quality writing about the Adirondacks or other places similar in geography and spirit. We publish fiction, poetry, personal essays, book reviews and oral history for those interested in the Adirondacks, nature in general, and well-crafted writing." Annually. Estab. 1979. Circ. 700.

Needs: Adventure, contemporary, humor/satire, literary, prose poem, regional, reminiscences, oral history and nature/outdoors. Receives 8-10 unsolicited fiction mss/month. Accepts 6-8 mss/issue. Does not read January-August. Publishes ms 3-6 months after acceptance. Published fiction by Jeffrey Clapp. Published new writers within the last year. Length: 500 words minimum; 3,000 words maximum; 2,500 words average. Also publishes literary essays, poetry. Occasionally critiques rejected mss. Sometimes recommends other markets.

How to Contact: Send complete ms with SASE (IRCs) and brief bio. Submit mss Aug. 1-Nov. 30. Reports in 2-10 weeks. Reports in 2-10 weeks. Sample copy for $5.75. Fiction guidelines for 5×10 SAE with 1 first-class stamp.

Payment: Pays 1 contributor's copy. Charges $3 each for 3 or more extra copies.

Terms: Acquires first rights.

Advice: "We look for concise, clear, concrete prose that tells a story and touches upon a universal theme or situation. We prefer realism to romanticism but will consider nostalgia if well done. Pay attention to grammar and syntax. Avoid murky language, sentimentality, cuteness or folksiness. We would like to see more good fiction related to the Adirondacks. Please include short biography and word count. If manuscript has potential, we work with author to improve and reconsider for publication. Our readers prefer fiction to poetry (in general) or reviews. Write from your own experience, be specific and factual (within the bounds of your story) and if you write about universal features such as love, death, change, etc., write about them in a fresh way. Triteness and mediocracy are the hallmarks of the majority of stories seen today."

BOGG, A Magazine of British & North American Writing, (II), Bogg Publications, 422 N. Cleveland St., Arlington VA 22201. (703)243-6019. U.S. Editor: John Elsberg. Magazine: 6×9; 64-68 pages; 60 lb. white paper; 70 lb. cover stock; line illustrations. "American and British poetry, prose poems and other experimental short 'fictions,' reviews, and essays on small press." Published triannually. Estab. 1968. Circ. 750.

Needs: Very short experimental and prose poem. "We are always looking for work with British/ Commonwealth themes and/or references." Receives 25 unsolicited fiction mss/month. Accepts 1-2 mss/issue; 3-6 mss/year. Publishes ms 3-18 months after acceptance. Published 50% new writers within the last year. Length: 300 words maximum. Also publishes literary essays, literary criticism, poetry. Occasionally critiques rejected mss.

How to Contact: Query first or send ms (2-6 pieces) with SASE (IRCs). Reports in 1 week on queries; 2 weeks on mss. Sample copy for $3.50 or $4.50 (current issue). Reviews novels and short story collections.

Payment: Pays 2 contributor's copies. Reduced charge for extras.

Terms: Acquires one-time rights.

Advice: "Read magazine first. We are most interested in prose work of experimental or wry nature to supplement poetry."

‡BOHEMIAN CHRONICLE, It's Not for Everyone, (I, II), P.O. Box 387, Largo FL 34649-0387. Editor: Emily Skinner. Assistant Editor: Ellen Williams. Magazine: 8×11 (folded); 12 pages; standard paper; illustrations and photographs. "Experimental, quality works, anything that *isn't* mainstream!" Monthly. Estab. 1991. Circ. 500.

Needs: Adventure, childrens/juvenile (written by children only), ethnic/multicultural, experimental, gay, humor/satire, literary, mystery/suspense (experimental), psychic/supernatural/occult, romance (conversational), science fiction (light), serialized novel. Receives 100 mss/month. Accepts 5 mss/issue; 60 mss/year. Does not read mss from October-November. Publishes ms 1-10 months after acceptance. Length: 500-1,000 words preferred. Publishes short shorts. Also publishes literary essays, literary criticism and poetry. Always critiques or comments on rejected mss.

How to Contact: Send complete ms with a cover letter. Should include estimated word count. Reports in 1-2 months. Send SASE (or IRC) for reply, return of ms or send a disposable copy of ms. No simultaneous or reprint submissions. Sample copy for 6×9 SAE and $1 with 1 first-class stamp (IRC). Fiction guidelines for #10 SAE and 1 first-class stamp.

Payment: Pays $5 and 5 contributor's copies.

Terms: Pays on publication for all rights, first rights or first North American serial rights.

Advice: "Don't write long introduction letters and don't send clips. Stick to the suggested length." Would like to see more "humor! Satire (non-political)!" No "romance—as in traditional romance."

BOTH SIDES NOW, An Alternative Journal of New Age/Aquarian Transformations, (II), Free People Press, 10547 State Highway 110 N., Tyler TX 75704-9537. (903)592-4263. Editor: Elihu Edelson. Magazine: 8½×11; 10 pages; bond paper and cover; b&w line illustrations; photos (screened for newsprint). Estab. 1969.

Needs: Material with new-age slant, including fantasy, feminist, humor/satire ("including political"), psychic/supernatural, spiritual, religious/inspirational, ecological fables, parables. "No violence (including S/M), prurience (pornography), or fascistic views." Length: "about 2 magazine pages at most." Also publishes some poetry. Occasionally critiques rejected mss with "brief note."

How to Contact: Send complete ms with SASE (IRCs). Simultaneous submissions and previously published work OK. Reports in 3 months on mss. Sample copy for $1. Reviews "New Age and counterculture fiction."

Payment: Pays 5 contributor's copies. Charges $1 each for extra copies.

Terms: "Authors retain rights."

Advice: "Heed our editorial interests. Keep it short."

BOTTOMFISH MAGAZINE, (II), Bottomfish Press, Language Arts Division, De Anza College, 21250 Steven Creek Blvd., Cupertino CA 95014. (408)864-8538. Editor-in-Chief: Robert Scott. Magazine: 7×8½; 80-100 pages; White Bristol vellum cover; b&w high contrast illustrations and photos. "Contemporary poetry, fiction, b&w graphics and photos for literary and writing community." Annually. Estab. 1976. Circ. 500.

Needs: Experimental, literary and prose poem. "Literary excellence is our only criteria. We will consider all subjects." Receives 50-100 unsolicited fiction mss/month. Accepts 5-6 mss/issue. Length: 500 words minimum; 5,000 words maximum; 2,500 words average.

How to Contact: "Submission deadline: February 1; publication date: end of March." Send complete ms with cover letter, brief bio and SASE. No simultaneous submissions or reprints. Reports in 3-4 months. Publishes ms an average of 6 months-1 year after acceptance. Sample copy $4.

Payment: Pays 2 contributor's copies.

Terms: Acquires one-time rights.

Advice: "Strive for orginality and high level of craft; avoid clichéd or stereotyped characters and plots. We don't print slick, commercial fiction, regardless of quality."

BOULEVARD, (III), Opojaz Inc., P.O. Box 30386, Philadelphia PA 19103-8386. (215)561-1723. Editor: Richard Burgin. Magazine: 5½ × 8½; 150-225 pages; excellent paper; high-quality cover stock; illustrations; photos. "*Boulevard* aspires to publish the best contemporary fiction, poetry and essays we can print." Published 3 times/year. Estab. 1986. Circ. about 2,800.

- *Small Magazine Review*, a new publication by Dustbooks, Inc. selected *Boulevard* for its "Small Magazine Club."

Needs: Contemporary, experimental, literary, prose poem. Does not want to see "anything whose first purpose is not literary." Receives over 400 mss/month. Buys about 8 mss/issue. Does not accept manuscripts between May 1 and October 1. Publishes ms less than 1 year after acceptance. Agented fiction ⅓-¼. Length: 5,000 words average; 10,000 words maximum. Publishes short shorts. Published work by Lee K. Abbott, Francine Prose, Alice Adams. Also publishes literary essays, literary criticism, poetry. Sometimes critiques rejected mss and recommends other markets.

How to Contact: Send complete ms with cover letter. Reports in 2 weeks on queries; 3 months on mss. SASE. Simultaneous submissions OK. Sample copy for $6 and SAE with 5 first-class stamps (IRCs).

Payment: Pays $50-250; contributor's copies; charges for extras.

Terms: Pays on publication for first North American serial rights. Does not send galleys to author unless requested.

Advice: "We are open to different styles of imaginative and critical work and are mindful of Nabokov's dictum 'There is only one school, the school of talent.' Above all, when we consider the very diverse manuscripts submitted to us for publication, we value original sensibility, writing that causes the reader to experience a part of life in a new way. Originality, to us, has little to do with a writer intently trying to make each line or sentence odd, bizarre, or eccentric, merely for the sake of being 'different.' Rather, originality is the result of the character or vision of the writer; the writer's singular outlook and voice as it shines through in the totality of his or her work."

MARION ZIMMER BRADLEY'S FANTASY MAGAZINE, (II, IV), Box 249, Berkeley CA 94701. (510)644-9222. Editor and Publisher: Marion Zimmer Bradley. Magazine: 8½ × 11; 64 pages; 60 lb. text paper; 10 lb. cover stock; b&w interior and 4 color cover illustrations. "Fantasy only; strictly family oriented." Quarterly.

- This magazine is named for and edited by one of the pioneers of fantasy fiction. Bradley is perhaps best known for the multi-volume Darkover series.

Needs: Fantasy. May include adventure, contemporary, humor/satire, mystery/suspense and young adult/teen (10-18) (all with fantasy elements). "No avant garde or romantic fantasy. No computer games!" Receives 50-200 unsolicited mss/week. Buys 8-10 mss/issue; 36-40 mss/year. Publishes 3-12 months after acceptance. Agented fiction 5%. Length: 3,000-4,000 words average; 7,000 words maximum. Publishes short shorts.

How to Contact: Send complete ms. SASE. Reports in 10 days. No simultaneous submissions. Sample copy $3.50. Fiction guidelines for #10 SASE (IRC).

Payment: Pays 3-10¢/word; contributor's copies.

Terms: Pays on acceptance. $25 kill fee "if held 12 months or more." Buys first North American serial rights.

Advice: "If I want to finish reading it, I figure other people will too. A manuscript stands out if I care whether the characters do well, if it has a rhythm. Make sure it has characters *you* care about. If you don't care about them, how do you expect me to? Read guidelines *before* sending ms."

‡**(the) BRAVE NEW TICK, (I, IV),** Graftographic Press, P.O. Box 24, S. Grafton MA 01560. (508)799-3769. Editor: Paul Normal Dion. Newsletter: 8½ × 11; 10 pages; standard paper; b&w illustrations. "Civil rights for all, focus on gay rights, activism. Would very much like to publish gay fiction—no porn." Monthly. Estab. 1993. Circ. 75-100.

Needs: Erotica (gay), gay, lesbian, psychic/supernatural/occult. Receives 1-2 unsolicited mss/month. Length: 1 or 2 pages typed maximum. Publishes short shorts. Also publishes literary essays, literary criticism and poetry.
How to Contact: Open to any method of submission. Should include bio. Send SASE (or IRC) for return of ms. Simultaneous, reprint and electronic submissions OK (IBM compatible, ASCII files accepted and preferred). Sample copy for #10 SAE and 52¢ postage plus 2-3 loose first-class stamps.
Payment: Pays contributor's copies.
Terms: "Rights remain with contributor."
Advice: Looks for fiction "related to gay rights, well written, thought provoking, visually interesting. Hard core porn is not what I'm looking for."

BRAVO MUNDO NUEVO, Alternative Literature for a Brave New World, (I, II), La Sombra Publishing, P.O. Box 285, Hondo TX 78861. (210)426-5453. Editor: E.D. Santos. Newsletter: 8½ × 11; 8 pages; 70 lb. paper; illustrations. "Lesser known fiction writers are encouraged to submit to *BMN*. Fantasy, science fiction, social awareness type material are most welcome." Quarterly. Estab. 1990.
Needs: Fantasy, science fiction (soft/sociological), "social awareness" material. No "how-to; editorials; racist material; socially or environmentally flammable material." Publishes annual special fiction issue. Receives 5 unsolicited mss/month. Accepts 5 mss/issue; 20 mss/year. Publishes ms 6-9 months after acceptance. Recently published work by Angela deHoyos. Length: 600 words preferred; 20 words minimum; 1,200 words maximum. Publishes short shorts. Sometimes critiques rejected mss and recommends other markets.
How to Contact: Send complete ms with cover letter. Cover letter should include previous publications, if any, length of experience in writing, preferred genre of writing, current address and phone number. Reports in 2 months on mss. SASE. Simultaneous and reprint submissions OK. Sample copy free. Fiction guidelines for #10 SAE and 1 first-class stamp (IRCs).
Payment: Pays subscription to magazine.
Terms: Acquires one-time rights.
Advice: Looks for "originality and a gift for spontaneous storytelling as the principal criteria in choosing fiction for this publication. A manuscript need not be 'polished' to stand out; in point of fact, the more unrefined, the more authentic and genuinely appealing it is."

THE BRIDGE, A Journal of Fiction & Poetry, (II), The Bridge, 14050 Vernon St., Oak Park MI 48237. Editor: Jack Zucker. Fiction Editor: Helen Zucker. Magazine: 5½ × 8½; 160 pages; 60 lb. paper; heavy cover. "Fiction and poetry for a literary audience." Semiannually. Estab. 1990.
Needs: Ethnic, mainstream, regional. Receives 80 unsolicited mss/month. Acquires 5-10 mss/issue; 10-14 mss/year. Publishes ms within one year of acceptance. Length: 3,000 words average; 7,500 words maximum. Publishes short shorts. Length: 1,000 words. Also publishes some short essays, some criticism, poetry.
How to Contact: Send complete manuscript with cover letter. Reports in 1 week on queries; 2-4 months on mss. SASE (IRCs). Simultaneous submissions OK. Sample copy for $5 ($8 for 2). Reviews novels and short story collections.
Payment: Pays in contributor's copies.
Terms: Acquires first North American serial rights.
Advice: "Don't give us fiction intended for a popular/commercial market—we'd like to get 'real literature.' "

BRILLIANT STAR (II), National Spiritual Assembly of the Baha'is of the U.S., Baha'i National Center, Wilmette IL 60091. Managing Editor: Pepper Peterson Oldziey. Magazine: 8½ × 11; 33 pages; matte paper; glossy cover; illustrations; photos. "A magazine for Baha'i children about the history, teachings and beliefs of the Baha'i faith. Manuscripts should reflect spiritual principles of the Baha'i faith." For children approx. 5-12 years old. Bimonthly. Estab. 1969. Circ. 2,300.
Needs: Adventure, children's/juvenile, ethnic, historical (general), humor/satire, mystery/suspense, spiritual, young adult/teen (10-18 years). "Accepts inspirational fiction if not overtly preachy or moralistic and if not directly Christian and related directly to Christian holidays." Upcoming themes: "Courage" (March-April); "100th Anniversary of the Faith in America" (May-June); "Starship" (July-August); "The Darkest Hour" (Sept.-Oct.); "Press on to Meet the Dawn" (Nov.-Dec.); "The First Prejudice-Free Generation" (Jan.-Feb. 1995). Receives 30 unsolicited mss/month. Accepts 3-4 mss/issue; 18-24 mss/year. Publishes ms no sooner than 6 months after acceptance. Recently published work by Susan Pethick and John Paulits; published new writers within the last year. Length: 100 words minimum; 600 words maximum. "Length should correlate with intended audience—very short mss for

young readers, longer mss must be for older readers (ages 10-12), and intended for their interests." Publishes short shorts. Also publishes poetry.

How to Contact: No queries. Send complete ms. Cover letter not essential. Reports in 6-10 weeks on mss. SASE. Simultaneous submissions OK "but please make a notation that it is a simultaneous sub." Sample copy for 9×12 SAE and 5 oz. postage. Fiction guidelines for #10 SAE with 1 first-class stamp.

Payment: Pays in contributor's copies (two); charges for extras.

Terms: "Writer can retain own copyright or grant to the National Spiritual Assembly of the Baha'is of the U.S."

Advice: "We enjoy working with beginning writers and try to develop a constructive collaborative relationship with those who show promise and sensitivity to our aims and focus. We feel that the children's market is open to a wide variety of writers: fiction, nonfiction, science, photo-essays. Our needs for appealing fiction especially for pre-schoolers and young readers make us a good market for new writers. *Please*, have a story to tell! The single main reason for rejection of manuscripts we review is lack of plot to infuse the story with energy and make the reader want to come along, as well as length to age/interest level mismatch. Longer stories must be intended for older children. Only very short stories are useable for young audiences. Seeking writers from Afro-American, Hispanic, Asian and Native American backgrounds to increase multi-ethnic focus of our magazine."

BROOMSTICK, A National, Feminist Periodical by, for, and About Women Over Forty, (II, IV), 3543 18th St. #3, San Francisco CA 94110. Editors: Mickey Spencer and Polly Taylor. Magazine: 8½×11; 40 pages; line drawings. "Our first priority in selecting and editing material is that it convey clear images of women over 40 that are positive, that it show the author's commitment against the denigration of midlife and long-living women which pervades our culture, and that it offer us alternatives which will make our lives better." For "women over 40 interested in being part of a network which will help us all develop understanding of our life situations and acquire the skills to improve them." Quarterly. Estab. 1978. Circ. 3,000.

Needs: Feminist experience in political context, old women, age and agism, humor, ethnic. No mss of "romantic love, nostalgic, saccharine acceptance, by or about men or young women." Receives 10 unsolicited fiction mss/month. Accepts 12-15 mss/year. Published work by Astra, Wilma Elizabeth McDaniel, Ruth Harriet Jacobs; published new writers within the last year. Recommends magazine subscription before sending ms. Critiques rejected mss.

How to Contact: Send complete mss with 2 SASEs (IRCs). Simultaneous and previously published submissions OK. Reports in 3 months on queries and mss. Sample copy for $5. Writer's guidelines for 50¢ or SASE.

Payment: Pays 2 contributor's copies; $5 charge for extras.

Advice: "Don't use stereotypes to establish character. Give protagonists' names, not just roles (e.g. 'mother'). Avoid using 'you,' which sounds preachy. Read our editorials."

BROWNBAG PRESS, (II), Hyacinth House Publications, P.O. Box 120, Fayetteville AR 72702-0120. Editors: Shannon Frach, Randal Seyler. Magazine: 30-55 pages; 20 lb. paper; cardstock cover; b&w illustrations. "*Brownbag Press* is a digest of poetry, fiction, and experimental writing that is seeking avant-garde, forceful, and often bizarre literature for a literate, adult audience that is bored to death with the standard offerings of modern mainstream fiction." Semiannually. Estab. 1989. Circ. 375.

● Hyacinth House Publications also publishes *Psychotrain* listed in this book. No need to send to both publications, says the editor, as submissions will be considered for both.

Needs: Condensed/excerpted novels, contemporary, erotica, ethnic, experimental, feminist, gay, humor/satire, lesbian, literary, prose poem, psychic/supernatural/occult, translations, "Punk, psychedelia, fringe culture, Dada, surrealism. A sense of dark humor is definitely a plus. No religious, romance, or criminally boring mainstream. No tedious formula fiction. No yuppie angst. Nothing saccharine." Receives 150 unsolicited ms/month. Acquires 4-6 ms/issue. Publishes ms 1 year after acceptance. Recently published work by Brooks Caruthers, Bill Eakin, Laura White Schuett and Alfred Schwaid. Length: 100-4,000 words. Publishes short shorts. Length: 100 words or longer. Sometimes critiques rejected mss and recommends other markets.

How to Contact: Send complete ms with or without cover letter. "Don't use a cover letter to brag about how great you are; if you're that good, I guarantee we'll have heard of you." Reports in 2-6 months on ms. SASE. Simultaneous and reprint submissions OK. Sample copy for $3 and 4 first-class stamps. Make checks out to "Hyacinth House Publications". Cash is also OK. Fiction guidelines for #10 SAE and 1 first-class stamp (IRC).

Payment: No payment.
Terms: Acquires one-time rights.
Advice: "We're getting a lot of fiction that reads as if it were penned by the living dead. What we need, instead, is writing that is vigorous, unrepentant, and dynamically *alive*. We'd like to see *Brownbag* become more forceful and intense with every issue. Send us the strongest, most compelling material you've got. Keep the weak stuff at home. Short, tight stories always beat long, rambling ones. International writers should try their best to obtain U.S. stamps for SASEs. Using IRCs will seriously delay response time. Also, we're receiving too many submissions with postage due. Canadian writers should pause a few seconds to meditate upon the fact that Canadian stamps do not work on SASEs mailed from the U.S. A great deal of time and postage could be saved by writers if they would actually take the time to read market listings carefully. We receive material every day from people who claim to have seen our entries here, but who could not possibly have read them past the initial address."

‡**BUKOWSKI AND SERIAL KILLERS, (I, IV),** Homemade Ice Cream Press, P.O. Box 470186, Fort Worth TX 76147. Editor: Robert W. Howington. Magazine: 8½×11; 52 pages; 20 lb. bond paper; colored bond cover stock; illustrations and photographs. "The magazine is dedicated to LA poet Charles Bukowski and serial killers. It contains articles, fiction, poems, drawings, photos, etc. about Bukowski and serial killers. Only these two subjects are considered." Published irregularly. Estab. 1992. Circ. 150.
  • Yes, this is exactly what the editor says it is—information on Bukowski and lots of material (fiction and nonfiction) on serial killers. Not for the squeamish. Homemade Ice Cream Press also publishes *Flaming Envelopes*; write for details.
Needs: Humor/satire, literary. Editorial calender available for SASE. Receives 10-12 mss/month. Accepts 40-50 mss/issue. Publishes ms 6-12 months after acceptance. Recently published work by Todd Moore, Justice Howard, Lyn Lifshin, Frank Cotolo. Length: 500 words preferred; 50 words minimum; 1,000 words maximum. Publishes short shorts. Length: 50-500 words. Also publishes literary essays, literary criticism and poetry.
How to Contact: Send complete ms with a cover letter. Should include 1-page bio. Reports in 1-3 months. Send SASE (or IRC) for return of ms. Simultaneous and reprint submissions OK. Sample copy for $5. (Make checks payable to Robert W. Howington.) Fiction guidelines for #10 SAE and 1 first-class stamp (2 IRCs).
Payment: Pays 1 contributor's copy; additional copies for $4.
Terms: Buys one-time rights.
Advice: Looks for "sex and violence, guts, honesty, guns, real life, Bukowski-esque."

BYLINE, (I, II), Box 130596, Edmond OK 73013. (405)348-5591. Editor-in-Chief: Marcia Preston. Managing Editor: Kathryn Fanning. Monthly magazine "aimed at encouraging and motivating all writers toward success, with special information to help new writers." Estab. 1981.
  • *Byline* is fast becoming known as an excellent starting place for new writers. For more information check out our interview with the editor in the 1991 edition of this book. The magazine is ranked #40 in the latest *Writer's Digest* Fiction 50 list. The magazine also sponsors the *Byline* Literary Awards listed in this book.
Needs: Literary, genre and general fiction. Receives 75-100 unsolicited fiction mss/month. Buys 1 ms/issue, 12 mss/year. Recently published work by Brenda Burnham and Michael Bugeja; published many new writers within the last year. Length: 4,000 words maximum; 2,000 words minimum. Also publishes poetry.
How to Contact: Send complete ms with SASE (IRCs). Simultaneous submissions OK, "if notified." "For us, no cover letter is needed." Reports in 1-2 months. Publishes ms an average of 3 months after acceptance. Sample copy, guidelines and contest list for $3.50.
Payment: Pays $50 and 2 contributor's copies.
Terms: Pays on acceptance for first North American rights.
Advice: "We're very open to new writers. Submit a well-written, professionally prepared ms with SASE. No erotica or senseless violence; otherwise, we'll consider most any theme. We also sponsor short story and poetry contests."

CALLALOO, A Journal of African-American and African Arts and Letters, (II, IV), Dept. of English, University of Virginia, Charlottesville VA 22903. (804)924-6637. Editor: Charles H. Rowell. Magazine: 7×10; 250 pages. Scholarly magazine. Quarterly. Plans special fiction issue in future. Estab. 1976. Circ. 1,500.
  • One of the leading voices in African-American literature, *Callaloo* received first prize for

Special Issues from the Council of Editors of Literary Journals (CELJ), for the two-volume Haitian Issue "Haiti: the Literature and Culture, Parts I and II."

Needs: Contemporary, ethnic (black culture), feminist, historical (general), humor/satire, literary, prose poem, regional, science fiction, serialized/excerpted novel, translations. Also publishes poetry and drama. Upcoming themes: 1994: Cultural Criticism: The Body & Sexuality; Contemporary African American Writers; Ishmael Reed Special Section; Wilson Ham's Special Issue; Native American Writing; 1995: Ann Petry Special Section; The Literature of Jamaica; Maryse Condé Special Issue; Gay/Lesbian Special Issue; James Baldwin Special Issue; Australian Aboriginal Literature. Acquires 3-5 mss/issue; 10-20 mss/year. Length: no restrictions.

How to Contact: Submit complete ms in duplicate and cover letter with name, address and SASE (IRCs). Reports on queries in 2 weeks; 2-3 months on mss. Simultaneous submissions OK. Previously published work accepted "occasionally." Sample copy $8.

Payment: Pays in contributor's copies.

Terms: Acquires all rights. Sends galleys to author.

CALLIOPE, (II, IV), Creative Writing Program, Roger Williams University, Bristol RI 02809. (401)254-3217. Co-ordinating Editor: Martha Christina. Magazine: 5½ × 8½; 40-56 pages; 50 lb. offset paper; vellum or 60 lb. cover stock; occasional illustrations and photos. "We are an eclectic little magazine publishing contemporary poetry, fiction, and occasionally interviews." Semiannually. Estab. 1977. Circ. 400.

Needs: Literary, contemporary, experimental/innovative. "We try to include at least 2 pieces of fiction in each issue." Receives approximately 10-20 unsolicited fiction mss each month. Does not read mss mid-March to mid-August. Published new writers within the last year. Length: open. Publishes short shorts under 20 pages. Critiques rejected mss when there is time.

How to Contact: Send complete ms with SASE. Reports immediately or up to 3 months on mss. Sample copy $2.

Payment: Pays 2 contributor's copies and one year's subscription beginning with following issue.

Terms: Rights revert to author on publication.

Advice: "We are not interested in reading anyone's very first story. If the piece is good, it will be given careful consideration. Reading a sample copy of *Calliope* is recommended. Let the characters of the story tell their own story; we're very often (painfully) aware of the writer's presence. Episodic is fine; story need not (for our publication) have traditional beginning, middle and end."

CALYX, A Journal of Art & Literature by Women, (II), Calyx, Inc., P.O. Box B, Corvallis OR 97339. (503)753-9384. Managing Editor: Margarita Donnelly. Editorial Coordinator: Beverly McFarland. Editors: Linda Varsell Smith, Micki Reaman, Lois Cranston, Dorothy Mack, Amy Agnello. Magazine: 7 × 8; 128 pages per single issue, 250 per double; 60 lb. coated matte stock paper; 10 pt. chrome coat cover; original art. Publishes prose, poetry, art, essays, interviews and critical and review articles. "*Calyx* editors are seeking innovative and literary works of exceptional quality." Biannually. Estab. 1976. Circ. 3,000.

● *Calyx* received an Honorable Mention for editorial content and First Place for cover design in 1993 from the American Literary Magazine Awards.

Needs: Accepts 6-10 prose mss/issue, 9-15 mss/year. Receives approximately 300 unsolicited fiction mss each month. Reads mss only October 1-November 15 each year. Submit only during these periods. Recently published works by Beth Bosworth, Eleonora Chiavetta, Ellen Frye; published new writers within the last year. Length: 5,000 words maximum. Also publishes literary essays, literary criticism, poetry.

How to Contact: Send ms with SASE (IRCs) and biographical notes. Simultaneous submissions OK. Reports in up to 6 months on mss. Publishes ms an average of 6 months after acceptance. Sample copy $8 plus $1.50 postage. Reviews novels and short story collections.

Payment: Pays in copies and subscriptions.

Advice: Most mss are rejected because "the writers are not familiar with *Calyx*—writers should read *Calyx* and be familiar with the publication."

✸THE CAPILANO REVIEW, (II), 2055 Purcell Way, North Vancouver, British Columbia V7J 3H5 Canada. (604)984-1712. Editor: Robert Sherrin. Magazine: 6 × 9; 80-100 pages. Magazine of "fresh, innovative art and literature for literary/artistic audience." Quarterly. Estab. 1972. Circ. 1,000.

Needs: Contemporary, experimental, literary and prose poem. Receives 30 unsolicited mss/month. Buys 1-2 mss/issue; 4 mss/year. Published works by Bill Gaston, Sharon Thesen and Myrna Kostash. Published "lots" of new writers within the last three years. Length: 2,000-6,000 words. Publishes short

shorts. Also publishes literary essays. Occasionally recommends other markets.
How to Contact: Send complete ms with cover letter and SASE (IRCs). Sample copy for $8 (Canadian).
Payment: Pays $160 maximum ($40/page), 2 contributor's copies and one year subscription.
Terms: Pays on publication.

THE CARIBBEAN WRITER, (IV), The University of the Virgin Islands, RR 02, Box 10,000—Kingshill, St. Croix, Virgin Islands 00850. (809)778-0246. Editor: Erika Waters. Magazine: 6×9; 160 pages; 60 lb. paper; glossy cover stock; illustrations and photos. *"The Caribbean Writer* is an international magazine with a Caribbean focus. The Caribbean should be central to the work, or the work should reflect a Caribbean heritage, experience or perspective." Annually. Estab. 1987. Circ. 1,500.
Needs: Contemporary, historical (general), humor/satire, literary, mainstream and prose poem. Receives 400 unsolicited mss/year. Acquires 10 mss/issue. Length: 300 words minimum. Also accepts poetry.
How to Contact: Send complete ms with cover letter. "Blind submissions only. Send name, address and title of ms on separate sheet. Title only on ms. Mss will not be considered unless this procedure is followed." Reports "once a year." SASE. Simultaneous submissions OK. Sample copy for $5 and $2 postage. Fiction guidelines for SASE (IRCs).
Payment: Pays 2 contributor's copies. Annual prizes for best story ($400); for best poem ($250).
Terms: Acquires one-time rights.
Advice: Looks for "fiction which reflects a Caribbean heritage, experience or perspective."

CAROLINA QUARTERLY, (II), Greenlaw Hall CB #3520, University of North Carolina, Chapel Hill NC 27599-3520. (919)962-0244. Editor-in-Chief: Amber Vogel. Fiction Editors: Betina Entzminger, Brenda Thissen. Literary journal: 70-90 pages; illustrations. Triannually. Estab. 1948. Circ. 1,000.
Needs: Literary. Receives 150-200 unsolicited fiction mss/month. Acquires 5-7 mss/issue; 15-20 mss/ year. Publishes ms an average of 12 weeks after acceptance. Recently published work by Barry Hannah, Nanci Kincaid, Doris Betts. Published new writers within the last year. Length: 7,000 words maximum; no minimum. Also publishes short shorts, literary essays, poetry. Occasionally critiques rejected mss.
How to Contact: Send complete ms with cover letter and SASE (IRCs) to fiction editor. No simultaneous submissions. Reports in 2-4 months. Sample copy for $5; Writer's guidelines for SASE and 1 first-class stamp.
Payment: Pays in contributor's copies.
Terms: Acquires first rights.

✿CAROUSEL LITERARY ARTS MAGAZINE, (I, II), Room 273, University Centre, University of Guelph, Guelph, Ontario N1G 2W1 Canada. Editors: Michael Carbert, Gregory Ferguson. Magazine: 5½×8½; 80 pages; illustrations and photographs. Annually. Estab. 1985. Circ. 500.
Needs: Contemporary, literary. Receives 5 unsolicited mss each month. Accepts 3-4 mss per issue. Publishes ms 1-2 months after acceptance. Recently published work by Leon Rooke, Clark Blaise, John Metcalf, Hugh Hood, Constance Rooke, Diane Schoemperlen. Length: 3,000 words maximum. Also publishes literary essays, interviews, poetry.
How to Contact: Send complete ms. Include bio with manuscript. No simultaneous submissions. Reports in 2 months on queries; 4 months on mss. SASE (IRCs). Sample copy $7 (Canadian).
Payment: Pays in contributor's copies.
Terms: Acquires one-time rights.
Advice: "We want work which takes chances in style, point of view, characterization. We are open to new writers."

CATALYST, A Magazine of Heart & Mind, (II, IV), Catalyst, Inc., #400, 236 Forsyth St. SW, Atlanta GA 30303-3700. (404)730-5785. Editor: Pearl Cleage. Magazine: 8×11; 130 pages; newsprint; photographs. "Seeks to stimulate the worldwide flow of ideas. Publishes fiction, drama, short stories, poetry and criticism for a general audience." Semiannually. Estab. 1986. Circ. 5,000.
   ● Catalyst was voted "Best Literary Boost" by *Atlanta Magazine* in 1991.
Needs: Open. Publishes annual special fiction issue. Receives 100-200 unsolicited mss/month. Buys 75-100 mss/issue. Publishes ms 6 months after acceptance. Recently published work by Lois Lyles, Zaron Burnett, Jr. Length: 3,000 words maximum. Publishes short shorts. Recommends other markets.

How to Contact: Query first. Simultaneous submissions OK. Reports in 1 week on queries; 6 months on mss. SASE. Sample copy for $2.50 and 9 × 12 SASE. Fiction guidelines for #10 SASE (IRCs).
Payment: Pays $10-200, contributor's copies. Charges for extras.
Terms: Pays on publication. Rights remain with author.
Advice: "Attend workshops; join a writing organization; read a variety of different writers' works; learn good writing skills; and seek advice from established writers."

‡**CAT'S EAR, Poetry and Fiction, (II)**, Galliard Group Publishers, P.O. Box 946, Kirksville MO 63501. (816)627-2210. Editor: Tim Rolands. Fiction Editors: Tim Rolands and Jack Holcomb. Magazine: 5½ × 8½; 64-96 pages; 50 lb. recycled paper; one cover photo. "Poetry and fiction for intelligent readers, though not exclusively academic." Annual. Estab. 1992. Circ. 100.
Needs: Experimental, horror, humor/satire, literary, mainstream/contemporary, psychic/supernatural/ occult, science fiction (soft/sociological). Plans special fiction issue or anthology in the future. Receives 3-5 unsolicited mss/month. Accepts 1 ms/issue. Recently published work by Alfred Schwaid. Length: 3,000 words average. Publishes short shorts. Length: 500 words.
How to Contact: Send complete ms with a cover letter. Should include estimated word count and list of publications (optional). Reports in 1 month on queries; 3 months on mss. Send SASE (or IRC) for reply, return of ms or send a disposable copy of ms. No simultaneous submissions. Electronic submissions OK. Sample copy for $5. Fiction guidelines for #10 SAE and 1 first-class stamp or IRC.
Payment: Pays 2 contributor's copies; additional copies for $4.
Terms: Acquires first North American serial rights. Sends galleys to author.

‡**CEMETARY PLOT, (I, IV)**, Tellstar Productions, P.O. Box 1264, Huntington WV 25714. Editor: Shannon Bridget Murphy. Magazine: 8 × 11; b&w illustrations, glossy color and b&w photographs. "*Cemetary Plot* is a magazine devoted to horror and the supernatural. The magazine staff includes a psychic. *Cemetary Plot* is primarily fiction for all ages." Triannually. Estab. 1993. Circ. 500.
• The magazine *Ghost Town*, listed in this book, also is published by Tellstar Productions.
Needs: Experimental, horror, humor/satire, mystery/suspense, psychic/supernatural/occult, young adult/teen. Publishes annual special fiction issue. Receives 5-10 unsolicited mss/month. Accepts 2-4 mss/issue. Time between acceptance of ms and publication varies. Length: 1,500-3,500 words preferred. Publishes short shorts. Length: 500 words or less. Also publishes literary essays and poetry. Always critiques or comments on rejected ms.
How to Contact: Send complete ms with a cover letter. Should include estimated word count, bio (500 words) and list of publications. Reports in 6 weeks. Send a disposable copy of ms. Simultaneous, reprint and electronic submissions OK. Sample copy for $8. Fiction guidelines for $1. Reviews novels and short story collections.
Payment: "Payment depends upon budget." Pays 1 contributor's copy.
Terms: Buys first rights and one-time rights.
Advice: "I am looking for fiction that is interesting and includes the elements of suspense, humor/ satire, mystery/suspense. Supernatural nonfiction is welcome if it is realistic. Beginning fiction writers should experiment and be creative." Would like to see more work from "young writers—high school and college. Please do not send 'blood and guts' stories. Write for details about contests and annual photography competition."

CHAMINADE LITERARY REVIEW, (II, IV), Chaminade Press, 3140 Waialae Ave., Honolulu HI 96816. (808)735-4723. Editor: Loretta Petrie. Magazine: 6 × 9; 175 pages; 50 lb. white paper; 10 pt. C1S cover; photographs. "Multicultural, particularly Hawaii—poetry, fiction, artwork, criticism, photos, translations for all English-speaking internationals, but primarily Hawaii." Semiannually. Estab. 1987. Circ. 350.
Needs: Excerpted novel, ethnic, experimental, humor/satire, literary, religious/inspirational, translations. "We have published a variety including translations of Japanese writers, a fishing story set in Hawaii, fantasy set along the Amazon, but the major point is they are all 'literary.' No erotica, horror, children's or young adult, confession, lesbian, gay." Receives 8 unsolicited mss/month. Acquires 5-8 mss/issue. Publishes ms 3-6 months after acceptance. "We haven't published short shorts yet, but would depending on quality." Sometimes critiques rejected ms.
How to Contact: Send complete ms with cover letter. Include short contributor's note. Reporting time depends on how long before deadlines of May 15 and December 15. SASE. Reprint submissions OK. Sample copy for $5.

Payment: Pays subscription to magazine.
Terms: Acquires one-time rights.
Advice: "We look for good writing; appeal for Hawaii audience and writers everywhere. *CLR* was founded to give added exposure to Hawaii's writers, both here and on the mainland, and to juxtapose Hawaii writing with mainland and international work."

CHANGING MEN, Issues in Gender, Sex, & Politics, (II), Feminist Men's Publications, Inc., 306 N. Brooks, Madison WI 53715. (608)256-2565. Editor: Michael Biernbaum. Fiction Editor: Paul Matalucci. Magazine: 8½×11; 72 pages; bond paper; glossy card stock cover; illustrations and photographs. "Issues in gender, sex and politics for pro-feminist men (largely)." Biannual. Estab. 1979. Circ. 6,000.
 • Focusing on the changing roles of men in our society, this publication was nominated for the *Utne Reader* Alternative Press Award in both 1991 and 1992.
Needs: Contemporary, erotica, experimental, feminist, gay, humor/satire, lesbian, literary, sports. "Fiction should be pro-feminist or pro-gay/lesbian or deal with issues in leftist/radical politics." Upcoming themes: "Undoing Gender." Receives 5-10 unsolicited mss/month. Acquires 1-2 mss/issue. Publishes ms 6-12 months after acceptance. Published work by Bob Shelby, S. Kolankiewicz, Keith Kelly. Length: 1,500-2,000 words average; 1,000 words minimum; 4,000 words maximum. Sometimes critiques rejected mss.
How to Contact: Send complete ms with cover letter. Include brief description of work enclosed. Reports in 6 months on mss. SASE. "May consider" simultaneous submissions. Sample copy for $6. Fiction guidelines for SASE (IRCs).
Payment: Pays contributor's copies.
Terms: Acquires first North American serial rights. Sends galleys to author.
Advice: "Fresh perspectives on feminist, gay/lesbian and political issues. Writer should ideally be familiar with our magazine, know our spheres of interest and know what we have recently published to avoid excessive similarity/duplication."

THE CHARITON REVIEW, (II), Northeast Missouri State University, Kirksville MO 63501. (816)785-4499. Editor: Jim Barnes. Magazine: 6×9; 100+ pages; 60 lb. paper; 65 lb. cover stock; photographs on cover. "We demand only excellence in fiction and fiction translation for a general and college readership." Semiannually. Estab. 1975. Circ. 700+.
Needs: Literary, contemporary and translations. Buys 3-5 mss/issue; 6-10 mss/year. Published work by Steve Heller, John Deming, Eve Shelnutt; published new writers within the last year. Length: 3,000-6,000 words. Also publishes literary essays, poetry. Critiques rejected mss when there is time. Sometimes recommends other markets.
How to Contact: Send complete ms with SASE (IRCs). No book-length mss. No simultaneous submissions. Reports in less than 1 month on mss. Publishes ms an average of 6 months after acceptance. Sample copy for $3 with SASE. Reviews novels and short story collections.
Payment: Pays $5/page up to $50 maximum; contributor's copy; $3.50 for extras.
Terms: Pays on publication for first North American serial rights; rights returned on request.
Advice: "Do not ask us for guidelines: the only guidelines are excellence in all matters. Write well and study the publication you are submitting to. We are interested only in the very best fiction and fiction translation. We are not interested in slick material. We do not read photocopies or carbon copies. Know the simple mechanics of submission—SASE, no paper clips, no odd-sized SASE, etc. Know the genre (short story, novella, etc.). Know the unwritten laws."

THE CHATTAHOOCHEE REVIEW, (II), DeKalb College, 2101 Womack Rd., Dunwoody GA 30338. (404)551-3166. Editor: Lamar York. Magazine: 6×9; 150 pages; 70 lb. paper; 80 lb. cover stock; illustrations; photographs. Quarterly. Estab. 1980. Circ. 1,250.
Needs: Literary, mainstream. No juvenile, romance, sci-fi. Receives 500 unsolicited mss/month. Accepts 5 mss/issue. Published work by Leon Rooke, R.T. Smith; published new writers within the last year. Length: 2,500 words average. Also publishes literary essays, literary criticism, poetry. Sometimes critiques rejected mss and recommends other markets.
How to Contact: Send complete ms with cover letter, which should include sufficient bio for notes on contributors' page. Reports in 2 months. SASE (IRCs). May consider simultaneous submission "reluctantly." Sample copy for $4. Fiction guidelines available on request. Reviews novels and short story collections.

Payment: Pays in contributor's copies.
Terms: Acquires first rights.
Advice: "Arrange to read magazine before you submit to it." Known for publishing southern regional fiction.

CHELSEA (II), Chelsea Associates, Inc., Box 5880, Grand Central Station, New York NY 10163. Editor: Sonia Raiziss. Magazine: 6×9; 185-235 pages; 60 lb. white paper; glossy cover stock; artwork; occasional photos. "We have no consistent theme except for single special issues. Otherwise, we use general material of an eclectic nature: poetry, prose, artwork, etc., for a sophisticated, literate audience interested in avant-garde literature and current writing, both national and international." Annually. Estab. 1958. Circ. 1,300.

• *Chelsea* sponsors the Chelsea Awards also listed in this book. Entries to that contest will also be considered for the magazine, but writers may submit directly to the magazine as well. The magazine was the recipient of an NEA grant and a New York State Council for the Arts grant in 1992.

Needs: Literary, contemporary, poetry and translations. No humorous, scatological, purely confessional or child/young-adult experiences. Receives approximately 100 unsolicited fiction mss each month. Approximately 1% of fiction is agented. Published work by Susan Sonde, Josip Novakovich, Roberta Allen. Length: not over 25 printed pages. Publishes short shorts of 4-6 pages. Critiques rejected mss when there is time.
How to Contact: Send complete ms with with SASE (IRCs) and succinct cover letter with previous credits. No simultaneous submissions. Reports in 3 months on mss. Publishes ms within a year after acceptance. Sample copy $5 plus postage.
Payment: Pays contributor's copies, $5 per printed page; annual Chelsea Award, $500 (send SASE for guidelines).
Terms: Buys first North American serial rights plus one-time non-exclusive reprint rights.
Advice: "Familiarize yourself with issues of the magazine for character of contributions. Manuscripts should be legible, clearly typed, with minimal number of typographical errors and cross-outs, sufficient return postage. Most mss are rejected because they are conventional in theme and/or style, uninspired, contrived, etc. We see far too much of the amateurish love story or romance. Writers should say something that has never been said before or at least say something in a unique way. There is too much focus on instant fame and not enough attention to craft. Our audience is sophisticated, international, and eclectic and expects freshness and originality."

CHICAGO REVIEW, 5801 S. Kenwood Ave., Chicago IL 60637. Fiction Editor: Andy Winston. Magazine for a highly literate general audience: 6½×9; 96 pages; offset white 60 lb. paper; illustrations; photos. Quarterly. Estab. 1946. Circ. 2,200.
Needs: Literary, contemporary and experimental. Accepts up to 5 mss/issue; 20 mss/year. Receives 80-100 unsolicited fiction mss each month. No preferred length, except will not accept book-length mss. Also publishes literary essays, literary criticism, poetry. Sometimes critiques rejected mss "upon request." Sometimes recommends other markets.
How to Contact: Send complete ms with cover letter. SASE. Simultaneous submissions OK. Reports in 4-5 months on mss. Sample copy for $5. Guidelines with SASE (IRCs). Reviews novels and short story collections. Send books to Book Review Editor.
Payment: Pays 3 contributor's copies and subscription.
Advice: "We look with interest at fiction that addresses subjects inventively, work that steers clear of clichéd treatments of themes. We're always eager to read writing that experiments with language, whether it be with characters' viewpoints, tone or style."

CHIPS OFF THE WRITER'S BLOCK, (I), Box 83371, Los Angeles CA 90083. Editor: Wanda Windham. Newsletter. "Freelancer's forum, the beginner's chance to be published." Bimonthly.
• While the name for this publishing company is *Chips Off the Writer's Block*, and work should be sent there, there are actually three magazines published. *Fiction Forum* is the magazine featuring short fiction.
Needs: "We will consider all categories of fiction, as our publication gives writers a chance to be 'critiqued' by fellow writers." No pornographic or offensive material. Published new writers within the last year. "Always" critiques rejected mss.
How to Contact: Submit complete ms. "Cover letters are not necessary. Please note the word count on the first page of the story." Reports in 6 weeks to 2 months. SASE. Simultaneous submissions OK. Sample copy for $5. Fiction guidelines for #10 SAE and 1 first-class stamp (IRCs).

Payment: Pays in contributor's copies.
Advice: "The editor works directly with the author if editing is necessary or if the story needs to be reworked. The writer's peer group also sends in comments, suggestions, etc., once the story is in print. The comments are discussed in later issues."

CHIRICÚ, (II, IV), Ballantine Hall 849, Indiana University, Bloomington IN 47405. Editor: Sean T. Dwyer. "We publish essays, translations, poetry, fiction, reviews, interviews and artwork (illustrations and photos) that are either by or about Latinos. We have no barriers on style, content or ideology, but would like to see well-written material." Annually. Estab. 1976. Circ. 500.
Needs: Contemporary, ethnic, experimental, fantasy, feminist, humor/satire, literary, mainstream, prose poem, science fiction, serialized/excerpted novel, translations. No fiction that has nothing to do with Latinos (when not written by one). Published work by Ricardo Lindo, Eduardo Galeano; published new writers within the last year. Length: 7,000 words maximum; 3,000 words average. Occasionally critiques rejected mss. Sometimes recommends other markets.
How to Contact: Send complete ms with cover letter. "Include some personal information along with information about your story." SASE. No simultaneous submissions. Reports in 5 weeks. Publishes ms 6-12 months after acceptance. Sample copy for $5. Guidelines for #10 SASE (IRCs).
Advice: "Realize that we are a Latino literary journal so that if you are not Latino, then your work must reflect an interest in Latino issues or have a Latino bent to it in literature." Mss rejected "because beginning writers force their language instead of writing from genuine sentiment, because of multiple grammatical errors and because writers think that naming a character José gives their story a Latino slant."

CHRYSALIS, Journal of the Swedenborg Foundation, (II), The Swedenborg Foundation, P.O. Box 549, West Chester PA 19381-0549. (215)430-3222. Send mss to: Rt. 1, Box 184, Dillwyn VA 23936. (804)983-3021. Editor-in-Chief: Carol S. Lawson. Fiction Editor: Phoebe Loughrey. Magazine: 7½×10; 80 pages; archival paper; coated cover stock; illustrations; photos. "A literary magazine centered around one theme per issue. Publishes fiction, articles, poetry, book and film reviews for intellectually curious readers interested in spiritual topics." Triannually. Estab. 1985. Circ. 3,000.
Needs: Adventure (leading to insight), contemporary, experimental, historical (general), literary, mainstream, mystery/suspense, science fiction, spiritual, sports. No religious, juvenile, preschool. Upcoming themes: "The Future of Religion" (Spring 1994); "Music" (Summer 1994); "Order" (Autumn 1994); "Windows" (Spring 1995); "Play" (Summer 1995); "The Good Life" (Autumn 1995). Receives 40 mss/month. Buys 4-5 mss/issue; 12-18 mss/year. Publishes ms within 12 months of acceptance. Published work by Larry Dossey, Frances Vaughan, John Hitchcock, Perry Martin; published new writers within the last year. Length: 1,500 words minimum; 2,500 words maximum. Publishes short shorts. Also publishes literary essays, literary criticism, poetry. Sometimes critiques rejected mss and recommends other markets.
How to Contact: Query first and send SASE (IRCs) for guidelines. Reports in 2 months. SASE. No simultaneous, reprinted or inpress material. Sample copy for $5. Fiction guidelines for #10 SAE and 1 first-class stamp.
Payment: Pays $75-250 and 5 contributor's copies.
Terms: Pays on publication for one-time rights. Sends galleys to author.
Advice: Looking for "1. *Quality*; 2. appeal for our audience; 3. relevance to/illumination of an aspect of issue's theme."

CICADA, (II, IV), 329 "E" St., Bakersfield CA 93304. (805)323-4064. Editor: Frederick A. Raborg, Jr. Magazine: 5½×8¼; 24 pages; Matte cover stock; illustrations and photos. "Oriental poetry and fiction related to the Orient for general readership and haiku enthusiasts." Quarterly. Estab. 1985. Circ. 600.
● *Cicada* is edited by Frederick A. Raborg, Jr., who is also editor of *Amelia* and *SPSM&H* listed in this book. See also the listing for the *Amelia* Magazine Awards.
Needs: *All with Oriental slant*: Adventure, contemporary, erotica, ethnic, experimental, fantasy, feminist, historical (general), horror, humor/satire, lesbian, literary, mainstream, mystery/suspense, psychic/supernatural/occult, regional, contemporary romance, historical romance, young adult romance, science fiction, senior citizen/retirement and translations. "We look for strong fiction with Oriental (especially Japanese) content or flavor. Stories need not have 'happy' endings, and we are open to the experimental and/or avant-garde. Erotica is fine (the Japanese love their erotica); pornography, no." Receives 30+ unsolicited mss/month. Buys 1 ms/issue; 4 mss/year. Publishes ms 6 months-1 year after acceptance. Agented fiction 5%. Recently published work by Gilbert Garand, Frank Holland and Jim Mastro. Length: 2,000 words average; 500 words minimum; 3,000 words maximum. Critiques rejected

ms when appropriate. Always recommends other markets. Also publishes poetry.
How to Contact: Send complete ms with cover letter. Include Social Security number and appropriate information about the writer in relationship to the Orient. Reports in 2 weeks on queries; 3 months on mss (if seriously considered). SASE. Sample copy $4.50. Fiction guidelines for #10 SAE and 1 first-class stamp (IRCs).
Payment: Pays $10-25 plus contributor's copies; charge for extras.
Terms: Pays on publication for first North American serial rights. $5 kill fee.
Advice: Looks for "excellence and appropriate storyline. Strong characterization and knowledge of the Orient are musts. Neatness counts high on my list for first impressions. A writer should demonstrate a high degree of professionalism."

CIMARRON REVIEW, (II), Oklahoma State University, 205 Morrill, Stillwater OK 74078-0135. (405)744-9476. Editor: Gordon Weaver. Managing Editor: Paul Bowers. Magazine: 6×9; 100 pages; illustrations on cover. "Poetry and fiction on contemporary themes; personal essay on contemporary issues that cope with life in the 20th century, for educated literary readers. We work hard to reflect quality." Quarterly. Estab. 1967. Circ. 700.
Needs: Literary and contemporary. No collegiate reminiscences or juvenilia. Buys 6-7 mss/issue, 24-28 mss/year. Published works by Peter Makuck, Mary Lee Settle, W. D. Wetherell, John Timmerman; published new writers within the last year. Also publishes literary essays, literary criticism, poetry. Sometimes recommends other markets.
How to Contact: Send complete ms with SASE (IRCs). "Short cover letters are appropriate but not essential, except for providing *CR* with the most recent mailing address available." No simultaneous submissions. Reports in 8-10 weeks on mss. Publishes ms within 12 months after acceptance. Sample copy with SASE and $3. Reviews novels, short story collections, and poetry collections.
Payment: Pays one-year subscription to author, plus $50 for each prose piece and $15 for each poem.
Terms: Buys all rights on publication. "Permission to reprint granted freely."
Advice: "Short fiction is a genre uniquely suited to the modern world. *CR* seeks an individual, innovative style that focuses on contemporary themes."

‡✹THE CLAREMONT REVIEW, The Contemporary Magazine of Young Adult Writers, (I,IV), The Claremont Review Publishers, 4980 Wesley Rd., Victoria, British Columbia V8Y 1Y9 Canada. (604)658-5221. Fax: (604)658-5387. Editors: Terence Young, Bill Stenson. Magazine: 6×9; 110-120 pages; book paper; soft gloss cover; b&w illustrations. "We are dedicated to publishing emerging young writers aged 13-19 from anywhere in the English-speaking world, but primarily Canada and the U.S." Published twice/year. Estab. 1992. Circ. 350.
Needs: Young adult/teen ("their writing, not writing for them"). Plans to publish special fiction issue or anthology. Receives 5-6 unsolicited mss/month. Accepts 4-5 mss/issue; 10-12 mss/year. Publishes ms 3 months after acceptance. Length: 1,500-3,000 words preferred; 5,000 words maximum. Publishes short shorts. Also publishes prose poetry. Always comments on rejected mss.
How to Contact: Send complete ms with cover letter. Include 2-line bio, list of publications and SASE (IRCs). Reports in 6 weeks-3 months. Simultaneous submissions OK. Sample copy for $5 with 6×9 SAE and $2 Canadian postage. Fiction guidelines free with SAE.
Payment: Pays $5 minimum plus 1 contributor's copy. Additional copies for $5.
Terms: Pays on publication for first North American serial rights and one-time rights.
Advice: Looking for "good concrete narratives with credible dialogue and solid use of original detail. It must be unique, honest and a glimpse of some truth. Send an error-free final draft with a short covering letter and bio; please, read us first to see what we publish."

CLIFTON MAGAZINE , (II), University of Cincinnati Communications Board, 204 Tangeman University Center, ML 136, Cincinnati OH 45221. (513)556-6379. Editor: Rob Hartzell (1993-94). Editors change each year. "Send future correspondence to 'Editor.' " Magazine: 8×11; 48 pages; 70 lb. enamel coated paper; illustrations; photos. "*Clifton* is the magazine of the University of Cincinnati, presenting fiction, poetry and feature articles of interest to the University community. It is read by a highly literate audience of students, academics and professionals looking for original and exciting ideas presented in our award-winning format." Quarterly. Estab. 1972. Circ. 30,000.
 ● This student-run college magazine has won numerous awards over the years, including the Columbia Scholastic Gold Crown Award in 1992 and the Silver Crown in 1991.
Needs: Literary, contemporary, science fiction (soft/sociological), fantasy, feminist, erotica, horror, prose poem, regional and ethnic. "Will consider anything we haven't read a thousand times before. We try to have no preconceptions when approaching fiction." Receives approximately 30 unsolicited

fiction mss each month. Accepts 1-2 mss/issue, 5 mss/year. Length: 5,000 words maximum. Publishes short shorts. Also publishes poetry.

How to Contact: Send complete ms with SASE (IRCs). Simultaneous submissions OK. Reports in 6-8 weeks on mss. Sample copy $2.75. Guidelines with #10 SASE. Reviews novels. Send books to Fiction Editor.

Payment: Pays 3 contributor's copies.

Terms: Acquires first rights.

Advice: "There is a trend in literature to overglorify the mundane, resulting in bland stories with lukewarm themes. Too often we find ourselves rejecting well-written stories that have no punch to them. Literary does not necessitate navel gazing. Literature is a mirror (usually the funhouse variety) to the world, and is just as dirty, ugly and sweaty, if not more so. Good writing feels right, like an expensive steak, and takes as long to eat. Don't be afraid to be different. Don't be different for the sake of being different. We read manuscripts first as readers, then as editors. If we as readers are bored, we as editors don't waste our time. A story should be mechanically sound, intricate, concise and lyrical. New and young writers are encouraged to submit. Work by UC students, grads and faculty is especially welcome. Regional writers given top priority, but writers outside Ohio are also considered. In the end, it's the quality of the story that decides whether or not it is published."

CLOCKWATCH REVIEW, A Journal of the Arts, (II), Dept. of English, Illinois Wesleyan University, Bloomington IL 61702. (309)556-3352. Editor: James Plath. Magazine: 5½×8½; 64-80 pages; coated stock paper; glossy cover stock; illustrations; photos. "We publish stories which are *literary* as well as alive, colorful, enjoyable—stories which linger like shadows," for a general audience. Semiannually. Estab. 1983. Circ. 1,500.

Needs: Contemporary, experimental, humor/satire, literary, mainstream, prose poem and regional. Receives 50-60 unsolicited mss/month. Accepts 2 mss/issue; 4 mss/year. Published work by Ellen Hunnicutt, Beth Brandt, Charlotte Mandel; published new writers within the last year. Length: 2,500 words average; 1,200 words minimum; 4,000 words maximum. Occasionally critiques rejected mss if requested.

How to Contact: Send complete ms. Reports in 2 months. SASE (IRCs). Publishes ms 3-12 months after acceptance. Sample copy for $4.

Payment: Pays 3 contributor's copies and small cash stipend. (Currently $50, but may vary).

Terms: Buys first serial rights.

Advice: "*Clockwatch* has always tried to expand the audience for quality contemporary poetry and fiction by publishing a highly visual magazine that is thin enough to invite reading. We've included interviews with popular musicians and artists in order to further interest a general, as well as academic, public and show the interrelationship of the arts. Give us characters with meat on their bones, colorful but not clichéd; give us natural plots, not contrived or melodramatic. Above all, give us your *best* work."

COCHRAN'S CORNER, (I), 225 Ralston, Converse TX 78109. (210)659-5062. Editor: Debra G. Tompkins. Magazine: 5½×8; 52 pages. "We publish fiction, nonfiction and poetry. Our only requirement is no strong language." For a "family" audience. Quarterly. Estab. 1986. Circ. 500.

Needs: Adventure, historical (general), horror, humor/satire, children's/juvenile, mystery/suspense, religious/inspirational, romance, science fiction and young adult/teen (10-18 years). "Mss must be free from language you wouldn't want your/our children to read." Plans a special fiction issue. Receives 50 mss/month. Accepts 4 mss/issue; 8 mss/year. Publishes ms by the next issue after acceptance. Published work by Juni Dunkin, Ruth Cox Anderson, Becky Knight. Length: 500 words preferred; 300 words minimum; 1,000 words maximum. Also publishes literary essays, literary criticism, poetry.

How to Contact: "Right now we are forced to limit acceptance to *subscribers only*." Send complete ms with cover letter. Reports in 3 weeks on queries; 3 months on mss. SASE (IRCs) for manuscript. Simultaneous and reprint submissions OK. Sample copy for $5, 9×12 SAE and 90¢ postage. Fiction guidelines for #10 SAE and 1 first-class stamp.

Read the Business of Fiction Writing section to learn the correct way to prepare and submit a manuscript.

Payment: Pays in contributor's copies.
Terms: Acquires one-time rights.
Advice: "I feel the quality of fiction is getting better. The public is demanding a good read, instead of having sex or violence carry the story. I predict that fiction has a good future. We like to print the story as the writer submits it if possible. This way writers can compare their work with their peers and take the necessary steps to improve and go on to sell to bigger magazines. Stories from the heart desire a place to be published. We try to fill that need."

‡**COLD-DRILL MAGAZINE, (IV),** English Dept., Boise State University, 1910 University Dr., Boise ID 83725. (208)385-1999. Editor: Rebekah Harvey. Magazine: box format; various perfect and non-perfect bound inserts; length: determined by submissions; illustrations, photos. Material submitted *must be by Idaho authors or deal with Idaho.* For adult audiences. Annually. Estab. 1970. Circ. 500.
* In the past *Cold-Drill* has included themed material, but the editor says the magazine is moving back to allowing submissions to dictate theme.
Needs: "For our 1993-94 issue we are looking for poems, short stories, nonfiction, essays, camera-ready artwork. We want material about the sweat and frustration, anger and satisfaction of a day's work."
How to Contact: Query first. SASE.
Payment: Pays in contributor's copies.
Terms: Acquires first rights.

COLLAGES AND BRICOLAGES, The Journal of International Writing, (II), P.O. Box 86, Clarion PA 16214. (814)226-5799. Editor: Marie-José Fortis. Magazine: 8×11; 100-150 pages; illustrations. "The theme, if there is any, is international cultures, with socio-political undertones. The magazine may include essays, short stories, short plays, poems that show innovative promise." Annually. Estab. 1987.
* The editor is no longer concentrating on post-modernism. Focus is now on "innovative, committed, literary fiction."
Needs: Contemporary, ethnic, experimental, feminist, humor/satire, literary, philosophical works. "Also symbolist, surrealist b&w designs/illustrations are welcome." Upcoming themes: "George Sand" (1994) (tentative). Receives about 30 unsolicited fiction mss/month. Publishes ms 6-9 months after acceptance. Recently published work by Marilou Awiakta, Diane Hamill Metzger, Eric Basso, Greg Boyd; published new writers within the last year. Publishes short shorts. Also publishes literary essays, literary criticism, poetry. Sometimes critiques rejected ms; recommends other markets when there is time.
How to Contact: Send complete ms with cover letter that includes a short bio. Reports in 2-3 months. SASE (IRCs). Simultaneous submissions OK. Sample copy $6. Reviews novels and short story collections. "How often and how many per issue depends on reviewers available."
Payment: Pays 2 contributor's copies.
Terms: Acquires first rights. Rights revert to author after publication.
Advice: "This is a fin-de-siecle—also the end of a millenium—with chaos, conflicts, cruelty, and confusion. The writer should be aware of these elements, and let them enter her every pore. Yet, paradoxically, she should write as if nothing else mattered."

‡**COLORADO REVIEW, (II),** English Department, Colorado State University, Fort Collins CO 80523. (303)491-7251. Editor: David Milofsky. Literary journal: 160 pages; 70 lb. book weight paper. Semiannually. Estab. as *Colorado State Review* 1966. Circ. 500.
Needs: Contemporary, ethnic, experimental, literary, mainstream, translations. Receives 300 unsolicited fiction mss/month. Accepts 3-4 mss/issue. Recently published work by Stanley Elkin, T. Alan Broughton, Gladys Swan; published new writers within the last year. Length: under 6,000 words. Does not read mss May-August. Also publishes literary essays, book reviews, poetry. Occasionally critiques rejected mss.
How to Contact: Send complete ms with SASE (IRCs) and brief bio with previous publications. Reports in 3 months. Publishes ms 6-12 months after acceptance. Sample copy for $5. Reviews novels or short story collections.

Payment: Pays $5/printed page for fiction; 2 free contributor's copies; extras for $5.

Terms: Pays on publication for first North American serial rights. "We assign copyright to author on request." Sends galleys to author.

Advice: "We are interested in manuscripts which show craft, imagination and a convincing voice. If a story has reached a level of technical competence, we are receptive to the fiction working on its own terms. The oldest advice is still the best: persistence. Approach every aspect of the writing process with pride, conscientiousness—from word choice to manuscript appearance."

‡**THE COLUMBUS LITERARY GAZETTE, A Paper for All Seasons, (I, II),** P.O. Box 141418, Columbus OH 43214. (614)262-4425. Editor: Bonnie Djouadi. Tabloid: 10×13; 16 pages; newsprint; illustrations, photographs and cartoons. "We strive to make the publishing process an enjoyable one for writers. This is a family paper, so we are looking for stories that are fun, make you cry, bring chills to the bone, or keep you on the edge of your seat. We have a featured short story, poetry corner, young readers, young writers, interviews, and an ongoing serial." Monthly. Estab. 1991. Circ. 950.

Needs: Adventure, childrens/juvenile, condensed novel, ethnic/multicultural, fantasy (children's fantasy, science fantasy), feminist, gay, historical, horror, humor/satire, lesbian, literary, mainstream/contemporary, mystery/suspense, psychic/supernatural/occult, regional, science fiction, serialized novel, westerns, young adult/teen. No "violence, sex, and profanity—we get enough of that on TV." Will consider holiday material. Publishes biannual special fiction issue or anthology. Receives 8-10 unsolicited mss/month. Accepts 3 mss/issue; 36 mss/year. Publishes ms 6-12 months after acceptance. Recently published work by William Allen, Mike Leasure, Donna Stuart, Aloysius Wald. Length: 2,500 words preferred; 500 words minimum; 3,500 words maximum. Publishes short shorts (mostly by young writers). Also publishes literary essays, literary criticism and poetry. Always critiques or comments on rejected mss.

How to Contact: Send complete ms with a cover letter. Should include estimated word count, name and address on typed ms. Reports in 4-6 months. Send a disposable copy of the ms. Simultaneous submissions OK. Sample copy for $1.50. Fiction guidelines free. Reviews novels and short story collections.

Payment: Pays 1 contributor's copy.

Terms: Writers retain all rights. Sends galleys to author.

Advice: "As stated previously, we need pieces that will affect emotions, keep one's attention and stir the reader. We often select pieces that have a moral to them as well as an entertaining aspect. We may publish pieces that others reject, because we often 'go out on a limb' for a story with merit. Find a serious writer's critique group to share your story with first. Don't trust your friend's and family's opinions—they'll love it! Don't be afraid to be asked for a rewrite. Someone who reworks their piece at the request of an editor gleans a lot of respect." Would like to see more "humor, humor and more humor! These days, the majority of humor received is from personal essays. We now have a backlog of poetry."

‡**COMMON LIVES/LESBIAN LIVES, A Lesbian Quarterly, (IV),** Box 1553, Iowa City IA 52244. "*CL/LL* seeks to document the experiences and thoughts of lesbians for lesbian audience." Magazine: 5×8½; 112-128 pages; illustrations; photos. Quarterly.

Needs: *All pertaining to lesbian culture*: Adventure, comics, contemporary, erotica, ethnic, experimental, fantasy, feminist, historical (general), humor/satire, juvenile, lesbian, prose poem, psychic/supernatural/occult, regional, romance, science fiction, senior citizen/retirement, suspense/mystery, western and young adult/teen. Length: 4-10 pages. Also publishes literary essays, literary criticism, poetry. Occasionally critiques rejected mss.

How to Contact: Send complete ms with cover letter; a short bio sketch is required. Reports in 4 months. SASE (IRCs). Publishes ms up to 4 months after acceptance. Published "many" new writers within the last year. Sample copy $5. Reviews novels and short story collections.

Payment: Pays 2 contributor's copies.

Advice: "Readers relate stories to their lives; fiction is an interesting and accessible way for lesbians to document their experience and express their opinions."

COMMUNITIES: JOURNAL OF COOPERATION, (II), Rt. 1, Box 155, Rutledge MO 63563. (816)883-5543. Business Manager: Laird Schaub. Editors change each issue. "Features articles on intentional communities, urban collectives, rural communes, politics, health, alternative culture and workplace democracy for people involved in cooperative ventures." Quarterly. Estab. 1973. Circ. 4,000.

Needs: Feminist, science fiction (soft/sociological), utopian and cooperative. Accepts "maybe 4 manuscripts per year (would do more if we got them)." Length: 1,000 words minimum; 5,000 words maximum. Generally critiques rejected mss.

How to Contact: Query first or send complete ms. Reports in 1 month on queries; 6 weeks on mss. Simultaneous and previously published submissions OK. Sample copy for $4.50.

Payment: Pays 1 year subscription and 3 contributor's copies.

Terms: Acquires one-time rights.

A COMPANION IN ZEOR, (I, II, IV), 307 Ashland Ave., McKee City NJ 08232. Editor: Karen Litman. Fanzine: 8½ × 11; 60 pages; "letter" paper; heavy blue cover; b&w line illustrations; occasional b&w photographs. Publishes science fiction based on the various Universe creations of Jacqueline Lichtenberg. Occasional features on Star Trek, and other interests, convention reports, reviews of movies and books, recordings, etc. Published irregularly. Estab. 1978. Circ. 300.

- *Companion in Zeor* is one of two fanzines devoted to the work and characters of Jacqueline Lichtenberg. Lichtenberg's work includes several future world, alien and group culture novels and series including the Sime/Gen Series and The Dushau trilogy. She's also penned two books on her own vampire character and she co-authored *Star Trek Lives*.

Needs: Fantasy, humor/satire, prose poem, science fiction. "No vicious satire. Nothing X-rated. Homosexuality prohibited unless *essential* in story. We run a clean publication that anyone should be able to read without fear." Occasionally receives one manuscript a month. Accepts "as much as can afford to print." Publication of an accepted ms "can take years, due to limit of finances available for publication." Occasionally critiques rejected mss and recommends other markets.

How to Contact: Query first or send complete ms with cover letter. "Prefer cover letters about any writing experience prior, or related interests toward writing aims." Reports in 1 month. SASE. Simultaneous submissions OK. Sample copy price depends on individual circumstances. Fiction guidelines for #10 SAE and 1 first-class stamp (IRC). "I write individual letters to all queries. No form letter at present." SASE for guidelines required. Reviews science fiction/fantasy collections or titles.

Payment: Pays in contributor's copies.

Terms: Acquires first rights.

Advice: "We take fiction based on any and all of Jacqueline Lichtenberg's published novels. The contributor should be familiar with these works before contributing material to my fanzine. Also accepts manuscripts on cassette from visually handicapped if submitted. 'Zines also on tape for those individuals."

‡✸COMPENIONS, The Quarterly Publication of the Writer's Club of Stratford, (I), P.O. Box 2511, St. Marys, Ontario N4X 1A3 Canada. (519)284-1675. Editor: Jerry Penner. President: Marco Balestrin. Magazine: 8½ × 11; 12-20 pages; bond paper; bond cover; computer graphics illustrations. "We are expanding the mandate of our magazine to include the work of outside writers. We would like to see serious beginning writers who give original twists to the old forms." Quarterly. Estab. 1983. Circ. 16 issues (to members).

- See listings for other writers clubs and organizations across the US and Canada in the Organizations and Resources section.

Needs: Adventure, ethnic/multicultural, experimental, fantasy (science fantasy), feminist, historical (general), horror, humor/satire, literary, mainstream/contemporary, mystery/suspense (amateur sleuth, private eye/hard-boiled, romantic suspense), psychic/supernatural/occult, regional, romance (contemporary, gothic), science fiction (hard science, soft/sociological), translations, westerns (frontier, traditional). "No pornography, ultra-religious or 'cutesy' stuff. We are considering thematic slants. However, we haven't nailed down any themes yet!" Receives 3 unsolicited mss/month. Accepts 5 mss/ issue; 15-20 mss/year. Does not read mss between June and August. Publishes ms 3 months after acceptance. Recently published work by Helene Gatschene, Jerry Penner, Marco Balestrin, Susan Chapman-Bossence. Length: 800-1,000 words preferred; 100 words minimum; 1,500 words maximum. Publishes short shorts. Length: 300-400 words preferred. Also publishes literary essays and poetry. Often critiques or comments on rejected mss.

How to Contact: *Charges $3.50 reading fee per manuscript* (up to 1,500 words). Send complete ms with a cover letter. Should include estimated word count, 1-page bio and "anything unusual that may be of interest." Reports in 2 months on queries; 3 months on mss. Send SASE (or IRC) for reply, return of ms or send a disposable copy of ms. Simultaneous, reprint and electronic submissions OK. Sample copy for $2, 9 × 12 SAE and 2 IRCs (if outside Canada).

Payment: Pays 2 contributor's copies; additional copies for $1.50 and 2 IRCs.
Terms: Buys one-time rights.
Advice: "A manuscript must be visceral, appeal to the guts. Must leave us either wincing from its intensity or guffawing because of its humour. Extremes are welcomed warmly." Would like to see "a genuine attempt to delve into the meaning of modern existence, a questioning of our world, using established genres to 'push the envelope'!"

COMPOST NEWSLETTER, (IV), Compost Coven, 729 Fifth Ave., San Francisco CA 94118. (415)751-9466. Editor: Valerie Walker. Newsletter: 7×8½; 28 pages; bond paper; illustrations and scanned photographs. Publishes "humor/satire from a pagan/punk perspective." Quarterly. Estab. 1981. Circ. under 100.
Needs: Experimental, fantasy, feminist, gay, humor/satire, lesbian, psychic/supernatural/occult, science fiction, serialized novel, pagan. No Christian. Publishes ms within 3 or 4 issues after acceptance. Length: 500 words minimum; 1,500 words maximum.
How to Contact: Query with clips of published work. Reports in 4 months. SASE (IRCs). Simultaneous and reprint submissions OK. Accepts electronic submissions via Macintosh disk. Sample copy $2.50. (Make checks/MO's out to Valerie Walker; mark "for CNL".)
Payment: Pays in contributor's copies.
Terms: Acquires one-time rights. Publication not copyrighted.
Advice: "If you don't like the magazine market, go out and make one of your own. Type single space on white paper, or send a Macintosh disk in MacWrite or Microsoft Word. Don't bother to format unless it's essential for the feel of the piece. Entertain us, even if you're serious. Get strange." Publishes ms "if it is funny, bizarre, or we agree with its politics."

CONCHO RIVER REVIEW, (I, II, IV), % English Dept., Angelo State University, San Angelo TX 76909. (915)657-4441. Editor: Terence A. Dalrymple. Magazine: 6½×9; 100-125 pages; 60 lb. Ardor offset paper; Classic Laid Color cover stock; b&w drawings. "We publish any fiction of high quality—no thematic specialties—contributors must be residents of Texas or the Southwest generally." Semiannually. Estab. 1987. Circ. 300.
● The magazine is considering featuring "guest editors" with each issue, but mss should still be sent to the editor, Terence A. Dalrymple.
Needs: Contemporary, ethnic, historical (general), humor/satire, literary, regional and western. No erotica; no science fiction. Receives 10-15 unsolicited mss/month. Accepts 3-6 mss/issue; 8-10 mss/year. Publishes ms 4 months after acceptance. Published work by Robert Flynn, Clay Reynolds, Roland Sodowsky. Length: 3,500 words average; 1,500 words minimum; 5,000 words maximum. Also publishes literary essays, poetry. Sometimes critiques rejected mss and recommends other markets.
How to Contact: Send complete ms with SASE (IRCs); cover letter optional. Reports in 3 weeks on queries; 3-8 weeks on mss. SASE for ms. Simultaneous submissions OK (if noted). Sample copy $4. Fiction guidelines for #10 SAE and 1 first-class stamp. Reviews novels and short story collections. Send books to Terence A. Dalrymple, % English Dept., Angelo State University, San Angelo TX 76909.
Payment: Pays in contributor's copies; $4 charge for extras.
Terms: Acquires first rights.
Advice: "We prefer a clear sense of conflict, strong characterization and effective dialogue."

CONFRONTATION, (II), English Dept., C.W. Post of Long Island University, Brookville NY 11548. (516)299-2391. Editor: Martin Tucker. Magazine: 6×9; 190-250 pages; 70 lb. paper; 80 lb. cover; illustrations; photos. "We like to have a 'range' of subjects, form and style in each issue and are open to all forms. Quality is our major concern. Our audience is literate, thinking people; formally or self-educated." Semiannually. Estab. 1968. Circ. 2,000.
● *Confrontation* has garnered a long list of awards and honors including the Editor's Award for Distinguished Achievement from CCLM (now the Council of Literary Magazines and Presses) and NEA. Work from the magazine has appeared in numerous anthologies including the *Pushcart Prize, Best American Short Stories* and *O. Henry Prize Stories*. Note payment rates have increased over 1993.
Needs: Literary, contemporary, prose poem, regional and translations. No "proseletyzing" literature. Upcoming themes: "New Southern Writing," "Emerging South Africa." Buys 30 mss/issue; 60 mss/year. Receives 400 unsolicited fiction mss each month. Does not read June-Sept. Approximately 10-15% of fiction is agented. Recently published work by Nadine Gordimer, Mario Vargas Llosa, Jayne Cortez; published many new writers within the last year. Length: 500-4,000 words. Publishes short

shorts. Also publishes literary essays, poetry. Critiques rejected mss when there is time. Sometimes recommends other markets.

How to Contact: Send complete ms with SASE (IRCs). "Cover letters acceptable, not necessary. We accept simultaneous submission but do not like it." Accepts diskettes if accompanied by computer printout submissions. Reports in 6-8 weeks on mss. Publishes ms 6-12 months after acceptance. Sample copy for $3. Reviews novels and short story collections.

Payment: Pays $20-$250; 1 contributor's copy; half price for extras.

Terms: Pays on publication for all rights "with transfer on request to author."

Advice: "Keep trying."

CORNFIELD REVIEW, (IV), The Ohio State University-Marion, 1465 Mt. Vernon Ave., Marion OH 43302. (614)389-2361. Editor: Stuart Lishan. Magazine: 5×7; 48-52 pages. "Work centered in the Midwest or by writers from the Midwest." Annually. Estab. 1975. Circ. 300.

• *Cornfield Review* has received grants from the Ohio Arts Council for the last four years.

Needs: Literary. Receives 50 unsolicited mss/month. Acquires 2-3 mss/year. Reads mss November-February only. Publishes ms 6 months after acceptance. Length: 2,000 words average; 500 words minimum; 3,000 words maximum. Publishes short shorts. Also publishes literary essays and poems.

How to Contact: Send complete ms with cover letter. Should include bio (50 words). SASE (or IRC) for return of the ms. No simultaneous submissions.

Payment: Pays contributor's copies.

Terms: Acquires one-time rights.

CORONA, Marking the Edges of Many Circles, (II), Department of History and Philosophy, Montana State University, Bozeman MT 59717. (406)994-5200. Co-Editors: Lynda Sexson, Michael Sexson. Managing Editor: Sarah Marrillo. Magazine: 7×10; 130 pages; 60 lb. "mountre matte" paper; 65 lb. Hammermill cover stock; illustrations; photos. "Interdisciplinary magazine—essays, poetry, fiction, imagery, science, history, recipes, humor, etc., for those educated, curious, with a profound interest in the arts and contemporary thought." Annually. Estab. 1980. Circ. 2,000.

Needs: Comics, contemporary, experimental, fantasy, feminist, humor/satire, literary, prose poem, regional. "Our fiction ranges from the traditional Talmudic tale to fiction engendered by speculative science, from the extended joke to regional reflection—if it isn't accessible and original, please don't send it." Receives varying number of unsolicited fiction mss/month. Accepts 6 mss/issue. Published work by Rhoda Lerman and Stephen Dixon; published new writers within the last year. Publishes short shorts. Also publishes literary essays, poetry. Occasionally critiques rejected mss. Sometimes recommends other markets.

How to Contact: Query. Reports in 6 months on mss. Sample copy $7.

Payment: Pays minimal honorarium; 2 free contributor's copies; discounted charge for extras.

Terms: Acquires first rights. Sends galleys to author upon request.

Advice: "Be knowledgeable of contents other than fiction in *Corona*; one must know the journal."

COSMIC LANDSCAPES, An Alternative Science Fiction Magazine, (I, IV), % Dan Petitpas, 19 Carroll Ave., Westwood MA 02090. (617)329-1344. Editor: Dan Petitpas. Magazine: 7×8½; 32-56 pages; white bond paper and cover stock; illustrations; photos occasionally. "A magazine which publishes science fiction for science-fiction readers; also articles and news of interest to writers and sf fans. Occasionally prints works of horror and fantasy." Annually. Estab. 1983. Circ. 150.

Needs: Science fiction (hard science, soft/sociological). Receives 10-15 unsolicited mss/month. Accepts 8 mss/issue. Published new writers in the last year. Length: 2,500 words average; 25 words minimum. Will consider all lengths. "Every manuscript receives a personal evaluation by the editor." Sometimes recommends other markets.

How to Contact: Send complete ms with info about the author. Reports usually in 1 week-3 months. SASE. Simultaneous submissions OK. Sample copy for $3.50. Fiction guidelines with SASE (IRCs).

Payment: Pays 2 contributor's copies; $2 for extras.

Terms: Acquires one-time rights.

Advice: "Writers should send a cover letter; include SASE and a return address. I'd like to know a little about you. Stories should have a beginning, middle and an ending, with an interesting character or two, and a strong idea central to its plot. Stay away from 'Twilight Zone' endings where the marauding aliens turn out to be from the Planet Earth, and elaborate jokes passing as stories. Don't get all your ideas from TV shows or movies. Study the manuscript format given in this book and make your submission as professional-looking as possible. New writers are particularly welcomed."

Literary Publishing: One Story at a Time

The Cream City Review began in 1975 as a small literary magazine. In the years following, the magazine grew to 300 pages, five times its original size. Divided in thirds, the magazine now features one-third fiction, one-third poetry and one-third non-fiction.

Patricia Montalbano came to *The Cream City Review* as an assistant fiction editor in the spring of 1992. When the fiction editor position opened up that fall, she was promoted. Most editors are graduate students so vacancies open up regularly as they move on.

The Cream City Review doesn't have a philosophy as such, but according to Montalbano, "We try to remain true to good fiction. We like pieces which are experimental, but only if there is substance behind the experiment. One of the trends I've noticed recently is cleverness for the sake of cleverness. I find

Patricia Montalbano

myself writing on the envelope: Is it enough merely to be clever and witty, to try things in an innovative style? I think along with the experiments in technique, one needs to remember the story itself. The way a story is told is worth something only when the story is worth telling in the first place. I think theme and style must work together in a piece."

Montalbano hesitates to make generalizations about what makes a good story. "I think each story must be evaluated on its own terms. Of course, every writer wants to know the formula, the secret for exactly the thing an editor is 'looking for,' but the truth is, we're looking for high-quality fiction, stories that resonate, that leave you thinking about them after the last sentence. There's no way to list the ingredients for a good story because the recipe can be so many different things."

When selecting work for an issue and measuring the stack they've chosen, the staff tries to ensure that the stories chosen are different enough thematically and stylistically for the readers to have a diverse read. "But mostly we judge each piece individually and stick with what knocks us over by its power (often quiet or subtle) or its originality of voice or approach.

"We do an awful lot of back and forth in our discussion of the finalists for an issue. Sometimes we fiction editors read the story three times each before we decide for or against it. It's a difficult process and we often have to send back work which we like very much. When you receive about 100 fiction submissions per week and can only publish 20 stories per year, you have to ask yourself, is this one of the best ten stories I will read in the next six months?"

Montalbano's favorite part of the job is being able to call someone to say their story has been accepted for the next issue of *The Cream City Review.* "As a writer myself, I know what a great feeling it is to receive that phone call, and it's nice to make someone's day like that. There's a relationship with that writer established instantly, an editor/writer bond that continues to grow as the issue goes through the stages of production."

— Donna Collingwood

COTTONWOOD, Magazine and Press, (II), 400 Kansas Union, Box J, University of Kansas, Lawrence KS 66045. (913)864-3777. Editor: George F. Wedge. Fiction Editors: Ben Accardi, Laurie Carlson. Magazine: 6×9; 112 pages; illustrations; photos. "Publish most types of 'literary' fiction. Intended audience: educated, sophisticated reader." Triannually. Estab. 1965. Circ. 500.
Needs: Ethnic/multicultural, experimental, literary, mainstream/contemporary, regional, science fiction. Receives 20 unsolicited mss/month. Acquires 5 mss/issue; 15 mss/year. Publishes ms 12-18 months after acceptance. Agented fiction less than 5%. Length: 2,500-4,000 words average; 500 words minimum; 8,000 words maximum. Also publishes poetry. Sometimes critiques or comments on rejected mss.
How to Contact: Send complete ms with cover letter. Should include bio (25 words), list of publications. Reports in 2 weeks on queries; 1-2 months on mss. SASE (or IRC) for return of ms. No simultaneous submissions. Sample copy for $3. Fiction guidelines for #10 SAE and 1 first-class stamp.
Payment: Pays 1 contributor's copy.
Terms: Acquires first rights. Fiction published in the magazine is eligible for annual Alice Carter Awards for the best fiction and poetry published in *Cottonwood.*

CRAZYHORSE, (II), Dept. of English, Univ. of Arkansas, Little Rock, AR 72204. (501)569-3160. Managing Editor: Zabelle Stodola. Fiction Editor: Judy Troy. Magazine: 6×9; 140 pages; cover illustration only. "Publishes original, quality literary fiction." Biannually. Estab. 1960. Circ. 1,000.
 • Stories appearing in *Crazyhorse* regularly appear in the *Pushcart Prize* and *Best American Short Stories* anthologies.
Needs: Literary. No formula (science-fiction, gothic, detective, etc.) fiction. Receives 100-150 unsolicited mss/month. Buys 3-5 mss/issue; 8-10 mss/year. Does not read mss in summer. Past contributors include Lee K. Abbott, Frederick Busch, Andre Dubus, Pam Durban, H.E. Francis, James Hannah, Gordon Lish, Bobbie Ann Mason and Maura Stanton; published new writers within the last year. Publishes short shorts. Also publishes literary essays, literary criticism, poetry. "Rarely" critiques rejected mss.
How to Contact: Send complete ms with cover letter. Reports in 1-3 months. SASE. No simultaneous submissions. Sample copy $5. Reviews novels and short story collections. Send books to fiction editor.
Payment: Pays $10/page and contributor's copies.
Terms: Pays on publication for first North American serial rights. *Crazyhorse* awards $500 to the author of the best work of fiction published in the magazine in a given year.
Advice: "Read a sample issue and submit work that you believe is as good as or better than the fiction we've published."

CRAZYQUILT, (II), P.O. Box 632729, San Diego CA 92163-2729. (619)688-1023. Editor: Jim Kitchen. Magazine: 5½×8½; 92 pages; illustrations and photos. "We publish short fiction, poems, nonfiction about writing and writers, one-act plays and b&w illustrations and photos." Quarterly. Estab. 1986. Circ. 175.
Needs: Contemporary, ethnic, fantasy, gay, historical, humor/satire, literary, mainstream, mystery/suspense, science fiction, excerpted novel. "Shorter pieces are preferred." Receives 85-100 unsolicited mss/quarter. Accepts 1-3 mss/issue; 4-12 mss/year. Publishes 1 year after acceptance. Published work by Louis Phillips, Geraldine Little, Judson Jerome; published new writers within the last year. Length: 1,500 words minimum; 4,000 words maximum. Also publishes literary essays, literary criticism, poetry. Occasionally critiques rejected mss.

How to Contact: Send complete ms with cover letter. Reports in 6 weeks on mss. Simultaneous submissions OK. Sample copy $4.50 ($2.50 for back issue). Fiction guidelines for SAE and 1 first-class stamp (IRC).
Payment: Pays 2 contributor's copies.
Terms: Acquires first North American serial rights or one-time rights.
Advice: "Write a story that is well constructed, develops characters and maintains interest."

THE CREAM CITY REVIEW, (II), University of Wisconsin-Milwaukee, Box 413, Milwaukee WI 53201. (414)229-9708. Editors: Mark Drechsler and Brian Jung. Fiction Editors: Patricia Montalbano, Kathleen Lester and Andrew Rivera. Editors rotate. Magazine: 5½×8½; 300 pages; 70 lb. offset/perfect-bound paper; 80 lb. cover stock; illustrations; photos. "General literary publication—an electric selection of the best we receive." Semiannually. Estab. 1975. Circ. 2,000.
• See the Insider Viewpoint featuring Patricia Montalbano in this edition.
Needs: Ethnic, experimental, humor/satire, literary, prose poem, regional and translations. Receives approximately 300 unsolicited fiction mss each month. Accepts 6-10 mss/issue. Published work by Eve Shelnutt, Stuart Dybek, Robley Wilson, William Kittredge and Marge Piercy; published new writers within the last year. Length: 1,000-10,000 words. Publishes short shorts. Also publishes literary essays, literary criticism, poetry. Critiques rejected mss when there is time. Recommends other markets "when we have time."
How to Contact: Send complete ms with SASE. Simultaneous submissions OK. Reports in 2 months. Sample copy $4.50. Reviews novels and short story collections.
Payment: Pays 2 contributor's copies.
Terms: Acquires first rights. Sends galleys to author. Rights revert to author after publication.
Advice: "Read as much as you write so that you can examine your own work in relation to where fiction has been and where fiction is going."

‡THE CREATIVE WOMAN, (I), TAPP Group, #119, 1212 S. Naper Blvd., Naperville IL 60540. (708)255-1232. Fax: (708)255-1243. Editor: Margaret Choudhury. Magazine: 8½×11; 54 pages; illustrations and b&w photos. "To celebrate the creative achievements of women in many fields, we publish nonfiction, fiction, poetry, book reviews, photography, original art, focusing on a special topic in each issue and presented from a feminist perspective." Quarterly. Estab. 1976. Circ. 369.
Needs: Feminist, gay, historical, humor/satire, lesbian, literary, mainstream/contemporary. Does not want to see animal stories. Upcoming themes: "Societies of Females" (Spring 1994); "Women in Engineering" (Summer 1994); "Latin American Women" (Autumn 1994); "Women in Classical Music" (Winter 1994/95). List of upcoming themes available for SASE. Receives 8-10 unsolicited mss/month. Accepts up to 3 mss/issue; 8 mss/year. Publishes ms within 1 year of acceptance. Recently published work by Hollis Seamon, Catherine Limbert, Bess Shapiro. Length: 2,000 words average; 100 words minimum; 3,000 words maximum. Publishes short shorts. Length: 300 words. Also publishes literary essays, literary criticism and poetry. Sometimes comments on rejected mss ("if requested").
How to Contact: Query first or send complete ms with cover letter. Should include estimated word count and short bio. Send SASE (or IRC) for reply, return of ms or send a disposable copy of ms. No simultaneous submissions or reprints. Electronic submissions OK. Sample copy $5. Fiction guidelines free. Reviews novels and short story collections; send review copies to Editor, Suite 288, 126 E. Wing, Arlington Heights IL 60004.
Payment: Pays $60 maximum plus 3 contributor's copies. Additional copies for $2.50.
Terms: Pays prior to publication for first rights.
Advice: "We are a magazine by, for, and about women. Not to say that men do not contribute—we welcome contributions from everyone. Look through back issues. Keep it short: know what you want to say, say it, and get out. If in doubt, query."

THE CRESCENT REVIEW, (II), The Crescent Review, Inc., 1445 Old Town Rd., Winston-Salem NC 27106-3143. (202)364-5939. Editor: Guy Nancekeville. Magazine: 6×9; 160 pages. Estab. 1983.
• Work appearing in *The Crescent Review* has been included in past editions of the *Best American Short Stories, Pushcart Prize, Black Southern Writers* anthologies, and in the *New Stories from the South*.
Needs: "All kinds of stories." Does not read submissions May-June; Nov.-Dec.
How to Contact: Reports in 2 weeks-4 months. SASE (IRCs). No simultaneous submissions. Sample issue for $5.
Payment: Pays 2 contributor's copies; discount for contributors.
Terms: Acquires first North American serial rights.

CRIME CLUB, (I), Suite 171, 6172 Bollinger Rd., San Jose CA 95129. (408)257-0442. Editors: Rob Oxoby and Marc Oxoby. Magazine. "Journal of poetry, prose and visual arts." Quarterly. Estab. 1991. Circ. 400.

Needs: Any genre. Adventure, experimental, fantasy, historical, humor/satire, literary, mainstream, mystery/suspense, psychic/supernatural/occult, regional, religious, science fiction, serialized novel, prose poem. Length: 5,000 words maximum. Publishes short shorts. Length: 200-500 words. Also accepts poetry.

How to Contact: Query first or send complete ms with cover letter. Simultaneous submissions OK. Accepts electronic submissions (query first). Reports in 2 months.

Payment: Pays 1 contributor's copy.

Terms: Acquires first North American serial rights.

Advice: "Be honest, be smart and have fun with it. We are serious but do this because we enjoy it. We'll publish anything of quality."

CRUCIBLE, (I, II), English Dept., Barton College, College Station, Wilson NC 27893. (919)399-6456. Editor: Terrence L. Grimes. Magazine of fiction and poetry for a general, literary audience. Annually. Estab. 1964. Circ. 500.

Needs: Contemporary, ethnic, experimental, feminist, gay, lesbian, literary, regional. Receives 12 unsolicited mss/month. Accepts 5-6 mss/year. Publishes ms 4-5 months after acceptance. Does not normally read mss from April 30 to December 1. Recently published work by William Hutchins, Guy Nancekeville. Length: 8,000 words maximum. Publishes short shorts.

How to Contact: Send 3 complete copies of ms unsigned with cover letter which should include a brief biography, "in case we publish." Reports in 2 weeks on queries; 4-5 months on mss (by June 15). SASE (IRCs). Sample copy for $5. Fiction guidelines free.

Payment: Pays contributor's copies.

Terms: Pays on publication for first rights.

Advice: "Write about what you know. Experimentation is fine as long as the experiences portrayed come across as authentic, that is to say, plausible."

CUTBANK, (II), English Department, University of Montana, Missoula MT 59812. Editors-in-Chief: C.N. Blakemore, Francesca Abbate. Fiction Editor: David Belman. Editors change each year. Terms run from June-June. After June 1994, address to "Fiction Editor." Magazine: 5½ × 8½; 115-130 pages. "Publishes highest quality fiction, poetry, artwork, for a general, literary audience." Semiannually. Estab. 1973. Circ. 600.

Needs: Receives 200 unsolicited mss/month. Accepts 6-12 mss/year. Does not read mss from February 28-August 15. Publishes ms up to 6 months after acceptance. Published new writers within the last year. Length: 40 pages maximum. Also publishes literary essays, literary criticism, poetry. Occasionally critiques rejected mss.

How to Contact: Send complete ms with cover letter, which should include "name, address, publications." Reports in 1-4 months on mss. SASE. Simultaneous submissions OK. Sample copy $4 (current issue $6.95). Fiction guidelines for SASE. Reviews novels and short story collections. Send books to fiction editor.

Payment: Pays 2 contributor's copies.

Terms: Rights revert to author upon publication, with provision that *Cutbank* receives publication credit.

Advice: "Strongly suggest contributors read an issue. We have published stories by David Long, William Kittredge, Rick DeMarinis, Patricia Henley, Melanie Rae Thon and Michael Dorris in recent issues, and like to feature new writers alongside more well-known names. Send only your best work."

CWM, (II, III, IV), 1300 Kicker Rd., Tuscaloosa AL 35404. (205)553-2284. Editor: David C. Kopaska-Merkel. Co-editor: Geof Huth, 317 Princeton Rd., Apt. 451, Schenectady NY 12306. (518)374-7143. Magazine: Variable size; pages, paper quality, cover variable; ink drawings or others possible. "Each issue has a theme. We publish fiction, art and poetry for anyone interested in something a little bit different." Estab. 1990.

Needs: "Any submission fitting the theme." Upcoming theme: "The Archaeology of the Soul" (issue #3, 1994). Receives 10-15 mss/month. Accepts 1-5 mss/issue; 2-10 mss/year. Publishes ms within 2 years of acceptance. Length: 10,000 words maximum. Publishes short shorts; any length is acceptable. Also publishes poetry. Sometimes comments on rejected mss and recommends other markets.

How to Contact: Query first or send complete manuscript with cover letter. Reports in 2-4 weeks on queries; 3-16 weeks on mss. SASE. No simultaneous submissions. Accepts computer printout submissions. Accepts electronic submissions via disk. Fiction guidelines for #10 SAE and 1 first-class stamp (IRC).
Payment: Pays contributor's copies.
Terms: Acquires one-time rights.
Advice: "A manuscript must meet our theme for the issue in question. It stands out if it begins well and is neatly and clearly prepared. Given a good beginning, the story must hold the reader's interest all the way to the end and not let go. It helps if a story haunts the reader even after it is put aside."

D.C., (I), % Katrina Kelly, 18 Taylor Ave., Earlville NY 13332. (717)697-8380. Editor: Katrina Kelly. Newsletter: 8½ × 11; 12-14 pages; illustrations. "*D.C.* is interested in funny and/or interesting materials, sick humor is good, too. Our audience is people of the punk genre and the sarcastically morbid." Monthly. Estab. 1988. Circ. 150.
Needs: Horror, humor/satire. Receives 10-15 unsolicited mss/month. Acquires 3 (depending on length) mss/issue. Publishes ms soon after acceptance. Published work by Katrina Kelly, Kevin Miller, James Shepard, Frank Hart. Length: 2,000 words average. Publishes short shorts.
How to Contact: Query first. Reports in 2-4 weeks. Simultaneous submissions OK. Sample copy for $1.50. Fiction guidelines for SAE and 2 first-class stamps (IRCs).
Payment: Pays subscription to magazine. Must write often to stay on mailing list.
Advice: "I like submissions that are well written, are *somewhat* logical and interest or amuse." Magazine known for fiction "of the disgusting, revolting kind."

DAGGER OF THE MIND, Beyond The Realms Of Imagination, (II), K'yi-Lih Productions (a division of Breach Enterprises), 1317 Hookridge Dr., El Paso TX 79925. (915)591-0541. Executive Editor: Arthur William Lloyd Breach. Assistant Editor: Sam Lopez. Magazine. 8½ × 11; 62-86 pages; hibright paper; high glossy cover; from 5-12 illustrations. Quarterly. Estab. 1990. Circ. 5,000.
Needs: Lovecraftian. Adventure, experimental, fantasy, horror, mystery/suspense (private eye, police procedural), science fiction (hard science, soft/sociological). "Nothing sick and blasphemous, vulgar, obscene, racist, sexist, profane, humorous, weak, exploited women stories and those with idiotic puns." Plans special paperback anthologies. Receives 300 unsolicited mss/month. 8-15 mss/issue; 90-100 mss/ year depending upon length. Publishes ms 1 year after acceptance. Agented fiction 30%. Published work by Sidney Williams, Jessica Amanda Salmonson, Donald R. Burleson. Length: 4,500 words average; 5,000 minimum; 10,000 words maximum. Publishes short shorts. Length: Under 1,000 words. Also publishes literary essays, literary criticism, poetry. Sometimes comments on rejected mss.
How to Contact: Send complete manuscript with cover letter. "Include a bio and list of previously published credits with tearsheets. I also expect a brief synopsis of the story." Reports in 3-3½ months on mss. SASE. Simultaneous submissions OK. Accepts electronic submissions. Sample copy for $3.50, 9 × 12 SAE and 5 first-class stamps. Fiction guidelines for #10 SAE and 1 first-class stamp.
Payment: Pays ½-1¢/word plus 1 contributor's copy.
Terms: Pays on publication for first rights (possibly anthology rights as well).
Advice: "I'm a big fan of the late H.P. Lovecraft. I love reading through Dunsanian and Cthulhu Mythos tales. I'm constantly on the lookout for this special brand of fiction. If you want to grab my attention immediately, write on the outside of the envelope 'Lovecratian submission enclosed.' There are a number of things which make submissions stand out for me. Is there any sensitivity to the tale? I like sensitive material, so long as it doesn't become mushy. Another thing that grabs my attention are characters which leap out of the pages at you. Then there are those old standards for accepting a manuscript: good imagery, story plot and originality. Move me, bring a tear to my eye; make me stop and think about the world and people around me. Frighten me with little spoken of truths about the human condition. In short, bring out all my emotions (except humor, I detest humor) and show me that you can move me in such a way as I have never been moved before."

Check the Category Indexes, located at the back of the book, for publishers interested in specific fiction subjects.

🐝**THE DALHOUSIE REVIEW, (II)**, Room 314, Dunn Building, Dalhousie University, Halifax, Nova Scotia B3H 3J5 Canada. Editor: Dr. Alan Andrews. Magazine: 15cm × 23cm; approximately 140 pages; photographs sometimes. Publishes articles, book reviews, short stories and poetry. Quarterly. Circ. 800.

Needs: Literary. Length: 5,000 words maximum. Also publishes essays on history, philosophy, etc., and poetry.

How to Contact: Send complete ms with cover letter. SASE (Canadian stamps). Sample copy $6.50 (Canadian) plus postage. Occasionally review novels and short story collections.

‡**DAN RIVER ANTHOLOGY, (I)**, Box 298, Thomaston ME 04861. (207)354-0998. Editor: R.S. Danbury III. Book: 5½ × 8½; 156 pages; 60 lb. paper; gloss 65 lb. full-color cover; b&w illustrations. For general/adult audience. Annually. Estab. 1984. Circ. 1,200.

• See also this publisher's new magazine, *Northwoods Journal* listed in this section and the Dan River Press in the Small Press section of this book.

Needs: Adventure, contemporary, ethnic, experimental, fantasy, historical (general), horror, humor/satire, literary, mainstream, prose poem, psychic/supernatural/occult, regional, romance (contemporary and historical), science fiction, senior citizen/retirement, suspense/mystery and western. No "evangelical Christian, pornography or sentimentality." Receives 20-30 unsolicited mss/month. Accepts about 8-10 mss/year. Reads "mostly in March." Length: 2,000-2,400 words average; 800 words minumum; 3,000 words maximum. Also publishes poetry.

How to Contact: *Charges reading fee: $1 for poetry; $3 for prose.* Send complete ms with SASE. Reports in April each year. Sample copy for $9.95 paperback, $19.95 cloth, plus $2.50 shipping. Fiction guidelines for #10 SASE (IRCs).

Payment: Pays $5/page, minimum *cash advance on acceptance* against royalties of 10% of all sales attributable to writer's influence: readings, mailings, autograph parties, etc., plus up to 50% discount on copies, plus other discounts to make total as high as 73%.

Terms: Acquires first rights.

Advice: "Also: The CAL Anthology—Same Guidelines. Acceptance/Rejection—November."

🐝**DANCE CONNECTION, A Canadian Dance Journal, (II, IV)**, 603, 815 1st St. SW, Calgary, Alberta, T2P 1N3 Canada. (403)237-7327. Editor: Heather Elton. Magazine: 8½ × 11; 56 pages; coated matte stock paper; colour cover; illustrations and b&w photographs. "Dance: Interview, essay, commentary, reviews for dance lovers, academics, educators, professionals, artists." Published 5 times per year. Estab. 1983. Circ. 5,000.

• *Dance Connection* has been nominated for 2 Western Canadian Magazine Awards. This magazine has published only one piece of dance fiction so far because "few people query with dance fiction." They also publish dance-related poetry.

Needs: Dance. "Do not send anything not related to dance. No poems about ballet." Plans special fiction issue. Upcoming themes: "Dance & the Sacred," "Dance & Technology." Receives 10 unsolicited mss/month. Buys 1 mss/issue; 3 mss/year. Publishes ms 3 months after acceptance. Length: 1,100 words average; 400 words minimum; 2,500 words maximum. Publishes short shorts. Length: 800 words.

How to Contact: Query with clips of published work or send complete manuscript with cover letter. Reports in 2 months. SASE (IRCs). Simultaneous and reprint submissions OK. Accepts electronic submissions; prefers Macintosh disk (Microsoft Word). Sample copy for 9 × 12 SAE. Fiction guidelines for #10 SAE.

Payment: Pays $25-250 (Canadian), subscription to magazine and contributor's copies.

Terms: Pays on publication for first rights or one-time rights.

🐝**DANDELION MAGAZINE, (II)**, Dandelion Magazine Society, 922 9th Ave., Calgary, Alberta T2C 0S4 Canada. (403)265-0524. Fiction Editors: Elena Malterre, Beth Everest. Magazine: 100 pages. Semiannually. Estab. 1972. Circ. 800.

Needs: Literary. Receives 50 unsolicited mss/month. Accepts 5 mss/issue; 10 mss/year. Publishes ms 6 months after acceptance. Publishes short shorts. Sometimes critiques rejected mss.

How to Contact: Send complete ms with cover letter. Reports in 6 months on mss. SASE (IRCs). Reviews novels and short story collections by Alberta authors. Sample copy for $6. Fiction guidelines for SAE.

Payment: Pays $125/mss.
Terms: Acquires one-time rights.
Advice: "The best way to understand what we publish is by reading *Dandelion*. We invite you to subscribe. We publish reviews of books by Alberta authors, poetry, visual arts, short fiction and the occasional article. We try to be eclectic in what we publish. Please remember that since we only publish twice a year this sometimes gives rise to a delay in returning manuscripts. For our June issue we consider manuscripts during January through to the end of March. For our December issue we consider manuscripts during July through to the end of September. Manuscripts without SASE, or without sufficient postage will not be returned."

‡**DARK REGIONS, (II),** P.O. Box 6301, Concord CA 94524. (510)254-7442. Fax: (510)254-6419. Editor: Joe Morey. Fiction Editors: Joe Morey, Mike Olson and John Rosenman. Magazine: digest-sized; 100 pages; white paper; 100 lb. gloss cover; 10 illustrations/issue; photographs occasionally. "We're dedicated to putting out a quality product, on time, which will entertain as well as make the reader think. Publishing weird fantasy and horror, and occasionally weird science fiction. Intended for mature readers." Quarterly. Estab. 1985. Circ. 500.
   • *Dark Regions* is a member of the Small Press Writers and Artists Organization and recently received SPWAO's Best Fiction Award for the story "Darby's Bone," by Albert J. Manachino.
Needs: Fantasy (weird), horror, science fiction (weird). Upcoming themes: "Virtual Reality/Computers" (June 1994). List of upcoming themes available for SASE. Publishes special fiction issue or anthology. Receives 100 unsolicited mss/month. Accepts 8-10 mss/issue; 36-40 mss/year. Does not read mss October 15 through January 1. Publishes ms 6-12 months after acceptance. Recently published work by Elizabeth Massie, Kevin J. Anderson, Ardath Mayhar, Bruce Boston. Length: 3,000 words average; 1,000 words minimum; 5,000 words maximum. Publishes short shorts. Also publishes poetry. Often critiques rejected mss.
How to Contact: Send complete ms with a cover letter. Should include estimated word count, brief bio and list of publications. Reports in 1 week on queries; 2-4 weeks on mss. Send SASE (or IRC) for reply, return of ms or send a disposable copy of ms. No simultaneous submissions. Sample copy for $3.95 and 3 first-class stamps or IRCs. Fiction guidelines for #10 SAE and 1 first-class stamp or IRC.
Payment: Pays ¼-1¢/word and 1 contributor's copy; additional copies $2 (plus 3 first-class stamps).
Terms: Pays on publication for first North American serial rights.
Advice: "We want weird fiction with good short story elements, good short story structure. The more original the better." Looks for "original ideas. Stories that move through action/description. Stories that employ elements of suspense. Inventive tales which push the boundaries of weirdness." Avoid "overused themes such as Friday the 13th, Conan, invaders from Mars. Also: werewolves, vampires (unless highly original). No racism, no hard pornography and definitely no children in sexual situations."

DARK TOME, (I, IV), P.O. Box 705, Salem OR 97308. Editor: Michelle Marr. (503)391-7729. Magazine: 5½×8½; 30-80 pages; 20 lb. paper; 60 lb. cover; illustrations. "We publish horror fiction for mature readers who are not easily offended." Bimonthly. Estab. 1990. Circ. 150.
Needs: Horror, psychic/supernatural/occult. "I want original nightmares, not classic ghost stories." Receives 50 unsolicited mss/month. Acquires 6-10 mss/issue; 30-60 mss/year. Publishes manuscript 2-4 months after acceptance. Length: 1,500 words average; 4,000 words maximum. Especially looking for short shorts (to 1,000 words).
How to Contact: Send complete manuscript with cover letter. Reports in 2-5 weeks. SASE. Sample copy for $2.75 payable to Michelle Marr. Fiction guidelines for #10 SASE (IRCs).
Payment: Pays in contributor's copies and small cash payment.
Terms: Buys first North American serial rights.
Advice: "I am looking for stories with vivid images that will remain in the mind of the reader, and horrors that affect only a small number of people."

‡**DAUGHTERS OF NYX, A Magazine of Goddess Stories, Mythmaking, and Fairy Tales, (I, IV),** Ruby Rose's Fairy Tale Emporium, P.O. Box 1187, White Salmon WA 98672. Fiction Editor: Kim Antieau. Magazine: 8½×11; 32 pages; illustrations. "We are a woman-centered publication, interested in stories that retell legends, myths and fairy tales from a matristic viewpoint. Feminist, women's spirituality, pagan." Quarterly. Estab. 1993. Circ. 2,000.
Needs: Ethnic/multicultural, fantasy, feminist, lesbian, literary, mainstream/contemporary, psychic/supernatural/occult, science fiction, goddess stories, fairy tales, myths. No "anti-woman, slasher, violent" material. Receives 10 unsolicited mss/month. Accepts 7-10 mss/issue; 40 mss/year. Publishes ms

within 24 months after acceptance. Length: 5,000 words preferred; 1,000 words minimum; 7,000 words maximum. Also publishes literary essays. Sometimes critiques or comments on rejected mss.

How to Contact: Send complete ms with a cover letter. Should include estimated word count, short bio and list of publications. Reports in 3-12 weeks. Send SASE (or IRC) for reply, return of ms or send a disposable copy of ms. Simultaneous and reprint submissions OK, "but please tell us." Sample copy for $4.50. Fiction guidelines for #10 SAE and 1 first-class stamp or IRC. Reviews novels and short story collections.

Payment: Pays ¼¢/word; $5 minimum; 2 contributor's copies.

Terms: Pays on publication for first North American serial rights.

Advice: A manuscript stands out "if the author understands goddess stories and their power for women. Read the field—Starhawk, Merlin Stone, Barbara Walker, Z. Budapest." Avoid sending "sword and sorcery fantasy masquerading as retellings of fairy tales."

DAUGHTERS OF SARAH, (II, IV), 2121 Sheridan Rd., Evanston IL 60201. (708)866-3882. Editor: Reta Finger. Magazine: 5½ × 8½; 64 pages; illustrations and photos. "Christian feminist publication dealing with Christian theology, history, women and social issues from a feminist point of view." Quarterly. Estab. 1974. Circ. 5,000.

● *Daughters of Sarah* has received awards for its poetry and Second Place for Literary Magazines awarded by Chicago Women in Publishing in 1993.

Needs: Historical, religious/inspirational, feminist and spiritual (Christian feminist). "No subjects unrelated to feminism from Christian viewpoint." Upcoming themes: "Women and Violence" (deadline: March 15, 1994); "Twentieth Anniversary Issue" (deadline: June 15, 1994). Receives 10-20 unsolicited fiction mss/month. Buys 2 fiction mss/year. Recently published work by Rosemary Radford Ruetner, Toinette M. Eugene and Mary Cartledge-Hayes. Length: 1,800 words maximum. Publishes short shorts. Also publishes poetry. Occasionally critiques rejected mss "if related and close to acceptance."

How to Contact: Query first with description of ms and SASE (IRCs). Include cover letter stating why ms was written; short biography of author. Simultaneous and previously published submissions OK "but won't pay." Reports in 1 month on queries. Publishes "most" mss 3 months to 1 year after acceptance. Sample copy for $4.50. Reviews novels and short story collections. Send books and review queries to Dulcie Gannett.

Payment: Pays $15/printed page; 3 free contributor's copies. Offers kill fee of one-half stated fee.

Terms: Pays upon publication for first North American serial or one-time rights.

Advice: "Make sure topic of story fits with specific theme of publication. We get many stories that are either Christian stories, women's stories, Christian women's stories, but not necessarily feminist. We believe that the Christian gospel was meant to be radically egalitarian and we try to integrate it with feminist insights and analysis available today."

‡DEAD OF NIGHT™ MAGAZINE, (II), Suite 228, 916 Shaker Road, Longmeadow MA 01106-2416. (413)567-9524. Editor: Lin Stein. Magazine: 8½ × 11; 64-96 pages; newsprint paper; slick b&w cover stock; illustrations, and occasionally photographs. "*Dead of Night Magazine* publishes horror, fantasy, mystery, sci-fi and vampire-related fiction. If we had a 'motto' it might be 'horror/fantasy/mystery/sci-fi in a different vein'." Semiannually. Estab. 1989. Circ. 1,000.

● The editor of *Dead of Night Magazine* is a member of the Small Press Writer's and Artist's Organization and Horror Writers of America. The editor advises writers to obtain a sample copy first. If $5 is beyond the writer's budget, he says, back issues for $2.50 may be available.

Needs: Condensed novel, fantasy (science fantasy, sword and sorcery), horror, mystery/suspense (mysteries need supernatural element), psychic/supernatural/occult, science fiction (soft/sociological). "We don't care for fantasy with an overabundance of elves, wizards, etc." Receives 90 unsolicited mss/month. Accepts 8-12 mss/issue; 16-24 mss/year. Does not read mss during June, July, August. Publishes mss 6-18 months after acceptance. Recently published work by Janet Fox, J.N. Williamson, Mort Castle, Gary Braunbeck. Length: 2,500-2,800 words preferred; 500 words minimum; 2,800 words maximum. Publishes literary essays, literary criticism and poetry. Often critiques or comments on rejected mss.

How to Contact: Send complete ms with a cover letter. Should include estimated word count, bio (1-2 paragraphs), Social Security number and list of publications (if available). Reports in 3 weeks on queries; 4-6 weeks on mss. Send SASE (or IRC) for reply, return of ms or send a disposable copy of ms. No simultaneous submissions. "No reprints except novel/book excerpts." Sample copy for $5. Fiction guidelines for #10 SAE and 1 first-class stamp. Reviews novels or short story collections.

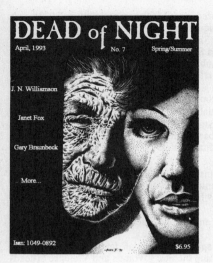

DEAD of NIGHT

April, 1993   No. 7   Spring/Summer

J. N. Williamson

Janet Fox

Gary Braunbeck

More...

Issn: 1049-0892 $6.95

According to Lin Stein, editor/publisher of Dead of Night, this cover "represents the dark, brooding, mysterious and even somewhat ambiguous nature of the fiction we publish." Since the magazine publishes "horror stories of all sorts, as well as classic tales of vampirism," Stein felt that this illustration by Allen Koszowski fit the publication perfectly. "Allen Koszowski's artwork is well-known in the small press, and many of our readers are great fans of his work. He is a most talented and well-respected artist, with a style that is haunting and unique."

Payment: Pays 2¢/word minimum; 3¢/word maximum; 1 contributor's copy (cover artists: 2); additional copies for 10% discount off cover price.
Terms: Pays on publication for one-time rights.
Advice: "We look for truly frightening horror, believable fantasy, mysteries with some 'mysteriousness' and character oriented sf. Vampire tales should add some fresh or unique slant to the legend. Good writing is what makes a ms 'stand out.' We'd like to see stories that are not so 'media-influenced'; that is, tales that don't re-hash the latest horror movie/thriller the writer has seen at the box office or on television. Horror fantasy/mystery/sci-fi fiction is not the same as h/f/m/sf films. We see too much 'splatter' that doesn't do a thing to advance the story line. (We see this in h/f/m/sf—horror doesn't have an 'exclusive' on gratuitous gore.) Also, we see too many vampire stories in which the writer tries to take the gothic atmosphere too far; as examples, writers sometimes try to make their vampire characters speak in 'Olde English'—annoying, and often poorly done."

DEATHREALM, (II), 3223-F Regents Park, Greensboro NC 27455. (919)288-9138. Editor: Mark Rainey. Magazine: 8½ × 11; 50-60 pages; 20 lb. bond paper; 8 pt. glossy coated cover stock; pen & ink, screened illustrations; b&w photos. Publishes "fantasy/horror," for a "mature" audience. Quarterly. Estab. 1987. Circ. 1,200.
● This horror and dark fantasy magazine won the Small Press Writers and Artists Organization's "Best Magazine" award and the editor won the "Best Editor" award in the same year (1990). Right now the editor is looking for fiction with supernatural-based plots.
Needs: Experimental, fantasy, horror, psychic/supernatural/occult and science fiction. "Sci-fi tales should have a horror slant. *Strongly* recommend contributor buy a sample copy of *Deathrealm* before submitting." Receives 200-300 mss/issue; 30 mss/year. Publishes ms within 1 year of acceptance. Published work by Joe R. Lansdale, Fred Chappell, Kevin J. Anderson, Jessica Amanda Salmonson. Length: 5,000 words average; 10,000 words maximum. Publishes short shorts. Also publishes literary criticism, poetry. Sometimes critiques rejected mss and recommends other markets.
How to Contact: Send complete ms with cover letter, which should include "publishing credits, some bio info, where they heard about *Deathrealm*. Never reveal plot in cover letter." May accept simultaneous submissions, but "not recommended." Reports in 2 weeks on queries; 9-12 weeks on ms. SASE. Sample copy for $4 and $1 postage. Fiction guidelines for #10 SAE and 1 first-class stamp. Reviews novels and short story collections. Send books to Randy Johnston, 3114 NW 41, Oklahoma City OK 73112.
Payment: Pays ½¢/word; higher rates for established professionals; contributor's copies.
Advice: "Concentrate on characterization; development of ideas; strong atmosphere, with an important setting. I frown on gratuitous sex and violence unless it is a mere side effect of a more sophisticated story line. Stay away from overdone themes—foreboding dreams come true; being a frustrated writer;

using lots of profanity and having a main character so detestable you don't care what happens to him."

DENVER QUARTERLY, (II, III), University of Denver, Denver CO 80208. (303)871-2892. Editor: Donald Revell. Magazine: 6×9; 144-160 pages; occasional illustrations. "We publish fiction, articles and poetry for a generally well-educated audience, primarily interested in literature and the literary experience. They read *DQ* to find something a little different from a strictly academic quarterly or a creative writing outlet." Quarterly. Estab. 1966. Circ. 1,000.
Needs: "We are now interested in experimental fiction (minimalism, magic realism, etc.) as well as in realistic fiction." Also publishes poetry.
How to Contact: Send complete ms with SASE (IRCs). Does not read mss May-September 15. Do not query. Reports in 3 months on mss. Publishes ms within a year after acceptance. Recently published work by Joyce Carol Oates, T.M. McNally, Charles Baxter; published new writers within the last year. No simultaneous submissions. Sample copy $5 with SASE.
Payment: Pays $5/page for fiction and poetry, 2 free author's copies.
Terms: Buys first North American serial rights.
Advice: "We'll be looking for serious, realistic and experimental fiction. Nothing so quickly disqualifies a manuscript as sloppy proofreading and mechanics. Read the magazine before submitting to it. Send clean copy and a *brief* cover letter. We try to remain eclectic and I think we do, but the odds for beginners are bound to be long considering the fact that we receive nearly 8,000 mss per year and publish only about 10 short stories."

✿DESCANT, (II), Box 314, Station P, Toronto, Ontario M5S 2S8 Canada. (416)603-0223. Editor: Karen Mulhallen. Magazine: 5¾×8¾; 100-300 pages; heavy paper; good cover stock; illustrations and photos. "High quality poetry and prose for an intelligent audience who wants to see a broad range of literature." Quarterly. Estab. 1970. Circ. 1,200.
 • In past years *Descant* has won Canada's National Magazine Award for both poetry and fiction.
 Work published in *Descant* was selected for the *Journey Prize* anthology.
Needs: Literary, contemporary, translations. "Although most themes are acceptable, all works must have literary merit." Upcoming theme: "Japan" (1994-5; check for issue date). Receives 100-200 unsolicited mss/month. Recently published work by Michael Ondaatje, Douglas Glover, Margaret Atwood. Publishes short shorts. Also publishes literary essays, poetry. Critiques rejected mss when there is time.
How to Contact: Send complete ms with cover letter. SAE, IRC. Simultaneous submissions OK ("but we only print unpublished material"). Reports in 3 months on mss. Sample copy for $7.50 plus $2 for postage to U.S.
Payment: Pays a modest honorarium and 1 year subscription. Extra contributor's copies at discount.
Advice: "*Descant* has plans for several special issues in the next two years. Unsolicited work is less likely to be accepted in the coming months, and will be kept on file for longer before it appears."

DESCANT, (II), Department of English, Texas Christian University, Fort Worth TX 76129. (817)921-7240. Editors: Betsy Colquitt, Stanley Trachtenberg, Harry Opperman, Steve Sherwood. "*Descant* uses fiction and poetry. No restriction on style, content or theme. *Descant* is a 'little' literary magazine, and its readers are those who have interest in such publications." Semiannually. Estab. 1955. Circ. 500.
Needs: Literary, contemporary and regional. No genre or category fiction. Receives approximately 50 unsolicited fiction mss each month. Does not read mss in summer. Published new writers within the last year. Length: 1,500-5,000 words. Publishes short shorts. Sometimes recommends other markets. Also publishes poetry.
How to Contact: Send complete ms with SASE (IRCs). Reports usually within 6 weeks on ms. Sample copy $8 (old copy).
Payment: Pays 2 contributor's copies; charges $8 for extra copies.
Advice: "Submit good material. Even though a small publication, *Descant* receives many submissions, and acceptances are few compared to the total number of mss received." Mss are rejected because they "are badly written, careless in style and development, shallow in characterization, trite in handling and in conception. We offer a $500 annual prize for fiction—the Frank O'Connor Prize. Award is made to the story considered (by a judge not connected to the magazine) to be the best published in a given volume of the journal."

DEUTERIUM, A Digest of Poems, Prose, and Art, (I), P.O. Box 20013, Dayton OH 45420-0013. (513)252-5784. Editor: Randy Watts. Magazine: 5½×8½; 16 pages; some illustrations. "For beginning, thought provoking writers." Semiannually. Estab. 1991. Circ. 100.

Needs: Confession, contemporary, experimental, fantasy, gay, historical (general), mainstream, prose poem, regional, romance (contemporary, historical), science fiction, mystery/suspense. Length: Open. Publishes short shorts. Also accepts poetry. Recommends other markets.
How to Contact: Query first. Simultaneous and reprint submissions OK. Sample copy free.
Payment: Pays contributor's copies.
Terms: Acquires one-time rights.
Advice: "I like down-to-earth writers. Don't write over the average American head."

‡**DIS, Southeastern Culture Quarterly, (IV),** Fez Press, P.O. Box 2453, Tallahassee FL 32316. (904)561-6519. Editor: Kim MacQueen. Magazine: 7×8; 44 pages; 20 lb. white paper; white card cover; illustrations and photographs. "*DIS* is mainly interested in humor of literally any type, but especially socially or culturally oriented. We accept essays, poetry, fiction, line drawings, photography and comics." Quarterly. Estab. 1991. Circ. 500.
Needs: Humor/satire: adventure, condensed novel, ethnic/multicultural, experimental, feminist, gay, historical (general), horror, lesbian, literary, mainstream/contemporary, mystery/suspense, psychic/supernatural/occult, regional, romance, translations. "Make it funny." No New Age. "We're open to theme suggestions from our readers." Plans special fiction issue or anthology in the future. Receives 1-2 unsolicited mss/month. Accepts 1 ms/issue; 3 mss/year. Publishes ms 2 months after acceptance. Recently published work by Mark Hinson, Jamie Granger, Joe Straub. Length: open. Publishes short shorts. Also publishes literary essays and poetry. Often critiques or comments on rejected mss.
How to Contact: Query with clips of published work. Should include list of pubications. Reports in 2-3 months. SASE (or IRC) for reply or send a disposable copy of the ms. Simultaneous, reprint and electronic submissions OK. Sample copy for $3. Fiction guidelines for #10 SAE and 1 first-class stamp or IRC. Reviews novels and short story collections.
Payment: Pays 5 contributor's copies. No charge up to 15 additional copies.
Terms: Acquires first rights.
Advice: "If it's well-written, free of cliché and funny we'll take it, usually, although the editor prefers to eschew most overly introspective ranting stuff."

‡**DOGWOOD TALES MAGAZINE, For the Fiction Lover in all of us, (I),** Two Sisters Publications, P.O. Box 172068, Memphis TN 38187. Editor: Linda Ditty. Fiction Editor: Peggy Carman. Magazine: 5½×8½; 50-75 pages; 20 lb. paper; 60 lb. cover stock; illustrations. "Interesting fiction that would appeal to all groups of people. Each issue will have a Special Feature Story about a Southern person, place or theme." Bimonthly. Estab. 1993.
Needs: Adventure, mainstream/contemporary, mystery/suspense (amateur sleuth, cozy, police procedural, private eye/hard-boiled, romantic suspense), romance (contemporary, gothic, historical); Southern person, place, theme in any genre listed above. No erotica, science fiction, children, westerns. Accepts 5-7 mss/issue; 30-42 mss/year. Publishes ms 2-6 months after acceptance. Length: 1,350 words preferred; 200 words minimum; 2,500 words maximum. Publishes short shorts. Length: 200-500 words. Sometimes critiques or comments on rejected mss.
How to Contact: Send complete ms with a cover letter. Should include estimated word count and list of publications. Reports in 8-10 weeks on mss. Send SASE (or IRC) for reply, return of ms or send a disposable copy of ms. Simultaneous submissions OK. Sample copy for $2.25. Fiction guidelines for #10 SAE and 1 first-class stamp.
Payment: Pays 1 contributor's copy; special feature pays 2 copies; additional copies for $1.50.
Terms: Buys first North American serial rights. Not copyrighted.
Advice: "We like fresh and action moving stories with a strong ending. Must be tightly written and reach out and grab the reader. Revise and send your best. Don't be afraid to submit. Don't be discouraged by rejections. Try other publishers."

‡**DOWNSTATE STORY, (I, IV),** 1825 Maple Ridge, Peoria IL 61614. (309)688-1409. Editor: Elaine Hopkins. Magazine: illustrations. "Short fiction—some connection with Illinois." Annually. Estab. 1992. Circ. 1,000.
 ● *Downstate Story* was the recipient of a 1993 grant from The Puffin Foundation.
Needs: Adventure, erotical, ethnic/multicultural, experimental, historical (general), horror, humor/satire, literary, mainstream/contemporary, mystery/suspense, psychic/supernatural/occult, regional, romance, science fiction, westerns. Accepts 10 mss/issue. Publishes ms up to 1 year after acceptance. Length: 300 words minimum; 2,000 words maximum. Publishes short shorts. Also publishes literary essays.

How to Contact: Send complete ms with a cover letter. Reports "ASAP." SASE for return of ms. Simultaneous submissions OK. Sample copy for $8. Fiction guidelines for SAE and 1 IRC.
Payment: Pays $50 maximum.
Terms: Pays on acceptance for first rights.

DREAM INTERNATIONAL/QUARTERLY, (I, II, IV), U.S. Address: Charles I. Jones, #N-3, 411 14th St., Ramona CA 92065. Australia address: Dr. Les Jones, 256 Berserker St., No. Rockhampton, Queensland 4701, Australia. Editors: Les and Chuck Jones. Magazine: 5 × 7; 60-90 pages; Xerox paper; parchment cover stock; some illustrations and photos. "Publishes fiction and nonfiction that is dream-related or clearly inspired by a dream. Also dream-related fantasy." Quarterly. Estab. 1981. Circ. 80-100.
Needs: Adventure, confession, contemporary, erotica, ethnic, experimental, fantasy, historical (general), horror, humor/satire, literary, mainstream, mystery/suspense, prose poem, psychic/supernatural/occult, romance, science fiction, translations, young adult/teen (10-18). Upcoming themes: "We are planning to solicit and encourage subjects related to the paranormal . . . possibly a contest associated with such subject sometime early in 1993." Receives 20-30 unsolicited mss/month. Publishes ms 6-8 months after acceptance. Length: 1,000 words minimum; 1,500 words maximum. Published new writers within the last year. Publishes short shorts. Length: 500-800 words. Also publishes literary essays, poetry (poetry submissions to Tim Scott, 4147 N. Kedvale Ave., #2B, Chicago IL 60641; send SASE for poetry guidelines). Occasionally critiques rejected mss. Sometimes recommends other markets.
How to Contact: Reports in 6 weeks on queries; 3 months on mss. SASE. Simultaneous and reprint submissions OK. Sample copy for $6.50 (add $1.50 to single copy purchases to cover postage and handling), SAE and 2 first-class stamps (IRCs). Guidelines for $1.50 SAE and 1 first-class stamp. "Accepted mss will not be returned unless requested at time of submission."
Payment: Pays in contributor's copies (contributors must pay $1.50 for postage and handling); sometimes offers magazine subscription.
Terms: Acquires one-time rights.
Advice: "Use your nightly dreams to inspire you to literary flights. Avoid stereotypes and clichés. When contacting U.S. editor, make all checks, money orders, and overseas drafts payable to *Charles Jones.*"

DREAMS & NIGHTMARES, The Magazine of Fantastic Poetry, (IV), 1300 Kicker Rd., Tuscaloosa AL 35404. (205)553-2284. Editor: David C. Kopaska-Merkel. Magazine: 5½ × 8½; 20 pages; ink drawing illustrations. "*DN* is mainly a poetry magazine, but I *am* looking for short-short stories. They should be either fantasy, science fiction, or horror." Estab. 1986. Circ. 200.
• *Dreams & Nightmares* received a 1993 cash award from the Professional Book Center for "advancing the field of speculative poetry."
Needs: Experimental, fantasy, horror, humor/satire, science fiction. "Try me with anything *except*: senseless violence, misogyny or hatred (unreasoning) of any kind of people, sappiness." Receives 4-8 unsolicited fiction mss/month. Buys 1-2 mss/issue; 1-5 mss/year. Publishes ms 1-9 months after acceptance. Published work by Ron McDowell, D.F. Lewis. Length: 500 words average; 1,000 words maximum. Publishes short shorts. Length: 500 or fewer words. Sometimes critiques rejected mss and recommends other markets. Also publishes poetry.
How to Contact: Send complete manuscript. Reports in 1-3 weeks on queries; 1-6 weeks on mss. SASE. No simultaneous submissions. Accepts electronic submissions. Sample copy for $1.50 in stamps. Fiction guidelines for #10 SAE and 1 first-class stamp (IRCs).
Payment: Pays $3 and 2 contributor's copies.
Terms: Pays on acceptance for one-time rights.
Advice: "A story must grab the reader and hold on to the end. I want to be *involved.* Start with a good first line, lead the reader where you want him/her to go and end with something that causes a reaction or provokes thought."

✹DREAMS & VISIONS, New Frontiers in Christian Fiction, (II), Skysong Press, RR1, Washago, Ontario L0K 2B0 Canada. Editor: Steve Stanton. Fiction Editor: Wendy Stanton. Magazine: 5½ × 8½; 52 pages; 20 lb. bond paper; Mayfair Fancy cover; illustrations on cover. "Contemporary Christian fiction in a variety of styles for adult Christians." Triannually. Estab. 1989. Circ. 300.
Needs: Contemporary, experimental, fantasy, humor/satire, literary, religious/inspirational, science fiction (soft/sociological). "All stories should portray a Christian world view or expand upon Biblical themes or ethics in an entertaining or enlightening manner." Receives 20 unsolicited mss/month.

Accepts 7 mss/issue; 21 mss/year. Publishes ms 2-6 months after acceptance. Length: 2,500 words; 2,000 words minimum; 6,000 words maximum.

How to Contact: Send complete ms with cover letter. "Bio is optional: degrees held and in what specialties, publishing credits, service in the church, etc." Reports in 1 month on queries; 8-10 weeks on mss. SASE. Simultaneous submissions OK. Sample copy for $3.95. Fiction guidelines for SAE and 1 IRC.

Payment: Pays in contributor's copies; extras at ⅓ discount.

Terms: Acquires first North American serial rights and one-time, non-exclusive reprint rights.

Advice: "In general we look for work that has some literary value, that is in some way unique and relevant to Christian readers today. Our first priority is technical adequacy, though we will occasionally work with a beginning writer to polish a manuscript. Ultimately, we look for stories that glorify the Lord Jesus Christ, stories that build up rather than tear down, that exalt the sanctity of life, the holiness of God, and the value of the family."

‡THE DUCKABUSH JOURNAL, (I), P.O. Box 390, Hansville WA 98104. Editor: Tom Snyder. Fiction Editor: Gary Parks. Magazine: 5½ × 8½; 75 pages; recycled 70 lb. paper; matte card linen finish cover; illustrations. "Literary audience, mostly on the Olympic Peninsula and the Seattle area. We are open in terms of theme, but are interested in the evolving ways in which humans relate to nature and to each other." Semiannual. Estab. 1988. Circ. 400.

Needs: Erotica, ethnic/multicultural, experimental, gay, humor/satire, literary, mainstream/contemporary. Nothing "strict genre like young adult, science fiction, romance, mystery, etc." Receives 10 unsolicited mss/month. Accepts 2-3 mss/issue; 4-6 mss/year. Publishes ms 3-4 months after acceptance. Recently pubished work by Annie Hanson, Anton Wishik. Length: 5,000 words maximum. Publishes short shorts. Also publishes (very occasionally) literary essays, poetry. Sometimes critiques or comments on rejected mss.

How to Contact: Send complete ms with a cover letter. Should include a short bio, list of publications. Reports in 2 months on mss. SASE (or IRC) for return of ms or a disposable copy of ms. Simultaneous, reprint and electronic submissions OK. Sample copy for $4 and SASE.

Payment: Pays 1 contributor's copy.

Terms: Acquires one-time rights.

Advice: "We like good language—poets turned fiction writers—though the stories should still show a sense of movement, of plot."

EAGLE'S FLIGHT, A Literary Magazine, (I), #822, 2501 Hunters Hill Dr., Enid OK 73703. Editor: Shyamkant Kulkarni. Fiction Editor: Rekha Kulkarni. Tabloid: 8½ × 11; 4-8 pages; bond paper; broad sheet cover. Publication includes "fiction and poetry for a general audience." Quarterly.

Needs: Literary, mainstream, mystery/suspense, romance. Plans to publish special fiction issue in future. Accepts 2-4 mss/year. Does not read mss June-December. Recently published work by Bal Swami, Anee H. Baker, Nancy Sweetland, O'Bannan M. Cook. Length: 1,500 words preferred; 1,000 words minimum; 2,000 words maximum. Publishes short shorts. Also publishes literary criticism, poetry.

How to Contact: Query first. Reports in 6 weeks on queries; 3-4 months on mss. SASE. Sample copy or fiction guidelines for $1 and #10 SAE and 1 first-class stamp (IRCs). Reviews novels and short story collections.

Payment: Pays $5-20 or subscription to magazine, contributor's copies; charge for extras.

Terms: Pays on publication for first North American serial rights or one-time rights.

Advice: "We look for form, substance and quality. Read and study what one wants to write and work at. Annual Best Story Award is given to the best short story published during previous year in March/April."

EARTH'S DAUGHTERS, (I, II), A Feminist Arts Periodical, Box 41, Central Park Station, Buffalo NY 14215. (716)835-8719. Collective editorship. Business Manager: Bonnie Johnson. Magazine: usually 5½ × 8½; 50 pages; 60 lb. paper; coated cover; 2-4 illustrations; 2-4 photos. "We publish poetry and short fiction; also graphics, art work and photos; our focus is the experience and creative expression of women." For a general/women/feminist audience. Quarterly. Published special topical issues last year; plans more this year. Estab. 1971. Circ. 1,000.

Needs: Contemporary, erotica, ethnic, experimental, fantasy, feminist, humor/satire, literary, prose poem. "Keep the fiction short." Send SASE in April for current themes. Receives 25-50 unsolicited fiction mss/month. Accepts 2-4 mss/issue; 8-12 mss/year. Published work by Gabrielle Burton, Mary Jane Markell, Meredith Sue Willis and Julia Alvarez; published several new writers within the last year. Length: 400 words minimum; 1,000 words maximum; 800 words average. Occasionally critiques rejected mss and recommends other markets.

How to Contact: Send complete ms. SASE (IRCs). Simultaneous submissions OK. Reports in 3 weeks on queries; 3 weeks to 3 months on mss. Publishes ms an average of 1 year after acceptance. Sample copy for $4.

Payment: Pays 2 contributor's copies, additional copies half price.

Terms: Acquires first rights. Copyright reverts to author upon publication.

Advice: "We require work of technical skill and artistic intensity; we welcome submissions from unknown writers. Send SASE in April of each year for themes of upcoming issues. Please do not inquire as to the status of your work too soon or too often—the US Mail is dependable, and we have yet to lose a manuscript."

ECHOES, (II), The Hudson Valley Writers Association, Box 7, LaGrangeville NY 12540. Editor: Marcia Grant. Fiction Editor: Don Monaco. Magazine: 5½ × 8½; 44 pages; illustrations. Quarterly. Estab. 1985. Circ. 350.

 • *Echoes* is also known as *Hudson Valley Echoes*.

Needs: "We do not categorize material—we consider material of *all* types." Receives 15-30 unsolicited mss/month. Acquires 2-5 mss/issue; 8-20 mss/year. Publishes ms 8-12 weeks after acceptance. Published work by Arnold Lipkind, C.C. Doucette; "often encourages promising authors." Length: 1,500 words preferred; 750 words minimum; 3,000 words maximum. Publishes short shorts. Sometimes critiques rejected mss and recommends other markets.

How to Contact: Send complete ms with cover letter. Reports in 8-16 weeks. SASE. Simultaneous submissions and reprints OK, if author owns rights. Sample copy for $4.50. Back issues $3. Fiction guidelines for SASE (IRCs).

Payment: Pays 1 contributor's copy.

Terms: Acquires one-time rights.

Advice: "Suggest reading a sample copy. We look for quality writing, engaging ideas and writing that we can get excited about."

EIDOS: Sexual Freedom and Erotic Entertainment for Women, Men & Couples, (IV), Box 96, Boston MA 02137-0096. (617)262-0096. Editor: Brenda Loew Tatelbaum. Tabloid: 10 × 14; 72 pages; web offset printing; illustrations; photos. Magazine of erotica for women, men and couples of all sexual orientations, preferences and lifestyles. "Explicit material regarding language and behavior formed in relationships, intimacy, moment of satisfaction—sensual, sexy, honest. For an energetic, well informed, international erotica readership." Quarterly. Estab. 1984. Circ. 7,000.

Needs: Erotica. Humorous or tongue-in-cheek erotic fiction is especially wanted. Publishes at least 4 pieces of fiction/year. Published new writers within the last year. Length: 1,000 words average; 500 words minimum; 2,000 words maximum. Also publishes literary criticism, poetry. Occasionally critiques rejected mss and recommends other markets.

How to Contact: Send complete ms with SASE (IRCs). "Cover letter with history of publication or short bio is welcome." Reports in 1 month on queries; 2 months on mss. Simultaneous submissions OK. Sample copy $10. Fiction guidelines for #10 envelope with 1 first-class stamp. Reviews novels and short story collections, "if related to subject of erotica (sex, politics, religion, etc.)."

Payment: Pays in contributor's copies.

Terms: Acquires first North American serial rights.

Advice: "We receive more erotic fiction manuscripts now than in the past. Most likely because both men and women are more comfortable with the notion of submitting these manuscripts for publication as well as the desire to see alternative sexually explicit fiction in print. Therefore we can publish more erotic fiction because we have more material to choose from. There is still a lot of debate as to what erotic fiction consists of. This is a tough market to break into. Manuscripts must fit our editorial needs and it is best to order a sample issue prior to writing or submitting material. Honest, explicitly pro-sex, mutually consensual erotica lacks unwanted power, control and degradation—no coercion of any kind."

‡1812, A Literary Arts Magazine, (I, II), P.O. Box 1812, Amherst NY 14226-7812. Fiction Editor: Richard Lynch. Magazine: 4¼ × 11; 150+ pages; coated cover stock; illustrations and photographs. "We want to publish work that we believe is deserving. This includes reprints—anything that has some *bang*." Annually. Estab. 1994.

Needs: Experimental, humor/satire, literary, mainstream/contemporary, translations. Also publishes literary essays, literary criticism and poetry. Sometimes critiques or comments on rejected mss.
How to Contact: Send complete ms with a cover letter. Should include brief list of publications and short cover letter. Reports in 1 month. SASE (IRCs) for return of ms. Simultaneous and reprint submissions OK. Reviews novels and short story collections.
Payment: Payment is "arranged."
Terms: Buys one-time rights.
Advice: "Our philosophy can be summed up in the following quote from Beckett: 'I speak of an art turning from it in disgust, weary of its puny exploits, weary of pretending to be able, of being able, of doing a little better the same old thing, of going a little further along a dreary road.' Too many writers copy. We want to see writing by those who aren't on the 'dreary road.' "

ELDRITCH TALES (II, IV), Yith Press, 1051 Wellington Rd., Lawrence KS 66049. (913)843-4341. Editor-in-Chief: Crispin Burnham. Magazine: 6×9; 120 pages (average); glossy cover; illustrations; "very few" photos. "The magazine concerns horror fiction in the tradition of the old *Weird Tales* magazine. We publish fiction in the tradition of H.P. Lovecraft, Robert Bloch and Stephen King, among others, for fans of this particular genre." Semiannually. Estab. 1975. Circ. 1,000.
Needs: Horror and psychic/supernatural/occult. "No mad slasher stories or similar nonsupernatural horror stories." Receives about 8 unsolicited fiction mss/month. Buys 12 mss/issue, 24 mss/year. Published work by J.N. Williamson, William F. Wu and Charles Grant. Published new writers within the last year. Length: 50-100 words minimum; 20,000 words maximum; 10,000 words average. Occasionally critiques rejected mss. Sometimes recommends other markets.
How to Contact: Send complete ms with SASE (IRCs) and cover letter stating past sales. Previously published submissions OK. Prefers letter-quality submissions. Reports in 4 months. Publication could take up to 5 years after acceptance. Sample copy $6 and $1 for postage and handling.
Payment: ¼¢/word; 1 contributor's copy. $1 minimum payment.
Terms: Pays in royalties on publication for first rights.
Advice: "Buy a sample copy and read it thoroughly. Most rejects with my magazine are because people have not checked out what an issue is like or what type of stories I accept. Most rejected stories fall into one of two categories: non-horror fantasy (sword & sorcery, high fantasy) or non-supernatural horror (mad slasher stories, 'Halloween' clones, I call them). When I say that they should read my publication, I'm not whistling Dixie. We hope to up the magazine's frequency to a quarterly. We also plan to be putting out one or two books a year, mostly novels, but short story collections will be considered as well."

ELF: ECLECTIC LITERARY FORUM, (II), P.O. Box 392, Tonawanda NY 14150. (716)693-7006. Editor: C.K. Erbes. Magazine: 8½×11; 56 pages; 60 lb. white offset paper; coated cover; 2-3 illustrations; 2-3 photographs. "Well-crafted short stories, poetry, essays on literary themes for a sophisticated audience." Quarterly. Estab. 1991. Circ. 5,000.
Needs: Adventure, contemporary, ethnic, fantasy, feminism, historical (general), humor/satire, literary, mainstream, mystery/suspense (private eye), prose poem, regional, science fiction (hard science, soft/sociological), sports, western. No violence and obscenity (horror/erotica). Accepts 4-6 mss/issue; 16-24 mss/year. Publishes ms up to 1 year after acceptance. Recently published work by W. Edwin Verbecke, Sandra Gould Ford, Charles J. Lincoln, Esq., Jim Nichols, Tara Menon, Alyce Ingram. Length: 3,500 words average. Publishes short shorts. Length: 500 words. Sometimes critiques rejected mss and recommends other markets.
How to Contact: Send complete ms with optional cover letter. Reports in 4-6 weeks on mss. SASE. Simultaneous submissions OK (if so indicated). Sample copy for $4.50 ($6 foreign). Fiction guidelines for #10 SAE and 1 first-class stamp (IRCs).
Payment: Pays contributor's copies.
Terms: Acquires first North American serial rights.
Advice: "Short stories stand out when dialogue, plot, character, point of view and language usage work together to create a unified whole on a significant theme, one relevant to most of our readers. We also look for writers whose works demonstrate a knowledge of grammar and how to manipulate it effectively in a story. Each story is read by an Editorial Board comprised of English professors who teach creative writing and are published authors."

‡EMRYS JOURNAL, (I, II), The Emrys Foundation, Box 8813, Greenville SC 29604. (803)288-5154. Editor: Robin Visel. Magazine: 6×9; 100 pages; 60 lb. paper and cover stock; calligraphy illustrations. "We publish short fiction, poetry, and essays. We are particularly interested in hearing from women and other minorities. We are mindful of the southeast but not limited to it." Annually. Estab. 1984. Circ. 300.

Needs: Contemporary, feminist, literary, mainstream and regional. "We read only during August-September. During reading periods we receive around 1,000 manuscripts." Accepts 3-7 stories per issue. Publishes ms 2 months after acceptance. Length: 3,500 words average; 2,500 word minimum; 6,000 word maximum. Publishes short shorts. Length: 1,600 words. Sometimes recommends other markets. Also publishes poetry.

How To Contact: Send complete ms with cover letter. "No queries." Reports in 4 months. SASE. Sample copy $10 and 7×10 SAE with 4 first-class stamps. Fiction guidelines for #10 SAE and 1 first-class stamp (IRCs).

Payment: Pays in contributor's copies.

Terms: Acquires first rights. "Send to managing editor for guidelines."

Advice: Looks for "fiction by women and minorities, especially but not exclusively southeastern."

EPIPHANY: The OgaLaLa Review, (II), P.O. Box 2699, University of Arkansas, Fayetteville AR 72701. Editors: Gordon Grice, Tracy Hyatt Grice. Magazine: digest-sized; 80-120 pages; flat-spined; laser-printed; matte card cover. "Mainstream literature for a general and academic audience." Semiannually. Estab. 1990. Circ. 400.

● The magazine is now primarily interested in mainstream or experimental literary fiction. Note changed subtitle.

Needs: Mainstream literary fiction. Receives 30-50 unsolicited mss/month. Buys 3 mss/issue. Publishes ms 1 year after acceptance. Length: Up to 10,000 words. Publishes short shorts. Also publishes poetry and essays.

How to Contact: Send complete ms with SASE (IRCs). "Cover letter OK but not required." Reports in 2 months. "Considers simultaneous submissions, but writer should notify us promptly of acceptance elsewhere. No previously published material." Sample copy for $5.

Payment: Pays in contributor's copies, plus small honorarium when funds are available.

Terms: Acquires first rights.

Advice: "We get many stories about adultery and even more about child abuse. It will be increasingly difficult to sell us a story on one of these subjects. Besides mainstream fiction, we use much material that is hard to place in mainstream markets—long stories, prose poems, unusual subjects and approaches."

EPOCH MAGAZINE, (II), 251 Goldwin Smith Hall, Cornell University, Ithaca NY 14853. (607)255-3385. Editor: Michael Koch. Submissions should be sent to Michael Koch. Magazine: 6×9; 80-100 pages; good quality paper; good cover stock. "Top level fiction and poetry for people who are interested in good literature." Published 3 times a year. Estab. 1947. Circ. 1,000.

● Work originally appearing in this quality literary journal has appeared in numerous antholog-ies including *Best American Short Stories, Best American Poetry, Pushcart Prize, The O. Henry Prize Stories, Best of the West* and *New Stories from the South.* Note that *Epoch* no longer rotates editors.

Needs: Literary, contemporary and ethnic. Buys 4-5 mss/issue. Receives approximately 100 unsolicited fiction mss each month. Does not read in summer. Published work by Denis Johnson, Harriet Doerr, Lee K. Abbott; published new writers in the last year. Length: 10-30 typed, double-spaced pages. Also publishes literary essays (usually solicited), poetry. Critiques rejected mss when there is time. Sometimes recommends other markets.

How to Contact: Send complete ms with SASE (IRCs). May accept simultaneous submissions if indicated in cover letter ("but prefer not to"). Reports in 2-8 weeks on mss. Publishes ms an average of 3 months after acceptance. Sample copy for $5.

Terms: Pays on publication for first North American serial rights.

Advice: "Read the journals you're sending work to."

EROTIC FICTION QUARTERLY, (I, II, IV), EFQ Publications, Box 424958, San Francisco CA 94142. Editor: Richard Hiller. Magazine: 5×8; 186 pages; perfect-bound; 50 lb. offset paper; 65 lb. cover stock. "Small literary magazine for thoughtful people interested in a variety of sexual themes. Irregularly published."

Needs: Any style heartfelt, intelligent erotica. Also, stories not necessarily erotic whose subject is some aspect of authentic sexual experience. No standard pornography; no "men's magazine" stories; no contrived plots or gimmicks; no broad satire, parody or obscure "literary" writing. Length: 500 words minimum; 5,000 words maximum; 1,500 words average. Occasionally critiques rejected ms.

How to Contact: Send complete ms only. Send SASE (IRCs) for return, or send a disposable copy with SASE for reply. Fiction guidelines for SASE.
Payment: Pays $50.
Terms: Pays on acceptance for first rights.
Advice: "Wanted: unpublished as well as published writers who have something to say regarding sexual attitudes, emotions, roles, etc. Story ideas should come from real life, not media; characters should be real people. There are essentially no restrictions regarding content, style, explicitness, etc."

‡**THE ESCAPIST, A Biannual Literary Journal for Fans of C.S. Lewis, (I),** 6861 Catlett Rd., St. Augustine FL 32095. Editor: T.M. Spell. Magazine: 8½×11; 4-16 pages; 20-50 lb. paper; 20-50 lb. cover. "Escapism is viewed in a very positive light here, and stories in some way related to this theme are welcome. Looking for stories in the Lewisian tradition, or work that evokes what Lewis defined as 'Joy.' For teens to seniors who enjoy Christian fiction without the didactics, and who aren't afraid to ask themselves the tough questions about reality." Estab. 1990. Circ. 700.
Needs: Adventure, ethnic, experimental, fantasy, humor/satire, literary, prose poem, religious/inspirational, science fiction, suspense/mystery, translations. Receives 15-25 unsolicited mss/month. Accepts 4-10 mss/issue; 8-20 mss/year. Publishes ms 6 months to 1 year after acceptance. Published work by Linda Foss, Timothy Scott, Don Hornbostel, Ron Blizzard. Length: 2,500 words average; 25 words minimum; 3,000 words maximum. Publishes short shorts. Sometimes critiques rejected mss and recommends other markets.
How to Contact: "If you would like me to comment on or critique your submission, just ask." Reports in 1-3 weeks on queries; 4-12 weeks on mss. SASE. Simultaneous and reprint submissions OK. Sample copy for $2. Fiction guidelines for #10 SAE and 1 first-class stamp (IRCs).
Payment: Pays 2 contributor's copies.
Terms: Acquires first North American serial rights or one-time rights (if a reprint).
Advice: "Traditional themes and styles are welcome here, as always, but I'm also very interested in publishing cutting-edge work, fiction that takes chances, that shakes people up, and makes them reexamine what Christianity is all about. Is it about praying your way to prosperity and turning church attendance into an end in itself? Or is it about going out into the world where the real pain needs hands on healing? It's about being spiritually resurrected by someone who's been physically resurrected—Jesus Christ. Write to wake the dead!"

✸**EVENT, (II),** Douglas College, Box 2503, New Westminster, British Columbia V3L 5B2 Canada. Editor: Dale Zieroth. Fiction Editor: Maurice Hodgson. Assistant Editor: Bonnie Bauder. Magazine: 6×9; 136 pages; quality paper and cover stock; illustrations; photos. "Primarily a literary magazine, publishing poetry, fiction, reviews, rarely plays and graphics; for creative writers, artists, anyone interested in contemporary literature." Triannually. Estab. 1970. Circ. 1,000.
Needs: Literary, contemporary, feminist, humor, regional. No technically poor or unoriginal pieces. Buys 6-8 mss/issue. Receives approximately 100 unsolicited fiction mss/month. Recently published work by Tom Wayman, George Woodcock, Heather Spears; published new writers within the last year. Length: 5,000 words maximum. Also publishes poetry. Critiques rejected mss "when there is time."
How to Contact: Send complete ms with SASE and bio (*must* be Canadian postage or IRC). Reports in 1-4 months on mss. Publishes ms an average of 6-12 months after acceptance. Sample copy $5.
Payment: Pays $22/page and 2 contributor's copies.
Terms: Pays on publication for first North American serial rights.
Advice: "A good narrative arc is hard to find."

THE EVERGREEN CHRONICLES, A Journal of Gay & Lesbian Literature, (II), Box 8939, Minneapolis MN 55408. Managing Editors: Jim Berg, Susan Raffo. Magazine: 5½×8½; 90-100 pages; linen bond paper; b&w line drawings and photos. "No one theme, other than works must have a lesbian or gay appeal. Works sensual and erotic are considered. We look for poetry and prose, but are open to well-crafted pieces of nearly any genre." Semiannually. Estab. 1985. Circ. 400.
 • The magazine plans to hold a novella contest and will spotlight various themes this year. Check with them for details.
Needs: Gay or lesbian: adventure, confession, contemporary, ethnic, experimental, fantasy, feminist, humor/satire, literary, romance (contemporary), science fiction, serialized/excerpted novel, suspense/mystery. "We are interested in works by gay/lesbian artists in a wide variety of genres. The subject matter need not be specifically lesbian or gay-themed, but we do look for a deep sensitivity to that experience. Accepts 1-2 mss/issue; 12-15 mss/year. Publishes ms approx. 2 months after acceptance.

Published work by Terri Jewel, Lev Raphael and Ruthann Robson; published new writers in the last year. Length: 3,500-4,500 words average; no minimum; 5,200 words maximum. 25 pages double-spaced maximum on prose. Publishes short shorts. Sometimes comments on rejected mss.
How to Contact: Send 4 copies of complete ms with cover letter. "It helps to have some biographical info included." Reports on queries in 3 weeks; on mss in 3-4 months. SASE. Sample copy for $8, 6×9 SAE and $1 postage. Fiction guidelines for #10 SAE and 1 first-class stamp.
Payment: Pays in contributor's copies.
Terms: Acquires one-time rights.
Advice: "Perseverance is on a par with skill at the craft."

EXPERIMENTAL (BASEMENT), (I), eXpErImENtAL (bAsEemEnT) pReSs, # A-191, 3740 N. Romero Rd., Tucson AZ 85705. (602)293-3287. Editor: Charles L. Champion. Magazine or newsletter; 25-75 pages; black and white illustrations and photographs. "Much of our philosophy is a branch off of the classic DaDaist thoughts." Published: spontaneously (3-5 issues, depending on funds). Estab. 1990. Circ. 250.
• Note that this magazine spells its name eXpErImENtAL (bAsEmEnT).
Needs: Experimental. "Constructivist fiction, visualature, conceptual fiction." Publishes special fiction issue or anthology. Receives 2-5 mss/month. Acquires 1-2 mss/issue; 7 mss/year. Publishes ms 1 month after acceptance. Recently published work by Karl Kempton, Jeff Skeates, Richard Kostelanetz. Length: "no longer than 12 legal size pieces of paper." Publishes short shorts. Also publishes literary essays, literary criticism and poetry. Often critiques rejected mss.
How to Contact: Send complete ms with a cover letter. "If writer is not familiar with the term 'vizlation' it would be wise to send an SASE or $1 for info." Reports in 1 month. SASE (IRCs). Simultaneous submissions OK. Sample copy $3. Reviews novels and short story collections.
Payment: Pays 1 contributor copy.
Terms: Not copyrighted.
Advice: Looks for "an author who extends the beauty of a language by experiment."

EXPLORATIONS '94, (I, II), University of Alaska Southeast, 11120 Glacier Highway, Juneau AK 99801. (907)789-4418. Editor: Art Petersen. Magazine: 5½ × 8¼; 44 pages; heavy cover stock; illustrations and photographs. "Poetry, prose and art—we strive for artistic excellence." Annually. Estab. 1980. Circ. 500.
Needs: Experimental, humor/satire, traditional quality fiction, poetry, and art. Receives 1,000 mss/year.
How to Contact: Send complete ms with cover letter, which should include bio. Name and address on *back* of first page of each submission. All submissions entered in contest. Reading/entry fee $4/story required. Submission deadline is March 21, postmarked by. Reports in 2-3 months. Mss cannot be returned. Simultaneous and reprint submissions OK. Sample copy $4 ($3 for back issues).
Payment: Pays 2 contributor's copies. *Charges $4 reading fee for non-UAS fiction contributors.* Also awards 5 annual prizes of $500 for prose, $500 for poetry and $125 for art ($100, $50 and $25). Judges: '91, Bill Hotchkiss; '92, Charles Bukowski; '93, James B. Hall. Write for guidelines.
Terms: Acquires one-time rights (rights remain with the author).
Advice: "Concerning poetry and prose, standard form as well as innovation are encouraged; appropriate and fresh *imagery* (allusions, metaphors, similes, symbols . . .) as well as standard or experimental form draw editorial attention. 'Language really spoken by men' and women and authentically rendered experience are encouraged. Unfortunately, requests for criticism usually cannot be met. The prizes for 1994 will be awarded by novelist, short story writer and poet James B. Hall."

EXPLORER MAGAZINE, (I), Flory Publishing Co., Box 210, Notre Dame IN 46556. (219)277-3465. Editor: Ray Flory. Magazine: 5¹/₂ × 8¹/₂; 20-32 pages; 20 lb. paper; 60 lb. or stock cover; illustrations. Magazine with "basically an inspirational theme including love stories in good taste." Christian writing audience. Semiannually. Estab. 1960. Circ. 200+.
• The editor has created The Joseph Flory Memorial Award in honor of his late father, a writer and editor and recipient of several Freedom Foundation Awards.
Needs: Literary, mainstream, prose poem, religious/inspirational, romance (contemporary, historical, young adult) and science fiction. No pornography. Buys 2-3 mss/issue; 5 mss/year. Length: 600 words average; 300 words minimum; 900 words maximum. Also publishes literary essays. Occasionally critiques rejected mss.

How to Contact: Send complete ms with SASE (IRCs). Reports in 1 week. Publishes ms up to 3 years after acceptance. Simultaneous submissions OK. Sample copy $3. Fiction guidelines for SAE and 1 first-class stamp.
Payment: Pays up to $25.
Terms: Cash prizes of $25, $20, $15 and $10 based on subscribers' votes. A plaque is also awarded to first place winner. Joseph Flory Memorial Award is chosen by editor; $10 plus a plaque.
Advice: "See a copy of magazine first; have a good story to tell—in *good* taste! Most fiction sent in is too *long*! Be yourself! Be honest and sincere in your style. Write what you know about. Our philosophy is to reach the world with Christian literature, drawing others closer to God and nature."

‡EXPLOSIVE DECOMPRESSION, The Magazine of Adventure, Science Fiction, Horror and Role Playing, (I, II), Willowood Publishing, P.O. Box 660085, Miami Springs FL 33266-0085. (305)889-2881. Editor: Kris Williamson. Magazine: 8½ × 11; 60-80 pages; 20 lb. bond paper; 67 lb. Bristol cover; b&w illustrations. "We believe that the writer should retain the rights to his or her work, which is not usually the case with many of the pro Role Playing Game magazines. *Explosive Decompression* is also geared toward a mature, primarily male readership." Semiannually. Estab. 1993. Circ. 300.
• Willowood Publishing also publishes *Shadow Sword*, listed in this book.
Needs: Adventure, fantasy (dark real world), horror, science fiction (hard science, military). No "sociological sf, horror without a supernatural element, media related stories, murder stories." Upcoming themes: possible science fiction anthology; query for details. Publishes special fiction issue or anthology. Receives 30-110 unsolicited mss/month. Accepts 6-10 mss/issue; 12-20 mss/year. Publishes ms 2 months-1 year after acceptance. Recently published work by Gerard D. Houarner, William Marden, Frank O. Dodge, Buzz Lovko, Barbara Custer. Length: 800 words minimum; 10,000 + words maximum. Also publishes literary criticism. Always critiques or comments on rejected mss.
How to Contact: Send complete ms with a cover letter. Should include estimated word count, bio (200 words), list of publications. Reports in 1-2 weeks on queries; 1-3 months on mss. Send SASE (IRCs) for reply, return of ms or send a disposable copy of ms. Simultaneous and reprint submissions OK (query for reprints). Sample copy for $3.25. Fiction guidelines for SASE. Reviews novels and short story collections.
Payment: Pays 1 contributor's copy; additional copies for $3.
Terms: Buys one-time or reprint rights.
Advice: "Read the guidelines carefully and be certain that what is being submitted is appropriate. Never be afraid to send your story to me." Would like to see more "supernatural horror, psychic, occult and military sf as well as war-based adventures, especially Vietnam and WWII." Avoid sending "slasher and serial killer-type horror, sociological sf and war-based horror or 'Twilight Zone' type stories."

EYES, (I), Apt. 301, 2715 S. Jefferson Ave., Saginaw MI 48601. (517)752-5202. Editor: Frank J. Mueller, III. Magazine: 8½ × 11; 28+ pages; 20 lb. paper; Gilbert Laid 65 lb. cover. "No specific theme. Hopefully, horror-related; surrealism most welcome. For a general, educated, not necessarily literary audience." Estab. 1991. Circ. 30-40.
Needs: Contemporary, experimental, fantasy (dark), horror, mainstream, prose poem, romance (gothic). Nothing pornographic; no preachiness; children's fiction discouraged. As of now receives average of 10-11 unsolicited mss/month. Accepts 4-6 mss/issue. Publishes ms up to 1 year after acceptance. Length: 3,500 words preferred; 6,000 words maximum. Sometimes critiques rejected mss.
How to Contact: Query first or send complete ms. Reports in 1 month (or less) on queries; 4-6 weeks on mss. SASE. No simultaneous submissions. Sample copy for $3. Fiction guidelines for #10 SAE and 1 first-class stamp (IRCs).
Payment: No payment.
Terms: Acquires one-time rights.
Advice: "Write and write again. If rejected, try again. If you have a manuscript you like and would like to see it in *Eyes*, send it to me. I may agree with you. Try to have your manuscript say something."

THE FARMER'S MARKET, (II), Midwestern Farmer's Market, Inc., Box 1272, Galesburg IL 61402. Editor: Jean C. Lee. Magazine: 5½ × 8½; 100-200 pages; 60 lb. offset paper; 65 lb. cover; b&w illustrations and photos. Magazine publishing "quality fiction, poetry, nonfiction, author interviews, etc., in the Midwestern tradition for an adult, literate audience." Semiannually. Estab. 1982. Circ. 500.
• *The Farmer's Market* has received numerous grants and awards including Illinois Arts Council Literary Awards for 1985-1991 and Illinois Arts Council grants for 1983-1993. Work published in the magazine has been selected for the *O. Henry Prize* anthology.

Needs: Contemporary, feminist, humor/satire, literary, regional and excerpted novel. "We prefer material of clarity, depth and strength; strong plots, good character development." No "romance, juvenile, teen." Accepts 10-20 mss/year. Published work by Mary Maddox, David Williams; published new writers within the last year. Also publishes literary essays, poetry. Occasionally critiques rejected mss or recommends other markets.

How to Contact: Send complete ms with SASE (IRCs). Reports in 1-3 months. No simultaneous submissions. Publishes ms 4-8 months after acceptance. Sample copy for $4.50 and $1 postage and handling.

Payment: Pays 2 contributor's copies. (Other payment dependent upon grants).

Terms: Authors retain rights.

Advice: "We're always interested in regional fiction but that doesn't mean cows and chickens and home-baked apple pie, please. We are publishing more fiction and we are looking for exceptional manuscripts. Read the magazines before submitting. If you don't want to buy it, ask your library. We receive numerous mss that are clearly unsuitable. We're not sweet; we're not cute and we're not 'precious!' "

FAT TUESDAY, (II), RD2, Box 4220, Manada Gap Rd., Grantville PA 17028. Editor-in-Chief: F.M. Cotolo. Editors: B. Lyle Tabor and Thom Savion. Associate Editors: Lionel Stevroid and Kristen vonOehrke. Journal: 8½×11 or 5×8; 27-36 pages; good to excellent paper; heavy cover stock; b&w illustrations; photos. "Generally, we are an eclectic journal of fiction, poetry and visual treats. Our issues to date have featured artists like Patrick Kelly, Charles Bukowski, Joi Cook, Chuck Taylor and many more who have focused on an individualistic nature with fiery elements. We are a literary mardi gras—as the title indicates—and irreverancy is as acceptable to us as profundity as long as there is fire! Our audience is anyone who can praise literature and condemn it at the same time. Anyone too serious about it on either level will not like *Fat Tuesday*." Annually. Estab. 1981. Circ. 700.

Needs: Comics, erotica, experimental, humor/satire, literary, prose poem, psychic/supernatural/occult, serialized/excerpted novel and dada. "Although we list categories, we are open to feeling out various fields if they are delivered with the mark of an individual and not just in the format of the particular field." Receives 20 unsolicited fiction mss/month. Accepts 4-5 mss/issue. Published new writers within the last year. Length: 1,000 words maximum. Publishes short shorts. Occasionally critiques rejected mss and usually responds with a personal note or letter.

How to Contact: Send complete ms with SASE (IRCs). "No previously published material considered." No simultaneous submissions. Reports in 1 month. Publishes ms 3-10 months after acceptance. Sample copy for $5.

Payment: Pays 1 contributor's copy.

Terms: Acquires one-time rights.

Advice: "As *Fat Tuesday* enters its second decade, we find that publishing small press editions is more difficult than ever. Money remains a problem, mostly because small press seems to play to the very people who wish to be published in it. In other words, the cast is the audience, and more people want to be in *Fat Tuesday* than want to buy it. It is through sales that our magazine supports itself. This is why we emphasize buying a sample issue ($5) before submitting. We have calculated that if only 25% of the submissions we received in the last year had bought sample issues, we could have published four or five issues in 1991 as opposed to the one we struggled to release. As far as what we want to publish—send us shorter works. 'Crystals of thought and emotion which reflect your individual experiences. As long as you dig into your guts and pull out pieces of yourself. Your work is your signature . . . Like time itself, it should emerge from the penetralia of your being and recede into the infinite region of the cosmos,' to coin a phrase, and remember *Fat Tuesday* is mardi gras—so fill up before you fast. Bon soir."

‡**FATHERS, BROTHERS, SONS, (II, IV),** F.J. McLaughlin Newsletter Network, 1346 Joan Dr., Southampton PA 18966-4341. Editor: Mark McLaughlin. Newsletter: 8½×11; 8 pages; 20 lb. bond paper. "To promote appreciation and awareness of the positive effect our contact with men provides. To publish heart-warming, enjoyable stories for people who are tired of all the negative press about men." Quarterly. Estab. 1993. Circ. under 500.
Needs: "Must have a male interest or focus. Male or female writers accepted." Ethnic/multicultural, humor/satire, literary, mainstream/contemporary, senior citizen/retirement. No "negative, brutal, violent or degrading stories." Receives 3 unsolicited mss/month. Accepts 2 mss/issue; 8 mss/year. Publishes ms within 1-2 issues after acceptance. Recently published work by Mike Lopiccolo, Chuck Smith, Larry Bratt. Length: 500 words preferred; 100 words minimum; 1,000 words maximum. Publishes short shorts. Length: open. Also publishes literary essays, literary criticisms and poetry. Always critiques or comments on rejected ms.
How to Contact: Query first. Submissions should include estimated word count and Social Security number. Reports in 2-4 weeks on queries; 4-6 weeks on mss. Send SASE (or IRC) for reply, return of ms or send a disposable copy of ms. Simultaneous, reprint and electronic submissions OK. Sample copy for $3. Fiction guidelines for #10 SAE. Reviews novels and short story collections.
Payment: Pays subscription and 4 contributor's copies; additional copies for $1.
Terms: Acquires one-time rights.
Advice: "The story must create an emotional response: joy, laughter, or sadness—in clear writing." Would like to see more "stories of relationships and experiences with male mentors, teachers and friends."

FELICITY, (I), Weems Concepts, HCR-13, Box 21AA, Artemas PA 17211. (814)458-3102. Editor: Kay Weems-Winter. Newsletter: 8½×11; 20 lb. bond paper; illustrations. "Publishes articles, poetry and short stories. Poetry has different theme each issue. No theme for stories." Bimonthly. Estab. 1988. Circ. 200.
Needs: Open. Short stories, any genre in good taste. No erotica, translations. All submissions treated as contest entries. Entry fee is $5 and the deadline is the 30th of each month. Length: 800-2,500 words. Publishes short shorts. Length up to 800 words; entry fee $2. Editor will consider stories that do not win for *My Legacy* or recommends other markets. Publishes ms 3-4 months after acceptance.
How to Contact: Send complete ms with cover letter or enter bimonthly contests. "Send SASE for return of ms or tell me to destroy it if not accepted." Reports in 4-5 months. SASE. Simultaneous and reprint submissions OK as long as author still retains rights. Sample copy for $2, #10 SAE and 65¢ postage. Fiction guidelines for #10 SAE and 1 first-class stamp (IRCs) or check *The Bottom Line*, market listing for contests.
Payment: Pays in contributor's copies and ½ of entry fee collected for Short Story Contest. All entries receive copy of the issue.
Terms: Acquires one-time rights. Copyrighted. "We sponsor bimonthly contests. Winner receives half of entry fees collected for the short story contest. Submit ms along with entry fee and you will be entered in the contest. Deadline is the 30th of each month. Read both of our publications—*Felicity* and *The Bottom Line Publications*. Our contests are listed there."
Advice: Looks for "good opening sentence, realistic characters, nice descriptions, strong plot with believable ending. Use natural conversations. Let me *feel* your story. Keep me interested until the end. Keep trying. A lot of mss I read are from new writers. Personally I enjoy stories and articles which will create a particular emotion, build suspense, or offer excitement or entertainment. Don't spell out everything in detail—keep me guessing."

FEMINIST STUDIES, (II), Women's Studies Program, University of Maryland, College Park MD 20742. (301)405-7413, 7415. Editor: Claire G. Moses. Fiction Editor: Alicia Ostriker. Magazine: journal-sized; about 200 pages; photographs. "Scholarly manuscripts, fiction, book review essays for professors, graduate/doctorial students; scholarly interdisciplinary feminist journal." Triannually. Estab. 1974. Circ. 7,500.
Needs: Contemporary, ethnic, feminist, gay, lesbian. Receives about 15 poetry and stories/month. Acquires 2-3 mss/issue. "We review fiction twice a year. Deadline dates are May 1 and December 1. Authors will receive notice of the board's decision by June 30 and January 30, respectively." Publishes short shorts. Sometimes comments on or critiques a rejected ms and recommends other markets.
How to Contact: Send complete ms with cover letter. SASE (IRCs). No simultaneous submissions. Sample copy for $10. Fiction guidelines free.
Payment: Pays 2 contributor's copies and 10 tearsheets.
Terms: Send galleys to authors.

FICTION, (II), % Dept. of English, City College, 138th St. & Convent Ave., New York NY 10031. (212)650-6319/650-6317. Editor: Mark Jay Mirsky. Managing Editor: Allan Aycock. Magazine: 6×9; 150-250 pages; illustrations and occasionally photos. "As the name implies, we publish *only* fiction; we are looking for the best new writing available, leaning toward the unconventional. *Fiction* has traditionally attempted to make accessible the unaccessible, to bring the experimental to a broader audience." Biannually. Estab. 1972. Circ. 3,000.
  • Stories first published in *Fiction* have been selected for inclusion in the *Pushcart Prize* and *Best of the Small Presses* anthologies.
Needs: Contemporary, experimental, humor/satire, literary and translations. No romance, science-fiction, etc. Receives 200+ unsolicited mss/month. Acquires 12-20 mss/issue; 24-40 mss/year. Does not read mss May-October. Publishes ms 1-12 months after acceptance. Agented fiction 10-20%. Recently published work by Harold Brodkey, Joyce Carol Oates, Peter Handke, Max Frisch, Susan Minot and Adolfo Bioy-Casares. Length: 6,000 words maximum. Publishes short shorts. Sometimes critiques rejected mss and recommends other markets.
How to Contact: Send complete ms with cover letter. Reports in 3+ months on mss. SASE (IRCs). Simultaneous submissions OK, but please advise. Sample copy $5. Fiction guidelines free.
Payment: Pays in contributor's copies.
Terms: Acquires first rights.
Advice: "The guiding principle of *Fiction* has always been to go to terra incognita in the writing of the imagination and to ask that modern fiction set itself serious questions, if often in absurd and comic voices, interrogating the nature of the real and the fantastic. It represents no particular school of fiction, except the innovative. Its pages have often been a harbor for writers at odds with each other. As a result of its willingness to publish the difficult, experimental, unusual, while not excluding the well known, *Fiction* has a unique reputation in the U.S. and abroad as a journal of future directions."

FICTION INTERNATIONAL, (II), English Dept., San Diego State University, San Diego CA 92182. (619)594-6220. Editor: Harold Jaffe. "Serious literary magazine of fiction, extended reviews, essays." Magazine: 200 pages; illustrations; photos. "Our twin biases are progressive politics and post-modernism." Biannually. Estab. 1973. Circ. 2,500.
Needs: Literary, political and innovative forms. Receives approximately 300 unsolicited fiction mss each month. Unsolicited mss will be considered only from September 1 through December 15 of each year. Published new writers within the last year. No length limitations but rarely use manuscripts over 25 pages. Portions of novels acceptable if self-contained enough for independent publication.
How to Contact: Send complete ms with SASE (IRCs). Reports in 1-3 months on mss. Sample copy for $9: query Harry Polkinhorn, managing editor.
Payment: Pays in contributor's copies.
Advice: "Study the magazine. We're highly selective. A difficult market for unsophisticated writers."

✿THE FIDDLEHEAD, (I, II), University of New Brunswick, Campus House, Box 4400 Fredericton, New Brunswick E3B 5A3 Canada. (506)453-3501. Editor: Don McKay. Fiction Editors: Diana Austin, Banny Belyea, Ted Colson and Linda McNutt. Magazine: 6×9; 104-128 pages; ink illustrations; photos. "No criteria for publication except quality. For a general audience, including many poets and writers." Quarterly. Estab. 1945. Circ. 1,000.
  • *The Fiddlehead* celebrates its 50th Anniversary in 1995. The editors are looking for writers who had their *first* publication in the magazine.
Needs: Literary. No non-literary fiction. Receives 100-150 unsolicited mss/month. Buys 4-5 mss/issue; 20-40 mss/year. Publishes ms up to 1 year after acceptance. Small percent agented fiction. Recently published work by Sharon Pywell; published new writers within the last year. Length: 50-3,000 words average. Publishes short shorts. Occasionally critiques rejected mss.
How to Contact: Send complete ms with cover letter. SASE. "*Canadian* stamps or international reply coupons!" for mss. Reprint submissions OK. No simultaneous submissions. Reports in 3-6 months. Sample copy for $6.50 (US). Reviews novels and short story collections—*Canadian only*.
Payment: Pays $10-12 (Canadian)/published page and 1 contributor's copy.
Terms: Pays on publication for first or one-time rights.
Advice: "Less than 5% of the material received is published."

FIGHTING WOMAN NEWS, (IV), 6741 Tung Ave. West, Theodore AL 36582. Editor: Debra Pettis. Magazine: 8½×11; 24 pages; 60 lb. offset bond paper; slick cover; illustrations; photos. "Women's martial arts, self defense, combative sports. Articles, reviews, etc., related to these subjects. Well-educated adult women who are actually involved with martial arts read us because we're there and we're good." Quarterly. Estab. 1975. Circ. 3,500.

Needs: Science fiction, fantasy, feminist, adventure, mystery/suspense (police procedural, private eye) and translations. "No material that shows women as victims, incompetents, stereotypes; no 'fight scenes' written by people who don't know anything about fighting skills." Receives very few unsolicited fiction mss. Recently published work by Dee Powers, Cathy D. Better. Length: 2,500 words.

How to Contact: Query with clips of published work with SASE (IRCs). Enclose cover letter with ms. Simultaneous submissions OK, but "we must know if it is a simultaneous submission." Reports as soon as possible on queries and mss. Sample copy $3.50. Specify "fiction" when asking for samples. Guidelines for #10 SASE.

Payment: Pays contributor's copies and subscription.

Terms: Acquires one-time rights. Will print author's copyright if desired.

Advice: "We are now getting unsolicited mss from published writers who have what we want; i.e., a good, competent story that's just a bit too martial-arts oriented for their regular markets. Our readers have expressed a strong preference for more technique and theory with a few specific complaints about too much fiction or poetry. So even with a more regular publication schedule and corresponding increase in total pages, we are not likely to use more fiction. Read the magazine before submitting. I also think the theme of death in combat can do with a rest."

FIGMENT MAGAZINE, Tales from the Imagination, (I, II, IV), P.O. Box 3128, Moscow ID 83843-0477. Editors: Barb & J.C. Hendee. Magazine: 5½×8½; 60 pages; slick stock cover; illustrations. "Poetry/stories/vignettes/novelettes in genres of sf, fantasy, and sf/f related horror, for adults." Quarterly. Estab. 1989.

- *Figment Magazine* was rated #35 on the latest *Writer's Digest* Fiction 50 list. J.C. Hendee's article on working with editors, "Eating Your Eggshells," was included in the 1993 edition of *Novel & Short Story Writer's Market*.

Needs: Fantasy, science fiction (hard science, soft/sociological). "We're open to standard plotting through slightly experimental, as long as the story is interesting, comprehensible and always *entertaining*." Receives 400+ mss/month. Buys 8-12 mss/issue; 32-48 mss/year. Publishes ms within 9 months after acceptance. Recently published work by Nina Kiriki Hoffman, K.D. Wentworth, Karl Schroeder, James Glass. Length: 100-10,000 words; 3,000 words preferred. Also publishes poetry. Sometimes critiques rejected mss and recommends other markets.

How to Contact: "Send for guidelines first." Send complete ms with cover letter; include Social Security number, bio, SASE (IRCs) and listing of publishing credits (year to date only) including where and when. Reports in 2 weeks on queries; 1 month average on mss. No simultaneous submissions. Encourages disk submissions. Sample copy for $4. Fiction guidelines for #10 SASE. Reviews novels and short story collections. Send to J.P. McLaughlin, reviewer.

Payment: Pays ½-1¢/word (for fiction).

Terms: Pays within 30 days of acceptance for first North American serial rights only. Sends galleys to author.

Advice: "Looks for original ideas or original methods used with old ideas. Cutting edge material that is fantastical and far-reaching but always entertaining! Don't tell us what your story is about in your cover letter; if we can't figure it out from the manuscript, then some more work needs to be done before you submit. We expect professional submissions in the proper format."

FINE MADNESS, (II), Box 31138, Seattle WA 98103-1138. Magazine: 5×8; 64 pages; 65 lb. paper; 60 lb. cover stock. Estab. 1981. Circ. 800.

Needs: Contemporary, experimental, literary, prose poem and translations. Receives 30 unsolicited mss/month. Accepts 1-2 mss/issue; 2-4 mss/year. Publishes ms no more than 1 year after acceptance. Published work by Naomi Nye, David Downing, Hillel Schwarz and Michael Novak. Length: "approx. 12 pages max." Publishes short shorts. Also "would like to see" literary essays.

How to Contact: Send complete ms with cover letter. No simultaneous submissions. Reports in 3 months on mss. Sample copy $4. Guidelines free.

Payment: Pays subscription to magazine and contributor's copies.

Terms: Acquires first North American serial rights. Copyright reverts to author upon publication.

♣FIREWEED, A Feminist Quarterly, Box 279, Station B, Toronto, Ontario M5T 2W2 Canada. (416)323-9512. Editors: The Fireweed Collective. Women's literary and cultural journal, with an emphasis on race, class and sexuality. Quarterly. Estab. 1978. Circ. 2,000.

Needs: Fiction, poetry, nonfiction, articles, lesbian, working class, and women of color content. No "women's formula style." Receives 60 unsolicited fiction mss/month. Buys 30 mss/issue; 120 mss/year. Length: 1,200 words minimum; 18,000 words maximum; 6,000 words average. Occasionally critiques rejected ms.
How to Contact: Query first with SASE (IRCs). Photocopied submissions OK. Reports in 6 months on queries. Sample copy $5 in Canada, $6 in U.S.
Payment: "Please inquire."
Terms: Copyright held jointly by *Fireweed* and author.

FISH DRUM MAGAZINE, (II), % 626 Kathryn Ave., Santa Fe NM 87501. Editor: Robert Winson. Magazine: 5½×8½; 40-odd pages; glossy cover; illustrations and photographs. "Lively, emotional vernacular modern fiction, art and poetry." Published 2-4 times/year. Estab. 1988. Circ. 500.
Needs: Contemporary, erotica, ethnic, experimental, fantasy, gay, lesbian, literary, prose poem, regional, science fiction. "We're interested in material by New Mexican writers; also on the practice of Zen. Most of the fiction we've published is in the form of short, heightened prose-pieces." Receives 6-10 unsolicited mss/month. Accepts 1-2 mss/issue; 2-8 mss/year. Publishes ms 6 months-1 year after acceptance. Also publishes literary essays, literary criticism, poetry. Recommends other markets.
How to Contact: Send complete manuscript. No simultaneous submissions. Reports on mss in 1-3 months. SASE. Sample copy for $3. Reviews novels and short story collections.
Payment: Pays in contributor's copies. Charges for extras.
Terms: Acquires first North American serial rights. Sends galleys to author.

FLIPSIDE, (II), Professional Writing Program, Dixon 110, California University, California PA 15419. (412)938-4082. Editors: Jim Black, J.E. Novak. Tabloid: 11¹/₂×17; 45-60 pages; illustrations; photos. "Emphasis on 'new journalism.' Fiction, nonfiction, poetry, humor." Semiannually. Estab. 1987. Circ. 5,000.
• *Flipside* received First Place with a Special Merit Award from the American Scholastic Press Association in 1992.
Needs: Contemporary, experimental, literary. No genre fiction. Receives 5-6 unsolicited mss/month. Accepts 2-3 mss/issue; 6-8 mss/year. Does not read June-August. Publishes ms 1-6 months after acceptance. Length: 1,000-5,000 words average; 10,000 words maximum. Also publishes literary essays, literary criticism, some poetry.
How to Contact: Send complete manuscript with cover letter. Reports in 2-4 weeks on queries; 1-2 months on mss. SASE. Simultaneous submissions OK. Sample copy and fiction guidelines for 9×12 SAE and $1.24 postage (IRCs).
Payment: Pays 3 contributor's copies.
Terms: Acquires first North American serial rights.
Advice: "Experimental and alternative fiction are always welcome here. Traditional fiction, darkly executed, is also encouraged."

THE FLORIDA REVIEW, (II), Dept. of English, University of Central Florida, Orlando FL 32816. (407)823-2038. Contact: Russell Kesler. Magazine: 5½×8½; 128 pages. Semiannually. Estab. 1972. Circ. 1,000.
• Work from this quality literary journal was selected for the *Editor's Choice III: Fiction, Poetry & Art From the US Small Presses* (1984-1990), published by the Spirit That Moves Us Press.
Needs: Contemporary, experimental and literary. "We welcome experimental fiction, so long as it doesn't make us feel lost or stupid. We aren't especially interested in genre fiction (science fiction, romance, adventure, etc.), though a good story can transcend any genre." Receives 120 mss/month. Acquires 8-10 mss/issue; 16-20 mss/year. Publishes ms within 3-6 months of acceptance. Published work by Stephen Dixon, Richard Grayson and Liz Rosenberg. Publishes short shorts. Also publishes literary criticism, poetry.
How to Contact: Send complete ms with cover letter. Reports in 2-4 months. SASE (IRCs). Simultaneous submissions OK. Sample copy for $4.50; free fiction guidelines. Reviews novels and short story collections.
Payment: Pays in contributor's copies. Small honorarium occasionally available.
Terms: "Copyright held by U.C.F.; reverts to author after publication. (In cases of reprints, we ask that a credit line indicate that the work first appeared in the *F.R.*)"
Advice: "We publish fiction of high 'literary' quality—stories that delight, instruct, and aren't afraid to take risks."

FOLIO: A LITERARY JOURNAL, (II), Literature Department, American University, Washington DC 20016. (202)885-2971. Editor changes yearly. Send mss to attention: editor. Magazine: 6 × 9; 64 pages. "Fiction is published if it is well written. We look for language control, skilled plot and character development." For a scholarly audience. Semiannually. Estab. 1984. Circ. 400.
Needs: Contemporary, literary, mainstream, prose poem, translations, essay, b&w art or photography. No pornography. Occasional theme-based issues. See guidelines for info. Receives 150 unsolicited mss/month. Accepts 3-5 mss/issue; 6-40 mss/year. Does not read mss during May-August or December-January. Published work by Henry Taylor, Kermit Moyer, Linda Pastan; publishes new writers. Length: 2,500 words average; 4,500 words maximum. Publishes short shorts. Occasionally critiques rejected mss.
How to Contact: Send complete ms with cover letter, which should include a brief bio. Reports in 1-2 weeks on queries; 1-2 months on mss. SASE. Simultaneous and reprint submissions OK (if noted). Sample copy for $5. Guidelines for #10 SAE and 1 first-class stamp (IRCs).
Payment: Pays in contributor's copies.
Terms: Acquires first North American rights. "$75 award for best fiction and poetry. Query for guidelines."

FOOTWORK, The Paterson Literary Review, (I, II), Passaic County Community College, One College Blvd., Paterson NJ 07505. (201)684-6555. Editor: Maria Mazziotti Gillan. Magazine: 8 × 11; 200 pages; 60 lb. paper; 70 lb. cover; illustrations; photos. Plans fiction issue in future.
• *Footwork* was chosen by *Library Journal* as one of the 10 best literary magazines in the US.
Needs: Contemporary, ethnic, experimental. "We are interested in quality short stories, with no taboos on subject matter." Receives about 60 unsolicited mss/month. Publishes ms about 6 months-1 year after acceptance. Published new writers within the last year. Length: 2,500-3,000 words. Also publishes literary essays, literary criticism, poetry.
How to Contact: Reports in 1 year or less on mss. SASE (IRCs). Simultaneous submissions OK. Sample copy $5. Reviews novels and short story collections.
Payment: Pays in contributor's copies.
Terms: Acquires first North American rights.
Advice: "We look for original, vital, powerful work. The short story is—when successful—a major achievement. Because we publish relatively little work, we cannot consider stories which are slight, however charming."

THE FOUR DIRECTIONS, American Indian Literary Quarterly, (II, IV), Snowbird Publishing Company, P. O. Box 729, Tellico Plains TN 37385. (615)982-7261. Senior Editor: Joanna Meyer. Assistant Editor: William Meyer. Magazine: 8 × 11; 68 pages; 70 lb. paper; 100+ lb. cover; 10-20 illustrations; 2-6 photographs. "All writing must be by American Indian authors. We prefer writing that furthers the positive aspects of the American Indian spirit. We publish poetry, fiction, essays and reviews." Quarterly. Estab. 1992. Circ 1,200.
Needs: American Indian only: adventure, children's/juvenile; erotica; ethnic/multicultural; experimental; fantasy; feminist; historical (general); horror; humor/satire; literary; mystery/suspense; psychic/supernatural/occult; regional; science fiction; sports; transalations; westerns; young adult/teen (10-18 years). "Writing should reflect Indian issues and views in all categories." Upcoming themes: "All-Women's Issue" (Vol. I, No. 4); "Indian Prisoners' Issue (Vol. II, No. 2); "Children's Issue" (Vol. II, No. 4). Will publish special fiction issue or anthology. Receives 10 mss/month. Buys 8-12 mss/issue; 32-48 mss/year. Publishes ms 2-9 months after acceptance. Recently published Lise McCloud, Mary Lockwood, Joe Bruchac. Length: 2,000 words; 300 words minimum; 6,000 words maximum. Publishes short shorts. Length: 350 words. Also publishes literary essays, criticism, poetry. Often critiques rejected mss.
How to Contact: Query with clips of published work or send complete ms with a cover letter. Should include estimated word count, 1-page or less bio, list of publications, tribal affiliation. Reports in 2-6 weeks on queries; 2-10 weeks on mss. Send SASE (IRC) for reply, return of ms, or send a disposable copy of the ms. Simultaneous, reprint or electronic submissions OK. Sample copy for 8½ × 11 SAE and 4 first-class stamps or IRCs. Fiction guidelines for #10 SAE and 1 first-class stamp.
Payment: Pays 2¢/word plus 4 contributor's copies.
Terms: Pays on publication for one-time rights. Sends galleys to author, when schedule allows.
Advice: "Writing we'll consider must be relevant, creative, original and of interest to a wide readership, both Indian and non-Indian. We seek professional quality writing, and work, if *about* Indians, that is accurate and authentic. We want work that shows positive spiritual strengths. We've not seen

enough theater scripts/drama. We'd like to see more. And we *know* there's more humorous writing than has been submitted."

FRICTION, Wampus Multimedia 9893 Burke Pond Court, Burke VA 22015. (703)250-6010. Editor: Mark W. Doyon. Magazine: 8½×11; 12-16 pages; 70 lb. patina matte text; line art and photos. "Thematically linked fiction . . . ." Quarterly. Estab. 1989.
Needs: Contemporary, humor/satire, literary. "*No genre fiction.*" Upcoming themes: send for editorial calendar. Receives 10-15 unsolicited mss/month. Accepts 3-5 mss/issue; 12-20 mss/year. Publishes ms 2-6 months after acceptance. Recently published work by Robyn Parnell, George K. Rosenstock, Matthew Shields and Kevin Kerr. Length: 1,500-2,000 words average; 500 words minimum; 2,500 words maximum. Publishes short shorts. Sometimes critiques rejected mss and recommends other markets.
How to Contact: Send complete ms with cover letter. Reports in 2 weeks on queries; 6 weeks on mss. SASE. Simultaneous submissions OK. Accepts electronic submissions via disk (PC-formatted). Sample copy for $2, 9×12 SAE and 3 first-class stamps (IRCs). Fiction guidelines free.
Payment: Pays subscription to magazine.
Terms: Acquires one-time rights.
Advice: "We look for mss with strong thematic and editorial content. The writing should be concise and linear, but ultimately it's a strong point-of-view that makes or breaks a piece. If a submission reflects a strong vision, we'll often edit the language as necessary. Ultimately a ms must complement the issue's stated THEME (e.g. 1993 themes were: Debtors' Prison, Outward Bound, Revised Expectations, World in Flux). Make sure that you have *something to say*. And then say it as concisely and elegantly as possible. Stay away from 'cute' or 'wacky' characterizations. Avoid 'clever' language. Present complex themes in a simple way."

‡FRONTIERS (II), A Journal of Women Studies, Mesa Vista Hall 2142, University of New Mexico, Albuquerque NM 87131. Editor: Jane Slaughter. Magazine: 6×9; 200 pages; photos. "Women studies; academic articles in all disciplines; criticism, book and film reviews; exceptional creative work (art, short fiction, photography, poetry)."
Needs: Feminist, lesbian. Receives 15 unsolicited mss/month. Accepts 7-12 mss/issue. Publishes ms 6 months to 1 year after acceptance. Sometimes critiques rejected mss and recommends other markets.
How to Contact: Send complete ms with cover letter. Reports in 1 month on queries; 3-6 months on mss. SASE (IRCs). Sample copy for $8.
Payment: Pays 2 contributor's copies.
Terms: Acquires first North American serial rights.
Advice: "We are a *feminist* journal. *FRONTIERS* aims to make scholarship in women studies, and *exceptional* creative work, accessible to a cross-disciplinary audience inside and outside the university."

‡FUEL MAGAZINE, (II), Anaconda Press, P.O. Box 146640, Chicago IL 60614. Editor: Andy Lowry. Magazine: 5½×8½; 70 pages; 60# offset paper; 10 pt. cast coat cover stock; illustrations. "*Fuel* is a very eccentric, eclectic magazine. We do not consider ourselves an academic publication; rather, we prefer to publish underground lesser-known writers." Quarterly. Estab. 1992. Circ. 5,000.
Needs: Ethnic/multicultural, experimental, feminist, literary. No science fiction, romance, horror, humor/satire. List of upcoming themes available for SASE. Publishes special fiction issue or anthology. Receives 50 unsolicited mss/month. Accepts 5 mss/issue; 20-25 mss/year. Publishes ms 3-5 months after acceptance. Recently published work by Nicole Panter, Larry Oberc, CC Chapman, Sesshu Foster. Length: 1,500 words preferred; 500 words minimum; 3,000 words maximum. Publishes short shorts. Length: 250 words. Also publishes poetry.
How to Contact: Query first. Should include estimated word count and list of publications. Reports in 4 weeks on queries; 6 weeks on mss. SASE (or IRC). No simultaneous submissions. Reprint and electronic submissions OK. Sample copy for $3. Fiction guidelines for #10 SAE and 1 first-class stamp or IRC. Reviews novels and short story collections.
Payment: Pays contributor's copies; additional copies at cost.
Terms: Acquires one-time rights.
Advice: "We are not your normal publication—we want intelligent, cutting edge, strongly written works."

FUGUE, Literary Digest of the University of Idaho, (I), Brink Hall, Rm. 200, University of Idaho, Moscow ID 83843. Executive Editor: Mark K. Coen. Editors change each year. Send to Executive Editor. Magazine: 5½×8½; 40-60 pages; 20 lb. stock paper. "We are interested in all classifications of fiction—we are not interested in pretentious 'literary' stylizations. We expect stories to be written in a manner engaging for anyone, not just academics and the pro-literatae crowd." Semiannually. Estab. 1990. Circ. 200+.

Needs: Adventure, ethnic/multicultural, experimental, fantasy, historical (general), horror, humor/satire, literary, mainstream/contemporary, mystery/suspense, regional, romance, science fiction, sports, westerns. Receives 50+ unsolicited mss/month. Buys 4-8 mss/issue; 8-16 mss/year. Does not read May-September. Publishes ms 3-5 months after acceptance. Length: 3,000 words average; 50 words minimum; 7,000 words maximum. Publishes short shorts. Also publishes literary essays and poetry. Sometimes critiques or comments on rejected mss.

How to Contact: Send complete ms with cover letter. "Obtain guidelines first." Should include estimated word count, Social Security number and list of publications. Report in 2 weeks on queries; 2 months on mss. SASE (or IRC) for a reply to a query or return of ms. No simultaneous submissions. Sample copy for $3. Fiction guidelines for #10 SAE and 1 first-class stamp or IRC.

Payment: Pays ½¢/word plus 1 contributor's copy. Additional copies $4.

Terms: Pays on publication for first North American serial rights.

Advice: Looks for "competent writing, clarity and consideration for the reader above stylism. Do not send us the traditional themes considered to be 'literary'.

‡GAIA, A Journal of Literary and Environmental Arts, (II), Whistle Press, Inc., P.O. Box 709, Winterville GA 30683. (706)549-1810. Editor: Robert S. King. Fiction Editor: Marina Roscher. Magazine: 8½×11; 36-60 pages; 50% recycled paper; b&w illustrations and photographs. "High-quality fiction and science fiction on any subject, although preference is given to work on environmental, social, or political themes. No escapist literature." Quarterly. Estab. 1993. Circ. 500.

Needs: Condensed novel, literary, science fiction (soft/sociological). "No superficial plots or mass market romances." Publishes special fiction issue or anthology. Receives 125 unsolicited mss/month. Accepts 3 mss/issue; 12 mss/year. Publishes ms 6-10 months after acceptance. Recently published work by Donn Irving, Ellen LaConte, Lawrence Millman. Length: 2,500 words preferred; 10,000 words maximum. Publishes short shorts. Also publishes literary essays, literary criticism and poetry. Sometimes critiques or comments on rejected mss.

How to Contact: Send complete ms with a cover letter. Should include estimated word count and bio (short paragraph). Reports in 2 weeks on queries; 2 months on mss. Send SASE (or IRC) for reply, return of ms or send a disposable copy of ms. No simultaneous submissions. Reprints and electronic submissions OK. Sample copy for $4 (single issue); $6 (double). Fiction guidelines for #10 SAE. Reviews novels and short story collections; send to Max Wheat, review editor.

Payment: Pays subscription and 2 contributor's copies; additional copies for 40% off cover price.

Terms: Acquires all rights. Sends galleys to author.

Advice: "We seek tightly written, compelling, provocative work with depth of character and meaning. Stories on environmental themes stand the best chance, though we will not reject a well-written piece on any subject. Would love to see more attention paid to the language; e.g., turn of phrase, succinct use of words to generate a high energy level."

‡GALAXY CLASS, (I, IV), Mindset Press, P.O. Box 7000-822, Redondo Beach CA 90277. Editor: Christopher Simmons. Magazine: 8½×11; 64 pages; recycled bond paper; vellum bristol cover stock; illustrations and photographs. "Specifically published for fans of the TV series, 'Star Trek: The Next Generation'." Semiannually. Estab. 1987. Circ. 1,500.

Needs: Adventure, erotica, romance, science fiction. Publishes special fiction issue or anthology. Receives 5+ unsolicited mss/month. Accepts 5-7 mss/issue; 25 mss/year. Does not read mss at end of year/holidays. Publishes ms 6-12 months after acceptance. Recently published work by Andra Marie Mueller, Sherry Hopper, Yvonne Harrison. Length: 10,000-15,000 words preferred; 1,000 words minimum; 30,000 words maximum. Also publishes literary criticism and poetry. Sometimes critiques or comments on rejected mss.

How to Contact: Send complete ms with a cover letter. Should include estimated word count, bio, list of publications and plot outline. Reports in 1-3 months. Send a disposable copy of ms. Electronic submissions OK. Sample copy for $4. Fiction guidelines for #10 SAE and 1 first-class stamp (IRCs). Reviews novels and short story collections.

Payment: Pays subscription and 2-5 contributor's copies; additional copies for 50% off cover price.

Terms: Acquires first rights.

Advice: Looks for "well-written work, knowledge of characters within genre, believable dialogue."

GASLIGHT, Tales of the Unsane, (II), Strait-Jacket Publications, P.O. Box 21, Cleveland MN 56017-0021. Editor: Melissa Gish. Magazine: 5½ × 8½; 44-52 pages; 60 lb. white paper; 100 lb. color cover; illustrations. "Highly imaginative sci-fi, fantasy, macabre fiction borne out of the darkest recesses of the creator's mind. Eager to work with new and/or unpublished writers." Triannually (April, August, December). Estab. 1992. Circ. 150.

Needs: Experimental, fantasy (horror, science), horror, mystery/suspense (macabre), science fiction (hard science, horror, soft/sociological). Upcoming themes: "Cronomopsychosis—new slants on time travel" (April 1994); "Popcorn Issue—movies or the movie industry" (December 1994); "Under the Bigtop" Circus and Freak Show issue (April 1995); "Feathers and Fur" Shapeshifting issue (December 1995). Details of upcoming themes available for SASE. Publishes annual special fiction issue or anthology. Receives 100-125 unsolicited mss/month. Buys 10-12 mss/issue; 40-50 mss/year. Publishes ms 2-3 months or less after acceptance. Published work by D.F. Lewis, Lenora K. Rogers, Joshua Waterman. Length: 2,500 words average; 150 words minimum; 3,000 words maximum. Publishes short shorts. Length: 300 words. Also publishes poetry. Often critiques or comments on rejected mss.

How to Contact: Send complete ms with cover letter. Should include estimated word count, brief bio, list of recent publications, request for workshopping of ms. Reports in 2 weeks on queries; 3-4 weeks on mss. Send SASE (IRCs) for reply, return of mss or send a disposable copy of the ms. Simultaneous and reprint submissions OK. Sample copy for $4.25; $5 Canada; $6 overseas. Fiction guidelines for #10 SAE and 1 first-class stamp or IRC. Reviews novels and short story collections.

Payment: Pays 2¢/word maximum, subscription to the magazine (featured author only), 1 contributor's copy plus 15% discount on additional copies.

Terms: Pays on acceptance for first North American serial rights or reprint rights, if ms is a reprint. Sponsors Annual Fiction Chapbook Contest, send #10 SASE (29¢) for application and guidelines.

Advice: "Ideas must be fresh. Prose must be clean and tight with a good command of grammar. Original plots, well-developed characters. Individual style must be apparent—no rehash or copycat material." Looks for "visits from other beings—fresh ideas for alien cultures. New slants on dragon themes. Militaristic sci-fi. Good blends of horror/sci-fi or of fantasy/horror. Please, no serial killers, no stripper-hooker murders, no sexism, no racism, no specism, no heavy profanity, blood and slime is only acceptable if it is relevant to the plot. No monster movie rip-offs, no cliché or ambiguous endings."

GAY CHICAGO MAGAZINE (II), Ultra Ink, Inc. 3121 N. Broadway, Chicago IL 60657-4522. (312)327-7271. Publisher: Ralph Paul Gernhardt. Associate Publisher: Jerry Williams. Magazine: 8½ × 11; 80-144 pages; newsprint paper and cover stock; illustrations; photos. Entertainment guide, information for the gay community.

Needs: Erotica (but no explicit hard core), lesbian, gay and romance. Receives "a few" unsolicited mss/month. Acquires 10-15 mss/year. Published new writers within the last year. Length: 1,000-3,000 words.

How to Contact: Send complete ms with SASE (IRCs). Accepts disk submissions compatible with Merganthaler Crtronic 200. Must have hard copy with disk submissions. Reports in 4-6 weeks on mss. Free sample copy for 9 × 12 SAE and $1.45 postage.

Payment: Minimal. 5-10 free contributor's copies; no charge for extras "if within reason."

Terms: Acquires one-time rights.

Advice: "I use fiction on a space-available basis, but plan to use more because we have doubled our format size to 8½ × 11."

GEORGETOWN REVIEW, (II), G & R Publications, Box 227, 400 East College St., Georgetown KY 40324. (502)863-8308. Editor: Steven Carter. Magazine: 6 × 9; 85-100 pages; 60 lb. offset paper; 80 lb. cover. "We want to publish quality fiction and poetry. Our audience is people who are interested in reading quality fiction and poetry." Published twice a year. Estab. 1993. Circ. 1,000.

Needs: Literary. No romance, juvenile, fantasy. Receives 500-700 mss/year. Does not read mss May-August. Publishes 3-6 months after acceptance. Length: open. Publishes short shorts. Length: 400-500 words. Also publishes poetry.

How to Contact: Send complete ms with a cover letter. Reports in 3-4 months on mss. SASE (IRC). Simultaneous submissions OK. Sample copy $5, 9 × 12 SAE and 5 first-class stamps.

Payment: Pays 2 contributor's copies.

Terms: Acquires first North American serial rights. Sends galleys to author.

Advice: "We simply look for quality work, no matter what the subject or style."

THE GEORGIA REVIEW, (I, II, III), The University of Georgia, Athens GA 30602-9009. (706)542-3481. Editor-in-Chief: Stanley W. Lindberg. Associate Editor: Stephen Corey. Journal: 7×10; 208 pages (average); 50 lb. woven old style paper; 80 lb. cover stock; illustrations; photos. *"The Georgia Review,* winner of the 1986 National Magazine Award in Fiction, is a journal of arts and letters, featuring a blend of the best in contemporary thought and literature—essays, fiction, poetry, graphics and book reviews—for the intelligent nonspecialist as well as the specialist reader. We seek material that appeals across disciplinary lines by drawing from a wide range of interests." Quarterly. Estab. 1947. Circ. 6,200.
  • This magazine has an excellent reputation for publishing high-quality fiction.
Needs: Experimental and literary. "We're looking for the highest quality fiction—work that is capable of sustaining subsequent readings, not throw-away pulp magazine entertainment. Nothing that fits too easily into a 'category.' " Receives about 400 unsolicited fiction mss/month. Buys 3-4 mss/issue; 12-15 mss/year. Does not read unsolicited mss in June, July or August. Would prefer *not* to see novel excerpts. Published work by Lee K. Abbott, Marjorie Sandor, John Edgar Wideman; published new writers within the last year. Length: Open. Also publishes literary essays, literary criticism, poetry. Occasionally critiques rejected mss.
How to Contact: Send complete ms with SASE (IRCs). No multiple submissions. Reports in 2-3 months. Sample copy $6; guidelines for #10 SAE with 1 first-class stamp. Reviews short story collections.
Payment: Pays minimum: $35/printed page; 1 year complimentary subscription; 1 contributor's copy, reduced charge for extra.
Terms: Pays on publication for first North American serial rights. Sends galleys to author.

THE GETTYSBURG REVIEW, (II), Gettysburg College, Gettysburg PA 17325. (717)337-6770. Editor: Peter Stitt. Assistant Editor: Jeff Mock. Magazine: 6³/₄×10; approx. 170 pages; acid free paper; full color illustrations and photos. "Quality of writing is our only criterion; we publish fiction, poetry and essays." Quarterly. Estab. 1988. Circ. 4,500.
  • *The Gettysburg Review* won a Gold Ozzie Award for Best Design, Scholarly Education Journal and has published four works reprinted in the 1993 *Pushcart Prize* anthology. Editor Peter Stitt also received the 1993 Nora Magi Award for Editorial Excellence. This was the first time this award, sponsored by PEN, was given.
Needs: Contemporary, experimental, historical(general), humor/satire, literary, mainstream, regional and serialized novel. "We require that fiction be intelligent, and aesthetically written." Receives approx. 125 mss/month. Buys approx. 4-6 mss/issue; 16-24 mss/year. Publishes ms within 3-6 months of acceptance. Recently published work by Joyce Carol Oates, Frederick Busch. Length: 3,000 words average; 1,000 words minimum; 20,000 words maximum. Occasionally publishes short shorts. Also publishes literary essays, some literary criticism, poetry. Sometimes critiques rejected mss.
How to Contact: Send complete ms with cover letter, which should include "education, credits." Reports in 3-6 months. SASE (IRCs). No simultaneous submissions. Sample copy for $7 (postage paid). Does not review books per se. "We do essay-reviews, treating several books around a central theme." Send review copies to editor.
Payment: Pays $25/printed page plus subscription to magazine, contributor's copy. Charge for extra copies.
Terms: Pays on publication for first North American serial rights.
Advice: "Reporting time can take more than three months. It is helpful to look at a sample copy of *The Gettysburg Review* to see what kinds of fiction we publish before submitting."

‡GHOST TOWN, (I, IV), Tellstar Productions, P.O. Box 1264, Huntington WV 25714. Editor: Shannon Bridget Murphy. Magazine: 8×11; b&w illustrations; glossy color photographs. *"Ghost Town* focuses on ghost towns primarily in the southwest and Mexico, although other sites are considered." Triannually. Estab. 1993.
  • Tellstar Productions also publishes *Cemetary Plot,* also a new listing in this book.
Needs: Adventure, regional, westerns, young adult/teen, special interest (ghost towns and western historic sites). "Although fiction is occasionally accepted it must be realistic or have an historic basis." List of upcoming themes available for SASE. Publishes special fiction issue or anthology. Receives 2-4 unsolicited mss/month. Accepts 1-2 mss/issue. Time between acceptance of ms and publication varies. Length: 1,500-2,500 words preferred. Publishes short shorts; 500 words or less preferred. Also publishes literary essays, literary criticism and poetry. Always critiques or comments on rejected mss.
How to Contact: Send complete ms with a cover letter. Should include estimated word count, bio (500 words) and list of publications. Reports in 6 weeks. Send a disposable copy of ms. Simultaneous, reprint and electronic submissions OK. Sample copy for $8. Fiction guidelines for $1.

Payment: "Payment depends upon budget." Pays 1 contributor's copy.
Terms: Buys first rights or one-time rights.
Advice: Looks for "fiction that is realistic, creative. Fiction with a historic basis preferred. Short short stories have the best chance of being published in *Ghost Town*. Fiction written by young writers is needed." Write to *Ghost Town* for details about contests.

‡GLIMMER TRAIN STORIES, (II), Glimmer Train Press, #1205, 812 SW Washington St., Portland OR 97205. Editors: Susan Burmeister and Linda Davies. Magazine: 6¾ × 9¼; 168 pages; recycled, acid-free paper; 20 illustrations; 12 photographs. Quarterly. Estab. 1991. Circ. 21,000.
● The magazine also sponsors an annual short story contest for new writers. See listing in the Contests and Awards section.
Needs: Literary. Plans to publish special fiction issue or anthology. Receives 3,000 unsolicited mss/month. Accepts 10 mss/issue; 40 mss/year. Reads in January, April, July, October. Publishes ms 4-9 months after acceptance. Agented fiction 20%. Recently published work by Joyce Thompson, Richard Bausch, Stephen Dixon, Joyce Carol Oates, Mary McGarry Morris, Charles Baxter, Ann Beatty, Louise Erdrich. Length: 1,200 words minimum; 6,000 words maximum.
How to Contact: Send complete ms with a cover letter. Should include estimated word count and list of publications. Reports in 3 months. Send SASE (or IRC) for return or send a disposable copy of ms (with stamped postcard or envelope for notification). Simultaneous submissions OK. Sample copy for $9. Fiction guidelines for #10 SAE and 1 first-class stamp.
Payment: Pays $300 and 10 contributor's copies.
Terms: Pays on acceptance for first rights.

‡GLIMPSES MAGAZINE, Science Fiction, Fantasy & Horror, (II), Quick Glimpse Press, P.O. Box 751, Bowling Green OH 43402. Editors: Michael F. Haynes and Leslie Ann Conner. Magazine: 5½ × 8½; 72 pages; 20 lb. paper; 10 pt. glossy cover stock; illustrations. "We publish science fiction, fantasy and horror with adult sensibilities and themes, but not necessarily adult language or 'situations'." Quarterly. Estab. 1992. Circ. 500.
● The editor of *Glimpses* is a member of the Small Press Writers and Artists Organization.
Needs: Experimental, fantasy (science fantasy, sword and sorcery), horror, mystery/suspense (supernatural preferred), science fiction. Publishes special fiction issue or anthology. Receives 75-125 unsolicited mss/month. Accepts 10 mss/issue; 40 mss/year. Publishes ms 3-18 months after acceptance. Agented fiction 1%. Recently published work by Jacie Ragan, Don D'Ammassa, K.D. Wentworth. Length: 1,500-4,000 words preferred; 6,000 words maximum. Also publishes poetry and poetry chapbooks. Often critiques or comments on rejected mss.
How to Contact: Send complete ms with a cover letter. Should include estimated word count, brief bio and list of publications (also brief). Reports in 1-4 months. Send SASE (or IRC) for reply, return of ms or send a disposable copy of ms. No simultaneous submissions. Reprint submissions OK. Sample copy for $4.50. Fiction guidelines for #10 SAE and 1 first-class stamp. Reviews novels and short story collections.
Payment: Pays 1-2¢/word.
Terms: Pays on acceptance for first North American serial rights. Sends galleys to author.
Advice: "Manuscripts which stand out are those with traditional narrative styles but original plots. 'Experimental' fiction can be a thing of wonder and delight but too often is merely undecipherable writing and a weak plot."

GOLDEN ISIS MAGAZINE, (I, IV), P.O. Box 525 , Ft. Covington NY 12937. Editor: Gerina Dunwich. Magazine: Digest-sized; approx. 8 pages; 20 lb. stock; paper cover; illustrations. "*Golden Isis* is a mystical New Age literary magazine of occult fiction, Goddess-inspired poetry, Pagan artwork, Wiccan news, letters, occasional book reviews and classified ads." Quarterly. Estab. 1980. Circ. 4,000 (including 2 libraries).
Needs: Psychic/supernatural/occult, bizarre humor, fantasy and mystical Egyptian themes. "Please do not send us pornographic, religious, racist or sexist material. We will not consider stories written in present tense." Receives 100+ mss/month. Acquires 1-2 mss/issue; 4-8 mss/year. Published fiction by Rod R. Vick, Cary G. Osborne and Gypsy Electra; published many new writers within the last year. Length: 1,500 words maximum. Publishes short shorts. Also publishes poetry. Occasionally critiques rejected mss and often recommends other markets.

How to Contact: Send complete ms. SASE. Simultaneous submissions OK. Reports in up to 1 month. Sample copy $2.95. Fiction guidelines for #10 SAE and 1 first-class stamp (IRCs).

Payment: Payment varies from 1 contributor's copy to $10.

Terms: Pays on publication for first North American serial rights.

Advice: "Submit short fiction that is well-written, atmospheric and equipped with a good surprise ending. Originality is important. Quality writing is a must. Avoid clichés, poor grammar, predictable endings, unnecessary obscenity and run-on sentences, for these things will only bring you a fast rejection slip. Also publishes chapbooks: $5 reading fee (returned upon publication); length up to 50 pages; query first or send complete ms. Sample chapbook $5."

GOTTA WRITE NETWORK LITMAG, (I, II), Maren Publications, 612 Cobblestone Circle, Glenview IL 60025. Editor: Denise Fleischer. Fax: (708)296-7631 after 6 pm or call to set up Fax appointment. Magazine: 8½×11; 48+ pages; saddle-stapled ordinary paper; matte card or lighter weight cover stock; illustrations. Magazine "serves as an open forum to discuss new markets, successes and difficulties. Gives beginning writers their first break into print and promotionally supports established professional novelists." Distributed through the US, Canada and England. Semiannually. Estab. 1988. Circ. 200.

● In addition to publishing fiction, *Gotta Write Network Litmag* includes articles on writing techniques, small press market news, writers' seminar reviews, science fiction convention updates, and features a "Behind the Scenes" section in which qualified writers can conduct mail interviews with small press editors and professional writers. Writers interviewed in this manner in the past have included Frederik Pohl, Jody Lynn Nye, Gregory L. Norris.

Needs: Adventure, contemporary, fantasy, historical, humor/satire, literary, mainstream, prose poem, romance (gothic), science fiction (hard science, soft/sociological). "Currently seeking work with a clear-cut message or a twist at the very end. All genres accepted with the exception of excessive violence, sexual overtones or obscenity. Interested in seeing more offbeat stories. Open to life's challenges, science fiction/fantasy/horror." Receives 75-150 unsolicited mss per month. Accepts 1-6 mss per issue; up to 20 mss a year. Publishes mss 6-12 months after acceptance. Length: 10 pages maximum for short stories. Also publishes poetry. Recommends other markets.

How to Contact: Send complete ms with cover letter. Include "who you are, type of work submitted, previous publications and focused area of writing." Reports in 1-2 months (later during publication months). SASE. No simultaneous submissions or reprints. Sample copy for $5. Fiction guidelines for SASE (IRCs).

Payment: Pays for short stories, $10 or 2 contributor's copies.

Terms: Buys first North American serial rights.

Advice: "If I still think about the direction of the story after I've read it, I know it's good. Organize your thoughts on the plot and character development (qualities, emotions) before enduring 10 drafts. Make your characters come alive by giving them a personality and a background and then give them a little freedom. Let them take you through the story."

GRAFFITI OFF THE ASYLUM WALLS, An Illiterary Journal, (II, IV), P.O. Box 515, Fayetteville AR 72702-0515. Curator: Bryan Westbrook. Magazine: Digest-sized; 28 pages; colored paper cover; illustrations. "The stuff you would be afraid to show your mother, priest and/or psychiatrist. Humor preferred." Publishes "whenever enough material is available." Estab. 1992. Circ. 200.

Needs: Erotica, experimental, feminist, horror, humor/satire, psychic/supernatural/occult, political (anti-Republican). "Nothing pro-religious, pro-animal rights, anything high fallutin'." Recently published work by Robert W. Howington, Allen Renfro, Marc Swan. Length: 1-1,000 words. Also publishes literary essays and poetry. Often critiques or comments on rejected mss.

How to Contact: Send complete ms with cover letter. Should include bio (personal bio, not publication list). Reports within 2 months. Send SASE (IRCs) for reply, return of ms or send a disposable copy of ms. Simultaneous and reprint submissions OK. Sample copy for $3. Reviews novels and short story collections.

Payment: Pays 1 contributor's copy.

Terms: Acquires one-time rights.

Advice: "If it can make me laugh (not an easy task) or shock me (also a challenge) it will make it. Non-narrative stories have a harder time here. Forget everything you've ever read in school or been told in writing classes. I want to hear from the real you."

✸**GRAIN, (I, II)**, Saskatchewan Writers' Guild, Box 1154, Regina, Saskatchewan S4P 3B4 Canada. Editor: Geoffrey Ursell. Fiction Editor: Edna Alford. Literary magazine: 6×9; 144 pages; Chinook offset printing; chrome-coated stock; illustrations; some photos. "Fiction and poetry for people who enjoy high quality writing." Quarterly. Estab. 1973. Circ. 1,800-2,000.

• *Grain*, known as one of the most prestigious Canadian journals, won the Western Magazine Award for Fiction (in Canada) for both 1991 and 1992. The Saskatchewan Writers' Guild also sponsors the annual Short Grain Contest listed in the Contests and Awards section of this book.

Needs: Contemporary, experimental, literary, mainstream and prose poem. "No propaganda—only artistic/literary writing." No mss "that stay *within* the limits of conventions such as women's magazine type stories, science fiction; none that push a message." Receives 80 unsolicited fiction mss/month. Buys 8-12 mss/issue; 32-48 mss/year. Agented fiction approximately 1%. Recently published 2 short stories by emerging writers selected for the third *Journey Prize Anthology*. Length: "No more than 50 pages." Also publishes poetry. Occasionally critiques rejected mss.

How to Contact: Send complete ms with SAE, IRC and brief letter. "Let us know if you're just beginning to send out." No simultaneous submissions. Reports within 6 months on ms. Publishes ms an average of 4 months after acceptance. Sample copy $5.

Payment: Pays $30-100; 2 contributor's copies.

Terms: Pays on publication for one-time North American rights. "We expect acknowledgment if the piece is republished elsewhere."

Advice: "Submit a story to us that will deepen the imaginative experience of our readers. *Grain* has established itself as a first-class magazine of serious fiction. We receive submissions from around the world. If Canada is a foreign country to you, we ask that you *do not* use US postage stamps on your return envelope. If you live outside Canada and neglect the International Reply Coupons, we *will not* read or reply to your submission."

GRAND STREET, (II), 131 Varick St., #906, New York NY 10013. (212)807-6548. Fax (212)807-6544. Editor: Jean Stein. Magazine: 7×9; 220-240 pages; illustrations; photographs. "We seek new fiction and nonfiction of all types. We welcome experimental work. The only real criterion for acceptance is quality." Quarterly. Estab. 1981. Circ. 5,000.

Needs: Fiction, poetry, essays, translations. Receives 400 unsolicited mss/month. Buys 8 mss/issue; 32 mss/year. Time between acceptance of the ms and publication varies. Agented fiction 90%. Recently published work by David Foster Wallace, David Holper, Beth Nugent, Yehudit Katzir, Stephen Millhauser, David Gates, Duong Thu Huong, William T. Vollman. Length: 6,000 words average; 1,000 words minimum; 9,000 words maximum. Sometimes critiques or comments on rejected mss.

How to Contact: Send complete ms with a cover letter. Reports in 6 weeks on mss. Send SASE (or IRC) for return of the ms or a disposable copy of the ms. Simultaneous and electronic submissions OK. Sample copy for $12; $15 overseas and Canada.

Payment: Pays $250-1,200 and 2 contributor's copies. Additional copies at a reduced rate of $5.

Terms: Pays on publication for first North American serial rights. Sends galleys to author.

Advice: What magazine looks for is "hard to say, other than first-rate writing. We are fairly eclectic in our publishing policies. Look at a copy of the magazine first. That will give you a good idea of what we're looking for."

GRASSLANDS REVIEW, (I, II), Mini-Course—University of North Texas, N.T. Box 13706, Denton TX 76203. Editor: Laura B. Kennelly. Magazine: 6×9; 80 pages. *Grasslands Review* prints creative writing of all types; poetry, fiction, essays for a general audience. Semiannually. Estab. 1989. Circ. 300.

Needs: Adventure, contemporary, ethnic, experimental, fantasy, horror, humor/satire, literary, mystery/suspense, prose poem, regional, science fiction and western. Nothing pornographic or overtly political or religious. Accepts 5-8 mss/issue. Reads only in October and March. Publishes ms 6 months after acceptance. Recently published work by Therese Arceneaux, Paul Foreman, Antler, David Alpaugh, Bayla Winter. Length: 1,500 words average; 100-3,500 words. Publishes short shorts (100-150 words). Also publishes poetry. Sometimes critiques rejected mss and recommends other markets.

How to Contact: Send complete ms in October or March *only* with cover letter. No simultaneous submissions. Reports on mss in 3 months. SASE (IRCs). Sample copy for $2. May review novels or short story collections.

Payment: Pays in contributor's copies.

Terms: Acquires one-time rights. Publication not copyrighted.

Advice: "We are looking for fiction which leaves the reader with a strong feeling or impression — or a new perspective on life. The *Review* began as an in-class exercise to allow experienced creative writing students to learn how a little magazine is produced. We now wish to open it up to outside submissions so that our students can gain an understanding of how large the writing community is in the United States and so that they may have experience in working with other writers."

‡**GREAT RIVER REVIEW (II)**, 211 W. 7th, Winona MN 55987. Fiction Editor: Pamela Davies. Magazine: 6×8; 150 pages. Literary publication of fiction, poetry, art and book reviews. Semiannually. Estab. 1977.

 • *Great River Review* was honored as "Best Literary Magazine in Your State (Minnesota)" by *Clockwatch* at the 1993 Hemingway Days Festival.

Needs: "Quality fiction. No slick or sub-genre fiction." Prints 6-7 stories/issue. Receives approximately 40 unsolicited fiction mss each month. Published new writers within the last year. Length: 2,000-10,000 words.

How to Contact: Send complete mss with SASE (IRCs). Publishes mss 3-6 months after acceptance. Sample copy $6.

Advice: "Our editors seek work that reflects basic human values and that displays the care and craft at the core of good art." Priority to Midwestern writers and Midwestern settings.

GREEN EGG/HOW ABOUT MAGIC?, (IV), Church of All Worlds, Box 1542, Ukiah CA 95482. (707)485-7787. Editor: Diane Darling. Magazine: 8½×11; 72 pages; *H.A.M.* 12-16 pages; recycled paper; 4 color glossy cover; b&w illustrations; and photographs. "Magical fantasy, ecological, historical having to do with pagan civilizations." Quarterly. Estab. 1988. Circ. 8,000.

 • *Green Egg* won Silver Awards in 1990 and 1991 from the Wiccan Pagan Press Alliance.

Needs: Magical, Pagan and ecological themes: adventure, children's/juvenile (5-9 and 10-12 years), erotica, ethnic/multicultural, experimental, fantasy (science fantasy, sword and sorcery, children's fantasy), historical (general), humor/satire, psychic/supernatural/occult, religious/inspirational (Pagan). "No porn, mystery, sports, western, modern life, Christian, evil and painful." Upcoming themes: "Interreligious Dialogue" (Winter 1993); "Rites of Passage" (Spring 1994). Receives 2-3 unsolicited mss/month. Acquires 4 mss/year. Recently published work by Ivo Dominguez, Tim Waggoner, Starhawk, Daniel Blair Stewart, Bill Beattie. Length: 600 words minimum; 2,000 words maximum. Publishes short shorts. Length: 500 words. Also publishes poetry. Sometimes critiques or comments on rejected mss.

How to Contact: Send complete ms with cover letter. Should include estimated word count and bio (1 paragraph — 50 words). Reports in 2 months. Send SASE for reply, return of ms or send disposable copy of the ms. Include photo of author, if possible, and graphics, if available. Simultaneous, reprint and electronic submissions OK. Sample copy of *Green Egg* $6.75; sample copy of *H.A.M.* $2.25. Fiction guidelines for SAE and 1 first-class stamp or IRC. Reviews novels and short story collections.

Payment: Pays subscription to the magazine or contributor's copies.

Terms: Acquires one-time rights.

Advice: "Looks for economy of prose, artistic use of language, but most important is that the subject matter be germaine to our Pagan readership. Magical stories teaching ethics for survival as healthy biosphere heroines, human/animal/otherworld interface; transformative experiences; tidy plots; good grammar, spelling, punctuation; humor; classical deities and ethnic stuff."

GREEN MOUNTAINS REVIEW, (II), Johnson State College, Box A-58, Johnson VT 05656. (802)635-2356, ext. 339. Editor: Neil Shepard. Fiction Editor: Tony Whedon. Magazine: Digest-sized; 125-150 pages. Semiannually. Estab. 1975 (new series, 1987). Circ. 1,000.

 • *Green Mountains Review* received an NEA grant and a Vermont Council of the Arts grant for 1993.

Needs: Adventure, contemporary, experimental, humor/satire, literary, mainstream, serialized/excerpted novel, translations. Upcoming themes: "Our Winter/Spring 1994 issue will be devoted to women's issues, with an interview with Grace Paley." Receives 30 unsolicited mss/month. Accepts 5 mss/issue; 10 mss/year. Publishes ms 4-6 months after acceptance. Length: 25 pages maximum. Publishes short shorts. Also publishes literary criticism, poetry. Sometimes critiques rejected mss.

How to Contact: Send complete ms with cover letter. Reports in 1 month on queries; 3-4 months on mss. SASE (IRCs). Simultaneous submissions OK. Sample copy for $7.50.
Payment: Pays in contributor's copies.
Terms: Acquires first North American serial rights. Sends galleys to author upon request.
Advice: "The editors are open to a wide spectrum of styles and subject matter, as is apparent from a look at the list of fiction writers who have published in its pages: Walter Wetherell, Julia Alvarez, Ellen Lesser, Susan Hubbard, Phillip Kimball and Gladys Swan. One issue was devoted to Vermont fiction writers, and another issued filled with new writing from the People's Republic of China. The Fall/Winter 1992-93 issue was devoted to multicultural writing."

✦GREEN'S MAGAZINE, Fiction for the Family, (II), Green's Educational Publications, Box 3236, Regina, Saskatchewan S4P 3H1 Canada. Editor: David Green. Magazine: 5¼×8; 100 pages; 20 lb. bond paper; matte cover stock; line illustrations. Publishes "solid short fiction suitable for family reading." Quarterly. Estab. 1972.
Needs: Adventure, fantasy, humor/satire, literary, mainstream, mystery/suspense and science fiction. No erotic or sexually explicit fiction. Receives 20-30 mss/month. Accepts 10-12 mss/issue; 40-50 mss/year. Publishes ms within 3-6 months of acceptance. Agented fiction 2%. Published work by Solomon Pogarsky, Ann Beacham, Hélène Scheffler-Mason. Length: 2,500 words preferred; 1,500 words minimum; 4,000 words maximum. Also publishes poetry. Sometimes critiques rejected mss and recommends other markets.
How to Contact: Send complete ms. "Cover letters welcome but not necessary." Reports in 2 months. SASE. "Must include international reply coupons." No simultaneous submissions. Sample copy for $4. Fiction guidelines for #10 SAE and international reply coupon. Reviews novels and short story collections.
Payment: Pays in contributor's copies.
Terms: Acquires first North American serial rights.

GREENSBORO REVIEW, (II), University of North Carolina at Greensboro, Dept. of English, Greensboro NC 27412. (919)334-5459. Editor: Jim Clark. Fiction Editor: Julianna Baggott. Fiction editor changes each year. Send future mss to the editor. Magazine: 6×9; approximately 136 pages; 60 lb. paper; 65 lb. cover. Literary magazine featuring fiction and poetry for readers interested in contemporary literature. Semiannually. Circ. 600.
Needs: Contemporary and experimental. Accepts 6-8 mss/issue, 12-16 mss/year. Published work by Jill McCorkle, Robert Morgan and Peter Taylor. Published new writers within the last year. Length: 7,500 words maximum.
How to Contact: Send complete ms with SASE (IRCs). No simultaneous submissions. Unsolicited manuscripts must arrive by September 15 to be considered for the winter issue and by February 15 to be considered for the summer issue. Manuscripts arriving after those dates may be held for the next consideration. Reports in 2 months. Sample copy for $4.
Payment: Pays in contributor's copies.
Terms: Acquires first North American serial rights.
Advice: "We want to see the best being written regardless of theme, subject or style. Recent stories from *The Greensboro Review* have been included in *The Best American Short Stories*, *Prize Stories: The O. Henry Awards*, *New Stories from the South* and *Best of the West*, anthologies recognizing the finest short stories being published."

GRUE MAGAZINE, (II, IV), Hell's Kitchen Productions, Box 370, New York NY 10108. Editor: Peggy Nadramia. Magazine: 5½×8½; 96 pages; 60 lb. paper; 10 pt. C1S film laminate cover; illustrations; photos. "Quality short fiction centered on horror and dark fantasy—new traditions in the realms of the gothic and the macabre for horror fans well read in the genre, looking for something new and different, as well as horror novices looking for a good scare." Triannually. Estab. 1985.
Needs: Horror, psychic/supernatural/occult. Receives 250 unsolicited fiction mss/month. Accepts 10 mss/issue; 25-30 mss/year. Publishes ms 1-2 years after acceptance. Published work by Thomas Ligotti, Joe R. Lansdale, Don Webb; published new writers within the last year. Length: 4,000 words average; 6,500 words maximum. Sometimes critiques rejected ms and recommends other markets.
How to Contact: Send complete ms with cover letter. "I like to hear where the writer heard about *Grue*, his most recent or prestigious sales, and maybe a word or two about himself." Reports in 3 weeks on queries; 4 months on mss. SASE (IRCs) for ms. Sample copy $4.50. Fiction guidelines for #10 SAE and 1 first-class stamp.

Payment: Pays 2 contributor's copies plus ½¢ per word.
Terms: Pays on publication for first North American serial rights.
Advice: "Editors actually vie for the work of the better writers, and if your work is good, you will sell it—you just have to keep sending it out. But out of the 250 mss I read in September, maybe three of them will be by writers who cared enough to make their plots as interesting as possible, their characterizations believable, their settings unique, and who took the time to do the rewrites and polish their prose. Remember that readers of *Grue* are mainly seasoned horror fans, and *not* interested or excited by a straight vampire, werewolf or ghost story—they'll see all the signs, and guess where you're going long before you get there. Throw a new angle on what you're doing; put it in a new light. How? Well, what scares *you*? What's *your* personal phobia or anxiety? When the writer is genuinely, emotionally involved with his subject matter, and is totally honest with himself and his reader, then we can't help being involved, too, and that's where good writing begins and ends."

GULF COAST, A Journal of Literature & Art, (II), Dept. of English, University of Houston, 4800 Calhoun Rd., Houston TX 77204-5641. (713)749-3431. Contact: Fiction Editors. Editors change each year. Magazine: 6×9; 108 pages; stock paper, gloss cover; illustrations and photographs. "Fiction on the cusp for the literary-minded." Estab. 1984. Circ. 1,500.
Needs: Excerpted novel, contemporary, ethnic, experimental, humor/satire, literary, regional, translations, special interest: *translations* from emerging literatures, South America, Africa, China, etc. No children's, religious/inspirational. Receives 40 unsolicited mss/month. Accepts 5-6 mss/issue; 6-8 mss/year. Publishes ms 6 months-1 year after acceptance. Agented fiction 5%. Published work by Larry Woiwode, John Hawkes and Oscar Hijuelos. Length: No limit. Publishes short shorts. Sometimes critiques rejected mss.
How to Contact: Send complete manuscript with cover letter. "As few words as possible; please notify us if the submission is being considered elsewhere." Reports in 1-3 months. Simultaneous submissions OK ("but prefer not to"). Sample copy for $7, 9×12 SAE and 4 first-class stamps. Fiction guidelines for #10 SAE and 1 first-class stamp (IRCs).
Payment: Pays contributor's copies.
Terms: Acquires one-time rights.
Advice: "We are most intrigued by those who take risks, experiment with language."

GULF STREAM MAGAZINE, (II), Florida International University, English Dept., North Miami Campus, N. Miami FL 33181. (305)940-5599. Editor: Lynne Barrett. Associate Editor: Chris Gleason. Assistant Editor: Blythe Nobleman. Editors change every 1-2 years. Magazine: 5½×8½; 96 pages; bond paper; laminate (1 color, b&w) cover; cover illustrations only; cover photographs only. "We publish *good quality*—fiction, nonfiction and poetry for a predominately literary market." Semiannually. Estab. 1989. Circ. 500.
Needs: Contemporary, literary, mainstream. Nothing "radically experimental." Plans special issues. Receives 80 unsolicited mss/month. Acquires 5 mss/issue; 10 mss/year. Does not read mss during the summer. Publishes ms 6 weeks-3 months after acceptance. Published work by Alan Cheuse, Ann Hood. Length: 5,000 words average; 7,500 words maximum. Publishes short shorts. Also publishes poetry. Sometimes critiques rejected mss.
How to Contact: Send complete manuscript with cover letter including "previous publications/short bio." Reports in 3 months. SASE (IRCs). Simultaneous submissions OK "if noted." Sample copy $4. Free fiction guidelines.
Payment: Pays subscription and 2 contributor's copies.
Terms: Acquires first North American serial rights.
Advice: "Looks for good concise writing—well plotted; interesting characters."

GYPSY, Die Sympathische Alternative, (II), Vergin Press, 10708 Gay Brewer, El Paso TX 79935. (915)592-3701. Editors: Belinda Subraman and S. Ramnath. Magazine: 8½×11; 84 pages; 20-60 lb. offset paper; 60 lb. card cover; drawings; sometimes photographs. "Quality writing, occasionally limited to theme, for the literary and artistic community." Semiannually. Estab. 1984. Circ. 1,000.
 • Editor Belinda Subraman was interviewed for the 1993 *Novel & Short Story Writer's Market*.
Needs: Experimental, feminist, literary, serialized novel, translations. Receives 100 unsolicited fiction mss/month. Accepts 2-4 mss/issue; 6-10 mss/year. Publishes ms 1-8 months after acceptance. Length: "open, but short is better—perhaps 500-2,500 words." Publishes short shorts. Also publishes literary essays, literary criticism, poetry. Sometimes critiques or comments on rejected mss. Sometimes recommends other markets.

How to Contact: Query first or send complete ms with cover letter. Reports in 2-4 months. SASE. Reprint submissions sometimes OK. May accept simultaneous submissions if noted, but "prefer not to." Sample copies for $7. Fiction guidelines for #10 SAE and 1 first-class stamp (IRCs).
Payment: Pays in contributor's copies.
Terms: Acquires one-time rights.

HABERSHAM REVIEW, (I, II), Piedmont College, P.O. Box 10, Demorest GA 30535. (404)778-2215. Editors: David L. Greene, Lisa Hodgens Lumpkin. Magazine. "General literary magazine with a regional (Southeastern U.S.) focus for a literate audience." Semiannually. Estab. 1991.
Needs: Contemporary, experimental, literary, mainstream, regional. Receives 100 unsolicited mss/ month. Acquires 6-10 mss/issue. Publishes short shorts. Sometimes critiques rejected mss.
How to Contact: Send complete ms with cover letter. Reports in 6 months on mss. SASE (IRCs). No simultaneous submissions. Sample copy for $6.
Payment: Pays in contributor's copies.
Terms: Acquires first rights.

HALF TONES TO JUBILEE, (II), English Dept. Pensacola Junior College, 1000 College Blvd., Pensacola FL 32504. (904)484-1416. Editors: Allan Peterson and Walter Spara. Magazine: 6×9; approx. 100 pages; 70 lb. laid stock; 80 lb. cover. "No theme, all types published." Annually. Estab. 1985. Circ. 500.
Needs: Open. Receives 4-6 unsolicited mss/month. Accepts approx. 6 mss/issue. "We publish in September." Recently published work by Rachel Cann, Dusty Sklar, Jorie Green, Mark Spencer. Length: 1,500 words average. Publishes short shorts. Also publishes poetry. Sometimes critiques rejected mss and recommends other markets.
How to Contact: Send complete ms with cover letter. SASE (IRCs). Sample copy $4. Free fiction guidelines.
Payment: Pays 2 contributor's copies.
Terms: Acquires one-time rights.

HARD ROW TO HOE DIVISION, (II), Misty Hill Press, P.O. Box 541-I, Healdsburg CA 95448. (707)433-9786. Editor: Joe Armstrong. Newspaper: 8½×11; 12 pages; 60 lb. white paper; illustrations and photos. "Book reviews, short story and poetry of rural USA including environmental and nature subjects." Triannually. Estab. 1982. Circ. 150.
● See the listing for Misty Hill Press in the Small Press section of this book. *Hard Row to Hoe* was called "one of 10 best literary newsletters in the U.S." by *Small Press* magazine in their Summer 1992 issue.
Needs: Rural America. Receives 8-10 unsolicited mss/month. Acquires 1 ms/issue; 3-4 mss/year. Publishes ms 6-9 months after acceptance. Length: 1,500 words average; 2,000-2,200 words maximum. Publishes short shorts. Sometimes critiques rejected mss and tries to recommend other markets.
How to Contact: Send complete ms with cover letter. Reports in 3-4 weeks on mss. SASE. Simultaneous submissions OK. Sample copy for $2. Fiction guidelines for legal-size SAE and 1 first-class stamp (IRCs).
Payment: Pays 3 contributor's copies.
Terms: Acquires one-time rights.
Advice: "Be certain the subject fits the special need."

HARDBOILED, (I,II), Gryphon Publications, Box 209, Brooklyn NY 11228-0209. Editor: Gary Lovisi. Magazine: Digest-sized; 100 pages; offset paper; color cover; illustrations. Publishes "cutting edge, hard, noir fiction with impact! Query on nonfiction and reviews." Quarterly. Estab. 1988.
Needs: Mystery/suspense (private eye, police procedural, noir). Receives 40-60 mss/month. Buys 20-25 mss/year. Publishes ms within 6 months-2 years of acceptance. Recently published work by Andrew Vachss, Joe Lansdale, Richard Lupoff, Frank Grubber, Eugene Izzi; published many new writers within the last year. Length: 2,000 words minimum; 4,000 words maximum. Sometimes critiques rejected mss and recommends other markets.
How to Contact: Query first or send complete ms with cover letter. Query with SASE (IRCs) only on anything over 3,000-4,000 words. No full-length novels. Reports in 2 weeks on queries; 2-6 weeks on mss. SASE. Simultaneous submissions OK, but query first. Sample copy $6.
Payment: Pays $5-50 and 2 contributor's copies.
Terms: Pays on publication for first North American serial rights. Copyright reverts to author.

HAUNTS, Tales of Unexpected Horror and the Supernatural, (II, IV), Nightshade Publications, Box 3342, Providence RI 02906. (401)781-9438. Editor: Joseph K. Cherkes. Magazine: 6×9 digest; 80-100 pages; 50 lb. offset paper; perfect-bound; pen and ink illustrations. "We are committed to publishing only the finest fiction in the genres of horror, fantasy and the supernatural from both semi-pro and established writers. We are targeted towards the 18-35 age bracket interested in tales of horror and the unknown." Quarterly. Plans special fiction issue. Estab. 1984. Circ. 1,200.
Needs: Fantasy, horror, psychic/supernatural/occult. No pure adventure, explicit sex, or blow-by-blow dismemberment. Receives 700-750 unsolicited fiction mss/month. Buys 10-12 mss/issue; 50-75 mss/year. Published work by Mike Hurley, Kevin J. Anderson, Frank Ward; published new writers within the last year. Length: 3,500 words average; 1,000 words minimum; 8,500 words maximum. Critiques rejected mss and recommends other markets when possible.
How to Contact: Query first. "Cover letters are a nice way to introduce oneself to a new editor." Open to submissions January 1 to June 1, inclusive. Reports in 2-3 weeks on queries; 3-4 months on mss. SASE (IRCs) for query. Accepts magnetic media (IBM PC-MS/DOS Ver 2.0 or higher), and most major word processing formats. Sample copy $3.95 plus $1 postage and handling. Fiction guidelines for #10 SASE.
Payment: Pays $5-50 (subject to change), contributor's copies, charge for extras.
Terms: Pays on publication for first North American serial rights.
Advice: "Follow writers' guidelines closely. They are a good outline of what your publisher looks for in fiction. If you think you've got the 'perfect' manuscript, go over it again—carefully. Check to make sure you've left no loose ends before sending it out. Keep your writing *concise*. If your story is rejected, don't give up. Try to see where the story failed. This way you can learn from your mistakes. Remember, success comes to those who persist. We plan to open to advertising on a limited basis, also plan a media campaign to increase subscriptions and distributed sales."

HAWAII PACIFIC REVIEW, (II), Hawaii Pacific University, 1060 Bishop St., Honolulu HI 96813. (808)544-0214. Editor: Elizabeth Fischel. Magazine: 6×9; 100-150 pages; quality paper; glossy cover; illustrations and original artwork. "The *Review* seeks to reflect the cultural diversity that is the hallmark of Hawaii Pacific University. Consequently, we welcome material on a wide variety of themes and we encourage experimental styles and narrative techniques. Categories: fiction, poetry, personal essays." Annually. Estab. "nationwide in 1988."
Needs: Adventure, contemporary, ethnic, experimental, fantasy, humor/satire, literary, mainstream, regional, science fiction, translations. No romance, confessions, religious or juvenile. Receives approx. 50 unsolicited fiction mss/month. Accepts 4-8 mss/issue. Deadline for the Spring annual issue is January 1. Does not read in summer. Publishes ms 3-12 months after acceptance. Published new writers within the last year. Length: 5,000 words maximum. Publishes short shorts. Also publishes literary essays, poetry. Sometimes critiques rejected mss or recommends other markets.
How to Contact: Send complete manuscript with cover letter, which should include a brief bio. Reports in 3 months. SASE. Simultaneous submissions OK. Fiction guidelines for #10 SAE and 1 first-class stamp (IRCs).
Payment: Pays in contributor's copies.
Terms: Acquires first North American serial rights. Rights revert to author upon publication.
Advice: "As more publication opportunities arise and more writers become visible, a new writer must find fresh, innovative ways of storytelling to truly stand out and move the genre forward. We look specifically for fiction that presents a strong voice—be it cultural, ethnic, etc."

HAWAII REVIEW, (II), University of Hawaii English Dept., 1733 Donaghho Rd., Honolulu HI 96822. (808)956-3030. Editor: Carrie Hoshino. Magazine: 6½×9½; 150-170 pages; illustrations; photos. "We publish short stories as well as poetry and reviews by new and experienced writers. As an international literary journal, we hope to reflect the idea that cultural diversity is of universal interest." For residents of Hawaii and non-residents from the continental US and abroad. Triannually. Plans special fiction issue on environmental concerns. Estab. 1972. Circ. 5,000.
Needs: Contemporary, ethnic, experimental, humor/satire, literary, prose poem, regional and translations. Receives 50-75 mss/month. Buys no more than 40 mss/issue; 130 mss/year. Published work by William Pitt Root, Ursule Molinaro and Ian Macmillan; published new writers within the last year. Length: 4,000 words average; no minimum; 8,000 words maximum. Occasionally critiques mss. Also publishes poetry. Recommends other markets.

How to Contact: Send complete ms with SASE (IRCs). Reports in 3-4 months on mss. Sample copy for $5. Fiction guidelines for SASE.

Payment: Payment "varies depending upon funds budgeted. Last year, we paid $35-70 per story;" 2 contributor's copies.

Terms: Pays on publication for all rights. Sends galleys to author upon request. After publication, copyright reverts to author upon request.

HAYDEN'S FERRY REVIEW, (II), Arizona State University, Matthews Center ASU, Tempe AZ 85287-1502. (602)965-1243. Managing Editor: Salima Keegan. Editors change every 1-2 years. Magazine: 6 × 9; 128 pages; fine paper; illustrations and photographs. "Contemporary material by new and established writers for a varied audience." Semiannually. Estab. 1986. Circ. 600.

● Work from *Hayden's Ferry Review* was selected for inclusion in the *Pushcart Prize* anthology in 1992.

Needs: Contemporary, ethnic, experimental, fantasy, feminist, gay, historical (general), humor/satire, literary, mainstream, prose poem, psychic/supernatural/occult, regional, romance (contemporary), science fiction, senior citizen/retirement. Possible special fiction issue. Receives 150 unsolicited mss/month. Accepts 5 mss/issue; 10 mss/year. Publishes mss 3-4 months after acceptance. Published work by Raymond Carver, Ken Kesey, Rita Dove, Chuck Rosenthal and Rick Bass. Length: No preference. Publishes short shorts. Also publishes literary essays.

How to Contact: Send complete ms with cover letter. No simultaneous submissions. Reports in 2-3 months from deadline on mss. SASE (IRCs). Sample copy for $6. Fiction guidelines for SAE.

Payment: Pays 2 contributor's copies.

Terms: Buys first North American serial rights. Sends galleys to author.

HEART ATTACK MAGAZINE, Myocardial Infarction Horror, (I, IV), Coronary Press, 518 Lowell St., Methuen MA 01844. (508)685-2342. Co-editors: David Gordon, Michael Thomas Dillon. Magazine: 8½ × 11; 60-80 pages; 20 lb. bond paper; card stock/color gloss cover; illustrations; photographs. "Horror, sci-fi, dark fantasy. Mostly publish horror. Humor is good too (especially black). Audience ranges from 16 years-70 years." Quarterly. Estab. 1991. Circ. 1,000.

● *Heart Attack* was nominated by the Small Press Writers and Artists Organization as "Best New Magazine/Editor" in 1991.

Needs: Erotica, fantasy (science fantasy), horror, humor/satire, mystery/suspense (horror slant), psychic/supernatural/occult, romance (gothic), science fiction (hard science, soft/sociological). "All stories should have a horror slant. No pornography or racism but sex and profanity is okay." Receives 150-200 unsolicited mss/month. Acquires 10-12 mss/issue; 48 mss/year. Publishes ms 6-10 months after acceptance. Agented fiction 5%. Published work by John B. Rosenman, Brad J. Boucher, Marthayn Pelegrimas, Gregory L. Norris. Length: 2,000 words preferred; 150 words minimum; 3,000 words maximum. Publishes short shorts. Length: 400 words. Also publishes literary criticism, poetry. *Always* critiques or comments on rejected mss.

How to Contact: Send complete ms with cover letter or send for guidelines. Include estimated word count, bio (2 paragraphs), list of publications (if any). Reports in 1 week on queries; 4-6 weeks on mss. Send SASE for reply, return of mss or disposable copy of the ms. No simultaneous submissions. Sample copy for $4. Fiction guidelines for #10 SAE and 1 first-class stamp or IRC. Reviews novels and short story collections. Send published book (horror and sf only) review copies to Brad Boucher, P.O. Box 750, E. Hampstead NH 03826.

Payment: Pays 1 contributor's copy.

Terms: Acquires first North American serial rights.

Advice: Looks for "good plot, constant suspense, detail, enjoyable characters. Traditional horror (monsters, aliens, etc.) are okay as long as it is written well. Personally, friendliness is important, but also professionalism. Know that the editor is the boss even if you don't agree. Remember that an editor's policy is mainly built on his opinion. Take an editor's critique into consideration, but don't accept it as *law*, unless it is grammatical errors. Just be kind and professional and able to accept constructive criticism. Most manuscripts lately have seemed to be lacking in great suspense. We like to be captivated almost immediately, but also to be held there throughout the story. Also, we don't see enough sci-fi, dark fantasy or dark humor. All we get mostly is horror."

THE HEARTLANDS TODAY, (II), The Firelands Writing Center, Firelands College of BGSU, Huron OH 44839. (419)433-5560. Editors: Larry Smith and Nancy Dunham. Magazine: 6 × 9; 160 pages; b&w illustrations; 25-30 photographs. Material must be set in the Midwest . . . prefer material that reveals life in the Midwest today for a general, literate audience. Annually. Estab. 1991.

Needs: Ethnic, humor, literary, mainstream, regional (Midwest). Upcoming theme: "Community" (Midwest location). Receives 15 unsolicited mss/month. Buys 6 mss/issue. Does not read mss August-December. Publishes ms 6 months after acceptance. Published work of Wendell Mayo, Tony Tomassi, Gloria Bowman. Length: 4,500 words maximum. Also publishes literary essays, poetry. Sometimes critiques rejected mss and recommends other markets.

How to Contact: Send complete ms with cover letter. Reports in 2 months on mss. SASE for ms, not needed for query. Simultaneous submissions OK, if noted. Sample copy for $5.

Payment: Pays $20-25 and 2 contributor's copies.

Terms: Pays on publication for first rights.

Advice: "We look for writing that connects on a human level, one that moves us with its truth and opens our vision of the world. If writing is a great escape for you, don't bother with us. We're in it for the joy, beauty or truth of the art. We look for a straight, honest voice dealing with human experiences. We do not define the Midwest, we hope to be a document of the Midwest. If you feel you are writing from the Midwest, send. We look first at the quality of the writing."

HEAVEN BONE, (IV), Heaven Bone Press, Box 486, Chester NY 10918. (914)469-9018. Editors: Steven Hirsch, Kirpal Gordon. Magazine: $8^{1}/_{2} \times 11$; 49-78 pages; 60 lb. recycled offset paper; full color cover; computer clip art, graphics, line art, cartoons, halftones and photos scanned in tiff format. "New consciousness, expansive, fine literary, earth and nature, spiritual path. We use current reviews, essays on spiritual and esoteric topics, creative stories and fantasy. Also: reviews of current poetry releases and expansive literature." Readers are "spiritual seekers, healers, poets, artists, musicians, students." Semiannually. Estab. 1987. Circ. 2,500.

Needs: Experimental, fantasy, psychic/supernatural/occult, esoteric/scholarly, regional, religious/inspirational, spiritual. "No violent, thoughtless or exploitive fiction." Receives 45-110 unsolicited mss/month. Accepts 5-15 mss/issue; 12-30 mss/year. Publishes ms 2 weeks-10 months after acceptance. Published work by Fielding Dawson, Janine Pommy-Vega, Charles Bukowski, Marge Piercy; published new writers within the last year. Length: 3,500 words average; 1,200 words minimum; 6,000 words maximum. Publishes short shorts. Also publishes literary essays, literary criticism, poetry. Sometimes critiques rejected mss and may recommend other markets.

How to Contact: Send complete ms with cover letter, which should include short bio of recent activities. Reports in 2 weeks on queries; 2 weeks-6 months on mss. SASE (IRCs). Reprint submissions OK. Accepts electronic submissions via "Apple Mac versions of Macwrite, Microsoft Word v. 5.1 or Writenow v. 3.0." Sample copy $6. Fiction guidelines free. Reviews novels and short story collections.

Payment: Pays in contributor's copies; charges for extras.

Terms: Acquires first North American serial rights. Sends galleys to author, if requested.

Advice: "Our fiction needs are temperamental, so please query first before submitting. We prefer shorter fiction. Do not send first drafts to test them on us. Please refine and polish your work before sending. Always include SASE. We are looking for the unique, unusual and excellent."

‡HELIOCENTRIC NET, (II), Three-Stones Publications Ltd., P.O. Box 68817, Seattle WA 98168-0817. Editor: Lisa Jean Bothell. Magazine: $8^{1}/_{2} \times 11$; 40 pages; 20 lb. offset white paper; 67 lb. cardstock cover; illustrations. "Horror/dark fantasy fiction; poetry and publishing-oriented nonfiction. Adult audience. Philosophy—we look for horrific/dark fantasy themes based on boundary-pushing experiences and ideas—paranormal, supernatural, mystical, mythical. Eclectic." Quarterly. Estab. 1992.

● The editor is a member of the Small Press Writers and Artists Organization. In addition to the magazine, Three-Stones Publications also publishes a quarterly newsletter.

Needs: Experimental (horror and dark fantasy), feminist (constructive only), horror, psychic/supernatural/occult, romance (dark fantasy related), science fiction (horrific). "No nihilistic horror; no erotica, pornography, intentionally discriminatory." Plans to publish chapbooks. Receives 75-100 unsolicited mss/month. Publishes mss 5 months maximum after acceptance. Recently published work by D.F. Lewis, David Addleman, Greg Norris, Jeffrey Stadt. Length: 2,000 words preferred; 2,500 words maximum. Publishes short shorts. Also publishes poetry. Always comments on rejected mss.

How to Contact: Send complete ms with a cover letter. Query first on all reprint proposals. Should include estimated word count, bio (50 or so words) list of publications, mention where you heard of *Heliocentric Net*. Reports in 2-3 weeks on queries; 3-5 weeks on mss. Send SASE (or IRCs) for reply, return of ms or send a disposable copy of ms. Simultaneous, reprint and electronic submissions OK (with query). Sample copy for $3.50 and 2 first-class stamps for copy of newsletter only. Fiction guidelines for SAE and 1 first-class stamp. Reviews novels, magazines and short story collections.

Payment: Acquires 1 contributor's copy.

Terms: Buys first North American serial, one-time rights or as author requests. Sends galleys to author (if author sends SASE).

Advice: "We look for fiction with a constructive outlook and with ideas of real depth and insight, strong plotlines, realistic and believable characters, and complete story boundaries and resolutions. Don't be afraid to send thoughtful and intelligent horror/dark fantasy as opposed to the common action, shock value, and nihilistic horror that is flooding the market. Ms stands out when readers *care about and empathize* with characters, and when concept is unique."

🍁**HERSPECTIVES, The Dialogue of the Common Woman for Wise Women, Strong Women, Healers, & Peacemakers, (II, IV),** Box 2047, Squamish, British Columbia V0N, 3G0 Canada. (604)892-5723. Editor: Mary E. Billy. Magazine: 8½×11; 50-60 pages; bond paper; b&w illustrations and photographs. "Feminist; ecology; spirituality; poetry; articles; cartoons; graphics; letters; short short fiction for women. Quarterly. Estab. 1989. Circ. 500.

Needs: Confession, contemporary, erotica, ethnic, experimental, fantasy, feminist, humor/satire, juvenile, lesbian, mainstream, prose poem, senior citizen/retirement, young adult/teen (10-18 years) (for women). "No sexist, racist, homophobic; prefer positive perspective." Receives 3 unsolicited mss/month. Accepts 2-4 mss/issue; 6 mss/year. Publishes ms 3-24 months after acceptance. Length: open. Publishes short shorts. Sometimes critiques rejected mss.

How to Contact: Send complete ms with cover letter. Include "where you heard about or read *Herspectives*, international coupons for ms return if outside of Canada. Reports in 2-6 weeks. SASE. Simultaneous and reprint submissions OK. Sample copy for $5. Writer's guidelines for #10 SAE and 1 first-class Canadian stamp or IRC.

Payment: Pays 1 contributor's copy.

Terms: Acquires first rights. Not copyrighted.

Advice: Looks for "clean tight writing, ring of honesty and guts, humor, a positive attitude without sounding Pollyanaish. Absolutely no violence."

HIGH PLAINS LITERARY REVIEW, (II), Suite 250, 180 Adams Street, Suite 250, Denver CO 80206. (303)320-6828. Editor-in-Chief: Robert O. Greer, Jr. Magazine: 6×9; 135 pages; 70 lb. paper; heavy cover stock. "The *High Plains Literary Review* publishes poetry, fiction, essays, book reviews and interviews. The publication is designed to bridge the gap between high-caliber academic quarterlies and successful commercial reviews." Triannually. Estab. 1986. Circ. 1,100.

Needs: Most pressing need: outstanding essays, serious fiction, contemporary, humor/satire, literary, mainstream, regional. No true confessions, romance, pornographic, excessive violence. Receives approximately 300 unsolicited mss/month. Buys 4-6 mss/issue; 12-18 mss/year. Publishes ms usually 6 months after acceptance. Published work by Richard Currey, Joyce Carol Oates, Nancy Lord and Rita Dove; published new writers within the last year. Length: 4,200 words average; 1,500 words minimum; 8,000 words maximum; prefers 3,000-6,000 words. Also publishes literary essays, literary criticism, poetry. Occasionally critiques rejected mss. Sometimes recommends other markets.

How to Contact: Send complete ms with cover letter, which should include brief publishing history. Reports in 6 weeks. SASE (IRCs). Simultaneous submissions OK. Sample copy for $4.

Payment: Pays $5/page for prose and 2 contributor's copies.

Terms: Pays on publication for first North American serial rights. "Copyright reverts to author upon publication." Sends copy-edited proofs to the author.

Advice: "*HPLR* publishes *quality* writing. Send us your very best material. We will read it carefully and either accept it promptly, recommend changes or return it promptly. Do not start submitting your work until you learn the basic tenets of the game including some general knowledge about how to develop characters and plot and how to submit a manuscript. I think the most important thing for any new writer interested in the short story form is to have a voracious appetite for short fiction, to see who and what is being published, and to develop a personal style."

 The maple leaf symbol before a listing indicates a Canadian publisher.

HILL AND HOLLER: Southern Appalachian Mountains, (II), Seven Buffaloes Press, Box 249, Big Timber MT 59011. Editor: Art Cuelho. Magazine: 5½ × 8½; 80 pages; 70 lb. offset paper; 80 lb. cover stock; illustrations; photos rarely. "I use mostly rural Appalachian material: poems and stories. Some folklore and humor. I am interested in heritage, especially in connection with the farm." Annually. Published special fiction issue. Estab. 1983. Circ. 750.

• Art Cuelho of Seven Buffaloes Press also edits *Azorean Express, Black Jack* and *Valley Grapevine* listed in this book. See also the listing for the publishing company for more information.

Needs: Contemporary, ethnic, humor/satire, literary, regional, rural America farm. "I don't have any prejudices in style, but I don't like sentimental slant. Deep feelings in literature are fine, but they should be portrayed with tact and skill." Receives 10 unsolicited mss/month. Accepts 4-6 mss/issue. Publishes ms 6 months-1 year after acceptance. Length: 2,000-3,000 words average. Also publishes short shorts of 500-1,000 words.

How to Contact: Query first. Reports in 2 weeks on queries. SASE (IRCs). Sample copy $6.75.

Payment: Pays in contributor's copies; charge for extras.

Terms: Acquires first North American serial rights "and permission to reprint if my press publishes a special anthology." Sometimes sends galleys to author.

Advice: "In this Southern Appalachian rural series I can be optimistic about fiction. Appalachians are very responsive to their region's literature. I have taken work by beginners that had not been previously published. Be sure to send a double-spaced clean manuscript and SASE. I have the only rural press in North America; maybe even in the world. So perhaps we have a bond in common if your roots are rural."

HIS GARDEN MAGAZINE, (II, IV), 216 N. Vine St., Kewanee IL 61443. (309)852-0332. Editor: Margi L.Washburn. Magazine: 8½ × 11; 32 pages; 20 lb. white paper; 20 lb. color cover; illustrations. "*His Garden* is an inspirational publication. I like to print a good variety of uplifting material. If I can bring a smile or make someone aware of the good things in life, that will be my goal." Triannually. Estab. 1992. Circ. 150.

Needs: Fantasy (spiritual warfare). No erotica, horror, science fiction, mystery. Receives 35+ unsolicited mss/month. Buys 3-5 mss/issue; 10-15 mss/year. Publishes ms 4-6 months after acceptance. Recently published work by Lois Hayn, Nathaniel Johnson, Jr. Length: 250 words minimum; 2,500 words maximum. Publishes short shorts. Also publishes poetry. Always critiques or comments on rejected mss.

How to Contact: Send complete ms with cover letter. Should include estimated word count, bio and list of publications. Reports in 3 weeks on queries; 2 months on mss. Send SASE (IRCs) for reply, return of ms or send a disposable copy of the ms. Simultaneous and reprint submissions OK. Sample copy for $3.50. Fiction guidelines for SASE. Reviews novels and short story collections.

Payment: Pays $5 and 1 contributor's copy. Additional copies $2.

Terms: Buys one-time rights. Not copyrighted.

Advice: "I need to feel emotion of some kind. If a writer can make me care what happens to the character(s) in a story, I'll consider acceptance. I love subtle messages that really touch my heart. I'd like to see more written about how our changing world has affected our values, our children, the family and the elderly."

HOB-NOB (I), 994 Nissley Rd., Lancaster PA 17601. Editor/Publisher: Mildred K. Henderson. Magazine: 8½ × 11; 76+ pages; 20 lb. bond paper; 20 lb. (or heavier) cover stock; b&w illustrations; few photos. "*Hob-Nob* is a small (one-person), amateur publication currently with a literary emphasis on original prose and poetry. This publication is directed toward amateur writers and poets, but many of them would like to be professional. For some, appearance in *Hob-Nob* is simply an opportunity to be published somewhere, while others possibly see it as a springboard to bigger and better things." Semiannually. Estab. 1969. Circ. 450.

Needs: Literary, adventure, contemporary, humor, fantasy, psychic/supernatural/occult, prose poem, regional, romance (gothic), religious/inspirational, science fiction, spiritual, sports, mystery (amateur sleuth, English cozy), juvenile, young adult, senior citizen/retirement, western (frontier, young adult), very brief condensed novels, excerpts from novels. "Upbeat" subjects are preferred. Family emphasis. "Clean only. No erotica, works with excessive swearing or blatantly sexual words, gross violence, suicide, etc." Accepts 25-35 mss/issue. Does not read new contributor's submissions March 1-December 31, to prevent a backlog; any received before January will be returned. Receives 8-10 fiction mss each month. Recently published work by Patrick Cauchi, Bernard Hewitt, Howard Giordano, Lisa Jean Shientag; published many new writers within the last year. Length: preferably 500-2,000 words.

Sometimes serializes a longer story (2 installments). Critiques rejected mss when there is time. Sometimes recommends other markets.
How to Contact: Send complete ms with SASE. No simultaneous submissions. Reports in several months on acceptance, "less for rejections." Publishes ms at least 1½-2 years after acceptance. Sample copy for $3.50 or $3 for a back issue.
Payment: Pays 1 contributor's copy for first appearance only. $3.50 for one extra, $3 each for additional. Readers' choice contest every issue—votes taken on favorite stories and poems. Small prizes up to $10.
Terms: Acquires first rights. Reprint rights revert to author.
Advice: "Include name and address on at least the first page, and name on others. State 'original and unpublished.' I especially appreciate the 'light' touch in both fiction and nonfiction—family stories and light romance (*no* erotica); offbeat, whimsical, humorous, maybe even cornball at times." Includes "some recurring humorous characters from certain established contributors. Occasional two-part stories (*under* 5,000 words total)."

HOBSON'S CHOICE (I), Starwind Press, Box 98, Ripley OH 45167. (513)392-4549. Editor: Susannah West. Magazine: 8½×11; 16 pages; 60 lb. offset paper and cover; b&w illustrations; line shot photos. "Science fiction and fantasy for young adults and adults with interest in science, technology, science fiction and fantasy." Monthly. Estab. 1974. Circ. 2,000.
Needs: Fantasy, science fiction (hard science, soft/sociological). "We like SF that shows hope for the future and protagonists who interact with their environment rather than let themselves be manipulated by it." No horror, pastiches of other authors, stories featuring characters created by others (i.e. Captain Kirk and crew, Dr. Who, etc.). Receives 50+ unsolicited mss/month. Buys 2-4 mss/issue; 16-24 mss/year. Publishes ms between 4 months-2 years after acceptance. Recently published work by Robert Gray, Stuart Napier, Doug Beason; published new writers within the last year. Length: 3,000-8,000 words average; 2,000 words minimum; 8,000 words maximum. Also publishes literary criticism and "occasionally" literary essays. Occasionally critiques rejected mss.
How to Contact: Send complete ms. Reports in 2-3 months. "If an author hasn't heard from us by 4 months, he/she should feel free to withdraw." SASE (IRCs) for ms. No simultaneous submissions. Accepts electronic submissions via disk for the IBM PC or PC compatible in ASCII format and Macintosh. Sample copy $2.25; issue #2-5 $2.50 each. Fiction guidelines for #10 SAE and 1 first-class stamp. Tipsheet packet (all guidelines plus tips on writing science fiction) for $1.25 and SASE.
Payment: Pays 1-4¢/word and contributor's copies.
Terms: Pays 25% on acceptance; 75% on publication. "25% payment is kill fee if we decide not to publish story." Rights negotiable. Sends galleys to the author.
Advice: "I certainly think a beginning writer can be successful if he/she studies the publication *before* submitting, and matches the submission with the magazine's needs. Get our guidelines and study them *before* submitting. Don't submit something *way over* or *way under* our word length requirements. Be understanding of editors; they can get swamped very easily, *especially* if there's only one editor handling all submissions. You don't need to write a synopsis of your story in your cover letter—the story should be able to stand on its own."

‡HOME OFFICE OPPORTUNITIES, (I, IV), Deneb Publishing, P.O. Box 780, Lyman WY 82937. (307)786-4513. Editor: Diane Wolverton. Magazine: 6½×10; 24 pages; newsprint paper; illustrations and photographs. "Bimonthly digest of help, information and nurturing for people who operate home office." Bimonthly. Estab. 1989. Circ. 500.
• Deneb also publishes the popular *Housewife Writer's Forum*, also listed in this book. The *Housewife Writer's Forum* Short Fiction Contest is listed in the Contest and Awards section.
Needs: "Business-oriented fiction. Strong business savvy, central character." Accepts 1 ms/issue; 6 mss/year. Publishes ms 3-6 months after acceptance. Length: 1,500-2,000. Publishes short shorts.
How to Contact: Send complete ms with cover letter. Should include estimated word count, bio (35-50 words), and list of publications. Reports in 4-8 weeks. Send SASE (or IRC) for reply, return of ms or send a disposable copy of ms. Simultaneous, reprint and electronic submissions OK. Sample copy for $2. Fiction guidelines for business size SAE and 1 first-class stamp.
Payment: Pays 1¢/word minimum; 5 contributor's copies; additional copies for $1.50 each.
Terms: Pays on acceptance for first rights or one-time rights.
Advice: "We are a very open market to new writers—we don't care as much about publication credits as we do about finding writers who can send us fiction that makes our readers feel good about being in business." Looking for more "writers who have a real sense of what it means to be in business—

who understand what it's like to make payroll, file tax forms and deal with competitors. Communicate some of that in a short story and you'll have a winner with us."

HOME PLANET NEWS, (II), Home Planet Publications, P. O. Box 415, New York NY 10009. (718)769-2854. Tabloid: 11½×16; 24 pages; newsprint; illustrations; photos. *"Home Planet News* publishes mainly poetry along with some fiction, as well as reviews (books, theater and art), and articles of literary interest. We see *HPN* as a quality literary journal in an eminently readable format—and in content urban, urbane and politically aware." Triannually. Estab. 1979. Circ. 1,000.
• Poetry by Daniel Berrigan and Frank Murphy appearing in *HPN* has been included in the *Pushcart Prize* and *Editor's Choice* anthologies.
Needs: Ethnic/multicultural, experimental, feminist, gay, historical (general), lesbian, literary, mainstream/contemporary, science fiction (soft/sociological). No "children's or genre stories (except rarely for some SF)." Upcoming themes: "AIDS." Publishes special fiction issue or anthology. Receives 12 mss/month. Buys 1 ms/issue; 3 mss/year. Publishes 1 year after acceptance. Recently published Maureen McNeil, B.Z. Niditch, Layle Silbert. Length: 2,500 words average; 500 words minimum; 3,000 words maximum. Publishes short shorts. Also publishes literary criticism, poetry.
How to Contact: Send complete ms with a cover letter. Reports in 3-6 months on mss. Send SASE (IRC) for reply, return of ms or send a disposable copy of the ms. Sample copy $3. Fiction guidelines for SAE.
Payment: Pays 4 contributor's copies; additional copies $1.
Terms: Acquires one-time rights.
Advice: "We use very little. It just has to grab us. We need short pieces of some complexity." Looking for "well-written, well-plotted stories with well-developed, believable characters."

THE HOPEWELL REVIEW 1994: New Work by Indiana's Best Writers, (III, IV), Arts Indiana, Inc., #701, 47 S. Pennsylvania St., Indianapolis IN 46204. (317)632-7894. Editor: Michael Wilkerson. Magazine: 5½×8½; 128 pages; perfect bound. *"The Hopewell Review* is an annual anthology of fiction and poetry. The primary criterion for selection is high literary quality." Annually. Estab. 1989.
• *The Hopewell Review* was awarded the Indiana Governor's Award in 1993.
Needs: Condensed/excerpted novel, contemporary, experimental, humor/satire, literary, prose poem, regional, translations. "Writers must currently live in Indiana or have an extraordinary tie." Receives 1,200 unsolicited mss/year. Buys 4-6 mss/issue. Publishes annually (September). Recently published work by Scott Russell Sanders, Yusef Komunyaka and Roger Mitchell. Length: 4,000 words maximum. Sometimes critiques rejected mss.
How to Contact: Send complete ms with cover letter which should include brief biography. Annual deadline: March 1. Notification: June. SASE. Simultaneous submissions OK with notification. Sample copy for $6.95 and $2 postage. Fiction guidelines for SAE and 1 first-class stamp (IRCs).
Payment: Pays $125-625 ($500 award of excellence. Juror for *Hopewell Review 1993* fiction was Jonathan Galassi, editor for Farrar, Straus & Giroux, Inc.); and 2 contributor's copies. Charges for extras.
Terms: Pays on publication for first rights, one-time rights.
Advice: "Fresh perspectives and use of the English language make a ms stand out."

HOPSCOTCH: THE MAGAZINE FOR GIRLS, (II), The Bluffton News Publishing & Printing Co., P.O. Box 164, Bluffton OH 45817. (419)358-4610. Fax: (419)358-5027. Editor: Marilyn Edwards. Magazine: 7×9; 50 pages; enamel paper; pen & ink illustrations; photographs. Bimonthly. Estab. 1989. Circ. 9,000.
• *Hopscotch* is indexed in the *Children's Magazine Guide* and *Ed Press* and received a Parents' Choice Gold Medal Award in 1992.
Needs: Children's/juvenile (5-9, 10-12 years): adventure, ethnic/multicultural, fantasy, historical (general), sports. Upcoming themes: "Helping Animals" (April/May 1994); "What To Do In the Summer" (June/July 1994); "Horses" (August/September 1994); "Poetry" (October/November 1994); "Dolls" (December/January 1994/1995). Receives 300-400 unsolicited mss/month. Buys 20-40 mss/year. Agented fiction 2%. Recently published work by Lois Grambling, Betty Killion, Jean Patrick, VaDonna Jean Leaf. Length: 700-1,000 words preferred; 300 words minimum; 1,000 maximum. Publishes short shorts. Length: 250-400 words. Also publishes poetry, puzzles, hidden pictures and crafts. Always comments on rejected mss.
How to Contact: Send complete ms with cover letter. Should include estimated word count, 1-page bio, Social Security number, list of publications. Reports in 2-4 weeks on queries; 6-10 weeks on mss. Send SASE for reply, return of ms or send disposable copy of the ms. Simultaneous and reprint

submissions OK. Sample copy for $3. Fiction guidelines for #10 SASE. Reviews novels and short story collections.

Payment: Pays 5-10¢/word (extra for usable photos or illustrations) and 1-2 contributor's copies. Additional copies $3; $2 for 10 or more.

Terms: Pays before publication for first North American serial rights.

Advice: Looks for "age of girl involved (6-12 years), length under 1,000 words, typewritten — having been proofread."

HOR-TASY, (II, IV), Ansuda Publications, Box 158-J, Harris IA 51345. Editor/Publisher: Daniel R. Betz. Magazine: 5½ × 8½; 72 pages; mimeo paper; index stock cover; illustrations on cover. "*Hor-Tasy* is bringing back actual *horror* to horror lovers tired of seeing so much science fiction and SF passed off as horror. We're also very much interested in true, poetic, pure fantasy."

Needs: Fantasy and horror. "Pure fantasy: Examples are trolls, fairies and mythology. The horror we're looking for comes from the human mind — the ultimate form of horror. It must sound real — so real that in fact it could very possibly happen at any time and place. We must be able to feel the diseased mind behind the personality. No science fiction in any way, shape or form. We don't want stories in which the main character spends half his time talking to a shrink. We don't want stories that start out with: 'You're crazy,' said so and so." Accepts 6 mss/issue. Receives 15-20 unsolicited fiction mss each month. Critiques rejected mss "unless it's way off from what we're looking for." Sometimes recommends other markets.

How to Contact: Send complete ms with SASE (IRCs). Simultaneous submissions OK ("if we know about it.") "If not interested (in ms), we return immediately. If interested, we may keep it as long as 2 months." Publishes ms an average of 1 year after acceptance. Sample copy for $2.95.

Payment: Pays 2 contributor's copies. Extras at cover price less special discount rates.

Terms: Acquires first North American serial rights.

Advice: "Most stories rejected are about spooks, monsters, haunted houses, spacemen, etc. Because *Hor-Tasy* is a unique publication, I suggest the potential writer get a sample copy. Only unpublished work will be considered."

HOUSEWIFE-WRITER'S FORUM, (I), P.O. Box 780, Lyman WY 82937. (307)786-4513. Editor: Diane Wolverton. Fiction Editor: Bob Haynie. Magazine: 6½ × 10; 32-48 pages; glossy cover; illustrations. "Support for the woman who juggles writing with family life. We publish short fiction, poetry, essays, nonfiction, line drawings, humor and hints. For women of all ages; house husbands who write." Bimonthly. Estab. 1988. Circ. over 1,500.

• This magazine also includes fiction marketing tips and information. It is ranked #48 on the latest *Writer's Digest* Fiction 50 list and also won first place in the Wyoming Media Professionals annual contest for regularly published magazines. See also our listing for the contest sponsored by the magazine, *Housewife Writer's Forum* Short Story Contest. See the listing for *Home Office Opportunities*, also by this publisher.

Needs: Contemporary, experimental, historical (general), humor/satire, literary, mainstream, mystery/suspense, romance (contemporary, historical). No pornographic material. Receives 100-200 mss/month. Buys 1-2 mss/issue; 6-12 mss/year. Publishes ms within 6 months-1 year after acceptance. Recently published work by Elaine McCormick, Carol Shenold and Carole Bellacera. Length: 1,500 words preferred; 500 words minimum; 2,000 words maximum. Publishes short shorts. Publishes critiques of accepted mss.

How to Contact: Send complete ms with cover letter. Reports in 3-4 months on mss. SASE "with *adequate* postage." Simultaneous and reprint submissions OK. Sample copy for $4. Fiction guidelines for #10 SAE and 1 first-class stamp (IRCs).

Payment: Pays 1¢/word, plus 1 contributor's copy. Half price for extra copies.

Terms: Pays on acceptance for first North American rights. Sponsors awards for fiction writers. "We sponsor occasional contests geared to the interests of housewife-writers. First place winners are published in the magazine. Entry fees: $4. Prize: $30. Send #10 SAE with 1 first-class stamp for guidelines and further information."

Advice: "All mss are read and sometimes suggestions are offered on the rejections. All published materials are printed with Fiction Editor Bob Haynie's critiques. Here are a few samples to show you what he's looking for: 'Life is made up of small details. Writing often consists of finding the right ones out of the thousands that make up even the briefest moment and using them to convey information to the reader. There's more to this than just a bunch of required items and small details, though. There is also believable dialogue, controlled pacing, and a fine ending that fits the tone and the action and the narrator just right. I look for the overall effect of the story — the product of its theme, its narrative skill, its handling of detail and pace and dialogue, its felicity of beginning, transition and ending. The degree to which all these things mesh and contribute to a whole meaning that surpasses the mere sum of the constituents is the degree to which a story succeeds.' "

THE HUNTED NEWS, (II), The Subourban Press, P.O. Box 9101, Warwick RI 02889. (401)739-2279. Editor: Mike Wood. Magazine: 8½ × 11; 25-30 pages; photocopied paper. "I am looking for good writers, in the hope that I can help their voices be heard. Like most in the small press scene, I just wanted to create another option for writers who otherwise might not be heard." Triannually. Estab. 1991. Circ. 200.
Needs: Children's/juvenile (1-4 and 10-12 years), erotica, experimental, gay, humor/satire, lesbian, literary, mainstream/contemporary, serialized novel, translations. No science fiction; politically-biased; romance. Publishes annual special fiction issue or anthologies. Receives 5-10 unsolicited mss/month. Acquires 1-2 mss/issue; 6 mss/year. Publishes ms within 3 months after acceptance. Recently published work by Darryl Smyers, Robert Howington. Length: 500 words minimum; 900 words maximum. Publishes short shorts. Length: 300 words +. Also publishes literary essays, literary criticism and poetry. Always critiques or comments on rejected mss.
How to Contact: Send complete ms with cover letter. Should include bio. Reports in 1 month. Send SASE (IRCs) for reply, return of ms or send disposable copy of the ms. Simultaneous and reprint submissions OK. Sample copy for 8½ × 11 SAE and 3 first-class stamps. Fiction guidelines free. Reviews novels or short story collections.
Payment: Pays up to 5 contributor's copies.
Terms: Acquires one-time rights.
Advice: "I look for an obvious love of language and a sense that there is something at stake in the story, a story that somehow needs to be told. Write what you need to write, say what you think you need to say, no matter the subject, and take a chance and send it to me; a writer will always find an audience if the work is true."

HYPERBOLE, The Art of Digital Storytelling, (I, II), Suite 204, 1756 114th Ave. S.E., Bellevue WA 98004. (206)451-7751. Editor: Greg Roach. Fiction Editor: Paul Wayne Hiaumet. Computer disk magazine: illustrations and photographs. "Published on computer disks—no general theme—fiction, poetry, graphics." Quarterly. Estab. 1990. Circ. 350.
Needs: Adventure, condensed/excerpted novel, contemporary, erotica, experimental, fantasy, historical (general), horror, humor/satire, literary, mainstream, mystery/suspense, prose poem, science fiction, serialized novel, translations. Plans special fiction issue. Receives 4 unsolicited mss/month. Buys 1-3 mss/issue; 10-20 mss/year. Publishes ms 2-4 months after acceptance. Recently published work by Michael Banks, Christopher Woods, Hanz Doppler, Dave Christner. Length: Open. Publishes short shorts. Also publishes poetry. Sometimes critiques rejected mss and recommends other markets.
How to Contact: Send complete ms with cover letter. Include Social Security number. Reports in 2 weeks on queries; 1 month on mss. SASE. Reprint submissions OK. Sample copy for $3. Fiction guidelines for #10 SAE and 1 first-class stamp.
Payment: Pays $5 flat or $1/page and contributor's copies.
Terms: Pays on publication for first rights.
Advice: "Hypermedia opens up new doors for fiction writers—it's a whole new genre. *Hyperbole* is a disk based publication—no printed paper is involved. While *Hyperbole* runs on computers (Macintosh & IBM) it is not about computers. We are dedicated to exploring interactive media (the integration of text, graphics, music, animation and sound on a computer) as a legitimate mode of communication and a viable opportunity for artists and writers."

HYPHEN MAGAZINE, Chicago's Magazine of the Arts, (I), Shoestring Publications, P.O. Box 516, Somonauk IL 60552-0516. (815)498-3547. Editor: Eduardo Cruz Eusebio. Fiction Editors: Margaret Lewis, Dave Mead. Magazine: 8½ × 11; 72 pages; white bond paper; glossy cover; illustrations and photos. Purpose is "to bring the arts together, and to present the arts to the people in a format that is inviting, intriguing and attractive. We publish interviews, fiction and nonfiction about the arts, artists, and anything that might interest artists and art supporters." Quarterly. Estab. 1991. Circ. 2,000.
● *Hyphen Magazine* received "Best of Show" from Chicago Communications '92.
Needs: Erotica, ethnic/multicultural, experimental, feminist, gay, historical (general), humor/satire, lesbian, literary, mainstream/contemporary, psychic/supernatural/occult, regional, science fiction, serialized novel, translations. No romance. Publishes special fiction issue or anthology. Receives 45 unsolicited mss/month. Buys 4 mss/issue; 16 mss/year. Publishes ms 2-4 months after acceptance. Published work by Phillip Brooks, Jennifer Sheridan, Zoe Keithley. Length: 2,500 words average; 4,000 words

maximum. Publishes short shorts. Length: 400 words. Also publishes literary essays and poetry. Often critiques or comments on rejected mss.

How To Contact: Send complete ms with cover letter. Should include a one paragraph bio with submission. Reports in 1 month on queries; 4-5 months on mss. Send SASE (IRC) for reply, return of ms or send disposable copy of ms. Simultaneous, reprint submissions OK. Sample copy for $4. Fiction guidelines for #10 SAE and 1 first-class stamp. Reviews novels and short story collections.

Payment: Pays 2 contributor's copies, subscription. Additional copies for $3.

Terms: Pays on publication for first North American serial rights or one-time rights.

Advice: Looks for "committed and vigorous writing. Never send a first draft, but never forget your first impulse. If the story doesn't move you, it will not move anyone else."

THE ICONOCLAST, (II), Wagner Labs & Enterprises, 1675 Amazon Rd., Mohegan Lake NY 10547. Editor: Phil Wagner. Newsletter: 8½ × 11; 12-16 pages; 20 lb. white paper; 20 lb. cover stock; illustrations. "*The Iconoclast* is a self-supporting, independent, unaffiliated general interest magazine with an appreciation of the profound, absurd and joyful in life. Material is limited only by *its* quality and *our* space. We want readers who are open-minded, unafraid to think, and actively engaged with the world." Published 8/year. Estab. 1992. Circ. 250.

Needs: Adventure, ethnic/multicultural, humor/satire, literary, mainstream/contemporary, science fiction, sports. "Nothing militant, solipsistic, or silly." Receives 20 unsolicited mss/month. Accepts 1-2 mss/issue; 10-15 mss/year. Publishes ms 1 week-6 months after acceptance. Length: 1,500 words preferred; 100 words minimum; 2,000 words maximum. Publishes short shorts. Also publishes literary essays, literary criticism and poetry. Often critiques or comments on rejected mss.

How to Contact: Send complete ms. Reports in 1 month. Send SASE (IRCs) for reply, return of mss or send a disposable copy of the ms. Simultaneous and reprint submissions OK. Sample copy for $1.50. Reviews novels and short story collections.

Payment: Pays 1-2 contributor's copies; additional copies 90¢ (40% discount).

Terms: Acquires one-time rights.

Advice: "We like fiction that has something to say (and not about its author). We hope for work that is observant, intense and multi-leveled. Follow Pound's advice—'make it new.' Write what you want in whatever style you want—then pray there's someone who can appreciate your sensibility."

‡THE ILLINOIS REVIEW, (II), Illinois Writers, Inc., 4240/English Dept., Illinois State University, Normal IL 61790-4240. Editor: Jim Elledge. Magazine: 5½ × 8½; 56-64 pages; glossy cover stock; cover illustrations only. "We're open to any work of literary merit by unknown or established authors. Mainstream and alternative works are equally desired. Marginalized individuals are welcomed. Our only bias is for excellence." Semiannually. Estab. 1993. Circ. 300.

• *The Illinois Review* replaces the *Illinois Writers Review*. First issue was published Fall 1993.

Needs: Ethnic/multicultural, experimental, feminist, gay, lesbian, literary and mainstream/contemporary. Length: open. Publishes short shorts. Also publishes literary essays, literary criticism and poetry.

How to Contact: Send complete ms with a cover letter. "Cover letters are not required but are read. An author may mention anything in his/her cover letter, but the piece will be accepted only if it's good." Reports in 1-2 weeks on queries; 2 months on mss. Send SASE (or IRC) for reply, return of ms or send a disposable copy of ms. Sample copy for $6. Fiction guidelines for #10 SAE and 1 first-class stamp.

Payment: Free subscription to the magazine and 2 contributor's copies.

Terms: Acquires first North American serial rights.

Advice: "Excellence is our only bias. Buy a sample and see the varied styles of the work published in our pages." Avoid sending "religious, romance, nostalgia, sentimental" work.

IMMANENT FACE MAGAZINE, (I), P.O. Box 890, Allston MA 02134. Editor: Carl Quesnel. Magazine: 8½ × 11; 20-25 pages; 25 lb. paper; 60 lb. cover; illustrations and photographs. "Theme: Exploration of the psyche and the confused world of interpersonal relationships." Quarterly. Estab. 1987. Circ. 250.

• The editor says the magazine is accepting less fiction these days so submissions must be of high quality.

Needs: Condensed/excerpted novel, contemporary, experimental, fantasy, literary, prose poem, science fiction (hard science, soft/sociological), serialized novel, translations. "We do *not* want to see material that is not final-draft quality." Receives 40 unsolicited mss/month. Accepts 3 mss/issue; 12 mss/year. Publishes ms 1-3 months after acceptance. Recently published work by D. Castleman, Lyn

Lifshin. Length: 1,750 words preferred; 3,000 words maximum. Publishes short shorts. Sometimes comments on rejected mss and recommends other markets.

How to Contact: Send complete ms with cover letter. Include "name, address, greeting, how the writer heard of our magazine, biographical tidbit maybe, *not* a list of previous publications." Reports in 1 month on queries; 2 months on mss. SASE. Simultaneous and reprint submissions OK. Accepts electronic submissions via disk. Sample copy for $1.50 (all checks payable to Carl Quesnel). Fiction guidelines for #10 SAE and 1 first-class stamp (IRCs).

Payment: Pays contributor's copies.

Terms: Not copyrighted.

Advice: "Manuscripts that stand out make me feel strongly—either positive or negative—or else they capture an atmosphere really well. Description is very important."

INDIANA REVIEW, (II), 316 N. Jordan Ave., Indiana University, Bloomington IN 47405. (812)855-3439. Editor: Gretchen Knapp. Associate Editor: Cara Diaconoff. Editors change every 2 years. Send future submissions to "Fiction Editor." Magazine: 6×9; 224 pages; 60 lb. paper; Glatfelter cover stock. "Magazine of contemporary fiction and poetry in which there is a zest for language, some relationship between form and content, and awareness of the world. For fiction writers/readers, followers of lively contemporary poetry." Biannually. Estab. 1976. Circ. 650.

Needs: Literary, contemporary, experimental, mainstream. "We are interested in innovation, logic, unity, a social context, a sense of humanity. All genres that meet some of these criteria are welcome. We would also consider novellas, novel excerpts and 'suites' of 3 related stories." Buys 3-4 mss/issue. Recently published work by Ursula LeGuin, David Michael Kaplan, Ann Packer; published new writers within the last year. Length: 1-35 magazine pages. Also publishes literary essays, poetry.

How to Contact: Send complete ms with cover letter. "Don't describe or summarize the story." SASE (IRCs). No simultaneous submissions. Reports in 3 months. Publishes ms an average of 2-10 months after acceptance. Sample copy $7.

Payment: Pays $5/page.

Terms: Buys North American serial rights.

Advice: "Refrain from the chatty cover letter. Send one story at a time (unless they're really short), and no simultaneous submissions."

INFINITY LIMITED, A Journal for the Somewhat Eccentric, (II), The Infinity Group, P.O. Box 2713, Castro Valley CA 94546-0546. (510)581-8172. Editor: Genie Lester. Magazine: 8½×11; 40 pages; bond paper; parchment cover; illustrations and photos. "Stories with plots. No vulgar language, senseless violence, or graphic sex please." Quarterly. Estab. 1988. Circ. 1,000.

Needs: Adventure, contemporary, ethnic, experimental, fantasy, historical (general), humor/satire, literary, mystery/suspense, prose poem, psychic/supernatural/occult, regional, romance (contemporary, historical), science fiction, translations. "No pretentious prose, erotica, horror (unless *very* well done); stories without a plot or point, war recollections." Upcoming themes: "Music, Romance, Flowers" (Spring); "War, Water" (Summer); "People, Philsophy" (Fall). Plans to publish annual special fiction issue or anthology. Receives 50+ unsolicited mss/month. Acquires 5-7 mss/issue; 20-28 mss/year. Does not read mss June-August, December 15-January 15. Publishes ms 2 months-1 year after acceptance. Recently published work by Daniel Green, Thomas Kretz, I.B. Nelson, Andrew Kong Knight, Ken Johnson. Length: 10,000 words maximum. Publishes short shorts. Sometimes critiques rejected mss and recommends other markets.

How to Contact: Send complete ms with cover letter. Include brief bio. Reports in 2-3 months on mss. SASE. Simultaneous submissions OK. Accepts electronic submissions. Sample copy for $3.95 and 9×12 SAE. Fiction guidelines for #10 SAE and 1 first-class stamp (IRCs).

Payment: Pays in contributor's copies.

Terms: Acquires one-time and reprint rights. Sends galleys to author.

Advice: "Our editorial board is a group of volunteers of widely-varying ages, political and religious persuasions, ethnic groups, races and professions. If they agree on a manuscript, we are fairly sure that our readers will find it acceptable. If one of us gets excited about a work, the rest usually agree to its publication. Make sure your manuscript is readable, accompanied by an SASE, identified with your name on every page, and *not* stapled. Please have patience with us. We try to respond promptly, but we are volunteers spending our own money and time."

‡THE INKSLINGER, Magazine of Southwest Books & Authors, (II, IV), 101½ Cienega St., Santa Fe NM 87501. (505)988-2099. Editor: Michael W. Eliseuson. Fiction Editor: Anthony Moreland. Tabloid: 10×15¾; 24 pages; electrobright paper; illustrations and photographs. "Southwest focus:

West Texas to Southern California, to cover the book and author trade throughout the Southwest. All genres published. Heavy on book reviews and author interviews." Bimonthly. Estab. 1992. Circ. 5,000.

Needs: Adventure, childrens/juvenile, condensed novel, ethnic/multicultural, experimental, fantasy, feminist, gay, historical (Southwest), humor/satire, lesbian, literary, mainstream/contemporary, mystery/suspense, psychic/supernatural/occult, regional (Southwest), religious/inspirational, romance, science fiction, senior citizen/retirement, serialized novel, sports, translations, westerns, young adult/ teen. Publishes special fiction issue. Receives 15 unsolicited mss/month. Accepts 4 mss/issue; 25-30 mss/year. Publishes ms 3-6 months after acceptance. Agented fiction 15%. Recently published work by N. Scott Momaday, John Nichols, Roger Zelazny, Raphael Hayes. Length: 2,500 words preferred; 1,000 words minimum; 2,500 words maximum. Publishes short shorts. Length: 500 words. Also publishes literary essays, literary criticism and poetry. Sometimes critiques or comments on rejected mss.

How to Contact: Send complete ms with a cover letter. Should include estimated word count, bio (100 words), Social Security number, list of publications and b&w photo. Reports in 2 weeks on queries; 4 weeks on mss. Send SASE (or IRC) for reply, return of ms or send a disposable copy of ms. Simultaneous, reprint and electronic submissions OK. Sample copy for $1.75, 10×15 SAE and 3 first-class stamps. Fiction guidelines for #10 SAE and 1 first-class stamp. Reviews novels and short story collections.

Payment: Pays 2 contributor's copies; additional copies for $2.

Terms: Acquires one-time rights.

Advice: Looks for "fresh literary conceit."

INNISFREE, (I, II), Box 277, Manhattan Beach CA 90266. (213)772-5558. Fax: (310)546-5862. Editors: Rex Winn and Arlene J. Pollack. Magazine: 8½×11; 50+ pages; 90 lb. cover stock; illustrations and photos. Publishes "fiction, poetry, essays—open forum." Bimonthly. Estab. 1981. Circ. 350.

Needs: Adventure, contemporary, ethnic, fantasy, literary, mainstream, mystery/suspense (private eye, police procedural), regional and science fiction. "No political or religious sensationalism." Accepts 12-15 mss/issue; approx. 80 mss/year. Publishes ms within 12 months of acceptance. Recently published work by Ron Fleshman, Elisabeth Lockwood, L. Glen Wadsworth and A. David Sydney. Length: 3,000 words average. Publishes short shorts. Sometimes critiques rejected mss.

How to Contact: Send complete mss with cover letter. Reports in 6-8 weeks. SASE (IRCs). May accept simultaneous submissions, but "reluctantly." Accepts electronic submissions via IBM disk. Sample copy for $5. Free fiction guidelines.

Payment: No payment. Prizes offered.

Terms: Acquires one-time rights.

Advice: "Fiction market is on the decline. This is an attempt to publish writers who take pride in their work and have some talent."

INTERIM, (II), Dept. of English, University of Nevada, Las Vegas NV 89154. (702)739-3172. Editor and Founder: A. Wilber Stevens. Magazine: 6×9; 48-64 pages; heavy paper; glossy cover; cover illustrations. Publishes "poetry and short fiction for a serious, educated audience." Semiannually. Estab. 1944; revived 1986. Circ. 600-800.

Needs: Contemporary and experimental, literary. Accepts 2-3 mss/issue. Publishes ms within 6 months-1 year of acceptance. Recently published work by Gladys Swan and James B. Hall. Length: 4,000 words preferred; 7,500 words maximum. Also publishes poetry.

How to Contact: Send complete ms with cover letter. Reports on mss in 2 months. SASE (IRCs). Sample copy $5.

Payment: Pays in contributor's copies and two-year subscription to magazine.

‡INTERNATIONAL QUARTERLY, Essays, Fiction, Drama, Poetry, Art, Reviews, (II), P.O. Box 10521, Tallahassee FL 32302-0521. (904)224-5078. Fax: (904)224-5127. Editor: Van K. Brock. Magazine: 7½×10; 176 pages; 50 lb. text paper; 60 lb. gloss cover; fine art illustrations. *"International Quarterly* seeks to bridge boundaries between national, ethnic and cultural identities, and among creative disciplines, by providing a venue for dialogue between exceptional writers and artists and discriminating readers. We look for work that reveals character and place from within." Quarterly. Estab. 1993.

Needs: Ethnic/multicultural, experimental, humor/satire, literary, mainstream/contemporary, regional, translations. "We would consider work in any of the genres that transcends the genre through quality of language, characterization and development. Our sympathies are strongly feminist. Many of the genre categories imply simplistic and limited literary purposes. Any genre can transcend its limits." Upcoming themes: "The Middle East and the Africas" (Winter 1994); "The Faces of the

Americas" (Spring 1994). "Summer 1994 we will begin a series on themes such as the 'Emergence of Freedoms,' 'Religion and Polity' and the 'Forms of Experience in Contemporary Literature and Art.' No issue is limited to work on its regional or thematic focus." Receives 10-15 unsolicited mss/month. Accepts 5 mss/issue; 20 mss/year. "We read all year, but fewer readers are active in July and August." Publishes ms 3-9 months after acceptance. Recently published work by Edmund Keeley, Iván Mándy, Gary Corseri, S.P. Elledge. Publishes short shorts. Also publishes literary essays, literary criticism (for general readers), poetry. Sometimes critiques or comments on rejected mss.

How to Contact: Query first or send complete ms with a cover letter. Should include estimated word count, bio, list of publications. Include rights available. "We prefer first rights for all original English texts." Reports in 1-2 weeks on queries; 2-4 months on mss. Send SASE (or IRC) for reply, return of ms or send a disposable copy of ms. Simultaneous, reprint (please specify) and electronic submissions OK. Sample copy for $5 (a reduced rate) and 4 first-class stamps or IRCs. Fiction guidelines for #10 SAE and 1 first-class stamp. Reviews novels and short story collections. Send books to Book Review Editor.

Payment: Pays free subscription to magazine and 1 contributor's copy.

Terms: Acquires first North American serial rights. Sends galleys to author ("in most cases").

Advice: "Read the four varied stories in our first issue. Also the two nonfiction 'stories' in the Essay section by Anneliese Wagner and Wayne Brown, which would have been accepted if they had been offered as stories. We like their quality of language, skill and discipline, sensitivity, wit or seriousness, and their careful, effortless-seeming development. And read a wide range of other good fiction. If you are really a beginning writer, persistently seek out and listen to the suggestions of other intelligent, practiced readers and writers. We would like to see more fiction break out of conventional thinking and set fictional modes without straining or trying to shock. Also fiction that presents the world of its characters from inside the skin of the culture, rather than those outside of the culture, tourists or short-termers as it were, commenting on the world of a story's subjects from outside, lamenting that it has fallen into our consumerist ways, etc., lamentable as that may be. Works we publish do not have to be foreign, they may arise out of a profound understanding of any culture or locale, as long as they provide the reader with an authentic experience of that locale, whatever the origin of the author. We have no taboos, but we want writing that understands and creates understanding, writers who want to go beyond cultural givens."

THE IOWA REVIEW, (II), University of Iowa, 308 EPB, Iowa City IA 52242. (319)335-0462. Editor: David Hamilton. Magazine: 6 × 9; 200 pages; first grade offset paper; Carolina C1S-10 pt. cover stock. "Stories, essays, poems for a general readership interested in contemporary literature." Triannually. Estab. 1970. Circ. 1,200.

● Work published in *Iowa Review* regularly has been selected for inclusion in the *Pushcart Prize* and *Best American Short Stories* anthologies.

Needs: Receives 150-200 unsolicited fiction mss/month. Agented fiction less than 10%. Buys 4-5 mss/issue, 12-16 mss/year. Does not read mss May-August. Published work by Mary Swander, Charles Baxter and Donald Hall; published new writers within the last year. Also publishes literary essays, literary criticism, poetry.

How to Contact: Send complete ms with SASE (IRCs). "Don't bother with queries." Simultaneous submissions OK. Reports in 4 months on mss. Publishes ms an average of 4-12 months after acceptance. Sample copy $5. Reviews novels and short story collections (3-6 books/year).

Payment: Pays $10/page; 2 contributor's copies; charge for extras: 30% off cover price.

Terms: Pays on publication for first North American serial rights. Hardly ever buys reprints.

Advice: In cover letters, "be moderate. Be decent. Be brief."

IOWA WOMAN, P.O. Box 680, Iowa City IA 52244. Editor: Marianne Abel. Nonprofit magazine "dedicated to encouraging and publishing women writers and artists internationally." Quarterly. Estab. 1979. Circ. 2,500.

● *Iowa Woman* has received numerous awards and honors including Iowa Community Cultural Grant Awards (1991, 1992 and 1993). The magazine has also had essays and fiction included in *Best American Essays* and *Best American Short Stories*. See the *Iowa Woman* Writing Contest listed also in this book. The magazine also received an Iowa Arts Council grant to put together a pilot documentary video on Iowa women writers and poets.

Needs: Historical, literary, regional, women's. Upcoming theme: "Personal essays reflecting women's publishing experiences as a way to celebrate our 15th anniversary of publishing women's work." Receives 200 unsolicited mss/month. Buys 3 mss/issue; 12 mss/year. Length: 6,500 words maximum. Also publishes literary essays, literary criticism, and sponsors contest.

How to Contact: Send complete ms. Reports in 3 months. SASE. Sample copy for $6. Fiction or contest guidelines for SAE with 1 first-class stamp (IRCs). Reviews novels and short story collections. Send books to Coleen Maddy, Books Editor.

Payment: Pays 2 contributor's copies; $4 charge for extras, $5 per published page; advertising discounts to published writers or artists in our magazine.

Terms: Buys first serial rights.

Advice: "Our editorial collective often responds critically with rejections. Our guidelines are clear, but we still get stories without women or women's experience as the center. New writers have a better chance with regular submissions than with our annual writing contest which is quite competitive."

‡**IRIS, A Gay Men's Literary Review, (II, IV),** P.O. Box 7263, Atlanta GA 30057. (404)237-0061. Editor: Dennis Adams. Fiction Editor: Glenn Crawford. Magazine: 8½×11; 70 pages; illustrations and photographs. "A quality literary review that describes the world of gay men. Not confined to gay writers, but works should illustrate topics of interest to gay men." Quarterly. Estab. 1993. Circ. 1,500.

Needs: Gay: erotica, literary. List of upcoming themes available for SASE. Publishes annual special fiction issue or anthology. Receives 50 unsolicited mss/month. Accepts 5 mss/issue; 60 mss/year. Publishes ms 3-6 months after acceptance. Recently published work by Bill Bagwell, Chris Woods, G. Crawford, Robert K. Engler. Length: 4,500 words maximum. Also publishes poetry. Sometimes critiques or comments on rejected mss.

How to Contact: Send complete ms with a cover letter. Should include estimated word count, 3 line bio. Reports in 6 weeks on queries; 3 months on mss. Send a disposable copy of ms. Simultaneous, reprint and electronic submissions OK. Sample copy for $1 and 9×12 SAE.

Payment: Pays $100, free subscription, 5 contributor's copies; additional copies for $3.

Terms: Pays on acceptance. Buys one-time rights, retains rights for anthology.

Advice: Looks for "original, thought provoking fiction that illustrates what it is to be gay, how one interacts in the gay community." Would like to see more erotica. Avoid sending AIDS-related stories.

IRIS: A Journal About Women, (II, IV), Box 323 HSC, University of Virginia, Charlottesville VA 22908. (804)924-4500. Editor: Rebecca Hyman. Fiction Editor: Kristen Staby Rembold. Magazine: 8½×11; 72 pages; glossy paper; heavy cover; illustrations and photographs. "Material of particular interest to women. For a feminist audience, college educated and above." Semiannually. Estab. 1980. Circ. 2,500.

● *Iris* received the Best in Virginia Award for a black-and-white magazine in 1992. An interview with Kristen Staby Rembold appears in this book.

Needs: Experimental, feminist, lesbian, literary, mainstream. "I don't think what we're looking for particularly falls into the 'mainstream' category—we're just looking for well-written stories of interest to women (particularly feminist women)." Receives 300 unsolicited mss/year. Accepts 5 mss/year. Publishes ms within 1 year after acceptance. Length: 4,000 words average. Sometimes critiques rejected mss.

How to Contact: Send complete ms with cover letter. Include "previous publications, vocation, other points that pertain. Make it brief!" Reports in 3 months on mss. SASE. Simultaneous submissions OK. Accepts electronic submissions via disk or modem. Sample copy for $5. Fiction guidelines for #10 SAE and 1 first-class stamp.

Payment: Pays in contributor's copies and 1 year subscription.

Terms: Acquires one-time rights.

Advice: "I select mss which are lively imagistically as well as in the here-and-now; I select for writing which challenges the reader. My major complaint is with stories that don't elevate the language above the bland sameness we hear on the television and everyday. Read the work of the outstanding women writers, such as Alice Munroe and Louise Erdrich."

ITALIAN AMERICANA, (II, IV), URI/CCE 199 Promenade St., Providence RI 02908-5090. (401)277-3824. Editor: Carol Bonomo Albright. Magazine: 7×9; 150 pages; varnished cover; photographs. "Italian experience in America; historical articles; fiction; memoirs all concerning Italian experience in the Americas." Semiannually. Estab. 1974. Circ. 1,000.

Needs: Italian American: literary. Publishes special fiction issue or anthology. Receives 10 mss/month. Buys 3 mss/issue; 6-7 mss/year. Publishes up to 1 year after acceptance. Agented fiction 5%. Recently published Salvatore LaPuma; Rita Ciresi, Maria Bruno. Length: 20 double spaced pages. Publishes short shorts. Also publishes literary essays, literary criticism, poetry. Often critiques rejected mss.

Looking for Fiction With Possibilities

"Diversity of viewpoints is something the staff of *Iris* always considers when pulling together an issue," says Kristen Staby Rembold, fiction editor of that publication, but all material must remain true to the magazine's title. *Iris: A Journal About Women* was started in 1980 at the University of Virginia by a band of volunteers—primarily writers and artists—who wanted to provide a forum for poetry, visual art and fiction for and about women. Today, *Iris* has succeeded in that regard and in others. The magazine won a Best in Virginia Award in 1992 and has been quoted by *Ms.* and the *Utne Reader*.

Kristen Staby Rembold

This success brings in approximately 600 fiction manuscripts annually, and despite the small staff, each is examined carefully. "We read every piece that is submitted to us, and we comment if we can and if we feel that a piece is deserving. Most editors are writers," Rembold says, and are sensitive to writers' needs.

When choosing the four to six stories *Iris* publishes each year, Rembold looks for fiction that works on a metaphorical level. "We get too many flat, two-dimensional stories devoid of imagery," she says. "I look for something that sticks with me and will be memorable." Rembold tries to find women's stories that don't have a chance to be published in mainstream magazines, and she has a preference for realistic stories. Rembold says she agrees with Mark Twain's statement that "fiction is obliged to stick to possibilities; truth isn't."

Rembold prefers well-developed stories, usually 2,500-4,000 words. She doesn't like short shorts (under 500 words) because the format doesn't allow for complete development. And, although Rembold is willing to publish novel excerpts, she rarely does because too often excerpts are not sufficiently self-contained.

Although *Iris* is for women, men's submissions are given equal consideration. "Men are welcome to submit fiction," explains Rembold, "as long as it follows the criterion of being about women." Additionally, she says she would like to see women's fiction reaching a wider audience, including more men. Currently, *Iris*'s audience is composed mostly of educated women, many of whom are writers. Rembold thinks a great benefit of submitting to *Iris* is that "you'll be read by a sympathetic audience; I'm referring to the editors *and* the readers."

Iris provides an alternative to the mainstream magazines, where Rembold believes

there is a problem with women's work being accepted. If it addresses women's issues, Rembold says, "it's often seen as feminist," and therefore not suitable. In the future, Rembold says, "I hope the fiction that we're publishing now in *Iris* and in a few other magazines such as *Iowa Woman* and *Calyx*, will have a place in the mainstream. It's starting to happen, and I hope the trend is going to continue."
—*Elizabeth Johnson*

How to Contact: Send complete manuscript (in triplicate) with a cover letter. Should include 3-5 line bio, list of publications. Reports in 1 month on queries; 2-4 months on manuscripts. Send SASE (IRC) for reply, return of ms or send a disposable copy of ms. No simultaneous submissions. Sample copy $5. Fiction guidelines for SAE and 1 first-class stamp. Reviews novels and short story collections. Send books to Professor John Paul Russo, English Dept., Univ. of Miami, Coral Gables, FL 33124.
Payment: Pays $50, plus 1 contributor copy and free subscription to magazine; additional copies $7.
Terms: Pays on publication for first North American serial rights.
Advice: "Please individualize characters, instead of presenting types (i.e., lovable uncle, aunt, etc.). No nostalgia pieces."

JAPANOPHILE, (I, II, IV), Box 223, Okemos MI 48864. (517)349-1795. Editor-in-Chief: Earl Snodgrass. Magazine: 5¼ × 8½; 58 pages; illustrations; photos. Magazine of "articles, photos, poetry, humor, short stories about Japanese culture, not necessarily set in Japan, for an adult audience, most with college background; travelers." Quarterly. Estab. 1974. Circ. 600.
• Note that because of the mandatory entry fee for the contest, published stories not winning the contest net $15 of the $20 payment. However, the winning story receives $100. See the *Japanophile* Short Story Contest listed in this book.
Needs: Adventure, historical (general), humor/satire, literary, mainstream, and mystery/suspense. Published special fiction issue last year; plans another. Receives 40-100 unsolicited fiction mss/month. Buys 12 ms/issue, 20-30 mss/year. Recently published work by Mimi Hinman, Pearl Solomon, Gerald Y. Kinro; published new writers within the last year. Length: 2,000 words minimum; 9,000 words maximum; 4,000 words average. Also publishes literary essays, literary criticism, poetry. Sometimes recommends other markets.
How to Contact: Send complete ms with SASE and cover letter with brief author bio and information about story. Simultaneous and reprint submissions OK. Reports in 3 months on mss. Sample copy for $4; guidelines for #10 SAE and 1 first-class stamp (IRCs).
Payment: Pays $20 on publication, for short stories. All stories submitted to the magazine are entered in the annual contest. *A $5 entry fee must accompany each submission*. Prizes include $100 plus publication for the best short story. Deadline December 31.
Terms: Pays on publication for all rights, first North American serial rights or one-time rights (depends on situation).
Advice: "Short stories usually involve Japanese and 'foreign' (non-Japanese) characters in a way that contributes to understanding of Japanese culture and the Japanese people. However, a *good* story dealing with Japan or Japanese cultural aspects anywhere in the world will be considered, even if it does not involve this encounter or meeting of Japanese and foreign characters. Some stories may also be published in an anthology."

JEWISH CURRENTS MAGAZINE, (IV), 22 E. 17th St., New York NY 10003. (212)924-5740. Editor-in-Chief: Morris U. Schappes. Magazine: 5½ × 8½; 48 pages. "We are a progressive monthly, broad in our interests, printing feature articles on political and cultural aspects of Jewish life in the US and elsewhere, reviews of books and film, poetry and fiction, Yiddish translations; regular columns on Israel, US Jewish community, current events, Jewish women today, secular Jewish life. Monthly themes include Holocaust and Resistance, Black-Jewish relations, Jewish Book Month, Jewish Music Month, etc. National audience, literate and politically left, well educated." Monthly. Estab. 1946. Circ. 2,600.
• This magazine may be slow to respond. They are backlogged through 1994.
Needs: Contemporary, ethnic, feminist, historical (general), humor/satire, literary, senior citizen/retirement, translations. "We are interested in *authentic* experience and readable prose; Jewish themes; humanistic orientation. No religious, political sectarian; no porn or hard sex, no escapist stuff. Go easy on experimentation, but we're interested." Receives 6-10 unsolicited fiction mss/month.

Accepts 0-1 ms/issue; 8-10 mss/year. Recently published work by Morton Stavis, Mayor David N. Dinkins; published new writers within the last year. Length: 1,000 words minimum; 3,000 words maximum; 1,800 words average. Also publishes literary essays, literary criticism, poetry.

How to Contact: Send complete ms with cover letter. "Writers should include brief biographical information, especially their publishing histories." SASE. No simultaneous submissions. Reports in 2 months on mss. Publishes ms 2 months-2 years after acceptance. Sample copy for $2 with SASE and 3 first-class stamps (IRCs). Reviews novels and short story collections.

Payment: Pays complimentary one-year subscription; 6 contributor's copies.

Terms: "We readily give reprint permission at no charge." Sends galleys to author.

Advice: Noted for "stories about Jewish family life, especially intergenerational relations, and personal Jewish experience — e.g., immigrant or holocaust memories, assimilation dilemmas, etc. Matters of character and moral dilemma, maturing into pain and joy, dealing with Jewish conflicts OK. Space is increasingly a problem. Tell the truth, as sparely as possible."

THE JOURNAL, (II), Dept of English, Ohio State University, 164 W. 17th St., Columbus OH 43210. (614)292-4076. Editors: Kathy Fagan (poetry); Michelle Herman (fiction). Magazine: 6×9; 80 pages. "We are open to all forms of quality fiction." For an educated, general adult audience. Semiannually. Estab. 1973. Circ. 1,300.

Needs: "Interested in all literary forms." No romance or religious/devotional. Accepts 2 mss/issue. Receives approximately 100 unsolicited fiction mss each month. "Usually" publishes ms within 1 year of acceptance. Agented fiction 10%. Published work by Liza Wieland, M.V. Clayton; published new writers within the last year. Length: Open. Also accepts poetry. Critiques rejected mss when there is time.

How to Contact: Send complete ms with cover letter. Reports "as soon as possible," usually 3 months. SASE. Sample copy $5.50; fiction guidelines for SASE (IRCs).

Payment: Pays $25 stipend when funds are available; contributor's copies; $5.50 charge for extras.

Terms: Acquires First North American serial rights. Sends galleys to author.

Advice: Mss are rejected because of "lack of understanding of the short story form, shallow plots, undeveloped characters. Cure: read as much well-written fiction as possible. Our readers prefer 'psychological' fiction rather than stories with intricate plots. Take care to present a clean, well-typed submission."

THE JOURNAL, (II), Poetry Forum, 5713 Larchmont Dr., Erie PA 16509. (814)866-2543. Fax: (814)866-2543 (Faxing hours: 8-10 a.m. and 5-8 p.m.) Editor: Gunvor Skogsholm. Newspaper: 7×8½; 18-20 pages; card cover; photographs. "Good writing — material on writing for late teens to full adulthood." Quarterly. Estab. 1989. Circ. 200.

● *The Journal* is edited by Gunvor Skogsholm, the editor of *Poetry Forum Short Stories*. Although this magazine is not strictly a pay-for-publication, she really means it when she says "subscribers come first." See the listing for *Poetry Forum Short Stories*.

Needs: Mainstream. Plans annual special fiction issue. Receives 25-30 unsolicited mss/month. Accepts 1 ms/issue; 7-10 mss/year. Publishes mss 2 weeks-7 months after acceptance. Agented .1% . Length: 500 words preferred; 300 words average; 150 words minimum. Publishes short shorts. Length: 400 words.

How to Contact: Send complete ms. Reports in 2 weeks to 7 months on mss. SASE. Simultaneous submissions OK. Accepts electronic submission via disk. Sample copy for $3. Fiction guidelines for SASE (IRCs).

Payment: No payment.

Terms: Acquires one-time rights. Not copyrighted.

Advice: "Subscribers come first!" Looks for "a good lead stating a theme, support of the theme throughout and an ending that rounds out the story or article. 1.) Let it be believable; 2.) Please don't preach; 3.) Avoid propaganda; 4.) Don't say: 'This is a story about a retarded person.' Instead prove it by your writing."

JOURNAL OF POLYMORPHOUS PERVERSITY, (I), Wry-Bred Press, Inc., 10 Waterside Plaza, Suite 20-B, New York NY 10010. (212)689-5473. Editor: Glenn Ellenbogen. Magazine: 6¾×10; 24 pages; 60 lb. paper; antique india cover stock; illustrations with some articles. "*JPP* is a humorous and satirical journal of psychology, psychiatry, and the closely allied mental health disciplines." For "psychologists, psychiatrists, social workers, psychiatric nurses, *and* the psychologically sophisticated layman." Semiannually. Estab. 1984.

Needs: Humor/satire. "We only consider materials that are 1) funny, 2) relate to psychology *or* behavior." Receives 50 unsolicited mss/month. Acquires 8 mss/issue; 16 mss/year. Most writers published last year were previously unpublished writers. Length: 1,500 words average; 4,000 words maximum. Comments on rejected mss.

How to Contact: Send complete ms *in triplicate*. Reports in 1-3 months on mss. SASE. Sample copy for $7. Fiction guidelines for #10 SAE and 1 first-class stamp (IRCs).

Payment: Pays 2 contributor's copies; charge for extras: $7.

Advice: "We will *not* look at poetry. We only want to see intelligent spoofs of scholarly psychology and psychiatry articles written in scholarly scientific language. Take a look at *real* journals of psychology and try to lampoon their *style* as much as their content. There are few places to showcase satire of the social sciences, thus we provide one vehicle for injecting a dose of humor into this often too serious area. Occasionally, we will accept a piece of creative writing written in the first person, e.g. 'A Subjective Assessment of the Oral Doctoral Defense Process: I Don't Want to Talk About It, If You Want to Know the Truth' (the latter being a piece in which Holden Caulfield shares his experiences relating to obtaining his Ph.D. in Psychology). Other creative pieces have involved a psychodiagnostic evaluation of The Little Prince (as a psychiatric patient) and God being refused tenure (after having created the world) because of insufficient publications and teaching experience."

JOURNAL OF REGIONAL CRITICISM, (II), Arjuna Library Press, 1025 Garner St. D, Space 18, Colorado Springs CO 80905. Editor: Dr. Joseph A. Uphoff, Jr. Pamphlet: size variable; number of pages variable; Xerox paper; Bristol cover stock; b&w illustrations and photos. "Surrealist and dreamlike prose poetry and very short surrealist stories to illustrate accompanying mathematical, theoretical material in the fine arts for a wide ranging audience interested in philosophical sophistication and erudite language." Variable frequency. Estab. 1979.

Needs: Adventure, contemporary, ethnic, experimental, fantasy, historical (general), horror, humor/satire, literary, mainstream, prose poem, psychic/supernatural/occult, regional, religious/inspirational, contemporary romance, science fiction. Upcoming theme: "English as a Second Language (for those confused by irony)." Receives 0-1 unsolicited fiction ms/month. Accepts 1-5 mss/issue. Recently published work by Janice Lynne Young, Celestine Frost, Timothy Hodor. Short short stories preferred. Also publishes literary criticism, poetry. Sometimes critiques rejected mss and recommends other markets.

How to Contact: Send complete ms with cover letter. Manuscript will *not* be returned. Cover letter should include goals, behind-the-scenes explanation, and biographical material or résumé, date of birth, degrees, awards, offices and publications. SASE (IRCs) for query. Simultaneous and reprint submissions OK. Sample copy, if and when available, for $1 postage. Reviews novels and short story collections.

Payment: Pays by contract after profit; contributor's copies.

Terms: Acquires "prototype presentation rights." Publication copyrighted—limited edition procedure copyrights.

Advice: "Piles of manuscripts contain undifferentiated nonentities. A story is like any work of art. It is a picture. These are ambitiously composed and buried by writers who are afraid to reread them, or they are courageously studied through readings separated by days, weeks or months. When the artist can stand the repeated sight of a polished image it is ready to be read aloud in public. It helps if the editor has some biographical knowledge of the author, a picture or a philosophical statement."

JUST A MOMENT, (I, II), Pine Grove Press, P.O. Box 40, Jamesville NY 13078. (315)423-9268. Editor: Gertrude S. Eiler. Magazine: 5½×8½; 75+ pages; 60 lb. offset paper; 65 lb. cover stock. "Our aim from the beginning has been to publish work of quality by authors with talent and ability whether previously published or not." Quarterly. Estab. 1990. Circ. 300.

• In the past few years *Just a Moment* has held a contest for college students, deadline each February. If interested, contact them to find out if there will be one planned for 1995.

Needs: Adventure, ethnic/multicultural, experimental, fantasy, historical, horror, humor/satire, literary, mainstream/contemporary, mystery/suspense, psychic/supernatural/occult, regional, romance, science fiction, senior citizen/retirement, sports, westerns (adult western, frontier, traditional). Receives 40 unsolicited mss/month. Acquires 9-10 mss/issue; 40 mss/year. Publishes ms up to 1 year after acceptance. Length: 3,500 words maximum. Publishes short shorts. Also publishes poetry. Often critiques or comments on rejected mss.

How to Contact: Send complete ms with cover letter. Should include estimated word count, bio, Social Security number (optional), list of publications (nice but optional). Reports in 2 weeks on queries; up to 6 months on mss. Send SASE (IRCs) for reply, return of ms, or disposable copy of the ms. No simultaneous submissions. Sample copy for $3.50. Fiction guidelines for any size SAE and 1 first-class stamp.

Payment: Pays subscription to the magazine or 4 contributor's copies.

Terms: Acquires one-time rights.

Advice: Looks for "quality writing, unusual subject matter, fresh and imaginative slant. Don't over-write! Don't be afraid to cut! Would like to see more Action! Adventure! Humor!"

KALEIDOSCOPE: International Magazine of Literature, Fine Arts, and Disability, (II, IV), 326 Locust St., Akron OH 44302. (216)762-9755. Editor-in-Chief: Darshan Perusek, Ph.D. Senior Editor: Gail Willmott. Magazine: 8½ × 11; 56-64 pages; non-coated paper; coated cover stock; illustrations (all media); photos. "*Kaleidoscope* creatively explores the experiences of disability through fiction, essays, poetry, and visual arts. Challenges and transcends stereotypical and patronizing attitudes about disability." Semiannually. Estab. 1979. Circ. 1,500.

Needs: Personal experience, drama, fiction, essay, artwork. Upcoming themes: "War-Related Disabilities (March 1994); "Disability and the Media" (August 1994). Receives 20-25 unsolicited fiction mss/month. Buys 10 mss/year. Approximately 1% of fiction is agented. Recently published work by Andre Dubus, Margaret Robison, Diana Hume George. Published new writers within the last year. Length: 5,000 words maximum. Also publishes poetry.

How to Contact: Query first or send complete ms and cover letter, which should include SASE (IRCs), author's educational and writing background, if author has a disability, how the disability has influenced the writing. Simultaneous submissions OK. Reports in 1 month on queries; 6 months on mss. Sample copy for $4. Guidelines for #10 SAE and 1 first-class stamp.

Payment: Pays cash ranging from $10-125; 2 contributor's copies; charge for extras: $4.50.

Terms: Pays on publication for first rights. Reprints are permitted with credit given to original publication.

Advice: "Read the magazine and get submission guidelines. We prefer that writers with a disability offer original perspectives about their experiences; writers without disabilities should limit themselves to our focus in order to solidify a connection to our magazine's purpose."

KALLIOPE, A Journal of Women's Art, (II), Florida Community College at Jacksonville, 3939 Roosevelt Blvd., Jacksonville FL 32205. (904)381-3511. Editor: Mary Sue Koeppel. Magazine: 7¼ × 8¼; 76-88 pages; 70 lb. coated matte paper; Bristol cover; 16-18 halftones per issue. "A literary and visual arts journal for women, *Kalliope* celebrates women in the arts by publishing their work and by providing a forum for their ideas and opinions." Short stories, poems, plays, essays, reviews and visual art. Triannually. Estab. 1978. Circ. 1,250.

● Kalliope received the Frances Buck Sherman Award in 1993 from the local branch of the National League of Pen Women.

Needs: "Quality short fiction by women writers." Upcoming themes: "Women's Spirituality" and "Making a Home of Wherever You Are" (deadline April 1994). Accepts 2-4 mss/issue. Receives approximately 100 unsolicited fiction mss each month. Published work by Layle Silbert, Robin Merle, Claudia Brinson Smith, Colette; published new writers within the last year. Preferred length: 750-3,000 words, but occasionally publishes longer (and shorter) pieces. Also publishes poetry. Critiques rejected mss "when there is time and if requested."

How to Contact: Send complete ms with SASE (IRCs) and short contributor's note. No simultaneous submissions. Reports in 2-3 months on ms. Publishes ms an average of 1-6 months after acceptance. Sample copy: $7 for current issue; $4 for issues from '78-'88. Reviews novels and short story collections.

Payment: Pays 3 contributor's copies or year's subscription. $7 charge for extras, discount for 4 or more.

Terms: Acquires first rights. "We accept only unpublished work. Copyright returned to author upon request."

Advice: "Read our magazine. The work we consider for publication will be well written and the characters and dialogue will be convincing and have strength and movement. We like a fresh approach and are interested in new or unusual forms. Make us believe your characters; give readers an insight which they might not have had if they had not read you. We would like to publish more work by minority writers." Manuscripts are rejected because "1) nothing *happens!*, 2) it is thinly disguised autobiography (richly disguised autobiography is OK), and 3) ending is either too pat or else just trails off."

KANSAS QUARTERLY, (I, II), Kansas Quarterly Association, English Dept., Kansas State University, Manhattan KS 66506-0703. (913)532-6716. Editors: Harold Schneider (emeritus), Ben Nyberg, John Rees, G.W. Clift and Jonathan Holden. Magazine: 6 × 9; 104-356 pages; 70 lb. offset paper; Frankcote 8 pt. coated cover stock; illustrations occasionally; unsolicited photos rarely. "A literary and cultural arts magazine publishing fiction and poetry. Special material on selected, announced topics in literary criticism, art history, folklore and regional history. For well-read, general and academic audiences." Quarterly. Published double and single fiction issues last year; plans repeat. Estab. 1968. Circ. 1,300.
Needs: "We consider most categories as long as the fiction is of sufficient literary quality to merit inclusion, though we have no interest in children's literature. We resist translations and parts of novels, but do not absolutely refuse them." Accepts 30-50 mss/year. Limited reading done in summer. Agented fiction approximately 1%. Published work by Stephen Dixon, D.E. Steward and Jerry Bumpus; published new writers within the last year. Length: 350-12,000 words. Sometimes recommends other markets.
How to Contact: Send complete ms with SASE (IRCs). Reports in 3 months+ on mss. Publishes ms an average of 18-24 months after acceptance. Sample copy $6.
Payment: Pays 2 contributor's copies and annual awards to the best of the stories published.
Terms: Acquires all rights. Sends galleys to author. "We reassign rights on request at time of republication." Sponsors awards: *KQ*/KAC (national); Seaton awards (for Kansas natives or residents). Each offers 6-10 awards from $25-$250.
Advice: "Always check a sample copy of the magazine to which you wish to send your stories—note its editors' likes and interests."

KARAMU, (II), English Dept., Eastern Illinois University, Charleston IL 61920. (217)581-5614. Editor: Peggy L. Brayfield. Magazine: 5 × 8; 60 pages; cover illustrations. "We like fiction that builds around real experiences, real images and real characters, that shows an awareness of current fiction and the types of experiments that are going on in it, and that avoids abstraction, sentimentality, over-philosophizing and fuzzy pontifications. For a literate, college-educated audience." Annually. Estab. 1967. Circ. 500.
  ● *Karamu* received two Illinois Arts Council Awards in 1990.
Needs: Literary, contemporary. Receives approximately 20-30 unsolicited fiction mss/month. Accepts 5-8 mss/issue. Recently published work by Emilio DeGrazia, Jefferson Humphries, Jere Hoar, Ellen Winter. Published new writers within the last year. Length: 2,000-7,000 words. Also publishes literary essays, poetry. Critiques rejected mss when time permits.
How to Contact: Send complete ms with SASE (IRCs). "Initial screening within 1 month, surviving mss may be held until May or June." Publishes ms an average of 1 year after acceptance. Sample copy $3; 2 issues for $5.
Payment: Pays 1 contributor's copy; half price charge for extras.
Advice: "Send for a sample copy, read it, and send a complete ms if your stories seem to match our taste. Please be patient—we sometimes get behind in our reading, especially between May and September. Mss submitted between January and June have the shortest waiting time, if they survive initial screening. We feel that much of the best writing today is being done in short fiction."

KELSEY REVIEW, (II, IV), Mercer County College, P.O. Box B, Trenton NJ 08690. (609)586-4800. Editor: Robin Schore. Magazine: 8 × 14; 64 pages; glossy paper; soft cover. "Must live or work in Mercer County, NJ." Annually. Estab. 1988. Circ. 1,000.
Needs: Open. Regional (Mercer County only). Receives 100 unsolicited mss/year. Acquires 24 mss/issue. Reads mss only in May. Publishes ms 1-2 months after acceptance. Length: 2,000 words maximum. Publishes short shorts. Also publishes literary essays, literary criticism and poetry. Always critiques or comments on rejected mss.
How to Contact: Send complete ms with cover letter. SASE or IRC for return of ms. No simultaneous submissions. Reports in 1-2 months. Sample copy free. Reviews "anything."
Payment: Pays 5 contributor's copies.
Terms: Acquires rights, revert to author on publication.
Advice: Looks for "quality: intellect, grace and guts."

KENNESAW REVIEW, (II), Kennesaw State College, English Dept., P.O. Box 444, Marietta GA 30061. (404)423-6297. Editor: Dr. Robert W. Hill. Magazine: "Just good fiction, all themes, for a general audience." Semiannually. Estab. 1987.

Needs: Condensed/excerpted novel, contemporary, ethnic, experimental, fantasy, feminist, gay, horror, humor/satire, literary, mainstream, psychic/supernatural/occult, regional. No romance. Receives 25-60 mss/month. Accepts 2-4 mss/issue. Publishes ms 6-12 months after acceptance. Recently published work by Julie Brown, Stephen Dixon, Robert Morgan, Carolyn Thorman. Length: 9-30 pages. Publishes short shorts. Length: 500 words. Occasionally comments on or critiques rejected mss.

How to Contact: Send complete ms with cover letter. Include previous publications. Reports in 2 months on mss. SASE (IRCs). Simultaneous submissions OK. Sample copy and fiction guidelines free.

Payment: Pays in contributor's copies.

Terms: Acquires first publication rights only. Acknowledgment required for subsequent publication.

Advice: "Use the language well and tell an interesting story. Send it on. Be open to suggestions."

KENTUCKY WRITING, (II), Somerset Community College, 808 Monticello St., Somerset KY 42501. (606)679-8501. Editors: Betty Peterson, Wanda Fries. Magazine: 5½ × 9½; 80 pages; illustrations; photographs. "We publish poetry, short fiction, literary essays, cartoons, drawings, black-and-white photos. We also publish one anthology of Kentucky student work, K-12, once a year." Annually. Estab. 1985. Circ. 1,500.

Needs: Mainstream/contemporary. Publishes annual special fiction issue or anthology. Receives 25 unsolicited mss/month. Acquires 20 mss/issue; 40 mss/year. Does not read mss in summer. Publishes ms 6 months-1 year after acceptance. Recently published work by Gurney Norman, Meredith Sue Willis. Length: 7,000 words maximum. Publishes short shorts. Also publishes literary essays and poetry. Sometimes critiques or comments on rejected mss.

How to Contact: Send complete ms with cover letter. Should include bio. Reports in 3-12 months on mss. SASE (IRCs) for return of ms. No simultaneous submissions. Sample copy for $5. Fiction guidelines for #10 SAE and 1 first-class stamp.

Payment: Pays 1 contributor's copy.

Terms: Acquires first North American serial rights.

Advice: "We look for strong characterization, vivid detail, a strong sense of place, conflict and resolution." Would like to see more "authentic voice; a genuine exploration of place, rather than reliance on clichés and stereotypes." Avoid sending "sentimental treatment of Appalachian themes."

THE KENYON REVIEW, (II), Kenyon College, Gambier OH 43022. (614)427-3339. Editor: Marilyn Hacker. "Fiction, poetry, essays, book reviews." Quarterly. Estab. 1939. Circ. 4,500.

- Work published in the *Kenyon Review* has been selected for inclusion in the *Pushcart Prize* anthology and the prestigious Iowa Short Fiction Award went to a collection of stories by a writer whose title story from the book was first published in *Kenyon Review*. The editor is well-known poet Marilyn Hacker.

Needs: Condensed/excerpted novel, contemporary, ethnic, experimental, feminist, gay, historical, humor/satire, lesbian, literary, mainstream, translations. Receives 300 unsolicited fiction mss/month. Does not read mss April-August. Publishes ms 12-18 months after acceptance. Length: 3-15 (typeset) pages preferred. Rarely publishes short shorts. Sometimes comments on rejected ms.

How to Contact: Send complete ms with cover letter. Reports on mss in 2-3 months. SASE (IRCs). No simultaneous submissions. Sample copy for $7.

Payment: Pays $10/page for fiction.

Terms: Pays on publication for one-time rights and option on anthology rights. Sends copy-edited version to author for approval.

Advice: "Read several issues of our publication. We remain invested in encouraging/reading/publishing work by (in particular) writers of color, writers expanding the boundaries of their genre, unpredictable voices and points of view."

85% of the information in Novel & Short Story Writer's Market *is updated from year to year. If you're still using this book and it is 1995 or later, buy the new edition at your favorite bookstore or order directly from Writer's Digest Books.*

KESTREL, A Journal of Literature and Art in the New World, (II), Division of Language and Literature, Fairmont State College, 1201 Locust Ave., Fairmont WV 26554. (304)367-4717. Editors: Martin Lammon, Valerie N. Colander, John King. Magazine: 6 × 9; photographs. "An eclectic journal publishing the best fiction, poetry, creative nonfiction and artwork for a literate audience. We strive to present contributors' work in depth." Semiannually. Estab. 1993. Circ. 500.
Needs: Ethnic/multicultural, experimental, feminist, literary, mainstream/contemporary, regional, translations. "No pornography, children's literature, romance fiction, pulp science fiction—formula fiction in general." Receives 30 unsolicited mss/month. Acquires 3-5 mss/issue; 6-10 mss/year. Publishes ms 6-12 months after acceptance. Length: 5,000 words maximum. Publishes short shorts. Also publishes literary essays and poetry. Sometimes critiques or comments on rejected mss.
How To Contact: Send complete ms with cover letter. Should include estimated word count, brief bio and list of publications with submission. Reports in 3 weeks on queries; 3 months on mss. SASE (or IRC) for return of ms or disposable copy of ms. No simultaneous submissions. Sample copy $5. Fiction guidelines for #10 SAE and 1 first-class stamp or IRC.
Payment: Pays 2 contributor's copies.
Terms: Rights revert to contributor on publication.

KIOSK, (II), English Department, S.U.N.Y. at Buffalo, 302 Clemens Hall, Buffalo NY 14260. (716)636-2570. Editor: M. Obropta. Fiction Editor: Robert Rebein. Magazine: 5½ × 8½; 100 pages; card stock cover. "We seek innovative, non-formula fiction and poetry." Annually (may soon be Biannually). Estab. 1986. Circ. 750.
Needs: Excerpted novel, short story, prose poem and translations. "No genre or formula fiction; we seek fiction that defies categorization—lush, quirky, flippant, challenging, etc. Stretch the boundaries." Receives 50 mss/month. Accepts 10-20 mss/issue. Publishes ms within 6 months of acceptance. Recently published work by Ray Federman, Carol Berge, Dennis Tedlock; published new writers within last year. Length: 3,000 words preferred; 7,500 words maximum. Publishes short shorts. Also publishes poetry. Sometimes critiques rejected mss; rarely recommends other markets.
How to Contact: Send complete mss with cover letter. Does not read from May to September. Reports in 2-3 months on mss. "Most sooner; if we keep it longer, we're considering it seriously." SASE (IRCs). Simultaneous and reprint submissions OK. Sample copy for $5. Guidelines for SAE.
Payment: Pays in contributor's copies.
Terms: Acquires one-time rights.
Advice: "First and foremost *Kiosk* is interested in sharp writing. There's no need to be dogmatic in terms of pushing a particular style or form, and we aren't. At the same time, we get tired of reading the same old story, the same old poem. Make it new, but also make it worth the reader's effort. Style without substance is a bugaboo. No gratuitous obscurity, but don't be afraid to take real chances. Though we consider all types, we definitely lean towards the experimental. Literary magazine writing is exciting when editors take chances and offer a place for writers who find other avenues closed."

‡KOKOPELLI NOTES, Transportation Choices for a Greener Planet, (IV), Kokopelli Council, Inc., P.O. Box 8186, Asheville NC 28814. (704)683-4844. Editor: Patrick Clark. Magazine: 8½ × 11; 32 pages; off-set recycled paper; 10 illustrations and photographs. "Stories about traveling by foot, bicycle, canoe, horse, train, or hitchhiking. We look for stories which reveal a spiritual depth as well as just plain exuberance for adventure. Using 'self-propelled' transportation in daily life also." Quarterly. Estab. 1991. Circ. 1,500.
• For more info on this magazine see the review section of *Utne Reader*'s July/August 1993 issue.
Needs: Environmental and deep ecology: adventure, historical (general), regional. "We are very specialized. Writers should get a review copy before submitting." Plans specific themes for upcoming issues. List of upcoming themes available for SASE. Receives 3 unsolicited mss/month. Accepts 1 ms/issue; 5 mss/year. Publishes ms up to 1 year after acceptance. Length: 500 words preferred; 250 words minimum; 1,000 words maximum. Publishes short shorts. Also publishes literary essays and poetry.
How to Contact: Query with clips of published work. Should include estimated word count and bio (50-100 words). Reports in 1 month. Send SASE (or IRC) for reply, return of ms or send a disposable copy of ms. Simultaneous, reprint and electronic submissions OK. Sample copy for $4. Fiction guidelines free.
Payment: Pays free subscription; additional copies for $3.
Terms: Acquires first North American serial rights.
Advice: "We look for stories about walking, bicycling, or other outdoor adventure which explore a deeper level of experience." Looks for "stories about connection to the earth and love of one's place."

KUMQUAT MERINGUE, "Dedicated to the Memory of Richard Brautigan", (I, II, IV), P.O. Box 5144, Rockford IL 61125. (815)968-0713. Editor: Christian Nelson. Magazine: Digest-sized; 32 pages; some illustrations and photographs. "Mostly poetry but always needing short, quirky, maybe sexy prose, preferably under 400 words. Unusual facets of love and sex. Like writing that puts us in the mood of Richard Brautigan." Published irregularly, approx. every 6-7 months. Estab. 1991. Circ. 500.

● Richard Brautigan's works include *Trout Fishing in America*, *The Hawkline Monster* and *In Watermelon Sugar*.

Needs: Adventure, erotica, ethnic/multicultural, experimental, feminist, gay, humor/satire, lesbian, literary, mainstream/contemporary, regional. No inspirational or regular science fiction. Receives 20 unsolicited mss/month. Acquires 2-4 mss/issue; 4-10 mss/year. Publishes ms 6-9 months after acceptance. Recently published work by Robert W. Howington, Tamara Moan, Howard Fine, Terry J. Fox. Length: 600 words maximum. Publishes short shorts. Also publishes literary essays and poetry. Often critiques or comments on rejected mss.

How to Contact: Send complete ms with cover letter. Reports in 1-2 months on mss. SASE (IRCs) for ms or send disposable copy of ms. Simultaneous submissions or reprints OK. Sample copy for $4. Fiction guidelines for #10 SAE.

Payment: Pays 1 contributor's copy.

Terms: Acquires first rights.

Advice: "*Kumquat Meringue* publishes literary works of uncommon and unusual virtue. We're very open to beginning or unpublished writers, but our editorial policy is an anomalous one. We never presume to judge whether a submitted piece is 'good' or 'bad.' The only judgment is whether or not we like it, and how it fits in with the feel of the magazine. And admittedly, we're hard to please. We do like concentration on the smaller details of everyday life, especially about love . . . and sex. We like to read about love gone wrong and love gone right. But we want the quirky side. So please, no hearts and flowers and none of that old worn out stuff about how much you love that certain someone. And no June moons or sleeping like spoons. We also like reading things 'to' or 'for' Richard Brautigan."

LACTUCA, (I, II), Box 621, Suffern NY 10901. Editor: Mike Selender. Magazine: Folded 8½ × 14; 72 pages; 24 lb. bond; soft cover; saddle-stapled; illustrations. Publishes "poetry, short fiction and b&w art, for a general literary audience." Published 2-3 times/year. Estab. 1986. Circ. 700.

Needs: Adventure, condensed/excerpted novel, confession, contemporary, erotica, literary, mainstream, prose poem and regional. No "self-indulgent writing or fiction about writing fiction." Receives 30 or more mss/month. Accepts 3-4 mss/issue; 10-12 mss/year. Publishes ms within 3-12 months of acceptance. Published work by Douglas Mendini, Tom Gidwitz, Ruthann Robson; published new writers within the last year. Length: around 12-14 typewritten double-spaced pages. Publishes short shorts. Often critiques rejected mss and recommends other markets.

How to Contact: Query first or send complete ms with cover letter. Cover letter should include "just a few brief notes about yourself. Please no long 'literary' résumés or bios. The work will speak for itself." Reports usually within 6 weeks. No longer than 3 months. SASE. No simultaneous or previously published work. Accepts electronic submissions via "MS DOS formatted disk. We can convert most word-processing formats." Sample copy for $4. Fiction guidelines for #10 SAE and 1 first-class stamp (IRCs).

Payment: Pays 2-5 contributor's copies, depending on the length of the work published.

Terms: Acquires first North American serial rights. Sends galleys to author. Copyrights revert to authors.

Advice: "We want fiction coming from a strong sense of place and/or experience. Work with an honest emotional depth. We steer clear of self-indulgent material. We particularly like work that tackles complex issues and the impact of such on people's lives. We are open to work that is dark and/or disturbing."

THE LAMPLIGHT, (II), Beggar's Press, 8110 N. 38 St., Omaha NE 68112. (402)455-2615. Editor: Richard R. Carey. Fiction Editor: Sandy Johnsen. Magazine: 8½ × 11; 40 pages; 20 lb. bond paper; 65 lb. stock cover; some illustrations; a few photographs. "Our purpose is to establish a new literature drawn from the past. We relish foreign settings in the 19th century when human passions transcended computers and fax machines. We are literary but appeal to the common intellect and the mass soul of humanity." Semiannually.

● Beggar's Press publishes *Raskolnikov's Cellar*, which alternates with *The Lamplight*, and also publishes *Beggar's Folios* and *The Beggar's Review*. Write them for information on these other publications.

Needs: Historical (general), humor/satire, literary, mystery/suspense (literary), romance (gothic, historical). "Settings in the past. Psychological stories." Plans special fiction issue or anthology in the future. Receives 10-15 unsolicited mss/month. Acquires 2 mss/issue; 4 mss/year. Publishes ms 4-12 months after acceptance. Recently published work by Fredrick Zydek, John J. McKernan. Length: 2,000 words preferred; 500 words minimum; 3,500 words maximum. Publishes short shorts. Length: 300 words. Also publishes literary criticism and poetry. Sometimes critiques or comments on rejected mss.

How to Contact: Send complete ms with cover letter. Should include estimated word count, bio (a paragraph or two) and list of publications. Reports in 1 month on queries; 2½ months on mss. SASE. Simultaneous and reprint submission OK. Sample copy for $7, 9×12 SAE and 2 first-class stamps (IRCs). Fiction guidelines for $1, #10 SAE and 1 first-class stamp. Reviews novels and short story collections.

Payment: Pays 2 contributor's copies. Additional copies at a reduced rate of 40% discount up to 5 additional copies.

Terms: Acquires first North American serial rights.

Advice: "We deal in classical masterpieces. Every piece must be timeless. It must live for five centuries or more. We judge on this basis. These are not easy to come by. But we want to stretch authors to their fullest capacity. They will have to dig deeper for us, and develop a style that is different from what is commonly read in today's market."

LANGUAGE BRIDGES QUARTERLY, Polish-English Literary Magazine, (II, IV), Box 850792, Richardson TX 75085-0792. (214)530-2782. Editor: Eva Ziem. Fiction Editor: Zofia Przebindowska-Tousty. Magazine: 8½×11; 20+ pages; 60 lb. paper; 65 lb. cover; illustrations. "Today's Poland and Polish spirit are the main subject; a picture of life in Poland, with emphasis on the recent Polish emigration wave problems, however topics of general nature are being accepted. For both English and Polish speaking readers." Quarterly. Estab. 1989. Circ. 300.

Needs: Condensed/excerpted novel, fantasy, historical (general), humor/satire, literary, prose poem, religious/inspirational, translations, young adult/teen (10-18 years). "No horror, no vulgar language." Receives 1 unsolicited ms/month. Accepts one fiction ms every second issue. Publishes ms 3-6 months after acceptance. "Length does not matter. The longer works are broken into parts." Publishes short shorts. Sometimes critiques rejected mss and recommends other markets.

How to Contact: Send complete ms with cover letter. Reports in 2-3 months on mss. Simultaneous and reprint submissions OK. Accepts electronic submissions via disk. Free sample copy and fiction guidelines.

Payment: Pays contributor's copies.

Terms: Pays for one-time rights. Sends galleys to author.

Advice: "*LBQ* is the only fully bilingual Polish-English literary magazine in the U.S. It obviously helps Polish newcomers to learn English and Polish Americans to brush up on their Polish. Consequently, through translated Polish literary works, *LBQ* introduces the English-speaking reader to Polish culture and problems of Poles in Poland and abroad. *LBQ* creates a bridge between Polish and American writers as well as the readers. As the bilingual population of Polish Americans has recently grown in the U.S.A., *LBQ* also fulfills the increasing demand for crosscultural dialogue in seeking common roots and discovering differences."

THE LAUREL REVIEW, (II), Northwest Missouri State University, Dept. of English, Maryville MO 64468. (816)562-1265. Co-editors: Craig Goad, David Slater and William Trowbridge. Associate Editors: Nancy Vieira Covto, Randall R. Freisinger, Steve Heller. Magazine: 6×9; 124-128 pages; good quality paper. "We publish poetry and fiction of high quality, from the traditional to the avant-garde. We are eclectic, open and flexible. Good writing is all we seek." Biannually. Estab. 1960. Circ. 800.

Needs: Literary and contemporary. Accepts 3-5 mss/issue, 6-10 mss/year. Receives approximately 60 unsolicited fiction mss each month. Approximately 1% of fiction is agented. Length: 2,000-10,000 words. Sometimes publishes literary essays; also publishes poetry. Critiques rejected mss "when there is time." Reads September to May.

How to Contact: Send complete ms with SASE (IRCs). No simultaneous submissions. Reports in 1-4 months on mss. Publishes ms an average of 1-12 months after acceptance. Sample copy for $3.50.

Payment: Pays 2 contributor's copies, 1 year subscription.

Terms: Acquires first rights. Copyright reverts to author upon request.

Advice: Send $3.50 for a back copy of the magazine.

THE LEADING EDGE, Magazine of Science Fiction and Fantasy, (II, IV), 3163 JKHB, Provo UT 84604. Editor: Michael Carr. Magazine: 5 × 8; 120-144 pages; 20 lb. bond paper; 40 lb. card stock; 15-20 illustrations. "We are a magazine dedicated to the new and upcoming author, poet, and artist involved in the field of science fiction and fantasy. We are for the upcoming professional." Triannually. Circ. 500.
Needs: Adventure, experimental, fantasy, humor/satire, prose poem, science fiction (hard science, soft/sociological). "We are very interested in experimental sf and humorous stories, but all pieces should fall within the category of sf and fantasy. No graphic sex, violence, dismemberment, etc. No outrageous religious commentary. No fannish/media stories; i.e., no Star Wars, Star Trek, Dr. Who, etc." Receives 40 unsolicited mss/month. Buys 6-8 mss/issue; 20-30 mss/year. Publishes ms 1-4 months after acceptance. Recently published work by Jane Yolen, Michael R. Collings, Dave Wolverton, Ben Bova. Length: 5,000 words; 500 words minimum; 17,000 words maximum. Publishes short shorts. Also publishes literary essays, literary criticism, poetry. Critiques rejected mss.
How to Contact: Send complete ms. Include name and address, phone number and title of story. Reports in 3-4 months on mss. SASE. Simultaneous submissions OK. Sample copy for $3.50. Fiction guidelines for #10 SAE and 1 first-class stamp (IRCs). Sometimes reviews novels and short story collections.
Payment: Pays 1¢/word up to $100 for fiction.
Terms: Pays on publication for first North American serial rights. Sends galleys to author.
Advice: "All fiction must be original, innovative and interesting. We are very familiar with the body of sf and fantasy work, and look for new stories. Too many writers of sf and fantasy rely on existing cliché and convention. Humor, hard science, and experimental fantasy have the best chance for publication. Accurate science, vivid imagery, and strong characterization will impress the editors. We want stories about people with problems; the setting is there to illustrate the problem, not vice versa. Proofread!!! Please send clean, proofread copy. Just because we're small doesn't mean we're sloppy. Research! Be accurate. Our readers are *very* aware of science and history. We do not publish graphic violence or sex. Violence is okay if it is necessary to the story."

THE LEDGE POETRY AND FICTION MAGAZINE, (II), 64-65 Cooper Ave., Glendale NY 11385. Editor: Timothy Monaghan. Magazine: 5½ × 8¾; 80 pages; typeset and perfect-bound; gloss cover; cover art. "Our only criteria is material of high literary merit." Semiannually. Estab. 1988. Circ. 750.
  • *The Ledge Poetry and Fiction Magazine* received a grant from the Queens Council on the Arts, through the New York State Council on the Arts.
Needs: "Stories which possess a gritty, arresting and/or provocative quality that makes us sit up and take notice; stories grounded in contemporary and/or urban experience." Receives approx. 40 unsolicited fiction mss/month. Accepts 3 mss/issue; 6 mss/year. Publishes mss 2-6 months after acceptance. Recently published work by Ezra Zonana, Mitch Levenberg, Diana Chang, Joyce Stewart. Length: "up to 15 pages, double-spaced." Publishes short shorts. Also publishes poetry. Comments on or critiques rejected mss occasionally, if warranted.
How to Contact: Send complete ms with cover letter (optional). Reports in 1-2 weeks on queries; 3 months or less on mss. SASE (IRCs). Sample copy for $5. Fiction guidelines for #10 SASE.
Payment: Pays 1 contributor's copy.
Terms: Acquires one-time rights.
Advice: "We are open to all schools and slants, but especially value a story written in prose that demonstrates mastery of the English language, an original slant on its theme, and an ending, whether loud or muted, naive or ironical, of some consequence."

LEFT BANK, (II, IV), Blue Heron Publishing, 24450 NW Hansen Rd., Hillsboro OR 97124. (503)621-3911. Editor: Linny Stovall. Book Form: 6 × 9; 160 pages; book paper; illustrations; photographs. "We only publish NW writers (OR, MT, ID, WA, AK, British Columbia and Alberta) and take only a few short stories—mostly essay format." Published in December and June. Estab. 1991. Circ. 7,000.
  • The publishers of *Left Bank* also publish the *Writer's Northwest Handbook* (by Media Weavers). It's chock full of market and writing information for the northwestern US.
Needs: Ethnic/multicultural, feminist, gay, humor/satire, lesbian, literary, mainstream/contemporary, regional. "Each issue is themed. Guidelines must be sent for since each issue is thematic. We also take excerpts from books in progress or recently in print (latter particularly if well-known author). List of upcoming themes available for SASE. Buys 2-6 fiction mss/issue. Publishes ms 4-6 months after acceptance. Agented fiction 50%. Recently published work by Ursula Le Guin, Ken Kesey. Length: 2,500 words preferred; 1,500-3,000 words maximum. Also publishes literary essays.

How to Contact: Query first and get guidelines for SASE. Should include bio (1 page maximum), list of publications. Reports in 2-3 weeks on queries; 2 months on mss. SASE (IRCs) for a reply to a query or send a disposable copy of the ms. Simultaneous and electronic submissions OK. Sample copy for $9.95 plus $2 (postage and handling). Fiction guidelines for SASE.
Payment: Pays $50-150 and 1 contributor's copy.
Terms: Buys first North American serial rights or one-time rights.

♣LEGEND, A "Robin of Sherwood" Fanzine, (I, II, IV), 1036 Hampshire Rd., Victoria, British Columbia V85 4S9 Canada. Editor: Janet P. Reedman. Magazine: Size varies; 200+ pages; bond paper; color print cover; illustrations. "Fantasy: Based on TV series 'Robin of Sherwood.' Annually. Estab. 1989. Circ. 200+.
Needs: Adventure, fantasy, historical, retold myths/legends. "All material must be based on 'Robin of Sherwood' in these genres. Nothing excessively violent/sexual, though adult themes are fine. Nothing sticky-sweet and saccharine, either!" Receives 2-3 unsolicited mss/month. Accepts 15-20 mss/issue; 15-20 mss/year. Publishes ms 4-18 months after acceptance. Length: 3,000 words preferred; 150 words minimum; 20,000 words maximum. Also publishes poetry. Sometimes critiques rejected mss and recommends other markets.
How to Contact: Query first. (I'll accept mss without queries, but it might be wise to write and ask if we're still open, overstocked, etc.). Reports in 2 months on queries; 2 months on mss. SASE. "Will accept loose stamps or IRCs, as I can use stamps from other countries." No simultaneous submissions. Fiction guidelines for #10 SAE and 1 loose first-class stamp.
Payment: Pays in contributor's copies for material over 3 pages long.
Terms: Acquires first North American serial rights.
Advice: "Please support small publications, so they can *survive* to publish your work! *Read* a sample copy, so you don't waste postage and the editor's time! We have had handwritten mss, juveniles, no SASE, satires, experimental fiction, 5 stories crammed in one envelope . . . *despite explicit* guidelines! Also, *please, no* phone calls unless you are invited to phone via the mail first!! *Legend* may undergo a change of publisher, although I will remain as editor."

THE LETTER PARADE, (I), Bonnie Jo Enterprises, P.O. Box 52, Comstock MI 49041. Editor: Bonnie Jo. Newsletter: legal/letter-sized; 6 pages. Monthly. Estab. 1985. Circ. 113.
Needs: "Anything short." Receives 5-6 unsolicited mss/month. Acquires 1-2 mss/issue. Publishes ms up to a year after acceptance. Recently published work by Mimi Lipson, Ann Keniston, Chuck Jones. Length: 250-750 words preferred; 1,000 words maximum. Publishes short shorts. Also publishes literary essays.
How to Contact: Send complete ms with a cover letter. "Please single space so I can publish pieces in the form I receive them." Send disposable copy of ms. Simultaneous and reprint submissions OK. Sample copy for $1. Reviews novels or short story collections. Send review copies to Christopher Magson.
Payment: Pays subscription to magazine.
Terms: Not copyrighted.
Advice: "My publication is small, so stories have got to be short. Comfortable writing makes a manuscript stand out."

LIBIDO, The Journal of Sex and Sensibility, (II, IV), Libido, Inc., P.O. Box 146721, Chicago IL 60614. (312)281-5839. Editors: Jack Hafferkamp and Marianna Beck. Magazine: 5½×8½; 80 pages; 70 lb. non-coated; b&w illustrations and photographs. "Erotica is the focus. Fiction, poetry, essays, reviews for literate adults." Quarterly. Estab. 1988. Circ. 7,500.
• Specializing in "literary" erotica, this journal has attracted a number of top-name writers.
Needs: Condensed/excerpted novel, confession, erotica, gay, lesbian. No "dirty words for their own sake, violence, sexual exploitation." Receives 25-50 unsolicited mss/month. Buys about 5/issue; about 20 per year. Publishes ms up to 1 year after acceptance. Published work by Marco Vassi, Anne Rampling (Ann Rice), Larry Tritten. Length: 1,000-3,000 words; 300 words minimum; 3,000 words maximum. Also publishes literary essays, literary criticism. Sometimes critiques rejected ms and recommends other markets.
How to Contact: Send complete ms with cover letter including Social Security number and brief bio for contributor's page. Reports in 3 months on mss. SASE (IRCs). No simultaneous submissions. Reprint submissions OK. Accepts electronic submissions via disk. Sample copy for $7. Free fiction guidelines. Reviews novels and short story collections.

Payment: Pays $15-50 and 2 contributor's copies.
Terms: Pays on publication for one-time or anthology rights.
Advice: "Humor is a strong plus. There must be a strong erotic element, and it should celebrate the joy of sex."

‡LIFE ENRICHMENT, (II), FJ McLaughlin Newsletter Network, 1346 Joan Dr., Southampton PA 18966-4341. (215)322-1346. Editor: Flo McLaughlin. Newsletter: 8½×11; 8 pages; 20 lb. bond paper. "Enrich your life by sharing your positive experiences. Read articles and stories about positive, upbeat people and events. Read by men and women who enjoy other folks' adventures and challenges." Quarterly. Estab. 1987. Circ. under 1,000.
Needs: Ethnic/multicultural, humor/satire, literary, mainstream/contemporary, regional, religious/inspirational, senior citizen/retirement. No material that is "dull, depressing, overly religious or agenda pushing." Receives 2-3 unsolicited mss/month. Accepts 1 ms/issue; 4 mss/year. Publishes ms usually within 1 or 2 issues after acceptance. Recently published work by Kathy Black, Peggy Boudin, Mary Bontempo. Length: 500 words preferred; 100 words minimum; 1,000 words maximum. Publishes short shorts. Also publishes literary essays, literary criticism and poetry. Always critiques or comments on rejected mss.
How to Contact: Query first. Should include estimated word count. Reports in 2-4 weeks on queries; 4-6 weeks on ms. Send SASE (or IRC) for reply, return of ms or send disposable copy of ms. Simultaneous, reprint and electronic submissions OK. Sample copy for $3. Fiction guidelines for SAE.
Payment: Pays subscription and 4 contributor's copies; additional copies for $1.
Terms: Acquires one-time rights.
Advice: "How do I react to the story and how clear is the writing? Is it positive? The story must make me think or create an emotional response." Looking for "stories of people who overcome adversity. Stories of families and the strength of parents teaching lifelong character."

‡LIGHT QUARTERLY, (II), P.O. Box 7500, Chicago IL 60680. Editor: John Mella. Magazine: 8½×11; 32-40 pages; Finch opaque (60 lb.) paper; 65 lb. variable color cover; illustrations. "Light and satiric verse and prose, witty but not sentimental. Audience: intelligent, educated, usually but not always 'professional.' " Quarterly. Estab. 1992. Circ. 1,000.
Needs: Humor/satire, literary. Receives 10-20 unsolicited fiction mss/month. Accepts 2-4 mss/issue. Publishes ms 6 months-2 years after acceptance. Recently published work by X.J. Kennedy, J.F. Nims, John Updike. Length: 1,200 words preferred; 600 words minimum; 2,000 words maximum. Publishes short shorts. Also publishes literary essays, literary criticisms and poetry. Sometimes critiques or comments on rejected mss.
How to Contact: Query first. Should include estimated word count and list of publications. Reports in 1 month on queries; 2-4 months on mss. Send SASE (or IRC) for reply, return of ms or send a disposable copy of ms. No simultaneous submissions. Electronic submissions OK. Sample copy for $3. Fiction guidelines for #10 SAE and 1 first-class stamp. Reviews novels and short story collections. Send review copies to review editor.
Payment: Pays contributor's copies (2 for domestic; 1 for foreign).
Terms: Pays on publication for first North American serial rights. Sends galleys to author (for long pieces).
Advice: Looks for "high literary quality; wit, allusiveness, a distinct (and distinctive) style. Read guidelines first."

LIMESTONE: A LITERARY JOURNAL, (II), University of Kentucky, Dept. of English, 1215 Patterson Office Tower, Lexington KY 40506-0027. (606)257-7008. Contact: Editorial Committee. Magazine: 6×9; 50-75 pages; standard text paper and cover; illustrations; photos. "We publish a variety of styles and attitudes, and we're looking to expand our offering." Annually. Estab. 1981. Circ. 1,000.
Needs: "Quality poetry and short fiction, literary, mainstream, thoughtful. No fantasy or science fiction. No previously published work." Receives 200 mss/year. Acquires 15 mss/issue. Does not read mss May-Sept. Publishes ms an average of 6 months after acceptance. Publishes new writers every year. Length: 3,000-5,000 words preferred; 5,000 words maximum. Publishes short shorts. Sometimes critiques rejected mss.
How to Contact: Send complete ms with cover letter, which should include publishing record and brief bio. Reports in 1 month on queries; 7 months or longer on mss. SASE (IRCs). Simultaneous submissions OK. Sample copy $3.
Payment: Pays 2 contributor's copies.
Terms: Rights revert to author.

LINDEN LANE MAGAZINE, (IV), Linden Lane Magazine and Press, 103 Cuyler Rd., P.O. Box 2384, Princeton NJ 08543-2384. (609)921-7943. Fax (609)921-7943. Editor: Belkis Cuza-Malé. Tabloid: 28 pages; newsprint; illustrations and photographs. "Latin-American and American writers, in Spanish or English." Quarterly. Estab. 1982. Circ. 3,000.

Needs: Ethnic/multicultural, experimental, literary, mainstream/contemporary. Special interest: Latin American authors in US. Publishes special fiction issue or anthology. Receives 30 unsolicited mss/month. Acquires 20 mss/year. Publishes ms 6 months after acceptance. Recently published work by Guillermo Cabrera Infante, Heberto Padilla, Blanca Varela, Lydia Cabrera. Length: 800 words average. Also publishes literary essays, literary criticism and poetry. Sometimes critiques or comments on rejected mss.

How to Contact: Send complete ms with cover letter. Should include list of publications with submission. Reports on mss in 3 months. Send SASE (or IRC) for return of ms or a disposable copy of the ms. Will consider simultaneous submissions. Sample copy $2 with 8×11 SAE. Reviews novels and short story collections.

Payment: Pays 10 contributor's copies. Additional copies for $1.

LINES IN THE SAND, (I, II), LeSand Publications, 890 Southgate Ave., Daly City CA 94015. (415)992-4770. Editor: Nina Z. Sanders. Fiction Editors: Nina Z. Sanders and Barbara J. Less. Magazine: 5½×8½; 32 pages; 20 lb. bond; King James cost-coated cover; illustrations. "Stories should be well-written, entertaining and suitable for all ages. Our readers range in age from 7 to 90. No particular slant or philosophy." Bimonthly. Estab. 1992. Circ. 100.

● The editor would like to see shorter stories, especially 250-1,200 words.

Needs: Adventure, children's/juvenile (10-12 years), experimental, fantasy (science fantasy, children's fantasy), horror, humor/satire, literary, mainstream/contemporary, mystery/suspense (private eye/hard-boiled, amateur sleuth, cozy, romantic suspense), science fiction (soft/sociological), senior citizen/retirement, westerns (traditional, frontier, young adult western), young adult/teen (10-18 years). "No erotica, pornography." Receives 40-50 unsolicited mss/month. Buys 8-10 mss/issue; 50-60 mss/year. Publishes ms 2-4 months after acceptance. Recently published work by Timothy Martin, Anthony P. McAnulla, Mel Tharp, Roxanna Chalmers. Length: 1,200 words preferred; 250 words minimum; 2,000 words maximum. Publishes short shorts. Length: 250 words. Also publishes poetry. Often critiques or comments on rejected mss.

How to Contact: Send complete ms with cover letter. Should include estimated word count, bio (3-4 sentences). Reports in 2-6 months on mss. Send SASE (IRCs) for reply, return of ms or disposable copy of themes. Simultaneous and reprint submissions OK. Sample copy for $3.50. Fiction guidelines for #10 SAE and 1 first-class stamp.

Payment: Pays $3-10 and 2 contributor's copies.

Terms: Pays on publication. Buys first North American serial rights. Sends galleys to author. Sponsors contests. To enter contest submit 2 copies of story, 2,000 words maximum, double-spaced typed and $5 reading fee for each story submitted.

Advice: "Use fresh, original approach, show, don't tell,' conform to guidelines, use dialogue when appropriate, be grammatically correct. Stories should have some type of conflict. Read a sample copy (or two). Study the guidelines. Use plain language; avoid flowery, 'big' words unless appropriate in dialogue."

LININGTON LINEUP, (IV), Elizabeth Linington Society, 1223 Glen Terrace, Glassboro NJ 08028-1315. Editor: Rinehart S. Potts. Newsletter: 8½×11; 16 pages; bond paper and cover stock; illustrations and photographs. "For those interested in the publications of Elizabeth Linington (a/k/a Lesley Egan, Egan O'Neill, Anne Blaisdell, Dell Shannon)—historical fiction and detective mysteries—therefore material must relate in some way thereto." Bimonthly. Plans special fiction issue. Estab. 1984. Circ. 400.

● Elizabeth Linington wrote 90 books under her many pen names. Among the mysteries she wrote as Del Shannon are *The Dispossessed*, *Destiny of Death* and *Chaos of Crime*. As Lesley Egan she wrote several books including *Little Boy Lost* and *The Miser*.

Needs: *Charges reading fee of $1. Requires magazine subscription of $12 before reading.* Historical (general), literary, mystery/suspense. Upcoming themes: LAPD in Fiction, Delia Riordan, RIP. Receives 3-4 fiction mss/month. Accepts 1 ms/issue; 6 mss/year. Publishes ms 3 months after acceptance. Publishes short shorts. Also publishes literary essays, literary criticism, poetry. Sometimes comments on rejected mss.

How to Contact: Query first. Reports in 1 month. SASE (IRCs). No simultaneous submissions. Reprint submissions OK. Sample copy for $3. Reviews novels, short story collections and reference books/criticism in mystery field.

Payment: Pays subscription to magazine.

Terms: Acquires first rights.

Advice: "Become familiar with Miss Linington's books and continuing characters. We have been receiving material which completely disregards the information cited above."

LITE, The Journal of Satire and Creativity, (I, II), P.O. Box 26162, Baltimore MD 21210. (410)719-7792. Editor: David W. Kriebel. Tabloid: 8½×11; 4 pages; 30 lb. newsprint paper; 2-4 illustrations; some photographs. "Satire, poetry, short fiction, occasional nonfiction pieces. Our audience is intelligent, literate, and imaginative. They have the ability to step back and look at the world from a different perspective." Monthly. Estab. 1989. Circ. 10,000.

● Due to the tremendous response to their listing, the magazine has increased its response time and will not be considering stories again until Summer 1994. Note, too, their format change from magazine to tabloid.

Needs: Experimental, fantasy, historical (general), horror, humor/satire, literary, mystery/suspense (private eye), psychic/supernatural/occult, science fiction (hard science, soft/sociological). "No erotica, gay, lesbian. Nothing demeaning to any ethnic or religious group. No stories with an obvious or trite 'message.' No violence for its own sake." Receives 20-30 unsolicited mss/month. Accepts 1-2 mss/issue; 12-18 mss/year. Publishes mss 1-3 months after acceptance. Recently published work by Richard Gardner, Bill Jones. Length: 1,500 words preferred; 2,500 words maximum (however, will consider serializing longer pieces). Publishes short shorts. Also publishes poetry. Sometimes comments on or critiques rejected mss.

How to Contact: Request guidelines, then send ms and cover letter. Include "information on the writer, focusing on what led him to write or create visual art. We want to know the person, both for our contributors guide 'Names in Lite' and to help build a network of creative people." Reports in 6-12 months. SASE. Simultaneous submissions OK, but prefer them not to be sent to other Baltimore publications. Sample copy for 9×12 SAE and 3 first-class stamps (IRCs). Fiction guidelines for #10 SAE and 1 first-class stamp.

Payment: Pays 5 contributor's copies; 5 extras for 9×12 SASE with 4 first-class stamps.

Terms: Acquires one-time rights.

Advice: "We first look for quality writing, then we look at content and theme. It's not hard to tell a dedicated writer from someone who only works for money or recognition. Fiction that resonates in the heart makes us take notice. It's a joy to read such a story." Known for "offbeat, creative, but not overtly sexual or violent. We like characterization and the play of ideas. We don't like contrived plots or political propaganda masquerading as literature."

‡LITERARY FRAGMENTS, (I, II, IV), Sauvie Island Press, P.O. Box 751, Beaverton OR 97075. (503)626-4237 (modem only). Editor: Susan Roberts. Electronic magazine. "*Literary Fragments* accepts unpublished writers and is distributed worldwide through several BBS networks. New, unpublished writers are the mainstay of our electronic magazine." Estab. 1980.

Needs: Open. Publishes special fiction issue or anthology. Publishes ms 90 days after acceptance. Length: 300 words and up preferred. Publishes short shorts.

How to Contact: Send complete ms with cover letter with ASCII text on diskette or upload to BBS (NW Literary Consortium 8am-5pm Pacific Standard Time (503)626-4237). Should include estimated word count, bio (200 words maximum), Social Security number. Reports in 4-6 weeks (if selected). Send a disposable copy of ms. No simultaneous submissions. Electronic submissions required. Fiction guidelines for #10 SASE (IRCs).

Payment: Payment depends on grant/award money available or no payment.

Terms: Buys one-time rights.

Advice: "Electronic text has an incredible market for readers and writers. To see a copy of *Literary Fragments*, call your local text BBS and request LitFrag.* If your SysOp doesn't have it, he can request it via FIDO point address 1:105/290.3."

THE LITERARY REVIEW, An International Journal of Contemporary Writing, Fairleigh Dickinson University, 285 Madison Ave., Madison NJ 07940. (201)593-8564. Editor-in-Chief: Walter Cummins. Magazine: 6×9; 128-152 pages; illustrations; photos. "Literary magazine specializing in fiction, poetry, and essays with an international focus." Quarterly. Estab. 1957. Circ. 2,000.

● Guest editor for the Lebanese issue is Elise Manganare and guest editor for the Latin American issue is Ilán Stavans. This magazine has received grants from a wide variety of international sources including the Spanish Consulate General in New York, the Program for Cultural Cooperation Between Spain's Ministry of Culture and U.S. Universities, Pro Helvetia, the Swiss Center Foundation. Work published in *The Literary Review* has been included in *Editor's Choice* and the Pushcart Prize anthologies.

Needs: Works of high literary quality only. Upcoming themes: "Lebanese Writing" (Spring 1994), "Latin American Detective and Science Fiction" (Fall 1994). Receives 50-60 unsolicited fiction mss/month. Approximately 1-2% of fiction is agented. Recently published Susan Moon, Peter Lars Sandberg, Susan Daitch; published new writers within the last year. Acquires 10-12 mss/year. Also publishes literary essays, literary criticism, poetry. Occasionally critiques rejected mss. Sometimes recommends other markets.

How to Contact: Send complete ms with SASE (IRCs). "Cover letter should include publication credits." Reports in 3 months on mss. Publishes ms an average of 1-1½ years after acceptance. Sample copy for $5; guidelines for SASE. Reviews novels and short story collections.

Payment: Pays 2 contributor's copies; 25% discount for extras.

Terms: Acquires first rights.

Advice: "Too much of what we are seeing today is openly derivative in subject, plot and prose style. We pride ourselves on spotting new writers with fresh insight and approach."

THE LITTLE MAGAZINE, (III), State University of New York at Albany, English Department, Albany NY 12222. Editors: David Coogan, Nancy Dunlop. Magazine: 5½×8½; 200 pages; 70 lb. Nikusa paper; 10 pt. high gloss cover; illustrations. "Fiction and poetry for a literary audience." Annually. Estab. 1965.

Needs: Experimental, feminist, humor/satire, literary, multi-genre, omnicultural, prose poem. No romance. Receives "roughly" 600 mss/issue over a 3-month reading period. Accepts 10 mss/issue. Reads only from September 1 to December 15. Publishes ms 6 months after acceptance. Recently published work by Eugene Garber, Lydia Davis, Ralph Lombreglia. Length: 3,000 words. Publishes short shorts.

How to Contact: Send complete ms with SASE (IRCs), but only send between September 1 and December 15. Reports in 2 months on queries; in 4 months on mss. Simultaneous and reprint submissions OK. Sample copy for $7.

Payment: Pays 2 contributor's copies.

Terms: Acquires first North American serial rights.

Advice: "We like a wide variety of work from traditional to experimental."

LIVING WATER MAGAZINE, A Magazine by, for, and about Christians, (I, II, IV), Sonshine Ministries, P.O. Box 750996, Houston TX 77275-0996. (713)944-6441. Editor: Lew Engle. Magazine: 8½×11; 20 pages; 20 lb. bond paper; pulp cover; 1-3 illustrations. "The philosophy is that all Christians have something to share—*Living Water* is that place where they can share it. We use fiction, nonfiction and poetry. Audience is Christians world-wide. Bimonthly. Estab. 1990. Circ. 75.

Needs: "Almost any fiction with a strong Christian slant." Adventure, children's/juvenile (10-12 years), historical (general), mainstream/contemporary, mystery/suspense (amateur sleuth, young adult), religious/inspirational, romance (contemporary, historical, young adult), young adult/teen (10-18 years). "Nothing humanistic, New Age, anti-Judeo-Christian." Receives 8-10 unsolicited mss/month. Buys 2-3 mss/issue; 12-18 mss/year. Publishes ms 2-6 months after acceptance. Length: 1,000 words preferred; 25 words minimum; 2,100 words maximum. Publishes short shorts. Length: 100 words. Also publishes poetry. Often critiques or comments on rejected mss.

How to Contact: Query first or send complete ms with cover letter. Should include estimated word count, bio (100 words), Social Security number. Reports in 1 month on queries; 2 months on mss. Send SASE (IRCs) for reply, return of ms or send disposable copy of the ms. Simultaneous submissions OK. Sample copy for 9×12 SAE and 3 first-class stamps. Fiction guidelines for #10 SAE and 1 first-class stamp. Reviews novels and short story collections.

Payment: Pays subscription and 3 contributor's copies. Obtain up to 10 additional copies for any donation.

Terms: Acquires first North American serial rights. Not copyrighted.

Advice: Looks for work that is "sound in its use of the Scriptures, and has *real* people dealing with *real* life. Get a sample copy—write from your heart—let your honesty show in your work. Write what you feel God has given you—not what you think someone might expect—but still follow all basic writing rules (good grammar, punctuation, etc.)."

LIZARD'S EYELID MAGAZINE, (I), MDF Productions, French Quarter, Suite 84, 999 SW 16th Avenue, Gainesville FL 32601. (904)338-9259. Fax: (407)746-1055. Editor: Sterling Sandow. Newsletter: 8 ½ × 11; 28-32 pages; illustrations and photos. "Political, underground music magazine aimed at 16-30 year olds." Quarterly. Estab. 1989. Circ. 5,000.
   ● *Lizard's Eyelid* was selected "Overall Best 'Zine" by the Florida Chapter of United Surrealist Street Artists in 1993.
Needs: Ethnic/multicultural, experimental, feminist, horror, humor/satire, psychic/supernatural/occult. Receives 30 unsolicited mss/month. Acquires 1-2 mss/issue; 4-6 mss/year. Publishes 2-3 months after acceptance. Recently published work by Charles Bukowski, Brooke Beetler, Asiamus Nonamet. Length: 500 words average; 50 words minimum; 1,500 words maximum. Publishes short shorts. Length: 250 words. Also publishes literary essays, literary criticism and poetry. Often critiques or comments on rejected mss.
How to Contact: Send complete ms with cover letter. Should include word count and bio (½ page or less). Reports on mss in 3 weeks. Send SASE (or IRC) for ms. Will consider simultaneous submissions. Sample copy $2. Fiction guidelines for #10 SAE and 1 first-class stamp or IRC. Reviews novels and short story collections.
Payment: Pays 5-10 contributor's copies. Additional copies for $1.
Terms: Acquires one-time rights. Sends galleys to author.
Advice: "We are always looking for the type of manuscript that is entirely uncensored and uninhibited. The type of story that makes you stop and think. Write what you feel, use the words and expressions that you mean."

LLAMAS MAGAZINE, The International Camelid Journal, (IV), Clay Press Inc., Box 100, Herald CA 95638. (209)223-0469. Editor: Cheryl Dal Porto. Magazine: 8½ × 11; 128+ pages; glossy paper; 80 lb. glossy cover stock; illustrations and pictures. For llama owners and lovers. 8 issues/year. Estab. 1979. Circ. 5,500.
Needs: Adventure, historical, humor. Receives 15-25 unsolicited fiction mss/month. Accepts 3-6 mss/issue; 12-24 mss/year. Publishes ms usually 3-4 months after acceptance. 15% of fiction is agented. Length: 1,500-3,000 words average. Publishes short shorts 300-1,000 words in length.
How to Contact: Query first. Reports in 1 month. Reprint submissions OK. Accepts electronic submissions via Apple 2 disk. Fiction guidelines free.
Payment: Pays $25-500, subscription to magazine and contributor's copies.
Terms: Pays on publication for first rights, first North American serial rights and one-time rights.

THE LONG STORY, (II), 11 Kingston St., North Andover MA 01845. *May be change of address in coming year. Please watch writing periodicals for notice.* (508)686-7638. Editor: R.P. Burnham. Magazine: 5½ × 8½; 150-200 pages; 60 lb. paper; 65 lb. cover stock; illustrations (b&w graphics). For serious, educated, literary people. No science fiction, adventure, romance, etc. "We publish high literary quality of any kind, but especially look for stories that have difficulty getting published elsewhere — committed fiction, working class settings, left-wing themes, etc." Annually. Estab. 1983. Circ. 900.
Needs: Contemporary, ethnic, feminist and literary. Receives 30-40 unsolicited mss/month. Accepts 6-7 mss/issue. Length: 8,000 words minimum; 20,000 words maximum. Sometimes recommends other markets.
How to Contact: Send complete ms with a brief cover letter. Reports in 2+ months. Publishes ms an average of 3 months to 1 year after acceptance. SASE (IRCs). May accept simultaneous submissions ("but not wild about it"). Sample copy for $5.
Payment: Pays 2 contributor's copies; $4 charge for extras.
Terms: Acquires first rights.
Advice: "Read us first and make sure submitted material is the kind we're interested in. Send clear, legible manuscripts. We're not interested in commercial success; rather we want to provide a place for long stories, the most difficult literary form to publish in our country."

‡THE LONGNECK, (I), North Bank Writer's Group, 208 S. Crawford Rd., Vermillion SD 57069. (605)624-4837. Editor: J.D. Erickson. Editors change each year. Tabloid: 11 × 17; 32-40 pages; 50 lb. news white paper; b&w illustrations and photographs. "We want your best short fiction, poetry, and essays. *The Longneck* speaks to a broad spectrum of college-educated readers. We have a sense of humor, with room for good, serious writing." Annually. Estab. 1993. Circ. 1,000.
Needs: Adventure, erotica, ethnic/multicultural, experimental, fantasy (science fantasy, sword and sorcery), feminist, gay, historical (general), horror, humor/satire, lesbian, literary, mainstream/contemporary, mystery/suspense (amateur sleuth, private eye/hard-boiled, romantic suspense, young adult

mystery), psychic/supernatural/occult, regional. No religious material. Accepts 10-20 mss/year. Publishes ms 6 weeks after acceptance. Recently published work by Vincent S. Green. Publishes short shorts. Length: 250-500 words. Also publishes literary essays and poetry. Sometimes critiques or comments on rejected mss.

How to Contact: Send complete ms with a cover letter. Should include estimated word count, bio and list of publications. Reports in 3 months on mss. Send a disposable copy of ms. Simultaneous, reprint and electronic submissions OK. Sample copy for $2.50.

Payment: Pays 2 contributor's copies.

Terms: Acquires first North American serial rights.

Advice: "If we see a beginning, middle, and end with qualities of passion or conviction, we might work with the author. A story that defines/affects its characters will get our attention. We assume you believe in your work. A brief cover letter with SASE will help us help you."

LOONFEATHER (II), Bemidji Arts Center, 426 Bemidji Ave., Bemidji MN 56601. (218)751-4869. Editors: Betty Rossi, Marsh Muirhead, Elmo Heggie. Magazine: 6 × 9; 48 pages; 60 lb. Hammermill Cream woven paper; 65 lb. vellum cover stock; illustrations; occasional photos. A literary journal of short prose, poetry and graphics. Mostly a market for Northern Minnesota, Minnesota and Midwest writers. Semiannually. Estab. 1979. Circ. 300.

Needs: Literary, contemporary, prose and regional. Accepts 2-3 mss/issue, 4-6 mss/year. Published new writers within the last year. Length: 600-1,500 words (prefers 1,500).

How to Contact: Send complete ms with SASE (IRCs), and short autobiographical sketch. Reports within 4 months of submission deadlines (January 31 and July 31). Sample copy $2 back issue; $5 current issue.

Payment: Free author's copies.

Terms: Acquires one-time rights.

Advice: "Send carefully crafted and literary fiction. Because of increase in size of magazine, we can include more, slightly longer fiction.The writer should familiarize himself/herself with the type of fiction published in literary magazines as opposed to family magazines, religious magazines, etc."

LOST AND FOUND TIMES, (II), Luna Bisonte Prods, 137 Leland Ave., Columbus OH 43214. (614)846-4126. Editor: John M. Bennett. Magazine: 5¹/₂ × 8¹/₂; 56 pages; good quality paper; good cover stock; illustrations; photos. Theme: experimental, avant-garde and folk literature, art. Published irregularly. Estab. 1975. Circ. 375.

Needs: Literary, contemporary, experimental, prose poem. Prefers short pieces. Also publishes poetry. Accepts approximately 2 mss/issue. Published work by Spryszak, Steve McComas, Willie Smith, Rupert Wondolowski, Al Ackerman; published new writers within the last year. Sometimes recommends other markets.

How to Contact: Query with clips of published work. SASE (IRCs). No simultaneous submissions. Reports in 1 week on queries, 2 weeks on mss. Sample copy for $5.

Payment: Pays 1 contributor's copy.

Terms: Rights revert to authors.

‡LOST CREEK LETTERS, (I, II), Lost Creek Publications, RR2, Box 373A, Rushville MO 64484. Editor: Pamela Montgomery. Magazine: 5½ × 8½; 40-44 pages; copy bond paper. Quarterly. Estab. 1990. Circ. 200.

Needs: Contemporary, ethnic, experimental, fantasy, feminist, humor/satire, literary, science fiction, surrealism. No romance, western, religious, juvenile. Publishes captionless cartoons. Receives 100+ unsolicited mss/month. Buys 3-5 mss/issue; 12-20 mss/year. Publishes ms 1-6 months after acceptance. Published work by John Weston and J.L. Lauinger. Length: 3,000 words average; 200 words minimum; 3,000 words maximum. Publishes short shorts. Also may publish essays; publishes poetry. Rarely critiques rejected ms; sometimes recommends other markets.

How to Contact: "Send for submission guidelines before submitting." Send complete manuscript with *no cover letter*. "Please *never* query." SASE. Simultaneous and photocopied submissions OK. Accepts computer printout submissions. Sample copy for $4.75. Fiction guidelines for #10 SAE and 1 first-class stamp, affixed (IRCs).

Payment: Pays $2-5 or contributor's copies.

Terms: Pays on publication for one-time rights. "We are read for *Best American Short Stories*. I nominate stories for the Pushcart Prize."

Advice: "A ms stands out if it is *rich* in detail and its characters are fully developed. A fine story is meaningful on more than an obvious superficial level. Polish is absolutely essential and can be achieved only by dedicated revising. Do *not* write a cover letter: stories are like jokes; if they're good, they need no explanation. Send the ms only, with your name and address on the first page, your name on each subsequent page. *A ms with no SASE goes directly into the trash unread."*

LOST WORLDS, The Science Fiction and Fantasy Forum, (I, IV), HBD Publishing, P.O. Box 605, Concord NC 28025. (704)933-7998. Editor: Holley B. Drye. Newsletter: 8½ × 11; 24 pages; 24 lb. bond paper; b&w illustrations. "General interest science fiction and fantasy, as well as some specialized genre writing. For a broad-spectrum age groups, anyone interested in newcomers." Monthly. Estab. 1988. Circ. 150.

Needs: Experimental, fantasy, horror, psychic/supernatural/occult, science fiction (hard science, soft/ sociological), serialized novel. Publishes annual special fiction issue. Receives 7-15 unsolicited mss/ month. Accepts 7-10 mss/issue; 100 and up mss/year. Publishes ms 3 months after acceptance (unless otherwise notified). Length: 3,000 words preferred; 2,000 words minimum; 5,500 words maximum. Publishes short shorts. Sometimes critiques rejected mss and recommends other markets. "Although we do not publish every type of genre fiction, I will, if asked, critique anyone who wishes to send me their work. There is no fee for reading or critiquing stories."

How to Contact: Query first. "Cover letters should include where and when to contact the author, a pen name if one is preferred as well as their real name, and whether or not they wish their real names to be kept confidential." Reports in 1 month on queries; 2 months on mss. SASE or IRCs (only if they wish return of their ms.) Simultaneous and reprint submissions OK. Accepts electronic submissions via disk or modem. Sample copy for $2. Fiction guidelines free.

Payment: Pays contributor's copies.

Terms: Acquires one-time rights.

Advice: "I look for originality of story, good characterization and dialogue, well-written descriptive passages, and over-all story quality. The presentation of the work also makes a big impression, whether it be good or bad. Neat, typed manuscripts will always have a better chance than hand-written or badly typed ones. All manuscripts are read by either three or four different people, with an eye towards development of plot and comparison to other material within the writer's field of experience. Plagiarism is not tolerated, and we do look for it while reading a manuscript under consideration. If you have any questions, feel free to call—we honestly don't mind. Never be afraid to send us anything, we really are kind people."

LOUISIANA LITERATURE, A Review of Literature and Humanities, (II, IV), Southeastern Louisiana University, SLU 792, Hammond LA 70402. (504)549-5022. Editor: David Hanson. Magazine: 6¾ × 9¾; 100 pages; 70 lb. paper; card cover; illustrations; photos. "We publish literary quality fiction and essays by anyone. Essays should be about Louisiana material, and preference is given to fiction with Louisiana and Southern themes, but creative work can be set anywhere." Semiannually. Estab. 1984. Circ. 400 paid; 700 printed.

    ● *Louisiana Literature* received an Honorable Mention for Editorial Content from the American Literary Magazine Awards in 1993.

Needs: Literary, mainstream, regional. No sloppy ungrammatical manuscripts. Upcoming themes: "Kate Chopin" (essays and reviews) (Spring 1994); "Acadian music and storytelling" (Fall 1994). Receives 100 unsolicited fiction mss/month. Buys mss related to special topics issues. Does not read mss June-July. Publishes ms 6 months maximum after acceptance. Published work by Kelly Cherry and Louis Gallo; published new writers within the last year. Length: 3,500 words preferred; 1,000 words minimum; 6,000 words maximum. Also publishes literary essay (Louisiana themes), literary criticism, poetry. Sometimes comments on rejected mss.

How to Contact: Send complete ms. Reports in 1-3 months on mss. SASE (IRCs). Sample copy for $5. Reviews novels and short story collections by Louisiana authors only.

Payment: Pays up to $100 and contributor's copies.

Terms: Pays on publication for one-time rights.

Advice: "Cut out everything that is not a functioning part of the story. Make sure ms is professionally presented. Use relevant specific detail in every scene."

"To keep costs down, we use 19th century engravings reflecting our primary mission as a forum for Louisiana and Southern regional writing," says Louisiana Literature *Editor David Hanson. "At present we cannot afford original art; however, our plans for upcoming issues may involve original covers—special issues on Creole writing, the Jewish experience in Louisiana, Kate Chopin and other Louisiana-related topics."* Louisiana Literature *uses approximately four stories per issue, and Hanson says that although they are moving toward special themes with each issue, "we will always welcome—and publish—unsolicited work from writers at all stages of their careers."*

Louisiana Literature

A REVIEW OF LITERATURE AND THE HUMANITIES

Spring 1993   Volume 10, Number 1

THE SEVENTH ANNUAL *LOUISIANA LITERATURE* PRIZE FOR POETRY

THE LOUISVILLE REVIEW, (II), Department of English, University of Louisville, Louisville KY 40292. (502)588-6801. Editor: Sena Naslund. General Editor: Karen S. Mann. Magazine: 6 × 8³/₄; 100 pages; Warren's Old Style paper; cover photographs. Semiannually. Estab. 1976. Circ. 750.
Needs: Contemporary, experimental, literary, prose poem. Receives 30-40 unsolicited mss/month. Acquires 6-10 mss/issue; 12-20 mss/year. Publishes ms 2-3 months after acceptance. Published work by Maura Stanton, Patricia Goedicke, Michael Cadnum. Length: 50 pages maximum. Publishes short shorts.
How to Contact: Send complete ms with cover letter. Reports on queries in 2-3 weeks; 2-3 months on mss. SASE. Sample copy for $4. Fiction guidelines for #10 SAE and 1 first-class stamp (IRCs).
Payment: Pays in contributor's copies.
Terms: Acquires first North American serial rights.
Advice: Looks for "original concepts, fresh ideas, good storyline, engaging characters, a story that works."

‡LUNA NEGRA, (II), S.P.P.C., Kent State University, Box 26, Student Activities, Kent OH 44242. Editor: James Hrusovsky. Magazine: 8½ × 11; 50 pages; b&w illustrations and photographs. "The *NKQ* is a poetry, short story, photography and art biannual." Estab. 1975. Circ. up to 2,000.
Needs: Open. Receives 3-4 unsolicited mss/month. Does not read mss in summer months. Publishes short shorts. Sometimes comments on rejected mss and recommends other markets.
How to Contact: Send complete ms with cover letter. SASE. Simultaneous, photocopied and reprint submissions OK. Accepts computer printout submissions. Free sample copy. Fiction guidelines for #10 SAE.
Payment: Pays in contributor's copies.
Terms: Acquires one-time rights. Rights revert to author after 60 days.

THE MACGUFFIN, (II), Schoolcraft College, Department of English, 18600 Haggerty Rd., Livonia MI 48152. (313)462-4400, ext. 5292 or 5327. Editor: Arthur J. Lindenberg. Fiction Editor: Elizabeth Hebron. Magazine: 5½ × 8½; 128 pages; 60 lb. paper; 110 lb. cover; b&w illustrations and photos. "*The MacGuffin* is a literary magazine which publishes a range of material including poetry, nonfiction and fiction. Material ranges from traditional to experimental. We hope our periodical attracts a variety of people with many different interests." Triannual. Quality fiction a special need. Estab. 1984. Circ. 500.
   • *The MacGuffin* received an honorable mention for editorial content in the American Literary Magazine awards.

Needs: Adventure, contemporary, ethnic, experimental, fantasy, historical (general), humor/satire, literary, mainstream, prose poem, psychic/supernatural/occult, science fiction, translations. No religious, inspirational, confession, romance, horror, pornography. Upcoming theme: "Literature, Art and the New Technology" (June 1994). Receives 25-40 unsolicited mss/month. Accepts 5-10 mss/issue; 10-30 mss/year. Does not read mss between July 1 and August 15. Publishes 6 months to 2 years after acceptance. Agented fiction: 10-15%. Published work by Arlene McKanic, Joe Schall, Joseph Benevento; published new writers within the last year. Length: 2,000-2,500 words average; 400 words minimum; 4,000 words maximum. Publishes short shorts. Length: 400 words. Also publishes literary essays. Occasionally critiques rejected mss and recommends other markets.
How to Contact: Send complete ms with cover letter, which should include: "1. *Brief* biographical information; 2. Note that this *is not* a simultaneous submission." Reports in 2-3 months. SASE (IRCs). Reprint submissions OK. Sample copy for $4; current issue for $4.75. Fiction guidelines free.
Payment: Pays 2 contributor's copies.
Terms: Acquires one-time rights.
Advice: "Be persistent. If a story is rejected, try to send it somewhere else. When we reject a story, we may accept the next one you send us. When we make suggestions for a rewrite, we may accept the revision. There seems to be a great number of good authors of fiction, but there are far too few places for publication. However, I think this is changing. Make your characters come to life. Even the most ordinary people become fascinating if they live for your readers."

THE MADISON REVIEW, (II), Department of English, Helen C. White Hall, 600 N. Park St., University of Wisconsin, Madison WI 53706. (608)263-3800. Rotating Editors. Magazine: 6×9; 180 pages. "Magazine of fiction and poetry with special emphasis on literary stories and some emphasis on Midwestern writers." Published semiannually. Estab. 1978. Circ. 500.
Needs: Experimental and literary stories, prose poems and excerpts from novels. Receives 50 unsolicited fiction mss/month. Acquires 7-12 mss/issue. Published work by Richard Cohen, Fred Chappell and Janet Shaw. Published new writers within the last year. Length: no preference. Also publishes poetry.
How to Contact: Send complete ms with cover letter and SASE (IRCs). "The letters should give one or two sentences of relevant information about the writer—just enough to provide a context for the work." Reports in 2 months on mss. Publishes ms an average of 4 months after acceptance. "We often do not report on mss during the summer." Sample copy $4.
Payment: Pays 2 contributor's copies; $2.50 charge for extras.
Terms: Acquires first North American serial rights.

MAGIC CHANGES, (II), Celestial Otter Press, P.O. Box 658, Warrenville IL 60555. (708)416-3111. Editor: John Sennett. Magazine: 8¹/₂×11; 110 pages; 60 lb. paper; construction paper cover; illustrations; photos. "Theme: transformation by art. Material: poetry, songs, fiction, stories, reviews, art, essays, etc. For the entertainment and enlightenment of all ages." Biannually. Estab. 1979. Circ. 500.
Needs: Literary, prose poem, science fiction (soft/sociological), sports fiction, fantasy and erotica. "Fiction should have a magical slant." Upcoming theme: "Music, Time, Magic." Accepts 8-12 mss/year. Receives approximately 15 unsolicited fiction mss each month. Published work by J. Weintraub, David Goodrum, Anne F. Robertson; published new writers within the last year. Length: 3,500 words maximum. Also publishes literary essays, literary criticism, poetry.
How to Contact: Send complete ms with SASE (IRCs). Simultaneous submissions OK. Accepts disk submissions compatible with IBM or Macintosh; prefers hard copy with disk submissions. Reports in 3 months. Publishes ms an average of 8 months after acceptance. Sample copy $5. Make check payable to John Sennett. Reviews novels and short story collections.
Payment: Pays 1-2 contributor's copies; $5 charge for extras.
Terms: Acquires first North American serial rights.
Advice: "Write about something fantastic in a natural way, or something natural in a fantastic way. We need good stories—like epic Greek poems translated into prose."

‡THE MAGIC MOUNTAIN, The Quarterly Journal of Growth and Expression, (II), P.O. Box 7161, Syracuse NY 13261. (315)422-3954. Editor: Greg Carter. Magazine: 7×8½; 40 pages; quality bond paper; heavy cover stock; illustrations. "Art, poetry, fiction, and essays related to individual growth. No group-related dogma will be accepted." Quarterly. Estab. 1993. Circ. 500.
Needs: Erotica, humor/satire, science fiction (soft/sociological). "Am not interested in academic or politically correct fiction." Receives 10 unsolicited mss/month. Accepts 2-3 mss/issue; 12 mss/year. Publishes ms 1-3 months after acceptance. Recently published work by Ron Androla, Aggie O'Shay,

M. Kettner. Length: 1,250 words preferred; 250 words minimum; 2,000 words maximum. Publishes short shorts. Also publishes literary essays, literary criticism and poetry. Often critiques or comments on rejected ms.
How to Contact: Send complete ms with a cover letter. Should include bio (1 paragraph). Reports in 2-4 weeks. Send SASE (or IRC) for reply, return of ms or disposable copy of ms. Simultaneous and reprint submissions OK. Sample copy for $2, 9 × 12 SAE and 4 first-class stamps. Fiction guidelines free with sample copy. Reviews novels and short story collections.
Payment: Pays 2 contributor's copies.
Terms: Acquires one-time rights.
Advice: "I urge both my readers and prospective contributors to think and feel for themselves."

MAGIC REALISM, (III, IV), Pyx Press, P.O. Box 620, Orem UT 84059-0620. Editors: C. Darren Butler and Julie Thomas. Magazine: 5½ × 8½; 80 pages; 20 lb. paper; card stock or bond cover; b&w illustrations. "Magic realism, exaggerated realism, some genre fantasy/dark fantasy, literary fantasy, occasionally glib fantasy of the sort found in folk, fairy tales and myths; for a general, literate audience." Triannually. Estab. 1990. Circ. 600.
• See the listing for Pyx Press in the Small Press section and their related magazine *A Theater of Blood* in this section.
Needs: Experimental, fantasy, literary, magic realism. "No sorcery/wizardry, witches, sleight-of-hand magicians, or occult." Receives 200 unsolicited mss/month. Accepts 5-12 mss/issue; 20-30 mss/year. Publishes ms 4-24 months after acceptance. Recently published work by Robert Pope, Daniel Quinn, Jessica Amanda Salmonson. Length: 4,000 words preferred; 100 words minimum; 8,000 words maximum; query for more than 8,000 words. Publishes short shorts. Length: 500-1,500 words. Rarely critiques rejected mss and recommends other markets.
How to Contact: Send complete ms with cover letter. Include bio, list of credits. "Response time is generally within 3 months, but acceptance can take up to 6 months." SASE. Simultaneous submissions OK. "Rarely accepts reprints." Back issue: $4.95; current issue: $5.95. Fiction guidelines for SAE and 1 first-class stamp (IRCs).
Payment: Pays $2/magazine page for prose.
Terms: Pays on publication for first North American serial rights or one-time rights and nonexclusive reprint rights "in case we want to use the work in an anthology."
Advice: "I like finely controlled feats of association; works wherein the human imagination defines reality. Magic realism subverts reality by shaping it into a human mold; bringing it closer to the imagination and to the subconscious. For example, people used to believe that swans migrated to the moon in autumn or that high-speed vehicles would be useless because human bodies would break apart at high speeds."

‡MAJESTIC BOOKS, (I, IV), P.O. Box 19097A, Johnston RI 02919. Fiction Editor: Cindy MacDonald. Bound soft cover short story anthologies; 5½ × 8½; 112 pages; 60 lb. paper; lcs cover stock. "Majestic Books is a small press which was formed to give children an outlet for their work. We publish soft cover bound anthologies of fictional stories by children, for children and adults who enjoy the work of children." Triannually. Estab. 1993. Circ. 250.
• Although Majestic Books is a small publisher, they are in the market for short fiction for their anthologies. They do a book of stories by children and plan one by adults.
Needs: Stories written on any subject by children (under 18) only. Childrens/juvenile (5-9 years, 10-12 years). Receives 20 unsolicited mss/month. Accepts 80 mss/year. Publishes ms 1 year maximum after acceptance. Recently published work by Michael Gordon, Tara Ruggieri, Elisha O'Mara, Maxwell Wright. Length: 100 words minimum; 7,500 words maximum. Publishes short shorts. Also publishes literary essays. Always critiques or comments on rejected mss.
How to Contact: Send complete ms with a cover letter. Should include estimated word count and age. Reports in 3 weeks. Send SASE (or IRC) for reply, return of ms or send a disposable copy of ms. Simultaneous submissions OK. Sample copy for $3. Fiction guidelines for #10 SAE and 1 first-class stamp.
Payment: Pays $2 and 1 contributor's copy.
Terms: Pays on publication for first rights.
Advice: "We judge our manuscripts against other manuscripts we have received from the same age group. Since we have received hundreds of entries thus far from kids ranging in age from 6-17, we use anything that is considered good for that age. We love all types of stories. Be original. We have received some manuscripts of shows we have seen on television or books we have read, just changing names

and some of the wording. Write from inside you and you'll be surprised at how much better your writing will be. Use *your* imagination."

MANOA, A Pacific Journal of International Writing, (II), English Dept., University of Hawaii Press, Honolulu HI 96822. (808)948-8833. Editors: Robert Shapard, Frank Stewart. Fiction Editor: Ian MacMillan. Magazine: 7×10; 240 pages. "An American literary magazine, emphasis on top US fiction and poetry, but each issue has a major guest-edited translated feature of recent writings from an Asian/Pacific country." Semiannually. Estab. 1989.
 • See the interview with Editor Robert Shapard in the 1992 *Novel & Short Story Writer's Market*. *Manoa* has received numerous awards and work published in the magazine was selected for prize anthologies.
Needs: Excerpted novel, contemporary, literary, mainstream and translation (from nations in or bordering on the Pacific). "Part of our purpose is to present top US fiction from throughout the US, not only to US readers, but to readers in Asian and Pacific countries. Thus we are not limited to stories related to or set in the Pacific—in fact, we do not want exotic or adventure stories set in the Pacific, but good US literary fiction of any locale." Accepts 10-12 mss/issue; 20-24/year. Publishes ms 6 months-1 year after acceptance. Agented fiction 10%. Published work by Anne Beattie, Ron Carlson and W.S. Merwin. Publishes short shorts. Also publishes literary essays, literary criticism, poetry.
How to Contact: Send complete ms with cover letter or through agent. Reports in 6 weeks. SASE (IRCs). Simultaneous submissions OK. Sample copy $7. Reviews novels and short story collections. Send books to Reviews Editor.
Payment: "Highly competitive rates paid so far." Pays contributor copies.
Terms: Pays for first North American serial, plus one-time reprint rights. Sends galleys to author.
Advice: "Hawaii has come of age literarily and wants to contribute to the best of US mainstream. It's readership is (and is intended to be) mostly national, not local. It also wants to represent top US writing to a new international market, in Asia and the Pacific. Altogether we hope our view is a fresh one; that is, not facing east toward Europe but west toward 'the other half of the world.' We mostly run short stories."

MARK, A Journal of Scholarship, Opinion, and Literature, (II), University of Toledo, 2801 W. Bancroft SU2514, Toledo OH 43606. (419)537-2318. Editors: Danielle Demuche. Magazine: 6×9; 72 pages; acid-free paper; some illustrations; photographs. Annual. Estab. 1967. Circ. 3,500.
Needs: Contemporary, ethnic, humor/satire, literary, regional and science fiction. Also accepts pen and ink drawings and b&w photos. "We do not have the staff to do rewrites or heavy copyediting—send clean, legible mss only." No "typical MFA first-person narrative—we like stories, not reportage." Receives 20-25 unsolicited fiction mss/month. Acquires 7-10 mss/year. Does not read June to September. Publishes ms 6 months after acceptance. Publishes short shorts.
How to Contact: Send complete ms with cover letter, name, address and phone. Reports in January each year. Sample copy $3 plus 7x10 SAE with 72¢ postage (IRC).
Payment: Pays 2 contributor's copies.
Terms: Acquires one-time rights.

THE MARYLAND REVIEW, Department of English and Modern Languages, University of Maryland Eastern Shore, Princess Anne MD 21853. (410)651-6552. Editor: Chester M Hedgepeth. Magazine: 6×9; 100-150 pages; quality paper stock; heavy cover; illustrations; "possibly" photos. "We have a special interest in black literature, but we welcome all sorts of submissions. Our audience is literary, educated, well-read." Annually. Estab. 1986. Circ. 500.
Needs: Contemporary, humor/satire, literary, mainstream, black literature. No genre stories; no religious, political or juvenile material. Accepts approx. 12-15 mss/issue. Publishes ms "within 1 year" after acceptance. Published work by John K. Crane, David Jauss; published new writers within the last year. Publishes short shorts. "Length is open, but we do like to include some pieces 1,500 words and under." Also publishes poetry.
How to Contact: Send complete ms with cover letter, which should include a brief autobiography. Reports "as soon as possible." SASE (IRCs), *but does not return mss.* No simultaneous submissions. "No fax copies, please." Sample copy for $6.
Payment: Pays in contributor's copies.
Terms: Acquires all rights.
Advice: "Think primarily about your *characters* in fiction, about their beliefs and how they may change. Create characters and situations that are utterly new. We will give your material a careful and considerate reading. Any fiction that is flawed by grammatical errors, misspellings, etc. will not have a chance."

We're seeing a lot of fine fiction these days, and we approach each story with fresh and eager eyes. Ezra Pound's battle-cry about poetry refers to fiction as well: 'Make it New!' "

THE MASSACHUSETTS REVIEW, (II), Memorial Hall, University of Massachusetts, Amherst MA 01002. (413)545-2689. Editors: Mary Heath, Jules Chametzky, Paul Jenkins. Magazine: 6×9; 172 pages; 52 lb. paper; 65 lb. vellum cover; illustrations and photos. Quarterly.
Needs: Short stories. Does not read mss June 1-October 1. Published new writers within the last year. Approximately 5% of fiction is agented. Critiques rejected mss when time permits.
How to Contact: Send complete ms. No ms returned without SASE (IRCs). Simultaneous submissions OK, if noted. Reports in 2 months. Publishes ms an average of 9-12 months after acceptance. Sample copy $5.50. Guidelines available for SASE.
Payment: Pays $50 maximum.
Terms: Pays on publication for first North American serial rights.
Advice: "Shorter rather than longer stories preferred (up to 28 pages). There are too many stories about 'relationships,' domestic breakups, etc."

‡MEDLEY OF PENS, (II), Writers' Craft Guild, 110 Monroe St., Columbia KY 42728. Editor: Joy Arnold. Fiction Editor: Jerry Bratten. Magazine: 5½×8½; 32+ pages; offset paper; 65 lb. cover stock; illustrations and photographs. "We wish to encourage and support writers by publishing previously unpublished work for a general audience—poems, short stories and essays." Semiannually. Estab. 1990. Circ. 250.
Needs: Adventure, childrens/juvenile, ethnic/multicultural, fantasy, feminist, historical (general), horror, humor/satire, literary, mainstream/contemporary, mystery/suspense, psychic/supernatural, regional, religious/inspirational, romance, science fiction, senior citizen/retirement, sports, translations, westerns, young adult/teen. No pornography. Upcoming themes: "Halloween," "Christmas." Publishes special fiction issue or anthology. Receives 80 unsolicited mss/month. Accepts 20+ mss/issue. Publishes ms 2-6 months after acceptance. Recently published work by Joy Arnold, Jerry Bratten, and Barry Bright. Length: 3,000 words maximum. Publishes short shorts. Also publishes literary essays and poetry. *Charges $5 fee with SASE for comments.*
How to Contact: Send complete ms with a cover letter. Should include estimated word count, bio (25 word maximum) and Social Security number. Reports in 6-8 weeks. SASE (or IRC) for return of ms. No simultaneous submissions. Sample copy for $3. Fiction guidelines for #10 SAE.
Payment: Pays 5 contributor's copies; additional copies for $2.50.
Terms: Acquires one-time rights.
Advice: Looks for "originality of style and treatment of the subject matter."

‡MEME-SHOT MAGAZINE, (I), 19528 Ventura Blvd., #367, Tarzana CA 91356. Editor: Reverend Matthew A. Carey. Magazine: 8½×11; 15-30 pages; card or paper cover stock; many illustrations. "The intended audience is Overmen, Überwomen, SubGenii and anyone else who pays attention. We are genetic and Memeic Mutants forcing our way of life upon the world." Annually. Estab. 1993. Circ. 35-100.
Needs: Adventure, erotica, experimental, fantasy, horror, humor/satire, psychic/supernatural/occult, science fiction (hard science, soft/sociological, cyberpunk); "seeking some New Journalism type writing if any is out there." Publishes special fiction issue or anthology. Accepts 2-3 mss/issue. Publishes ms 6-9 months after acceptance. Recently published work by Dan Clarke, Ralse Skull. Length: 230 words preferred; 23 words minimum; 555 words maximum. Publishes short shorts. "I prefer short-short to all other fiction, so ... no story is too small." Also publishes literary essays, literary criticism and poetry. Sometimes critiques or comments on rejected mss.
How to Contact: Query first, query with clips of published work or "fire at will. If the total weight of your submission is less than 1 oz. then forgo the query." Should include estimated word count, bio and list of publications. Reports in 1 month. Send SASE (or IRC) for reply, return of ms or send a disposable copy of ms. Simultaneous and reprint submissions OK. Sample copy for $3.53. Fiction guidelines for #10 SAE and 1 first-class stamp. Reviews novels and short story collections.
Payment: Pays subscription and contributor's copies; additional copies for postage.
Terms: Author retains all rights. Sends galleys to author. Not copyrighted.
Advice: "Criteria #1: Will it fit? #2: Did it make me laugh? #3: Did the writer sound like he was getting off on the process of writing? Make friends, make enemies, take liberties, make mistakes and write every day. If your life is messy, write messy. If your life is neat and tidy—wake up!"

‡MEN AS WE ARE, A Celebration of Men, (II), 581 10th St., Brooklyn NY 11215-4401. (718)499-2829. Editor: Jonathan Running Wind. Magazine: 8⅜ × 10⅞; 48 pages; 100% post-consumer recycled paper; illustrations and photographs. "Honest, vulnerable portrayal of the male experience in all its forms. Types of material: essay, fiction, poetry, journalism, drama excerpts, photography, illustration, fine art. Intended audience: men and women interested in examining and transforming the male gender roles in North American cultures, and in reading fine literature." Quarterly. Estab. 1991. Circ. 5,000.
Needs: Ethnic/multicultural, literary, mainstream/contemporary, regional, translations. Upcoming themes: "Gay and straight and everything in between"; "Fiction of Personal Recollection." Publishes special fiction issue or anthology. Receives 50-100 unsolicited mss/month. Accepts 2-3 mss/issue; 8-12 mss/year. Publishes ms 3-9 months after acceptance. Recently published work by Rick Derby, Bob Gates, Paul Milenski. Length: 1,500-3,000 words preferred; 500 words minimum; 9,000 words maximum. Publishes short shorts. Also publishes literary essays and poetry. Sometimes critiques or comments on rejected mss.
How to Contact: Send complete ms with a cover letter. Should include estimated word count, bio (200 words) and list of publications. Reports in 1 month on queries; 3-6 months on mss. Send SASE (or IRC) for reply, return of ms or send a disposable copy of ms. Simultaneous, reprint and electronic submissions OK. Sample copy for $5, 9 × 12 SAE and 75¢ postage. Fiction guidelines for #10 SASE. Reviews novels and short story collections.
Payment: Pays $0-50 and 3 contributor's copies.
Terms: Pays on publication for first rights, first North American serial rights or one-time rights.
Advice: A manuscript stands out with "original and simple use of language, engrossing stories and characters; relationships that change (epiphanies), moments of self-realization and knowledge; original and descriptive metaphor; simple and convincing evocation of time and place; stories that make me laugh, cry or that leave me bewildered, hopeful and confused." Would like to see more "non-white ('minority') and gay characters and writers; stories about infant, adolescent, and elder (50+) characters; stories that do more than describe and celebrate traditional self-destructive male behavior. Yes, we can be very self-destructive as men, but why, and is there hope for change?"

MERLYN'S PEN, The National Magazines of Student Writing, Grades 7-12, (IV), Box 1058, East Greenwich RI 02818. (401)885-5175. Editor: R. Jim Stahl. Magazines: 8⅛ × 10⅞; 36 pages; 50 lb. paper; 70 lb. gloss cover stock; illustrations; photos. Student writing only—grades 7 through 12, for libraries, homes and English classrooms. Bimonthly (September-April). Estab. 1985. Circ. 30,000 (combined).
● *Merlyn's Pen* now comes in two editions: Intermediate for grades 7-10 and Senior for grades 9-12.
Needs: Adventure, experimental, fantasy, historical (general), horror, humor/satire, literary, mainstream, mystery/suspense, regional, romance, science fiction, western, young adult/teen, editorial reviews, puzzles, word games, poetry. Must be written by students in grades 7-12. Receives 500 unsolicited fiction mss/month. Accepts 25 mss/issue; 100 mss/year. Publishes ms 3 months to 1 year after acceptance. Length: 1,500 words average; 25 words minimum; 4,000 words maximum. Publishes short shorts. Responds to rejected mss.
How to Contact: Send complete ms and cover letter with name, grade, age, home and school address, home and school telephone number, supervising teacher's name and principal's name. Reports in 10-12 weeks. SASE for ms. Sample copy for $3.
Payment: Pays 3 contributor's copies, charge for extras. Each author published receives a free copy of *The Elements of Style*.
Terms: Published works become the property of Merlyn's Pen, Inc.
Advice: "Write what you *know*; write where you are."

METROPOLITAN, (II), City of Light Publications, 6307 N. 31st St., Arlington VA 22207. Editor: J.L. Bergsohn. Magazine: 5½ × 8½; 50 pages; illustrated cover. "*Metropolitan* is primarily geared toward showcasing the talents of Washington area writers." Quarterly. Estab. 1991. Circ. 250.
● *Metropolitain* has changed the spelling of its name to *Metropolitan*.
Needs: Contemporary, literary. Receives 75 unsolicited mss/month. Accepts 4 mss/issue; 16 mss/year. Publishes ms up to 1 year after acceptance. Length: 5,000 words maximum. Publishes short shorts. Also publishes poetry. Sometimes comments on or critiques rejected mss.
How to Contact: Send complete ms with cover letter. Include brief bio with list of publication credits. Reports in 2 weeks on queries; 1 month on mss. SASE (IRCs). Simultaneous and reprint submissions OK. Accepts computer printout submissions. Sample copy for $5.

Payment: Pays 1 contributor's copy; charges for extras.
Terms: Acquires one-time rights.
Advice: "We look for stories with contemporary urban settings and realistic situations. We like simplicity and humor."

MICHIGAN QUARTERLY REVIEW, University of Michigan, 3032 Rackham, Ann Arbor MI 48109-1070. (313)764-9265. Editor: Laurence Goldstein. "An interdisciplinary journal which publishes mainly essays and reviews, with some high-quality fiction and poetry, for an intellectual, widely read audience." Quarterly. Estab. 1962. Circ. 1,800.
Needs: Literary. No "genre" fiction written for a "market." Upcoming themes: "Male Body" issue (Fall 1993); "Cuban theme" (Spring-Summer 1994). Receives 200 unsolicited fiction mss/month. Buys 2 mss/issue; 8 mss/year. Published work by Charles Baxter, Joan Silber and Jay Neugeboren; published new writers within the last year. Length: 1,500 words minimum; 7,000 words maximum; 5,000 words average. Also publishes poetry, literary essays.
How to Contact: Send complete ms with cover letter. "I like to know if a writer is at the beginning, or further along, in his or her career. Don't offer plot summaries of the enclosed story, though a background comment is welcome." Reports in 6-8 weeks. SASE. No simultaneous submissions. Sample copy for $2.50 and 2 first-class stamps (IRCs).
Payment: Pays $8-10/printed page.
Terms: Pays on publication for first rights. Awards the Lawrence Foundation Prize of $1,000 for best story in *MQR* previous year.
Advice: "Read back issues to get a sense of tone; level of writing. *MQR* is very selective; only send the very finest, best-plotted, most-revised fiction."

MID-AMERICAN REVIEW, (II), Department of English, Bowling Green State University, Bowling Green OH 43403. (419)372-2725. Fiction Editor: Ellen Behrens. Magazine: 5½×8½; 200 pages; 60 lb. bond paper; coated cover stock. "We publish serious fiction and poetry, as well as critical studies in contemporary literature, translations and book reviews." Biannual. Estab. 1981.
● *Mid-American Review* sponsors the Sherwood Anderson Short Fiction Prize listed in this book. Works published in the magazine have been reprinted in *Best American Short Stories* and *O. Henry Award Series*. *Mid-American Review* has also received a NEA grant for 1993-1994 and regularly receives grants from the Ohio Arts Council.
Needs: Experimental, traditional, literary, prose poem, excerpted novel and translations. Upcoming theme: "Fall 1993 issue was expected to be devoted to work by Asian-Americans." Receives about 120 unsolicited fiction mss/month. Buys 5-6 mss/issue. Does not read June-August. Approximately 5% of fiction is agented. Recently published work by Steven Schwartz, Eve Shelnutt, Philip Graham, William Goyen, Dan O'Brien; published new writers within the last year. Also publishes literary essays, literary criticism, poetry. Occasionally critiques rejected mss. Sometimes recommends other markets.
How to Contact: Send complete ms with SASE (IRCs). No simultaneous submissions. Reports in about 3 months. Publishes ms an average of 6 months after acceptance. Sample copy for $5. Reviews novels and short story collections. Send books to reviews editor.
Payment: Pays $8/page up to $50; 2 contributor's copies; $3 charge for extras.
Terms: Pays on publication for one-time rights.
Advice: "We just want *quality* work of whatever vision and/or style. We are not a regional publication. We are now looking for more translated fiction."

MIDLAND REVIEW, (II), Oklahoma State University, English Dept., Morrill Hall, Stillwater OK 74078. Editors change every year. Send to "Editor." Magazine: 6½×9½; 128 pages; 80 lb. paper; perfect bond cover stock; illustrations; photos. "A mixed bag of quality work." For "anyone who likes to read and for those that want news that folks in Oklahoma are alive. Publishes 30-40% OSU student material." Annual. Estab. 1985. Circ. 500.
Needs: Ethnic, experimental, feminist, historical (general), literary, prose poem, regional, translations. Receives 15 unsolicited fiction mss/month. Accepts 4 mss/issue. Publishes ms 6-10 months after acceptance. Published work by Jene Friedemann, Steffie Corcoran, Bruce Michael Gans; published new writers within the last year. Length: 4-10 pages double-spaced, typed. Publishes short shorts of 2-4 pages. Also publishes literary essays, literary criticism, poetry.
How to Contact: Send complete ms with cover letter. Reports in 6-8 weeks on queries. SASE (IRCs) for ms. Simultaneous submissions OK. Sample copy for $5 plus 90¢ postage and 9×12 SAE. Fiction guidelines for #10 SAE and 1 first-class stamp.

Payment: Pays 1 contributor's copy.
Terms: Copyright reverts to author.
Advice: "We want to encourage good student stories by giving them an audience with more established writers."

MIDNIGHT ZOO, (I), Experiences Unlimited, P.O. Box 8040, Walnut Creek CA 94596. (510)682-9662. Editor: Jon L. Herron. Fiction Editor: Elizabeth Martin-Burk. Magazine: 11×17; 64 pages; 20 lb. bond paper; 100 lb. glossy cover; b&w illustrations and photographs. "Horror, science fiction and fantasy stories and poems plus science fact, interviews, reviews, writer's information, profiles, strange happenings for all ages interested in this genre." Monthly. Estab. 1990. Circ. 3,000.
• The Small Press Writers and Artists Organization nominated "Best Poet," "Best New Writer" and "Best Editor" from the magazine in 1992. Jon L. Herron also edits *Aberations* listed in this book.
Needs: Fantasy, horror, prose poem, psychic/supernatural/occult, science fiction (hard science, soft/sociological). Upcoming themes: "All Science Fiction Issue" (June 1994); "All Horror Issue" (October 1994); "Christmas Issue" (December 1994). We will accept stories up to 10,000 words. Receives 120 unsolicited mss/month. Buys 15 mss/issue. 180 mss/year. Recently pubished work by Ardath Mayhar, T. Jackson King, Don Hornbostel. Length: 3,000 words preferred; 500 words minimum; 10,000 words maximum (except for anthology—15,000). Publishes short shorts. Sometimes critiques rejected mss and recommends other markets.
How to Contact: Send complete ms with cover letter. Include Social Security number, telephone number and a short bio. Reports in 2 months on queries; 4 months on mss. SASE (IRCs). Simultaneous and reprint (very few) submissions OK. Accepts electronic submissions via disk or modem (MicroSoft Word, Word Perfect or ASCII). Sample copy for $6. Fiction guidelines for SAE and 1 first-class stamp.
Payment: Pays subscription to magazine; contributor's copies; reduced charge for extras.
Terms: Pays on publication for first North American serial rights. Sometimes sends galleys to author.
Advice: "First a ms must be well written and have an original idea or an original twist on an established idea. Good spelling and grammar are important. However, we work with writers who we feel show potential and in many cases have gone through 5 or 6 re-writes in order to get the best possible story from the writer. We remain dedicated to assisting new and under-published writers attain publication through our magazine and have even assisted writers in getting published in other magazines."

THE MILWAUKEE UNDERGRADUATE REVIEW, (I), UWM Honors Program, P.O. Box 413, Milwaukee WI 53201. Editor: Dean Andrade. Fiction Editor: Jennifer Dunajski. Magazine: 5½×8; 50 pages; 70 lb. glossy paper; 67 lb. card stock cover; b&w illustrations. Semiannually. Estab. 1989. Circ. 1,000.
Needs: Adventure, ethnic/multicultural, experimental, fantasy (science fantasy, sword and sorcery), feminist, gay, historical, horror, humor/satire, lesbian, literary, mainstream/contemporary, mystery/suspense (private eye/hard-boiled, amateur sleuth, cozy, police procedural, romantic suspense), psychic/supernatural/occult, regional, religious/inspirational, romance (contemporary, gothic, historical), science fiction (hard science, soft/sociological), sports, westerns (traditional, adult, frontier). Receives 10-20 unsolicited mss/month. Acquires 6-8 mss/issue; 12-16 mss/year. Publishes 10-12 weeks after acceptance. Published work by Christopher Grimes, Ottillia Willis, Peter J. Theis. Length: 2,000 words average; 200 words minimum; 5,000 words maximum. Publishes short shorts. Length: 400 words. Also publishes literary essays, literary criticism and poetry. Often critiques or comments on rejected mss.
How to Contact: Send complete ms with cover letter. Should include 200 word bio, electronic copy (if available) with submission. Reports on queries in 2 weeks; 8-10 weeks on mss. Send SASE (IRC) for reply, return of ms or send disposable copy of the ms. Will consider simultaneous, electronic submissions. Sample copy $2.50. Fiction guidelines for #10 SAE and 1 first-class stamp or IRC.
Payment: Pays 2 contributor's copies.
Terms: Acquires first North American serial rights.
Advice: Looks for "detail, resonance, compression, originality, ambiguity. Work that is well-informed yet subtle."

MIMSY MUSING, A Journal on Nursing, Illness, and the Care of Children, (I, IV), Box 161613, Sacramento CA 95816. Editor: David Hutchinson, RN. Newsletter: 8½×11; 16-20 pages; 20 lb. bond paper; 20 lb. bond cover; pen & ink illustrations. "For health care professionals, parents, anyone with an interest in kids, nursing *or* literature/ideas." Published 2 times/year. Estab. 1991. Circ. 400.

Needs: Humor/satire, mainstream, young adult/teen (10-18 years). "Nursing, pediatrics, medicine, hospital life, life and death, pain. No erotic; horror; lit-school experimental." Length: 1,000 words average; 5,000 words maximum. Publishes short shorts. Sometimes critiques or comments on rejected mss. Sometimes recommends other markets.

How to Contact: Send complete ms with cover letter. Include "author's interest or background relative to kids/nursing/medicine. Something personal perhaps, or at least complementary to the story." Reports in 2 weeks on queries; 1 month on mss. SASE. Simultaneous and reprint submissions OK. Sample copy for $2.50, 5×7 SAE and 2 first-class stamps. Fiction guidelines for #10 SAE and 1 first-class stamp (IRCs).

Payment: Pays $20 maximum and contributor's copies.

Terms: Pays on acceptance for one-time rights. Sometimes sends galleys to author.

Advice: "Work should be on a topic close to the author's heart (or mind). Every manuscript stands out in its own way; and each author has to find his/her own path to the rare land of polished writing. Honest effort is the minimum requirement; improvement generally follows."

MINAS TIRITH EVENING-STAR, (IV), W.W. Publications, Box 373, Highland MI 48357-0373. (813)585-0985. Editor: Philip Helms. Magazine: 8½×11; 40+ pages; typewriter paper; black ink illustrations; photos. Magazine of J.R.R. Tolkien and fantasy—fiction, poetry, reviews, etc. for general audience. Quarterly. Published special fiction issue; plans another. Estab. 1967. Circ. 500.
- *Minas Tirith Evening-Star* is the official publication of the American Tolkein Society. Contact the magazine for information on joining. The publisher, W.W. Publications, also appears in this book in the small press section.

Needs: "Fantasy and Tolkien." Upcoming theme: "J.R.R. Tolkien's 100th Birthday!" Receives 5 unsolicited mss/month. Accepts 1 ms/issue; 5 mss/year. Published new writers within the last year. Length: 1,000-1,200 words preferred; 5,000 words maximum. Publishes short shorts. Also publishes literary essays, literary criticism, poetry. Occasionally critiques rejected ms.

How to Contact: Send complete ms and bio. Reports in 1-2 months. SASE (IRCs). No simultaneous submissions. Reprint submissions OK. Sample copy for $1. Reviews novels and short story collections.

Terms: Acquires first rights.

Advice: Goal is "to expand knowledge and enjoyment of J.R.R. Tolkien's and his son Christopher Tolkien's works and their worlds."

MIND IN MOTION, A Magazine of Poetry and Short Prose, (II), Box 1118, Apple Valley CA 92307. (619)248-6512. Editor: Céleste Goyer. Magazine: 5½×8½; 60 pages; 20 lb. paper; 50 lb. cover. "We prefer to publish works of substantial brilliance that engage and encourage the readers' mind." Quarterly. Estab. 1985. Circ. 350.

Needs: Experimental, fantasy, humor/satire, literary, prose poem, science fiction. No "mainstream, romance, nostalgia, un-poetic prose; anything with a slow pace or that won't stand up to re-reading." Receives 50 unsolicited mss/month. Acquires 10 mss/issue; 40 mss/year. Publishes ms 2 weeks to 3 months after acceptance. Recently published work by Robert E. Brimhall, Margarita Guy, Tim J. Schaefer. Length: 2,000 words preferred; 250 words minimum; 3,500 words maximum. Also publishes poetry. Sometimes critiques rejected mss and occasionally recommends other markets.

How to Contact: Send complete ms. "Cover letter or bio not necessary." SASE. Simultaneous (if notified) submissions OK. Sample copy for $3.50. Fiction guidelines for #10 SAE and 1 first-class stamp (IRCs).

Payment: One contributor's copy when financially possible; charge for extras.

Terms: Acquires first North American serial rights.

Advice: "We are now able to take more stories per issue, and they may be a bit longer than previously, due to a format modification. *Mind in Motion* is noted for introspective, philosophical fiction with a great deal of energy and originality."

MIND MATTERS REVIEW, (I,II), Box 234, 2040 Polk St., San Francisco CA 94109. (415)775-4545. Editor: Carrie Drake. Magazine: 8 1/2×11; 30-64 pages; illustrations and photos. "*MMR* is basically a philosophical publication. We have published two short stories that were written in the form of parables." Audience is "conservative intellectually, but liberal fiscally." Quarterly. Estab. 1988. Circ. 1,000.

Needs: Historical (general), literary, prose poem. No "utopian" fiction. Buys 1 ms/issue; 4 mss/year. Publishes ms 6-12 months after acceptance. Published Manuel Dominguez and Charles Corry. Length: 800 words preferred; 400 words minimum; 2,000 words maximum.

How to Contact: Query first. Reports in 3 weeks. SASE (IRC). Simultaneous and reprint submissions OK. Sample copy for $3.50. Fiction guidelines for SASE.

Payment: Pays contributor's copies.

Terms: Acquires one-time rights. Sends galleys to author.

Advice: "A beginning fiction writer for *MMR* should first be familiar with the overall frame of reference of *MMR* and its range of flexibility and limitations. We seek writers who are able to tap moral principles as a source of imagination and inspiration. The moral principle can be atheistic or Christian or Buddhist—whatever—as long as there is a logical structure. Characters and plots do not have to be complex or have strong emotional appeal as long as they draw attention to life experiences that give the reader something to think about."

THE MINNESOTA REVIEW, A Journal of Committed Writing, (II), Dept. of English, East Carolina University, Greenville NC 27858. (919)757-6388. Editor: Jeffrey Williams. Fiction Editor: Fred Pfeil. Magazine: 5¼×8; approximately 200 pages; some illustrations; occasional photos. "We emphasize socially and politically engaged work." Semiannually. Estab. 1960. Circ. 1,500.

Needs: Experimental, feminist, gay, historical (general), lesbian, literary. Receives 50-75 mss/month. Accepts 3-4 mss/issue; 6-8 mss/year. Publishes ms within 6 months to 1 year after acceptance. Published work by Harold Jaffe, Linda Schor, John Berger. Length: 1,500-6,000 words preferred. Publishes short shorts. Also publishes literary essays, literary criticism, poetry. Occasionally critiques rejected mss and recommends other markets.

How to Contact: Send complete ms with optional cover letter. Reports in 2-3 weeks on queries; 2-3 months on mss. SASE (IRCs). Simultaneous submissions OK. Reviews novels and short story collections. Send books to book review editor.

Payment: Pays in contributor's copies. Charge for extra copies.

Terms: Acquires first rights.

Advice: "We look for socially and politically engaged work, particularly work that stretches boundaries."

‡MINUS 7 MAGAZINE, (I), E&R Enterprises, Suite 33, 1723 Murray Ave., Pittsburgh PA 15217. (412)521-0744. Editor: Erik Scott Rosen. Magazine: 8½×11; 20 pages; 80 lb. glossy paper; card stock glossy cover; illustrations and photographs. "While the magazine has a regional focus (nonfiction), we are open to any fiction so long as it doesn't pander to our readers. Our readers are college-aged, young, going through transitions in their own life that match the transitions our society is experiencing." Monthly. Estab. 1993. Circ. 5,000.

Needs: Ethnic/multicultural, experimental, literary, mainstream/contemporary, regional (Pittsburgh), also some erotica. No "genre fiction (fantasy/sci-fi, western), historical (unless it has a strong Pittsburgh bent)." Publishes special fiction issue or anthology. Accepts 14-20 mss/year. Publishes ms 1-4 months after acceptance. Length: 2,500 words preferred; 5,000 words maximum. Publishes short shorts. Length: 200-500 words. Also publishes poetry. Sometimes critiques or comments on rejected mss.

How to Contact: Send complete ms with cover letter. Should include estimated word count and brief bio. Reports in 3 months. Send SASE (or IRC) for reply, return of ms or send a disposable copy of ms. Simultaneous, reprint and disk submissions OK. Sample copy for $1. Fiction guidelines for #10 SAE and 1 first-class stamp.

Payment: Pays $25 and 6 contributor's copies on publication.

Terms: Buys first North American serial rights.

Advice: Looks for "strong sense of characters, tight pacing, realistic dialogue. Revise, revise, revise—then proofread 8 or 10 times. Nothing turns an editor off more than receiving a manuscript with numerous spelling errors or coffee stains. We are eager to see tight, experimental short-shorts."

---

‡ *The double dagger before a listing indicates that the listing is new in this edition. New markets are often the most receptive to submissions by new writers.*

‡THE MIRACULOUS MEDAL, (IV), The Central Association of the Miraculous Medal, 475 E. Chelten Ave., Philadelphia PA 19144. (215)848-1010. Editor: Rev. John W. Gouldrick, C.M. Magazine. Quarterly.
Needs: Religious/inspirational. Receives 25 unsolicited fiction mss/month; accepts 2 mss/issue; 8 mss/year. Publishes ms up to two years or more after acceptance.
How to Contact: Query first with SASE. Sample copy and fiction guidelines free.
Payment: Pays 2¢/word minimum.
Terms: Pays on acceptance for first rights.

MISSISSIPPI REVIEW, (I, II), University of Southern Mississippi, Box 5144, Hattiesburg MS 39406-5144. (601)266-4321. Editor: Frederick Barthelme. "Literary publication for those interested in contemporary literature—writers, editors who read to be in touch with current modes." Semiannually. Estab. 1972. Circ. 1,500.
Needs: Literary, contemporary, fantasy, humor, translations, experimental, avant-garde and "art" fiction. No juvenile. Buys varied amount of mss/issue. Does not read mss in summer. Length: 100 pages maximum.
How to Contact: Send complete ms with SASE (IRCs) including a short cover letter. Sample copy for $8.
Payment: Pays in contributor's copies.
Terms: Acquires first North American serial rights.

MISSISSIPPI VALLEY REVIEW, (III), Western Illinois University, Dept. of English, Simpkins Hall, Macomb IL 61455. Editors: John Mann and Tama Baldwin. Magazine: 96 pages; original art on cover. "A small magazine, *MVR* has won 16 Illinois Arts Council awards in poetry and fiction. We publish stories, poems and essays." Biannually. Estab. 1971. Circ. 800.
Needs: Literary, contemporary. Does not read mss in summer. Published work by Ray Bradbury, Gwendolyn Brooks, Louise Erdrich, Al Hirschfeld. Also publishes poetry.
How to Contact: Send complete ms with SASE (IRCs). Reports in 3 months. Sample copy for $6.
Payment: Pays 2 contributor's copies.
Terms: Individual author retains rights.
Advice: "Persistence."

THE MISSOURI REVIEW, (II), 1507 Hillcrest Hall, University of Missouri, Columbia MO 65211. (314)882-4474. Editors: Speer Morgan, Greg Michalson. Magazine: 6×9; 256 pages. Theme: fiction, poetry, essays, reviews, interviews, cartoons. "All with a distinctly contemporary orientation. For writers, and the general reader with broad literary interests. We present nonestablished as well as established writers of excellence. The *Review* frequently runs feature sections or special issues dedicated to particular topics frequently related to fiction." Published 3 times/academic year. Estab. 1977. Circ. 4,500.
● An interview with Editor Speer Morgan appeared in the 1992 *Novel & Short Story Writer's Market*.
Needs: Literary, contemporary; open to all categories except juvenile, young adult. Receives approximately 300 unsolicited fiction mss each month. Buys 6-8 mss/issue; 18-25 mss/year. Published new writers within the last year. No preferred length. Also publishes personal essays, poetry. Critiques rejected mss "when there is time."
How to Contact: Send complete ms with SASE (IRCs). Reports in 10 weeks. Sample copy for $6.
Payment: Pays $20/page minimum.
Terms: Pays on signed contract for all rights.
Advice: Awards William Peden Prize in fiction; $1,000 to best story published in *Missouri Review* in a given year. Also sponsors Editors' Prize Contest with a prize of $1,000.

‡MIXED MEDIA, (I, II), Mental Press % Paul Semel, 33 Aspen Road, West Orange NJ 07052. Editor: Paul Semel. Magazine: 8½×11; 32 pages; heavy stock cover; illustrations and photographs. "We are open to all styles and subject matter. Experimental, avante-garde, traditional; anything goes. Our stories have ranged from 3 lines to 3 pages." Annually. Estab. 1992. Circ. 150.
Needs: Adventure, erotica, ethnic/multicultural, experimental, fantasy (science fantasy), feminist, gay, horror, humor/satire, lesbian, literary, mainstream/contemporary, mystery/suspense (private eye/hardboiled), psychic/supernatural/occult, romance (gothic). No "unrealistically happy stories, greeting card sentimentality." List of upcoming themes or editorial calendar available for SASE. "Mss are accepted

in June; published in October." Recently published work by Rollins, Jeff DeSmedt, Prabu Vasan. Length: 4 pages, double-spaced maximum. Also publishes poetry.
How to Contact: Send complete ms with a cover letter. Should include bio (1 paragraph). Reporting time varies. Send SASE (or IRC) for reply, return of ms or send a disposable copy of ms. Simultaneous, reprint and electronic submissions OK. Sample copy for $3. Fiction guidelines for SASE.
Payment: Pays 1 contributor's copy.
Terms: Acquires one-time rights.
Advice: "Something must grab us immediately, and show us something we haven't seen."

MOBIUS, The Journal of Social Change, (II), 1149 E. Mifflin, Madison WI 53703. (608)255-4224. Editor: Fred Schepartz. Magazine: 8½ × 11; 16-32 pages; 60 lb. paper; 60 lb. cover. "Looking for fiction which uses social change as either a primary secondary theme. This is broader than most people think. Need social relevance in one way or another. For an artistically and politically aware and curious audience." Quarterly. Estab. 1989. Circ. 150.
Needs: Contemporary, ethnic, experimental, fantasy, feminist, gay, historical (general) horror, humor/satire, lesbian, literary, mainstream, prose poem, science fiction. "No porn, no racist, sexist or any other kind of ist. No Christian or spiritually proselytizing fiction." Receives 15 unsolicited ms/month. Accepts 2-3 mss/issue. Publishes ms 3-9 months after acceptance. Length: 3,500 words preferred; 500 words minimum; 5,000 words maximum. Publishes short shorts. Length: 300 words. Sometimes critiques rejected mss.
How to Contact: Send complete ms with cover letter. Reports in 2-3 months. SASE. Simultaneous and reprint submissions OK. Sample copy for $2, 9 × 12 SAE and 3 first-class stamps. Fiction guidelines for 9 × 12 SAE and 4-5 first-class stamps (IRCs).
Payment: Pays contributor's copies.
Terms: Acquires one-time rights.
Advice: Looks for "first and foremost, good writing. Prose must be crisp, polished, story must pique my interest and make me care due to a certain intellectual, emotional aspect. Second, *Mobius* is about social change. We want stories that make some statement about the society we live in, either on a macro or micro level. Not that your story needs to preach from a soapbox (actually, we prefer that it doesn't) but your story needs to have *something* to say."

THE MONOCACY VALLEY REVIEW, (II), Mt. St. Mary's College, Emmitsburg MD 21727. (301)447-6122. Editor: William Heath. Fiction Editor: Roser Camiacals-Heath. Magazine: 8½ × 11; 72 pages; high-quality paper; illustrations and photographs. For readers in the "Mid-Atlantic region; all persons interested in literature." Annual. Estab. 1986. Circ. 500.
Needs: Adventure, contemporary, experimental, historical, humor/satire, literary, mainstream, prose poem reviews. "We would not exclude any categories of fiction, save pornographic or obscene. Our preference is for realistic fiction that dramatizes things that matter." Receives 20-25 unsolicited mss/month. Buys 3-5 mss/issue. Published work by Ann Knox; Maxine Combs; Doris Selinsky. Length: 3,000-4,000 words preferred; no minimum; 10,000 words maximum. Also publishes poetry. Sometimes critiques rejected mss.
How to Contact: Send 50-word bio. SASE (IRC). Simultaneous submissions OK. Sample copy for $5. Fiction guidelines for #10 SAE and 1 first-class stamp. Reviews novels and short story collections.
Payment: Pays $10-25 and contributor's copies.
Terms: Pays on publication.
Advice: "Send mss in December and January. Responses are sent out by May, at the latest."

THE MONTHLY INDEPENDENT TRIBUNE TIMES JOURNAL POST GAZETTE NEWS CHRONICLE BULLETIN, The Magazine to Which No Superlatives Apply, (II), 1630 Allston Way, Berkeley CA 94703. Editor: T.S. Child. Fiction Editor: Denver Tucson. Magazine: 5½ × 8; 8 pages; 60 lb. paper; 60 lb. cover; illustrations and photographs. "Our theme is the theme of utter themelessness. In the past, we have published short stories, short short stories, the world's shortest story, plays, game show transcriptions, pictures made of words, teeny-weeny novelinis." Published irregularly. Estab. 1983. Circ. 500.
Needs: Adventure, experimental, humor/satire, mystery/suspense (private eye, amateur sleuth), psychic/supernatural/occult. "If it's serious, literary, perfect, well-done or elegant, we don't want it. If it's wacky, bizarre, unclassifiable, funny, cryptic or original, we might." Nothing "pretentious; serious; important; meaningful; honest." Receives 10 unsolicited mss/month. Accepts 1-2 mss/issue. Accept manuscripts published in next issue. Length: 400 words preferred. 1,200 words maximum. Publishes short shorts. Length: 400 words. Sometimes critiques rejected mss.

How to Contact: Send complete ms with cover letter. Reports in 1 month. SASE. "May" accept simultaneous submissions. Sample copy $.50, any size SAE and 1 first-class stamp (IRCs).
Payment: Pays subscription (2 issues); 3 contributor's copies.
Terms: Not copyrighted.
Advice: "First of all, work must be *short*—1,200 words maximum, but the shorter the better. It must make me either laugh or scratch my head, or both. Things that are slightly humorous, or written with any kind of audience in mind are returned. We want writing that is spontaneous, unconscious, boundary-free. If you can think of another magazine that might publish your story, send it to them, not us. Send us your worst, weirdest stories, the ones you're too embarrassed to send anywhere else."

THE MOODY STREET REVIEW, (I, II), Apt. 19L, 205 E. 78th St., New York NY 10021. Editor: David Gibson. Magazine: 8×8; 90 lb. cover; illustrations and photographs. "This is a magazine of fiction, poetry, and nonfiction for literary and artistic down to earth, bare-bones types. Inspired by writers of the Beat Generation and their literary forebears: Blake, Wordsworth, Emerson, etc. If you're not familiar with this tradition, don't send." Semiannually. Estab. 1988. Circ. 1,000.
  • Note the editor is now looking at shorter stories.
Needs: Contemporary, ethnic, literary, mainstream, regional, memoirs, translations (especially from French). Receives 50-75 unsolicited mss/month. Publishes "as many good ones as I can get my hands on; at least 3 mss/issue." Reads mss all year long, but does not respond August-January. Recently published work by Rod Kessler, Catherine Gammon, Janice Levy, Jim Morgan. Length: 5,000 words. Sometimes critiques rejected mss and suggests alternative markets.
How to Contact: Reports in 1 month on queries; 3 months on mss. SASE (IRCs) for all submissions. Sample copy $5 (payable to David Gibson).
Payment: *Charges $1 reading fee.* Pays 2 contributor's copies.
Terms: Not copyrighted.
Advice: "Prospective contributors should be familiar with literary magazines in general. Some of my favorites are *Alaska Quarterly Review*, *Threepenny Review*, *Southern Review*, *Ontario Review*. I most enjoy stories in which the overall effect (use of vivid imagery, sentence rhythm, authorial or 'psychic' distance, etc.) is achieved immediately, so that the reader may enjoy the unfolding of events, or psychological development of characters' viewpoints, without being necessarily distracted from what John Gardner calls the 'vivid and continuous fictional dream.' *MSR* is also interested in receiving studies and criticism on any writers of the Beat Generation, their sources of inspiration, etc."

‡MOSTLY MAINE, A Writer's Journal, (I), Susan Jo Publishing, P.O. Box 8805, Portland ME 04104. Editor: Peter McGinn. Magazine: 5½×8; 32-40 pages; 20 lb. stock paper. "Our goal is to support and encourage writers, especially beginners. Two of the best forms of encouragements are seeing your work in print, and receiving feedback from other writers. We want to provide both." Quarterly. Estab. 1992. Circ. 60.
Needs: Adventure, fantasy (science fantasy, sword and sorcery), feminist, gay, historical (general), humor/satire, lesbian, literary, mainstream/contemporary, mystery/suspense (amateur sleuth, private eye/hard-boiled, romantic suspense), psychic/supernatural/occult, regional, romance (contemporary, gothic), science fiction (hard science, soft/sociological), sports, westerns (frontier, traditional). No erotica, violent horror. Accepts 4-6 mss/issue; 16-24 mss/year. Publishes ms 1-6 months after acceptance. Recently pubilshed work by Susan Johnson, Michele Jacques. Length: 6,000 words maximum. Publishes short shorts. Also publishes literary essays, literary criticism, poetry. Always critiques or comments on rejected mss.
How to Contact: Send complete ms with a cover letter. Should include bio with submission. Reports in 1-3 weeks on queries; 1-3 month on mss. Send a disposable copy of ms. Simultaneous and reprint submissions OK. Sample copy for $1.50. Fiction guidelines for #10 SAE and 1 first-class stamp (IRC).
Payment: Pays 1 contributor's copy to first-time submitters only; additional copies for $1.50.
Terms: Acquires one-time rights. Sends galleys to author (upon request only).
Advice: "We're looking for crisp writing—vivid images, realistic dialogue, characters we can believe in. We want old fashion storytelling that achieves some sort of closure. It's that simple. *Mostly Maine* is a magazine without an ego. We are writers first and editors second. So don't send us stilted cover letters and formal bios. Be creative and natural. Treat us like that supportive writers' group you never have time to join. Looks for stories with humor in them, in large or small doses. We all enjoy a mix of humor in our lives. Why shouldn't our fictional characters?"

THE MOUNTAIN LAUREL, Quarterly Journal of Mountain Life, P.O. Box 562, Wytheville VA 24382. (703)228-7282. Editor: Susan M. Thigpen. Tabloid: 32 pages; newsprint; illustrations and photographs. "Everyday details about life in the Blue Ridge Mountains of yesterday, for people of all ages interested in folk history." Quarterly. Estab. 1983. Circ. 50,000.
Needs: Historical, humor, regional. "Stories must fit our format—we accept seasonal stories. There is always a shortage of good Christmas stories. A copy of our publication will be your best guideline as to what we want. We will not even consider stories containing bad language, sex, gore, horror." Receives approximately 40 unsolicited fiction mss/month. Accepts up to 15 mss/issue; 60 mss/year. Publishes ms 2-6 months after acceptance. Length: 500-600 words average; no minimum; 1,000 words maximum. Publishes short shorts. Length: 300 words. Sometimes critiques rejected mss. Recommends other markets.
How to Contact: Send complete ms with cover letter, which should include "an introduction to the writer as though he/she were meeting us in person." Reports in 1 month. SASE (IRCs). Simultaneous submissions OK. Sample copy for 9 × 12 SAE and 5 first-class stamps. Fiction guidelines for #10 SAE and 1 first-class stamp.
Payment: Pays in contributor's copies.
Terms: Acquires one-time rights.
Advice: "Tell a good story. Everything else is secondary. A tightly written story is much better than one that rambles. Short stories have no room to take off on tangents. *The Mountain Laurel* has published the work of many first-time writers as well as works by James Still and John Parris. First publication ever awarded the Blue Ridge Heritage Award."

MUSE PORTFOLIO, (I, II), 25 Tannery Rd., Unit Box 8, Westfield MA 01085. Editor: Haemi Balgassi. Magazine: 5½ × 8½; 29 pages; 20 lb. paper; color or heavier stock cover; illustrations. "*M.P.* welcomes submissions from sincere, eloquent freelancers who crave the opportunity to share and support one another's writing through a casual forum. *M.P.* is a non-profit publication." Published 2-4 times/year. Estab. 1992. Circ. 200.
Needs: Ethnic/multicultural, feminist, historical (general), literary, mainstream/contemporary, mystery/suspense (amateur sleuth, cozy, romantic suspense, general), regional, romance (contemporary, young adult, anything tasteful), senior citizen/retirement, young adult/teen (10-18 years). No pornography, vulgarity, excessive violence, profanity. Receives 25 unsolicited mss/month. Acquires 3-5 fiction mss/issue; 6-20 mss/year. Publishes ms 6-15 months after acceptance. Recently published work by Joseph Balgassi, J. Ray Condren, Ellie Cobb. Length: 1,000 words preferred; 300 words minimum; 2,500 words maximum. Publishes short shorts. Length: 300-500 words. Also publishes literary essays and poetry. Sometimes critiques or comments on rejected mss.
How to Contact: Send complete ms with cover letter. "No phone queries, please." Should include estimated word count, bio (short paragraph), list of publications (optional). Reports in 2 weeks on queries; 5 to 10 weeks on mss. SASE (IRCs) for a reply to query or return of ms. Reprint submissions OK. Sample copy for $2.50 and 6×9 or larger SAE with 2 first-class stamps. Fiction guidelines for #10 SAE and 1 first-class stamp.
Payment: Pays 1 contributor's copy.
Terms: Acquires one-time rights. Not copyrighted, but author copyright notices included in issues.
Advice: "We are eager to review the 'personal best' efforts of sincere, earnest writers of all levels. We especially encourage the beginning freelancer, and also appreciate submissions from more experienced writers who are willing to share their work with newer colleagues. Be sincere, and treat yourself, your writing and the freelance process with respect. Remember the 'three P's': Be *patient, persistent* and *professional*. Develop as *polished* a voice as possible. We are excited and appreciative when we discover the rare creative gem that has obviously been polished through *necessary revisions*."

MYSTERY NOTEBOOK (Ashenden), (II, IV), Box 1341, F.D.R. Station, New York NY 10150. Editor: Stephen Wright. Journal and Newsletter: 8½ × 11; 10-16 pages and occasional double issues; photocopied; self cover; illustrations and photos sometimes. "Mystery books, news, information; reviews and essays. Ashenden section is devoted to Somerset Maugham and his works." For mystery readers and writers and for Maugham readers and scholars. Quarterly. Estab. 1984. Circ. (approx.) 1,000.
Needs: Excerpted novel (mystery/suspense). Receives few unsolicited mss. Length: brief. Short shorts considered. Also publishes articles and essays (brief) on Maugham and his works. Occasionally comments on rejected ms.
How to Contact: Query. Reports in 3 weeks on queries; 1 month on mss. SASE (IRCs) for ms. Simultaneous and previously published submissions OK (if query first). Sample copies or back issues $7.50, double issues $15.

Payment: None. "If author is a regular contributor, he or she will receive complimentary subscription. Usually contributor receives copies of the issue in which contribution appears."
Advice: "Mystery magazines use all kinds of stories in various settings. This is also true of mystery books except that no matter what kind of detective is the protagonist (private eye, amateur, police, female operative) the novel must be the best of its kind — even for consideration. Mystery fiction books have increased in demand — *but* the competetion is more keen than ever. So only those with real talent *and* a superb knowledge of mystery-writing craft have *any* chance for publication. Do try to get the reader interested in the first few pages. It also helps if you know and understand the current market."

MYSTERY TIME, An Anthology of Short Stories, (I), Box 2907, Decatur IL 62524. Editor: Linda Hutton. Booklet: 5½×8½; 44 pages; bond paper; illustrations. "Annual collection of short stories with a suspense or mystery theme for mystery buffs." Estab. 1983.
Needs: Mystery/suspense only. Receives 10-15 unsolicited fiction mss/month. Buys 10-12 mss/year. Recently published work by Harold Gauer, Kristin Neri, Sylvia Roberts. Published new writers within the last year. Length: 1,500 words maximum. Occasionally critiques rejected mss and recommends other markets.
How to Contact: Send complete ms with SASE (IRCs). "No cover letters." Simultaneous and previously published submissions OK. Reports in 1 month on mss. Publishes ms an average of 6-8 months after acceptance. Sample copy for $3.50. Fiction guidelines for #10 SAE and 1 first-class stamp.
Payment: Pays ¼¢/word minimum; 1¢/word maximum; 1 contributor's copy; $2.50 charge for extras
Terms: Buys one-time rights. Buys reprints.
Advice: "Study a sample copy and the guidelines. Too many amateurs mark themselves as amateurs by submitting blind."

‡**MYSTIC FICTION, (II),** P.O. Box 40625, Bellevue WA 98015-4625. (206)649-0926. Editor: Su Llewellyn. Magazine: 8½×11; 32-56 pages; 60 lb. bond glossy paper; self-cover. "*MF* publishes short stories of almost any genre that demonstrate transformation, especially psychological and emotional. We reject stories with static characters." Quarterly. Estab. 1993.
Needs: Adventure, erotica, ethnic/multicultural, experimental, fantasy (science fantasy, sword and sorcery), feminist, historical (general), horror, humor/satire, literary, mainstream/contemporary, mystery/suspense, psychic/supernatural/occult, science fiction, westerns (frontier, traditional). No romance. Publishes special fiction issue or anthology. Receives 12-15 unsolicited mss/month. Accepts 7-13 mss/issue; 28-52 mss/year. Publishes ms 6 months to a year after acceptance. Recently published work by Mike James, Carol Meredith, Sheryll Watt, Joe Murphy, Mark McLaughlin. Length: 5,000 words preferred; 500 words minimum; 10,000 words maximum. Publishes short shorts. Length: 450 words. Also publishes poetry. Always critiques or comments on rejected mss.
How to Contact: Send complete ms with a cover letter. Should include estimated word count, Social Security number and "a few words justifying how the main character changes in cover letter." Reports in 1-2 weeks on queries; 2 months on mss. Send SASE (or IRC) for reply, return of ms or send a disposable copy of ms. No simultaneous submissions. Reprint and electronic submissions OK. Sample copy for $4. Fiction guidelines for SASE.
Payment: Pays $2 minimum; $20 maximum; 2 contributor's copies; additional copies for $2.50.
Terms: Pays on acceptance for first North American serial rights or one-time rights (in the case of a reprint).
Advice: Looks for: "character transformation demonstrated; writing craft/thorough line editing; distinctive characters. Read William Sloane's *The Craft of Writing!*" Would like to see more "careful attention to prose — too often writers talk *at* us, the reader is constantly aware of the author. Writers should ask themselves if the sentence, word, paragraph is coming from the author — would the character think of that? Remember — scene is not scenery!"

THE MYTHIC CIRCLE, (I), The Mythopoeic Society, Box 6707, Altadena CA 91001. Co-Editors: Tina Cooper and Christine Lowentrout. Magazine: 8½×11; 50 pages; high quality photocopy paper; illustrations. "A tri-quarterly fantasy-fiction magazine. We function as a 'writer's forum,' depending heavily on letters of comment from readers. We have a very occasional section called 'Mythopoeic Youth' in which we publish stories written by writers still in high school/junior high school, but we are not primarily oriented to young writers. We have several 'theme' issues (poetry, American fantasy) and plan more of these in the future. We give subscribers' submissions preference." Triquarterly. Estab. 1987. Circ. 150.

Needs: Short fantasy. "No erotica, no graphic horror, no 'hard' science fiction." Receives 25 unsolicited ms/month. Accepts 19-20 mss/issue. Publishes ms 1-2 years after acceptance. Published work by Charles de Lint, Gwyneth Hood, Angelee Sailer Anderson; published new writers within the last year. Length: 3,000 words average. Publishes short shorts. Length: 8,000 words maximum. Always critiques rejected mss; may recommend other markets."

How to Contact: Send complete ms with cover letter. "We give each ms a personal response. We get many letters that try to impress us with other places they've appeared in print—that doesn't matter much to us." Reports in 3 months. SASE (IRCs). No simultaneous submissions. Accepts electronic submissions, IBM or MAC floppies. Sample copy for $6.50; fiction guidelines for #10 SASE.

Payment: Pays in contributor's copies; charges for extras.

Terms: Acquires one-time rights.

Advice: "There are very few places a fantasy writer can send to these days. *Mythic Circle* was started because of this; also, the writers were not getting any kind of feedback when (after nine or ten months) their mss were rejected. We give the writers personalized attention—critiques, suggestions—and we rely on our readers to send us letters of comment on the stories we publish, so that the writers can see a response. Don't be discouraged by rejections, especially if personal comments/suggestions are offered."

NAHANT BAY, (II), What Cheer Press, #2, 29 Front St., Marblehead MA 01945. (617)639-1889. Editors: Kim A. Pederson and Kalo Clarke. Magazine: 5¼×8½; 60-65 pages; 20 lb. bond paper; illustrations and photographs. "Short stories, essays and poetry for those interested in quality fiction." Annually. Estab. 1990.

Needs: Adventure, condensed/excerpted novel, contemporary, erotica, ethnic, experimental, fantasy, feminist, gay, historical, horror, humor/satire, lesbian, literary, mainstream, mystery/suspense, prose poem, psychic/supernatural/occult, regional, science fiction, translations. No romance, juvenile, teen, religious, confession. Receives 5-10 unsolicited mss/month. Accepts 2-3 mss/issue. Length: 1,250 words minimum; 2,500 words maximum. Publishes short shorts. Sometimes critiques rejected mss and recommends other markets.

How to Contact: Send complete ms with cover letter. Include brief biographical information. Reports in 4-6 months on mss. SASE. Simultaneous submissions OK. Accepts electronic submissions via disk or modem. Sample copy for $6, SAE and 5 first-class stamps (IRCs). Fiction guidelines for #10 SAE and 1 first-class stamp.

Payment: Pays 1 contributor's copy. Charge for extras.

Terms: Acquires first North American serial rights.

Advice: Looks for striking use of language; compelling characters and story; sense of humor; sense of irony.

NASSAU REVIEW, (I, II), Nassau Community College, State University of New York, Stewart Ave., Garden City NY 11596. (516)222-7186. Editor: Paul A. Doyle. Fiction Editor: Virginia A. Moran. Magazine: 5½×8½; 80-120 pages; heavy stock paper; b&w illustrations and photographs. For "college teachers, libraries, educated college-level readers." Annually. Estab. 1964.

Needs: Contemporary, fantasy, historical (general), literary, mainstream, serialized novel. Receives 500 unsolicited mss/year. Accepts 15 mss/issue. Does not read mss January-August. Publishes ms 6 months after acceptance. Published work by Dick Wimmer, Louis Phillips, Norbert Petsch. Length: 800-1,500 words preferred; 1,000 words minimum; 1,500 words maximum. Publishes short shorts.

How to Contact: Send complete ms with cover letter. Include basic publication data. Reports in 1 month on queries; 8 months on mss. SASE (IRCs). No simultaneous submissions. Sample copy for 9×12 SAE.

Payment: No payment.

Terms: Acquires first rights or one-time rights.

Advice: Looks for "imaginative, concrete writing on interesting characters and scenes." Send story ms before October 15, $150 prize to best story published each year.

THE NATIONAL GAY & LESBIAN READER, (I, IV), (formerly *The Northwest Gay & Lesbian Reader*), Suite #1169, 1202 E. Pike St., Seattle WA 98122. (206)322-4609. Editor: Ron Whiteaker. Magazine: 8½×11; 48 pages; newsprint paper, illustrations, photographs. "A wide range of formats reflecting the gay/lesbian/bisexual experience." Quarterly. Estab. 1989. Circ. 4,000.

● Big changes for this publication including a name change, new address, new format and a national focus.

Needs: Gay, lesbian, bisexual. "Light erotica OK. No hard-core erotica, or 'abusive attitude' fiction." Receives 10 unsolicited mss/month. Accepts 4 mss/issue. Publishes ms 2 months after acceptance. Published work by William Freeberg, Aubrey Hart Sparks, Jill Sunde. Length: 2,000 words preferred; 1,000 words minimum; 3,500 words maximum. Publishes short shorts.
How to Contact: Send complete ms with cover letter. Include "a bit about the story and its author." Reports in 2 months on queries; 3 months on mss. SASE. Accepts electronic submissions—IBM compatible disk in generic (ASCII) word processing format. Sample copy for $3.95, 9×12 SAE and 4 first-class stamps. Fiction guidelines for #10 SAE and 1 first-class stamp (IRCs).
Payment: Pays in contributor's copies and free subscription.
Terms: Acquires one-time rights.
Advice: "A story that is clever and well-written and contains original ideas is considered first, rather than the hackneyed, over-done story lines containing redundant dogma and irritating buzzwords. Reflect the gay/lesbian/bisexual experience."

NCASA JOURNAL, A Publication of the National Coalition Against Sexual Assault, (I, IV), Suite 500, 123 S. 7th St., Springfield IL 62701. (217)753-4117. Editor: Becky Bradway. Newsletter: 8½×11; 12-16 pages; illustrations and photographs. "*NCASA Journal* is a forum for commentary, information and creative work concerning sexual assault and the anti-sexual assault movement." Quarterly. Estab. 1985. Circ. 1,500.
Needs: Condensed/excerpted novel, contemporary, ethnic, experimental, feminist, gay, humor/satire, literary, prose poem, regional, serialized novel, translations. Fiction and poetry are included in a special section, "Voices of Survivors." Work should be written by survivors of rape or incest. "All fiction must be grounded in a feminist perspective." Accepts 1-2 mss/issue; 4-6 mss/year. Publishes ms up to 1 year after acceptance. Length: 2,000 words average; 500 words minimum; 3,000 words maximum. Publishes short shorts. Sometimes critiques rejected mss and recommends other markets.
How to Contact: Send complete manuscript with cover letter. Reports in 2 weeks on mss. SASE. Simultaneous and reprint submissions OK. Sample copy $4. Fiction guidelines for SASE and 1 first-class stamp (IRCs).
Payment: Pays 3 contributor's copies.
Terms: Acquires first rights.
Advice: "*NCASA Journal* is looking for well-written, thoughtful fiction and poetry from survivors of rape and incest. Fiction may be based upon personal experience, but should utilize the mechanics of the story form: plot, characterization, dialogue, etc. Stories should have fully realized characters who ring true as fiction. Personal exploration should be done within the context of the story. Please do not be discouraged by rejection; this magazine has very limited space for creative work."

NEBO, A Literary Journal, (II), Arkansas Tech University, Dept. of English, Russellville AR 72801. (501)968-0256. Editors change each year. Contact Editor or Advisor: Dr. Michael Karl Ritchie. Literary, fiction and poetry magazine: 5×8; 50-60 pages. For a general, academic audience. Annually. Estab. 1983. Circ. 500.
Needs: Literary, mainstream, reviews. Receives 20-30 unsolicited fiction mss/month. Accepts 2 mss/issue; 6-10 mss/year. Does not read mss May 1-Sept. 1. Published new writers within the last year. Length: 3,000 words maximum. Also publishes literary essays, literary criticism, poetry. Occasionally critiques rejected mss.
How to Contact: Send complete ms with SASE (IRCs) and cover letter with bio. Simultaneous submissions OK. Reports in 3 months on mss. Publishes ms an average of 6 months after acceptance. Sample copy $5. "Submission deadlines for all work are Nov. 15 and Jan. 15 of each year." Reviews novels and short story collections.
Payment: Pays 1 contributor's copy.
Terms: Acquires one-time rights.
Advice: "A writer should carefully edit his short story before submitting it. Write from the heart and put everything on the line. Don't write from a phony or fake perspective. Frankly, many of the manuscripts we receive should be publishable with a little polishing. Manuscripts should *never* be submitted with misspelled words or on 'onion skin' or colored paper."

THE NEBRASKA REVIEW, (II), University of Nebraska at Omaha, Omaha NE 68182-0324. (402)554-2771. Fiction Editor: James Reed. Magazine: 5½×8½; 72 pages; 60 lb. text paper; chrome coat cover stock. "*TNR* attempts to publish the finest available contemporary fiction and poetry for college and literary audiences." Publishes 2 issues/year. Estab. 1973. Circ. 500.
- *The Nebraska Review* has published a number of award-winning writers.

Needs: Contemporary, humor/satire, literary and mainstream. Receives 40 unsolicited fiction mss/month. Acquires 4-5 mss/issue, 8-10 mss/year. Does not read April 1-September 1. Recently published work by Elizabeth Evans, Stephen Dixon, Stewart O'Nan, E.S. Goldman, and Stephen Pett; published new writers within the last year. Length: 5,000-6,000 words average. Also publishes poetry.
How to Contact: Send complete ms with SASE (IRCs). Reports in 1-3 months. Publishes ms an average of 6-12 months after acceptance. Sample copy $2.50.
Payment: 2 free contributor's copies plus 1 year subscription; $2 charge for extras.
Terms: Acquires first North American serial rights.
Advice: "Write 'honest' stories in which the lives of your characters are the primary reason for writing and techniques of craft serve to illuminate, not overshadow, the textures of those lives. Sponsors a $300 award/year—write for rules."

‡NEGATIVE CAPABILITY (II), A Literary Quarterly, 62 Ridgelawn Dr. E., Mobile AL 36608. (205)661-9114. Editor-in-Chief: Sue Walker. Managing Editor: Richard G. Beyer. Magazine: 5½×8½; 160 pages; 70 lb. offset paper; 4 color/varnish cover stock; illustrations; photos. Magazine of short fiction, prose poems, poetry, criticism, commentaries, journals and translations for those interested in contemporary trends, innovations in literature. Triquarterly. Estab. 1981. Circ. 1,000.
Needs: Adventure, contemporary, ethnic, experimental, fantasy, feminist, historical (general), literary, mystery/suspense, prose poem, psychic/supernatural/occult, regional, romance (contemporary, gothic/historical), science fiction, senior citizen/retirement, translations. Accepts 2-3 mss/issue, 6-10 mss/year. Does not read July-Sept. Publishes short shorts. Published work by A.W. Landwehr, Gerald Flaherty and Richard Moore; published new writers within the last year. Length: 1,000 words minimum. Also publishes literary essays, literary criticism. Sometimes recommends other markets.
How to Contact: Query or send complete ms. SASE (IRCs). Reports in 2 weeks on queries; 6 weeks on mss. Publishes ms an average of 6 months after acceptance. Sample copy $5. Reviews novels and short story collections.
Payment: Pays 2 contributor's copies.
Terms: Acquires first rights, first North American serial rights or one-time rights. Sends galleys to author.
Advice: "We consider all manuscripts and often work with new authors to encourage and support. We believe fiction answers a certain need that is not filled by poetry or nonfiction." Annual fiction competition. Deadline Dec. 1.

THE NEW CRUCIBLE, A Magazine About Man and His Environment, (I), RRI, Box 76, Stark KS 66775-9802. Editor: Garry De Young. Magazine: 8½×11; variable number of pages; 20 lb. paper; soft cover; illustrations and photographs. Publishes "environmental material—includes the total human environment." Bimonthly. Estab. 1964.
Needs: Atheist. "Keep material concise, use clear line drawings. Environmentalists must be Materialists because the environment deals with matter. Thus also evolutionists. Keep this in mind. Manuscripts not returned. Will not accept religious or other racist or sexist material." Upcoming theme: "Dynamics of Discriminatory Practice." Length: concise preferred. Publishes short shorts. Also publishes literary criticism, poetry. Sometimes critiques rejected mss. Publishes original cartoons.
How to Contact: Send complete ms with cover letter. Cover letter should include "biographical sketch of author." SASE. Simultaneous and reprint submissions OK. Sample copy for $5, 9×12 SAE and 4 first-class stamps (IRCs).
Payment: Pays in contributor's copies.
Terms: *Charges $1/page reading fee.* "Will discuss rights with author."
Advice: "Be gutsy! Don't be afraid to attack superstitionists. Attack those good people who remain so silent—people such as newspaper editors, so-called scientists who embrace superstition such as the Jesus myth or the Virgin Mary nonsense. We publish the works of Elbert Hubbard and also the Haldeman-Julius Little Blue Books which were the forerunners of the present paperbacks. Many are considered taboo by local libraries. We also solicit material critical of Zionist expansionism."

NEW DELTA REVIEW, (II), English Dept./Louisiana State University, Baton Rouge LA 70803. (504)388-5922. Editors: Randi Gray, Nicola Mason, Catherine Williamson. Fiction Editor: Matt Clark. Magazine: 6×9; 75-125 pages; high quality paper; glossy card cover; illustrations; photographs. "No theme or style biases. Poetry, fiction primarily; also creative essays, literary interviews and reviews." Semi-annual. Estab. 1984.
• *New Delta Review* also sponsors the Eyster Prizes for fiction and poetry. See the listing in the

Contest and Awards Section of this book. Work from the magazine has been included in the *Pushcart Prize* anthology.

Needs: Contemporary, experimental, humor/satire, literary, mainstream, prose poem, translations. Receives 120 unsolicited mss/ month. Accepts 4-8 mss/issue. Recently published work by Sibbie O'Sullivan, Edward J. Delaney, James T. English, Michael A. Griffith; published new writers within the last year. Length: 20 ms pages average; 250 words minimum. Publishes short shorts. Also publishes poetry. Sometimes critiques rejected mss.

How to Contact: Send complete ms with cover letter. Cover letter should include "credits, if any; no synopses, please." No simultaneous submissions. Reports on mss in 2-3 months. SASE (IRCs). Mss deadlines September 1 for fall; February 15 for spring. Sample copy $4. Reviews novels and short story collections.

Payment: Pays in contributor's copies. Charge for extras.

Terms: Acquires first North American serial rights. Sponsors award for fiction writers in each issue. Eyster Prize-$50 plus notice in magazine. Mss selected for publication are automatically considered.

Advice: "The question we are asked most is still what *kind* of fiction we like. We answer: the good kind. Be brave. Explore your voice. Make sparks fly off your typewriter. Send your best work, even if others have rejected it. Don't let our address mislead you: We like fiction and poetry that explore national and international sensibilities, not just Southern regionalism. And don't forget the SASE if you want a response."

NEW ENGLAND REVIEW, (III), Middlebury College, Middlebury VT 05753. (802)388-3711, ext. 5075. Editors: David Huddle, Devon Jersild and William Lychack. Magazine: 6×9; 180 pages; 70 lb paper; coated cover stock; illustrations; photos. A literary quarterly publishing fiction, poetry and essays on life and the craft of writing. For general readers and professional writers. Quarterly. Estab. 1977. Circ. 2,000.

• *New England Review* has long been associated with Breadloaf Writer's Conference, held at Middlebury College.

Needs: Literary. Receives 250 unsolicited fiction mss/month. Accepts 5 mss/issue; 20 mss/year. Does not read ms June-August. Recently published work by Robert Olen Butler, Grace Paley, Charles Baxter, Joyce Carol Oates and Marge Piercy; published new writers within the last year. Publishes ms 3-9 months after acceptance. Agented fiction: less than 5%. Publishes short shorts. Sometimes critiques rejected mss.

How to Contact: Send complete ms with cover letter. "Cover letters that demonstrate that the writer knows the magazine are the ones we want to read. We don't want hype, or hard-sell, or summaries of the author's intentions. Will consider simultaneous submissions, but must be stated as such." Reports in 8-10 weeks on mss. SASE (IRCs).

Payment: Pays $10/page; subscription to magazine; contributor's copies; charge for extras.

Terms: Pays on publication. Acquires first rights and reprint rights. Sends galleys to author.

Advice: "It's best to send one story at a time, and wait until you hear back from us to try again."

NEW FRONTIER, (IV), 101 Cuthbert St., Philadelphia PA 19106. (215)627-5683. Editor: Sw. Virato. Magazine: 8×10; 48-60 pages; pulp paper stock; illustrations and photos. "We seek new age writers who have imagination yet authenticity." Monthly. Estab. 1981. Circ. 60,000.

Needs: New age. "A new style of writing is needed with a transformation theme." Receives 10-20 unsolicited mss/month. Accepts 1-2 mss/issue. Publishes ms 3 months after acceptance. Agented fiction "less than 5%." Published work by John White, Laura Anderson; published work by new writers within the last year. Length: 1,000 words average; 750 words minimum; 2,000 words maximum. Publishes short shorts. Length: 150-500 words. Occasionally critiques rejected mss and recommends other markets.

How to Contact: Send complete ms with cover letter, which should include author's bio and credits. Reports in 2 months on mss. SASE (IRCs) for ms. Simultaneous and reprint submissions OK. Sample copy for $2. Fiction guidelines for #10 SAE and 1 first-class stamp.

Terms: Acquires first North American serial rights and one-time rights.

Advice: "The new age market is ready for a special kind of fiction and we are here to serve it. Don't try to get an A on your term paper. Be sincere, aware and experimental. Old ideas that are senile don't work for us. Be fully alive and aware—tune in to our new age audience/readership."

NEW LAUREL REVIEW, (II), 828 Lesseps St., New Orleans LA 70117. (504)947-6001. Editor: Lee Meitzen Grue. Magazine: 6×9; 120 pages; 60 lb. book paper; Sun Felt cover; illustrations; photo essays. Journal of poetry, fiction, critical articles and reviews. "We have published such internationally known writers as James Nolan, Tomris Uyar and Yevgeny Yevtushenko." Readership: "Literate, adult audiences as well as anyone interested in writing with significance, human interest, vitality, subtlety, etc." Annually. Estab. 1970. Circ. 500.

Needs: Literary, contemporary, fantasy and translations. No "dogmatic, excessively inspirational or political" material. Acquires 1-2 fiction mss/issue. Receives approximately 50 unsolicited fiction mss each month. Length: about 10 printed pages. Also publishes literary essays, literary criticism, poetry. Critiques rejected mss when there is time.

How to Contact: Send complete ms with SASE (IRCs). Reports in 3 months. Sample copy $6. Reviews novels and short story collections.

Payment: Pays 1 contributor's copy.

Terms: Acquires first rights.

Advice: "We are interested in international issues pointing to libraries around the world. Write fresh, alive 'moving' work. Not interested in egocentric work without any importance to others. Be sure to watch simple details such as putting one's name and address on ms and clipping all pages together. Caution: Don't use overfancy or trite language."

NEW LETTERS MAGAZINE, (I, II), University of Missouri-Kansas City, 5100 Rockhill Rd., Kansas City MO 64110. (816)235-1168. Fax: (816)235-2611. Editor: James McKinley. Magazine: 14 lb. cream paper; illustrations. Quarterly. Estab. 1971 (continuation of *University Review*, founded 1935). Circ. 2,500.

Needs: Contemporary, ethnic, experimental, humor/satire, literary, mainstream, translations. No "bad fiction in any genre." Upcoming theme: New Letters Literary Awards Issue (Winter 1994). Recently published work by Tess Gallagher, Jimmy Carter and Amiri Barak; published work by new writers within the last year. Agented fiction: 10%. Also publishes short shorts. Occasionally critiques rejected mss.

How to Contact: Send complete ms with cover letter. Does not read mss May 15-October 15. Reports in 3 weeks on queries; 6-8 weeks on mss. SASE (IRCs) for ms. No simultaneous or multiple submissions. Sample copy: $8.50 for issues older than 5 years; $5.50 for 5 years or less.

Payment: Pays honorarium—depends on grant/award money; 2 contributor's copies. Sends galleys to author.

Advice: "Seek publication of representative chapters in high-quality magazines as a way to the book contract. Try literary magazines first."

‡NEW METHODS, The Journal of Animal Health Technology, (IV), Box 22605, San Francisco CA 94122-0605. (415)664-3469. Editor: Ronald S. Lippert, AHT. Newsletter ("could become magazine again"): 8½ × 11; 4-6 pages; 20 lb. paper; illustrations; "rarely" photos. Network service in the animal field educating services for mostly professionals in the animal field; e.g. animal health technicians. Monthly. Estab. 1976. Circ. 5,608.

● *New Methods* is connected with New Methods Distributing, a pet care products distributor.

Needs: Animals: adventure, condensed novel, contemporary, experimental, historical, mainstream, regional. No stories unrelated to animals. Receives 12 unsolicited fiction mss/month. Buys one ms/issue; 12 mss/year. Length: Open. "Rarely" publishes short shorts. Occasionally critiques rejected mss. Recommends other markets.

How to Contact: Query first with theme, length, expected time of completion, photos/illustrations, if any, biographical sketch of author, all necessary credits or send complete ms. Report time varies (up to 4 months). SASE (IRCs) for query and ms. Simultaneous submissions OK. Sample copy and fiction guidelines $2.90.

Payment: No payment.

Terms: Acquires one-time rights.

Advice: Sponsors contests: theme changes but generally concerns the biggest topics of the year in the animal field. "Emotion, personal experience—make the person feel it. We are growing."

NEW ORLEANS REVIEW, (II), Box 195, Loyola University, New Orleans LA 70118. (504)865-2294. Editor: John Biguenet. Magazine: 8½ × 11; 100 pages; 60 lb. Scott offset paper; 12 + King James C1S cover stock; photos. "Publishes poetry, fiction, translations, photographs, nonfiction on literature and film. Readership: those interested in current culture, literature." Quarterly. Estab. 1968. Circ. 1,000.

Needs: Literary, contemporary, translations. Buys 9-12 mss/year. Length: under 40 pages.

How to Contact: Send complete ms with SASE (IRCs). Does not accept simultaneous submissions. Accepts disk submissions; inquire about system compatibility. Prefers hard copy with disk submission. Reports in 3 months. Sample copy $9.

Payment: "Inquire."

Terms: Pays on publication for first North American serial rights. Sends galleys to author.

THE NEW PRESS LITERARY QUARTERLY, (II), 53-35 Hollis Court Blvd., Flushing NY 11365. (718)229-6782. Publisher: Bob Abramson. Magazine: 8½ × 11; 40 pages; medium bond paper and thick cover stock; illustrations and photographs. "Poems, short stories, commentary, personal journalism. Original, informative and entertaining." Quarterly. Estab. 1984.

Needs: Adventure, confession, ethnic, experimental, fantasy, humor/satire, literary, mainstream, prose poem, serialized/excerpted novel, spiritual, sports, translations. No gratuitous violence. Upcoming themes: "Recreation/the flesh" (summer); "Education/the spirit" (winter). Receives 25 unsolicited mss/month. Accepts 5 mss/issue; 20 mss/year. Publishes ms 12 months after acceptance. Published new writers within the last year. Length: 4,000 words maximum; 100 words minimum. Also publishes literary essays, literary criticism, poetry. Sometimes critiques rejected mss and recommends other markets.

How to Contact: Send complete ms with cover letter. Reports in 2 months. SASE. Simultaneous and reprint submissions OK. Sample copy $4; fiction guidelines for SASE (IRCs). $15 for one-year (4 issues) subscription.

Payment: Pays 3 contributor's copies, $15 for each prose piece and $100 for the best essay and short story entered in the contests for each issue with a $5 entry fee.

Terms: Buys one-time rights.

the new renaissance, (II), 9 Heath Rd., Arlington MA 02174. Fiction Editors: Louise T. Reynolds, Harry Jackel and Patricia Michaud. Magazine: 6 × 9; 144-208 pages; 70 lb. paper; laminated cover stock; artwork; photos. "An international magazine of ideas and opinions, emphasizing literature and the arts, *tnr* takes a classicist position in literature and the arts. Publishes a variety of very diverse, quality fiction, always well crafted, sometimes experimental. *tnr* is unique among literary magazines for its marriage of the literary and visual arts with political/sociological articles and essays. We publish the beginning as well as the emerging and established writer." Biannually. Estab. 1968. Circ. 1,500.

● Work published in *the new renaissance* has been chosen for inclusion in *Editor's Choice III* and *Editor's Choice IV*.

Needs: Literary, humor, prose poem, translations, off-beat, quality fiction and, occasionally, experimental fiction. "We don't want to see heavily plotted stories with one-dimensional characters or heavily academic or 'poetic' writing, or fiction that is self-indulgent." Buys 5-6 mss/issue, 8-13 mss/year. Receives approximately 75-130 unsolicited fiction mss each month. Reads only from January 2 thru April 30. Agented fiction approx. 8-12%. Recently published work by Philip Greene, Kurt Kusenberg, Jacqueline Merriam-Paskow, Tom Ruane, Lauren Hahn (translator). Published new writers within the last year. Length of fiction: 3-36 pages. Also publishes literary essays, literary criticism, poetry. Comments on rejected mss "when there is time and when we want to encourage the writer or believe we can be helpful. If you prefer we not comment, say so with ms."

How to Contact: Send complete ms with SASE (IRCs) of sufficient size for return. "Inform us if multiple submission. If you query, enclose SASE, IRC or stamped post card." Reluctantly accepts simultaneous submissions. Reports in 1-5 weeks on queries; 6-9 months on mss. Publishes ms an average of 15-20 months after acceptance. Sample copy $6.75 for 2 back issues, $7.50 or $9 for recent issue. Reviews novels and short story collections, also biography, poetry collections, etc.

Payment: Pays $40-80 after publication; 1 contributor's copy. Query for additional copies, discount with 5 or more copies.

Terms: Buys all rights in case of a later *tnr* book collection; otherwise, rights return to the writer.

Advice: "We represent one of the best markets for writers because we publish a greater variety (of styles, statements, tones) than most magazines, small or large. Study *tnr* and then send your best work; we will read 2 manuscripts *only* if they are 4 pages or less; for mss 6 pages or more, send only one ms. Manuscripts are rejected because writers do not study their markets but rather send out indiscriminately. Fully one-third of our rejected manuscripts now fall into this category; others are from tyro writers who haven't yet mastered their craft or writers who are not honest or who haven't fully thought their story through or from writers who are careless about language. Also, many writers feel compelled to 'explain' their stories to the reader instead of letting the story speak for itself. Overwritten mss are becoming more and more common. Learn to edit your own work."

NEW VIRGINIA REVIEW, (II), 2A, 1306 E. Cary St., Richmond VA 23219. (804)782-1043. Editor: Mary Flinn. Magazine: 6½ × 10; 180 pages; high quality paper; coated, color cover stock. "Authors are serious writers of contemporary fiction." Published January, May and October. Estab. 1978. Circ. 2,000.

Needs: Contemporary, experimental, literary, mainstream, serialized/excerpted novel. No blue, science fiction, romance, children's. Receives 50-100 unsolicited fiction mss/month. Accepts an average of 15 mss/issue. Does not read from April 1 to September 1. Publishes ms an average of 6-9 months after acceptance. Length: 5,000-6,500 words average; no minimum; 8,000 words maximum. Also publishes poetry. Sometimes critiques rejected mss.
How to Contact: Send complete ms with cover letter, name, address, telephone number, brief biographical comment. Reports in 6 weeks on queries; up to 6 months on mss. "Will answer questions on status of ms." SASE (IRCs). Sample copy $7 and 9×12 SAE with 5 first-class stamps.
Payment: Pays $10/printed page; contributor's copies; charge for extras, ½ cover price.
Terms: Pays on publication for first North American serial rights. Sponsors contests and awards for Virginia writers only.
Advice: "Try to write good strong fiction, stick to it, and try again with another editor."

NEW VOICES IN POETRY AND PROSE, (I), New Voices Publishing, P.O. Box 52196, Shreveport LA 71135. (318)797-8243. Editor: Cheryl White. Magazine: 8½×11; 16-24 pages; linen paper; illustrations. "Dedicated to publishing new writers; appreciate many types of fiction." Semiannually. Estab. 1991. Circ. 400.
   • *New Voices* also sponsors a contest listed in this book.
Needs: Adventure, fantasy, historical (general), horror, humor/satire, literary, mainstream/contemporary, mystery/suspense, psychic/supernatural/occult, regional, religious/inspirational, romance, science fiction (soft/sociological). No "controversial themes; political; racist." Receives 20 unsolicited mss/month. Buys 3 ms/issue; 6-8 mss/year. Publishes ms 6 months after acceptance. Recently published work by Dan Schwala, Joan Shaw, Susan Vreeland. Length: 4,000 words maximum. Publishes short shorts. Also publishes poetry. Often critiques or comments on rejected mss.
How to Contact: Send complete ms with cover letter. Should also send estimated word count, very brief bio and list of publications with submission. Reports in 2 months on mss. Send SASE (IRC) for return of ms. Will consider simultaneous submissions and reprints. Sample copy $5. Fiction guidelines free. Reviews novels and short story collections.
Payment: Pays 1 contributor's copy.
Terms: Acquires one-time rights.
Advice: "A short story appeals to us when it *really tells a story* about human nature, or offers up a basic lesson about life. Develop characters well, so they are fleshed-out and real to life. Complicated plots can be a hindrance; stick to the simple."

‡NEW WRITING, A Literary Magazine for New Writers, (I, II), P.O. Box 1812, Amherst NY 14226-7812. Editor: Sam Meade. Magazine: 150+ pages; coated cover stock; illustrations and photographs. "We want to publish work that we believe is deserving." Annually. Estab. 1994.
Needs: Work by new writers: experimental, humor/satire, literary, mainstream/contemporary, translations. Length: open. Publishes short shorts. Sometimes critiques or comments on rejected mss.
How to Contact: Send complete ms with a cover letter. Should include *brief* list of publications and *short* cover letter. Reports in 1 month. Send SASE (or IRC) for return of ms. Simultaneous submissions OK. Reviews novels and short story collections.
Payment: Pays 2 contributor's copies.
Terms: Acquires one-time rights.
Advice: "Don't send first copies of *any* story. Always read over, and rewrite!" Avoid "stories with characters who are writers."

✤NeWEST REVIEW (II, IV), Box 394, R.P.O. University, Saskatoon, Saskatchewan S7N 9Z9 Canada. Editor: Gail Youngberg. Magazine: 40 pages; book stock; illustrations; photos. Magazine devoted to western Canada regional issues; "fiction, reviews, poetry for middle- to high-brow audience." Bimonthly (6 issues per year). Estab. 1975. Circ. 1,000.
Needs: "We want fiction of high literary quality, whatever its form and content. But we do have a heavy regional emphasis." Receives 15-20 unsolicited mss/month. Buys 1 ms/issue; 10 mss/year. Length: 2,500 words average; 1,500 words minimum; 5,000 words maximum. Sometimes recommends other markets.
How to Contact: "We like *brief* cover letters." Reports very promptly in a short letter. SAE, IRCs or Canadian postage. No multiple submissions. Sample copy $3.50.
Payment: Pays $100 maximum.
Terms: Pays on publication for one-time rights.
Advice: "Polish your writing. Develop your story line. Give your characters presence. If we, the readers, are to care about the people you create, you too must take them seriously."

NEXT PHASE, (I, II), Phantom Press, 33 Court St., New Haven CT 06511. (203)772-1697. Editor: Kim Means. 8½×11; 32 pages. "Features the best of fiction, poetry and illustration by up-and-coming writers and artists. We publish quality work as long as it is environmentally and humanely oriented." Quarterly. Estab. 1989. Circ. 1,000.
Needs: Experimental, fantasy. Receives 10-15 unsolicited mss/month. Accepts 6 mss/issue; 20 mss/year. Publishes short shorts. Also publishes poetry (but poetry should be sent to Holly Day, P.O. Box 284, Huntington Beach CA 92648). Critiques rejected mss and recommends other markets.
How to Contact: Send complete manuscript with cover letter. SASE (IRCs). Simultaneous and reprint submissions OK. Reports in 3 weeks. Sample copy for $3 per issue includes postage.
Payment: Pays contributor's copies.
Terms: Acquires one-time rights.
Advice: "We are now accepting a broader range of fiction at longer lengths—up to 2,000 words. Environmentally-oriented fiction or fantasy, experimental pieces encouraged."

NIGHT OWL'S NEWSLETTER, (II, IV), P.O. Box 488, La Porte TX 77572-0488. (713)470-8748. Editor: Robin Parker. Newsletter: 8½×11; 16 pages; 20 lb. copy paper; cartoons. A newsletter for "night owls—people who can't sleep through much of the hours between midnight and 6 a.m. and often want to sleep late in the morning." Quarterly. Estab. 1990.
Needs: Excerpted novel, experimental, fantasy, humor/satire, literary. "All variations must relate to the subject of night and/or night owls. No erotica." Upcoming themes: "Shift Work," "Safe Treatments for 'Insomnia'," "Sleep Treatments," " 'Insomnia' and Depression," "Naps," "When Night and Day People Marry." Accepts 1-2 mss/issue; 4-10 mss/year. Publishes ms 1 year after acceptance. Recently published work by Catharine Mason. Length: 500-700 words preferred; 250 words minimum; 1,000 words maximum. Publishes short shorts. Critiques or comments on rejected mss.
How to Contact: Send complete ms with cover letter. Include short bio and credits. Reports in 2-3 months. SASE. Simultaneous and reprint submissions OK. Sample copy for $3.50. Fiction guidelines for #10 SAE and 1 first-class stamp (IRCs).
Payment: Pays $1 minimum plus 1 contributor's copy; charges for extras.
Terms: Buys one-time rights.
Advice: "We are most interested in a humorous and intelligent approach to the problem of people not being able to get to sleep or stay asleep at night and/or unable to wake up in the morning. This means the writer must understand the problem and have information to help others (besides suggesting drugs, alcohol or sex) or offer support."

NIMROD, International Journal of Prose and Poetry, (II), Arts & Humanities Council of Tulsa, 2210 S. Main, Tulsa OK 74114. Editor-in-Chief: Francine Ringold. Magazine: 6×9; 160 pages; 60 lb. white paper; illustrations; photos. "We publish one thematic issue and one awards issue each year. "A recent theme was 'Australia,' a compilation of poetry, prose and fiction by authors from Australia. We seek vigorous, imaginative, quality writing." Published semiannually. Estab. 1956. Circ. 3,000+.
• Look for the interview with *Nimrod's* Editor-in-Chief Francine Ringold in the 1993 edition of *Novel & Short Story Writer's Market.*
Needs: "We accept contemporary poetry and/or prose. May submit adventure, ethnic, experimental, prose poem, science fiction or translations." Upcoming theme: "Canadian Literature" (1994). Receives 120 unsolicited fiction mss/month. Published work by Janette Turner Hospital, Josephine Jacobson, Alice Walker, Francois Camoin, Gish Jen; published new writers within the last year. Length: 7,500 words maximum. Also publishes poetry.
How to Contact: Reports in 3 weeks-3 months. Sample copy: "to see what *Nimrod* is all about, send $4.50 for a back issue. To receive a recent awards issue, send $6.90 (postage incl.)
Payment: Pays 2 contributor's copies, plus $5/page up to $25 total per author per issue.
Terms: Buys one-time rights.
Advice: "Read the magazine. Write well. Be courageous. No superfluous words. No clichés. Keep it tight but let your imagination flow. Read the magazine. Strongly encourage writers to send #10 SASE for brochure for annual literary contest with prizes of $1,000 and $500."

NO IDEA MAGAZINE, (I), P.O. Box 14636, Gainesville FL 32604-4636. Editor: Var Thëlin. Magazine: 8½×11; 64 pages, 16 four-color pages; 37 lb. newsprint; illustrations and photographs. Each issue comes with a hard-vinyl 7-inch record. "Mostly underground/punk/hardcore music and interviews, but we like delving into other art forms as well. We publish what we feel is good—be it silly or moving." Sporadically. Estab. 1985.

Needs: Adventure, contemporary, experimental, fantasy, horror, humor/satire, mystery/suspense (amateur sleuth, private eye), science fiction. "Humor of a strange, odd manner is nice. We're very open. No poetry, please." Receives 5-10 mss/month. Publishes ms up to 6 months after acceptance. Publishes mostly short shorts. Length: 1-6 pages typed.
How to Contact: Send complete manuscript with cover letter. Simultaneous submissions OK. Sample copy $3. Checks to Var Thëlin. Reviews novels and short story collections.
Payment: Pays in contributor's copies.
Terms: Acquires one-time rights.
Advice: "A query with $3 will get you a sample of our latest issue and answers to any questions asked. Just because we haven't included a writer's style of work before doesn't mean we won't print their work. Perhaps we've never been exposed to their style before."

THE NOCTURNAL LYRIC, (I), Box 77171, San Francisco CA 94107-7171. (415)621-8920. Editor: Susan Moon. Digest: 5½ × 8½; 40 pages; illustrations. "We are a non-profit literary journal, dedicated to printing fiction by new writers for the sole purpose of getting read by people who otherwise might have never seen their work." Bimonthly. Estab. 1987. Circ. 150.
Needs: Experimental, fantasy, horror, humor/satire, psychic/supernatural/occult, science fiction, poetry. "We will give priority to unusual, creative pieces." Receives approx. 50 unsolicited mss/month. Publishes ms 6-10 months after acceptance. Publishes short shorts. Length: 2,000 words maximum. Also publishes poetry.
How to Contact: Send complete ms with cover letter. Cover letter should include "something about the author, what areas of fiction he/she is interested in." Reports in 1 week on queries; 2-3 months on mss. SASE. Simultaneous and reprint submissions OK. Sample copy $2 (checks made out to Susan Moon, editor). Fiction guidelines for #10 SAE and 1 first-class stamp (IRCs).
Payment: Pays in gift certificates for subscription discounts.
Terms: Publication not copyrighted.
Advice: "Please stop wasting your postage sending us things that are in no way bizarre. We're getting more into strange, surrealistic horror and fantasy, or silly, satirical horror. If you're avant-garde, we want you! We're mainly accepting things that are bizarre all the way through, as opposed to ones that only have a surprise bizarre ending."

NOISY CONCEPT, The Journal of Voluntary Insanity, (I), 1216 Lincoln Ave., Cuyahoga Falls OH 44223. (216)678-1576. Editor: Keith Robb. Magazine: Digest-sized; bond paper; bond cover; illustrations. "Generally we intend to promote voluntary insanity, currently through such topics as hemp legalization, animal rights, anti-authoritarianism, vegetarianism and music. All viewpoints are considered, yet stupidity is ridiculed." Quarterly. Estab. 1989. Circ. 200-500.
Needs: Adventure, erotica, experimental, fantasy (science fantasy), feminist, horror, humor/satire, literary, mainstream/contemporary, mystery/suspense, psychic/supernatural/occult, science fiction (hard science, soft/sociological), young adult/teen (10-18 years). Does not want to see "anything that promotes fascism, oppression or the capitalist machine." Buys 1 ms/issue; 6 ms/year. Publishes ms up to 1 year after acceptance. Length: 400 words average; 500 words maximum. Publishes short shorts. Also publishes poetry.
How To Contact: Send complete ms. Reports in 2 months on ms. Send SASE (IRC) for reply, return of ms or send disposable copy of ms. Will consider simultaneous submissions and reprints. Sample copy $1. Reviews novels and short story collections.
Payment: Pays 1 contributor's copy. Additional copies 25¢ each/10 or more.
Terms: Acquires one-time rights. Not copyrighted.
Advice: "Insanity is a label attached to a person who is different. It is synonymous with 'originality,' 'creativity,' and 'individuality.' I make no rules and I expect writers not to follow them. Don't read a sample copy first. Just write from the heart. Too many writers want to fit into a mold because too many publications have too many rules."

NOMOS, Studies in Spontaneous Order, (II, IV), Nomos Press, Inc., 257 Chesterfield, Glen Ellyn IL 60137. (708)858-7184. Editor: Carol B. Low. 8½ × 11; 32 pages; original illustrations. "Essays, poems, fiction, letters relating to Libertarian concepts and culture for a Libertarian audience." Quarterly. Estab. 1982. Circ. 450 paid; 1,000 total.
Needs: Historical (general), humor/satire, mystery/suspense (police procedurals), science fiction (hard science). "We are a strictly hard-core Libertarian magazine and only consider relevant fiction. Reviews of novels also accepted." Receives 1 unsolicited ms/month. Accepts 1 ms/issue; 4 mss/year.

Publishes ms 4-8 months after acceptance. Length: 500-2,000 words average; 2,000 words maximum. Publishes short shorts. Occasionally critiques rejected mss.
How to Contact: Send complete manuscript with cover letter. Reports in 5-6 months on mss. SASE (IRCs). No simultaneous submissions. Accepts electronic submissions. Sample copy $4.50. Fiction guidelines for #10 SASE. Reviews novels.
Payment: Pays choice of subscription to magazine or contributor's copies.
Terms: Acquires one-time rights. Sends galleys or letter detailing edits or desired corrections to author.

THE NORTH AMERICAN REVIEW, University of Northern Iowa, Cedar Falls IA 50614. (319)273-6455. Editor: Robley Wilson. Publishes quality fiction. Bimonthly. Estab. 1815. Circ. 4,500.
Needs: "We will not be reading any new material until January, 1994, due to backlog."
How to Contact: Send complete ms with SASE (IRCs). Sample copy $4.
Payment: Pays approximately $20/printed page; 2 contributor's copies. $3.50 charge for extras.
Terms: Pays on publication for first North American serial rights.
Advice: "We stress literary excellence and read 3,000 manuscripts a year to find an average of 35 stories that we publish. Please *read* the magazine first."

NORTH ATLANTIC REVIEW, (I), North Eagle Corp. of NY, 15 Arbutus Lane, Stony Brook NY 11790. (516)751-7886. Editor: John Gill. Magazine: 7 × 9; 200 pages; glossy cover. "General interest." Estab. 1989. Circ. 1,000.
● *North Atlantic Review* tends to accept traditional fiction.
Needs: General fiction. Has published special fiction issue. Accepts 40 mss/year. Publishes ms 6-10 months after acceptance. Length: 3,000-7,000 words average. Publishes short shorts. Sometimes critiques rejected mss and recommends other markets.
How to Contact: Send complete ms with cover letter. Reports in 4-6 months on queries. SASE (IRCs). Simultaneous and photocopied submissions OK. Sample copy for $10.

NORTH DAKOTA QUARTERLY, (II), University of North Dakota, Box 7209, University Station, Grand Forks ND 58202. (701)777-3321. Editor: Robert W. Lewis. Fiction Editor: William Borden. Poetry Editor: Jay Meek. Magazine: 6 × 9; 200 pages; bond paper; illustrations; photos. Magazine publishing "essays in humanities; some short stories; some poetry." University audience. Quarterly. Estab. 1910. Circ. 800.
● Work published in *North Dakota Quarterly* was selected for inclusion in *Prize Stories 1993: The O. Henry Awards*.
Needs: Contemporary, ethnic, experimental, feminist, historical (general), humor/satire and literary. Plans an annual anthology or special edition. Receives 20-30 unsolicited mss/month. Acquires 4 mss/issue; 16 mss/year. Recently published work by Jerry Bumpus, Carol Shields, Rilla Askew, Chris Mazza; published new writers within the last year. Length: 3,000-4,000 words average. Also publishes literary essays, literary criticism, poetry. Sometimes critiques rejected mss.
How to Contact: Send complete ms with cover letter. "But they need not be much more than hello; please read this story; I've published (if so, best examples) . . ." SASE (IRCs). Reports in 3 months. Publishes ms an average of 6-8 months after acceptance. Sample copy $5. Reviews novels and short story collections.
Payment: Pays 5 contributor's copies; 20% discount for extras; year's subscription.
Terms: Acquires one-time rights.
Advice: "Read widely. Write, write; revise, revise."

NORTHEAST ARTS MAGAZINE, (II), Boston Arts Organization, Inc., J.F.K. Station, P.O. Box 6061, Boston MA 02114. Editor: Mr. Leigh Donaldson. Magazine: 6½ × 9½; 32-40 pages; matte finish paper; card stock cover; illustrations and photographs. Bimonthly. Estab. 1990. Circ. 750.
Needs: Ethnic, gay, historical (general), literary, mystery/suspense (private eye), prose poem. No obscenity, racism, sexism, etc. Upcoming themes: "the culinary arts, window-dressing, unique boat building, jazz history . . ." Receives 50 unsolicited mss/month. Accepts 1-2 mss/issue; 5-7 mss/year. Publishes ms 2-4 months after acceptance. Agented fiction 20%. Length: 750 words preferred. Publishes short shorts. Sometimes critiques rejected mss.
How to Contact: Send complete ms with cover letter. Include short bio. Reports in 1 month on queries; 2-4 months on mss. SASE (IRCs). Simultaneous submissions OK. Sample copy for $4.50, SAE and 75¢ postage. Fiction guidelines free.

INSIDER VIEWPOINT

Voice, Rhythm and Imagery: Essentials for Literary Excellence

Hannah Wilson says *Northwest Review*'s only criterion for publication is "excellence." For this literary journal, published since 1957 under the auspices of the University of Oregon in Eugene, Oregon, that means she and her staff look for three key elements in submissions they receive: a distinct voice, a certain rhythm and convincing imagery.

The *Northwest Review* has a staff of seven which is almost entirely volunteer, with the exception of John Witte, the journal's overall editor. Wilson was offered the position of fiction editor four years ago. Having just left her teaching job, she accepted with some hesitation.

"I did not have experience in editing, although I think teaching helps one to edit. I'm also a writer and I did not want the critical eye to become the first one

Hannah Wilson

I saw my own work with. But then I decided it was time to get back to reading more analytically."

And, ironically, the "critical eye" has become an inherent part of the magazine's editing process. *Northwest Review*'s editors have become known for actually nourishing writers whose work is submitted to them. "We offer a lot of critical, editorial help" to writers, says Wilson. They often send submissions back to writers and request revisions before publication.

The journal is seasonal, published three times a year. The editors receive an average of 100 submissions each month, and choose from that number three or four stories an issue, along with nonfiction essays and a mix of personal and analytical essays and poetry.

Although the editors accept a wide variety of work, including translations, they rarely publish genre work such as science fiction. They are open to short submissions, under 500 words, "if it works." Often, if the writer sends a short piece, Wilson will contact the writer and request a similar short piece to pair with it. On the other hand, she discourages submissions exceeding 40 pages.

The magazine's main concern is, of course, the quality of the prose. A strong voice is an important element because it can reveal depth of character, says Wilson. "We need to feel that there is a human being that we can care about in that voice, and it's not a machine talking to us."

Wilson also looks for a certain rhythm which she calls a "prose rhythm, a certain pacing that, if we read it aloud, we would like what we hear." Convincing imagery is also essential, she says. "The imagery needs to emerge naturally from the story," rather than seem "slathered on for effect.

"We want a story in which we can discern a line of tension in which the story can move ... it need not be a traditional plot line, but there needs to be some kind of narrative tension."

Lastly, Wilson warns writers not to be daunted by the magazine's reputation or stated criterion of "excellence." Spending too much time and effort on trying to fit a magazine's standards is the wrong approach, she says, and too often results in a lopsided story. Instead, writers should trust themselves. "The writer has to believe in what the story is about and what's happening in the story."

— Heather K. Hardy

Payment: Pays 2 contributor's copies.
Terms: Acquires first North American serial rights. Sometimes sends galleys to author.
Advice: Looks for "creative/innovative use of language and style. Unusual themes and topics."

NORTHWEST REVIEW, (II), 369 PLC, University of Oregon, Eugene OR 97403. (503)346-3957. Editor: John Witte. Fiction Editor: Hannah Wilson. Magazine: 6 × 9; 140-160 pages; high quality cover stock; illustrations; photos. "A general literary review featuring poems, stories, essays and reviews, circulated nationally and internationally. For a literate audience in avant-garde as well as traditional literary forms; interested in the important younger writers who have not yet achieved their readership." Triannually. Estab. 1957. Circ. 1,200.
   ● See the interview with Fiction Editor Hannah Wilson in this section.
Needs: Literary, contemporary, feminist, translations and experimental. Accepts 4-5 mss/issue, 12-15 mss/year. Receives approximately 100 unsolicited fiction mss each month. Published work by Susan Stark, Madison Smartt Bell, Maria Flook, Charles Marvin; published new writers within the last year. Length: "Mss longer than 40 pages are at a disadvantage." Also publishes literary essays, literary criticism, poetry. Critiques rejected mss when there is time. Sometimes recommends other markets.
How to Contact: Send complete ms with SASE (IRCs). "No simultaneous submissions are considered." Reports in 3-4 months. Sample copy $3.50. Reviews novels and short story collections. Send books to John Witte.
Payment: Pays 3 contributor's copies and a one-year subscription; 40% discount on extras.
Terms: Acquires first rights.
Advice: "Persist. Copy should be clean, double-spaced, with generous margins. Careful proofing for spelling and grammar errors will reduce slowing of editorial process." Mss are rejected because of "unconvincing characters, overblown language, melodramatic plot, poor execution."
Needs: Adventure, condensed/excerpted novel, contemporary, ethnic, experimental, fantasy, horror, humor/satire, literary, prose poem, psychic/supernatural/occult, romance (contemporary), science fiction, serialized novel, suspense/mystery, translations. Nothing religious, children stories, heavy political. Receives 10-15 unsolicited mss/month. Buys 3-6 mss/issue. Publishes ms 1 year after acceptance. Recently published work by Diane Mapps, Kay Kinghammer. Length: 3,500 words average. Publishes short shorts. Rarely (for a fee) critiques rejected mss.
How to Contact: Send complete manuscript with cover letter. Reports in 3 months on mss. SASE. Photocopied and reprint submissions OK. Accepts computer printout submissions. Sample copy $3 each with 9 × 12 SAE and $1 postage. Fiction guidelines for #10 SAE and 1 first-class stamp.
Payment: Pays $150 maximum plus contributor's copies. Charge for extras.
Terms: Pays on publication for one-time rights.

‡NORTHWOODS JOURNAL, A Magazine for Writers, (I), Conservatory of American Letters, P.O. Box 298, Thomaston ME 04861. (207)354-0998. Editor: R.W. Olmsted. Fiction Editor: R.S. Danbury III. Magazine: 5½ × 8½; 32-64 pages; white paper; 65 lb. card cover; some illustrations and photographs. "No theme, no philosophy—for people who read for entertainment." Quarterly. Estab. 1993. Circ. 1,000.

- Conservatory of American Letters is also connected with *Dan River Anthology* listed in this section and the Dan River Press listed in the Small Press section.

Needs: Adventure, erotica, experimental, fantasy (science fantasy, sword and sorcery), literary, mainstream/contemporary, mystery/suspense (amateur sleuth, police procedural, private eye/hard-boiled, romantic suspense), psychic/supernatural/occult, regional, romance (gothic, historical), science fiction (hard science, soft/sociological), sports, westerns (frontier, traditional). Publishes special fiction issue or anthology. Receives 50 unsolicited mss/month. Accepts 12-15 mss/year. Length: 2,500 words maximum. Also publishes literary essays, literary criticism and poetry.

How to Contact: "Get guidelines first" then send complete ms with a cover letter. Should include estimated word count and list of publications. Reports in 1-2 days on queries; by next deadline plus 5 days on mss. Send SASE (or IRC) for reply, return of ms or send a disposable copy of ms. No simultaneous submissions. Electronic submissions OK. Sample copy for $6.50. Fiction guidelines for #10 SAE and 1 first-class stamp. Reviews novels and short story collections. Send books to James A. Freeman, review editor.

Payment: Varies, "minimum $5/published page."

Terms: Pays on publication for all rights. Sends galleys to author.

Advice: "Read guidelines, read the things we've published. Know your market."

NOW & THEN, (IV), Center for Appalachian Studies and Services, East Tennessee State University, Box 70556, Johnson City TN 37614-0556. (615)929-5348. Editor: Pat Arnow. Magazine: 8½×11; 36-52 pages; coated paper and cover stock; illustrations; photographs. Publication focuses on Appalachian culture, present and past. Readers are mostly people in the region involved with Appalachian issues, literature, education." Triannually. Estab. 1984. Circ. 1,000.

Needs: Ethnic, literary, regional, serialized/excerpted novel, prose poem, spiritual and sports. "Absolutely has to relate to Appalachian theme. Can be about adjustment to new environment, themes of leaving and returning, for instance. Nothing unrelated to region." Upcoming themes: "Appalachian Celebrations" (summer 1994, deadline March 1994), "Center for Appalachian Studies and Services 10th Anniversary" (fall 1994, deadline July 1). Buys 2-3 mss/issue. Publishes ms 3-4 months after acceptance. Published work by Lee Smith, Pinckney Benedict, Gurney Norman, George Ella Lyon; published new writers within the last year. Length: 3,000 words maximum. Publishes short shorts. Also publishes literary essays, poetry.

How to Contact: Send complete ms with cover letter. Reports in 3 months. Include "information we can use for contributor's note." SASE (IRCs). Simultaneous submissions OK, "but let us know when it has been accepted elsewhere right away." Sample copy $3.50. Reviews novels and short story collections.

Payment: Pays up to $50 per story, contributor's copies, one year subscription.

Terms: Buys first-time rights.

Advice: "We're emphasizing Appalachian culture, which is not often appreciated because analysts are so busy looking at the trouble of the region. We're doing theme issues. Beware of stereotypes. In a regional publication like this one we get lots of them, both good guys and bad guys: salt of the earth to poor white trash. Sometimes we get letters that offer to let us polish up the story. We prefer the author does that him/herself." Send for list of upcoming themes.

NUCLEAR FICTION, (II,V), P.O. Box 49019, Austin TX 78765. (512)478-7262. Editors: Brian Martin, Jennifer Ragan. Magazine. "A bimonthly magazine of sci-fi, fantasy and horror. Includes film and book reviews, art, poetry." Estab. 1988.

Needs: Horror, fantasy and science fiction.

How to Contact: Send complete ms; cover letter optional. Reports in 4-6 weeks on average. Sample copy for $3. Reviews novels and short story collections. Send books to Brian Martin, Editor, 2518 Leon St. #107, Austin TX 78705.

Payment: Pays ½¢/word for fiction and reviews. (Minimum payment $7.50.)

Terms: Pays on acceptance for first North American serial rights.

Advice: "Be mindful of the fundamentals of story telling. Otherwise, no strict requirements here; good work is to be found in all types of imaginative fiction."

THE OAK, (I), 1530 7th St., Rock Island IL 61201. (309)788-3980. Editor: Betty Mowery. 8½×11; 8-14 pages. "Anything of help to writers." Bimonthly. Estab. 1991. Circ. 385.
Needs: Adventure, contemporary, experimental, historical (general), humor/satire, mainstream, mystery/suspense, prose poem, regional, romance (gothic). No erotica. Receives about 12 mss/month. Accepts up to 6 mss/issue. Publishes ms within 3 months of acceptance. Published new writers within the last year. Length: 500 words maximum. Publishes short shorts. Length: 200 words.
How to Contact: Send complete ms. Reports in 1 week. SASE (IRCs). Simultaneous and reprint submissions OK. Sample copy $2. Subscription $10 for 6 issues.
Payment: Pays in contributor's copies.
Terms: Acquires first rights.
Advice: "Just send a manuscript, but first read a copy of our publication to get an idea of what type of material we take. Please send SASE. If not, manuscripts *will not* be returned. Be sure name and address is on the manuscript."

‡OASIS, A Literary Magazine, (I, II), P.O. Box 626, Largo FL 34649-0626. (813)587-9552. Editor: Neal Storrs. Magazine: 70 pages. "Literary magazine first, last and always—looking for styles that please, delight and amaze, that are polished and poised. Next to that, content considerations relatively unimportant—open to all." Bimonthly. Estab. 1992. Circ. 200.
Needs: Experimental, literary, mainstream/contemporary. Receives 150 unsolicited mss/month. Accepts 5 mss/issue; 30 mss/year. Publishes ms 4 months after acceptance. Recently published work by Vijay Dan Detha, Alberto Fuguet, Gabriel Gersh, Gregory Fitzgerald. Length: 3,000 words preferred; 100 words minimum; 7,000 words maximum. Publishes short shorts. Also publishes literary essays and poetry. Often critiques or comments on rejected mss.
How to Contact: Send complete ms with or without a cover letter. Reports in 1-2 weeks. Send SASE (or IRC) for reply, return of ms or send a disposable copy of ms. Simultaneous and reprint submissions OK. Sample copy for $6.50. Fiction guidelines for #10 SAE.
Payment: Pays $15-50 and 1 contributor's copy.
Terms: Pays on publication for first rights.

‡OBSIDIAN II: BLACK LITERATURE IN REVIEW (II, IV), Dept. of English, North Carolina State University, Raleigh NC 27695-8105. (919)515-4153. Editor: Gerald Barrax. Fiction Editor: Susie R. Powell. Magazine: 6×9; approx. 130 pages. "Creative works in English by Black writers, scholarly critical studies by all writers on Black literature in English." Published 2 times/year (spring/summer, fall/winter). Estab. 1975. Circ. 500.
Needs: Ethnic (pan-African), feminist. No poetry, fiction or drama mss not written by Black writers. Accepts 7-9 mss/year. Published new writers within the last year. Length: 1,500-10,000 words.
How to Contact: Send complete ms in duplicate with SASE (IRCs). Reports in 3 months. Publishes ms an average of 4-6 months after acceptance. Sample copy $5.
Payment: Pays in contributor's copies.
Terms: Acquires one-time rights. Sponsors contests occasionally; guidelines published in magazine.

OFFICE NUMBER ONE, (I, II), 2111 Quarry Rd., Austin TX 28703. (512)320-8243. Editor: Carlos B. Dingus. Magazine: 8½×11; 12 pages; 60 lb. standard paper; b&w illustrations and photos. "I look for short stories or essays (100-800 words) that can put a reader on edge—but *not* because of profanity or obscenity, rather because the story serves to jolt the reader away from a consensus view of the world." Quarterly. Estab. 1989. Circ. 1,000.
Needs: Fictional news articles, experimental, fantasy, horror, humor/satire, literary, psychic/supernatural/occult, also fictional reviews. Upcoming themes: "I have a generic bad news page, and generic good news. Need articles about escaping from somewhere or something, or capturing and defeating through transformation. Limericks about fishing and fish, harvests & dogs." Receives 4 unsolicited mss/month. Buys 1-3 mss/issue; 6 mss/year. Publishes ms 4-6 months after acceptance. Recently published work by Jim Sullivan. Length: 30 word minimum; 800 words maximum. Also publishes literary essays, literary criticism and poetry. Sometimes critiques or comments on rejected mss.
How to Contact: Send complete ms with optional cover letter. Should include estimated word count and summary of article and intent ("How does this reach who?") with submission. Reports in 4-6 weeks on mss. Send SASE (IRC) for reply, return of ms or send disposable copy of ms. Will consider simultaneous submissions, reprints. Sample copy for $2 with SAE and 3 first-class stamps or 3 IRCs. Fiction guidelines for SAE and 1 first-class stamp or 1 IRC.

Payment: Pays 23¢/word and 1 contributor's copy. Additional copies for $1 plus postage.
Terms: Payment on publication. Purchases one-time rights.
Advice: "Clean writing, no unnecessary words, perfect word choice, clear presentation of an idea. Make the piece perfect. Express *one* good idea. Write for an audience that you can identify. Be able to say why you write what you write. I'm planning to publish more *shorter* fiction. I plan to be more up-beat and to focus on a journalistic style—but I will broaden what can be accomplished within this style."

‡OFFWORLD, The All-New Illustrated Magazine of Science Fiction and Fantasy, (II), Graphic Image Press, Inc., P.O. Box 1109, Murray Hill Station, New York NY 10156-0604. Fax: (212)570-2493. Editor: Arnaldo Lopez. Magazine: 6⅝ × 10⅛; 64 pages; quality bond paper; heavy glossy cover; illustrations and few photographs. "We see our magazine as the type of publication that can be enjoyed by readers from 8 to 80 years old. The stories are sophisticated, entertaining—the art is colorful, beautiful, sometimes haunting. The science fiction or fantasy stories we accept must not contain gratuitous profanity, no explicit sex. There are other publications for that." Quarterly. Estab. 1993. Circ. 8,000.
Needs: Fantasy (science fantasy, sword & sorcery), science fiction (hard science, soft/sociological). No horror. Plans special fiction issue or anthology. Receives approximately 120 unsolicited mss/month. Accepts 4-6 mss/issue; 16-24 mss/year. Publishes ms approximately 6 months after acceptance. Recently published work by Nat Gertler, Franklin Delano Carr, Oriana W. Damascus. Length: 3,500 words preferred; 2,000 words minimum; 6,000 words maximum. Publishes short shorts. Length: 1,000-1,500 words. Also publishes poetry. Often critiques rejected mss.
How to Contact: Send complete ms with cover letter. Should include estimated word count, 1 page bio, Social Security number, list of publications. Reports in 4-8 months. Send SASE (IRCs) for reply, return of ms or send disposable copy of ms. Simultaneous and electronic submissions OK. Sample copy for $3.95 with 7 × 11 SAE and 2 first-class stamps. Fiction guidelines for legal-size SAE and 1 first-class stamp.
Payment: Pays $100 minimum; $300 maximum; 3 contributor's copies.
Terms: Pays on acceptance for first rights.
Advice: Looks for "a manuscript that's professionally submitted with a SASE and dark, clean type; a story that is actually science fiction or fantasy, a story that is tightly constructed. Since we use a lot of art, try to make your story as visual as possible. Remember the market, we're science fiction and fantasy. Do not use profanity or vivid descriptions of genitalia as a vehicle for covering up holes in a story. Try to be as professional as possible."

THE OHIO REVIEW, (II), 209C Ellis Hall, Ohio University, Athens OH 45701-2979. (614)593-1900. Editor: Wayne Dodd. Assistant Editor: Robert Kinsley. Magazine: 6 × 9; 144 pages; illustrations on cover. "We attempt to publish the best poetry and fiction written today. For a mainly literary audience." Triannually. Estab. 1971. Circ. 2,000.
Needs: Contemporary, experimental, literary. "We lean toward contemporary on all subjects." Receives 150-200 unsolicited fiction mss/month. Buys 3 mss/issue. Does not read mss June 1-August 31. Publishes ms 6 months after acceptance. Agented fiction: 1%. Also publishes poetry. Sometimes critiques rejected mss and/or recommends other markets.
How to Contact: Query first or send complete ms with cover letter. Reports in 6 weeks. SASE. Sample copy $4.25. Fiction guidelines for #10 SASE (IRCs).
Payment: Pays $5/page, free subscription to magazine, 2 contributor's copies.
Terms: Pays on publication for first North American serial rights. Sends galleys to author.
Advice: "We feel the short story is an important part of the contemporary writing field and value it highly. Read a copy of our publication to see if your fiction is of the same quality. So often people send us work that simply doesn't fit our needs."

OLD HICKORY REVIEW, (II), Jackson Writers Group, Box 1178, Jackson TN 38302. (901)668-3717 or (901)664-5959. President: William Nance, Jr.. Fiction Editors: Dorothy Stanfill and William Nance, Jr. Magazine: 8½ × 11; approx. 90 pages. "Usually 3-4 short stories and 75-80 poems—nothing obscene or in poor taste. For a family audience." Semiannually. Estab. 1969. Circ. 300.
Needs: Contemporary, experimental, fantasy, literary, mainstream. Receives 50 unsolicited fiction mss/month. Acquires 4 mss/issue; 8 mss/year. Publishes within 1 year of acceptance. Length: 2,500-3,000 words. Publishes short shorts. Also publishes poetry. Sometimes critiques rejected mss and recommends other markets.

How to Contact: Send complete ms with cover letter, which should include "credits." Reports on queries in 2-3 weeks; on mss in 1-2 months. SASE (IRCs). Sample copy available. Fiction guidelines for SAE.
Payment: Pays 2 contributor's copies; charge for extras. Sponsors contests for fiction writers, "advertised in literary magazine and with fliers."
Advice: "We are tired of war, nursing homes, abused children, etc. We are looking for original thought. No pornographic fiction. Our publication goes into schools, libraries, etc."

THE OLD RED KIMONO, (II), Box 1864, Rome GA 30162. (706)295-6312. Editors: Ken Anderson and Jonathan Hershey. Magazine: 8 × 11; 65-70 pages; white offset paper; 10 pt. board cover stock. Annual. Estab. 1972. Circ. 1,200.
Needs: Literary. "We will consider good fiction regardless of category." Receives 20-30 mss/month. Accepts 6-8 mss/issue. Does not read mss March 15-September 1. "Issue out in May every year." Published work by Thomas Feeny, David Huddle, Peter Huggins. Length: 2,000-3,000 words preferred; 5,000 words maximum. Publishes short shorts. "We prefer short fiction." Also publishes poetry.
How to Contact: Send complete ms with cover letter. Reports in 2 weeks on queries; 2-3 months on mss. SASE (IRCs). Simultaneous submissions OK, but "we would like to be told." Fiction guidelines for #10 SAE and 1 first-class stamp.
Payment: Pays in contributor's copies.
Terms: Acquires first rights.

‡THE OLYMPIA REVIEW, (II), 1404 E. 7th Ave., Olympia WA 98501. Editor: Michael McNeilley. Fiction Editor: Frank Till. Magazine: 5½ × 8½; 50 pages; 60 lb. text paper; 65 lb. vellum cover; illustrations and photos. "Our motto 'Barrier-free writing for the 90s.' Educated, intelligent audience, in our community and nationwide. Bartenders, attorneys, teachers, librarians, gillnetters, hard rock miners, artists, city council members, cashiers, computer operators and member of congress." Semiannually. Estab. 1993. Circ. 500.
Needs: Adventure, erotica, ethnic/multicultural, experimental, feminist, historical (general), humor/satire, literary, mainstream/contemporary, regional, science fiction (speculative fiction), translations. "No religious, genre, formula fiction, MFA minimalist auto journalism, first drafts." Publishes anthology. Accepts 1-2 mss/issue; 2-4 mss/year. Publishes ms up to 6 months after acceptance. Length: 3,500 words maximum. Publishes short shorts. Also publishes literary essays, literary criticism, poetry.
How to Contact: Send complete ms with a cover letter. Should include estimated word count, bio (25-50 words), Social Security number, list of publications with submission. Reports in 2 months on mss. Send SASE (or IRC) for reply, return of ms. Simultaneous, reprint (say where, when) and electronic submissions (MS-Word for MS-DOS) OK. Sample copy for $4.25. Fiction guidelines for #10 SAE and 1 first-class stamp. Reviews novels and short story collections.
Payment: Pays 1 contributor's copy; additional copies for $2.50.
Terms: Acquires one-time rights. Sends galleys to author.
Advice: "I look for fiction that draws me in. An authentic voice. An interesting character, setting, situation. A story I want to read over again. There are no set criteria. Make your own critera . . . let the excellence of your writing speak for itself. *Or* promise to listen. We recommend patience. Giving everything a thorough reading takes time. Take time yourself—in manuscript preparation, in editing and proofreading, to make sure your story says exactly what you mean it to say. Wait a bit after completing it before sending it out—sometimes new meanings appear in time that ask for further development. Patience."

ONCE UPON A WORLD, (IV), Route 1, Box 110A, Nineveh IN 46164. Editor: Emily Alward. Magazine: 8½ × 11; 80-100 pages; standard white paper; colored card stock cover; pen & ink illustrations. "A science fiction and fantasy magazine with emphasis on alternate-world cultures and stories of idea, character and interaction. Also publishes book reviews and a few poems for an adult audience, primarily readers of science fiction and fantasy. We are known for science fiction and fantasy stories with excellent worldbuilding and a humanistic emphasis." Annually. Estab. 1988. Circ. 100.
- This magazine is now also accepting essays on the work of specific science fiction and fantasy authors.
Needs: Fantasy, science fiction. No realistic "stories in contemporary settings"; horror; stories using Star Trek or other media characters; stories with completely negative endings." Receives 20 unsolicited mss/month. Accepts 8-12 mss/issue; per year "varies, depending on backlog." Publishes ms from 2 months to 1½ years after acceptance. Published work by Janet Reedman and Mark Andrew Garland. Length: 3,000 words average; 400 words minimum; 10,000 words maximum. Publishes short shorts.

Also publishes poetry. Sometimes critiques rejected mss and recommends other markets.
How to Contact: Send complete manuscript. Reports in 2-4 weeks on queries; 2-16 weeks on mss. SASE (IRCs). "Reluctantly" accepts simultaneous submissions, if noted. Sample copy $8.50; checks to Emily Alward. Fiction guidelines for #10 SAE and 1 first-class stamp. Reviews novels and short story collections.
Payment: Pays contributor's copies.
Terms: Acquires first rights. "Stories copyrighted in author's name; copyrights not registered."
Advice: "Besides a grasp of basic fiction technique, you'll need some familiarity with the science fiction and fantasy genres. We suggest reading some of the following authors whose work is similar to what we're looking for: Isaac Asimov, Poul Anderson, Norman Spinrad, David Brin, Anne McCaffrey, Marion Zimmer Bradley, Mercedes Lackey, Katharine Kimbriel."

ONIONHEAD, (II), Literary Quarterly, Arts on the Park, Inc., 115 N. Kentucky Ave., Lakeland FL 33801. (813)680-2787. Editors: Charles Kersey, Dennis Nesheim, Dudley Uphoff. Editorial Assistant: Anna Wiseman. Magazine: Digest-sized; 40 pages; 20 lb. bond; glossy card cover. "Provocative political, social and cultural observations and hypotheses for a literary audience—an open-minded audience." Estab. 1989. Circ. 250.
Needs: Contemporary, ethnic, experimental, feminist, gay, humor/satire, lesbian, literary, prose poem, regional. "Must have a universal point (International)." Publishes short fiction in each issue. Receives 100-150 unsolicited titles/month. Acquires approximately 28 mss/issue; 100 titles (these numbers include: poetry, short prose and essays)/year. Publishes ms within 18 months of acceptance. Published work by Lyn Lifshin, A.D. Winans, Jessica Freeman, Laurel Speer. Length: 3,000 words average; 4,000 words maximum. Publishes short shorts. Also publishes poetry.
How to Contact: Send complete manuscript with cover letter that includes brief bio and SASE (IRCs). Reports in 2 weeks on queries; 2 months on mss. No simultaneous submissions. Sample copy $3 postpaid. Fiction guidelines for #10 SAE and 1 first-class stamp.
Payment: Pays in contributor's copy. Charge for extras.
Terms: Acquires first North American serial rights.
Advice: "Review a sample copy of *Onionhead* and remember *literary quality* is the prime criterion. Avoid heavy-handed approaches to social commentary—be subtle, not didactic."

‡ORANGE COAST REVIEW, (II), Dept. of English, 2701 Fairview Rd., Orange Coast College, Costa Mesa CA 92628-5005. (714)432-5043. Editor: Greg Hammond. Fiction Editor: Angela Powell. Editors change every 6 months. Magazine: 5½ × 8½; 70 pages; 60 lb. paper; medium/heavy cover; illustrations and photos. "We look for quality, of course. The genre, style, and format take second place to intelligence and depth. Our largest audience consists of students and writers." Annual. Estab. 1990. Circ. 750.
Needs: Condensed novel, ethnic/multicultural, experimental, feminist, gay, humor/satire, lesbian, literary, mainstream/contemporary, serialized novel, translations. No mainstream short fiction and poetry. Receives 100 unsolicited mss/month. Accepts 5-10 mss/issue. Does not read mss May-September inclusive. Publishes ms 6 months after acceptance. Recently published work by Jo-Ann Mapson, Meredith Moore, Mark Seyi. Length: Open. Publishes short shorts. Also publishes literary essays, poetry. Sometimes critiques or comments on rejected mss.
How to Contact: Send complete ms with a cover letter. Should include estimated word count, short paragraph bio, list of publications with submission. Reports in 2-3 weeks on queries; 2-3 months on mss. SASE (or IRC) for return ms. Simultaneous submissions OK. Sample copy for $4. Fiction guidelines for #10 SAE and 1 first-class stamp.
Payment: Pays $1/published page fiction, 2 contributor's copies.
Terms: Pays on publication for one-time rights.
Advice: "A manuscript stands out when it actually has a beginning, middle and end; a coherent theme that isn't vague or preachy; and characters that come to life. Check your grammar, punctuation, and spelling—three times. If you don't care about the easy stuff, why should we expect you to have cared about the story or poem. Never single space." Looks for "writing that involves their own voice or style, not Raymond Carver's or whoever else impresses them."

OTHER VOICES, (II), The University of Illinois at Chicago, Dept of English (M/C 162), Box 4348, Chicago IL 60680. (312)413-2209. Editors: Sharon Fiffer and Lois Hauselman. Magazine: 5⅞ × 9; 168-205 pages; 60 lb. paper; coated cover stock; occasional photos. "Original, fresh, diverse stories and novel excerpts" for literate adults. Semiannually. Estab. 1985. Circ. 1,500.

Needs: Contemporary, experimental, humor/satire, literary, excerpted novel. No taboos, except ineptitude and murkiness. No fantasy, horror, juvenile, psychic/occult. Receives 300 unsolicited fiction mss/month. Accepts 20-23 mss/issue. Recently published work by Lynne Sharon Schwartz, Karen Karbo, James McManus, Terry McMillan; published new writers within the last year. Length: 4,000 words average; 5,000 words maximum.

How to Contact: Send mss with SASE (IRCs) or submit through agent October 1 to April 1, only. Mss received during non-reading period are returned unread. Cover letters "should be brief and list previous publications. Also, list title of submission. Most beginners' letters try to 'explain' the story—a big mistake." Simultaneous submissions OK. Reports in 10-12 weeks on mss. Sample copy $7 (includes postage). Fiction guidelines for #10 SAE and 1 first-class stamp.

Payment: Pays in contributor's copies and modest cash gratuity (when possible).

Terms: Acquires one-time rights.

Advice: "There are so *few* markets for *quality* fiction! We—by publishing 40-45 stories a year—provide new and established writers a forum for their work. Send us your best voice, your best work, your best best."

OTHER WORLDS, The Paperback Magazine of Science Fiction-Science Fantasy, (II), Gryphon Publications, Box 209, Brooklyn NY 11228. Editor: Gary Lovisi. Magazine: 5×8; 100+ pages; offset paper; card cover; perfect-bound; illustrations and photographs. "Adventure—or action-oriented science fiction—stories that are fun to read." Annually. Estab. 1988. Circ. 300.

Needs: Science fiction (hard science, sociological) "with impact." No fantasy, sword and sorcery. Receives 24 unsolicited mss/month. Accepts 4-6 mss/issue. Publishes ms 1-2 years (usually) after acceptance. Length: 3,000 words maximum. Publishes short shorts. Length: 500 words. Sometimes critiques rejected mss and recommends other markets.

How to Contact: Send complete ms with cover letter. Simultaneous submissions OK. Reports in 2 weeks on queries; 1 month on mss. SASE (IRCs). Sample copy $9.95 (100 pages perfect bound).

Payment: Pays 2 contributor's copies.

Terms: Acquires first North American serial rights. Copyright reverts to author.

Advice: Looks for "harder sf stories, with *impact*!"

OTTERWISE, For Kids into Saving Animals and the Environment, (II, IV), P.O. Box 1374, Portland ME 04104. Editor: Cheryl Miller. Fiction Editor: Marianne Matte. Newsletter: 8½×11; 16 pages; recycled paper; illustrations; photographs. "For kids 8-13, short stories about animal welfare and saving the environment." Quarterly. Estab. 1988. Circ. 3,000.

Needs: Children's/Juvenile (8-13 years): animal welfare, environmental. "Vegetarianism, endangered animals;" spay/neuter issues (pet overpopulation); "natural gardening." Receives 10 unsolicited mss/month. Acquires 1 ms/issue; 4 mss/year. Publishes ms up to 3 months after acceptance. Length: 500 words preferred; 100 words minimum; 800 words maximum. Publishes short shorts.

How to Contact: Send complete ms with cover letter. Reports in 1 month. Send SASE (IRCs) for reply, return of ms or send disposable copy of the ms. Simultaneous, reprint and electronic submissions OK. Sample copy for $2. Fiction guidelines free.

Payment: No payment.

Terms: Acquires one-time rights.

Advice: Looks for "stories written from animal's point of view that show action on part of kids—well written. Don't write 'down' to kids. Don't be too obvious and corny."

OUTERBRIDGE, (II), English A-323, The College of Staten Island (CUNY), 715 Ocean Terr., Staten Island NY 10301. (718)390-7779. Editor: Charlotte Alexander. Magazine: 5½×8½; approx. 110 pages; 60 lb. white offset paper; 65 lb. cover stock. "We are a national literary magazine publishing mostly fiction and poetry. To date, we have had several special focus issues (the 'urban' and the 'rural' experience, 'Southern,' 'childhood,' 'nature and the environment,' 'animals'). For anyone with enough interest in literature to look for writing of quality and writers on the contemporary scene who deserve attention. There probably is a growing circuit of writers, some academics, reading us by recommendations." Annually. Estab. 1975. Circ. 500-700.

Needs: Literary. "No *Reader's Digest* style; that is, very popularly oriented. We like to do interdisciplinary features, e.g., literature and music, literature and science and literature and the natural world." Upcoming themes: "Animal World;" "Farms and Farming;" "Send-ups of PC," (politically correct language). Accepts 8-10 mss/year. Does not read in July or August. Published work by William Davey, Ron Berube, Patricia Ver Ellen; published new writers within the last year. Length: 10-25 pages. Also publishes poetry. Sometimes recommends other markets.

How to Contact: Query. Send complete ms with cover letter. "Don't talk too much, 'explain' the work, or act apologetic or arrogant. If published, tell where, with a brief bio." SASE (IRCs). Reports in 8-10 weeks on queries and mss. Sample copy $5 for annual issue.

Payment: Pays 2 contributor's copies. Charges ½ price of current issue for extras to its authors.

Terms: Acquires one-time rights. Requests credits for further publication of material used by *OB*.

Advice: "Read our publication first. Don't send out blindly; get some idea of what the magazine might want. A *short* personal note with biography is appreciated. Competition is keen. Read an eclectic mix of classic and contemporary. Beware of untransformed autobiography, but *everything* in one's experience contributes."

‡OVER MY DEAD BODY!, The Mystery Magazine, (I, II), P.O. Box 1778, Auburn WA 98071-1778. (206)473-4650. Editor: Cherie Jung. Magazine: 8½ × 11; 48-60 pages; glossy cover stock; b&w illustrations and photographs. "We publish a broad range of mystery, detective and crime fiction from traditional cozy to hardboiled and everything in between." Quarterly. Estab. 1993. Circ. 1,000.

Needs: Mystery/suspense. If mystery-related: adventure, feminist, gay, horror, lesbian, psychic/supernatural/occult; if related to mystery/crime we also publish cross-over (sci-fi, westerns, etc.). Upcoming themes available for SASE. Publishes special fiction issue or anthology. Receives 400 unsolicited mss/month. Accepts 10-15 mss/issue; 150 mss/year. Publishes ms within 1 year after acceptance. Recently published work by J.J. Lamb, Mary Bowen Hall. Length: 2,000 words preferred; 500 words minimum; 4,000 words maximum. Publishes short shorts. Length: 250-500 words. Often critiques or comments on rejected mss.

How to Contact: Send complete ms with a cover letter. Should include estimated word count, bio (50 words or less), list of publications. Reports in 6 weeks on queries; 3 months on mss. Send SASE (or IRC) for reply, return of ms or send a disposable copy of ms. Simultaneous and electronic submissions OK. Sample copy for $5 (include postage). Fiction guidelines for #10 SAE and 1 first-class stamp. Reviews novels and short story collections.

Payment: Pays 1¢/word; 2 contributor's copies; additional copies for $2.

Terms: Buys first North American serial rights. Sends galleys to author.

Advice: "We're willing to work with writers on stories that have potential. Some of the stories we've purchased have been rewritten 3 or 4 times before acceptance. However, sloppy presentation (typos, missing pages, copy that is difficult to read) doesn't stand a chance."

OWEN WISTER REVIEW, (II), ASUW Student Publications Board, P.O. Box 4238, University of Wyoming, Laramie WY 82071. (307)766-3819. Fax: (307)766-4027. Editor: Georgette Hartley. Fiction Editors: "Fiction Selection Committee." Editors change each year. After 1993, contact selection committee. Magazine: 6 × 9; 92 pages; 60 lb. matte paper; 80 lb. glossy cover; illustrations; photographs. "Though we are a university publication, our audience is wider than just an academic community." Semiannually. Estab. 1978. Circ. 500.

● *Owen Wister Review* has won numerous awards and honors far surpassing many student-run publications. Nine poems from *OWR* were nominated for inclusion in the *Pushcart Prize* anthology (1992-1993). The magazine received Best of Show award from the Associated Collegiate Press/College Media Advisors and six individual Gold Circle Awards from the Columbia Scholastic Press Association.

Needs: Ethnic/multicultural, experimental, humor/satire, literary, translations. No science fiction or fantasy. Plans special fiction issue or anthology.

Receives 12-15 unsolicited mss. Acquires 3 mss/issue; 6-8 mss/year. "Summer months are generally down time for *OWR*." Publishes ms 2-3 months after acceptance. Published work by Mark Jenkins, John Bennet, the Kunstwaffen art collaborative, Sue Thornton. Length: 1,300 words average; 3,500 words maximum. Publishes short shorts. Also publishes literary essays, literary criticism and poetry.

How to Contact: Send complete ms with cover letter. Should include estimated word count, bio, list of publications. Reports in 2-3 weeks on queries; 2-3 months on mss. Send SASE (IRCs) for reply, return of ms or send disposable copy of the ms. Simultaneous submissions OK. Sample copy for $5. Free fiction guidelines.

Payment: Pays 1 contributor's copy. 10% off additional copies.

Terms: Acquires one-time rights.

Advice: "In the last few issues we have geared the material toward what we think of as 'underpublished' groups—minorities, veterans, the gay community—survivor groups. This has broadened our audience to include just about anyone who wishes to be challenged by their reading material. Our committee likes to hear a fresh voice. Experimental fiction is encouraged. Consistency is very important. We look for and encourage young writers but insist on quality. Metafiction and short humor

This cover illustration by Dave Swartout was selected by the editors of Oxalis to "represent spring. We usually have a poetry contest and publish the winners in the spring issue," says Fiction Editor Mildred Barker. Swartout was a winner of a 1992 art contest held by Oxalis, and his work has appeared in other issues of the publication. On the subject of fiction, Barker says, "We have used about 12 stories each year. We like to see good stories on social issues, as well as humorous work, though we will publish whatever we like."

stand out among the longer works. We want to be hooked and not let go; regardless of subject matter, the approach should be compelling and relentless."

OXALIS, A Literary Magazine, (II), Stone Ridge Poetry Society, P.O. Box 3993, Kingston NY 12401. (914)687-7942. Editor: Shirley Powell. Fiction Editor: Mildred Barker. Magazine: 8½×11; 48-60 pages; 60 lb. recycled paper; 65 lb. recycled cover. "A selection of the best in poetry and fiction presented in an attractive package. For people interested in good writing." Annual. Estab. 1988. Circ. 350.
Needs: Adventure, contemporary, erotica, ethnic, experimental, fantasy, feminist, gay, historical, horror, humor/satire, lesbian, literary, mainstream, mystery/suspense, prose poem, regional, romance (contemporary, historical), science fiction, senior citizen/retirement, sports, western (frontier stories), contemporary issues: environment, human rights. "Nothing sentimental or preachy." No children's literature. Receives 10 unsolicited mss/month. (Magazine is about half poetry, half fiction.) Publishes ms 6-15 months after acceptance. Recently published work by Mitch Grabois, Iqbal Pittalwala, Don Stockard, Lucy Honig. Length: 4,000 words maximum. Publishes short shorts. Also publishes poetry.
How to Contact: "*Oxalis* will go dormant during the 1994 winter. Staff will emerge in spring eager to select poems, stories and art from May 1 to August 30." Include "2 or 3 sentence bio suitable for Contributors' Page." Reports in up to 3 months. SASE (IRCs). May accept simultaneous submissions, but "prefer not to." Sample copy for $5. Fiction guidelines for #10 SAE and 1 first-class stamp.
Payment: Pays 2 contributor's copies.
Terms: Acquires first rights or one-time rights.
Advice: Looks for "something different from anything I've read before. Something that changes my mind or shakes me up. Fiction I can't forget. Read *Oxalis* and acquaint yourself with contemporary writing. Then write something better."

OXFORD MAGAZINE, (II), Bachelor Hall, Miami University, Oxford OH 45056. (513)529-5256. Fiction Editor: Keith Banner. Editors change every year. Send future submissions to "Fiction Editor." Magazine: 6×9; 85-100 pages; illustrations. Biannually. Estab. 1985. Circ. 500-1,000.
● This college literary has published work selected for the *Pushcart Prize* anthology in 1991.
Needs: Ethnic, experimental, feminist, gay, humor/satire, lesbian, literary, translations. Receives 50-60 unsolicited mss/month. Does not read mss May through August. Published new writers within the last year. Length: 2,000-3,000 words average; 4,000 words maximum. Publishes short shorts. Also publishes literary essays, literary criticism, poetry.
How to Contact: Send complete ms with cover letter, which should include a short bio or interesting information. No simultaneous submissions. Reports in 3-4 months on mss. SASE. Sample copy for $5, 10×12 SAE and 4 first-class stamps (IRCs).

Payment: Pays in contributor's copies.
Terms: Acquires one-time rights.
Advice: "We look for writing that makes sense: fiction that makes you put down your spoon and reread the page until your soup goes cold. *Oxford Magazine* is looking for fiction that moves the mind. Unfortunately, this is a quality which eludes definition. We are interested in fresh voices, not educated imitations of other authors. Call us optimistic, but we believe that literature has a place in modern (post-modern?) culture, and we like our magazine to reflect that. That doesn't mean stories which end happily; it means stories which are significant. We are interested in providing a forum for voices which don't normally receive one, and in subject matters which reflect the potential of those voices."

‡**OXYGEN, A Literary Quarterly, (II),** #1010, 535 Geary St., San Francisco CA 94102. (415)776-9681. Editor: Richard Hack. Magazine: 8½×11; 32-38 pages; bond paper; 67 lb. color cover. "We are an eclectic, very diverse quarterly looking for vivid, meaningful writing. We welcome fiction and poetry in modes realistic, surreal, expressionistic, beat, devotional, erotic, satiric, and invective. We stand for inclusive, democratic values and social equality." Quarterly. Estab. 1991. Circ. 150-200.
Needs: Erotica, ethnic/multicultural, experimental, feminist, literary, mainstream/contemporary, religious/inspirational, translations (especially from Spanish; bilingual contributions preferred). "Nothing overly commercial, insincere, or mocking, though we enjoy satire and 'black humor'." Receives 8 unsolicited mss/month. Accepts 3-4 mss/issue; 12-16 mss/year. Publishes ms up to 3 or 4 months after acceptance. Recently published work by Richard Hack, Eugene Wildman, David Fisher, Jamie Sanbonmatsu. Length: 500-7,500 words. Publishes short shorts. Also publishes literary essays, literary criticism and poetry.
How to Contact: Send complete ms with a cover letter. Should include bio (1-2 paragraphs), list of publications (not necessary). Reports in 2-8 weeks. Send SASE (or IRC) for reply or return of ms. Simultaneous, reprint and electronic submissions OK. Sample copy for $3 (make check out to Richard Hack, not to *Oxygen*). Fiction guidelines for #10 SAE and 1 first-class stamp.
Payment: Pays 2 contributor's copies.
Terms: All rights revert to contributors.
Advice: "We want vivid, efficient, honest fiction. It can be a short story, tale, fragment, experimental piece, or an excerpt from a novel. We like meaningful writing with inclusive values, hopefully rich and suggestive writing, or a style with a nice feel to it. Does it believe in something, does it love life? Does it satirize injustice and abuse? We are more interested in low life than in upper-class life. What kind of personal quality does it demonstrate?"

PABLO LENNIS, The Magazine of Science Fiction, Fantasy and Fact, (I, IV), Deneb Press, Fandom House, 30 North 19th St., Lafayette IN 47904. Editor: John Thiel. Magazine: 8½×11; 22 pages; standard stock; illustrations and "occasional" photos. "Science fiction, fantasy, science, research and mystic for scientists and science fiction and fantasy appreciators." Monthly.
Needs: Fantasy, science fiction. Receives 25 unsolicited mss/year. Accepts 3 mss/issue; 35 mss/year. Publishes ms 6 months after acceptance. Published work by P.M. Fergusson, Michael Kube-McDowell, Darrin Kidd; published new writers within the last year. Length: 1,500 words average; 3,000 words maximum. Also publishes literary criticism, poetry. Occasionally critiques rejected mss and recommends other markets.
How to Contact: "Method of submission is author's choice but he might prefer to query. No self-statement is necessary." No simultaneous submissions. Reports in 2 weeks. Does not accept computer printouts.
Payment: Pays 1 contributor's copy.
Terms: Publication not copyrighted.
Advice: "I have taboos against unpleasant and offensive language and want material which is morally or otherwise elevating to the reader. I prefer an optimistic approach, and favor fine writing. With a good structure dealt with intelligently underlying this, you have the kind of story I like. I prefer stories that have something to say to those which have something to report."

‡**PACIFIC COAST JOURNAL, (I, II),** French Bread Publications, P.O. Box 355, Campbell CA 95009-0355. Editor: John S. French. Fiction Editor: Stephanie Kylkis. Magazine: 5½×8⅛; 56 pages; 20 lb. paper; 67 lb. cover; illustrations. "We just want quality material. Slight focus towards western US/ Pacific Rim." Quarterly (or "whenever we have enough money"). Estab. 1992. Circ. 200.
Needs: Ethnic/multicultural, experimental, feminist, historical (general), humor/satire, literary, science fiction (soft/sociological, magical realism). Upcoming themes: "Visual/Conceptual" (August '94). Receives 20-30 unsolicited mss/month. Accepts 3-4 mss/issue; 10-12 mss/year. Publishes ms 6-18

months after acceptance. Length: 2,500 words preferred; 5,000 words maximum. Publishes short shorts. Also publishes literary essays and poetry. Sometimes critiques or comments on rejected mss.
How to Contact: Send complete ms with a cover letter. Should include bio (less than 50 words) and list of publications. Reports in 4 months. Send SASE (or IRC) for reply, return of ms or send a disposable copy of ms. Simultaneous, reprint and electronic submissions OK. Sample copy for $2.50, 6×9 SAE and 1 first-class stamp. Reviews novels and short story collections.
Payment: Pays 1 contributor's copy.
Terms: Acquires one-time rights.
Advice: "Plot is not important. Characterization is the main thing that will make a story demand to be read."

PACIFIC REVIEW (II), Dept. of English and Comparative Lit., San Diego State University, San Diego CA 92182-0295. (619)594-5443. Contact: Editor. Magazine: 6×9; 100-150 pages; book stock paper; paper back, extra heavy cover stock; illustrations, photos. "There is no designated theme. We publish high-quality fiction, poetry, and familiar essays: academic work meant for, but not restricted to, an academic audience." Biannual. Estab. 1973. Circ. 1,000.
Needs: "We do not restrict or limit our fiction in any way other than quality. We are interested in all fiction, from the very traditional to the highly experimental. Acceptance is determined by the quality of submissions." Does not read June-August. Published new writers within the last year. Publishes short shorts. Length: 4,000 words max.
How to Contact: Send original ms with SASE (IRCs). No unsolicited submissions. Reports in 3-5 months on mss. Sample copy $6.
Payment: 1 contributor's copy.
Terms: "First serial rights are *Pacific Review*'s. All other rights revert to author."

PAINTED BRIDE QUARTERLY, (II), Painted Bride Art Center, 230 Vine St., Philadelphia PA 19106. (215)925-9914. Editor: Kathy Volk-Miller. Literary magazine: 6×9; 96-100 pages; illustrations; photos. Quarterly. Estab. 1975. Circ. 1,000.
Needs: Contemporary, ethnic, experimental, feminist, gay, lesbian, literary, prose poem and translations. Published new writers within the last year. Length: 3,000 words average; 5,000 words maximum. Publishes short shorts. Also publishes literary essays, literary criticism, poetry. Occasionally critiques rejected mss.
How to Contact: Send complete ms. Reports in 3 weeks-3 months. SASE (IRCs). Sample copy $5. Reviews novels and short story collections. Send books to editor.
Payment: Pays 1 contributor's copy, 1 year free subscription, 50% off additional copies.
Terms: Acquires first North American serial rights.
Advice: "We want quality in whatever—we hold experimental work to as strict standards as anything else. Many of our readers write fiction; most of them enjoy a good reading. We hope to be an outlet for quality. A good story gives, first, enjoyment to the reader. We've seen a good many of them lately, and we've published the best of them."

‡PALO ALTO REVIEW, A Journal of Ideas, (I, II), Palo Alto College, 1400 West Villaret, San Antonio TX 78224. (210)921-5255 (or 921-5017). Fax: (210)921-5277. Editor: Bob Richmond and Ellen Shull. Magazine: 8½×11; 60 pages; 60 lb. natural white paper (50% recycled); illustrations and photographs. "Not too experimental nor excessively avant-garde, just good stories (for fiction). Ideas are what we are after. We are interested in connecting the college and the community. We would hope that those who attempt these connections will choose startling topics and interesting angles with which to investigate the length and breadth of the teaching/learning spectrum." Semiannually (spring and fall). Estab. 1992. Circ. 500-600.
Needs: Adventure, ethnic/multicultural, experimental, fantasy, feminist, historical (general), humor/satire, literary, mainstream/contemporary, mystery/suspense, regional, romance, science fiction, translations, westerns. Also "education—in its broadest sense." Upcoming themes: "Parents (& Children)" (spring 1994); "Books" (fall 1994). Upcoming themes available for SASE. Receives 100 unsolicited mss/month. Accepts 2-4 mss/issue; 4-8 mss/year. Does not read mss March-April and October-November when putting out each issue. Publishes ms 2-15 months after acceptance. Recently published work by Sonia Gernes, Jo LeCoeur, Craig Loomis. Length: 3,500 words preferred; 4,500 words maximum. Publishes short shorts. Also publishes literary essays, literary criticism and poetry. Always critiques or comments on rejected mss.

How to Contact: Send complete ms with a cover letter. "Request sample copy and guidelines." Should include brief bio and brief list of publications. Reports in 3-4 months. Send SASE (or IRC) for reply, return of ms or send a disposable copy of ms. Simultaneous and electronic (Macintosh disk) submissions OK. Sample copy for $5. Fiction guidelines for #10 SAE and 1 first-class stamp.
Payment: Pays 2 contributor's copies; additional copies for $5.
Terms: Acquires first North American serial rights.
Advice: "Good short stories have interesting characters confronted by a dilemma working toward a solution. Generally, the characters are interesting because the readers can identify with them and know much about them. Edit judiciously. Cut out extraneous verbage. Set up a choice that has to be made. Then create tension—who wants what and why they can't have it."

THE PAPER BAG, (I, II), Box 268805, Chicago IL 60626-8805. (312)285-7972. Editor: Michael H. Brownstein. Magazine: 5½×8½; 25-40 pages; cardboard cover stock; illustrations. Quarterly. Estab. 1988. Circ. 300.
Needs: Adventure, contemporary, erotica, ethnic, experimental, fantasy, feminist, horror, literary, mainstream, mystery/suspense, prose poem and western. Plans to publish special fiction or anthology issue in the future. Receives 10 unsolicited mss/month. Accepts 2-4 mss/issue; 36-60 mss/year. Publishes mss 3 months to 1 year after acceptance. Under 500 words preferred; 500 words maximum. "Has to be under 500 words." Sometimes critiques rejected mss and recommends other markets.
How to Contact: Send complete ms with cover letter. "Include brief bio for our contributor's page." Reports in 1 week on queries; 1 week to 3 months on mss. SASE. Sample copy $3. Fiction guidelines for SAE and 1 first-class stamp (IRCs).
Payment: Pays in contributor's copies.
Terms: Acquires first rights. Sometimes sends pre-publication galleys to the author.

PAPER RADIO, (I,II), P.O. Box 4646, Seattle WA 98104-0646. Editor: N.S. Kvern. Magazine: 48-64 pages; photocopied and/or offset paper and cover; illustrations; b&w photographs. "We're open to anything, but it has to be short—usually less than 2,500 words." Readers are "mostly people who are interested in avant garde, political, bizarre, surrealism, cyberpunk, literary/experimental writing and computers." Published 2-3 times/year. Estab. 1986. Circ. 2,000.
Needs: Erotica, experimental, fantasy, literary, prose poem, science fiction. Receives 50 unsolicited fiction mss/month. Accepts 4-5 mss/issue; 12-15 mss/year. Publishes ms an average of 2-3 months after acceptance. Length: 2,000 words average; 3,500 words maximum. Publishes short shorts. Sometimes critiques rejected mss.
How to Contact: Send complete ms with cover letter. "Some autobiographical information is helpful—one or two paragraphs—and I like to know where they heard about our magazine." Reports in 2 months. SASE (IRCs). Simultaneous submissions OK. Sample copy $4.
Payment: Pays contributor's copies.
Terms: Acquires first rights, "artist can publish material elsewhere simultaneously."
Advice: "We are devoted to the cause of experimentation and literature and we like a wide variety of fiction. Best to see a sample copy. Our publication is orderly in its chaos, wild and untameable in its order."

PARAGRAPH, A Magazine of Paragraphs, (II), 18 Beach Point Dr., East Providence RI 02906. (401)437-9573. Co-Editors: Walker Rumble and Karen Donovan. Magazine: 4¼×5½; 38 pages. "No particular theme—we publish collections of paragraphs for a general audience." Published 3 times/year. Estab. 1985. Circ. 700.
Needs: "Any topic is welcome, including experimental writing. Our only requirement is that paragraphs must be 200 words or less." Receives 30-40 unsolicited mss/month. Accepts 30-33 mss/issue; 90 mss/year. Publishes mss 2-3 months after acceptance. Recently published work by Lisa Shea, Laurel Speer, Conger Beasley Jr., Deborah Bayer, Gary Fincke. Length: 200 words. Also publishes literary essays, but 200 words maximum, of course. Sometimes critiques rejected mss.
How to Contact: Send complete ms with cover letter. Reports in 1 week on queries; 2 months on mss. SASE. Simultaneous submissions OK. Sample copy $3. Fiction guidelines for SAE and 1 first-class stamp (IRCs).
Payment: Pays contributor's copies and charges for extras.
Terms: Acquires first rights. Sends galleys to author.

THE PARIS REVIEW (II), 45-39 171 St. Pl., Flushing NY 11358 (*business office only, send mss to address below*). Editor: George A. Plimpton. Managing Editor: James Linville. Magazine: 5¼×8½; about 240 pages; illustrations and photographs (unsolicited artwork not accepted). "Fiction and poetry of superlative quality, whatever the genre, style or mode. Our contributors include prominent, as well as less well-known and previously unpublished writers. 'The Art of Fiction' interview series includes important contemporary writers discussing their own work and the craft of writing." Quarterly.
- George Plimpton, editor of the well-respected *Paris Review*, also edits a popular series of interviews with well-known writers whose work has appeared in the magazine.
Needs: Literary. Receives about 1,000 unsolicited fiction mss each month. Published work by Raymond Carver, Elizabeth Tallent, Rick Bass, John Koethe, Sharon Olds, Derek Walcott, Carolyn Kizer, Tess Gallagher, Peter Handke, Denis Johnson, Bobbie Ann Mason, Harold Brodkey, Joseph Brodsky, John Updike, Andre Dubus, Galway Kinnell, E.L. Doctorow and Philip Levine. Published new writers within the last year. No preferred length. Also publishes literary essays, poetry.
How to Contact: *Send complete ms with SASE (IRCs) to Fiction Editor, 541 E. 72nd St., New York NY 10021.* Simultaneous submissions OK. Sample copy $8.
Payment: Pays for material.
Terms: Pays on publication for first North American serial rights. Sends galleys to author.

PARTING GIFTS, (II), 3413 Wilshire, Greensboro NC 27408. Editor: Robert Bixby. Magazine: 5×8; 40 pages. "High quality insightful fiction, very brief and on any theme." Semiannually. Estab. 1988.
Needs: "Brevity is the second most important criterion behind literary quality." Summer fiction issue planned. Publishes ms within one year of acceptance. Length: 250 words minimum; 1,000 words maximum. Also publishes poetry. Sometimes critiques rejected mss.
How to Contact: Send complete ms with cover letter. Simultaneous submissions OK. Reports in 1 day on queries; 1-7 days on mss. SASE (IRCs).
Payment: Pays in contributor's copies.
Terms: Acquires one-time rights.
Advice: "Read the works of Amy Hempel, Jim Harrison, Kelly Cherry, C.K. Williams and Janet Kauffman, all excellent writers who epitomize the writing *Parting Gifts* strives to promote. I need more than ever for my authors to be better read. I sense that many unaccepted writers have not put in the hours reading."

PARTISAN REVIEW, (II), 236 Bay State Rd., Boston MA 02215. (617)353-4260. Editor: William Phillips. Executive Editor: Edith Kurzweil. Magazine: 6×9; 160 pages; 40 lb. paper; 60 lb. cover stock. "Theme is of world literature and contemporary culture: fiction, essays and poetry with emphasis on the arts and political and social commentary, for the general intellectual public; scholars." Quarterly. Estab. 1934. Circ. 8,000.
Needs: Contemporary, experimental, literary, prose poem, regional and translations. Receives 100 unsolicited fiction mss/month. Buys 2 mss/issue; 8 mss/year. Published work by José Donoso, Isaac Bashevis Singer, Doris Lessing; published new writers within the last year. Length: open. Publishes short shorts.
How to Contact: Send complete ms with SASE (IRCs) and cover letter listing past credits. No simultaneous submissions. Reports in 4 months on mss. Sample copy for $5 and $1.50 postage.
Payment: Pays $25-200; 1 contributor's copy.
Terms: Pays on publication for first rights.
Advice: "Please, research the type of fiction we publish. Often we receive manuscripts which are entirely inappropriate for our journal. Sample copies are available for sale and this is a good way to determine audience."

PASSAGER, A Journal of Remembrance and Discovery, (II, IV), University of Baltimore, 1420 N. Charles, Baltimore MD 21201-5779. Editor: Kendra Kopelke. Fiction Editor: Sally Darnowsky. Magazine: 8¼ square; 32-36 pages; 70 lb. paper; 80 lb. cover; photographs. "We publish stories and novel excerpts to 4,000 words, poems to 50 lines, interviews with featured authors." Quarterly. Estab. 1990. Circ. 750.
Needs: "Special interest in discovering new older writers, but publishes all ages." Receives 200 unsolicited mss/month. Accepts 3-4 prose mss/issue; 12-15/year. Publishes ms up to 1 year after acceptance. Recently published work by Thomas Fitzsimmons, Will Inman, Wayne Karlin, Hilda Morley, Ruth Daigon. Length: 250 words minimum; 4,000 words maximum. Publishes short shorts. Also publishes personal essays, poetry. Often critiques rejected mss.

How to Contact: Send complete ms with cover letter. Reports in 3 months on mss. SASE. Simultaneous submissions OK, if noted. Sample copy for $3.50. Fiction guidelines for #10 SAE and 1 first-class stamp (IRCs).
Payment: Pays subscription to magazine and contributor's copies.
Terms: Acquires first North American serial rights. Sometimes sends galleys to author.
Advice: "*Get a copy* so you can see the quality of the work we use. We often reject beautifully written work that is bland in favor of rougher work that has the spark we're looking for. In those cases, we try to work with the author to bring the work to a publishable condition—if possible."

PASSAGES NORTH, (II), Kalamazoo College, 1200 Academy St., Kalamazoo MI 49006-3295. Editor: Michael Barrett. Magazine: 6×9; 100 pages; original art and photography. "*Passages North* publishes quality fiction, poetry and creative nonfiction by emerging and established writers and outstanding work from the programs at the doctorate, masters, and bachelor levels." Readership: General and literary. Semiannual. Estab. 1979. Circ. 1,500.
Needs: "Excellence is our only criterion. We seek the best fiction regardless of subject, form or style." Accepts 5-10 mss/year. Does not read June-August. Recently published works by Susan Straight, Gary Gildner, Alison Baker; published new writers within the last year. Length: open. Critiques returned mss when there is time.
How to Contact: Send complete ms with SASE (IRCs) and brief letter of previous publication, awards. Simultaneous submissions OK, if writer's phone number is included and writer phones *Passages North* immediately if work is taken elsewhere. Reports in 3 weeks to 2 months. Publishes an average of 3-6 months after acceptance. Sample copy $5.
Payment: Pays 2 contributor's copies and 1-year subscription.
Terms: Rights revert to author on publication.

‡PBW, (I), 130 W. Limestone, Yellow Springs OH 45387. (513)767-7416. Editor: Richard Freeman. Electronic disk magazine: 700 pages; illustrations. "*PBW* is an experimental floppy disc and B.B. publication that 'prints' strange and 'unpublishable' in above-ground-sense writing." Quarterly. Estab. 1988.
● *PBW* is an electronic magazine which can be read using MacWrite (Mac disk) or it is available over modem on BBS. Write for details.
Needs: Erotica, experimental, gay, lesbian, literary. No "conventional fiction of any kind." Receives 3 unsolicited mss/month. Accepts 40 mss/issue; 160 mss/year. Publishes ms within 3 months after acceptance. Recently published work by Lisa B. Herskovits, Susan Wolf, Marie Markoe, Susannah Manley, Jeff Jarvie. Length: open. Publishes short shorts and novels in chapters. Publishes literary essays, literary criticisms and poetry. Always critiques or comments on rejected mss.
How to Contact: Send complete ms with a cover letter. Reports in 2 weeks. Send SASE (or IRC) for reply, return of ms or send a disposable copy of ms. Simultaneous, reprint and electronic (Mac) submissions OK. Sample copy for $2. Reviews novels and short story collections.
Payment: Pays 1 contributor's copy.
Terms: All rights revert back to author. Not copyrighted.

PEARL, A Literary Magazine, (II, IV), Pearl, 3030 E. Second St., Long Beach CA 90803. (310)434-4523. Editors: Joan Jobe Smith, Marilyn Johnson and Barbara Hauk. Magazine: 5½×8½; 72 pages; 60 lb. bond paper; 80 lb. gloss cover; b&w drawings and graphics. "We are primarily a poetry magazine, but we do publish some *very short* fiction and nonfiction. We are interested in lively, readable prose that speaks to *real* people in direct, living language; for a general literary audience." Triannually. Estab. 1974 ("folded" after 3 issues but began publishing again in 1987). Circ. 500.
Needs: Contemporary, humor/satire, literary, mainstream, prose poem. "We will only consider short-short stories up to 1,200 words. Longer stories (up to 4,000 words) may only be submitted to our short story contest. All contest entries are considered for publication. Although we have no taboos stylistically or subject-wise, obscure, predictable, sentimental, or cliché-ridden stories are a turn-off." Publishes an all fiction issue each year. Receives 5-10 unsolicited mss/month. Accepts 1-10 mss/issue; 12-15 mss/year. Publishes ms 6 months to 1 year after acceptance. Recently published work by MacDonald

---

● *A bullet introduces comments by the editor of* Novel & Short Story Writer's Market *indicating special information about the listing.*

Harris, Josephine Marshall, Gerald Locklin, Lisa Glatt, Charles Harper Webb. Length: 1,000 words average; 500 words minimum; 1,200 words maximum. Also publishes poetry.
How to Contact: Send complete ms with cover letter including publishing credits and brief biographical information. No simultaneous submissions. Reports in 6-8 weeks on mss. SASE. Sample copy $6 (postpaid). Fiction guidelines for #10 SAE and 1 first-class stamp (IRCs).
Payment: Pays 2 contributor's copies.
Terms: Acquires first North American serial rights. Sends galleys to author. "*Pearl* holds an annual short story contest. Submission period: December 1-March 1. Award: $50, publication in *Pearl*, 10 copies. $5 entry fee. Maximum length: 4,000 words. Send SASE for complete guidelines."
Advice: "We look for vivid, *dramatized* situations and characters, stories written in an original 'voice,' that make sense and follow a clear narrative line. What makes a manuscript stand out is more elusive, though—more to do with feeling and imagination than anything else . . ."

THE PEGASUS REVIEW, (I, IV), Box 134, Flanders NJ 07836. (201)927-0749. Editor: Art Bounds. Magazine: 5½×8½; 6-8 pages; illustrations. "Our magazine is a bimonthly, entirely in calligraphy, illustrated. Each issue is based on specific themes." Estab. 1980. Circ. 280.
• Because *The Pegasus Review* is done in calligraphy, submissions must be very short. Two pages, says the editor, is the ideal length.
Needs: Humor/satire, literary, prose poem and religious/inspirational. Upcoming themes: "Beginnings" (January/February); "Environment" (March/April); "Family" (May/June); "War" (July/August); "Creativity" (September/October); "Future" (November/December). "Themes may be approached by humor, satire, inspirational, autobiographical, prose. Try to avoid the obvious." Receives 50 unsolicited mss/month. Accepts "about" 70 mss/year. Published work by new writers within the last year. Publishes short shorts of 2-3 pages; 500 words. Themes are subject to change, so query if in doubt. "Occasional brief critiques."
How to Contact: Send complete ms. SASE (IRCs) "a must." Brief cover letter with author's background and full name—no initials. Simultaneous submissions acceptable, if so advised. Reports in 1 month. Sample copy $2. Fiction guidelines for SAE.
Payment: Pays 2 contributor's copies. Occasional book awards.
Terms: Acquires one-time rights.
Advice: "Adhere to guidelines. Let the brevity of the piece become part of your creative discipline. Cover letter not necessary, but it is informative and should be brief. Get involved with a local writers group—experience can be invaluable. Use *Writer's Digest* and similar publications as additional marketing sources."

PEMBROKE MAGAZINE, (I, II), Box 60, Pembroke State University, Pembroke NC 28372. (919)521-4214, ext. 433. Editor: Shelby Stephenson. Fiction Editor: Stephen Smith. Magazine: 9×10; 225 pages; illustrations; photos. Magazine of poems and stories plus literary essays. Annually. Estab. 1969. Circ. 500.
Needs: Open. Receives 120 unsolicited mss/month. Publishes short shorts. Published work by Fred Chappell, Robert Morgan; published new writers within the last year. Length: open. Occasionally critiques rejected mss and recommends other markets.
How to Contact: Send complete ms. No simultaneous submissions. Reports in up to 3 months. SASE (IRCs). Accepts computer printout submissions. Sample copy $5 and 9×10 SAE.
Payment: Pays 1 contributor's copy.
Advice: "Write with an end for *writing*, not publication."

‡PENDRAGON, A Literary Magazine, (II), Valdosta State University, English Department, Valdosta GA 31698. (912)244-4673. Editors: William Fuller and Kathleen Morgan. Editors change every 1-2 years. Current editor, Kathleen Morgan (1993-1994). Magazine: 5¾×8¾; 100 pages; 60 lb. paper. "We have no particular bias. We publish the best fiction we can find. We do not normally use fantasy or genre fiction." Annually. Estab. 1991. Circ. 750.
Needs: Gay, historical (general), lesbian, literary, mainstream/contemporary, regional. No romance, religious, fantasy, science fiction. Receives 10-12 unsolicited mss/month. Accepts 4-5 mss/issue. "We read year round but much slower in summer." Publishes ms 6 months after acceptance. Agented fiction 1%. Recently published work by Janice Daugherty, Dirk van Nouhuys. Length: 3,000-4,000 words preferred; 1,500 words minimum; 5,000 words maximum. Also publishes literary essays and poetry. Sometimes critiques or comments on rejected ms.

238 Novel & Short Story Writer's Market '94

How to Contact: Send complete ms with a cover letter. Should include estimated word count and brief bio. Reports in 2-4 months. Send SASE (or IRC) for reply, return of ms or a disposable copy of ms. No simultaneous submissions. Sample copy for $4.

Payment: Pays 2 contributor's copies. "All submissions are considered for 'Best of Issue' prize of $50."

Terms: Acquires first North American serial rights.

PENNSYLVANIA ENGLISH, (II), English Department, Penn State University—Erie, Humanities Division, Erie PA 16563. Editor: Dean Baldwin. Fiction Editor: Chris Dubbs. Magazine: 7 × 8½; 100 pages; 20 lb. bond paper; 65 lb. matte cover. For "teachers of English in Pennsylvania at the high school and college level." Semiannually. Estab. 1985. Circ. 300.

Needs: Literary, contemporary mainstream. Does not read mss from May to August. Publishes ms an average of 6 months after acceptance. Length: 5,000 words maximum. Publishes short shorts. Also publishes literary essays, literary criticism, poetry. Sometimes critiques rejected mss.

How to Contact: Send complete ms with cover letter. Reports in 2 months. SASE (IRCs). Simultaneous submissions OK.

Payment: Pays in contributor's copies.

Terms: Acquires first North American serial rights.

PENNSYLVANIA REVIEW, University of Pittsburgh, 526 C.L./English Dept., Pittsburgh PA 15260. (412)624-0026. Managing Editor: Julie Parson-Nesbitt. Magazine: 7 × 10; 70-100 pages. Magazine of fiction, poetry, nonfiction, interviews, reviews, novel excerpts, long poems for literate audience. Semiannually. Estab. 1985. Circ. 1,000.

Needs: Ethnic, experimental, feminist, gay, humor/satire, lesbian, literary, prose poem, regional, translations. "High quality!" Receives 75 unsolicited fiction mss/month. Accepts 3-5 mss/issue; 6-10 mss/year. Mss not read in summer months (May-August). Recently published work by Cynthia Kadohata, Joyce Carol Oates; published new writers within the last year. Length: 5,000 maximum words for prose. Comments on rejected mss "rarely and only if we've had some interest."

How to Contact: Send complete ms. Reports in 2 weeks on queries; 3-6 months on mss. SASE (IRCs) for ms. Simultaneous submissions OK, if informed when ms is accepted elsewhere. Sample copy $6. Fiction guidelines for #10 SAE and 1 first-class stamp.

Payment: Pays 2 contributor's copies.

Advice: "Don't be discouraged when your work is returned to you. Returns are not necessarily a comment on the quality of the writing. Keep trying."

PEOPLENET, "Where People Meet People," (IV), Box 897, Levittown NY 11756. (516)579-4043. Editor: Robert Mauro. Newsletter: 8½ × 11; 18 pages; 20 lb. paper; 20 lb. cover stock. "Romance stories featuring disabled characters." Triannual. Estab. 1987. Circ. 200.

Needs: Romance, contemporary and disabled. Main character must be disabled. Upcoming theme: "Marriage between disabled and non-disabled." Accepts 1 ms/issue; 3 mss/year. Publishes ms up to 2 years after acceptance. Length: 500-1,000 words; 800-1,000 average. Publishes short shorts. Also publishes literary criticism, poetry. Especially looking for book reviews on books dealing with disabled persons.

How to Contact: Send complete ms and SASE (IRCs). Reports in 1 month *"only* if SASE there." No simultaneous submissions. Sample copy $3. Fiction guidelines for #10 SAE and 1 first-class stamp.

Payment: Pays 1¢/word on acceptance.

Terms: Acquires first rights.

Advice: "We are looking for stories of under 1,000 words on romance with a disabled man or woman as the main character. No sob stories or 'super crip' stories. Just realistic romance. No porn. Love, respect, trust, understanding and acceptance are what I want."

PERCEPTIONS, (I), 1530 Phillips, Missoula MT 59802. (406)543-5875. Editor: Temi Rose. Magazine: 4 × 5; 20 pages. Publishes "primarily women's perceptions," for readers of "all ages, both sexes." Triannually. Estab. 1982. Circ. 100.

● Work published in *Perceptions* has been selected regularly to appear in the *Pushcart Prize* anthology. The magazine is also included in *Ms* magazine's list of feminist publications.

Needs: Adventure, condensed/excerpted novel, confession, contemporary, experimental, fantasy, feminist, mystery/suspense, prose poem, psychic/supernatural/occult, religious/inspirational, science fiction. Publishes short shorts. Collected by University of Wisconsin, Madison Serials Library; UMI microfilm: Alternative Press Collection; produces poetry videos with permission of writers. Critiques rejected mss "only if requested."

How to Contact: Query first. Reports in 6 weeks. SASE. Simultaneous and reprint submissions OK. Accepts electronic submissions via disk or modem. Sample copy $5. Fiction guidelines for SAE and 1 first-class stamp (IRCs).

Payment: Pays in contributor's copies.

PERCEPTIONS, The Journal of Imaginative Sensuality, (I, II, IV), Sensuous SIG, Inc., P.O. Box 2867, Toledo OH 43606-0867. Editor: Victoria. Magazine: 5½ × 8½; 52 pages; 20 lb. bond paper; 60 lb. cover; illustrations; photographs. "*Perceptions* is a journal celebrating the nature of sensuality. We celebrate a realization that virtually everything sexual is sensual, but that sensuality's diversity far exceeds only a sexual purview." Quarterly. Estab. 1988. Circ. 250.

Needs: Erotica, experimental, gay, humor/satire, lesbian, psychic/supernatural/occult, science fiction (soft/sociological). "Any fiction with a sensual slant. We do not accept pornography or graphically obscene fiction." Receives 10 unsolicited mss/month. Acquires 4-5 mss/issue; 20 mss/year. Publishes ms 2-6 months after acceptance. Published work by Vlasa Glen, Bud Martin, Bart Geraci, Alan Schwartz. Length: 800 words preferred; 400 words minimum; 1,600 words maximum (unless serialized). Publishes short shorts. Length: 400-800 words. Also publishes literary essays, literary criticism and poetry. Always critiques or comments on rejected mss.

How to Contact: US writers send $3 for 44-page sample issue and submission guidelines (cost is $4 to Canada and Mexico, and $6 overseas). Should include 3-4 sentence bio. Reports in 2 weeks on queries; 2 months on mss. Send SASE (IRCs) for reply, return of ms or send disposable copy of ms. Simultaneous and reprint submissions OK. Electronic submission preferred.

Payment: Pays 1 contributor's copy. Additional copies $2.

Terms: Acquires one-time rights.

Advice: "We prefer fiction that has an original or unusual story or angle. We attempt to publish fiction from a variety of viewpoints. Steer away from the temptation to depict sexuality or erotic issues in a graphic or obscene way. We prefer more sensual or 'intellectual' stories."

PEREGRINE, The Journal of Amherst Writers and Artists, (II), Amherst Writers and Artists Press, Box 1076, Amherst MA 01004. (413)253-3307. Fiction Editor: Cynthia Kennison. Fiction editors change every year. Send future submissions to Pat Schneider, editor. Magazine: 5 × 7; 90 pages; sturdy matte white paper; heavier cover stock. "Poetry and prose—short stories, short short stories, and occasionally prose fantasies or reflections that are fiction yet are not stories." Annual.

• *Peregrine* has been awarded grants from the Massachusetts Cultural Council for the past several years.

Needs: "No specific 'category' requirements; we publish what we love." Accepts 2-4 mss/issue. Publishes ms an average of 6 months after acceptance. Published work by Anna Kirwan Vogel, Jane Yolen, Barbara VanNoord; published new writers within the last year. Length: 1,000-2,500 words preferred. Publishes short shorts. "Short pieces have a better chance of publication."

How to Contact: Send complete ms with cover letter, which should include brief biographical note. Reports in 3-6 months. SASE (IRCs). Simultaneous submissions are encouraged. Sample copy $3 plus $2 postage.

Payment: Pays contributor's copies.

Terms: All rights return to writer upon publication.

Advice: "Every manuscript is read by 3 or more readers. We publish what we love most—and it has varied widely."

PHOEBE, An Interdisciplinary Journal of Feminist Scholarship, (II, IV), Theory and Aesthetics, Women's Studies Program, State University of New York, College at Oneonta, Oneonta NY 13820. (607)431-2014. Editor: Kathleen O'Mara. Fiction Editor: Marilyn Wesley. Journal: 7 × 9; 140 pages; 80 lb. paper; illustrations and photos. "Feminist material for feminist scholars and readers." Semiannually. Estab. 1989. Circ. 400.

Needs: Feminist: ethnic, experimental, gay, humor/satire, lesbian, literary, translations. Receives 6 unsolicited mss/month. "One-third to one-half of each issue is short fiction and poetry." Does not read mss in summer. Publishes ms 3-4 months after acceptance. Length: 1,500-2,500 words preferred. Publishes short shorts. Sometimes critiques rejected mss and recommends other markets.

How to Contact: Send complete ms with cover letter. Reports in 1 month on queries; 15 weeks on mss. Sample copy for $7.50. Fiction guidelines free.
Payment: Pays in contributor's copies.
Terms: Acquires one-time rights.
Advice: "We look for writing with a feminist perspective. *Phoebe* was founded to provide a forum for cross-cultural feminist analysis, debate and exchange. The editors are committed to providing space for all disciplines and new areas of research, criticism and theory in feminist scholarship and aesthetics. *Phoebe* is not committed to any one conception of feminism. All work that is not sexist, racist, homophobic, or otherwise discriminatory, will be welcome. *Phoebe* is particularly committed to publishing work informed by a theoretical perspective which will enrich critical thinking."

PHOEBE, A Journal of Literary Arts, (II), George Mason University, 4400 University Dr., Fairfax VA 22030. (703)993-2915. Editors: Charles Fox, Kurt Olsson. Fiction Editors: Jamy Bond, Jason Ellison. Editors change each year. Magazine: 6×9; 116 pages; 80 lb. quality paper; 0-5 illustrations per issue; 0-10 photographs per issue. "We publish fiction, poetry, photographs, illustrations and some reviews." Published 2 times/year. Estab. 1972. Circ. 3,000.
Needs: "Looking for a broad range of poetry, fiction and essays. Encourage writers and poets to experiment, to stretch the boundaries of genre." No romance, western, juvenile, erotica. Receives 20 mss/month. Accepts 3-5 mss/issue. Does not read mss in summer. Deadlines for mss are: October 1 for Winter issue; March 1 for Summer issue. Publishes ms 3-6 months after acceptance. Length: no more than 35 pages. Also publishes literary essays, literary criticism, poetry.
How to Contact: Send complete ms with cover letter. Include "name, address, phone. Brief bio." SASE (IRCs). Simultaneous submissions OK. Sample copy $4.
Payment: Pays 4 contributor's copies.
Terms: Acquires one-time rights. All rights revert to author.
Advice: "We are interested in a variety of fiction, poetry and nonfiction. We suggest potential contributors study previous issues. Each year *Phoebe* sponsors poetry and fiction contests, with $500 awarded to the winning poem and short story. The deadline for the Greg Grummer Award in Poetry is October 1; the deadline for the Phoebe Fiction Prize is March 1. Those interested in entering should write for full contest guidelines."

PIG IRON, (II), Box 237, Youngstown OH 44501. (216)747-6932. Editor: Jim Villani. Magazine. 8½×11; 128 pages; 60 lb. offset paper; 85 pt. coated cover stock; b&w illustrations; b&w 120 line photographs. "Contemporary literature by new and experimental writers." Annually. Estab. 1975. Circ. 1,000.
Needs: Literary and thematic. No mainstream. Upcoming theme: "The Family: Tradition & Possibility" (Dec. 1994), "Jazz Tradition" (Oct. 1995). Buys 10-20 mss/issue. Receives approximately 75-100 unsolicited fiction mss each month. Recently published work by Helen Ruggieri, Claudia Ricci, Coco Gordon, Gary Fincke, James Bertolino, Bob Fox, Terry Wright. Length: 8,000 words maximum. Also publishes literary nonfiction, poetry.
How to Contact: Send complete ms with SASE (IRCs). No simultaneous submissions. Reports in 3 months. Sample copy $4.
Payment: Pays $5/printed page; 2 contributor's copies; $5 charge for extras.
Terms: Pays on publication for first North American serial rights.
Advice: "Looking for works psychological, new critical, aggressive, poised for a new century unfolding, unveiling." Rejects manuscripts "lacking modern style, experimental style. Editors look for stylistic innovation."

THE PIKESTAFF FORUM, (II), Box 127, Normal IL 61761. (309)452-4831. Editors: Robert D. Sutherland, James Scrimgeour, James McGowan and Curtis White. Tabloid: 11½×17½; 40 pages; newsprint paper; illustrations; photos. "*The Pikestaff Forum* is a general literary magazine publishing poetry, prose fiction, drama." Readership: "General literary with a wide circulation in the small press world. Readers are educated (but not academic) and have a taste for excellent serious fiction." Published irregularly—"whenever we have sufficient quality material to warrant an issue." Estab. 1977. Circ. 1,000.
Needs: Literary and contemporary with a continuing need for good short stories or novel excerpts. "We welcome traditional and experimental works from established and non-established writers. We look for writing that is clear, concise and to the point; contains vivid imagery and sufficient concrete detail; is grounded in lived human experience; contains memorable characters and situations. No confessional self-pity or puffery; self-indulgent first or second drafts; sterile intellectual word games or

five-finger exercises or slick formula writing, genre-pieces that do not go beyond their form (westerns, mysteries, gothic, horror, science fiction, swords-and-sorcery fantasy), commercially oriented mass-market stuff, violence for its own sake, racist or sexist material or pornography (sexploitation)." Accepts 1-4 mss/issue. Receives approximately 15-20 unsolicited fiction mss each month. Published work by Constance Pierce, Linnea Johnson; published new writers within the last year. Length: from 1 paragraph to 4,000 or 5,000 words. Also publishes poetry. Critiques rejected mss when there is time.
How to Contact: Query. Send complete ms. SASE (IRCs). "Reluctantly" accepts simultaneous submissions. Reports in 3 weeks on queries, 3 months on mss. Publishes ms up to 1 year after acceptance. Sample copy $2.
Payment: Pays 3 contributor's copies. Cover price less 50% discount for extras.
Terms: Acquires first rights. Copyright remains with author.
Advice: "We are highly selective, publishing only 3% of the stories that are submitted for consideration. Read other authors with an appreciative and critical eye; don't send out work prematurely; develop keen powers of observation and a good visual memory; get to know your characters thoroughly; don't let others (editors, friends, etc.) define or 'determine' your sense of self-worth; be willing to learn; outgrow self-indulgence. Develop discipline. Show, don't tell; and leave some work for the reader to do. Write for the fun of it (that way there's a sure return for the investment of time and effort). Always write to achieve the best quality you can; be honest with yourself, your potential readers, and your story. Learn to become your own best editor: know when you've done well, and when you haven't done as well as you can. Remember: there's a lot of competition for the available publication slots, and editorial bias is always a factor in what gets accepted for publication. Develop a sense of humor about the enterprise."

THE PINEHURST JOURNAL, Pinehurst Press, P.O. Box 360747, Milpitas CA 95036. (510)440-9259. Editor: Michael K. McNamara. Contributing Editor: Kathleen M. McNamara. Magazine: 8½ × 11; 44 pages; recycled 24 lb. paper; 67 lb. cover; illustrations. "Fiction, nonfiction and poetry for an educated audience appreciative of polished, thought-provoking work." Quarterly. Estab. 1990. Circ. 300.
Needs: Contemporary, experimental, feminist, gay, historical (general), horror, humor/satire, lesbian, literary, mainstream, mystery/suspense, prose poem. "No hard sci-fi, fantasy, occult, swords and sorcery, slasher or porn, travel or religious. No formula western or romance." Receives 80 mss/month. Accepts 17 mss/issue; 65-70 mss/year. Publishes ms 1-4 months after acceptance. Length: 2,000 words average; 750 words minimum; 4,000 words maximum. Publishes literary essays, some literary and poetry criticism. Critiques mss and recommends other markets.
How to Contact: Send complete ms with cover letter and short bio which includes publishing successes, if any. Indicate whether piece is a simultaneous submittal. Reports in 1 month or less on queries; 2 months or less on mss. SASE. Simultaneous submissions OK. Sample copy for $5. Guidelines for #10 SAE and 1 first-class stamp (IRCs).
Payment: Pays $5 and 1 contributor's copy for fiction (contributor's copy for poetry). Charge for extras.
Terms: Buys one-time rights.
Advice: "Try to make each word pull its own weight and polish, polish, polish then punctuate, punctuate, punctuate."

‡THE PIPE SMOKER'S EPHEMERIS, (I, II, IV), The Universal Coterie of Pipe Smokers, 20-37 120 St., College Point NY 11356. Editor: Tom Dunn. Magazine: 8½ × 11; 54-66 pages; offset paper and cover; illustrations; photos. Pipe smoking and tobacco theme for general and professional audience. Irregular quarterly. Estab. 1964.
Needs: Historical (general), humor/satire, literary, pipe smoking related. Publishes ms up to 1 year after acceptance. Length: 2,500 words average; 5,000 words maximum. Also publishes short shorts. Occasionally critiques rejected mss.
How to Contact: Send complete ms with cover letter. Reports in 2 weeks on mss. Simultaneous and reprints OK. Sample copy for 8½ × 11 SAE and 6 first-class stamps (IRCs).
Terms: Acquires one-time rights.

PIRATE WRITINGS, The Best of it All! (II), Pirate Writings Publishing, 53 Whitman Ave., Islip NY 11751. Editor: Edward J. McFadden. Magazine: digest; perfect-bound. "We are looking for poetry and short stories that entertain." Semiannually. Estab. 1992. Circ. 500.
● Pirate Writings Publishing recently published *Starfleet Mysteries*, a collection of Star Trek mystery stories.

Needs: Adventure, fantasy (science fantasy, sword and sorcery), literary, mystery/suspense, science fiction. Plans to publish special fiction issue or anthology in the future. Receives 30-40 unsolicited mss/month. Buys 8 mss/issue; 16-20 mss/year. Publishes ms 6 months-1 year after acceptance. Length: 1,500 words average; 500 words minimum; 2,500 words maximum. Also publishes poetry. Sometimes critiques or comments on rejected mss.

How to Contact: Send complete ms with cover letter. Should include estimated word count, 1 paragraph bio, Social Security number, list of publications with submission. Reports in 1 week on queries; 2 months on mss. Send SASE (or IRC) for reply or return of ms or disposable copy of ms. Will consider simultaneous submissions. Sample copy $3.50 (make check payable to Edward McFadden). Fiction guidelines for #10 SAE.

Payment: Pays 1 contributor's copy.

Terms: Acquires first North American serial rights.

Advice: "My goal is to provide a diverse, entertaining and thought provoking magazine featuring all the above stated genres in every issue. Hints: I love a good ending. Move me, make me laugh, surprise me, and you're in. Read *PW* and you'll see what I mean. Pirate Writings Publishing also publishes books and chapbooks. Query for more info."

PLÉIADES MAGAZINE/PHILAE (I), Box 357, Suite D, 6677 W. Colfax, Lakewood CO 80215. John Moravec, Pléiades Productions. Magazine: 8½ × 11; 30-50 pages; 30 lb. paper; illustrations. "We want well thought out material; no sex stories, and good rhymed poetry and carefully written prose. We want articles about national issues." Both magazines will, in the future, be published twice a year; *Philae* more often depending on material. *Philae* estab. 1947, *Pléiades*, estab. 1984. Circ. 10,000.

Needs: Literary, fantasy, horror, mystery/suspense, senior citizen/retirement, serialized/excerpted novel, western. Receives 50-100 unsolicited mss/month. Publishes ms 3 months or less after acceptance. Length: 1,200-1,800 words average; 500-800 words minimum.

How to Contact: Send complete ms with short cover letter. SASE. Reports in 2-3 weeks. Simultaneous submissions OK. Sample copy $3.75. (Checks made out to John L. Moravec). Fiction guidelines for #10 SAE and 1 first-class stamp (IRCs).

Payment: Pays in contributor's copies, awards, trophies.

Advice: "Learn to write, and take lessons on punctuation. Shorter fiction and articles considered first."

PLOUGHSHARES, (II), Emerson College, 100 Beacon St., Boston MA 02116. (617)578-8753. Executive Director: DeWitt Henry. "Our theme is new writing (poetry, fiction, personal essays) that addresses contemporary adult readers who look to fiction and poetry for help in making sense of themselves and of each other." Triquarterly. Estab. 1971. Circ. 4,200.

 • *Ploughshares* also sponsors a writing seminar in Holland. See the 1991 *Novel & Short Story Writer's Market* for an article on the conference as well as the listing in the Conferences and Workshops section of this edition.

Needs: Literary, prose poem. "No genre (science fiction, detective, gothic, adventure, etc.), popular formula or commercial fiction whose purpose is to entertain rather than to illuminate." Buys 25+ mss/year. Receives approximately 400-600 unsolicited fiction mss each month. Published work by Rick Bass, Joy Williams, Andre Dubus; published new writers within the last year. Length: 300-6,000 words.

How to Contact: "Query with #10 SASE for guidelines and examine a sample issue. Reading period: August 1 to April 1. Cover letter should include "previous pubs." SASE (IRCs). Reports in 3-5 months on mss. Sample copy $8.95. (Please specify fiction issue sample.)

Payment: Pays $10/page plus copies and a subscription. Offers 50% kill fee for assigned ms not published.

Terms: Pays on publication for first North American serial rights.

Advice: "Be familiar with our fiction issues, fiction by our writers and by our various editors (e.g., Rosellen Brown, Tim O'Brien, Jay Neugeboren, Jayne Anne Phillips, James Alan McPherson) and more generally acquaint yourself with the best short fiction currently appearing in the literary quarterlies, and the annual prize anthologies (*Pushcart Prize, O. Henry Awards, Best American Short Stories*). Also realistically consider whether the work you are submitting is as good as or better than—in your own opinion—the work appearing in the magazine you're sending to. What is the level of competition? And what is its volume? (In our case, we accept about 1 ms in 200.) Never send 'blindly' to a magazine, or without carefully weighing your prospect there against those elsewhere. Always keep a copy of work you submit."

POETIC SPACE, Poetry & Fiction, (I, II), P.O. Box 11157, Eugene OR 97440. Editor: Don Hildenbrand. Fiction Editor: Thomas Strand. Magazine: 8×11; 16 pages; light paper; medium cover; b&w art. "Social, political, avant-garde, erotic, environmental material for a literary audience." Biannual (September and March). Estab. 1983. Circ. 600.
Needs: Contemporary, erotica, ethnic, experimental, fantasy, feminist, gay, humor/satire, lesbian, literary, prose poem, regional, serialized novel, translations. No sentimental, romance, mainstream. Plans first chapbook, Summer '93. Receives 10-12 unsolicited mss/month. Accepts 2 mss/issue; 4-6 mss/year. Publishes ms 3-4 months after acceptance. Published work by Nathan Versace and Louise A. Blum. Length: 1,500-2,000 words average. Publishes short shorts. Also publishes literary essays, literary criticism, poetry. Sometimes critiques rejected mss and recommends other markets.
How to Contact: Send complete ms with cover letter that includes basic info/credits. Reports in 1-2 weeks on queries; 1-2 months on mss. SASE. No simultaneous submissions. Sample copy for $3, 4×9 SAE and 45¢ postage. Fiction guidelines for #10 SAE and 1 first-class stamp (IRCs). Reviews novels and short story collections. Send books to Don Hildenbrand.
Payment: Pays contributor's copies.
Terms: Acquires one-time rights or "reserves anthology rights."

POETRY FORUM SHORT STORIES, (I, II), Poetry Forum, 5713 Larchmont Dr., Erie PA 16509. (814)866-2543. Fax: (814)866-2543 (fax hours 8-10 a.m., 5-8 p.m.). Editor: Gunver Skogsholm. Newspaper: 7×8½; 34 pages; card cover; illustrations. "Human interest themes (no sexually explicit or racially biased or blasphemous material) for the general public—from the grassroot to the intellectual." Quarterly. Estab. 1989. Circ. 400.
 ● Note the publication policy charging for membership to the magazine for publication and, says the editor, "subscribers come first!"
Needs: Confession, contemporary, ethnic, experimental, fantasy, feminist, historical, literary, mainstream, mystery/suspense, prose poem, religious/inspirational, romance, science fiction, senior citizen/retirement, young adult/teen. "No blasphemous, sexually explicit material." Publishes annual special fiction issue. Receives 50 unsolicited mss/month. Accepts 12 mss/issue; 40 mss/year. Publishes ms 6 months after acceptance. Agented fiction less than 1%. Length: 2,000 words average; 500 words minimum; 5,000 words maximum. Also publishes literary essays, literary criticism, poetry.
How to Contact: *This magazine charges a "professional members" fee of $36.* The fee entitles you to publication of a maximum of 3,000 words. Send complete ms with cover letter. Reports in 3 weeks to 2 months on mss. SASE. Simultaneous and reprint submissions OK. "Accepts electronic submissions via disk gladly." Sample copy $3. Fiction guidelines for SAE and 1 first-class stamp (IRCs). Reviews novels and short story collections.
Terms: Preference given to submissions by subscribers. Acquires one-time rights.
Advice: Also sponsors contest.

POETRY MOTEL, (II), Suburban Wilderness Press, 1619 Jefferson, Duluth MN 55812. Editor: Pat McKinnon. Fiction Editor: Bud Backen. Magazine: 7×8½; 50-80 pages; 20 lb. paper; various cover; various amount of illustrations and photographs. "We're wide open though we lean toward wry satire and hilarity." 1-2 times annually. Estab. 1984. Circ. 750.
Needs: Condensed/excerpted novel, contemporary, erotica, ethnic, fantasy, feminist, gay, humor/satire, lesbian, literary, prose poem, science fiction. "Nothing along the popular/genre lines." Receives 2-5 unsolicited mss/month. Accepts 2-5 mss/issue; 2-10 mss/year. Publishes ms 1 month to 2 years after acceptance. Published work by Willie Smith, Gregory Burnham, Hugh Knox. Length: 300 words average; 25 words minimum; 1,500 words maximum. Publishes short shorts. Length: 300-500 words. Also publishes literary essays, literary criticism, poetry. Sometimes critiques rejected mss.
How to Contact: Send complete ms with cover letter. Reports in 1 week on queries; 1 week to 1 month on mss. SASE. Simultaneous and reprint submissions OK. Sample copy $5.95. Fiction guidelines for #10 SAE and 1 first-class stamp (IRCs). Reviews novels and short story collections.
Payment: Pays contributor's copies. Charge for extras.
Terms: Acquires one-time rights.
Advice: "Read what we print first since it is beyond description and never what you might imagine."

THE POINTED CIRCLE, (II), Portland Community College-Cascade, 705 N. Killingsworth St., Portland OR 97217. (503)244-6111 ext. 5230. Editors: Student Editorial Staff. Magazine: approx. 80 pages; b&w illustrations and photographs. "Anything of interest to educationally/culturally mixed audience." Annually. Estab. 1980.

Needs: Contemporary, ethnic, literary, prose poem, regional. "We will read whatever is sent, but encourage writers to remember we are a quality literary/arts magazine intended to promote the arts in the community." Acquires 3-7 mss/year. Accepts submissions only December 1-February 15, for October 1 issue. Length: 3,000 words maximum.
How to Contact: Send complete ms with cover letter and brief bio. SASE. Sample copy for $3.50. Fiction guidelines for #10 SAE and 1 first-class stamp (IRCs).
Payment: Pays in contributor's copies.
Terms: Acquires one-time rights.
Advice: "Looks for quality—topicality—nothing trite. The author cares about language and acts responsibly toward the reader, honors the reader's investment of time and piques the reader's interest."

THE PORTABLE WALL, (II), Basement Press, 215 Burlington, Billings MT 59101. (406)256-3588. Editor: Daniel Struckman. Magazine: 6×9¼; 40 pages; cotton rag paper; best quality cover; line engravings; illustrations. "We consider all kinds of material. Bias toward humor." Semiannually. Estab. 1977. Circ. 400.
Needs: Adventure, contemporary, ethnic, experimental, feminist, historical, humor/satire, literary, mainstream, prose poem, regional, science fiction, senior citizen, sports, translations. "We favor short pieces and poetry." Receives 5-10 unsolicited mss/month. Accepts 3-4 mss/issue; 6-8 mss/year. Publishes ms 6 months to a year after acceptance. Published works by Gray Harris, Wilbur Wood. Length: 2,000 words preferred. Publishes short shorts. Also publishes literary essays, literary criticism, poetry. Sometimes critiques rejected mss.
How to Contact: Send complete ms with cover letter. No simultaneous submissions. Reports in 2-4 weeks on mss. SASE (IRCs). Sample copy $6.50.
Payment: Pays subscription to magazine.
Terms: Acquires one-time rights.
Advice: "We like language that evokes believable pictures in our minds and that tells news."

BERN PORTER INTERNATIONAL, Bern Porter Books, 22 Salmond St., Belfast ME 04915. (207)338-6798. Editor: Bern Porter. Magazine: 8½×11; 98-132 pages; illustrations and photographs. "High literary quality with international flavor." Bimonthly. Estab. 1991.
Needs: Experimental, literary, prose poem, translations, international. Publishes special fiction issue. Receives 30-50 unsolicited mss/month. Buys 10-15 mss/issue. Publishes ms immediately after acceptance. Length: open. Publishes short shorts. Comments on or critiques rejected mss and recommends other markets.
How to Contact: Query first. Reports in 1 week. SASE (IRCs). Simultaneous and reprint submissions OK. Sample copy and fiction guidelines free.
Payment: Pays 6¢/word.
Terms: Pays on publication. Buys world rights. Sends galleys to author.

‡PORTLAND REVIEW, (I, II), Portland State University, Box 751, Portland OR 97207. (503)725-4533. Editor: Milla Gay Walker. Magazine: 9×12; 80 pages; 40 lb. paper; 60 lb. cover stock; b&w drawings and photos. "We seek to publish fiction in which content takes precedence over style." Published 2 times/year. Estab. 1955. Circ. 1,500.
Needs: Contemporary, literary, regional, humor/satire, experimental. "No porno, sci fi, mood pieces/vignettes, or material which advocates political or religious ideologies." Publishes within 1 year of acceptance. Length: 3,500 words average; 5,000 words maximum. Critiques ms when time allows. Also publishes critical essays, poetry, drama, interviews and reviews.
How to Contact: Submit complete ms with short bio and publishing credits. SASE. Simultaneous submissions OK (if noted). Reports in 6-8 weeks. Sample copy for $5 plus $1 postage.
Payment: Pays 1 contributor's copy.
Terms: Acquires one-time rights.
Advice: "Our editors, and thus our tastes/biases change annually, so keep trying us."

POSKISNOLT PRESS, Yesterday's Press, (I, II, IV), Yesterday's Press, JAF Station, Box 7415, New York NY 10116-4630. (718)680-3899. Editor: Patricia D. Coscia. Magazine: 7×8½; 20 pages; regular typing paper. Estab. 1989. Circ. 100.
Needs: Contemporary, erotica, ethnic, experimental, fantasy, feminist, gay, humor/satire, lesbian, literary, mainstream, prose poem, psychic/supernatural/occult, romance, senior citizen/retirement, western, young adult/teen (10-18 years). "X-rated material is not accepted!" Plans to publish a special fiction issue or anthology in the future. Receives 50 unsolicited mss/month. Accepts 30 mss/issue;

100+ mss/year. Publishes ms 6 months after acceptance. Length: 200 words average; 100 words minimum; 500 words maximum. Publishes short shorts. Length: 100-500 words. Sometimes critiques rejected mss and recommends other markets.

How to Contact: Query first with clips of published work or send complete manuscript with cover letter. Reports in 1 week on queries; 6 months on mss. SASE. Accepts simultaneous submissions. Sample copy for $4 with #10 SAE and $2 postage. Fiction guidelines for #10 SAE and $2 postage (IRCs).

Payment: Pays with subscription to magazine or contributor's copies; charges for extras.

Terms: Acquires all rights, first rights or one-time rights.

THE POST, (II), Publishers Syndication International, Suite 856, 1377 K St., Washington DC 20005. Editor: A.P. Samuels. Newspaper: 8½×11; 32 pages. Monthly. Estab. 1988.

Needs: Adventure, mystery/suspense (private eye), romance (romantic suspense), western (traditional). "No explicit sex, gore, extreme violence or bad language." Receives 75 unsolicited mss/month. Buys 1 ms/issue; 12 mss/year. Time between acceptance and publication varies. Agented fiction 10%. Length: 10,000 words average.

How to Contact: Send complete ms with cover letter. Reports on mss in 5 weeks. No simultaneous submissions. Fiction guidelines for #10 SAE and 1 first-class stamp (IRCs).

Payment: Pays ½¢ to 4¢/word.

Terms: Pays on acceptance for all rights.

‡POSTMODERN CULTURE, (IV), Oxford UF, Box 8105, North Carolina State University, Raleigh NC 27695. (919)515-2687. Fax: (919)515-3628. Co-Editor: Eyal Amiran. Magazine. "Works that are postmodern." Triannual. Estab. 1990. Circ. 2,500.

Needs: Postmodern, any genre. Publishes annual special fiction issue or anthology. Accepts 3 mss/year. Publishes ms 3 months after acceptance. Agented fiction 25%. Recently published work by Robert Coover, Kathy Acker, Richard Vollman. Length: 10,000 words maximum. Publishes short shorts. Also publishes literary essays, literary criticism, poetry. Often critiques or comments on rejected mss.

How to Contact: Send complete ms with a cover letter. Use E-mail—send to pmc@unity.ncsu.edu. Reports in 6 weeks on mss. Send a disposable copy of ms. Simultaneous and electronic submissions OK. Sample copy free.

Payment: Free subscription to the magazine.

Terms: Usually author holds copyright. Sends galleys to author.

POTATO EYES, (II), Nightshade, Box 76, Troy ME 04987. (207)948-3427. Editors: Carolyn Page and Roy Zarucchi. Fiction Editor: Dr. Ted Holmes. Magazine: 5½×8½; 108 pages; 60 lb. text paper; 80 lb. Curtis flannel cover. "We tend to showcase Appalachian talent from Alabama to Quebec, and in doing so, we hope to dispel hackneyed stereotypes and political borders. However, we don't limit ourselves to this area, publishing always the best that we receive. Our subscribers have included: boat builder, teacher, dairy farmer, college prof, doctor, lawyer, world traveler, lumberman, archaeologist and cab driver." Estab. 1988. Circ. 800.
- The publishers of *Potato Eyes* were featured in an interview in the 1991 *Novel & Short Story Writer's Market*. They also operate Nightshade Press listed in the Small Press section of this book.

Needs: Contemporary, humor/satire, literary, mainstream, regional and ecological themes. Published a *1992 Nightshade Short Story Reader*. Receives 250 unsolicited mss/month. Accepts 5 mss/issue; 10 mss/year. Publishes ms 2 months-2 years after acceptance. Recently published work by Ann Williams, Pat Carr, Edward M. Holmes, Robert Chute and Steven Lewis. Length: 3,000 words maximum; 2,000 average. Publishes short shorts. Length: 450 words. Also publishes poetry (looking for English/French translations of Franco poems) plus one or two novels. Sometimes critiques rejected mss and recommends other markets.

How to Contact: Send complete ms with cover letter. Reports in 4 weeks-4 months on mss. SASE. Sample copy $5, including postage. Fiction guidelines with #10 SAE.

Payment: Pays in contributor's copies.

Terms: Acquires first North American serial rights.

Advice: "We care about the larger issues, including pollution, ecology, bio-regionalism, uncontrolled progress and 'condominia,' as well as the rights of the individual. We care about television, the great sewer pipe of America, and what it is doing to America's youth. We are exploring these issues with writers who have originality, a reordered perspective, and who submit to us generous sprinklings of humor and satire. Although we do occasionally comment on valid fiction, we have walked away un-scathed from the world of academia and refuse to correct manuscripts. We respect our contributors and treat them as professionals, however, and write personal responses to every submission if given a SASE. We expect the same treatment—clean copy without multi folds or corrections. We like brief non-Narcissistic cover letters containing the straight scoop. We suggest that beginning fiction writers spend the money they have set aside for creative writing courses or conferences and spend it instead on subscriptions to good little literary magazines."

POTPOURRI, (II), P.O. Box 8278, Prairie Village KS 66208. (913)642-1503. Editor: Polly W. Swafford. Newspaper: 12×14; 28 pages. "Literary magazine: short stories, verse, essays, travel, prose-poetry for a general adult audience." Monthly. Estab. 1989. Circ. 6,000.
  • *Potpourri* offers annual awards (of $100 each) in fiction and poetry; more depending on grants received. Potpourri Publications Co. also publishes *Potpourri Petites*, "little books," and a new biannual magazine, *Republish*, of selected reprints from literary publications across the US.
Needs: Adventure, contemporary, ethnic, experimental, fantasy, historical (general), humor/satire, literary, mainstream, mystery/suspense (private eye), prose poem, romance (contemporary, historical, romantic suspense), science fiction (soft/sociological), western (frontier stories). "*Potpourri* accepts a broad genre; hence its name. Guidelines specify no religious, confessional, racial, political, erotic, abusive or sexual preference materials unless fictional and necessary to plot." Publishes annual special all-fiction issue. Receives 75 unsolicited mss/month. Accepts 6-8 mss/issue; 60-80 mss/year. Publishes ms 3-6 months after acceptance. Agented fiction 1%. Recently published work by Thomas E. Kennedy, David Ray, Layle Silbert, Lloyd van Brunt, C. Marcus Parr, Arthur Winfield Knight. Length: 2,500 words maximum. Also publishes poetry. Sometimes critiques on rejected mss and recommends other markets.
How to Contact: Send complete ms with cover letter. Include "complete name, address, phone number, brief summary statement about submission, short bio on author." Reports in 3-6 weeks on queries; 2-4 months on mss. SASE. Simultaneous submissions OK. Sample copy for 9×12 SAE and 4 first-class stamps. Fiction guidelines for #10 SAE and 1 first-class stamp (IRCs).
Payment: Pays contributor's copies (up to 20).
Terms: Acquires first rights.
Advice: "We look for stories of literary value and stories with reader appeal. First, does the manuscript spark immediate interest and the introduction create the effect that will dominate? Second, does the action in dialogue or narration tell the story? Third: does the conclusion leave something with the reader to be long remembered? We look for the story with an original idea and an unusual twist."

✸PRAIRIE FIRE, (II), Prairie Fire Press Inc., Room 423, 100 Arthur St., Winnipeg, Manitoba R3B 1H3 Canada. (204)943-9066. Managing Editor: Andris Taskans. Magazine: 6×9; 128 pages; offset bond paper; sturdy cover stock; illustrations; photos. "Essays, critical reviews, short fiction and poetry. For writers and readers interested in Canadian literature." Published 4 times/year. Estab. 1978. Circ. 1,500.
Needs: Literary, contemporary, experimental, prose poem, reviews. "We will consider work on any topic of artistic merit, including short chapters from novels-in-progress. We wish to avoid gothic, confession, religious, romance and pornography." Upcoming theme: "Summer (1994) will be special, double-sized issue on science fiction. Canadian contributors only." Buys 3-6 mss/issue, 12-24 mss/year. Does not read mss in summer. Recently published work by David Arnason, Patrick Roscoe, Diane Schoemperlen; published new writers within the last year. Receives 70-80 unsolicited fiction mss each month. Publishes short shorts. Length: 7,000 words maximum; 2,500 words average. Also publishes literary essays, literary criticism, poetry. Critiques rejected mss "if requested and when there is time." Sometimes recommends other markets.
How to Contact: Send complete ms with IRC w/envelope and short bio. No simultaneous submissions. Reports in 4-6 months. Sample copy for $8 (Canadian). Reviews novels and short story collections. Send books to Andris Taskans.
Payment: Pays $45 for the first page, $30 for each additional page; 1 contributor copy; 60% of cover price for extras.
Terms: Pays on publication for first North American serial rights. Rights revert to author on publication.
Advice: "We are publishing more fiction, and we are commissioning illustrations. Read our publication before submitting. We prefer Canadian material. Most mss are not ready for publication. Be neat, double space, and put your name and address on everything! Be the best writer you can be."

‡✿THE PRAIRIE JOURNAL OF CANADIAN LITERATURE, (I, II, IV), Prairie Journal Press, Box 61203, Brentwood Postal Services, 217K-3630 Brentwood Rd. NW, Calgary, Alberta T2L 2K6 Canada. Editor: A.E. Burke. Journal: 7×8½; 50-60 pages; white bond paper; Cadillac cover stock; cover illustrations. Journal of creative writing and scholarly essays, reviews for literary audience. Semiannually. Published special fiction issue last year. Estab. 1983.
• This magazine received a Canadian National Magazine Award in 1993. See the listing for their press in this book.
Needs: Contemporary, literary, prose poem, regional, excerpted novel, novella, typed single space. Canadian authors given preference. No romance, erotica, pulp. Publishes genre series open to submissions: *Prairie Journal Poetry II* and *Prairie Journal Fiction III*. Receives 20-40 unsolicited mss each month. Accepts 10-15 mss/issue; 20-30 mss/year. Suggests sample issue before submitting ms. Published work by Nancy Ellen Russell, Carla Mobley, Patrick Quinn; published new writers within the last year. Length: 2,500 words average; 100 words minimum; 3,000 words maximum. Also publishes literary essays, literary criticism, poetry. Sometimes critiques rejected mss and recommends other markets.
How to Contact: Send complete ms. Reports in 1 month. SASE or SAE and IRC. Photocopied submissions OK. Accepts computer printout submissions. Sample copy $6 (Canadian) and SAE with $1.10 for postage or IRC. Include cover letter of past credits, if any. Reply to queries for SAE with 48¢ for postage or IRC. No American stamps. Reviews novels and short story collections.
Payment: Pays contributor's copies and modest honoraria.
Terms: Acquires first North American serial rights. In Canada author retains copyright.
Advice: Interested in "innovational work of quality. Beginning writers welcome. There is no point in simply republishing known authors or conventional, predictable plots. Of the genres we receive fiction is most often of the highest calibre. It is a very competitive field. Be proud of what you send. You're worth it."

PRAIRIE SCHOONER, (II), University of Nebraska, English Department, 201 Andrews Hall, Lincoln NE 68588-0334. (402)472-3191. Editor: Hilda Raz. Magazine: 6×9; 144 pages; good stock paper; heavy cover stock. "A fine literary quarterly of stories, poems, essays and reviews for a general audience that reads for pleasure." Quarterly. Estab. 1927. Circ. 3,000.
• *Prairie Schooner*, one of the oldest publications in this book, has garnered several awards and honors over the years. Work appearing in the magazine has been selected for various anthologies. See the interview with the editor in the 1993 *Writer's Market*.
Needs: Good fiction. Upcoming theme: "Fall 1993 was 'Canadian Women Writers' – a special issue of *Prairie Schooner*." Accepts 4-5 mss/issue. Receives approximately 150 unsolicited fiction mss each month. Recently published work by Leo Litwak, Ursula Hegi, Wayne Karlin, Kyoko Mori; published new writers within the last year. Length: varies. Also publishes poetry.
How to Contact: Send complete ms with SASE (IRCs) and cover letter listing previous publications – where, when. Reports in 3 months. Sample copy $3.50. Reviews novels and short story collections.
Payment: Pays in contributor's copies and prize money awarded.
Terms: Acquires all rights. Will reassign rights upon request after publication.
Advice: "*Prairie Schooner* is eager to see fiction from beginning and established writers. Be tenacious. Accept rejection as a temporary setback and send out rejected stories to other magazines. *Prairie Schooner* is not a magazine with a program. We look for good fiction in traditional narrative modes as well as post modernist, meta-fiction or any other form or fashion a writer might try." Annual prize of $500 for best fiction, $500 for best new writer (poetry or fiction), $500 for best poetry; additional prizes, $250-1,000.

PRIMAVERA, (II, IV), Box 37-7547, Chicago IL 60637. (312)324-5920. Editorial Board. Magazine: 5½×8½; 100 pages; 60 lb. paper; glossy cover; illustrations; photos. Literature and graphics reflecting the experiences of women: poetry, short stories, photos, drawings. Readership: "an audience interested in women's ideas and experiences." Annually. Estab. 1975. Circ. 1,000.
• *Primavera* has won grants from the Illinois Arts Council and from Chicago Women in Publishing.
Needs: Literary, contemporary, science fiction, fantasy, feminist, gay/lesbian and humor. "We dislike slick stories packaged for more traditional women's magazines. We publish only work reflecting the experiences of women, but also publish mss by men." Accepts 6-10 mss/issue. Receives approximately 40 unsolicited fiction mss each month. Recently published work by S.L. Marin, Cathryn Camper, Elizabeth Woodbury, Birthalene Miller; published new writers within the last year. Length: 25 pages maximum. Also publishes poetry. Critiques rejected mss when there is time. Often gives suggestions

for revisions and invites re-submission of revised ms. Occasionally recommends other markets.
How to Contact: Send complete ms with SASE (IRCs). Cover letter not necessary. No simultaneous submissions. Reports in 1 week—5 months on mss. Publishes ms up to 1 year after acceptance. Sample copy $5; $9 for recent issues. Guidelines for SASE.
Payment: Pays 2 contributor's copies.
Terms: Acquires first rights.

★PRISM INTERNATIONAL, (I, II), E462-1866 Main Mall, University of British Columbia, Vancouver, British Columbia V6T 1Z1 Canada. (604)822-2514. Executive Editors: Patricia Gabin, Vigeland B. Rubin. Editor: Anna Nobile. Magazine: 6×9; 72-80 pages; Zephyr book paper; Cornwall, coated one side cover; photos on cover. "A journal of contemporary writing—fiction, poetry, drama, creative non-fiction and translation. *Prism*'s audience is world-wide, as are our contributors." Readership: "Public and university libraries, individual subscriptions, bookstores—an audience concerned with the contemporary in literature." Quarterly. Estab. 1959. Circ. 1,200.
● *Prism International* has received a Canadian National Magazine Award.
Needs: Literary, contemporary, prose poem or translations. "Most any category as long as it is *fresh*. No overtly religious, overtly theme-heavy material or anything more message- or category-oriented than self-contained." Buys approximately 70 mss/year. Receives 50-100 unsolicited fiction mss each month. Published new writers within the last year. Length: 5,000 words maximum "though flexible for outstanding work." Publishes short shorts. Also publishes poetry. Critiques rejected mss when there is time.
How to Contact: Send complete ms with SASE or SAE, IRC and cover letter with bio, information and publications list. "Keep it simple. US contributors take note: US stamps are not valid in Canada and your ms will not likely be returned if it contains US stamps. Send International Reply Coupons instead." Reports in 6 months. Sample copy $5 (U.S./Canadian).
Payment: Pays $20 (Canadian)/printed page, 1 year's subscription.
Terms: Pays on publication for first North American serial rights.
Advice: "Too many derivative, self-indulgent pieces; sloppy construction and imprecise word usage. There's not enough attention to voice and not enough invention. We are committed to publishing outstanding literary work in all genres. We are on the lookout for strong, believable characters; real 'voices'; interesting ideas/plots. We *do not* want 'genre' fiction (i.e., romance, horror) . . . which does not mean genres should be avoided . . . rather, they should be integrated." Sponsors annual short fiction contest. Contest issue comes out in April. Grand prize is $2,000 (Canadian). Send SASE (IRC) for details.

PRISONERS OF THE NIGHT, An Adult Anthology of Erotica, Fright, Allure and . . . Vampirism, (II, IV), MKASHEF Enterprises, P.O. Box 688, Yucca Valley CA 92286-0688. Editor: Alayne Gelfand. Magazine: 8½×11; 50-80 pages; 20 lb. paper; slick cover; perfect-bound; illustrations. "An adult, erotic vampire anthology of original character stories and poetry. Heterosexual and homosexual situations included." Annually. Estab. 1987. Circ. approx. 5,000.
Needs: "All stories must be vampire stories, with unique characters, unusual situations." Adventure, contemporary, erotica, experimental, fantasy, feminist, gay, lesbian, literary, mystery/suspense, prose poem, psychic/supernatural/occult, romance (gothic, romantic suspense), science fiction (soft/sociological), western (adult). No fiction that deals with anyone else's creations, i.e., no "Dracula" stories. Receives 30-50 unsolicited fiction mss/month. Buys 5-12 mss/issue. Publishes ms 1-11 months after acceptance. Recently published work by M.C. Sumner, Nancy Kilpatrick, James S. Dorr, Kevin Kirk; published new writers within the last year. Length: under 10,000 words. Publishes short shorts. Sometimes critiques rejected mss. Recommends other markets.
How to Contact: Send complete ms with short cover letter. "A brief introduction of author to the editor; name, address, *some* past credits if available." Reports in 1-3 weeks on queries; 2-4 months on mss. Reads *only* September-March. SASE. No simultaneous submissions. Accepts electronic submissions via IBM Word Perfect (4.2 or 5.1) disk. Sample copy #1-4, $15; #5, $12; #6, $9.95; #7, $9.95. Fiction guidelines for #10 SAE and 1 first-class stamp (IRCs).
Payment: Pays 1¢/word for fiction.
Terms: Pays on publication for first North American serial rights.
Advice: "Let's face it, there's not much that's completely 'new,' 'unique' or 'daring' left to write about anymore. Especially not in such a limited genre as vampires. But *POTN* is looking for stories that approach themes with a new slant, a different angle, an alien eye. *POTN* wants to hear new voices, new tones to the old tunes, imaginative points of view. Counts and Countesses are definitely out. The pick up at the single's bar has been done to death. The hitchhiker on the road is last decade's news.

And, although it's a contemporary topic, we prefer not to address the issue of AIDS as it relates to vampires. *POTN* wants to read your story and be surprised, delighted, intrigued. *POTN* does *not* want to be put off by pornography or obscenity. Please don't add sex to an already finished story; sex must be an integral part of the tale. Explicitness is not necessary, but it is acceptable. *POTN* stresses the romantic aspects of the vampire as opposed to the bloody, gory, horrific aspects. No 'slasher' stories here, please! And it's an absolute must that you send for guidelines before submitting."

PROCESSED WORLD, (II), #1829, 41 Sutter St., San Francisco CA 94104. (415)626-2979. Editor: collective. Magazine: 8½×11; 64 pages; 20 lb. bond paper; glossy cover stock; illustrations; photos. "Magazine about work, office work, computers and hi-tech (satire)." Biannually. May publish special fiction issue. Estab. 1981. Circ. 5,000.
Needs: Comics, confession, "tales of toil," contemporary, fantasy, humor/satire, literary, science fiction. Acquires 1-2 mss/issue; 3-6 mss/year. Recently published work by James Pollack. Published new writers within the last year. Length: 1,250 words average; 100 words minimum; 1,500 words maximum. Occasionally critiques rejected ms.
How to Contact: Send complete ms. Reports in 4 months. SASE (IRCs). Simultaneous submissions OK. Sample copy $5.
Payment: Pays subscription to magazine.
Terms: Acquires one-time rights.
Advice: "Make it real. Make it critical of the status quo. Read the magazine before you send us a story."

PROPHETIC VOICES, An International Literary Journal, (II), Heritage Trails Press, 94 Santa Maria Dr., Novato CA 94947. (415)897-5679. Editor: Goldie L. Morales. Fiction Editors: Ruth Wildes Schuler and Jeanne Leigh Schuler. Magazine: 6¾×8¼; 100-144 pages; bond paper; textured cover; illustrations and photographs. "Material with a social awareness/ecology slant for an adult audience. Interested in material from other countries." Semiannually.
Needs: Historical (general) and prose poem. "We want gripping material that is also educational." No religious, sexual, juvenile, sports, young adult. Receives 10 unsolicited mss/month. Acquires 1 or 2 mss/issue; 3 or 4 mss/year. Publishes ms 1-3 years after acceptance. Published work by P. Raja, Denver Stull and Kirpal Gordon. Publishes short shorts. Recommends other markets.
How to Contact: Send complete ms. Reports in 5 weeks on queries; 3 months on mss. SASE (IRCs). Simultaneous and reprint submissions OK. Sample copy $6.
Payment: Pays contributor's copy.
Terms: Acquires one-time rights.
Advice: "A story should be different, educational—one that a reader is not likely to forget. Material must have universal and timeless appeal. We are not interested in trendy stories or those appealing only to a limited region or geographical locale."

PROVINCETOWN ARTS, (II), Provincetown Arts, Inc., 650 Commercial St., P.O. Box 35, Provincetown MA 02657. (508)487-3167. Editor: Christopher Busa. Magazine: 9×12; 184 pages; 60 lb. uncoated paper; 12 pcs. cover; illustrations and photographs. "*PA* focuses broadly on the artists, writers and theater of America's oldest continuous art colony." Annually. Estab. 1985. Circ. 8,000.
  • This large-format arts publication has had work included in the *Pushcart Prize* anthology, *Best American Poetry* and *Best American Essays*. It also won First Place for Editorial Content and Cover Design from the American Literary Magazine Awards in 1992.
Needs: Plans special fiction issue. Receives 300 unsolicited mss/year. Buys 5 mss/issue. Publishes ms 3 months after acceptance. Recently published work by Carole Maso and Hilary Masters. Length: 3,000 words average; 1,500 words minimum; 8,000 words maximum. Publishes short shorts. Length: 1,500-8,000 words. Also publishes literary essays, literary criticism, poetry. Sometimes critiques rejected mss and recommends other markets.
How to Contact: Send complete ms with cover letter including previous publications. No simultaneous submissions. Reports in 2 weeks on queries; 3 months on mss. SASE (IRCs). Sample copy $7.50. Reviews novels and short story collections.
Payment: Pays $75-300.
Terms: Pays on publication for first rights. Sends galleys to author.

PSI, (II), Suite 856, 1377 K Street NW, Washington DC 20005. Editor: A.P. Samuels. Magazine: 8½ × 11; 32 pages; bond paper; self cover. "Mystery and romance." Bimonthly. Estab. 1987.
Needs: Romance (contemporary, historical, young adult), mystery/suspense (private eye), western (traditional). Receives 35 unsolicited mss/month. Buys 1-2 mss/issue. Length: 10,000 words average. Critiques rejected mss "only on a rare occasion."
How to Contact: Send complete ms with cover letter. Reports in 2 weeks on queries; 1 month on mss. SASE (IRCs). No simultaneous submissions. Accepts electronic submissions via disk.
Payment: Pays 1-4¢/word plus royalty.
Terms: Pays on acceptance for first North American serial rights.
Advice: "Manuscripts must be for a general audience. Just good plain story telling (make it compelling). No explicit sex or ghoulish violence."

PSYCHOTRAIN, (II), Hyacinth House Publications, P.O. Box 120, Fayetteville AR 72702-0120. Editor: Shannon Frach. Magazine: 8½ × 11; 25-35 pages; 20 lb. paper; cardstock; illustrations. "*PsychoTrain* is a journal of poetry, fiction, and art that welcomes intense, earthy, decadent, and often risqué work from a wide array of authors, including both beginners and more established. I publish for a generally left-of-center audience that appreciates humor noir, radical writing, and tough, edgy fiction." Estab. 1991. Circ. 200.
• Hyacinth House Publications also publishes *Brownbag Press*. There is no need to submit to both, says the editor, because manuscripts will be considered for all.
Needs: Condensed/excerpted novel, erotica, ethnic, experimental, feminist, gay, humor/satire, lesbian, literary, prose poem, psychic/supernatural/occult, translations, "Pagan, Dada/surrealism, counterculture, subcultural writing of any and all persuasions." No candy-coated, dandyfied fiction here. Just pure, old-fashioned decadence. Nothing didactic. No hand-wringing sentimentalism. No whining unless it's really damned funny." Plans special fiction issue. Receives 175 unsolicited mss/month. Accepts 5-7 mss/issue. Publishes ms 1 year after acceptance. Recently published work by Gomez Robespierre, C.F. Roberts, Joseph Benzola, Aldo Alvarez. Length: 50 words minimum; 3,500 words maximum; 1,000-3,000 preferred. Publishes short shorts. Sometimes critiques rejected mss and recommends other markets.
How to Contact: Send complete ms with cover letter. "A cover letter is not necessary. If you send one, don't give me a mere list of credits or whine about how nobody understands you because you're a sensitive artist. A friendly note always beats a cold, pedantic, computerized form letter. And no plot synopses, please. Reports in 2-6 months on mss. SASE. Simultaneous and reprint submissions OK. Sample copy for $3 and 4 first-class stamps. Fiction guidelines for #10 SAE and 1 first-class stamp (IRCs).
Payment: Acquires one-time rights.
Terms: Acquires one-time rights.
Advice: "*Psychotrain* is a publication that we're attempting to make more outrageous with each issue. Given this, it makes little sense to keep sending us tame, boring, sterile manuscripts. We get mountains of them, especially from writing programs. We're glad that the academic crowd has discovered us and is showing their undying support by flooding us with unsolicited manuscripts, but please realize that any story that is conformist enough to be pounded like hamburger through the average McWorkshop isn't going to make it past the first cut. Be as sinister and twisted as possible. Take your most bizarre story out from under your mattress and ask yourself how you can make it even wilder. Write up that draft, and then do a mindbendingly weird rewrite of it. Then send it in. Be sure your name and address is on the manuscript itself, as well as an approximate word count. Please tell us whether or not your ms is disposable."

PUCK!, The Unofficial Journal of the Irrepressible, (II), Permeable Press, Studio 15, 900 Tennessee, San Francisco CA 94107-3014. (415)648-2175. Editor: Brian Clark. Fiction Editor: Kurt Putnam. Magazine: 8½ × 11; 80 pages; recycled uncoated paper; coated cover; illustrations and photos. "Our audience does not accept mainstream media as presenting anything even vaguely resembling reality. We publish poetry, prose and dozens of reviews in our humble attempt to counteract the hogwash of *Time, Paris Review,* et al." Triannually. Estab. 1984. Circ. 2,500.
Needs: Condensed novel, erotica, ethnic/multicultural, experimental, fantasy (science fantasy), feminist, gay, historical (general), horror, humor/satire, lesbian, literary, psychic/supernatural/occult, regional, religious/inspirational, science fiction (hard science, soft/sociological, cyberpunk), translations. Upcoming themes: Plans a 10th Anniversary Issue (October 1994). List of upcoming themes available for SASE. Receives 100 unsolicited mss/month. Buys 3-10 mss/issue; 25 mss/year. Publishes ms within 6 months after acceptance. Agented fiction 10%. Published work by Stan Henry, Hugh Fox, Belinda

Subraman. Publishes short shorts. Also publishes literary essays, literary criticism, poetry. Sometimes critiques or comments on rejected mss.
How to Contact: Send complete ms with cover letter. Should include bio (under 50 words), list of publications. Reports in 2 months. Send SASE (IRC) for reply or return of ms. No simultaneous submissions. Accepts reprints and electronic (disk or modem) submissions. Sample copy $6.50. Fiction guidelines for #10 SAE and 2 first-class stamps or IRCs. Reviews novels and short story collections. Send review copies to Attn: Reviews Editor at above address.
Payment: Pays 2 or more contributor's copies plus honorarium (40%)
Terms: Payment on publication. Buys first North American serial rights.
Advice: Looks for "a certain 'je ne sais quois' — as if the work has been channeled or written in a fit of brilliant rage. Keep trying to pull your head out of this ocean of bogus media we're being drowned in. Subscribe." E-mail address: bcclark@igc.apc.org.

PUCKERBRUSH REVIEW, (I, II), Puckerbrush Press, 76 Main St., Okono ME 04473. (207)866-4868/ 581-3832. Editor: Constance Hunting. Magazine: 9×12; 80-100 pages; illustrations. "We publish mostly new Maine writers; interviews, fiction, reviews, poetry for a literary audience." Semiannually. Estab. 1979. Circ. approx. 500.
Needs: Experimental, gay (occasionally), literary, belles-lettres. "Nothing cliché." Receives 30 unsolicited mss/month. Accepts 6 mss/issue; 12 mss/year. Publishes ms 1 year after acceptance. Recently published work by Deborah Pease, James Kelman. Sometimes publishes short shorts. Also publishes literary essays, literary criticism, poetry. Sometimes critiques rejected mss and recommends other markets.
How to Contact: Send complete ms with cover letter. Reports in 2 months. SASE. Simultaneous submissions OK. Sample copy $2. Fiction guidelines for SASE (IRCs). Sometimes reviews novels and short story collections.
Payment: Pays in contributor's copies.
Advice: "Just write the story as it would like you to do."

PUERTO DEL SOL, (I), New Mexico State University, Box 3E, Las Cruces NM 88003. (505)646-3931. Editors: Antonya Nelson and Kevin McIlvay. Magazine: 6×9; 200 pages; 60 lb. paper; 70 lb. cover stock; photos sometimes. "We publish quality material from anyone. Poetry, fiction, art, photos, interviews, reviews, parts-of-novels, long poems." Semiannual. Estab. 1961. Circ. 1,500.
Needs: Contemporary, ethnic, experimental, literary, mainstream, prose poem, excerpted novel and translations. Receives varied number of unsolicited fiction mss/month. Acquires 8-10 mss/issue; 12-15 mss/year. Does not read mss May-August. Recently published work by Ricard Augilar Melantzon, Steven Schwartz and Judith Ortiz Cofer; published new writers within the last year. Also publishes poetry. Occasionally critiques rejected mss.
How to Contact: Send complete ms with SASE (IRCs). Simultaneous submissions OK. Reports in 2 months. Sample copy $7.
Payment: Pays 2 contributor's copies.
Terms: Acquires one-time rights (rights revert to author).
Advice: "We are open to all forms of fiction, from the conventional to the wildly experimental, as long as they have integrity and are well written. Too often we receive very impressively 'polished' mss that will dazzle readers with their sheen but offer no character/reader experience of lasting value."

PULPHOUSE, A Fiction Magazine, (I, II), Box 1227, Eugene OR 97440. Publisher: Dean Wesley Smith. Editor: Jonathan Bond. Magazine: 8½×11; 64 pages; saddle-stitched; web-printed. Estab. 1988. Has 10,000 copies in print.
   ● Pulphouse Publishing has several lines of books, mostly featuring short stories or novellas by single authors. Submissions are by invitation *only. Pulphouse* magazine ranked #3 on the *Writer's Digest* Fiction 50 list. In both 1991 and 1992 *Pulphouse* was nominated for a Hugo Award for Best Magazine of its size.
Needs: Fantasy, horror, science fiction, speculative fiction. Published work by Harlan Ellison, Kate Wilhelm, Michael Bishop, Charles de Line, George Alec Effinger; published new writers within the last year. Length: 7,500 words maximum.
How to Contact: Send complete ms with cover letter "that gives publication history, work history, or any other information relevant to the magazine. Don't tell us about the story. The story will tell us about the story." SASE. Reports in 2 months. Sample copy for $3.95. Fiction guidelines for #10 SAE and 1 first-class stamp (IRCs).

Payment: Pays 4-7¢/word.
Terms: Pays on acceptance for first serial rights.
Advice: "*Pulphouse* needs fiction that takes risks, that presents viewpoints not commonly held in the field. Although such fiction can include experimental writing, it is usually best served by clean, clear prose. We are looking for strong characterization, fast-moving plot, and intriguing settings."

QUANTA, (I), #S919, 3003 Van Ness St. NW, Washington DC 20008. Editor: Daniel K. Appelquist. Electronic magazine: 8½×11; 35-40 pages; illustrations; photos. "*Quanta* is primarily an electronic publication, distributed across computer networks to an international audience. It is dedicated to bringing the works of new and amateur authors to a wide readership." Bimonthly. Estab. 1989. Circ. 2,200.
  • *Quanta* was runner-up for "Best Regular Literary Publication" in the Disktop Publishing Associations' Digital Quill Awards.
Needs: Fantasy (science fantasy), psychic/supernatural/occult, science fiction (hard science, soft/sociological). Plans special fiction issue or anthology. Receives 20 mss/month. Accepts 5 mss/issue; 20 mss/year. Publishes 1-2 months after acceptance. Published work by J. Palmer Hall, Michael C. Berch, Jason Suell and Phillip Nolte. Publishes short shorts. Also publishes literary essays, literary criticism, poetry. Always critiques rejected manuscripts.
How to Contact: Send complete ms with a cover letter; send ms in electronic form (disk or E-mail). Should include estimated word count, short bio and list of publications. Reports in 3 weeks on queries; 2 months on manuscripts. Send SASE (IRCs) for reply, return of ms or send disposable copy of ms. Simultaneous, reprint and electronic submissions OK. Sample copy for SAE and 5 first-class stamps. Fiction guidelines for 8½×11 SAE.
Payment: Pays 1 contributor copy.
Terms: Acquires one-time rights.
Advice: "Interesting or novel narratorial style or good content. I shy away from 'formula' pieces (e.g., hack 'n' slash fantasy). Send electronic manuscript if possible."

✱QUARRY, (II), Quarry Press, Box 1061, Kingston, Ontario K7L 4Y5 Canada. (613)548-8429. Editor: Steven Heighton. Magazine: 7¼×9¼; 120 pages; #1 book 120 paper; 160 lb. Curtis Tweed cover stock; illustrations; photos. "Quarterly anthology of new Canadian poetry, prose. Also includes graphics, photo essays, travelogues, photographs and book reviews. We seek readers interested in vigorous, disciplined, new Canadian writing." Published special fiction issue; plans another. Estab. 1952. Circ. 1,100.
Needs: Experimental, fantasy, literary, serialized/excerpted novel and translations. "We do not want highly derivative or clichéd style." Receives 80-100 unsolicited fiction mss/month. Buys 4-5 mss/issue; 20 mss/year. Does not read in July. Less than 5% of fiction is agented. Published work by Diane Schoemperlen, David Helwig, Joan Fern Shaw; published new writers within the last year. Length: 3,000 words average. Publishes short shorts. Usually critiques rejected mss and recommends other markets.
How to Contact: Send complete ms with SAE, IRC and brief bio. Publishes ms an average of 3-6 months after acceptance. Sample copy $5 with 4×7 SAE and 46¢ Canadian postage or IRC.
Payment: Pays $10/page; 1 year subscription to magazine and 1 contributor's copy.
Terms: Pays on publication for first North American serial rights.
Advice: "Read previous *Quarry* to see standard we seek. Read Canadian fiction to see Canadian trends. We seek aggressive experimentation which is coupled with competence (form, style) and stimulating subject matter. We also like traditional forms. Our annual prose issue (spring) is always a sellout. Many of our selections have been anthologized. Don't send US stamps or SASE (if outside Canada). Use IRC. Submit with brief bio."

QUARTERLY WEST, (II), University of Utah, 317 Olpin Union, Salt Lake City UT 84112. (801)581-3938. Editor: Marty Williams. Fiction Editors: Lawrence Coates, Jan Stucki and Kirsten Scott. Editors change periodically. Magazine: 6×9; 150+ pages; 60 lb. paper; 5-color cover stock; illustrations and photographs. "We try to publish a variety of fiction and poetry from all over the country based not so much on the submitting author's reputation but on the merit of each piece. Our publication is aimed primarily at an educated audience interested in contemporary literature and criticism." Semiannual. "We sponsor a biennial novella competition." Estab. 1976. Circ. 1,000.
Needs: Literary, contemporary, translations. Buys 4-6 mss/issue, 10-12 mss/year. Receives approximately 100 unsolicited fiction mss each month. Published work by Andre Dubus and Chuck Rosenthal; published new writers within the last year. No preferred length; interested in longer, "fuller" short

stories. Critiques rejected mss when there is time. Sometimes recommends other markets.
How to Contact: Send complete ms. Cover letters welcome. SASE. Simultaneous submissions OK.
Reports in 2 months; "sooner, if possible." Sample copy for $6.50.
Payment: Pays $15-300.
Terms: Pays on publication for first North American serial rights.
Advice: Mss are rejected because of "poor style, formula writing, clichés, weak characterization. We solicit quite frequently, but tend more toward the surprises—unsolicited. Don't send more than one story per submission, but submit as often as you like."

QUEEN OF ALL HEARTS, (II), Queen Magazine, Montfort Missionaries, 26 S. Saxon Ave., Bay Shore NY 11706. (516)665-0726. Managing Editor: Roger M. Charest, S.M.M. Magazine: 7¾×10¾; 48 pages; self cover stock; illustrations; photos. Magazine of "stories, articles and features on the Mother of God by explaining the Scriptural basis and traditional teaching of the Catholic Church concerning the Mother of Jesus, her influence in fields of history, literature, art, music, poetry, etc." Bimonthly. Estab. 1950. Circ. 5,000.
• *Queen of All Hearts* received a second-place award for "Best Catholic Magazine on Prayer and Spirituality" from the Catholic Press Association.
Needs: Religious/inspirational. "No mss not about Our Lady, the Mother of God, the Mother of Jesus." Length: 1,500-2,000 words. Sometimes recommends other markets.
How to Contact: Send complete ms with SASE (IRCs). No simultaneous submissions. Reports in 1 month on mss. Publishes ms 6-12 months after acceptance. Sample copy for $2.50 with 9×12 SAE.
Payment: Varies. Pays 6 contributor's copies.
Advice: "We are publishing stories with a Marian theme."

✿QUEEN'S QUARTERLY, A Canadian Review, (II, IV), Queen's University, Kingston, Ontario K7L 3N6 Canada. (613)545-2667. Editor: Boris Castel. Magazine: 6×9; 800 pages/year; illustrations. "A general interest intellectual review, featuring articles on science, politics, humanities, arts and letters. Book reviews, poetry and fiction." Published quarterly. Estab. 1893. Circ. 3,000.
Needs: Adventure, contemporary, experimental, fantasy, historical (general), humor/satire, literary, mainstream, science fiction and women's. "*Special emphasis on work by Canadian writers.*" Buys 2 mss/issue; 8 mss/year. Published work by Janette Turner Hospital; published new writers within the last year. Length: 5,000 words maximum. Also publishes literary essays, literary criticism, poetry.
How to Contact: "Send complete ms and a copy on disk in Wordperfect—only one at a time—with SASE (IRCs)." No simultaneous or multiple submissions. Reports within 3 months. Sample copy for $6.50. Reviews novels and short story collections.
Payment: Pays $100-300 for fiction, 2 contributor's copies and 1-year subscription; $5 charge for extras.
Terms: Pays on publication for first North American serial rights. Sends galleys to author.

RADIO VOID, (II), P.O. Box 5983, Providence RI 02903. Publisher: Brian T. Gallagher. Fiction Editor: Christopher Pierson. Magazine: 5½×8½; 112 pages; offset; illustrations and photographs (varies). "Conflicting, themeless variety...an eclectic blend in which, when sifted, can be found a common literary thread." Annual. Estab. 1986. Circ. 1,000.
Needs: Open to all types of fiction. Receives approximately 20 unsolicited fiction mss/month. Accepts 8-10 mss/issue; 100-150 mss/year. Publishes ms 6-7 months after acceptance. Published work by Eric Getz and Laurie Lindop. Length: Open. Publishes short shorts. Also publishes literary essays, literary criticism, poetry. Critiques or comments on rejected mss.
How to Contact: Send complete ms with a cover letter. Include name, address, biographical paragraph. No simultaneous submissions. Reports in 2 months on queries; 3-6 months on mss. SASE (IRCs). Sample copy for $5. Fiction guidelines for #15 SAE and 1 first-class stamp. Reviews novels and short story collections. Send books to Zoë Pierson.
Payment: Pays in contributor's copies and free business card-size ad.
Terms: "We do not purchase rights--author offers us a loan."

RAFALE, Supplement Littéraire, (II, IV), Franco-American Research Organization Group, University of Maine, Franco American Center, Orono ME 04473-1581. (207)581-3775. Fax: (207)581-1455. Editor: Rhea Robbins. Tabloid size, magazine format: 4 pages; illustrations and photos. Publication was founded to stimulate and recognize creative expression among Franco-Americans, all types of readers, including literary and working class. Monthly except July and August. Estab. 1986. Circ. 5,000.

Needs: "We will consider any type of short fiction, poetry and critical essays having to do with Franco-American experience. They must be of good quality in French as well as English. We are also looking for Canadian writers with French-North American experiences." Receives about 10 unsolicited mss/month. Accepts 2-4 mss/issue. Published work by Robert Cormier; published new writers within the last year. Length: 1,000 words average; 750 words minimum; 2,500 words maximum. Occasionally critiques rejected mss.

How to Contact: Send complete ms with cover letter, which should include a short bio and list of previous publications. Reports in 3 weeks on queries; 1 month on mss. SASE (IRCs). Simultaneous and reprint submissions OK.

Payment: Pays $10 and 3 copies.

Terms: Buys one-time rights.

Advice: "Write honestly. Start with a strongly felt personal Franco-American experience and develop it with a beginning, middle and end. If you make us feel what you have felt, we will publish it."

RAG MAG, (II), Box 12, Goodhue MN 55027. (612)923-4590. Publisher/Editor: Beverly Voldseth. Magazine: 6×9; 60-112 pages; varied paper quality; illustrations; photos. "We are eager to print poetry, prose and art work. We are open to all styles." Semiannual. Estab. 1982. Circ. 300.

Needs: Adventure, comics, contemporary, erotica, ethnic, experimental, fantasy, feminist, literary, mainstream, prose poem, regional. "Anything well written is a possibility. No extremely violent or pornographic writing." Receives 100 unsolicited mss/month. Accepts 4 mss/issue. Published work by Egon Ludowese, Rusty McKenzie, Spencer Reece and Tracy Nordstrom; published new writers within the last year. Length: 1,000 words average; 2,200 words maximum. Occasionally critiques rejected mss. Sometimes recommends other markets.

How to Contact: Send 3-6 pages. Reports in 3-4 weeks. SASE (IRCs). Simultaneous and previously published submissions OK. Single copy for $6.

Payment: Pays 1 contributor's copy; $4.50 charge for extras.

Terms: Acquires one-time rights.

Advice: "Submit clean copy on regular typing paper (no tissue-thin stuff). We want fresh images, sparse language, words that will lift us out of our chairs. I like the short story form. I think it's powerful and has a definite place in the literary magazine."

‡RAJAH (I, II), The Rackham Journal of the Arts and Humanities, 411 Mason Hall, University of Michigan, Ann Arbor MI 48109-1027. Fiction Editor: Anna Dalby. Magazine: 6×9; approx. 100 pages; 60 lb off-white stock; 10 pt, perfect bound cover; illustrations and photos. "Our interest is in quality poetry, short fiction, essays, criticism and translations by new and established authors who are mostly graduate students at the University of Michigan, for an educated reading public." Annually. Estab. 1971. Circ. 500.

Needs: Adventure, confession, contemporary, ethnic, experimental, fantasy, feminist, historical (general), horror, humor/satire, lesbian, literary, mainstream, regional, serialized/excerpted novel, translations. No children's, pornographic or obscene fiction. Receives 2 unsolicited mss/month. Accepts approximately 1 ms/issue from author outside University of Michigan. Publishes ms no more than 2 years after acceptance. Length: 2,500 words average; 5,000 words maximum. Critiques rejected mss. Also publishes literary essays, literary criticism, poetry. Occasionally recommends other markets.

How to Contact: Send complete ms with cover letter, which should include date, brief bio, publications record (if any). Reports on mss in 6-10 months. SASE (IRCs). Accepts electronic submissions compatible with Apple Macintosh (preferred), or IBM compatible floppy disk using Microsoft Word. Sample copy for $1.50, 6½×9½ SAE and 95¢ postage.

Advice: "We are especially interested in material focusing on social issues and current culture, and we are always on the lookout for manuscripts by unpublished authors. We believe that both fiction and scholarly articles reflect that kind of work being produced by talented young people around the world. *RaJAH* is primarily a graduate student publication but accepts a limited number of manuscripts from unsolicited authors."

RANDOM REALITIES, (II), 1304 Pirkle Rd., Norcross GA 30093. Editor: Jeff Dennis. Magazine: 5½×8½; 68-76 pages; 60 lb. cream offset paper; semi-gloss 65 lb. cover; b&w illustrations and photographs. "Science fiction, horror, and fantasy for a literate audience of 25 and up. Our readers are interested in commercial fiction that is unique, often blending styles from several genres. Our aim is a wide variety of speculative fiction in every issue." Triannual. Estab. 1992. Circ. 400.

Needs: Fantasy (children's fantasy, science fantasy, sword and sorcery), horror (psychological, supernatural), science fiction (hard science, soft/sociological). No "Star Trek, possessed or abused children, or blatant slasher stories. No mindless violence or unnecessary gore." We publish very little with children or teenage protagonists—most of our fiction centers around adult themes. Receives 125-200 unsolicited mss/month. Acquires 6-10 mss/issue; 20-30 mss/year. Publishes ms 3-12 months after acceptance. Length: 2,000-4,000 words preferred; no minimum; 7,000 words maximum. No unsolicited poetry.

How to Contact: Send complete ms with cover a letter. Should include estimated word count, 50-100 word bio, list of publications. Reports in 6-10 weeks on mss. Proper SASE (IRCs) for reply or return of ms. No simultaneous submissions and please, only one story submission at a time. Sample copy for $4.50 plus $1 postage and handling. (Checks/money orders payable to Random Realities Publications.) Fiction guidelines for #10 SASE.

Payment: Pays ½¢/word and 1 contributor's copy on publication.

Terms: Buys first North American serial rights. Sends galleys to author.

Advice: "We like to showcase the work of new and established writers, so publishing credits are not as important as effective storytelling. Your stories should center around the human condition and contain some form of human interaction so that our readers can identify with the characters. Give your characters intriguing occupations or interests, put them in mysterious and/or dangerous situations, and place them in exotic and bizarre settings. If it's horror, make us shiver with fright. If it's science fiction, give us a reality that is awe inspiring, but don't bog the story down with too much high technology. If it's fantasy, dazzle us with magic and imagery. Above all, make your tales unique. The only way you'll know if you have a unique concept is to read, read, read, in your area(s) of interest. Buy a sample copy or subscription—this will tell you far more about our editorial tastes than will even the most detailed of fiction guidelines. We like a good mix of dialogue and narrative. Pull us into your world on that first page, keep the story moving, add a twist or two along the way, and you've probably got a sale."

THE RAVEN CHRONICLES, a Magazine of Multicultural Art, Literature and the Spoken Word, (II), The Raven Chronicles, P. O. Box 95918, Seattle WA 98145. (206)543-0249. Editors: Annie Hansen and Arthur Tulee. Magazine: 8½ × 11; 48-64 pages; 50 lb. book paper; glossy cover; b&w illustrations; photos. *"The Raven Chronicles* is designed to promote multicultural art, literature and the spoken word." Triannual. Estab. 1991. Circ. 1,000-2,500.
  • This magazine is a frequent winner of Bumbershoot Bookfair awards.

Needs: Ethnic/multicultural, literary, regional. Receives 45-50 mss/month. Buys 2-3 mss/issue; 8 mss/ year. Publishes 3-6 months after acceptance. Recently published work by David Romtvedt, Sherman Alexie, D.L. Birchfield and Bill Ransom. Length: 2,000 words average; 2,500 words maximum. Publishes short shorts. Length: 300-500 words. Also publishes literary essays, literary criticism, poetry. Sometimes critiques rejected mss.

How to Contact: Send complete ms with a cover letter. Should include estimated word count. Reports in 3-6 months on manuscripts. Send SASE (IRCs) for return of ms. Simultaneous submissions OK. Sample copy for $2 plus $1.21 postage. Fiction guidelines for #10 SAE and 1 first-class stamp.

Payment: Pays $10-25 plus 2 contributor's copies; additional copies at half cover cost.

Terms: Pays on publication for first North American serial rights. Sends galleys to author.

Advice: Looks for "clean, direct language, written from the heart. Read sample copy, or look at *Before Columbus* anthologies, *Greywolf Annual* anthologies."

RE ARTS & LETTERS [REAL], (II), "A Liberal Arts Forum," Stephen F. Austin State University, P.O. Box 13007, Nacogdoches TX 75962. (409)568-2101. Editor: Lee Schultz. Academic journal: 6 × 10; perfect-bound; 120-150 pages; "top" stock. "65-75% of pages composed of fiction (2-4 stories per issue), poetry (20-60 per issue), an occasional play, book reviews (assigned after query) and interviews. Other 25-35% comprised of articles in scholarly format. Work is reviewed based on the intrinsic merit of the scholarship and creative work and its appeal to a sophisticated international readership (U.S., Canada, Great Britain, Ireland, Brazil, Puerto Rico, Italy)." Semiannual. Estab. 1968. Circ. 400.

Needs: Adventure, contemporary, genre, feminist, science fiction, historical, experimental, regional. No beginners. Receives 35-70 unsolicited mss per month. Accepts 2-5 fiction mss/issue. Reads mss September-April. Publishes 1-6 months after acceptance; one year for special issues. Published work by Joe R. Lansdale, Lewis Shiner, Walter McDonald, Peter Mattheisson. Length 1,000-7,000 words. Occasionally critiques rejected mss and conditionally accepts on basis of critiques and changes. Recommends other markets.

How to Contact: Send complete ms with cover letter. No simultaneous submissions. Reports in 2 weeks on queries; 3-4 weeks on mss. SASE (IRCs). Sample copy and writer's guidelines $5. Guidelines for SASE.
Payment: Pays 1 contributor's copy; charges for extras.
Terms: Rights revert to author.
Advice: "Please study an issue. Have your work checked by a well-published writer—who is not a good friend."

‡REACH MAGAZINE, (Successor to Breakthrough! Magazine), (I, II), P.O. Box 134/Drawer 194, Pearl Harbor HI, 96860-5181. (808)484-2214. Editor: Jessie Porter. Magazine: 8½ × 11; 25 pages; bond paper; illustrations. "Families, adult and children general interest throughout North America and Canada. *Reach Magazine* has positive approach in regards to realistic views about life, love, death, friendship etc. . . . ." Quarterly. Estab. 1993. Circ. 1,500.
Needs: Adventure, children's/juvenile (10-12 years), ethnic/multicultural, humor/satire, literary, mainstream/contemporary, mystery/suspense (romantic suspense, young adult mystery), regional, religious/inspirational, romance (contemporary, young adult), senior citizen/retirement, sports, young adult/teen. No erotica, gay, feminist, horror, lesbian. Plans annual special fiction issue or anthology. Receives 5 unsolicited mss/month. Accepts 10 mss/issue; 40 mss/year. Publishes ms 3 months after acceptance. Length: 500 words minimum; 2,500 words maximum. Also publishes literary essays, literary criticism, poetry. Always critiques or comments on rejected mss.
How to Contact: Send complete ms with a cover letter. Should include estimated word count, a one-page bio with submission. Reports in 1 month. SASE (or IRCs) for return ms. Simultaneous and reprint submissions OK. Sample copy for $3, 9 × 12 SAE. Fiction guidelines for 9 × 12 SAE.
Payment: Pays 1 contributor's copy.
Terms: Acquires first North American serial rights. Not copyrighted (copyright in process at this time).
Advice: "I look for a positive approach from writer to reader, high moral standards, family togetherness and youths in a positive role. No preachy or negative overtones. Individual style and creativity. Honesty, dedication, style and creativity must never take the backseat for quick profit. Let your own creativity and style shine through your work. Remember the responsibility of the writer to the reader is much greater than simply entertainment."

RED CEDAR REVIEW, (II), Dept. of English, 17C Morrill Hall, Michigan State University, East Lansing MI 48825. (517)355-9656. Editors change. Editor until June 1994 is N. Barkiewicz. After that, contact Fiction Editor. Magazine: 5½ × 8½; 50-80 pages. Theme: "literary—poetry, fiction, book reviews, artwork." Biannual. Estab. 1963. Circ. 400.
Needs: Literary, feminist, regional and humorous. Accepts 3-4 mss/issue, 6-10 mss/year. Published new writers within the last year. Length: 500-5,000 words. Also publishes poetry, 4 poems per submission.
How to Contact: Query with unpublished ms with SASE (IRCs). No simultaneous submissions. Reports in 2-3 months on mss. Publishes ms up to 4 months after acceptance. Sample copy for $3.50.
Payment: Pays 2 contributor's copies. $5 charge for extras.
Terms: Acquires first rights.
Advice: "Read the magazine and good literary fiction. There are many good writers out there who need a place to publish, and we try to provide them with that chance for publication."

‡RED DANCEFLOOR, (I, II), Red Dancefloor Press, P.O. Box 7392, Van Nuys CA 91409-7392. Editor: David Goldschlag. Fiction Editor: Liz Ziemba. Magazine: 5½ × 8½; 100-110 pages; 60 lb. white offset paper; glossy cover stock; photos. "We have no themes; if it's good we print it. Do not publish religious material. Experimental avante garde work is welcome." Triannual. Estab. 1990. Circ. 300-400.
Needs: Experimental, feminist, literary. Accepts 7-8 mss/year. Does not read mss June-August. Publishes ms 1 year after acceptance. Recently published work by Jeff Weltman and Colleen O'Driscoll. Length: 3,500 words preferred; 5,000 words maximum. Publishes short shorts. Also publishes literary essays, literary criticism, reviews and poetry. Sometimes critiques or comments on rejected mss, if requested and time allows.
How to Contact: "Due to frequent backlogs, it would be a good idea to query first." Send complete ms with a cover letter. Should include estimated word count and 3-4 line bio. Reports in 2 weeks on queries; 8 weeks on mss. Send SASE (or IRC) for reply, return of ms or send a disposable copy of ms. Simultaneous and reprint submissions OK. Electronic (Wordperfect 5.1) submissions plus hard copy

OK. Sample copy for $6. Fiction guidelines for #10 SAE and 1 first-class stamp. Reviews novels and short story collections.
Payment: Pays 1 contributor's copy; additional copies at 20% off.
Terms: Acquires one-time rights. Sends galleys to author.

REDCAT MAGAZINE, (I), 6309 Wiley St., Hollywood FL 33023. (305)983-5684. Editor: Jim Pettit. Magazine: 5½ × 8½; 50-90 pages; 20 lb. bond paper; 90 lb. cover. "Easy reading, fright-provoking, non-pretentious horror for the masses. Consider us a training ground." Quarterly. Estab. 1991. Circ. 150.
Needs: Fantasy (dark), horror. No "gothic horror; no sword and sorcery; no science fiction; no movie rip-offs." Receives 45 unsolicited submissions/month. Buys 4-8 mss/issue; 16-32 mss/year. Publishes ms 3 months maximum after acceptance. Recently published work by Gregory Nyman, T.W. Kriner and Terry Campbell. Length: 3,500 words preferred; 2,000 words minimum; 10,000 words maximum. Always critiques or comments on rejected mss.
How to Contact: Send complete ms with cover letter. "Disk submissions *encouraged*. Any IBM format, 3.5″ or 5.25″ is OK. To save paper and postage costs, no hardcopy printout is necessary if submitting via disk." Should include estimated word count, Social Security number. "Not absolutely *necessary* but we'd like to know a *little* about you." Reports in 2 months on mss. SASE (IRCs) or send disposable copy of the ms. No simultaneous submissions. Sample copy for $4. Fiction guidelines for #10 SAE and 1 first-class stamp.
Payment: Pays $5 and 1 contributor's copy.
Terms: Pays on publication for one-time rights. Not copyrighted.
Advice: "Write to please yourself. You can't produce good work if you're not having fun trying. Good horror—at least as defined by us— comes when everyday people find themselves neck deep in some negative situation that's totally beyond their control. And remember—we're not the ultimate arbiters of taste. A rejection by us may be due more to our lack of taste than your lack of talent. Keep trying. And please—read us before submitting. We like easy-reading, fright-provoking, non-pretentious horror. A lot of writers need to expand a bit and realize that horror doesn't appear only in the dark and moldy bowels of a Transylvanian castle or on the fog-shrouded moors at midnight under a crescent moon; evil and death can just as easily show up in the middle of Disneyworld at high noon, or at the mall during the Christmas shopping rush."

THE REDNECK REVIEW OF LITERATURE, (I, II), 2919 N. Donner Ave., Milwaukee WI 53211. (414)332-6881. Editor: Penelope Reedy. Magazine: 8½ × 11; 80 pages; offset paper; cover varies from semi-glossy to felt illustrations; photos. "I consider *Redneck* to be one of the few—perhaps the only— magazines in the West seeking to bridge the gap between literate divisions. My aim is to provide literature from and to the diverse people in the western region. Readership is extremely eclectic including ranchers, farmers, university professors, writers, poets, activists, civil engineers, BLM conservation officers, farm wives, attorneys, judges, truck drivers." Semiannual. Estab. 1975. Circ. 500.
Needs: "Publishes poetry, fiction, plays, essays, book reviews and folk pieces." Upcoming theme: "Death in the West" (Spring 1994). Receives 30 "or so" unsolicited mss/month. Receives 4-5 mss/ issue. Published work by Rafael Zepeda, Clay Reynolds and Gerald Haslam; published new writers within the last year. Length: 1,500 words minimum; 2,500 words maximum. Also publishes literary essays, literary criticism, poetry.
How to Contact: Send complete ms. SASE (IRCs). May accept simultaneous submissions. Reprint submissions from established writers OK. Reports in 2-8 weeks. Sample copy for $6 with $1 postage.
Payment: Pays in contributor's copies.
Terms: Rights returned to author on publication.
Advice: "Give characters action, voices. Tell the truth rather than sentimentalize. *Redneck* deals strictly with a contemporary viewpoint/perspective, though the past can be evoked to show the reader how we got here. Nothing too academic or sentimental reminiscences. I am not interested in old-time wild west gunfighter stories."

REFLECT, (II, IV), 3306 Argonne Ave., Norfolk VA 23509. (804)857-1097). Editor: W.S. Kennedy. Magazine: 5½ × 8½; 48 pages; pen & ink illustrations. "Spiral Mode fiction and poetry for writers and poets—professional and amateur." Quarterly. Estab. 1979.
Needs: Spiral fiction. "The four rules to the Spiral Mode fiction form are: (1) The story a situation or condition. (2) The outlining of the situation in the opening paragraphs. The story being told at once, the author is not overly-involved with dialogue and plot development, may concentrate on *sound*, *style*, *color*—the superior elements in art. (3) The use of a concise style with euphonic wording. Good

poets may have the advantage here. (4) The involvement of Spiral Fiction themes—as opposed to Spiral Poetry themes—with love, and presented with the mystical overtones of the Mode." No "smut, bad taste, anarchist. . ." Accepts 2-6 mss/issue; 8-24 mss/year. Publishes ms 3 months after acceptance. Published work by Ruth Wildes Schuler, B.Z. Niditch, Patricia Anne Treat. Length: 1,500 words average; 2,500 words maximum. Publishes short shorts. Sometimes critiques rejected mss and recommends other markets.

How to Contact: Send complete ms with cover letter. Reports in 2 months on mss. SASE (IRCs). No simultaneous submissions. Sample copy $2. Free fiction guidelines.

Payment: Pays contributor's copies.

Terms: Acquires one-time rights. Publication not copyrighted.

Advice: "Subject matter usually is not relevant to the successful writing of Spiral Fiction, as long as there is some element or type of *love* in the story, and provided that there are mystical references. (Though a dream-like style may qualify as 'mystical.')"

REJECTS, The Magazine for Rejected Dark Fantasy, (I), P.O. Box 12193, Eugene OR 97440-4393. (503)683-8326. Fiction Editor: Kenneth Brady. Magazine: digest-sized; 40-50 pages; 20 lb. white paper; card cover; illustrations. "Fiction and poetry with a dark slant." Quarterly. Estab. 1992. Circ. 150.

Needs: Rejected mss. "Must be accompanied by 5 rejection slips from other publications. Fantasy (high or dark), horror, psychic/supernatural/occult, science fiction. Buys 6-8 mss/issue; 24-32/year. Publishes 2-6 months after acceptance. Length: 3,000 words maximum; query if longer. Publishes short shorts. Also publishes poetry. Always comments on rejected mss.

How to Contact: Send complete ms with a cover letter ("must have some deep wisdom of life"). Should include estimated word count, brief bio, list of publications (if any) and 5 rejection slips from other publications. Reports in 2 months. SASE (IRCs). No simultaneous submissions. Accepts electronic submissions (MS DOS ASCII format). Sample copy for $2.50 (payable to Kenneth Brady). Fiction guidelines for #10 SAE and 1 first-class stamp.

Payment: Pays 2 contributor's copies additional at ½ price.

Terms: Acquires first North American serial rights.

Advice: "*Rejects* is a publication for stories and poetry on the dark side that have met with no success so far. That doesn't mean they're not good stories—maybe the right editor has yet to see them. I would like to see more submissions in the fantasy genre. So far, I've published mostly horror. And while I like horror, I would also like a mix of more science fiction and fantasy."

RENEGADE, (II), Box 314, Bloomfield MI 48303. (313)972-5580. Editor: Michael E. Nowicki. Co-editors: Larry Snell and Miriam Jones. Magazine: 5½×8½; 32 pages; 4-5 illustrations. "We are open to all forms except erotica and we publish whatever we find good." Estab. 1988. Circ. 100.

Needs: Adventure, condensed/excerpted novel, contemporary, experimental, fantasy, feminist, historical (general), horror, humor/satire, literary, mainstream, mystery/suspense, prose poem, psychic/supernatural/occult, religious/inspirational, romance, science fiction, translations and western. Receives 40-50 unsolicited mss/month. Accepts 2 mss/issue; 4 mss/year. Publishes ms 6 months after acceptance. Published work by Sam Astrachan. Length: 400-4,000 words; 3,000 average. Publishes short shorts. Length: 400 words. Also publishes literary essays, literary criticism, poetry. Sometimes critiques rejected mss and recommends other markets.

How to Contact: Send complete ms with a cover letter. Simultaneous submissions OK. Reports in 2 weeks-1 month on queries; 3 weeks-6 months on mss. SASE (IRCs). Sample copy for $3. Fiction guidelines for #10 SAE and 1 first-class stamp. Reviews novels and short story collections.

Payment: Pays in contributor's copies.

Terms: All rights revert to author. Publication not copyrighted.

Advice: "We look for characters which appear to be real and deal with life in a real way, as well as the use of plot to forefront the clash of personalities and the theme of the work. Take advice cautiously and apply what works. Then submit it. We are always happy to critique work we read."

RENOVATED LIGHTHOUSE PUBLICATIONS, (II), P.O. Box 340251, Columbus OH 43234-0251. Editor: R. Allen Dodson. 5½×8½; 56 pages; card cover; illustrations and photographs. "Trying to define the cutting edge of literary—what modern society wants to read in quality work. Not the stuffy image of a coffee table publication, but engaging articles and stories, poetry and reviews, that is liberal and in good taste." Estab. 1986. Circ. 200.

Needs: Adventure, experimental, fantasy, historical (general), literary, mainstream, prose poem, regional, science fiction (soft/sociological), New Age. Receives 30 unsolicited mss/month. Buys 36 mss/year. Publishes ms 1½ years average after acceptance. Also publishes literary essays, literary criticism,

For a publication named Reno-vated Lighthouse, this cover has an obvious connection. "On the surface, this cover reflects the title of our magazine," says Editor R. Allen Dodson. "On a deeper level, it represents the changing nature of modern literature; old forms reworked for a new audience." Regarding the role that fiction plays in the magazine, Dodson says, "Fiction sells our magazine. People read Renovated Lighthouse to be entertained for a moment. We always try to choose work that also incorporates an important social comment or idea." The cover art is by David Drew Longey of Amherst, Massachusetts, a freelance artist and owner of Eye Food Designs.

RENOVATED LIGHTHOUSE
LITERARY MAGAZINE

MAY 1993

poetry. Sometimes critiques rejected mss and sometimes recommends other markets.
How to Contact: Query with cover letter and credits, when applicable. "Personal information and comments about the story—I like to get to know my writers." Reports in 2 months. SASE (IRCs). Rarely use previously published work and no simultaneous submissions. Sample copy for $4. Guidelines available.
Payment: Pays $1.25 and 1 contributor's copy.
Terms: Acquires first rights.

REVIEW, LATIN AMERICAN LITERATURE AND ARTS, 680 Park Ave., New York NY 10021. (212)249-8950. Editor: Alfred Mac Adam. Managing Editor: Daniel Shapiro. "Magazine of Latin American fiction, poetry and essays in translation for academic, corporate and general audience." Biannual.
Needs: Literary. No political or sociological mss. Upcoming themes: "Latin American Travelers" (Fall 1993); "Latin American Women's Writing" (Spring 1994); "Cuban Literature and Arts" (Spring 1995). Receives 5 unsolicited mss/month. Buys 8 mss/issue; 16 mss/year. Length: 1,500-2,000 words average. Occasionally critiques rejected mss.
How to Contact: Query first or send complete ms. Reports in 8 weeks. Previously published submissions OK if original was published in Spanish. Simultaneous submissions OK, if notified of acceptance elsewhere. Sample copy free. Reviews novels and short story collections. Send books to Daniel Shapiro, Managing Editor.
Payment: Pays $50-200, and 2-3 contributor's copies.
Terms: Pays on publication.
Advice: "We are always looking for good translators."

RFD, A Country Journal for Gay Men Everywhere, (I, II, IV), Short Mountain Collective, P.O. Box 68, Liberty TN 37095. (615)536-5176. Contact: The Collective. Magazine: 8½ × 11; 64-80 pages. "Focus on radical faeries, gay men's spirituality—country living." Quarterly. Estab. 1974. Circ. 3,000.
Needs: Gay: Erotica, ethnic/multicultural, experimental, fantasy, feminist, humor/satire, literary, mainstream/contemporary, mystery/suspense, psychic/supernatural/occult, regional, romance. Receives 10 unsolicited mss/month. Acquires 3 mss/issue; 12 mss/year. Length: open. Publishes short shorts. Also publishes literary essays, literary criticism and poetry.
How to Contact: Send complete ms with cover letter. Should include estimated word count. Usually reports in 6-9 months. Send SASE (IRCs) for reply, return of ms or send disposable copy of ms. Sample copy for $5. Free fiction guidelines.
Payment: Pays 1 or 2 contributor's copies.
Terms: Not copyrighted.

‡**RIVER CITY, Memphis State Review, (II),** Dept. of English, Memphis State University, Memphis TN 38152. (901)678-8888. Editor: Sharon Bryan. Magazine: 6 × 9; 100 pages. National review of poetry, fiction and nonfiction. Semiannual. Estab. 1980. Circ. 1,200.
Needs: Novel excerpts, short stories. Published work by Fred Busch; published new writers within the last year.
How to Contact: Send complete ms with SASE (IRCs). Sample copy for $4.
Payment: Annual $100 prize for best poem or best short story and 2 contributor's copies. "We pay if grant monies are available."
Terms: Acquires first North American serial rights.
Advice: "We're soliciting work from writers with a national reputation, and are occasionally able to pay, depending on grants received. I would prefer no cover letter. *River City* Writing Awards in Fiction: $2,000 1st prize, $500 2nd prize, $300 3rd prize. See magazine for details."

RIVER STYX, (II), Big River Association, 14 S. Euclid, St. Louis MO 63108. (314)361-0043. Contact: Editor. Magazine: 6 × 8; 90 pages; b&w visual art. "No theme restrictions, high quality, intelligent work." Triannual. Estab. 1975.
Needs: Excerpted novel chapter, contemporary, ethnic, experimental, feminist, gay, satire, lesbian, literary, mainstream, prose poem, translations. "Avoid 'and then I woke up' stories." Receives 15 unsolicited mss/month. Buys 1-3 mss/issue; 3-8 mss/year. Reads only in September and October. Recently published work by John High, Fanny Howe and Constance Urdang. Length: no more than 20-30 manuscript pages. Publishes short shorts. Also publishes poetry. Sometimes critiques rejected mss and recommends other markets.
How to Contact: Send complete manuscript with name and address on every page. Reports in 4 months on mss. Simultaneous submissions OK. Sample copy for $7. Fiction guidelines for #10 SAE and 1 first-class stamp.
Payment: Pays $8/page maximum and contributor's copies.
Terms: Pays on publication for first North American serial rights.
Advice: Looks for "writer's attention to the language and the sentence; responsible, controlled narrative."

‡**RIVERSEDGE, A Journal of Art & Literature, (II),** UT-PA, 1201 W. University Dr., CAS 266, Edinburg TX 78539-2999. (210)381-3638. Fax: (210)381-2177. Editor: Dorey Schmidt. Magazine: 100 pages; b&w illustrations and photos. "As a 'Third Coast' publication, *RiverSedge* prints regional and national creative voices whose origin or content speaks specifically to the unique multi-cultural reality of the southwest, while retaining a commitment to the universality of quality art and literature." Semiannual. Estab. 1972. Circ. 300.
Needs: Ethnic/multicultural, experimental, feminist, historical (general), literary, mainstream/contemporary, regional, translations. Upcoming themes: "Rural/Urban" (deadline Nov. 15). List of upcoming themes available for SASE. Plans special fiction issue or anthology in the future. Receives 10-12 unsolicited mss/month. Accepts 6-8 mss/issue; 12-16 mss/year. Does not read mss in summer. Publishes ms 4-6 weeks after acceptance. Length: 1,600 words preferred; 100 words minimum; 2,600 words maximum. Also publishes literary essays and poetry. Sometimes critiques or comments on rejected mss.
How to Contact: Send complete ms with a cover letter. Should include bio (not over 200 words with submission). Reports in 3 months on mss. Send SASE (or IRC) for reply, return of ms or send a disposable copy of ms. No simultaneous submissions. Accepts electronic submissions (disk or modem) via Macintosh. Sample copy for SAE.
Payment: Pays 2 contributor's copies; additional copies for $4.
Terms: Acquires one-time rights.
Advice: Looks for "general literaryness—a sense of language as link, not lectern. Characters who look and act and speak in believable ways. Stories which are not simply outpourings of human angst, but which acknowledge both ying/yang of life. Read several issues of the publication first!" Would like to

---

Market categories: (I) Open to new writers; (II) Open to both new and established writers; (III) Interested mostly in established writers; (IV) Open to writers whose work is specialized.

see more "stories which do not depend on excessive profanity, violence, pain and sexist attitudes. If everyone is screaming at a high pitch, no one hears anything. How about just a few quiet helpful whispers?"

RIVERSIDE QUARTERLY, (II,IV), Box 958, Big Sandy TX 75755. (903)636-5505. Editor: Leland Sapiro. Fiction Editor: Redd Boggs. Magazine: 5½ × 8½; 64 pages; illustrations. Quarterly. Estab. 1964. Circ. 1,100.
Needs: Fantasy and science fiction (hard science, soft/sociological). Accepts 1 ms/issue; 4 mss/year. Publishes ms 6 months after acceptance. Length: 3,500 words maximum; 3,000 words average. Publishes short shorts. Also publishes literary essays, literary criticism, poetry. Critiques rejected mss.
How to Contact: *Send directly to fiction editor, Redd Boggs, P.O. Box 44, El Verano CA 95433.* Send complete ms with a cover letter. Reports in 2 weeks. SASE (IRCs). Simultaneous submissions OK. Accepts electronic submissions. Sample copy for $2.50. Reviews novels and short story collections.
Payment: Pays in contributor's copies.
Terms: Acquires one-time rights. Sends galleys to author.
Advice: "Would-be contributors are urged to first inspect a copy or two of the magazine (available at any major college or public library) to see the *kind* of story we print."

RIVERWIND, (I, II), General Studies/Hocking College, Nelsonville OH 45764. (614)753-3591 (ext. 2375). Editors: Audrey Naffziger and C.A. Dubielak. Fiction Editor: Robert Clark Young. Magazine: 7 × 7; 60 lb. paper; cover illustrations. "College press, small literary magazine." Annual. Estab. 1975.
● In addition to receiving funding from the Ohio Arts Council since 1985, *Riverwind* won the Septa Award in 1992 and a Sepan Award in 1993.
Needs: Contemporary, erotica, ethnic, feminist, historical (general), horror, humor/satire, literary, mainstream, prose poem, spiritual, sports, regional, translations, western. No juvenile/teen fiction. Receives 30 mss/month. Does not read during the summer. Published work by Roy Bentley and Greg Anderson; published new writers within the last year. Sometimes critiques rejected mss.
How to Contact: Send complete ms with a cover letter. No simultaneous submissions. Reports on mss in 1-4 months. SASE (IRCs).
Payment: Pays in contributor's copies.
Advice: "Your work must be strong, entertaining. It helps if you are an Ohio/West Virginia writer. We hope to print more fiction. We now publish mainly regional writers (Ohio, West Virginia, Kentucky)."

ROANOKE REVIEW, (II), English Department, Roanoke College, Salem VA 24153. (703)375-2500. Editor: Robert R. Walter. Magazine: 6 × 9; 40-60 pages. Semiannual. Estab. 1967. Circ. 300.
Needs: Receives 30-40 unsolicited mss/month. Accepts 2-3 mss/issue; 4-6 mss/year. Publishes ms 6 months after acceptance. Length: 2,500 words minimum; 7,500 words maximum. Publishes short shorts. Occasionally critiques rejected mss.
How to Contact: Send complete ms with a cover letter. Reports in 1-2 weeks on queries; 8-10 weeks on mss. SASE (IRCs) for query. Sample copy for $2.
Payment: Pays in contributor's copies.

‡ROCK FALLS REVIEW, (I, II), Unicorn Tree Press, P.O. Box 104, Stamford NE 68977. (308)868-3545. Editor: Diana L. Lambson. Magazine: 8½ × 11; 20-24 pages; 20-24 lb. bond paper; 60-80 lb. bond cover; b&w illustrations. "We are a general interest publication. We accept poetry (short is better for us), short fiction, nonfiction articles, essays, science fiction, fantasy, reviews, how-tos, puzzles (occasionally). We are roughly seasonal but not hidebound about it. Most of our readers are middle of the road, average folks. We are expanding our readership." Quarterly. Estab. 1989. Circ. 50.
● *Rock Falls Review* is affiliated with Authors' Ink and the Great Plains Writer's Club.
Needs: Adventure, ethnic/multicultural, fantasy (science fantasy, sword and sorcery), historical (general), humor/satire, mainstream/contemporary, mystery/suspense (amateur sleuth, cozy, police procedural, private eye/hard-boiled, romantic suspense), regional, religious/inspirational, romance (contemporary, gothic, historical), science fiction (hard science, soft/sociological), senior citizen/retirement, sports, westerns (frontier, traditional). No gay, lesbian, occult, erotica, experimental. Publishes special fiction issue or anthology. Receives 1-5 unsolicited mss/month. Accepts 1-4 mss/issue; 12-16 mss/year. Publishes ms "usually next issue, or following issue" after acceptance. Recently published work by Tom Brown, Lynn Stearns, Jeff Lacey and Richard Shepherd. Length: 1,500-2,500 words preferred; 500 words minimum; 2,500 words maximum. Also publishes literary essays and poetry. Often critiques or comments on rejected mss.

How to Contact: Send complete ms with a cover letter. Should include estimated word count and bio ("brief but newsy. We want to know the real person."). Reports in 1-2 weeks on queries; 3-5 weeks or 1-3 months on ms (depends on the editor's work load). Send SASE (or IRC) for reply, return of ms or send a disposable copy of ms. Simultaneous and reprint submissions OK (with proper credits). Sample copy for $3.50 and 9½×11 SAE. Fiction guidelines for #10 SAE and 1 first-class stamp. Reviews novels and short story collections.
Payment: Pays 1 contributor's copy.
Terms: Acquires one-time rights. Not copyrighted.
Advice: "Even though we encourage beginners that does not mean they don't need to be professional. Edit, don't be afraid to re-write and tighten. Have a destination in mind. Don't just put pen to paper and wander for no reason. We've had a nice balance so far with the exception of western. It would be good to have some of that genre and also mysteries."

‡**ROCKET LITERARY QUARTERLY, (I,II),** P.O. Box 672, Water Mill NY 11976. (516)287-4233. Editor: Darren Johnson. Magazine: 4¼×11; 24-40 pages; white 24 lb. paper; color 67 lb. cover. "A Rocket is a transcendental, celestial traveler—innovative and intelligent fiction and poetry aimed at opening minds—even into the next century." Quarterly (plus one special issue). Estab. 1993. Circ. 300-500.
Needs: Erotica, ethnic/multicultural, experimental, humor/satire, literary, science fiction (literary, soft/sociological), special interests (narrative verse, prose poetry). "No genre, autobiographical fiction, writing without a story, anything derivative in the least." Publishes special fiction issue or anthology. Receives 5 unsolicited mss/month. Accepts 2-4 mss/issue; 8-16 mss/year. Recently published work by Leslie Scalapino, Darren Johnson. Length: 1,500 words average; 500 words minimum; 5,000 words maximum. Publishes short shorts. Length: 400 words. Also publishes poetry. Always critiques or comments on rejected mss.
How to Contact: Send complete ms with a cover letter. Should include estimated word count and bio (100 words) with submission. Reports in 2 weeks on queries; 1 month on mss. Send SASE (or IRC) for reply, return of ms or send a disposable copy of ms. Simultaneous submissions OK. Sample copy for $1.50. Reviews novels and short story collections. Send books to editor.
Payment: Pays $0-50, free subscription to the magazine; additional copies for $1.
Terms: Pays on publication for one-time rights.
Advice: Looks for "a unique voice, an original situation though believable; sentence rhythms. The editor sold his first novel at the age of 23, just after graduation, so he's empathetic to newcomers. A strength of character, expansive mind, ability to hear music—these things will appear in the Prose." Would like to see more "fiction with the beats and word play of good experimental poetry and logic and substance of traditional fiction."

THE ROCKFORD REVIEW, (II), The Rockford Writers Guild, Box 858, Rockford IL 61105. Editor-in-Chief: David Ross. Magazine: 5⅜×8½; 96 pages; b&w illustrations; b&w photos. "We look for prose and poetry with a fresh approach to old themes or new insights into the human condition." Annual. Estab. 1971. Circ. 500.
● The Rockford Writers Guild publishes this and *Tributary*, also listed in this book.
Needs: Ethnic, experimental, fantasy, humor/satire, literary, regional, science fiction (hard science, soft/sociological). Upcoming theme: "The Next Decade"—How the human condition is apt to change in the future. Published work by David Olsen, Judith Beth Cohen, Thomas E. Kennedy and Michael Driver. Length: Up to 2,500 words. Also publishes one-acts and essays.
How to Contact: Send complete ms. "Include a short biographical note—no more than four sentences." Simultaneous submissions OK. Reports in 6-8 weeks on mss. SASE (IRCs). Sample copy for $6. Fiction guidelines for SASE.
Payment: Pays contributor's copies. "Two $50 editor's choice cash prizes per issue."
Terms: Acquires first North American serial rights.
Advice: "Any subject or theme goes as long as it enhances our understanding of our humanity."

‡✲**ROOM OF ONE'S OWN (II),** Growing Room Collective, Box 46160, Station D, Vancouver, British Columbia V6J 5G5 Canada. Editors: Editorial Collective. Magazine: 5×6; 100 pages; bond paper; bond cover stock; b&w illustrations and photos. Feminist literary: fiction, poetry, criticism, reviews. Readership: general, nonscholarly. Quarterly. Estab. 1975. Circ. 1,200.
Needs: Literary, feminist and lesbian. No "sexist or macho material." Buys 6 mss/issue. Receives approximately 40 unsolicited fiction mss each month. Agented fiction 2%. Published work by Janette Turner Hospital, Anne E. Norman and Judith Monroe; published new writers within the last year. Length: 3,000 words preferred. "No critiques except under unusual circumstances."

How to Contact: Send complete ms with SASE or SAE and IRC. "Please include cover letter. State whether multiple submission or not (we don't consider multiple submissions) and whether previously published." Reports in 3-6 months. Publishes mss within a year after acceptance. Sample copy for $8. "Mss without SASE Canadian or SAE and IRCs will *not* be returned."
Payment: Pays 2 contributor's copies.
Terms: Acquires first rights.
Advice: "Write well and unpretentiously." Mss are rejected because they are "unimaginative."

‡**THE ROUND TABLE (II, IV), A Journal of Poetry and Fiction,** 375 Oakdale Dr., Rochester NY 14618. Editors: Alan and Barbara Lupack. Magazine: 6×9; 64 pages. "We publish serious poetry and fiction based on or alluding to the Arthurian legends." Annual. Estab. 1984. Circ. 150.
Needs: "Any approach with a link to Arthurian legends. The quality of the fiction is the most important criterion." Accepts 3-7 mss/year. Published new writers within the last year. Publishes ms 9 months after acceptance. Publishes short shorts.
How to Contact: Send complete ms with cover letter. Reports usually in 2-3 months, but stories under consideration may be held longer. SASE (IRCs) for ms. Simultaneous submissions OK—if notified immediately upon acceptance elsewhere. Sample copy $4 (specify fiction issue). Fiction guidelines for SAE and 1 first-class stamp.
Payment: Contributor's copy, reduced charge for extras.

‡**S.L.U.G.FEST, LTD., A Magazine of Free Expression, (I, II),** P.O. Box 536, Leominster MA 01453. (508)537-2534. Editor: M.T. Nowak. Fiction Editor: George Carlson. Magazine: 8½×11; 60-80 pages; b&w illustrations. "We are dedicated to publishing the best poetry and fiction we can find from writers who have yet to be discovered." Quarterly. Estab. 1990. Circ. 300.
Needs: Adventure, ethnic/multicultural, experimental, historical (general), horror, humor/satire, literary, mainstream/contemporary, psychic/supernatural/occult, regional, religious/inspirational, "philosophies, ramblings." Receives 20-25 unsolicited mss/month. Accepts 5-6 mss/issue; 20-25 mss/year. Publishes mss 4 months maximum after acceptance. Length: 2,500-4,000 words preferred. Publishes short shorts. Also publishes literary essays, literary criticism, and poetry. Often critiques and comments on rejected mss.
How to Contact: Send complete ms with a cover letter. Should include estimated word count. Reports in 2 weeks on queries; 4 months on mss. Send SASE (or IRC) for reply, return of ms or send a disposable copy of ms. Simultaneous and reprint submissions OK. Sample copy for $5. Fiction guidelines free. Reviews novels and short story collections.
Payment: Pays 1 contributor's copy.
Terms: Rights revert to author upon publication.
Advice: "Style and content must grab our editors. Strive for a humorous or unusual slant on life."

SALMON MAGAZINE, (I, II), P.O. Box 440313, Somerville MA 02144. Editor: Andrew Tang. Fiction Editor: Anna Watson. Magazine: 5½×8; 150-200 pages; glossy cardstock cover; illustrations and photographs. For "a literary audience." Published 1-2 times a year. Estab. 1991.
Needs: Excerpted novel, contemporary, erotica, ethnic, experimental, fantasy (as long as there's no unicorn), feminist, gay, horror, lesbian, literary, mystery/suspense, prose poem, regional, science fiction, senior citizen/retirement, translation. No "pornography, religious fiction, men's adventure, political propaganda." Receives 50-100 unsolicited mss/month. Accepts 12-14 mss/issue; 24-28 mss/year. Does not read mss July and August. Accepted manuscripts published in next issue. Published work by Edwidge Danticat, Katherine Min and Val Gerstle. Length: 3,000 words. Submit "one story at a time." Publishes short shorts. Sometimes critiques rejected ms and recommends other markets.
How to Contact: Send complete ms with or without cover letter. Reports in 1-2 weeks on queries; 1-4 months on mss. SASE (IRCs). Simultaneous (if noted) and reprint submissions OK.
Payment: Pays 1 contributor's copy. Charges for extras; 40% discount.
Terms: Acquires one-time rights. Sends pre-publication galleys to the author "on occasion—we check before changing anything big."
Advice: "The most important quality is emotional honesty. If a manuscript lacks integrity, if it is manipulative, I become uninterested. I like writing that makes me see words and phrases in a new light; I'm interested in stories incorporating questions of gender, race . . . identity. I like to be surprised, shocked, moved . . . ."

SALT LICK PRESS, (II), Salt Lick Foundation, #15, 1416 ME 21st Ave., Portland OR 97232-1507. (503)249-1014. Editor: James Haining. Magazine: 8½ × 11; 100 pages; 70 lb. offset stock; 65 lb. cover; illustrations and photos. Irregularly. Estab. 1969.
Needs: Contemporary, erotica, ethnic, experimental, feminist, gay, lesbian, literary. Receives 25 unsolicited mss each month. Accepts 2 mss/issue. Length: open. Occasionally critiques rejected mss.
How to Contact: Send complete ms with cover letter. Reports in 2 weeks on queries; 1 month on mss. SASE (IRCs). Simultaneous and reprint submissions OK. Sample copy for $5, 9 × 12 SAE and 3 first-class stamps.
Payment: Pays in contributor's copies.
Terms: Acquires first North American serial rights. Sends galleys to author.

SAN GABRIEL VALLEY MAGAZINE, (IV), Miller Books, 2908 W. Valley Blvd., Alhambra CA 91803. (213)284-7607. Editor: Joseph Miller. Magazine: 5¼ × 7¼; 48 pages; 60 lb. book paper; vellum bristol cover stock; illustrations; photos. "Regional magazine for the Valley featuring local entertainment, dining, sports and events. We also carry articles about successful people from the area. For upper-middle-class people who enjoy going out a lot." Bimonthly. Published special fiction issue last year; plans another. Estab. 1976. Circ. 3,000.
Needs: Contemporary, inspirational, psychic/supernatural/occult, western, adventure and humor. No articles on sex or ERA. Receives approximately 10 unsolicited fiction mss/month. Buys 2 mss/issue; 20 mss/year. Length: 500-2,500 words. Also publishes short shorts. Recommends other markets.
How to Contact: Send complete ms with SASE (IRCs). Reports in 2 weeks on mss. Sample copy for $1 with 9 × 12 SASE.
Payment: Pays 5¢/word; 2 contributor's copies.
Terms: Payment on acceptance for one-time rights.

SAN JOSE STUDIES, (II), San José State University, One Washington Square, San José CA 95192-0090. Editors: John Engell and D. Mesher. Magazine: digest-sized; 112-144 pages; good paper and cover; occasional illustrations and photos. "A journal for the general, educated reader, with a particular focus on California and Bay Area cultures. Covers a wide variety of materials: fiction, poetry, interviews, interdisciplinary essays. Local and California contributors are especially welcome, as are works of prose and poetry dealing with or set in California, or of particular interest to the region." Triannual. Estab. 1975. Circ. 500.
Needs: Social and political, literary, humor, ethnic and regional. Upcoming theme: "Memorial issue on César Chavez" (June 1994). Receives approximately 20 unsolicited fiction mss each month. Published work by Molly Giles and Richard Flanagan. Length: 2,500-5,000 words. Also publishes literary essays, literary criticism, poetry. Critiques rejected mss when there is time. Sometimes recommends other markets.
How to Contact: Send complete ms with SASE (IRCs). No simultaneous submissions. Reports in 2-3 months. Publishes ms an average of 6-12 months after acceptance. Sample copy for $5.
Payment: Pays 2 contributor's copies. Annual $100 award for best story, essay or poem.
Terms: Acquires first rights. Work must be submitted on disk after acceptance.
Advice: "Name should appear *only* on cover sheet. We seldom print beginning writers of fiction or poetry."

SAN MIGUEL WRITER, (I, II), Aldama #43, San Miguel de Allende, GTO Mexico 37700. (011)52-465-22225. Editor: Carl Selph. Magazine: 5½ × 8½; 80 pages; illustrations. "We accept fiction, nonfiction, poetry, etc., based on 'literary' quality definable only as it is perceived by a group of 3 well-read editors sensitive to a community of artists of all kinds and professionals—many retired—from all fields." Semiannual. Estab. 1989. Circ. 250.
  ● Even though this magazine is published in Mexico, work is primarily in English and since it is based in North America we included it here rather than in the foreign section.
Needs: Adventure, ethnic/multicultural, experimental, fantasy (science fantasy, sword and sorcery), feminist, gay, historical (general), humor/satire, lesbian, literary, mystery/suspense (police procedural, romantic suspense), psychic/supernatural/occult, regional, romance (contemporary, historical), science fiction (soft/sociological), senior citizen/retirement, serialized novel, translations. "Our special interest is manuscripts in Spanish from Latino writers." Nothing pornographic unless with redeeming literary quality; no simplistic action. Receives 30 unsolicited mss/month. Acquires 3-6 mss/issue. Publishes ms 3-5 months after acceptance. Published work by Ann Ireland, Alice K. Barten and Madelene Carr. Length: 6,000 words maximum. Publishes short shorts. Also publishes literary essays, literary criticism and poetry.

How to Contact: Send complete ms with cover letter. Should include estimated word count, one-paragraph bio, list of publications. Reports in 3 months on mss. SASE (IRCs) for return of ms or send disposable copy of ms. No simultaneous submissions. Electronic submissions OK.

Payment: Pays 1 contributor's copy.

Terms: Rights remain with author. Writers can participate in contest "simply by submitting their work for acceptance. $100 prize each for the best selection in poetry and prose, English or Spanish, chosen annually."

Advice: "Though principally an English-language publication, we relish our presence in San Miguel and eagerly solicit work in Spanish. The editors impose no restrictions on subject and style but stipulate that, in their judgment, manuscripts be of literary merit and of interest to our readers. San Miguel, a town with an unrelenting flow of painters, writers, musicians — artists of all kinds and people representing careers of all kinds — provides a challenging readership for contributors to the *San Miguel Writer*. Our editors, attuned to such an environment, are not only discriminating but, yes, elitist — in the most serious sense of that word — about the calibre of the magazine they are producing."

SANSKRIT, Literary Arts Publication of UNC Charlotte, (II), University of North Carolina at Charlotte, Highway 49, Charlotte NC 28223. (704)547-2326. Co-editors: Jeff Byers and Jeff Bane. Fiction Editor: Scott Buchanan. Magazine: 9 × 15, 60-90 pages. "We are a general lit/art mag open to all genres, if well written, for college students, alumni, writers and artists across the country." Annual. Estab. 1968.

- *Sanskrit* has received the Pacemaker Award, Associated College Press, Gold Crown Award and Columbia Scholastic Press award.

Needs: Contemporary, erotica, ethnic, experimental, feminist, gay, humor/satire, lesbian, literary, mainstream, prose poem, regional, translations. No formula, western, romance. Receives 2-4 unsolicited mss/month. Acquires 3-6 mss/issue. Does not read mss in summer. Publishes in late March. Published work by Nann Budd, P.L. Thomas, Jerry Saviano. Length: 250 words minimum; 5,000 words maximum. Publishes short shorts. Also publishes poetry. Sometimes critiques rejected mss.

How to Contact: Send complete manuscript with cover letter. SASE (IRCs). Simultaneous submissions OK. Sample copy $6. Fiction guidelines for #10 SAE.

Payment: Pays contributor's copies.

Terms: Acquires one-time rights. Publication not copyrighted.

Advice: "A tight cohesive story, in an often shattered world, wins my heart. I like quirkiness just to the point of self indulgence. There is a fine line . . . there are many fine lines . . . walk as many as you can."

SANTA MONICA REVIEW, (III), Santa Monica College, 1900 Pico Blvd., Santa Monica CA 90405. (213)450-5150. Editor: James Krusoe. Magazine: 5½ × 8; 140 pages, rag paper. Semiannual. Estab. 1988. Circ. 1,000.

Needs: Contemporary, literary. Accepts 5 mss/issue; 10 mss/year. Publishes mss varying amount of time after publication. Published work by Ann Beattie, Arturo Vivante, Guy Davenport and Barry Hannah.

How to Contact: Send complete ms with cover letter. Reports in 3 months on mss. SASE (IRCs). Simultaneous submissions OK. Sample copy for $7.

Payment: Pays subscription to magazine, contributor's copies.

Terms: Acquires one-time rights.

Advice: "We are *not* actively soliciting beginning work. We want to combine high quality West Coast, especially Los Angeles, writing with that from the rest of the country."

‡SCIFANT (I), Box 398, Suisun CA 94585. Editor: Paul Doerr. Magazine: 8½ × 11; 98 pages (microfiche only); illustrations and photos. "We publish science fiction, fantasy, horror, space fiction and space high technology." Monthly.

- Paul Doerr edits a variety of periodicals and books on microfiche and paper. His company is called Luna Ventures.

Needs: Adventure, experimental, fantasy, historical (general), horror, humor/satire, romance, science fiction, serialized/excerpted novel, suspense/mystery. Upcoming themes: "Harems"; "WWIII and After." Receives 50 unsolicited mss/month. Buys 30 mss/issue. Publishes ms 2 months-2 years after acceptance. Publishes short shorts of a half page and up. Occasionally critiques rejected mss and recommends other markets.

How to Contact: Send complete ms with cover letter. Ms must be single spaced with margins no greater than a half inch and proofread (camera ready). Reports in 1 month. SASE (IRCs). Simultaneous and reprint submissions OK. Accepts electronic submissions via Apple II. Fiction guidelines for #10 SASE. Sample copy for $3. (Copy in microfiche.)
Payment: Payment schedule on spec sheet.
Terms: Pays percentage of sales profit.
Advice: "Send me something! Would like to see more fiction on topics of WW II and space colonization."

SCREAM OF THE BUDDHA, (III), Buddha Rose Publications, P.O. Box 548, Hermosa Beach CA 90254. (310)543-3809. Fax: (310)543-9673. Editor-in-Chief: Scott Shaw, Ph.D. Editor: Elliot Sebastian. Magazine: 8½ × 11; 30 pages; card cover; illustrations; photos. "To publish the abstract, the literally obscene, the mystical, the erotic, the powerful. We here are literary anarchists." Bimonthly. Estab. 1988. Circ. 1,000.
  ● *Scream of the Buddha* now only accepts submissions through an agent.
Needs: Adventure, erotica, experimental, literary, psychic/supernatural/occult, science fiction. "Not boring, traditional junk." Receives 800 mss/month. Buys 3 mss/issue; 12-15 mss/year. Publishes 8 months after acceptance. Agented fiction 100%. Published Charles Bukowski, Scott Shaw, Hae Won Shin and James F. Spezze III. Length: 1,000 words. Publishes short shorts. Also publishes literary essays, literary criticism, poetry. Sometimes critiques rejected mss.
How to Contact: Submit through an agent. Should include minimal bio. Reports in 1 month. Send SASE (IRCs) for reply. Simultaneous reprint submissions OK. Sample copy for $5. Reviews novels and short story collections.
Payment: Pays 1 contributor's copies.
Terms: Acquires first rights.
Advice: Looks for "a ms that screams a form of passion that we have never read before. So often, we see the same old ego-filled material; telling someone else where it is at, from one individual's point of view. Junk. Some people love us—most hate us—WE DON'T CARE! Forget structure. Forget all that you have been taught. Forget what the 'masters' have written, because that is all nonsense. Scream your own vision and an audience will come to you."

THE SEATTLE REVIEW, (II), Padelford Hall GN-30, University of Washington, Seattle WA 98195. (206)543-9865. Editor: Donna Gerstenberger. Fiction Editor: Charles Johnson. Magazine: 6×9. "Includes general fiction, poetry, craft essays on writing, and one interview per issue with a Northwest writer." Semiannual. Published special fiction issue. Estab. 1978. Circ. 1,000.
Needs: Contemporary, ethnic, experimental, fantasy, feminist, gay, historical, horror, humor/satire, lesbian, literary, mainstream, prose poem, psychic/supernatural/occult, regional, science fiction, excerpted novel, mystery/suspense, translations, western. "We also publish a series called Writers and their Craft, which deals with aspects of writing fiction (also poetry)—point of view, characterization, etc., rather than literary criticism, each issue." Does not want to see "anything in bad taste (porn, racist, etc.)." Receives about 100 unsolicited mss/month. Buys about 3-6 mss/issue; about 4-10 mss/year. Does not read mss June-August. Agented fiction 25%. Published work by David Milofsky, Lawson Fusao Inada and Liz Rosenberg; published new writers within the last year. Length: 3,500 words average; 500 words minimum; 10,000 words maximum. Publishes short shorts. Sometimes critiques rejected mss. Occasionally recommends other markets.
How to Contact: Send complete ms. "If included, cover letter should list recent publications or mss we'd seen and liked, but been unable to publish." Reports in 6-8 months. SASE (IRCs). Sample copy "half-price if older than one year." Current issue for $5; some special issues $5.50−6.50.
Payment: Pays 0-$100, free subscription to magazine, 2 contributor's copies; charge for extras.
Terms: Pays on publication for first North American serial rights. Copyright reverts to writer on publication; "please request release of rights and cite *SR* in reprint publications." Sends galleys to author.
Advice: "Beginners do well in our magazine if they send clean, well-written manuscripts. We've published a lot of 'first stories' from all over the country and take pleasure in discovery."

THE SECRET ALAMEDA, (II), P.O. Box 527, Alameda CA 94501. (510)521-5597. Editor: Richard Whittaker. Magazine: 8½ × 11; 64-72 pages; 70 lb. coated paper; illustrations and photographs. "We're a magazine put together by artists. We publish art portfolios, interviews, articles, and fiction." Audience is "hard to define. We think we have an educated audience, probably over 30 years old for the most part. People who appreciate the visual arts as well as the literary arts." Triquarterly. Estab. 1991. Circ. 1,500-2,500.

Needs: "Literary work—sometimes serious, sometimes humorous—but always work of substance and depth. We prefer honest, personal work based on lived experience. Will consider nonfiction along these lines also. Not interested in most 'genres' of writing." Published work by George Lakoff, Barbara Minton, Wm. Dudley and Ronald Hobbs. Length: 500-2,500 words. Sometime critiques rejected mss.

How to Contact: Send complete ms with cover letter. Reports in 4-6 weeks. SASE (IRCs). Simultaneous and reprint submissions OK. Sample copy for $5.

Payment: Pays subscription and contributor's copies.

Terms: Acquires one-time rights.

Advice: "Read a copy of the magazine."

SEEMS, (II), Lakeland College, Sheboygan WI 53081. (414)565-3871. Editor: Karl Elder. Magazine: $7 \times 8\frac{1}{2}$; 40 pages. "We publish fiction and poetry for an audience which tends to be highly literate. People read the publication, I suspect, for the sake of reading it." Published irregularly. Estab. 1971. Circ. 300.

Needs: Literary. Accepts 4 mss/issue. Receives 12 unsolicited fiction mss each month. Published work by John Birchler; published new writers within the last year. Length: 5,000 words maximum. Publishes short shorts. Also publishes poetry. Critiques rejected mss when there is time.

How to Contact: Send complete ms with SASE. Reports in 2 months on mss. Publishes ms an average of 1-2 years after acceptance. Sample copy $4.

Payment: Pays 1 contributor's copy; $3 charge for extras.

Terms: Rights revert to author.

Advice: "Send clear, clean copies. Read the magazine in order to help determine the taste of the editor." Mss are rejected because of "lack of economical expression, or saying with many words what could be said in only a few. Good fiction contains all of the essential elements of poetry; study poetry and apply those elements to fiction. Our interest is shifting to story poems, the grey area between genres."

SEMIOTEXT(E), (II), Autonomedia, P.O. Box 568, Brooklyn NY 11211. (718)387-6471. Editor: Jim Fleming. Fiction Editor: Pete Wilson. Magazine: 7×10; 160 pages; 50 lb. paper; 10 pf cover; illustrations and photos. "Radical/marginal for an arts/academic audience." Annual. Estab. 1974. Circ. 8,000.

Needs: Erotica, ethnic, experimental, fantasy, feminist, gay, literary, psychic/supernatural/occult, science fiction, translations. Published work by Kathy Acker, William Burroughs. Publishes short shorts. Sometimes recommends other markets.

How to Contact: Query first. Reporting time varies. SASE (IRCs) for ms. Simultaneous submissions OK. Accepts electronic submissions. Sample copy for $10.

Payment: Pays in contributor's copies.

Terms: Acquires first North American serial rights. Sends galleys to author.

SENSATIONS MAGAZINE, (I,II), A5, 2 Radio Ave., Secaucus NJ 07094. Founder: David Messineo. Magazine: $8\frac{1}{2} \times 11$; 50-70 pages; 20 lb. inside paper, 67 lb. cover paper; vellum cover; black ink line illustrations. "We publish short stories and poetry, no specific theme, for a liberal, worldly audience who reads for pleasure." Magazine also includes the Rediscovering America in Poetry research series. Semiannual. Estab. 1987.

Needs: Adventure, contemporary, fantasy, gay, historical, horror, humor/satire, lesbian, literary, mainstream, mystery/suspense (private eye), prose poem, regional, romance (historical), science fiction, western (traditional). "We're not into gratuitous profanity, pornography, or violence. Sometimes these are needed to properly tell the tale. We'll read anything unusual, providing it is submitted in accordance with our submission policies. No abstract works only the writer can understand." Upcoming theme: " A theme issue on Coney Island's amusement parks is anticipated for the summer of 1995." Submit Coney Island themed stories during 1994; send SASE first for submission information. Accepts 2-4 mss/issue. Publishes ms 2 months after acceptance.

How to Contact: "Send name, address, a paragraph of background information about yourself, a paragraph about what inspired the story. We'll send submission guidelines when we are ready to judge material." Reports in 1-2 weeks on queries; 4-6 weeks on mss. SASE (IRCs) for brochure. Simultaneous submissions OK. Accepts electronic submissions (Macintosh only). *Must first purchase* sample copy $8. Check payable to David Messineo. *"Do not submit material before reading submission guidelines."* Next deadline: August 1, 1994.

Payment: No payment.
Terms: Acquires one-time rights.
Advice: "Each story must have a strong beginning that grabs the reader's attention in the first two sentences. Characters have to be realistic and well-described. Readers must like, hate, or have some emotional response to your characters. Setting, plot, construction, attention to detail—all are important. We work with writers to help them improve in these areas, but the better the stories are written before they come to us, the greater the chance for publication. Purchase sample copy first and read the stories, then determine which of your stories is most appropriate to submit. Our research project offers the first collection of poetry written in and about America in the 1500s and 1600s, which may also be of interest to you."

‡SEQUOIA, Stanford Literary Magazine, Storke Publications Bldg., Stanford CA 94305. Poetry and Managing Editor: Carlos Rodriguez. Fiction Editor: Mark Clevenger. "Literary journal ranges from traditional to avant-garde for newly published to established writers." Semiannual. Estab. 1887. Circ. 500.
Needs: "Literary excellence is the primary criterion. We prefer literary, ethnic, experimental, and 'short' short fiction." Receives 50 mss/month. Accepts 2-3 mss/issue; 24-30 mss/year. Publishes ms 2-8 weeks after acceptance. Length: 8,000 words or 20 pages maximum.
How to Contact: Send complete ms with SASE (IRC). Tries to report in 3 months "during academic year." Sample copy for $6.
Payment: Pays 1-2 contributor's copies. Contributor's rates on request.
Terms: Author retains rights.

THE SEWANEE REVIEW, (III), University of the South, Sewanee TN 37383. (615)598-1245. Editor: George Core. Magazine: 6×9; 192 pages. "A literary quarterly, publishing original fiction, poetry, essays on literary and related subjects, book reviews and book notices for well-educated readers who appreciate good American and English literature." Quarterly. Estab. 1892. Circ. 3,000.
Needs: Literary, contemporary. No translations, juvenile, gay/lesbian, erotica. Buys 10-15 mss/year. Receives 100 unsolicited fiction mss each month. Does not read mss June 1-August 31. Published new writers within the last year. Length: 6,000-7,500 words. Critiques rejected mss "when there is time." Sometimes recommends other markets.
How to Contact: Send complete ms with SASE (IRCs) and cover letter stating previous publications, if any. Reports in 1 month on mss. Sample copy $6 plus 50¢ postage.
Payment: Pays $10-12/printed page; 2 contributor's copies; $3.50 charge for extras. Writer's guidelines for SASE.
Terms: Pays on publication for first North American serial rights and second serial rights by agreement.
Advice: "Send only one story at a time, with a serious and sensible cover letter. We think fiction is of greater general interest than any other literary mode."

‡SHADOW SWORD, The Magazine of Fantasy Fiction and Role Playing, (I, II, IV), Willowood Publishing, P.O. Box 660085, Miami Springs FL 33266-0085. (305)889-2881. Editor: Glenda Woodrum. Magazine: 8½×11; 50-60 pages; 20 lb. bond paper; 67 lb. Bristol or glossy 80 lb. cover stock; b&w illustrations. "*Shadow Sword* is geared to a mature audience which is primarily male." Quarterly. Estab. 1993. Circ. 300.
 ● Willowood Publishing also publishes *Explosive Decompression* listed in this book.
Needs: Fantasy (heroic fantasy, sword and sorcery). "No modern world fantasy, romance oriented fantasy, 'cute' stories, stories with evil wizards. Every January I release a heroines of fantasy issue which features all female lead characters." List of upcoming themes available for SASE. Publishes special fiction issue or anthology. Receives 30-110 unsolicited mss/month. Accepts 6-10 mss/issue; 32-40 mss/year. Publishes ms 2 months-1 year after acceptance. Recently published work by William Marden, Buzz Lovko, Gerard D. Houarner, Ann Ambrosio and Mark Rich. Length: 5,000 words preferred; 800 words minimum; 10,000 words maximum. Also publishes literary essays and literary criticism. Always critiques or comments on rejected mss.
How to Contact: Send complete ms with a cover letter. Query first if the work is a reprint. Should include estimated word count, 200 word bio and list of publications. Reports in 1-2 weeks on queries; 1-4 months on mss. Send SASE (or IRC) for reply, return of ms or send a disposable copy of ms. Simultaneous and reprint submissions OK. Sample copy for $3.25. Fiction guidelines for SASE. Reviews novels and short story collections. Send review copies to ATTN: Review Staff (address same).

Payment: Pays 1 contributor's copy; additional copies for $3.
Terms: Acquires one-time rights and reprint rights.
Advice: "Read the guidelines carefully. A large portion of my rejections are due to the writer submitting an inappropriate work to my publication." Looks for "stories with larger than life heroes/heroines. Avoid evil sorcerers/sorceresses out to conquer the world and sociological plots that contain no real conflict."

SHATTERED WIG REVIEW, (I, II), Shattered Wig Productions, 523 E. 38th St., Baltimore MD 21218-1930. (301)243-6888. Editor: Collective. Magazine: 70 pages; "average" paper; cardstock cover; illustrations and photos. "Open forum for the discussion of the absurdo-miserablist aspects of everyday life. Fiction, poetry, graphics, essays, photos." Semiannual. Estab. 1988. Circ. 500.
Needs: Confession, contemporary, erotica, ethnic, experimental, feminist, gay, humor/satire, juvenile (5-9 years), lesbian, literary, preschool (1-4 years), prose poem, psychic/supernatural/occult, regional, young adult/teen (10-18), meat, music, film, art, pickles, revolutionary practice. Does not want "anything by Ann Beattie or John Irving." Receives 15-20 unsolicited mss/month. Publishes ms 2-4 months after acceptance. Published work by Al Ackerman, Jake Berry and Bella Donna; published new writers within the last year. Publishes short shorts. Also publishes literary criticism, poetry. Sometimes critiques rejected mss and recommends other markets.
How to Contact: Send complete ms with cover letter or "visit us in Baltimore." Reports in 1 month. SASE (IRCs) for ms. Simultaneous and reprint submissions OK. Sample copy for $4.
Payment: Pays in contributor's copies.
Terms: Acquires one-time rights.
Advice: "The arts have been reduced to imploding pus with the only material rewards reserved for vapid stylists and collegiate pod suckers. The only writing that counts has no barriers between imagination and reality, thought and action. Send us at least 3 pieces so we have a choice."

❋SHIFT MAGAZINE, (II), Solomon-Heintzman, 88 Roxborough St. East, Toronto, Ontario M4W 1V8 Canada. (416)868-6565. Fax: (416)360-5694. Editors: Evan Solomon, Andrew Heintzman. Magazine: 8½ × 11; 48-60 pages; 20 lb. glossy paper; 80 lb. glossy cover; illustrations; photographs. "Writers are encouraged to send submissions with an insider's feel to media culture: emphasis on independent media." Quarterly. Estab. 1992. Circ. 2,500.
Needs: Adventure, condensed novel, erotica, ethnic/multicultural, experimental, feminist, gay, historical, humor/satire, lesbian, literary, mainstream/contemporary, regional, serialized novel, translations. Nonfiction also needed. No pornography. Plans special fiction issue or anthology in the future. Receives 50-80 unsolicited fiction mss/month. Acquires 5-9 mss/issue; 20-35 mss/year. Publishes ms 1-5 months after acceptance. Recently published work by Michael Coren, Eliza Clark, Evan Solomon, John Sullivan. Length: 4,000 words maximum. Publishes short shorts. Also publishes essays and literary commentary. Often critiques or comments on rejected mss.
How to Contact: Send complete ms with cover letter. Should include estimated word count, bio (2 lines), list of publications. Reports in 2 weeks on queries; 2 months on mss. SASE (IRC). Simultaneous submissions, reprint (if noted) and electronic submissions (3.5 disks with hard copy) OK. Sample copy for $4 (Canadian) and 8½ × 11 SAE. Fiction guidelines for 8½ × 11 SAE. Reviews novel and short story collections.
Payment: Pays 1 contributor's copy.
Terms: Acquires one-time rights.
Advice: Looks for "new, exciting stories on media-related subjects which speak to generation X culture. It should be clearly written. No jargon. Loose but informative feel is encouraged. *But* all styles are examined. Story must be good on its own terms."

SHOCKBOX, The Literary/Art Magazine with Teeth, (II), P.O. Box 7226, Nashua NH 03060. (603)888-8549. Editor: C.F. Roberts. Magazine: digest-sized; 44 pages. "We publish raw, jarring experimental literary fiction. For generally alternative art/literary, underground audience." Quarterly. Estab. 1991.
Needs: Experimental, humor/satire, literary. "No slick, watered-down prose. No contrived TV-Movie-of-the-Week fodder." Receives 10 unsolicited mss/month. Accepts 3 mss/issue; 20 mss/year. Time varies between acceptance and publication. Recently published work by Skip Rhudy, Shannon Frach, Charles Frenoy and Randal Seyler. Length: 1,000 words or less preferred. Publishes short shorts. Sometimes comments on rejected mss and recommends other markets.

How to Contact: Query first. Include name, address, short bio. Reports in 2 weeks on queries; 2-3 months on mss. SASE (IRCs). Simultaneous and reprint submissions OK. Sample copy for $2.50. Fiction guidelines for #10 SAE. Make check payable to C.F. Roberts.
Payment: Pays in contributor's copies.
Terms: Acquires first rights or one-time rights.
Advice: "More and more nowadays, I find that I am bored and annoyed by mainstream 'literature' and all the preconceived ideas associated with it. Please do step out of these bounds and give me something startling and unusual to read. I want to hedge away from the status quo and all it entails. SURPRISE ME."

SHORT FICTION BY WOMEN, (II, IV), Box 1276, Stuyvesant Station, New York NY 10009. Editor: Rachel Whalen. Magazine: journal-sized; illustrations and photographs on cover only. "*Short Fiction By Women* publishes very readable fiction which meets standards of literary excellence. For everyone who enjoys fine fiction." Triannual. Estab. 1991.
Needs: Excerpted novel, contemporary, ethnic, experimental, feminist, gay, lesbian, literary, translations. "Stories do *not* need a 'feminist slant' to be acceptable; nor do they need to be about women or have a woman narrator. We are interested in all good stories by women writers. No romance, horror, mystery, erotica, Christian/inspirational." Receives 150-200 unsolicited mss/month. Buys 5-15 mss/issue; 15-45 mss/year. Publishes ms 6 months after acceptance. Recently published work by Edwidge Danticat, Louisa Peck, Patricia Halloff and Timea K. Szell. Length: 5,000 words preferred; 20,000 words maximum. Also publishes plays. Sometimes critiques rejected mss and recommends other markets.
How to Contact: Send complete ms with cover letter. If unsure, send for writers's guidelines. Reports in 6 weeks on mss. SASE (IRCs) for ms. Simultaneous submissions OK. Sample copy for $6. Fiction guidelines for #10 SAE and 1 first-class stamp.
Payment: "Payment is based on length of story and funds available. Our long-term goal is to pay writers a 'living wage.' "
Terms: Pays on publication for first serial rights.
Advice: "Proofread, rewrite, clarify. Read and analyze literature. Study the many excellent books available on fiction writing."

SHORT STUFF MAGAZINE FOR GROWN-UPS, (II), Bowman Publications, P.O. Box 7057, Loveland CO 80537. (303)669-9139. Editor: Donna Bowman. Magazine: 8½ × 11; 40 pages; bond paper; enamel cover; b&w illustrations and photographs. "Nonfiction is regional—Colorado and adjacent states. Fiction and humor must be tasteful, but can be any genre, any subject. We are designed to be a 'Reader's Digest' of fiction. We are found in professional waiting rooms, etc." Monthly.
● The editor says she'd like to see more young (25+) humor and finds "clean" humor "hard to come by."
Needs: Adventure, contemporary, historical (general), humor/satire, mainstream, mystery/suspense (amateur sleuth, English cozy, police procedural, private eye, romantic suspense), regional, romance (contemporary, gothic, historical), western (frontier). No erotica. "We use holiday themes." Receives 150 unsolicited mss/month. Buys 9-12 mss/issue; 76 mss/year. Publishes accepted work immediately. Published work by Dean Ballenger. Length: 1,000 words average; 1,500 words maximum.
How to Contact: Send complete ms with cover letter. SASE (IRCs). Reports in 3-6 months. Sample copies with SAE and 98¢ postage. Fiction guidelines for SAE.
Payment: Pays $10-50 and subscription to magazine.
Terms: Pays on publication for first North American serial rights.
Advice: "We seek a potpourri of subjects each issue. A new slant, a different approach, fresh viewpoints—all of these excite us. We don't like gore, salacious humor or perverted tales. Prefer third person. Be sure it is a story with a beginning, middle and end. It must have dialogue. Many beginners do not know an essay from a short story. Essays occasionally used if *humorous*."

SIDE SHOW, Short Story Annual, (II), Somersault Press, P.O. Box 1428, El Cerrito CA 94530-1428. (510)215-2207. Editor: Shelley Anderson, Kathe Stolz and Marjorie K. Jacobs. Book (paperback): 5½ × 8½; 300 pages; 50 lb. paper. "Quality short stories for a general, literary audience." Annual. Estab. 1991. Circ. 500.
● Work published in *Side Show* was selected for inclusion in the 1993 Pushcart Prize anthology.
Needs: Contemporary, ethnic, feminist, gay, humor/satire, lesbian, literary, mainstream. Nothing genre, religious, pornographic. Receives 50-60 unsolicited mss/month. Buys 25-30 mss/issue. Does not read mss in August. Publishes ms up to 9 months after acceptance. Published work by Dorothy Bryant,

Molly Giles and Jonis Agee. Length: Open. Publishes short shorts. Critiques rejected mss and recommends other markets.

How to Contact: All submissions entered in contest. *$10 entry fee* (includes subscription to 1994 *Side Show*). Deadline: June 30, 1994. No guidelines. Send complete ms with cover letter and entry fee. Reports in 2-3 weeks on mss. SASE (IRCs). Simultaneous submissions OK. Sample copy for $10 and $2 postage and handling ($.83 sales tax CA residents).

Payment: Pays $5/printed page.

Terms: Pays on publication for first North American serial rights. Sends galleys to author. All submissions entered in our contest for cash prizes $30 (1st); $25 (2nd); $20 (3rd).

Advice: Looks for "readability, vividness of characterization, coherence, inspiration, interesting subject matter, point of view, originality, plausibility."

✸**SIDETREKKED, (I, IV)**, Science Fiction London, 785 Northmile Rd., London, Ontario N6H 2X9 Canada. (519)471-1574. Editor: Douglas McKay. Editors change by election. Newspaper: 7 × 8½; 36-40 pages; bond paper; b&w drawings, halftone photographs. "Science fiction for science fiction readers, mostly adults." Quarterly. Estab. 1980. Circ. 200.

Needs: Fantasy, science fiction (hard science, soft/sociological). "We will consider any story with a science fictional slant. Because science fiction tends to be all-embracing, that could include horror, humor/satire, romance, suspense, feminist, gay, ethnic, etc. — yes, even western — but the science fiction classification must be met, usually by setting the story in a plausible, futuristic universe." Receives 3-5 unsolicited fiction mss/month. Accepts 3-8 mss/issue. Time between acceptance and publication varies. Published work by Joe Beliveau, Dave Seburn. Length: 1,000-5,000 words preferred. "No hard-and-fast rules, but we can't accommodate novelettes or novellas." Publishes short shorts. Critiques or comments on rejected mss, if requested by the author. Recommends other markets on occasion.

How to Contact: Send complete ms with cover letter. No simultaneous submissions. Reports in 3 weeks on queries; in 1 month on mss. SASE (IRCs). Sample copy for $2 (Canadian) and 9 × 10 SAE.

Payment: Pays in contributor's copies.

Terms: Acquires first North American serial rights.

Advice: "We are more forgiving than most fiction markets and we try to work with new writers. What makes us want to work with a writer is some suggestion that he or she understands what makes a good story. What makes a manuscript stand out? Tell a good story. The secondary things are fixable if the story is there, but if it is not, no amount of tinkering can fix it."

SIDEWALKS, (II), P.O. Box 321, Champlin MN 55316. (612)421-3512. Editor: Tom Heie. Magazine: 5½ × 8½; 60-75 pages; 60 lb. paper; textured recycled cover. "*Sidewalks* . . . place of discovery, of myth, power, incantation . . . places we continue to meet people, preoccupied, on our way somewhere . . . tense, dark, empty places . . . place we meet friends and strangers, neighborhood sidewalks, place full of memory, paths that bring us home." Semiannual. Estab. 1991. Circ. 500.

Needs: Experimental, humor/satire, literary, mainstream/contemporary, regional. No violent, pornographic kinky material. Acquires 6-8 mss/issue; 12-16 mss/year. Work is accepted for 2 annual deadlines: May 31 and December 31. Publishes ms 1-1½ months after deadline. Published work by Lin Enger and Paul Hintz. Length: 2,500 words preferred; 3,000 words maximum. Publishes short shorts. Also publishes poetry.

How to Contact: Send complete ms with cover letter. Should include estimated word count, very brief bio, list of publications. Reports in 1 week on queries; 2-3 months on mss. Send SASE (IRCs) for reply, return of ms or send a disposable copy of the ms. No simultaneous submissions. Accepts electronic submissions. Sample copy for $5.

Payment: Pays 1 contributor's copy. Additional copies $4.

Terms: Acquires one-time rights.

Advice: "We look for a story with broad appeal, one that is well-crafted and has strong narrative voice, a story that leaves the reader thinking after the reading is over."

SIGN OF THE TIMES, A Chronicle of Decadence in the Atomic Age, (II), P.O. Box 70672, Seattle WA 98107. (206)323-6764. Editor: Mark Souder. Tabloid: 8 × 10; 32 pages; book paper; 120 lb. cover stock; illustrations; photos. "Decadence in all forms for those seeking literary amusement." Semiannual. Published special fiction issue last year; plans another. Estab. 1980. Circ. 750.

Needs: Comics, erotica, experimental, gay, lesbian. No religious or western manuscripts. Receives 6 unsolicited mss/month. Buys 10 mss/issue; 20 mss/year. Published work by Gary Smith, Willie Smith, Ben Satterfield. Length: 3,000 words average; 500 words minimum, 5,000 words maximum. Publishes short shorts. Sometimes comments on rejected mss and recommends other markets.

How to Contact: Send complete ms with cover letter and bio. Reports in 6 weeks on mss. SASE (IRCs). Sample copy $3.50. Fiction guidelines for #10 SASE.
Payment: Pays up to $20, subscription to magazine, 2 contributor's copies; 1 time cover price charge for extras.
Terms: Pays on publication for first rights plus anthology in the future.

‡**THE SILVER WEB, (II),** Buzzcity Press, Box 38190, Tallahassee FL 32315. Send submissions to Box 38190. Editor: Ann Kennedy. Magazine: 8½ × 11; 64 pages; 20 lb. paper; glossy cover; b&w illustrations and photographs. "Speculative fiction for those that seek to be challenged—all ages." Semiannual. Estab. 1989.
  ● Work published in *The Silver Web* has appeared in *The Year's Best Horror* (DAW Books). In 1992, the magazine was nominated for "Best Magazine" and "Best New Magazine" by the Small Press Writers and Artists Organization.
Needs: Experimental, horror, humor/satire, psychic/supernatural/occult, science fiction. "No slash n' gore, no predictable endings." Receives 30-40 unsolicited mss/month. Accepts 8-12 mss/issue. Publishes ms 6-12 months after acceptance. Length: 2,500 words; 8,000 words maximum. Publishes short shorts. Also publishes poetry. Sometimes critiques rejected ms and recommends other markets.
How to Contact: "Get guidelines, or better yet, a copy of our magazine, and then submit." Reports in 2-3 weeks on queries; 2 months on mss. SASE (IRCs). Sample copy for $4.75 plus $1 postage and handling. Fiction guidelines for #10 SAE and 1 first-class stamp.
Payment: Pays 1-3¢/word plus 1 contributor's copy. Discount to writers for additional copies.
Terms: Acquires first North American serial rights, reprint rights or one time rights.
Advice: "The kind of work I look for is a piece that will stay with me long after I've finished reading it. It must paint pictures in my mind that are not easily erased. Read a copy of our magazine, at least— get our Writer's Guidelines. *The Silver Web* publishes surrealistic fiction and poetry. Work too bizarre for mainstream, but perhaps too literary for genre. NOTE: This is not a straight horror/sci-fi magazine. No typical storylines."

SILVERFISH REVIEW, (II), Silverfish Press, Box 3541, Eugene OR 97403. (503)344-5060. Editor: Rodger Moody. High quality literary material for a general audience. Published in July and December. Estab. 1979. Circ. 750.
Needs: Literary. Accepts 1-2 mss/issue. Also publishes literary essays, poetry, interview, translations.
How to Contact: Send complete ms with SASE (IRCs). No simultaneous submissions. Reports in 2-3 months on mss. Sample copy for $4 and $1.50 postage.
Payment: Pays 5 contributor's copies; $5/page when funding permits.
Terms: Rights revert to author.
Advice: "We publish primarily poetry; we will, however, publish good quality fiction. *SR* is mainly interested in the short short story (one-minute and three-minute)."

SING HEAVENLY MUSE!, (II), Box 13320, Minneapolis MN 55414. Editor: Sue Ann Martinson. Magazine: 6 × 9; 125 pages; 55 lb. acid-free paper; 10 pt. glossy cover stock; illustrations; photos. Women's poetry, prose and artwork. Annual. Estab. 1977.
Needs: Literary, feminist, prose poem and ethnic/minority. Receives approximately 30 unsolicited fiction mss each month. Published work by Helene Cappuccio, Erika Duncan and Martha Roth. Publishes short shorts. Also publishes literary essays, poetry. Sometimes recommends other markets.
How to Contact: Query for information on theme issues, reading periods or variations in schedule. Include cover letter with "brief writing background and publications." No simultaneous submissions. Reports in 1-6 months on queries and mss. Publishes ms an average of 1 year after acceptance. Sample copy for $4.
Payment: Pays 2 contributor's copies and honorarium, depending on funding.
Terms: Acquires first rights.
Advice: "Try to avoid preaching. Look for friends also interested in writing and form a mutual support-and-criticism group."

THE SINGLE SCENE (II, IV), Box 30856, Gahanna OH 43230. (614)476-8802. Editor: Jeanne Marlowe. Magazine: 8 × 11; 24 pages; illustrations; photos. Single living, male-female relationship topics covered for single adults. Bimonthly. Estab. 1985. Circ. 7,000.
Needs: Confession, contemporary, experimental, fantasy, humor/satire, mainstream, mystery/suspense. Buys 6-12 mss/year. Upcoming theme: "Using Myers-Briggs Personality Theory (MBTI) to Build Better Relationships." Publication time varies "now that I have a backlog." Published work by

Paul Wolf and J.C. Reagan; published new writers within the last year. Length: 3,000 words maximum; "shorter mss more likely to be accepted." Publishes short shorts. Occasionally critiques rejected mss.

How to Contact: Send complete ms with a statement granting one-time rights in exchange for copies. Reports in 2 weeks on queries; 1 month on mss. SASE (IRCs) for ms, "unless you don't want ms returned." Simultaneous and reprint submissions OK, "if not from regional publications (OH)." Sample copy for $2. Reviews novels and short story collections.

Payment: Contributor's copies and advertising trade for most; $25 plus advertising trade maximum.

Terms: Pays on publication for one-time rights.

Advice: "My readers are primarily interested in meeting people, dating/relating to the other sex. I like to include a biographical note about my contributors' relation to singles. Although I have little space, I like to tackle tough problems and integrate fiction with editorial and personal experience. I don't shy away from the controversial, but reject the superficial."

SINISTER WISDOM, (IV), Box 3252, Berkeley CA 94703. Editor: Elana Dykewomon. Magazine: 5½×8½; 128-144 pages; 55 lb. stock; 10 pt C1S cover; illustrations; photos. Lesbian-feminist journal, providing fiction, poetry, drama, essays, journals and artwork. Quarterly. Past issues included "Lesbians of Color," and "Resistance." Estab. 1976. Circ. 3,000.

Needs: Lesbian: adventure, contemporary, erotica, ethnic, experimental, fantasy, feminist, historical, humor/satire, literary, prose poem, psychic, regional, science fiction, sports, translations. No heterosexual or male-oriented fiction; nothing that stereotypes or degrades women. Receives 50 unsolicited mss/month. Accepts 25 mss/issue; 75-100 mss/year. Publishes ms 1 month to 1 year after acceptance. Published work by Sapphire, Melanie Kaye/Kantrowitz, Adrienne Rich, Terri L. Jewell and Gloria Anzaldúa; published new writers within the last year. Length: 2,000 words average; 500 words minimum; 4,000 words maximum. Publishes short shorts. Also publishes literary essays, literary criticism, poetry. Occasionally critiques rejected mss. Sometimes recommends other markets.

How to Contact: Send 2 copies of complete ms with cover letter, which should include a brief author's bio to be published when the work is published. Simultaneous submissions OK, if noted. Reports in 2 months on queries; 9 months on mss. SASE (IRCs). Sample copy $6.25. Reviews novels and short story collections. Send books to "Attn: Book review."

Payment: Pays in contributor's copies.

Terms: Rights retained by author.

Advice: The philosophy behind *Sinister Wisdom* is "to reflect and encourage the lesbian movements for social change, especially change in the ways we use language."

SKYLARK, (I), Purdue University, 2200 169th St., Hammond IN 46323. (219)989-2262. Editor: Pamela Hunter. Magazine: 8½×11; 100 pages; illustrations; photos. Fine arts magazine—short stories, poems and graphics for adults. Annual. Estab. 1971. Circ. 600-1,000.

● This college magazine has received three Columbia Scholastic Press Association awards for its essays and poetry.

Needs: Contemporary, ethnic, experimental, fantasy, feminist, humor/satire, literary, mainstream, mystery/suspense (English cozy), prose poem, regional, romance (gothic), science fiction, serialized/excerpted novel, spiritual, sports and western (frontier stories). Upcoming theme: Water (submit November 1993-May 1994). Receives 15 mss/month. Accepts 12-15 mss/issue. Recently published work by James I. Huston, Julie Demboski, Althea E. Rhodes and Chris Dubbs; published new writers within the last year. Length: 4,000 words maximum. Also publishes essays, poetry.

How to Contact: Send complete ms. SASE (IRCs) for ms. Reports in 12 weeks. Sample copy for $5; back issue for $3.

Payment: Pays 1 contributor's copy.

Terms: Acquires first rights. Copyright reverts to author.

Advice: "The goal of *Skylark* is to encourage *creativity* and give beginning and published authors showcase for their work. Manuscripts *must* be carefully prepared and proofread."

SLATE AND STYLE, Magazine of the National Federation of the Blind Writers Division, (IV), NFB Writer's Division, 2704 Beach Dr., Merrick NY 11566. (516)868-8718. Fax: (516)868-9076. Editor: Loraine E. Stayer. Fiction Editor: Loraine Stayer. Newsletter: 8×10; 32 print/40 Braille pages; cassette and large print. "Articles of interest to writers, and resources for blind writers." Quarterly. Estab. 1982. Circ. 200.

Needs: Adventure, contemporary, fantasy, humor/satire, blindness. No erotica. "Avoid theme of death and handicapped." Does not read June, July. Length: 1,000 words average. Publishes short shorts. Also publishes literary criticism, poetry. Critiques rejected mss only if requested. Sometimes recommends other markets.

How to Contact: Send ms with cover letter. Reports in 3 months. Sample copy $2.50 and cassette mailer if tape requested. Large print copies also available. "Sent Free Matter For The Blind. If not blind, send 2 stamps (IRCs)."

Payment: Pays in contributor's copies.

Terms: Acquires one-time rights. Publication not copyrighted. Sponsors contests for fiction writers.

Advice: "Keep a copy. Editors can lose your work. Consider each first draft as just that and review your work before you send it. SASE a must."

‡SLIPPERY WHEN WET, A Magazine of Sex & Fun, (IV), More! Productions, P.O. Box 3101, Berkeley CA 94703. Editor: Suuah Cherwin. Magazine: 8½ × 11; 48 pages; bond paper; illustrations and photos. "Sex is fun; the scene is fun. Here's how to publish; open to erotica, humor, observations and how-tos; interested parties." Quarterly. Estab. 1991. Circ. 2,000.

Needs: Erotica. Receives 5-10 unsolicited mss/month. Acquires 3 mss/issue; 12 mss/year. Publishes ms 3 months after acceptance. Recently published work by Carol Queen, Mark Pritchard and Kris Kovick. Length: 750 words minimum; 5,000 words maximum. Publishes short shorts. Also publishes literary essays, literary criticism and poetry. Often critiques or comments on rejected mss.

How to Contact: Send complete ms with a cover letter and diskette for Mac. Should include estimated word count and bio (1 paragraph). Reports in 1 month on queries; 2 months on mss. Send SASE (or IRC) for reply, return of ms or send a disposable copy of ms. Simultaneous, reprint and electronic (Mac diskette preferred with/hard copy) submissions OK. Sample copy for $7. Fiction guidelines free. Reviews novels and short story collections.

Payment: Pays 2-5 contributor's copies.

Terms: Acquires one-time rights.

Advice: Looks for "hot, funny, new ideas. Ask yourself, 'what does the *reader* discover?' "

SLIPSTREAM, (II, IV), Box 2071, New Market Station, Niagara Falls NY 14301. (716)282-2616. Editor: Dan Sicoli. Fiction Editors: R. Borgatti, D. Sicoli and Livio Farallo. Magazine: 7 × 8½; 100-120 pages; high quality paper and cover; illustrations; photos. "We use poetry and short fiction with a contemporary urban feel." Estab. 1981. Circ. 300.

Needs: Contemporary, erotica, ethnic, experimental, humor/satire, literary, mainstream and prose poem. No religious, juvenile, young adult or romance. Receives over 75 unsolicited mss/month. Accepts 2-8 mss/issue; 6-12 mss/year. Length: under 15 pages. Publishes short shorts. Recently published work by John Richards, Gerald Locklin and Jennie Kaufman. Rarely critiques rejected mss. Sometimes recommends other markets.

How to Contact: "Query before submitting." Reports within 2 months. SASE (IRCs). Sample copy for $5. Fiction guidelines for #10 SASE.

Payment: Pays 2 contributor's copies.

Terms: Acquires one-time rights on publication.

Advice: "Writing should be honest, fresh; develop your own style. Check out a sample issue first. Don't write for the sake of writing, write from the gut as if it were a biological need. Write from experience and mean what you say, but say it in the fewest number of words."

THE SMALL POND MAGAZINE, (II), Box 664, Stratford CT 06497. (203)378-4066. Editor: Napoleon St. Cyr. Magazine: 5½ × 8½; 42 pages; 60 lb. offset paper; 65 lb. cover stock; illustrations (art). "Features contemporary poetry, the salt of the earth, peppered with short prose pieces of various kinds. The college educated and erudite read it for good poetry, prose and pleasure." Triannual. Estab. 1964. Circ. 300.

Needs: "Rarely use science fiction or formula stories you'd find in *Cosmo, Redbook, Ladies Home Journal,* etc." Buys 10-12 mss/year. Longer response time in July and August. Receives approximately 50 unsolicited fiction mss each month. Length: 200-2,500 words. Critiques rejected mss when there is time. Sometimes recommends other markets.

How to Contact: Send complete ms with SASE (IRCs) and short vita. Reports in 2 weeks-3 months. Publishes ms an average of 2-12 months after acceptance. Sample copy for $3; $2.50 for back issues. **Payment:** Pays 2 contributor's copies; $2.50/copy charge for extras. **Terms:** Acquires all rights. **Advice:** "Send for a sample copy first. All mss must be typed. Name and address and story title on front page, name of story on succeeding pages and paginated." Mss are rejected because of "tired plots and poor grammar; also over-long — 2,500 words maximum. Don't send any writing conference ms unless it got an A or better."

SNAKE NATION REVIEW, (II), Snake Nation Press, Inc., 110, #2 West Force St., Valdosta GA 31601. (912)249-8334. Editor: Roberta George. Fiction Editor: Nancy Phillips. 6×9; 110 pages; acid free 70 lb. paper; 90 lb. cover; illustrations and photographs. "We are interested in all types of stories for an educated, discerning, sophisticated audience." Semiannual. Estab. 1989. Circ. 1,000.
  • *Snake Nation Review* receives funding from the Georgia Council of the Arts, the Georgia Humanities Council and the Porter/Fleming Foundation for Literature.
Needs: "Short stories of 5,000 words or less, poems (any length), art work that will be returned after use." Condensed/excerpted novel, contemporary, erotica, ethnic, experimental, fantasy, feminist, gay, horror, humor/satire, lesbian, literary, mainstream, mystery/suspense, prose poem, psychic/supernatural/occult, regional, science fiction, senior citizen/retirement. "We want our writers to have a voice, a story to tell, not a flat rendition of a slice of life." Plans annual anthology. Receives 50 unsolicited mss/month. Buys 8-10 mss/issue; 20 mss/year. Publishes ms 3-6 months after acceptance. Agented fiction 1%. Published work by Judith Oitiz Cofer and Victor Miller. Length: 3,500 words average; 300 words minimum; 5,500 words maximum. Publishes short shorts. Length: 500 words. Also publishes literary essays, poetry. Sometimes critiques rejected mss and recommends other markets.
How to Contact: Send complete ms with cover letter. Reports on queries in 3 months. SASE (IRCs). Sample copy for $5, 8×10 SAE and 90¢ postage. Fiction guidelines for SAE and 1 first-class stamp. **Payment:** Pays $100 maximum and contributor's copies. **Terms:** Buys first rights. Sends galleys to author. **Advice:** "Looks for clean, legible copy and an interesting, unique voice that pulls the reader into the work." Spring contest: short stories (5,000 words); $300 first prize, $200 second prize, $100 third prize; entry fee: $5 for stories, $1 for poems. Contest Issue with every $5 fee.

SNAKE RIVER REFLECTIONS, (I), 1863 Bitterroot Dr., Twin Falls ID 83301. (208)734-0746 (evenings). Editor: William White. Newsletter: 5½×8½; 6 pages; illustrations. "General interest newsletter with social commentary." Published 10 times/year. Estab. 1990. Circ. 300.
  • *Snake River Reflections* was selected to be included in the Hemingway Western Studies Center exhibition "Some Zines, Newsletters and Apas" in 1992.
Needs: Literary, regional and humor/satire. No erotica, gay, lesbian or occult fiction. Accepts 1 ms/issue; 5 mss/year. Publishes ms within 1 month of acceptance. Length: 1,500 words maximum. Also publishes literary essays, literary criticism, poetry. Sometimes critiques rejected mss and recommends other markets.
How to Contact: Submit complete ms with SASE (IRCs). No simultaneous submissions. Sample copy for 60¢. Fiction guidelines for #10 SASE. **Payment:** Pays 2 contributor's copies. **Terms:** Acquires first rights. **Advice:** "Be persistent. Study a sample of our publication. Make your story exciting."

SNOWY EGRET, (II), The Fair Press, P.O. Box 9, Bowling Green IN 47833. (812)829-1910. Editors: Karl Barnebey, Mike Aycock. Magazine: 8½×11; 50 pages; text paper; heavier cover; illustrations. "Literary exploration of the abundance and beauty of nature and the ways human beings interact with it." Semiannual. Estab. 1922. Circ. 500.
Needs: Nature writing, including 'true' stories, eye-witness accounts, descriptive sketches and traditional fiction. "We are particularly interested in fiction that celebrates abundance and beauty of nature, encourages a love and respect for the natural world, and affirms the human connection to the environment. No works written for popular genres: horror, science fiction, romance, detective, western, etc." Receives 25 unsolicited ms/month. Buys up to 6 mss/issue; up to 12 mss/year. Publishes ms 6 months-1 year after acceptance. Published works by Jane Candia Coleman, Stephen Lewandowski and Margarita Mondrus Engle. Length: 1,000-3,000 words preferred; 500 words minimum; 10,000 words maximum. Publishes short shorts. Length: 400-500 words. Sometimes critiques rejected mss and recommends other markets.

How to Contact: Send complete ms with cover letter. "Cover letter optional: do not query." Reports in 2 months. SASE (IRCs). Simultaneous submissions OK if noted. Sample copy for $8, 9×12 SAE. Send #10 SASE for writer's guidelines.
Payment: Pays $2/page; 2 contributor's copies; charge for extras.
Terms: Pays on publication. Purchases first North American serial rights. Sends galleys to author. Publication copyrighted.
Advice: Looks for "honest, freshly detailed pieces with plenty of description and/or dialogue which will allow the reader to identify with the characters and step into the setting. Characters who relate strongly to nature, either positively or negatively, and who, during the course of the story, grow in their understanding of themselves and the world around them."

SOUNDINGS EAST, (II), English Dept., Salem State College, Salem MA 01970. (508)741-6270. Advisory Editor: Claire Keyes. Magazine: 5½×8½; 64 pages; illustrations; photos. "Mainly a college audience, but we also distribute to libraries throughout the country." Biannual. Estab. 1973. Circ. 3,000.
Needs: Literary, contemporary, prose poem. No juvenile. Publishes 4-5 stories/issue. Receives 30 unsolicited fiction mss each month. Submissions limited to 2 fiction pieces, 5 poems, and/or 5 photos/illustrations. Does not read April-August. Deadlines: November 20, Fall/Winter issue; April 20, Spring/Summer issue. Published work by James Brady, Terry Farish and Christina Shea; published new writers within the last year. 250-4,000 words. "We are open to short pieces as well as to long works."
How to Contact: Send complete ms with SASE (IRCs) between September and March. Accepts partial novels and multiple submissions if notified. Reports in 1-3 months on mss. Sample copy for $3.
Payment: Pays 2 contributor's copies.
Terms: All publication rights revert to author.
Advice: "We're impressed by an excitement—coupled with craft—in the use of the language. It also helps to reach in and grab the reader by the heart."

‡SOUTH CAROLINA REVIEW, (II), Clemson University, Clemson SC 29634-1503. (803)656-3229. Editors: R.J. Calhoun, Frank Day and Carol Johnston. Managing Editor: Mark Winchell. Magazine: 6×9; 200 pages; 60 lb. cream white vellum paper; 65 lb. cream white vellum cover stock; illustrations and photos rarely. Semiannual. Estab. 1967. Circ. 700.
Needs: Literary, contemporary, humor and ethnic. Receives 50-60 unsolicited fiction mss each month. Does not read mss June-August or December. Published work by Joyce Carol Oates, Rosanne Coggeshall, Stephen Dixon; published new writers within the last year. Rarely critiques rejected mss.
How to Contact: Send complete ms with SASE (IRCs). Reports in 6-9 months on mss. Sample copy $5.
Payment: Pays in contributor's copies.
Advice: Mss are rejected because of "poorly structured stories, or stories without vividness or intensity. The most celebrated function of a little magazine is to take a chance on writers not yet able to get into the larger magazines—the little magazine can encourage promising writers at a time when encouragement is vitally needed. (We also publish 'name' writers, like Joyce Carol Oates, Stephen Dixon, George Garrett.) Read the masters extensively. Write and write more, with a *schedule*. Listen to editorial advice when offered. Don't get discouraged with rejections. Read what writers say about writing (e.g. *The Paris Review* interviews with George Plimpton; Welty's *One Writer's Beginnings*, etc). Take courses in writing and listen to, even if you do not follow, the advice."

SOUTH DAKOTA REVIEW, (II), University of South Dakota, Box 111, University Exchange, Vermillion SD 57069. (605)677-5966. Editor: John R. Milton. Associate Editor: Brian Bedard. Magazine: 6×9; 150 pages; book paper; glossy cover stock; illustrations sometimes; photos on cover. "Literary magazine for university and college audiences and their equivalent. Emphasis is often on the West and its writers, but will accept mss from anywhere. Issues are generally fiction and poetry with some literary essays." Quarterly. Estab. 1963. Circ. 500.
Needs: Literary, contemporary, ethnic, experimental, excerpted novel, regional and translations. "We like very well-written stories. Contemporary western American setting appeals, but not necessary. No formula stories, sports or adolescent 'I' narrator." Receives 30 unsolicited fiction mss/month. Accepts about 10-20 mss/year, more or less. Assistant editor accepts mss in June-July, sometimes August. Agented fiction 5%. Publishes short shorts of 5 pages double-spaced typescript. Published work by Ed Loomis, Max Evans and Dennis Lynds; published new writers within the last year. Length: 1,300 words minimum; 6,000 words maximum. (Has made exceptions, up to novella length.) Sometimes recommends other markets.

How to Contact: Send complete ms with SASE (IRCs). "We like cover letters that are not boastful and do not attempt to sell the stories but rather provide some personal information about the writer." No multiple submissions. Reports in 5-7 weeks. Publishes ms an average of 1-6 months after acceptance. Sample copy for $5.
Payment: Pays 2-4 contributor's copies, depending on length of ms; $3 charge for extras.
Terms: Acquires first rights and second serial rights.
Advice: Rejects mss because of "careless writing; often careless typing; stories too personal ('I' confessional), adolescent; working manuscript, not polished; subject matter that editor finds trivial. We are trying to use more fiction and more variety. We would like to see more sophisticated stories. Do not try to outguess editors and give them what you think they want. Write honestly. Be yourself."

SOUTHEASTERN FRONT, (I, II), Southeastern Front Organization, 565 17th St. NW, Cleveland TN 37311. Editor: Robin Merritt. Magazine: 8½×11; 40-60 pages; glossy cover; illustrations and photos. "*Southeastern FRONT* is an artists and writers representation/presentation service, a gallery in a magazine. Our aim is to provide exposure for artists and writers from all over the US and abroad. We hope to create an excellent medium of presentation for artists from isolated geographic areas." Estab. 1986. Circ. 1,500.
Needs: "There are no stylistic limitations on submissions or subject matter. We are interested in finding high quality new work by new and/or emerging artists and writers and helping them to obtain exposure. No pieces which are devoid of intellectual or aesthetic merit, nor strictly commercially designed work." Receives 12-20 unsolicited mss/month. Accepts 5-8 mss/issue; 18-20 mss/year. Published new writers within the last year. Length: no restrictions. Publishes short shorts. Critiques rejected mss. Recommends other markets.
How to Contact: Send complete ms with cover letter. Reports in 2-4 months on queries and mss. SASE (IRCs) for ms. Simultaneous and reprint submissions OK *if authors retain rights.* Write for information on availability of sample copies. Fiction guidelines for SAE and 1 first-class postage.
Payment: Pays contributor's copies; charge for extras at wholesale rates for more than 5 copies.
Terms: Writers retain all rights.
Advice: "Allow yourself total creative and intellectual freedom, but never forget to be an artist, a craftsman who is conscious of aesthetic values. Be sure to include substantial human experience in your plots."

SOUTHERN CALIFORNIA ANTHOLOGY, (II), Master of Professional Writing Program—USC, MPW-WPH 404 USC, Los Angeles CA 90089-4034. (213)740-3252. Contact: Sarah Pearson. Magazine: 5½×8½; 142 pages; semi-glossy cover stock. "The *Southern California Anthology* is a literary review that is an eclectic collection of previously unpublished quality contemporary fiction, poetry and interviews with established literary people, published for adults of all professions; of particular interest to those interested in serious contemporary literature." Annual. Estab. 1983. Circ. 1,500.
Needs: Contemporary, ethnic, experimental, feminist, historical (general), humor/satire, literary, mainstream, regional, serialized/excerpted novel. No juvenile, religious, confession, romance, science fiction. Receives 30 unsolicited fiction mss each month. Accepts 10-12 mss/issue. Does not read February-September. Publishes ms 4 months after acceptance. Length: 10-15 pages average; 2 pages minimum; 25 pages maximum. Publishes short shorts.
How to Contact: Send complete ms with cover letter or submit through agent. Cover letter should include list of previous publications. Reports on queries in 1 month; on mss in 4 months. SASE (IRCs). Sample copy $4. Fiction guidelines for #10 SAE and 1 first-class stamp.
Payment: Pays in contributor's copies.
Terms: Acquires first rights.
Advice: "The *Anthology* pays particular attention to craft and style in its selection of narrative writing."

SOUTHERN EXPOSURE, (II, IV), Institute for Southern Studies, P.O. Box 531, Durham NC 27702. (919)419-8311. Editor: Eric Bates. Magazine: 8½×11; 64 pages. "Southern politics and culture—investigative reporting, oral history, fiction for an audience of Southern changemakers—scholars, journalists, activists." Quarterly. Estab. 1972. Circ. 5,000.
  • *Southern Exposure* has won numerous awards for its reporting including the Sidney Hillman Award for reporting on racial justice issues.
Needs: Contemporary, ethnic, feminist, gay, humor/satire, lesbian, literary, regional. Receives 50 unsolicited mss/month. Buys 1 mss/issue; 4 mss/year. Publishes ms 3-6 months after acceptance. Agented fiction 25%. Published work by Clyde Egerton, Jill McCorkle and Larry Brown. Length: 3,500 words preferred.

How to Contact: Send complete ms with cover letter. No simultaneous submissions. Reports in 4-6 weeks on mss. SASE (IRCs) for ms. Sample copy for $4, 8½×11 and $1.85 postage. Fiction guidelines for #10 SAE and 1 first-class stamp.
Payment: Pays $100, subscription to magazine and contributor's copies.
Terms: Pays on publication for first rights.

SOUTHERN HUMANITIES REVIEW, (II, IV), Auburn University, 9088 Haley Center, Auburn University AL 36849. Co-editors: Dan R. Latimer and R.T. Smith. Magazine: 6×9; 96 pages; 60 lb. neutral pH, natural paper, 65 lb. neutral pH med. coated cover stock; occasional illustrations and photos. "We publish essays, poetry, fiction and reviews. Our fiction has ranged from very traditional in form and content to very experimental. Literate, college-educated audience. We hope they read our journal for both enlightenment and pleasure." Quarterly. Estab. 1967. Circ. 800.
• *Poet's Market* 1993 features an interview with R.T. Smith, poet and co-editor of *SHR.*
Needs: Serious fiction, fantasy, feminist, humor and regional. Receives approximately 25 unsolicited fiction mss each month. Accepts 1-2 mss/issue, 4-6 mss/year. Slower reading time in summer. Published work by Anne Brashler, Heimito von Doderer and Ivo Andric; published new writers within the last year. Length: 3,500-5,000 words. Also publishes literary essays, literary criticism, poetry. Critiques rejected mss when there is time. Sometimes recommends other markets.
How to Contact: Send complete ms (one at a time) with SASE (IRCs) and cover letter with an explanation of topic chosen—special, certain book, etc., a little about author if they have never submitted. Reports in 90 days. Sample copy for $5. Reviews novel and short story collections.
Payment: Pays 2 contributor's copies; $5 charge for extras.
Terms: Acquires all rights. Sends galleys to author.
Advice: "Send us the ms with SASE. If we like it, we'll take it or we'll recommend changes. If we don't like it, we'll send it back as promptly as possible. Read the journal. Send a typewritten, clean copy carefully proofread. We also award annually the Hoepfner Prize of $100 for the best published essay or short story of the year. Let someone whose opinion you respect read your story and give you an honest appraisal. Rewrite, if necessary, to get the most from your story."

THE SOUTHERN REVIEW, (II), Louisiana State University, 43 Allen Hall, Baton Rouge LA 70803. (504)388-5108. Editors: James Olney and Dave Smith. Magazine: 6¾×10; 240 pages; 50 lb. Glatfelter paper; 65 lb. #1 grade cover stock; occasional photos. "A literary quarterly publishing critical essays, poetry and fiction for a highly intellectual audience." Quarterly. Published special fiction issue. Estab. 1935. Circ. 3,000.
• This quality literary journal was ranked #50 on the latest *Writer's Digest* Fiction 50 list.
Needs: Literary and contemporary. "We emphasize style and substantial content. No mystery, fantasy or religious mss." Buys 7-8 mss/issue. Receives approximately 100 unsolicited fiction mss each month. Agented fiction 5%. Recently published work by Gloria Naylor, Wendell Berry and Jill McCorkle; published new writers within the last year. Length: 2,000-10,000 words. Also publishes literary essays, literary criticism, poetry. Sometimes recommends other markets.
How to Contact: Send complete ms with cover letter and SASE (IRCs). "Prefer brief letters giving information on author concerning where he/she has been published before, biographical info and what he/she is doing now." Reports in 2 months on mss. Publishes ms an average of 1-2 years after acceptance. Sample copy for $5. Reviews novels and short story collections.
Payment: Pays $12/printed page; 2 contributor's copies.
Terms: Pays on publication for first North American serial rights. "We transfer copyright to author on request." Sends galleys to author.
Advice: "Develop a careful style with characters in depth." Sponsors annual contest for best first collection of short stories published during the calendar year.

SOUTHWEST REVIEW, (II), Box 374, 307 Fondren Library West, Southern Methodist University, Dallas TX 75275. (214)768-1037. Editor: Willard Spiegelman. Magazine: 6×9; 144 pages. "The majority of our readers are college-educated adults who wish to stay abreast of the latest and best in contemporary fiction, poetry, literary criticism and books in all but the most specialized disciplines." Quarterly. Estab. 1915. Circ. 1,600.
Needs: "High literary quality; no specific requirements as to subject matter, but cannot use sentimental, religious, western, poor science fiction, pornographic, true confession, mystery, juvenile or serialized or condensed novels." Upcoming theme: "New and Familiar Voices in American Fiction." Receives approximately 200 unsolicited fiction mss each month. Recently published work by Janet Peery, Anne West, Askold Melnyczuk, Brad Conard and Millicent Dillon. Length: prefers 3,000-5,000 words.

Also publishes literary essays, poetry. Occasionally critiques rejected mss. Sometimes recommends other markets.

How to Contact: Send complete ms with SASE (IRCs). Reports in 6 months on mss. Publishes ms 6-12 months after acceptance. Sample copy for $5. Guidelines for SASE.

Payment: Payment varies; writers receive 3 contributor's copies.

Terms: Pays on publication for first North American serial rights. Sends galleys to author.

Advice: "We have become less regional. A lot of time would be saved for us and for the writer if he or she looked at a copy of the *Southwest Review* before submitting. We like to receive a cover letter because it is some reassurance that the author has taken the time to check a current directory for the editor's name. When there isn't a cover letter, we wonder whether the same story is on 20 other desks around the country."

SOU'WESTER, (II), Southern Illinois University-Edwardsville, Edwardsville IL 62026-1438. (618)692-3190. Managing Editor: Fred W. Robbins. Magazine: 6×9; 88 pages; Warren's Olde Style paper; 60 lb. cover. General magazine of poetry and fiction. Triannual. Estab. 1960. Circ. 300.

Needs: Receives 40-50 unsolicited fiction mss/month. Accepts 3 mss/issue; 9 mss/year. Published work by Robert Wexelblatt and Robert Solomon; published new writers within the last year. Length: 10,000 words maximum. Also publishes poetry. Occasionally critiques rejected mss.

How to Contact: Send complete ms with SASE (IRCs). Simultaneous submissions OK. Reports in 4 months. Publishes ms an average of 6 months after acceptance. Sample copy for $5.

Payment: Pays 2 contributor's copies; $5 charge for extras.

Terms: Acquires first serial rights.

‡SPECTRUM, (II), Box 14800, University of California, Santa Barbara CA 93107. Editor: Robert Cruzen. Magazine: 6×9; 100-150 pages; illustrations and photos. "Interested in quality work. Poetry, fiction and essay." Annual. Estab. 1957. Circ. 750.

Needs: Literary. No science fiction. Does not read mss January 15-August. Publishes short shorts. Also publishes literary essays, literary criticism, poetry.

How to Contact: Send complete ms. SASE (IRCs). Simultaneous submissions OK. Sample copy for $4 and 7×10 SAE. Fiction guidelines for #10 SASE.

Payment: Contributor's copies.

SPECTRUM, (II), Box 72-C, Anna Maria College, Sunset Lane, Paxton MA 01612. (617)849-3450. Editor: Robert H. Goepfert. Magazine: 6×9; 64 pages; illustrations and photos. "An interdisciplinary publication publishing fiction as well as poetry, scholarly articles, reviews, art and photography. Submissions are especially encouraged from those affiliated with liberal arts colleges." Semiannual. Estab. 1985. Circ. 1,000.

Needs: Contemporary, experimental, historical, literary, mainstream. No western, mystery, erotica, science fiction. Receives an average of 15 unsolicited fiction ms/month. Accepts 4-6 mss/issue. Publishes ms approximately 6 months after acceptance. Length: 2,000-5,000 words preferred; 3,000 words average; 10,000 words maximum. Publishes short shorts. Also publishes literary essays, literary criticism, poetry. Sometimes critiques rejected mss and recommends other markets.

How to Contact: Send complete ms with cover letter. Reports in 6 weeks. SASE (IRCs) for ms. No simultaneous submissions. Sample copy for $3. Fiction guidelines with SASE.

Payment: Pays $20 and 2 contributor's copies.

Terms: Pays on publication for first North American serial rights. Sends pre-publication galleys to author. Publication not copyrighted.

Advice: "Our chief aim is diversity."

‡SPECTRUM•TXT, (II), Spectrum Press, Inc., Box 109, 3023 N. Clark St., Chicago IL 60657. Editor: D.P. Agin. Electronic disk magazine. "*Spectrum.txt* is an intellectual review published on floppy disks. We publish only on computer disks, no print media publishing at all. Our disks are floppy disks and not CD-ROM and are available in both PC (all disk sizes) and Macintosh (1.44 M disks only) formats." Estab. 1993.

• See the interview with Spectrum Press Editor D.P. Agin in the Small Press section of this edition.

Needs: Open. Publishes short shorts. Also publishes literary essays and poetry.

How to Contact: Query first or submit on floppy disks, PC/DOS formatted, ASCII or WordPerfect (DOS) texts. Mac disks can be submitted, provided disks or HD (1.44m) and text is plain Mac ASCII. Send SASE (or IRC) for reply, return of disk. Simultaneous and reprint submissions OK (if author has electronic rights). "A typical PC Spectrum.txt disk (comes with simple text reader) has a retail price of $6." Fiction guidelines free.

Payment: Pays 1 contributor's copy.

Terms: All rights revert to author on publication and author retains all print media rights prior to publication.

‡**SPELLBOUND, Tales of Myth, Magic and Mayhem, (I, II, IV)**, 7705 Mountain Creek Way, Douglas-ville GA 30134. (404)949-2404. Editor: Cathy Shanks. Magazine: 8½ × 11; 80-100 pages; bond paper; hi-gloss cover stock; b&w illustrations. "Fantasy of all types: heroic, sword and sorcery, high, western, humor. Myths from traditional mythology. Gay themes okay. This is an adult publication, where tales of heroes and gods provide old-fashioned action adventure entertainment." Semiannual. Estab. 1993. Circ. 500.

Needs: Fantasy (contemporary, sci-fantasy, sword and sorcery); "must contain strong elements of mythology or active magic." No "horror, hard sci-fi, no 'dead children' stories, no bleak endings." Receives 60-100 unsolicited mss/month. Accepts 14-20 ms/issue; 40 mss/year maximum. Publishes ms 6-18 months after acceptance. Length: 5,000 words preferred; 300 words minimum; 10,000 words maximum. Publishes short shorts. Length: 400 words. Also publishes poetry. Always critiques or comments on rejected mss.

How to Contact: Send complete ms with a cover letter. Should include estimated word count and short bio. Reports in 2 months on queries. Send SASE (or IRC) for reply, return of ms or send a disposable copy of ms. Electronic submissions OK. Sample copy for $6 (postpaid). Fiction guidelines for #10 SAE and 1 first-class stamp.

Payment: Pays minimum of 1 contributor's copy; additional copies for $5.

Terms: Acquires one-time rights.

Advice: "Looking for upbeat, not sappy, stories that emphasize the basic heroic nature of people. Fast-paced action adventure with strong dialogue. Magic should be central to story; mythology from traditional myths. New writers, send something reasonably short—2,500 to 3,500 words. READ: what's already been overdone in fantasy won't find a home in *Spellbound*. Keep the story moving—I love action stories." Would like to see more "traditional, male sword and sorcery; Native American myths; contemporary or futuristic fantasy in a cyberpunk vein but with strong magic—something similiar to the 'Shadow Run' series."

THE SPIRIT THAT MOVES US, (II), Box 820-N, Jackson Heights NY 11372-0820. (718)426-8788. Editor: Morty Sklar. Publishes fiction, essays, poetry and artwork. "We want feeling and imagination, work coming from the human experience." Annual. Estab. 1975. Circ. 1,500-2,000.

● The Spirit That Moves Us Press (also listed in this book) publishes the *Editor's Choice* anthologies, featuring selections from the small press.

Needs: "SASE (IRCs) first to find out what our needs are." Literary and contemporary—"anything goes, if it is fiction, poetry or art." Upcoming theme: "Phoenix: Stories, Essays & Poetry from Former Drug Addicts." Buys 5-6 mss/issue and about 15 mss for special fiction issues. Receives approximately 90 unsolicited fiction mss each month. Published work by W.P. Kinsella, Julia Alvarez, Bhararti Mukh-erJee, Jaime Manrique; published new writers within the last year. Length: 10,000 words maximum. Also publishes literary essays, poetry. Critiques rejected mss when there is time.

How to Contact: Send SASE first for theme and plans. "A cover letter sort of makes the exchange more personal." Simultaneous submissions OK, if noted. Reports in 1 week-1 month on mss. Publishes ms an average of 6 months after acceptance. Sample copy $5.50 for *Free Parking*, our 15th Anniversary collection.

Payment: Pays cash and free cloth copy, 40% discount for paperbacks; 25% on all other publications.

Terms: Acquires first rights. Buys reprints for anthology issue.

Advice: "Query first for theme with SASE. We're small but good and well-reviewed. Send the work you love best. Write from yourself and not from what you feel is the fashion or what the editor wants. This editor wants what you want if it has heart, imagination and skill. Aside from the obvious reason for rejection, poor writing, the main reason for rejection is lack of human concerns—that is, the writer seems to be concerned with style more than content. Read a copy of the magazine you'll be submitting work to. Don't rely on your writing for money unless you're in it for the money. Have time to write, as much time as you can get (be anti-social if necessary). Do not send a manuscript to be 'tossed' if we can't use them. We want writers to recycle/resend them."

SPIT: A JOURNAL OF THE ARTS, (I), #7, 240 E. Ninth St., New York NY 10003. (212)505-9590. Magazine: 8½×11; 50-75 pages; illustrations and photographs. "We are a magazine for emerging artists as well as for more established artists who support our work. We consider fiction/prose of all styles. Audience is varied, though at the moment, mostly avant-garde." Published every 6-9 months. Estab. 1990. Circ. 400.
Needs: Contemporary, erotica, ethnic, experimental, feminist, gay, historical (general), humor/satire, lesbian, literary, prose poem, regional, senior citizen/retirement, translations. Receives 30 unsolicited mss/month. Accepts 4-5 mss/issue. Publishes ms up to 6 months after acceptance. Published work by Jennifer Blowdryer, Steven Schrader and Jeremy Stoljar. Length: 2,500 words average; 6,000 words maximum. Publishes short shorts. Sometimes critiques rejected mss.
How to Contact: Send complete ms with cover letter. Include a brief biographical statement. Reports in 2 weeks on queries; up to 9 months on mss. SASE (IRCs). Simultaneous and reprint submissions OK. Sample copy for $3; current issue for $4. Fiction guidelines for any size SAE and 1 first-class stamp.
Payment: Pays in contributor's copies.
Terms: Acquires one-time rights.
Advice: "We are interested in discovering and supporting new writers of all styles, experiences, backgrounds and orientations. It is not necessary that our writers be thoroughly developed or polished; a unique voice, vision or use of language will draw our editors to a work of fiction or prose."

SPITBALL (I), 6224 Collegevue Place, Cincinnati OH 45224. (513)541-4296. Editor: Mike Shannon. Magazine: 5½×8½; 96 pages; 55 lb. Glatfelter Natural, Neutral, pH paper; 10 pt. C1S cover stock; illustrations; photos. Magazine publishing "fiction and poetry about *baseball* exclusively for an educated, literary segment of the baseball fan population." Quarterly. Estab. 1981. Circ. 1,000.
Needs: Confession, contemporary, experimental, historical, literary, mainstream and suspense. "Our only requirement concerning the type of fiction written is that the story be *primarily* about baseball." Receives "100 or so" unsolicited fiction mss/year. Accepts 12-16 mss/year. Published work by Dallas Wiebe, Michael Gilmartin and Rick Wilber. Published new writers within the last year. Length: 20 typed double spaced pages. The longer it is, the better it has to be.
How to Contact: Send complete ms with SASE (IRCs), and cover letter with brief bio about author. Reporting time varies. Publishes ms an average of 3 months after acceptance. Sample copy for $5.
Payment: "No monetary payment at present. We may offer nominal payment in the near future." 2 free contributor's copies per issue in which work appears.
Terms: Acquires first North American serial rights. Buys reprints "if the work is good enough and it hasn't had major exposure already."
Advice: "Our audience is mostly college educated and knowledgeable about baseball. The stories we have published so far have been very well written and displayed a firm grasp of the baseball world and its people. In short, audience response has been great because the stories are simply good as stories. Thus, mere use of baseball as subject is no guarantee of acceptance. We are always seeking submissions. Unlike many literary magazines, we have no backlog of accepted material. Consult *The Best of Spitball* (1988) by Pocket Books, Div. of Simon & Schuster. Still in print even if not in local bookstores. Fiction is a natural genre for our exclusive subject, baseball. There are great opportunities for writing in certain areas of fiction, baseball being one of them. Baseball has become the 'in' spectator sport among intellectuals, the general media and the 'yuppie' crowd. Consequently, as subject matter for adult fiction it has gained a much wider acceptance than it once enjoyed."

SPOOFING!, Yarns and Such, (I, IV), Creative With Words Publications, Box 223226, Carmel CA 93922. Editor: Brigitta Geltrich. Editors rotate. Booklet: 5½×8½; approximately 60 pages; bond paper; illustrations. Folklore. Annual. Estab. 1975. Circ. varies.
Needs: Ethnic, humor/satire, mystery/suspense (amateur sleuth, private eye), regional, folklore. "Once a year we publish an anthology of the writings of young writers, titled: *We are Writers Too!*" No violence or erotica, religious fiction. Upcoming themes: "Animals," "Cartoons," "Impossible Loves (clean family reading)." Receives 100 unsolicited fiction mss/month. Does not read mss July-August. Publishes ms 2-6 months after acceptance. Publishes after set deadlines: after July 31 or December 31 of any given year. Published new writers within the last year. Length: 1,000 words average. Critiques rejected mss "when requested, *then we charge $20/prose, up to 1,000 words.*"
How to Contact: Query first or send complete ms with cover letter and SASE (IRCs). "Reference has to be made to which project the manuscript is being submitted. Unsolicited mss without SASE will be destroyed after holding them 1 month." Reports in 2 weeks on queries; 2 months on mss; longer on specific seasonal anthologies. No simultaneous submissions. Accepts electronic submissions

Blending Genres Can Make Work Fresh

Square One Editor Bill Gagliani is living proof that editing a small press magazine is a labor of love. His work requires not only great dedication with few rewards, but also, admittedly, a little insanity.

Square One began as a student publication at the University of Wisconsin in 1984. Since then, the magazine's goal has been to publish good fiction, regardless of its classification.

No longer associated with the university, *Square One* is now a one-person operation. Gagliani squeezes the magazine into his busy schedule that includes, among other projects, a fulltime job and his own writing.

Gagliani receives 40-50 manuscripts per month and only publishes 6-12 per year. He says he tries to reply to every submission, although this sometimes takes him nearly a year.

"As a writer, I like to know if I struck out totally, or if I was close, or if there was something I could fix that they would like better, so I try to do that," he says.

Over half the submissions he receives— and half of those published— are by new writers. Although Gagliani says he doesn't base decisions on how many published credits a writer has, he advises writers to rigorously pursue publication, and to be "persistent and polite.

"Publishing in the small press allows newer writers to build a body of work," he says. "It's a good experience, even though there's not a lot of money in it. And the small press can be a stepping stone for writers hoping to advance to the paying publications."

Gagliani says he reads many manuscripts with great beginnings that are ruined when the writer changes point of view. Narrow focus is the key.

"An author shouldn't try to get at all those background facts by hitting me in the head with them in big lumps, especially at the beginning of the story," he says. "I'd rather look at what is happening within the story than at all the things that led up to it."

The protagonist in a good story in any genre should change during the course of the story, he says. "I don't believe in epiphany stories per se, but if the character is exactly the same at the end of the story as he was at the beginning, chances are I'm not going to like it very much."

He adds that he gets a lot of stories that resemble TV scripts. "I get a lot of middle-of-the-road stuff where the writer really hasn't thought through 'what would the character do next?' It's as if they're looking at their watch and thinking, 'six minutes to go, time to wrap it up.' "

What does he want to see more of? Genre-blending. "I think if people did more genre blending we wouldn't have genres anymore, and that would be great. A mainstream story with a slight fantasy element is great. I want magic realism. I like things like urban fantasy, mysteries that are quirky. I love many of the subcategories of science fiction, because they're hard-edged, they're today . . . I see too much of the same old thing."

His apartment, he says, is a sea of paper. Sometimes weeding through the manuscripts is a chore. The hardest part is getting started. And of course, he jokes, he's not getting rich doing it.

So why does he keep it up?

"I don't know. It's crazy, really. Maybe it's a vicarious thrill of giving other people the opportunity to get published, sometimes to the detriment of my own work. I guess the only way to explain it is that I love writing and I love reading. Whether I'm reading the newest novel by a big-name writer or stories by people who are hoping to get published, I love it."

—*Argie Manolis*

---

via Radio Shack Model 4/6 disk and Macintosh. Sample copy price $5 for children's issues, $6 for adult issues. Fiction guidelines for #10 SASE.
Payment: No payment. 20% reduction on each copy ordered.
Terms: Acquires one-time rights.

SPSM&H, (II, IV), *Amelia* Magazine, 329 "E" St., Bakersfield CA 93304. (805)323-4064. Editor: Frederick A. Raborg, Jr. Magazine: 5½×8¼; 24 pages; Matte cover stock; illustrations and photos. "*SPSM&H* publishes sonnets, sonnet sequences and fiction, articles and reviews related to the form (fiction may be romantic or Gothic) for a general readership and sonnet enthusiasts." Quarterly. Estab. 1985. Circ. 600.
● This magazine is edited by Frederick A. Raborg, Jr., who is also editor of *Amelia* and *Cicada*. See also the listing for the *Amelia* Magazine Awards.
Needs: Adventure, confession, contemporary, erotica, ethnic, experimental, fantasy, feminist, gay, historical (general), horror, humor/satire, lesbian, literary, mainstream, mystery/suspense, regional, contemporary and historical romance, science fiction, senior citizen/retirement, translations and western. All should have romantic element. "We look for strong fiction with romantic or Gothic content, or both. Stories need not have 'happy' endings, and we are open to the experimental and/or avantgarde. Erotica is fine; pornography, no." Receives 30 unsolicited mss/month. Buys 1 ms/issue; 4 mss/year. Publishes ms 6 months-1 year after acceptance. Agented fiction 5%. Recently published work Brad Hooper, Mary Louise R. O'Hara and Clara Castelar Bjorlie. Length: 2,000 words average; 500 words minimum; 3,000 words maximum. When appropriate critiques rejected ms; recommends other markets.
How to Contact: Send complete ms with cover letter. Should include Social Security number. Reports in 2 weeks. SASE (IRCs). Sample copy for $4.50. Fiction guidelines for #10 SAE and 1 first-class stamp.
Payment: Pays $10-25; contributor's copies; charge for extras.
Terms: Pays on publication for first North American serial rights.
Advice: "A good story line (plot) and strong characterization are vital. I want to know the writer has done his homework and is striving to become professional."

SQUARE ONE, A Magazine of Fiction, (I, II), Tarkus Press, Box 11921, Milwaukee WI 53211-0921. Editor: William D. Gagliani. Magazine: 7×8½; 75-90 pages; 20 lb. white bond paper; 80 lb. colored linen cover; illustrations; pen and ink drawings or any black on white. "There is no specific theme at *Square One*, but we publish only fiction and illustrations. Aimed at a general literate audience—people who *enjoy* reading fiction." Annual. Estab. 1984. Circ. 250.
● See the interview with Editor William Gagliani in this book.

Needs: Open to all categories including mainstream, mystery, science fiction, horror (all subgenres), fantasy, magic realism, suspense, etc. "We like exciting stories in which things happen and characters *exist*." Receives 40-50 unsolicited fiction mss/month. Does not read mss between May and September. Accepts 6-12 mss/issue, depending on lengths; 6-12 mss/year. Publishes ms generally 1-14 months after acceptance. Published new writers within the last year. Length: 3,000 words average; 7,500 words maximum. Occasionally publishes short shorts but not vignettes. "It is editorial policy to comment on at least 75% of submissions rejected, but *please* be patient—we have a very small staff."

How to Contact: Send complete ms with cover letter. "Too many letters explain or describe the story. Let the fiction stand on its own. If it doesn't, the letter won't help. We like a brief bio and a few credits, but some writers get carried away. Use restraint and plain language—don't try to impress (it usually backfires)." Reports in 1-14 months on mss. SASE (IRCs) for ms. Simultaneous (if so labeled) and reprint submissions OK. Can accept electronic submissions via disk, "DS/DD, 3.5" Atari Mega ST Disks (using WordPerfect 4.1 for Atari) and HD or DS/DD 3.5" disks (using Microsoft Word 5.0, Works, or WordPerfect 2.0+ for Macintosh). Hard copy should accompany any electronic submissions." Sample copies of older issues, $2.50, 9 × 12 SAE and 7 first-class stamps. Fiction guidelines for #10 SAE and 1 first-class stamp. Please make checks payable to William D. Gagliani.

Payment: Pays 2 contributor's copies.

Terms: Acquires one-time rights.

Advice: "*Square One* is not a journal for beginners, despite what the name may imply. Rather, the name refers to the back-to-basics approach that we take—fiction must first and foremost be compelling. We want to see stories that elicit a response from the reader. We are currently seeking more horror/dark fantasy (all subgenres welcome), but still like to see variety—strong fiction in any genre remains an overall theme. We must stress that, since we are an irregular publication, contributors should expect long response lags. Our staff is small and *Square One* is a part-time endeavor. Patience is the best advice we can offer. Financial difficulties have delayed our new issue several times, but it is in production and we are reading for future issues. Also, we oppose the absurdity of asking that writers subscribe to every magazine they would like to write for, especially given most writers' financial state. Check local public and college libraries and bookstores to see what's going on in the small press and literary markets, and—as a matter of dignity—consider carefully before submitting to magazines that routinely charge reading fees."

STARLIGHT, Star Books, Inc., 408 Pearson St., Wilson NC 27893. (919)237-1591. Editor: Allen W. Harrell. Magazine: digest-sized 5½ × 7½; 64 pages; 20 lb. paper; b&w illustrations and photographs. "Christian inspirational material for men and women of all ages, some children." Quarterly. Estab. 1987.

Needs: Religious/inspirational. Wants "any genre, for any age, as long as it is exciting, God-honoring, in conformity with biblical truth." Publishes ms less than 3 months after acceptance. Published work by Anthony Chiarilli and John R. Price. Length: "10-12 double-spaced pages but open to longer or shorter." Also publishes poetry. Sometimes critiques rejected mss and suggests rewrite.

How to Contact: Send complete ms with cover letter. No simultaneous submissions. Reports in 2-4 months. SASE (IRCs). Sample copy for $4. Fiction guidelines for #10 SAE and 2 first-class stamps.

Payment: Pays 3 contributor's copies.

Terms: Acquires first rights.

Advice: "We want to see the surprises the Lord assigns to His people. First-person, personal, pro-life."

STARRY NIGHTS, (I, II, IV), Merry Men Press, 274 Roanoke Road, El Cajon CA 92020. Editor: Robin Hood. Magazine: 8½ × 11; 100 pages; 20 lb. paper; 90 lb. cover stock. Erotic science fiction/fantasy, art "for a mature audience." Estab. 1990.

Needs: Erotica: mystery (romantic suspense), romance (gothic), science fiction (hard science). "See guidelines for definition of erotica. There's a big difference between *E* and *pornography*." Has published special fiction issue in the past. Receives 7 unsolicited mss per month; buys up to 15 mss per issue. Publishes ms 1-11 months after acceptance. "Will accept multiple stories from same author. Comments on rejected mss and recommends other markets.

How to Contact: Reports in 1 week on queries; 1 month on mss. SASE (IRCs). No simultaneous submissions. Accepts electronic submissions, "hard copy must be included." Fiction guidelines for SAE and 1 first-class stamp.

Payment: Pays 1¢/word and 1 contributor's copy.

Terms: Pays on publication for first North American serial rights.

STONE SOUP, The Magazine By Children, (I, IV), Children's Art Foundation, Box 83, Santa Cruz CA 95063. (408)426-5557. Editor: Gerry Mandel. Magazine: 6×8¾; 48 pages; high quality paper; Sequoia matte cover stock; illustrations; photos. Stories, poems, book reviews and art by children through age 13. Readership: children, librarians, educators. Published 5 times/year. Estab. 1973. Circ. 17,000.
- This is known as "the literary journal for children." *Stone Soup* has previously won the Edpress Golden Lamp Honor Award and the Parent's Choice Award.
Needs: Fiction by children on themes based on their own experiences, observations or special interests. No clichés, no formulas, no writing exercises; original work only. Receives approximately 1,000 unsolicited fiction mss each month. Accepts approx. 15 mss/issue. Published new writers within the last year. Length: 150-2,500 words. Also publishes literary essays, poetry. Critiques rejected mss upon request.
How to Contact: Send complete ms with cover letter. "We like to learn a little about our young writers, why they like to write, and how they came to write the story they are submitting." SASE (IRCs). No simultaneous submissions. Reports in 1 month on mss. Publishes ms an average of 1-6 months after acceptance. Sample copy for $4. Guidelines for SASE. Reviews children's books.
Payment: Pays $10 plus 2 contributor's copies; $2 charge for extras.
Terms: Buys all rights.
Advice: Mss are rejected because they are "derivatives of movies, TV, comic books; or classroom assignments or other formulas."

STORY, (II), F&W Publications, 1507 Dana Ave., Cincinnati OH 45207. (513)531-2222. Editor: Lois Rosenthal. Magazine: 6¼×9½; 128 pages; uncoated, recycled paper; uncoated index stock. "We publish finest quality short stories. Will consider unpublished novel excerpts if they are self-inclusive." Quarterly. Estab. 1931.
- *Story* won the National Magazine Award for Fiction in 1992. Note payment has increased.
Needs: Literary, experimental, humor, mainstream, translations. No genre fiction—science fiction, detective, young adult, confession, romance, etc. Buys approximately 12 mss/issue. Agented fiction 50-60%. Published work by Joyce Carol Oates, Bobbie Ann Mason, Tobias Wolff, Madison Smartt Bell, Rick DeMarinis, Antonya Nelson, Rick Bass, Charles Baxter, Hortense Calisher, Robert Olmstead and Melissa Pritchard; published new writers within the last year. Length: up to 8,000 words.
How to Contact: Send complete ms with or without cover letter, or submit through agent. SASE (IRCs) necessary for return of ms and response. May accept simultaneous submissions (reluctantly). Sample copy for $5.95, 9×12 SAE and $2.40 postage. Fiction guidelines for #10 SAE and 1 first-class stamp.
Payment: Pays $400 plus 5 contributor's copies.
Terms: Pays on acceptance for first North American serial rights. Sends galleys to author.
Advice: "We accept fiction of the highest quality, whether by established or new writers. Since we receive over 300 submissions each week, the competition for space is fierce. We look for original subject matter told through fresh voices. Read issues of *Story* before trying us."

STORYQUARTERLY, (II), Box 1416, Northbrook IL 60065. (312)433-0741. Co-editors: Anne Brashler and Diane Williams. Magazine: approximately 6×9; 130 pages; good quality paper; illustrations; photos. A magazine devoted to the short story and committed to a full range of styles and forms. Semiannual. Estab. 1975. Circ. 3,000.
Needs: Accepts 12-15 mss/issue, 20-30 mss/year. Receives 200 unsolicited fiction mss/month. Published new writers within the last year.
How to Contact: Send complete ms with SASE (IRCs). Simultaneous submissions OK. Reports in 3 months on mss. Sample copy for $4.
Payment: Pays 3 contributor's copies.
Terms: Acquires one-time rights. Copyright reverts to author after publication.
Advice: "Send one manuscript at a time, subscribe to the magazine, send SASE."

‡STRANGE DAYS, Bizarre Tales and Illustrations of the Imagination, (II), Broken Arrow Publishing, P.O. Box 564, Worcester MA 01613. Editor: Peter Bianca. Magazine: 8½×11; 56 pages; white 50 lb. offset paper; glossy cover; illustrations. "Horror, science fiction, fantasy, mystery." Quarterly. Estab. 1991. Circ. 3,500.
Needs: Fantasy, horror, humor/satire, mystery/suspense, psychic/supernatural/occult, science fiction. Receives 50-75 unsolicited mss/month. Accepts 8-12 mss/issue. Publishes ms 3-6 months after acceptance. Recently published work by Jeffry Thomas, Mark Gado, Mike Thorne and Bruce Boston.

Length: 3,500 words preferred; 1,000 words minimum; 5,000 words maximum.
How to Contact: Send complete ms with a cover letter. Should include estimated word count and short bio. Reports in 2-3 weeks on queries; 8-12 weeks on ms. Send SASE (or IRC) for reply, return of ms or send a disposable copy of ms. No simultaneous submissions. Electronic submissions OK. Sample copy for $5.95. Fiction guidelines free.
Payment: Pays 1¢/word; 1 contributor's copy; additional copies for 20% off.
Terms: Buys first North American serial rights.
Advice: Looks for "originality and ability to grasp reader's attention in such a small amount of space (word count), as our average length story is only 3,500 words. Read a copy of our publication and see firsthand what type of fiction we are publishing. Don't be afraid to experiment with your stories—if at first you don't succeed, try us again." Would like to see more "originality—too often we receive stories that have been done before in some way or other, i.e., revenge story, died and gone to Heaven—which is really Hell, serial killers of prostitutes, etc."

STROKER MAGAZINE, (II), #3, 124 N. Main St., Shavertown PA 18708. Editor: Irving Stettner. Magazine: 5½×8½; average 48 pages; medium paper; 80 lb. good cover stock; illustrations; photos. "*An un-literary* literary review interested in sincerity, verve, anger, humor and beauty. For an intelligent audience—non-academic, non-media dazed in the US and throughout the world." Published 3-4 times/year. Estab. 1974, 50 issues to date. Circ. 600.
Needs: Literary, contemporary. Published new writers within the last year. Also publishes poetry. No academic material. Length: "3-8 pages preferred but not essential."
How to Contact: Send complete ms with SASE (IRCs). Simultaneous submissions OK. Reports in 4 weeks. Sample copy for $4.50.
Payment: Pays 2 contributor's copies. $1 charge for extras.
Terms: Acquires one-time rights.
Advice: "We're a financial failure, but the best mag in the United States."

STRUGGLE, A Magazine of Proletarian Revolutionary Literature, (IV), Marxist-Leninist Party USA, Detroit Branch, Box 13261, Harper Station, Detroit MI 48213-0261. Editor: Tim Hall. Magazine: 5½×8½; 24-48 pages; 20 lb. white bond paper; colored cover; illustrations; occasional photographs. Publishes material related to "the struggle of the working class and all progressive people against the rule of the rich—including their war policies, racism, exploitation of the workers, oppression of women, etc." Quarterly. Estab. 1985.
Needs: Contemporary, ethnic, experimental, feminist, historical (general), humor/satire, literary, mystery/suspense, prose poem, regional, science fiction, senior citizen/retirement, translations, young adult/teen (10-18). "The theme can be approached in many ways, including plenty of categories not listed here." No romance, psychic, western, erotica, religious. Receives 5-6 unsolicited fiction mss/month. Publishes ms 3 months or less after acceptance. Recently published work by Willie Abraham Howard, Jr., Judy Fitzgerald, Sherrie Tucker and Victor A. Gallis; published new writers within the last year. Length: 1,000-3,000 words average; 5,000 words maximum. Publishes short shorts. Normally critiques rejected mss.
How to Contact: Send complete ms; cover letter optional but helpful. "Tries to" report in 3 months. SASE (IRCs). Simultaneous and reprint submissions OK. Sample copy for $1.50. Checks to Tim Hall-Special Account.
Payment: Pays 2 contributor's copies.
Terms: No rights acquired. Publication not copyrighted.
Advice: "Write about the oppression of the working people, the poor, the minorities, women, and if possible, their rebellion against it—we are not interested in anything which accepts the status quo. We are not too worried about plot and advanced technique (fine if we get them!)—we would probably accept things others would call sketches, provided they have life and struggle. Just describe for us a situation in which some real people confront some problem of oppression, however seemingly minor. Observe and put down the real facts. We have increased our fiction portion of our content in the last 2 years. We get poetry and songs all the time. We want 1-2 stories per issue."

STUDIO ONE, (II, IV), College of St. Benedict, St. Joseph MN 56374. Editor: Julie Jasken. Magazine: 7×10; 76-100 pages; illustrations (7-10/issue); photographs (10-15/issue). "Studio One is a regional magazine for literary and visual art. We publish photographs, drawings, paintings, poetry, essays and short fiction for the academic community in the Midwest, particularly for the College of St. Benedict and St. John's University." Annually. Estab. 1976. Circ. 1,500.

Needs: Contemporary, ethnic, feminist, humor/satire, literary, mainstream, prose poem, regional. "We will consider all work submitted and we welcome submissions. The categories above reflect what we tend to publish annually." Receives "maybe 1" unsolicited fiction ms/month. Acquires "5 out of 20" mss/year. Does not read mss in summer. Publishes ms 1-2 months after acceptance. Length: 500-1,000 words preferred; 2,000 words maximum. Publishes short shorts.

How to Contact: Send complete ms with cover letter. Include "return address, phone number and brief history of the work submitted (whether it has been published before)." Reports in 2-3 weeks on queries; 1-6 months on mss. SASE (IRCs). Simultaneous and reprint submissions OK.

Payment: Pays in contributor's copies.

Terms: Acquires all rights (or reprint rights).

Advice: "If the story strikes us as interesting, we consider it. But manuscripts that arrest us with their color, word choice, form or message are the manuscripts we publish. It is so difficult to define what we look for in a work other than quality. Usually the work simply tells us that it intends to be published. Please be patient with acceptance letters. If you submitted, we will respond before publication. Our deadline is always in February, so please submit by then."

⚜SUB-TERRAIN (I,II), Anvil Press, Box 1575, Stn. A, Vancouver BC V6C 2P7 Canada. (604)876-8710. Fiction Editors: D.E. Bolen and P. Pitre. Magazine: 7 × 10; 32 pages; offset printed paper; illustrations; photos. "*Sub-Terrain* provides a forum for work that pushes the boundaries in form or content." Estab. 1988.

Needs: "We are looking for work that expresses the experience of urban existence as we approach the closing of the century. Primarily a literary magazine; also interested in erotica, experimental, humor/satire." Receives 20-30 unsolicited mss/month. Accepts 15-20 mss/issue. Publishes ms 1-4 months after acceptance. Length: 200-3,000 words; 400-500 average. Publishes short shorts. Length: 200 words. Also publishes literary essays, literary criticism, poetry. Sometimes critiques rejected mss and "at times" recommends other markets.

How to Contact: Send complete ms with cover letter. Simultaneous submissions OK, if notify when ms is accepted elsewhere. Reports in 3-4 weeks on queries; 2-3 months on mss. SASE (IRCs). Sample copy for $3. Occasionally reviews novels and short story collections. Send books marked "Review Copy, Managing Editor."

Payment: Pays in contributor's copies.

Terms: Acquires one-time rights.

Advice: "We look for something special in the voice or style. Not simply something that is a well-written story. A new twist, a unique sense or vision of the world. The stuff that every mag is hoping to find. Write about things that are important to you: issues that *must* be talked about; issues that frighten, anger you. The world has all the cute, well-made stories it needs."

THE SUN, (II), The Sun Publishing Company, Inc., 107 N. Roberson St., Chapel Hill NC 27516. (919)942-5282. Editor: Sy Safransky. Magazine: 8½ × 11; 40 pages; offset paper; glossy cover stock; illustrations; photos. "*The Sun* is a magazine of ideas. We publish all kinds of writing — fiction, articles, poetry. Our only criteria are that the writing make sense and enrich our common space. We direct *The Sun* toward interests which move us, and we trust our readers will respond." Monthly. Estab. 1974. Circ. 20,000.

Needs: Open to all fiction. Accepts 3 ms/issue. Receives approximately 400 unsolicited fiction mss each month. Recently published work by Richard Duggin, Sharon Claybough and Miles Harvey; published new writers within the last year. Length: 10,000 words maximum. Also publishes poetry.

How to Contact: Send complete ms with SASE (IRCs). Reports in 6 months. Publishes ms an average of 6-12 months after acceptance. Sample copy for $3.

Payment: Pays up to $100 on publication, plus 2 contributor's copies and a complimentary subscription.

Terms: Acquires one-time rights. Publishes reprints.

SUN DOG: THE SOUTHEAST REVIEW, (II), English Department, 406 Williams, Florida State University, Tallahassee FL 32306. (904)644-4230. Editor: Ron Wiginton. Magazine: 6 × 9; 60-100 pages; 70 lb. paper; 10 pt. Krome Kote cover; illustrations; photos. Biannual. Estab. 1979. Circ. 2,000.

Needs: "We want stories which are well written, beautifully written, with striking images, incidents and characters. We are interested more in quality than in style or genre." Accepts 20 mss/year. Receives approximately 60 unsolicited fiction mss each month. Reads less frequently during summer. Critiques rejected mss when there is time. Occasionally recommends other markets (up to 5 poems or 1 story.)

How to Contact: Send complete ms with SASE (IRCs). "Short bio or cover letter would be appreciated." Publishes ms an average of 2-6 months after acceptance. Sample copy for $4.
Payment: Pays 2 contributor's copies. $2 charge for extras.
Terms: Acquires first North American serial rights which then revert to author.
Advice: "Avoid trendy experimentation for its own sake (present-tense narration, observation that isn't also revelation). Fresh stories, moving, interesting characters and a sensitivity to language are still fiction mainstays. Also publishes winner and runners-up of the World's Best Short Short Story Contest sponsored by the Florida State University English Department."

SWIFT KICK, (II), 1711 Amherst St., Buffalo NY 14214. (716)837-7778. Editor: Robin Kay Willoughby. Magazine: size; number of pages, paper quality, cover stock vary; illustrations; photos, b&w line art, xerographs. "Specializes in unusual formats, hard-to-classify works, visual poetry, found art, etc. for pataphysical, rarified audience." Published special fiction issue; plans another. Estab. 1981. Circ. 100.
Needs: Open. "If it doesn't seem to fit a regular category, it's probably what we'd like! No boring, slipshod, everyday stuff like in mass-market magazines." Receives 5 unsolicited fiction mss/month. Accepts 1-2 mss/issue. Does not read just before Christmas. Publishes ms depending on finances (6 months-1 year) after acceptance. Publishes short shorts of 1,000 words (or 1 picture). Sometimes recommends other markets.
How to Contact: Query first for longer works or send complete ms with cover letter for short work. Reports in 2 months to 1 year. SASE ("or include reply card with OK to toss enclosed work"). Simultaneous submissions OK. Will consider reprints of astoundingly good work (out of print). Sample copy for $7; make checks payable to the editor; "sample purchase recommended to best understand magazine's needs."
Payment: Pays in contributor's copies; half price for extras.
Terms: Acquires one-time rights. Rights revert to artists/authors. Sends galleys to author if requested.
Advice: "We always get less fiction than poetry—if a story is good, it has a good chance of publication in little mags. Editorially, I'm a snob, so don't write like anyone else; be *so* literate your writing transcends literature and (almost) literacy. Don't submit over 10 pages first time. Submit a 'grabber' that makes an editor ask for more. Don't neglect the stories in your own life for someone else's castles-in-the-air."

SYCAMORE REVIEW, (II), Department of English, Purdue University, West Lafayette IN 47907. (317)494-3783. Editor: Michael Manley. Fiction Editor: Scott Kallstrom. Editors change every two years. Send future submissions to "Fiction Editor." Magazine: 5½ × 8½; 130 pages; heavy, textured, uncoated paper; heavy matte cover. "Journal devoted to contemporary literature. We publish both traditional and experimental fiction, personal essay and poetry." Semiannual. Estab. 1989. Circ. 1,000.
  • Work published in *Sycamore Review* was selected for inclusion in the 1993 *Pushcart Prize* anthology. The magazine was also selected as "The Best Magazine in Indiana" for the PEN Hemingway Days Festival's "50 Magazines from 50 States."
Needs: Contemporary, experimental, humor/satire, literary, mainstream, regional, translations. "We generally avoid genre literature, but maintain no formal restrictions on style or subject matter. No science fiction, romance, children's." Publishes ms 3 months-1 year after acceptance. Length: 3,750 words preferred; 250 words minimum. Also publishes poetry. Sometimes critiques rejected mss and recommends other markets.
How to Contact: Send complete ms with cover letter. Cover letter should include previous publications, address changes. Reports in 2 months. SASE (IRCs). Simultaneous submissions OK. Sample copy for $5. Fiction guidelines for #10 SAE and 1 first-class stamp.
Payment: Pays in contributor's copies; charge for extras.
Terms: Acquires one-time rights.
Advice: "We publish both new and experienced authors but we're always looking for stories with strong emotional appeal, vivid characterization and a distinctive narrative voice; stories that appeal to the heart more than the head. Avoid gimmicks and trite, predictable outcomes. Write stories that have a ring of truth, the impact of felt emotion. Don't be afraid to submit, send your best."

‡TAILS OF WONDER, (I, II), Sharptooth Productions, P.O. Box 23, Franklin Park NJ 08823. Editor: Maritza DiSciullo. Publisher/Fiction Editor: Nicolas Samuels. Magazine: 8½ × 11; 40-50 pages; 50 lb. bond paper; glossy cover; b&w illustrations. Semiannual. Estab. 1993. Circ. 500.
Needs: Fantasy (dark fantasy, science fantasy, sword and sorcery), romance (sf/fantasy mix only), science fiction (hard science, horror/sf mix, soft/sociological). "Nothing overly erotic or religious." List of upcoming themes available for SASE. Publishes special fiction issue or anthology. Receives 30-40

unsolicited mss/month. Accepts 7-12 mss/issue; 14-30 mss/year. Publishes ms within 2 issues after acceptance. Recently published work by C.A. Zraik, Samuel Stember and Edo van Belkom. Length: 3,000 words preferred; 2,000 words minimum; 6,000 words maximum. Publishes short shorts. Also publishes literary criticism and poetry. Always critiques or comments on rejected mss.
How to Contact: *Charges $5 reading fee to nonsubscribers.* Send complete ms with a cover letter. Should include estimated word count, 1 paragraph bio, and list of publications. Reports in 2-3 weeks on queries; 2-3 months on mss. Send SASE (or IRC) for reply or send a disposable copy of ms. Simultaneous, reprint and electronic submissions OK. Sample copy for $5. Fiction guidelines for #10 SAE and 1 first-class stamp. Reviews novels or short story collections.
Payment: Pays $5 (sometimes more for established professionals). Pays for short shorts at ¼¢/word. Also pays 1 contributor copy; additional copies at $1 off regular rate. In addition to payment, the reading fee is returned if the story is accepted for publication.
Terms: Buys first and reprint rights.
Advice: "We give each story careful consideration. A manuscript that stands out is a well-written one, in *proper* manuscript format. Our best advice to you is that we are looking for stories that challenge the 'cutting edge' of the genre. By 'cutting edge' we mean new innovative ideas, or older themes with an innovative twist." Would like to see more "characters that are 'real.' Most characters seem two dimensional. A short story doesn't have to cut on the quality of the characters."

‡**TALES OF THE HEART, LA's Finest Fiction Magazine, (I, II),** #739, 8424A Santa Monica Blvd., Los Angeles CA 90069. (213)650-4246. Editors: Maxine Nunes, Leslie Paxton and Tracy Tynan. Magazine: 8½×11; 64 pages; book stock paper; glossy cover. "Good, compelling, risky, alive fiction. Fine fiction for a general audience. Intelligent but not 'literary'." Quarterly. Estab. 1993. Circ. 10,000.
Needs: Literary, mystery/suspense (police procedural, private eye/hard-boiled), science fiction, serialized novel, translations; also some erotica, ethnic/multicultural, fantasy, humor/satire. "We also publish cartoons. No romance, only well above-average for other categories—must be a superb example of a genre." Accepts 12-15 mss/issue; 48-60 mss/year. Publishes ms up to 1 year after acceptance. Agented fiction 50%. Length: 500 words minimum; 5,000 words maximum. Publishes short shorts. Occasionally publishes poetry.
How to Contact: Send complete ms with a cover letter or submit through an agent. Should include 1 paragraph bio, list of publications and how you heard about us. Reports in up to 6 months. Send SASE (or IRC) for reply, return of ms or send a disposable copy of ms. Simultaneous and electronic (only with hard copy) submissions OK. Sample copy for $3.50 and 8½×11 SAE. Reviews novels and short story collections.
Payment: Pays $25 maximum.
Terms: Pays on publication for first rights (also non-exclusive reprint rights, promotional and publication rights). "Author can approve text changes."
Advice: Looks for "emotional authenticity, craft, risk, a compelling and original voice. We would like more work representing a variety of races and ways of life."

‡**TALL TALES & SHORT STORIES, Denver's Fiction Paper, (II),** Dragamon Publishing, P.O. Box 16188, Denver CO 80216. (303)355-5811. Editor: C.P. Lowe. Magazine: 8½×11; 16-32 pages; newsprint paper. "We buy stories with a good plot, well-written and under 3,000 words (usually). We have subscription members from all over the country, but mostly deliver free to the Denver area. Our paper/magazine is 95% supported by advertisers." Bimonthly, but "we will be going to monthly soon." Estab. 1993. Circ. 10,000.
Needs: Adventure, condensed novel (only a few for serial), ethnic/multicultural, fantasy (science fantasy, sword and sorcery), feminist, gay, historical (general), horror, humor/satire, lesbian, mainstream/contemporary, mystery/suspense (amateur sleuth, cozy, police procedural, private eye/hard-boiled, romantic suspense), psychic/supernatural/occult, regional (Colorado stories), inspirational, romance (contemporary, gothic, historical), science fiction (hard science, soft/sociological), senior citizen/retirement, sports, westerns (frontier, traditional), young adult/teen (10-18 years). No "erotica and graphic and senseless violence. Some violence is needed at times but slasher material is never accepted. Receives 30 unsolicited mss/month. Accepts 3-4 ms/issue; 8-18 mss/year. Does not read mss in December and July. Publishes ms 6 months-1½ years after acceptance. Recently published work

---

Read the Business of Fiction Writing section to learn the correct way to prepare and submit a manuscript.

by Kathryn Beyerle, Howard Goldsmith and Linda Broggi. Length: 2,000 words preferred; 500 words minimum; 10,000 words maximum. Publishes short shorts. Sometimes critiques or comments on rejected mss.

How to Contact: Send complete ms with a cover letter. Should include estimated word count, 1 paragraph bio, Social Security number, phone number, address. Reports in 2 months on queries; 2-6 months on mss. Send SASE (or IRC) for reply, return of ms or send a disposable copy of ms. Simultaneous, reprint and electronic (Macintosh on the programs QuarkExpress or MacWrite2) submissions OK. Sample copy for 9 × 12 SAE and 3 first-class stamps. Fiction guidelines for #10 SAE and 1 first-class stamp.

Payment: Pays $35 minimum (depends on number of words); 1-5 contributor's copies on request; additional copies for SASE.

Terms: Pays on acceptance for one-time rights.

Advice: Looks for "good plot. If it takes place in Colorado, we take special notice. Well written, story must flow well. Can't be predictable. If the reader or editor can figure out the end before we finish the story, we won't buy."

TAMAQUA, (I, II), C120, Humanities Dept., Parkland College, Champaign IL 61821. (217)351-2217. Editor-in-Chief: James McGowan. Magazine: 5½ × 8½; 160-256 pages; 80 lb. paper; 12 point cover; some illustrations; 12-40 photos every issue. "No theme; top quality fiction, poetry, nonfiction (reviews, thoughtful essays, autobiography, biography, insightful travel, etc.) for a literate audience." Semiannual. Estab. 1990. Circ. 1,500.

Needs: Literary, condensed/excerpted novel, contemporary, ethnic, experimental, feminist, gay, humor/satire, prose poem, regional. "No stupid writing, no polemics, no demagogues, no zipperheads— that is, we want good, solid, intelligent, *professional* writing." Publishes special fiction issues (Native American issue, Pan American issue). Buys 4-10 mss/issue; 8-20 mss/year. Publishes ms 6 months after acceptance. Published work by Gerald Vizenor, Ralph Salisbury and Lisa McCloud. Length: 10,000 words maximum. Publishes short shorts. Length: under 1,000 words. Sometimes critiques rejected mss.

How to Contact: Send complete ms with cover letter. Reports in 3-4 weeks on queries; 6-8 weeks on mss. SASE (IRCs). Simultaneous submissions OK. Prefers electronic submissions. Sample copy for $6, 8½ × 11 SAE and 72¢ postage. Fiction guidelines for #10 SAE and 1 first-class stamp.

Payment: Pays $10-50, subscription to magazine, contributor's copies; charge for extras.

Terms: Pays on publication for first North American serial rights.

Advice: "The most influential ingredient for the growing market in fiction (as well as all other writing) is the reduced costs of production because of desk-top publishing. Purchase a copy and *study* the magazine, or others of similar quality, to distinguish between good, solid professional writing and that which is not."

TAMPA REVIEW, (III), 401 W. Kennedy Blvd., Box 19F, University of Tampa, Tampa FL 33606-1490. (813)253-3333, ext. 6266. Editor: Richard Mathews. Fiction Editor: Andy Solomon. Magazine: 7½ × 10½; approximately 70 pages; acid-free paper; visual art; photos. "Interested in fiction of distinctive literary quality." Semiannual. Estab. 1988.

Needs: Contemporary, ethnic, experimental, fantasy, historical, humor/satire, literary, mainstream, prose poem, translations. "We are far more interested in quality than in genre. Nothing sentimental as opposed to genuinely moving, nor self-conscious style at the expense of human truth." Buys 4-5 mss/issue. Publishes ms within 7 months-1 year of acceptance. Agented fiction 60%. Recently published work by Elizabeth Spencer, Lee K. Abbott, Lorrie Moore, Tim O'Connor, Scott Bradfield. Length: 1,000 words minimum; 6,000 words maximum. Publishes short shorts "if the story is good enough." Also publishes literary essays (must be labeled nonfiction), poetry. Sometimes critiques rejected mss and recommends other markets.

How to Contact: Send complete mss with cover letter. Should include brief bio and publishing record. Include Social Security number. No simultaneous submissions. SASE (IRCs). Reads September-December; reports January-March. Sample copy for $5 (includes postage) and 9 × 12 SAE. Fiction guidelines for #10 SAE and 1 first-class stamp.

Payment: Pays $10/printed page.

Terms: Pays on publication for first North American serial rights. Sends galleys to author—upon request.

Advice: "There are more good writers publishing in magazines today than there have been in many decades. Unfortunately, there are even more bad ones. In T. Gertler's *Elbowing the Seducer*, an editor advises a young writer that he wants to hear her voice completely, to tell (he means 'show') him in a story the truest thing she knows. We concur. Rather than a trendy workshop story or a minimalism that actually stems from not having much to say, we would like to see stories that make us believe they mattered to the writer and, more importantly, will matter to a reader. Trim until only the essential is left, and don't give up belief in yourself. And it might help to attend a good writers' conference, e.g. Wesleyan or Bennington."

‡**TAPROOT LITERARY REVIEW, (I, II),** Taproot Writer's Workshop, Inc., 302 Park Rd., Ambridge PA 15003. (412)266-8476. Editor: Tikvah Feinstein. Magazine: 5½ × 10½; 80 pages; #20 paper; glossy cover; illustrations and photographs. "We select on quality, not topic. We have published excellent work other publications have rejected due to subject matter, style or other bias. Variety and quality are our appealing features." Annual. Estab. 1987. Circ. 500.
Needs: Literary. Upcoming themes available for SASE. Publishes special fiction issue or anthology. Receives 20 unsolicited mss/month. Accepts 6 mss/issue. Publishes mss 3 months after acceptance. Recently published work by Sally Levin, Judith Robinson, Rex Downie Jr. and Martha Harris. Length: 2,000 words preferred; 250 words minimum; 3,000 words maximum (no longer than 10 pages, double-spaced maximum). Publishes short shorts. Length: 300 words preferred. Sometimes critiques or comments on rejected mss.
How to Contact: Send complete ms with a cover letter. Send for guidelines first. Should include estimated word count and bio. Reports in 6 months. Send SASE (or IRC) for return of ms or send a disposable copy of ms. No simultaneous submissions. Sample copy for $5, 6 × 12 SAE and 5 first-class stamps. Fiction guidelines for #10 SAE and 1 first-class stamp.
Payment: Awards prize money for winners each issue; free subscription; 1 contributor copy.
Terms: Buys first rights.
Advice: "If the story speaks in its own voice and reveals something about us that's important and memorable, we publish it."

TEMPORARY CULTURE, (II), P.O. Box 43072, Upper Montclair NJ 07043. Editor: H. Wessells. 4½ × 11; 24-32 pages; b&w illustrations. "Creating new mythologies from the bankrupt post-industrial landscapes. Pushing language to new terrain." Annual. Estab. 1988. Circ. 250.
Needs: Experimental, prose poem, science fiction, ecological. "No workshop confessionals and narrow-minded egocentric visions of the world. No self indulgence or senseless violence." Issue #9, 1994, will be "tribal" in its focus: anthropological or totemic artifacts, forest cults, bloodlines, and other tribal themes manifested in fiction. Receives 2-7 unsolicited mss/month. Acquires 8 mss/year. Publishes short shorts. Sometimes critiques or comments on rejected mss.
How to Contact: Send complete ms with cover letter. Reports in under 1 month. SASE (IRCs). Simultaneous submissions OK. Sample copy for $5.
Payment: Pays in contributor's copies.
Terms: Acquires one-time rights. Sometimes sends galleys to author.

‡**TERMINAL FRIGHT, (I),** P.O. Box 100, Black River NY 13612. Editor: Kenneth E. Abner Jr. Magazine: 8½ × 11; 52 pages; 60 lb. white paper; 80 lb. cover stock. "Traditional gothic and modern occult horror." Bimonthly. Estab. 1993.
● This is a new publication. At press time plans were for late 1993 launch.
Needs: Horror, supernatural/occult. Publishes ms 4 months after acceptance. Length: 1,500 words minimum; 10,000 words maximum.
How to Contact: Send complete ms with a cover letter. Should include estimated word count and 1-2 page bio; if available, on IBM compatible floppy disk (preferred). Reports in 6-8 weeks. Send SASE (or IRC) for return of ms or send a disposable copy of ms. Simultaneous submissions OK. Sample copy for $5. Fiction guidelines for #10 SASE.
Payment: Pays $15-100 (1¢/word); 1 contributor copy.
Terms: Pays on publication for first North American serial rights.
Advice: "The most important thing is to truly scare me. Stories should be unique, well-thought out and well-written. I highly discourage excessive vulgarity, explicit sex and graphic gore. All have their place in horror but only if used sparingly and with purpose, not as a crutch to an otherwise weak story."

‡**TERROR TIME AGAIN, (I, II),** Nocturnal Publications, 11 W. Winona St., St. Paul MN 55107. (612)227-6958. Editor: Donald L. Miller. Magazine: 5 × 8; 52-60 pages; 20 lb. paper; 67 lb. cover stock; illustrations. "*Terror Time Again*'s objective is to provoke a sense of fear in our readers." Quarterly. Estab. 1987. Circ. 200.

Needs: Only wants fear-inducing stories. No science fiction or sword and sorcery. Receives up to 35 unsolicited mss/month. Accepts 15-20 mss/issue. Publishes ms in 4-6 months. Published work by Steve Berman, D.A. Sale, Michael Floyd, Bob Madia and Steve Vernon; published new writers within the last year. Length: 1,000 words average; 250 words minimum; 2,000 words maximum. Publishes short shorts. Length: 250-700 words. Also publishes poetry. Sometimes critiques rejected mss; recommends other markets.

How to Contact: Send complete ms with brief bio about yourself. Reports in 2-4 weeks on mss. Remember to enclose a SASE (IRCs). Simultaneous and reprint submissions OK. Sample copy $4.50; fiction guidelines free. Reviews novels and short story collections in newsletter (see below).

Payment: Pays ½¢/word on acceptance.

Terms: Acquires one-time and reprint rights. Sponsors contest for writers through *The Nightmare Express.* "*Terror Time Again* has a cover contest via *The Nightmare Express* in which the cover illustration of the July/August issue of *TNE* is used by the writer to develop a story under 2,000 words. *TNE* is a newsletter for horror writers and is published bimonthly. A sample copy of *Nightmare Express* is $1.50."

THE TEXAS REVIEW, (II), Sam Houston State University Press, Huntsville TX 77341. (713)294-1423. Editor: Paul Ruffin. Magazine: 6 × 9; 148-190 pages; best quality paper; 70 lb. cover stock; illustrations; photos. "We publish top quality poetry, fiction, articles, interviews and reviews for a general audience." Semiannual. Estab. 1976. Circ. 700.

Needs: Literary and contemporary fiction. "We are eager enough to consider fiction of quality, no matter what its theme or subject matter. No juvenile fiction." Accepts 4 mss/issue. Receives approximately 40-60 unsolicited fiction mss each month. Does not read June-August. Published work by George Garrett, Ellen Gilchrist and Fred Chappell; published new writers within the last year. Length: 500-10,000 words. Critiques rejected mss "when there is time." Recommends other markets.

How to Contact: Send complete ms with cover letter. SASE (IRCs). Reports in 3 months on mss. Sample copy for $3.

Payment: Pays contributor's copies plus one year subscription.

Terms: Acquires all rights. Sends galleys to author.

‡A THEATER OF BLOOD, (III, IV), Pyx Press, P.O. Box 620, Orem UT 84059-0620. Editor: C. Darren Butler. Associate Editor: Lisa S. Laurencot. Book: 100-180-page limited edition, annual book serial. "This will appear in a numbered run of about 300 copies. Numbers 1-75 are planned as hardbound, hand-sewn books, on acid-free paper with other extras. Numbers 76—will be in trade paperback format, in signatures but not sewn." Estab. 1990. Circ. 300.

 ● *A Theater of Blood* has recently switched to a new book format. Their old magazine format will continue for 2 or 3 more issues. The first of the new format will appear in 1995. See also the Pyx Press listing in the Small Press section and *Magic Realism* in this section.

Needs: Horror. "All types of horror fiction: cosmic, dark fantasy, quiet, supernatural (though not using Lovecraft's creations). It is unlikely that I will accept any purely realistic horror; an otherworldly or fantasy element should be included. I have a bias against excessive gore or anything gratuitous." Receives 80 unsolicited mss/month. Accepts 8-15 mss/book. Publishes ms 4-24 months after acceptance. No reprints. Length: 3,000-20,000 words. Rarely critiques or comments on rejected mss.

How to Contact: Query first for works over 8,000 words or send complete ms with a cover letter. Should include estimated word count, 1 paragraph bio and list of publications. Reports in 2 months on queries; 3-6 months on mss. Send SASE (or IRC) for reply, return of ms or send a disposable copy of ms. Simultaneous submissions OK. Sample copy for $2.50 (old format). Fiction guidelines for #10 SAE and 1 first-class stamp.

Payment: Pays $2-10, "unless piece is very long and 1 copy of the trade-paperback."

Terms: Acquires first rights.

THEATRE OV THE NIGHT, (I), Nuclear Trenchcoated Subway Prophets Ministries, Box 162 Hampshire Col., Amherst MA 01002-5001. Internet E-mail: LVajra @Hamp. Hampshire.edu. Editrix: Ms. Lake Vajra. Magazine: 52 pages; ivory fetisch paper; pen & ink and collage illustrations; photographs. "Writings and art celebrating the beauty ov darkness and the night. Includes in-depth inquisitions with the darkest creative minds ov the Gothik underworld: dark musikal entities, artists, poets, dansers . . . focuses on nocturnal ethereal musiks, some induštrial. Published irregularly. Estab. 1793. Cir. varies.

Needs: "Decadent surreal macabre. Melancholy decay and dark romanticism. Sensual, multi-dimensional in form & meaning, elegant, ethereal, haunting, sinister, moody, somber, lurid, lush, voluptuous, intense longing, dark introversion, religious imagery, apokalyptik imagery, morbid, mysterious, self-affirming, sex-positive, homoerotic, pro-transgenderist, pro-vampirism: (dark fantasy/horror)." Receives 80 unsolicited mss/month. Acquires 5 mss/issue. Publishes short shorts. Also publishes literary essays, reviews (music, concert publications, books, film, wine), art/photography and poetry.

How to Contact: Send complete ms with cover letter. Reports in 1-2 months if like. "If completely unsuitable, we toss. See sample copy. No SASE no reply." Simultaneous submissions, reprints and electronic submissions OK. Sample copy for $6. Detailed submission guidelines for $1. Reviews novel and short story collections.

Payment: Pays contributor's copies; additional copies $6.

Terms: All rights belong to the creators.

Advice: "Subjects: decadence, witchcraft, crucifixion ecstasy, angels, vampires, water (drowning), the holy virgin, bondage, sirens, the night, fin-de-siècle grotesque, dreames, trance creation, lilith, hekate, ophelia, visions, dark night of the soul, night gardens, innocence, purity, maenads, erotic hallucinations, folklore, death as a rapture, tantra, beautiful sacred sexuality, LOVE, dreame-dialogue, elegant goth drag queens, sweet transvestites, pretty Victorian boys, preraphaelite girls, omni-sexual." Please do not send: "pessimistic, misogynist, suicidal, sappy, sentimental, nihilistic, crude, gross porn, road kill, violence towards women, male voyeurism ov lesbianism, country musik lyriks, baseball stories, cheesy vampire stories, anti-vampire, overt sleaziness, racist, sexist, homophobic, heterophobic, sex-negative, etc. . . . these will be tossed."

THEMA, (II,IV), Box 74109, Metairie LA 70033-4109. Editor: Virginia Howard. Magazine: 5½ × 8½; 200 pages; Grandee Strathmore cover stock; b&w illustrations. "Different specified theme for each issue — short stories, poems, b&w artwork must relate to that theme." Triannual. Estab. 1988.

• *Thema* editor, Virginia Howard, was featured in an interview in the 1991 *Novel & Short Story Writer's Market*. The magazine ranks #32 on the latest *Writer's Digest* Fiction 50 list.

Needs: Adventure, contemporary, experimental, humor/satire, literary, mainstream, mystery/suspense, prose poem, psychic/supernatural/occult, regional, science fiction, sports, western. "Each issue is based on a specified premise — a different unique theme for each issue. Many types of fiction acceptable, but must fit the premise. No pornographic, scatologic, erotic fiction." Upcoming themes: "The waiting room" (deadline February 1); "It is a fossil, Higgins?" (deadline May 1); "Three by a tremor tossed" (deadline August 1). Publishes ms within 3-4 months of acceptance. Recently published work by Carol Del Col, Caitlin Burke, Julie Hill Alger and Florri McMillan. Length: fewer than 6,000 words preferred. Publishes short shorts "if very clever." Length: 300-900 words. Also publishes poetry. Sometimes critiques rejected mss and recommends other markets.

How to Contact: Send complete ms with cover letter, which should include "name and address, brief introduction, specifying the intended target issue for the mss." Simultaneous submissions OK. Reports on queries in 1 week; on mss in 4 months after deadline for specified issue. SASE (IRCs). Sample copy for $8. Free fiction guidelines.

Payment: Pays $25.

Terms: Pays on acceptance for one-time rights.

Advice: "Do not submit a manuscript unless you have written it for a specified premise. If you don't know the upcoming themes, send for guidelines first, before sending a story. We need more stories told in the Mark Twain/O. Henry tradition in magazine fiction."

THIN ICE, (II), 379 Lincoln Ave., Council Bluffs IA 51503. Editor/Publisher: Kathleen Jurgens. Magazine: digest-sized; 95-104 pages; 16-20 lb. paper; enamel cover; b&w, pen and ink illustrations. "Horror and dark fantasy — short stories, poetry, interviews, art." Triannual. Estab. 1987. Circ. 250.

• Editor Kathleen Jurgens was voted "Best Editor" by the Small Press Writers and Artists Organization in 1991.

Needs: Fantasy (dark), horror, black humor/satire, poetry, psychic/supernatural/occult. No "racist, preachy, straight porn for shock value." Receives 50-100 unsolicited mss/month. Accepts approx. 10 mss/issue; approx. 40 mss/year. Publishes ms 1-2½ years after acceptance. Recently published work by Bentley Little, Judith Holman, John Ames, Wayne Allen Sallee, Rodger Gerberding and Denise Dumars. Length: 1,000-4,000 words preferred. Also publishes poetry. Critiques rejected mss.

How to Contact: Send complete ms with cover letter. Cover letter should include "a personal introduction, mention a few prior 'sales' if desired (though not necessary), where the writers heard of *Thin Ice*." SASE (IRCs) required. No simultaneous submissions. Reports in 3 weeks on queries; 1-2 months on mss. Sample copy for $4.50 and SASE to Kathleen Jurgens ($6 outside of the U.S.). Fiction guidelines with #10 SASE.

Payment: Pays in contributor's copies.
Terms: Acquires first North American serial rights.
Advice: "Invest in a copy of the magazine and read it from cover to cover. Get a 'feel' for the overall mood, tone, and subject matter. Don't apologize for misspellings or coffee stains on the manuscript—retype it. While I prefer informal query letters, I become quite irate when potential contributors treat me unprofessionally. I respond to all submissions personally, frequently offering editorial commentary. Always include a SASE with the correct amount of postage. Give me the full 2 months to respond. Absolutely no simultaneous or multiple submissions considered. Please, do not summarize the story in your cover letter."

13TH MOON, A Feminist Magazine, (IV), Dept. of English, SUNY-Albany, Albany NY 12222. (518)442-4181. Editor: Judith Johnson. Magazine: 6×9; 200 pages; 50 lb. paper; heavy cover stock; photographs. "Feminist literary magazine for feminist women and men." Annual. Estab. 1973. Circ. 1,500.
Needs: Excerpted novel, experimental, feminist, lesbian, literary, prose poem, science fiction, translations. No fiction by men. Accepts 1-3 mss/issue. Does not read mss May-September. Time varies between acceptance and publication. Published work by F.R. Lewis, Jan Ramjerdi and Wilma Kahn. Length: Open. Publishes short shorts. Also publishes poetry. Sometimes critiques rejected mss.
How to Contact: Send complete ms with cover letter and SASE (IRCs). Reports in 1 month on queries; 4 months on mss. SASE. Accepts electronic submissions via disk (WordPerfect 5.1 only). Sample copy for $10.
Payment: Pays 2 contributor's copies.
Terms: Acquires first North American serial rights.
Advice: Looks for "*unusual* fiction with feminist appeal."

✱THIS MAGAZINE, (II), Red Maple Foundation, 16 Skey Lane, Toronto, Ontario M6J 3S4 Canada. (416)588-6580. Editor: Moira Farr. Fiction Editor: Phil Hall. Magazine: 8½×11; 42 pages; bond paper; coated cover; illustrations and photographs. "Alternative general interest magazine." Estab. 1973. Circ. 12,000.
Needs: Ethnic, contemporary, experimental, fantasy, feminist, gay, lesbian, literary, mainstream, prose poem, regional. No "commercial/pulp fiction." Receives 15-20 unsolicited mss/month. Buys 1 mss/issue; 8 mss/year. Published work by Margaret Atwood and Peter McGehee. Length: 1,500 words average; 2,500 words maximum. Sometimes critiques rejected mss.
How to Contact: Query with clips of published work. Reports in 6 weeks on queries; 3-6 months on mss. SASE. No simultaneous submissions. Sample copy $4 (plus GST). Fiction guidelines for #9 SASE with Canadian stamps or IRC.
Payment: Pays $100 (Canadian) fiction; $25/poem published.
Terms: Buys one-time rights.
Advice: "It's best if you're familiar with the magazine when submitting work; a large number of mss that come into the office are inappropriate. Style guides are available. Manuscripts and queries that are clean and personalized really make a difference. Let your work speak for itself—don't try to convince us."

THE THREEPENNY REVIEW, (II), P.O. Box 9131, Berkeley CA 94709. (510)849-4545. Editor: Wendy Lesser. Tabloid: 10×17; 40 pages; Electrobrite paper; white book cover; illustrations. "Serious fiction." Quarterly. Estab. 1980. Circ. 8,000.
• *The Threepenny Review* has received GE Writers Awards, CLMP Editor's Awards, NEA grants, Lila Wallace grants and inclusion of work in the Pushcart Prize Anthology. It was ranked #36 on the latest *Writer's Digest* Fiction 50 List.
Needs: Literary. "Nothing 'experimental' (ungrammatical)." Receives 300-400 mss/month. Buys 3 mss/issue; 12 mss/year. Publishes 6-12 months after acceptance. Agented fiction 5%. Published work by Sigrid Nunez, Dagobato Gilb, Ann Packer and Leonard Michaels. Length: 5,000 words maximum. Publishes short shorts. Also publishes literary essays, literary criticism, poetry.
How to Contact: Send complete ms with a cover letter. Reports in 2-4 weeks on queries;1-2 months on mss. Send SASE (IRCs) for reply, return of ms or send a disposable copy of the ms. No simultaneous submissions. Sample copy for $6. Fiction guidelines for #10 SAE and 1 first-class stamp. Reviews novels and short story collections.
Payment: Pays $200 plus free subscription to the magazine; additional copies at half price.
Terms: Pays on acceptance. Acquires first North American serial rights. Sends galleys to author.

THRUST, Experimental and Underground Prose, (II), Experimental Chapbook Press, P.O. Box 1602, Austin TX 78767. Editor: Skip Rhudy. Magazine: digest-sized; 50-70 pages; 60 lb. offset paper; 65 lb. card cover; illustrations on cover. *"Thrust* is a magazine for writers and readers bored with the standard offerings of university-affiliated magazines, which pump out mainstream stories by the dumpster-full." Semiannual. Estab. 1992. Circ. 100.
Needs: Experimental, translations. "Absolutely no mainstream." Plans anthology in the future. Receives 30 unsolicited mss/month. Acquires 5-10 mss/issue; 15-30 mss/year. Publishes ms 6 weeks-6 months after acceptance. Recently published work by C.F. Roberts, Shannon Frach and Alfred Schwaid. Length: nothing over 25 pages. Publishes short shorts.
How to Contact: Send complete ms with a cover letter. Should include 1 paragraph bio. Reports in 2 weeks on queries; 1-2 months on mss. Send SASE (IRCs). Simultaneous submissions OK. Sample copy for $3.50. Reviews experimental novels and short story collections.
Payment: Pays 1 contributor's copy.
Terms: Acquires one-time rights.
Advice: "Material should be experimental in nature; we will consider anything that is not clearly mainstream. That means we will not consider genre work of any kind, *unless* the writer incorporates experimental elements in the language or perspective. Short, tightly-written prose stands the best chance of acceptance at *Thrust*. No strict guidelines regarding subject matter exist, but we are most interested in controversial themes generally disregarded or avoided by establishment literary magazines. We want to see more fiction set in the alternative culture scene. Read Julio Cortazar's short story collections and submit material that tells a story in an experimental mode: shifting first person perspectives; intertwined separate stories with similar themes (like in *All Fires The Fire*), dialogue that melts into internal reflection, dadaism, surrealism, and more. Above all: don't inhibit your creativity with the standardized, narrow guidelines of current mainstream aesthetics."

✸**TICKLED BY THUNDER, (II), A Newsmagazine for Writers**, Tickled by Thunder Pub. Co., 7385 129th St., Surrey, British Columbia V3W 7B8 Canada. (604)591-6095 (phone, voice or fax). Editor: Larry Lindner. Magazine: Digest-sized; bond paper; bond cover; illustrations and photographs. "Totally open. For writers." Quarterly. Estab. 1990. Circ. 150.
Needs: Adventure, contemporary, fantasy, humor/satire, literary, mainstream, mystery/suspense, prose poem, psychic/supernatural, religious/inspirational, science fiction, western. "No pornography." Receives 40 unsolicited mss/month. Buys 1-4 mss/issue; 4-16 mss/year. Publishes ms next issue after acceptance. Length: 1,500 words average; 2,000 words maximum. Publishes short shorts. Length: No preference. Also publishes poetry. Sometimes critiques rejected mss and recommends other markets.
How to Contact: Query with clips of published work, if any, including "brief resume/history of writing experience, photo, credits, etc." Reports in 2 months. SASE. Simultaneous submissions OK. Sample copy $2.50 (Canadian) or 3 IRCs. Fiction guidelines for legal SAE and 1 first-class stamp.
Payment: Pays $1 maximum.
Terms: Buys first rights.
Advice: "Send for guidelines, read a sample copy and ask questions. Send SASE for info on contest for fiction and poetry."

TIMBERLINES, (II), Lake City Writers Forum, P.O. Box 38, Lake City CO 81235. Contact: Editorial Panel. Magazine: 6½×9½; 55-100 pages; line drawings. "Contemporary, general fiction, poetry. While all themes and styles will be considered, *Timberlines'* orientation is toward quality work reflecting western, mountain or outdoor ambience or theme."Annual. Estab. 1991. Circ. 1,000.
Needs: Adventure, ethnic/multicultural, historical (general), humor/satire, literary, mainstream/contemporary, regional, senior citizen/retirement, young adult/teen. Receives 200 unsolicited mss/year. Reads mss only from September-December. Publishes short shorts. Also publishes literary essays.
How to Contact: Send complete ms with cover letter. Should include 1 paragraph bio and list of publications. SASE (IRCs) for return of ms or send a disposable copy of the ms. Sample copy for $4, 7×10 or larger SAE and 5 first-class stamps.
Payment: Pays 3 contributor's copies. Additional copies at our cost (it varies).
Terms: Acquires one-time rights. Not copyrighted.
Advice: Looks for "good writing—interesting story line, general appeal. Original approach. Learn what makes a good story and how to put it together."

TOMORROW, Speculative Fiction, (II), Unifont Co., P.O. Box 6038, Evanston IL 60204. (708)864-3668. Editor and Publisher: Algis Budrys. Magazine: 8¼×10¾; 80 pages; newsprint; slick cover; illustrations. "Any good science fiction, fantasy and horror, for an audience of fiction readers." Bimonthly. Estab. 1992.
Needs: Fantasy, horror, science fiction. Receives 100 mss/month. Buys 8-12 mss/issue; 48-82 mss/year. Publishes 2-3 issues after acceptance. Agented fiction 5%. Recently published Gene Wolfe, M. Shayne Bell, Rob Chilson and Norman Spinrad. Length: 4,000 words average. Publishes short shorts. Always critiques rejected mss.
How to Contact: Send complete ms with cover letter. Should include estimated word count, 25-word bio, Social Security number. Reports in 2 weeks. Send SASE (IRCs) for reply, return of ms or send a disposable copy of the ms. No simultaneous submissions. Sample copy for $4 plus postage.
Payment: $75 minimum; 7¢/word maximum plus 3 contributor's copies.
Terms: Pays between acceptance and publication. Acquires first North American serial rights. Sends galleys to author.
Advice: "Read my ongoing series on writing in the magazine."

‡**TOUCHSTONE LITERARY JOURNAL, (II)**, P.O. Box 8308, Spring TX 77387-8308. Editor/Publisher: William Laufer. Managing Editor: Guida Jackson. Magazine: 5½×8½; 40-104 pages; linen paper; kramkote cover; perfect bound; b&w illustrations; occasional photographs. "Literary and mainstream fiction, but enjoy experimental work and multicultural. Audience middle-class, heavily academic. We are eclectic and given to whims—i.e., two years ago we devoted a 104-page issue to West African women writers." Annual (with occasional special supplements). Estab. 1976. Circ. 1,000.
• Touchstone Press also publishes a chapbook series. Send a SASE for guidelines.
Needs: Humor/satire, literary, mainstream/contemporary, translations. No erotica, religious, juvenile, "stories written in creative writing programs that all sound alike." List of upcoming themes available for SASE. Publishes special fiction issue or anthology. Receives 20-30 mss/month. Accepts 2-10 mss/issue. Does not read mss in December. Publishes ms within the year after acceptance. Recently published work by Lynn Bradley, Roy Fish and Julia Mercedes Castilla. Length: 2,500 words preferred; 250 words minimum; 5,000 words maximum. Publishes short shorts. Length: 300 words. Also publishes literary essays, literary criticism and poetry. Sometimes critiques or comments on rejected mss.
How to Contact: Send complete ms with a cover letter. Should include estimated word count and 3 sentence bio. Reports in 2 months. Send SASE (or IRC) for return of ms. Simultaneous and electronic submissions OK. Sample copy for $3 or 10 first-class stamps. Fiction guidelines for #10 SAE and 1 first-class stamp.
Payment: Pays 2 contributor's copies; additional copies at 40% discount.
Terms: Acquires one-time rights. Sends galleys to author (unless submitted on disk).
Advice: "We like to see fiction that doesn't read as if it had been composed in a creative writing class. If you can entertain, edify, or touch the reader, polish your story and send it in. Don't worry if it doesn't read like our other fiction."

TRANSLATION, (II), The Translation Center, Columbia University, 412 Dodge, New York NY 10027. (212)854-2305. Director: Frank MacShane. Editors change each year. (One guest each issue). Magazine: 6×9; 200-300 pages; coated cover stock; photos. Semiannual. Estab. 1972. Circ. 1,500.
Needs: Literary translations only. Upcoming themes: Czech, Venezualan and African issues. Not accepting unsolicited mss. The Center serves as a clearing house for inquiries involving the publication of translations.
How to Contact: Call (212)854-4500. Sample copy $9.
Advice: "We are particularly interested in translations of previously untranslated work. Annual awards of $1,000 for outstanding translation of a substantial part of a book-length literary work. Translator must have letter of intent to publish from a publisher. Write for description and application for awards program."

TRIBUTARY, (II), The Rockford Writers Guild, Box 858, Rockford IL 61105. Editor: David Ross. Magazine: 5⅜×8½; b&w illustrations and photographs. "Devices with a fresh approach to old themes or new insights into the human condition whether prose or poetry." Quarterly supplement to annual *Rockford Review*. Estab. 1990. Circ. 200.
• The Rockford Writers Guild publishes this and *The Rockford Review*, also listed in this book.

Bringing Good Work to the Fore

George Witte

"Our goal is to be a bridge between the little magazine world and the book publishing world," George Witte, *Turnstile* editor, says. "We want to bring our writers to publishers' attention."

Founded in 1986, the spirit of *Turnstile* has been to seek out new writers who are not getting the opportunity to have work published, and use the expertise of the staff members to help them get nominated for awards and noticed by mainstream publishers.

While this vision may not be unique in the world of small literary magazines, the staff of *Turnstile* is. *Publishers Weekly* describes them as a group of "unpaid and idealistic young publishing professionals." Witte explains, "We work strictly on a volunteer basis." While not affiliated with any publishing house, *Turnstile*'s staff is comprised of a diverse group of about a dozen publishing professionals, including editors, literary agents, advertising professionals and graduate students, all working and meeting on their own time.

Witte stresses that he is "an editor," not "The Editor," of *Turnstile*, speaking just as a representative of the group. "There's no single voice on the magazine that has veto power. No one says 'We will do this.' We have a democratic staff."

Turnstile receives more than 1,000 submissions yearly, of which they publish about ten. Witte urges writers to read the magazines that they're interested in. "We get a lot of submissions from writers who've chosen us just because they've gotten to the 'Ts' in the market book," he says, "Most magazines will say they publish new writers. Read two or three copies of the magazine—see what we publish.

"You shouldn't submit too early. Learning to write well is analogous to learning to play a musical instrument really well, or learning to play professional tennis really well. Writers who keep writing and writing over the course of time have a good chance of eventually being published," he says.

As far as criteria for the fiction they publish, there's no one quality or style that Witte looks for. "Over the years, we've published traditional narrative. That said, there's also been variety in the magazine. We've published comic stories, darker stories, contemporary. We're not closed to anything," he says, "But obviously, we wouldn't do this if we didn't really want to publish things that were wonderful. That's why we've held together for so long."

—*Alice P. Buening*

Needs: Ethnic, experimental, fantasy, humor/satire, science fiction (hard science, soft/sociological). Publishes short shorts up to 500 words.

How to Contact: Send complete ms. Simultaneous submissions OK, if noted. Reports in 6-8 weeks. SASE (IRCs). Sample copy for $2.50. Fiction guidelines for #10 SAE and 1 first-class stamp.

Payment: Pays in contributor's copies. Submissions considered for $25 Readers' Poll prize.

Terms: Acquires first North American serial rights.

TRIQUARTERLY, (II), Northwestern University, 2020 Ridge Ave., Evanston IL 60208. (708)491-7614. Fiction Editors: Reginald Gibbons and Susan Hahn. Magazine: 6×9¼; 240 pages; 60 lb. paper; heavy cover stock; illustration; photos. "A general literary quarterly especially devoted to fiction. We publish short stories, novellas or excerpts from novels, by American and foreign writers. Genre or style is not a primary consideration. We aim for the general but serious and sophisticated reader. Many of our readers are also writers." Triannual. Estab. 1964. Circ. 5,000.

- In 1991 the publishers of *TriQuarterly* published *Fiction of the '80s*, a collection of the best fiction published in the magazine during the 1980s. The magazine ranks #49 on the latest *Writer's Digest* Fiction 50 list.

Needs: Literary, contemporary and translations. "No prejudices or preconceptions against anything *except* genre fiction (romance, science fiction, etc.)." Buys 10 mss/issue, 30 mss/year. Receives approximately 500 unsolicited fiction mss each month. Does not read April 1-September 30. Agented fiction 10%. Published work by Stanley Elkin, Chaim Potok and Alice Fulton; published new writers within the last year. Length: no requirement. Publishes short shorts.

How to Contact: Send complete ms with SASE (IRCs). No simultaneous submissions. Reports in 3-4 months on mss. Publishes ms an average of 6-12 months after acceptance. Sample copy for $4.

Payment: Pays $20/page (fiction); 2 contributor's copies. Cover price less 40% discount for extras.

Terms: Pays on publication for first North American serial rights. Sends galleys to author.

TUCUMCARI LITERARY REVIEW, (I, II), 3108 W. Bellevue Ave., Los Angeles CA 90026. Editor: Troxey Kemper. Magazine: 5½×8½; 32 pages; 20 lb. bond paper; 110 lb. cover stock; few illustrations; Xerox photographs. "Old-fashioned fiction that can be read and reread for pleasure; no weird, strange pipe dreams." Bimonthly. Estab. 1988. Circ. small.

Needs: Adventure, contemporary, ethnic, historical (general), humor/satire, literary, mainstream, mystery/suspense, regional (southwest USA), senior citizen/retirement, western (frontier stories). No science fiction, drugs/acid rock, pornography, horror, martial arts. "No talking animals or plants. No talking with God or telling what He told you." Accepts 6 or 8 mss/issue; 35-40 mss/year. Publishes ms 2-6 months after acceptance. Length: 400-1,200 words preferred. Also publishes rhyming poetry.

How to Contact: Send complete ms with or without cover letter. Reports in 2 weeks. SASE (IRCs). Simultaneous and reprint submissions OK. Sample copy for $1.50 plus 50¢ postage. Fiction guidelines for #10 SAE and 1 first-class stamp.

Payment: Pays in contributor's copies.

Terms: Acquires one-time rights. Publication not copyrighted.

Advice: "Do not try to copy the horror/violence/sex/big explosions/dirty words/loose morals you see in movies and on TV. I keep reading somewhere that those things have about run their course, anyway."

TURNSTILE, (II), Suite 2348, 175 Fifth Ave., New York NY 10010. Editor: George Witte. Magazine: 6×9; 128 pages; 55 lb. paper; 10 pt. cover; illustrations; photos. "Publishing work by new writers." Biannual. Estab. 1988. Circ. 1,000.

- *Turnstile* has received grants from the New York State Council of the Arts for the last three years, as well as a grant from the National Endowment for the Arts in 1993-94. See the interview with Editor George Witte in this section.

Needs: Contemporary, experimental, humor/satire, literary, regional. No genre fiction. Receives approximately 100 unsolicited fiction mss/month. Publishes approximately 5 short story mss/issue. Published work by James Applewhite and Richard Russo; published new writers within the last year. Length: 2,000 words average; 4,000 words maximum. Also publishes poetry, nonfiction essays, and interviews with well-known writers. Sometimes comments on rejected mss.

How to Contact: Query first or send complete ms with cover letter. Reports on queries in 3-4 weeks; on mss in 6-10 weeks. SASE (IRCs). Simultaneous submissions OK. Sample copy for $6.50 and 7×10 SAE; fiction guidelines for #10 SAE and 1 first-class stamp.

Payment: Pays in contributor's copies; charge for extras.
Terms: Acquires one-time rights.
Advice: "More than ever we're looking for *well-crafted* stories. We're known for publishing a range of new voices, and favor stories that rely on traditional narrative techniques (e.g. characterization, plot, effective endings)."

TWISTED, P.O. Box 1249, Palmetto GA 30268-1249. (404)463-1458. Editor: Christine Hoard. Magazine: 8½ × 11; 152 pages; 60 lb. paper; 67 lb. cover stock; illustrations; photos. "Emphasis on contemporary horror and fantasy, anything on the dark side of reality." For readers of horror, "weird," fantasy, etc. Published irregularly. Estab. 1985. Circ. 300.
Needs: "We are mostly interested in adult-oriented horror." Fantasy, horror, prose poem, psychic/supernatural/occult. "No hard science fiction, no sword and sorcery. Graphic horror or sex scenes OK if tastefully done. Sexist-racist writing turns me off." Receives approximately 30 unsolicited fiction mss/month. Accepts 10 mss/issue. Publishes ms 2 months - 2 years after acceptance. Published work by David Bruce, Joe Faust, Bentley Little and Kathleen Jurgens; publishes new writers. Length: 2,000 words average; 200 words minimum; 5,000 words preferred. Sometimes critiques rejected mss and recommends other markets.
How to Contact: Reporting time varies, usually 2-3 months. Cover letters not necessary but appreciated. No simultaneous or multiple submissions. Sample copy for $6. Fiction guidelines for #10 SAE and 1 first-class stamp.
Payment: Pays in contributor's copies.
Terms: Acquires first rights.
Advice: "Sometimes we are overstocked or temporary closed for submissions so probably best to inquire first."

2 AM MAGAZINE, (I, II, IV), Box 6754, Rockford IL 61125-1754. Editor: Gretta M. Anderson. Magazine: 8½ × 11; 60 or more pages; 60 lb. offset paper; 70 lb. offset cover; illustrations; photos occasionally. "Horror, science fiction, fantasy stories, poetry, articles and art for a sophisticated adult audience." Quarterly. Summer fiction issue planned. Estab. 1986. Circ. 2,000.
● This horror, science fiction and fantasy magazine ranks #16 on the latest *Writer's Digest* Fiction 50 list.
Needs: Experimental, fantasy, horror, humor/satire, mystery/suspense (police procedurals, romantic suspense), prose poem, psychic/supernatural/occult, romance (gothic), science fiction (hard science, soft/sociological). No juvenile. Receives 400 unsolicited mss/month. Buys 12-14 mss/issue; 50 mss/year. Publishes ms an average of 6-9 months after acceptance. Recently published work by Darrel Schweitzer, Auram Davidson, John Coyne and Larry Tritten; published new writers within the last year. Length: 3,000 words average; 500 words minimum; 5,000 words maximum. Publishes short shorts. Sometimes critiques rejected mss and recommends other markets.
How to Contact: Send complete ms with cover letter (cover letter optional). Simultaneous submissions OK. Reports in 1 month on queries; 10-12 weeks on mss. SASE (IRCs). Sample copy for $4.95 and $1 postage. Fiction guidelines for #10 SASE.
Payment: Pays ½¢/word minimum, negotiable maximum; 1 contributor's copy; 40% discount on additional copies.
Terms: Pays on acceptance for one-time rights with non-exclusive anthology option. Sends prepublication galleys to author.
Advice: "Publishing more pages of fiction, more science fiction, and mystery, as well as horror. Put name and address on ms, double-space, use standard ms format. Pseudonym should appear under title on first ms page. True name and address should appear on upper left on first ms page."

‡TWO-TON SANTA (I), Box 1332, Portsmouth NH 03801. (603)427-0631. Editor: Guy Capecelatro III. Magazine: 5¾ × 8¼; 4 pages. "Because of its size, only four pages, the material must be fairly short. Most tend to be stories and poems about real people dealing with somehow, ironic situations." Weekly. Estab. 1988. Circ. 200.
Needs: Condensed/excerpted novel, contemporary, erotica, experimental, feminist, gay, horror, humor/satire, juvenile (5-9 years), lesbian, preschool (1-4 years), prose poem, religious/inspirational and senior citizen/retirement. "We do not encourage writing styles that tend to alienate people. The language should not detract from or overwhelm the story itself." Publishes annual fiction issue. Receives 400 unsolicited mss/month. Accepts 2 mss/month; 112 mss/year. Publishes ms 2-4 weeks after acceptance. Published work by Russell Edson, Ray Halliday, Nancy Krygowski and Pagan Kennedy.

Length: 3-700 words; 100-300 words average. Also publishes poetry. Sometimes critiques rejected mss and recommends other markets.
How to Contact: Query first. Reports in 2-3 weeks. Simultaneous and reprint submissions OK.
Payment: Pays in contributor's copies.
Terms: Acquires one-time rights.
Advice: "The stories that stand out are ones that provide a glimpse into real life. They are imaginative in their presentation of how we exist. Stories don't necessarily follow a logical progression, but should invoke some sort of feeling within the reader. Each scene should work at being a part of the whole, if only in setting or voice. The language should not hinder an idea but be used merely as a presentation."

✸**UNDERPASS, (II),** Underpass Press, #574-21, 10405 Jasper Ave., Edmonton, Alberta T5J 3S2 Canada. Editor: Barry Hammond. Magazine: 5¼ × 8¼; pages vary; 60 lb. bond paper; Mayfair cover; some illustrations. "Mainly a poetry annual for an adult audience." Annual. Estab. 1987. Circ. 200-300.
Needs: Contemporary, experimental, literary, prose poem. "We have only published a few short stories. We are mainly a poetry annual. No religious or nature poetry." Receives 6 mss/month. Buys 1 or 2 mss/issue. Does not read mss November-January. Publishes ms within 6 months after acceptance. Published work by Wade Bell. Length: 2,000 words average; 500 words minimum; 6,000 words maximum. Publishes short shorts. Length: No preference. Sometimes critiques rejected mss.
How to Contact: Send complete ms with cover letter including "brief bio and publishing history (if any)." Reports in 6 weeks. "Our deadline is August 31st each year." SASE (IRCs). Simultaneous submissions OK. Sample copy for $6.95, 6 × 9 SAE and 2 first-class stamps. Fiction guidelines for #10 SAE and 1 first-class stamp.
Payment: Pays $10 minimum and contributor's copies.
Terms: Buys one-time rights. Sends galleys to author.
Advice: "Try poetry before submitting prose."

‡**THE UNFORGETTABLE FIRE, (IV),** P.O. Box 388, Lyndhurst NJ 07071. Editor: Jordan O'Neill. Newsletter: 8½ × 11; 28 pages; illustrations. "Feminist, humanist publication, by, for and about women. We do accept submissions from men, however." Quarterly. Estab. 1992. Circ. 3,000.
Needs: Ethnic/multicultural, feminist, gay, humor/satire, lesbian. "Nothing sexist, racist, homophobic, violent, pornographic." Publishes special fiction issue or anthology. Receives 10-15 unsolicited mss/month. Accepts 2 mss/issue; 10 mss/year. Recently published work by Lynn Stearns and Khris Reynhout. Length: 1,500 words maximum. Publishes short shorts. Publishes literary essays, literary criticism and poetry. Always critiques and comments on rejected mss.
How to Contact: Send complete ms with a cover letter. Should include 1 paragraph bio. Reports in 1 week on queries; 3-4 weeks on mss. Send SASE (or IRC) for reply, return of ms or send a disposable copy of ms. Simultaneous, reprint and electronic submissions OK. Sample copy and fiction guidelines free. Reviews novels and short story collections.
Payment: Pays 1-2 contributor's copies.
Terms: Pays on acceptance.
Advice: Looks for work "usually with a strong feminist/humanist tone — compassionate stories pertaining to everyday life — stories related to overcoming hardships and, most importantly, empowerment. Write from the heart with a female angle, writing, speaking to and about other women so our readers feel connected to the story."

UNIVERSITY OF PORTLAND REVIEW, (II), University of Portland, 5000 N. Willamette Blvd., Portland OR 97203. (503)283-7144. Editor-in-Chief: Thompson M. Faller. Magazine: 5 × 8; 40-55 pages. "Magazine for the college-educated layman of liberal arts background. Its purpose is to comment on the human condition and to present information in different fields with relevance to the contemporary scene." Semiannual. Established 1948. Circ. 1,000.
Needs: "Only fiction that makes a significant statement about the contemporary scene will be employed." Receives 4 unsolicited mss/month. Acquires 2-3 mss/issue, 4-6 mss/year. Published new writers within the last year. Length: 1,500 words minimum; 3,500 words maximum; 2,000 words average. Sometimes recommends other markets.

Check the Category Indexes, located at the back of the book, for publishers interested in specific fiction subjects.

How to Contact: Send complete ms with SASE (IRCs). Reports in 3 weeks on queries; 6 months on mss. Publishes ms up to 1 year after acceptance. Sample copy for 50¢.
Payment: Pays 5 contributor's copies; 50¢ charge for extras.
Terms: Acquires all rights.

UNMUZZLED OX, (III), Unmuzzled Ox Foundation Ltd., 105 Hudson St., New York NY 10013. Editor: Michael Andre. Tabloid. "Magazine about life for an intelligent audience." Quarterly. Estab. 1971. Circ. 20,000.
● The next few issues of this magazine include poetry, essays and art only. You may want to check before sending submissions or expect a long response time.
Needs: Contemporary, literary, prose poem and translations. No commercial material. Receives 20-25 unsolicited mss/month. Also publishes poetry. Occasionally critiques rejected mss.
How to Contact: "Cover letter is significant." Reports in 1 month. SASE (IRCs). Sample copy for $7.50.
Payment: Contributor's copies.

UNREALITY, (II), P.O. Box 1155, Columbia SC 29202-1155. Editor: David Schindler. Magazine: 7×8½; 40-60 pages; 20 lb. paper; b&w illustrations. "The theme of the magazine is the overlapping of reality and the unreal. The philosophy is to allow writers the freedom to explore dark or fantastic themes without having to pander to the requirements of any particular genre." Quarterly. Estab. 1992.
Needs: Fantasy, horror, literary/mainstream, psychic/supernatural/occult. "I'm open to anything so long as it has a dark or unreal slant." Receives 50 unsolicited mss/month. Acquires 6-10 mss/issue; 30-40 mss/year. Publishes ms 3-6 months after acceptance. Published work by D.F. Lewis, Lenora K. Rogers and Bobby G. Warner. Length: 4,000 words maximum. Also publishes poetry. Often critiques or comments on rejected mss.
How to Contact: Send complete ms with a cover letter. Should include brief bio. Reports in 4-6 weeks on mss. Send SASE (IRCs) for reply, return of ms or send a disposable copy of the ms. Simultaneous submissions OK, if identified as such. Sample copy for $3.50 (payable to David Schindler). Fiction guidelines for #10 SAE and 1 first-class stamp.
Payment: Pays 1-2 contributor's copies for stories. Additional copies at a discount.
Terms: Acquires first North American serial rights.
Advice: Looks for "a well-written, intelligent story, not just a good scare. Send for my guidelines and read them carefully before you submit. They're very detailed and will help you avoid sending inappropriate material."

‡THE URBANITE, A Journal of City Fiction & Poetry, (II, IV), Urban Legend Press, P.O. Box 4737, Davenport IA 52808. Editor: Mark McLaughlin. Magazine. "We look for quality fiction in an urban setting with a surrealistic tone . . . we prefer character-driven storylines. Our audience is urbane, culture-oriented and hard to please! We only select fiction that we feel will still be considered fascinating a hundred years from now." Published irregularly. Estab. 1991. Circ. 500.
● A story by M.R. Scofidio published in *The Urbanite* was selected for inclusion in the *Year's Best Fantasy and Horror* (No.6). Three other stories from the same issue received Honorable Mentions in the anthology.
Needs: Experimental, fantasy (dark fantasy), horror, humor/satire, literary, psychic/supernatural/occult, science fiction (soft/sociological). "We love horror, but please, no tired, gore-ridden horror plots. Horror submissions must be subtle and sly." List of upcoming themes available for SASE. Receives 20 unsolicited mss/month. Accepts 8-10 mss/issue; 25 mss/year. Publishes ms 6 months after acceptance. Recently published work by M.R. Scofidio, Pamela Briggs, Terri Willits and Barbara Toner. Length: 2,000 words preferred; 500 words minimum; 3,000 words maximum. Publishes short shorts. Length: 350 words preferred. Also publishes poetry. Sometimes critiques or comments on rejected mss.
How to Contact: Query first; each issue has its own theme and guidelines for that theme. Should include estimated word count, 4-5 sentence bio, Social Security number and list of publications. Reports in 1 month on queries; 4-5 months on mss. Send SASE (or IRC) for reply, return of ms or send a disposable copy of ms. Sample copy for $5. Fiction guidelines for #10 SAE and 1 first-class stamp.
Payment: Pays 2¢/word and 2 contributor's copies.
Terms: Pays on acceptance for first North American serial rights and non-exclusive rights for public readings.
Advice: "The tone of our magazine is unique, and we strongly encourage writers to read an issue to ascertain the sort of material we accept. We want to see more surrealism and more bizarre (yet urbane and thought-provoking) humor. We also want to see more subtle, sly horror. Writers must query to find out our future themes."

URBANUS/RAIZIRR, (II), Urbanus Press, P.O. Box 192561, San Francisco CA 94119. Executive Editor: Rose Mok. Magazine: 5½ × 8½; 48 pages; 60 lb. offset paper; 10 pt. coated cover; illustrations; a few photographs. "We seek writing for an audience that is generally impatient with mainstream writing—at the same time, not falling into the underground literary mode." Semiannual. Estab. 1988. Circ. 800.
Needs: Erotica, ethnic/multicultural, experimental, feminist, gay, horror, humor/satire, lesbian, literary, mainstream/contemporary, science fiction (soft/sociological). "Nothing generic slice-of-life—far too much of it out there." Receives 100-150 unsolicited mss/month. Buys 10 mss/year. Publishes ms 6-18 months after acceptance. Length: 5,000 words maximum. Publishes short shorts. Also publishes poetry. Sometimes comments on or critiques rejected mss.
How to Contact: Send complete ms with a cover letter. Should include estimated word count, list of publications (3-5 sentences). Reports in 2-4 weeks on queries; 1-3 months on mss. Send SASE (IRCs) for reply, return of ms or send a disposable copy of the ms. No multiple or simultaneous submissions. Sample copy for $5. Writer's guidelines available for #10 SAE and 1 first-class stamp.
Payment: Pays ½¢/word and 1 contributor's copy.
Terms: Pays on publication for first North American serial rights.
Advice: "Firstly, we do not appreciate receiving more than one story at a time; if we pass a submitter's first effort, unless we state otherwise, we do not wish to be inundated with numerous approaches in the months to come. Wait to get our attention with a *very good* story. Sample a copy, if possible, though we understand writers are strapped enough by the cost of postage and other intangibles; at the very least *read* and *subscribe* to a few alternative magazines to get a sense for what angles interest a small cross section of editors."

US1 WORKSHEETS, (II), Postings, Box 1, Ringoes NJ 08551. (908)782-6492. Editor: Rotating board. Magazine: 11½ × 17; 20-25 pages. Publishes poetry and fiction. Annual. Estab. 1973.
Needs: "No restrictions on subject matter or style. Good story telling or character deliniation appreciated. Audience does not include children." Recently published work by Alicia Ostriker, Richard Kostelanetz, Geraldine C. Little, Robin Clippers Sethe, J.A. Perkins, Cynthia Goodling and Judith McNally. Publishes short shorts.
How to Contact: Query first. Reports on queries "as soon as possible." SASE (IRCs). Sample copy $4.
Payment: Pays in contributor's copies.
Terms: Acquires one-time rights. Copyright "reverts to author."

VALLEY GRAPEVINE, (I, IV), Seven Buffaloes Press, Box 249, Big Timber MT 59011. Editor/Publisher: Art Cuelho. Theme: "poems, stories, history, folklore, photographs, ink drawings or anything native to the Great Central Valley of California, which includes the San Joaquin and Sacramento valleys. Focus is on land and people and the oil fields, farms, orchards, Okies, small town life, hobos." Readership: "Rural and small town audience, the common man with a rural background, salt-of-the-earth. The working man reads *Valley Grapevine* because it's his personal history recorded." Annual. Estab. 1978. Circ. 500.
● *Valley Grapevine* is published by Art Cuelho of Seven Buffaloes Press. He also publishes *Azorean Express, Black Jack, Hill and Holler,* listed in this book. See also his listing for the press.
Needs: Literary, contemporary, western and ethnic (Arkie, Okie). No academic, religious (unless natural to theme), or supernatural material. Receives approximately 4-5 unsolicited fiction mss each month. Length: 2,500-10,000 (prefers 5,000) words.
How to Contact: Query. SASE (IRCs) for query, ms. Reports in 1 week. Sample copy available to writers for $5.75.
Payment: Pays 1-2 contributor's copies.
Terms: Acquires first North American serial rights. Returns rights to author after publication, but reserves the right to reprint in an anthology or any future special collection of Seven Buffaloes Press.
Advice: "Buy a copy to get a feel of the professional quality of the writing. Know the theme of a particular issue. Some contributors have 30 years experience as writers; most 15 years. Age does not matter; quality does."

VeriTales®, Short Stories for the Evolving Spirit, (II), Fall Creek Press, P.O. Box 1127, Fall Creek OR 97438. (503)744-0938. Editor: Helen Wirth. Trade paperback anthologies: 5½ × 8½; 192 pages; recycled, uncoated 50-70 lb. paper; 10 pt C1S recycled cover. "Description of a veri-tale: Through a well-developed and forward-moving short story, the reader is sensitized to an opportunity for spiritual growth. Fiction with substance, for 'thinking' adults." Publishes 2 titles/year with varying publication dates. Estab. 1993.

Needs: Adventure, ethnic/multicultural, experimental, fantasy (science fantasy, sword and sorcery), feminist, gay, historical, humor/satire, lesbian, literary, mainstream/contemporary, mystery/suspense (amateur sleuth, cozy, romantic suspense), psychic/supernatural/occult, regional, religious/inspirational, romance (contemporary, gothic, historical), science fiction (soft/sociological), senior citizen/retirement, sports, westerns (adult western, frontier, traditional)."We publish exclusively anthologies of short stories which meet the criteria of VeriTales." Receives 40-60 unsolicited synopses/month. Buys 8-15 mss/book; 16-30 mss/year. Publishes ms a maximum of 3 years after acceptance. Length: 9,000 words maximum. Publishes short shorts. Sometimes critiques or comments on rejected mss.
How to Contact: Query first; request author guide; enclose #10 SASE (IRCs); identify where you learned of Fall Creek Press. "After reviewing author guide, submit synopsis per guidelines and SASE for reply. Reports in 1 month. Simultaneous submissions OK. Samples of our trade paperbacks will be available at list price plus shipping."
Payment: Pays royalties and 1 contributor's copy. Additional copies 40% discount from list.
Terms: Buys all rights. Sends galleys to author.
Advice: Looks for "short stories that 'go somewhere.' The protagonists are not the same people at the end that they were at the beginning. Their lives are changed because of the experience contained within the story. We look for stories that address a new subject or that apply a new treatment to an old subject, frequently ending with an unexpected 'twist.' All stories must demonstrate specific choices by the protagonist which open doors to spiritual growth."

VIDEOMANIA, The Video Collectors Newspaper, (I, II), LegsOfStone Publishing Co., Box 47, Princeton WI 54968. (414)295-4377. Editor: Bob Katerzynske. Tabloid; 10½ × 16; 32 pages; newsprint paper; ground wood cover; b&w/color illustrations and photographs. "Slanted towards the home entertainment buff, individuals with a *real* interest in home video and entertainment. Publishes *anything* we feel is of interest to our readers — fiction and non-fiction. Audience is mostly male (90%), but female readership is always increasing." Bimonthly. Estab. 1982. Circ. 5-6,000.
Needs: Movie-related themes. Experimental, fantasy, feminist, horror, humor/satire, lesbian, mainstream, science fiction (soft/sociological), video/film. Receives 3-4 unsolicited mss/month. Buys 1-2 mss/issue; 6-9 mss/year. Publishes ms 2-6 months after acceptance. Publishes short shorts. Length: 300-500 words. Sometimes critiques rejected mss and recommends other markets.
How to Contact: Send complete ms with cover letter. No simultaneous submissions. Reports in 1-2 months. SASE (IRCs). Sample copy for $2.50, 9 × 12 SAE and $1 postage. Fiction guidelines for #10 SAE and 1 first-class stamp.
Payment: Pays $2.50 token payment in certain cases; contributor's copies.
Terms: Pays on publication for all rights or as writer prefers.
Advice: "If the editor likes it, it's in. A good manuscript should not be too heavy; a *touch* of humor goes a long way with us. Don't expect to get rich off of us. On the other hand, we're more willing than other publications to look at the first-time, non-published writer. We've published established writers in the past that wanted to use our publication as sort of a sounding board for something experimental."

THE VILLAGER, 135 Midland Ave., Bronxville NY 10707. (914)337-3252. Editor: Amy Murphy. Fiction Editor: Mrs. Ahmed Hazzah. Magazine: 28-40 pages. "Magazine for a family audience." October-June. Estab. 1928. Circ. 1,000. Upcoming theme: "Black History Month" (February 1994).
Needs: Adventure, historical, humor/satire, literary, prose poem, romance (historical), mystery/suspense. Length: 1,500-1,800 words. Also publishes poetry.
How to Contact: Send complete ms with cover letter. SASE (IRCs). Sample copy for $1.25.
Payment: Pays 2 contributor's copies.

THE VINCENT BROTHERS REVIEW, (II), Vincent Brothers Publishing, 4566 Northern Circle, Mad River Twp., Dayton OH 45424. Editor: Kimberly Willardson. Magazine: 5½ × 8½; 64-84 pages; 60 lb. white coated paper; 60 lb. Oxford (matte) cover; b&w illustrations and photographs. "We publish two theme issues per year. Writers must send SASE for information about upcoming theme issues. Each issue of *TVBR* contains poetry, b&w art, at least 3 short stories and usually 1 nonfiction piece. For a mainstream audience looking for an alternative to the slicks." Triannual. Estab. 1988. Circ. 400.
 • Ranked #37 on the latest *Writer's Digest* Fiction 50 list, *Vincent Brothers Review* has also received grants from the Ohio Arts Council for the last four years. For more information see the interview with Editor Kimberly Willardson in the 1993 edition of this book. The magazine plans a fall fiction contest; deadline in October. Contact them for details.

Needs: Adventure, condensed/excerpted novel, contemporary, ethnic, experimental, feminist, historical (general), humor/satire, literary, mainstream, mystery/suspense (amateur sleuth, cozy, private eye), prose poem, regional, science fiction (soft/sociological), senior citizen/retirement, serialized novel, translations, western (adult, frontier, traditional). We focus on the way the story is presented rather than the genre of the story. No racist, sexist, fascist, etc. work." Send SASE (IRCs) for themes. Receives 200-250 unsolicited mss/month. Buys 3-5 mss/issue; 9-15 mss/year. Publishes ms 2-4 months after acceptance. Recently published work by Doris Read, Don Stockard and Susan Streeter Carpenter. Length: 2,500 words average; 250 words minimum; 3,500 words maximum. Publishes short shorts. Length: 250-1,000 words. Also publishes literary essays, literary criticism, poetry. Often critiques rejected mss and sometimes recommends other markets.
How to Contact: "Send query letter *before* sending novel excerpts or condensations! Send only 1 short story at a time — unless sending short shorts." Send complete ms with cover letter. Include Social Security number. "Include previous publications; if the manuscript should be returned (SASE must be included) or if the manuscript is photocopied." Simultaneous submissions OK, but not preferred. Reports in 3-4 weeks on queries; 1-2 months on mss. SASE. Sample copy for $4.50. Fiction guidelines for #10 SAE and 1 first-class stamp. Reviews novels and short story collections.
Payment: Pays $10 minimum and 2 contributor's copies. Charge (discounted) for extras.
Terms: Buys one-time rights.
Advice: "*TVBR* editorial staff is developing a keen and growing interest in "flash" fiction (750 words maximum) and "sudden" fiction (usually acknowledged as having 1,000 words maximum). We're eager to read well-crafted short short stories and prose poems."

VINTAGE NORTHWEST, (I, IV), Northshore Senior Center, Box 193, Bothell WA 98041. (206)487-1201. Editor: Lawrence T. Campbell. Magazine: 7×8½; 64 pages; illustrations. "A senior literary magazine published by and for seniors. All work done by volunteers except printing." For "all ages who are interested in seniors' experiences." Published winter and summer. Estab. 1980. Circ. 500.
Needs: Adventure, comedy, condensed novel (1,000 words maximum), fantasy, historical, humor/satire, inspirational, mystery/suspense, poetry, senior citizen/retirement, western (frontier). No religious or political mss. Upcoming themes: "A Zest for Living" (Summer 1994). Receives 2-3 unsolicited mss/month. Accepts 2 mss/issue. Published work by Dave Kneeshaw and Sylvia Tacker; published new writers within the last year. Length: 1,000 words maximum. Also publishes literary essays. Occasionally critiques rejected mss.
How to Contact: Send complete ms. SASE (IRCs). Simultaneous and previously published submissions OK. Reports in 3-6 months. Sample copy for $2.75. Fiction guidelines with SASE.
Payment: Pays 1 contributor's copy.
Advice: "Our only requirement is that the author be over 50 or physically handicapped when submission is written."

VIRGIN MEAT, (I), 2325 W.K 15, Lancaster CA 93536. (805)722-1758. Editor: Steve Blum. Digest: 5×8½; 26 pages. Published irregularly. Estab. 1987. Circ. 350.
Needs: Horror. Receives 3-4 mss/day. Length: 2,000 words maximum. Also publishes poetry.
How to Contact: Send complete ms with cover letter. Reports in 1 month. Simultaneous and reprint submissions OK. Sample copy for $2. Reviews novels and short story collections.
Payment: Pays in contributor's copies.
Terms: Acquires one-time rights. Publication not copyrighted.
Advice: "Horror fiction should be horrific all the way through, not just at the end. Avoid common settings, senseless violence and humor."

VIRGINIA QUARTERLY REVIEW, (III), One West Range, Charlottesville VA 22903. (804)924-3124. Editor: Staige Blackford. "A national magazine of literature and discussion. A lay, intellectual audience; people who are not out-and-out scholars but who are interested in ideas and literature." Quarterly. Estab. 1925. Circ. 4,500.
Needs: Literary, contemporary, feminist, romance, adventure, humor, ethnic, serialized novels (excerpts) and translations. "No pornography." Buys 3 mss/issue, 20 mss/year. Length: 3,000-7,000 words.
How to Contact: Query or send complete ms. SASE (IRCs). No simultaneous submissions. Reports in 2 weeks on queries, 2 months on mss. Sample copy $5.
Payment: Pays $10/printed page. Offers Emily Clark Balch Award for best published short story of the year.
Terms: Pays on publication for all rights. "Will transfer upon request."
Advice: "Because of the competition, it's difficult for a nonpublished writer to break in."

WAGONS OF STEEL MAGAZINE, (II, IV), P. O. Box 1435, Vashon WA 98070. Editor: Gaffo Jones. Fiction Editor: Natalie Kosovac. Newsletter: 5½×8½. "A magazine of humor and satire with an emphasis on the station wagon. Anecdotes, essays, fiction, photos, comics for mostly Seattle-area collegians and young urbanites." Quarterly. Estab. 1990. Circ. 500.
Needs: Adventure, erotica, experimental, fantasy (automotive), horror, humor/satire, psychic/supernatural/occult. Receives 50 mss/month. Buys 3 mss/issue; 12 mss/year. Published B.B. Cunningham, Doug Ingle. Length: open. Publishes *short shorts*. Also publishes poetry. Sometimes critiques rejected mss.
How to Contact: Send complete ms with a cover letter. Should include very short bio. Reports in 4-6 weeks on manuscripts. Send SASE (IRC) for reply, return of ms or send a disposable copy of the ms. Simultaneous submissions OK. Sample copy $3 and postage. Fiction guidelines for #10 SAE.
Payment: Pays 1 contributor's copy; additional copies $2.
Terms: Acquires first rights.
Advice: Looks for "originality, humor, irreverance, a basic understanding of what we're trying to do here."

‡✹**WASCANA REVIEW, (II),** University of Regina, Regina, Saskatchewan S4S 0A2 Canada. Editor: Kathleen Wall. "Literary criticism, fiction and poetry for readers of serious fiction." Semiannual. Estab. 1966. Circ. 500.
Needs: Literary and humor. Buys 6 mss/year. Receives approximately 20 unsolicited fiction mss/month. Agented fiction 5%. Length: no requirement. Occasionally recommends other markets.
How to Contact: Send complete ms with SASE (IRCs). Reports in 2 months on mss. Publishes ms an average of 1 year after acceptance. Sample copy $4. Guidelines with SAE, IRC.
Payment: Pays $3/page for prose; $10/page for poetry; 2 contributor's copies.
Terms: Pays on publication for all rights.
Advice: "Stories are often technically incompetent or deal with trite subjects. Usually stories are longer than necessary by about one-third. Be more ruthless in cutting back on unnecessary verbiage."

WASHINGTON REVIEW, (II, IV), Friends of the Washington Review of the Arts, Box 50132, Washington DC 20091. (202)638-0515. Fiction Editor: Jeff Richards. "We publish fiction, poetry, articles and reviews on all areas of the arts. We have a particular interest in the interrelationships of the arts and emphasize the cultural life of the DC area." Readership: "Artists, writers and those interested in cultural life in this area." Bimonthly. Estab. 1975. Circ. 12,000.
Needs: Literary. Accepts 1-2 mss/issue. Receives approximately 50-100 unsolicited fiction mss/month. Length: Prefers 3,000 words or less. Critiques rejected mss when there is time.
How to Contact: Send complete ms with SASE (IRCs). Reports in 2 months. Publishes ms an average of 6 months after acceptance. Copy for tabloid-sized SASE and $2.50.
Payment: Pays contributor's copies plus small payment whenever possible.
Terms: Pays on publication for first North American serial rights.
Advice: "Edit your writing for redundant adjectives. Make sure everything makes sense: the plot, character, motivation. Try to avoid clichés."

WEBSTER REVIEW, (II), Webster Review, Inc., Webster University, 470 E. Lockwood, Webster Groves MO 63119. (314)432-2657. Editor: Nancy Schapiro. Magazine: 5×8; 120 pages; 60 lb. white paper; 10pt. C1S; cover illustrations and photographs. "Literary magazine, international, contemporary. We publish many English translations of foreign fiction writers for academics, writers, discriminating readers." Annual. Estab. 1974.
Needs: Contemporary, literary, translations. No erotica, juvenile. Receives 100 unsolicited mss/month. Accepts 3-5 mss/issue; 6-10 mss/year. Publishes ms one year or more after acceptance. Agented fiction less than 1%. Published work by David Williams and Anjana Appachana. Publishes short shorts. Sometimes critiques rejected mss.
How to Contact: Send complete manuscript with cover letter. Reports in 2-4 months on mss. SASE (IRCs). Simultaneous submissions OK. Sample copy for 6×9 SAE and 2 first-class stamps.
Payment: Pays contributor's copies.
Terms: Acquires first rights.

WEST, (II), Bluestone Press, P.O. Box 1186, Hampshire College, Amherst MA 01002. Editors: J. Horoschak, J.Beckman. Magazine: 5½×8½; 150 pages; laid or equivalent paper; 80 lb. matte cover; illustrations; photographs. "We consider traditional as well as 'avant-garde' material, including picto-

WEBSTER REVIEW

Number sixteen   Fall, 1992

"We chose this cover because the photograph displayed not only visual artistry, but seemed to us to represent some of the literary qualities that we value," says Nancy Schapiro, editor and publisher of Webster Review. "The image . . . manifests a complexity and coherence which we treasure in the fiction and poetry we publish, as well as in our cover art." About half of the 128 pages in each issue of Webster Review are devoted to fiction. "We place no length restrictions and have published novel excerpts as well as short stories, prose poems and translations." The cover's photographer, Frank Ferrario, is on the fine arts faculty at Fontbonne College in St. Louis.

rial essays, artist's books, letters, artwork, etc. Audience is mostly writers, but also a substantial number of institutions plus libraries." Quarterly. Estab. 1990. Circ. 300.

Needs: Condensed novel, erotica, ethnic/multicultural, experimental, feminist, gay, historical, humor/satire, lesbian, literary, mainstream/contemporary, regional, translations. "We accept submissions of any style, but do not frequently publish genre fiction." List of upcoming themes available for SASE. Publishes special fiction issue or anthology. Receives 60 unsolicited mss/month. Acquires 5 mss/issue; 20 mss/year. Publishes ms usually 1 month after acceptance. Agented fiction 5%. Published work by Alice Mattison, Louise Blum, Paul Beckman. Length: 2,000-3,000 words preferred. Publishes short shorts. Also publishes literary essays, literary criticism and poetry. Sometimes critiques or comments on rejected mss.

How to Contact: Send complete ms with cover letter. Should include one-paragraph bio, list of publications. Reports in 1 month on queries; 3 months on mss. Send SASE (IRCs) for reply, return of ms or send a disposable copy of ms. Simultaneous and electronic submissions OK. Sample copy for $6. Fiction guidelines for #10 SASE.

Payment: Pays 1 contributor's copy.

Terms: Acquires first North American serial rights. Sponsors annual fiction contest. Write for entry guidelines, include SASE.

Advice: "In general, we look for fiction that combines a compelling theme with control of language. Manuscripts that challenge traditional formats or uses of language stand out. However, we do always respect a well-written piece in a more traditional vein."

WEST BRANCH, (II), Bucknell Hall, Bucknell University, Lewisburg PA 17837. Editors: K. Patten and R. Taylor. Magazine: 5½ × 8½; 96-120 pages; quality paper; illustrations; photos. Fiction and poetry for readers of contemporary literature. Biannual. Estab. 1977. Circ. 500.

Needs: Literary, contemporary, prose poems and translations. No science fiction. Accepts 3-6 mss/issue. Recently published work by Chuck Martin, David Milofsky and Sharon Sheehe Stark; published new writers within the last year. No preferred length.

How to Contact: Send complete ms with cover letter, "with information about writer's background, previous publications, etc." SASE (IRCs). No simultaneous submissions. Reports in 6-8 weeks on mss. Sample copy $3.

Payment: Pays 2 contributor's copies and one-year subscription; cover price less 25% discount charge for extras.

Terms: Acquires first rights.

Advice: "Narrative art fulfills a basic human need—our dreams attest to this—and storytelling is therefore a high calling in any age. Find your own voice and vision. Make a story speak to your own mysteries. Cultivate simplicity in form and in theme. Look and listen through your characters."

‡❋WEST COAST LINE, A Journal of Contemporary Writing & Criticism, (II), 2027 E. Academic Annex, Simon Fraser University, Burnaby, British Columbia V5A 1S6 Canada. (604)291-4287. Fax: (604)291-5737. Editor: Roy Miki. Magazine: 6×9; 128-144 pages. "Poetry, fiction, criticism—modern and contemporary, North American, cross-cultural. Readers include academics, writers, students." Triannual. Estab. 1990. Circ. 500.
Needs: Ethnic/multicultural, experimental, feminist, gay, literary. "We do not publish journalistic writing or strictly representational narrative." Upcoming themes: (Spring 1994) "Colour. An Issue," cross-cultural writing/theory. Receives 30-40 unsolicited mss/month. Accepts 2-3 mss/issue; 3-6 mss/year. Publishes ms 2-6 months after acceptance. Recently published work by Damian Lopes, Beverley Daurio, Michael Winter and Wang Pingy. Length: 3,000-4,000 words. Publishes short shorts. Length: 250-400 words. Also publishes literary essays and literary criticism.
How to Contact: Send complete ms with a cover letter. "We supply an information form for contributors." Reports in 3 months. Send SASE (or IRC) for return of ms. No simultaneous submissions. Electronic submissions OK. Sample copy for $10 (Canadian). Fiction guidelines free.
Payment: Pays $3/page minimum; $4/page maximum (Canadian); subscription; 1 contributor copy; additional copies for $6-8/copy, depending on quantity ordered.
Terms: Pays on publication for one-time rights.
Advice: "Special concern for contemporary writers who are experimenting with, or expanding the boundaries of conventional forms of poetry, fiction and criticism; also interested in criticism and scholarship on Canadian and American modernist writers who are important sources for current writing. We recommend that potential contributors send a letter of enquiry before submitting a manuscript."

‡WESTERN TALES, (II), P.O. Box 33842, Granada Hills CA 91394. (818)881-6821. Editor: Dorman Nelson. Magazine: 8½×11; 100 pages; 60 lb. cover stock; b&w illustrations. Looks for "western stories and poetry for a family audience of all ages." Quarterly. Estab. 1993.
Needs: Westerns (frontier, traditional, young adult western). No porn or hard core violence. Upcoming themes: Women Writer's Issue (fall 1994); Edgar Rice Burroughs issue (summer 1994). Publishes special fiction issue or anthology. Receives 150-200 mss/month. Accepts 26 mss/issue; 100 mss/year. Publishes ms 6 months after acceptance. Agented fiction 10%. Length: 4,000-5,000 words preferred. Publishes short shorts. Length: 1,000 words. Also publishes poetry.
How to Contact: Query first, send complete ms with a cover letter or submit through an agent. Should include short bio and social security number. Reports in 6 weeks. Send SASE (or IRC) for reply, return of ms or send a disposable copy of ms. Simultaneous and reprint submissions OK. Sample copy $6. Fiction guidelines for #10 SAE.
Payment: Pays $100 (story); $25 (poetry); 1 contributor's copy.
Terms: Pays on acceptance for first North American serial rights.

WESTVIEW, A Journal of Western Oklahoma, (II), Southwestern Oklahoma State University, 100 Campus Dr., Weatherford OK 73096-3098. (405)774-3168. Editor: Fred Alsberg. Magazine: 8½×11; up to 44 pages; 24 lb. paper; slick cover; illustrations and photographs. Quarterly. Estab. 1981. Circ. 800.
● The editor was inducted into the Western Oklahoma Historical Society Hall of Fame for his work on *Westview*.
Needs: Adventure, contemporary, ethnic (especially Native American), humor, literary, mainstream, prose poem, science fiction, mystery/suspense, western. No pornography, violence, or gore. No overly sentimental. "We use themes related to Western Oklahoma, as well as non-thematic work of quality." Upcoming themes: Flora and Fauna; Hard Times/Good Times; Terrain—Rivers, Lakes, Hills; Yesterday, Today, Tomorrow. Receives 2-5 unsolicited mss/month. Accepts 10 ms/issue; 40 mss/year. Publishes ms 1 month-2 years after acceptance. Recently published work by Mark Spencer, Keith Long and Pamela Rodgers. Length: 2,000 words average; 100 words minimum; 3,000 words maximum. Also

publishes literary essays, literary criticism, poetry. Occassionally critiques rejected mss and sometimes recommends other markets.

How to Contact: Simultaneous submissions OK. Send complete ms with SASE (IRCs). Reports in 1-2 months. "We welcome submissions on a 3.5 disk formatted for WordPerfect 5.0, IBM or Mackintosh. Please include a hard copy printout of your submission."

Payment: Pays contributor's copies.

Terms: Acquires first rights.

Advice: "Write for a copy of our stylesheet and for our list of themes for future issues. Don't neglect the SASE."

❀**WHETSTONE, (II),** English Dept., University of Lethbridge, Lethbridge, Alberta T1K 3M4 Canada. (403)329-2373. Contact: Professor Martin Oordt. Magazine: 6×9; 48-64 pages; superbond paper; photos. Magazine publishing "poetry, prose, drama, prints, photographs and occasional music compositions for a university audience." Biannual. Estab. 1971. Circ. 500.

Needs: Experimental, literary, mainstream. "Interested in works by native writers/artists. Interested in multi-media works by individuals or collaborators. Accepts 1-2 ms/issue, 3-4 mss/year. Does not read May-August. Published new writers within the last year. Length: 12 double-spaced pages maximum. Also publishes literary essays, literary criticism, poetry.

How to Contact: Send complete ms with SASE, or SAE with IRC and cover letter with author's background and experience. No simultaneous submissions. Reports in 5 months on mss. Publishes ms an average of 3-4 months after acceptance. Sample copy $5 (Canadian) and 7½ × 10½ or larger SAE and 2 Canadian first-class stamps or IRCs.

Payment: Pays 1 contributor's copy.

Terms: Acquires no rights.

Advice: "We seek most styles of quality writing. Avoid moralizing."

WHISKEY ISLAND MAGAZINE, (II), University Center 7, Cleveland State University, Cleveland OH 44115. (216)687-2056. Contact: Fiction Editor. Editors change each year. Magazine of fiction and poetry, including experimental works, with no specific theme. Published 1-2 times/year. Estab. 1978. Circ. 2,500.

Needs: Receives 20-30 unsolicited fiction mss/month. Acquires 3-4 mss/issue. Length: 6,500 words maximum. Also publishes poetry (poetry submissions should contain no more than 10 pages).

How to Contact: Send complete ms with SASE (IRCs). No simultaneous or previously published submissions. Reports in 2-4 months on mss. Sample copy $3.

Payment: Pays 2 contributor's copies.

Terms: Acquires one-time rights.

Advice: "Please include brief bio."

WHISPER, (II), Scream Press, 509 Enterprise Dr., Rohnert Park CA 94928. Editor: Anthony Boyd. Magazine: 8½×11; 20 pages; 20 lb. paper; 60 lb. cover; illustrations and photographs. "Horror is *not* a theme. *Whisper* is general interest. Audience: youngest reader 11, oldest reader 55 – all ages, all professions." Semiannual. Estab. 1987. Circ. 250.

Needs: Adventure, contemporary, fantasy, humor/satire, mystery/suspense, science fiction. "No gore, no porn." Receives 2 unsolicited mss/month. Accepts 1 ms/issue; 2 mss/year. Publishes ms 6-12 months after acceptance. Length: 1,500-1,750 words.

How to Contact: Send complete ms with cover letter. Include "a short bio, a few publication credits, and anything else I may find interesting. Tell me a joke so I'm in a good mood to read your story." Reports in 1 week on queries; 1 month on mss. SASE (IRCs). Reprint submissions OK, if stated. No simultaneous submissions. Sample copy for $3.

Payment: Pays in contributor's copies.

Terms: Acquires one-time rights.

Advice: "I like a lot of what *Pandora* publishes, good plot, and some strong twists. I look for neatness, and appropriateness – I'm not interested in crude, violent drivel and stories that don't follow guidelines (length, etc.) are sent back unread."

THE JAMES WHITE REVIEW, A Gay Men's Literary Quarterly, (II, IV), The James White Review Association, 3356 Butler Quarter Station, Minneapolis MN 55403. (612)291-2913 or (612)339-8317. Editor: Collective of 3. Tabloid: 17×26; 16 pages; illustrations; photos. "We publish work by *male* gay writers – any subject for primarily gay and/or gay sensitive audience." Quarterly. Estab. 1983. Circ. 4,000.

• *The James White Review* won an award for Publisher Service from the Lambda Literary Awards in 1990.
Needs: Contemporary, adventure, experimental, gay, humor/satire, literary, prose poem, translations. No pornography. Receives 50 unsolicited fiction mss/month. Buys 3 mss/issue; 12 mss/year. Publishes ms 3 months or sooner after acceptance. Published work by Felice Picano and George Stambolian; published new writers within the last year. Length: 30 pages, double-spaced. Sometimes critiques rejected mss. Recommends other markets "when we can."
How to Contact: Send complete ms with cover letter and short bio. SASE (IRCs). No simultaneous submissions. Reports in 2-3 months. Sample copy $3. Fiction guidelines $1.
Payment: Pays 2 contributor's copies and $50.
Terms: Buys one-time rights; returns rights to author.
Advice: "We are publishing longer stories and serializing."

✷WHITE WALL REVIEW, 63 Gould St., Toronto, Ontario M5B 1E9 Canada. Editors change annually. Send mss to "Editors." Magazine: 5¾ × 8¾; 160 pages; Zephyr Antique paper; soft cover, glossy; two-tone illustrations; b&w photographs. "Book of poetry, prose, art and photography. Publishes unknown, international and professional writers. For international audience." Annual. Estab. 1976. Circ. 500.
Needs: "No content 'requirements.'" Must be reasonably short. Nothing "spawning hate, prejudice or obscenity." Accepts 100+ mss/book. Accepts mss from September to 1st week in December of a given year. Published work by Steven Heighton, Robert Hough, Ruth Olsen Latta; published new writers within the last year. Also publishes poetry.
How to Contact: Send complete ms with cover letter. "The cover letter should contain important information about why the writer is submitting to our publication, where he/she saw our information and some biographical information." Reports on mss "when accepted, by May of each year." SASE or SAE and IRC for ms. No simultaneous submissions. Sample copy $8.
Payment: Pays 1 contributor's copy.
Terms: Acquires first or one-time rights.
Advice: "Keep it *short*. We look for creativity but not to the point of obscurity."

WICKED MYSTIC, (I, II, IV), P.O. Box 3087, Astoria NY 11103. (718)545-6713. Editor: Andre Schelu-chin. Magazine: digest-sized; 80 pages; 20 lb. paper; 28 lb. cover. "Horror, gothic, gore, vampires, violence, blood, death." Bimonthly. Estab. 1990. Circ. 1,000.
Needs: Erotica, horror, psychic/supernatural/occult, vampires. No romance. Receives 30 unsolicited mss/month. Acquires 10 mss/issue; 60 mss/year. Time between acceptance of the ms and publication varies. Published work by Kim Elizabeth, Michael Arnzen, Gregory Nyman and Mark Fewell. Length: 2,000 words preferred; 500 words minimum; 3,000 words maximum. Also publishes literary essays, literary criticism and poetry.
How to Contact: Send complete ms with cover letter. Should include estimated word count, short and basic bio, list of publications. Reports in 2-4 weeks. Send SASE (IRCs) for reply, return of mss or send a disposable copy of the ms. Simultaneous and electronic submissions OK. Sample copy for $4. Free fiction guidelines.
Payment: Pays 1 contributor's copy.
Terms: Acquires first rights.
Advice: Looks for "more originality. Take a topic that either has not been done before or take one that has been done before and give it a new and bizarre twist. I don't like stories that are too predictable."

WIDENER REVIEW, (II), Widener University, One University Place, Chester PA 19013. (215)499-4341. Fiction Editor: Michael Clark. Magazine: 5¼ × 8½; 80 pages. Fiction, poetry, essays, book reviews for general audience. Annual. Estab. 1984. Circ. 250.
Needs: Contemporary, experimental, literary, mainstream, regional, serialized/excerpted novel. Receives 15 unsolicited mss/month. Publishes 3-4 mss/issue. Does not read mss in summer. Publishes ms 3-9 months after acceptance. Length: 1,000 words minimum; 5,000 words maximum. Occasionally critiques rejected mss.
How to Contact: Send complete ms with cover letter. Reports in 3 months on mss. Deadline for submission: March 15, notification by June 15. SASE (IRCs) for ms. No simultaneous submissions or reprints. Sample copy for $4. Fiction guidelines for #10 SAE and first-class stamp.
Payment: Pays 1 contributor's copy; charge for extras.
Terms: Acquires first serial rights.

‡WILDE OAKS, (II, IV), Billy DeFrank Lesbian/Gay Community Center, 175 Stockton Ave., San Jose CA 95126. (408)293-2429. Editor: Bill Olver. Magazine: 8½×5¼; 100 pages; 20 lb. white paper; glossy cover stock; 5-10 photographs/issue. "Wilde Oaks publishes work with lesbian, gay, bisexual or transgender themes only. With that in mind, we remain wide open to all genre, subjects, and forms. We seek work that speaks to our lives in all our diversity, appeals to our many interests, enlightens and entertains." Semiannual. Estab. 1992. Circ. 300.

Needs: Gay and lesbian: adventure, erotica, ethnic/multicultural, experimental, fantasy (science fantasy, sword and sorcery), feminist, humor/satire, literary, mainstream/contemporary, mystery/suspense, psychic/supernatural/occult, regional, science fiction, westerns. "We are not especially interested in children's/young adult—nothing dogmatically religious." List of upcoming themes available for SASE (IRCs). Accepts 2-4 mss/issue; 6-8 mss/year. Does not read mss May, June, July, November, December, January. Publishes ms 1-2 months after acceptance. Recently published work by Klaus Merrell, Florence Pontius, Marc Lynx and Jason Whitaker. Length: 3,000 words preferred; Publishes short shorts. Also publishes literary essays and poetry; also photography, artwork, comics/cartoons. Sometimes critiques or comments on rejected mss.

How to Contact: Send complete ms with a cover letter. Should include estimated word count, 50-75 word bio and list of publications. Reports in 4 weeks on queries; 3 months on mss. Send a disposable copy of ms. Reprint and electronic submissions OK. Sample copy for $10. Fiction guidelines for #10 SAE and 2 first-class stamps.

Payment: Pays 1 contributor's copy; additional copies for $8.

Terms: Acquires one-time rights.

Advice: "We look for excellence. We appreciate work that knows its target, aims squarely for it, and hits it. We do not judge detective fiction on the same scale as erotica or literary prose, etc." Looks for "work that reveals the person inside the writer while avoiding the 'see me/feel me clichés.' Honesty is very attractive, but whining is not. We prefer literary work, but genre work is OK. We'd like more humor. We don't see near enough from people of color."

THE WILLIAM AND MARY REVIEW, (II), P.O. Box 8795, Campus Center, The College of William and Mary, Williamsburg VA 23187-8795. Editor: Andrew Zawacki. Magazine: 110 pages; graphics; photography. "We publish high quality fiction, poetry, essays, interviews with writers, and art. Our audience is primarily academic." Annual. Estab. 1962. Circ. 3,500.

• This magazine has received numerous honors from the Columbia Scholastic Press Association's Golden Circle Awards.

Needs: Literary, contemporary and humor. Receives approximately 90 unsolicited fiction mss/month. Accepts 9 mss/issue. Recently published work by Paul Wood, W.S. Penn, Amy Clampitt, Robert Hershon and Dana Gioia; published new writers within the last year. Length: 7,000 words maximum. Also publishes poetry. Usually critiques rejected mss.

How to Contact: Send complete ms with SASE (IRCs) and cover letter with name, address and phone number. "Cover letter should be as brief as possible." Simultaneous submissions OK. Reports in 2-4 months. All departments closed in June, July and August. Sample copy $5.50. May review novels, poetry and short story collections.

Payment: Pays 5 contributor's copies; discounts thereafter.

Terms: Acquires first rights.

Advice: "We want original, well written stories. Staff requests names be attached separately to individual works. Page allotment to fiction will rise in relation to quality fiction received. The most important aspect of submitting ms is to be familiar with the publication and the types of material it accepts. For this reason, back copies are available."

WILLOW REVIEW, (II), College of Lake County, 19351 W. Washington St., Grayslake IL 60030. (708)223-6601 ext. 2550 or 2956. Editor: Paulette Roeske. Magazine: 6×9; 68-76 pages; 70 lb. paper; 80 lb. 4-color cover. "*Willow Review* is nonthematic and publishes short fiction, memoirs and poetry. For a general and literary adult audience." Annual. Estab. 1969. Circ. 1,000.

Needs: Contemporary, ethnic, experimental, feminist, historical, humor/satire, literary, prose poem, regional. "There is no bias against a particular subject matter, although there is a clear editorial preference for literary fiction." No "popular genre fiction; children/young adult." Plans special fiction issue. Receives 50 unsolicited mss/month. Buys 7-8 mss/issue. Does not read mss June-August. Accepted mss published in April of each year. Recently published work by Gregory Orr, Lisel Mueller, Gloria Naylor. Length: 1,500 words minimum; 3,500 words maximum. Publishes short shorts. Length: 500 words. Sometimes comments on rejected mss and recommends other markets.

How to Contact: Send complete ms with cover letter. Include Social Security number, complete mailing address, telephone number, list of several previous publications, other recognition (awards, etc. if applicable). Reports in 1-2 months on mss. SASE or IRCs (if writer would like it returned). Sample copy for $3. Fiction guidelines for #10 SAE and 1 first-class stamp.
Payment: All manuscripts are automatically considered for the annual *Willow Review* awards: $100 for first place, $50 for second and $25 for third.
Terms: Pays on publication for first North American serial rights. Not copyrighted.
Advice: *"Willow Review*, because of its 68-76 page length, is forced to make word count a factor although we would publish an exceptional story which exceeds our recommended length. Beyond that, literary excellence is our sole criteria. Perhaps voice, more than any other factor, causes a manuscript to stand out. Study the craft—read the best little magazines, subscribe to them, maintain contact with other writers through writer's groups or informally, attend fiction readings and ask the writers questions in the discussion periods which typically follow. Read Eudora Welty's *One Writer's Beginnings* or John Gardner's *On Becoming a Novelist* or Flannery O'Connor on writing fiction or the articles in *Poets & Writers*. Consider writing a discipline, a field of study—it won't kill 'inspiration' or 'creativity' but will augment it to help you write the best story you can write."

‡**WIND MAGAZINE, (II),** P.O. Box 24548, Lexington KY 40524. (606)885-5342. Co-editors: Steven R. Cope and Charlie G. Hughes. Magazine: 5½×8½; 100 pages. "Eclectic literary journal with stories, poems, book reviews from small presses, essays. Readership is students, professors, housewives, literary folk, adults." Semiannual. Estab. 1971. Circ. 450.
Needs: Literary, mainstream/contemporary, translations. "We have an adult target audience, but this does not mean we'll consider porn; save your postage." Publishes special fiction issue or anthology. Accepts 8 fiction mss/issue; 16 mss/year. Publishes ms less than 1 year after acceptance. Recently published work by Carolyn Osborn, Jane Stuart, David Shields, Lester Goldberg and Elisabeth Stevens. Length: 5,000 words maximum. Publishes short shorts. Length: 300-400 words. Also publishes literary essays, literary criticism and poetry. Sometimes critiques or comments on rejected mss.
How to Contact: Send complete ms with a cover letter. Should include estimated word count and bio (50 words). Reports in 2 weeks on queries; 2 months on mss. Send SASE (or IRC) for reply, return of ms or send a disposable copy of ms. No simultaneous submissions. Sample copy for $3.50. Fiction guidelines for SAE. Reviews novels and short story collections from small presses.
Payment: Pays 1 contributor copy; additional copies for $3.
Terms: Acquires first North American serial rights and anthology reprint rights.
Advice: "The writing must have an impact on the reader; the reader must come away changed, perhaps haunted, or maybe smiling. There is nothing I like better than to be able to say 'I wish I had written that.' Unfortunately, a boring and messy manuscript also stands out."

WISCONSIN ACADEMY REVIEW, (II, IV), Wisconsin Academy of Sciences, Arts & Letters, 1922 University Ave., Madison WI 53705. (608)263-1692. Editor-in-Chief: Faith B. Miracle. Magazine: 8½×11; 48-52 pages; 75 lb. coated paper; coated cover stock; illustrations; photos. "The *Review* reflects the focus of the sponsoring institution with its editorial emphasis on Wisconsin's intellectual, cultural, social and physical environment. It features short fiction, poetry, essays and Wisconsin-related book reviews for people interested in furthering regional arts and literature and disseminating information about sciences." Quarterly. Estab. 1954. Circ. 2,000.
Needs: Experimental, historical (general), humor/satire, literary, mainstream, prose poem. "Author must have lived or be living in Wisconsin or fiction must be set in Wisconsin." Receives 5-6 unsolicited fiction mss/month. Accepts 1-2 mss/issue; 6-8 mss/year. Published new writers within the last year. Length: 1,000 words minimum; 4,000 words maximum; 3,000 words average. Also publishes poetry; "will consider" literary essays, literary criticism.
How to Contact: Send complete ms with SAE and state author's connection to Wisconsin, the prerequisite. Sample copy $2. Fiction guidelines for SAE and 1 first-class stamp. Reviews books on Wisconsin themes.
Payment: Pays 3-5 contributor's copies.
Terms: Acquires on publication for first rights.
Advice: "Manuscript publication is at the discretion of the editor based on space, content, and balance. We do not use previously published poetry and fiction or genre fiction. We publish emerging as well as established authors; fiction and poetry, without names attached, are sent to reviewers for evaluation."

THE WISCONSIN RESTAURATEUR, (I, II), Wisconsin Restaurant Association, #300, 31 S. Henry, Madison WI 53703. (608)251-3663. Editor: Jan LaRue. Magazine: 8½×11; 80 pages; 80 lb. enamel cover stock; illustrations; photos. "Published for foodservice operators in the state of Wisconsin and for suppliers of those operations. Theme is the promotion, protection and improvement of the foodservice industry for foodservice workers, students, operators and suppliers." Monthly except December/January combined. Estab. 1933. Circ. 4,200.
Needs: Literary, contemporary, feminist, science fiction (soft/sociological), regional, western, mystery (amateur sleuth, private eye, young adult), adventure, humor, juvenile and young adult. "Only exceptional fiction material used. No stories accepted that put down persons in the foodservice business or poke fun at any group of people. No off-color material. No religious, no political." Buys 1-2 mss/issue, 12-24 mss/year. Receives 15-20 unsolicited fiction mss/month. Length: 500-2,500 words. Critiques rejected mss "when there is time."
How to Contact: Send complete ms with SASE (IRCs). Simultaneous submissions OK. Reports in 1-2 months. Sample copy for 9×12 SASE. Guidelines for SASE.
Payment: Pays $2.50-$20; contributor's copy; 50¢ charge for extra copy.
Terms: Pays on acceptance for first rights and first North American serial rights.
Advice: "Make sure there is some kind of lesson to be learned, a humorous aspect, or some kind of moral to your story." Mss are rejected because they are not written for the restaurateur/reader.

WISCONSIN REVIEW, (II), University of Wisconsin, Box 158, Radford Hall, Oshkosh WI 45901. (414)424-2267. Editor: Troy Schoultz. Editors change every year. Send submissions to "Fiction Editor." Magazine: 6×9; 60-100 pages; illustrations. Literary prose and poetry. Triannual. Estab. 1966. Circ. 2,000.
Needs: Literary and experimental. Receives 30 unsolicited fiction mss each month. Published new writers within the last year. Length: up to 5,000 words. Publishes short shorts. Critiques rejected mss when there is time. Occasionally recommends other markets.
How to Contact: Send complete ms with SASE (IRCs) and cover letter with bio notes. Simultaneous submissions OK. Reports in 2-4 months. Publishes ms an average of 1-2 months after acceptance. Sample copy $2.
Payment: Pays in contributor's copies.
Terms: Acquires first rights.
Advice: "We look for well-crafted work with carefully developed characters, plots and meaningful situations. The editors highly appreciate work of original and fresh thought when considering a piece of experimental fiction."

‡WOLFRIDGEREVIEW, (II), Route One, Box 7X, Harrison ID 83833. Editor/Publisher: Judith Shannon Paine. Magazine: 6½×9; 60 pages; 50 lb. paper; 65 lb. cover; illustrations; photos occasionally. "Themes will vary. The material must be lively, well-developed. For adult audience interested in contemporary, literary, avant garde." Annual. Estab. 1989. Circ. 200.
Needs: Contemporary, experimental, humor/satire, prose poem, romance (contemporary), western. "No religious, political rant, juvenile, pornography, occult." Plans special fiction issue in the future. Acquires 5-10 mss/issue; 30-40 mss/year. Length: 250 words preferred; 1,000 words maximum. Publishes short shorts. Length: 350 words. Sometimes critiques rejected mss and recommends other markets.
How to Contact: Send complete ms with cover letter and SASE (IRCs) sufficient for its return. Reports in 2 weeks-3 months on mss. No simultaneous submissions. Sample copy for $4. (Make checks payable to Judith Shannon Paine).
Payment: Pays 1 contributor's copy.
Terms: Acquires one-time rights. Rights revert to author.
Advice: "Seek pride and pleasure by doing your very very best. A manuscript must be finely crafted, lively, original, from start to finish, neat, well-spelled and syntaxically acceptable. A fresh, funny, warm, bold or gripping manuscript will get my attention. Like fine wine, it should have its very own bouquet and have time to breathe. Be your own meanest editor. Don't be afraid. I don't bite. Have fun when you write. Structure is important. Get naked. I want to see the bare bones in your work, please."

‡WONDERDISK, International Science Fiction, Fantasy & Horror Magadisk, (I, II), Wonder Digital Press, P.O. Box 58367, Louisville KY 40268-0367. Editor: Walter Gammons. Electronic Disk Magazine (800K Macintosh format). "Seeking quality science fiction, fantasy, horror short stories (sexual themes OK if integral to plot) from international authors (in English)." Quarterly. Estab. 1993. Circ. 1,000.

- Submissions may also be made through CompuServe and GEnie E-mail. CompuServe address: ID #75000,445. GEnie address: W.Gammons.

Needs: Erotica, experimental, fantasy (mythological, science fantasy, sword and sorcery), horror, science fiction (hard science, soft/sociological). No "horror with unnecessary gore or violence, gay, sex that is not tastefully done, no pure porno." Upcoming themes available for SASE. Publishes special fiction issue or anthology. Receives 50-60 unsolicited mss/month. Accepts 10-15 mss/issue; 40-60 mss/year. Publishes ms 3-6 months after acceptance. Length: 4,000-5,000 preferred; 2,500 words minimum; 9,500 words maximum. Also publishes literary essays, literary criticism and poetry. Always critiques or comments on rejected mss.

How to Contact: Send complete ms with a cover letter. Send ms on disk 800K Macintosh format. Should include short bio and list of publications. Reports in 2-4 weeks on queries; 2 months on mss. Send SASE (or IRC) for reply, return of ms or send a disposable copy of ms. Sample copy for $8. Fiction guidelines for #10 SAE and 3 first-class stamps. $4 for *Galactic Gazette*, our newsletter on disk, with complete guidelines, etc.

Payment: Pays $10-75; subscription; 5 contributor's copies; additional copies for $4.

Terms: Buys one-time rights or first world rights.

Advice: Looks for "well-written, quality science fiction, fantasy or horror; more stories from foreign countries like Asia and eastern Europe—Russia, etc."

THE WORCESTER REVIEW, Worcester Country Poetry Association, Inc., 6 Chatham St., Worcester MA 01609. (508)797-4770. Editor: Rodger Martin. Magazine: 6×9; 60-100 pages; 60 lb. white offset paper; 10 pt. C1S cover stock; illustrations and photos. "We like high quality, creative poetry, artwork and fiction. Critical articles should be connected to New England." Semiannual. Estab. 1972. Circ. 1,000.

- Work published in *The Worcester Review* was nominated for inclusion in the *Pushcart Prize* anthology for 1993.

Needs: Literary, prose poem. "We encourage New England writers in the hopes we will publish at least 30% New England but want the other 70% to show the best of writing from across the US." Receives 10-20 unsolicited fiction mss/month. Accepts 2-4 mss/issue. Publishes ms an average of 6 months to 1 year after acceptance. Agented fiction less than 10%. Published work by Debra Friedman and Carol Glickfeld. Length: 2,000 words average; 1,000 words minimum; 4,000 words maximum. Publishes short shorts. Also publishes literary essays, literary criticism, poetry. Sometimes critiques rejected mss and recommends other markets.

How to Contact: Send complete ms with cover letter. Reports in 2 weeks on queries; 4-5 months on mss. SASE (IRCs). Simultaneous submissions OK if other markets are clearly identified. Sample copy $4; fiction guidelines free.

Payment: Pays 2 contributor's copies and honorarium if possible.

Terms: Acquires one-time rights.

Advice: "Send only one short story—reading editors do not like to read two by the same author at the same time. We will use only one. We generally look for creative work with a blend of craftsmanship, insight and empathy. This does not exclude humor. We won't print work that is shoddy in any of these areas."

WORDS OF WISDOM, (II), 612 Front St. East, Glendora NJ 08029-1133. (609)863-0610. Editor: J.M. Freiermuth. Newsletter: 5½×8½; 36-48 pages; copy paper; some illustrations and photographs. "Fiction, satire, humorous poetry and travel for a general audience —80% of readers have B.A." Monthly. Estab. 1981. Circ. 180.

Needs: Adventure, contemporary, ethnic, feminist, historical (general), humor/satire, mainstream, mystery/suspense (cozy, private eye), regional, western (adult, frontier, traditional). No religion, children's, gay, romance. Plans second "All Woman Author" issue (August 1994) and "All New Jersey Author" issue (Nov. 1994). Receives 30-40 unsolicited mss/month. Accepts 10-12 mss/issue; 100-150 mss/year. Publishes ms 2-6 months after acceptance. Recently published work by James Kelleher, Don Stockard, Mary M. Schmidt, Yvonne M. Dupes, Janice Levy and Thomas Wells; published first time writers last year. Length: 2,000-3,000 words average; 1,200 words minimum; 9,000 words maximum. Publishes short shorts. Length: "Long enough to develop a good bite." Sometimes critiques rejected mss and recommends other markets.

How to Contact: Send complete manuscript copy and/or DOS floppy with cover letter including "name, address, SASE." Reports in 3-6 weeks on mss. SASE (IRCs). Simultaneous and reprint submissions OK. Accepts electronic submissions. Sample copy for $2 post paid. Reviews novels and short story collections.
Payment: Pays subscription to magazine for first publication and contributor's copies for subsequent publications.
Terms: Acquires one-time rights. Publication not copyrighted.
Advice: "If your story has a spark of life or a degree of humor that brings a smile to my face, you have a chance here. Most stories lack these two ingredients. Don't send something you wrote ten years ago."

WORM, (II), Macronex, 115 Grand St., Brooklyn NY 11211-4123. Fax: (718)782-0747. Editor: Kit Blake. Newsletter: 8½×11; 20 pages; 20 lb. paper; colored paper cover; computer graphics, illustrations and photographs. "Cultural media magazine for a modern audience." Monthly. Estab. 1991.
Needs: Contemporary, erotica, ethnic, experimental, gay, historical, lesbian, literary, science fiction (hard science, soft/sociological, techno). No fantasy, romance, sports. Publishes special fiction issue. Upcoming themes: Exploring the present and potential political power of minor media (i.e., camcorders, indie labels, small press, etc.); evolution, both physical and social, in an age of biotechnology and instant communication. Receives 2 unsolicited mss/month. Accepts 1 mss/issue; 12 mss/year. Recently published work by Ian Keldoulis and David Brody. Length: 2,000 words preferred; 300 words minimum; 3,000 words maximum. Publishes short shorts. Length: 300-500 words. Recommends other markets.
How to Contact: Send complete ms with cover letter. Reports in 3 weeks on queries; 3 months on mss. SASE (IRCs). Simultaneous and reprint submissions OK. Recommends electronic submissions via disk or modem (Mac format preferred). Sample copy for $2.
Payment: Pays contributor's copies.
Terms: Acquires one-time rights. Not copyrighted.
Advice: Looks for "otherworldliness. Make a micro model for a macro world."

THE WORMWOOD REVIEW, (II, IV), P.O. Box 4698, Stockton CA 95204. (209)466-8231. Editor: Marvin Malone. Magazine: 5½×8½; 48 pages; 60 lb. matte paper; 80 lb. matte cover; illustrations. "Concentrated on the prose-poem specifically for literate audience." Quarterly. Estab. 1959. Circ. 700.
Needs: Prose poem. No religious or inspirational. Receives 500-600 unsolicited mss/month. Buys 30-40 mss/issue; 120-160 mss/year. Publishes ms 6-18 months after acceptance. Published work by Charles Bukowski and Dan Lenihan. Length: 300 words preferred; 1,000 words maximum. Critiques or comments on rejected mss.
How to Contact: Send complete ms with cover letter. Reports in 1-2 months. SASE (IRCs). No simultaneous submissions. Sample copy for $4. Fiction guidelines for #10 SAE and 1 first-class stamp.
Payment: Pays $12-140 or equivalent in contributor's copies.
Terms: Acquires all rights, but reassigns rights to author on written request.
Advice: A manuscript that stands out has "economical verbal style coupled with perception and human values. Have something to say—then say it in the most economical way. Do *not* avoid wit and humor."

WRITERS' FORUM, (II), University of Colorado at Colorado Springs, Colorado Springs CO 80933-7150. Editor: Dr. Alex Blackburn. "Ten to fifteen short stories or self-contained novel excerpts published once a year along with 25-35 poems. Highest literary quality only: mainstream, avant-garde, with preference to western themes. For small press enthusiasts, teachers and students of creative writing, commercial agents/publishers, university libraries and departments interested in contemporary American literature." Estab. 1974.
● Ohio University Press and Swallow Press published an anthology in October 1993 titled *Higher Elevations: Stories From The West, a Writer's Forum Anthology.*
Needs: Literary, contemporary, ethnic (Chicano, Native American, not excluding others) and regional (West). Receives approximately 40 unsolicited fiction mss each month and will publish new as well as experienced authors. Published fiction by Robert Olen Butler, Charles Baxter and Gladys Swan; published many new writers within the last year. Length: 1,500-8,500 words. Also publishes literary essays, literary criticism, poetry. Critiques rejected mss "when there is time and perceived merit."

How to Contact: Send complete ms and letter with relevant career information with SASE (IRCs). Prefers submissions between September and February. Simultaneous submissions OK. Reports in 3-5 weeks on mss. Publishes ms an average of 6 months after acceptance. Sample back copy $7 to *NSSWM* readers. Current copy $10. Check payable to "University Press of Colorado/Writers' Forum." **Payment:** Pays 2 contributor's copies. Cover price less 60% discount for extras.

Terms: Acquires one-time rights. Rights revert to author.

Advice: "Read our publication. Be prepared for constructive criticism. We especially seek submissions that show immersion in place (trans-Mississippi West) and development of credible characters. Turned off by slick content. Probably the TV-influenced fiction with trivial dialogue and set-up plot is the most quickly rejected. Our format — a 5½ × 8½ professionally edited and printed paperback book — lends credibility to authors published in our imprint."

WRITERS' OPEN FORUM, (I), Bristol Publishing, P.O. Box 516, Tracyton WA 98393. Editor: Sandra E. Haven. Magazine: 5½ × 8½; 32 pages; slick cover; illustrations. *"Writers' Open Forum* is is the only international magazine specifically designed to help new writers improve their marketability and writing skills through our unique peer critique process. We offer detailed information on writing, market listings plus print several stories and articles per issue. Some critiques on our printed stories are published; all are mailed on to originating author." Bimonthly. Estab. 1990.

Needs: Adventure, childrens/juvenile (5-9 years, 10-12 years), fantasy, historical (general), humor/satire, mainstream/contemporary, mystery/suspense, psychic/supernatural/occult, regional, romance (contemporary, young adult), science fiction, senior citizen/retirement, sports, westerns, young adult/teen. "No graphic sex, violence, slice-of-life or wildly experimental formats." Plans special fiction issue or anthology. Buys 4-7 mss/issue; 30-42 mss/year. Publishes ms 4 months after acceptance. Length: 100 words minimum; 2,000 words maximum. Publishes short shorts. Always comments on rejected mss "that have followed our guidelines."

How to Contact: Send complete ms with a cover letter. Should include brief bio. Reports in 2 months on mss. Send SASE (IRCs) for reply, return of ms or send a disposable copy of the ms. Sàmple copy for $3. Fiction guidelines for #10 SAE and 1 first-class stamp.

Payment: Pays $5 minimum plus 1 contributor's copy; additional copies $2.50 each for 1-5, $2 each for 6 or more.

Terms: Pays on acceptance. Acquires first rights.

Advice: "We will not consider any manuscript with graphic sex, violence, or slice-of-life or experimental formats. We prefer stories with a protagonist the reader can care about, a problem to resolve, complications along the way, and a resolution resulting from the protagonist's decision or action. It may be a chapter from a book or journal, but must be so stated in the cover letter and still suit our requirements."

‡WRITING FOR OUR LIVES, Creative Expressions in Writing by Women, (I, IV), Running Deer Press, 647 N. Santa Cruz Ave., Annex, Los Gatos CA 95032. (408)354-8604. Editor: Janet M. McEwan. Magazine: 5¼ × 8¼; 80 pages; 70 lb. recycled white paper; 80 lb. recycled cover. *"Writing For Our Lives* is a periodical which serves as a vessel for poems; short fiction; stories; letters; autobiographies; and journal excerpts from the life stories, experiences and spiritual journeys of women. Audience is women and friends of women." Semiannual. Estab. 1992. Circ. 700.

Needs: Ethnic/multicultural, experimental, feminist, humor/satire, lesbian, literary, translations, "autobiographical, breaking personal or historical silence on any concerns of women's lives. Women writers only, please." Receives 5-10 unsolicited mss/month. Accepts 10 mss/issue; 20 mss/year. Publishes ms 2-18 months after acceptance. Length: 2,100 words maximum. Publishes short shorts. Also publishes poetry. Sometimes critiques or comments on rejected mss.

How to Contact: Send complete ms with a cover letter. Should include SAS postcard. Reports in 1-8 months. "Publication dates are May and November. Closing dates for mss are 2/15 and 8/15. I report on mss within 2 months following each closing date." Send SASE (or IRC) for reply, and also sufficient for return of ms if desired. Simultaneous and reprint submissions OK. Sample copy for $6 (in California add 8.25% sales tax), $8 overseas. Fiction guidelines for #10 SAE and 1 first-class stamp.

Payment: Pays 2 contributor's copies; additional copies for 50% discount and 1 year subscription at 50% discount.

Terms: Acquires one-time rights in case of reprints and first world-wide English language serial rights.

Advice: "I welcome your writing. I like many more pieces than I can print. If I don't select yours this time, try again!"

‡**THE WRITING ON THE WALL, (I)**, P.O. Box 8, Orono ME 04473. Editor: Scott D. Peterson. Magazine: 8½×11; 22 pages; 70 lb. paper; 70 lb. cover; illustrations and photographs. "Our goal is to combat the negativity of the mass media, build community, and provide a voice for the 20-something generation." Triannual. Estab. 1992. Circ. 100.
Needs: Literary, mainstream/contemporary. Will also consider novel excerpts. List of upcoming themes available for SASE. Receives 20-30 unsolicited mss/month. Accepts 3-4 mss/issue; 10-12 mss/year. Publishes ms 2-3 months after acceptance. Recently published work by Lenore Baeli Wang, Carolee Brockmann and Greg Laughlin. Length: 2,000 words preferred; 500 words minimum; 3,000 words maximum. Publishes short shorts. Publishes literary essays, literary criticism and poetry. Sometimes critiques or comments on rejected mss.
How to Contact: Send complete ms with a cover letter. Should include estimated word count and bio (less than 50 words). Reports in 2 weeks on queries; 3 months on mss. Send SASE (or IRC) for reply, return of ms or send a disposable copy of ms. Reprint and electronic submissions OK. Sample copy for $3. Fiction guidelines for #10 SAE and 1 first-class stamp.
Payment: Pays 2 contributor's copies; additional copies for $2.
Terms: Acquires one-time rights.
Advice: "We're looking for fiction that edifies as well as entertains—especially stories that send readers away with a sense of positive action. Write honestly and examine your stuff for TV sitcom or movie plot/characters."

‡**WYRD, Science Fiction & Fantasy for the Alternate Realities Continuum, (II)**, P.O. Box 7903, Athens GA 30604-7903. (706)543-4435. Editor: Genelle D. Helms. Magazine: 5×8; 14 pages; standard paper. Quarterly. Estab. 1991. Circ. 100.
Needs: Fantasy (science fantasy, sword and sorcery), horror, humor/satire, mystery/suspense (private eye/hard-boiled), psychic/supernatural/occult, science fiction (hard science, soft/sociological). No religious, romance, sports, experimental. Receives 5-8 unsolicited mss/month. Accepts 2 mss/issue; 8 mss/year. Publishes mss 3-5 months after acceptance. Recently published work by Alan M. Schwarz, Cheryl Fannon and Dan McGirt. Length: 500-10,000 words. Publishes short shorts. Length: 200 words. Also publishes poetry. Often critiques or comments on rejected mss.
How to Contact: Query with clips of published work. Should include estimated word count, and (brief) bio. Reports in 3 weeks on queries; 3 months on mss. Send SASE (or IRC) for reply, return of ms or send a disposable copy of ms. Simultaneous and reprint submissions. Sample copy for $1.50. Fiction guidelines for $1, #10 SAE and 1 first-class stamp. Reviews novels and short story collections.
Payment: Pays subscription (5 months) or 10 contributor's copies; additional copies for $1.
Terms: Acquires one-time rights.
Advice: Looks for "strong, definitive endings—clever plot twists—well-defined characters—fast-paced, intellectually stimulating action and dialogue." Would like to see more "stories based on role-playing game campaigns; strong, capable female heroes; comedic fiction (tongue-in-cheek fantasy, witty sci-fi); the beginning of myth (Where do faeries come from? What do dragons do with all that cash? What happens when Odin and the gang play stickball?)."

XAVIER REVIEW, (I, II), Xavier University, Box 110C, New Orleans LA 70125. (504)486-7411, ext. 7481. Editor: Thomas Bonner, Jr. Magazine of "poetry/fiction/nonfiction/reviews (contemporary literature) for professional writers/libraries/colleges/universities." Semiannual. Estab. 1980. Circ. 500.
Needs: Contemporary, ethnic, experimental, historical (general), literary, Latin-American, prose poem, Southern, religious, serialized/excerpted novel, translations. Receives 30 unsolicited fiction mss/month. Accepts 2 mss/issue; 4 mss/year. Length: 10-15 pages. Occasionally critiques rejected mss.
How to Contact: Send complete ms. SASE (IRCs). Sample copy $5.
Payment: Pays 2 contributor's copies.

‡**XIB, (I, II)**, P.O. Box 262112, San Diego CA 92126. Editor: Tolek. Magazine· 7×8½; 56 pages; offset basis 70 paper; 12 point gloss cover; 25-30 illustrations; 15-20 b&w photos. "Audience mostly of poets, hence prefer fiction concise and compact, more like prose-poem form." Semiannual. Estab. 1991. Circ. 500.
Needs: Erotica, ethnic/multicultural, experimental, fantasy (science fantasy, sword and sorcery), feminist, gay, historical (general), horror, humor/satire, lesbian, literary, psychic/supernatural/occult, regional, science fiction (hard science, soft/sociological), senior citizen/retirement, translations. No children's or romance. List of upcoming themes available for SASE. Receives 5-10 unsolicited mss/month. Accepts 2-3 mss/issue; 4-6 mss/year. Publishes ms 1-6 months after acceptance. Recently published work by Robert Nagler, D.F. Lewis, David Comfort. Length: 1,500 words average; 2,500 words maxi-

mum. Publishes short shorts. Also publishes poetry. Often critiques or comments on rejected mss.
How to Contact: Send complete ms with a cover letter. Reports in 2-3 weeks. Send SASE (or IRC) for reply, return of ms or send a disposable copy of ms. Sample copy for $5. Fiction guidelines for #10 SAE and 1 first-class stamp.
Payment: Pays 1 contributor's copy; additional copies for $3 each plus $2 s&h.
Terms: Acquires one-time rights.

‡XTREME, The Magazine of Extremely Short Fiction, P.O. Box 678383, Orlando FL 32867-8383. Editors: Ian Io and Rho Wiley. Magazine: 8½×11. "Xtreme, the magazine of extremely short fiction, publishes fiction of EXACTLY 250 words. Fiction is considered on the basis of merit only. We feel that the 250 word format affords an opportunity for all writers to push the limits of the language." Semiannual. Estab. 1993. Circ. 500.
Needs: Experimental, literary, mainstream/contemporary. Publishes special fiction issue or anthology. Accepts 10-20 mss/issue; 20-40 mss/year. Publishes ms 6 months after acceptance. Recently published work by Patti Magee, Bob Garick, Jeanne Mahaffey, Sophia Kowalski, -K. and The Black Shakespeare. Length: exactly 250 words. Sometimes critiques or comments on rejected mss.
How to Contact: Send complete ms with a cover letter. Reports in 4 weeks on queries; up to 6 months on mss. Send SASE (or IRC) for reply or return of ms. Simultaneous and electronic submissions OK. Sample copy for 9×12 SAE and 2 first-class stamps. Fiction guidelines for SAE.
Payment: Pays contributor's copies.
Terms: All rights revert back to author upon publication. Sends galleys to author.
Advice: Looks for "the ability to tell a complete story in the boundaries of the 250 word format. A succinct use of the language always stands out. Work with the form. Try to push the limits of what can happen in only 250 words."

YELLOW SILK: Journal of Erotic Arts, (II), Verygraphics, Box 6374, Albany CA 94706. (510)644-4188. Editor/Publisher: Lily Pond. Magazine: 8½×11; 60 pages; matte coated stock; glossy cover stock; 4-color illustrations; photos. "We are interested in nonpornographic erotic literature: joyous, mad, musical, elegant, passionate. 'All persuasions; no brutality' is our editorial policy. Literary excellence is a priority; innovative forms are welcomed, as well as traditional ones." Quarterly. Estab. 1981. Circ. 16,000.
   • The editor of *Yellow Silk* is developing a new publication, *Green Magazine*. Write for details.
Needs: Comics, erotica, ethnic, experimental, fantasy, feminist/lesbian, gay, humor/satire, literary, prose poem, science fiction and translations. No "blow-by-blow" descriptions; no hackneyed writing except when used for satirical purposes. Nothing containing brutality. Buys 4-5 mss/issue; 16-20 mss/year. Published work by William Kotzwinkle, Gary Soto; published new writers within the last year. Length: no preference. Occasionally critiques rejected ms.
How to Contact: Send complete ms with SASE (IRCs) and include short, *personal* bio notes. No queries. No pre-published material. No simultaneous submissions. Name, address and phone number on each page. Submissions on disk OK *with* hard copy only. Reports in 3 months on mss. Publishes ms up to 3 years after acceptance. Sample copy $7.50.
Payment: Pays 3 contributor's copies plus competitive payment.
Terms: Pays on publication for all periodical and anthology rights for one year following publication, at which time rights revert back to author; and nonexclusive reprint and anthology rights for the duration of the copyright.
Advice: "Read, read, read! Including our magazine—plus Nabokov, Ntozake Shange, Rimbaud, Virginia Woolf, William Kotzwinkle, James Joyce. Then send in your story! Trust that the magazine/editor will not rip you off—they don't. As they say, 'find your own voice,' then trust it. Most manuscripts I reject appear to be written by people without great amounts of writing experience. It takes years (frequently) to develop your work to publishable quality; it can take many rewrites on each individual piece. I also see many approaches to sexuality (for my magazine) that are trite and not fresh. The use of language is not original, and the people do not seem real. However, the gems come too, and what a wonderful moment that is. Please don't send me anything with blue eye shadow."

‡YOUNG JUDAEAN, (IV), Hadassah Zionist Youth Commission, 50 W. 58th St., New York NY 10019. (212)247-9210. Contact: Editor. Magazine: 8½×11; 16 pages; illustrations. "*Young Judaean* is for members of the Young Judaea Zionist youth movement, ages 8-12." Triannual. Estab. 1910. Circ. 4,000.

Needs: Children's fiction including adventure, ethnic, fantasy, historical, humor/satire, juvenile, prose poem, religious, science fiction, suspense/mystery and translations. "All stories must have Jewish relevance." Receives 10-15 unsolicited fiction mss/month. Publishes ms up to 2 years after acceptance. Buys 1-2 mss/issue; 10-20 mss/year. Length: 500 words minimum; 800 words maximum.
How to Contact: Send complete ms with SASE (IRCs). Reports in 3 months on mss. Sample copy for 75¢. Free fiction guidelines.
Payment: Pays 5¢/word up to $50; 2 free contributor's copies; 75¢ charge for extras.
Terms: Pays on publication for first rights.
Advice: "Stories must be of Jewish interest—lively and accessible to children without being condescending."

YOUNG VOICES MAGAZINE, The Magazine of Young People's Creative Work, (I, II, IV), Box 2321, Olympia WA 98507. (206)357-4863. Editor: Steve Charak. Magazine: "All materials are by elementary through high school students for children and adults interested in children's work." Bimonthly. Estab. 1988. Circ. 1,000.
Needs: Adventure, experimental, historical (general), humor/satire, juvenile (5-18), literary, mainstream, mystery/suspense (young adult), prose poem, science fiction and sports. "Everything must be written by elementary, middle or high school students. (12th grade is the limit.)" No excessive violence or sexual content. Plans a special fiction issue or anthology in the future. Receives 200 unsolicited mss/month. Buys 30 mss/issue; 160-200 mss/year. Publishes ms 4-6 months after acceptance. Recently published work by Steven Shetterly and Jarrett Roux Horne. Length: 500 words average. Publishes short shorts. Also publishes poetry. Always critiques rejected mss and recommends other markets.
How to Contact: Make sure age, grade and school are in the letter. Simultaneous and reprint submissions OK. Sample copy for $4. Fiction guidelines for SASE (IRCs).
Payment: Pays $3-5 and contributor's copies.
Terms: Pays on acceptance for one-time rights.
Advice: "Query, explaining story idea. Do not submit unsolicited manuscripts. Suggestion: Read the magazine. Look at what we publish."

ZERO HOUR, "Where Culture Meets Crime," (I, II, IV), Box 766, Seattle WA 98111. (206)621-8829. Editor: Jim Jones. Tabloid: 11×16; 36 pages; newsprint paper; illustrations and photos. "We are interested in fringe culture. We publish fiction, poetry, essays, confessions, photos, illustrations and interviews, for young, politically left audience interested in current affairs, non-mainstream music, art, culture." Semiannual. Estab. 1988. Circ. 3,000.
Needs: Confessions, erotica, ethnic, experimental, feminist, gay, humor/satire, psychic/supernatural/occult and translations. "Each issue revolves around an issue in contemporary culture: cults and fanaticism, addiction, pornography, etc." No romance, inspirational, juvenile/young, sports. Receives 5 unsolicited mss/month. Accepts 3 mss/issue; 9 mss/year. Publishes ms 2-3 months after acceptance. Published work by Jesse Bernstein and Mike Allmayer. Length: 1,200 words average; 400 words minimum; 1,500 words maximum. Publishes short shorts. Length: 400 words. Also publishes literary essays, literary criticism, poetry. Sometimes critiques rejected mss.
How to Contact: Query first. Reports in 2 weeks on queries; 1 month on mss. SASE (IRCs). Simultaneous submissions OK. Sample copy for $3, 9×12 SAE and 5 first-class stamps. Fiction guidelines free. Reviews novels and short story collections.
Payment: Pays in contributor's copies.
Terms: Acquires one-time rights. Sends galleys to author.
Advice: "Does it fit our theme? Is it well written, from an unusual point of view or on an unexplored/underexplored topic?"

ZOIKS!, "Chunka Chunka Chunka," (I, II, IV), P.O. Box 33561, Raleigh NC 27636. Editor: Skip Elsheimer. Fiction Editor: David Jordan. Magazine: illustrations and photos. "*Zoiks!* is interested in new ideas and new ways of thinking. Or at least using old ideas in a new way. The pen is mightier than the sword and not as heavy." Estab. 1986.
Needs: Experimental, humor/satire, psychic/supernatural/occult, translations, underground literature, conspiracy-oriented fiction. "No fiction that is pretentious, lacking humor." Upcoming themes: "Zoiks! coffeehouse" (about heavenly coffee and hellish coffeehouses); "Zoiks! sexual deviance" (when the human mind can be the most creative); "Zoiks! Scooby Doo" (a deep analysis of one of the most important cartoons of our time); "Zoiks! food" (stories involving food, stories with recipes as a bonus!). Receives 2-3 unsolicited mss/week. Accepts 1-2 mss/issue; 6-12 mss/year. Published work by Harrison Nutkins and B.Z. Niditch; published new writers within the last year. Publishes short

shorts. Sometimes critiques rejected mss or recommends other markets.

How to Contact: Query first with clips of published work or send complete ms with cover letter, which should include address. Should tell something about the author. Reports in 2 months. Simultaneous and reprint submissions OK. Accepts electronic submissions via Macintosh 800K and IBM 720K and modem. Sample copy $1.50. Make checks payable to Skip Elsheimer.

Payment: Pays in contributor's copies; charges for extras at cost plus postage.

Terms: Publication not copyrighted. Work belongs to the author.

Advice: "We're exposing the clockwork of our society and laughing hard at the shoddy craftsmanship. We're not doing this to make money, we want to (dis)color people's ideas and perceptions. We're looking for writers who have that same desire."

‡ZUZU'S PETALS QUARTERLY, A Journal of the Written Arts, (II), P.O. Box 4476, Allentown PA 18102. (215)821-1324. Editor: T. Dunn. Magazine: 8½ × 11; 50-60 pages; 20 lb. paper; 64 lb. cover stock; black and white illustrations and photographs. "Arouse the senses; stimulate the mind." Quarterly. Estab. 1992. Circ. 350.

Needs: Ethnic/multicultural, feminist, gay, humor/satire, lesbian, literary, regional. No "romance, sci-fi, the banal, TV style plotting." Receives 110 unsolicited mss/month. Accepts 1-3 mss/issue; 4-12 mss/year. Publishes ms 4-6 months after acceptance. Agented fiction 10%. Recently published work by Norah Labiner, Jean Erhardt and Thomas Michael McDade. Length: 1,000 words minimum; 4,000 words maximum. Publishes short shorts. Length: 350 words. Also publishes literary essays, literary criticism and poetry. Sometimes critiques or comments on rejected mss.

How to Contact: Send complete ms with a cover letter. Should include estimated word count and list of publications. Reports in 2 weeks on queries; 2 weeks-2 months on mss. Send SASE (or IRC) for reply, return of ms or send a disposable copy of ms. Simultaneous and electronic submissions OK. Sample copy for $5. Fiction guidelines free. Reviews novels and short story collections. Send to Doug DuCap, Reviewer.

Payment: Pays 1 contributor's copy; additional copies for $5.

Terms: Acquires one-time rights.

Advice: Looks for "strong plotting and a sense of vision. Original situations and true to life reactions."

ZYZZYVA, the last word: west coast writers & artists, (II, IV), Suite 1400, 41 Sutter St., San Francisco CA 94104. (415)255-1282. Editor: Howard Junker. Magazine: 6 × 9; 144 pages; graphics; photos. "Literate" magazine. Quarterly. Estab. 1985. Circ. 4,000.

Needs: Contemporary, experimental, literary, prose poem. West Coast writers only. Receives 300 unsolicited mss/month. Buys 5 fiction mss/issue; 20 mss/year. Agented fiction: 10%. Recently published work by Peter Bacho, David Shields, Kathryn Trueblood and William T. Vollmann; published new writers within the last year. Length: varies. Also publishes literary essays.

How to Contact: Send complete ms. "Cover letters are of minimal importance." Reports in 2 weeks on mss. SASE (IRCs). No simultaneous submissions or reprints. Sample copy for $5. Fiction guidelines on masthead page.

Payment: Pays $50-250.

Terms: Pays on acceptance for first North American serial rights.

Advice: "Keep the faith."

International literary and small circulation magazines

The following is a list of literary and small circulation publications from countries outside the U.S. and Canada that accept or buy short fiction in English (or in the universal languages of Esperanto or Ido).

Before sending a manuscript to a publication in another country, it's a good idea to query first for information on the magazine's needs and methods of submission. Send for sample copies, or try visiting the main branch of your local library, a nearby college library or bookstore to find a copy.

All correspondence to markets outside your own country must include International Reply Coupons, if you want a reply or material returned. You may find it less expensive to send copies of your manuscript for the publisher to keep and just enclose a return postcard with one IRC for a reply. Keep in mind response time is slow for many overseas publishers, but don't hesitate to send a reply postcard with IRC to check the status of your submission. You can obtain IRCs from the main branch of your local post office. The charge for one in U.S. funds is 95¢.

THE ABIKO QUARTERLY LITERARY RAG, 8-1-8 Namiki, Abiko-Shi, Chiba-Ken 270-11 Japan. Tel./ Fax: (0471)84-7904. Editors: Anna Livia Plurabelle, Laurel Tycks. Fiction Editor: D.C. Palter. Quarterly. Circ. 500. Publishes 4 stories/issue. "We are a semi-bilingual (Japanese/English) magazine for Japanese and foreigners living in Japan." Needs: contemporary, erotica, experimental, historical, humor, literary, mainstream, regional. Length: 3,000 average; 5,000 maximum. Send entire manuscript with SAE and IRCs. Pays in 2 contributor's copies. "Stories influenced by James Joyce wanted. A story submitted in both English and Japanese receives special consideration. I look for strong character development as well as a good plot. Most stories I receive are exclusively character development or plot, but both are necessary to stand a good chance of being published." Follow proper format and submission procedures. Sponsors contest ($750). Write for details. Sample copy for $10 and $3 postage.

AQUARIUS, Flat 10, Room-A, 116 Sutherland Ave., Maida-Vale, London W9 England. Fiction Editor: Sean Glackin. Editor: Eddie Linden. Circ. 5,000. Publishes 5 stories/issue. Interested in humor/satire, literary, prose poem and serialized/excerpted novels. "We publish prose and poetry and reviews." Payment is by agreement. "We only suggest changes. Most stories are taken on merit." Price in UK £5 plus postage and packing; in US $18 plus $3 postage.

AUGURIES, 48 Anglesey Road, Alverstoke, Gosport, Hampshire P012 2EQ England. Editor: Nik Morton. Circ. 300. Averages 30-40 stories/year. "Science fiction and fantasy, maximum length 4,000 words." Pays £2 per 1,000 words plus complimentary copy. "Buy back issues, then try me!" Sample copy $10. Subscription (4 issues) $30 to 'Morton Publishing.' Member of the New SF Alliance.

‡BBR MAGAZINE, P.O. Box 625, Sheffield, S1 3GY, UK. Editor: Chris Reed. Semiannually. Circ. 3,000. Publishes 20,000-30,000 words/issue. "BBR is a magazine of new speculative fiction. We are particularly interested in material that is too adventurous or thought-provoking for big publishers to handle, but that is no justification for explicit sex and/or violence irrelevant to the story. Plot is of paramount importance. We receive too many stories that contain very good ideas which are weakly and loosely handled, especially with endings that are meaningless or irrelevant to the rest of the story." Length: 2,000 words minimum; 10,000 words maximum. "If word-processed, do not use right justification or proportional spacing, as the variable spacing of words is harder to read. Dot-matrix printout must be clearly legible, especially if photocopied. Never send your only copy! Mark the first sheet clearly with the number of words, plus your name and address. Number each subsequent sheet of the manuscript. Submissions will also be accepted on 3½" or 5¼" diskettes suitable for IBM compatibles, or 3½" Apple Mac diskettes. Alternatively, you can e-mail your submission % C.S.Reed@sheffield.ac.uk. In each case, please use a straightforward single column ASCII text file. Pays £5/1,000 words or equivalent in US dollars and contributor's copies. "Obtain and read guidelines, and consult recent issues to see what we're publishing." Enclose a SASE for the return of your manuscript if it is not accepted. We are unable to reply to writers who do not send return postage. We recommend IRCs plus disposable copy for overseas submissions. One US dollar is an acceptable (and cheaper!) alternative to IRCs. Sample copy available in US for $5 from Anne Marsden, 1052 Calle del Cerro, #708, San Clemente CA 92672-6068. (Checks payable to Anne Marsden).

CAMBRENSIS, 41 Heol Fach, Cornelly, Bridgend, Mid-Glamorgan, CF33 4LN Wales. Editor: Arthur Smith. Quarterly. Circ. 500. "Devoted solely to the short story form, featuring short stories by writers born or resident in Wales/or with some Welsh connection; receives grants from the Welsh Arts' Council and the Welsh Writers' Trust; uses art-work — cartoons, line-drawings, sketches etc." Length: 2,500 words maximum. Writers receive 3 copies of magazine. Writer has to have some connection with Wales. SAE and IRCs or similar should be enclosed "Air mail" postage to avoid long delay. Send IRCs for a sample copy. Subscriptions via Blackwell's Periodicals, P.O. Box 40, Hythe Bridge Street, Oxford, OX1 2EU, UK or Faxon Europe, P.O. Box 297, 10000A D Amsterdam, Holland.

CHAPMAN, 4 Broughton Place, Edinburgh EH1 3RX Scotland. Fiction Editor: Joy Hendry. Quarterly. Circ. 2,000. Publishes 4-6 stories/issue. "Founded in 1970 *Chapman*, Scotland's quality literary magazine, is a dynamic force in Scotland, publishing poetry, fiction, criticism, reviews; articles on theatre, politics. language and the arts." Length: 1,000 words minimum; 6,000 words maximum. Include SAE and return postage (IRCs) with submissions. Pays £8-50/page.Sample copy available for £3.50 (includes postage).

CONTRAST, Box 3841, Cape Town 8000 South Africa. Editors: Stephen Watson, Mike Nicol, Jill Gallimore, Michael King, Mtutuzeli Matshoba, Daniel Hugo, Damon Galgut. Circ. 1,000. Averages 6-8 short stories/year. "A literary journal of Southern Africa; emphasis on publishing short stories (max 6,500 words), poetry, literary articles and essays." No payment—contributor's copies sent. "Include self-addressed envelope."

CREATIVE FORUM, Bahri Publications, 997A Gobindpuri Kalkaj, P.O. Box 4453, New Delhi 110019 India. Telephones: 011-6445710, 011-6448606. Fax: 91.11-6460796. Fiction Editor: U.S. Bahri. Circ. 1,800. Publishes 8-12 stories annually. "We accept short stories for our journal, *Creative Forum* in addition to poetry and criticism on fiction and poetry (contemporary only). Novels/novellas accepted if suitable subsidy is forthcoming from the author." Length: 2,000-3,000 words. Pays in copies. Manuscripts should be "neatly typed and not beyond 200 sheets." Subscriptions $50 US. "Short stories accompanied with $25 US towards annual subscription of the journal are given preferential treatment and priority."

DILIMAN REVIEW, Rm. 208 Palma Hall Annex (Phan), University of the Phillippines, Diliman, Quezon City 3004 Philippines. Editor: Lilia Quindoza Santiago.

‡EDINBURGH REVIEW, 22 George Square, Edinburgh EH8 Scotland. Circ. 2,000. Publishes 16 stories/year. "An international journal of ideas and literature. Interested in all stories, especially the experimental and unorthodox." Pays for published fiction and provides contributor's copies. "We take 5 months to give a decision. We are especially interested in translations and interviews of some length."

‡FIRE RAISERS', 64 Lugar Place, Troon, Strathclyde, KA10 7EA, UK. Fiction Editor: Mr. Alistar Fitchett. Published irregularly—usually semiannually. Circ. 1,000. Publishes 2-4 stories/issue. "*Fire Raisers* is a collection of writings on a wide variety of topics—music,media, film, politics, art etc. Fiction is imaginative and provokative, modern and sharp." Length: 3,000 words maximum. Pays 1 contributor's copy. "It should be concise, imaginative prose. Stylistic experiments are welcomed, as long as content is not sub-ordinated. Don't try to write what you think another country/culture might be interested in. Write what you know." Send SASE (IRCs) to the contact address. No guidelines available—we like people to take a risk.

FOOLSCAP, 78 Friars Road, East Ham, London E6 1LL England. Fiction and Poetry Editor: Judi Benson. Published 2 times/year. Publishes 2-3 stories/issue. "We are primarily poetry though can handle short fiction of up to 5 pages. This could include a scene from a novel. We are looking for strong quality work but will give careful consideration to all submissions. Any subject considered, also nonfiction." Length: 420-2,000 words. Pays 1 contributor's copy. "Do not send work exceeding 10 typed pages as the magazine does not have the space. Send manuscript in typed form with SAE and enough IRCs for return." Sample copy available for $6.

FORESIGHT (IV), 44 Brockhurst Rd., Hodge Hill, Birmingham B36 8JB England. Editor: John Barklam. Fiction Editor: Judy Barklam. Quarterly. Magazine including "new age material, world peace, psychic phenomena, research, occultism, spiritualism, mysticism, UFOs, philosophy, etc. Shorter articles required on a specific theme related to the subject matter of *Foresight* magazine." Length: 300-1,000 words. Pays in contributor's copies. Send SAE with IRC for return of ms. Sample copy for 30p and 35p postage.

FRANK, An International Journal of Contemporary Writing and Art, 104 rue Edouard Vaillant, 93100 Montreuil France. Editor: David Applefield. Semiannual. "Eclectic, serious fiction, favors innovative works that convey social, political, environmental concern—all styles, voices—and translations, novel extracts" for literary international audience. "Send your best work, consult a copy of the journal before submitting." Published in Paris in English. Published work by Frederick Barthelme, Robert Coover, Rita Dove, Italo Calvino, Vaclav Havel, Sony Labou Tansi. Special foreign dossiers of work little known to American readers. Including: The Congo, Pakistan, Phillippines, Belgium, Vietnam (1994). Length: 3,000 words maximum. Pays 2 copies and $5 (US)/printed page. "Send work that conveys a sense of necessity and soulfulness." Sample copy $8 (US).

GLOBAL TAPESTRY JOURNAL, (II), BB Books, 1 Spring Bank, Longsight Rd., Copster Green, Blackburn, Lancashire BB1 9EU England. Editor: Dave Cunliffe. "Post-underground with avant-garde, experimental, alternative, counterculture, psychedelic, mystical, anarchist etc. fiction for a bohemian and counterculture audience." Recently published fiction by Bill Holdsworth, Steve Walker, Maria Mitchelli; published work by new writers within the last year. Sample copy $4 (Sterling Cheque, British Money Order or dollar currency).

GRANTA, 2/3 Hanover Yard, Noel Road, Islington, London N1 8BE England. U.S. Associate Publisher: Anne Kinard. Editor: Bill Buford. U.S. office: Suite 1316, 250 W. 57th St., New York NY 10107. Quarterly. "Paperback magazine (256 pages) publishing fiction (including novellas and works-in progress), essays, political analysis, journalism, etc." Potential contributors *must* be familiar with the magazine.

THE HARDCORE, P.O. Box 1899, London N9 8JT England. Fiction Editor: J. Nuit. Quarterly. Circ. 500. Publishes 3 stories/issue. "The magazine at the edge of contemporary culture. We print high speed, hard edged, glitteringly intellegent stories set in the absolute present or near future." Length: 1,500 words minimum; 10,000 words maximum. "Complimentary copy always sent to writer/artist. Payment by share of profits in English pounds." Write to enquire. Send $4 US to editorial address.

HECATE, Box 99, St. Lucia Q4067 Australia. Fiction Editor: Carole Ferrier. Circ. 2,000. Publishes 5-8 stories annually. "Socialist feminist; we like political stories (broadly defined)." Writers receive $50 (Australian) and 5 copies. "We only rarely publish non-Australian writers of fiction."

THE HONEST ULSTERMAN, 14 Shaw Street, Belfast BT4 1PT, Northern Ireland. Fiction Editor: Tom Clyde. Circ. 1,000. Publishes 3-4 stories/year. "Mainly poetry, book review, socio-political comment, short stories, novel extracts, etc. Main interest is Ireland/Northern Ireland." Writers receive small payment and two contributor's copies. For 4 issues send UK £14 airmail or sample issue US $7. "Contributors are strongly advised to read the magazine before submitting anything."

‡**HORIZON**, Stationsstraat 232A, 1770 Liedekerke Belgium. Fiction Editor: Johnny Haelterman. Bimonthly. Circ. 200. Publishes at least 1 story/issue. "*Horizon* is a cultural magazine for a general public, therefore fiction should be suitable for a general public. Preference is given to stories which can happen, although slightly fantastic fiction is sometimes accepted." Length: 450 words minimum; 8,000 words maximum. "Enclose money or IRCs if you want your work back. Payment in Belgian funds for original fiction in Dutch only. No payment for fiction in other languages but the writers receive two copies in that case. English fiction can be translated into Dutch without payment (two copies). Submitting outside your country is mainly the same as in your own country, except that the postage costs are higher. Puns are usually not translatable, so avoid writing stories with a plot or an essential part based on puns if you want your work to be translated. For a few dollars (or equal amount in other foreign money) anyone can have a sample copy."

HRAFNHOH, 32 Strŷd Ebeneser, Pontypridd Mid Glamorgan CF37 5PB Wales. Fiction Editor: Joseph Biddulph. Circ. 300-500. Published irregularly. "Now worldwide and universal in scope. Suitable: fictionalized history, local history, family history. Explicitly Christian approach. Well-written stories or general prose opposed to abortion and human embryo experimentation particularly welcome. No payment made, but free copies provided. Be brief, use a lot of local colour and nature description, in a controlled, resonant prose or in dialect. Suitable work accepted in esperanto, français, español, and other languages, including Creole. "US stamps are of no use to me, but US banknotes acceptable." IRC will cover a brief response. But mss however small are expensive to return, so please send copy." Sample copy free, but 3 IRCs would cover real cost of sending it overseas.

ILLUMINATIONS, Radley College, Abingdon, Oxon, OX14 2HR England or % Dept. of English, University of Florida, Gainesville, Florida, 32611, U.S.A. Annual. Circ. 500. Publishes 1-2 short pieces (c. 2,000 words/issue). "*Illuminations* is an international magazine of contemporary writing, concentrating on poetry, very open to translation, taking only a limited amount of fiction. All material is read on its own merits; we have no genre or formula expectations." Length: 3,000 words maximum. Pays 2 contributor's copies plus 1 subsequent issue. Sample copies ($5) available from address given.

IMAGO, School of Communication, QUT, GPO Box 2434, Brisbane 4001 Australia. Contact: Dr. Philip Neilsen or Helen Horton. Published 3 times/year. Circ. 750. 30-50% fiction. *Imago* is a literary magazine publishing short stories, poetry articles, interviews and book reviews. "While content of articles and interviews should have some relevance either to Queensland or to writing, stories and poems may be on any subject. The main requirement is good writing." Length: 1,000 words minimum; 3,000 words maximum; approximately 2,000 words preferred. Pays on publication in accordance with Australia Council rates: short stories, $A80 minimum; articles, $A80 minimum; reviews, $A50. Also provides contributor's copy. "Contributions should be typed double-spaced on one side of the paper, each page bearing the title, page number and author's name. Name and address of the writer should appear on a cover page of longer mss, or on the back, or bottom, of single page submissions. A SASE (SAE and IRCs) with sufficient postage to cover the contents, should be sent for the return of ms or for notification of acceptance or rejection. No responsibility is assumed for the loss of or damage to unsolicited manuscripts." Sample copy available for $A7. Guidelines, as above, available on request.

INDIAN LITERATURE, Sahitya Akademi, National Academy of Letters, Rabindra Bhavan, 35 Ferozeshah Rd., New Delhi 110 001 India. Editor: Professor K. Sachidanandan. Circ. 4,100. Publishes 6 issues/year; 144-200 pages/issue. "Presents creative work from 22 Indian languages including Indian English." Sample copy $7.

‡INDIAN WRITER, C-23, Anna Nagar East, Madras-600102 India. Quarterly. Publishes about 10 pages of fiction/issue. "This is a quarterly journal of the Writers Club of India. We carry poems, short stories, synopsis of novels and book reviews." Length: 800 words maximum. "The ms should be written observing MLA style handbook or Chicago Manual of style, typed in double space. Writers should establish contacts with journals and publishers and find out their requirements, philosophy of publication, including subject, style, length, political colours and so on and then only submit their manuscripts for consideration."

‡INKSHED, 387 Beverly Road, Hull HU5 1LS England. Fiction Editor: Sue Wilsea. Circ. 500. Publishes approx. 10 stories/year. "Small press literary magazine. Any type of fiction used up to 2,500 words." Writers receive a complimentary copy. "Just keep it neat, typed, well-spaced with name and address on front sheet." Please send IRCs for response.

IRON MAGAZINE, (II), Iron Press, 5 Marden Ter., Cullercoats, North Shields, Tyne & Wear NE30 4PD England. Editor: Peter Mortimer. Circ. 1,000. Published 3 times/year. Publishes 14 stories/year. "Literary magazine of contemporary fiction, poetry, articles and graphics." Length: 6,000 words maximum. Pays approx. £10/page. No simultaneous submissions. Five poems, two stories/submission the limit. Sample copy for $10 (US) (no bills-no checks). "Please see magazine before submitting and don't submit to it before you're ready! Many stories submitted are obviously only of interest to the domestic market of the writer. Always try there first! And do try to find something out about the publication, or better, see a sample copy, before submitting."

‡JEWISH QUARTERLY, P.O. Box 1148, London NW5 2AZ, England. Fiction Editors: Colin Shindler or Morij Farhi. Quarterly. Publishes 1 contribution of fiction/issue. "It deals in the broadest sense with all issues of Jewish interest." Length: 2,000 words minimum; 5,000 words maximum. "We are fixing new payment levels for short story writers. Work should have either a Jewish theme in the widest interpretation of that phrase or a theme which would interest our readership. The question which contributors should ask is 'Why should it appear in the *Jewish Quarterly* and not in another periodical?' "

LA KANCERKLINIKO, (IV), 162 rue Paradis, 13006 Marseille France. Phone: 91-3752-15. Fiction Editor: Laurent Septier. Circ. 300. Quarterly. Publishes 40 pages of fiction annually. "An esperanto magazine which appears 4 times annually. Each issue contains 32 pages. *La Kancerkliniko* is a political and cultural magazine. General fiction, science fiction, etc. Short stories or very short novels. The short story (or the very short novel) must be written only in esperanto, either original or translation from any other language." Length: 15,000 words maximum. Pays in contributor's copies. Sample copy on request with 3 IRCs from Universal Postal Union.

LANDFALL/OXFORD UNIVERSITY PRESS, (formerly *Landfall/Caxton Press*), P.O. Box 11-149, Ellerslie, Auckland 5 New Zealand. Editor: Chris Price. Publishes fiction, poetry, commentary and criticism. Length: maximum 10,000 words. Pays NZ $11 per page for fiction. "Without wishing to be unduly nationalist, we would normally give first preference to stories which contain some kind of New Zealand connection."

‡**LINQ (II), Literature in North Queensland,** English Language and Literature Association, English Dept., James Cook University of North Queensland, Townsville 4811 Australia. Editor-in-Chief: Elizabeth Perkins. Magazine of articles, stories, poems, reveries on literature, history, for academic and general audience.

LONDON MAGAZINE, 30 Thurloe Place, London SW7 England. Editor: Alan Ross. Bimonthly. Circ. 5,000. Publishes 3-4 stories/issue. "Quality is the only criteria." Length: 1,500-5,000 words. Pays £50-100, depending on length, and contributor's copy. "Send only original and literary, rather than commercial, work."

MANUSHI, A Journal About Women and Society, C/202 Lajpat Nagar 1, New Delhi 110024 India. Editor: Madhu Kishwar. Bimonthly. Circ. up to 8,000. Publishes one fiction story/issue. "*Manushi* is a magazine devoted to human rights and women's rights issues with a focus on the Indian subcontinent and the situation of Indian communities settled overseas. It includes poetry, fiction, historical and sociological studies, analysis of contemporary politics, review of mass media and literature, biographies, profiles and histories of various movements for social change." Length: 12,000 words maximum. Duplicate mss preferred.

‡**MARANG,** Dept. of English, University of Botswana, P/B 0022, Gaborone Botswana. Editor: A.N. Mensah. Circ. 200. "Departmental journal featuring poems, short stories and critical articles from colleagues in the Southern African region." Writers are not paid for work used; writers receive copies of the publication in which work appears.

MASSACRE, BCM 1698, London WC1N 3XX United Kingdom. Editor: Roberta McKeown. Annual. Circ. 300. Published 19 stories in 1992 (from 1,000 to 5,000 words each). *Massacre* is "an annual anthology (paperback, perfect-bound) dedicated to anti-naturalistic and marginal writings. Looking for the subjective – satire, parodies, surrealism, the 'absurd' are particularly welcome. No slice-of-life stories, sci-fi or poetry, please." Length: 2,000 words maximum. "SAE a must (IRCs). No simultaneous submissions, please." Pays 1 contributor's copy plus 50% discount on further copies (plus postage). "*Massacre* is quirky and many mss submitted are not suitable. Try to read a sample copy before submitting. This magazine is not for everybody." Sample copy from Indelible Inc., BCM 1698, London WC1N 3XX UK. Price: £6.50 (in sterling, checks payable to Indelible Inc.) or $13 (in dollars, cheques payable to R. McKeown).

MEANJIN, University of Melbourne, Parkville, Victoria 3052 Australia. Fiction Editor: Jenny Lee. Circ. 3,500. "*Meanjin*'s emphasis is on publishing a wide range of writing by new and established writers. Our primary orientation is toward Australian writers, but material from overseas sources is also published." Writer receives approx. $60 (Australian)/1,000 words and 2 copies. "Please submit typed manuscript and enclose return addressed envelope with IRCs."

‡**MIDNIGHT IN HELL (WEIRDEST TALES OF FANDOM),** The Cottage, Smithy Brae, Kilmacolm, Renfrewshire, PA134EN, Scotland. Fiction Editor: George N. Houston. Quarterly. Circ. 200. Publishes 6-10 stories (short)/issue. "We accept fiction, art and poetry within the horror/science fiction/fantasy genres and any crossover thereof. We exist to give the fan writer an outlet with which to stretch their talents and maybe make it to the professional writing scene! . . . Not forgetting keeping people abreast of the cult film world . . . ." Length: 500 words minimum; 4,000 words maximum. "Fiction described above should be accompanied by a return envelope with the correct postage." Pays 1 contributor's copy. "Don't censor yourself in any way! Keep plugging at it, and send out to as many as possible!" Write for guidelines.

‡**THE MOWER,** % Memoria Pulp, Postbox 101710, 88647 Ueberlingen Germany. Tel: 49-7551-2869. Contact: Oliver Ruts or Andrea Schuler. Published irregularly. Averages 20-50 short stories/issue. "The stranger – the better." No limits on length. Pays 1 copy; contributors can get further copies for reduced price. "Every *Mower* magazine has one special subject or theme. There are no limitations on creativity and no *censorship*. Interested writers should get in touch with us first by fax or phone (or by letter)."

NEW HOPE INTERNATIONAL, 20 Werneth Ave., Hyde, SK14 5NL England. Fiction Editor: Gerald England. Circ. 750. Publishes 2-6 stories annually. Publishes "mainly poetry. Fiction used must be essentially literary but not pretentious. Only short fiction used (max 2,000 words). Would use more fiction but the standard submitted (in comparison to the poetry) has been rather poor." Payment: 1 complimentary copy. Guidelines available for IRC. Sample copy: $5 (cash, if cheque, send $10, due to bank charges).

THE NEW WELSH REVIEW, 49 Park Place, Cardiff Wales CF1 3AT UK. Editor: Robin Reeves. *"NWR,* a literary quarterly, publishes stories, poems and critical essays." Accepts 16-20 mss/year. Pays "cheque on publication and one free copy." Length: 2,000-3,000 words.

NORTHERN PERSPECTIVE, Box 41246, Casuarina 0811 Australia. Editor: Penny Lane. Circ. 1,000. Semiannual. Publishes about 200 pages of fiction annually. "Publishes short stories, poems, book reviews, articles. *Northern Perspective* is a liberal arts/literary magazine." Length: 1,500-4,000 words. Writers are paid $10 (Australian)/1,000 words and receive contributor's copies. "Strive for 'form' and style in short story; image in poetry."

OUTRIDER, Journal of Multicultural Literare, P.O. Box 210, Indooroopilly, Queensland 4068, Australia. Fiction Editor: Manfred Jurgensen. Circ. 1,000. Publishes approx. 20 short stories plus other prose features annually. *"Outrider* aims to extend the concept of Australian literature. It publishes literary prose, poetry and articles dealing wth literature in Australia. Translated works are welcome." Pays $10/1,000 words. "We expect a professional presentation of manuscripts (enclose self-addressed stamped envelope!). There are no restrictions on what we publish, provided it is good writing."

PANURGE, (I), Crooked Holme Farm Cottage, Brampton, Cumbria CA8 2AT UK. Tel. 06977-41087. Fiction Editor: John Murray. Circ. 1,000. Published twice/year. Perfect-bound, 120 pages. "Dedicated to short fiction by new and up-and-coming names. Each issue features several previously unpublished names. Several *Panurge* writers have been included in major anthologies, approached by agents, offered contracts by publishers. All lengths, styles and attitudes given serious consideration. US submissions welcomed. New editor is founder-editor and winner of the Dylan Thomas Award 1988. We now promote a regular Worldwide Fiction Comp (SAE for details) with £500 prize. We are also bringing back hard-hitting features on fiction publishing; third world fiction etc." Pays 1 month after publication, 1 contributor's copy. Pays £10/3 printed pages. Overseas subscription $15; Airmail $20. Sample copy $7.

PARIS TRANSCONTINENTAL, A Magazine of Short Stories, Institut des Pays Anglophones, Sorbonne Nouvelle, 5, rue de l'Ecole de Médecine, 75006 Paris, France. Fiction Editors: Claire Larrière, Albert Russo and Devorah Goldberg. Semiannually. Circ. 500. Publishes short stories exclusively; no poetry, nonfiction or artwork. *"Paris Transcontinental,* purports to be a forum for writers of excellent stories whose link is the English language, wherever it is spoken. It purports thus to be global in scope and to introduce the best among today's authors, whether they hail from Europe or the Americas, from Oceania, Africa or Asia, for new literatures are evolving that reflect our post-colonial and computerized societies in ways that do not necessarily converge but certainly enrich our common space, hopefully also spurring our mutual understanding." Length: 2,000 words minimum; 4,000 words maximum. "Submitters should send us no more than 3 unpublished stories at a time, along with a few lines about themselves and their work (approx. 100 words), one IRC to let them know of our decision, and *extra* IRCs (at least 3) for the return of their manuscripts. (No stamps please!)" Pays 2 contributor's copies. "Have an authentic voice and be professional. Write with your gut and read from all quarters. Author's featured include Stephen Dixon, Herbert Liebman, Jayanta Mahapatra, Joyce Carol Oates, Albert Russo, Alan Sillitoe and Michael Wilding." Send IRC for guidelines. For a sample copy, send a check for FF65 (or 65 French Francs) drawn on your own local bank.

PLANET-THE WELSH INTERNATIONALIST, P.O. Box 44, Aberystwyth, Dyfed, Cymru/ Wales UK. Fiction Editor: John Barnie. Bimonthly. Circ. 1,300. Publishes 1-2 stories/issue. "A literary/cultural/ political journal centered on Welsh affairs but with a strong interest in minority cultures in Europe and elsewhere." Length: 1,500-4,000 words maximum. No submissions returned unless accompanied by an SAE. Writers submitting from abroad should send at least 3 IRCs. Writers receive 1 contributor's copy. Payment is at the rate of £40 per 1,000 words (in the currency of the relevant country if the author lives outside the UK). "We do not look for fiction which necessarily has a 'Welsh' connection, which some writers assume from our title. We try to publish a broad range of fiction and our main criterion is quality. Try to read copies of any magazine you submit to. Don't write out of the blue to a magazine which might be completely inappropriate to your work. Recognize that you are likely to

PARIS TRANSCONTINENTAL

A MAGAZINE OF SHORT STORIES

This cover drawing, titled "Displacement and Crossing Over," is descriptive of the characteristics of Paris Transcontinental, according to Fiction Editor Claire Larriere. "The quality of the stories published in the magazine bridges the gap of their authors' different backgrounds and inspiration," says Larriere. Submissions are welcomed from "all short story writers who write in English, famous or yet unknown, from all over the world, without limitations of theme." The cover art seen here is by French sculptor Henri Larriere, whose works have been exhibited in galleries and museums in the U.S. and elsewhere.

have a high rejection rate, as magazines tend to favor writers from their own countries." Sample copy: cost (to USA & Canada) £2.87. Writers' guidelines for SAE.

THE PLAZA, A Space for Global Human Relations, U-Kan Inc., Yoyogi 2-32-1, Shibuya-Ku, Tokyo Japan 151. Tel: (81)3-3379-3881. Fax: (81)3-3379-3882. Editor: Joel Baral. Fiction Editor: Taylor Mignon. Quarterly. Circ. 8,000. Publishes about 3 stories/issue. "*The Plaza* is an intercultural and bilingual magazine (English and Japanese). Our focus is the 'essence of being human.' All works are published in both Japanese and English (translations by our staff if necessary). The most important criteria is artistic level. We look for works that reflect simply 'being human.' Stories on intercultural (not international) relations are desired. *The Plaza* is devoted to offering a spiritual *Plaza* where people around the world can share their creative work. We introduce contemporary writers and artists as our generation's contribution to the continuing human heritage." Length: 200-1,200 words, minimalist short stories are welcomed. Send complete ms with cover letter. Sample copy and guidelines free.

‡PLURILINGUAL EUROPE/EUROPE PLURILINGUE, % Nadine Dormoy, 44, rue Perronet, 92200 Neuilly, France. Fiction Editors: Nadine Dormoy, Albert Russo. Semiannually. Circ. 1,000. 20% of published content/issue is fiction. "Fiction in English must involve or be set in one of the 12 nations of the European Community. "Plurilingual Europe" is a pluridisciplinary review that purports to foster understanding between the countries of the EC. All articles, essays and literary work should be written in any of the EC's 10 official languages. High specialization is required for the non-literary material. Excellence in every field always considered." Length: 500 words minimum; 2,000 words maximum. Pays 2 contributor's copies. "Have a good knowledge of the country's customs they describe or at least an original viewpoint of that country and its people. Recent contributors: George Steiner, Umberto Eco, Hugo Claus, Albert Russo, Jacques Darras, Renzo Titone, Eduardo Lourenço, etc." Subscription rate: US $22 (for 2 issues, postage included). U.S. check made out and sent to Liliane Lazar, 37 Hill Lane, Roslyn Heights, NY 11517, U.S.A.

PRINTED MATTER, Hikari Biru 303, 3-7-10 Takadanobaba, Shinjuku-ku, Tokyo 169 Japan. Editor: Stephen Forster. Quarterly. Circ. 600. About 1/3 of each issue is fiction. "*Printed Matter* is an English-language literary journal that features fiction, poetry, reviews, interviews, essays and artwork, now in its seventeenth year of publication. Though based in Japan, the magazine has an international outlook: we are not especially looking for a backdrop of cherry blossoms and Mt. Fuji. Any type of fiction is acceptable; the sole criterion is quality." Length: up to 5,000 words. Pays 2 contributor's copies. "As with submissions anywhere, study the magazine first. Submit clearly typed manuscripts together with the usual enclosures (SASE or IRCs)." Sample copy: 600 yen; £3; US $5; Australian $6.

QUADRANT, Box 1495, Collingwood, Victoria 3066 Australia. Fiction Editor: Mr. Les Murray. Monthly. Circ. 5,000. Publishes 1-2 stories/issue. "Magazine of current affairs, culture, politics, economics, the arts, literature, ideas; stories: general and varied." Length: 4,000 words maximum. Pays contributor's copies and a minimum of $80 (Australian). For sample copy "write to us, enclosing cheque (or equivalent) for $10 (Australian)."

ROMANIAN REVIEW, Redactia Publicatiilor Pentru Strainatate, Piata Presei Libere NR1, 71341 Bucuresti Romania. Fiction Editor: Mrs. Andreea Ionescu. Monthly. Fiction 40%. "Our review is scanning the Romanian history and cultural realities, the cooperation with other countries in the cultural field and it is also a mean of acquaintance with Romanian and overseas writers. We publish the *Romanian Review* in six languages (English, German, French, Spanish, Russian, Chinese). Fiction related to Romanian civilization may enter the pages of the *Review*." Length: 2,000 words minimum; 5,000 words maximum. "As we do not have the possibility of payment in foreign currency, we can only offer "lei" 800-2,000/story, depending on its length and qualities. The exchange may be done on the writer's account." Sample copies available; write for information.

‡SCRIPSI, Ormond College, University of Melbourne, Parkville, Victoria 3052 Australia. Fiction Editors: Owen Richardson, Andrew Rutherford. Circ. 2,500. Publishes 4-8 stories/year. *Scripsi* publishes Australian and international fiction, poetry and criticism. Pays in contributor's copies. Payment nominal.

SEPIA, Poetry & Prose Magazine, (I), Kawabata Press, Knill Cross House, Knill Cross, Millbrook, Nr Torpoint, Cornwall England. Editor-in-Chief: Colin David Webb. Published 3 times/year. "Magazine for those interested in modern un-clichéd work." Contains 32 pages/issue. Length: 200-4,000 words (for short stories). Pays 1 contributor's copy. Always include SAE with IRCs. Send $1 for sample copy and guidelines.

SF NEXUS, P.O. Box 1123 Brighton BN1 6EX England. Fiction Editor: P. Brazier. Quarterly. Circ. 2,000. Publishes 3 stories/issue. "Science fiction and related genre. Light or humorous work is favoured." Length: 2,000 words minimum; 4,000 words maximum. Pays 2 contributor's copies and £50, per 1,000 words. "Subscribe to the magazine and read several issues first. We always read subscribers manuscripts ahead of unknown submissions."

SMOKE, (II), Windows Project, 40 Canning St., Liverpool L8 7NP England. Contact: Dave Ward. Magazine of poetry, fiction, art, long poems, collages, concrete art, photos, cartoons. "N.B. Fiction up to 2,000 words."

SOCIAL ALTERNATIVES, % Dept. of Government, University of Queensland, St. Lucia, Queensland 4072 Australia. Fiction Editor: David Myers. Circ. 3,000. Quarterly. Publishes verse and 2-3 stories in each quarterly issue. "The journal is socio-political, but stories of any theme or style will be considered. The criterion is excellence." Length: 1,000-3,000 words. Pays writers "if we have money—we usually don't." Writers receive one contributor's copy. Send "3 copies of story, immaculately presented so no sub-editing is necessary. SASE (IRCs) for return."

STAPLE, Tor Cottage 81, Cavendish Rd., Matlock DE4 3HD U.K.. Fiction Editor: Don Measham. Published 3 times/year. Circ. up to 600. Publishes up to 50% fiction. Staple is "90+ pages, perfect-bound; beautifully designed and produced. Stories used by *Staple* have ranged from social realism (through autobiography, parody, prequel, parable) to visions and hallucinations. We don't use unmodified genre fiction, i.e. adventure, crime or westerns. We are interested in extracts from larger works—provided author does the extraction." Length: 200 words minimum; 5,000 words maximum. Adequate IRCs and large envelope for return, if return is required. Otherwise IRC for decision only. Pays complimentary copy plus subscription for US contributors. Get a specimen copy of one of the issues with strong prose representation. Send 10 IRCs for airmail dispatch, 5 IRCs for surface mail. The monograph series *Staple First Editions* has been re-launched. IRC for details. Closing date March 1994. For guidelines: editorials of *Staple 22* and Staple 26 designed to guide prose writers. Send appropriate cash or draft.

STUDIO: A JOURNAL OF CHRISTIANS WRITING, (II), 727 Peel St., Albury 2640 Australia. Managing Editor: Paul Grover. Circ. 300. Quarterly. Averages 20-30 stories/year. "*Studio* publishes prose and poetry of literary merit, offers a venue for new and aspiring writers, and seeks to create a sense of community among Christians writing." Length: 500-5,000 words. Pays in copies. Sample copy $8 (Australian). Subscription $40 (Australian) for 4 issues (1 year). International draft in Australian dollars. SASE (IRCs) required.

SUNK ISLAND REVIEW, P.O. Box 74, Lincoln LN1 1QG England. Fiction Editor: Michael Blackburn. Biannual. "A biannual magazine of new fiction, poetry, translations. Articles and graphics. Short stories, science fiction and excerpts from novels, novellas are all welcome not romance, historical fiction etc." Length: Open. Send cover letter and no more than 2 short stories at a time. Pays on publication. "Read the magazine first. We prefer disposable mss. All mss must be accompanied by adequate number of IRCs for reply or return."

TEARS IN THE FENCE, (II), 38 Hod View, Stourpaine, Nr. Blandford Forum, Dorset DT11 8TN England. Editor: David Caddy. Semiannual. A magazine of poetry, fiction and graphics, "blended with a conservation section to develop the concepts of ecology and conservation beyond their present narrow usage." Publishes 1-2 stories/issue. Pays £7.50 per story plus complimentary copy of the magazine. Sample copy $5 (US).

THE THIRD HALF MAGAZINE, "Amikeco," 16, Fane Close, Stamford, Lincolnshire PE9 1H9 England. Fiction Editor: Kevin Troop. Published irregularly (when possible). "*The Third Half* literary magazine publishes mostly poetry, but editorial policy is to publish as much *short* short story writing as possible in each issue. Short stories especially for children, for use in the classroom, with 'questions' and 'work to do' are occasionally produced, along with poetry books, as separate editions. I wish to expand on this." Length: 1,800 words maximum. Pays in contributor's copies.

TOGETHER, For All Concerned with Christian Education, The National Society, Church House, Great Smith St., London SW1P 3NZ England. Editor-in-Chief: Mrs. D. Jamal. Magazine of forward-looking Christian education for children under 12. Short stories, plays, services, projects, etc. Also songs, carols, occasional poems. Readers are primary school and Sunday school teachers, clergy.

VERANDAH, Deakin University, %TAS, 336 Glenferrie Rd., Hawthorn, Victoria 3144 Australia. Circ. 1,000. Publishes 6-8 stories annually. "*Verandah* is an annual publication published by TAS (Toorak Association of Student's and Deakin University's Faculty of Arts). *Verandah* is edited by students of Victoria College who are majoring in writing and literature. We publish contemporary fiction (no science fiction), poetry and nonfiction and graphics. Writers and artists receive 2 copies of each issue and $5-20 (Australian) per published item. Mss should be " typed, presented on A4-sized paper, double-spaced and, if author wants ms returned, a stamped, self-addressed envelope with sufficient postage must be included. We accept submissions from January to late May, and *Verandah* is published in September."

‡VIGIL, (II), Vigil Publications, 12 Priory Mead, Bruton, Somerset BA10 0DZ England. Editor: John Howard Greaves. Estab. 1979. Circ. 250. "Simply the enjoyment of varied forms of poetry and literature with an informed view of poetic technique." Plans special fiction issue. Needs: experimental, literary, regional. Length: 500-1,500 words. Pays in contributor's copies. "Most of the stories we receive are work in progress rather than finished pieces. Well structured, vibrantly expressed work is a delight when it arrives. Freshness and originality must always find an audience." Contributor guidelines available for IRC.

WASAFIRI, P.O. Box 195, Canterbury, Kent CT2 7BX England. Fiction Editor: Ms. Susheila Nasta. Semi-annual. Circ. 700. Publishes 2-3 short stories/issue. "Publishes critical articles, interviews, fiction and poetry by and about African, Asian, Carribbean, Pacific and Black British writers." Length: 500 words miminum; 2,000 words maximum. Pays contributor's copies. "We welcome any writing for consideration which falls into our areas of interest. Work from writers outside Britain is a major part of our interest. Articles should be double-spaced and follow MLA guidelines."

WEBBER'S, 15 McKillop St., Melbourne, Victoria 3000 Australia. Contact: The Editor. Biannual. "*Webber's* is a relatively new literary magazine specializing in short fiction, poetry, reviews, essays and interviews. It attempts to encourage new writers as well as established ones." Length: 2,000 words maximum. Material submitted must be previously unpublished and include SAE with IRCs. Pays approximately $60-75 (Australian) and 1 contributor's copy. "We are always interested in receiving new manuscripts and consider each contribution carefully. In writing about what *they* know, writers from other countries will be providing Australian readers with material about which they do not know. This is always very positive."

WESTERLY, English Dept., University of Western Australia, Nedlands, 6009 Australia. Caroline Horobin, Administrator. Quarterly. Circ. 1,000. "A quarterly of poetry, prose, reviews and articles of a literary and cultural kind, giving special attention to Australia and Southeast Asia." Pays $50 (AUS) minimum and 1 contributor's copy. Sample copy for $6 (AUS).

‡WESTWORDS, 15 Trelawney Rd., Peverell, Plymouth, Devon PL3 4JS U.K. Editor: D. Woolley. Annual. Circ. 300-400. Publishes 2-3 short stories/issue. "Short stories only so far, but will consider short extracts from novels in progress." Length: 2,500 words maximum. Pays 2 contributor's copies only. Sample copy available for £1 plus IRC equal to £1.

‡WORKS, 12 Blakestones Rd., Slaithwaite, Huddersfield HD7 5UQ England. Fiction Editor: D. Hughes. Circ. 1,000. 70% of content is fiction. "52 pages speculative and imaginative fiction (science fiction) with poetry, illustrated." Quarterly. Price: Enclose IRC. £5 *cash only* for 1 issue, £20 *cash* or check in pounds sterling for 4 issues. Member of the New Science Fiction Alliance. Pays in copies. "All manuscripts should be accompanied by a SASE (in the UK). USA send 2 IRC's with ms, if disposable or 4 IRCs, if not. Usual maximum is 4,500 words."

Literary and small circulation magazines/'93-'94 changes

The following literary magazines appeared in the 1993 edition of *Novel & Short Story Writer's Market* but are not in the 1994 edition. Those publications whose editors did not respond to our request for an update of their listings may not have done so for a variety of reasons — they may be out of business, for example, or they may be overstocked with submissions. These "no responses" are listed with no additional explanation below. If an explanation was given, it appears in parentheses next to the listing name. Some responded too late for inclusion and this is indicated.

Agora (asked to be left out this year)
Aldebaran
The Amaranth Review
The Amherst Review
Anarchy (asked to be left out this year)
Anything That Moves
The Asymptotical World (asked to be left out this year)
The Atavachron and All Our Yesterdays
Atlantis
Aura Literary/Arts Review
The Barrelhouse (asked to be deleted)
La Bella Figura
Beyond . . . Science Fiction & Fantasy (out of business)
The Black Scholar
Black Writer Magazine
The Blizzard Rambler
Bluff City
BLUR, Boston Literary Review
Breakthrough! (ceased publication)
Chalk Talk
Chapter One
The Coe Review
Collections

Colorado-North Review (ceased publication)
Columbia: A Magazine of Poetry & Prose
Conjunctions
Crab Creek Review
Diffusions
Door County Almanak (ceased publication)
Eldritch Science (ceased publication)
11th Street Ruse
EOD (The Esoteric Order of Dagon) Magazine (out of business)
Exit
Fag Rag
Feminist Baseball (out of business)
Five Fingers Review
Forbidden Lines (ceased publication)
Fritz
The G.W. Review
The Gingerbread Diary
Happiness Holding Tank (not accepting submissions this year)
Heresies
Howling Dog

Hurricane Alice
Indian Youth of America Newsletter (suspended publication)
ipsissima verba/the very words (asked to be left out this year)
Jeopardy
Kola
Lighthouse
The Limberlost Review
Long Shot
Lost (asked to be deleted)
Lynx (no fiction)
Mati (no unsolicited fiction)
Meshuggah (asked to be left out this year)
Middle Eastern Dancer (ceased publication)
Mindscapes (suspended publication)
Mioritam
Moon
Mystery Street
Neophyte (unable to contact)
New Anglican Review (complaints)
New Catholic Review (complaints)
New Mexico Humanities Re-

view (asked to be deleted)
The New Quarterly
Nightsun
Nostoc Magazine
La Nuez (out of business)
Oregon East
Ouroboros
P.I. Magazine (no fiction)
The P.U.N. (asked to be deleted)
Painted Hills Review
Palace Corbie (unable to locate)
Pandora (asked to be left out this year)
The Panhandler
Peckerwood
The Plowman
Poetry Magic Publications (suspended publication)
Portable Lower East Side
The Pottersfield Portfolio
Primal Voices (unable to locate)
Pulsar (unable to locate)

Quarry West
Rainbow City Express
Reconstructionist (ceased publication)
Response
Rhino
Rohwedder
Ruby's Pearls
Salad
Salome: A Journal for the Performing Arts (no unsolicited fiction)
Shooting Star Review
The Short Story Digest (out of business)
The Signal
Sonoma Mandala
Sonora Review
Sozoryoku (out of business)
Spindrift
Tal
Tradeswomen
The Twopenny Porringer (out of business)
The Ultimate Writer (com

plaints)
The Unsilenced Voice (asked to be deleted)
Valley Women's Voice
Vandeloecht's Fiction Magazine (ceased publication)
Verve
Viet Nam Generation
The Village Idiot (ceased publication)
Vision (out of business)
Weirdbook (asked to be left out this year)
Willow Springs
Witness
The Wittenberg Review (ceased publication)
The Wolske's Bay Star (undergoing reorganization)
Wordsmith
Working Classics
Writ Magazine
Writers' Rendezvous

International literary and small circulation magazines/'93-'94 changes

Acumen
EOD (The Esoteric Order of Dagon) Magazine (out of business)
Going Down Swinging
Island
Krax Magazine (no fiction)

New Outlook, Middle East Magazine
The New Welsh Review
Nutshell Quarterly
Passport Magazine
Phlogiston
Scarp

Stand Magazine
Tak Tak Tak (asked to be deleted)
Takahe, Quarterly Literary Magazine
The Writers' Rostrum (out of business)

Commercial Periodicals

Redbook, Highlights, Good Housekeeping, Esquire — these are the magazines many of us grew up with, the ones in which those of us who write short fiction dream of being published. And it is in this section, Commercial Periodicals, where you will find listings for these and other popular publications including *Seventeen, Boys' Life* and *Harper's Magazine*. This section includes nearly 200 magazines with circulations of more than 10,000.

In terms of payment, exposure and prestige, commercial periodicals make excellent markets for fiction — but there is a catch. Because these magazines are well-known and often pay well, the competition for publication is very tough. Most commercial publications buy one or two stories an issue, yet every year — every month, in fact — thousands of writers submit to these popular magazines. For this reason detailed information from a few other well-known publications, such as *Playboy*, is pointedly missing from this section. They declined a listing in an effort to avoid receiving more submissions than their staff can reasonably handle. Still others, such as *McCall's*, do not include complete information because, while they printed fiction in the past, they no longer do so.

Despite the odds, however, some talented new writers do break into print through the pages of many of the magazines listed here. Well-respected publications such as *The Atlantic Monthly* and *The New Yorker* continue their listings from year to year and say they are open to both new and established writers. Careful research, professional presentation and, of course, top-quality prose are the keys necessary to help you break into this market.

Types of magazines

We mentioned some of the better-known commercial publications above. In this section you will find a number of popular publications, some for a broad-based, general-interest readership and others for large but select groups of readers — children, women, men, seniors and teenagers. You'll also find several regional publications such as *Buzz* for the Los Angeles area, *The Rhode Islander* for folks in that state and *Lethbridge Magazine*, covering that city and the rest of southern Alberta.

Several large religious magazines are listed here, including the Catholic publication, *Liguorian* and *The Lutheran Journal* and a number of magazines devoted to the interests of particular cultures and outlooks such as the Zionist journal, *Midstream* and the African-American news monthly, *Emerge Magazine*.

This section also includes the top markets for genre fiction and many of these have excellent records for publishing new writers. For example, mystery markets listed in this section include *Ellery Queen's Mystery Magazine, Hitchcock Mystery Magazine* and *New Mystery*. For science fiction, you'll find *Omni, Amazing Stories* and several others. There's even a new market for western stories, the *Louis L'Amour Western Magazine*. These magazines are known to book publishers as fertile ground for budding novelists.

Choosing your market

Unlike smaller journals and publications, most of the magazines listed in this section are available at newsstands and bookstores. Many can also be found in the library and guidelines and sample copies are almost always available by mail. Start your search, then, by familiarizing yourself with the fiction included in the magazines that interest you.

Don't make the mistake of thinking, just because you are familiar with a magazine, that its fiction isn't any different today than when you first saw it. Nothing could be farther from the truth—commercial magazines, no matter how well established, are constantly revising their fiction needs as they strive to reach new readerships and expand their audience base.

If you write a particular type of fiction, you may want to look that subject up in the Category Index for this section. There you will find a list of markets looking for that particular subject. Last year we further refined subject categories within listings so writers can tell more about the specific needs of a publication. For example, a magazine may be listed in the Category Index as taking mystery fiction, but check the listing to find out if only a particular subcategory interests them such as hard-boiled detective stories or police procedurals or English-style cozies.

You may want to use our ranking codes as a guide, especially if you are a new writer. At the end of this introduction is a list of the Roman numeral codes and how we use them.

About the listings

See How to Get the Most out of This Book for information about the material common to all listings in this book. In this section in particular, pay close attention to the number of submissions a magazine receives in a given period and how many they publish in the same period. This will give you a clear picture of how stiff your competition can be.

While many of the magazines listed here take one or two pieces of fiction an issue, some also publish special fiction issues once or twice a year. We have indicated this in the listing information. We also note if the magazine is open to novel excerpts as well as short fiction and we advise novelists to query first before submitting long work.

The Business of Fiction Writing in this book provides the basics of submitting your work. As with all markets listed, professional presentation is a must. Editors at commercial magazines are especially busy and anything you can do to make your manuscript easy-to-read and accessible will help your chances. Most magazines want to see complete manuscripts, but watch for publications in this section who require a query first.

More about the listings

As in the previous section, we've included our own comments in many of the listings here, set off by a bullet (•). Whenever possible, we list the publication's recent awards and honors. We've also included any special information about the publication we feel will help you in determining whether a particular market interests you.

We've used a number of sources for this information including our readers, industry experts and the magazines themselves. One source is *Writer's Digest*'s Fiction 50 list, published in the magazine every other year. The editors select 50 of the top markets for magazine fiction using a wide range of criteria including openness to new writers, amount of fiction published, payment, prestige, treatment of writers and other factors. The next Fiction 50 list appears in the June 1994 issue.

Some of the publishers whose magazines are listed in this section publish more than one publication. We've cross-referenced these so you can easily find sister magazines and any contests sponsored by the magazine also listed in this book.

This year we've added another symbol to our listings. We've identified Canadian listings with a maple leaf (🍁). All North American listings are grouped together first and you'll find a list of commercial publications from other countries following the main section. Remember to use International Reply Coupons rather than stamps when you want a reply from a country other than your own.

For more information

For more on trends in commercial fiction, see our Commercial Fiction Trends Report earlier in this book. For more on commercial magazines in general, see issues of *Writer's Digest* and industry trade publications such as *Folio*, available in larger libraries.

For news about some of the genre publications listed here and information about a particular field, there are a number of magazines devoted to genre topics, including *Mystery Scene*, *Locus* (for science fiction) and *Science Fiction Chronicle*. Addresses for these and other industry magazines can be found in the section Publications of Interest to Fiction Writers.

Membership in the national groups devoted to specific genre fields is not restricted to novelists and can be valuable to writers of short fiction in these fields. Many include awards for "Best Short Story" in their annual contests. For information on groups such as the Mystery Writers of America, the Romance Writers of America and the Science Fiction and Fantasy Writers of America see the Organizations and Resources section.

The ranking system we've used in this section is as follows:

I   **Periodical encourages beginning or unpublished writers to submit work for consideration and publishes new writers regularly.**

II **Periodical publishes work by established writers and by new writers of exceptional talent.**

III **Magazine does not encourage beginning writers; prints mostly writers with previous publication credits and publishes very few new writers.**

IV **Special-interest or regional magazine, open only to writers on certain topics or from certain geographical areas.**

ABORIGINAL SCIENCE FICTION, (II, IV), Box 2449, Woburn MA 01888-0849. Editor: Charles C. Ryan. Magazine: 8½×11; 100-116 pages; 40 lb. paper; 60 lb. cover; 4-color cover and b&w interior illustrations; photos. "*Aboriginal Science Fiction* is looking for good science fiction stories. While 'hard' science fiction will get the most favorable attention, *Aboriginal Science Fiction* also wants good action-adventure stories, *good* space opera, humor and science fantasy for adult science fiction readers." Quarterly. Estab. 1986. Circ. 21,000+.
  • This leading science fiction magazine ranked #43 on the Writer's Digest Fiction 50 list.
Needs: Science fiction. Original, previously unpublished work only. "No fantasy, sword and sorcery, horror, or Twilight-Zone type stories." Receives 250 unsolicited mss/week. Buys 12 mss/issue; 48 mss/ year. Publishes ms 1 year after acceptance. Agented fiction 5%. Published work by Larry Niven, David Brin and Walter Jon Williams; published many new writers within the last year. Length: 2,500 words minimum; 6,000 words maximum. Some shorter material accepted, but "no shorter than 1,500-2,000 words for fiction. Jokes may be 50-150 words." Always comments on rejected mss.
How to Contact: Send complete ms. Reports in 2-3 months. SASE, (IRCs). Sample copy for $4.95 (double issue) plus $1.05 postage and handling. Fiction guidelines for #10 SAE and 1 first-class stamp. Reviews novels and short story collections. Send books to Janice M. Eisen, Apt. 454, 225 State St., Schenectady NY 12305 or Darrell Schweitzer, 113 Deepdale Rd., Strafford PA 19087.
Payment: Pays "$250 flat" and 2 contributor's copies.
Terms: Pays on publication for first North American serial rights and non-exclusive reprint and foreign options.
Advice: "Stories with the best chance of acceptance will make unique use of the latest scientific theories; science ideas; have lively, convincing characters; an ingenious plot; a powerful and well integrated theme, and use an imaginative setting. Read all the science fiction classics and current magazines to understand the field and to avoid clichés."

AIM MAGAZINE, (I, II), 7308 S. Eberhart Ave., Chicago IL 60619. (312)874-6184. Editor: Ruth Apilado. Fiction Editor: Mark Boone. Newspaper: 8½×11; 48 pages; slick paper; photos and illustrations. "Material of social significance: down-to-earth gut. Personal experience, inspirational." For "high school, college and general public." Quarterly. Estab. 1973. Circ. 10,000.

● *Aim* sponsors an annual short story contest listed in this book.

Needs: Open. No "religious" mss. Published special fiction issue last year; plans another. Receives 25 unsolicited mss/month. Buys 15 mss/issue; 60 mss/year. Published work by Thomas J. Cottle, Karl Damgaard, Richie Zeiler; published new writers within the last year. Length: 800-1,000 words average. Publishes short shorts. Sometimes comments on rejected mss.

How to Contact: Send complete ms. SASE (IRCs) with cover letter and author's photograph. Simultaneous submissions OK. Reports in 1 month. Sample copy for $3.50 with SAE (9 × 12) and $1 postage. Fiction guidelines for #10 envelope and 1 first-class stamp. Reviews novels and short story collections occasionally. Send books to fiction editor.

Payment: Pays $15-25.

Terms: Pays on publication for first rights.

Advice: "Search for those who are making unselfish contributions to their community and write about them. Our objective is to purge racism from the human bloodstream. Write about your own experiences." Known for "stories with social significance, proving that people from different ethnic, racial backgrounds are more alike than they are different."

ALOHA, The Magazine of Hawaii and the Pacific, (IV), Davick Publishing Co., Suite 309, 49 S. Hotel St., Honolulu HI 96813. (808)523-9871. Fax: (808)533-2055. Editorial Director: Cheryl Tsutsumi. Magazine about the 50th state. Upscale demographics. Bimonthly. Estab. 1977. Circ. 65,000.

● The publisher of *ALOHA* has published a coffee table book, *The Best of ALOHA*, which won the Grand Award of Excellence in the Hawaii Visitors Bureau Travel Journalism Awards Competition.

Needs: "Only fiction that illuminates the true Hawaiian experience. No stories about tourists in Waikiki or contrived pidgin dialogue." Receives 6 unsolicited mss/month. Publishes ms up to 1 year after acceptance. Length: 1,000-2,500 words average.

How to Contact: Send complete ms. No simultaneous submissions. Reports in 2 months. SASE (IRCs). Sample copy for $2.95.

Payment: Pays between $200-500.

Terms: Pays on publication for first-time rights.

Advice: "Submit only fiction that is truly local in character. Do not try to write anything about Hawaii if you have not experienced this culturally different part of America."

AMAZING® STORIES, (II), TSR, Inc., Box 111, Lake Geneva WI 53147. (414)248-3625. Editor: Mr. Kim Mohan. Magazine: 8⅜ × 10¾; 96 (or more) pages; 80 lb. enamel; 100 lb. Northcote cover stock; perfect-bound; color illustrations; rarely photos. Magazine of science fiction, fantasy and horror fiction stories for adults and young adults. Monthly. Estab. 1926. Circ. 20,000.

● *Amazing Stories* ranked #5 on the latest *Writer's Digest* Fiction 50 list. See our listing for TSR's *Dragon* and for the press listing in this book. An interview with Editor Kim Mohan appears in this section.

Needs: Science fiction (hard science, soft sociological), fantasy, horror. "We prefer science fiction to dominate our content, but will not turn away a well-written story regardless of genre. Low priority to heroic, pseudo-Medieval fantasy; no hack-'n'-slash or teen exploitation horror." Receives 700-1,000 unsolicited fiction mss/month. Buys 8-10 mss/issue; 100-120 mss/year. Publishes ms 4-8 months after acceptance. Agented fiction approximately 5%. Recently published work by Thomas M. Disch, Ursula K. LeGuin, Barry B. Longyear, Jack Dann and Jack Williamson; published new writers within the last year. Length: 1,000 words minimum; 25,000 words maximum; will consider serialization of or excerpts from longer works. Usually critiques rejected mss.

How to Contact: Send complete ms with cover letter (list other professional credits in science fiction, fantasy or horror). Reports in 1-2 months. SASE (IRCs). No simultaneous submissions. Sample copy for $5. Fiction guidelines for #10 SASE.

● *A bullet introduces comments by the editor of* Novel & Short Story Writer's Market *indicating special information about the listing.*

Payment: Pays 6-10¢/word.
Terms: Pays on acceptance for first worldwide rights in the English language. Sends prepublication galleys to author.
Advice: "*AMAZING® Stories* is interested in all forms of science fiction, with an emphasis on strong plot lines and believable characterization. Avoid rehashes of old ideas and stereotypical story lines or characters. We encourage writers to experiment with innovative styles and approaches, but not at the expense of comprehensibility. All of that advice holds true for fantasy and horror as well. Read the magazine and others of its type, to get an idea of the competition you're up against before trying to write for it. Send us a story that deserves to be called Amazing, and we'll find a place for it."

AMERICAN ATHEIST, A Journal of Atheist News and Thought, (II, IV), American Atheist Press, P.O. Box 2117, Austin TX 78768-2117. Editor: R. Murray-O'Hair. Magazine: 8½×11; 56 pages; 40 lb. offset paper; 80 lb. glossy cover; illustrations and photographs. "The *American Atheist* is devoted to the history and lifestyle of atheism, as well as critiques of religion. It attempts to promote an understanding of atheism, while staying aware of religious intrusions into modern life. Most of its articles are aimed at a general—but atheistic—readership. Most readers are college or self-educated." Monthly. Estab. 1958. Circ. 30,000.
Needs: Contemporary, feminist, historical (general), humor/satire, atheist, anti-religious. "All material should have something of particular interest to atheists." No religious fiction; no erotica. Receives 0-6 mss/month. "We would like to publish 1 story per issue; we do *not* receive enough quality mss to do so." Publishes mss "1-3 months" after acceptance. Length: 2,000-3,000 words preferred; 800 words minimum; 5,000 words maximum. Sometimes critiques rejected mss.
How to Contact: Send complete ms with cover letter and biographical material. Reports in 3 months. SASE. Accepts electronic submissions, "WordPerfect compatible or in ASCII. Should be accompanied by printout." Sample copy for 9×12 SAE or label. Fiction guidelines for #10 SASE (IRCs). Reviews novels and short story collections. Send books to book review editor.
Payment: Pays $15/1,000 words, free subscription to the magazine and contributor's copies.
Terms: Pays on acceptance for one-time rights.
Advice: "Submit material carefully after reviewing the publication in question. We receive a lot of submissions that are entirely inappropriate, and this slows down our ability to respond."

THE AMERICAN CITIZEN ITALIAN PRESS, 13681 "V" St., Omaha NE 68137. Editor: Diana C. Failla. Magazine. Quarterly.
Needs: Ethnic, historical (general), sports, celebrity, human interest, mainstream and translations. Receives 4-5 unsolicited mss/month. Buys 1-2 mss/issue. Length: 80 words minimum; 1,200 words maximum. Publishes short shorts.
How to Contact: Send complete ms with cover letter. Reports in 1 month on queries. Simultaneous submissions OK. Sample copy and fiction guidelines for 9×12 SAE (IRCs).
Payment: Pays $20-25.
Terms: Pays on publication for one-time rights.

‡**THE AMERICAN NEWSPAPER CARRIER, (II)**, Box 2225, Kernersville NC 27285. (919)788-4336. Editor: Will H. Lowry. Newsletter: 9×12; 4 pages; slick paper; b&w illustrations and photos. "A motivational newsletter publishing upbeat articles—mystery, humor, adventure and inspirational material for newspaper carriers (younger teenagers, male and female)." Monthly. Estab. 1927.
Needs: Adventure, comics, humor/satire, inspirational, suspense/mystery and young adult/teen. No erotica, fantasy, feminist, gay, juvenile, lesbian, preschool, psychic/supernatural or serialized/excerpted novel. Receives approximately 12 unsolicited mss/month. Buys 1 ms/issue; 12 mss/year. Publishes ms 3-6 months after acceptance. "About all" of fiction is agented. Published new writers within the last year. Length: approximately 1,000 words average; 800 words minimum; 1,200 words maximum. Rarely critiques rejected mss.
How to Contact: Send complete ms. Reports in 1 month. SASE (IRCs). Free sample copy and fiction guidelines with #10 SAE and 1 first-class stamp for each.
Payment: Pays $25.
Terms: Pays on acceptance for all rights.
Advice: "We could use some stories dealing with motor route carriers and adult carriers."

ANALOG SCIENCE FICTION & FACT, (II), Dell Magazines Fiction Group, 1540 Broadway, New York NY 10036. (212)782-8532. Editor: Stanley Schmidt. Magazine: 5³/₁₆×7³/₈; 178 pages; illustrations (drawings); photos. "Well-written science fiction based on speculative ideas and fact articles on topics

INSIDER VIEWPOINT

No More Men on Venus

First published in 1926, *Amazing Stories* is the oldest magazine devoted to science fiction in continuous publication up until today, says Editor Kim Mohan. TSR, the Wisconsin-based book and role-playing game publisher, took over publication in 1982 and in 1991 decided on a change in format from a small, pulp-style magazine to a large, glossy, full-color publication. Along with that change the publisher also decided on a change of editors.

Kim Mohan

"I've always been a science fiction fan—I cut my teeth on Heinlein, Silverberg and Asimov, so it was great when TSR offered me the job," he says. "And it's been a wonderful trip ever since."

Writing and, in fact, editing science fiction are perhaps not as easy today as they were when the magazine first started, says Mohan. "Why? It's occurred to me that a part of the reason is that back in the '20s, '30s, '40s and even the '50s the task was easier because there were lots of things you could imagine . . . men on Venus, men on Jupiter. Now, because we know so much more, these stories don't work anymore."

Mohan adds that he sees a lot more fantasy writing being published these days than science fiction, because "fantasy is open-ended; unlike science fiction it doesn't have to be based in reality. Science fiction can be limiting because there are rules and constraints." On the other side of the coin, he says, we're doing things now in real-world science that are opening up new horizons for writers. "We're learning about nanotechnology, genetic manipulation . . . things that were inconceivable only a few years ago.

"Science fiction readers today are a lot more discerning, a lot more discriminating," he says. "Writers have to do more homework to keep up with what's going on."

Mohan subscribes to the weekly *Science News* to keep in touch with the latest scientific developments in the news, but he says one of the best sources for science information is the newspaper. Writers should subscribe to at least one news weekly, and technical journals and science magazines such as *Omni* can be helpful, too.

Amazing Stories publishes "as much of the legitimate science fiction genre as we can find," says Mohan, but he also is open to some nontraditional fantasy and keeps an open mind about what he considers science fiction.

"It's hard to say what I consider good. It's not preordained. I know what I like, but I try to have no preference for subject matter. The type of presentation or style of work we publish is pretty eclectic. I look for an original idea, but we might even use a story based on an idea that has been used before if it is so well-written we can't turn it down. Basically, we're looking for writers who've done the best job with the best idea."

When asked about the value of science fiction conventions, Mohan says they are good for networking, but their function is mostly social. "The best way to go for a writer is to attend a workshop, one in which a few people bring work and it is critiqued back and forth. These workshops are led by established professionals and you usually get one-on-one help. Writers' groups are good, too. Any feedback you can get from your contemporaries is valuable. You should do this [get feedback] before you show your work to an editor."

The magazine receives 100 to 125 manuscript submissions each week and there are three editors on staff who read them. "I reserve for myself, as first reader, manuscripts by writers with significant credentials, those with stories already published in the field. This is about a quarter of the stories in our slush pile."

The other two editors on staff read the rest of the submissions first and make recommendations. Because there are so many good established writers, the magazine publishes a very small percentage of work from unpublished writers—maybe one story every six to eight months.

Yet, Mohan says, "We try to be open-minded when reading any piece of work. I read everybody's story expecting and hoping it will be a story I want to buy. We want to publish new writers; we make this part of a conscious effort."

Despite the competition, he says, short story writing is the best place to start in the science fiction field. "Many writers who start with short stories go on to six-figure novel contracts. I'd say there are almost no novelists [in this field] today who were not published first in magazines."

—Robin Gee

on the present and future frontiers of research. Our readership includes intelligent laymen and/or those professionally active in science and technology." Thirteen times yearly. Estab. 1930. Circ. 85,000.

● *Analog* is considered one of the leading science fiction publications. The magazine has won a number of Hugos and Nebula Awards. It ranked #6 on the latest *Writer's Digest* Fiction 50 list. *Asimov's* (also listed in this book) is the Dell Magazines' other science fiction publication.

Needs: Science fiction (hard science, soft sociological) and serialized novels. "No stories which are not truly science fiction in the sense of having a plausible speculative idea *integral to the story*. We do two double-size issues per year (January and July)." Receives 300-500 unsolicited fiction mss/month. Buys 4-8 mss/issue. Agented fiction 30%. Published work by Lois McMaster Bujold, Anne McCaffrey, Jerry Oltion, Timothy Zahn and Charles Sheffield; published new writers within the last year. Length: 2,000-80,000 words. Publishes short shorts. Critiques rejected mss "when there is time." Sometimes recommends other markets.

How to Contact: Send complete ms with SASE (IRCs). Cover letter with "anything that I need to know before reading the story, e.g. that it's a rewrite I suggested or that it incorporates copyrighted material. Otherwise, no cover letter is needed." Query with SASE only on serials. Reports in 1 month on both query and ms. No simultaneous submissions. Fiction guidelines for SASE. Sample copy for $2.50. Reviews novels and short story collections. Send books to Tom Easton.

Payment: Pays 5-8¢/word.

Terms: Pays on acceptance for first North American serial rights and nonexclusive foreign rights. Sends galleys to author.

Advice: Mss are rejected because of "inaccurate science; poor plotting, characterization or writing in general. We literally only have room for 1-2% of what we get. Many stories are rejected not because of anything conspicuously *wrong*, but because they lack anything sufficiently *special*. What we buy must stand out from the crowd. Fresh, thought-provoking ideas are important. Familiarize yourself with the magazine—but don't try to imitate what we've already published."

APPALACHIA JOURNAL, (II, IV), Appalachian Mountain Club, 5 Joy St., Boston MA 02108. (617)523-0636. Editor: Sandy Stott. Magazine: 6×9; 160 pages; 50 lb. recycled paper; 10 pt. C1S cover; 5-10 illustrations; 20-30 photographs. "*Appalachia* is the oldest mountaineering and conservation journal in the country. It specializes in backcountry recreation and conservation topics (hiking, canoeing, cross-country skiing, etc.) for outdoor (including armchair) enthusiasts." Semiannual. Estab. 1876. Circ. 10,000.
Needs: Prose, poem, sports. Receives 5-10 unsolicited mss/month. Buys 1-4 mss/issue; 2-8 mss/year. Publishes ms 6-12 months after acceptance. Length: 500-4,000 words average. Publishes short shorts.
How to Contact: Send complete ms with cover letter. No simultaneous submissions. Reports in 1 month on queries; 2 months on mss. SASE (IRCs) for query. Sample copy for $5. Fiction guidelines for #10 SAE.
Payment: Pays contributor's copies. Occasionally pays $100-300 for a feature—usually assigned.
Advice: "All submissions should be related to conservation, mountaineering, and/or backcountry recreation both in the Northeast and throughout the world. Most of our journal is nonfiction. The fiction we publish is mountain-related and often off-beat."

ARIZONA COAST, (II), Hale Communications, Inc., 912 Joshua, Parker AZ 85344. (602)669-6464. Editor: Jerry Hale. Magazine: 5½×8½; 40 pages; 70 lb. gloss; illustrations; photos. Publication prints stories about tourism, old West, lifestyle for young travel-oriented family audiences, snowbirds and senior citizens. Bimonthly. Estab. 1988. Circ. 15,000.
Needs: Condensed/excerpted novel, historical (general), senior citizen/retirement, serialized novel, western. Receives 1 unsolicited ms/month. Accepts 1 ms/issue; 6 mss/year. Publishes ms 6 months after acceptance. Publishes short shorts. Sometimes critiques rejected mss and recommends other markets.
How to Contact: Send complete ms with cover letter. Reports in 2 months. Simultaneous submissions OK. Accepts electronic submissions. Sample copy free. Reviews novels and short story collections.
Payment: Pays free subscription to magazine.
Terms: Acquires one-time rights.
Advice: "Don't give up!"

ART TIMES, A Cultural and Creative Journal, (II), CSS Publications, Inc., 16 Fite Rd., Saugerties NY 12477. (914)246-6944. Fax: Same. Editor: Raymond J. Steiner. Magazine: 12×15; 20 pages; Jet paper and cover; illustrations; photos. "Arts magazine covering the disciplines for an over 40, affluent, arts-conscious and literate audience." Monthly. Estab. 1984. Circ. 15,000.
Needs: Adventure, contemporary, ethnic, fantasy, feminist, gay, historical, humor/satire, lesbian, literary, mainstream and science fiction. "We seek quality literary pieces. Nothing violent, sexist, erotic, juvenile, racist, romantic, political, etc." Receives 30-50 mss/month. Buys 1 ms/issue; 11 mss/year. Publishes ms within 18-24 months of acceptance. Length: 1,500 words maximum. Publishes short shorts.
How to Contact: Send complete ms with cover letter. Simultaneous submissions OK. Reports in 6 months. SASE (IRCs). Sample copy for $1.75, 9×12 SAE and 3 first-class stamps. Fiction guidelines for #10 SAE and 1 first-class stamp.
Payment: Pays $15, free subscription to magazine (one year); 6 contributor's copies.
Terms: Pays on publication for first North American serial rights.
Advice: "Competition is greater (more submissions received), but keep trying. We print new as well as published writers."

ASIMOV'S SCIENCE FICTION, (II), Dell Magazines, 380 Lexington Ave., New York NY 10168-0035. Editor: Gardner Dozois. Managing Editor: Sheila Williams. Magazine: 5³/₁₆×7³/₈ (trim size); 192 pages; 29 lb. newspaper; 70 lb. to 8 pt. C1S cover stock; illustrations; rarely photos. Magazine consists

The double dagger before a listing indicates that the listing is new in this edition. New markets are often the most receptive to submissions by new writers.

of science fiction and fantasy stories for adults and young adults. Published 13 issues/year. Estab. 1977. Circ. 120,000.

● Named for a science fiction "legend," *Asimov's* ranked #2 on the latest *Writer's Digest* Fiction 50 list and regularly receives Hugo and Nebula Awards. Editor Gardner Dozois has received several awards for editing including Hugos and those from *Locus* and *Science Fiction Chronicle* magazines. *Locus* also named *Asimov's* "Best Magazine" in 1993. Dell Magazines' other science fiction magazine is *Analog* also listed in this book.

Needs: Science fiction (hard science, soft sociological) and fantasy. No horror or psychic/supernatural. "We have two double-issues per year (April and November)." Receives approximately 800 unsolicited fiction mss each month. Buys 10 mss/issue. Publishes ms 6-12 months after acceptance. Agented fiction 30%. Published work by George Alec Effinger, Connie Willis, Walter Jon Williams, Gregory Benford and Judith Moffett; published new writers in the last year. Length: up to 20,000 words. Publishes short shorts. Critiques rejected mss "when there is time." Sometimes recommends other markets.

How to Contact: Send complete ms with SASE (IRCs). No simultaneous submissions. Reports in 1-2 months. Fiction guidelines for #10 SASE. Sample copy for $3.50 and 9 × 12 SASE. Reviews novels and short story collections. Send books to book reviewer.

Payment: Pays 6-8¢/word for stories up to 7,500 words; 5¢/word for stories over 12,500; $450 for stories between those limits.

Terms: Pays on acceptance for first North American serial rights plus specified foreign rights, as explained in contract. Very rarely buys reprints. Sends galleys to author.

Advice: "We are looking for character stories rather than those emphasizing technology or science. New writers will do best with a story under 10,000 words. Every new science fiction or fantasy film seems to 'inspire' writers — and this is not a desirable trend. Be sure to be familiar with our magazine and the type of story we like; workshops and lots of practice help. Try to stay away from trite, cliched themes. Start in the middle of the action, starting as close to the end of the story as you possibly can."

THE ASSOCIATE REFORMED PRESBYTERIAN, (II, IV), The Associate Reformed Presbyterian, Inc., 1 Cleveland St., Greenville SC 29601. (803)232-8297. Editor: Ben Johnston. Magazine: 8½ × 11; 32-48 pages; 50 lb. offset paper; illustrations; photos. "We are the official magazine of our denomination. Articles generally relate to activities within the denomination — conferences, department work, etc., with a few special articles that would be of general interest to readers." Monthly. Estab. 1976. Circ. 6,300.

Needs: Contemporary, juvenile, religious/inspirational, spiritual and young adult/teen. "Stories should portray Christian values. No retelling of Bible stories or 'talking animal' stories. Stories for youth should deal with resolving real issues for young people." Receives 30-40 unsolicited fiction mss/month. Buys 1 ms/some months; 10-12 mss/year. Publishes ms within 1 year after acceptance. Recently published work by Lawrence Dorr, J. Michael Sharman and Louise Carroll. Length: 300-750 words (children); 1,250 words maximum (youth). Sometimes critiques rejected mss. Occasionally recommends other markets.

How to Contact: Query and cover letter preferred. Reports in 6 weeks on queries and mss. Simultaneous submissions OK. Sample copy for $1.50; fiction guidelines for #10 SAE and 1 first-class stamp (IRCs).

Payment: Pays $20-50 and contributor's copies.

Terms: Buys first rights.

Advice: "We are using less. Instead of children's short stories of a general nature, we now have a 'theme page' for children."

THE ATLANTIC MONTHLY, (II), (formerly *The Atlantic*), 745 Boylston St., Boston MA 02116. (617)536-9500. Editor: William Whitworth. Senior Editors: Michael Curtis, Jack Beatty. Managing Editor: Cullen Murphy. General magazine for the college educated with broad cultural interests. Monthly. Estab. 1857. Circ. 500,000.

● *The Atlantic Monthly* ranks #1 on the latest *Writer's Digest* Fiction 50 list.

Needs: Literary and contemporary. "Seeks fiction that is clear, tightly written with strong sense of 'story' and well-defined characters." Buys 15-18 stories/year. Receives approximately 1,000 unsolicited fiction mss each month. Published work by Alice Munro, E.S. Goldman, Charles Baxter and T.C. Boyle; published new writers within the last year. Preferred length: 2,000-6,000 words.

How to Contact: Send cover letter and complete ms with SASE (IRCs). Reports in 2 months on mss.
Payment: Pays $2,500/story.
Terms: Pays on acceptance for first North American serial rights.
Advice: When making first contact, "cover letters are sometimes helpful, particularly if they cite prior publications or involvement in writing programs. Common mistakes: melodrama, inconclusiveness, lack of development, unpersuasive characters and/or dialogue."

THE BABY CONNECTION NEWS JOURNAL, (IV), Parent Education for Infant Development, P.O. Drawer 13320, San Antonio TX 78213. Editor: G. Morris-Boyd. Newspaper: 35" web press; 10¾×16; 24 pages; newsprint paper; newsprint cover; illustrations and photographs. "Material on pregnancy, infant sensory development, birthing and breastfeeding for new and expectant parents, midwives, nurses, ob/gyn's." Quarterly. Estab. 1986. Circ. 45,000.
Needs: Humor/satire, mainstream, pregnancy, parenting, romance (contemporary). Receives 40-60 unsolicited mss/month. Accepts 6-7 mss/quarter; 24 mss/year. Publishes ms 2-3 months after acceptance. Published work by Susan Ludington, Vicki Lansky. Length: 800 words average; 800 words minimum; 1,100 words maximum. Publishes short shorts.
How to Contact: Query with clips of published work. Send complete manuscript with cover letter. "Always include a brief personal bio—not all about works published but info on the writer personally. Married? Children? Hobbies? Our readers like to feel they know the writers personally." Simultaneous submissions OK. Reports in 6-9 months. Sample copy for 10×13 SAE with 3 first-class stamps (IRCs) and $3. Fiction guidelines for #10 SAE and 1 first-class stamp and $1.50.
Payment: Pays in contributor's copies. Charges for extras.
Terms: Acquires first rights.
Advice: "Our needs are definitely more focused. We need fiction based on human experience and prefer writing which allows our readers a window to view humanity clearly. Never call an editor to see if work is received. Always send a letter with a SASE if you have any questions regarding your submission. Remember, thousands of reviews are being catalogued at any given time. A phone call shuts down systems."

BALLOON LIFE, The Magazine for Hot Air Ballooning, (II,IV), 2145 Dale Ave., Sacramento CA 95815. (916)922-9648. Editor: Tom Hamilton. Magazine: 8½×11; 48+ pages; 80 lb. Tahoe Gloss; color, b&w photos. "Sport of hot air ballooning. Readers participate in hot air ballooning as pilots, crew, official observers at events and spectators."
Needs: Humor/satire, sports and hot air ballooning. "Manuscripts should involve the sport of hot air ballooning in any aspect." Buys 4-6 mss/year. Publishes ms within 3-4 months after acceptance. Published work by Carl Kohler and Lorna Powers; published new writers within the last year. Length: 800 words minimum; 1,500 words maximum; 1,200 words average. Publishes 400-500 word shorts. Sometimes critiques rejected mss and recommends other markets.
How to Contact: Send complete ms with cover letter that includes Social Security number. Reports in 3 weeks on queries; 2 weeks on mss. SASE (IRCs). Simultaneous and reprint submissions OK. Sample copy for 9×12 SAE and $1.90 postage. Fiction guidelines for #10 SAE and 1 first-class stamp.
Payment: Pays $25-75 and contributor's copies.
Terms: Pays on publication for first North American serial, one-time or other rights. 50-100% kill fee.
Advice: "Generally the magazine looks for humor pieces that can provide a light-hearted change of pace from the technical and current event articles. An example of a work we used was titled 'Balloon Astrology' and dealt with the character of a hot air balloon based on what sign it was born (made) under."

BALTIMORE JEWISH TIMES, (II, IV), 2104 N. Charles St., Baltimore MD 21218. (410)752-3504. Local News Editor: Barbara Pash. Magazine: 160 pages; illustrations; photos. Magazine with subjects of interest to Jewish readers. Weekly. Estab. 1918. Circ. 20,000.
Needs: Contemporary Jewish themes only. Receives 7-10 unsolicited fiction mss/month. Buys 10-15 mss/year. Length: 3,500 words maximum (or 6-15 typed pages). Occasionally critiques rejected mss.
How to Contact: Send complete ms. Simultaneous and previously published submissions OK "on occasion." Reports in 2 months on mss. Sample copy $2 and #10 envelope.
Payment: Pays $35-150.
Terms: Pays on publication.

BECKETT BASEBALL CARD MONTHLY, (IV), Statabase, 15850 Dallas Parkway, Dallas TX 75244. (214)991-6657. Editor: Dr. James Beckett. Fiction Editor: Mike Payne. Magazine: $8^{1}/_{2} \times 11$; 128 pages; coated glossy paper; 8 pt. Sterling cover; 12 illustrations; 100+ photographs. "Collecting baseball cards is a leisure-time avocation. It's wholesome and something the entire family can do together. We emphasize its positive aspects. For card collectors and sports enthusiasts, 6-60." Monthly. Estab. 1984. Circ. 800,000+ paid.

Needs: Humor/satire, sports, young adult/teen (10-18 years). "Sports hero worship; historical fiction involving real baseball figures; fictionalizing specific franchises of national interest such as the Yankees, Dodgers or Mets." No fiction that is "unrealistic sportswise." Publishes ms 4-6 months after acceptance. Length: 1,500 words average; 2,500 words maximum. Publishes short shorts. Sometimes comments on rejected mss or recommends other markets "if we feel we can help the reader close the gap between rejection and acceptance."

How to Contact: Send complete ms with cover letter. Include Social Security number. Reports in 6 weeks. SASE. Will consider reprints "if prior publication is in a very obscure or very prestigious publication." Sample copy for $3. Fiction guidelines free.

Payment: Pays $80-400.

Terms: Pays on acceptance for first rights.

Advice: "Fiction must be baseball oriented and accessible to both pre-teenagers and adults; fiction must stress redeeming social values; fictionalization must involve the heroes of the game (past or present) or a major-league baseball franchise with significant national following. The writer must have a healthy regard for standard English usage. A prospective writer must examine several issues of our publication prior to submission. Our publication is extremely successful in our genre, and our writers must respect the sensitivities of our readers. We are different from other sports publications, and a prospective writer must understand our distinctiveness to make a sale here."

BEPUZZLED, (II, IV), Lombard Marketing, Inc., 22 E. Newberry Rd., Bloomfield CT 06002. (203)769-5700. Editors: Luci Seccareccia and Susan Braun. "Mystery jigsaw puzzles . . . includes short mystery story with clues contained in puzzle picture to solve the mystery for preschool, 8-12 year olds, adults." Estab. 1987.

● Most of the large bookstore chains and specialty shops carry *bePuzzled* and other mystery puzzles. See "Off the Beaten Path" in the 1991 *Novel & Short Story Writer's Market* for more on *bePuzzled*.

Needs: Mystery: Adventure, juvenile, mainstream, preschool, suspense, young adult—all with mystery theme. Receives 3 unsolicited fiction mss/month. Buys 20 mss/year. Publishes ms 6-18 months after acceptance. Recently published work by John Lutz, Matt Christopher, Alan Robbins, Henry Slesar, Katherine Hall Page. Length: 4,000 words preferred; 3,000 words minimum; 4,000 words maximum. Sometimes recommends other markets.

How to Contact: Query for submission guidelines. Reports in 2 months. SASE (IRCs). Simultaneous submissions OK. Fiction guidelines free.

Payment: Pays $200 minimum.

Terms: Payment is made on delivery of final ms. Buys all rights.

Advice: "Thoughtful, challenging mysteries that can be concluded with the visual element of a puzzle. Many times we select certain subject matter and then send out these specifics to our pool of writers . . . List clues and red herrings. Then write the story containing supporting information. Play one of our mystery thrillers so you understand the relationship between the story and the picture."

BIKE REPORT, (I, IV), Bikecentennial, Box 8308, Missoula MT 59807. (406)721-1776. Editor: Daniel D'Ambrosio. Magazine on bicycle touring: $8^{3}/_{8} \times 10^{7}/_{8}$; 24 pages; coated paper; self cover; illustrations and b&w photos. Published 9 times annually. Estab. 1974. Circ. 25,000.

Needs: Adventure, fantasy, historical (general), humor/satire, regional and senior citizen/retirement with a bicycling theme. Buys variable number of mss/year. Published new writers within the last year. Length: 2,000 words average; 1,000 words minimum; 2,500 words maximum. Publishes short shorts. Occasionally comments on a rejected ms.

How to Contact: Send complete ms with SASE (IRCs). Reports in 6 weeks. Simultaneous and previously published submissions OK. Accepts electronic submissions; prefers hard copy with disk submission. Sample copy for $1, 9×12 SAE and 60¢ postage. Fiction guidelines for #10 SAE and 1 first-class stamp.

Payment: Pays $25-65/published page.

Terms: Pays on publication for first North American serial rights.

BLACK BELT, (II), Rainbow Publications, Inc., 24715 Ave. Rockefeller, Valencia CA 91355. (805)257-4066. Executive Editor: Jim Coleman. Magazine: 112 pages. Emphasizes "martial arts for both practitioner and layman." Monthly. Circ. 100,000.
Needs: Martial arts-related, historical and modern-day. Buys 1-2 fiction mss/year. Publishes ms 3 months to 1 year after acceptance. Published work by Glenn Yancey.
How to Contact: Query first. Reports in 2-3 weeks.
Payment: Pays $100-200.
Terms: Pays on publication for first North American serial rights; retains right to republish.

BOMB MAGAZINE, (II), New Art Publications, Suite 1002A, 594 Broadway, New York NY 10012. (212)431-3943. Editor: Betsy Sussler. Magazine: 11 × 14; 100 pages; 70 lb. gloss cover; illustrations and photographs. "Artist-and-writer-edited magazine." Quarterly. Estab. 1981.
• *Bomb* ranked #47 on the latest *Writer's Digest* Fiction 50 list.
Needs: Contemporary, experimental, serialized novel. Publishes "Summer Reading" issue. Receives 40 unsolicited mss/week. Buys 6 mss/issue; 24 mss/year. Publishes ms 3-6 months after acceptance. Agented fiction 20%. Recently published work by Jim Lewis, AM Homes, Sandra Cisneros, Leslie Dick. Length: 10-12 pages average. Publishes interviews.
How to Contact: Send complete manuscript with cover letter. Simultaneous submissions OK. Reports in 4 months on mss. SASE (IRCs). Sample copy $4 with $2.50 postage.
Payment: Pays $100 and contributor's copies.
Terms: Pays on publication for first or one-time rights. Sends galleys to author.

BOSTON REVIEW, (II), Boston Critic Inc., 33 Harrison Ave., Boston MA 02111. Publisher/Editor: Joshua Cohen. "A bimonthly magazine of politics, arts and culture." Tabloid: 11 × 17; 40 pages; jet paper. Estab. 1975. Circ. 20,000.
• *Boston Review* sponsors a fiction contest. See the listing in Contests and Awards.
Needs: Contemporary, ethnic, experimental, literary, prose poem, regional, and translations. Receives 100+ unsolicited fiction mss/month. Buys 4-6 mss/year. Publishes ms an average of 4 months after acceptance. Recently published work by Joyce Carol Oates, Yasunari Kawabata, Stephen Dixon, Heidi Jon Schmidt, Alice Mattison. Length: 4,000 words maximum; 2,000 words average. Publishes short shorts. Occasionally critiques rejected ms.
How to Contact: Send complete ms with cover letter and SASE (IRCs). "You can almost always tell professional writers by the very thought-out way they present themselves in cover letters. But even a beginning writer should find some link between the work (its style, subject, etc.) and the publication—some reason why the editor should consider publishing it." Reports in 2-4 months. Simultaneous submissions OK (if noted). Sample copy for $4. Reviews novels and short story collections. Send books to Kim Cooper, managing editor.
Payment: Pays $50-100 and 5 contributor's copies.
Terms: Pays after publication for first rights.
Advice: "We believe that original fiction is an important part of our culture—and that this should be represented by the *Boston Review*."

✿**BOWBENDER, Canada's Archery Magazine, (II, IV),** Suite 600, 237 8th Ave. S.E., Calgary, Alberta T2G 5C3 Canada. (403)264-3270. Fax: (403)264-3276. Editor: Chris Matisajk. Magazine: 8¼ × 10⅞; 48 pages; 60 lb. gloss stock; 100 lb. gloss cover; illustrations; photos. "We publish material dealing with hunting, wildlife, conservation, equipment, nature and Olympic team coverage etc., for outdoorsmen, especially hunters and competitive archers." Published 6 times/year. Estab. 1984. Circ. 25,000.
Needs: Adventure, sports and western. "*Might* publish fiction if it concerns (bow) hunting, archery or traveling in the Canadian outdoors." Does not want to see anything veering off the topic of archery in Canada. Publishes ms within 1 year after acceptance. Length: 1,200 words average; 500 words minimum; 2,000 words maximum.
How to Contact: Query first or send complete ms with cover letter, which should include a brief autobiography (archery) to be included in the magazine. Reports in 1 week on queries; 3 weeks on mss. SASE (IRCs) for ms. Sample copy for $2.95 (Canadian), 9 × 12 SAE and $1.34 (Canadian postage). Editorial/Photography guidelines for #10 SAE and 42¢ (Canadian), 30¢ (U.S.) postage.
Payment: Pays $300 maximum. (Roughly 10¢/word depending on regularity of submission, quality photo complement, etc.) Free contributor's copies; charge for extras.
Terms: Pays on publication for first North American serial rights, or first Canadian if requested and acceptable.
Advice: "Fiction remains a 'big' maybe. Write for guidelines and review a sample copy first."

BOWHUNTER MAGAZINE, The Magazine for the Hunting Archer, (IV), Cowles Magazines, Inc., Box 8200, Harrisburg PA 17105. (717)657-9555. Fax: (717)657-9526. Editor: M.R. James. Publisher: Dave Canfield. Managing Editor: Richard Cochran. Magazine: 8¼×10¾; 150 pages; 75 lb. glossy paper; 150 lb. glossy cover stock; illustrations and photographs. "We are a special interest publication for people who hunt with the bow and arrow. We publish hunting adventure and how-to stories. Our audience is predominantly male, 30-50, middle income." Bimonthly. Circ. 200,000.
Needs: Bowhunting, outdoor adventure. "Writers must expect a very limited market. We buy only one or two fiction pieces a year. Writers must know the market—bowhunting—and let that be the theme of their work. No 'me and my dog' types of stories; no stories by people who have obviously never held a bow in their hands." Receives 1-2 unsolicited fiction mss/month. Buys 1-2 mss/year. Publishes ms 3 months to 2 years after acceptance. Length: 1,500 words average; 500 words minimum; 2,000 words maximum. Publishes short shorts. Length: 500 words. Sometimes critiques rejected mss and recommends other markets.
How to Contact: Query first or send complete ms with cover letter. Reports in 2 weeks on queries; 4 weeks on mss. Sample copy for $2 and 8½×11 SAE (IRCs) with appropriate postage. Fiction guidelines for #10 SAE and 1 first-class stamp.
Payment: Pays $100-350.
Terms: Pays on acceptance for first North American serial rights.
Advice: "We have a resident humorist who supplies us with most of the 'fiction' we need. But if a story comes through the door which captures the essence of bowhunting and we feel it will reach out to our readers, we will buy it. Despite our macho outdoor magazine status, we are a bunch of English majors who love to read. You can't bull your way around real outdoor people—they can spot a phony at 20 paces. If you've never camped out under the stars and listened to an elk bugle and try to relate that experience without really experiencing it, someone's going to know. We are very specialized; we don't want stories about shooting apples off people's heads or of Cupid's arrow finding its mark. James Dickey's *Deliverance* used bowhunting metaphorically, very effectively . . . while we don't expect that type of writing from everyone, that's the kind of feeling that characterizes a good piece of outdoor fiction."

BOYS' LIFE, For All Boys, (II), Boy Scouts of America, Magazine Division, Box 152079, 1325 Walnut Hill Lane, Irving TX 75015-2079. (214)580-2000. Fiction Editor: Kathleen V. DaGroomes. Magazine: 8×11; 68 pages; slick cover stock; illustrations; photos. "*Boys' Life* covers Boy Scout activities and general interest subjects for ages 8 to 18, Boy Scouts, Cub Scouts and others of that age group." Monthly. Estab. 1911. Circ. 1,300,000.
• *Boys' Life* ranked #20 on the latest *Writer's Digest* Fiction 50 list. The magazine has received numerous awards including First Place in the 1991 Merit Magazine Award Competition sponsored by the Society of Children's Book Writers and Illustrators.
Needs: Adventure, humor/satire, mystery/suspense (young adult), science fiction, sports and western (young adult). "We publish short stories aimed at a young adult audience and frequently written from the viewpoint of a 10- to 16-year-old boy protagonist." Receives approximately 150 unsolicited mss/month. Buys 12-18 mss/year. Recently published work by Donald J. Sobol, Geoffrey Norman, G. Clifton Wisler and Marlys Stapelbroek; published new writers within the last year. Length: 500 words minimum; 1,500 words maximum; 1,200 words average. "Very rarely" critiques rejected ms.
How to Contact: Send complete ms with SASE (IRCs). "We'd much rather see manuscripts than queries." Reports in 6 weeks. Simultaneous submissions OK. For sample copy "check your local library." Writer's guidelines available; send SASE.
Payment: Pays $500 and up, "depending on length and writer's experience with us."
Terms: Pays on acceptance for one-time rights.
Advice: "*Boys' Life* writers understand the readers. They treat them as intelligent human beings with a thirst for knowledge and entertainment. We tend to use some of the same authors repeatedly because their characters, themes, etc., develop a following among our readers."

‡BREAD (II), Church of the Nazarene, 6401 The Paseo, Kansas City MO 64131. (816)333-7000. Fax: (816)333-1683. Editor: Karen De Sollar. Magazine: 8½×11; 34 pages; illustrations; photos. Christian leisure reading magazine for junior and senior high students. Monthly. Circ. 18,000.
Needs: Fiction and how-to stories on Christian living. Themes should be school and church oriented, but without sermonizing. Buys 25 mss/year. Published work by Alan Cliburn, Jeanette D. Gardner, Betty Everette and Mike LaCrosse; published new writers within the last year.

How to Contact: Send complete ms with SASE (IRCs). Reports in 6 weeks on mss. Sample copy for $1, 9 × 12 SAE and 45¢ postage. Free guidelines for SASE.
Payment: Pays 4¢/word for first rights and 3.5¢/word for second rights.
Terms: Pays on acceptance for first rights and second serial rights. Accepts simultaneous submissions. Byline given.
Advice: "Our readers clamor for fiction."

BUFFALO SPREE MAGAZINE, (II, IV), Spree Publishing Co., Inc., 4511 Harlem Rd., Buffalo NY 14226. (716)839-3405. Editor: Johanna V. Shotell. "City magazine for professional, educated and above-average income people." Quarterly. Estab. 1967. Circ. 21,000.
Needs: Literary, contemporary, feminist, mystery, adventure, humor and ethnic. No pornographic or religious. Buys about 15 mss/issue; 60 mss/year. Length: 2,500 words maximum.
How to Contact: Send complete ms with SASE (IRCs). Reports within 3-6 months. Sample copy for $2, 9 × 12 SASE and $2.40 postage.
Payment: Pays $80-150; 1 contributor's copy.
Terms: Pays on publication for first rights.

‡BUGLE, Journal of Elk and the Hunt, (II, IV), Rocky Mountain Elk Foundation, P.O. Box 8249, Missoula MT 59807-8249. (406)523-4568. Fax: (406)523-4550. Editor: Dan Crockett. Magazine: 8½ × 11; 114-156 pages; 55 lb. Escanaba paper; 80 lb. Sterling cover; b&w, 4-color illustrations and photographs. "The Rocky Mountain Elk Foundation is a nonprofit conservation organization, established in 1984 to help conserve critical habitat for elk and other wildlife. *Bugle*, the Foundation's quarterly magazine specializes in articles, research, stories (fiction and nonfiction), art and photography pertaining to the world of elk and elk hunting." Quarterly. Estab. 1984.
Needs: Adventure, childrens/juvenile (5-9 years, 10-12 years), historical (general), westerns (frontier). Receives 1-5 unsolicited mss/month. Accepts 1 ms/issue; 4-8 mss/year. Publishes ms 6 months after acceptance. Recently published work by Don Burgess and Mike Logan. Length: 2,500 words preferred; 1,500 words minimum; 5,000 words maximum. Publishes short shorts. Also publishes literary essays and poetry. Sometimes critiques or comments on rejected mss.
How to Contact: Query first or send complete ms with a cover letter. Should include estimated word count and bio (100 words). Reports in 2-4 weeks on queries; 4-6 weeks on ms. Send SASE (IRCs) for reply, return of ms or send a disposable copy of ms. Simultaneous, reprint and electronic submissions OK. Sample copy for $5. Writers guidelines free.
Payment: Pays 15¢/word maximum or 3 contributor's copies.
Terms: Pays on acceptance for one-time rights.
Advice: "We accept fiction and nonfiction stories about elk that show originality, and respect for the animal and its habitat. No 'formula' outdoor writing. No how-to writing."

BUZZ, The Talk of Los Angeles, (II, IV), Buzz Inc., 11835 W. Olympic #450, Los Angeles CA 90064. (310)473-2721. Fax: (310)473-2876. Editor: Allan Mayer. Fiction Editor: Renée Vogel. Magazine: 9 × 10⅞; 96-120 pages; coated paper. Published 10 times/year. Estab. 1990. Circ. 70,000.
Needs: Literary, mainstream/contemporary, regional. Receives 75-100 unsolicited mss/month. Buys 1 ms/issue; 10 mss/year. Published work by Frederic Raphael, Charles Bukowski, Barry Gifford, Amy Gerstler. Length: 2,000 words minimum; 5,000 words maximum. Also publishes literary essays. Sometimes critiques or comments on rejected mss.
How to Contact: Send complete ms with a cover letter. Reports on mss in 2 months. SASE (IRCs) for return of ms. Simultaneous and electronic submissions OK. Sample copy for $2.50, 11 × 14 SAE and $2.90 postage. Fiction guidelines for SASE. Send books to Renée Vogel.
Payment: Pays $500-3,000 and contributor's copies.
Terms: Buys first North American serial rights. Sends galleys to author.
Advice: "Only interested in fiction by L.A. writers or about L.A."

‡CALLIOPE, World History for Young People, (II, IV), Cobblestone Publishing, Inc., 7 School St., Peterborough NH 03458. Editor-in-Chief: Carolyn P. Yoder. Department. Magazine. "*Calliope* covers world history (east/west) and lively, original approaches to the subject are the primary concerns of the editors in choosing material. For 8-14 year olds." Bimonthly. Estab. 1990. Circ. 12,000.
● Cobblestone Publishing also publishes the children's magazines *Cobblestone, Faces* and *Odyssey* listed in this book. An interview with Carolyn P. Yoder appeared in the 1993 *Children's Writer's and Illustrator's Market*.

"Our covers always feature celebrities who embody some aspect of the sensibility that we feel characterizes the new reality of Los Angeles—a city that is no longer just an entertainment capital, but a bona fide world capital," says Buzz Literary Editor Renee Vogel. Actress Barbara Hershey, featured on this cover, is "articulate, intelligent and outspoken—just like the city in which she lives," says Vogel. Buzz's fiction section, "L.A. Tales," features local writers. Vogel says the purpose is to help these writers develop their talents and "encourage the growing West Coast literary sensibility." (Cover photo by Firooz Zahedi. Photo copyright © 1993 Buzz Inc.)

Needs: Material must fit upcoming theme; write for themes and deadlines. Childrens/juvenile (8-14 years). "Authentic historical and biographical fiction, adventure, retold legends, etc. relating to the theme." Published after theme deadline. Length: 800 words maximum. Publishes short shorts. Also publishes poetry.

How to Contact: Query first or query with clips of published work (if new to *Calliope*). Should include estimated word count and 1-page outline explaining information to be presented, extensive bibliography of materials used. Reports in several months (if interested, response 5 months before publication date). Send SASE (IRCs) for reply (writers may send a stamped reply postcard to find out if query has been received). Sample copy for $3.95, 7½ × 10½ SAE and $1.05 postage. Guidelines for #10 SAE and 1 first-class stamp.

Payment: Pays 10-17¢/word.

Terms: Pays on publication for all rights.

CAMPUS LIFE MAGAZINE, (II), Christianity Today, Inc., 465 Gundersen Drive, Carol Stream IL 60188. (312)260-6200. Fax: (708)260-0114. Editor: James Long. Senior Editor: Christopher Lutes. Magazine: 8¼ × 11¼; 100 pages; 4-color and b&w illustrations; 4-color and b&w photos. "General interest magazine with a Christian point of view." Articles "vary from serious to humorous to current trends and issues, for high school and college age readers." Monthly except combined May-June and July-August issues. Estab. 1942. Circ. 130,000.

● *Campus Life* regularly receives awards from the Evangelical Press Association.

Needs: Condensed novel, humor/satire, prose poem, serialized/excerpted novel. "All submissions must be contemporary, reflecting the teen experience in the 90s. We are a Christian magazine but are *not* interested in sappy, formulaic, sentimentally religious stories. We *are* interested in well crafted stories that portray life realistically, stories high school and college youth relate to. Nothing contradictory of Christian values. If you don't understand our market and style, don't submit." Buys 5 mss/year. Reading and response time slower in summer. Recently published work by Barbara Durkin, Tracy Dalton; published new writers within the last year. Length: 1,000-3,000 words average, "possibly longer." Publishes short shorts.

How to Contact: Query with short synopsis of work, published samples and SASE (IRCs). Does not accept unsolicited mss. Reports in 4-6 weeks on queries. Sample copy $2 and 9½ × 11 envelope.

Payment: Pays "generally" $250-400; 2 contributor's copies.

Terms: Pays on acceptance for one-time rights.

Advice: "We print finely crafted fiction that carries a contemporary teen (older teen) theme. First person fiction often works best. Ask us for sample copy with fiction story. Fiction communicates to our reader. We want experienced fiction writers who have something to say to or about young people without getting propagandistic."

☘CANADIAN MESSENGER, (IV), Apostleship of Prayer, 661 Greenwood Ave., Toronto, Ontario M4J 4B3 Canada. (416)466-1195. Editors: Rev. F.J. Power, S.J.; Alfred De Manche. Magazine: 7×10; 32 pages; glossy paper; self cover; illustrations; photos. Publishes material with a "religious theme or a moral about people, adventure, heroism and humor, for Roman Catholic adults." Monthly. Estab. 1891. Circ. 17,000.
  ● The Apostleship of Prayer also publishes *Messenger of the Sacred Heart* listed in this book.
Needs: Religious/inspirational. Receives 10 mss/month. Buys 1 ms/issue. Publishes ms within 1-1½ years of acceptance. Length: 500 words minimum; 1,500 words maximum.
How to Contact: Send complete ms with cover letter. No simultaneous submissions. Reports on mss in "a few" weeks. SASE (IRCs). Sample copy for $1. Fiction guidelines for $1 and 7½×10½ SAE.
Payment: Pays 4¢/word.
Terms: Pays on acceptance for first North American rights.

CAPPER'S, (II), Stauffer Communications 1503 S.W. 42nd St., Topeka KS 66609-1265. (913)274-4300. Fax: (913)274-4305. Editor: Nancy Peavler. Magazine: 24-48 pages; newsprint paper and cover stock; photos. A "clean, uplifting and nonsensational newspaper for families from children to grandparents." Biweekly. Estab. 1879. Circ. 375,000.
  ● Stauffer Communications also publishes *Grit* listed in this book.
Needs: Serialized novels. "We accept only novel-length stories for serialization. No fiction containing violence, sexual references or obscenity." Receives 2-3 unsolicited fiction mss each month. Buys 2-3 stories/year. Published work by Juanita Urbach, Colleen L. Reece, John E. Stolberg; published new writers within the last year.
How to Contact: Send complete ms with SASE (IRCs). Cover letter and/or synopsis helpful. Reports in 5-6 months on ms. Sample copy for $1.
Payment: Pays $75-400 for one-time serialization and contributor's copies (1-2 copies as needed for copyright).
Terms: Pays on acceptance for second serial (reprint) rights and one-time rights.
Advice: "Please proofread and edit carefully. We've seen major characters change names partway through the manuscript."

CAREER FOCUS, COLLEGE PREVIEW, DIRECT AIM, JOURNEY, VISIONS, (IV), Communications Publishing Group, Inc., 106 W. 11th St., #250, Kansas City MO 64105-1806. Editor: Georgia Clark. Magazines: 70 pages; 50 lb. paper; gloss enamel cover; 8×10 or 5×7 (preferred) illustrations; camera ready photographs. *Career Focus*, "For Today's Professionals" includes career preparation, continuing education and upward mobility skills for advanced Black and Hispanic college students and college graduates. Annually. *College Preview*, "For College-Bound Students" is designed to inform and motivate Black and Hispanic high school students on college preparation and career planning. *Direct Aim*, "A Resource for Career Strategies," is designed for Black and Hispanic college students. Discusses career preparation advancement and management strategies as well as life-enhancement skills. Quarterly. Circ. 600,000. *Journey*, "A Success Guide for College and Career-Bound Students" is for Asian American high school and college students who have indicated a desire to pursue higher education through college, vocational/technical or proprietary schools. Semiannually. *Visions*, "A Success Guide for Career-Bound Students" is designed for Native American students who want to pursue a higher education through college, vocational/technical or proprietary schools. Semiannually. Specialized publication limited to certain subjects or themes.
Needs: Adventure, condensed/excerpted novel, contemporary, ethnic, experimental, historical (general), humor/satire, prose poem, romance (contemporary, historical, young adult), science fiction, sports, suspense/mystery. Receives 2-3 unsolicited mss/month. Buys 2-4 mss/year. After acceptance of ms, time varies before it is published. Length: 1,000 words minimum; 4,000 words maximum. Publishes short shorts. Does not usually comment on rejected ms.
How to Contact: Query with clips of published work (include Social Security number) or send copy of resume and when available to perform. Reports in 4-6 weeks. SASE (IRCs). Simultaneous and reprint submissions OK. Sample copy and fiction guidelines for 9×10 SASE.

 The maple leaf symbol before a listing indicates a Canadian publisher.

Payment: Pays 10¢ per word.
Terms: Pays on acceptance for first rights and second serial (reprint) rights.
Advice: "Today's fiction market is geared toward stories that are generated from real-life events because readers are more sophisticated and aware of current affairs. But because everyday life is quite stressful nowadays, even young adults want to escape into science fiction and fairytales. Fiction should be entertaining and easy to read. Be aware of reader audience. Material should be designed for status-conscious young adults searching for quality and excellence. Do not assume readers are totally unsophisticated and avoid casual mention of drug use, alcohol abuse or sex. Avoid overly ponderous, overly cute writing styles. We are an ethnic market so fiction cannot be obviously anglo. Query describing the topic and length of proposed article. Include samples of published work if possible. Must be typed, double spaced on white bond paper (clean copy only)."

CAT FANCY, (IV), Fancy Publications, P.O. Box 6050, Mission Viejo CA 92690. (714)855-8822. Editor: Debbie Phillips-Donaldson. General cat and kitten magazine, for "people interested in the responsible care of their pets." Monthly. Circ. 298,000.
Needs: Cat-related themes only. "Stories should focus on a cat or cats, not just be about people who happen to have a cat." Receives approximately 40 unsolicited fiction mss/month. Accepts 3-4 mss/year. Publishes ms 2-10 months after acceptance. Agented fiction 10%. Published work by Barbara L. Diamond, Edward W. Clarke and Sandi Fisher; published new writers within the last year. Length: 3,000 words maximum. Sometimes recommends other markets.
How to Contact: "Please query first, and enclose copies of published clips, if available." No simultaneous submissions. Reports in 2-3 months. SASE (IRCs). Sample copy for $4.50. Fiction guidelines for SASE.
Payment: Pays 5-10¢/word and 2 contributor's copies.
Terms: Rarely buys reprints.
Advice: "Don't let rejections discourage you. We reject many well-written stories because we simply don't have space for them all. At the same time, don't assume your story is beyond reproach. Seek out the opinions of teachers and of writers you respect—and not just those who will be kind to you. Do the best you can to 'develop backbone' and to look hard at your work. Then consider the market of the magazine in which you want to be published. Send out your story and if rejected, revise or choose another market and try, try again. Remember: You never really fail until you stop trying."

CHANGES, The Magazine for Personal Growth, (II), U.S. Journal Inc., 3201 SW 15th St., Deerfield Beach FL 33442. (305)360-0909. Managing Editor: Jeffrey Laign. Magazine: 8½ × 11; 92 pages; slick paper; glossy cover; illustrations; photos. "Fiction often deals with growth and recovery from painful past, or character change through realization." Bimonthly. Estab. 1986. Circ. 100,000.
Needs: "Quality, professional fiction, typed, double-spaced." Receives 50 mss/month. Buys 6 mss/year. Publishes ms within several months of acceptance. Agented fiction 5%. Recently published work by Carol Konek, Elizabeth Benedict. Length: 2,000 words maximum. Publishes short shorts.
How to Contact: Query with clips of published work or send complete ms with cover letter which should include Social Security number and "a short professional bio." Reports in 3 months. SASE. No simultaneous submissions. Sample copy for $3.95 and SASE. Fiction guidelines for #10 SAE and 1 first-class stamp.
Payment: Pays 15¢/word.
Terms: Pays on publication for first North American serial rights. Publication copyrighted.
Advice: "Too much of the fiction we read is superficial and imitative. We're looking for bold new writers who have something to say."

❋CHICKADEE, The Magazine for Young Children from OWL, (II), Young Naturalist Foundation, Suite 306, 56 The Esplanade, Toronto, Ontario M5E 1A7 Canada. (416)868-6001. Fax: (416)868-6009. Editor: Lizann Flatt. Magazine: 8½ × 11¾; 32 pages; glossy paper and cover stock; illustrations and photographs. "*Chickadee* is created to give children under nine a lively, fun-filled look at the world around them. Each issue has a mix of activities, puzzles, games and stories." Monthly except July and August. Estab. 1979. Circ. 130,000.
 • *Chickadee* has won several awards including the 1991 EDPRESS Golden Lamp Honor award and the Parents' Choice Golden Seal Award.
Needs: Juvenile. No religious or anthropomorphic material. Buys 1 ms/issue; 10 mss/year. Publishes ms an average of 1 year after acceptance. Published new writers within the last year. Length: 300 words minimum; 800 words maximum; 500 words average.

How to Contact: Send complete ms and cover letter with $1 to cover postage and handling. Simultaneous submissions OK. Reports in 2 months. Sample copy for $4.50. Free fiction guidelines for SAE.
Payment: Pays $25-250 (Canadian); 2 contributor's copies.
Terms: Pays on acceptance for all rights. Occasionally buys reprints.
Advice: "Read back issues to see what types of fiction we publish. Common mistakes include: loose, rambling and boring prose; stories that lack a clear beginning, middle and end; unbelievable characters; and overwriting."

CHILD LIFE, (IV), Children's Better Health Institute, Box 567, 1100 Waterway Blvd., Indianapolis IN 46206. (317)636-8881. Editor: Stan Zukowski. Juvenile magazine for youngsters ages 9-11. Looking for adventure, humor, contemporary situations, folk and fairy tales and especially stories that deal with an aspect of health, nutrition, exercise (sports) or safety.
  ● The Children's Better Health Institute also publishes *Children's Digest, Children's Playmate, Humpty Dumpty, Jack and Jill* and *Turtle* magazines listed in this book.
Needs: Juvenile. No adult or adolescent fiction. Published work by Nancy Sweetland, Ben Westfried, Joseph Sherman and Eileen Spinelli; published new writers within the last year. Length: 1,000 words maximum.
How to Contact: Send complete ms with SASE (IRCs). Reports in 8-10 weeks. Sample copy $1.25. Writer's guidelines for SASE.
Payment: Approximately 10¢/word for all rights.
Terms: Pays on publication.
Advice: "Always keep in mind your audience's attention span and interests: grab their attention quickly, be imaginative, and try to make your dialogue free and as natural as possible. We are staying away from heavy narrative. Writers who make liberal use of dialogue to expound situations are more likely to be taken seriously."

CHILDREN'S DIGEST, (II, IV), Children's Better Health Institute, P.O. Box 567, 1100 Waterway Blvd., Indianapolis IN 46206. Editor: Elizabeth A. Rinck. Magazine: 6½ × 9; 48 pages; reflective and preseparated illustrations; color and b&w photos. Magazine with special emphasis on health, nutrition, exercise and safety for preteens.
  ● Other magazines published by Children's Better Health Institute and listed in this book are *Child Life, Children's Playmate, Humpty Dumpty, Jack and Jill* and *Turtle.*
Needs: "Realistic stories, short plays, adventure and mysteries. We would like to see more stories that reflect today's society: concern for the environment, single-parent families and children from diverse backgrounds. Humorous stories are highly desirable. We especially need stories that *subtly* encourage readers to develop better health or safety habits. Stories should not exceed 1,500 words." Receives 40-50 unsolicited fiction mss each month. Recently published work by Judith Josephson, Pat McCarthy, Sharen Liddell; published new writers within the last year.
How to Contact: Send complete ms with SASE (IRCs). "A cover letter isn't necessary unless an author wishes to include publishing credits and special knowledge of the subject matter." Reports in 10 weeks. Sample copy for $1.25. Guidelines with SASE.
Payment: Pays 10¢/word minimum with up to 10 contributor's copies.
Terms: Pays on publication for all rights.
Advice: "We try to present our health-related material in a positive—not a negative—light, and we try to incorporate humor and a light approach wherever possible without minimizing the seriousness of what we are saying. Fiction stories that deal with a health theme need not have health as the primary subject but should include it in some way in the course of events. Most rejected health-related manuscripts are too preachy or they lack substance. Children's magazines are not training grounds where authors learn to write 'real' material for 'real' readers. Because our readers frequently have limited attention spans, it is very important that we offer them well-written stories."

CHILDREN'S PLAYMATE, (IV), Children's Better Health Institute, P.O. Box 567, 1100 Waterway Blvd., Indianapolis IN 46206. (317)636-8881. Editor: Elizabeth A. Rinck. Magazine: 6¹/₂×9; 48 pages; preseparated and reflective art; b&w and color illustrations. Juvenile magazine for children ages 6-8 years.
  ● *Child Life, Children's Digest, Humpty Dumpty, Jack and Jill* and *Turtle* magazines are also published by Children's Better Health Institute and listed in this book.
Needs: Juvenile with special emphasis on health, nutrition, safety and exercise. "Our present needs are for short, entertaining stories with a subtle health angle. Seasonal material is also always welcome." No adult or adolescent fiction. Receives approximately 150 unsolicited fiction mss each month. Re-

cently published work by Batta Killion, Ericka Northrop, Elizabeth Murphy-Melas; published new writers within the last year. Length: 700 words or less.
How to Contact: Send complete ms with SASE (IRCs). Indicate word count on material. Reports in 8-10 weeks. Sample copy for $1.25.
Payment: Pays up to 15¢/word and up to 10 contributor's copies.
Terms: Pays on publication for all rights.
Advice: "Stories should be kept simple and entertaining. Study past issues of the magazine—be aware of vocabulary limitations of the readers."

CHRISTIAN SINGLE, (II), Baptist Sunday School Board, 127 Ninth Ave, North, MSN 140, Nashville TN 37234. (615)251-2228. Magazine: 8½×11; 50 pages; illustrations; photographs. "We reflect the doctrine and beliefs of evangelical Christian single adults. We prefer positive, uplifting, encouraging fiction written from the single perspective." Monthly. Estab. 1979. Circ. 75,000.
Needs: Religious/inspirational. Receives 1 unsolicited ms/month. Buys 1 ms/issue; 4-5 mss/year. Length: 600-1,200 words average. Publishes short shorts and poetry.
How to Contact: Send query with SASE (IRCs). Should include estimated word count and opening paragraph. Reports in 1-2 weeks on queries; 3-6 weeks on mss. Send SASE for reply, return of ms or send a disposable copy of the ms. No simultaneous submissions. Accepts reprint and electronic submissions. Sample copy for 9×12 SAE and 4 first-class stamps.
Payment: Payment is "negotiable."
Terms: Pays on acceptance. Buys all rights, first rights, first North American serial rights or one-time rights.
Advice: Looks for mss intended for a single audience that are not preachy. Write to evoke an emotion. No Pollyanna stories please. I want stories of "real" life with "real" people finding real answers using biblical principles."

CLUBHOUSE, Your Story Hour, (II), Box 15, Berrien Springs MI 49103. (616)471-3701. Editor-in-Chief: Elaine Trumbo. Magazine: 8½×11; 8 pages; 60 lb. offset paper; self cover stock; illustrations and some photos. "A Christian magazine designed to help young people feel good about themselves. Our primary goal is to let them know there is a God and that He loves kids. Stories are non-moralistic in tone and full of adventure." Readers are "children 9-14 years old. Stories are selected for the upper end of the age range. Primary audience—kids without church affiliation." Published 12 times/year. Estab. 1951 under former name *The Good Deeder*. Circ. 6,000.
Needs: Adventure, contemporary, historical (general), religious, young adult/teen. No Christmas stories that refer to Santa, elves, reindeer, etc. No Halloween/occult stories. Receives 250 unsolicited fiction mss/month. Buys 2-3 mss/issue, 24-30 mss/year. Reads mss in March and April only. Publishes ms 6-18 months after acceptance. Published new writers within the last year. Length: 1,000-1,200 words. Occasionally critiques rejected mss and recommends other markets.
How to Contact: Send complete ms in March and April. Reports in 2 months. SASE (IRCs) always. Simultaneous submissions and previously published work OK. Sample copy with 6×9 SAE and 3 first-class stamps. Fiction guidelines for #10 SAE and 1 first-class stamp.
Payment: Pays $25-35 and contributor's copies.
Terms: Pays within 6 months for any rights offered. Buys reprints.
Advice: "Especially interested in stories in which children are responsible, heroic, kind, etc., not stories in which children are pushed into admitting that a parent, sibling, friend, etc., was right all along. I want upbeat, fun, exciting stories. Do not mention church, Sunday School, etc., just because this is a Christian magazine. General tone of the magazine is warmth, not criticism. Remember that a story should follow a plot sequence and be properly wrapped up at the end. Most stories I reject involve kids who have regrettable turns of behavior which they finally change, appeal to a too-young age group, are preachy, are the wrong length or lack sparkle. Fiction can be more exact than truths, because details can be fashioned to complete the plot which might by necessity be omitted if the account were strictly factual."

‡COBBLESTONE, The History Magazine for Young People, (IV), 7 School St., Peterborough NH 03458. Magazine. "Historical accuracy and lively, original approaches to the subject are primary concerns of the editors in choosing material. For 8-14 year olds." Monthly (except July and August). Estab. 1979. Circ. 42,000.
 ● *Calliope, Faces* and *Odyssey*, other children's magazines published by Cobblestone Publishing, Inc, are also listed in this book.

Needs: Material must fit upcoming theme; write for theme list and deadlines. Childrens/juvenile (8-14 years). "Authentic historical and biographical fiction, adventure, retold legends, etc., relating to the theme." Upcoming themes available for SASE (IRCs). Published after theme deadline. Accepts 1-2 fiction mss/issue. Length: 800 words maximum. Publishes short shorts. Also publishes poetry.

How to Contact: Query first or query with clips of published work (if new to *Cobblestone*). Should include estimated word count. "Include detailed outline explaining the information to be presented in the article and bibliography of material used." Reports in several months. If interested, response to queries five months before publication date. Send SASE (IRCs) for reply or send self-addressed postcard to find out if query was received. Sample copy for $3.95, 7½×10½ SAE and $1.05 postage. Fiction guidelines for #10 SAE and 1 first-class stamp.

Payment: Pays 10-17¢/word.

Terms: Pays on publication for all rights.

Advice: Writers may send $8.95 plus $3 shipping for *Cobblestone*'s index for a listing of subjects covered in back issues.

✱THE COMPANION OF ST. FRANCIS AND ST. ANTHONY, (II), Conventual Franciscan Friars, Box 535, Postal Station F, Toronto, Ontario M4Y 2L8 Canada. (416)463-5442. Editor: Fr. Rick Riccioli, OFM. Conv. Managing Editor: Betty McCrimmon. Publishes material "emphasizing religious and human values and stressing Franciscan virtues—peace, simplicity, joy." Monthly. Estab. 1936. Circ. 10,000.

● *The Companion of St. Francis and St. Anthony* received 3 honorable mentions from the Canadian Church Press in 1993.

Needs: Adventure, humor, mainstream, religious. Canadian settings preferred. Receives 50 unsolicited fiction mss/month. Buys 2/issue. Time varies between acceptance and publication. Length: 800 words minimum; 1,500 words maximum. Publishes short shorts, 200 words preferred.

How to Contact: Send complete mss. Reports in 3 weeks to 1 month on mss. SASE with "cash to buy stamps" or IRCs. Sample copy and fiction guidelines free.

Payment: Pays 6¢/word (Canadian funds).

Terms: Pays on publication for first North American serial rights.

CONTACT ADVERTISING, (IV), Box 3431, Ft. Pierce FL 34948. (407)464-5447. Editor: Herman Nietzche. Magazines and newspapers. Publications vary in size, 56-80 pages. "Group of 26 erotica, soft core publications for swingers, single males, married males." Bimonthly, quarterly and monthly. Estab. 1975. Circ. combined is 2,000,000.

● This is a group of regional publications with *very* explicit sexual content, graphic personal ads, not for the easily offended.

Needs: Erotica, fetish, fantasy, feminist, gay and lesbian. Receives 8-10 unsolicited mss/month. Buys 1-2 mss/issue; 40-50 mss/year. Publishes ms 1-3 months after acceptance. Length: 2,000 words minimum; 3,500 words maximum; 2,500-3,500 words average. Sometimes critiques rejected mss and recommends other markets.

How to Contact: Query first, query with clips of published work or send complete ms with cover letter. Reports in 1-2 weeks on queries; 3-4 weeks on mss. SASE (IRCs). Simultaneous and reprint submissions OK. Sample copy for $6. Fiction guidelines free.

Payment: 1st submission, free subscription to magazine; subsequent submissions $25-75; all receive three contributor's copies.

Terms: Pays on publication for all rights or first rights. Sends galleys to author if requested.

Advice: "Know your grammar! Content must be of an adult nature but well within guidelines of the law. Fantasy, unusual sexual encounters, swinging stories or editorials of a sexual bend are acceptable."

CORNERSTONE MAGAZINE, (II), Cornerstone Communications, Inc., 939 W. Wilson Ave., Chicago IL 60640. (312)989-2080. Fax (312)989-2076. Editor: Dawn Herrin. Fiction Editor: Jennifer Ingerson. Magazine: 8½×11; 64 pages; 35 lb. coated matie paper; self cover; illustrations and photos. "For young adults, 18-35. We publish nonfiction (essays, personal experience, religious), music interviews, current events, film and book reviews, fiction, poetry. *Cornerstone* challenges readers to look through the window of biblical reality. Known as avant-garde, yet attempts to express orthodox belief in the language of the nineties." Approx. bimonthly. Estab. 1972. Circ. 60,000.

● *Cornerstone Magazine* has won numerous awards from the Evangelical Press Association. It has also received a number of design awards, including one from *Print* magazine.

Needs: Ethnic/multicultural, fantasy (science fantasy, sword and sorcery), humor/satire, literary, mainstream/contemporary, religious/inspirational. Special interest in "issues pertinent to contemporary society, seen with a biblical worldview." No "pornography, cheap shots at non-Christians, unrealistic or syrupy articles." Upcoming theme: "Racism." Receives 60 unsolicited mss/month. Buys 1 mss/issue; 3-4 mss/year. Does not read mss during Christmas/New Year's week and the first week of July. Published work by Dave Cheadle, C.S. Lewis, J.B. Simmonds. Length: 1,200 words average; 250 words minimum; 2,500 words maximum. Publishes short shorts. Length: 250-450 words. Also publishes literary essays, literary criticism, poetry.

How to Contact: Send complete ms. Should include estimated word count, bio (50-100 words), list of publications, and name, address, phone and fax number on every item submitted. Send disposable copy of the ms. Will consider simultaneous submissions, reprints and electronic (disk or modem) submissions. Reports in 2-3 months. Sample copy for 8½×11 SAE and 6 first-class stamps or IRCs. Reviews novels and short story collections.

Payment: Pays 8-10¢/word maximum; also 6 contributor's copies. Additional copies for $1.

Terms: Payment on publication. Purchases first serial rights.

Advice: "Articles may express Christian world view but shouldn't be unrealistic or syrupy. We're looking for high-quality fiction with skillful characterization and plot development and imaginative symbolism." Looks for "mature Christian short stories, as opposed to those more fit for church bulletins. We want fiction with bite and an edge but with a Christian worldview."

COSMOPOLITAN MAGAZINE, (III), The Hearst Corp., 224 W. 57th St., New York NY 10019. (212)649-2000. Editor: Helen Gurley Brown. Fiction Editor: Betty Kelly. Associate Fiction Editor: Suzanne Bober. Most stories include male-female relationships, traditional plots, characterizations. Single career women (ages 18-34). Monthly. Circ. just under 3 million.

 • *Cosmopolitan* ranks #22 on the latest *Writer's Digest* Fiction 50 list.

Needs: Adventure, contemporary, mystery and romance. "Stories should include a romantic relationship and usually a female protagonist. The characters should be in their 20s or 30s (i.e., same ages as our readers). No highly experimental pieces. Upbeat endings." Buys 1 short story plus a novel or book excerpt/issue. Agented fiction 98%. Published excerpts by Danielle Steel, Pat Booth and Belva Plain; published new writers within the last year. Length: short shorts (1,500 words); longer (2,000-4,000 words). Occasionally recommends other markets.

How to Contact: Send complete ms with SASE (IRCs). Guidelines for #10 SASE. Reports in 8-10 weeks. "We cannot contact you unless you enclose a #10 SASE." Publishes ms 6-18 months after acceptance.

Payment: Pays $750-2,000.

Terms: Pays on acceptance for first North American serial rights. Buys reprints.

Advice: "It is rare that unsolicited mss are accepted. We tend to use agented, professional writers. The majority of unsolicited short stories we receive are inappropriate for *Cosmo* in terms of characters used and situations presented, or they just are not well written."

COUNTRY WOMAN, (IV), Reiman Publications, Box 643, Milwaukee WI 53201. (414)423-0100. Editor: Ann Kaiser. Managing Editor: Kathleen Pohl. Magazine: 8½×11; 68 pages; excellent quality paper; excellent cover stock; illustrations and photographs. "Articles should have a rural theme and be of specific interest to women who live on a farm or ranch, or in a small town or country home, and/or are simply interested in country-oriented topics." Bimonthly. Estab. 1971.

Needs: Fiction must be upbeat, heartwarming and focus on a country woman as central character. "Many of our stories and articles are written by our readers!" Published work by Lori Ness, Wanda Luttrell and Dixie Laslett Thompson; published new writers within last year. Publishes 1 fiction story/issue. Length: 750-1,000 words.

How to Contact: All manuscripts should be sent to Kathy Pohl, Managing Editor. Reports in 2-3 months. Include cover letter and SASE (IRCs). Simultaneous and reprint submissions OK. Sample copy and writer's guidelines for $2 and SASE. Guidelines for #10 SASE.

Payment: Pays $90-125.

Terms: Pays on acceptance for one-time rights.

Advice: "Read the magazine to get to know our audience. Send us country-to-the-core fiction, not yuppie-country stories—our readers know the difference! Very traditional fiction—with a definite beginning, middle and end, some kind of conflict/resolution, etc."

CREATIVE KIDS, (I, IV), GCT, Inc., Box 6448, Mobile AL 36660. (205)478-4700. Editor: Fay L. Gold. Magazine: 8½×11; 32 pages; illustrations; photos. Material by children for children. Published 8 times/year. Estab. 1980. Circ: 20,000.
   • *Creative Kids* featuring work by children has won Edpress and Parents' Choice Gold Awards.
Needs: "We publish work by children ages 5-18." Juvenile (5-9 years); young adult/teen (10-18 years). No sexist, racist or violent material. Upcoming themes: Environment (March); Spring/Flowers (April); Summer/Sports (May); Fall/Halloween/School (October); International Issue (potpourri) (November); Winter/Sports (December); Animals (January); People/Feelings/Friends (February). Accepts 8-10 mss/issue; 60-80 mss/year. Publishes ms up to one year after acceptance. Published new writers within the last year. Publishes short shorts.
How to Contact: Send complete ms with cover letter, which should include name, age, home address, school name and address, statement of originality signed by teacher or parent. Reports in 2 weeks on queries; 1 month on mss. SASE (IRCs). No simultaneous submissions. Sample copy for $3.
Payment: Pays contributor's copy only.
Terms: Acquires all rights.
Advice: "Ours is a magazine to encourage young creative writers to use their imaginations, talent and writing skills. Type the manuscript—double space. Include all vital information about author. Send to one magazine at a time."

CRICKET MAGAZINE, (II), Carus Corporation, P.O. Box 300, Peru IL 61354. (815)224-6656. Editor-in-Chief: Marianne Carus. Magazine: 7×9; 64 pages; illustrations; photos. Magazine for children, ages 7-14. Monthly. Estab. 1973. Circ. 100,000.
   • *Cricket* ranked #34 on the latest *Writer's Digest* Fiction 50 List and has received a Parents' Choice Award, a Paul A. Witty Short Story Award and awards from Edpress. Carus Corp. also publishes *Ladybug* listed in this book.
Needs: Juvenile: adventure, contemporary, ethnic, fantasy, historic fiction, folk and fairytales, humorous, mystery, science fiction and translations. No adult articles. All issues have different "mini-themes." Receives approximately 1,100 unsolicited fiction mss each month. Publishes ms 6-24 months or longer after acceptance. Buys 180 mss/year. Agented fiction 1-2%. Published work by Peter Dickinson, Mary Stolz, Jane Yolen; published new writers within the last year. Length: 500-1,500 words.
How to Contact: Do not query first. Send complete ms with SASE (IRCs). List previous publications. Reports in 3 months on mss. Sample copy for $2; Guidelines for SASE.
Payment: Pays up to 25¢/word; 2 contributor's copies; $2 charge for extras.
Terms: Pays on publication for first rights. Sends edited mss for approval. Buys reprints.
Advice: "Do not write *down* to children. Write about well-researched subjects you are familiar with and interested in, or about something that concerns you deeply. Children *need* fiction and fantasy. Carefully study several issues of *Cricket* before you submit your manuscript." Sponsors contests for children, ages 5-14.

CRUSADER MAGAZINE, (II), Calvinist Cadet Corps, Box 7259, Grand Rapids MI 49510. (616)241-5616. Fax: (616)241-5558. Editor: G. Richard Broene. Magazine: 8½×11; 24 pages; 50 lb. white paper and cover stock; illustrations; photos. Magazine to help boys ages 9-14 discover how God is at work in their lives and in the world around them. 7 issues/year. Estab. 1958. Circ. 12,000.
Needs: Adventure, comics, juvenile, religious/inspirational, spiritual and sports. Receives 60 unsolicited fiction mss/month. Buys 3 mss/issue; 18 mss/year. Publishes ms 4-11 months after acceptance. Published work by Sigmund Brouwer, Alan Cliburn and Betty Lou Mell. Length: 800 words minimum; 1,500 words maximum; 1,200 words average. Publishes short shorts.
How to Contact: Send complete ms and SASE (IRCs) with cover letter including theme of story. Reports in 4-8 weeks. Simultaneous and previously published submissions OK. Sample copy with a 9×12 SAE and 3 first-class stamps. Fiction guidelines for #10 SAE and 1 first-class stamp.
Payment: Pays 2-5¢/word; 1 contributor's copy.
Terms: Pays on acceptance for one-time rights. Buys reprints.
Advice: "On a cover sheet list the point your story is trying to make. Our magazine has a theme for each issue, and we try to fit the fiction to the theme."

DETROIT JEWISH NEWS, (IV), 27676 Franklin Rd., Southfield MI 48034. (313)354-6060. Editor: Phil Jacobs. Associate Editor: Alan Hitsky. Newspaper: 120+ pages; illustrations and photos. Jewish news. Weekly. Estab. 1942. Circ. 20,000.
   • *Detroit Jewish News* has received the Rockover Award for Jewish Journalism an average of four times each year for the last several years.

Needs: "For fiction, we prefer articles on any subject with a Jewish flavor." Receives 3-4 unsolicited mss/month. Buys 6 mss/year. Publishes ms 2-3 months after acceptance. Length: 1,000-2,000 words averge. Publishes short shorts. Sometimes critiques rejected mss.
How to Contact: Send complete ms with cover letter that includes Social Security number. Reports in 2 weeks on queries; 1 month on mss. SASE (IRCs). Simultaneous and reprint submissions OK. Sample copy for $1.
Payment: Pays $40-100 and contributor's copies; charge for extras.
Terms: Pays on publication for one-time rights. Offers kill fee.

DIALOGUE, The Magazine for the Visually Impaired, (I, II), Blindskills Inc., P.O. Box 5181, Salem OR 97304. (503)581-4224. Editor/Publisher: Carol McCarl. Magazine: 9×11; 115 pages; matte stock. Publishes information on blind-related technology and human interest articles for blind, deaf-blind and visually impaired adults. Quarterly. Estab. 1961. Circ. 50,000.
Needs: Adventure, contemporary, humor/satire, literary, mainstream, regional, senior citizen/retirement and suspense/mystery. No erotica, religion, confessional or experimental. Receives approximately 10 unsolicited fiction mss/month. Buys 3 mss/issue, 12 mss/year. Publishes ms an average of 6 months after acceptance. Published work by Patrick Quinn, Marieanna Pape and John Dasney; published new writers within the last year. Length: 1,500 words average; 500 words minimum; 2,000 words maximum. Publishes short shorts. Occasionally critiques rejected mss. Sometimes recommends other markets. "We give top priority to blind or visually impaired (legally blind) authors."
How to Contact: Query first or send complete ms with SASE (IRCs). Also send statement of visual handicap. Reports in 2 weeks on queries; 6 weeks on mss. Reprint submissions OK. Accepts electronic submissions on disk; IBM and compatible; Word Perfect preferred. Sample copy for $5 and #10 SAE with 1 first-class stamp; free to visually impaired. Fiction guidelines free.
Payment: Pays $5-50 and contributor's copy.
Terms: Pays on acceptance for first rights. "All fiction published in *Dialogue* automatically enters the Victorin Memorial Award Contest held annually. One winner per year.
Advice: "Study the magazine. This is a very specialized field. Remember the SASE!"

DISCOVERIES, (II), WordAction Publishing Company, 6401 The Paseo, Kansas City MO 64131. Editor: Latta Jo Knapp. Story paper: 8½×11; 4 pages; illustrations. "Committed to reinforce the Bible concept taught in Sunday School curriculum, for ages 8-10 (grades 3-4)." Weekly.
• Other WordAction-affiliated publications include *Standard* and *Teens Today* listed in this book.
Needs: Religious, puzzles, Bible trivia, 100-200 words. Buys 1-2 stories and 1-2 puzzles/issue. Publishes ms 1-2 years after acceptance. Length: 500-700 words.
How to Contact: Send complete ms with cover letter and SASE (IRCs). Send SASE for sample copy and guidelines.
Payment: Pays 5¢/word for multiple rights.
Terms: Pays on acceptance or on publication.
Advice: "Stories should vividly portray definite Christian emphasis or character building values, without being preachy."

DRAGON MAGAZINE, The Monthly Adventure Role-Playing Aid, (IV), TSR, Inc., P.O. Box 111, Lake Geneva WI 53147. (414)248-3625. Editor: Roger E. Moore. Fiction Editor: Barbara G. Young. Magazine: 8½×11; 120 pages; 50 penn. plus paper; 80 lb. northcote cover stock; illustrations; rarely photos. "*Dragon* contains primarily nonfiction—articles and essays on various aspects of the hobby of fantasy and science fiction role-playing games. One short fantasy story is published per issue. Readers are mature teens and young adults; over half our readers are under 18 years of age. The majority are male." Monthly. Estab. 1976. Circ. 85,000.
• TSR also has a listing in the Commercial Publishers section of this book. See also TSR's other publication, *Amazing Stories* in this book.
Needs: "We are looking for all types of fantasy (not horror) stories. We are *not* interested in fictionalized accounts of actual role-playing sessions." Upcoming themes: "fantasy humor" (April 1994); Underground Adventuring (November 1994); "gothic horror" (October 1994). Receives 50-60 unsolicited

---

Read the Business of Fiction Writing section to learn the correct way to prepare and submit a manuscript.

fiction mss/month. Buys 10-12 mss/year. Publishes ms 6-12 months after acceptance. Published work by Lois Tilton, Heather Lynn Sarik, Jean Lorrah; published new writers within the last year. Length: 1,500 words minimum; 8,000 words maximum; 3,000-4,000 words average. Occasionally critiques rejected mss.

How to Contact: Send complete ms, estimated word length, SASE (IRCs). List only credits of professionally published materials within genre. No simultaneous submissions. Reports in 4-6 weeks. Sample copy for $4.50. Fiction guidelines for #10 SAE and 1 first-class stamp. Reviews fantasy and science fiction novels for their application to role-playing games.

Payment: Pays 5-8¢/word; 2 free contributor's copies; $2 charge for extras.

Terms: Pays on acceptance for fiction only for first worldwide English language rights.

Advice: "It is *essential* that you actually see a copy (better, several copies) of the magazine to which you are submitting your work. Do not rely solely on market reports, as stories submitted to the wrong publication waste both your time and the editor's. We see *lots* of stories about dragons—try a less conventional fantasy creature: ogre, pixie, dwarf."

DRUMMER, (II, IV), Desmodus, Inc., Box 410390, San Francisco CA 94141. (415)252-1195. Editor: Marcus-Jay Wonacott. Magazine: 8½×11; 84 pages; glossy full-color cover; illustrations and photos. "Gay male erotica, fantasy and mystery with a leather, SM or other fetish twist." Monthly. Estab. 1975. Circ. 20,000.

Needs: Adventure, erotica, fantasy, gay, horror, humor/satire, mystery/suspense, science fiction and western. "Fiction must have an appeal to gay men." Receives 20-30 unsolicited fiction mss/month. Accepts 3 mss/issue. Publishes ms 6-8 months after acceptance.

How to Contact: Send complete ms with cover letter. SASE (IRCs). Simultaneous submissions OK. Reprints OK "only if previously in foreign or very local publications." Accepts electronic submissions compatible with IBM PC. Reports in approximately 3 months. Sample copy for $5. Fiction guidelines for #10 SASE. Reviews novels and short story collections.

Payment: Pays $100 and contributor's copies.

Terms: Pays on publication for first North American serial rights.

EMERGE MAGAZINE, Black America's News Magazine (III), Suite 2200, 1700 N. Moore St., Arlington VA 22209. (703)875-0430. Editor: George E. Curry Managing Editor: Ms. Florestine Purnell. 8⅛×10⅞; 84 pages; 40 lb. paper; 70 lb. cover stock; 5-6 illustrations; 45 photographs. "*Emerge* is an African American news monthly that covers news, politics, arts and lifestyles for the college educated, middle class African American audience." Estab. 1989.

Needs: Ethnic, fantasy, humor/satire, literary. "*Emerge* is looking for humorous, tightly written fiction no longer than 2,000 words about African Americans."

How to Contact: Submit ms through agent only. Reviews novels and short story collections. Send to Ms. Florestine Purnell, managing editor.

Payment: Pays $1,000-2,000 and contributor's copies.

Terms: Pays 25% kill fee. Buys first North American serial rights.

Advice: "*Emerge* stories must accomplish with a fine economy of style what all good fiction must do: make the unusual familiar. The ability to script a compelling story is what has been missing from most of our submissions."

‡ESQUIRE, The Magazine for Men, (III), Hearst Corp., 250 W. 55th St., New York NY 10019. (212)649-4020. Editor: Terry McDonell. Fiction Editor: Will Blythe. Magazine. Monthly. Estab. 1933. Circ. 750,000.

● *Esquire* is well-respected for its fiction and has received several National Magazine Awards.

Needs: No "pornography, science fiction or 'true romance' stories." Receives "hundreds" of unsolicited mss/month. Rarely accepts unsolicited fiction. Recently published work by Cormac McCarthy, Richard Ford, Ann Beattie, Jayne Ann Phillips, James Sauer, Jim Harrison.

How to Contact: Send complete ms with cover letter or submit through an agent. Simultaneous submissions OK. Fiction guidelines for SASE (IRCs) and first-class stamps.

Payment: Pays in cash, amount undisclosed.

Terms: Pays on acceptance.

Advice: Submit one story at a time.

EVANGEL, (IV), Light & Life Press, P.O. Box 535002, Indianapolis IN 46253-5002. (317)244-3660. Editor: Carolyn B. Smith. Sunday school take-home paper for distribution to adults who attend church. Fiction involves couples and singles coping with everyday crises, making decisions that show growth.

Magazine: 5½×8½; 8 pages; 2-color illustrations; b&w photos. Weekly. Estab. 1896. Circ. 35,000.

Needs: Religious/inspirational. "No fiction without any semblance of Christian message or where the message clobbers the reader." Receives approximately 75 unsolicited fiction mss/month. Buys 1 ms/issue, 52 mss/year. Published work by C. Ellen Watts, Jeanne Zornes and Betty Steele Everett. Length: 1,000-1,200 words.

How to Contact: Send complete ms with SASE (IRCs). Reports in 1 month. Sample copy and writer's guidelines with #10 SASE.

Payment: Pays 4¢ per word for first rights; $3/word for reprints and 2 contributor's copies; charge for extras.

Terms: Pays on publication for simultaneous, first, second serial (reprint), first North American serial or one-time rights.

Advice: "Choose a contemporary situation or conflict and create a good mix for the characters (not all-good or all-bad heroes and villains). Don't spell out everything in detail; let the reader fill in some blanks in the story. Keep him guessing." Rejects mss because of "unbelievable characters and predictable events in the story."

‡**EXPANSE® MAGAZINE, (II),** Suite 49, 7982 Honeygo Blvd., Baltimore MD 21236-5948. Fiction Editor: Steven E. Fick. Magazine: 8½×11; 80 pages; 60 lb. paper; 80 lb. cover stock; illustrations. "We strive to publish the best in science fiction and publish it in the best possible way for an intelligent readership with developed tastes. Seeing ourselves as a kind of gallery of fine literature, we use innovative design to 'frame' each story and best present its unique style." Quarterly. Estab. 1993. Circ. 13,000.

Needs: Science fiction. "We do not publish fantasy or horror. And we're not interested in 'cross-over' pieces that attempt to meld the attributes of science fiction with other genres." Receives 100 unsolicited mss/month. Accepts 8-10 mss/issue; 40 mss/year. Pubilshes ms 18 months after acceptance. Agented fiction 5%. Recently published work by L. Sprague DeCamp, Stanley G. Weinbaum, Don D'Ammassa, Mark Rich, Jacie Ragan. Length: 6,500 words average; 2,500 words minimum; 10,000 words maximum. Publishes short shorts. Length: 1,500 words or less. Also publishes literary essays, poetry. Sometimes critiques or comments on rejected mss.

How to Contact: Send complete ms with cover letter. Should include estimated word count, one page bio, Social Security number, list of publications and phone number. Reports on mss in 2-3 months. SASE (IRCs). Sample copy $5 (overseas: add $2) payable in US funds only. Fiction guidelines for #10 SAE and 1 first-class stamp.

Payment: Pays 5-8¢/word; additional copies at 50% discount. Pays on acceptance. Buys first North American serial rights and non-exclusive world English-language serial rights.

Advice: "We look for original ideas and a captivating style that makes those ideas come alive on paper. *Read* a lot of good science fiction. Subscribe to the various sf publications . . . that's the only way to truly know what 'original' is. Whatever you do, don't follow trends and don't get your concept of sf from television! More than what sf *is*, understand what it should *do*. Good science fiction is a means of exploring the unknown. It should capture that sense of wonder and discovery, the excitement and adventure of human progress . . ."

‡**FACES, The Magazine About People, (II, IV),** Cobblestone Publishing, Inc., 7 School St., Peterborough NH 03458. (603)924-7209. Fax: (603)924-7380. Editor-in-Chief: Carolyn P. Yoder. Magazine. *Faces* is a magazine about people for 8-14 year olds. "All manuscripts are reviewed by the American Museum of Natural History in New York before being accepted." Estab. 1984. Circ. 15,000. Monthly, except June, July and August.

● Cobblestone Publishing also publishes *Calliope, Cobblestone* and *Odyssey* listed in this book.

Needs: All material must relate to theme; send for theme list. Childrens/juvenile (8-14 years), "retold legends, folk tales, stories from around the world, etc., relating to the theme." Length: 800 words preferred. Publishes short shorts.

How to Contact: Query first or query with clips of published work (send query 6-9 months prior to theme issue publication date). Should include estimated word count and bio (2-3 lines). Reports 4 months before publication date. Send SASE (or IRC) for reply. Sample copy for $3.95, 7½×10½ SAE and 98¢ postage. Fiction guidelines for SASE.

Payment: Pays 10-17¢/word.

Terms: Pays on publication for all rights.

‡**FAITH 'N STUFF: The Magazine For Kids, (III)**, Guideposts Association, Inc., 16 E. 34th St., New York NY 10016. (212)251-8100. Fax: (212)684-0679. Editor: Mary Lou Carvey. Fiction Editor: Lurlene McDaniel. Magazine: 8¼×10¾; 32 pages. "Value-centered bimonthly for kids 7-12 years old. Bible-based; not preachy; concerned with contemporary issues." Bimonthly. Estab. 1990. Circ. 100,000.
Needs: Children's/juvenile: fantasy, historical (general), humor, mystery/suspense, religious/inspirational, westerns. "No 'adult as hero' or 'I-prayed-I-got' stories." Upcoming themes: Choices, Animals, Humor, Courage. Receives 50-75 unsolicited mss/month. Accepts 1-2 mss/issue; 6-10 mss/year. Recently published work by Lurlene McDaniel, Judy Baer, Cameron Judd. Length: 1,300 words preferred; 600 words minimum; 1,500 words maximum. Publishes short shorts. Also publishes small amount of poetry. Sometimes critiques rejected mss; "only what shows promise."
How to Contact: Send complete ms with cover letter. Should include estimated word count, Social Security number, phone number and SASE. Reports in 6-8 weeks. Send SASE (IRCs) for reply, return of ms or send disposable copy of ms. Simultaneous submissions OK. Sample copy for $3.25, 10×13 SAE and $1.21 postage (in US). Fiction guidelines for #10 SAE and 1 first-class stamp.
Payment: $100-300 maximum and 2 contributor's copies. Additional copies available.
Terms: Pays on acceptance for all rights.

THE FAMILY, (II, IV), Daughters of St. Paul, 50 St. Paul's Ave., Boston MA 02130. (617)522-8911. Managing Editor: Sr. Theresa Frances FSP. Magazine: 8½×11; 40 pages; glossy paper; self-cover; illustrations and photos. Family life—themes include parenting issues, human and spiritual development, marital situations for teen-adult, popular audience predominantly Catholic. Monthly, except July-Aug. Estab. 1953. Circ. 10,000.
• Another magazine published by the Daughters of St. Paul is *My Friend* listed in this book.
Needs: Religious/inspirational. "We favor upbeat stories with some sort of practical or moral message." No sex, romance, science fiction, horror, western. Receives about 100 unsolicited mss/month. Buys 3-4 mss/issue; 30-40 mss/year. Publishes ms 4-6 months after acceptance. Length: 800 words minimum; 1,500 words maximum; 1,200 words average.
How to Contact: Send complete ms with cover letter that includes Social Security number and list of previously published works. Reports in 2 months on mss. SASE (IRCs). No simultaneous submissions. Reprint submissions OK. Sample copy for $1.75, 9×12 SAE and 5 first-class stamps. Guidelines for #10 SAE and 1 first-class stamp.
Payment: Pays $50-100.
Terms: Pays on publication for first North American serial or one-time rights (reprints). Sends galleys to author "only if substantive editing was required."
Advice: "We look for 1) message; 2) clarity of writing; 3) realism of plot and character development. If seasonal material, send at least 7 months in advance. We're eager to receive submissions on family topics. And we love stories that include humor."

FIFTY SOMETHING MAGAZINE, "For the Fifty-and-Better," Media Trends Publications, 8250 Tyler Blvd., Mentor OH 44060. (216)974-9594. Editor: Linda L. Lindeman. Magazine: 8×11; 32-48 pages; #50 gloss paper; illustrations and photos. "Light-hearted issues on aging. 50+ is the best time of your life. Positive approach to getting older. Tradition—how things used to be." Bimonthly. Estab. 1990. Circ. 25,000.
Needs: Adventure, historical (general), humor/satire, romance (historical), senior citizen/retirement, westerns. Nothing "high tech." Receives 60 unsolicited mss/month. Buys 4 mss/issue; 24 mss/year. Published work by Patricia Mote, Ron DeCarlo, Caryl Jost. Length: 1,000 words average; 400 words minimum. Publishes short shorts. Also publishes literary essays and poetry. Always critiques or comments on rejected mss.
How To Contact: Send complete ms with cover letter. Should include estimated word count with submission. Reports in 2 weeks on queries; 5 weeks on mss. Send SASE (IRCs) for reply, return of ms or send disposable copy of ms. Will consider simultaneous submissions, reprints and electronic (disk or modem) submissions. Sample copy for 9×12 SAE and $1.21 postage. Fiction guidelines for #10 SAE and 1 stamp or IRCs. Reviews novels and short story collections.
Payment: Pays 10 contributor's copies. Additional copies for postage.
Terms: Acquires one-time rights.
Advice: "Photos always help make the story more interesting. Just go for it!"

FIRST, (II), For Women, Heinrich Bauer North America Inc., 270 Sylvan Ave., Englewood Cliffs NJ 07632. (201)569-6699. Editor: Jane Travlsen. Magazine: 150 pages; slick paper; illustrations and photos. "Women's service magazine for women age 18 up—no upper limit—middle American audience." Estab. 1989. Circ. 2 million.

• This magazine ranks #11 on the latest *Writer's Digest* Fiction 50 list. Heinrich Baur North America also publishes *Woman's World Magazine*, listed in this book.

Needs: Contemporary, literary, mainstream and regional. "No experimental, romance, formula fiction, fantasy or sci-fi stories." Receives 200 unsolicited mss/month. Buys 1 ms/issue; 16 mss/year. Time between acceptance and publication varies. Recently published work by Lynn Coulter, Tima Smith and P.J. Platz. Length: 1,500 words minimum; 2,200 words maximum.

How to Contact: Send complete ms with cover letter. "Cover letter should be brief, mention previous publications and agent, if any, and tell us if material is seasonal. No queries please." Reports in 8-10 weeks on mss. SASE (IRCs) for ms or reply. Fiction guidelines for #10 SAE and 1 first-class stamp. Send seasonal material 6 months in advance.

Payment: Pays $1,500.

Terms: Pays on acceptance for first North American serial rights.

Advice: "We especially like a strong voice and fresh sensibility on themes of interest to contemporary women. Read at least 3 issues of the magazine. Send us the story you had to write for yourself, not one you concocted 'especially for *First.*' "

FIRST HAND, Experiences for Loving Men, (II, IV), First Hand Ltd., Box 1314, Teaneck NJ 07666. (201)836-9177. Fax: (201)836-5055. Editor: Bob Harris. Magazine: digest size; 130 pages; illustrations. "Half of the magazine is made up of our readers' own gay sexual experiences. Rest is fiction and columns devoted to health, travel, books, etc." Monthly. Estab. 1980. Circ. 60,000.

• First Hand Ltd. also publishes *Guys* listed in this book.

Needs: Erotica, gay. "Should be written in first person." No science fiction or fantasy. Erotica should detail experiences based in reality. Receives 75-100 unsolicited mss/month. Buys 6 mss/issue; 72 mss/ year. Publishes ms 9-18 months after acceptance. Published work by John Hoff, Rick Jackson, Jack Sofelot; published new writers within the last year. Length: 3,000 words preferred; 2,000 words minimum; 3,750 words maximum. Sometimes critiques rejected mss.

How to Contact: Send complete ms with cover letter which should include writer's name, address, telephone and Social Security number and "should advise on use of pseudonym if any. Also whether selling all rights or first North American rights." No simultaneous submissions. Reports in 3-4 months. SASE (IRCs). Sample copy for $5. Fiction guidelines for #10 SAE and 1 first-class stamp.

Payment: Pays $100-150.

Terms: Pays on publication for all rights or first North American serial rights.

Advice: "Avoid the hackneyed situations. Be original. We like strong plots."

FLORIDA WILDLIFE, (IV), Florida Game & Fresh Water Fish Commission, 620 S. Meridian St., Tallahassee FL 32399-1600. (904)488-5563. Editor: Dick Sublette. Assistant Editor: Janisse Ray. Magazine: 8½×11; 52 pages. "Conservation-oriented material for an 'outdoor' audience." Bimonthly. Estab. 1947. Circ. 30,000.

Needs: Adventure, sports. "Florida-related adventure or natural history only. We rarely pubilsh fiction." Buys 3-4 mss/year. Length: 1,200 words average; 500 words minimum; 1,500 words maximum.

How to Contact: Send complete ms with cover letter including Social Security number. "We prefer to review article. Response time varies with amount of material on hand." Sample copy for $1.25.

Payment: Pays $50 per published page.

Terms: Pays on publication for one-time rights.

Advice: "Send your best work. It must *directly* concern Florida wildlife."

FREEWAY, (II), Box 632, Glen Ellyn IL 60138. (708)668-6000 (ext. 3210). Editor: Amy J. Cox. Magazine: 8½×11; 4 pages; newsprint paper; illustrations; photos. Weekly Sunday school paper "specializing in first-person true stories about how God has worked in teens' lives," for Christian teens ages 15-21.

• Another magazine for teens by this publisher, *Teen Power*, is listed in this book. *Freeway* received an Award of Excellence in 1992 from the Evangelical Press Association.

Needs: Comics, humor/satire, spiritual, allegories and parables. Length: 1,000 words average; 1,200 words maximum. Occasionally critiques rejected mss.
How to Contact: Send complete ms with SASE (IRCs). Reports in 2-3 months. Simultaneous submissions OK. Sample copy or fiction guidelines available for SASE.
Payment: Pays 6-10¢/word.
Terms: Pays on acceptance for one-time rights.
Advice: "Send us humorous fiction (parables, allegories, etc.) with a clever twist and new insight on Christian principles. Do *not* send us typical teenage short stories. Watch out for cliché topics and approaches." Looks for "true-to-life, contemporary. Our fiction must have a 'take-away value'—a biblical principle for Christian living the reader can apply to his or her life."

THE FRIEND MAGAZINE, (II), The Church of Jesus Christ of Latter-day Saints, 23rd Floor, 50 E. North Temple, Salt Lake City UT 84150. (801)240-2210. Editor: Vivian Paulsen. Magazine: 8½ × 10½; 50 pages; 40 lb. coated paper; 70 lb. coated cover stock; illustrations; photos. Publishes for 3-11 year-olds. Monthly. Estab. 1971. Circ. 220,000.
 • The Church of Jesus Christ of Latter-Day Saints also publishes *New Era* listed in this book.
Needs: Adventure, ethnic, some historical, humor, mainstream, religious/inspirational, nature. Length: 1,000 words maximum. Publishes short shorts. Length: 250 words.
How to Contact: Send complete ms. "No query letters please." Reports in 6-8 weeks. SASE (IRCs). Sample copy for 9½ × 11 SAE and $1 postage.
Payment: Pays 9-10¢/word.
Terms: Pays on acceptance for all rights.
Advice: "The *Friend* is particularly interested in stories with substance for tiny tots. Stories should focus on character-building qualities and should be wholesome without moralizing or preaching. Boys and girls resolving conflicts is a theme of particular merit. Since the magazine is circulated worldwide, the *Friend* is interested in stories and articles with universal settings, conflicts, and character. Other suggestions include rebus, picture, holiday, sports, and photo stories, or manuscripts that portray various cultures. Very short pieces (up to 250 words) are desired for younger readers and preschool children. Appropriate humor is a constant need."

GALLERY MAGAZINE, (I), Montcalm Publishing Corporation, 401 Park Avenue South, New York NY 10016. (212)779-8900. Editor: Barry Janoff. Fiction Editor: Rose Rubin Rivera. Magazine: 130 pages; illustrations and photographs. Magazine for men, 18-45. Monthly. Estab. 1972. Circ. 425,000.
 • In addition to a new fiction editor, *Gallery Magazine* has increased its need for fiction from 6 to 13 manuscripts per year.
Needs: Adventure, erotica, humor/satire, literary, mainstream, suspense/mystery. Receives 100 unsolicited fiction mss/month. Accepts 13 mss/year. Publishes ms 5 months after acceptance. Less than 10% of fiction is agented. Length: 1,500-3,000 words average; 1,000 words minimum; 3,500 words maximum. Sometimes critiques rejected mss and recommends other markets.
How to Contact: Send complete ms. Reports in 2 months. SASE (IRCs). Accepts electronic submissions, if Mac or compatible disk available. Sample copy $6.25. Fiction guidelines for #10 SAE and 1 first-class stamp.
Payment: Pays $500, contributor's copies.
Terms: Pays on publication. Buys first North American serial rights.
Advice: Fiction is "slightly off-beat, but always reflecting some aspect of life that our readers can relate to. We reject all manuscripts regarding UFOs, sci-fi, horror, and prostitution. All of the manuscripts that we publish are extremely well written, but not overly polished—we prefer pieces that are rough around the edges. We also give special consideration to writers who have never been published or only have minor publishing credits. Don't assume anything. *Gallery* is a men's magazine, but we do not publish the 'typical' men's magazine fiction. Check each market carefully by reading several issues of each particular magazine, always ask for fiction guidelines before submitting a manuscript, and never send a cover letter that has the line, 'My friends loved this piece and I know it is perfect for your magazine.' Also, we are not impressed if someone submitting a manuscript tells us that his professor in college called him 'a future Hemingway.' "

Market categories: (I) Open to new writers; (II) Open to both new and established writers; (III) Interested mostly in established writers; (IV) Open to writers whose work is specialized.

THE GEM, (II), Churches of God, General Conference, Box 926, Findlay OH 45839. (419)424-1961. Editor: Kathy Rodabaugh. Magazine: 6×9; 8 pages; 50 lb. uncoated paper; illustrations (clip art). "True-to-life stories of healed relationships and growing maturity in the Christian faith for senior high students through senior citizens who attend Churches of God, General Conference Sunday Schools." Weekly. Estab. 1865. Circ. 8,000.
Needs: Adventure, feminist, humor, mainstream, religious/inspirational, senior citizen/retirement. Nothing that denies or ridicules standard Christian values. Receives 30 unsolicited fiction mss/month. Buys 1 ms every 2-3 issues; 20-25 mss/year. Publishes ms 4-12 months after submission. Published work by Betty Steele Everett, Todd Lee and Betty Lou Mell. Length: 1,500 words average; 1,000 words minimum; 1,700 words maximum.
How to Contact: Send complete ms with cover letter ("letter not essential, unless there is information about author's background which enhances story's credibility or verifies details as being authentic"). Reports in 6 months. SASE (IRCs). Simultaneous and reprint submissions OK. Sample copy and fiction guidelines for #10 SAE and 1 first-class stamp. "If more than one sample copy is desired along with the guidelines, will need 2 oz. postage."
Payment: Pays $10-15 and contributor's copies. Charge for extras (postage for mailing more than one).
Terms: Pays on publication for one-time rights.
Advice: "Competition at the mediocre level is fierce. There is a dearth of well-written, relevant fiction which wrestles with real problems involving Christian values applied to the crisis times and 'passages' of life. Humor which puts the daily grind into a fresh perspective and which promises hope for survival is also in short supply. Write from your own experience. Avoid religious jargon and stereotypes. Conclusion must be believable in terms of the story—don't force a 'Christian' ending. Avoid simplistic solutions to complex problems. Listen to the storytelling art of Garrison Keillor. Feel how very particular experiences of small town life in Minnesota become universal."

‡GENRE MAGAZINE, (II, IV), 725 Superba Ave., Venice CA 90291. Editor: Judy Wieder. Magazine: 116 pages; glossy paper; illustrations and photographs. "Short stories revolving around gay life—no porno." Bimonthly. Estab. 1990. Circ. 100,000.
● This is a very upscale, slick magazine for gay men. *Genre*'s fiction was nominated for a Maggie Award.
Needs: Gay: adventure, fantasy (science fantasy), lesbian, mainstream/contemporary, mystery/suspense, romance (contemporary), sports, westerns (frontier). Publishes special fiction issue or anthology. Receives 50 unsolicited mss/month. Publishes ms several months after acceptance. Recently published work by Tyler St. Mark, Robert Bahr. Length: 3,000 words preferred. Sometimes critiques or comments on rejected mss.
How to Contact: Send complete ms with a cover letter. Should include estimated word count and bio. Reports in several months. Send SASE (IRCs) for return of ms or send a disposable copy of ms. Electronic (IBM 3½″ disc, Microsoft Wd5 and hard copy) submissions OK. Reviews novels and short story collections.
Payment: Pays $200 maximum; contributor's copies.
Terms: Pays on publication for all rights or one-time rights.

GENT, (II), Dugent Publishing Corp., Suite 600, 2600 Douglas Rd., Coral Gables FL 33134. (305)443-2378. Editor: Bruce Arthur. "Men's magazine designed to have erotic appeal for the reader. Our publications are directed to a male audience, but we do have a certain percentage of female readers. For the most part, our audience is interested in erotically stimulating material, but not exclusively." Monthly. Estab. 1959. Circ. 175,000.
Needs: Erotica: contemporary, science fiction, horror, mystery, adventure and humor. *Gent* specializes in "D-Cup cheesecake," and fiction should be slanted accordingly. "Most of the fiction published includes several sex scenes. No fiction that concerns children, religious subjects or anything that might be libelous." Receives approximately 30-50 unsolicited fiction mss/month. Buys 2 mss/issue; 26 mss/year. Publishes ms an average of 3 months after acceptance. Agented fiction 10%. Published new writers within the last year. Length: 2,000-3,500 words. Critiques rejected mss "when there is time."
How to Contact: Send complete ms with SASE (IRCs). Reports in 1 month. Sample copy for $5. Fiction guidelines for #10 SASE.
Payment: Pay starts at $200; 1 contributor's copy.
Terms: Pays on publication for first North American serial rights.
Advice: "Since *Gent* magazine is the 'Home of the D-Cups,' stories and articles containing either characters or themes with a major emphasis on large breasts will have the best chance for consideration. Study a sample copy first." Mss are rejected because "there are not enough or ineffective erotic

sequences, plot is not plausible, wrong length, or not slanted specifically for us."

‡GENTLEMAN'S BLACK COMPANION (I), Gentleman's Black Companion, Inc., Box 447, Voorhees NJ 08003. (212)564-0112. Editor: J.H. Hartley. Magazine: 8½×11; 96 pages; 50 lb coated paper; 80 lb cover stock; illustrations; photos. Men's magazine, sexually oriented material of a heavily erotic nature, geared to swinging concepts. Monthly. Published special fiction issue. Estab. 1976. Circ. 175,000.
Needs: Erotica, fantasy. No non-erotic fiction. Receives 20 unsolicited fiction mss/month; accepts 2 fiction mss/issue. Publishes ms 6 weeks to 6 months after acceptance. Length: 1,000-2,500 words.
Payment: Payment is negotiable.
How to Contact: Send complete ms with cover letter. SASE (IRCs). Reports in 1 month on queries. Sample copy $4.95 and 8½×11 SAE with 2 first-class stamps. Fiction guidelines for $3.95 and 8½×11 SAE with 2 first-class stamps.
Terms: Pays on publication. Acquires all rights.

THE GIFTED CHILD TODAY, (IV), GCT Inc., P.O. Box 6448, Mobile AL 36660. (205)478-4700. Editor: Marvin Gold. Magazine: 8½×11; 64 pages; coated paper; self-cover; illustrations and photographs. "Focuses on materials about gifted, creative, and talented children and youth. For parents and professionals." Bimonthly. Estab. 1978. Circ. 10,000.
• *The Gifted Child Today* has won several Ed Press awards, the most recent in 1993. GCT, Inc. also publishes books. Contact them for details.
Needs: "As long as the subject matter deals with gifted, creative, and/or talented individuals in some way, material will be considered." Does not want to see "protagonist(s) and/or antagonist(s) that are not gifted, creative and/or talented individuals." Receives 3-4 unsolicited mss each month. Accepts 1 ms/issue. Publishes ms 1-2 years after acceptance. Length: 1,800 words average; 1,000 words minimum; 5,000 words maximum. Publishes short shorts. Length: 500 words.
How to Contact: Send complete ms with cover letter. No simultaneous submissions. Reports in 1 month on queries; 2 months on mss. SASE (IRCs). Sample copy for $5. Reviews novels and short story collections "only if material deals with gifted individuals as subject."
Payment: Pays in contributor's copies. Charges for extras.
Terms: Acquires first rights.

GOLD AND TREASURE HUNTER, (II), (formerly *Modern Gold Miner and Treasure Hunter*), P.O. Box 47, Happy Camp CA 96039. (916)493-2029. Editor: Dave McCracken. Fiction Editor: Janice Trombetta. Magazine: 8×10⅞; 56 pages; 50 lb. coated #5 paper; 80 lb. Sterling Web cover; pen-and-ink illustrations; photographs. "Recreational and small-scale gold mining, treasure and relic hunting. All stories must be related to these topics. For recreational hobbyists, adventure loving, outdoor people." Bimonthly. Estab. 1988. Circ. 50,000.
Needs: Adventure, experimental, historical, humor, mystery/suspense, senior citizen/retirement. "Futuristic stories OK, but not sci-fi. No erotica, gay, lesbian--absolutely no 'cussing!' " Buys 1-2 mss/issue; 6-16 mss/year. Publishes ms 4-6 months after acceptance. Published work by Ken Hodgson and Michael Clark. Length: 2,000 words preferred; 900 words minimum; 2,700 words maximum. Publishes short shorts. Length: 400-500 words. Sometimes critiques or comments on rejected mss.
How to Contact: Send complete ms with cover letter. Include Social Security number, "brief outline of the story and something about the author." Reports in 2 weeks on queries; 4-6 weeks on mss. SASE (IRCs) for mss. Accepts electronic submissions. Sample copy for $2.95 (U.S.), $3.95 (Canada). Free fiction guidelines.
Payment: Pays 3¢/word minimum and contributor's copy.
Terms: Pays on publication for all rights.
Advice: Looks for "as always, quality writing. We can edit small changes but the story has to grab us. Our readers love 'real life' fiction. They love exploring the 'that could happen' realm of a good fiction story. Keep your story geared to gold mining or treasure hunting. Know something about your subject so the story doesn't appear ridiculous. Don't try to dazzle readers with outlandish adjectives and keep slang to a minimum." Sponsors fiction contest—look for rules in upcoming issues.

GOLF JOURNAL, (II), United States Golf Assoc., Golf House, Far Hills NJ 07931. (908)234-2300. Managing Editor: David Earl. Magazine: 48 pages; self cover stock; illustrations and photos. "The magazine's subject is golf—its history, lore, rules, equipment and general information. The focus is on amateur golf and those things applying to the millions of American golfers. Our audience is generally professional, highly literate and knowledgeable; presumably they read *Golf Journal* because of an interest in the game, its traditions, and its noncommercial aspects." Published 8 times/year. Estab. 1948. Circ. 310,000.

Needs: Humor. "Fiction is very limited. *Golf Journal* has had an occasional humorous story, topical in nature. Generally speaking, short stories are not used. Golf jokes will not be used." Buys 20+ mss/year. Published new writers within the last year. Length: 1,000-2,000 words. Recommends other markets. Critiques rejected mss "when there is time."

How to Contact: Send complete ms with SASE (IRCs). Reports in 2 months on mss. Sample copy for SASE.

Payment: Pays $500-1,000; 1-10 contributor's copies.

Terms: Pays on acceptance.

Advice: "Know your subject (golf); familiarize yourself first with the publication." Rejects mss because "fiction usually does not serve the function of *Golf Journal*, which, as the official magazine of the United States Golf Association, deals chiefly with nonfiction subjects."

GOOD HOUSEKEEPING, (II), 959 Eighth Ave., New York NY 10019. Editor: John Mack Carter. Fiction Editor: Lee Quarfoot. Magazine: 8×10; approximately 250 pages; slick paper; thick, high-gloss cover; 4-color illustrations, b&w and color photos. Homemaking magazine of informational articles, how-to's for homemakers of all ages. Monthly. Circ. 20 million.

• *Good Housekeeping* ranked #10 on the latest *Writer's Digest* Fiction 50 list.

Needs: "*Good Housekeeping* looks for stories of emotional interest to women—courtship, romance, marriage, family, friendship, personal growth, coming-of-age. The best way to know if your story is appropriate for us is to read several of our recent issues. (We are sorry but we do not furnish free sample copies of the magazine.)" Buys 1 short story/issue. Agented fiction 90%. Length: 1,000-3,000 words.

How to Contact: Send complete disposable ms with cover letter. *Unsolicited manuscripts will not be returned* (see Advice). Simultaneous submissions OK. Reports in 4-6 weeks. Publishes ms an average of 6 months after acceptance.

Payment: Pays standard magazine rates.

Terms: Pays on acceptance for first North American serial rights.

Advice: "It is now our policy that all submissions of unsolicited fiction received in our offices will be read and, if found to be unsuitable for us, destroyed by recycling. If you wish to introduce your work to us, you will be submitting material that will not be critiqued or returned. The odds are long that we will contact you to inquire about publishing your submission or to invite you to correspond with us directly, so please be sure before you take the time and expense to submit it that it is our type of material."

‡GRAND TIMES, Exclusively for Active Retirees, (II), P.O. Box 9493, Berkeley CA 94709. (510)848-0456. Editor: Kira Albin. Magazine: 8½×11; 32 pages; illustrations and photographs. "All items must be upbeat in tone and written on subjects of interest to an older audience, i.e. active retirees. The style of writing must be entertaining, succint and clear; comparable with that in *Reader's Digest*." Bimonthly. Estab. 1992. Circ. 20,000.

Needs: Senior citizen/retirement: adventure, historical (general), humor/satire, mainstream/contemporary, mystery/suspense (mature adult), romance (mature adult), sports. "All pieces should be of special interest to reader's aged 70+." Receives 5-15 unsolicited mss/month. Buys 1 ms/issue; 6-8 mss/year. Publishes ms 1 year after acceptance. Published work by Jane Bosworth and Ted Carroll. Length: 800-1,200 average; 250 words minimum; 1,700 words maximum. Publishes short shorts. Length: 250-500 words. Also publishes poetry.

How to Contact: "It is recommended that manuscripts be submitted only after obtaining Writers' Guidelines." Send complete ms with a cover letter. Should include estimated word count and very short bio. Reports in 1-4 weeks on queries; 2-3 months on mss. SASE (IRCs) for return of ms or send a disposable copy of ms. Simultaneous and reprint submissions OK. Sample copy for $3.50. Writers' guidelines for #10 SAE and 1 first-class stamp.

Payment: Pays 1 contributor's copy. "The amount of additional payment is dependent on subject matter, quality and length."

Terms: Pays on acceptance. Buys one-time rights.

Advice: "The characters or plot need to have some relevance to active retirees. Don't lose the focus/theme of the story by bringing in too many ideas. Make sure characters are really developed and bring meaning to the story. *Please* obtain Writers' Guidelines before making a submission. Remember that Grand Times is for active retirees—stories should be geared specifically. Beware of any condescension, ageism or stereotyping."

GRIT, America's Family Magazine, (II), Stauffer Communications, Inc., 1503 S.W. 42nd St., Topeka KS 66609-1265. (913)274-4300. Editor-in-Chief: Roberta J. Peterson. Note on envelope: Attn: Fiction Department. Tabloid: 50 pages; 30 lb. newsprint; illustrations and photos. "*Grit* is a 'good news' publication and has been since 1882. Fiction should be approx. 2,500 words and interesting, inspiring, perhaps compelling in nature. Audience is *conservative*; readers tend to be 40+ from smaller towns, rural areas." Biweekly. Estab. 1882. Circ. 400,000.

  • *Grit* is considered one of the leading family-oriented publications. Stauffer Communications also publishes *Cappers*, listed in this book.

Needs: Adventure, condensed novelette, mainstream/contemporary (conservative), mystery/suspense, light religious/inspirational, romance (contemporary, historical), science fiction, westerns (frontier, traditional). Buys 1 mss/issue; 26 mss/year. Length: 2,500 words average; 2,300 words minimum; 2,700 words maximum. Also publishes poetry.

How to Contact: Send complete ms with cover letter. Should include estimated word count, brief bio, social security number, list of publications with submission. Reports in 2 months. Send SASE (IRC) for reply, return of ms or send disposable copy of ms. No simultaneous submissions. Will consider electronic (disk or modem) submissions (Macintosh). Sample copy $1.50 plus postage/appropriate SASE.

Payment: $150 minimum; $225 maximum.

Terms: Purchases first North American serial rights.

Advice: Looks for "well-written, simple and readable; fresh approach; strong start."

GUIDE MAGAZINE, (I, II, IV), Review & Herald Publishing Association, 55 W. Oak Ridge Dr., Hagerstown MD 21740. (301)791-7000. Fax: (301)791-7012. Editor: Jeannette Johnson. Magazine: 6×9; 32 pages; glossy (coated) paper; illustrations; photographs. "*Guide* is a weekly Christian journal geared toward 10- to 14-year-olds. Stories and other features presented are relevant to the needs of today's young person, and emphasize positive aspects of Christian living." Weekly. Estab. 1953. Circ. 40,000.

  • Affiliated with the Seventh-day Adventist Church, *Guide* has won awards from the Protestant Church Publishing Association, Associated Church Press and Evangelical Church Press.

Needs: Religious/inspirational: adventure (10-14 years), humor, sports. No romance, science fiction, horror, etc. "We use four general categories in each issue: spiritual/devotional; personal growth; adventure/nature; humor." Receives 80-100 unsolicited mss/month. Buys 2-3 mss/issue; 150 mss/year. Publishes ms 3-12 months after acceptance. Length: 1,000-1,200 words average. Publishes short shorts. Often critiques or comments on rejected mss.

How to Contact: Send complete ms. Should include estimated word count, Social Security number. Reports in 2 weeks. SASE (IRCs) for return of ms or send disposable copy. Simultaneous and reprint submissions OK. Sample copy for #10 SAE and 2 first-class stamps. Fiction guidelines for #10 SAE and 1 first-class stamp.

Payment: Pays 3-5¢/word and 3 contributor's copies. Additional copies 50¢ each.

Terms: Pays on acceptance. Buys first, first North American serial, one-time, reprint or simultaneous rights.

Advice: "The aim of *Guide* magazine is to reflect in creative yet concrete ways the unconditional love of God to young people 10 to 14 years of age. Believing that an accurate picture of God is a prerequisite for wholeness, our efforts editorially and in design will be focused on accurately portraying His attributes and expectations."

‡GUYS, First Hand Ltd., Box 1314, Teaneck NJ 07666. (201)836-9177. Fax: (201)836-5055. Editor: William Spencer. Magazine: digest size; 160 pages; illustrations; photos. "Fiction and informative departments for today's gay man. Fiction is of an erotic nature, and we especially need short shorts and novella-length stories." Published 10 times/year. Estab. 1988.

  • *First Hand*, another magazine by this publisher, also is listed in this book.

Needs: Gay. "Should be written in first person. No science fiction or fantasy. No four-legged animals. All characters must be over 18. Stories including members of ethnic groups or the disabled are especially welcome. Erotica should be based on reality." Upcoming themes: "Jock Tales," "Seafood Tales," "Prison Tales," "Campus Tales," "Uniform Tales." Buys 6 mss/issue; 66 mss/year. Publishes ms 6-12 months after acceptance. Published work by Rick Jackson, Kenn Richie, Jay Shaffer; published new writers within the last year. Length: 3,000 words average; 2,000 words minimum; 3,750 words maximum. For novellas: 7,500-8,600 words. Publishes short shorts. Length: 750-1,250 words. Sometimes critiques rejected mss and recommends other markets.

How to Contact: Send complete ms with cover letter, which should include writer's name, address, telephone and Social Security number and whether selling all rights or first North American serial rights. Reports in 6-8 weeks on ms. SASE (IRCs). Accepts computer printout submissions. Sample copy for $5. Fiction guidelines for #10 SAE and 1 first-class stamp. Reviews novels and short story collections.
Payment: Pays $100-150; $75 for short shorts (all rights); $250 for novellas (all rights).
Terms: Pays on publication or in 240 days, whichever comes first, for all rights or first North American serial rights.
Advice: "Use language that you would normally use. Don't get poetic or rhapsodic. Sex is a basic act. Use basic language."

HADASSAH MAGAZINE, (IV), 50 W. 58th St., New York NY 10019. Executive Editor: Alan M. Tigay. Senior Editor: Zelda Shluker. Jewish general interest magazine: 8½×11; 48-70 pages; coated and uncoated paper; slick, medium weight coated cover; drawings and cartoons; photos. Primarily concerned with Israel, the American Jewish community, Jewish communities around the world and American current affairs. Monthly except combined June/July and August/September issues. Circ. 375,000.
 • *Hadassah* was nominated for a National Magazine Award in 1992 and has received several Rockover Awards for Excellence in Jewish Journalism.
Needs: Ethnic (Jewish). Receives 20-25 unsolicited fiction mss each month. Recently published fiction by Joanne Greenberg, Anita Desai and Lori Ubell; published new writers within the last year. Length: 1,500-2,000 words.
How to Contact: Query first with writing samples. Reports in 3-4 months on mss. "Not interested in multiple submissions or previously published articles." Must submit appropriate size SASE (IRCs).
Payment: Pays $300 minimum.
Terms: Pays on publication for U.S. publication rights.
Advice: "Stories on a Jewish theme should be neither self-hating nor schmaltzy."

HARPER'S MAGAZINE, (II, III), 11th Floor, 666 Broadway, New York NY 10012. (212)614-6500. Editor: Lewis H. Lapham. Magazine: 8×10³/₄; 80 pages; illustrations. Magazine for well educated, widely read and socially concerned readers, college-aged and older, those active in political and community affairs. Monthly. Circ. 200,000.
 • This is considered a top but tough market for contemporary fiction. The magazine was a National Magazine Award Finalist for fiction in 1991.
Needs: Contemporary and humor. Stories on contemporary life and its problems. Does a summer reading issue usually in August. Receives approximately 300 unsolicited fiction mss/month. Published new writers within the last year. Length: 1,000-5,000 words.
How to Contact: Query to managing editor, or through agent. Reports in 6 weeks on queries.
Payment: Pays $500-1,000.
Terms: Pays on acceptance for rights, which vary on each author and material. Negotiable kill fee. Sends galleys to author.
Advice: Buys very little fiction but *Harper's* has published short stories traditionally.

HI-CALL, (II), Gospel Publishing House, 1445 Boonville Ave., Springfield MO 65802-1894. (417)862-2781. Editor: Tammy Bicket. Take-home Sunday school paper for teenagers (ages 12-17). Weekly. Estab. 1936. Circ. 80,000.
 • *Hi-Call* may change its name later this year; however, writers will still be able to reach the magazine at the above address.
Needs: Religious/inspirational, mystery/suspense, adventure, humor, spiritual and young adult, "with a strong but not preachy Biblical emphasis." Receives approximately 100 unsolicited fiction mss/month. Published work by Betty Steele Everett, Alan Cliburn and Michelle Starr. Published new writers within the last year. Length: up to 1,500 words.
How to Contact: Send complete ms with SASE. Reports in 1-3 months. Simultaneous and reprint submissions OK. Free sample copy and guidelines.
Payment: Pays 2-3¢/word.
Terms: Pays on acceptance for one-time rights.
Advice: "Most manuscripts are rejected because of shallow characters, shallow or predictable plots, and/or a lack of spiritual emphasis. Send seasonal material approximately 18 months in advance."

HIGH ADVENTURE, (II), General Council Assemblies of God (Gospel Publishing Co.), 1445 Boonville, Springfield MO 65802. (417)862-2781, ext. 4178. Editor: Marshall Bruner. Magazine: 8⁵/₁₆×11⅛; 16 pages; Lancer paper; self cover; illustrations; photos. Magazine for adolescent boys. "Designed to provide boys with worthwhile, enjoyable, leisure reading; to challenge them in narrative form to higher ideals and greater spiritual dedication; and to perpetuate the spirit of the Royal Rangers program through stories, ideas and illustrations." Quarterly. Estab. 1971. Circ. 86,000.
Needs: Adventure, historical (general), religious/inspirational, suspense/mystery and western. Published new writers within the last year. Length: 1,200 words minimum. Publishes short shorts to 1,000 words. Occasionally critiques rejected mss.
How to Contact: Send ms with SASE (IRCs). Include Social Security number. Reports in 2 months. Simultaneous and reprint submissions OK. Free sample copy and fiction guidelines for 9×12 SASE.
Payment: Pays 2-3¢/word (base) and 3 contributor's copies.
Terms: Pays on acceptance for first rights and one-time rights.
Advice: "Ask for list of upcoming themes."

HIGHLIGHTS FOR CHILDREN, 803 Church St., Honesdale PA 18431. (717)253-1080. Editor: Kent L. Brown, Jr. Address fiction to: Beth Troop, Manuscript Coordinator. Magazine: 8½×11; 42 pages; uncoated paper; coated cover stock; illustrations; photos. Monthly. Circ. 2.8 million.
• *Highlights* is very supportive of writers. The magazine sponsors a contest and a workshop each year at Chautauqua (New York). See the listings for these and for their press, Boyds Mills Press in other sections of this book. The magazine ranked #24 on the latest *Writer's Digest* Fiction 50 list. Several authors published in *Highlights* have received SCBWI Magazine Merit Awards.
Needs: Juvenile (ages 2-12). Unusual stories appealing to both girls and boys; stories with good characterization, strong emotional appeal, vivid, full of action. "Begin with action rather than description, have strong plot, believable setting, suspense from start to finish." Length: 400-900 words. "We also need easy stories for very young readers (100-400 words)." No war, crime or violence. Receives 600-800 unsolicited fiction mss/month. Buys 6-7 mss/issue. Also publishes rebus (picture) stories of 125 words or under for the 3-to 7-year-old child. Recently published work by Virginia Kroll, Judith Logan Lehne and Steven Sweeney; published new writers within the last year. Critiques rejected mss occasionally, "especially when editors see possibilities in story."
How to Contact: Send complete ms with SASE (IRCs) and include a rough word count and cover letter "with any previous acceptances by our magazine; any other published work anywhere." No simultaneous submissions. Reports in 4 weeks. Free guidelines on request.
Payment: Pays 14¢ and up per word.
Terms: Pays on acceptance for all rights. Sends galleys to author.
Advice: "We accept a story on its merit whether written by an unpublished or an experienced writer. Mss are rejected because of poor writing, lack of plot, trite or worn-out plot, or poor characterization. Children *like* stories and learn about life from stories. Children learn to become lifelong fiction readers by enjoying stories. Feel passion for your subject. Create vivid images. Write a child-centered story; leave adults in the background."

ALFRED HITCHCOCK MYSTERY MAGAZINE, (I, II), Dell Magazines Fiction Group, 1540 Broadway., New York NY 10036. (212)782-8532. Editor: Cathleen Jordan. Mystery fiction magazine: 5¹/₁₆×7³/₈; 160 pages; 28 lb. newsprint paper; 60 lb. machine-/coated cover stock; illustrations; photos. Published 13 times/year. Estab. 1956. Circ. 225,000.
• Stories published in *Alfred Hitchcock Mystery Magazine* have won Edgar Awards for "Best Mystery Story of the Year," Shamus Awards for "Best Private Eye Story of the Year" and Robert L. Fish Awards for "Best First Mystery Short Story of the Year." It ranks #14 on the latest *Writer's Digest* Fiction 50 list. See *Ellery Queen's Mystery Magazine* also listed in this book.
Needs: Mystery and detection (amateur sleuth, cozy, private eye, police procedural). No sensationalism. Number of mss/issue varies with length of mss. Length: up to 14,000 words. Also publishes short shorts.
How to Contact: Send complete ms and SASE (IRCs). Simultaneous submissions OK, if indicated. Reports in 2 months. Guideline sheet for SASE.
Payment: Pays 6½¢/word on acceptance.

"I think the cover indicates that there's a lot of fun to be had inside this publication," says Coordinating Editor Richard Wallace of Highlights for Children. "Les Gray's wacky, busy covers always have high kid-appeal." Wallace says there are at least five short stories per issue, with an emphasis on "stories that will entertain and—without being didactic—show kids something about the world." Covers have the same "Fun with a Purpose" theme as the rest of the magazine, says Wallace, "even if that 'purpose' is as simple as tweaking the imagination, as with Gray's penguin carpenters." (Artwork by Les Gray. © 1993 Highlights for Children.)

HOME TIMES, (I, II, IV), Neighbor News, Inc., P.O. Box 16096, West Palm Beach FL 33416. (407)439-3509. Editor: Dennis Lombard. Newspaper: tabloid; 24-32 pages; newsprint; illustrations and photographs. "Interdenominational Christian news, views, fiction, poetry, sold to general public, *not* through churches." Weekly. Estab. 1980. Cicr. 10,000.
Needs: Adventure, historical (general), humor/satire, literary, mainstream, religious/inspirational, romance, sports. "All fiction needs to be related to the publication's focus on current events and Christian perspective—we feel you must examine a sample issue because *Home Times* is *different*." Nothing "preachy or doctrinal." Receives 50 unsolicited mss/month. Buys 10-20 mss/issue. Publishes ms 1-6 months after acceptance. Recently published work by Chuck Colsen, James Dobson, Walt Williams. Length: 700 words average; 500 words minimum; 900 words maximum.
How to Contact: Send complete manuscript with cover letter including Social Security number and word count. "Absolutely no queries." "1-2 sentences on what the piece is and on who you are." Reports on mss in 1 week. SASE (IRCs). Simultaneous and reprint submissions OK. Sample copy for $1, 9 × 12 SAE and 3 first-class stamps. Guidelines for #10 SAE and 1 first-class stamp.
Payment: Pays $5-35.
Terms: Buys one-time rights.
Advice: "Read our newspapers—get the drift of our rather unusual interdenominational non-doctrinal content. Looks for "historical, issues, or family orientation; also like creative nonfiction.""

HUMPTY DUMPTY'S MAGAZINE, (II), Children's Better Health Institute, Box 567, 1100 Waterway Blvd., Indianapolis IN 46206. Editor: Christine French Clark. Magazine: 6½ × 9⅛; 48 pages; 35 lb. paper; coated cover; illustrations; rarely photos. Children's magazine stressing health, nutrition, hygiene, exercise and safety for children ages 4-6. Publishes 8 issues/year.
• Children's Better Health Institute also publishes *Child Life, Children's Digest, Children's Playmate, Jack and Jill* and *Turtle* listed in this book.
Needs: Juvenile health-related material and material of a more general nature. No inanimate talking objects. Rhyming stories should flow easily with no contrived rhymes. Receives 250-300 unsolicited fiction mss/month. Buys 3-5 mss/issue. Length: 600 words maximum.
How to Contact: Send complete ms with SASE (IRCs). No queries. Reports in 8-10 weeks. Sample copy for $1.25. Editorial guidelines for SASE.
Payment: Pays minimum 10-20¢/word for stories plus 2 contributor's copies (more upon request).
Terms: Pays on publication for all rights. (One-time book rights returned when requested for specific publication.)
Advice: "In contemporary stories, characters should be up-to-date, with realistic dialogue. We're looking for health-related stories with unusual twists or surprise endings. We want to avoid stories and poems that 'preach.' We try to present the health material in a positive way, utilizing a light

humorous approach wherever possible." Most rejected mss "are too wordy. Cover letters should be included only if they give pertinent information—list of credits, bibliography, or mention of any special training or qualifications that make author an authority."

HUSTLER, Larry Flynt Publications, Suite 300, 9171 Wilshire Blvd., Beverly Hills CA 90210. Does not accept outside fiction; all fiction is staff written.

HUSTLER BUSTY BEAUTIES, (I, IV), HG Publications, Inc., Suite 300, 9171 Wilshire Blvd., Beverly Hills CA 90210. (310)858-7100. Editor: N. Morgen Hagen. Magazine: 8×11; 100 pages; 60 lb. paper; 80 lb. cover; illustrations and photographs. "Adult entertainment and reading centered around large-breasted women for an over-18 audience, mostly male." Monthly. Estab. 1988. Circ. 150,000.
Needs: Adventure, erotica, fantasy, mystery/suspense. All must have erotic theme. Receives 25 unsolicited fiction mss/month. Buys 1 ms/issue; 6-12 mss/year. Publishes mss 3-6 months after acceptance. Published work by Mike Dillon, H.H. Morris. Length: 1,600 words preferred; 1,000 words minimum; 2,000 words maximum.
How to Contact: Query first. Then send complete ms with cover letter. Reports in 2 weeks on queries; in 2-4 weeks on mss. SASE (IRCs). Sample copy for $5. Fiction guidelines free.
Payment: Pays $80-500.
Terms: Pays on publication for all rights.
Advice: Looks for "1. Plausible plot, well-defined characters, literary ingenuity. 2. Hot sex scenes. 3. Readable, coherent, grammatically sound prose."

IDEALS MAGAZINE, (II), Ideals Publications Inc., Suite 800, 565 Marriott Dr., Nashville TN 37210. (615)885-8270. Publisher: Patricia Pingry. Magazine: 8⁷/₁₆×10⁷/₈; 80 pages; illustrations; photos. "*Ideals* is a family-oriented magazine with issues corresponding to seasons and based on traditional values." Published 8 times a year. Estab. 1944.
Needs: Seasonal, inspirational, or nostalgic short, short fiction or prose poem. Length: 700 words maximum.
How to Contact: Send complete ms with SASE (IRCs). Reports in 3-4 months on mss.
Payment: Varies.
Terms: Pays on publication for one-time rights.
Advice: "We publish fiction that is appropriate to the theme of the issue and to our audience."

‡IN TOUCH FOR MEN, (IV), 13122 Saticoy St., North Hollywood CA 91605. (818)764-2288. Editor: D. DiFranco. Magazine: 8×10¾; 100 pages; glossy paper; coated cover; illustrations and photographs. "*In Touch* is a magazine for gay men. It features five to six nude male centerfolds in each issue, but is erotic rather than pornographic. We include fiction." Monthly. Estab. 1973. Circ. 70,000.
Needs: Confession, gay, erotica, romance (contemporary, historical). All characters must be over 18 years old. Stories must have an explicit erotic content. No heterosexual or internalized homophobic fiction. Buys 3 mss/month; 36 mss/year. Publishes ms 3 months after acceptance. Length: 2,500 words average; up to 3,500 words maximum. Sometimes critiques rejected mss and recommends other markets.
How to Contact: Send complete ms with cover letter, name, address and Social Security number. Reports in 2 weeks on queries; 2 months on mss. SASE (IRCs). Simultaneous and reprint submissions, if from local publication, OK. Sample copy for $5.95. Fiction guidelines free. Reviews novels and short story collections.
Payment: Pays $25-75 (except on rare occasions for a longer piece).
Terms: Pays on publication for one-time rights.
Advice: Publishes "primarily erotic material geared toward gay men. Periodically (but very seldom) we will run fiction of a non-erotic nature (but still gay-related), but that's not the norm. I personally prefer (and accept) manuscripts that are not only erotic/hardcore, but show a developed story, plot and concise ending (as opposed to just sexual vignettes that basically lead nowhere). If it's got a little romance, too, that's even better. Emphasis still on erotic, though. We're starting to fuse more 'safe sex' depictions in fiction, hoping that it becomes the standard for male erotica. Hopefully portraying responsible activity will prompt people to act responsibly, as well."

INDIA CURRENTS, (II,IV), The Complete Indian American Magazine, Box 21285, San Jose CA 95151. (408)274-6966. Fax: (408)274-2733. Editor: Arvind Kumar. Magazine: 8½×11; 104 pages; newsprint paper; illustrations and photographs. "The arts and culture of India as seen in America for Indians and non-Indians with a common interest in India." Monthly. Estab. 1987. Circ. 25,000.

• *India Currents* recently won an award for "Cultural Awareness Through Journalism" from the Federation of Indian American Associations.

Needs: All Indian content: contemporary, ethnic, feminist, historical (general), humor/satire, literary, mainstream, prose poem, regional, religious/inspirational, romance, translations (from Indian languages). "We seek material with insight into Indian culture, American culture and the crossing from one to another." Receives 12 unsolicited mss/month. Buys 1 ms/issue; 12 mss/year. Publishes ms 2-6 months after acceptance. Published work by Chitra Divakaruni, Jyotsna Sreenivasan, Mathew Chacko; published new writers within the last year. Length: 1,500 words average; 1,000 words minimum; 3,000 words maximum. Publishes short shorts. Length: 500 words.

How to Contact: Send complete ms with cover letter and clips of published work. Reports in 2-3 months on mss. SASE (IRCs). Simultaneous and reprint submissions OK. Accepts electronic submissions. Sample copy $3.

Payment: Pays in subscriptions.

Terms: Pays on publication for one-time rights.

Advice: "Story must be related to India and subcontinent in some meaningful way. The best stories are those which document some deep transformation as a result of an Indian experience, or those which show the humanity of Indians as the world's most ancient citizens."

INDIAN LIFE MAGAZINE, (II, IV), Intertribal Christian Communications, Box 3765, Station B, Winnipeg, Manitoba R2W 3R6 Canada. (204)661-9333 or (800)665-9275 in Canada only. Fax: (204)661-3982. Contact: Editor. Magazine: 8½ × 11; 24 pages; newsprint paper and cover stock; illustrations; full cover; photos. A nondenominational Christian magazine written and read mostly by North American Indians. Bimonthly. Estab. 1979. Circ. 30,000.

• *Indian Life Magazine* has won several awards for "Higher Goals in Christian Journalism" and "Excellence" from the Evangelical Press Association. The magazine also won awards from the Native American Press Association.

Needs: Ethnic (Indian), historical (general), juvenile, religious/inspirational, young adult/teen, native testimonies, bible teaching articles. Length: 1,000-1,200 words average.

How to Contact: Query letter preferred. Simultaneous submissions OK. Reports in 1 month on queries. IRC or SASE ("US stamps no good up here"). Sample copy $1 and 8½ × 11 SAE. Fiction guidelines for $1 and #10 SAE.

Advice: "Keep it simple with an Indian viewpoint at about a 7th grade reading level. Read story out loud. Have someone else read it to you. If it doesn't come across smoothly and naturally, it needs work."

INIQUITIES, The Magazine of Great Wickedness & Wonder, (I, II), Suite 1346, 235 E. Colorado Blvd., Pasadena CA 91101. Editors: J.F. Gonzalez and Buddy Martinez. Magazine: 8½/2 × 11; 96 pages; slick glossy paper; illustrations and photographs. "Horror fiction, nonfiction in relation to horror and relating subjects (see guidelines) for anybody who has an interest in horror (books, film, etc.)." Quarterly. Estab. 1990. Circ. 10,000.

Needs: Horror, mystery, (police procedural) psychic/supernatural/occult; suspense and science fiction (soft sociological). No sword and sorcery, romance, confessional, pornography. Receives 250 unsolicited mss/month. Buys 6-8 mss/issue; 30-35 mss/year. Publishes ms 6 months-1½ years after acceptance. Published work by Peter Straub, Clive Barker, Ray Bradbury. Length: 4,000-6,000 words preferred; 10,000 words maximum. Publishes short shorts. Sometimes critiques rejected mss and recommends other markets.

How to Contact: Send complete ms with cover letter. Include "credits, if any, name, address and phone number. I don't want the writer to tell me about the story in the cover letter." Reports in 1-3 weeks on queries; 3 months on mss. SASE (IRCs). Simultaneous and reprint submissions OK. Sample copy for $5.95. Fiction guidelines for #10 SAE and 1 first-class stamp.

Market conditions are constantly changing! If you're still using this book and it is 1995 or later, buy the newest edition of Novel & Short Story Writer's Market *at your favorite bookstore or order directly from Writer's Digest Books.*

Payment: Pays 3¢-5¢/word.
Terms: Offers kill fee of half the amount. Buys first North American serial rights. Sends galleys to author.
Advice: Looks for "believable characters and original ideas. Good writing. Fantastic writing. Make the words flow and count for the story. If the story keeps us turning the pages with bated breath, it has a great chance. If we get through the first two pages and it's sloppy, displays weak, or uninteresting characters or a contrived plot, we won't even finish it. Chances are the reader won't either. Know the genre and what's been done. *Invest in a sample copy.* While we are open to different styles of horror, we have high expectations for the fiction we publish. The only way a beginner will know what we expect is to buy the magazine and read what we've published."

INSIDE, The Magazine of the Jewish Exponent, (II), Jewish Federation, 226 S. 16th St., Philadelphia PA 19102. (215)893-5700. Editor-in-Chief: Jane Biberman. Magazine: 175-225 pages; glossy paper; illustrations; photos. Aimed at middle- and upper-middle-class audience, Jewish-oriented articles and fiction. Quarterly. Estab. 1980. Circ. 80,000.
Needs: Contemporary, ethnic, humor/satire, literary and translations. No erotica. Receives approximately 10 unsolicited fiction mss/month. Buys 1-2 mss/issue; 4-8 mss/year. Published new writers within the last year. Length: 1,500 words minimum; 3,000 words maximum; 2,000 words average. Occasionally critiques rejected mss.
How to Contact: Query first with clips of published work. Reports on queries in 3 weeks. SASE (IRCs). Simultaneous submissions OK. Sample copy for $3. Fiction guidelines for SASE.
Payment: Pays $100-600.
Terms: Pays on acceptance for first rights. Sometimes buys reprints. Sends galleys to author.
Advice: "We're looking for original, avant-garde, stylish writing."

INTERNATIONAL BOWHUNTER, (I, II, IV), P.O. Box 67, Pillager MN 56473-0067. (218)746-3333. Editor: Johnny Boatner. Magazine: 8¼ × 10¾; 68 pages; enamel paper; illustrations and photographs. "Bowhunting articles only for bowhunters." Published 6 times/year. Estab. 1990. Circ. 50,000 + .
Needs: Adventure and sports. "We want articles by people who are actually bowhunters writing about their experience." Receives 30 unsolicited mss/month. Buys 7-12 mss/issue; 49-84/year. Publishes ms 1-6 months after acceptance. Length: 1,200 words preferred; 600 words minimum; 4,000 words maximum. Publishes short shorts. Length: 500 words. Sometimes critiques rejected mss and recommends other markets.
How to Contact: Send complete ms with cover letter. Include Social Security number and bio. Reports on queries in 2 weeks. SASE (IRCs). Sample copy for $2, #10 SAE and 1 first-class stamp. Fiction guidelines for #10 SAE and 1 first-class stamp.
Payment: Pays $25-150 and contributor's copies; charge for extras.
Terms: Buys first rights.
Advice: "Read your guidelines."

‡**INTERRACE MAGAZINE, The Source for Interracial Living, (IV),** P.O. Box 12048, Atlanta GA 30355-2048. (404)364-9690. Editor: Candy Mills. Magazine: 8½ × 11; 40 + pages; gloss paper; 60 lb. gloss cover; illustrations and photos. "All submissions must have an interracial theme as this is a national magazine serving interracial couples/families, biracial/multiracial people and those who have transracially adopted." Published 9 times/year.
Needs: All submissions must have an interracial/multiracial theme!!! Adventure, condensed novel, fantasy (science fiction), humor/satire, literary, mainstream/contemporary, mystery/suspense, romance (contemporary), serialized novel, westerns (traditional), young adult. "Summer issue 1994 will be our literary issue which will highlight several short stories." List of upcoming themes available for SASE (IRCs). Publishes annual special fiction issue or anthology. Receives 5-10 unsolicited mss/month. Accepts 1 ms/issue; 9 mss/year. Publishes ms 4-8 months, occasionally 1 year after acceptance. Recently published work by Christopher Conlon, Frances Parker, Bob Slaymaker. Length: 2,400 words average; 1,600 words minimum; 4,000 words maximum. Publishes short shorts. Length: 500 words. Also publishes literary essays, literary criticism, poetry. Sometimes critiques or comments on rejected mss.
How to Contact: Send complete ms with cover letter and synopsis. Should include estimated word count, bio, Social Security number and list of publications. Reports in 2-4 weeks on queries; 1-2 months on mss. Send a disposable copy of ms. Simultaneous, reprint and electronic submissions OK. Sample copy for $2. Fiction and nonfiction guidelines for #10 SAE and 1 first-class stamp. Reviews novel and short story collections.

Payment: Pays $10-30, free subscription to magazine and up to 5 contributor's copies.
Terms: Pays on publication. Buys one-time rights.
Advice: "It's not so much how well-written the piece is but how 'smart' it is. In other words, the characters are continually evolving, the story holds your attention from start to finish and the storyline has a beginning, middle and end, always with a multicultural/interracial focus."

JACK AND JILL, (IV), The Children's Better Health Institute, Box 567, 1100 Waterway Blvd., Indianapolis IN 46206. (317)636-8881. Editor: Steve Charles. Children's magazine of articles, stories and activities many with a health, safety, exercise or nutritional-oriented theme, ages 6-8 years. Monthly except January/February, March/April, May/June, July/August. Estab. 1938.
● Other publications by this publisher listed in this book include *Child Life, Children's Digest, Children's Playmate, Humpty Dumpty* and *Turtle*.
Needs: Science fiction, mystery, sports, adventure, historical fiction and humor. Health-related stories with a subtle lesson. Published work by Peter Fernandez, Adriana Devoy and Myra Schomberg; published new writers within the last year. Length: 500-1,500 words.
How to Contact: Send complete ms with SASE. Reports in 10 weeks on mss. Sample copy 75¢. Fiction guidelines for SASE.
Payment: Pays 8¢/word.
Terms: Pays on publication for all rights.
Advice: "Try to present health material in a positive—not a negative—light. Use humor and a light approach wherever possible without minimizing the seriousness of the subject. We need more humor and adventure stories."

JUGGLER'S WORLD, (IV), International Juggler's Association, Box 443, Davidson NC 28036. (704)892-1296. Editor: Bill Giduz. Fiction Editor: Ken Letko. Magazine: 8½×11; 40 pages; 70 lb. paper and cover stock; illustrations and photos. For and about jugglers and juggling. Quarterly.
Needs: Historical (general), humor/satire, science fiction. No stories "that don't include juggling as a central theme." Receives "very few" unsolicited mss/month. Accepts 2 mss/year. Publishes ms an average of 6-12 months to 1 year after acceptance. Length: 2,000 words average; 1,000 words minimum; 2,500 words maximum. Sometimes critiques rejected mss.
How to Contact: Query first. Reports in 1 week. Simultaneous submissions OK. Prefers electronic submissions via IBM or Macintosh compatible disk. Sample copy for $2.50.
Payment: Pays $25-50, free subscription to magazine and 3 contributor's copies.
Terms: Pays on acceptance for first rights.

JUNIOR TRAILS, (I, II), Gospel Publishing House, 1445 Boonville Ave., Springfield MO 65802. (417)862-2781. Elementary Editor: Sinda S. Zinn. Magazine: 5½×8½; 8 pages; 36 lb. coated offset paper; art illustrations; photos. "A Sunday school take-home paper of nature articles and fictional stories that apply Christian principles to everyday living for 10-to 12-year-old children." Weekly. Estab. 1954. Circ. 70,000.
Needs: Contemporary, religious/inspirational, spiritual, sports and juvenile. Adventure stories are welcome. No Biblical fiction or science fiction. Buys 2 mss/issue. Published work by Betty Lou Mell, Mason M. Smith, Nanette L. Dunford; published new writers within the last year. Length: 1,200-1,500 words. Publishes short shorts.
How to Contact: Send complete ms with SASE (IRCs). Reports in 6-8 weeks. Free sample copy and guidelines.
Payment: Pays 3¢/word. 3 free author's copies.
Terms: Pays on acceptance.
Advice: "Know the age level and direct stories relevant to that age group. Since junior-age children (grades 5 and 6) enjoy action, fiction provides a vehicle for communicating moral/spiritual principles in a dramatic framework. Fiction, if well done, can be a powerful tool for relating Christian principles. It must, however, be realistic and believable in its development. Make your children be children, not overly mature for their age. We would like more stories with a *city* setting. Write for contemporary children, using setting and background that includes various ethnic groups."

KID CITY, (II), Children's Television Workshop, 1 Lincoln Plaza, New York NY 10023. (212)595-3456. Editor-in-Chief: Maureen Hunter-Bone. Magazine: 8½×11; 32 pages; glossy cover; illustrations; photos. General interest for children 6-10 "devoted to sparking kids' interest in reading and writing about the world around them." Published 10 times/year. Estab. 1974. Circ. 350,000.

Needs: Adventure, mystery, juvenile (6-10 years), science fiction. Publishes ms "at least" 6 months after acceptance. Length: 600-750 words average; 1,000 words maximum.
How to Contact: Send complete ms with cover letter. Reports in 1-2 months on mss. SASE. Sample copy for $1.50 and 9×12 SAE with 75¢ postage. Writers' guidelines for 9×12 SAE with 75¢ postage.
Payment: Pays $200-400 and contributor's copies.
Terms: Pays on acceptance for all rights (some negotiable).
Advice: "We look for bright and sparkling prose. Don't talk down. Don't stereotype. Don't use cutesy names, animals or plots. No heavy moralizing or pat dilemmas."

LADIES' HOME JOURNAL, (III), Published by Meredith Corporation, 100 Park Ave., New York NY 10017. Editor-in-Chief: Myrna Blyth. Fiction/Articles Editor: Jane Farrell. Magazine: 190 pages; 34-38 lb. coated paper; 65 lb. coated cover; illustrations and photos.
   • *Ladies Home Journal* has won several awards for journalism. It ranks #21 on the latest *Writer's Digest* Fiction 50 list.
Needs: Book mss and short stories, *accepted only through an agent.* Return of unsolicited material cannot be guaranteed. Published work by Fay Weldon, Anita Shreve, Jane Shapiro, Anne Rivers Siddons. Length: approximately 3,500 words.
How to Contact: Send complete ms with cover letter (credits). Simultaneous submissions OK. Publishes ms 4-12 months after acceptance.
Terms: Buys First North American rights.
Advice: "Our readers like stories, especially those that have emotional impact. Stories about relationships between people — husband/wife — mother/son — seem to be subjects that can be explored effectively in short stories. Our reader's mail and surveys attest to this fact: Readers enjoy our fiction, and are most keenly tuned to stories dealing with children. Fiction today is stronger than ever. Beginners can be optimistic; if they have talent, I do believe that talent will be discovered. It is best to read the magazine before submitting."

LADYBUG, (II, IV), Carus Corporation, P.O. Box 300, Peru IL 61354. (815)224-6643. Editor-in-Chief: Marianne Carus. Contact: Submissions Editor. Magazine: 8×10; 36 pages plus 4-page pullout section; illustrations. "*Ladybug* publishes original stories and poems and reprints written by the world's best children's authors. For young children, ages 2-6." Monthly. Estab. 1990. Circ. 130,000.
   • Carus Corporation's magazine for older children, *Cricket* is also listed in this book. *Ladybug* has received the Parent's Choice Award, the Golden Lamp Honor Award from the Educational Press Association and a Magazine Merit award from the Society of Children's Book Writers and Illustrators. Sources tell us Carus Corporation has just launched a new publication, *Spider*, for children in early grades. Check with them for details.
Needs: Juvenile, fantasy (children's), preschool, read-out-loud stories, picture stories, folk tales, fairy tales. Length: 300-750 words preferred. Publishes short shorts.
How to Contact: Send complete ms with cover letter. Include word count on ms (do not count title). Reports in 3 months. SASE (IRCs). Reprints are OK. Fiction guidelines for SAE and 1 first-class stamp. Sample copy: $2.
Payment: Pays up to 25¢/word (less for reprints).
Terms: Pays on publication for first publication rights or second serial (reprint) rights. For recurring features, pays flat fee and copyright becomes property of Carus Publishing.
Advice: Looks for "well-written stories for preschoolers: age-appropriate, not condescending. We look for rich, evocative language and sense of joy or wonder."

LADY'S CIRCLE, (II), Lopez Publications, Suite 906, 152 Madison Ave., New York NY 10016. (212)689-3933. Editor: Mary Bemis. Magazine. "A lot of our readers are in Midwestern states." Bimonthly. Estab. 1963. Circ. 100,000.
Needs: Historical, humor/satire, mainstream, religious/inspirational, senior citizen/retirement. Receives 100 unsolicited fiction mss/month. Buys about 3-4 fiction mss/year. Time between acceptance and publication "varies, usually works 6 months ahead." Length: 1,000 words minimum; 1,200 words maximum. Accepts short shorts "for fillers." Sometimes critiques rejected ms.
How to Contact: Query first. Reports in 3 months on queries. SASE (IRCs). Simultaneous and reprint submissions OK. Accepts electronic submissions via disk or modem. Sample copy for $3.95; fiction guidelines for SAE.
Payment: Pay varies, depending on ms.
Terms: Pays on publication for first North American serial rights.

‡**LOUIS L'AMOUR WESTERN MAGAZINE, (I, II, IV),** Bantam Doubleday Dell Magazines, 15th Floor, 1540 Broadway, New York NY 10036. (212)782-8532. Fax: (212)782-8338. Editor: Elana Lore. Magazine: 8 × 10¾; 80 pages; some groundwood paper, some coated stock; 100 lb. Sterling cover with UV coating; illustrations and photographs. "We publish western short stories for an audience that is about 70 percent male, 35-64 years old, largely non-urban, with a household income of $35,000 + ." Monthly. (First issue in January 1994. Magazine will be bi-monthly for first three issues, then monthly.) Estab. 1994.

● Bantam Doubleday Dell's magazine group also includes *Ellery Queen's Mystery Magazine*, *Alfred Hitchcock Mystery Magazine*, *Analog Science Fiction & Fact* and *Asimov's Science Fiction*.

Needs: Westerns (frontier, traditional). Receives 250 unsolicited mss/month. Accepts 6-9 mss/issue. Publishes ms 6 months after acceptance. Agented fiction 5%. Length: 5,000-7,000 preferred; 12,000 words maximum.

How to Contact: Send complete ms with a cover letter. Should include Social Security number and list of publications. Reports in 2 months. Send SASE (IRCs) for reply, return of ms or send a disposable copy of ms. Simultaneous and reprint submissions OK. Sample copy for $3. Fiction guidelines for #10 SAE and 1 first-class stamp.

Payment: Pays 8¢/word.

Terms: Pays on acceptance for first serial rights.

Advice: "Get a copy of our writers' guidelines before you submit. Read a copy of the magazine before you submit to see what kinds of things we're looking for." Looking for "original ideas that bring to life the people and places of the West. We don't want any shoot'em ups, any reworked Saturday morning TV show western stories."

LETHBRIDGE MAGAZINE, (I, II), 248684 Alberta Ltd., P.O. Box 1203, Lethbridge, Alberta T1J 4A4 Canada. (403)327-3200. Editor: Richard Burke. Magazine: 8 ½ × 11; 48 pages; glossy paper; illustrations and photos. "*Lethbridge Magazine* prints general interest topics relating to Lethbridge and Southern Alberta for an audience of all ages." Bimonthly. Estab. 1981. Circ. 17,218.

Needs: Adventure, historical (general), humor/satire, literary, regional. Receives 10 unsolicited mss/month. Buys 1 ms/year. Publishes ms 2 months after acceptance. Length: 1,500 words preferred; 1,000 words minimum; 2,000 words maximum. Publishes short shorts.

How to Contact: Query first with clips of published work or send complete ms with cover letter. Reports in 2 months. SASE (IRCs). Simultaneous and reprint submissions OK. Accepts electronic submissions (copy on disk). Sample copy for $2. Fiction guidelines for SASE.

Payment: Pays 5-12¢/word. Provides contributor's copies.

Terms: Pays on publication for first North American serial rights.

Advice: "Space requirements usually dictate if we can use a submission. Originality and quality of writing make a manuscript stand out. Keep the length short."

LIGUORIAN, (I, IV), "A Leading Catholic Magazine," Liguori Publications, 1 Liguori Dr., Liguori MO 63057. (314)464-2500. Editor-in-Chief: Allan Weinert, CSS.R. Managing Editor: Susan M. Schuster. Magazine: 5 × 8½; 64 pages; b&w illustrations and photographs. "*Liguorian* is a Catholic magazine aimed at helping our readers to live a full Christian life. We publish articles for families, young people, children, religious and singles — all with the same aim." Monthly. Estab. 1913. Circ. 400,000.

● *Liguorian* received Catholic Press Association awards for 1993 including Honorable Mention for Best Short Story and Best Cover and Second Place for General Excellence.

Needs: Religious/inspirational, young adult and senior citizen/retirement (with moral Christian thrust), spiritual. "Stories submitted to *Liguorian* must have as their goal the lifting up of the reader to a higher Christian view of values and goals. We are not interested in contemporary works that lack purpose or are of questionable moral value." Receives approximately 25 unsolicited fiction mss/month. Buys 12 mss/year. Recently published work by Sharon Helgens, Kathleen Choi, Shirley Anne Morgan, Beverly Sheresh; published new writers within the last year. Length: 1,500-2,000 words preferred. Also publishes short shorts. Occasionally critiques rejected mss "if we feel the author is capable of giving us something we need even though this story did not suit us." Occasionally recommends other markets.

How to Contact: Send complete ms with SASE (IRCs). Accepts disk submissions compatible with IBM or Macintosh, using a DOS program; prefers hard copy with disk submission. Reports in 6 weeks on mss. Sample copy and fiction guidelines for #10 SASE.

Payment: Pays 10-12¢/word and 6 contributor's copies. Offers 50% kill fee for assigned mss not published.
Terms: Pays on acceptance for all rights.
Advice: "First read several issues containing short stories. We look for originality and creative input in each story we read. Since most editors must wade through mounds of manuscripts each month, consideration for the editor requires that the market be studied, the manuscript be carefully presented and polished before submitting. Our publication uses only one story a month. Compare this with the 25 or more we receive over the transom each month. Also, many fiction mss are written without a specific goal or thrust, i.e., an interesting incident that goes nowhere is *not a story*. We believe fiction is a highly effective mode for transmitting the Christian message and also provides a good balance in an unusually heavy issue."

LILITH MAGAZINE, The Independent Jewish Women's Magazine, (I, II, IV), Suite 2432, 250 W. 57th St., New York NY 10107. (212)757-0818. Editor: Susan Weidman Schneider. Fiction Editor: Julia Wolf Mazow. Magazine: 8½×11; 32 pages; 80 lb. cover; b&w illustrations; b&w and color photos. Publishes work relating to Jewish feminism, for Jewish feminists, feminists and Jewish households. Quarterly. Estab. 1975. Circ. 10,000.
Needs: Ethnic, feminist, lesbian, literary, prose poem, psychic/supernatural/occult, religious/inspirational, senior citizen/retirement, spiritual, translation, young adult. "Nothing that does not in any way relate to Jews, women or Jewish women." Receives 15 unsolicited mss/month. Accepts 1 ms/issue; 3 mss/year. Publishes ms 2-10 months after acceptance. Published work by Leslea Newman and Fredelle Maynard. Publishes short shorts.
How to Contact: Send complete ms with cover letter, which should include a 2-line bio. Reports in 2 months on queries; 2-6 months on mss. SASE (IRCs). Simultaneous and reprint submissions OK. Sample copy for $5. Fiction guidelines for #10 SAE and 1 first-class stamp. Reviews novels and short story collections. Send books to Rachel Dobkin.
Payment: Varies.
Terms: Acquires first rights.

LIVE, (IV), Assemblies of God, 1445 Boonville, Springfield MO 65802-1894. (417)862-2781. Editor: Paul Smith. "A take-home story paper distributed weekly in young adult/adult Sunday school classes. *Live* is a fictional story paper primarily. True stories in narrative style are welcome. Poems, first-person anecdotes and humor are used as fillers. The purpose of *Live* is to present in short story form realistic characters who utilize biblical principles. We hope to challenge readers to take risks for God and to resolve their problems scripturally." Weekly. Circ. 155,000.
Needs: Religious/inspirational, prose poem and spiritual. "Inner city, ethnic, racial settings." No controversial stories about such subjects as feminism, war or capital punishment. Buys 2 mss/issue. Published work by Maxine F. Dennis, E. Ruth Glover and Larry Clark; published new writers within the last year. Length: 500-2,000 words.
How to Contact: Send complete ms. Social Security number and word count must be included. Simultaneous submissions OK. Reports in 12-18 months. Sample copy and guidelines for SASE (IRCs).
Payment: Pays 3¢/word (first rights); 2¢/word (second rights).
Terms: Pays on acceptance.
Advice: "Stories should go somewhere! Action, not just thought-life; interaction, not just insights. Heroes and heroines, suspense and conflict. Avoid simplistic, pietistic conclusions, preachy, critical or moralizing. We do not accept science or Bible fiction. The stories should be encouraging, challenging, humorous. Even problem-centered stories should be upbeat." Reserves the right to change titles, abbreviate length and clarify flashbacks in stories for publication.

LOLLIPOPS MAGAZINE, (II), Good Apple, Inc., Box 299, Carthage IL 62321. (217)357-3981. Editor: Donna Borst. Magazine: 8½×11; 64 pages; illustrations. "Preschool-2nd grade publication for teachers and their students. All educational material. Short stories, poems, activities, math, gameboards." Published 5 times/year. Circ. 18,000.
Needs: Preschool-grade 2. Submissions cover all areas of the curriculum. Seasonal materials considered. Receives 40-50 unsolicited mss/month. Number of fiction mss bought varies per issue. Published new writers within the last year. Occasionally accepts short stories (500-750 words).

How to Contact: Query first or write for guidelines and a free sample copy. Reports in 1 week on queries. SASE for ms.
Payment: Payment varies; depends on story.
Terms: Pays on publication for all rights.

THE LOOKOUT, (II), Standard Publishing, 8121 Hamilton Ave., Cincinnati OH 45231. (513)931-4050. Fax: (513)931-0904. Editor: Simon J. Dahlman. Magazine: 8½×11; 16 pages; newsprint paper; newsprint cover stock; illustrations; photos. "Conservative Christian magazine for adults." Weekly. Estab. 1894. Circ. 120,000.
• *The Lookout* has won awards from the Evangelical Press Association and placed #29 on the latest *Writer's Digest* Fiction 50 list. Standard Publishing also publishes *Radar* and *Seek* listed in this book.
Needs: Religious/inspirational. No predictable, preachy material. Taboos are blatant sex and swear words. Receives 50 unsolicited mss/month. Buys 40-45 mss/year. Publishes ms 2-12 months after acceptance. Published work by Bob Hartman, Myrna J. Stone, Dave Cheadle and Daniel Schantz; published new writers within the last year. Length: 1,200-2,000 words.
How to Contact: Send complete ms with SASE (IRCs). Reports in 3-4 months on ms. Simultaneous and reprint submissions OK. Sample copy for 50¢. Guidelines for #10 SASE.
Payment: Pays 5-7¢/word for first rights; 4-5¢/word for other rights and contributor's copies.
Terms: Pays on acceptance for one-time rights. Buys reprints.
Advice: "We would like to see a better balance between stories that focus on external struggles (our usual fare in the past) and those that focus on internal (spiritual, emotional, psychological) struggles. Send us good stories—not good sermons dressed up as stories. Keep stories in a contemporary setting with an adult's point of view. Many writers with a Christian viewpoint try to 'preach' in their stories. That is as deadly for our purposes as for anyone. Tell the story, and let the 'message' take care of itself."

THE LUTHERAN JOURNAL, (II), Outlook Publications, Inc., 7317 Cahill Rd., Minneapolis MN 55435. (612)941-6830. Editor: Rev. A.U. Deye. "A family magazine providing wholesome and inspirational reading material for the enjoyment and enrichment of Lutherans." Quarterly. Estab. 1936. Circ. 136,000.
Needs: Literary, contemporary, religious/inspirational, romance (historical), senior citizen/retirement and young adult. Must be appropriate for distribution in the churches. Buys 3-6 mss/issue. Length: 1,000-1,500 words.
How to Contact: Send complete ms with SASE (IRCs). Sample copy for SAE with 59¢ postage.
Payment: Pays $10-25 and 6 contributor's copies.
Terms: Pays on publication for all and first rights.

McCALL'S, 110 Fifth Ave., New York NY 10011-5603. No longer publishes fiction.

MADEMOISELLE MAGAZINE, Condé Nast Publications, Inc., 350 Madison Ave., New York NY 10017. No longer publishes fiction.

THE MAGAZINE FOR CHRISTIAN YOUTH!, (II, IV), The United Methodist Publishing House, 201 8th Avenue S., Nashville TN 37202. (615)749-6463. Contact: Editor. Magazine: 8½×11; 48 pages; slick, matte finish paper. "*The Magazine for Christian Youth!* tries to help teenagers develop Christian identity and live their faith in contemporary culture. Fiction and nonfiction which contributes to this purpose are welcome." Monthly. Estab. 1985. Circ. 30,000.
• *The Magazine for Christian Youth* has won awards from the Evangelical Press Association and The Associated Church Press. The United Methodist Publishing House also publishes *Mature Years* listed in this book.
Needs: Religious, young adult: adventure, contemporary, ethnic, fantasy, humor/satire, mystery/suspense, prose poem, science fiction, spiritual, translations. Upcoming themes: "Teen Writing Contest" (February-April 1994); "100% All Teen Issue," all fiction, articles, photos and illustrations done by teens. (November 1994). Receives 25-50 unsolicited mss/month. Buys 1-2 mss/issue; 12-24 mss/year. Publishes ms 9-12 months after acceptance. Length: 700-1,500 words.
How to Contact: Query or send complete ms with cover letter. Reports in 3-6 months. SASE (IRCs). Simultaneous and reprint submissions OK. Sample copy and fiction guidelines for 9½×12½ SAE and 5 first-class stamps. Fiction limited to teenaged writers.

Payment: Pays 5¢/word.
Terms: Pays on acceptance for first North American serial rights or one-time rights.
Advice: "Get a feel for our magazine first. Don't send in the types of fiction that would appear in Sunday school curriculum just because it's a Christian publication. Reflect the real world of teens in contemporary fiction. Don't preach; but story should have a message to help teenagers in some way or to make them think more deeply about an issue." Writing contest announced in March issue. Deadline is early April.

MAGAZINE OF FANTASY AND SCIENCE FICTION, (II), P.O. Box 11526, Eugene OR 97440. Editor: Kristine Kathryn Rusch. Magazine: illustrations on cover only. Publishes "science fiction and fantasy. Our readers are age 13 and up who are interested in science fiction and fantasy." Monthly. Estab. 1949.

• *Magazine of Fantasy and Science Fiction* has won numerous awards including two Nebulas in 1991. The magazine ranks 15 on the latest *Writer's Digest* Fiction 50 list.

Needs: Fantasy and science fiction. Receives "hundreds" of unsolicited fiction submissions/month. Buys 8 fiction mss/issue ("on average"). Time between acceptance and publication varies. Length: 20,000 words maximum. Publishes short shorts. Critiques rejected ms, "if quality warrants it." Sometimes recommends other markets.
How to Contact: Send complete ms with cover letter. Reports in 6-8 weeks. SASE (IRCs). No simultaneous submissions. Sample copy for $3 or $5 for 2. Fiction guidelines for SAE.
Payment: Pays 5-7¢/word.
Terms: Pays on acceptance for first North American serial rights; foreign, option on anthology if requested.

‡MASSAGE, Keeping You—In Touch, (IV), Noah Publishing Inc., P.O. Box 1500, Davis CA 95617. (916)757-6033. Fax: (916)757-6041. Senior Editor: Melissa Mower. Magazine: 8¼ × 11; 100 pages; 70 lb. gloss paper; 80 lb. gloss cover; illustrations and photographs. "The philosophy is to spread the good word about massage therapy and other healing arts. Material published includes pieces on technique, business advice, experiential pieces and interviews/profiles on pioneers/leaders in the field. Intended audience is those who practice massage and other allied healing arts." Bimonthly. Estab. 1985. Circ. 20,000.
Needs: All fiction unacceptable unless in a positive light about massage experience. Receives 10 unsolicited ms/month. Accepts 3 ms/issue; 10 mss/year. Publishes ms 1 year after acceptance. Recently published work by Erik Lee, Mary Bond. Length: 2,000 words preferred; 1,500 words minimum; 2,500 words maximum. Always critiques or comments on rejected mss.
How to Contact: Query first. Should include bio (2-3 sentences). Reports in 2 months. Send SASE (IRCs) for reply or send a disposable copy of ms. Sample copy for $5.50. Writer's guidelines free.
Payment: Pays $100 maximum; 2 contributor's copies; additional copies for $3.
Terms: Pays 30 days after publication for first rights.
Advice: Looks for "humor, detail, strong massage theme that's positive. Send it for consideration and I'll give honest feedback. I've never seen a massage mystery in short fiction and think it would be fun."

MATURE LIVING, (II), Sunday School Board of the Southern Baptist Convention, MSN 140, 127 Ninth Ave. N., Nashville TN 37234. (615)251-2191. Editor: Al Shackleford. Magazine: 8½ × 11; 48 pages; non-glare paper; slick cover stock; illustrations; photos. "Our magazine is Christian in content and the material required is what would appeal to 60+ age group: inspirational, informational, nostalgic, humorous. Our magazine is distributed mainly through churches (especially Southern Baptist churches) that buy the magazine in bulk and distribute it to members in this age group." Monthly. Estab. 1977. Circ. 360,000.
Needs: Contemporary, religious/inspirational, humor, prose poem, spiritual and senior citizen/retirement. Avoid all types of pornography, drugs, liquor, horror, science fiction and stories demeaning to the elderly. Buys 1 ms/issue. Publishes ms an average of 1 year after acceptance. Published work by Burndean N. Sheffy, Pearl E. Trigg, Joyce M. Sixberry; published new writers within the last year. Length: 425-900 words (prefers 900). "Also, please use 42 characters per line."

Check the Category Indexes, located at the back of the book, for publishers interested in specific fiction subjects.

How to Contact: Send complete ms with SASE. Reports in 2 months. Sample copy for $1. Guidelines for SASE.

Payment: Pays $21-73; 3 contributor's copies. 85¢ charge for extras.

Terms: Pays on acceptance. First rights 15% less than all rights, reprint rights 25% less. Rarely buys reprints.

Advice: Mss are rejected because they are too long or subject matter unsuitable. "Our readers seem to enjoy an occasional short piece of fiction. It must be believable, however, and present senior adults in a favorable light."

MATURE YEARS, (II), United Methodist Publishing House, 201 Eighth Ave. S., Nashville TN 37202. (615)749-6468. Editor: Marvin W. Cropsey. Magazine: 8½×11; 112 pages; illustrations and photos. Magazine "helps persons in and nearing retirement to appropriate the resources of the Christian faith as they seek to face the problems and opportunities related to aging." Quarterly. Estab. 1953.

• United Methodist Publishing House also publishes a magazine for teens, the *Magazine for Christian Youth*, listed in this book.

Needs: Religious/inspirational, nostalgia, humor, intergenerational relationships, prose poem, spiritual (for older adults). "We don't want anything poking fun at old age, saccharine stories or anything not for older adults." Buys 1 ms/issue, 4 mss/year. Publishes ms 1 year after acceptance. Published new writers within the last year. Length: 1,000-1,800 words.

How to Contact: Send complete ms with SASE (IRCs) and Social Security number. No simultaneous submissions. Reports in 2 months. Sample copy for 10½×11 SAE and $3.50 postage.

Payment: Pays 4¢/word.

Terms: Pays on acceptance.

Advice: "Practice writing dialogue! Listen to people talk; take notes; master dialogue writing! Not easy, but well worth it! Most inquiry letters are far too long. If you can't sell me an idea in a brief paragraph, you're not going to sell the reader on reading your finished article or story."

✿MESSENGER OF THE SACRED HEART, (II), Apostleship of Prayer, 661 Greenwood Ave., Toronto, Ontario M4J 4B3 Canada. (416)466-1195. Editors: Rev. F.J. Power, S.J. and Alfred DeManche. Magazine: 7×10; 32 pages; coated paper; self-cover; illustrations; photos. Magazine for "Canadian and U.S. Catholics interested in developing a life of prayer and spirituality; stresses the great value of our ordinary actions and lives." Monthly. Estab. 1891. Circ. 17,000.

• *Canadian Messenger*, also published by the Apostleship of Prayer, is listed in this book.

Needs: Religious/inspirational. Stories about people, adventure, heroism, humor, drama. No poetry. Buys 1 ms/issue. Published work by Ken Thoren, Rev. Charles Dickson, Ph.D. and Rev. John M. Scott, S.J.; published new writers within the last year. Length: 750-1,500 words. Recommends other markets.

How to Contact: Send complete ms with SAE or IRCs. No simultaneous submissions. Reports in 1 month. Sample copy for $1.50 (Canadian).

Payment: Pays 4¢/word, 3 contributor's copies.

Terms: Pays on acceptance for first North American serial rights. Rarely buys reprints.

Advice: "Develop a story that sustains interest to the end. Do not preach, but use plot and characters to convey the message or theme. Aim to move the heart as well as the mind. If you can, add a light touch or a sense of humor to the story. Your ending should have impact, leaving a moral or faith message for the reader."

METRO SINGLES LIFESTYLES, (I), Metro Publications, Box 28203, Kansas City MO 64118. (816)436-8424. Editor: Robert L. Huffstutter. Fiction Editor: Earl R. Stonebridge. Tabloid: 36 pages; 30. lb newspaper stock; 30 lb. cover; illustrations; photos. "Positive, uplifting, original, semi-literary material for all singles: widowed, divorced, never-married, of all ages 18 and over." Bimonthly. Estab. 1984. Circ. 25,000.

Needs: Humor/satire, literary, prose poem, religious/inspirational, romance (contemporary), special interest, spiritual, single parents. Receives 2-3 unsolicited mss/month. Buys 1-2 mss/issue; 12-18 mss/year. Publishes ms 2 months after acceptance. Length: 1,500 words average; 1,200 words minimum; 4,000 words maximum. Publishes short shorts. Published work by Patricia Castle, Libby Floyd, Donald G. Smith; published new writers within the last year. Length: 1,200. Occasionally critiques rejected mss. Recommends other markets.

How to Contact: Send complete ms with cover letter. Include short paragraph/bio listing credits (if any), current profession or job. Reports in 3 weeks on queries. SASE (IRCs). Sample copy $3.
Payment: Pays $25-50, free subscription to magazine and contributor's copies.
Terms: Payment on publication.
Advice: Looks for "singular way of life, problems and blessings of single parent families, the eternal search fopr the right mate—or the right date. Forget what society and the media says, write exactly how you feel about a certain subject and never worry about the negative responses ... If you can imagine it, it's probably possible."

MIDSTREAM, A Monthly Jewish Review, (I, IV), Theodor Herzl Foundation, 110 E. 59th St., New York NY 10022. (212)339-6021. Editor: Joel Carmichael. Magazine: 8½×11; 48 pages; 50 lb. paper; 65 lb. white smooth cover stock. "We are a Zionist journal; we publish material with Jewish themes or that would appeal to a Jewish readership." Monthly. Estab. 1955. Circ. 10,000.
• Work published in *Midstream* was included in the *O. Henry Prize* award anthology.
Needs: Historical (general), humor/satire, literary, mainstream, translations. Receives 15-20 unsolicited mss/month. Accepts 1 mss/issue; 10 mss/year. Publishes ms 6-18 months after acceptance. Agented fiction 10%. Published work by I. B. Singer, Anita Jackson, Enid Shomer. Length: 2,500 words average; 1,500 words minimum; 4,500 words maximum. Sometimes critiques rejected mss.
How to Contact: Send complete ms with cover letter, which should include "address, telephone, or affiliation of author; state that the ms is fiction." Reports in "up to 6 months." SASE (IRCs).
Payment: Pays 5¢/word and contributor's copies.
Terms: Pays on publication for first rights.
Advice: "Always include a cover letter and double space."

MILITARY LIFESTYLE, (II), Downey Communications, Inc., Suite 710, 4800 Montgomery Lane, Bethesda MD 20814-5341. Editor: Hope M. Daniels. Magazine: 8×10½; averages 84 pages; coated paper; illustrations and photos. Monthly magazine for military families worldwide. Publishes 12 issues per year. Estab. 1969. Circ. 100,000.
• See the listing for the *Military Lifestyle* Short Story Contest listed in the Contests and Awards Section.
Needs: Contemporary. "Fiction must deal with lifestyle or issues of particular concern to our specific military families audience." Receives 50 unsolicited mss/month. Buys 1-2 mss/issue; 10-15 mss/year. Published new writers within the last year. Length: 1,500 words average. Generally critiques rejected mss.
How to Contact: Send complete ms with cover letter, which should include information on writer and writing credits and history. No simultaneous or electronic submissions. Reports in 6-8 weeks on mss. SASE (IRCs) with proper postage. Sample copy for $1.50, 9×12 SAE and 4 first-class stamps. Fiction guidelines for #10 SASE and 1 first-class stamp. Reviews novels and short story collections.
Payment: Pays $400 minimum and 2 contributor's copies.
Terms: Pays generally on publication unless held more than 6 months; then on acceptance for first North American serial rights.
Advice: "Fiction is slice-of-life reading for our audience. Primarily written by family members or service members themselves, the stories deal with subjects very close to our readers: prolonged absences by spouses, the necessity of handling child-raising alone, the fear of accidents while spouses are on maneuvers or in dangerous situations, etc. We also like stories with a lighter touch—humorous, husband/wife relationships, parenting, etc. The important point: target the material to our audience—military families—and make the characters real, empathetic and believable. Read your copy over as an objective reader rather than as its author before submission. Better yet, read it aloud!"

MONTANA SENIOR CITIZENS NEWS, (II,IV), Barrett-Whitman Co., Box 3363, Great Falls MT 59403. (406)761-0305. Editor: Jack Love. Tabloid: 11×17; 60-80 pages; newsprint paper and cover; illustrations; photos. Publishes "everything of interest to seniors, except most day-to-day political items like Social Security and topics covered in the daily news. Personal profiles of seniors, their lives, times and reminiscences." Bimonthly. Estab. 1984. Circ. 25,000.
Needs: Historical, senior citizen/retirement, western (historical or contemporary). No fiction "unrelated to experiences to which seniors can relate." Buys 1 or fewer mss/issue; 4-5 mss/year. Publishes ms within 6 months of acceptance. Published work by Anne Norris, Helen Clark, Juni Dunklin. Length: 500-800 words preferred. Publishes short stories. Length: under 500 words.

"Military Lifestyle's *signature is young, active-duty military families and we make sure our monthly covers reflect that idea," says Editor Hope Daniels. "Rather than use models, we solicit requests from military families stationed in the Washington DC area to serve as our cover families," Daniels says. Cover families are also featured in a popular column inside the magazine which includes more photos and background on their lives. Fiction in* Military Lifestyle *generally consists of "short, contemporary slice-of-life stories the readers can fully identify with, on subjects they are intimately familiar with," says Daniels. (Photograph by Cameron Davidson for* Military Lifestyle.*)*

How to Contact: Send complete ms with cover letter and phone number. Only responds to selected mss. SASE (IRCs). Simultaneous and reprint submissions OK. Accepts electronic submission via WordPerfect disk. Sample copy for 9 × 12 SAE and $2 postage and handling.
Payment: Pays $2/column inch.
Terms: Pays on publication for first rights or one-time rights.

MOONLIGHT, 475 Park Ave. S., New York NY 10016. See Starlog Group in the Commercial Publishers section for more information.

MY FRIEND, The Catholic Magazine for Kids, (II), Daughters of St. Paul, 50 St. Paul's Ave., Boston MA 02130. (617)522-8911. Editor: Sister Anne Joan. Magazine: 8½ × 11; 32 pages; smooth, glossy paper and cover stock; illustrations; photos. Magazine of "religious truths and positive values for children in a format which is enjoyable and attractive. Each issue contains Bible stories, lives of saints and famous people, short stories, science corner, contests, projects, etc." Monthly during school year (September-June). Estab. 1979. Circ. 10,000.
 • Daughters of St. Paul also publishes *The Family* listed in this book. In 1993 *My Friend* received First Place for General Excellence (Specialized Interest Publication) and Best Cover from the Catholic Press Association.
Needs: Juvenile, religious/inspirational, spiritual (children), sports (children). Receives 30 unsolicited fiction mss/month. Accepts 3-4 mss/issue; 30-40 mss/year. Published work by Eileen Spinelli, Bob Hartman and M. Donaleen Howitt; published new writers within the past year. Length: 200 words minimum; 900 words maximum; 600 words average.
How to Contact: Send complete ms with SASE (IRCs). Reports in 1-2 months on mss. Publishes ms an average of 1 year after acceptance. Sample copy for 9 × 12 SAE and 90¢ postage.
Payment: Pays $20-150 (stories, articles).
Advice: "We prefer child-centered stories in a real-world setting. Children enjoy fiction. They can relate to the characters and learn lessons that they might not derive from a more 'preachy' article. We accept only stories that teach wholesome, positive values. We are particularly interested in science and media-related articles and in material for boys aged 8-10."

NA'AMAT WOMAN, Magazine of NA'AMAT USA, The Women's Labor Zionist Organization of America, (IV), 200 Madison Ave., New York NY 10016. (212)725-8010. Editor: Judith A. Sokoloff. "Magazine covering a wide variety of subjects of interest to the Jewish community — including political and social issues, arts, profiles; many articles about Israel; and women's issues. Fiction must have a Jewish theme. Readers are the American Jewish community." Published 5 times/year. Estab. 1926. Circ. 30,000.

Needs: Contemporary, literary. Receives 10 unsolicited fiction mss/month. Buys 3-5 fiction mss/year. Length: 1,500 words minimum; 3,000 words maximum. Also buys nonfiction.
How to Contact: Query first or send complete ms with SASE (IRCs). Reports in 3 months on mss. Free sample copy for 9 × 11½ SAE and 98¢ postage.
Payment: Pays 8¢/word; 2 contributor's copies.
Terms: Pays on publication for first North American serial rights; assignments on work-for-hire basis.
Advice: "No maudlin nostalgia or romance; no hackneyed Jewish humor and no poetry."

NEW ERA MAGAZINE, (II, IV), The Church of Jesus Christ of Latter-day Saints, 50 E. North Temple St., Salt Lake City UT 84150. (801)532-2951. Editor: Richard M. Romney. Magazine: 8 × 10½; 51 pages; 40 lb. coated paper; illustrations and photos. "We will publish fiction on any theme that strengthens and builds the standards and convictions of teenage Latter-day Saints ('Mormons')." Monthly. Estab. 1971. Circ. 200,000.
● This publisher also publishes *The Friend* listed in this book. *New Era* is a recipient of the Focus on Excellence Award from Brigham Young University. The magazine also sponsors a writing contest listed in this book.
Needs: Stories on family relationships, self-esteem, dealing with loneliness, resisting peer pressure and all aspects of maintaining Christian values in the modern world. "All material must be written from a Latter-day Saint ('Mormon') point of view—or at least from a generally Christian point of view, reflecting LDS life and values." Receives 30-35 unsolicited mss/month. Accepts 1 ms/issue; 12 mss/year. Publishes ms 3 months to 3 years after acceptance. Length: 1,500 words average; 250 words minimum; 2,000 words maximum.
How to Contact: Query letter preferred; send complete ms. Reports in 6-8 weeks. SASE (IRCs). Sample copy for $1 and 9 × 12 SAE with 2 first-class stamps. Fiction guidelines for #10 SASE.
Payment: Pays $50-375 and contributor's copies.
Terms: Pays on acceptance for all rights (reassign to author on request).
Advice: "Each magazine has its own personality—you wouldn't write the same style of fiction for *Seventeen* that you would write for *Omni*. Very few writers who are not of our faith have been able to write for us successfully, and the reason usually is that they don't know what it's like to be a member of our church. You must study and research and know those you are writing about. We love to work with beginning authors, and we're a great place to break in if you can understand us." Sponsors contests and awards for LDS fiction writers. "We have an annual contest; entry forms are in each September issue. Deadline is January; winners published in August."

‡NEW HAMPSHIRE LIFE, (II, IV), Masthead Communications, Inc., Box 1200, North Hampton NH 03862. (603)964-2121. Fiction Editor: John A. Meng. Magazine: 8½ × 11; 100 pages; coated freesheet paper; 65 lb. coated cover stock; color photographs, 75/issue. "Lifestyle magazine for and about New Hampshire. We publish fiction each issue plus regional events, investigative journalism, recipes, business, health, fashion and people articles for an upscale, well-educated audience, 25-50." Bimonthly. Estab. (as *Seacoast Life*) 1985. Circ. 20,000.
Needs: Adventure, contemporary, fantasy, humor/satire, literary, mainstream, regional, science fiction, senior citizen/retirement, serialized/excerpted novel, suspense/mystery and translations. "No radical fiction, i.e. homosexual, pornographic, etc. We promote literature that elicits an emotional response—not the type with a purpose to horrify or impress." Receives 20-30 unsolicited fiction mss/month. Accepts 1 mss/issue; 6 mss/year (including a holiday issue). Publishes ms 3-6 months after acceptance. Published work by Jules Archer, Sharon Helgens, Lawrence Millman and Robert Baldwin; published new writers within the last year. Length: 1,500-3,000 words average. Sometimes critiques rejected ms.
How to Contact: "Subject must be regional in order to submit—New Hampshire." Send complete ms with cover letter, writer's bio. Reports in 1 month. SASE (IRCs). Simultaneous and photocopied submissions OK. Accepts computer printout submissions. Sample copy for $2.50 and 9 × 12 SAE with $2.40 postage. Fiction guidelines for #10 SAE and 40¢ postage.
Payment: Pays $100 minimum; varies according to individual circumstances.
Terms: Pays 30 days after publication. Rights purchased negotiated with each individual writer.
Advice: "Our readership is highly educated, critical of shabby work and loves good fiction. Our readers love to read. Writers should be patient. We will read and reply to all submissions."

NEW MYSTERY, (III), The Best New Mystery Stories, #2001, 175 Fifth Ave., New York NY 10010. (212)353-1582. Editor: Charles Raisch. Magazine: 8½ × 11; 96 pages; illustrations and photographs. "Mystery, suspense and crime." Quarterly. Estab. 1990. Circ. 50,000.

• For more on *New Mystery* see the close-up interview with Editor Charles Raisch in the 1991 *Novel & Short Story Writer's Market*.

Needs: Mystery/suspense. Plans special annual anthology. Receives 150 unsolicited mss/month. Buys 6-10 ms/issue. Agented fiction 50%. Recently published work by Jerry Kennealy, Josh Pachter, Henry Slesar and Fred Breinersdorfer. Length: 3,000-5,000 words preferred. Sometimes critiques rejected mss and recommends other markets.

How to Contact: Send complete ms with cover letter. Reports on ms in 1 month. SASE (IRCs). Accepts electronic submissions. Sample copy for $5, 9 × 12 SAE and 4 first-class stamps.

Payment: Pays $25-250.

Terms: Pays on publication for all rights.

Advice: Stories should have "believable characters in trouble; sympathetic lead; visual language." Sponsors "Annual First Story Contest."

THE NEW YORKER, (III), The New Yorker, Inc., 20 W. 43rd St., New York NY 10036. (212)840-3800. Fiction Department. A quality magazine of interesting, well written stories, articles, essays and poems for a literate audience. Weekly. Estab. 1925. Circ. 750,000.

• *The New Yorker* received the National Magazine Award for Fiction in 1993.

How to Contact: Send complete ms with SASE (IRCs). Reports in 8-10 weeks on mss. Publishes 1-2 mss/issue.

Payment: Varies.

Terms: Pays on acceptance.

Advice: "Be lively, original, not overly literary. Write what you want to write, not what you think the editor would like. Send poetry to Poetry Department."

NOAH'S ARK, A Newspaper for Jewish Children, (II, IV), Suite 250, 8323 Southwest Freeway, Houston TX 77074. (713)771-7143. Editors: Debbie Israel Dubin and Linda Freedman Block. Tabloid: 4 pages; newsprint paper; illustrations; photos. "All material must be on some Jewish theme. Seasonal material relating to Jewish holidays is used as well as articles and stories relating to Jewish culture (charity, Soviet Jewry, ecology), etc." for Jewish children, ages 6-12. Monthly Sept.-June. Estab. 1979. Circ. 450,000.

Needs: Juvenile (6-12 years); religious/inspirational; ages 6-12 Jewish children. "Newspaper is not only included as a supplement to numerous Jewish newspapers and sent to individual subscribers but is also distributed in bulk quantities to religious schools; therefore all stories and articles should have educational value as well as being entertaining and interesting to children." Receives 10 unsolicited mss/month. Buys "few mss but we'd probably use more if more appropriate mss were submitted." Published new writers within the last year. Length: 600 words maximum.

How to Contact: Send complete ms with SASE (IRCs). "The cover letter is not necessary; the submission will be accepted or rejected on its own merits." Simultaneous submissions and reprints OK. Sample copy for #10 envelope and 1 first-class stamp. "The best guideline is a copy of our publication."

Payment: Varies; contributor's copies.

Terms: Pays on acceptance for one-time rights.

Advice: "Our newspaper was created by two writers looking for a place to have our work published. It has grown in only 10 years to nearly 1 million readers throughout the world. Beginners with determination can accomplish the impossible."

NORTHEAST, the Sunday Magazine of the Hartford Courant, (IV), 285 Broad St., Hartford CT 06115. (203)241-3700. Editor: Lary Bloom. Magazine: 10 × 11½; 32-100 pages; illustrations; photos. "A regional (New England, specifically Connecticut) magazine, we publish stories of varied subjects of interest to our Connecticut audience" for a general audience. Weekly. Published special fiction issue and a special college writing issue for fiction and poetry. Estab. 1981. Circ. 300,000.

• *Northeast* ranked #38 on the latest *Writer's Digest* Fiction 50 list.

Needs: Contemporary and regional. No children's stories or stories with distinct setting outside Connecticut. Receives 150 unsolicited mss/month. Buys 1 ms/issue; 2 mss/month. Publishes short shorts. Length: 750 words minimum; 3,500 words maximum.

How to Contact: Send complete ms with 10 × 12 SASE (IRCs). Reports in 6-8 weeks. Simultaneous submissions OK. No reprints or previously published work. Sample copy and fiction guidelines for 10 × 12 or larger SASE.

Payment: Pays $250-1,000.

Terms: Pays on acceptance for one-time rights.

‡NORTHWEST JOURNAL: The Magazine of the Interior Northwest, (II, IV), (formerly *Palouse Journal*), North Country Book Express, Box 9632, Moscow ID 83843. (208)882-0888. Editor: Ed Hughes. Magazine: 11×14; 24-40 pages; 34 lb. stock; gloss cover; illustrations; photos. "We are a regional general interest magazine, for an educated, literate audience." Bimonthly. Estab. 1981.
Needs: Regional. "We will consider good writing about our region." Buys 1 ms/issue at most; 2-6 mss/year. Published work by Robert Wrigley, Pat McManus, Mary Blew; published new writers within the last year. Length: 1,500 words maximum. Will consider short shorts as columns, up to 800 words. Occasionally critiques rejected mss.
How to Contact: Send complete ms with cover letter. Reports in 2-3 months. SASE (IRCs). Photocopied submissions OK. Accepts computer printout submissions. Sample copy for $2. Writers' guidelines for SASE. Reviews novels and short story collections "only if author, publisher or subject is of the interior Northwest."
Payment: Pays $25-75 for a full feature story.
Terms: Pays on publication for first North American serial rights.
Advice: "We look for good clean writing, a regional relevance. Manuscripts are often rejected because writer is obviously not familiar with the magazine and story lacks regional flavor. Read the publication first to see if your story fits! We only publish work about the Pacific and Intermountain West."

‡NUGGET, (II), Dugent Publishing Corp., Suite 600, 2600 Douglas Rd., Coral Gables FL 33134. (305)443-2378. Editor-in-Chief: Christopher James. A newsstand magazine designed to have erotic appeal for a fetish-oriented audience. Published 8 times a year. Estab. 1956. Circ. 100,000.
Needs: Offbeat, fetish-oriented material encompassing a variety of subjects (B&D, TV, TS, spanking, amputeeism, infantalism, catfighting, etc.). Most of fiction includes several sex scenes. No fiction that concerns children or religious subjects. Buys 2 mss/issue. Agented fiction 5%. Length: 2,000-3,500 words.
How to Contact: Send complete ms with SASE (IRCs). Reports in 1 month. Sample copy for $3.50. Guidelines for legal-sized SASE.
Payment: Pay starts at $200 and 1 contributor's copy.
Terms: Pays on publication for first rights.
Advice: "Keep in mind the nature of the publication, which is fetish erotica. Subject matter can vary, but we prefer fetish themes."

‡ODYSSEY, Science That's Out of this World, Cobblestone Publishing, Inc., 7 School St., Peterborough NH 03458. Editor: Elizabeth E. Lindstrom. Magazine. "Scientific accuracy, original approaches to the subject are primary concerns of the editors in choosing material. For 8-14 year olds." Monthly (except July and August). Estab. 1991. Circ. 40,000.
● Cobblestone Publishing also publishes *Calliope*, *Cobblestone* and *Faces*, listed in this book.
Needs: Material must match theme; send for theme list and deadlines. Childrens/juvenile (8-14 years), "authentic historical and biographical fiction, science fiction, retold legends, etc., relating to theme." List of upcoming themes available for SASE (IRCs). Length: 750 words maximum.
How to Contact: Query first or query with clips of published work (if new to *Odyssey*). Should include estimated word count and a detailed 1-page outline explaining the information to be presented; an extensive bibliography of materials authors plan to use." Reports in several months. Send SASE (IRCs) for reply or send stamped postcard to find out if ms has been received. Sample copy for $3.95, 7½×10½ SAE and $1.05 postage. Fiction guidelines for SASE.
Payment: Pays 10-17¢/word.
Terms: Pays on publication for all rights.
Advice: "We also include in-depth nonfiction, plays and biographies."

OMNI, (II), General Media, 1965 Broadway, New York NY 10023. Fiction Editor: Ellen Datlow. Magazine: 8½×11; 114-182 pages; 40-50 lb. stock paper; 100 lb. Mead off cover stock; illustrations; photos. "Magazine of science and science fiction with an interest in near future; stories of what science holds, what life and lifestyles will be like in areas affected by science for a young, bright and well-educated audience between ages 18-45." Monthly. Estab. 1978. Circ. 1,000,000.
● *Omni* has won numerous awards (see "Advice" below). They rank #25 on the latest *Writer's Digest* Fiction 50 list. Ellen Datlow also edits *The Year's Best Fantasy and Horror* (a reprint anthology).
Needs: Science fiction, contemporary fantasy and technological horror. No sword and sorcery or space opera. Buys 20 mss/year. Receives approximately 400 unsolicited fiction mss/month. Agented fiction 5%. Recently published work by Joyce Carol Oates, Terry Bisson, Harlan Ellison and Pat Cadigan.

Length: 2,000 words minimum, 10,000 words maximum. Critiques rejected mss that interest me "when there is time." Sometimes recommends other markets.

How to Contact: Send complete ms with SASE (IRCs). No simultaneous submissions. Reports within 3 weeks. Publishes ms 3 months to 2 years after acceptance.

Payment: Pays $1,250-2,250; 3 free contributor's copies.

Terms: Pays on acceptance for first North American serial rights with exclusive worldwide English language periodical rights and nonexclusive anthology rights.

Advice: "Beginning writers should read a lot of the best science fiction short stories today to get a feeling for what is being done. Also, they should read outside the field and nonfiction for inspiration. We are looking for strong, well written stories dealing with the next 100 years. Don't give up on a market just because you've been rejected several times. If you're good, you'll get published eventually. Don't ever call an editor on the phone and ask why he/she rejected a story. You'll either find out in a personal rejection letter (which means the editor liked it or thought enough of your writing to comment) or you won't find out at all (most likely the editor won't remember a form-rejected story)." Recent award winners and nominees: "Tower of Babylon," by Ted Chiang won the Nebula award for novelette and has been nominated for a Hugo. "They're Made out of Meat," by Terry Bisson, was nominated for the Nebula Award. Ellen Datlow has been nominated in Best Professional editor category of the Hugos 4 years running.

ON OUR BACKS, Entertainment for the Adventurous Lesbian, (II, IV), Blush Entertainment, 526 Castro St., San Francisco CA 94114. (415)861-4723. Editor: Heather Findlay. Magazine: 8½ × 11; 50 pages; slick paper; illustrations; photos. "Lesbian erotica, short stories, nonfiction, commentary, news clips, photos." Bimonthly. Estab. 1984. Circ. 30,000.

Needs: Erotica, fantasy, humor/satire, nonfiction of interest to lesbians. No "non-erotic, heterosexual" fiction. Receives 20 mss/month. Buys 2-3 mss/issue. Publishes ms within 1 year of acceptance. Published new writers within the last year. Length: 2,500 words minimum; 5,000 words maximum.

How to Contact: Send complete ms. Simultaneous submissions OK. Reports in 6 weeks. Accepts electronic submissions via (Mac) disk. Sample copy for $6. Fiction guidelines for #10 SAE and 1 first-class stamp.

Payment: Pays $20-100 and contributor's copies.

Terms: Pays on publication for first North American serial rights.

Advice: "Ask yourself—does it turn me on? Ask a friend to read it—does it turn her on as well? Is it as well-written as any well-crafted non-erotic story? We love to read things that we don't see all the time—originality is definitely a plus! We're looking for lesbian erotica that deals with relationship issues as well as sex, stories that have high literary merit."

ON THE LINE, (II), Mennonite Publishing House, 616 Walnut Ave., Scottdale PA 15683-1999. (412)887-8500. Editor: Mary Meyer. Magazine: 7 × 10; 8 pages; illustrations; b&w photos. "A religious take-home paper with the goal of helping children grow in their understanding and appreciation of God, the created world, themselves and other people." For children ages 10-14. Weekly. Estab. 1970. Circ. 10,000.

● *Purpose, Story Friends* and *With*, listed in this book, are also published by the Mennonite Publishing House.

Needs: Adventure and religious/inspirational for older children and young teens (10-14 years). Receives 50-100 unsolicited mss/month. Buys 1 ms/issue; 52 mss/year. Published work by Michael La-Cross, Betty Lou Mell, Virginia Kroll; published new writers within the last year. Length: 750-1,000 words.

How to Contact: Send complete ms noting whether author is offering first-time or reprint rights. Reports in 1 month. SASE (IRCs). Simultaneous and previously published work OK. Free sample copy and fiction guidelines.

Payment: Pays on acceptance for one-time rights.

Advice: "We believe in the power of story to entertain, inspire and challenge the reader to new growth. Know children and their thoughts, feelings and interests. Be realistic with characters and events in the fiction. Stories do not need to be true, but need to *feel* true."

OPTIONS, The *Bi*-Monthly, (I, II, IV), AJA Publishing, Box 470, Port Chester NY 10573. Associate Editor: Diana Sheridan. Magazine: digest-sized; 130 pages; newsprint paper; glossy cover stock; illustrations and photos. Sexually explicit magazine for and about bisexuals. 10 issues/year. Estab. 1982. Circ. 100,000.

382 *Novel & Short Story Writer's Market '94*

• Please see advice below—AJA Publishing also publishes *Beau* but it is not listed separately in this book.
Needs: Erotica, bisexual, gay, lesbian. "First person as-if-true experiences." Accepts 7 unsolicited fiction mss/issue. "Very little" of fiction is agented. Published new writers within the last year. Length: 2,000-3,000 words average; 2,000 words minimum. Sometimes critiques rejected mss.
How to Contact: Send complete ms with or without cover letter. No simultaneous submissions. Reports in approximately 3 weeks. SASE (IRCs). "Submissions on Macintosh disk welcome, but please include hard copy too." Sample copy for $2.95 and 6 × 9 SAE with 5 first-class stamps. Fiction guidelines for SASE.
Payment: Pays $100.
Terms: Pays on publication for all rights.
Advice: "Read a copy of *Options* carefully and look at our spec sheet before writing anything for us. That's not new advice, but to judge from some of what we get in the mail, it's necessary to repeat. We only buy 2 bi/lesbian pieces per issue; need is greater for bi/gay male mss. Though we're a bi rather than gay magazine, the emphasis is on same-sex relationships. If the readers want to read about a male/female couple, they'll buy another magazine. Gay male stories sent to *Options* will also be considered for publication in *Beau*, our gay male magazine. *Most important:* We *only* publish male/male stories that feature 'safe sex' practices unless the story is clearly something that took place pre-AIDS."

ORANGE COAST MAGAZINE, The Magazine of Orange County, (III), Suite 8, 245-D Fischer Ave., Costa Mesa CA 92626. (714)545-1900. Editor: Lynn Beresford. Managing Editor: Eve Belson. Associate Editor: Allison Joyce. Magazine: 8½ × 11; 175 pages; 50 lb. Sonoma gloss paper; Warrenflo cover; illustrations and photographs. *Orange Coast* publishes articles offering insight into the community for its affluent, well-educated Orange County readers. Monthly. Estab. 1974. Circ. 38,000.
• *Orange Coast* won First Place for Fiction from the Maggie Awards in 1990 and 1991.
Needs: All genres. Fiction submissions need not have Orange County setting or characters. Receives 30 unsolicited mss/month. Buys 2 mss/year. Publishes ms 4-6 months after acceptance. Published work by Robert Ray. Length: 2,500 words average; 1,500 words minimum; 3,000 words maximum.
How to Contact: Send complete ms with cover letter that includes Social Security number. Reports in 3 months. SASE (IRCs). Simultaneous submissions OK. Sample copy for 9 × 12 SASE.
Payment: Pays $250.
Terms: Pays on acceptance for first North American serial rights.

THE OTHER SIDE, (III), 300 W. Apsley St., Philadelphia PA 19144-4221. (215)849-2178. Editor: Mark Olson. Fiction Editor: Jennifer Wilkins. Magazine: 8½ × 11; 64 pages; illustrations and photographs. Magazine of justice rooted in discipleship for Christians with a strong interest in peace, social and economic justice. Bimonthly. Estab. 1965. Circ. 14,000.
• *The Other Side* has received awards from the Associated Church Press, including Best General Publication.
Needs: Contemporary, ethnic, experimental, feminist, humor/satire, literary, mainstream, mystery/suspense, spiritual. Receives 250 unsolicited fiction mss/year. Buys 6 mss/year. Publishes ms 6-15 months after acceptance. Published work by Laurie Skiba, James Schaap and Shirley Pendlebury. Length: 500 words minimum; 5,000 words maximum; 2,500 words average.
How to Contact: Send complete ms with SASE (IRCs). Reports in 6-8 weeks. No simultaneous submissions or pre-published material. Sample copy for $4.50.
Payment: Pays $50-250; free subscription to magazine; 6 contributor's copies.
Terms: Pays on acceptance for all or first rights.

OUI MAGAZINE, (II), 7th Floor, 28 W. 25th Ave., New York NY 10010. (212)647-0222. Editor: Mike Scott. Magazine: 8 × 11; 112 pages; illustrations; photos. Magazine for college-age males and older. Monthly. Estab. 1972. Circ. 1 million.
Needs: Contemporary, fantasy, lesbian, men's, mystery and humor. Buys 1 ms/issue; 12 mss/year. Receives 200-300 unsolicited fiction mss/month. Published new writers within the last year. Length: 1,500-3,000 words.
How to Contact: Send complete ms with SASE. Include cover letter with author background, previous publications, etc. Reports in 6-8 weeks on mss.
Payment: Pays $250 and up.
Terms: Pays on publication for first rights.
Advice: "Many mss are rejected because writers have not studied the market or the magazine. We want writers to take chances and offer us something out of the ordinary. Look at several recent issues to see what direction our fiction is headed."

OUTLAW BIKER, (II, IV), Outlaw Biker Enterprises, Box 447, Voorhees NJ 08003. Editor: Roy Sundance. Magazine: 8½ × 11; 96 pages; 50 lb. color paper; 80 lb. cover stock; illustrations; photos. "Motorcycle/biker lifestyle magazine." Published 10 times/year. Estab. 1984. Circ. 180,000.
• The publisher of this magazine also publishes *Skin Art* and *Tattoo Revue* listed in this book.
Needs: Biker fiction and humor. Receives 20 unsolicited mss/month. Accepts 1 fiction ms/issue. Publishes ms 2-8 months after acceptance. Length: 1,000-2,500 words.
How to Contact: Send complete ms with cover letter and SASE. Reports in 6 weeks. Sample copy $5.
Payment: Payment varies according to length and quality of work.
Terms: Pays on publication for all rights.

PILLOW TALK, (I, II), 801 2nd Ave., New York NY 10017. Editor: Asia Fraser. Magazine: digest-sized; 98 pages; photos. Bimonthly erotic letters magazine.
• This is also the publisher of *Private Letters* listed in this book.
Needs: Erotica, in letter form. "We use approximately 20 short letters of no more than six manuscript pages per issue, and five long letters of between seven and ten manuscript pages. We look for well-written, graphic erotica meant to sexually titillate by being sensual, not vulgar." Published new writers within the last year. Recommends other markets.
How to Contact: "We encourage unsolicited manuscripts. Writers who have proven reliable will receive assignments."
Payment: Pays $5/page for short letters and a $75 flat rate for long letters.
Terms: Pays on acceptance.
Advice: "Keep it short and sensual. We buy many more short letters than long ones. This is a 'couples-oriented' book; the sex should be a natural outgrowth of a relationship, the characters should be believable, and both male and female characters should be treated with respect. No S&M, bondage, male homosexuality, incest, underage characters or anal sex—not even in dialogue, not even in implication. No language that even implies sexual violence—not even in metaphor. No ejaculation on any part of a person's body. Romance is a big plus. Before sending in any material, request 'Submission Guidelines for Writers' to get a clear picture of what we're looking for, and how to present submissions."

PLAYBOY MAGAZINE, 680 N. Lake Shore Dr., Chicago IL 60611. Prefers not to share information.

POCKETS, Devotional Magazine for Children, (II), The Upper Room, Box 189, 1908 Grand Ave., Nashville TN 37202. (615)340-7333. Editor-in-Chief: Janet R. McNish. Magazine: 7 × 9; 32 pages; 50 lb. white econowrite paper; 80 lb. white coated, heavy cover stock; color and 2-color illustrations; some photos. Magazine for children ages 6-12, with articles specifically geared for ages 8 to 11. "The magazine offers stories, activities, prayers, poems—all geared to giving children a better understanding of themselves as children of God." Published monthly except for January. Estab. 1981. Estimated circ. 68,000.
• *Pockets* was nominated by *MagazineWeek* for an Excellence Award in 1991. The magazine has also received honors from the Educational Press Association of America. *Pockets* ranks #44 on the latest *Writer's Digest* Fiction 50 list.
Needs: Adventure, contemporary, ethnic, fantasy, historical (general), juvenile, religious/inspirational and suspense/mystery. "All submissions should address the broad theme of the magazine. Each issue will be built around several themes with material which can be used by children in a variety of ways. Scripture stories, fiction, poetry, prayers, art, graphics, puzzles and activities will all be included. Submissions do not need to be overtly religious. They should help children experience a Christian lifestyle that is not always a neatly wrapped moral package, but is open to the continuing revelation of God's will. Seasonal material, both secular and liturgical, is desired. No violence, horror, sexual and racial stereotyping or fiction containing heavy moralizing." Receives approximately 120 unsolicited fiction mss/month. Buys 2-3 mss/issue; 22-33 mss/year. Publishes short shorts. A peace-with-justice theme will run throughout the magazine. Published work by Peggy King Anderson, Angela Gibson and John Steptoe; published new writers last year. Length: 600 words minimum; 1,500 words maximum; 1,200 words average.
How to Contact: Send complete ms with SASE. Previously published submissions OK, but no simultaneous submissions. Reports in 2 months on mss. Publishes ms 1 year to 18 months after acceptance. Sample copy for $1.95. Fiction guidelines and themes with SASE. "Strongly advise sending for themes before submitting."

Payment: Pays 12¢/word and up and 2-5 contributor's copies. $1.95 charge for extras; $1 each for 10 or more.
Terms: Pays on acceptance for newspaper and periodical rights. Buys reprints.
Advice: "Do not write *down* to children." Rejects mss because "we receive far more submissions than we can use. If all were of high quality, we still would purchase only a few. The most common problems are overworked story lines and flat, unrealistic characters. Most stories simply do not 'ring true', and children know that. Each issue is theme-related. Please send for list of themes. Include SASE." Sponsors annual fiction writing contest. Deadline: Oct. (1,000-1,600 words.)

PORTLAND MAGAZINE, Maine's City Magazine, (II), 578 Congress St., Portland ME 04101. (207)775-4339. Editor: Colin Sargent. Magazine: 68 pages; 60 lb. paper; 80 lb. cover stock; illustrations and photographs. "City lifestyle magazine—style, business, real estate, controversy, fashion, cuisine, interviews, art." Monthly. Estab. 1986. Circ. 22,000.
Needs: Contemporary, historical, literary. Receives 20 unsolicited fiction mss/month. Buys 1 mss/ issue; 12 mss/year. Publishes short shorts. Published work by Janwillem Vande Wetering, Sanford Phippen, Mamene Medwood. Length: 3 double-spaced typed pages.
How to Contact: Query first. "Fiction below 700 words, please." Send complete ms with cover letter. Reports in 3 months. SASE (IRCs). Accepts electronic submissions.
Terms: Pays on publication for first North American serial rights.
Advice: "We publish ambitious short fiction featuring everyone from Frederick Barthelme to newly discovered fiction by Edna St. Vincent Millay."

PRIME TIME SPORTS AND FITNESS, (IV), Prime Time Publishing, P.O. Box 6097, Evanston IL 60204. (708)864-8113. Editor: Dennis Dorner. Fiction Editor: Linda Jefferson. Magazine; 8½×11; 40-80 pages; coated enamel paper and cover stock; 10 illustrations; 42 photographs. "For active sports participants." Estab. 1975. Circ. 67,000.
● *Prime Time Sports and Fitness* has won several awards for "recreational reporting."
Needs: Adventure, contemporary, erotica, fantasy, historical, humor/satire, mainstream, mystery/suspense (romantic suspense), sports, young adult/teen (10-18 years). No gay, lesbian. Receives 30-40 unsolicited mss/month. Buys 1-2 mss/issue; 20/year. Publishes ms 3-8 months after acceptance. Agented fiction 10%. Published work by Dennis Dorner, Sally Hammill. Length: 2,000 words preferred; 250 words minimum; 3,000 words maximum. Publishes short shorts. Length: 250-500 words. Sometimes critiques rejected ms and recommends other markets.
How to Contact: Send complete ms with cover letter, include Social Security number. "Do *not* include credits and history. We buy articles, not people." Reports in 1-3 months on queries; 1 week - 3 months on mss. SASE (IRCs). Simultaneous and reprint submissions OK. Sample copy for 10×12 SAE and $1.40 postage. Fiction guidelines free for SAE.
Payment: Pays $25-500.
Terms: Pays on publication for all rights, first rights, first North American serial rights, one-time rights; "depends on manuscript."
Advice: "Be funny, ahead of particular sports season, and enjoy your story. Bring out some human touch that would relate to our readers."

PRIVATE LETTERS, (I, II), 801 2nd Ave., New York NY 10017. Editor: Asia Fraser. Magazine: digest-sized; 98 pages; illustrations; photographs. "Adult erotica that is well-written, using graphic terms that excite the sexual nature of the reader in a pleasant, positive manner." Bimonthly letters magazine.
● The publisher of *Private Letters* also publishes *Pillow Talk* listed in this book.
Needs: Erotica, written in letter form. No S&M, incest, homosexuality, anal sex or sex-crazed women and macho, women-conquering studs. "We use approximately 20 short letters per issue of no more than six double-spaced manuscript pages and five long letters of about 10 double-spaced manuscript pages." Published work by Diana Shamblin, Frank Lee and Shirley LeRoy; published new writers within the last year. Recommends other markets.
How to Contact: Send complete ms (only after requesting guidelines). "The majority of the material is assigned to people whose writing has proven consistently top-notch. They usually reach this level by sending us unsolicited material which impresses us. We invite them to send us some more on spec, and we're impressed again. Then a long and fruitful relationship is hopefully established. We greatly encourage unsolicited submissions. We are now printing two additional issues each year, so naturally the demand for stories is higher."

Payment: Pays $5 per page for short letters; $75 for long (7-10 page) letters.
Terms: Pays on acceptance.
Advice: "If you base your writing on erotic magazines other than our own, then we'll probably find your material too gross. We want good characterization, believable plots, a little romance, with sex being a natural outgrowth of a relationship. (Yes, it can be done. Read our magazine.) Portray sex as an emotionally-charged, romantic experience—not an animalistic ritual. *Never* give up, except if you die. In which case, if you haven't succeeded as a writer yet, you probably never will. (Though there have been exceptions.) Potential writers should be advised that each issue has certain themes and topics we try to adhere to. Also, while the longer stories of more than 7 pages pay more, there are only about five of them accepted for each issue. We buy far more 4-6 page mss. Request with SASE (IRCs) our 'Submission Guidelines for Writers' to get a clear picture of what we're looking for, and how to present submissions."

PURPOSE, (II), Mennonite Publishing House, 616 Walnut Ave., Scottdale PA 15683-1999. (412)887-8500. Editor: James E. Horsch. Magazine: 5⅜ × 8⅜; 8 pages; illustrations; photos. "Magazine focuses on Christian discipleship—how to be a faithful Christian in the midst of tough everyday life complexities. Uses story form to present models and examples to encourage Christians in living a life of faithful discipleship." Weekly. Estab. 1968. Circ. 18,000.
• Mennonite Publishing House also publishes *On the Line*, *Story Friends* and *With* listed in this book.
Needs: Historical, religious/inspirational. No militaristic/narrow patriotism or racism. Receives 100 unsolicited mss/month. Buys 3 mss/issue; 40 mss/year. Recently published work by Joanne Lehman, Emily Sargent Councilman, Clare Miseles and Joyce Moyer Hostetter. Length: 600 words average; 900 words maximum. Occasionally comments on rejected mss.
How to Contact: Send complete ms only. Reports in 2 months. Simultaneous and previously published work OK. Sample copy for 6 × 9 SAE and 2 first-class stamps (IRCs). Writer's guidelines free with sample copy only.
Payment: Pays up to 5¢/word for stories and 2 contributor's copies.
Terms: Pays on acceptance for one-time rights.
Advice: Many stories are "situational—how to respond to dilemmas. Write crisp, action moving, personal style, focused upon an individual, a group of people, or an organization. The story form is an excellent literary device to use in exploring discipleship issues. There are many issues to explore. Each writer brings a unique solution. Let's hear them. The first two paragraphs are crucial in establishing the mood/issue to be resolved in the story. Work hard on developing these."

ELLERY QUEEN'S MYSTERY MAGAZINE, (II), Dell Magazines Fiction Group, 1540 Broadway, New York NY 10036. (212)782-8546. Editor: Janet Hutchings. Magazine: digest-sized; 160 pages with special 288-page issues in March and October. Magazine for lovers of mystery fiction. Published 13 times/year. Estab. 1941. Circ. 279,000.
• Dell Magazines other mystery publication is *Alfred Hitchcock Mystery Magazine* listed in this book. *Ellery Queen's* is ranked #18 on the latest *Writer's Digest* Fiction 50 list. The magazine has won numerous awards.
Needs: "We accept only mystery, crime, suspense and detective fiction." Receives approximately 300 unsolicited fiction mss each month. Buys 10-15 mss/issue. Publishes ms 6-12 months after acceptance. Agented fiction 50%. Published work by Clark Howard, Robert Barnard and Ruth Rendell; published new writers within the last year. Length: up to 7,000 words, occassionally longer. Publishes 2-3 short novels of up to 17,000 words/year by established authors; minute mysteries of 250 words; short mystery verse. Critiques rejected mss "only when a story might be a possibility for us if revised." Sometimes recommends other markets.
How to Contact: Send complete ms with SASE (IRCs). Cover letter should include publishing credits and brief biographical sketch. Simultaneous submissions OK. Reports in 3 months or sooner on mss. Fiction guidelines with SASE. Sample copy for $2.75.
Payment: Pays 3¢/word and up.
Terms: Pays on acceptance for first North American serial rights. Occasionally buys reprints.
Advice: "We have a Department of First Stories and usually publish at least one first story an issue—i.e., the author's first published fiction. We select stories that are fresh and of the kind our readers have expressed a liking for. In writing a detective story, you must play fair with the reader re clues

Over the last 53 years, Ellery Queen "has published the most creative writers in the field of crime fiction," says Editor Janet Hutchings. "This cover will suggest to many the hardboiled subgenre of mystery fiction, but it does not in this sense represent our magazine's philosophy or theme. We publish the full range of crime and detection, from psychological suspense to private-eye to police stories. Except for a book review column and mystery crossword puzzle, the magazine is entirely fiction." The cover art is by Richard Parisi, a freelance illustrator based in New York.

and necessary information. Otherwise you have a better chance of publishing if you avoid writing to formula."

R-A-D-A-R, (II), Standard Publishing, 8121 Hamilton Ave., Cincinnati OH 45231. (513)931-4050. Editor: Margaret Williams. Magazine: 12 pages; newsprint; illustrations; a few photos. "*R-A-D-A-R* is a take-home paper, distributed in Sunday school classes for children in grades 3-6. The stories and other features reinforce the Bible lesson taught in class. Boys and girls who attend Sunday school make up the audience. The fiction stories, Bible picture stories and other special features appeal to their interests." Weekly. Estab. 1978.
 • *Seek* and *The Lookout*, also published by Standard, are listed in this book.
Needs: Fiction—The hero of the story should be an 11- or 12-year-old in a situation involving one or more of the following: history, mystery, animals, prose poem, spiritual, sports, adventure, school, travel, relationships with parents, friends and others. Stories should have believable plots and be wholesome, Christian character-building, but not "preachy." No science fiction. Receives approximately 75-100 unsolicited mss/month. Published work by Betty Lou Mell, Betty Steele Everett and Alan Cliburn; published new writers within the last year. Length: 900-1,000 words average; 400 words minimum; 1,200 words maximum. Publishes short shorts.
How to Contact: Send complete ms. Reports in 2 weeks on queries; 6-8 weeks on mss. SASE (IRCs) for ms. No simultaneous submissions; reprint submissions OK. Free sample copy and guidelines.
Payment: Pays 3-7¢/word; contributor's copy.
Terms: Pays on acceptance for first rights, reprints, etc.
Advice: "Send for sample copy, guidesheet, and theme list. Follow the specifics of guidelines. Keep your writing current with the times and happenings of our world."

RADIANCE, The Magazine for Large Women, (II), Box 30246, Oakland CA 94604. (510)482-0680. Editor: Alice Ansfield. Fiction Editors: Alice Ansfield and Carol Squires. Magazine: 8½ × 11; 48-52 pages; glossy/coated paper; 70 lb. cover stock; illustrations; photos. "Theme is to encourage women to live fully now, whatever their body size. To stop waiting to live or feel good about themselves until they lose weight." Quarterly. Estab. 1984. Circ. 8,000. Readership: 30,000.
 • In 1991 *Radiance* was nominated for a "Best of the Alternative Press" award by the *Utne Reader* magazine.
Needs: Adventure, contemporary, erotica, ethnic, fantasy, feminist, historical, humor/satire, mainstream, mystery/suspense, prose poem, science fiction, spiritual, sports, young adult/teen. "Want fiction to have a larger-bodied character; living in a positive, upbeat way. Our goal is to empower women." Receives 80 mss/month. Buys 40 mss/year. Publishes ms within 1 year of acceptance. Recently published work by Marla Zarrow, Sallie Tisdale and Mary Kay Blakely. Length: 2,000 + words; 800

words minimum; 3,500 words maximum. Publishes short shorts. Sometimes critiques rejected mss and recommends other markets.

How to Contact: Query with clips of published work and send complete mss with cover letter. Reports in 2-3 months. SASE (IRCs). Reprint submissions OK. Sample copy for $3.50. Guidelines for #10 SASE. Reviews novels and short story collections ("with at least 1 large-size heroine.")

Payment: Pays $35-100 and contributor's copies.

Terms: Pays on publication for one-time rights. Sends galleys to the author if requested.

Advice: "Read our magazine before sending anything to us. Know what our philosophy and points of view are before sending a manuscript. Look around within your community for inspiring, successful and unique large women doing things worth writing about. At this time, prefer fiction having to do with a larger woman (man, child). *Radiance* is one of the leading resources in the size acceptance movement. Each issue profiles dynamic large women from all walks of life, along with articles on health, media, fashion and politics. Our audience is the 30 million American women who wear a size 16 or over. Feminist, emotionally-supportive, quarterly magazine."

RANGER RICK MAGAZINE, (II), National Wildlife Federation, 1400 16th St. NW, Washington DC 20036-2266. (703)790-4278. Editor: Gerald Bishop. Fiction Editor: Deborah Churchman. Magazine: 8 × 10; 48 pages; glossy paper; 60 lb. cover stock; illustrations; photos. "*Ranger Rick* emphasizes conservation and the enjoyment of nature through full-color photos and art, fiction and nonfiction articles, games and puzzles, and special columns. Our audience ranges in ages from 6-12, with the greatest number in the 7 to 10 group. We aim for a fourth grade reading level. They read for fun and information." Monthly. Estab. 1967. Circ. 900,000.

● *Ranger Rick* has won several Ed Press awards and was a runner up for the National Magazine Award for single issue in 1991.

Needs: Fantasy, mystery (amateur sleuth), adventure, science fiction, sports, and humor. "Interesting stories for kids focusing directly on nature or related subjects. Fiction that carries a conservation message is always needed, as are adventure stories involving kids with nature or the outdoors. Moralistic 'lessons' taught children by parents or teachers are not accepted. Human qualities are attributed to animals only in our regular feature, 'Adventures of Ranger Rick.' " Receives about 150-200 unsolicited fiction mss each month. Buys about 6 mss/year. Published fiction by Leslie Dendy. Length: 900 words maximum. Critiques rejected mss "when there is time."

How to Contact: Query with sample lead and any clips of published work with SASE (IRCs). May consider simultaneous submissions. Reports in 1-2 months on queries and mss. Publishes ms 8 months to 1 year after acceptance, but sometimes longer. Sample copy for $2. Guidelines for legal-sized SASE.

Payment: Pays $550 maximum/full-length ms.

Terms: Pays on acceptance for all rights. Very rarely buys reprints. Sends galleys to author.

Advice: "For our magazine, the writer needs to understand kids and that aspect of nature he or she is writing about—a difficult combination! Mss are rejected because they are contrived and/or condescending—often overwritten. Some mss are anthropomorphic, others are above our readers' level. We find that fiction stories help children understand the natural world and the environmental problems it faces. Beginning writers have a chance equal to that of established authors *provided* the quality is there. Would love to see more science fiction and fantasy, as well as mysteries."

REDBOOK, (II), The Hearst Corporation, 224 W. 57th St., New York NY 10019. Fiction Editor: Dawn Raffel. Magazine: 8 × 10³/₄; 150-250 pages; 34 lb. paper; 70 lb. cover; illustrations; photos. "*Redbook's* readership consists of American women, ages 25-44. Most are well-educated, married, have children and also work outside the home." Monthly. Estab. 1903. Circ. 4,000,000.

● For more information, see the interview with *Redbook* Fiction Editor Dawn Raffel in the 1993 edition of this book. Work published in *Redbook* has been selected for the *O. Henry Prize* anthology in 1992. The magazine is ranked #4 on the latest *Writer's Digest* Fiction 50 list.

Needs: "*Redbook* generally publishes one or two short stories per issue. Stories need not be about women exclusively; but must appeal to a female audience. We are interested in new voices and buy up to a quarter of our stories from unsolicited submissions. Standards are high: Stories must be fresh, felt and intelligent; no formula fiction." Receives up to 3,000 unsolicited fiction mss each month; published new writers within the last year. Length: up to 22 ms pages.

How to Contact: Send complete ms with SASE (IRCs). No queries, please. Simultaneous submissions OK. Reports in 4-6 weeks.
Terms: Pays on acceptance for first North American serial rights.
Advice: "Superior craftsmanship is of paramount importance: We look for emotional complexity, dramatic tension, precision of language. Note that we don't run stories that look back on the experiences of childhood or adolescence. Please read a few issues to get a sense of what we're looking for."

REFORM JUDAISM, (II), Union of American Hebrew Congregations, 838 5th Ave., New York NY 10021. (212)249-0100, ext. 400. Editor: Aron Hirt-Manheimer. Managing Editor: Joy Weinberg. Magazine: 8 × 10¾; 80 pages; illustrations; photos. "We cover subjects of Jewish interest in general and Reform Jewish in particular, for members of Reform Jewish congregations in the United States and Canada." Quarterly. Estab. 1972. Circ. 295,000.
Needs: Humor/satire, religious/inspirational. Receives 30 unsolicited mss/month. Buys 3 mss/year. Publishes ms 6 months after acceptance. Length: 1,200 words average; 600 words minimum; 3,000 words maximum.
How to Contact: Send complete ms with cover letter. Reports in 3 weeks. SASE (IRCs) for ms. Simultaneous submissions OK. Sample copy for $3.50.
Payment: Pays 10¢/word.
Terms: Pays on publication for first North American serial rights.

RHAPSODY, 475 Park Ave. S., New York NY 10016. See Starlog Group in the Commercial Publishers section for more information.

THE RHODE ISLANDER MAGAZINE, (IV), (formerly *Sunday Journal Magazine*), *The Providence Journal-Bulletin*, 75 Fountain St., Providence RI 02902. (401)277-7349. Editor: Elliot Krieger. Magazine: 10 × 11½; 28 pages; coated newsprint paper; illustrations; photos. "Magazine that has appeared weekly for 40 years in the *Providence Sunday Journal*." Circ. 280,000.
Needs: Regional. "We will accept fiction from or about Rhode Island only." Published fiction by Paul Watkins and Ann Hood; published new writers within the last year.
How to Contact: Submit with SASE (IRCs). Reports in 1 week.
Payment: Pays $175-400.
Terms: Buys one-time rights. Sponsors short-story contest for local writers.

ROAD KING MAGAZINE, (I), William A. Coop, Inc., Box 250, Park Forest IL 60466. (708)481-9240. Magazine: 5¾ × 8; 48-88 pages; 60 lb. enamel paper; 60 lb. enamel cover stock; illustrations; photos. "Bimonthly leisure-reading magazine for long-haul, over-the-road professional truckers. Contains short articles, short fiction, some product news, games, puzzles and industry news. Truck drivers read it while eating, fueling, during layovers and at other similar times while they are en route."
Needs: Truck-related, western, mystery, adventure and humor. "Remember that our magazine gets into the home and that some truckers tend to be Bible Belt types. No erotica or violence." Receives 200 unsolicited fiction mss each year. Buys 1 ms/issue; 6 mss/year. Publishes ms 1-2 months after acceptance. Published work by Forrest Grove and Dan Anderson. Length: 1,200 words, maximum.
How to Contact: Send complete ms with SASE (IRCs). No simultaneous submissions. Reports in 3-6 months. Sample copy for 6 × 9 SASE.
Payment: Pays $400 maximum.
Terms: Pays on acceptance for all rights.
Advice: "Don't phone. Don't send mss by registered or insured mail or they will be returned unopened by post office. Don't try to get us involved in lengthy correspondence. Be patient. We have a small staff and we are slow." Mss are rejected because "most don't fit our format . . . they are too long; they do not have enough knowledge of trucking; there is too much violence. Our readers like fiction. We are a leisure reading publication with a wide variety of themes and articles in each issue. Truckers can read a bit over coffee, in the washroom, etc., then save the rest of the magazine for the next stop. Know the trucker market. We are not interested in stereotypical image of truckers as macho, beer guzzling, women-chasing cowboys."

ST. ANTHONY MESSENGER, (II), 1615 Republic St., Cincinnati OH 45210-1298. Editor: Norman Perry, O.F.M. Magazine: 8 × 10¾; 56 pages; illustrations; photos. "*St. Anthony Messenger* is a Catholic family magazine which aims to help its readers lead more fully human and Christian lives. We publish articles which report on a changing church and world, opinion pieces written from the perspective of

Christian faith and values, personality profiles, and fiction which entertains and informs." Monthly. Estab. 1893. Circ. 325,000.

● This is a leading Catholic magazine, but has won awards for both religious and secular journalism and writing. In 1993 the magazine received 6 awards from the Catholic Press Association and 5 awards from the Cincinnati Editors Association. *St. Anthony Messenger* ranks #39 on the latest *Writer's Digest* Fiction 50 list.

Needs: Contemporary, religious/inspirational, romance, senior citizen/retirement and spiritual. "We do not want mawkishly sentimental or preachy fiction. Stories are most often rejected for poor plotting and characterization; bad dialogue—listen to how people talk; inadequate motivation. Many stories say nothing, are 'happenings' rather than stories." No fetal journals, no rewritten Bible stories. Receives 70-80 unsolicited fiction mss/month. Buys 1 ms/issue; 12 mss/year. Publishes ms up to 1 year after acceptance. Published work by Marjorie Franco, Joseph Pici, Joan Savro and Philip Gambone. Length: 2,000-2,500 words. Critiques rejected mss "when there is time." Sometimes recommends other markets.

How to Contact: Send complete ms with SASE (IRCs). No simultaneous submissions. Reports in 6-8 weeks. Sample copy and guidelines for #10 SASE. Reviews novels and short story collections. Send books to Barbara Beckwith, book review editor.

Payment: Pays 14¢/word maximum; 2 contributor's copies; $1 charge for extras.

Terms: Pays on acceptance for first North American serial rights.

Advice: "We publish one story a month and we get up to 1,000 a year. Too many offer simplistic 'solutions' or answers. Pay attention to endings. Easy, simplistic, deus ex machina endings don't work. People have to feel characters in the stories are real and have a reason to care about them and what happens to them. Fiction entertains but can also convey a point in a very telling way just as the Bible uses stories to teach."

ST. JOSEPH'S MESSENGER AND ADVOCATE OF THE BLIND, (II), Sisters of St. Joseph of Peace, 541 Pavonia Ave., Jersey City NJ 07306. (201)798-4141. Magazine: 8½×11; 16 pages; illustrations; photos. For Catholics generally but not exclusively. Theme is "religious—relevant—real." Quarterly. Estab. 1903. Circ. 20,000.

● *St. Joseph's Messenger and Advocate of the Blind* ranked #30 on the latest *Writer's Digest* Fiction 50 list.

Needs: Contemporary, humor/satire, mainstream, religious/inspirational, romance and senior citizen/retirement. Receives 30-40 unsolicited fiction mss/month. Buys 3 mss/issue; 20 mss/year. Publishes ms an average of 1 year after acceptance. Published work by Eileen W. Strauch; published new writers within the last year. Length: 800 words minimum; 1,800 words maximum; 1,500 words average. Occasionally critiques rejected mss.

How to Contact: Send complete ms with SASE (IRCs). Simultaneous and previously published submissions OK. Sample copy for #10 SAE and 1 first-class stamp. Fiction guidelines for SASE.

Payment: Pays $15-40 and 2 contributor's copies.

Terms: Pays on acceptance for one-time rights.

Advice: Rejects mss because of "vague focus or theme. Write to be read—keep material current and of interest. *Do not preach*—the story will tell the message. Keep the ending from being too obvious. Fiction is the greatest area of interest to our particular reading public."

SASSY MAGAZINE, (I, II, IV), Lang Communications, 230 Park Ave., New York NY 10169. (212)551-9500. Editor: Christina Kelly. Managing Editor: Virginia O'Brien. Magazine; 9½×11; 100-130 pages; glossy 40 lb. stock paper and cover; illustrations and photographs. "Lifestyle magazine for girls, ages 14-19, covering entertainment, fashion as well as serious subjects." Monthly. Estab. 1988. Circ. 650,000.

● *Sassy*, known for its gutsy approach to writing for young women, has received a *MagazineWeek* Award for Editorial Excellence in 1992 and was a finalist again in 1993. It ranked #9 on the

---

85% of the information in Novel & Short Story Writer's Market *is updated from year to year. If you're still using this book and it is 1995 or later, buy the new edition at your favorite bookstore or order directly from Writer's Digest Books.*

INSIDER VIEWPOINT

Writing for Teens not as Easy as it Seems

Fiction Editor Christina Kelly, who has been with *Sassy* magazine since its first issue in 1988, says there is no great secret to getting published in the magazine— she is just looking for "fiction that is genuine, that has the ring of truth to it."

But she adds that writing genuine fiction for a teenage audience is not an easy feat. "Many [writers] write in an adult's conception of what a teenage voice sounds like rather than a genuine teenage voice," Kelly says. "I'm not saying that older people can't write for teenagers, because a lot of good teenage fiction is written by older people. But if you're wondering how a teenager would talk, or what a teenage voice sounds like, then you shouldn't be writing it. If it comes really naturally to you, then do it."

Christina Kelly

© Matthew Hranek

Although she does not want typical teenage romance, she says she will accept realistic stories dealing with romance. "I don't have a problem with the subject of romance. In fact, a lot of our stories deal with that," Kelly says. "It just depends on the way it's handled . . . I don't want a story that says, 'like, I met this cute guy, and he's really cool, and I found out he likes me too!' I'm interested in quality fiction."

Despite the reputation *Sassy* has acquired for tackling controversial issues other teenage magazines wouldn't touch, Kelly says she has to reject overly controversial stories.

"Without getting into the long history of the controversy associated with the magazine, we just have to be careful," she says. "Sometimes, while writing about real life, fiction writers will write about drug use or sex. Say a character is smoking pot in a story. A teenage reader might see that as an endorsement of pot smoking rather than a documentation of pot smoking . . . If it were completely up to me, I'd probably print the story, but it's not. The owner of the magazine sometimes vetoes stories I'd like to print."

Sassy receives over 300 unsolicited manuscripts for every one the magazine can print. Other *Sassy* staff members screen the unsolicited manuscripts, and Kelly reads the best 25 percent and makes the final decision. But *Sassy* no longer has the staff to comment on every manuscript, Kelly says.

"We usually send a form letter, unless it's a story I really like," she says. "If I really like a story but can't use it, I'll either call or write to the writer to tell them what the story needs. Later, I've often printed the story."

Kelly also contacts writers who send well-written stories that are too long. "I'll ask them to cut their manuscripts in half," she says. "If they say no, then I have to reject them, because we just don't have the space. The ideal length for a story is about 2,000 words, and we rarely go over 3,000."

Most stories published in *Sassy* were written by previously unpublished writers, adds Kelly. "I may seem unapproachable to new fiction writers ... but I'm really committed to finding new voices as opposed to asking Joyce Carol Oates to shell something out for us," she says.

Writers should keep submitting, no matter what, Kelly says. Writers whose manuscripts were initially rejected have later submitted work that was accepted.

"In a way it's almost haphazard, what gets picked, so I would encourage writers to submit anything that they think might be interesting, and not to be discouraged by form letters," Kelly says.

—Argie Manolis

latest *Writer's Digest* Fiction 50 list. Look for the interview with editor Christina Kelly in this edition.

Needs: Contemporary, ethnic, experimental, feminist, gay, humor/satire, literary, mainstream, prose poem, young adult/teen (10-18 years). "No typical teenage romance." Publishes annual special fiction issue. Receives 300 unsolicited mss/month. Buys 1 ms/issue; 12 mss/year. Publishes ms 3-6 months after publication. Published Christina Kelly, John Elder, Elizabeth Mosier. Length: 2,000 words; 1,000 words minimum; 3,500 words maximum. Sometimes critiques rejected mss and recommends other markets.

How to Contact: Send complete manuscript with cover letter. Include social security number and address, brief background, perhaps one sentence on what story is about or like. Reports in 3 months. SASE (IRCs). Simultaneous submissions OK. Sample copy for $2. Fiction guidelines are free.

Payment: Pays $1,000 and contributor's copies.

Terms: Pays on acceptance. Offers 20% kill fee. Buys all rights or first North American serial righs. Send galleys to author (if requested and if time permits).

Advice: "We look for unusual new ways to write for teenagers. It helps if the story has a quirky, vernacular style that we use throughout the magazine. Generally our stories have to have a teenage protagonist but they are not typical teen fiction. In the end, our only real criterion is that a story is original, intelligent, well-crafted and moves us."

SEEK, (II), Standard Publishing, 8121 Hamilton Ave., Cincinnati OH 45231. Editor: Eileen H. Wilmoth. Magazine: 5½×8½; 8 pages; newsprint paper; art and photos in each issue. "Inspirational stories of faith-in-action for Christian young adults; a Sunday School take-home paper." Weekly. Estab. 1970. Circ. 40,000.

● Standard Publishing also publishes *R-A-D-A-R* and *The Lookout* listed in this book.

Needs: Religious/inspirational. Buys 150 mss/year. Publishes ms an average of 1 year after acceptance. Published new writers within the last year. Length: 500-1,200 words.

How to Contact: Send complete ms with SASE (IRCs). No simultaneous submissions. Reports in 2-3 months. Free sample copy and guidelines. Reviews "some" novels and short story collections.

Payment: Pays 5-7¢/word.

Terms: Pays on acceptance. Buys reprints.

Advice: "Write a credible story with Christian slant—no preachments; avoid overworked themes such as joy in suffering, generation gaps, etc. Most mss are rejected by us because of irrelevant topic or message, unrealistic story, or poor character and/or plot development. We use fiction stories that are believable."

SEVENTEEN, (II), III Magazine Corp., 850 3rd Ave., New York NY 10022. (212)407-9700. Fiction Editor: Joe Bargmann. Magazine: 8½×11; 125-400 pages; 40 lb. coated paper; 80 lb. coated cover stock; illustrations; photos. A general interest magazine with fashion, beauty care, pertinent topics such as current issues, attitudes, experiences and concerns of teenagers. Monthly. Estab. 1944. Circ. 1.9 million.

• *Seventeen* sponsors an annual fiction contest for writers age 13-21. See the listing for this in the Contests and Awards section.

Needs: High-quality literary fiction. Receives 350 unsolicited fiction mss/month. Buys 1 mss/issue. Agented fiction 50%. Published work by Margaret Atwood, Joyce Carol Oates; published new writers within the last year. Length: approximately 1,500-3,500 words. Also publishes short shorts.

How to Contact: Send complete ms with SASE (IRCs) and cover letter with relevant credits. Reports in 3 months on mss. Guidelines for submissions with SASE.

Payment: Pays $700-2,500.

Terms: Pays on acceptance for one-time rights.

Advice: "Respect the intelligence and sophistication of teenagers. *Seventeen* remains open to the surprise of new voices. Our commitment to publishing the work of new writers remains strong; we continue to read every submission we receive. We believe that good fiction can move the reader toward thoughtful examination of her own life as well as the lives of others—providing her ultimately with a fuller appreciation of what it means to be human. While stories that focus on female teenage experience continue to be of interest, the less obvious possibilities are equally welcome. We encourage writers to submit literary short stories concerning subjects that may not be immediately identifiable as 'teenage,' with narrative styles that are experimental and challenging. Too often, unsolicited submissions possess voices and themes condescending and unsophisticated. Also, writers hesitate to send stories to *Seventeen* which they think too violent or risqué. Good writing holds the imaginable and then some, and if it doesn't find its home here, we're always grateful for the introduction to a writer's work."

‡SHINING STAR, Practical Teaching Magazine for Christian Educators and Parents, (II), Box 299, Carthage IL 62321. Editor: Becky Daniel. Magazine: 8½×11; 80 pages; illustrations. "Biblical stories only for teachers and parents of children K-8th graders." Quarterly. Estab. 1982. Circ. 20,000.

Needs: Looking for ideas for ways to teach scripture to children age 4-12. Receives 100 unsolicited mss/month. Buys 3 mss/issue; 12 mss/year. Publishes ms 9-12 months after acceptance. Published new writers within the last year. Length: 500-1,000 words. Publishes short shorts.

How to Contact: Send complete ms with cover letter. Reports in 1 month. SASE (IRCs) for ms. Simultaneous submissions OK. Sample copy $2. Fiction guidelines with SASE.

Payment: Pays $20-50 and contributor's copies.

Terms: Pays on publication for all rights.

Advice: "Know the scriptures and be a teacher or person that has worked with and understands young children. Work should place emphasis on building positive self-concepts in children in Christian setting. Stories should be set in Biblical times and include characters and stories from the Bible."

SHOFAR, For Jewish Kids On The Move, (I, II, IV), 43 Northcote Dr., Melville NY 11747. (516)643-4598. Editor: Gerald H. Grayson, Ph.D. Magazine: 8½×11; 32-48 pages; 60 lb. paper; 80 lb. cover; illustration; photos. Audience: Jewish children in fourth through eighth grades. Monthly (October-May). Estab. 1984. Circ. 10,000.

Needs: Children's/juvenile (middle reader): cartoons, contemporary, humorous, poetry, puzzles, religious, sports. "All material must be on a Jewish theme. Receives 12-24 unsolicited mss/month. Buys 3-5 mss/issue; 24-40 mss/year. Published work by Caryn Huberman, Diane Claerbout and Rabbi Sheldon Lewis. Length: 500-700 words. Occasionally critiques rejected mss. Recommends other markets.

How to Contact: Send complete ms with cover letter. Reports in 6-8 weeks. SASE (IRCs). Simultaneous and reprint submissions OK. Sample copy for 9×12 SAE and 5 first-class stamps. Fiction guidelines for 3½×6½ SAE and 1 first-class stamp.

Payment: Pays 10¢/word and 5 contributor's copies.

Terms: Pays on publication for first North American serial rights.

Advice: "Know the magazine and the religious-education needs of Jewish elementary-school-age children. If you are a Jewish educator, what has worked for you in the classroom? Write it out; send it on to me; I'll help you develop the idea into a short piece of fiction. A beginning fiction writer eager to break into *Shofar* will find an eager editor willing to help."

THE SINGLE PARENT, Journal of Parents Without Partners, (IV), Parents Without Partners, Inc., 401 N. Michigan Ave., Chicago IL 60611. (312)644-6610, ext. 3226. Fax: (312)245-1082. Editor: Mercedes Vance. Magazine: "Members of PWP are single parents who are divorced, widowed or never married. *The Single Parent (TSP)* tries to look at the positive side of the single parent's situation and is interested in all aspects of parenting, particularly the 'single parent's' parenting situation. About 10 percent of material is aimed at juvenile audience." Quarterly. Estab. 1957. Circ. 90,000.

- *The Single Parent* won the 1990 Award for Excellence in magazine writing on children of divorce from the National Council of Children's Rights. Parents Without Partners is a national organization for single parents.

Needs: For children, adolescents and adult readers: contemporary, humorous, problem-solving, mystery/suspense, adventure. Stories with single parent angle only. No sad, sports, romance or religious material. Accompanying photos/graphics strongly encouraged. Length: 800-1,500 words.

How to Contact: Send complete ms with accompanying photos/graphics and author photo and biography. Mss must be submitted on WordPerfect/ASCII format on 3½" disk with hard copy. Mss not returned.

Payment: Pays in contributor's copies.

Terms: Pays on publication.

‡**SINGLES ALMANAC, (I)**, Bailey Associates, Inc., 51 Shelton Rd., Monroe CT 06468. (203)261-2908. Fax: (203)268-5794. Editor: Dave Faulknor. Magazine: 8 × 10¾; 36 pages; gloss paper. "Adult divorced, widowed, never married, parents without partners." Monthly. Estab. 1981. Circ. 75,000.

Needs: Condensed novel, erotica, experimental, historical (general), humor/satire, literary, mainstream/contemporary, mystery/suspense (amateur sleuth, cozy, private eye/hard-boiled, romantic suspense), psychic/supernatural/occult, regional, religious/inspirational, romance (contemporary, historical), science fiction (soft/sociological), serialized novel. No explicit sex. Receives 2-4 unsolicited mss/month. Accepts 1 ms/issue; 12 mss/year. Publishes ms 2-3 months after acceptance. Length: 650 words preferred; 500 words minimum; 1,200 words maximum. Publishes short shorts. Also publishes poetry.

How to Contact: Send complete ms with a cover letter. Should include estimated word count. Reports in 1 week on queries; 1 month on ms. Send a disposable copy of ms. Simultaneous, reprint and electronic submissions OK. Sample copy for 9 × 12 SAE and 75¢ postage. Fiction guidelines free.

Payment: Pays $30-60; contributor's copies.

Terms: Pays on publciation for first rights.

‡**680 MAGAZINE, (I)**, Northeast Consolidated, P.O. Box 2340, Walnut Creek CA 94595. (510)935-7673. Editor: Matt Van Fossen. Magazine: 8½ × 11; 96 pages; 60 lb. gloss paper; 80 lb. cover; 4 illustrations; 20 photos. "We want to publish material that is interesting to us. We want weird, coherent and sexy fiction." Quarterly. Estab. 1991. Circ. 10,000.

Needs: Open. "Anything is acceptable as long as it's good." Receives 2-5 unsolicited mss/month. Accepts 1 ms/issue; 4 mss/year. Does not read mss January-February. Length: 1,000 words average; 500 words minimum; 1,250 words maximum. Publishes short shorts. Also publishes literary criticism and poetry. Sometimes critiques or comments on rejected mss.

How to Contact: Query with clips of 1 published work. Reports in 3 months. Send a disposable copy of mss. Simultaneous and reprint submissions OK. Sample copy for $3, 8½ × 11 SAE and 5 first-class stamps. Fiction guidelines for #10 SAE and 1 first-class stamp. Reviews novels and short story collections. Send books to editor.

Payment: Pays 10¢/word.

Terms: Pays on publication for first North American serial rights.

Advice: "Clear, concise, interesting fiction always stands out. Find the underbelly of society. Contrast it with propriety."

‡**SKIN ART, (I, IV)**, Outlaw Biker Enterprises, Inc., Box 447, Voorhees NJ 08003. Editor: Michelle Delio. Magazine: 8½ × 11; 96 pages; 50 lb. coated paper; 80 lb. cover stock; illustrations; photos. "Art magazine devoted to showcasing the very best of modern tattooing." Published 10 times/year. Estab. 1988. Circ. 180,000.

- Outlaw Biker Enterprises publishes several other magazines including *Outlaw Biker* and *Tatoo Revue* listed in this book.

Needs: Fiction pertaining to subject matter (tatooing). Receives 20 unsolicited mss/month. Publishes 1 fiction ms/issue. Publishes mss 2-8 months after acceptance. Length: 1,000-2,500 words. "Very open to freelance writers and unpublished writers. Freelance photographers also needed send SASE (IRCs) for guidelines and needs."

How to Contact: Send complete ms with cover letter and SASE. Responds to queries within 6 weeks. Sample copy $5 and 8½ × 11 SAE with 2 first-class stamps.
Payment: Payment varies according to quality of work.
Terms: Pays on publication. Buys all rights.
Advice: "Very targeted market, strongly suggest you read magazine before submitting work."

SOJOURNER, A Women's Forum, (II, IV), 42 Seaverns, Jamaica Plain MA 02130. (617)524-0415. Editor: Karen Kahn. Magazine: 11 × 17; 48 pages; newsprint paper; illustrations; photos. "Feminist journal publishing interviews, nonfiction features, news, viewpoints, poetry, reviews (music, cinema, books) and fiction for women." Published monthly. Estab. 1975. Circ. 40,000.
Needs: Contemporary, ethnic, experimental, fantasy, feminist, lesbian, humor/satire, literary, prose poem and women's. Upcoming themes: "Fiction/Poetry Issue" (February); "Annual Health Supplement" (March). Receives 20 unsolicited fiction mss/month. Accepts 10 mss/year. Agented fiction 10%. Published new writers within the last year. Length: 1,000 words minimum; 4,000 words maximum; 2,500 words average. Recommends other markets.
How to Contact: Send complete ms with SASE (IRCs) and cover letter with description of previous publications; current works. Simultaneous submissions OK. Reports in 3-6 months. Publishes ms an average of 6 months after acceptance. Sample copy $3 with 10 × 13 SASE. Fiction guidelines for SASE.
Payment: Pays subscription to magazine and 2 contributor's copies, $15. No extra charge up to 5; $1 charge each thereafter.
Terms: Buys first rights only.
Advice: "Pay attention to appearance of manuscript! Very difficult to wade through sloppily presented fiction, however good. Do write a cover letter. If not cute, it can't hurt and may help. Mention previous publication(s)."

STANDARD, (I, II, IV), Nazarene International Headquarters, 6401 The Paseo, Kansas City MO 64131. (816)333-7000. Editor: Everett Leadingham. Magazine: 8½ × 11; 8 pages; illustrations; photos. Inspirational reading for adults. Weekly. Estab. 1936. Circ. 165,000.
● Other magazines listed in this book associated with the Nazarene are *Discoveries* and *Teens Today*.
Needs: Religious/inspirational, spiritual. Receives 350 unsolicited mss/month (both fiction and nonfiction). Accepts 240 mss/year. Publishes ms 14-18 months after acceptance. Published new writers within the last year. Length: 1,000 words average; 300 words minimum; 1,700 words maximum. Also publishes short shorts of 300-350 words.
How to Contact: Send complete ms with name, address and phone number. Reports in 2-3 months on mss. SASE (IRCs). Simultaneous submissions OK but will pay only reprint rates. Sample copy and guidelines for SAE and 1 first-class stamp.
Payment: Pays 3½¢/word; 2¢/word (reprint); contributor's copies.
Terms: Pays on acceptance for one-time rights.
Advice: "Too much is superficial; containing the same story lines. Give me something original, humorous, yet helpful. I'm also looking for more stories on current social issues. Make plot, characters realistic. Contrived articles are quick to spot and reject."

STORY FRIENDS, (II), Mennonite Publishing House, 616 Walnut Ave., Scottdale PA 15683. (412)887-8500. Editor: Marjorie Waybill. Sunday school publication which portrays Jesus as a friend and helper. Nonfiction and fiction for children 4-9 years of age. Weekly.
● *Story Friends* ranked #42 on the latest *Writer's Digest* Fiction 50 list. The Mennonite Publishing House listings in this book also include *On the Line*, *Purpose* and *With* magazines.
Needs: Juvenile. Stories of everyday experiences at home, in church, in school or at play, which provide models of Christian values. Length: 300-800 words.
How to Contact: Send complete ms with SASE (IRCs). Seasonal or holiday material should be submitted 6 months in advance. Free sample copy.
Payment: Pays 3-5¢/word.
Terms: Pays on acceptance for one-time rights. Buys reprints. Not copyrighted.
Advice: "It is important to include relationships, patterns of forgiveness, respect, honesty, trust and caring. Prefer exciting yet plausible short stories which offer different settings, introduce children to wide ranges of friends and demonstrate joys, fears, temptations and successes of the readers."

STRAIGHT, (II), Standard Publishing Co., 8121 Hamilton Ave., Cincinnati OH 45231. (513)931-4050. Editor: Carla Crane. "Publication helping and encouraging teens to live a victorious, fulfilling Christian life. Distributed through churches and some private subscriptions." Magazine: 6½ × 7½; 12 pages; newsprint paper and cover; illustrations (color); photos. Quarterly in weekly parts. Estab. 1951. Circ. 60,000.

  • *Straight* ranked #31 on the latest *Writer's Digest* Fiction 50 list.

Needs: Contemporary, religious/inspirational, romance, spiritual, mystery, adventure and humor—all with Christian emphasis. "Stories dealing with teens and teen life, with a positive message or theme. Topics that interest teenagers include school, family life, recreation, friends, church, part-time jobs, dating and music. Main character should be a 15- or 16-year-old boy or girl, a Christian and regular churchgoer, who faces situations using Bible principles." Receives approximately 100 unsolicited fiction mss/month. Buys 1-2 mss/issue; 75-100 mss/year. Publishes ms an average of 1 year after acceptance. Less than 1% of fiction is agented. Published work by Alan Cliburn, Marian Bray, Teresa Cleary; published new writers within the last year. Length: 800-1,200 words. Recommends other markets.

How to Contact: Send complete ms with SASE (IRCs) and cover letter (experience with teens especially preferred from new writers). Reports in 1-2 months. Sample copy and guidelines for SASE.

Payment: Pays 3-7¢/word.

Terms: Pays on acceptance for first and one-time rights. Buys reprints.

Advice: "Get to know us before submitting, through guidelines and sample issues (SASE). And get to know teenagers. A writer must know what today's teens are like, and what kinds of conflicts they experience. In writing a short fiction piece for the teen reader, don't try to accomplish too much. If your character is dealing with the problem of prejudice, don't also deal with his/her fights with sister, desire for a bicycle, or anything else that is not absolutely essential to the reader's understanding of the major conflict."

STREET NEWS, (II), Suite 8040, 543 W. 43rd St., New York NY 10036. News Editor: Janet Lickenhauer. Tabloid: 12 × 15; 20 pages; newsprint; illustrations. "*Street News* is published to be sold by the homeless. Philosophy is objectivist. We would publish short fiction, but we're not presently in a position to pay money for it. That may change later." Biweekly. Estab. 1989. Circ. 20,000.

Needs: Children's/juvenile (5-9 years, 10-12 years), ethnic/multicultural, humor/satire, literary, mainstream/contemporary, mystery/suspense (young adult), regional, senior citizen/retirement, serialized novel, sports, translations, young adult/teen (10-18 years), urban. "No erotica, no hard genre stuff. Will consider fantasy in here-and-now setting." Receives 1-2 unsolicited mss/month. Publishes ms 1-2 months after acceptance. Length: 400 words minimum; 2,000 words maximum. Also publishes poetry.

How to Contact: Send complete ms with cover letter. Should include estimated word count, bio (one or two sentences), and list of publications with submission. Reports in 1 month. Send SASE (IRCs) for reply, return of ms or send disposable copy of ms. Sample $2 or $1 and 9 × 12 SAE with 3 oz. postage.

Payment: Pays 3 contributor's copies. Additional copies for SAE.

Terms: Acquires one-time rights.

Advice: Looks for "an interesting point; a new, or even oddball, way of looking at things. When you've finished the first draft (or maybe better, the second draft), go back and look for ways to prepare your reader better for understanding your point. Read 'The Power of Plot Irony' and 'The Sport of Fiction' in October '92 *Writer's Digest*."

STUDENT LEADERSHIP JOURNAL, (IV), InterVarsity Christian Fellowship, P.O. Box 7895, 6400 Schroeder Rd., Madison WI 53707-7895. (608)274-9001. Editor: Jeff Yourison. "The journal is a networking and leadership development tool for audience described below. We publish articles on leadership, spiritual growth and evangelism. We publish occasional poetry, short stories and allegories. The audience is Christian student leaders on secular college campuses." Quarterly. Estab. 1988. Circ. 8,000.

  • *Student Leadership Journal* has received awards from the Evangelical Press Association. The editor says the magazine is currently running a serial, "Campus Exposure," in the vein of the "Northern Exposure" television series.

Needs: Religious/inspirational, prose poem. "The form of fiction is not nearly as important as its quality and content. Fiction published by *Student Leadership* will always reflect a Christian worldview." No romance or children's fiction. Receives 10-15 unsolicited fiction mss/month. Buys up to 1 ms/issue; 4 ms/year. Publishes ms up to 2 years after acceptance. Length: 2,000 words preferred; 200 words minimum; 2,500 words maximum.

How to Contact: Query first with clips of published work. "A good cover letter will demonstrate familiarity with the magazine and its needs and will briefly describe the submission and any relevant information." Reports in up to 3 months on queries; up to 6 months on mss. SASE. Simultaneous and reprint submissions OK. Sample copy for $3, 9×12 SAE and $1 postage. Fiction guidelines for #10 SAE and 1 first-class stamp. Reviews novels and short story collections "if they address our audience *and* contemporary cultures."
Payment: Pays $25-200.
Terms: Pays on acceptance for first or one-time rights. Sends pre-publication galleys to author.
Advice: "Read! Read! Read! The short story author must be an *artist* with words in so short a space. *Read* the best work of others. Observe it; get it into your bones. Just like a picture, a story must be vivid, colorful, well-balanced and eye-catching. Write! Write! Write! Don't be afraid to have at it! Picasso pitched many of his sketches. You'll pitch most of yours. But it's good practice, and it keeps your creative mind flowing."

SWANK MAGAZINE, (II, IV), Swank Publication, 63 Grand Ave., River Edge NJ 07661. Editor: Paul Gambino. Magazine: 8½×11; 116 pages; 20 lb. paper; 60 lb. coated stock; illustrations; photos. "Men's sophisticate format. Sexually-oriented material. Our readers are after erotic material." Published 13 times a year. Estab. 1952. Circ. 350,000.
Needs: High-caliber erotica. "Fiction always has an erotic or other male-oriented theme; also eligible would be mystery or suspense with a very erotic scene. Writers should try to avoid the clichés of the genre." Buys 1 ms/issue, 18 mss/year. Receives approximately 80 unsolicited fiction mss each month. Published new writers within the last year. Length: 1,500-2,750 words.
How to Contact: Send complete ms with SASE (IRCs) and cover letter, which should list previous publishing credits. No simultaneous submissions. Reports in 3 weeks on mss. Sample copy $5.95 with SASE.
Payment: Pays $300-500. Offers 25% kill fee for assigned ms not published.
Terms: Buys first North American serial rights.
Advice: "Research the men's magazine market." Mss are rejected because of "typical, overly simple storylines and poor execution. We're looking for interesting stories—whether erotic in theme or not— that break the mold of the usual men's magazine fiction. We're not only just considering strict erotica. Mystery, adventure, etc. with erotica passages will be considered."

SYNDICATED FICTION PROJECT, (I), (formerly PEN Syndicated Fiction Project), P.O. Box 15650, Washington DC 20003. (202)543-6322. Director: Caroline Marshall. "Fiction syndicate created to market quality short fiction to a broad, national audience via radio (The Sound of Writing, co-pro-duced with NPR), newspaper Sunday magazines and regional magazines (a varying group) and literary publications, including *American Short Fiction* published by the University of Texas Press."
● For more on this project see the interview with Director Caroline Marshall in the 1992 *Writer's Market* and "Off the Beaten Path" in the 1991 *Novel & Short Story Writer's Market*. Stories originally selected for the Syndicated Fiction Project have received recognition in various ways. For example a story selected for the project and published in *American Short Fiction* was chosen for the *1991 Annual Best* anthology and another story written for the project's radio broadcast by Robert Olin Butler was included in his Pulitzer-prize winning collection.
Needs: Literary. Receives 2,500-5,000 submissions/year. Buys 50 unpublished mss/year. Only reads in January. Length: 2,500 words maximum. Publishes short shorts.
How to Contact: Please send for guidelines first. Send 2 copies of complete ms with cover letter and brief bio. Up to 2 stories may be submitted at one time, but no one story may exceed 2,500 words. Decisions made by late May. SASE (IRCs). Fiction guidelines for #10 SASE.
Payment: Pays $500 plus $100/print publication. "Realistic possible potential: $1,000."
Terms: Pays $500 on return of contract; syndication fees paid on semiannual basis. Buys worldwide serial rights, audio and anthology rights.
Advice: "Newspaper and radio audiences prefer short pieces of general, topical or family interest. Submitters are encouraged to imagine seeing their work in a Sunday magazine with accompanying illustration or hearing it on the air to judge a story's suitability."

‡TATTOO REVUE, (I, IV), Outlaw Biker Enterprises, Inc., Box 447, Voorhees NJ 08003. Editor: Michelle Delio. Magazine: 8½×11, 96 pages; 50 lb. coated paper; 80 lb. cover stock; illustrations and photos. "Art magazine devoted to showcasing the very best of modern tattooing." Published 10 times/year. Estab. 1988. Circ. 180,000.
● The publisher of *Tattoo Revue* also publishes *Outlaw Biker* and *Skin Art* listed in this book.

Needs: Fiction pertaining to subject matter (tattooing). Receives 20 unsolicited mss/month. Publishes 1 fiction ms/issue. Publishes ms 2-8 months after acceptance. Length: 1,000-2,500 words. "Very open to freelance writers and unpublished writers. Freelance photographers also needed send SASE (IRCs) for guidelines and needs."
How to Contact: Send complete ms with cover letter and SASE. Responds to queries with 6 weeks. Sample copy is $5 and 8½×11 SAE with 2 first-class stamps.
Payment: Payment varies according to length and quality of work.
Terms: Pays on publication. Buys all rights.
Advice: "Very targeted market, strongly suggest you read magazine before submitting work."

'TEEN MAGAZINE, (II), Petersen Publishing Co., 8490 Sunset Blvd., Los Angeles CA 90069. Editor: Roxanne Camron. Magazine: 100-150 pages; 34 lb. paper; 60 lb. cover; illustrations and photos. "The magazine contains fashion, beauty and features for the young teenage girl. The median age of our readers is 16. Our success stems from our dealing with relevant issues teens face, printing recent entertainment news and showing the latest fashions and beauty looks." Monthly. Estab. 1957. Circ. 1.1 million.
Needs: Romance, adventure, mystery, humor and young adult. Every story, whether romance, mystery, humor, etc., must be aimed for teenage girls. The protagonist should be a teenage girl. No experimental, science fiction, fantasy or horror. Buys 1 ms/issue; 12 mss/year. Generally publishes ms 3-5 months after acceptance. Published work by Emily Ormand, Louise Carroll and Linda Bernson; published new writers within the last year. Length: 2,500-4,000 words. Publishes short shorts.
How to Contact: Send complete ms and short cover letter with SASE (IRCs). Reports in 10 weeks on mss. Sample copy for $2.50. Guidelines for SASE.
Payment: Pays $100.
Terms: Pays on acceptance for all rights.
Advice: "Try to find themes that suit the modern teen. We need innovative ways of looking at the age-old problems of young love, parental pressures, making friends, being left out, etc. Subject matter and vocabulary should be appropriate for an average 16-year-old reader. *'TEEN* would prefer to have romance balanced with a plot, re: a girl's inner development and search for self. Handwritten mss will not be read."

TEEN POWER, (IV), Scripture Press Publications, Inc., Box 632, Glen Ellyn IL 60138. (708)668-6000. Editor: Amy Cox. Magazine: 5⅜×8⅜; 8 pages; glossy paper and cover; illustrations and photographs. "*Teen Power* publishes true stories and fiction with a conservative Christian slant—must help readers see how principles for Christian living can be applied to everyday life; for young teens (11-16 years); many small town and rural; includes large readerships in Canada, England and other countries in addition to U.S." Estab. 1966.
● Another magazine by this publisher, *Freeway,* is listed in this book. *Teen Power* won an Award of Merit in 1992 from the Evangelical Press Association.
Needs: Adventure, humor/satire, religious/inspirational, young adult/teen (11-16 years). "All must have spiritual emphasis of some sort." Receives approximately 75-100 unsolicited mss/month. Buys 2 mss/issue; about 100 mss/year. Publishes ms at least 1 year after acceptance. Recently published work by Alan Cliburn, Betty Steele Everett and Marlys G. Stapelbroek; published new writers within the last year. Length: 1,000 words preferred; 250 words minimum; 1,100 words maximum. Publishes short shorts. Length: 300-500 words. Sometimes critiques rejected mss and recommends other markets.
How to Contact: Send complete ms with cover letter. Reports in 2-3 months. SASE (IRCs). Simultaneous and reprint submissions OK. Sample copy and fiction guidelines for #10 SAE and 1 first-class stamp.
Payment: Pays $20 minimum; $120 maximum; contributor's copies.
Terms: Pays on acceptance. Buys one-time rights.
Advice: "We look for spiritual emphasis (strong but not preachy), writing style, age appropriateness, creativity in topic choice and presentation. A writer for *Teen Power* must know something about young teens and what is important to them, plus have a working knowledge of basic principles for Christian living, and be able to weave the two together."

TEENS TODAY, (II), Church of the Nazarene, 6401 The Paseo, Kansas City MO 64131. (816)333-7000. Editor: Carol Gritten. Sunday school take-home paper: 8½×11; 8 pages; illustrations; photos. "For junior and senior high students involved with the Church of the Nazarene who find it interesting and helpful to their areas of life." Weekly. Circ. 60,000.
● Other Nazarene-affiliated magazines listed in this book are *Discoveries* and *Standard.*

Needs: Contemporary, religious/inspirational, romance, humor, juvenile, mystery/suspense (romantic suspense), science fiction (soft sociological), young adult and ethnic. "Nothing that puts teens down or endorses lifestyles not in keeping with the denomination's beliefs and standards." Buys 1-2 mss/ issue. Published new writers within the last year. Length: 1,000-1,500 words.
How to Contact: Send complete ms with SASE. Simultaneous submissions OK. Reports in 2 months on mss. Publishes ms 8-10 months after acceptance. Sample copy and guidelines for SASE.
Payment: Pays 4¢/word and 3½¢/word on second reprint.
Terms: Pays on acceptance for first and second serial rights. Buys reprints.
Advice: "Don't be too juvenile."

TEXAS CONNECTION MAGAZINE, (IV), Box 541805, Dallas TX 75220. (214)951-0316. Editor: Alan Miles. Magazine: 8½ × 11; 168 pages; book offset paper; 100 lb. enamel cover; illustrations and photographs. "Adult erotica, for adults only." Monthly. Estab. 1985. Circ. 50,000.
Needs: Erotica, erotic cartooning, sexual fantasy, feminist, gay, humor/satire and lesbian. "Publishes new quarterly digest—100% fiction." Receives 20-30 unsolicited mss/month. Buys 2-3 mss/issue. Publishes ms 2-3 months after acceptance. Length: 1,750 words preferred; 1,000 words minimum; 2,500 words maximum.
How to Contact: Send complete ms with cover letter. Cover letter must state writer/author's age (18 yrs. minimum). Reports in 4-6 weeks. SASE (IRCs) for ms, not needed for query. Simultaneous and reprint submissions OK. Sample copy for $8.50. Free fiction guidelines. Reviews erotic fiction only.
Payment: Pays $25-200, free subscription to magazine and contributor's copies.
Terms: Pays on publication. Purchases all rights on some, first rights on most.
Advice: "We publish an adult, alternative lifestyle magazine that is (uniquely) distributed both in the adult store market and mass-market outlets (convenience stores) throughout 5 states: Texas (main), Oklahoma, Arkansas, Louisiana, New Mexico. We are, of course, interested in fresh, erotic fiction only."

THRASHER, Skateboard Magazine, (I, II), High Speed Productions, P.O. Box 884570, San Francisco CA 94188-4570. (415)822-3083. Fax: (415)822-8359. Editor: Jake Phelps. Fiction Editor: Brian Brannon. Magazine: 20.5 × 27.7 cm; 88-114 pages; coated paper; 4-color and b&w illustrations and photographs. "*Thrasher* is a blunt and honest hardcore publication for youth, skateboarding and sincere music." Monthly. Estab. 1981. Circ. 200,000.
Needs: Must deal with teen culture in some manner. Receives 5-10 unsolicited mss/month. Buys 0-4 mss/issue; 8-15 mss/year. Publishes ms 3-36 months after acceptance. Published work by Mike Gumkowski, Don Redondo. Length: 500 words preferred; 25 words minimum; 1,500 words maximum. Publishes short shorts. Also publishes literary essays, criticism and poetry.
How to Contact: Send complete ms with a cover letter. Should include estimated word count, Social Security number, list of publications. SASE (IRCs) for return of ms or send a disposable copy of ms. No simultaneous submissions. Accepts electronic submissions. Sample copy for 9 × 12 SAE. Fiction guidelines for 9 × 12 SAE.
Payment: Pays 15¢/word and 5 contributor's copies, if requested.
Terms: Pays on publication. Buys first rights.
Advice: Looks for "creative thought involving skateboarding, music, snowboarding, fiction, youth culture. Keep submitting manuscripts whenever you have them. Our over-worked staff may not always reply, but we do read them."

TIKKUN, A Bimonthly Jewish Critique of Politics, Culture and Society, (III), Institute for Labor and Mental Health, 5100 Leona St., Oakland CA 94619. (510)482-0805. Editor: Michael Lerner. Magazine: 8 × 11; 96 pages; high quality paper. "*Tikkun* was created as the liberal alternative to *Commentary Magazine* and the voices of Jewish conservatism, but is not aimed just at a Jewish audience. Readers are intellectuals, political activists, Washington policy circles, writers, poets." Bimonthly.
Needs: Condensed/excerpted novel, contemporary, feminist, gay, historical (general), humor/satire, lesbian, literary, mainstream, translations, Jewish political. "No narrowly Jewish fiction—at least half of our readers are not Jewish—or anything that is not of highest quality." Receives 150 unsolicited mss/month. Buys 1 ms/issue. Publishes ms 6-9 months after acceptance. Agented fiction 50%. Published work by Amos Oz, Lynne Sharon Schwartz, E.M. Broner. Length: 4,000 words preferred. Publishes short shorts. Almost always critiques rejected mss.

"Thrasher's September 1993 cover of Karma Tsocheff lacerating a 180 degree nosegrind on a metal bar above a flight of steps represents the grace and freedom that skaters feel as they ride their boards on objects never designed for their craft," says Brian Brannon, Thrasher's *music/fiction editor. And the photo's relationship to the publication's overall philosophy? "Our philosophy is we have no philosophy." Regarding fiction, Brannon says, "We toe a fine line between reality and fiction whenever applicable in our publication." Cover photo by Sean Dolinsky.*

How to Contact: Send complete ms with cover letter. Reports in 2-3 months. SASE (IRCs). Sample copy for $7.50.
Payment: Pays $100-250.
Terms: Pays on publication for first rights.
Advice: Looks for creativity, sensitivity, intelligence, originality, profundity of insight. "Read *Tikkun*, at least 3-4 issues worth, understand the kinds of issues that interest our readers, and then imagine yourself trying to write fiction that delights, surprises and intrigues this kind of an audience. Do not write what you think will feel sweet or appealing to this audience—but rather that which will provoke, bring to life and engage them."

TOUCH, (II), Calvinettes, Box 7259, Grand Rapids MI 49510. (616)241-5616. Editor: Joanne Ilbrink. Magazine: 8½×11; 24 pages; 50 lb. paper; 50 lb. cover stock; illustrations and photos. "Our purpose is to lead girls into a living relationship with Jesus Christ. Puzzles, poetry, crafts, stories, articles, and club input for girls ages 9-14." Monthly. Circ. 16,000.
    ● *Touch* won fourth place for fiction from the Evangelical Press Association awards in 1992.
Needs: Adventure, ethnic, juvenile and religious/inspirational. "Articles must help girls discover how God is at work in their world and the world around them." Each issue has a theme; write for biannual update. Receives 50 unsolicited fiction mss/month. Buys 3 mss/issue; 30 mss/year. Recently published work by A.J. Schut; published new writers within the last year. Length: 500 words minimum; 1,000 words maximum; 1,000 words average.
How to Contact: Send complete ms with 8×10 SASE (IRCs). Prefers no cover letter. Reports in 4 months. Simultaneous and previously published submissions OK. Sample copy for 8×10 SASE. Free guidelines.
Payment: Pays 3-5¢/word.
Terms: Pays on acceptance for simultaneous, first or second serial rights.
Advice: "Try new and refreshing approaches. The one-parent, new girl at school is a bit overdone in our market. We have been dealing with issues like AIDS, abuse, drugs, and family relationships in our stories—more awareness-type articles."

TURTLE MAGAZINE FOR PRESCHOOL KIDS, (I, II), Children's Better Health Institute, Benjamin Franklin Literary & Medical Society, Inc., Box 567, 1100 Waterway Blvd., Indianapolis IN 46206. Editor: Christine French Clark. Magazine of picture stories and articles for preschool children 2-5 years old.
    ● Children's Better Health Institute also publishes magazines for older children including *Child Life, Children's Digest, Children's Playmate, Jack and Jill* and *Humpty Dumpty* listed in this book.

Turtle received a 1992 Edpress award for the photo story "Fall Cane" in its October/November issue.

Needs: Juvenile (preschool). Special emphasis on health, nutrition, exercise and safety. Also has need for "action rhymes to foster creative movement and retold folktales for use in 'Pokey Toes Theatre.'" Receives approximately 100 unsolicited fiction mss/month. Published work by Ginny Winter, Robin Krautbauer and Ann Devendorf; published new writers within the last year. Length: 8-24 lines for picture stories; 500 words for bedtime or naptime stories.

How to Contact: Send complete ms with SASE (IRCs). No queries. Reports in 8-10 weeks. Send SASE for Editorial Guidelines. Sample copy for $1.25.

Payment: Pays 10-20¢/word (approximate). Payment varies for poetry and activities.

Terms: Pays on acceptance for all rights. (One-time book rights may be returned when requested for specific publication.)

Advice: "Become familiar with past issues of the magazine and have a thorough understanding of the preschool child. You'll find we are catering more to our youngest readers, so think simply. Also, avoid being too heavy-handed with health-related material. First and foremost, health features should be fun! Because we have developed our own turtle character ('Pokey Toes'), we are not interested in fiction stories featuring other turtles."

‡TWN, South Florida's Weekly Gay Alternative, (IV), The Weekly News, Inc., 901 NE 79th St., Miami FL 33138. (305)757-6333 ext. 8910. Fax: (305)756-6488. Editor: Steven R. Biller. Tabloid: 52 pages; newsprint paper; color cover stock; b&w illustrations and photographs. "TWN is a gay newspaper with 92% male readership. No sex stories. We're interested in issue-oriented writing, particularly with South Florida in mind." Weekly. Estab. 1977. Circ. 34,000.

Needs: Experimental, feminist, gay, historical (general), humor/satire, lesbian, literary. Upcoming themes: "National Coming Out Day" (October), "Valentine's Day, Multiculturalism" (February), "Gay Pride" (June), "BAD (the Worst of South Florida)" (March). Plans to publish special fiction issue or anthology. Receives 3-5 unsolicited mss/month. Accepts 1 ms/issue; 8-12 mss/year. Publishes ms 2-3 months after acceptance. Agented fiction 50%. Length: 1,200 words preferred; 1,000 words minimum; 2,000 words maximum. Publishes short shorts. Length: 400-600 words. Also publishes literary essays and literary criticisms. Always critiques or comments on rejected mss.

How to Contact: Query with clips of published work. Should include estimated word count, bio (1 paragraph), social security number. Reports in 1 month on queries; 2 months on ms. Send SASE (or IRC) for reply, return of ms or send a disposable copy of ms. Simultaneous, reprint (must not have appeared for a local competitor's product.), and electronic submissions. Sample copy for $1.50. Fiction guidelines free. Reviews novels or short story collections.

Payment: Pays $75-500.

Terms: Pays on publication for one-time rights.

Advice: "We choose work that is timely and fits within a product that is mostly nonfiction and cultural analysis. Write tight. Word/page length not as important as conciseness, impact and timeliness."

VIRTUE, The Christian Magazine for Women, (II), D.C. Cook Foundation, Box 850, Sisters OR 97759-0850. (503)549-8261. Editor: Marlee Alex. Magazine: 8¹/₈ × 10⁷/₈; 80 pages; illustrations; photos. Christian women's magazine featuring food, fashion, family, etc. — "real women with everyday problems, etc." Published 6 times/year. Estab. 1978. Circ. 135,000.

Needs: Contemporary, humor, religious/inspirational and romance. "Must have Christian slant." Buys 1 ms/issue; 6 mss/year (maximum). Length: 1,000 words minimum; 1,500 words maximum; 1,200 words average.

How to Contact: Reports in 6-8 weeks on ms. Sample copy for 9 × 13 SAE and $1.50 postage (IRCs). Writer's guidelines for SASE.

Payment: Pays 15-25¢/published word.

Terms: Pays on publication for first rights or reprint rights.

Advice: "Read the magazine! Get to know our style. *Please* don't submit blindly. Send us descriptive, colorful writing with good style. *Please* — no simplistic, unrealistic pat endings or dialogue. We like the story's message to be implicit as opposed to explicit. Show us, inspire us — don't spell it out or preach it to us."

VISTA, (II), Wesley Press, Box 50434, Indianapolis IN 46953. (317)842-0444. Editor: Brenda Bratten. Magazine: 8½ × 11; 8 pages; offset paper and cover; illustrations and photos. "*Vista* is our adult take-home paper." Weekly. Estab. 1906. Circ. 50,000.

Needs: Humor/satire, religious/inspirational, senior citizen/retirement. Receives 100 unsolicited mss/month. Buys 4 mss/issue. Publishes ms 10 months after acceptance. Length: 500 words minimum; 1,300 words maximum.
How to Contact: Send complete ms with cover letter. Reports in 6-8 weeks. SASE (IRCs). Simultaneous and reprint submissions OK. Sample copy for 9×12 SAE.
Payment: Pays 2-4¢/word.
Terms: Pays on acceptance for first or reprint.
Advice: "Manuscripts for all publications must be in keeping with early Methodist teachings that people have a free will to personally accept or reject Christ. Wesleyanism also stresses a transformed life, holiness of heart and social responsibility. Obtain a writers' guidelines before submitting ms."

THE WASHINGTONIAN, (IV), Suite 200, 1828 L St. NW, Washington DC 20036. (202)296-3600. Editor: John A. Limpert. Submit ms to Assistant Editor: Carrie Harper. General interest, regional magazine. Magazine: 8¼×10⅞; 200 pages; 40 lb. paper; 80 lb. cover; illustrations; photos. Monthly. Estab. 1965. Circ. 157,055.
  • *The Washingtonian* has won the National Magazine Award once each in 5 categories for reporting, feature writing, public service, news reporting, service to the individual.
Needs: Short pieces set in Washington. Publishes a summer reading piece. Receives 8-10 unsolicited fiction mss/month. Buys 3 fiction mss/year. Length: 1,000 words minimum; 10,000 words maximum. Occasionally critiques rejected mss.
How to Contact: Send complete ms with SASE (IRCs). Reports in 2 months. Simultaneous submissions OK. Sample copy for $4.
Payment: Pays 50¢/published word.
Terms: Pays on publication for first North American rights. Negotiates kill fee for assigned mss not published.
Advice: Known for publishing "short pieces set in Washington. Note: We publish very little fiction."

WITH MAGAZINE, (II, IV), Faith & Life Press and Mennonite Publishing House, Box 347, Newton KS 67114. (316)283-5100. Magazine: 8½×11; 32 pages; 60 lb. coated paper and cover; illustrations and photos. "Our purpose is to help teenagers understand the issues that impact them and to help them make choices that reflect Mennonite-Anabaptist understandings of living by the Spirit of Christ. We publish all types of material—fiction, nonfiction, poetry, teen personal experience, etc." Published 8 times/year. Estab. 1968. Circ. 6,200.
  • *With* won several awards from the Associated Church Press and the Evangelical Press Association. Other Mennonite publications listed in this book include *On the Line*, *Purpose* and *Story Friends*.
Needs: Contemporary, ethnic, humor/satire, literary, mainstream, religious, young adult/teen (13-18 years). "We accept issue-oriented pieces as well as religious pieces. No religious fiction that gives 'pat' answers to serious situations." Receives about 50 unsolicited mss/month. Buys 1-2 mss/issue; 8-12 mss/year. Publishes ms up to 1 year after acceptance. Published new writers within the last year. Length: 1,500 words preferred; 400 words minimum; 2,000 words maximum. Rarely critiques rejected mss.
How to Contact: Send complete ms with cover letter, which should include short summary of author's credits and what rights they are selling. Reports in 1-2 months on mss. SASE (IRCs). Simultaneous and reprint submissions OK. Sample copy for 9×12 SAE and $1.21 postage. Fiction guidelines for #10 SAE and 1 first-class stamp.
Payment: Pays 2¢/word for reprints; 4¢/word for simultaneous rights (one-time rights to an unpublished story). Supplies contributor's copies; charge for extras.
Terms: Pays on acceptance for one-time rights.
Advice: "Write with a teenage audience in mind, but don't talk down to them. Treat the audience with respect. Real life isn't always like that and teens will perceive the story as unbelievable. Do include ethnic minorities in your stories; our audience is both rural and urban. Except for humorous fiction (which can be just for laughs) each story should make a single point that our readers will find helpful through applying it in their own lives."

WOMAN'S DAY, 1633 Broadway, New York NY 10019. No longer accepts fiction.

WOMAN'S WORLD MAGAZINE, The Woman's Weekly, (II), Heinrich Bauer North America, 270 Sylvan Ave., Englewood Cliffs NJ 07632. (201)569-0006. Editor: Dena Vane. Fiction Editor: Jeanne Muchnick. Magazine; 9½×11; 54 pages; newspaper quality. "The magazine for 'Mrs. Middle

America.' We publish short romances and mini-mysteries for all women, ages 18-68." Weekly. Estab. 1980. Circ. 1.5 million.
● *Woman's World* ranked #8 on the latest *Writer's Digest* Fiction 50 list. Heinrich Bauer NA also publishes *First* listed in this book.
Needs: Romance (contemporary), suspense/mystery. No humour, erotica. Receives 50 unsolicited mss/month. Buys 2 mss/issue; 104 mss/year. Publishes mss 6-10 weeks after acceptance. Agented fiction 2%. Published work by Tima Smith, P.J. Platz, Liza Albert and Fay Thompson. Length: romances — 1,900 words; mysteries — 1,000 words. Publishes short shorts. Sometimes critiques rejected mss and recommends other markets.
How to Contact: Send complete ms with cover letter. *"No queries."* Reports in 6-8 weeks. SASE. Sample copy for $1. Fiction guidelines free.
Payment: Romances — $1,000, mysteries — $500.
Terms: Pays on acceptance. Buys first North American serial rights only.

WOMEN'S AMERICAN ORT REPORTER, (III,IV), Women's American ORT, 315 Park Ave. S., New York NY 10010. (212)505-7700. Editor: Dana B. Asher. 8⅛×10⅞; glossy; photographs. "Jewish women's issues; education, for membership." Quarterly. Estab. 1966. Circ. 110,000.
Needs: Condensed/excerpted novel, ethnic, feminist, humor/satire and literary. Receives 2 unsolicited mss/month. Buys 2 mss/year. Publishes ms 3 months after acceptance. Agented fiction 50%. Length: 1,700 words. Published work by A.B. Yehoshua. Possibly publishes short shorts. Sometimes critiques rejected ms and recommends other markets.
How to Contact: Send complete ms with cover letter. Include Social Security number. Reports in 3 weeks. SASE (IRCs). Sample copy for SASE.
Payment: Varies.
Terms: Pays on publication for first North American serial rights.

WOMEN'S GLIB, A Collection of Women's Humor, (IV), Women's Glib™, P.O. Box 259, Bala Cynwyd, PA 19004. (215)668-4252. Editor: Rosalind Warren. Annual trade paperback book. 6×9; 200-300 pages; 60 lb. paper; (cartoons) and (photoessays). "Women's humor — humor written/drawn by women. Stories, essays, rhymed verse, cartoons, photoessays — short, hilarious feminist material." For "anybody who appreciates feminist humor." Annually. Estab. 1990. Circ. 45,000 in print (includes both *Women's Glib* and *Women's Glibber*.
● The first book in this series was a Lambda Literary Award finalist in 1992. Starting this year (1994) Warren will publish an annual collection of funny quips, quotes, anecdotes and one-liners by women titled *Glibquips*. It pays in copies, but she says it is a great break-in market.
Needs: Women's humor: Contemporary, ethnic, feminist, gay, humor/satire, lesbian, literary, mainstream. "I need mostly short, hilariously (laugh-out-loud) funny material — don't be safe, be outrageous! — *by women only*. No domestic humor. No diet or weight loss humor or material about how svelte a girl should be. No stories about how to catch or keep a man or about how men can't cook or do laundry. No homophobic, racist or sexist material. Female protagonists preferred." Receives 150 unsolicited mss/month. Buys 20 mss/issue. Publishes ms within a year after acceptance. Agented fiction 5%. Published work by Nora Ephron, Molly Ivins, Judy Tenuta and Lynda Barry. Length: 1,000 words preferred; 3,000 words maximum. Publishes short shorts. Sometimes critiques rejected mss and recommends other markets.
How to Contact: Query with clips of published work or send complete ms with cover letter. Reports in 2 weeks. SASE (IRCs). Simultaneous and reprint submissions OK. Sample copy for $11 (includes postage). (Make check payable to Roz Warren). Fiction guidelines for #10 SAE and 1 first-class stamp.
Payment: Pays $5/page and 2 contributor's copies.
Terms: Pays on publication for one-time, nonexclusive rights.
Advice: "If it makes me laugh I publish it. I prefer short (2-10 pages) material. Some of the most popular material in the first two books (*Women's Glib*) and *Women's Glibber* was by previously unpublished writers. Read the first two books in the series. I need humor pieces — material written to amuse the reader. I get a lot of good writing that I can't use because rather than being humor pieces they're short fiction, told with some wit, but basically they're stories."

WONDER TIME, (II), World Action Publications, 6401 The Paseo, Kansas City MO 64131. (816)333-7000. Editor: Lois Perrigo. Magazine: 8¼×11; 4 pages; self cover; color illustrations. Hand-out story paper published through WordAction Publications; stories should follow outline of Sunday School lessons for 6-8 year-olds. Weekly. Circ. 45,000.

Needs: Religious/inspirational and juvenile. Stories must have first- to second-grade readability. No fairy tales or science fiction. Receives 50-75 unsolicited fiction mss/month. Buys 1 ms/issue. Length: 200-350 words.
How to Contact: Send complete ms with SASE (IRCs). Reports in 6 weeks. Sample copy and curriculum guide with SASE.
Payment: Pays $25 minimum.
Terms: Pays on production (about 1 year before publication) for multi-use rights.
Advice: "We are looking for shorter stories (200-350 words) with a 1-2 grade readability. The stories need to apply to the weekly Sunday School lesson truths."

WY'EAST HISTORICAL JOURNAL, (II), Crumb Elbow Publishing, P.O. Box 294, Rhododendron OR 97049. (503)622-4798. Editor: Michael P. Jones. Journal: 5½×8½; 60 pages; top-notch paper; hardcover; illustrations and photographs. "Publishes historical or contemporary articles on the history of Oregon's Mt. Hood, the Columbia River, the Pacific NW, or the Old Oregon Country that includes Oregon, Washington, Idaho, Wyoming, Montana, Alaska, Northern California and British Columbia and sometimes other areas. For young adults to elderly." Quarterly. Estab. 1992. Circ. 10,000.
Needs: Open. Special interests include wildlife and fisheries, history of fur trade in Pacific Northwest, the Oregon Trail and Indians. "All materials should relate—somehow—to the region the publication is interested in." Plans to publish annual special fiction issue. Receives 10 unsolicited mss/month. Buys 1-2 mss/issue; 22-24 mss/year. Publishes ms up to one year after acceptance. Published work by Joel Palmer. Publishes short shorts. Recommends other markets. "We have several other publications through Crumb Elbow Publishing where we can redirect the material."
How to Contact: Query with clips of published work or send complete ms with cover letter. Reports in 2 months "depending upon work load." SASE (IRCs) (required or material will *not* be returned). Simultaneous and reprint submissions OK. Sample copy $7. Fiction guidelines for #10 SAE and 1 first-class stamp.
Payment: Pays contributor's copies.
Terms: Pays on publication. Buys one-time rights.
Advice: "A ms has to have a historical or contemporary tie to the Old Oregon Country, which was the lands that lay west of the Rocky Mountains to the Pacific Ocean, south to and including Northern California, and north to and including Alaska. It has to be about such things as nature, fish and wildlife, the Oregon Trail, pioneer settlement and homesteading, the Indian wars, gold mining, wild horses—which are only a few ideas. It has to be written in a non-offensive style, meaning please remove all four-letter words or passages dealing with loose sex. Do not be afraid to try something a little different. No prima donnas, please! Will not return long-distance calls. We wish to work with writers who are professionals, even if they haven't had any of their works published before. This is a great place to break into the publishing world as long as you are an adult who acts like an adult. Send copies only! And please note that we cannot be responsible for the U.S. Postal Service once you mail something to us, or we mail something to you. We are looking forward to working with those who love history and nature as much as we do."

XTRA MAGAZINE, Church-Wellesley Review (Literary Supplement) (IV, V), Pink Triangle Press, Box 7289, Stn. A, Toronto, Ontario M5W 1X9 Canada. (416)925-6665. Editor: Ken Popert. Fiction Editor: Dayne Ogilvie. Tabloid: 11½×17; 44-60 pages; newsprint paper; illustrations and photographs. "Gay/lesbian magazine, but fiction/poetry does not have to be about sexual orientation." Fiction supplement is annual. Estab. 1990 (supplement only). Circ. 27,500.
 ● *Xtra* recently received a Design Award from *Print Magazine*.
Needs: Gay, lesbian. Publishes annual special fiction issue. Receives 4-5 unsolicited mss/month. Buys up to 20 mss/year. Publishes mss spring after acceptance. Recently published work by Dale Peck (American novelist) and Sky Gilbert (Canadian playwright). Length: 1,500 words maximum. Publishes short shorts. Sometimes critiques rejected mss and recommends other markets.
How to Contact: Send complete manuscript with cover letter. Reports in 2-3 months on mss. SASE (IRCs). If notified, simultaneous and reprint submissions OK. Sample copy $1.
Payment: Pays 10¢/word (slightly more for poetry) up to $150 maximum.

YANKEE MAGAZINE, (II, III), Yankee, Inc., Dublin NH 03444. Editor: Judson D. Hale. Fiction Editor: Edie Clark. Magazine: 6×9; 176+ pages; glossy paper; 4-color glossy cover stock; illustrations; color photos. "Entertaining and informative New England regional on current issues, people, history, antiques and crafts for general reading audience." Monthly. Estab. 1935. Circ. 1,000,000.
 ● *Yankee* ranked #12 on the latest *Writer's Digest* Fiction 50 list.

Needs: Literary. Fiction is to be set in New England or compatible with the area. No religious/inspirational, formula fiction or stereotypical dialect, novels or novellas. Buys 6 mss/year. Published work by Andre Dubus, H. L. Mountzoures and Fred Bonnie; published new writers within the last year. Length: 2,500 words. Recommends other markets.

How to Contact: Send complete ms with SASE (IRCs) and previous publications. "Cover letters are important if they provide relevant information: previous publications or awards; special courses taken; special references (e.g. 'William Shakespeare suggested I send this to you . . . .')" Simultaneous submissions OK, "within reason." Reports in 6-8 weeks.

Payment: Pays $1,000.

Terms: Pays on acceptance; rights negotiable. Makes "no changes without author consent."

Advice: "Read previous 10 stories in *Yankee* for style and content. Fiction must be realistic and reflect life as it is—complexities and ambiguities inherent. Our fiction adds to the 'complete menu'—the magazine includes many categories—humor, profiles, straight journalism, essays, etc. Listen to the advice of any editor who takes the time to write a personal letter. Go to workshops; get advice and other readings before sending story out cold."

THE YOUNG CRUSADER, (II, IV), National Woman's Christian Temperance Union, 1730 Chicago Ave., Evanston IL 60201. (708)864-1396. Editor-in-Chief: Mrs. Rachel Bubar Kelly. Managing Editor: Michael C. Vitucci. "Character building material showing high morals and sound values; inspirational, informational nature articles and stories for 6-12 year olds." Monthly. Estab. 1887. Circ. 10,000.

Needs: Juvenile. Stories should be naturally written pieces, not saccharine or preachy. Buys 3-4 mss/issue; 60 mss/year. Length: 600-650 words. Also prose and poetry. Published work by Nadine L. Mellott, Gloria L. Sollid and Veronica McClearin.

How to Contact: Send complete ms with SASE (IRCs). Simultaneous submissions OK. Reports in 6 months or longer on mss. Sample copy for SASE.

Payment: Pays ½¢/word and contributor's copy. Pays ½¢/word for prose, 10¢/line for poetry.

Terms: "If I like the story and use it, I'm very lenient and allow the author to use it elsewhere. Don't write down to the child; the children of today are surprisingly bright and sophisticated." Mss/prose/poetry, if used, pays on publication. If not used mss/prose/poetry will be destroyed.

YOUNG SALVATIONIST/YOUNG SOLDIER, (II, IV), The Salvation Army, P.O. Box 269, 615 Slaters Lane, Alexandria VA 22313. (703)684-5500. Editor: Lt. Deborah Sedlar. Magazine: 8×11; 16 pages (*Young Salvationist*); illustrations and photos. Christian emphasis articles for youth members of The Salvation Army. Monthly. Estab. 1984. Circ. 50,000.

• Note *Young Salvationist* no longer publishes children's stories. Their focus is on teens and college-age young adults.

Needs: Religious/inspirational, young adult/teen. Receives 150 unsolicited mss/month. Buys 9-10 ms/issue; 90-100 mss/year. Publishes ms 3-4 months after acceptance. Length: 1,000 words preferred; 750 words minimum; 1,200 words maximum. Publishes short shorts. Sometimes critiques rejected mss and recommends other markets.

How to Contact: Send complete ms. Reports in 1-2 weeks on queries; 2-4 weeks on mss. SASE (IRCs). Simultaneous and reprint submissions OK. Sample copy for 9×12 SAE and 3 first-class stamps. Fiction guidelines and theme list for #10 SAE with 1 first-class stamp.

Payment: Pays 10¢/word.

Terms: Pays on acceptance for all rights, first rights, first North American serial rights and one-time rights.

Advice: "Don't write about your high school experience. Write about teens now."

International commercial periodicals

The following commercial magazines, all located outside the United States and Canada, also accept work in English from fiction writers. Countries represented here range from England, Ireland and Scotland to the Czech Republic, Germany and Italy. Also included are South Africa, Australia and China.

As with other publications, try to read sample copies. While some of these may be available at large newsstands, most can be obtained directly from the publishers. Write for guidelines as well. Whereas one editor may want fiction with some connection to his or her own country, another may seek more universal settings and themes. Watch, too, for payment policies. Many publications pay only in their own currencies.

In all correspondence, use self-addressed envelopes (SAEs) with International Reply Coupons (IRCs) for magazines outside your own country. IRCs may be purchased at the main branch of your local post office. In general, send IRCs in amounts roughly equivalent to return postage. When submitting work to these international publications, you may find it easier to include a disposable copy of your manuscript and only one IRC with a self-addressed postcard for a reply. This is preferred by many editors, and it saves you the added cost of having your work returned.

‡ANNABEL, D.C. Thomson & Co. Ltd., 80 Kingsway East, Dundee DD4 8SL Scotland. Contact: The Fiction Editor. Monthly. Circ. 90,000. Publishes 3 stories/issue. Average readers are "37-year-old women, professional or working a part-time, with children. We assume our readers are intelligent, with wide interests. Fiction should be an oasis of calm in their hectic lives. Focusing on relationships, strong emotional content. Believable characters. Romance, not sex. Magazine features two average-length stories and one mini story—the twist in the tale type but it must be clever, out of the ordinary." Length: 1,000 words minimum; 3,500 words maximum. SAE and IRCs required. "Typed in double spacing. Easily accessible, i.e., no plastic folders/sleeves." Payment by agreement in sterling on acceptance. Also pays 1 contributor's copy. "Make yourself familiar with the different habits, colloquiallisms and culture of the country. But don't write like a travelogue in an effort to show you've done your homework!" For sample copy send SAE to Subscribers Dept.; for guidelines send SAE to the Fiction Editor.

‡BELLA MAGAZINE, 25 Camden Road, London, England. Fiction Editor: Linda O'Byrne. Weekly. Circ. 1.2 million. Publishes 2 short stories/issue. "Women's magazine using one romance and one twist-ending story in each issue." Length: 1,200-3,000 words. Pays for published fiction and provides contributor's copies. "Read and study the magazine." Send SAE for guidelines.

‡COMMANDO, (IV), D. C. Thomson Co., Ltd., Albert Square, Dundee DD1 9QJ Scotland. Publishes 96 stories/year. "War stories (WW II) in pictures. Scripts wanted—send synopsis first." Pays for published fiction and provides contributor's copies. "Write to us for information sheet."

EROTIC STORIES, (IV), 4 Selsdon Way, City Harbour, London E14 9GL England. Editor: Joanna Payne. Deputy Editor: Dominic Collier. Published 13 times/year. Buys 300 stories/year. "*Erotic Stories* is Britain's only magazine devoted to short erotic fiction. We are looking for erotic stories in which plot and characterization are as important as erotic content." Length: 2,000-3,500 words. "Slightly longer stories are also acceptable. For guidelines send SAE with IRC." Pays 1 contributor copy.

FAIR LADY, (III), P.O. Box 1802, Cape Town 2000 South Africa. Editor: Liz Butler. Bi-monthly. Circ. 158,400. Publishes 1/issue. "We are a magazine chiefly for women of all ages, working mothers or pensioners, teenagers or homemakers. We try to keep a high standard of writing in our short stories, since our readers are well-educated and discerning." Length: 1,000 words minimum; 3,000 words maximum. "We will try to provide tearsheets on request. Payment varies, but can be made in US dollars in some circumstances. Include a short, informative covering letter so that we know you have given the submission of your story to us some thought. Don't just send the ms to everybody."

FORUM, Northern and Shell Tower, Box 381, City Harbour, London E14 9GL England. Fiction Editor: Elizabeth Coldwell. Circ. 30,000. Publishes 13 stories/year. "*Forum* is the international magazine of human relations, dealing with all aspects of relationships, sexuality and sexual health. We are looking for erotic stories in which the plot and characterisation are as important as the erotic content." Length: 2,000-3,000 words. Pays contributor's copy. "Try not to ask for the ms to be returned, just a letter of acceptance/rejection as this saves on your return postage. Anything which is very 'American' in language or content might not be as interesting to readers outside America. Writers can obtain a sample copy by saying they saw our listing."

‡IKARIE, (III, IV), Radlicka 61, 150 02 Praha 5, Czech Republic. Foreign Dept. Editor: Ivan Adamovič. Circ. 30,000. Publishes 70 short stories/year (50% classical, translations). "We are interested in good quality science fiction and dark fantasy, up to 25 manuscript pages, partly horror. We usually don't publish new, non-established writers. *Ikarie* is the only Czech professional monthly science fiction

magazine. Each issue contains more than 80,000 words. Royalties: $2 (US) per manuscript page."

INTERZONE: Science Fiction and Fantasy, (IV), 217 Preston Drove, Brighton BN1 6FL England. Editor: David Pringle. Monthly. Circ. 10,000. Publishes 5-6 stories/issue. "We're looking for intelligent science fiction in the 2,000-7,000 word range. Send 2 IRCs with 'overseas' submissions and a *disposable* ms." Pays £30 per 1,000 words on publication and 2 contributor's copies. "Please *read the magazine* — available through specialist science-fiction dealers or direct by subscription." Sample copies to USA: $5. Write for guidelines.

IRELAND'S OWN, (IV), 1 North Main St., Wexford Ireland. Fiction Editor: Austin Channing. Weekly. Circ. 56,000. Publishes 3 stories/issue. "*Ireland's Own* is a homely family-oriented weekly magazine with a story emphasis on the traditional values of Irish society. Short stories must be written in a straightforward nonexperimental manner with an Irish orientation." Length: 2,000-3,000 words. Pays £20-25 on publication and contributor's copies. "Study and know the magazine's requirements, orientation and target market. Guidelines and copies sent out on request."

‡LONDON REVIEW OF BOOKS, Tavistock House S., London, England. Assistant Editor: Andrew O'Hagan. Circ. 16,000. Publishes 3-6 stories annually. Publishes "book reviews with long essay-length reviews. Also publishes the occasional short story." Pays £200 per story and 6 contributor's copies.

LOVING MAGAZINE, Room 2735, IPC, King's Reach Tower, Stamford St., London SE1 9LS England. Editor: Lorna Read. Monthly. Circ. 40,000. Publishes 17 stories/issue. Needs "romantic fiction in first or third person, from male or female point of view. No school stories, no heroes/heroines under 16. We also have a 'Something Different' section for historical, crime or even science fiction stories, provided they have a romance at the core. Stories must be typed and double-spaced, and a word count must be given. Please advise if story is available on disk." Length: 1,000-5,000 words. Writers receive a contributor's copy. Payment is in authors' own currency and is on a sliding scale from £25-£50/1,000 words, according to how much editing work the story needs. Make plot universal enough to interest people in other countries and cultures. If a story is too parochial, it will alienate a foreign reader.

MY WEEKLY, 80 Kingsway East, Dundee DD4 8SL Scotland. Editor: Sandy Monks. "*My Weekly* is a widely read magazine aimed at 'young' women of all ages. We are read by busy young mothers, active middle-aged wives and elderly retired ladies." Fiction (romance and humor) "should deal with real, down-to-earth themes that relate to the lives of our readers. Our rates compare favourably with other British magazines. Complete stories can be of any length from 1,500 to 4,000 words. Serials from 3 to 10 installments."

NOVA SF, (IV), Perseo Libri srl, Box 1240, I-40100 Bologna Italy. Fiction Editor: Ugo Malaguti. Bimonthly. Circ. 5,000. "Science fiction and fantasy short stories and short novels." Pays $100-600, depending on length, and 2 contributor's copies on publication. "No formalities required, we read all submissions and give an answer in about 20 weeks. Buys first Italian serial rights on stories."

‡OVERSEAS!, (II), Kolpingstr. 1, Leimen 6906 Germany. Editor: Greg Ballinger. Published 10 times/ year. "*Overseas!* is published for the US military personnel stationed in Europe. It is the leading military magazine in Europe, directed to all members of the military." Needs humorous but factual travel-in-Europe stories. Length: 1,000-2,000 words maximum. Writers receive contributor's copies. Pay is negotiated. Sample copy and writer's guidelines available. "Send query and 4 IRCs. No American postage."

PEOPLE'S FRIEND, 80 Kingsway East, Dundee DD4 8SL Scotland. Fiction Editor: W. Balnave. Weekly. Circ. 566,000. Publishes 5 stories/issue. Length: 1,000-3,000 words. Pays $75-85 and contributor's copies. "British backgrounds preferred by our readership." Sample copy and guidelines available on application.

REALITY MAGAZINE, 75 Orwell Rd., Rathgar, Dublin 6 Ireland. Editor: Fr. Gerard R. Moloney, C.Ss.R. Monthly. Circ. 20,000. Publishes an average of 5 short stories annually. Length: 900-1,200 words. Pays £25-£35 (Ireland)/1,000 words and 2 contributor's copies. "Be clear, brief, to the point and practical. Write only about your own country. Sample copies supplied on request."

THE SCOTS MAGAZINE, (IV), 2 Albert Square, Dundee DD1 9QJ Scotland. Editor: John Rundle. Monthly. Circ. 85,000. "World's oldest popular periodical. We use well-written fiction in a Scottish setting with a specific Scottish content." Length: 1,000-4,000 words. Payment made in pounds sterling, also contributor's copies. "No ghosts of Culloden or Glen Coe, no haggis and no phoney Scots dialogue." Guidelines available on request.

‡TAKE A BREAK, 25-27 Camden Rd., London NW1 9LL England. (071)284-0909. Fax: (071)482-2777. Fiction Editor: Norah McGrath. Weekly. "Must have a strong plot and a good twist in the tail. We do not have a weekly serial so stories must be complete in themselves. Subject matter: almost anything, but avoid straightforward romance (i.e. boy meets girl and they live happily ever after); historical backgrounds; science fiction; stories told by animals or small children. *Take a Break* is a family magazine so graphic murders and sex crimes—especially those concerning children—are not acceptable. Because the stories are so short, it can be confusing if you have too many characters: a maximum of four is usually best. We prefer modern stories aimed at women in their mid-twenties and upwards." Length: 1,200 words average. No simultaneous submissions; previously unpublished work only. Pays £250 on acceptance for first British serial rights. "It can take up to four weeks before a decision is made concerning your manuscript, so please be patient. Should your story be rejected, it can be for any number of reasons. Sometimes we have already published or have in stock a similar story. More likely though, I feel it would not appeal to our readers. This does not necessarily mean I will not like another of your stories, so please don't lose heart. Stories intended for specific issues such as Christmas, Easter, Halloween, etc., should be sent a full three months in advance of issue date." Guidelines for SAE and IRC.

WOMAN'S REALM, IPC Magazines, King's Reach Tower, Stamford St., London SE1 9LS England. Fiction Editor: Sally Sheringham. Weekly. Circ. 530,000. Publishes 2 stories/issue. Appeals to practical, intelligent, family-minded women, age 25 upwards. High standard of writing required. Originality important. "Nearest US equivalent to our kind of fiction is probably *Redbook*." Length: 1,000-1,200 words and 2,800-3,000 words. Payment starts from approximately £150. *"Sadly, we are no longer able to accept unsolicited fiction."*

‡WOMAN'S WEEKLY, IPC Magazines, King's Reach, Stamford St., London SE1 9LS England. Fiction Editor: Gaynor Davies. Circ. 800,000. Publishes 1 serial and at least 2 short stories/week. "Short stories can be on any theme, but must have love as the central core of the plot, whether in a specific romantic context, within the family or mankind in general. Serials need not be written in installments. They are submitted as complete manuscripts and we split them up. Send first installment of serial (7,000 words) and synopsis of the rest." Length: 1,000-5,000 words for short stories; 14,000-42,000 words for serials. Short story payment starts at £220 and rises as writer becomes a more regular contributor. Serial payments start at around £400/installment. Writers also receive contributor's copies. "Read the magazine concerned and try to understand who the publication is aimed at." Writers' guidelines available. Write to "fiction department."

THE WORLD OF ENGLISH, P.O. Box 1504, Beijing China. Chief Editor: Chen Yu-lun. Circ. 300,000 +. "We welcome contributions of short and pithy articles that would cater to the interest of our reading public, new and knowledgeable writings on technological finds, especially interesting stories and novels, etc. As our currency is regrettably inconvertible, we send copies of our magazines as the compensation for contributions."

Commercial periodicals/'93-'94 changes

The following commercial magazines appeared in the 1993 edition of *Novel & Short Story Writer's Market* but are not in the 1994 edition. Those publications whose editors did not respond this year to our request for an update are listed below without further explanation. They may have done so for a variety of reasons—they may be out of business, they are no longer taking fiction or they may be overstocked with submissions. They may have responded too late for inclusion in this edition. If we received information about why a publication would not appear, we included the explanation next to its name below.

Alive Now! (asked to be deleted)

Atlantic Salmon Journal (no fiction)

Bear

Bostonia Magazine (asked to

be deleted)

Chess Life (asked to be deleted)

Chic

Common Touch Magazine (out of business)

Computoredge

Country America (no fiction)

Georgia Sportsman (asked to be deleted)

Gorezone (ceased publication)

The Guide: Gay Travel, Entertainment, Politics, and Sex (asked to be left out this year)

Gulfshore Life (no fiction)

The Home Altar (asked to be left out this year)

Home Life (using staff-written material only)

Horse Illustrated (uses very little fiction)

Hot 'n' Nasty

Hot Shots

I.D. (asked to be deleted)

InSights (inappropriate submissions)

Jive, Black Confessions, Black Romance, Bronze Thrills, Black Secrets

Kindergarten Listen (no unsolicited fiction until 1997)

Laf! (asked to be deleted)

Living with Teenagers (asked to be deleted)

Moment Magazine

Montana Senior Citizens News

Organica Quarterly (no fiction)

Out Magazine

Powerplay Magazine

Single Life Magazine (no fiction)

The Student

Sunshine Magazine (suspended publication)

Surfing Magazine

TQ (ceased publication)

The Vancouver Child (ceased publication)

Weird Tales (too many submissions)

International commercial periodicals/'93-'94 changes

Guide Patrol

New Woman

School Magazine

Superbike

Small Press

Before considering publication by a small press, take a look at our Small Press Roundtable article presented earlier in this book. We asked a number of successful small press publishers about their strengths and challenges and why writers should consider small press publication.

One thing everybody agreed on was that with all the bottom-line emphasis on "big books" and their authors, the large, commercial press is paying less attention to (and spending less money on) promoting the work of those they consider midlist authors or newer writers. And so, more and more of these writers are finding small press publication better suits their needs.

Introducing new writers to the reading public has become the most important role played by the small press today. Increasingly, too, small press publishers have devoted themselves to keeping accessible the work of talented fiction writers whose work has had limited exposure or who are not currently in the limelight. Many of the more successful small presses listed in this section, including Coffeehouse, Four Walls Eight Windows and Zoland Books, have built their reputations and their businesses on this and have become known for publishing prize-winning literary fiction.

Today, small press publishers have better technology, distribution, marketing and business savvy than ever before. Despite their size, they've become big competition for their larger counterparts. More and more readers looking for good literary or experimental fiction and new, talented writers are turning to the small press to find them.

The benefits of working with the small press

Despite the growth and success of several small presses, even the most successful are unable to afford the six-figure advances, lavish promotional budgets and huge press runs possible in the large, commercial houses. Yet, there are some very tangible benefits to working with the small press.

For one thing, they tend to keep books in print a lot longer than larger houses. And, in a way, there are no midlist or backlist authors. Since small presses publish a limited number of books, each one is equally important to the publisher and each one is promoted in much the same way and with the same commitment.

Small presses also offer a much closer and more personal relationship between author and editor. Many presses are owned and operated by only a few people. Editors stay longer because they have more of a stake in the business—often they own the business. Many small press publishers are writers themselves and know first-hand the importance of this type of editor-author or publisher-author relationship.

Types of small presses

We include close to 200 presses in this section, including 35 listings new to this edition. Most presses here publish only a handful of books each year, but a few publish up to 25 to 30 books per year. In this section we use the term "small press" in the broadest sense. Under this heading we include one- and two-person operations, small to mid-size independent presses, university presses and other nonprofit publishers.

The very small presses are sometimes called micropresses and are owned or operated by one to three people, usually friends or family members. Some are cooperatives of writers and most started out publishing their own books or books by their friends. These presses can easily be swamped with submissions, but writers published by them are usually treated as "one of the family."

Nonprofit presses depend on grants and donations to help meet operating costs. The economy is still in recovery, so many of these presses lost funding in recent years. Keep in mind, too, some of these presses are funded by private organizations such as churches or clubs, and books that reflect the backer's views or beliefs are most likely to be considered for publication.

Funding for university presses is often tied to government or private grants as well. Traditionally, universities tend to publish writers who are either affiliated with the university or whose work is representative of the region in which the school is located. Recently, however, university presses are trying their hand at publishing books without university connections aimed at the same readership as other publishers. This is mostly happening in nonfiction, but chances are university presses may start to publish more general fiction as well.

Many publishers in this section are independent literary and regional presses. Several have become highly sophisticated about competing in the marketplace and in carving out their own niche.

Selecting a small press

As with magazines, reading the listing should be just your first step in finding markets that interest you. It's best to familiarize yourself with a press's focus and line. Most produce catalogs or at least fliers advertising their books. Whenever possible, obtain these and writers' guidelines.

If possible, read some of the books published by a press that interests you. It is sometimes more difficult to locate books published by the small press (especially by micropress publishers). Some very small presses only sell through the mail. Literary and larger independent press books can be found at most independent bookstores and the number of books from these presses that make it into the large chain super stores is growing. Also try university bookstores and libraries.

Use the Category Index located near the end of this book. If you've written a particular type of novel, look in the Small Press section of the Category Index under the appropriate heading to find presses interested in your specific subject or area of interest.

We've also included Roman numeral ranking codes placed at the start of a listing to help you determine how open the press is to new writers. The explanations of these codes appear at the end of this introduction.

In addition to the double dagger (‡) indicating new listings, we include other symbols to help you in narrowing your search. This year we've added a maple leaf symbol (🍁) to identify Canadian presses. If you are not a Canadian writer, but are interested in a Canadian press, check the listing carefully. Many small presses in Canada receive grants and other funds from their provincial or national government and are, therefore, restricted to publishing Canadian authors.

Book packagers are marked with a box symbol (■). A packager, also known as a book producer, creates books and then sells them to a publisher. Normally, they buy all rights and the writer may or may not get a credit for it. Work is paid for by a flat sum rather than royalties.

You may also see an asterisk (*) at the start of a listing. This lets you know the press sometimes funds the publication of its books through a subsidy arrangement. By our definition, a subsidy press is one that requires writers to pay some or all of the costs of producing, marketing and distributing their books. Approach subsidy arrangements with caution. Find out exactly what type of production is involved and how many books will be produced. Check with a printer to find out how much it would cost you to have this type and amount of books printed yourself. Then, if the cost for the subsidy publication is more, find out what the extra money will pay for—how much and what type of marketing and distribution will be done. Don't hesitate to ask for a full accounting of any money to be spent, for copies of their other books (or where you can obtain them) and for any other information that will help you make an informed decision before you part with your money.

In the listings

How to Get the Most out of This Book outlines the material common to all listings and how it will help you in determining the right market for your work. Keep in mind many small presses do less than 10 books a year and have very small staffs. We've asked them to give a generous amount of response time in their listing, but note that it is not unusual for a smaller press to get behind. Add three or four weeks on to the reporting time listed before checking on the status of your submission.

As with commercial book publishers, we ask small presses to give us a list of recent titles each year. If they did not change their title list from last year, it may be that, because they do so few fiction titles, they have not published any new ones or they may be particularly proud of certain titles published earlier. If the recent titles are unchanged, we've altered the sentence to read "Published" rather than "Recently published."

The Business of Fiction Writing located earlier in this book gives the fundamentals of approaching book publishers. The listings include information on whether the publisher wishes to see sample chapters or an entire manuscript and any other material that must be included in a submission package.

Last year we added our own editorial comments set off by a bullet (●) within the listing. We've continued to do this, including awards and honors received by presses and other information we feel will help you make an informed decision, such as cross-referencing those presses which publish magazines or sponsor contests.

There are a number of publishing awards open to small presses or to their books. Many books published by the small press have received the Abby award, a special award given by booksellers (the American Booksellers Association) to books they most enjoyed selling over the last year. The Lambda Literary awards, given to books published by gay and lesbian presses, is another award often given to small press books. The Beyond Columbus Foundation awards the American Book Awards, given to books by American authors that reflect cultural diversity in American Writing and National Book Foundation honors one fiction book by an American author each year. Although most of these awards are open to all book publishers, books published by the small press have received several.

In addition to grants by states and national agencies, a few private and nonprofit organizations have stepped in to help fledgling small presses by providing funding and even guidance with the business side of their operations. We asked presses to give us this information and it sometimes appears in the editorial comments. One organization frequently mentioned was the Council of Literary Magazines and Presses with its Lila Wallace-*Reader's Digest* Literary Publishers Marketing Development Program.

For more information

For more small presses see the *International Directory of Little Magazines and Small Presses* published by Dustbooks (P.O. Box 100, Paradise CA 95967). To keep up with changes in the industry throughout the year, check issues of two major small press trade publications: *Small Press Review* (also published by Dustbooks) and *Small Press* (Small Press Inc., Kymbolde Way, Wakefield RI 02879).

The ranking codes used in this section are as follows:

   I **Publisher encourages beginning or unpublished writers to submit work for consideration and publishes new writers frequently.**

  II **Publisher accepts work by established writers and by new writers of exceptional talent.**

 III **Publisher does not encourage beginning writers; publishes mostly writers with extensive previous publication credits or agented writers and very few new writers.**

 IV **Special-interest or regional publisher, open only to writers on certain topics or from certain geographical areas.**

‡**ACCORD COMMUNICATIONS LTD., (IV),** Evergreen Pacific Publishing, Suite B, 18002 15th Ave. NE, Seattle WA 98155. (206)368-8157. Fax: (206)368-7968. Managing Editor: Karen Duncan. Estab. 1987. Small independent publisher. Publishes hardcover and paperback originals and paperback reprints. First novel print order: 3,000-5,000. Plans 2 first novels this year. Averages 3-4 total titles, 2-3 fiction titles each year. Sometimes comments on rejected ms.
   • This publisher's fiction series is new. They also publish several nonfiction, regional and fishing titles.
Needs: Mystery/suspense (amateur sleuth, cozy, malice domestic, police procedural). Publishes series detective fiction.
How to Contact: Accepts unsolicited mss. Submit outline/synopsis and 3 sample chapters. Include estimated word count, 1-page bio and list of publishing credits. Send SASE (or IRCs) for reply, return of ms or send a disposable copy of ms. Reports in 1 month on queries; 2 months on mss. Simultaneous submissions OK.
Terms: Pays royalties of 5% minimum; 15% maximum. Provides 10 author's copies. Time between acceptance of ms and publication varies.

ADVOCACY PRESS, (IV), Box 236, Santa Barbara CA 93102. Executive Director: Barbara Fierro Lang. Estab. 1983. Small publisher with 3-5 titles/year. Hardcover and paperback originals. Books: perfect or Smyth-sewn binding; illustrations; average print order: 5,000-10,000 copies; first novel print order: 5,000-10,000. Averages 2 children's fiction (32-48 pg.) titles per year.
   • Advocacy Press books have won the Ben Franklin Award (*My Way Sally*) and the Friends of American Writers Award (*Tonia the Tree*). The press also received the Eleanor Roosevelt Research and Development Award from the American Association of University Women for its significant contribution to equitable education.
Needs: Juvenile. Wants only feminist/nontraditional messages to boys or girls—picture books; self-esteem issues. Recently published *Minou*, by Mindy Bingham (picture book); *Kylie's Song*, by Patty Sheehan (picture book); *Nature's Wonderful World in Rhyme*, by William Sheehan. Publishes the World of Work Series (real life stories about work).

✚   *The double dagger before a listing indicates that the listing is new in this edition. New markets are often the most receptive to submissions by new writers.*

How to Contact: Submit complete manuscript with SASE (IRCs) for return. Reports in 10 weeks on queries. Simultaneous submissions OK.

Terms: Pays in royalties of 5-10%. Book catalog for SASE.

Advice: Wants "only fictional stories for children 4-12 years old that give messages of self sufficiency for little girls; little boys can nurture and little girls can be anything they want to be, etc. Please review some of our publications *before* you submit to us. Because of our limited focus, most of our titles have been written in-house."

*AEGINA PRESS, INC., (I,II), 59 Oak Lane, Spring Valley, Huntington WV 25704. (304)429-7204. Imprint is University Editions, Inc. Managing Editor: Ira Herman. Estab. 1984. Independent small press. Publishes paperback and hardcover originals and reprints. Books: 50 lb. white text/10 point high gloss covers; photo-offset printing; perfect binding; illustrations; average print order: 500-1,000. Plans 5-10 first novels this year. Averages 30 total titles, 15 fiction titles each year. Sometimes comments on rejected ms.

● See also the listing for University Editions in this book.

Needs: Adventure, contemporary, experimental, fantasy, historical, horror, literary, mainstream, regional, romance (gothic), science fiction (hard science, soft sociological), short story collections, mystery/suspense (romantic suspense, young adult), thriller/espionage. No racist, sexist, or obscene materials. Recently published *The Liberation of Bonner Child*, by Norman German (novel); *Tavern Tales*, by Alvin Roberts (short story collection); *Provoking the Power*, by Lynn Parkin Atkinson (fantasy novel). Published new writers within the last year.

How to Contact: Accepts unsolicited mss. Send outline/synopsis and 3 sample chapters or complete ms with cover letter. SASE (IRCs). Agented fiction 5%. Reports in 3 weeks on queries; 1-2 months on mss. Simultaneous submissions OK.

Terms: Pays 15% royalties. *Subsidy publishes most new authors.* "If the manuscript meets our quality standards but is financially high risk, self-publishing through the University Editions imprint is offered. All sales proceeds go to the author until the subsidy is repaid. The author receives a 40% royalty thereafter. Remaining unsold copies belong to the author." Sends galleys to author. Publishes ms 6-9 months after acceptance. Writer's guidelines for #10 SASE. Book catalog for 9×12 SAE, 4 first-class stamps and $2.

‡ALASKA NATIVE LANGUAGE CENTER, (IV), University of Alaska, Fairbanks AK 99775-0120. (907)474-6577. Editor: Tom Alton. Estab. 1972. Small education publisher limited to books in and about Alaska native languages. Generally nonfiction. Publishes hardcover and paperback originals. Books: 60 lb. book paper; offset printing; perfect binding; photos, line art illustrations; average print order: 500-1,000 copies. Averages 6-8 total titles each year.

Needs: Ethnic. Publishes original fiction only in native language and English by Alaska native writers. Recently published *Aleut Tales*, edited by Knut Bergsland and Moses Dirks; *K'Etetaalkanee*, by Catherine Attla; *Elnguq*, by Anna Jacobson.

How to Contact: Does not accept unsolicited mss. Electronic submissions via ASCII for modem transmissions or Macintosh compatible files on 3½″ disk.

Terms: Does not pay. Sends galleys to author.

ALYSON PUBLICATIONS, INC., (II), 40 Plympton St., Boston MA 02118. (617)542-5679. Fiction Editor: Sasha Alyson. Estab. 1977. Medium-sized publisher specializing in lesbian- and gay-related material. Publishes paperback originals and reprints. Books: paper and printing varies; trade paper, perfect-bound; average print order: 8,000; first novel print order: 6,000. Plans 4 first novels this year. Averages 15 total titles, 8 fiction titles each year.

● Alyson Publications received a New England Publishing Award in 1993 from the New England Booksellers Association.

Needs: "We are interested in all categories; *all* materials must be geared toward lesbian and/or gay readers." Recently published *Captain Swing*, by Larry Duplechan; *Tickled Pink*, edited by Richard Labonté; *Silver Saddles*, by Cap Iversen. Published new writers within the last year. Publishes anthologies. Authors may submit to them directly.

How to Contact: Query first with SASE (IRCs). Reports in 3 weeks on queries; 2 months on mss.

Terms: "We prefer to discuss terms with the author." Sends galleys to author. Book catalog for SAE and 3 first-class stamps.

AMERICAN ATHEIST PRESS, (IV), Gustav Broukal Press, Box 140195, Austin TX 78714-0195. Editor: Robin Murray-O'Hair, Estab. 1960. Paperback originals and reprints. Books: bond and other paper; offset printing; perfect bound; illustrations "if pertinent." Averages 6 total titles/year. Occasionally critiques or comments on rejected ms.
Needs: Contemporary, humor/satire, literary, science fiction. No "religious/spiritual/occult."
How to Contact: Query with sample chapters and outline. SASE (IRCs). Reports in 2 months on queries; 3 months on mss. Simultaneous submissions OK. Accepts electronic submissions via IBM-PC/Word-Perfect on disk.
Terms: Pays 8-11% royalties. Writers guidelines for #9 SAE and 1 first-class stamp. Book catalog free on request.
Advice: "We only publish fiction which relates to Atheism; we receive many queries for general interest fiction, which we do not publish."

✹ANNICK PRESS LTD., (IV), 15 Patricia Ave., Willowdale, Ontario M2M 1H9 Canada. (416)221-4802. Publisher of children's books. Publishes hardcover and paperback originals. Books: offset paper; full-color offset printing; perfect and library bound; full-color illustrations; average print order: 9,000; first novel print order: 7,000. Plans 18 first picture books this year. Averages approximately 20 titles each year, all fiction. Average first picture book print order 2,000 cloth, 12,000 paper copies. Occasionally critiques rejected ms.
Needs: Children's books only.
How to Contact: "Annick Press publishes only work by Canadian citizens or residents." Does not accept unsolicited mss. Query with SASE (IRCs). Free book catalog.
Terms: Sends galleys to author.
Advice: "Publishing more fiction this year, because our company is growing. But our publishing program is currently full."

‡ANOTHER CHICAGO PRESS, (II), Box 11223, Chicago IL 60611. Senior Editor: Lee Webster. Estab 1976. Small literary press, non-profit. Books: offset printing; perfect-bound, occasional illustrations; average print order 2,000. Averages 4 total titles, 3 fiction titles each year. Occasionally critiques or comments on rejected ms.
● Another Chicago Press published *Divine Days* which received Book of the Year from the *Chicago Sun-Times* and was a finalist for an award from the Society of Midland Authors.
Needs: Literary. No inspirational religious fiction. Recently published *Noble Rot*, by Richard Stern; *Divine Days*, by Leon Forest; *The Empty Lot*, by Mary Gray Hughes. Published new writers within the last year.
How to Contact: Does not accept or return unsolicited mss. Query first for books, then submit outline/synopsis and short excerpt (no more than 10 pages, unless more is requested). SASE (IRCs). Agented fiction 10%. Reports in 3 months. Simultaneous submissions OK.
Terms: Advance negotiable; pays royalties of 10%. Sends galleys to author.
Advice: "We publish novels and collections of short stories and poetry as our funds and time permit — and then probably only by solicitation. We publish literary fiction and poetry of substance and quality. We publish books that will entertain, enlighten or disturb. Our books, our authors will be read well into the 21st Century."

‡✹ANVIL PRESS, (I, II), Station "A", P.O. Box 1575, Vancouver, British Columbia V6C 2P7 Canada; or Lee Building, #204-A, 175 E. Broadway, Vancouver, British Columbia V5T 1W2 Canada. (604)876-8710. Managing Editor: Brian Kaufman. Fiction Editors: Brian Kaufman and Dennis E. Bolen. Estab. 1988. "1½ person operation with volunteer editorial board." Publishes paperback originals. Books: offset or web printing; perfect-bound; average print order: 1,000-1,500; first novel print order: 1,000. Plans 2 first novels this year. Averages 2-4 total titles, 1-2 fiction titles each year. Often comments on rejected ms. Also offers a critique service for a fee.

 The maple leaf symbol before a listing indicates a Canadian publisher.

Needs: Experimental, literary, short story collections. Recently published *Stupid Crimes*, by Dennis E. Bolen (literary novel); *A Circle of Birds*, by Hayden Trenholm (literary novella); *The Church on the Hill Is Leaking*, by Jo Leath (novella in prose and verse). Published new wrtiers within the last year. Publishes the Anvil Pamphlet series: shorter works (essays, political tracts, polemics, treatises and works of fiction that are shorter than novel or novella form).

How to Contact: Canadian writers only. Accepts unsolicited mss. Query first or submit outline/synopsis and 1-2 sample chapters. Include estimated word count and bio with submission. Send SASE (or IRC) for reply, return of ms or a disposable copy of ms. Reports in 1 month on queries; 2 months on mss. Simultaneous submissions OK (please note in query letter that manuscript is a simultaneous submission).

Terms: Pays royalties of 10-15% (of final sales). Average advance: $100-200. Sends galleys to author. Publishes ms within contract year. Book catalog for 6×9 SASE and 2 first-class stamps.

Advice: "We are a small literary press originally founded to publish *Sub-Terrain Magazine* – a literary magazine featuring the work of new and emerging North American Writers. We are on a title-to-title schedule. Approach all new projects with a fair deal of caution. Read our magazine or book or get hold of a catalogue. We are looking for contemporary, new voices."

APPLEZABA PRESS, Box 4134, Long Beach CA 90804. Editorial Director: Shelley Hellen. Estab. 1977. "We are a family-operated publishing house, working on a part-time basis. We plan to expand over the years." Publishes paperback originals. Averages 1 fiction title each year.

Needs: Contemporary, literary, experimental, feminist, gay, lesbian, fantasy, humor/satire, translations, and short story collections. No gothic, romance, confession, inspirational, satirical, black humor or slapstick. Published *Horse Medicine and Other Stories*, by Raephael Zepecha; *Nude*, by Judson Jerome.

How to Contact: Accepts unsolicited mss. Submit complete ms with SASE (IRCs). No simultaneous submissions. Reports in 2 months. Publishes ms 2-3 years after acceptance.

Terms: Pays in author's copies and 8-15% royalties; no advance. Free book catalog.

Advice: "Cover letter with previous publications, etc. is OK. Each book, first or twentieth, has to stand on its own. If a first-time novelist has had shorter works published in magazines, it makes it somewhat easier for us to market the book. We publish only book-length material."

ARIADNE PRESS, (I), 4817 Tallahassee Ave., Rockville MD 20853. (301)949-2514. President: Carol Hoover. Estab. 1976. Shoestring operation – corporation with 4 directors who also act as editors. Publishes hardcover and paperback originals. Books: 50 lb. alkaline paper; offset printing; Smyth-sewn binding; average print order 1,000; first novel print order 1,000. Plans 1 first novel this year. Averages 1 total title each year; only fiction. Sometimes critiques rejected ms. "We comment on selected mss of superior writing quality, even when rejected."

Needs: Adventure, contemporary, feminist, historical, humor/satire, literary, mainstream, psychological, family relations and marital, war. Looking for "literary-mainstream" fiction. No short stories, no science fiction, horror or mystery. Recently published *The Greener Grass*, by Paul Bourguignon; *A Rumor of Distant Tribes*, by Eugene Jeffers.

How to Contact: *Query first.* SASE (IRCs). Agented fiction 5%. Reports in 1 month on queries; 2 months on mss. Simultaneous submissions OK.

Terms: Pays royalties of 10%. No advance. Sends galleys to author. Writer's guidelines not available. List of books in stock for #10 SASE.

Advice: "We exist primarily for non-established writers. Try large, commercial presses first. Characters and story must fit together so well that it is hard to tell which grew out of the other."

ARJUNA LIBRARY PRESS, (II), Subsidiaries include: The Journal of Regional Criticism, Space 18, 1025 Garner St., Colorado Springs CO 80905-1774. Director: Dr. Joseph A. Uphoff, Jr.. Estab. 1979. "The Arjuna Library is an artist's prototype press." Publishes paperback originals. Books: 20 lb. paper; photocopied printing; perfect bound; b&w illustrations; average print order: 20. Averages 6 total titles, 3 fiction titles each year. Sometime comments on rejected ms.

● Arjuna Press has had exhibits at the Colorado Springs Fine Arts Center, KTSC Public Television (academic), University of Southern Colorado and The Poets House, New York, 1993.

Needs: Adventure, childrens/juvenile (fantasy), erotica, experimental, fantasy (surrealist), horror (supernatural), lesbian, romance (futuristic/time travel), science fiction (hard science/technological, soft/sociological poetry), young adult/teen (fantasy/science fiction). Nothing obscene or profane. Recently published *Deep Ellum*, by Robert W. Howington (surrealist); poetry broadsides by Megeen R. Mulholland, John Hulse and Lisa Harris.

How to Contact: Accepts unsolicited mss. Submit complete ms with cover letter, resume. Include list of publishing credits, a disposable copy of the ms to be filed; will return samples in envelopes. Simultaneous and electronic submissions OK.
Terms: Pays 1 author's copy, plus potential for royalties. Writer's guidelines for SASE (IRCs).
Advice: "New literature is not a reiteration of old ideas even when applied as relevance. Authors should be attempting to consider problems that are intractable in contemporary ideology. Such solutions appear unorthodox and require courageous defense; at this point, one need not worry about finding a subject for continuation."

‡ARTE PUBLICO PRESS, (II, IV), University of Houston, Houston TX 77204-2090. (713)749-4768. Publisher: Dr. Nicolas Kanellos. Estab. 1979. "Small press devoted to the publication of contemporary U.S. Hispanic literature." Publishes paperback originals and occasionally reprints. Average print order 2,000-5,000; first novel print order 2,500-5,000. Sometimes critiques rejected ms.
Needs: Contemporary, ethnic, feminist, literary, short story collections. Published *A Shroud in the Family*, by Lionel Garcia (satire); *This Migrant Earth*, by Rolando Hinojosa; *Taking Control*, by Mary Helen Ponce (short stories).
How to Contact: Accepts unsolicited mss. Submit outline/synopsis and sample chapters or complete ms with cover letter. Agented fiction 1%.
Terms: Average advance: $1,000. Provides 20 author's copies. Sends galleys to author. Book catalog free on request.
Tips: "All fiction, all paperback."

*ASYLUM ARTS, (II), P.O. Box 6203, Santa Maria CA 93456. (805)928-8774. Editor: Greg Boyd. Estab. 1985. Independent publisher. Publishes paperback originals. Books: acid-free paper; off-set printing; Smyth-sewn/wrapper binding; some illustrations; average print order: 2,000; first novel print order: 2,000. Averages 6-8 total titles, 4 fiction titles each year. Sometimes comments on rejected ms.
● Asylum Arts recently received a Gregory Kolovakos Seed Grant Award from the Council of Literary Magazines and Presses.
Needs: Erotica, experimental, literary, short story collections, translations. Plans anthology *French Romantic Reader* ; editors select stories. Recently published *Schooling the Spirit*, by Geoffrey Clark (stories); *City of Mazes*, by Cynthia Hendershot (stories); *Carnival Aptitude*, by Greg Boyd (stories). Publishes the *Asylum Annual*.
How to Contact: Accepts unsolicited mss. Query first. Include estimated word count, bio, list of publishing credits. SASE (IRCs) for a reply. Reports in 1 month on queries; 4 months on mss. No simultaneous submissions.
Terms: Pays royalties of 10% and author's copies. Also "individual arrangement, book by book; some cooperative projects." *Subsidy publishes 20%.* Sends galleys to author. Publishes ms 1-2 years after acceptance. Book catalog free.
Advice: "We are publishing more paperback originals as they are easier to distribute. We are a very small operation with no public funding. Hence our resources, both time and money, are limited."

THE ATLANTEAN PRESS, (II), 354 Tramway Dr., Milpitas CA 95035. (408)262-8478. Fax: (408)262-8478. Publisher: P. LeChevalier. Estab. 1990. "Very small (2-3 titles/year) independent; plans to expand in 1994." Publishes hardcover originals and reprints and paperback originals and reprints. Books: acid-free paper; Smyth-sewn case or sew and wrap; average print order: 2,000; first novel print order: 2,000. Averages 2-3 total titles, fiction and poetry, each year. Sometimes comments on rejected ms.
Needs: Adventure, childrens/juvenile, historical (general), literary, mainstream/contemporary, military/war, mystery/suspense (amateur sleuth, cozy, malice domestic, police procedural, private eye/hard boiled), short story collections, thriller/espionage, translations, western. Publishes quarterly literary magazine, *Atlantean Press Review*. Send for guidelines, enclosing a description of your work. Published *Whisper the Guns*, by Edward Cline (suspense).

The asterisk indicates a publisher who sometimes offers subsidy arrangements. Authors are asked to subsidize part of the cost of book production. See the introduction for more information.

How to Contact: Accepts unsolicited mss. Query first. Include estimated word count, 1 page bio, writing experience, ambitions and philosophy. SASE (IRCs). Reports in 3 months. Simultaneous and electronic submissions OK.

Terms: Pays royalties of 10% minimum; 25% maximum. Provides 5 or more author's copies. Pays honorarium ($15-100) or makes individual arrangement with author depending on the book. Sends galleys to author. Publishes ms 8-18 months after acceptance. Writer's guidelines for #10 SASE and 1 first-class stamp. Book brochure free.

Advice: "We are looking for good *romantic* fiction and drama. Not to be confused with "romance," this means serious fiction with a logical *plot*; strong, active motivated *characters* and a *theme*. Read Ayn Rand's *Romantic Manifesto*."

*AUTHORS UNLIMITED, (II), Imprints include Authors Unlimited and Military Literary Guild, 3324 Barham Blvd., Los Angeles CA 90068. (213)874-0902. Senior Editor: Renais J. Hill. Estab. 1983. Midsize independent publisher with plans to expand. Publishes hardcover and paperback originals. Books: 60 lb. paper; trade paper and hard cover binding; illustrations; average print order: 2,000. Plans 10 first novels this year. Averages 30 total titles, 15 fiction titles each year.

Needs: Adventure, contemporary, ethnic, fantasy, feminist, gay, glitz, historical, horror, humor/satire, lesbian, literary, mainstream, military/war, mystery/suspense (amateur sleuth, private eye, police procedural), psychic/supernatural/occult, regional, religious/inspirational, romance, science fiction, short story collections, spiritual, thriller/espionage, western. No pornography. Recently published *Mommy, Where Are You?*, by Joan E. Nelson; *Bonsai Society*, by Thomas Saxon; *Unbecoming Conduct*, by Bernice Bell. Published new writers within the last year.

How to Contact: Accepts unsolicited mss. Submit complete ms with cover letter. SASE (IRCs). Reports in 1 month. Simultaneous submissions OK.

Terms: *Subsidy publishes 10% of books* (cooperative terms, approx. 60/40%). No advance. Provides 50 author's copies. Sends galleys to author. Publishes ms 9 months after acceptance. Writer's guidelines, book catalog for 9 × 12 SAE and $1.25 postage.

Advice: "New authors should keep the action of the story moving constantly; do not let story drag or become repetitious; resolve the plot in a clear and concise way quickly; do not have too many subplots running through manuscript."

FREDERIC C. BEIL, PUBLISHER, INC., (II), 609 Whitaker St., Savannah GA 31401. Imprints include The Sandstone Press. President: Frederic C. Beil III. Estab. 1983. General trade publisher. Publishes hardcover originals and reprints. Books: acid-free paper; letterpress and offset printing; Smyth-sewn, hardcover binding; illustrations; average print order: 3,000; first novel print order: 3,000. Plans 2 first novels this year. Averages 14 total titles, 4 fiction titles each year.

Needs: Historical, literary, regional, short story collections, translations. Recently published *The Cup of Wrath: The Story of District Bonhoeffer's Resistance to Hitler*, by Mary Glazener; *Sudden Trees and Other Stories*, by H.E. Francis; *The Magicians*, by J.B. Priestley.

How to Contact: Does not accept unsolicited mss. Query first. Reports in 1 week on queries.

Terms: Payment "all negotiable." Sends galleys to author. Book catalog free on request.

BETHEL PUBLISHING, (IV), 1819 S. Main, Elkhart IN 46516.(219)293-8585. Contact: Senior Editor. Estab. 1903. Mid-size Christian book publisher. Publishes paperback originals and reprints. Averages 3-5 total titles per year. Occasionally critiques or comments on rejected manuscripts.

Needs: Religious/inspirational, young adult/teen. No "workbooks, cookbooks, coloring books, theological studies, pre-school or elementary-age stories."

How to Contact: Accepts unsolicited mss. Query first. Enclose SAE and 3 first-class stamps. Reports in 2 weeks on queries; 3 months on mss. Accepts simultaneous submissions. Publishes mss 8-16 months after acceptance.

Terms: Pays royalties of 10% and 12 author's copies. Writer's guidelines and book catalog free on request.

BILINGUAL PRESS/EDITORIAL BILINGÜE, (II, IV), Hispanic Research Center, Arizona State University, Tempe AZ 85287-2702. (602)965-3867. Editor: Gary Keller. Estab. 1973. "University affiliated." Publishes hardcover and paperback originals, and reprints. Books: 60 lb. acid-free paper; single sheet or web press printing; case-bound and perfect-bound; illustrations sometimes; average print order: 4,000 copies (1,000 case-bound, 3,000 soft cover). Plans 2 first novels this year. Averages 12 total titles, 6 fiction each year. Sometimes comments on rejected ms.

● A book published by Bilingual Press received an American Book Award from the Before Columbus Foundation in 1993.

Needs: Ethnic, literary, short story collections, translations. "We are always on the lookout for Chicano, Puerto Rican, Cuban-American or other U.S. Hispanic themes with strong and serious literary qualities and distinctive and intellectually important themes. We have been receiving a lot of fiction set in Latin America (usually Mexico or Central America) where the main character is either an ingenue to the culture or a spy, adventurer or mercenary. We don't publish this sort of 'Look, I'm in an exotic land' type of thing. Also, novels about the Aztecs or other pre-Columbians are very iffy." Recently published *The Mystery of Survival and Other Stories*, by Alicia Gaspar de Alba; *Pilgrims in Aztlán*, by Miguel Méndez (novel); and *Naked Ladies*, by Alma Luz Villanueva (novel). Published new writers within the last year.

How to Contact: Query first. SASE (IRCs). Include Social Security number with submission. Reports in 3 weeks on queries; 2 months on mss. Simultaneous submissions OK.

Terms: Pays royalties of 10%. Average advance $300. Provides 10 author's copies. Sends galleys to author. Publishes ms 1 year after acceptance. Writer's guidelines not available. Book catalog free.

Advice: "Writers should take the utmost care in assuring that their manuscripts are clean, grammatically impeccable, and have perfect spelling. This is true not only of the English but the Spanish as well. All accent marks need to be in place as well as other diacritical marks. When these are missing it's an immediate first indication that the author does not really know Hispanic culture and is not equipped to write about it. We are interested in publishing creative literature that treats the U.S. Hispanic experience in a distinctive, creative, revealing way. The kinds of books that we publish we keep in print for a very long time (certainly into the next century) irrespective of sales. We are busy establishing and preserving a U.S. Hispanic canon of creative literature."

‡BkMk PRESS, (II), UMKC, 107 University House, 5100 Rockhill Rd., Kansas City MO 64110-2499. (816)276-2558. Fiction Editor: Dan Jaffe. Estab. 1971. Publishes hardback and paperback originals. Books: standard paper; offset printing; perfect- and case-bound; average print order: 1,000; Averages 6 total titles; 1 fiction title each year.

Needs: Contemporary, ethnic, experimental, historical, literary, translations. "Fiction publishing limited to short stories and novellas. Ordinarily, prints anthologies or collections by one writer. BkMk Press does not publish commercial novels." Recently published *The Curandero*, by Daniel Curley; *Paper Crown* by Tom Hawkins.

How to Contact: Query first with SASE (IRCs). Reports in 3-4 months on queries.

Terms: Pays in royalties (approximately 10%, in copies and $50 adjustable by contract). Sends galleys to author. Free book catalog.

Advice: "We value the exceptional, rare, well-crafted and daring." Especially interested in Midwestern regional writers.

BLACK HERON PRESS, (I, II), P.O. Box 95676, Seattle WA 98145. Publisher: Jerry Gold. Estab. 1984. One-person operation; no immediate plans to expand. Publishes paperback and hardback originals. Average print order: 1,000; first novel print order: 500-1,500. Averages 4 fiction titles each year.

● Two books published by Black Heron Press have recently won awards from King County Arts Commission.

Needs: Adventure, contemporary, experimental, humor/satire, literary, science fiction. Vietnam war novel—literary. "We don't want to see fiction written for the mass market. If it sells to the mass market, fine, but we don't see ourselves as a commercial press." Recently published *When Bobby Kennedy Was a Moving Man*, by Robert Gordon; *The War Against Gravity*, by Kristine Rosemary; *The Remf Returns*, by David Willson.

How to Contact: Query and sample chapters only. Reports in 3 months on queries. Simultaneous submissions OK.

Terms: Pays standard royalty rates. No advance.

Advice: "A query letter should tell me: 1) number of words; 2) number of pages; 3) if ms is available on floppy disk; 4) if parts of novel been published; 5) if so, where? If you're going to submit to Black Heron, make the work as good as you can. I'm a good editor but I don't have the time to solve major problems with a manuscript."

✱BLACK MOSS PRESS, (II), Box 143 Station A, Windsor ON N9A-6L7 Canada. (519)252-2551. Fiction Editor: Marty Gervais. Estab. 1969. "Small independent publisher assisted by government grants." Publishes paperback originals. Books: Zephyr paper; offset printing; perfect binding; 4-color cover, b&w interior illustrations; average print order: 500. Averages 10-14 total titles, 7 fiction titles each year. Sometimes comments on rejected mss.

Needs: Humor/satire, juvenile (5-9 years, including easy-to-read, contemporary), literary, preschool/picture book, short story collections. "Usually open to children's material. Nothing religious, moralistic, romance." Recently published *The Failure of Love*, by Paul Vasey; *Ethel on Fire*, by Helen Humphreys; *Priest's Boy*, by Clive Doucet.

How to Contact: Accepts unsolicited mss. Submit outline/synopsis and 2 sample chapters. SASE. Reports in 1-3 months. *Canadian authors only.*

Terms: Pays for children's in royalties; literary in author's copies. Sends galleys to author. Publishes ms 1-2 years after acceptance. Book catalog for SASE.

Advice: "Generally, originality, well developed plots, strong, multi-dimensional characters and some unusual element catch my interest. It's rare that we publish new authors' works, but when we do, that's what we want. (We do publish short story collections of authors who have had some stories in lit mags.) Because we are assisted by government grants which place certain restrictions on us, we are unable to publish any material by anyone other than a Canadian citizen or immigrant landed in Canada."

BOOKS FOR ALL TIMES, INC., (III), Box 2, Alexandria VA 22313. Publisher/Editor: Joe David. Estab. 1981. One-man operation. Publishes hardcover and paperback originals. Books: 60 lb. paper; offset printing; perfect binding; average print order: 1,000. "No plans for new writers at present." Has published 1 fiction title to date. Occasionally critiques rejected ms.

Needs: Contemporary, literary, short story collections. "No novels at the moment; hopeful, though, of someday soon publishing a collection of quality short stories. No popular fiction or material easily published by the major or minor houses specializing in mindless entertainment. Only interested in stories of the Victor Hugo or Sinclair Lewis quality."

How to Contact: Query first with SASE (IRCs). Simultaneous submissions OK. Reports in 1 month on queries.

Terms: Pays negotiable advance. "Publishing/payment arrangement will depend on plans for the book." Book catalog free on request.

Advice: Interested in "controversial, honest books which satisfy the reader's curiosity to know. Read Victor Hugo, Fyodor Dostoyevsky and Sinclair Lewis, for example. I am actively looking for short articles (up to 5,000 words) on contemporary education. I prefer material critical of the public schools when documented and convincing."

✻BOREALIS PRESS, (I, IV), 9 Ashburn Dr., Ottawa, Ontario K2E 6N4 Canada. Imprint includes *Journal of Canadian Poetry*. Editor: Frank Tierney. Fiction Editor: Glenn Clever. Estab. 1970. Publishes hardcover and paperback originals and reprints. Books: standard book-quality paper; offset printing; perfect and cloth binding; average print order: 1,000. Buys juvenile mss with b&w illustrations. Average number of titles: 4.

* Borealis Press has a series, "New Canadian Drama," with six books in print. The series recently won Ontario Arts Council and Canada Council grants.

Needs: Contemporary, literary, juvenile, young adult. "Must have a Canadian content or author; query first." Recently published *Shenac's Work at Home*, by Margaret M. Robertson (Canadian novel of the 1800s); *Beyond the Snowstorm*, by Yvette Edmonds (Inuit tales); *New Canadian Drama: Feminist Plays*, edited by Rita Much.

How to Contact: Submit query with SASE (Canadian postage) or IRCs. No simultaneous submissions. Reports in 2 weeks on queries, 3-4 months on mss. Publishes ms 1-2 years after acceptance.

Terms: Pays 10% royalties and 3 free author's copies; no advance. Sends galleys to author. Free book catalog with SASE or IRC.

Advice: " Have your work professionally edited. We generally publish only material with a Canadian content or by a Canadian writer."

■BRYANS & BRYANS, (I) (Book Packager and Editorial Consultant), Box 121, Fairfield CT 06430. (203)330-1368. President: John B. Bryans. Fiction Editor: James A. Bryans. Arranges publication of paperback originals (packages). Books: paperback/mass market. *Critiques mss: $200 charge* "for 2-page evaluation only when this has been agreed upon in advance. Often I will offer comments and criticism at no charge where, based on a query, we have encouraged submission. Line-editing and ongoing consulting services to author and publishers."

Taking Readers Beyond the Horizons of Experience

"In the small press all writers are major writers," says Ronald Hatch, president of Cacanadadada, a small publishing house located in Vancouver, British Columbia. While resources for promoting a book are fewer than in a large press, he says, small press publishers spend equal amounts of time on each book.

"Big presses will spend big money on an established writer like Margaret Atwood, but newer or mid-range authors are often lost in terms of promotion. In the small press you have more intimacy, more input in your own book," he explains.

Hatch took over the press in 1989 after it was in operation about one year, but he has carried on the intent of the original owners. "The idea was to create an eclectic press, to specialize in poetry and short fiction first and move into longer works and local his-

Ronald Hatch

tory. I'm now moving into different areas: children's books, autobiographical fiction, works about the interior of British Columbia."

He started out looking for and publishing mostly experimental fiction, but "in fact, the manuscripts I've received have not always been experimental and I've been pleased with the more traditional works we've published such as [short story collections] *Black Light* and *Rapunzel, Rapunzel*. I've found the more conventional stories can work for us—those that have a hook in the beginning and an ending that is a clarification."

As with many small presses in Canada, Cacanadadada publishes mostly Canadian authors. A book recently published by the press, *Out of the Interior*, is in keeping with the press's commitment to publish books about Canadian history and British Columbia in particular. A semi-autobiographical account of a second-generation German's experience in the Canadian interior, the book is also a part of a growing trend to publish books exploring the ethnic experience in Canada, says Hatch.

"Many small ethnic communities are writing about an experience they've felt intensely and there is much good writing in this area, drawing on a whole background. Canada has tremendous resources of history and culture. There's also been more native writing as well, especially writing by first-nations people."

Overall, Hatch says he's seeing a lot of good fiction, but he also sees more work in which the writer does not seem to know much about the literary tradition. "It often strikes me that I see many manuscripts that suggest the writer has not read very much. They do not resonate the words, the phrases of earlier books. They're without a sense of past that echoes in good writing and creates a stronger chord in traditional work."

Hatch is very proud of the books he's published and refers to them often as examples of the type of things he likes to see. "*Black Light* is about whites and blacks in Africa and it's a collection of very powerful prose. That's what I look for—an energy in the writing. It has to grip you, move you. Not purple prose, but writing that involves the reader. I like stories that push boundaries, too: writing that gives a sense of moving beyond what you know, beyond the horizons of experience."

—*Robin Gee*

Needs: Adventure, contemporary, historical, horror, humor/satire, literary, mainstream, romance (contemporary, historical). Produced *Baton Rouge* (historical with romance elements); *Portland* and *Omaha*, by Lee Davis Willoughby (packaged by us for Knightsbridge Publishing, Los Angeles).
How to Contact: Does not accept unsolicited mss. Query first. SASE (IRCs). Agented fiction 50-90%. Reports in 2 weeks on queries; 1 month on mss. Electronic submissions OK via Microsoft Word on Macintosh disk.
Terms: Pays in royalties of 6-10%. Negotiable advance.
Advice: "Send us a letter, maximum 2 pages, describing the project and giving pertinent background info on yourself. Include an SASE and we will reply to let you know if we find the idea intriguing enough to see 3 sample chapters (the *first* three) and a detailed synopsis."

☘CACANADADADA, (I, II, IV), 3350 West 21 Ave., Vancouver, British Columbia V6S 1G7 Canada. (604)738-1195. President: Ronald B. Hatch. Estab. 1988. Publishes paperback originals. Books: 60 lb. paper; photo offset printing; perfect binding; average print order: 1,000; first novel print order: 1,000. Plans 1 first novel this year. Averages total titles, 3 fiction this year. Sometimes comments on rejected ms.
 • See the interview with Ronald Hatch in this edition.
Needs: Experimental and literary. Recently published *Worlds in Small*, by John Robert Columbo; *Nicolette*, by Robert Zend (experimental novel); *Rapunzel, Rapunzel*, by Jancis M. Andrews; *Black Light*, by Ron Shaw (short story collection).
How to Contact: *Canadian authors only.* Accepts unsolicited mss. Submit outline/synopsis and 1 or 2 sample chapters. SASE. Short story collections must have some magazine publication. Reports in 1 week on queries; 1 month on mss.
Terms: Pays royalties of 10%. Provides author's copies. Sends galleys to author. Publishes ms 6 months after acceptance.
Advice: "We publish both fiction and poetry. We are a Canadian publishing house and depend on a partial government subsidy to publish books. Thus, authors *must* be Canadian."

CADMUS EDITIONS, (III), Box 126, Tiburon CA 94920. (707)431-8527. Editor: Jeffrey Miller. Estab. 1979. Emphasis on quality literature. Publishes hardcover and paperback originals. Books: Approximately 25% letterpress; 75% offset printing; perfect and case binding; average print order: 2,000; first novel print order: 2,000. Averages 3-5 total titles, 3 fiction titles each year.
Needs: Literary. Published *The Wandering Fool*, by Yunus Emre, translated by Edouard Roditi and Guzin Dino; *The Hungry Girls*, by Patricia Eakins; *Zig-Zag*, by Richard Thornley.
How to Contact: Does not accept or return unsolicited mss. Query first. SASE. Photocopied submissions OK.
Terms: Royalties negotiated per book. Sends galleys to author.

 Listings marked with a solid box are book packagers. See the introduction for more information.

CALYX BOOKS, (II,IV), P.O. Box B, Corvallis OR 97339. (503)753-9384. Editor: M. Donnelly. Fiction Editor: Beverly McFarland. Estab. 1986. "We publish fine literature and art by women." Publishes hardcover and paperback originals. Books: offset printing; paper and cloth binding; average print order: 5,000-10,000 copies; first novel print order: 5,000. Published new writers within the last year. Averages 2-4 total titles each year.
   • *Calyx*, a literary journal by this publisher, is also listed in this book. Books published by Calyx have received the American Book Award, GLCA Fiction Award and Bumbershoot and other awards. They are not now working on an anthology but past anthologies include *Forbidden Stitch: An Asian-American Women's Anthology* and *Women and Aging.*
Needs: Contemporary, ethnic, experimental, feminist, lesbian, literary, short story collections, translations. Recently published *The Violet Shyness of Their Eyes: Notes from Nepal*, by Barbara J. Scot; *Raising the Tents*, by Frances Payne Adler; *Open Heart*, by Judith Mickel Sornberger. Published new writers within the last year.
How to Contact: Query first or submit outline/synopsis and 3 sample chapters. Include SASE (IRC). Open for submissions January-March. Reports in 1 month on queries; 6 months on mss.
Terms: Pays royalties of 10% minimum, author's copies, (depends on grant/award money). Sends galleys to author. Publishes ms 2 years after acceptance. Writer's guidelines for #10 SAE and 1 first-class stamp or IRC. Book catalog free on request.

CANE HILL PRESS, 11th Floor, 225 Varick St., New York NY 10014. (212)316-5513. Publisher: Steve Schrader. Estab. 1988. "Literary press—contemporary fiction." Publishes paperback originals. Average print order: 2,000. Plans 1 first novel this year. Averages 2-3 total titles, all fiction, each year. Sometimes comments on rejected ms.
   • For more information on Cane Hill Press, see the interview with Publisher Steve Schrader in the 1993 edition of *Novel & Short Story Writer's Market*.
Needs: Literary, short story collections. No genre. Published *Getting Jesus in the Mood*, by Anne Brashler (story collection); *Phoenix*, by Melissa Pritchard (novel); and *All Backs Were Turned*, by Marek Hlasko (translation from a Polish novel). Published new writers within the last year.
How to Contact: Accepts unsolicited mss. Query first. Agented fiction 50%. Reports in 1 week on queries; 1 month on mss. Simultaneous submissions OK.
Terms: Pays in advance; $2,000-3,000. Also 50 author's copies. Sends galleys to author. Publishes ms 18 months after acceptance. Book catalog free on request.

*CAROLINA WREN PRESS (II), 120 Morris St., Durham NC 27701. (919)560-2738. Imprints include Lollipop Power Books. Editor-in-Chief: Elaine Goolsby. Fiction Editor: Mary Lambeth Moore. "Small non-profit independent publishing company which specializes in women's and minority work and non-sexist, multi-racial children's books." Publishes paperback originals. Books: off-set printing; perfect and saddle-stitched binding; illustrations mainly in children's; average print order: 1,000 adult titles, 3,000 children's; first novel print order: 1,000. Published new writers within the last year. Plans 2 first novels this year. Averages 2-3 total titles each year. Sometimes comments on rejected mss.
Needs: Contemporary, ethnic, experimental, feminist, gay, juvenile (contemporary, easy-to-read), lesbian, literary, preschool/picture book, regional, short story collections, translations. No standard clichéd stuff, romances, etc. No animals (children's books). "We are currently looking for short stories by women, in particular; Southern and minority writers are *especially* encouraged to apply." Published *Love, Or a Reasonable Facsimile*, by Gloree Rogers (ethnic); *Brother and Keeper, Sister's Child*, by Margaret Stephens (literary).
How to Contact: Accepts unsolicited mss. Submit outline/synopsis and 1 or 2 sample chapters. SASE (IRCs). Reports in 6 months.
Terms: Pays in copies (10% of print run for adult titles, 5% for children's books). Pays cash advance if grants are available. Sends galleys to author. Publishes ms 2-3 years after acceptance. Writer's guidelines for #10 SAE and 2 first-class stamps. Book catalog for #10 SAE and 2 first-class stamps.
Advice: "We would like to see work from more black women writers."

● *A bullet introduces comments by the editor of* Novel & Short Story Writer's Market *indicating special information about the listing.*

CARPENTER PRESS, (III), Box 14387, Columbus OH 43214. Editorial Director: Robert Fox. Estab. 1973. One-man operation on part-time basis. Publishes paperback originals. Books: alkaline paper; offset printing; perfect or saddle stapled binding; illustrations sometimes; average print order: 500-2,500; first novel print order: 1,000.

• Due to budget considerations, the number of books Carpenter Press can produce is very limited, so the publisher has not been aggressively looking for new material. Yet he doesn't close the door entirely, saying he might hold onto something exceptional for future consideration.

Needs: Contemporary, literary, experimental, fantastical. "Literary rather than genre science fiction and fantasy." Published *Dawn of the Flying Pigs*, by Jerry Bumpus (short stories); and the 10th anniversary first novel contest winner, *The Three-Week Trance Diet*, by Jane Pirto. "Do not plan to publish more than one book/year including chapbooks, and this depends upon funding, which is erratic. Contemplating future competitions in the novel and short story."

How to Contact: Accepts unsolicited mss. Query. SASE (IRCs). Simultaneous submissions OK. Reports promptly.

Terms: Pays in author's copies or 10% royalties. "Terms vary according to contract." No cash advance. Free book catalog with 52¢ postage.

Advice: "Know what we've published. Don't try to impress us with whom you've studied or where you've published. Read as much as you can so you're not unwittingly repeating what's already been done. I look for freshness and originality. I wouldn't say that I favor experimental over traditional writing. Rather, I'm interested in seeing how recent experimentation is tying tradition to the future and to the work of writers in other countries. We encourage first novelists."

CATBIRD PRESS, (II), 16 Windsor Rd., North Haven CT 06473. Publisher: Robert Wechsler. Estab. 1987. Small independent trade publisher. Publishes hardcover and paperback originals and reprints. Books: acid-free paper; offset printing; cloth/paper binding; illustrations (where relevant). Average print order: 4,000; first novel print order: 3,000. Averages 5 total titles, 1-2 fiction titles each year.

Needs: Humor (specialty); literary, translations (specialty Czech, French and German read in-house). No thriller, historical, science fiction, or other genre writing; only writing with a fresh style and approach. Recently published *The Virtual Boss*, by Floyd Kemske.

How to Contact: Accepts unsolicited mss but no queries. Submit outline/synopsis with sample chapters. SASE (IRCs). Reports in 2-4 weeks on mss. Simultaneous submissions OK, but let us know if simultaneous.

Terms: Pays royalties of 7½-10%. Average advance: $2,000; offers negotiable advance. Sends galleys to author. Publishes ms approximately 1 year after acceptance. Terms depend on particular book. Writer's guidelines for #10 SAE with 1 first-class stamp.

Advice: "We are interested in quality fiction particularly with a comic vision. We are definitely interested in unpublished novelists who combine a sense of humor with a true knowledge of and love for language, a lack of ideology, care for craft and self-criticism."

CAVE BOOKS, (IV), Subsidiary of Cave Research Foundation, 756 Harvard Ave., St. Louis MO 63130. (314)862-7646. Editor: Richard A. Watson. Estab. 1957. Small press. Publishes hardcover and paperback originals and reprints. Books: acid-free paper; various printing methods; binding sewn in signatures; illustrations; average print order: 1,500; first novel print order: 1,500. Averages 4 total titles. Number of fiction titles varies each year. Critiques or comments on rejected ms.

• For years now Cave Books has been looking for realistic adventure novels involving caves. A writer with a *quality* novel along these lines would have an excellent chance for publication.

Needs: Adventure (cave exploration). Needs any realistic novel with caves as central theme. "No gothic, romance, fantasy or science fiction. Mystery and detective OK if the action in the cave is central and realistic. (What I mean by 'realistic' is that the author must know what he or she is talking about.)"

How to Contact: Accepts unsolicited mss. Submit complete ms with cover letter. Reports in 1 week on queries; 1 month on mss. Simultaneous submissions OK.

Terms: Pays in royalties of 10%. Sends galleys to author. Book catalog free on request.

Advice: Encourages first novelists. "We would like to publish more fiction, but we get very few submissions. Why doesn't someone write a historical novel about Mammoth Cave, Carlsbad Caverns, etc. . . . ?"

CENTER PRESS, (III), P.O. Box 16452, Encino CA 91416-6452. (818)377-4301. Publisher: Jana Cain. Estab. 1979. "Small three-person publisher with expansion goals." Publishes hardcover and paperback originals, especially poetry collections. Plans 1-2 novels this year. Averages 6 total titles. Occasionally critiques or comments on rejected ms; fee varies.

● Center Press sponsors the Masters Literary Awards listed in the Conference and Awards section.

Needs: Erotica, historical, humor/satire, literary, short story collections. *List for novels filled for next year or two.*

How to Contact: Query through agent only. SASE (IRCs). Agented fiction 90%. Reports in 2 months on queries. Simultaneous submissions OK.

Terms: Payment rate is "very variable." Sends galleys to author.

Advice: "Be competent, be solvent. Know who you are. Target your market."

‡*CHINA BOOKS, (IV), 2929 24th St., San Francisco CA 94110. (415)282-2994. Senior Editor: Wendy K. Lee. Estab. 1959. "Publishes books about China or things Chinese." Publishes hardcover and paperback originals. Books: letterpress, offset printing; perfect-bound; b&w illustrations; average print order: 5,000. Published new writers within the past year. Averages 6 total titles, 2 fiction titles each year. Sometimes critiques rejected mss.

Needs: Ethnic, subjects relating to China and translations from Chinese. Recently published *Beijinger in New York*, by Glen Cao.

How to Contact: Query first or submit outline/synopsis and 2 sample chapters. Reports in 2 weeks on queries; in 1 month on mss. Simultaneous submissions OK.

Terms: Pays royalties of 5-8%. Sends galleys to author. Publishes ms 1 year after acceptance. *Subsidy publishes 1%/year.* Writer's guidelines and book catalog free on request.

CLEAR LIGHT PUBLISHERS, (IV), 823 Don Diego, Santa Fe NM 87501. (505)989-9590. Publisher: Harmon Houghton. Estab. 1980. "Publish primarily on Southwest, traditional cultures." Publishes hardcover originals. Plans 3 first novels this year. Averages 10-12 total titles, 3 fiction titles each year. Sometimes comments on rejected ms.

Needs: Historical, humor/satire, regional, spiritual, western. Looking for "Southwest, western, native American."

How to Contact: Query first or submit outline/synopsis and sample chapters or sample of writing. SASE. Reports in 6-9 weeks on queries. Simultaneous submissions OK.

Terms: Pays 10-12.5% royalties, negotiable advance. Sends galleys to author. Publishes ms 3-6 months after acceptance. Book catalog free.

‡CLEIS PRESS, (I,II,IV), Box 14684, San Francisco CA 94114. Co-editor: Frédérique Delacoste. "Midsize independent women's press. Publishes paperback originals and reprints." Books: offset 50 lb. paper; offset printing; perfect binding; illustrations in some books; average print order: 3,000-5,000; first novel print order: 3,500. Published new writers within the past year. Averages 8 total titles, 3 fiction title each year.

Needs: Feminist, lesbian, literary, translations. "Particularly interested in translations of women's fiction." Recently published *In the Garden of Dead Cars*, by Sybil Claiborne (novel).

How to Contact: Submit complete ms. SASE (IRCs). Reports on mss in 3 months. Simultaneous submissions OK "with letter of explanation."

Terms: Pays negotiable royalties. Sends pre-publication galleys to author. Publishes 1-2 years after acceptance. Writer's guidelines and book catalog for #10 SAE and 2 first-class stamps.

Advice: Publishing more fiction than in the past. "We encourage new women writers."

‡✿COACH HOUSE PRESS, (II), #107, 50 Prince Arthur Ave., Toronto, Ontario M5R 1B5 Canada. (416)921-3910. Fax: (416)921-4403. Unsolicited Editor: Diane Martin. Estab. 1964. Midsize independent publisher. Publishes paperback originals. Plans 2 first novels this year. Averages 16 total titles, 5-10 fiction titles each year.

Needs: Feminist, gay, humor/satire, lesbian, literary, mainstream/contemporary. No mainstream romance, horror, science fiction. Publishes anthologies. Editors select stories. Recently published *Good Bones*, by Margaret Atwood (fiction); *Miss You Like Crazy*, by Eliza Clark (fiction/road); *An Aroma of Coffee*, by Dany Laferriére (translation). Published new writers within the last year.

How to Contact: Accepts unsolicited mss. Submit outline/synopsis and 3 sample chapters. Include 200 word bio and list of publishing credits with submission. Send SASE (or IRC) for reply or send a disposable copy of ms. Agented fiction 50%. Simultaneous submissions OK.

Terms: Pays royalties. Publishes ms 1 year after acceptance. Book catalog for SASE.

COFFEE HOUSE PRESS, (II), 27 N. 4th St., Minneapolis MN 55401. (612)338-0125. Editorial Assistant: Michael L. Wiegers. Fiction Editor: Allan Kornblum. Estab. 1984. "Nonprofit publisher with a small staff. We publish literary titles: fiction and poetry." Publishes paperback originals. Books: acid-free paper; offset and letterpress printing; Smyth-sewn binding; cover illustrations; average print order: 2,500; first novel print order: 3,000-4,000. Plans one first novel this year. Averages 10 total titles, 5-6 fiction titles each year. Sometimes critiques rejected ms.
  ● This successful nonprofit small press has received numerous grants from various organizations including NEA, the Mellon Foundation and Lila Wallace/*Reader's Digest*. Coffee House's award-winning author, Frank Chin, was interviewed for the 1992 *Novel & Short Story Writer's Market*. Another book, *Through the Arc of the Rainforest*, by Karen Tei Yamashita, received a Before Columbus Foundation Book Award, and it was the first small press book to receive the Janet Heidinger Kafka Prize.
Needs: Contemporary, ethnic, experimental, humor/satire, literary, short story collections. Looking for "non-genre, contemporary, high quality, unique material." No westerns, romance, erotica, mainstream, science fiction, mystery. Publishes anthologies, but they are closed to unsolicited submissions. Also publishes a series of short short collections called "Coffee to Go." Recently published *Brazil-Maru*, by Karen Tei Yamashita (our first hardcover edition); *For Keepsies*, by Gary Fincke (stories); *How I Learned*, by Gloria Frym (stories). Published new writers within the last year.
How to Contact: Accepts unsolicited mss. Submit samples with cover letter. SASE (IRCs). Agented fiction 10%. Reports in 3 months on queries; 9 months on mss.
Terms: Pays royalties of 8%. Average advance: $500. Provides 15 author's copies. Writer's guidelines for #10 SAE and 52¢ postage.
Advice: "Read excessively."

COLONIAL PRESS, (I, II), G 149 West Lake Lodge, Bessemer AL 35020. (205)428-2146. President: Bradley Twitty. Fiction Editor: Jo Barksdale. Editor: Tralelia Twitty. Children's Editor: Dr. Gaila Hodgen. Estab. 1954. "Small independent publisher." Publishes hardcover and paperback originals. Books: 50-60 lb. offset paper; perfect binding; average print order: 1,000-50,000. Plans 2 first novels this year. Averages 20-50 total titles, very few fiction titles each year. Always comments on rejected ms.
Needs: Childrens/juvenile (historical, series), historical, new age/mystic/spiritual, psychic/supernatural/occult, regional (South), religious inspirational (children's religious), short story collections, young adult/teen (historical).
How to Contact: Accepts unsolicited mss. Submit outline/synopsis and 1 sample chapter. Include bio. Send a disposable copy of the manuscript. Reports in 1 month on queries. Simultaneous submissions OK.
Terms: Pays royalties of 10-50%. Provides 10 author's copies. Also makes individual arrangements with author. Publishes ms 6 months-2 years after acceptance. Book catalog free.

CONFLUENCE PRESS INC., (II), Spalding Hall, Lewis-Clark State College, Lewiston ID 83501. (208)799-2336. Imprints: James R. Hepworth Books and Blue Moon Press. Fiction Editor: James R. Hepworth. Estab. 1976. Small trade publisher. Publishes hardcover and paperback originals and reprints. Books: 60 lb. paper; photo offset printing; Smyth-sewn binding; average print order: 1,500-5,000 copies. Averages 5 total titles each year. *Critiques rejected mss for $25/hour.*
  ● Books published by Confluence Press have received Western States Book Awards and awards from the Pacific Northwest Booksellers Association.
Needs: Contemporary, historical, literary, mainstream, short story collections, translations. "Our needs favor serious fiction, 1 novel and 1 short fiction collection a year, with preference going to work set in the contemporary western United States." Published *Angels and Others*, by Ken Smith; *Runaway*, by Mary Clearman Blew; *Passages West*, edited by Hugh Nichols. Published new writers within the last year.
How to Contact: Query first. SASE (IRCs) for query and ms. Agented fiction 50%. Reports in 6-8 weeks on queries and mss. Simultaneous submissions OK.
Terms: Pays royalties of 10%. Advance is negotiable. Provides 10 author's copies; payment depends on grant/award money. Sends galleys to author. Book catalog for 6×9 SASE.
Advice: "We are very interested in seeing first novels from promising writers who wish to break into serious print. We are also particularly keen to publish the best short story writers we can find. We are also interested in finding volume editors for our American authors series. Prospective editors should send proposals."

❀**COTEAU BOOKS, (IV),** Thunder Creek Publishing Co-operative Ltd., 401-2206 Dewdney Ave., Regina, Saskatchewan S4R 1H3 Canada. (306)777-0170. Managing Editor: Shelley Sopher. Estab. 1975. Small, independent publisher. Publishes hardcover and paperback originals. Books: #2 offset or 60 lb. hi-bulk paper; offset printing; perfect and Smyth-sewn binding; 4-color illustrations; average print order: 1,500-3,000; first novel print order: approx. 1,500. Plans 1 first novel this year. Publishes 9-11 total titles, 5-6 fiction titles each year. Sometimes comments on rejected mss.
  • Books published by Coteau Books have received Best First Book awards from the Common-wealth Writers Prize. The publisher does anthologies and these are announced when open to submissions.
Needs: No science fiction. Recently published *The Bonus Deal*, by Archie Crail; *Life Skills*, by Marlis Wesseler; *Sun Angel*, by Chris Fisher. Published new writers within the last year.
How to Contact: *Canadian writers only.* For children's literature, only publish Canadian Prairie Writers. Query first, then submit complete ms with cover letter. SASE (IRCs). No simultaneous or multiple submissions. Agented fiction 10%. Reports on queries in 3 weeks; on mss in 4 months.
Terms: "We're a co-operative who receives subsidies from the Canadian, provincial and local govern-ments. We do not accept payments from authors to publish their works." Sends galleys to author. Publishes ms 1-2 years after acceptance. Book catalog for 8½ × 11 SASE.
Advice: "We publish short-story collections, novels and poetry collections, as well as literary interviews and children's books. This is part of our mandate."

COUNCIL FOR INDIAN EDUCATION, (I,IV), 517 Rimrock Rd., Billings MT 59102. (406)252-7451. Editor: Hap Gilliland. Estab. 1963. Small, non-profit organization publishing Native American materi-als for schools. Publishes hardcover and paperback originals. Books: offset printing; perfect-bound or saddle-stitched binding; b&w illustrations; average print order: 1,000; first novel print order: 1,000. Published new writers within the last year; plans 3 first novels this year. Averages 5 total titles, 4 fiction titles each year. Usually critiques rejected ms.
Needs: All must be about Native Americans: adventure, ethnic, family saga, historical, juvenile (ad-venture, historical and others), preschool/picture book, regional, young adult/teen (easy-to-read, his-torical, mystery, western), western (frontier). Especially needs "short novels, and short stories accu-rately portraying Native American life past or present—fast moving with high interest." No sex emphasis. Published *Old Lop Ear Wolf*, by Royce Holland (3 stories); *Mi'ca—Buffalo Hunter*, by Jane Bendix (novel); *Search for Identity*, by various authors (short stories).
How to Contact: No manuscripts accepted between June 1 and October 1 each year. Accepts unsolic-ited mss. Submit complete ms with SASE (IRCs). Reports in 4 months. Simultaneous submissions OK.
Terms: Pays 10% of wholesale price or 1½¢/word. Sends galleys to author. Free writer's guidelines and book catalog.
Advice: Mostly publishes original fiction in paperback. "Be sure material is culturally authentic and good for the self-concept of the group about whom it is written. Send us only material on Native-Americans, make sure it is true to the culture and way of life of a particular tribe at a particular time, and that you don't downgrade any group."

CREATIVE ARTS BOOK CO., (II), 833 Bancroft Way, Berkeley CA 94710. (510)848-4777. Imprints: Creative Arts Communications Books, Creative Arts Life and Health Books and Saturday Night Specials. Editorial Production Manager: Donald Ellis. Estab. 1975. Small independent trade publisher. Publishes hardcover originals and paperback originals and reprints. Average print order: 2,500-10,000; average first novel print order: 2,500-10,000. Published new writers within the last year. Plans 3 first novels this year. Averages 10-20 titles each year.
  • Books published by Creative Arts have been finalists for the American Book Award and the press won *Bay Area Focus Magazine*'s Press of the Year award in 1990. They've published fiction by William Saroyan, Allen Ginsberg and Aldous Huxley.
Needs: Contemporary, erotica (literary), feminist, historical, literary, mystery/suspense (Saturday night specials), regional, short story collections, translations, western. Publishes anthologies, *Black Lizard Crime Fiction* (Vols. I & II). Recently published *Journey to Topaz* by Yoshiko Uchida; *Stolen Moments*, by Ed Michael Nagler; *Heaven*, by Al Young; *Miss Coffin & Mrs. Blood*, by Sandy Diamond.
How to Contact: Accepts unsolicited ms. Submit outline/synopsis and 3 sample chapters (approx. 50 pages). SASE (IRC). Agented fiction 50%. Reports in 2 weeks on queries; 1 month on mss. Simultane-ous submissions OK.
Terms: Pays royalties of 7½-15%; average advance of $1,000-10,000; 10 author's copies. Sends galleys to author. Writers guidelines and book catalog for SASE or IRC.

CREATIVE WITH WORDS PUBLICATIONS, (I), Box 223226, Carmel CA 93922. Editor-in-Chief: Brigitta Geltrich. Estab. 1975. One-woman operation on part-time basis. Books: bond and stock paper; mimeographed printing; saddle-stitched binding; illustrations; average print order varies. Publishes paperback anthologies of new and established writers. Averages 2 anthologies each year. *Critiques rejected mss; $10 for short stories; $20 for longer stories, folklore items; $5 for poetry.*
Needs: Humor/satire, juvenile (animal, easy-to-read, fantasy). "Editorial needs center on folkloristic items (according to themes): tall tales and such for annual anthologies." Needs seasonal short stories appealing to general public; "tales" of folklore nature, appealing to all ages, poetry and prose written by children. Recently published anthologies, "The Slavic People," "Christmas Stories," "Seasons and Holidays," "Tall Tales and Fairy Tales." Prose not to exceed 1,000 words.
How to Contact: Accepts unsolicited mss. Query first; submit complete ms (prose no more than 1,000 words) with SASE (IRCs) and cover letter. Reports in 1 month on queries; 2 months on mss. Publishes ms 1-6 months after acceptance. Writer's guidelines (1 oz.) for SASE. No simultaneous submissions.
Terms: Pays in 20% reduced author copies.
Advice: "Our fiction appeals to general public: children-senior citizens. Follow guidelines and rules of Creative With Words Publications and not those the writer feels CWW should have. We only consider fiction along the lines of folklore or seasonal genres. Be brief, sincere, well-informed and proficient!"

CREATIVITY UNLIMITED PRESS, (II), 30819 Casilina, Rancho Palos Verdes CA 90274. (310)377-7908. Contact: Rochelle Stockwell. Estab. 1980. One-person operation with plans to expand. Publishes paperback originals and self-hypnosis cassette tapes. Books: perfect binding; illustrations; average print order: 1,000; first novel print order 1,000 copies. Averages 1 title (fiction or nonfiction) each year.
Needs: Published *Insides Out*, by Shelley Stockwell (plain talk poetry); *Sex and Other Touchy Subjects*, (poetry and short stories): and *Timetravel: Do-It Yourself Past Life Regression Handbook*; *Overcoming Depression, Addiction and Compulsion*.
Advice: Write for more information.

CROSS-CULTURAL COMMUNICATIONS, (IV), 239 Wynsum Ave., Merrick NY 11566-4725. (516)868-5635. Fax: (516)379-1901. Editorial Director: Stanley H. Barkan. Estab. 1971. "Small/alternative literary arts publisher focusing on the traditionally neglected languages and cultures in bilingual and multimedia format." Publishes chapbooks, magazines, anthologies, novels, audio cassettes (talking books) and video cassettes (video books, video mags); hardcover and paperback originals. Publishes new women writers series, Holocaust series, Israeli writers series, Dutch writers series, Asian-, African- and Italian-American heritage writers series, Native American writers series.
Needs: Contemporary, literary, experimental, ethnic, humor/satire, juvenile and young adult folktales, and translations. "Main interests: bilingual short stories and children's folktales, parts of novels of authors of other cultures, translations; some American fiction. No fiction that is not directed toward other cultures. For an annual anthology of authors writing in other languages (primarily), we will be seeking very short stories with original-language copy (other than Latin script should be print quality 10/12) on good paper. Title: *Cross Cultural Review Anthology: International Fiction 1*. We expect to extend our *CCR* series to include 10 fiction issues: *Five Contemporary* (Dutch, Swedish, Yiddish, Norwegian, Danish, Sicilian, Greek, Israeli, etc.) *Fiction Writers*." Recently published *Sicilian Origin of the Odyssey*, by L.G. Pocock (bilingual English-Italian translations by Nat Scamacca); *Sikano L'Americano!* and *Bye Bye America*, by Nat Scammacca.
How to Contact: Accepts unsolicited mss. Query with SAE with $1 postage to include book catalog. "Note: Original language ms should accompany translations." Simultaneous and photocopied submissions OK. Reports in 1 month.
Terms: Pays "sometimes" 10-25% in royalties and "occasionally" by outright purchase, in author's copies—"10% of run for chapbook series," and "by arrangement for other publications." No advance.
Advice: "Write because you want to or you must; satisfy yourself. If you've done the best you can, then you've succeeded. You will find a publisher and an audience eventually. Generally, we have a greater interest in nonfiction novels and translations. Short stories and excerpts from novels written in one of the traditional neglected languages are preferred—with the original version (i.e., bilingual). Our kinderbook series will soon be in production with a similar bilingual emphasis, especially for folktales, fairy tales, and fables."

CRYSTAL RIVER PRESS, P.O. Box 1382, Healdsburg CA 95448. Publisher/Editor-in-Chief: Thomas Watson. Managing Editor: Ed Popp. Midsize independent childrens and young adult publisher. Publishes hardcover and paperback originals and paperback reprints. Average print order: 1,000-5,000. Averages 20-35 total titles each year. Sometimes comments on rejected ms.

Needs: Children's/juvenile, young adult/teen (10-18 years). Looking for environmental adventure—culture folklore. Publishes young adult shorts. Writers may submit to anthology editor. Recently published *Jenny's Locket*, by Christine Simpson; *Scruffy's Walk*, by Rebecca Chappell; *But Mom We Have No Chimney*, by Debra Schluter; *A Sheltered Christmas*, by Dr. Ken McKenzie. All children's subjects covered, fiction and nonfiction.

How to Contact: Accepts unsolicited mss. Query first then submit outline/synopsis and 3 sample chapters. Include estimated word count and bio. SASE (IRCs) for reply to query or return of ms. Agented fiction 15-30%. Reports in 1 week on queries; 1-2 months on mss. Simultaneous submissions OK.

Terms: Pays royalties of 8-12% first authors; first run advances are negotiable. Royalties go up on second printing. Provides 30 author's copies. Sends galleys to author. Publishes ms 6-10 months after acceptance. Writer's guidelines for #10 SAE and 1 first-class stamp.

✹HARRY CUFF PUBLICATIONS LTD., (IV), 94 LeMarchant Rd., St. John's, Newfoundland A1C 2H2 Canada. (709)726-6590. Managing Editor: Robert Cuff. Estab. 1981. "Small regional publisher specializing in Newfoundlandia." Publishes paperback originals. Books: offset printing; perfect binding; average print order: 1,000; first novel print order: 800. Averages 8 total titles, 1 fiction each year.

Needs: "Either about Newfoundland, or by a Newfoundlander, or both. No mainstream or erotica." Published *Collected Works of A.R. Scammell* (short story collection) and *Princes*, by Tom Finn (short story collection).

How to Contact: Accepts unsolicited mss. Submit outline/synopsis and 3 sample chapters. SASE (IRC) necessary for return of ms. Reports in 1 month on queries; 3-5 months on mss. Accepts electronic submissions via disk (query first).

Terms: Pays royalties of 10% minimum. Sends galleys to author. Publishes ms 6-18 months after acceptance. Writer's guidelines and book catalog free.

Advice: "I would like to see more good fiction, period, but it *has* to be about Newfoundland or by a Newfoundlander (note that these are entirely discrete categories) I don't want any more mss about the Vietnam War or running a radio station in Kansas City or the like! Our readers will not buy that from us."

*DAN RIVER PRESS, (I,II), Conservatory of American Letters, Box 298, Thomaston ME 04861. (207)354-0998. President: Robert Olmsted. Fiction Editor: R.S. Danbury III. Estab. 1976. Publishes hardcover and paperback originals. Books: 60 lb. offset paper; offset printing; perfect (paperback); hardcover binding; illustrations; average print order: 1,000; first novel print order: 1,000. Averages 4-5 total titles; 3 fiction titles last year.

• Dan River Press publishes *Dan River Anthology* and a new magazine, *Northwoods Journal*, listed in this book.

Needs: Adventure, contemporary, experimental, fantasy, historical, horror, humor/satire, literary, mainstream, military/war, psychic/supernatural/occult, regional, science fiction, short story collections, western. "We want good fiction that can't find a home in the big press world. No mindless stuff written flawlessly." Published *Bound*, by William Hoffman, (novel); *Blue Collar and Other Stories*, by Tom Laird (short story collection); *The Dreams are Dying*, by Everett Whealdon. Published new writers within the last year.

How to Contact: Accepts unsolicited mss, "but get guidelines. Large SASE (IRCs) please."

Terms: Pays $250 cash advance (minimum) on acceptance; 10% royalties on 1,000 copies, then 15%. Sends galleys to author. After acceptance, publication "depends on many things (funding, etc.). Probably in six months once funding is achieved." Writer's guidelines for #10 SAE and 2 first-class stamps. Book catalog for 6×9 SAE and 2 first-class stamps.

Advice: "Submit to us (and any other small press) when you have exhausted all hope for big press publication. Then, do not expect the small press to be a big press. We lack the resources to do things like 'promotion,' 'author's tours.' These things either go undone or are done by the author. When you give up on marketability of any novel submitted to small press, adopt a different attitude. Become humble, as you get to work on your second/next novel, grow, correct mistakes and create an audience. Remember . . . logic dictates that a small press can *not* market successfully. If they could, they'd be a large press, with no time for unknowns."

JOHN DANIEL AND COMPANY, PUBLISHERS, (I, II), Box 21922, Santa Barbara CA 93121. (805)962-1780. Fiction Editor: John Daniel. Estab. 1980; reestablished 1985. Small publisher with plans to expand. Publishes paperback originals. Books: 55-65 lb. book text paper; offset printing; perfect-bound paperbacks; illustrations sometimes; average print order: 2,000; first novel print order: 2,000. Plans 2 first novels this year. Averages 5 total titles, 2-3 fiction titles each year. Sometimes critiques rejected ms.
Needs: "I'm open to all subjects (including nonfiction)." Literary, mainstream, short story collections. No pornographic, exploitive, illegal or badly written fiction. Recently published *The Year of the Buck and Other Stories,* by Susan Harper; *Heaven Lies About, Southern Stories,* by Maclin Bocock; *Virgil Hunter, a novel,* by James M. Bellarosa. Published new writers within the last year.
How to Contact: Accepts unsolicited mss. Query first. SASE (IRCs). Submit outline/synopsis and 2 sample chapters. Reports in 3 weeks on queries; 2 months on mss. Simultaneous submissions OK.
Terms: Pays in royalties of 10% of net minimum. Sends galleys to author.
Advice: Encourages first novelists. "As an acquiring editor, I would never sign a book unless I were willing to publish it in its present state. Once the book is signed, though, I, as a developmental editor, would do hard labor to make the book everything it could become. Read a lot, write a lot, and stay in contact with other artists so you won't burn out from this, the loneliest profession in the world."

‡DARE TO DREAM BOOKS, (II), #112, 5062 S. 108th St., Omaha NE 68137-2314. (402)455-4946. Editor/Owner: Tony McCawley. Estab. 1993. "Two-person part-time publisher of personalized fictional novels." Paperback originals. Books: laser compatible paper; high speed laser printing; glue binding paperback; photograph on book cover. Plans 4 first novels this year. Averages 8 total titles each year. Often comments on rejected ms.
● This is a very new publisher with a unique approach. Books are "personalized" for the reader. A reader fills out information about him/herself and it is input into the book. Write for more details.
Needs: Adventure, fantasy (space fantasy, sword and sorcery), humor/satire, mystery/suspense (amateur sleuth, private eye/hardboiled), romance (contemporary, futuristic/time travel, gothic, historical, romantic suspense), western (frontier saga, traditional), young adult (adventure, fantasy/science fiction, mystery/suspense, sports, western). "Romance is our highest priority." No "children's or murders stories of any kind."
How to Contact: Accepts unsolicited mss. Submit outline/synopsis and first 3 sample chapters. Include estimated word count and detailed synopsis. Send a disposable copy of ms. Reports on mss in 1-2 months. Simultaneous submissions and electronic (disk or modem) submissions OK.
Terms: Pays $1,000-1,500 up front. Royalties paid starting with very first copy printed. Pays royalties of 35¢/copy. Sends galleys to author upon request. Publishes ms 6-12 months after acceptance. Writer's guidelines free.
Advice: "We want characters that are high profile, i.e. rich, powerful, famous, moviestars, ceos, presidents, etc. But also characters must be desirable and hero type. No murders—low violence characters who have only one lover, and no past lovers introduced into the book."

*MAY DAVENPORT PUBLISHERS, (I, II, IV), 26313 Purissima Rd., Los Altos Hills CA 94022. (415)948-6499. Editor/Publisher: May Davenport. Estab. 1975. One-person operation with independent subcontractors. Publishes hardcover and paperback originals. Books: 65-80 lb. paper; off-set printing; perfect binding/saddle-stitched/plastic spirals; line drawings; average print order 500-3,000; average first novel print order: 3,000. Plans 1-3 first novels this year. Averages 3-5 total titles/year (including coloring books/reprints); 2-5 fiction titles/year. Sometimes critiques rejected ms.
Needs: "Overstocked with picture book mss. Prefer drama for junior and senior high students. Don't preach. Entertain!" Recently published *Tug of War,* by Barbara A. Scott (novel); *A Fine Line,* by Constance D. Casserly (novel); *The Candy Heart,* by Carol De Wolf (children's story).
How to Contact: Query first with SASE (IRCs). Agented fiction 2%. Reports in 2-3 weeks.
Terms: Pays royalties of 10-15%; no advance. Sends galleys to author. "*Partial subsidy whenever possible in advance sales of 3,000 copies, which usually covers the printing and binding costs only.* The authors are usually teachers in school districts who have a special book of fiction or textbook relating to literature." Writer's guidelines free with SASE.
Advice: "Personal tip: Combat illiteracy by creating material which will motivate children/young adults to enjoy words and actions. Inquire first with SASE since we do not like to duplicate our animal narrators such as zoo animals or domestic pets. We already have enough of picture book stories. Try writing third person perspective novels for youg adults. Create youthful characters and make them come alive on the pages."

DAWNWOOD PRESS, (III, IV), 5th Floor, 387 Park Ave. S., New York NY 10016-8810. (212)532-7160. Fax: (212)213-2495. President: Kathryn Drayton. Fiction Editor: John Welch. Estab. 1984. Publishes hardcover originals. Books: 60 lb. Lakewood-white paper; offset litho printing; adhesive case binding; average print order: 5,000. Averages 1 fiction title each year.
Needs: Contemporary. "Our needs are taken care of for the next 2 years." No experimental. Published *History's Trickiest Questions*, by Paul Kuttner (history); *The Iron Virgin*, by Paul Kuttner.
How to Contact: Does not accept unsolicited mss. Submit through agent only. Reports in 2 weeks. Simultaneous submissions OK.
Terms: Advance negotiable. Sends galleys to author.
Advice: "Same advice since Dickens's days: Tell a story from the opening sentence in easily understood English, and if you must philosophize do so through action and colloquial dialogue."

✿DUNDURN PRESS, (II), #301, 2181 Queen St. E., Toronto, Ontario M4E 1E5 Canada. (416)698-0454. Editorial Contact Person: Kirk Howard. Estab. 1972. Subsidiaries include Hounslow Press and Simon & Pierre. Midsize independent publisher with plans to expand. Publishes hardcover and paperback originals.
Needs: Contemporary, literary.
How to Contact: Accepts unsolicited mss. Submit outline/synopsis and sample chapters. SASE for ms. Simultaneous submissions OK. Accepts electronic submissions.
Terms: Pays royalties of 10-15%; $1,000 average advance; 10 author's copies. Sends galleys to author. Publishes ms 6-9 months after acceptance. Writer's guidelines not available. Book catalog free on request for SASE.

E.M. PRESS, INC., (I, II), P.O. Box 4057, Manassas VA 22110. (703)754-0229. Editor: Beth Miller. Estab. 1991. "Small, traditional publishing company." Publishes paperback originals. Books: 50 lb. text paper; offset printing; perfect binding; illustrations; average print order: 1,200-5,000. Averages 3 total titles (all fiction) each year. If requested comments on rejected ms.
Needs: Adventure, childrens/juvenile, family saga, fantasy, horror, humor/satire, literary, mainstream/contemporary, military/war, mystery/suspense, romance, thriller/espionage. Recently published *Some Brief Cases of Inspector Alec Stuart of Scotland Yard*, by Archibald C. Wagner, MD (mystery); *The Search for Archerland*, by H.R. Coursen.
How to Contact: Accepts unsolicited mss. Submit outline/synopsis and sample chapters or complete ms with cover letter. Include estimated word count. Send a SASE (IRCs) for reply, return of ms or send a disposable copy of the ms. Agented fiction 10%. Reports in 1 month on queries; 2 months on mss. Simultaneous submissions OK.
Terms: Amount of royalties and advances vary. Sends galleys to author. Publishes ms 4-9 months after acceptance. Writer's guidelines for SASE.

EARTH-LOVE PUBLISHING HOUSE, (IV), Suite 353, 3440 Youngfield St., Wheatridge CO 80033. (303)233-9354. Fax: (303)233-9354. Director: Laodeciae Augustine. Estab. 1989. Small publisher. Publishes paperback originals and reprints. Books: 60 lb. paper; offset printing; sew and wrap binding; halftone illustrations; average print order: 5,000; first novel print order: 5,000. Averages 2 total titles, 1 fiction title each year. Often comments on rejected ms.
Needs: Adventure, metaphysical adventure, mystery/suspense (amateur sleuth), new age/mystic/spiritual.
How to Contact: Does not accept unsolicited mss. Query first. Include estimated word count and list of publishing credits with submission. SASE (IRCs). Reports in 3 weeks on queries; 5 weeks on mss. Simultaneous submissions OK. Accepts electronic (disk) submissions.
Terms: Pays royalties of 8% minimum; 12% maximum or 10% of run for author's copies. Publishes ms 6-10 months after acceptance.

THE ECCO PRESS, (II), 100 W. Broad St., Hopewell NJ 08525. (609)466-4748. Editor-in-Chief: Daniel Halpern. Estab. 1970. Small publisher. Publishes hardcover and paperback originals and reprints. Books: acid-free paper; offset printing; Smythe-sewn binding; occasional illustrations. Averages 25 total titles, 10 fiction titles each year. Average first novel print order 3,000 copies.
 • Ecco Press publishes the prestigious literary *Antaeus*, listed in this book.
Needs: Literary and short story collections. "We can publish possibly one or two original novels a year." No science fiction, romantic novels, western (cowboy). Recently published: *Where Is Here*, by Joyce Carol Oates; *Have You Seen Me*, by Elizabeth Graver; *Coming Up Down Home*, by Cecil Brown.

How to Contact: Accepts unsolicited mss. Query first, especially on novels, with SASE. Reports in 2 to 3 months, depending on the season.
Terms: Pays in royalties. Advance is negotiable. Writer's guidelines for SASE. Book catalog free on request.
Advice: "We are always interested in first novels and feel it's important that they be brought to the attention of the reading public."

THE EIGHTH MT. PRESS, (II, IV), 624 SE 29th Ave., Portland OR 97214. (503)233-3936. Publisher: Ruth Gundle. Estab. 1984. One-person operation on full-time basis. Publishes paperback originals. Books: acid-free paper; perfect-bound; average print order: 5,000. Averages 2 total titles, 1 fiction title each year.
Needs: Books written only by women. Ethnic, feminist, lesbian, literary, short story collections. Recently published *Cows and Horses*, by Barbara Wilson (feminist/literary); *Minimax*, by Anna Livia.
How to Contact: Accepts unsolicited mss. Query first. SASE (IRCs). Reports on queries in 2 weeks; on mss in 3 weeks.
Terms: Pays royalties of 8-10%. Sends galleys to author. Publishes ms within 1 year of acceptance.
Advice: "Query first! And present a clear and concise description of the project along with your publication credits, if any."

FABER AND FABER, INC., (I, II), 50 Cross St., Winchester MA 01890. Small trade house which publishes literary fiction and collections. Averages 4-6 fiction titles each year.
Needs: Literary. No mystery, romances, thrillers, juvenile, please. Allow 2 months for response. Recently published *The Loop*, by Joe Coomer; *Secret Language*, by Monica Wood; *Bluesman*, by Andre Dubus III.
How to Contact: Prefers query and one or two sample chapters with SASE (IRCs) for reply. Requires synopsis/description—cannot consider ms without this. Address to Publishing Assistant.
Advice: "Accepting very little original fiction at present."

FASA CORPORATION, (II, IV), B305, 1100 W. Cermac, Chicago IL 60608. Editor: Donna Ippolito. "Company responsible for science fiction, adventure games, to include adventures, scenarios, game designs and novels, for an audience high school age and up." Published new writers within the last year. Publishes 12 novels/year and 30 game products/year.
Needs: Adventure, science fiction. Publishes ms an average of 9 months to 1 year after acceptance. Occasionally critiques or comments on rejected ms. Recommends other markets.
How to Contact: Query first. Reports in 2-6 weeks. Simultaneous submissions OK. Accepts electronic submissions via IBM ASCII or Macintosh disks.
Terms: Pays on publication for all rights. Sends galleys to author.
Advice: "Must be familiar with our product and always ask about suitability before plunging into a big piece of work that I may not be able to use. Writers *must* write to spec. Interested in writers for line of fiction and in writing for game products."

THE FEMINIST PRESS AT THE CITY UNIVERSITY OF NEW YORK, 311 E. 94th St., New York NY 10128. (212)360-5790. Publisher: Florence Howe. Estab. 1970. "Nonprofit, tax-exempt, education organization interested in changing the curriculum, the classroom and consciousness." Publishes hardcover and paperback reprints. "We use a fine quality paper, perfect bind our books, four color covers; and some cloth for library sales if the book has been out of print for some time; we shoot from the original text when possible. We always include a scholarly and literary afterword, since we are introducing a text to a new audience; average print run: 4,000." Publishes no original fiction. Averages 8-10 total titles/year; 3-5 fiction titles/year (reprints of feminist classics only).
Needs: Contemporary, ethnic, feminist, gay, lesbian, literary, regional, science fiction, translations, women's.
How to Contact: Accepts unsolicited mss. Query first. Submit outline/synopsis and 1 sample chapter. SASE (IRC). Reports in 2 weeks on queries; 2 months on mss. Simultaneous submissions OK.
Terms: Pays royalties of 10% of net sales; $100 advance; 10 author's copies. Sends galleys to author. Book catalog free on request.

Read the Business of Fiction Writing section to learn the correct way to prepare and submit a manuscript.

FIRE ISLAND PRESS, (II, IV), Liberation Inc., Room 203B, 89 Robin Lane, Fairfield CT 06430-3939. (203)330-9596. President: Joseph Letendre. Estab. 1991. "Three-person operation." Publishes paperback originals. Books: 50 lb. paper; perfect binding; average print order: 4,000. Plans 4 first novels this year. Averages 6 titles, all fiction. Sometimes comments on rejected mss.
  • Other imprints of Liberation Inc. include Lavender Press and Marie's Books also listed in this section.
Needs: Erotica (gay and lesbian). Especially "a need for lesbian erotica. No S & M." Published *Flesh Fable*, by Aaron Travis (gay erotica) and *Bitter Beauties*, by Tripp Vandertord (gay erotica).
How to Contact: Does not accept unsolicited mss. Submit outline/synopsis and 3 sample chapters. Include estimated word count. SASE. Reports in 2 months. Simultaneous submissions OK.
Terms: Pays royalties of 10% minimum; 25% maximum. Average advance: $250. Sends galleys to author. Book catalog free.
Advice: "The demand for erotica has increased, I believe, due to the crisis of AIDS."

FIREBRAND BOOKS, (II), 141 The Commons, Ithaca NY 14850. (607)272-0000. Contact: Nancy K. Bereano. Estab. 1985. Publishes quality trade paperback originals. Averages 8-10 total titles each year.
Needs: Feminist, lesbian. Recently published *Cecile*, by Ruthann Robson (short stories); *The Gilda Stories*, by Jewelle Gomez (novel).
How to Contact: Accepts unsolicited mss. Submit outline/synopsis and sample chapters or send complete ms with cover letter. SASE (IRCs). Reports in 2 weeks on queries; 2 months on mss. Simultaneous submissions OK with notification.
Terms: Pays royalties.

*FLORIDA LITERARY FOUNDATION PRESS, (II), distributed by Woldt Corp., 2516 Ridge Ave., Sarasota FL 34235. (813)957-1281. Chairman: Virginia G. McClintock. Fiction Editor: Patrick J. Powers. Estab. 1989. "Nonprofit literary foundation." Publishes paperback originals. Books: quality trade paper. Averages 4-5 total titles, 1 anthology fiction title each year. Sometimes comments on rejected ms.
  • Woldt Corp. also distributes books by Starbooks listed in this book.
Needs: Literary. "Quality work on any subject—nothing clichéd." Recently published *The Princess' Lover*, by Elizabeth Clough (novel); *Whores of Suma-kand*, by Arpine K. Grenier (poetry).
How to Contact: Submit outline/synopsis and sample chapters. SASE (IRCs). Reports in 1 month on queries; 6 weeks on mss. Simultaneous submissions OK. Accepts electronic submissions.
Terms: Provides 10-50 author's copies, honorarium; payment depends on grant/award money. Individual arrangement with author depending on the book. *Specialists in subsidy publishing*. Sends galleys to author. Publishes ms 6-8 months after acceptance. Writer's guidelines free.

FOUR WALLS EIGHT WINDOWS, (II), #503, 39 W. 14th St., New York NY 10011. (212)206-8965. Co-Publishers: John Oakes/Dan Simon. Estab. 1986. "We are a small independent publisher." Publishes hardcover and paperback originals and paperback reprints. Books: quality paper; paper or cloth binding; illustrations sometimes; average print order: 3,000-7,000; first novel print order: 3,000-5,000. Averages 15 total titles/year; approximately 3-4 fiction titles/year.
  • Four Walls Eight Windows' books have received mention from the *New York Times* as "Notable Books of the Year" and have been nominated for *LA Times* fiction prizes.
Needs: Literary. Recently published *Flan*, by Stephen Tunney; *The Bodhrau Makers*, by John B. Keane; *Simple Passion*, by Annie Ernaux.
How to Contact: "Query letter accompanied by sample chapter and SASE is best. Useful to know if writer has published elsewhere, and if so, where." Accepts unsolicited mss. Submit outline/synopsis and 1 sample chapter. SASE (IRCs). Agented fiction 70%. Reports in 2 months on mss. Simultaneous submissions OK.
Terms: Pays standard royalties; advance varies. Sends galleys to author. Book catalog free on request.
Advice: "We get 2,000 or so submissions a year: 1. Learn what our taste is, first; 2. Be patient."

GAY SUNSHINE PRESS AND LEYLAND PUBLICATIONS, (IV), P.O. Box 410690, San Francisco CA 94141. (707)996-6082. Editor: Winston Leyland. Estab. 1970. Publishes hardcover and paperback originals. Books: natural paper; perfect-bound; illustrations; average print order: 5,000-10,000.
  • Gay Sunshine Press received a 1992 Lamba Book Award for *Gay Roots* (volume 1), named "Best Book by a Gay or Lesbian Press."

Needs: Literary, experimental, translations—all gay male material only. "We desire fiction on gay themes of *high* literary quality and prefer writers who have already had work published in literary magazines. We also publish erotica—short stories and novels." Published *Crystal Boys*, by Pai Hsien-yung (novel).
How to Contact: "Do not send an unsolicited manuscript." Query with SASE (IRCs). Reports in 3 weeks on queries; 2 months on mss. Send $1 for catalog.
Terms: Negotiates terms with author. Sends galleys to author. Pays royalties or by outright purchase.
Advice: "We continue to be interested in receiving queries from authors who have book-length manuscripts of high literary quality. We feel it is important that an author know exactly what to expect from our press (promotion, distribution, etc.) before a contract is signed. Before submitting a query or manuscript to a particular press, obtain critical feedback from knowledgeable people on your manuscript. If you alienate a publisher by submitting a manuscript shoddily prepared/typed, or one needing very extensive rewriting, or one which is not in the area of the publisher's specialty, you will surely not get a second chance with that press."

✹GOOSE LANE EDITIONS, (I, II, IV), 469 King St., Fredericton, New Brunswick E3B 1E5 Canada. (506)450-4251. Acquisitions Editor: Laurel Boone. Estab. 1957. Publishes hardcover and paperback originals and occasional reprints. Books: some illustrations; average print run: 2,000; first novel print order: 1,500. Averages 12 total titles, 2-4 fiction each year.
Needs: Contemporary, historical, literary, short story collections. "Not suitable for mainstream or mass-market submissions." Recently published *Fadimatu*, by Jennifer Mitton (novel); *Je t'aime Cowboy*, by T.F. Rigelhoff (stories); *Dawson City Seven*, by Don Reddick (novel).
How to Contact: Considers unsolicited mss; complete work, or "samples." Query first. SASE "with Canadian stamps, International Reply Coupons, cash, check or money order. No US stamps please." Reports in 6 months. Simultaneous submissions OK.
Terms: "We consider submissions from outside Canada only when they have a strong Canadian connection and exhibit outstanding literary skill." Pays royalties of 8% minimum; 12% maximum. Average advance: $100-200, negotiable. Sends galleys to author. Writers guidelines for 9×12 SAE and IRCs.

GRAYWOLF PRESS, (III), 2402 University Ave., St. Paul MN 55114. (612)641-0077. Publisher: Scott Walker. Estab. 1974. Growing small press, nonprofit corporation. Publishes hardcover and paperback originals and paperback reprints. Books: acid-free quality paper; offset printing; hardcover and soft binding; illustrations occasionally; average print order: 3,000-10,000; first novel print order: 2,000-6,000. Averages 18-20 total titles, 6-8 fiction titles each year. Occasionally critiques rejected ms. No genre books (romance, western, suspense).
- Graywolf Press books have won numerous awards. Most recently, *Cloud Street*, by Tim Winton received the Australian Miles Franklin Award; *Licorice*, by Abby Frucht received Quality Paperback Book's New Voices Award and *Skywater*, by Melinda Worth Popham received *Buzzworm*'s Edward Abbey Award. The press has recently started the Graywolf Discovery Series featuring reprint paperbacks of out-of-print "gems."
Needs: Literary, and short story collections. Published *The Last Studebaker*, by Robin Hemley (novel); *The Secret of Cartwheels*, by Patricia Henley (short stories); *Cloudstreet*, by Tim Winton (novel).
How to Contact: Query with SASE (IRCs). Reports in 2 weeks. Simultaneous submissions OK.
Terms: Pays in royalties of 7½-10%; negotiates advance and number of author's copies. Sends galleys to author. Free book catalog.

GRIFFON HOUSE PUBLICATIONS, Box 81, Whitestone NY 11357. (718)767-8380. President: Frank D. Grande. Estab. 1976. Small press. Publishes paperback originals and reprints.
Needs: Contemporary, literary, experimental, ethnic (open), translations, reprints, and multinational theory.
How to Contact: Query with SASE (IRCs). No simultaneous submissions. Reports in 1 month.
Terms: Pays in 6 free author's copies. No advance.

GRYPHON PUBLICATIONS, (I, II), Imprints include Gryphon Books, Gryphon Doubles, P.O. Box 209, Brooklyn NY 11228. (718)646-6126 (after 6 pm EST). Owner/Editor: Gary Lovisi. Estab. 1983. Small press. Publishes hardcover and paperback originals and trade paperback reprints. Books: bond paper; offset printing; perfect binding; average print order: 500-1,000. Published new writers within the last year. Plans 2 first novels this year. Averages 5-10 total titles, 4 fiction titles each year. Often comments on rejected ms.

Needs: Mystery/suspense (private eye/hardboiled, crime and true crime), science fiction (hard science/technological, soft/sociological), short story collections, thriller/espionage. No romance, westerns. Plans anthology of hardboiled crime fiction. Authors may submit story. Published *The Dreaming Detective*, by Ralph Vaughn (mystery-fantasy-horror); *The Woman in the Dugout*, by Gary Lovisi and T. Arnone (baseball novel); *A Mate for Murder*, by Bruno Fischer (hardboiled pulp). Publishes Gryphon Double novel series.

How to Contact: "I am not looking for novels now and *only* want to see a *1 page synopsis* with SASE (IRCs) for anything longer than 3,000 words." Include estimated word count, 50-word bio, short list of publishing credits, "how you heard about us." Send SASE for reply, return of ms or send a disposable copy of the ms. Agented fiction 5-10%. Reports in 2-4 weeks on queries; 2-6 weeks on mss. Simultaneous and electronic submissions OK (with hard copy—disk in ASCII).

Terms: For magazines, $5-45 on publication plus 2 contributor's copies; for novels/collections payment varies and is much more. Usually sends galleys to author. Publishes ms 1-3 years after acceptance. Writers guidelines and book catalog for SASE.

Advice: "I am looking for better and better writing, more cutting-edge material with *impact*! Keep it lean and focused."

✿**GUERNICA EDITIONS, (III, IV),** 3160 Avenue de Carignan, Montréal, Québec H1N 2Y5 Canada. Editor: Antonio D'Alfonso. Fiction Editor: Umberto Claudio. Editor for women's books: Julia Gualtieri. Estab. 1978. Publishes paperback originals. Books: offset printing; perfect/sewn binding; average print order: 1,000; average first novel print order: 1,000. Plans to publish 1 first novel this year. Publishes 16-20 total titles each year.

Needs: Contemporary, ethnic, literary, translations of foreign novels. Looking for novels about women and ethnic subjects. No unsolicited works. Published *Nice People: Dutch Short Stories*, edited by Gerri Bussink; *Benedetta in Guysterland*, by Giose Rimanellig; *Songs and Ballads*, by Federico Garcia Lorca.

How to Contact: Does not accept or return unsolicited mss. Query first. IRCs. 100% of fiction is agented. Reports in 6 months. Electronic submissions via IBM WordPerfect disks.

Terms: Pays royalties of 7-10% and 10 author's copies. Book catalog for SAE and $2 postage. (Canadian stamps only).

Advice: Publishing "more pocket books."

*****GUYASUTA PUBLISHER, (I,II),** Subsidiary of Lee Shore Agency, Sterling Bldg., 440 Friday Rd., Pittsburgh PA 15209. (412)821-6211. Imprint is One Foot on the Mountain Press. Acquisitions Manager: Anna Aivaliotis. Fiction Editor: Patrick Freeman. Estab. 1988. Publishes paperback originals. Books: offset printing; perfect-bound; illustrations; average print order: 750. Published new writers within the last year. Plans 4 first novels this year. Averages 30 total titles, 2 fiction titles each year. Sometimes comments on rejected ms.

Needs: Contemporary, erotica, short story collections. No "historical romances, experimental fiction, anything over 65,000 words."

How to Contact: Accepts unsolicited mss. Query first. SASE. Reports in 2 weeks on queries; 3 months on mss. Simultaneous submissions OK.

Terms: Pays royalties of 7% maximum. "We make individual arrangements with authors depending on the book. We do straight publishing and cooperative publishing. We send out press releases, include books in catalog, market mainly through mail and book conventions." Sends galleys to author. Publishes ms 6-9 months after acceptance. Writer's guidelines and book catalog for 4×9 SAE and 1 first-class stamp (IRCs).

Advice: "When submitting a manuscript do not send us your first draft. We will reject it. Work on your story, give it time to evolve. Read fiction and how-to books. Please type, double space and use healthy margins."

*****HEAVEN BONE PRESS, (II),** 86 Whispering Hills Dr., Chester NY 10918. (914)469-9018. Editor: Steve Hirsch. Estab. 1986. "Literary publisher." Publishes paperback originals. Books: paper varies; saddle or perfect binding; average print order: 2,000. Averages 4 total titles, 1 fiction title each year. Sometimes comments on rejected ms.

• See the listing for *Heaven Bone* magazine in this book.

Needs: Experimental, literary, new age/mystic spiritual, psychic/supernatural, science fiction (hard science/technological, soft/sociological).

How to Contact: Accepts unsolicited mss. Query first. Include estimated word count, short bio, list of publishing credits. SASE (IRCs). Agented fiction 10%. Reports in 1 month on queries; 6 months on mss. No simultaneous submissions. Accepts electronic submissions.

Terms: Pays author's copies (10% of press run); depends on grant/award money. "We also do cooperative arrangements or individual arrangement with author." Sends galleys to author. Publishes ms up to 18 months after acceptance. Writer's guidelines or book catalog for #10 SAE and 2 first-class stamps.
Advice: "Know our magazine, *Heaven Bone*, very well before attempting to be published by us. Looking for more experimental, surreal work—less workshop exercises."

HELICON NINE EDITIONS, (I,II), Subsidiary of Helicon Nine, Inc., 9000 W. 64th Terrace, Merrian KS 66202. (913)722-2999. Publisher/Editor: Gloria Vando Hickok. Estab. 1990. Small press publishing poetry, fiction, creative nonfiction and anthologies. Publishes paperback originals. Books: 70 lb. Vellum paper; offset printing; perfect-bound; 4-color cover; average print order: 1,000-5,000. Plans 8 total titles, 2-4 fiction titles this year.
Needs: Contemporary, ethnic, experimental, literary, short story collections, translations. "We're only interested in fine literature." Nothing "commercial." Recently published *Value of Kindness*, by Ellyn Bache; *Galaxy Girls: Wonder Women*, by Anne Whitney Pierce. Published new writers within the last year.
How to Contact: Does not accept unsolicited mss. Query first or submit outline/synopsis and sample chapter. SASE (IRCs). Reports in 1 week on queries; 3 months on mss.
Terms: Pays royalties, author's copies or honorarium. "Individual arrangement with author." Sends galleys to author. Publishes ms 1-6 months after acceptance. Writer's guidelines for SASE.
Advice: "Make it good. Check spelling and grammar before submitting. Be proud of your work. Submit a clean, readable copy in a folder or box—paginated with title and name on each page. Also, do not pre-design book, i.e. no illustrations—it's very amateurish. We'd like to see books that will be read 50-100 years from now. New classics."

‡HERBOOKS, (II,IV), P.O. Box 7467, Santa Cruz CA 95061. (408)425-7493. Contact: Irene Reti. Estab. 1984. "One-person lesbian feminist press, part-time basis." Publishes paperback originals. Books: 60 lb. paper; offset printing; perfect-bound; b&w photos and line drawings; average print order: 2,000; first novel print order: 1,500. Plans 2 total titles each year, 1 fiction title every other year. Sometimes comments on rejected ms "briefly."
Needs: Contemporary, ethnic, feminist, historical, lesbian. Looking for "Native-American lesbian fiction." No "sadomasochistic content; no work by men." Published new writers within the last year "in anthology form."
How to Contact: Accepts unsolicited mss. Query first. Reports in 2 weeks. Simultaneous submissions OK. Accepts electronic submissions via "Word 4.0 on disk for Mac."
Terms: Pays royalties of 10% minimum. Author's copies negotiable. Publishes ms 6-12 months after acceptance. Writer's guidelines and book catalog for #10 SAE with 45¢ postage.
Advice: "We primarily publish fiction in subject-oriented anthologies. Books by previously unpublished authors have not done well for us, and we can't afford to do many of them. Write for guidelines of current projects/anthologies. Look at other books published by HerBooks to see if you fit in our list. In 1994 HerBooks will sponsor our first lesbian novel contest. Write for details."

*HERITAGE PRESS, (II, IV), Box 18625, Baltimore MD 21216. (410)728-8521. President: Wilbert L. Walker. Estab. 1979. One-man operation, full-time basis; uses contractual staff as needed. Publishes hardcover originals. Books: 60 lb. white offset paper; offset printing; sewn hardcover binding; average print order: 2,000; first novel print order: 1,000. Averages 2 total titles, 1-2 fiction titles each year.
Needs: Ethnic (African-American). Interested in "fiction that presents a balanced portrayal of the black experience in America, from the black perspective. No fiction not dealing with African-Americans, or which views blacks as inferior." Published *Stalemate at Panmunjon* (the Korean War), and *Servants of All*, both by Wilbert L. Walker.
How to Contact: Does not accept unsolicited mss. Query first with SASE (IRCs). Simultaneous submissions OK. Reports in 2 weeks on queries; 2 months on mss. Publishes ms an average of 9 months after acceptance.
Terms: Must return advance if book is not completed or is unacceptable. *"We plan to subsidy publish only those works that meet our standards for approval.* No more than 1 or 2 a year. Payment for publication is based on individual arrangement with author." Book catalog free on request.
Advice: "Write what you know about. No one else can know and feel what it is like to be black in America better than one who has experienced our dichotomy on race." Would like to see new ideas with broad appeal. "First novels must contain previously unexplored areas on the black experience in

America. We regard the author/editor relationship as open, one of mutual respect. Editor has final decision, but listens to author's views."

‡HERMES HOUSE PRESS, (II), 113 Summit Ave., Brookline MA 02146. (617)566-9766. Publisher: Richard Mandell. Estab. 1980. Small press operation. Publishes paperback originals and reprints. Books: 70 lb. paper; offset printing; paper binding; illustrations; average print order: 1,000; first novel print order: 1,000. Plans 1-2 first novels this year. Averages 2 total titles, 1-2 fiction titles each year. Generally critiques rejected mss.

Needs: Contemporary, experimental, feminist, literary, short story collections, novellas and translations. No sexist, erotica, horror. Recently published *Three Stories*, by R.V. Cassill (short stories), *The Deadly Swarm & Other Stories*, by LaVerne Harrell Clark, *Bella B's Fantasy and Other Stories*, by Raymond Jean; and *O Loma! Constituting a Self*, by Kurt H. Wolff.

How to Contact: Not currently reading manuscripts. Reports in 3 weeks on queries; 2 months on mss. Publishes ms within 1 year after acceptance.

Terms: Pays in author's copies plus percentage above costs. Sends galleys to author.

Advice: Encourages first novelists. "We regard the author/editor relationship as open communication/ free dialogue. Be persistent."

✿HMS PRESS, (II), P.O. Box 340, Station B, London, Ontario N6A 4WI Canada. (519)434-4740. President: Wayne Ray. "One-person operation." Electronic Publisher (Books on Disc).

• HMS Press has changed its format from paperbound books to diskettes only.

Needs: Erotica, historical (general), humor/satire, literary, regional, essays, thesis, science fiction, war, crime, biography. Recently published *And Now We Meet* and *Desert*, by Robert McKay (science fiction); *In Flanders Fields*, by Planios/Malyon (essay).

How to Contact: Accepts unsolicited mss on disk. Query letter on disk or contact through FidoNet BBS, RelayNet BBS, CircuitNet BBS (Writer's Conference post to Wayne Ray). Send SASE (IRCs) for reply. Reports in 1 month. Simultaneous submissions OK. Accepts electronic submissions (IBM WP 5.1) only.

Terms: Pays royalties of 10% maximum or individual arrangement with author. Publishes upon acceptance. Book catalog free,

Advice: "Submit in Wordperfect of ASCII on 3" or 5" diskette well written mss any genre less than 350,000 words. Payment in kind."

*HOMESTEAD PUBLISHING, (I, II), Box 227, Moose WY 83012. (307)733-6248. Editor: Carl Schreier. Estab. 1980. Regional publishers for the Rocky Mountains, midsize firm. Publishes hardcover and paperback originals and reprints. Books: natural stock to enamel paper; web, sheet-feed printing; perfect or Smyth-sewn binding; b&w or color illustrations; average print order: 10,000; first novel print order: 2,000-5,000. Plans 1-2 first novels this year. Averages 16-20 total titles; 1-2 fiction titles each year. Sometimes critiques rejected ms.

Needs: Historical, juvenile (historical, wildlife), literary, preschool/picture book, short story collection, western, young adult/teen (10-18 years, historical). Looking for "good quality, well written and contemporary" fiction. Recently published *The Great Plains: A Young Reader's Journal*, by Bullock (children's natural history-adventure); *Tales of the Grizzly*, by Dr. Tim Clark and Denise Casey; *Murder in Jackson Hole*, by Jon Horton.

How to Contact: Accepts unsolicited mss. Query first. SASE (IRCs). Reports in 1 month. Sends galleys to author. Simultaneous submissions OK.

Terms: Pays royalties of 6-10%. Provides 6 author's copies. *Subsidy publishes "occasionally, depending on project."*

INDEPENDENCE PUBLISHERS OF GEORGIA INC., (I, II), 4771 E. Conway Dr., Atlanta GA 30327. (404)843-8084. Editor: Stanley Beitler. Associate Editor: Walter Sturdivant. Estab. 1992. Small press. Publishes hardcover originals. Books: offset, sheetfed printing; case binding; halftone and line illustrations and drawings; first novel print order: 2,500. Rarely critiques rejected ms.

Needs: Contemporary, experimental, historical, humor/satire, literary, mystery/suspense (cozy, private eye), regional, short story collections, thriller/espionage, translations, western (adult). Looks for "talented new and published writers of fiction and nonfiction." Published *Appalachian Patterns*, by Bo Ball (short-story collection).

How to Contact: Accepts unsolicited mss. Submit complete ms. SASE (IRCs) necessary for return of ms. Reports in 2 weeks on queries; 2 months on mss.
Terms: Pays royalties and advance.
Advice: Known for "quality fiction dealing with the human condition relative to one's environment. We are very flexible on themes and plots. We value a dramatic conflict involving characters that are deeply felt by the author. Essentially we look for good story telling and good to superior writing. We will work with an unpublished writer if we think he or she has superior talent."

INVERTED-A, INC., (II), 401 Forrest Hill, Grand Prairie TX 75051. (214)264-0066. Editors: Amnon and Aya Katz. Estab. 1977. A small press which evolved from publishing technical manuals for other products. "Publishing is a small part of our business." Publishes paperback originals. Books: bond paper; offset printing; illustrations; average print order: 250; first novel print order: 250. Publishes 2 titles a year, "in recent years mostly poetry; fiction is now about every other year." Also publishes a periodical *Inverted-A, Horn*, which appears irregularly and is open to very short fiction as well as excerpts from unpublished longer fiction.
Needs: "We are interested in justice and freedom approached from a positive and romantic perspective." Published *The Few Who Count*, by Aya Katz (novel); *Damned in Hell*, by A.A. Wilson (novella); *Inverted Blake* (collection); *Inverted Blake #2* (collection); *Undimmed by Tears* (collection).
How to Contact: Submit query with sample. SASE (IRCs). Reports in 6 weeks on queries; 3 months on mss. Simultaneous submissions OK. Accepts electronic submissions via modem or ASCII file on a pc MSDOS diskette. Electronic submission mandatory for final ms of accepted work.
Terms: "We do not pay except for author's copies." Sends galleys to author. For current list send SAE and 1 first-class stamp.
Advice: "Our volume is very small. You must hit home with subject and execution that are exceptional. We do not care about your credentials. We judge only by what we read."

‡■*IRONWOOD PRESS, INC., (I, II), P.O. Box 684, Winona MN 55987. (507)454-7524. Owner: Jack Larson. Estab. 1987. Book packager/manufacturer. Publishes paperback originals. Books: 60 lb. book paper; offset printing; perfect-bound; line illustrations/occasional photo; average print order: 1,000. Plans 3 first novels this year. Averages 5 total titles, 3 fiction titles each year. Often comments on rejected mss.
  ● This book manufacturer usually produces books for a fee, however, the owner is interested in producing his own anthologies and seeks short stories for inclusion. If a novel has merit, he may also consider co-publishing arrangements.
Needs: Short story collections: historical (general), humor/satire, literary, regional, religious/inspirational (general). Looking for human nature-interpersonal relationship (for anthology). Publishes anthology. Editors select stories by individual merit. Recently published *Just This Side of Fargo*, by Scott Olson (fiction); *Sylvia Plath is Dead, Pat's Last Portrait*, by R. Terry Syncoff (fiction). Publishes the Riverland Writer's Series. Published new writers within the last year.
How to Contact: Accepts unsolicited mss. Submit complete ms with cover letter. Include list of publishing credits. Reports in 6 weeks. Simultaneous submissions OK.
Terms: Pays royalties (negotiated), author's copies (negotiable) or makes individual arrangement on project basis. Usually pays in author copies. Will consider cooperative efforts. Will manufacture, but not with Ironwood imprint. Sends galleys to author. Writer's guidelines free for #10 SASE.
Advice: "Short, short, short. Stories, poetry and sharp commentary on timely issues. True human nature is not 'politically correct' and is not timely."

ISLAND HOUSE, (IV), 519½ Capp St., San Francisco CA 94110. (415)488-9002. Imprint: Cottage Books. Senior Editor: Susan Sullivan. Fiction Editor: Pat Healy. Estab. 1987. "Small Press, four person, full time." Publishes paperback originals. Books: acid-free paper; offset printing; perfect-bound; average print order: 2-3,000. Published new writers within the last year. Averages 3 total titles, 2 fiction titles each year. Sometimes comments on rejected ms; *$75 charge for critiques*.

Market categories: (I) Open to new writers; (II) Open to both new and established writers; (III) Interested mostly in established writers; (IV) Open to writers whose work is specialized.

Needs: Ethnic, experimental, faction, literary and short story collections. Looking for Irish-Celtic themes and quality. Published *The West*, by Ed Stack (short stories).
How to Contact: No unsolicited mss. Query first. Agented fiction 50%. Reports in 2 weeks on queries; 3 months on mss. Simultaneous submissions OK.
Terms: Pays royalties of 6-10%; offers negotiable advance. Sends galleys to author. Publishes ms 6-9 months after acceptance. Book catalog free.

ITALICA PRESS, (I, II, IV), #605, 595 Main St., New York NY 10044. (212)935-4230. Publishers: Eileen Gardiner and Ronald G. Musto. Estab. 1985. Small independent publisher. Publishes paperback originals. Books: 50-60 lb. natural paper; offset printing; Smythe-sewn binding; illustrations; average print order: 1,500. "First time translators published. We would like to see translations of Italian writers well-known in Italy who are not yet translated for an American audience." Publishes 6 total titles each year; 2 fiction titles. Sometimes critiques rejected mss.
Needs: Translations from Italian. Looking for "4 novels over next two years—exclusively translations of 20th Century Italian literature." Published *Dolcissimo*, by Giuseppe Bonaviri; *Man of Smoke*, by Aldo Palazzeschi; *Otronto*, by Maria Corti.
How to Contact: Accepts unsolicited mss. Query first. Reports in 3 weeks on queries; 2 months on mss. Simultaneous submissions OK. Electronic submissions via Macintosh disk.
Terms: Pays in royalties of 5-15% and 10 author's copies. Sends pre-publication galleys to author. Book catalog free on request.
Advice: "A *brief* call saves a lot of postage. 90% of the proposals we receive are completely off base—but we are very interested in things that are right on target. Send return postage if you want your manuscripts back."

✸JESPERSON PRESS LTD., (I), 39 James Lane, St. John's, Newfoundland A1E 3H3 Canada. (709)753-0633. Trade Editor: Albert Johnson. Midsize independent publisher. Publishes hardcover and paperback originals. Averages 7-10 total titles, 1-2 fiction titles each year. Sometimes comments on rejected ms.
Needs: Adventure, fantasy, humor/satire, juvenile (5-9 yrs. including: animal, easy-to-read, fantasy, historical, sports, spy/adventure, contemporary). Published *Daddy's Back*, by Barbara Ann Lane; *Fables, Fairies & Folklore of Newfoundland*, by Miké McCarthy and Alice Lannon; *Justice for Julie*, by Barbara Ann Lane. Published new writers within the last year.
How to Contact: Accepts unsolicited mss. Submit complete manuscript with cover letter. SASE (IRCs). Reports in 3 months on mss.
Terms: Pays negotiable royalties. Sends galleys to author. Book catalog free.

*JORDAN ENTERPRIZES PUBLISHING COMPANY, (II), P.O Box 15111, St. Louis MO 63110. Managing Editor: Patrique Quintahlen. Estab. 1990. Publishes hardcover and paperback originals and reprints. Books: 50-60 lb weight paper; perfect-bound; artists on staff for illustrations; average print order: 1,000-15,000. Averages 3 total titles; 2 fiction titles each year. *Offers editorial/publishing consultations services for new/unpublished writers for a fee.* Query for details.
Needs: Adventure, contemporary, ethnic, experimental, fantasy, historical, juvenile (animal, easy-to-read, fantasy, historical, contemporary), literary, mainstream, preschool/picture book, romance (contemporary, historical), science fiction, young adult/teen (easy-to-read, fantasy/science fiction, historical, problem novels, romance). "Looking for contemporary juvenile novels, interesting settings." No horror, gore, erotica, gay or occult novels. No sexism, racism or pornography. Published *The Strawberry Fox* (first reader), *The Strawberry Fox*, by Prentiss Van Daves illustrations by Nancy Dominique James (a play for children of all ages); *The Christmas Toy Welcome*.
How to Contact: Accepts unsolicited mss. Query first. Submit outline/synopsis with 3 sample chapters. SASE (IRCs). 50% of fiction is agented. Reports in 4 months on queries; in 6 months on mss. Accepts disk submissions from Macintosh Plus.
Terms: Pays royalties of 8-10%; average advance $500-5,000; advance is negotiable; advance is more for agented ms. Provides 50 author's copies. Sends galleys to author. *Subsidy publishes 1% of books each year.* Subsidy publishes books of poetry only, 50-150 pages. Subjects: love, psychology, philosophy, new male/female relationships, family.
Advice: "Devote 90% of your time to finding an agent. To save time and expense, it is recommended that authors learn as much as possible about not simply their writing craft, but also the very art of publishing. I recommend studying self publishing at some point after the author has completed several works, learning the actual book making process, book design, marketing, sales, distribution, and publishing and the money saving typesetting advantages of today's word processing and computer options."

This advice is to speed the 'submission-to-publication' process between author and small press operations. This is valuable in respect to new unpublished authors. The classical submissions methods of ms to major publishers still remains an important option to the author with a book with commercial value. For literary works of the highest quality small presses are the proven markets for success to the professional and the literary author."

KITCHEN TABLE: WOMEN OF COLOR PRESS (II, IV), Box 908, Latham NY 12110. Publisher: Barbara Smith. Estab. 1981. "Independent press with several paid employees, very good distribution." Publishes paperback originals. Books: 50 lb stock paper; offset/web press printing; perfect binding; some b&w graphic elements/designs; average print order: 5,000; first novel print order: 3,000. "All of our books are trade paperbacks, a few of which are bound for libraries." Averages 2 total titles each year; 1 fiction title every two years. Occasionally critiques rejected ms.
Needs: Ethnic, feminist, lesbian, literary, short story collections. "We do publish anthologies that are thematic. Writers may submit work in response to our specific calls for submissions for each title. Often because of the specialized nature of the subject matter, writers in the field are identified and contacted by the anthology editors." Needs for novels include novels by women of color—authors that reflect in some way the experiences of women of color. "We are looking for high quality, politically conscious writing and would particularly like to hear from Native American women fiction writers." Has published *Cuentos: Stories by Latinas*, edited by Alma Gómez, Cherríe Moraga; Mariana Romo-Carmona (short story anthology with selections in both English and Spanish); and *Seventeen Syllables and Other Stories*, by Hishye Yamamoto.
How to Contact: Accepts unsolicited mss. Query first. Submit outline/synopsis and 3 sample chapters. SASE (IRCs). Reports in 1 month on queries; 6 months on mss. Simultaneous submissions OK.
Terms: Pays in royalties of 7% minimum; 10% maximum and 10 author's copies. Sends galleys to author. Book catalog for 2 first-class stamps.
Advice: "One of the most common mistakes that our press tries to address is the notion that the first work a writer publishes should be a book as opposed to a submission to a periodical. Periodicals serve as a very valuable apprenticeship for a beginning writer. They should submit work to appropriate literary and other kinds of journals that publish fiction. By appropriate I mean appropriate for the kind of writing they do. Getting published in periodicals gives the writer experience and also creates a 'track record' that may interest the prospective book publisher."

KRUZA KALEIDOSCOPIX, INC., (IV), Box 389, Franklin MA 02038. (508)528-6211. Editor/President: J.A. Kruza. Fiction Editor: R. Burbank. Estab. 1976. Publishes hardcover and paperback originals. Books: 60-80 lb. coated paper; offset printing; saddle and perfect binding; illustrations; average print order: 10,000. Averages 12 total titles each year. Sometimes critiques rejected ms.
Needs: Historical (nautical); juvenile (5-9 yrs., including: animal, lesson teachings about work ethic, historical). "Stories for children, ages 3-7, with problem and characters who work out solution to problem, i.e. work ethic."
How to Contact: Accepts and returns unsolicited mss. Submit complete ms with cover letter. SASE (IRCs). Reports in 3 weeks on queries; 3 months on mss. Simultaneous submissions OK.
Terms: *Charges $3 reading fee.* Flat fee, depending on strength of story. Provides 10 author's copies. Writer's guidelines for #10 SAE with 1 first-class stamp.

LAVENDER PRESS, (II), Liberation Inc., Room 203A, 89 Robin Lane, Fairfield CT 06430-3939. Editor: Peter Daniels. Estab. 1990. "Three-person operation." Publishes paperback originals. Books: 50 lb. paper; stitch or perfect binding; average print order: 4,000; first novel print order: 4,500. Plans 3 first novels this year. Averages 6 total titles, all fiction, each year. Sometimes comments on rejected mss.
 • This press won the Lambda Gay Science Fiction Award for *Secret Matter*, by Toby Johnson, in 1990. Other imprints of Liberation Inc. include Fire Island and Marie's Books.
Needs: Gay, lesbian. Especially interested in "gay and lesbian science fiction, westerns. No gay romances." Recently published *Getting Life in Perspective*, by Toby Johnson (gay/spiritual/ghost); *We're Not Alone*, by Rik Isensee (gay/youth).
How to Contact: Does not accept unsolicited mss. Submit outline/synopsis and 3 sample chapters. Should include estimated word count. SASE (IRCs). Agented fiction 20%. Reports in 1 month on queries; 2 months on manuscripts.
Terms: Pays royalties of 10% minimum; 25% maximum. Average advance: $500. Sends galleys to author. Publishes up to 1 year after acceptance. Book catalog for #10 SAE and 1 first-class stamp.

LEE & LOW BOOKS, (I, II), 14th Floor, 228 E. 45th St., New York NY 10017. (212)867-6155. Fax: (212)338-9059. Publisher: Philip Lee. Estab. 1991. "Independent multicultural children's book publisher." Publishes hardcover originals. Averages 6 total titles, 4-6 fiction titles each year. Sometimes comments on rejected ms.
Needs: Children's/juvenile (preschool/picture book, historical, multicultural). Recently published *Abuela's Weave*, by Omar Castãneda (hardcover picture book); *Baseball Saved Us*, by Ken Mochizuki (hardcover picture book); *Joshua's Masai Mask*, by Dakari Hru (hardcover picture book).
How to Contact: Accepts unsolicited mss. Query first then submit outline/synopsis and 2 sample chapters, complete ms with cover letter or through an agent. Include estimated word count and bio (no more than one page). Send SASE for reply, return of ms or send a disposable of the ms. Agented fiction 30%. Reports in 3-5 weeks on queries; 4-6 weeks on mss. Simultaneous submissions OK.
Terms: Pays royalties. Offers advance. Sends galleys to author. Publishes ms 18 months after acceptance. Writer's guidelines for #10 SASE and 1 first-class stamp. Book catalog for SASE.
Advice: "Writers should familiarize themselves with the styles and formats of recently published children's books. Lee & Low Books is a multicultural children's book publisher. We would like to see more contemporary stories set in the U.S. Animal stories and folktales are discouraged."

‡✿**LES ÉDITIONS DE L'INSTANT MÊME, (I, II)**, C.P. 8, Succursale Haute-Ville, Québec City, Québec G1R 4M8 Canada. (418)527-8690. Fax: (418)681-6780. Directeur Littéraire (Publisher): Gilles Pellerin. Estab. 1986. "Small size independent literary publisher." Paperback originals (short story collections only). Plans 4 first novels this year. Averages 15-20 total titles each year. Always comments on rejected ms.
• The publisher has received the Prix Adrienne-Choquette de la Novelle for several years in a row, most recently for *Visa Pour le Réal* in 1993.
Needs: Short story collections: experimental, feminist, humor/satire, literary, mainstream contemporary, mystery/suspense (private eye/hardboiled), translations. Publishes anthologies of Mexican, Catalan, Irish short stories. Send stories to chargé de projet (editor and translator). Recently published *La Machine à Broyer les Petites Filles*, by Tonino Benacquista (hardboiled); *Visa Pour le Réal*, by Bertrand Bergeron (fantastic and science fiction); *La Déconvenue*, by Louise Cotnoir (feminist). Published new writers within the last year. Publishes collections (1 a year) of detective and hardboiled short stories.
How to Contact: Accepts unsolicited mss. Submit outline/synopsis and sample chapters or complete ms with cover letter. Include estimated word count. Send SASE (or IRC) for reply, return of ms or send a disposable copy of ms. Agented fiction 10%. Reports in 2 months on queries; 8 months on mss. Simultaneous submissions OK.
Terms: Pays royalties of 10-16%. Offers advance (only on collections). Sends galleys to author. Publishes ms 1 year after acceptance. Writer's guidelines free.
Advice: Accepting "more fiction than in our first years of publishing. Why? We've enlarged the publishing to short story writers out of Québec (Canada, France, Belgium, Catalogna, Mexico). Do not consider the short story as a kind of novel (and don't give us a listing of summaries and hope the book will be a best seller)."

✿**LESTER PUBLISHING LIMITED, (II)**, 507A, 56 The Esplanade, Toronto, Ontario M5E 1A7 Canada. (416)362-1032. Fax: (416)362-1647. Assistant Editor: Janice Weaver. Estab. 1991. Small independent publisher. Publishes hardcover and paperback originals. Published new writers within the last year. Plans 2 first novels this year. Averages 20 total titles, 3-5 fiction titles each year. Sometimes comments on rejected mss.
Needs: Children's/juvenile (preschool/picture book), historical (general), humor/satire, literary, mainstream/contemporary, short story collections, young adult/teen (adventure, historical, mystery/suspense, problem novels). No romance or science fiction. Recently published *The Rose Tree*, by Mary Walkin Keane (literary); *Hockey Night in the Dominion of Canada*, by Eric Zweig (historical); *Talking Power*, by David Lewis Stein (contemporary).
How to Contact: Accepts unsolicited mss. Submit outline/synopsis and 2-3 sample chapters. Should include estimated word count and cover letter. Send SASE (IRC) for reply, return of ms or send a disposable copy of the ms. Agented fiction 60-75%. Reports in 1 month on queries; 6 months on manuscripts.

Terms: Pays royalties, negotiable advance and 6-10 author's copies. Sends galleys to author. Publishes ms 6-18 months after acceptance. Writer's guidelines and catalog free.

Advice: "Fiction is a risky venture, especially in Canada. We publish very little and all in trade paperback (with the exception of young adult fiction, which we do as hardcover originals). I think we will, frankly, do less and less fiction and fewer first-time authors. Although we do not require them, an initial query letter is useful."

‡*LIBRA PUBLISHERS, INC., (II), Suite 383, 3089C Clairemont Dr., San Diego CA 92117. (619)571-1414. President: William Kroll. Estab. 1960. Small independent publisher. Hardcover and paperback originals. Books: 60 lb. offset paper; offset printing; hardcover—Smyth-sewn binding; paperback—perfect binding; illustrations occasionally; average print order 3,000; first novel print order 1,000+. Plans to publish 3 first novels this year. Averages approximately 15 total titles, 3-4 fiction titles each year.

Needs: "We consider all categories." Published *All God's Children*, by Alex LaPerchia (inspirational); *Seed of the Divine Fruit*, by Enrico Rinaldi (multi-generational about founding of Atlantic City); *Caveat Emptor*, by William Attias (racist takeover of a city).

How to Contact: Accepts unsolicited mss. Send complete ms with cover letter. SASE (IRCs). Reports on queries in 1 week; on mss in 2-3 weeks. Simultaneous submissions OK.

Terms: Pays 10-40% royalties. Sends galleys to author. Publishes ms an average of 6-12 months after acceptance. Book catalog for SAE with 5 first-class stamps.

Advice: "Libra publishes nonfiction books in all fields, specializing in the behavioral sciences. We also publish two professional journals: *Adolescence* and *Family Therapy*. We have published fiction on a royalty basis but because of the difficulty in marketing works by unknown writers, we are not optimistic about the chances of offering a standard contract. However, we shall continue to consider fiction in the hope of publishing on a standard basis books that we like and believe have good marketing potential. In addition, our procedure is as follows: Manuscripts we do not consider publishable are returned to the author. When we receive manuscripts which we feel are publishable but are uncertain of the marketability, we suggest that the author continue to try other houses. If they have already done so and are interested in self-publishing, we offer two types of services: (1) we provide editing, proofreading, book and cover design, copyrighting and production of the book; copies are then shipped to the author. (2) We provide these services plus promotion and distribution. In all cases, the problems and risks are spelled out."

‡LINCOLN SPRINGS PRESS (II), Box 269, Franklin Lakes NJ 07417. Editor: M. Gabrielle. Estab. 1987. Small, independent press. Publishes poetry, fiction, photography, high quality. Publishes paperback originals. Books: 65 lb paper; offset printing; perfect binding; average print order: 1,000. "Prefers short stories, but will publish first novels if quality high enough." Averages 4 total titles/year; 2 fiction titles.

Needs: Contemporary, ethnic, experimental, feminist, historical, literary, short story collections. No "romance, Janet Dailey variety." Recently published *Maybe It's My Heart*, by Abigail Stone (novel); *Confessions of a Joe Rock*, by Justin Vitiello.

How to Contact: Accepts unsolicited mss. Query first with 1 sample chapter. SASE (IRCs). Reports in 2 weeks-3 months. Simultaneous submissions OK.

Terms: Authors receive royalties of 5% minimum; 15% maximum "after all costs are met." Provides 10 author's copies. Sends galleys to author. Book catalog for SASE.

HENDRICK LONG PUBLISHING CO., (IV), Box 25123, Dallas TX 75225. (214)358-4677. Vice President: Joann Long. Estab. 1969. Independent publisher focusing on Texas and Southwest material geared primarily to a young audience. (K through high school). Publishes hardcover and paperback originals and hardcover reprints. Books: average print order: 2,000. Published new writers within the last year. Averages 8 total titles, 4 fiction titles each year. Sometimes comments on rejected ms.

Market conditions are constantly changing! If you're still using this book and it is 1995 or later, buy the newest edition of Novel & Short Story Writer's Market *at your favorite bookstore or order directly from Writer's Digest Books.*

Needs: Texas themes: historical, regional, for juvenile, young adult, teen. "No material not suitable for junior high/high school audience." Published *Boomer's Kids*, by Ruby C. Tolliver; *Johnny Texas*, by Carol Hoff (reprint); *Shipwrecked on Padre Island*, by Isabel Marvin.
How to Contact: Query first or submit outline/synopsis and sample chapters (at least 2—no more than 3). SASE (IRCs). Reports in 2 weeks on queries; 2 months on ms.
Terms: Offers advance. Sends galleys to author. Publishes ms 18 months after acceptance. Writer's guidelines for SASE. Book catalog for $1.

LONGSTREET PRESS, (III), Suite 118, 2140 Newmarket Pkwy., Marietta GA 30067. (404)980-1488. Senior Editor: John Yow. Associate Editor: Suzanne Comer Bell. Estab. 1988. "Small independent publisher with plans to grow." Publishes hardcover and paperback originals. Published new writers within the last year. Averages 20-25 total titles, 2-3 fiction titles each year. Sometimes comments on rejected ms.
  • For more information see the interview with Senior Editor John Yow in the 1993 edition.
Needs: Literary, mainstream. "Quality fiction." No "genre fiction, highly experimental work, ya, juvenile." Recently published *Whistling Woman*, by Louise Shivers; *This Old Heart of Mine*, by Merrill Joan Gerber (stories).
How to Contact: Agented or solicited mss only. Submit outline/synopsis and sample chapters. SASE (IRCs). Reports on queries in 6 weeks; on mss in 3 months. Simultaneous submissions OK (if told).
Terms: Pays in royalties; advance is negotiable; provides author's copies. Sends galleys to author. Publishes ms 6 months-1 year after acceptance. Writer's guidelines for #10 SAE and 1 first-class stamp. Book catalog for 9 × 12 envelope with 4 first-class stamps.
Advice: "Only a few slots for fiction here. Send samples of writing rather than plot summaries. Need agent or good credentials as previously published author."

‡LOONFEATHER PRESS, (II), 426 Bemidji Ave., Bemidji MN 56601. (218)751-4869. Editor/Publisher: Betty Rossi. Estab. 1979. "One-person staff with working board, also publish a literary magazine." Publishes paperback originals. Books: text paper; offset printing; perfect-bound; illustrations; average print order: 500-3,000. Plans are for 2 fiction and 1 poetry title this year. Often comments on rejected mss.
  • Loonfeather Press also publishes *Loonfeather* listed in the Literary/Small Circulation section. The press recently received a Minnesota Book Award for creative nonfiction and is now adding fiction to their line.
Needs: Ethnic/multicultural (Ojibwa, Native American), literary, regional (upper midwest), short story collections. No science fiction, western, romance. Publishes anthology. Writers may submit to anthology editor.
How to Contact: Accepts unsolicited mss. Query first. Include estimated word count and bio (maximum 1 page), Social Security number, list of publishing credits with submission. Send SASE (IRC) for reply, return of ms or send a disposable copy of ms. Reports in 3 weeks on queries; 3 months on mss. No simultaneous submissions.
Terms: Pays royalties of 10%. Advance is negotiable. Provides 20 author's copies. Sends galleys to author. Time between acceptance of the ms and publication is dependent on funding. Writer's guidelines for #10 SASE and 1 first-class stamp or IRC. Book catalog for #10 SASE and 1 first-class stamps or IRC.
Advice: "We have just started publishing and have done some anthologies which include fiction, and some poetry and creative nonfiction. As publisher of a literary magazine, we see a lot of bad fiction. Our publishing plans for the future are to do one anthology and one fiction (novel or short story collection) per year."

LUCKY HEART BOOKS, (I), Subsidiary of Salt Lick Press, #15, 1416 NE 21st Ave., Portland OR 97232-1507. (503)249-1014. Editor/Publisher: James Haining. Estab. 1969. Small press with significant work reviews in several national publications. Publishes paperback originals and reprints. Books: offset/bond paper; offset printing; hand-sewn or perfect-bound; illustrations; average print order: 500; first novel print order: 500. Sometimes comments on rejected ms.
Needs: Open to all fiction categories.
How to Contact: Accepts unsolicited mss. SASE (IRCs). Agented fiction 1%. Reports in 2 weeks - 4 months on mss.
Terms: Pays 10 author's copies. Sends galleys to author.
Advice: "Follow your heart. Use the head, but follow the heart."

MADWOMAN PRESS, (I, IV), P.O. Box 690, Northboro MA 01532. (508)393-3447. Editor/Publisher: Diane Benison. Estab. 1991. Independent small press publishing lesbian fiction. Publishes paperback originals. Books: perfect binding; average print order: 4,000-6,000. Averages 2-4 total titles, 2 fiction titles each year. Sometimes comments on rejected ms.

● Madwoman Press published *That's Ms. Bulldyke to You, Charlie!*, which was a 1993 Lambda Book Award finalist in the humor category.

Needs: "All must have lesbian themes: adventure, erotica, ethnic, feminist, mystery/suspense (amateur sleuth, private eye, police procedural), romance, science fiction (hard science, soft sociological), short story collection, thriller/espionage, western. Especially looking for lesbian detective stories." No horror. No gratuitous violence. Recently published *Sinister Paradise*, by Becky Bohan (novel); *Thin Fire*, by Nanci Little (novel).

How to Contact: Query first. Include brief statement of name, address, phone, previous publication and a 1-2 page precis of the plot. SASE (IRCs). Reports in 2 weeks on queries; 3 months on solicited mss. Simultaneous submissions OK.

Terms: Pays royalties of 8-15% "after recovery of publications costs." Provides 20 author's copies. Sends galleys to author. Publishes ms 1-2 years after acceptance. Writer's guidelines for #10 SAE and 1 first-class stamp.

Advice: "We're looking to form long-term relationships with writers, so talented first novelists are ideal for us. We want to publish an author regularly over the years, build an audience for her and keep her in print. We publish books by, for and about lesbians, books that are affirming for lesbian readers and authors."

MAGE PUBLISHERS, (IV), 1032 29th St. NW, Washington DC 20007. (202)342-1642. Editorial Contact: Amin Sepehari. Estab. 1985. "Small independent publisher." Publishes hardcover originals. Averages 4 total titles, 1 fiction title each year.

Needs: We publish *mainly* books on Iran. Ethnic (Iran) fiction.

How to Contact: Query first. SASE (IRC). Reports in 3 months on queries. Simultaneous submissions OK.

Terms: Pays royalties. Publishes ms 6-9 months after acceptance. Writer's guidelines for SASE. Book catalog free.

MARIE'S BOOKS, (II), Liberation Inc., Room 203C, 89 Robin Lane, Fairfield CT 06430-3939. (203)330-9596. Editor-in-Chief: Joseph Letendre. Estab. 1992. Publishes paperback originals. Books: perfect binding. Plans 4 first novels this year. Averages 4 total titles, all fiction.

● Liberation Inc.'s other imprints listed in this book are Lavender Press and Fire Island Press.

Needs: Lesbian, feminist. Plans ongoing series.

How to Contact: Accepts unsolicited mss. Submit outline/synopsis and 6 sample chapters. Should include estimated word count.

Terms: Pays royalties of 10% minimum; 25% maximum and 10 author's copies. Sends galleys to author.

‡*MAYHAVEN PUBLISHING, (I, II), P.O. Box 557, Mahomet IL 61853. (217)586-4493. Publisher: Doris R. Wenzel. "Full-time small publisher." Hardcover and paperback originals and reprints. Books: offset printing; illustrations; average print order: 2,000-5,000; first novel print order: 2,000. Plans 3 first novels this year. Averages 5-12 total titles. Sometimes comments on rejected ms; *$100 charge for critiques*.

Needs: Children's/juvenile (all types), historical (general), mystery/suspense, young adult. Recently published *Totally Trusting*, by Chas Lee (young adult); *An Honorable Spy*, by Warren Carrier (espionage); *Edge of Infinity*, by Jeff Groteboer (science fiction, space travel) and *Tantalizing Thai Cuisine*, by Vinita Atmiyandana Lawler.

How to Contact: Accepts unsolicited mss. Submit outline/synopsis and 3 sample chapters. Include ½ page bio and listing of publishing credits. Send SASE (or IRC) for reply, return of ms or send a disposable copy of ms. Reports in 3 months. No simultaneous submissions.

Terms: Pays royalties of 6-10%; offers $100 advance; provides 10 author's copies. Also individual arrangement with author depending on the book. "Because of many requests, we will be doing a few subsidy books—under alternate imprint, Wild Rose Publishing." Sends galleys to author. Publishes ms 6 months-2 years after acceptance. Book catalogs are free.

MERCURY HOUSE, (III), Suite 400, 201 Filbert St., San Francisco CA 94133. Executive Editor: Thomas Christensen. Publisher: William Brinton. Submissions Editor: Kirsten Janene-Nelson. Small, independent publisher of quality fiction and nonfiction. Publishes hardcovers and some paperback originals and reprints. Averages 12 titles annually. 25% of books from first-time authors.
Needs: Literary adult fiction, nonfiction and translations. Recently published *The Diary of Emily Dickenson*, by Jamie Fuller; *Story Earth*, compiled by the Inter Press Service; *City of Many Days*, by Shulamith Hareven.
How to Contact: No unsolicited mss. Submit query letter, 3 sample chapters, synopsis and SASE (IRCs). Reports in 3 months. Book catalog for 6½ × 9½ SAE and 52¢. No simultaneous submissions.

*MEY-HOUSE BOOKS, (II), Box 794, Stroudsburg PA 18360. (717)646-9556. Editorial contact: Ted Meyer. Estab. 1983. One-person, part-time operation with plans for at least 2 novels shortly. Publishes hardcover and paperback originals. Averages 1 title each year. Occasionally critiques or comments on rejected ms, "cost varies."
Needs: Adventure, contemporary, ethnic, science fiction. "No gay, erotic or lesbian fiction."
How to Contact: Accepts unsolicited mss. Query first. SASE (IRCs). Reports in 1 month on queries. Simultaneous submissions OK.
Terms: Payment "varies." Sends galleys to author. *Subsidy publishes "on an individual basis."*

MID-LIST PRESS, (I, II), Jackson, Hart & Leslie, Inc., 4324-12th Ave. S., Minneapolis MN 55407. (612)822-3733. Associate Publisher: Marianne Nora. Editors: Maria Ahrens, Jody Nolen, Lane Stiles. Estab. 1989. Small independent publisher. Publishes hardcover originals and paperback originals and hardcover reprints. Books: acid-free paper; offset printing; perfect or smyth-sewn binding; average print order: 2,000. Plans 1 first novel this year. Averages 3 total titles, 1 fiction title each year. Often comments on rejected ms.
Needs: Adventure, erotica, ethnic/multicultural, experimental, family saga, fantasy, feminist, gay, historical (general), horror, humor/satire, lesbian, literary, mainstream/contemporary, military/war, mystery/suspense, new age/mystic/spiritual, psychic/supernatural/occult, regional, science fiction, thriller/espionage, western. No childrens/juvenile, romance, young adult, religious. Recently published *Same Bed, Different Dreams*, by Hugh Gross (multicultural/literary); *News from Fort God*, by William Sutherland (the 1992 First Novel Series Award winner). Publishes First Novel Series Award.
How to Contact: Accepts unsolicited mss. Query first (for general fiction). For First Novel Series Award: query first for guidelines. Include #10 SASE (IRCs). Send SASE for reply, return of ms or send a disposable copy of the ms. Agented fiction 25%. Reports in 3 weeks on queries; 3 months on mss. Simultaneous submissions OK.
Terms: Pays royalty of 40% minimum; 50% maximum of profits. Average advance: $1,000 (for First Novel Series only). Sends galleys to author. Publishes ms 6-12 months after acceptance. Writer's guidelines for #10 SAE and 1 first-class stamp or IRC.
Advice: "Take the time to read some of the books the publisher you're submitting to has put out. And remember that first impressions are very important. If a query, cover letter, or first page is sloppily or ineptly written, an editor has little hope for the manuscript as a whole."

MILKWEED EDITIONS, Suite 400, 430 First Ave. N., Minneapolis MN 55401. (612)332-3192. Editor: Emilie Buchwald. Estab. 1980—*Milkweed Chronicle*/1984—*Milkweed Editions*. Nonprofit publisher with the intention of transforming culture through literature. Publishes hardcover and paperback originals. Books: book text quality—acid-free paper; offset printing; perfect or hardcover binding; average print order: 4,000; first novel print order depends on book. Averages 14 total titles/year. Number of fiction titles "depends on mss."
  ● For more on Milkweed, see the interview with Editor Emilie Buchwald in the 1990 *Novel & Short Story Writer's Market*.
Needs: For adult readers: literary fiction, nonfiction, poetry, essays; for children (ages 8-14): fiction and biographies. Translations welcome for both audiences. No legends or folktales for children. No romance, mysteries, science fiction. Recently published *Montana 1948*, by Larry Watson; *I Am Lavina Cumming*, by Susan Lowell; *Transforming a Rape Culture*, edited by Emilie Buchwald, Pamela Fletcher and Martha Roth.
How to Contact: Accepts unsolicited mss, send to the attention of Elisabeth Fitz, First Reader. Submit outline/synopsis and 2 sample chapters. SASE (IRCs). Reports in 1 month on queries; 2 months on mss. Simultaneous submissions OK. "Please send for guidelines. Must enclose SASE."

Terms: Authors are paid in royalties of 10%; advance is negotiable; 10 author's copies. Sends galleys to author. Book catalog for 3 first-class stamps.
Advice: "Read good contemporary fiction; find your own voice. Do not send us pornographic work, or work in which violence is done to women or children or men."

MISTY HILL PRESS, (II), 5024 Turner Rd., Sebastopol, CA 95472. (707)823-7437. Managing Editor: Sally S. Karste. Estab. 1985. Two person operation on a part-time basis. Publishes paperback originals. Books: illustrations; average print order: 2,000; first novel print order: 500-1,000. Plans 1 first novel this year. Publishes 1 title each year. Sometimes critiques rejected mss; *$15/hour charge for critiques*.
Needs: Juvenile (historical). Looking for "historical fiction for children, well researched for library market." Published *Trails to Poosey*, by Olive R. Cook (historical fiction); *Tales Fledgling Homestead*, by Joe Armstrong (nonfiction portraits).
How to Contact: Accepts unsolicited mss. Submit outline/synopsis and sample chapters. Reports within weeks. Simultaneous submissions OK.
Terms: Pays royalties of 5%. Sends prepublication galleys to author. Writer's guidelines and book catalog for SASE (IRCs).

MOTHER COURAGE PRESS, (I, IV), 1667 Douglas Ave., Racine WI 53404. (414)637-2227. Executive Editor: Barbara Lindquist. Estab. 1981. Small feminist press. Publishes paperback originals. Books: perfect-bound; sometimes illustrations; average print order: 3,000; first novel print order: 3,000. Averages 4 total titles, 1 fiction title each year.
Needs: Lesbian adventure, lesbian feminist/humor/satire, lesbian romance, lesbian science fiction, lesbian suspense/mystery. "Need strongly feminist, lesbian or women oriented, nothing written by men." No short stories. Published *Mega*, by B.L. Holmes (science fiction lesbian); *Hodag Winter*, by Deborah Wiese.
How to Contact: Accepts unsolicited mss. Query first with outline/synopsis and 2 sample chapters. SAE. Reports in 6 weeks on queries; 3 months on mss. Simultaneous submissions OK.
Terms: Pays in royalties of 10-15%. Average advance: $250. Sends galleys to author. Book catalog for SAE. No guidelines available.
Advice: "Write a good query letter, including, the plot of the novel, main characters, etc."

MOYER BELL LIMITED, Kymbolde Way, Wakefield RI 02879. (401)789-0074. President: Jennifer Moyer. Fiction Editor: Britt Bell. Estab. 1984. "Small publisher established to publish literature, reference and art books." Publishes hardcover and paperback originals and reprints. Books: Average print order 3,000; first novel print order: 3,000. Averages 18 total titles, 6 fiction titles each year. Sometimes comments on rejected ms.
Needs: Serious literary fiction. No genre fiction. Published *The Other Garden*, by Francis Wyndham (literary).
How to Contact: Accepts unsolicited mss. Submit outline/synopsis and 2 sample chapters. SASE (IRCs). Reports in 2 weeks on queries; 2 months on mss. Simultaneous and electronic submissions OK.
Terms: Pays royalties of 10% minimum. Average advance $1,000. Sends galleys to author. Publishes ms 9-18 months after acceptance. Book catalog free.

THE NAIAD PRESS, INC., (I, II, IV), Box 10543, Tallahassee FL 32302. (904)539-5965. Fax: (904)539-9731. Editorial Director: Barbara Grier. Estab. 1973. Books: 55 lb. offset paper; sheet-fed offset; perfect-bound; average print order: 12,000; first novel print order: 12,000. Publishes 24 total titles each year.
● The Naiad Press is one of the most successful and well-known lesbian publishers. Barbara Grier and Donna J. McBride recently received a Publisher's Service Award from the Lambda Literary Awards for 20 years of service and were featured speakers at the 1993 Gay Pride Rally in New York City.
Needs: Lesbian fiction, all genres. Recently published *The Cat Came Back*, by Hilary Mullins (novel); *Not Telling Mother: Stories From a Life*, by Diane Salvatore (novel); *The Romantic Naiad*, edited by Katherine V. Forrest and Barbara Grier.
How to Contact: Query first only. SASE (IRCs). Reports in 3 weeks on queries; 3 months on mss. No simultaneous submissions.
Terms: Pays 15% royalties using a standard recovery contract. Occasionally pays 7½% royalties against cover price. "Seldom gives advances and has never seen a first novel worthy of one. Believes authors are investments in their own and the company's future—that the best author is the author who produces a

book every 12-18 months forever and knows that there is a *home* for that book." Publishes ms 1-2 years after acceptance. Book catalog for legal-sized SASE.

Advice: "We publish lesbian fiction primarily and prefer honest work (i.e., positive, upbeat lesbian characters). Lesbian content must be accurate . . . a lot of earlier lesbian novels were less than honest. No breast beating or complaining. Our fiction titles are becoming increasingly *genre* fiction, which we encourage. Original fiction in paperback is our main field, and its popularity increases. We publish books BY, FOR AND ABOUT lesbians. We are not interested in books that are unrealistic. You know and we know what the real world of lesbian interest is like. Don't even try to fool us. Short, well written books do best. Authors who want to succeed and will work to do so have the best shot."

THE NAUTICAL & AVIATION PUBLISHING CO. OF AMERICA INC., (IV), 8 W. Madison St., Baltimore MD 21201. (410)659-0220. President: Jan Snouck-Hurgronje. Estab. 1979. Small publisher interested in quality military history and literature. Publishes hardcover originals and reprints. Averages 10 total titles, 1-4 fiction titles each year. Sometimes comments on rejected mss.

Needs: Military/war (especially military history and Civil War). Looks for "novels with a strong military history orientation." Recently published *New Guinea*, and *Checkfire*, by VADM William P. Mack.

How to Contact: Accepts unsolicited mss. Query first or submit complete mss with cover letter. SASE (IRCs) necessary for return of mss. Agented fiction "miniscule." Reports on queries in 2-3 weeks; on mss in 3 weeks. Simultaneous submissions OK.

Terms: Pays royalties of 14%. Advance negotiable. After acceptance publishes ms "as quickly as possible—next season." Book catalog free on request.

Advice: Publishing more fiction. Encourages first novelists. "We're interested in good writing—first novel or last novel. Keep it historical, put characters in a historical context. Professionalism counts. Know your subject. *Convince us.*"

NEW DIRECTIONS, (I, II), 80 Eighth Ave., New York NY 10011. (212)255-0230. Editor-in-Chief: Peter Glassgold. Small independent publisher. Publishes hardcover and paperback originals and reprints. Average print order: 1,000 hardback; 3,000 paperback. Sometimes critiques rejected ms.

Needs: "Mostly avant-garde; will look at everything, including poetry."

How to Contact: Accepts unsolicited mss. Query first with outline/synopsis and sample chapters. SASE (IRCs). Reports in 6-8 weeks on queries; 3-4 months on mss. No simultaneous submissions.

Terms: Pays royalties. Offers advance. Publishes ms at least 1 year after acceptance, "depends on type of book."

Advice: "Try to get published in a literary magazine first to establish a writing reputation and for the experience."

NEW RIVERS PRESS, Suite 910, 420 N. Fifth St., Minneapolis MN 55401. Publisher: C.W. Truesdale. Estab. 1968.

● See also the Minnesota Voices Project, sponsored by New Rivers Press, listed in the Contests and Awards section of this book. An interview with Publisher C.W. Truesdale appears in this section.

Needs: Contemporary, literary, experimental, translations. "No popular fantasy/romance. Nothing pious, polemical (unless other very good redeeming qualities). We are interested in only quality literature and always have been (though our concentration in the past has been poetry)." Published *Out Far, in Deep*, by Alvin Handleman (short stories); *Borrowed Voices*, by Roger Sheffer (short stories); *Suburban Metaphysics*, by Ronald J. Rindo (short stories).

How to Contact: Query. SASE (IRCs). Reports in 4-6 months on queries; within 4-6 months of query approval on mss. "No multiple submissions tolerated."

Terms: Pays 100 author's copies; also pays royalties; no advance. Minnesota Voices Series pays authors $500 plus 15% royalties on list price for second and subsequent printings. Free book catalog.

Advice: "We are not really concerned with trends. We read for quality, which experience has taught can be very eclectic and can come sometimes from out of nowhere. We are interested in publishing short fiction (as well as poetry and translations) because it is and has been a great indigenous American form and is almost completely ignored by the commercial houses. Find a *real* subject, something that

---

Check the Category Indexes, located at the back of the book, for publishers interested in specific fiction subjects.

belongs to you and not what you think or surmise that you should be doing by current standards and fads."

NEW VICTORIA PUBLISHERS, (I), Box 27, Norwich VT 05055. (802)649-5297. Editor: Claudia Lamperti. Publishes trade paperback originals. Averages 4-5 titles/year.
● Books published by New Victoria Publishers have been nominated for Lambda Literary Awards.
Needs: Lesbian/feminist: adventure, fantasy, historical, humor, mystery (amateur sleuth), romance, science fiction (soft sociological), thriller, western. Looking for "strong feminist characters, also strong plot and action. We will consider most anything if it is well written and appeals to a lesbian/feminist audience." Publishes anthologies or special editions. Recently published *Otherworld*, by Sarah Dreher; *Tell Me What You Like*, by Kate Allen; *Hers Was the Sky*, by Rebecca Béguin.
How to Contact: Submit outline/synopsis and sample chapters. SASE (IRCs). Reports in 2 weeks on queries; 1 month on mss. Disk submissions OK.
Terms: Pays royalties of 10%.
Advice: "We would particularly enjoy a humorous novel."

✹NEWEST PUBLISHERS LTD., (IV), #310, 10359 Whyte Ave., Edmonton, Alberta T6E 1Z9 Canada. General Manager: Liz Grieve. Editorial Coordinator: Eva Radford. Estab. 1977. Publishes paperback originals. Published new writers within the last year. Plans 1 first novel this year. Averages 8 total titles, 2 fiction titles each year. Sometimes offers brief comments on rejected ms.
● NeWest was chosen by the Alberta Book Industry Awards as Publisher of the Year in 1990. The publisher is continuing its Nunatak New Fiction Series featuring new western Canadian writers.
Needs: Literary. "Our press is most interested in western Canadian literature." Recently published *A Whiter Shade of Pale/Becoming Emma*, by Caterina Edwards (2 novellas); *Elephant Hook and Other Stories*, by Martin Sherman; *Ghost Works*, by Daphne Marlatt (collection).
How to Contact: Accepts unsolicited mss. Query first or submit outline/synopsis and 3 sample chapters. SASE (IRCs) necessary for return of manuscript. Reports in 1 month on queries; 3 months on mss. Accepts electronic submissions.
Terms: Pays royalties of 10% minimum. Sends galleys to author. Publishes ms at least 1 year after acceptance. Book catalog for 9×12 SASE or IRC.
Advice: "Keep in mind that we publish western Canadian writers only or topics applying to western Canada."

NIGHTSHADE PRESS, (II), Ward Hill, Troy ME 04987. (207)948-3427. Contact: Carolyn Page or Ted Holmes. Estab. 1988. "Fulltime small press publishing literary magazine, poetry chapbooks, 1 or 2 short story collections per year. Short stories *only, no novels please*." Publishes paperback originals. Books: 60 lb. paper; offset printing; saddle-stitched or perfect-bound; illustrations; average print order: 400. Published new writers within the last year. Averages about 10 total titles, 1 or more fiction titles each year, plus short history collection. Sometimes comments on rejected ms.
● Nightshade Press also publishes *Potato Eyes* listed in this book. For more see the interview with the publishers in the 1991 *Novel & Short Story Writer's Market*.
Needs: Contemporary, humor/satire, literary, mainstream, regional. No religious, romance, preschool, juvenile, young adult, fantasy, horror, psychic/occult. Recently published *The Nightshade Short Story Reader*, edited by Edward M. Holmes; *Wood Head: Stories from up North*, by Rebecca Rule; *Grass Creek Chronicles*, by Pat Carr.
How to Contact: Accepts unsolicited mss—short stories only. "Tend not to read agented material." Reports in 1 month on queries; 3-4 months on mss.
Terms: Pays 2 author's copies. Publishes ms about 1 year after acceptance. Writer's guidelines and book catalog for SASE (IRCs). Individual contracts negotiated with short story collection authors.
Advice: "Would like to see more real humor; less gratuitous violence—the opposite of TV. We have overdosed on heavily dialected southern stories which treat country people with a mixture of ridicule and exaggeration. We prefer treatment of characterization which offers dignity and respect for folks who make do with little and who respect their environment."

✹ORCA BOOK PUBLISHERS LTD., (I, IV), P.O. Box 5626, Station B, Victoria, British Columbia V8R 6S4 Canada. (604)380-1229. Publisher: R.J. Tyrrell. Estab. 1984. "Regional publisher of West Coast-oriented titles." Publishes hardcover and paperback originals. Books: quality 60 lb. book stock paper; illustrations; average print order: 3,000-5,000; first novel print order: 2,000-3,000. Plans 1-2 first novels

Expanding Opportunities in the Small Press

For Bill Truesdale of New Rivers Press and the Minnesota Voices Project, a small press is a deeply personal thing. "I got very interested in starting a small press myself because I had a hard time getting my first book published, so once I got a couple of books out I decided that maybe I'd do other young poets kind of a favor."

As Truesdale himself branched out into fiction, he began to include short story collections and short novels in his publishing program. New Rivers, which is celebrating its 25th anniversary this year, and Minnesota Voices, an annual competition of fiction and poetry which is 13 years strong, provide opportunities for new and emerging writers—opportunities Truesdale feels are dwindling each year.

C.W. Truesdale

"The prevailing attitude among many publishers is that they are so worried about the market that a lot of very good work never sees the light of day. I think that's an unforgivable sin and it's really horrible for writers. That's why I feel more and more strongly committed as the years go by to publishing those new writers."

In moving New Rivers Press from New York City to Minnesota in 1978, Truesdale says, "I was astounded to find that 25 percent of the manuscripts that had passed the preliminary reading stage were Minnesotan. My feeling was first, there was an awful lot of good writing out here and second, there were not many book publishing representatives in this area. We were really the first book publisher of national American fiction in the area."

Two years after arriving in Minnesota, Truesdale submitted a proposal to the Jerome Foundation, a small but very vigorous local arts foundation, to fund the Minnesota Voices Project. A slight misnomer, the Project publishes works by emerging artists from Minnesota, Wisconsin, Iowa and the Dakotas, currently bringing out three new writers and three new poets each year. "This will be the thirteenth year of doing it, and I can't believe the quality of the stuff we get. I think the fiction coming out of this area is just amazing."

Part of this is attributable to the long-term existence of the Minnesota Voices Project, Truesdale believes. Submissions have jumped from 95 three years ago to 207 this year. "One thing I do is write personal letters to whoever enters the competition. In at least two-thirds I get very specific, but I'm never judgmental. It doesn't square with my own experience, because people who start out writing schlock can turn out to be very good writers, and I don't think they should be discouraged."

Keeping the press smaller and more personal does have its difficulties. Truesdale describes funding as "very precarious, and at times very capricious." New Rivers did not get NEA funding in 1993, which forced him to scale back the national publishing program, placing a greater emphasis on regional publishing and anthologies.

Despite these difficulties, Truesdale remains enthusiastic and optimistic. "I think fiction in this country is very healthy, very strong. Basically what we're looking for is originality of voice and individuality—a voice that is involved in real subjects," Truesdale says, "and that's very hard to define. A good subject is important. It's partly background, partly genetic, partly other things. It's nothing that can be taught, although people can be taught how to bring it out. But the voice is essential."

—Kirsten Holm

---

this year. Averages 12 total titles, 2-3 fiction titles each year. Sometimes comments on rejected ms.
Needs: Contemporary, juvenile (5-9 years), literary, mainstream, young adult/teen (10-18 years). Looking for "contemporary fiction." No "romance, science fiction."
How to Contact: Query first, then submit outline/synopsis and 1 or 2 sample chapters. SASE (IRCs). Agented fiction 20%. Reports in 2 weeks on queries; 1-2 months on mss. Publishes Canadian authors only.
Terms: Pays royalties of 10%; $500 average advance. Sends galleys to author. Publishes ms 6 months-1 year after acceptance. Writer's guidelines for SASE (IRC). Book catalog for 8½ × 11 SASE (IRC).
Advice: "We are looking to promote and publish new West Coast writers, especially Canadians."

OUR CHILD PRESS, 800 Maple Glen Lane, Wayne PA 19087. (215)964-0606. CEO: Carol Hallenbeck. Estab. 1984. Publishes hardcover and paperback originals and reprints. Plans 2 first novels this year. Plans 2 titles this year. Sometimes comments on rejected ms.
Needs: Adventure, contemporary, fantasy, juvenile (5-9 yrs.), preschool/picture book and young adult/teen (10-18 years). Especially interested in books on adoption or learning disabilities. Published *Don't Call Me Marda*, by Sheila Welch (juvenile); *Oliver—An Adoption Story*, by Lois Wickstrom. Published new writers within the last year.
How to Contact: Does not accept unsolicited mss. Query first. Reports in 2 weeks on queries; 2 months on mss. Simultaneous submissions OK.
Terms: Pays royalties of 5% minimum. Publishes ms up to 6 months after acceptance. Book catalog free.

‡OUTRIDER PRESS, (II), Suite C-3, 1004 E. Steger Rd., Crete IL 60417. (708)672-6630. Fax: (708)672-6630. President: Phyllis Nelson. Fiction Editor: Whitney Scott. Estab. 1988. "One-person operation on part-time basis." Publishes paperback originals. Books: offset printing; perfect binding; average print order: under 5,000. Averages 1-2 total titles, 1 fiction title each year. Sometimes comments on rejected ms; *charges $2 double-spaced pages with 10-page minimum, prepaid and SASE for return.*
Needs: Feminist, lesbian, literary, New Age/mystic/spiritual, short story collection. Anthologies closed to outside submission.
How to Contact: Accepts unsolicited mss. Submit complete ms with cover letter (with short stories). Include estimated word count and list of publishing credits. SASE (IRCs) for return of ms. Reports in 1 month on queries; 2 months on mss. Simultaneous submissions OK. Accepts electronic submissions (3.5 IBM compatible—WordPerfect 5.1).
Terms: Payment depends on grant/award money. Sends galleys to author.
Advice: "We have a need for short and super-short fiction."

THE OVERLOOK PRESS, 149 Wooster St., New York NY 10012. (212)477-7162. Estab. 1972. Small-staffed, full-time operation. Publishes hardcover and paperback originals and reprints. Averages 30 total titles, 7 fiction titles each year. Occasionally critiques rejected mss.

Needs: Fantasy, juvenile (fantasy, historical, sports, contemporary), literary, psychic/supernatural/occult, regional (Hudson Valley), science fiction (hard science), thriller/espionage, translations. No romance or horror. Published *Divina Trace*, by Robert Antoni (novel); *The Diamond Lane*, by Karen Karbo (novel); *Cafe Berlin*, by Harold Nebenzal (novel).
How to Contact: Query first or submit outline/synopsis. SASE (IRCs). Allow up to 6 months for reports on queries. Simultaneous submissions OK.
Terms: Vary.

PADRE PRODUCTIONS, (II), Box 840, Arroyo Grande CA 93421-0840. (805)473-1947. Accepts fiction and poetry. See The Press of MacDonald and Reinecke.

PANDO PUBLICATIONS, (II), 5396 Laurie Lane, Memphis TN 38120. (901)682-8779. Editorial contact person: Andrew Bernstein. Estab. 1987. "Two person, full-time book publisher." Publishes hardcover and paperback originals. Books: 60 lb. paper; perfect-bound, Smyth-sewn or hardcover binding; average print order: 3,000-9,000. Averages 6-10 total titles each year. Rarely comments on rejected mss.
Needs: Adventure, historical, juvenile (animal, easy-to-read, historical, sports, contemporary), mainstream, military/war, mystery/suspense, regional, young adult/teen (easy-to-read, historical, problem novels, sports).
How to Contact: Accepts unsolicited mss. Submit outline/synopsis and 3 sample chapters. SASE (IRCs) for ms. Reports in 2 months on queries; 6 months on ms. Simultaneous submissions OK. Electronic submissions via WordPerfect preferred.
Terms: Pays royalties of 6-12½%. Average advance is about ⅓ of royalty of 1st run; negotiable. Sends galleys to author. Publishes ms within a year after acceptance.
Advice: Would like to see "more children's stories based on myth and legend, current happenings (world events, politics, demographic movements, social problems, ecological concerns, medical problems, growing up in a TV-VCR-cable-computer world, and so on). Read the ms out loud and see if it sounds right to you."

‡THE PAPER BAG PRESS, (I, II), P.O. Box 268805, Chicago IL 60626-8805. (312)285-7972. Editor: Michael H. Brownstein. Estab. 1988. "Small press with a small staff." Publishes paperback originals. Books: regular paper; Xerox printing; saddle-stapled binding; photocopy illustrations; average print order: 200. Published new writers within the last year. Averages 2 total titles, 1 fiction title each year. Always comments on rejected mss.
Needs: Adventure, contemporary, erotica, ethnic, experimental, fantasy, feminist, historical, horror, humor/satire, literary, mainstream, military/war, science fiction, short story collection, suspense/mystery, western. "We will only consider collections of short fiction. We never take short stories longer than 500 words."
How to Contact: Accepts unsolicited mss. Submit complete manuscript with cover letter. SASE (IRCs). Reports in 1 week-2 months on queries; 1 week-3 months on mss.
Terms: Provides author's copies "depends on press run;" honorarium; payment depends on grant/award money. Sometimes sends galleys to author. Writer's guidlines for SASE.
Advice: "Too often the fiction we get is sloppy, needs tremendous editing and does not follow our guidelines that all short stories be under 500 words."

PAPIER-MACHE PRESS, (IV), #14, 135 Aviation Way, Watsonville CA 95076. (408)763-1420. Editor/Publisher: Sandra Martz. Submissions Editor: Shirley Coe. Estab. 1984. "Specializes in women's issues; the art of growing older for both men and women." Publishes anthologies and "poetry and fiction" originals. Books: 60-70 lb. offset paper; perfect-bound or case-bound; photographs; average print order: 3,000-6,000. Publishes 4-6 total titles/year; 4-6 fiction/poetry titles/year.
- Papier-Mache Press publishes a number of well-received themed anthologies. Their anthology, *When I Am an Old Woman, I Shall Wear Purple*, received an ABBY Award in 1991 from the American Booksellers Association and a Benjamin Franklin Award in 1992.

Needs: Contemporary, feminist, short story collections, women's. Recently published fiction by Mary Ann Ashley and Randeane Tetu; *The Adventures of Stout Mama*, by Sibyl James. Published new writers within the last year.

How to Contact: Query first. SASE (IRCs). Reports in 2 months on queries; 6 months on mss. Simultaneous and photocopied submissions OK. Accepts computer printouts.
Terms: Standard royalty agreements for novels/fiction collections. Complimentary copies for anthology contributors; honorarium for contributors when anthologies go into second printings.
Advice: "Indicate with your manuscript whether or not you are open to revision suggestions. Always indicate on original submission if this is a simultaneous submission or a previously published work. We can handle either, but only if we know in advance. Absolutely essential to query first."

PATH PRESS, INC., (II), Suite 724, 53 W. Jackson, Chicago IL 60604. (312)663-0167. Fax: (312)663-0318. Editorial Director: Herman C. Gilbert. "Small independent publisher which specializes in books by, for and about Black Americans and Third World Peoples." Published new writers within the last year. Averages 6 total titles, 3 fiction titles each year. Occasionally critiques rejected ms.
Needs: Ethnic, historical, sports, and short story collections. Needs for novels include "black or minority-oriented novels of any genre, style or subject." Published *Brown Sky*, by David Covin (a novel of World War II); *Congo Crew*, by William Goodlett (a novel set in Africa during 1960-61).
How to Contact: Accepts unsolicited mss. Query first or submit synopsis and 5 sample chapters with SASE (IRCs). Reports in 2 months on queries; 4 months on mss. Simultaneous submissions OK.
Terms: Pays in royalties.
Advice: "Deal honestly with your subject matter and with your characters. Dig deeply into the motivations of your characters, regardless how painful it might be to you personally."

‡PEACHTREE PUBLISHERS, LTD., (II), 494 Armour Circle NE, Atlanta GA 30324. (404)876-8761. President: Margaret Quinlin. Estab. 1977. Small, independent publisher specializing in general interest publications, particularly of Southern origin. Publishes hardcover and paperback originals and hardcover reprints. Averages 20 total titles, 4 fiction titles each year. Average first novel print order 10,000-15,000.
Needs: Contemporary, literary, mainstream, regional, short story collections. "We are primarily seeking Southern fiction: Southern themes, characters, and/or locales." No science fiction/fantasy, young adult, horror, religious, romance, historical or mystery/suspense. Recently published *The Blue Valleys*, by Robert Morgan (stories); *The Song of Daniel*, by Philip Lee Williams; *The Girl Who Loved Elvis*, by Susie Mee; *To Dance with the White Dog*, by Terry Kay.
How to Contact: Accepts unsolicited mss. Query, submit outline/synopsis and 50 pages, or submit complete ms with SASE (IRCs). Reports in 1 month on queries; 3 months on mss. Simultaneous submissions OK.
Terms: Pays in royalties. Sends galleys to author. Free writer's guidelines and book catalog.
Advice: "We encourage original efforts in first novels."

PERMEABLE PRESS, (I), #15, 900 Tennessee, San Francisco CA 94107-3014. (415)648-2175. Imprints are Xerotic Ephemera, Puck! Publisher: Brian Clark. Editor: Kurt Putnam. Estab. 1984. "Small literary press with inhouse design and typesetting." Publishes hardcover and paperback originals and paperback reprints. Books: 60 lb. paper; offset printing; perfect-bound; illustrations; average print order: 3,500. Published new writers within the last year. Plans 1 first novel this year. Averages 3 total titles, all fiction, each year. Sometimes comments on rejected ms.
Needs: Erotica, experimental, feminist, gay, historical, juvenile, lesbian, literary, preschool/picture book, psychic/supernatural/occult, science fiction (hard science, soft sociological), short story collections, thriller/espionage. Looking for "cyberpunk; conspiracy. Should be challenging to read." No romance. Published *Shaman*, by Hugh Fox (experimental memoir); *The Royal Elephant*, by Lorraine Morrison (children's); *Shadow Self*, by Helen Duberstein (short stories).
How to Contact: Accepts unsolicited mss. Query first or submit outline/synopsis and 3 sample chapters. SASE (IRCs). Reports in 4-6 weeks on queries; 3 months on mss. Accepts electronic submissions.
Terms: Pays royalties of 5-20%. Author's copies vary. Honorarium depends on grant/award money. Sends galleys to author. Writer's guidelines and book catalog for 9 × 12 SAE and 4 first-class stamps.
Advice: "As a design firm our business has grown rapidly in several areas. Consequently we are currently looking for hot new titles as well as bargain reprint rights."

PIKESTAFF PUBLICATIONS, INC., (I, II), Box 127, Normal IL 61761. (309)452-4831. Imprints include The Pikestaff Press: Pikestaff Fiction Chapbooks; *The Pikestaff Forum*, general literary magazine. Editorial Directors: Robert D. Sutherland and James R. Scrimgeour. Estab. 1977. Small independent publisher with plans to expand gradually. Publishes hardcover and paperback originals. Books: paper varies; offset printing; b&w illustrations; average print order: 500-2,000. "One of the purposes of the press is to encourage new talent." Occasionally comments on rejected mss.

Needs: Contemporary, literary, and experimental. "No slick formula writing written with an eye to the commercial mass market or pure entertainment that does not provide insights into the human condition. Not interested in heroic fantasy (dungeons & dragons, swords & sorcery); science fiction of the space-opera variety; westerns; mysteries; love-romance; gothic adventure; or pornography (sexploitation)." Published fiction by Constance Pierce and Linnea Johnson.

How to Contact: Query or submit outline/synopsis and 1-2 sample chapters. "Anyone may inquire; affirmative responses may submit ms." SASE (IRCs). Reports in 1 month on queries; 3 months on mss. No simultaneous submissions.

Terms: Negotiates terms with author. Sends galleys to author. Publishes ms within 1 year after acceptance.

Advice: "Have fictional characters we can really *care* about; we are tired of disembodied characters wandering about in their heads unable to relate to other people or the world about them. Avoid too much TELLING; let the reader participate by leaving something for him or her to do. Yet avoid vagueness, opaqueness, personal or 'private' symbolisms and allusions. Here we regard the relationship between the writer and editor as a cooperative relationship—we are colleagues in getting the book out. The writer has an obligation to do the best self-editing job of which he or she is capable; writers should not rely on editors to make their books presentable. Don't give up easily; understand your reasons for wanting the work published (personal satisfaction? money? fame? to 'prove' something? to 'be a novelist'? etc.). Ask yourself honestly, Should it be published? What can it provide for a reader that makes it worth part of that reader's *lifetime* to read? Be prepared for shocks and disappointments; study contracts carefully and retain as many rights and as much control over the book's appearance as possible. Be prepared to learn how to be your own best promoter and publicist."

PINEAPPLE PRESS, (II, IV), P.O. Drawer 16008, Southside Station, Sarasota FL 34239. (813)952-1085. Executive Editor: June Cussen. Estab. 1982. Small independent trade publisher. Publishes hardcover and paperback originals and paperback reprints. Books: quality paper; offset printing; Smyth-sewn or perfect-bound; illustrations occasionally; average print order: 5,000; first novel print order: 2,000-5,000. Averages 12 total titles each year.

Needs: "In 1994 we prefer to see only Florida-related novels." Recently published two "Cracker Westerns" by Lee Grambling: *Riders of the Sewannee* and *Trail from St. Augustine*. Published new writers within the last year.

How to Contact: Prefers query, outline or one-page synopsis with sample chapters (including the first) and SASE (IRCs). Then if requested, submit complete ms with SASE. Reports in 2 months. Simultaneous submissions OK.

Terms: Pays royalties of 7½-15%. Advance is not usually offered. "Basically, it is an individual agreement with each author depending on the book." Sends galleys to author. Book catalog sent if label and 52¢ postage enclosed.

Advice: "We publish both Florida regional books and general trade fiction and nonfiction. Quality first novels will be published, though we usually only do one novel per year. We regard the author/editor relationship as a trusting relationship with communication open both ways. Learn all you can about the publishing process and about how to promote your book once it is published."

*POCAHONTAS PRESS, INC., (I, IV), Manuscript Memories, 832 Hulcheson Dr., Blacksburg VA 24060-3259. (703)951-0467. Editorial contact person: Mary C. Holliman. Estab. 1984. "One-person operation on part-time basis, with several part-time colleagues. Subjects not limited, but stories about real people are almost always required. Main intended audience is youth—young adults, ages 10-18." Books: 70 lb. white offset paper; offset litho printing; perfect binding; illustrations; average print order: 3,000-5,000. Averages 5 total titles. Usually critiques or comments on rejected mss.

● This press uses very little fiction. The publisher may consider making a short story into a short book, but does not generally publish novels or collections.

Needs: "Stories based on historical facts about real people." Contemporary, ethnic, historical, sports, regional, translations, western. "I will treat a short story as a book, with illustrations and a translation into Spanish or French and also Chinese someday." No fantasy or horror. Published *From Lions to Lincoln*, by Fran Hartman; *Mountain Summer*, by Bill Mashburn.

How to Contact: Accepts unsolicited mss. Query first. Reports in 1 month on queries; 1-2 months on mss. "I try to meet these deadlines but seldom succeed." Simultaneous submissions OK. "If simultaneous, I would need to know up front what other options the author is considering."

Terms: Pays royalties of 10% maximum. $50 advance negotiable. Sends galleys to author. "I will subsidy publish—but expect book and author to meet the same qualifications as a regular author, and will pay royalties on all copies sold as well as pay back the author's investment as books are sold."
Advice: "Tell a *story*—don't tell what happened, show it happening. Let your characters be real, squirm in their chairs, look out windows. Don't let them be so caught up in your idea or theme that you don't let the character be a person."

‡**THE POST-APOLLO PRESS, (I)**, 35 Marie St., Sausalito CA 94965. (415)332-1458. Publisher: Simone Fattal. Estab. 1982. Publishes paperback originals. Book: acid-free paper; lithography printing; perfect-bound; average print order: 3,000; first novel print order: 3,000. Published new writers within the last year. Averages 2 total titles, 1 fiction title each year. Sometimes comments on rejected ms.
Needs: Feminist, lesbian, literary, short story collections, spiritual and translations. No juvenile, horror, sports or romance. Published *Sitt Marie-Rose*, by Etel Adnan; *Home For The Summer*, by Georgina Kleege (psychological thriller); *Josef is Dying*, by Ulla Berkewicz.
How to Contact: Send query or complete ms with SASE (IRCs). Reports in 3 months.
Terms: Pays royalties of 6½% minimum or by individual arrangement. Sends galleys to author. Publishes ms 1½ years after acceptance. Book catalog free.

‡✿**PRAIRIE JOURNAL PRESS, (I, IV)**, Prairie Journal Trust, P.O. Box 61203, Brentwood Postal Services, 217K-360 Brentwood Rd. NW, Calgary, Alberta T2L 2K6 Canada. Estab. 1983. Small-press, noncommercial literary publisher. Publishes paperback originals. Books: bond paper; offset printing; stapled binding; b&w line drawings. Averages 2 total titles or anthologies each year. Occasionally critiques or comments on rejected ms if requested.
● See the listing for *The Prairie Journal of Canadian Literature* in the Literary/Small Circulation section of this book.
Needs: Literary, short stories. No romance, horror, pulp, erotica, magazine type, children's, adventure, formula, western. Published *Prairie Journal Fiction*, *Prairie Journal Fiction II* (anthologies of short stories) and *Solstice* (short fiction on the theme of aging).
How to Contact: Accepts unsolicited mss. Query first and send Canadian postage or IRCs and $3 for sample copy, then submit outline/synopsis and 1-2 stories with SASE (IRCs). Reports in 6 months.
Terms: Pays 1 author's copy; honorarium depends on grant/award provided by the government or private/corporate donations. Sends galleys to author. Book catalog free on request to institutions; SAE with IRC for individuals. "No U.S. stamps!"
Advice: "We wish we had the means to promote more new writers. We often are seeking theme-related stories. We look for something different each time and try not to repeat types of stories."

✿**THE PRAIRIE PUBLISHING COMPANY**, Box 2997, Winnipeg, Manitoba R3C 4B5 Canada. (204)885-6496. Publisher: Ralph Watkins. Estab. 1969. Buys juvenile mss with illustrations. Books: 60 lb. high-bulk paper; offset printing; perfect-bound; line-drawings; average print order: 2,000; first novel print order: 2,000.
Needs: Open. Published: *The Homeplace* (historical novel); *My Name is Marie Anne Gaboury* (first French-Canadian woman in the Northwest); and *The Tale of Jonathan Thimblemouse*. Published work by previously unpublished writers within the last year.
How to Contact: Query with SASE or IRCs. No simultaneous submissions. Reports in 1 month on queries, 6 weeks on mss. Publishes ms 4-6 months after acceptance. Free book catalog.
Terms: Pays 10% in royalties. No advance.
Advice: "We work on a manuscript with the intensity of a Max Perkins of Charles Scribner's Sons of New York. A clean, well-prepared manuscript can go a long way toward making an editor's job easier. On the other hand, the author should not attempt to anticipate the format of the book, which is a decision for the publisher to make. In order to succeed in today's market, the story must be tight, well written and to the point. Do not be discouraged by rejections."

✿**PRESS GANG PUBLISHERS, (II, IV)**, 603 Powell St., Vancouver, British Columbia V6A 1H2 Canada. (604)253-2537. Estab. 1974. Feminist press, 3 fulltime staff. Publishes paperback originals and reprints. Books: paperback; offset printing; perfect-bound; average print order: 3,500; first novel print order: 2,000. Plans 2 novels this year. Sometimes critiques rejected mss.
Needs: Looking for "feminist, mystery/suspense, short stories." Also accepts contemporary, erotica, ethnic (native women especially), humor/satire, lesbian, literary, science fiction. No children's/young adult/teen. Priority given to Canadian writers. Recently published *Paper, Scissors, Rock*, by Ann Decter (novel); *Sing Me No More*, by Lynette Dueck (novel); *Food & Spirits*, by Beth Brant (stories).

How to Contact: Accepts unsolicited mss. Query first. SASE (IRCs). Reports in 2 months on queries; 3-4 months on mss. Simultaneous submissions OK.

Terms: Pays 8-10% royalties. Sends galleys to author. Book catalog free on request.

‡**THE PRESS OF MACDONALD AND REINECKE (II,III)**, Padre Productions, Box 840, Arroyo Grande CA 93421-0840. (805)473-1947. Publisher: Lachlan P. MacDonald. Fiction Editor: Mack Sullivan. Estab. 1974. "Literary imprint of a small independent press." Publishes hardcover and paperback originals. Books: book paper; offset printing; Smyth-sewn, case-bound and perfect-bound; illustrations; average print order: 3,000; first novel print order: 500-3,000. Plans 1 first novel this year. Averages 6 total titles, 1-2 fiction titles each year. Sometimes comments on rejected mss.

Needs: Historical, humor/satire, literary, short story collections. Currently overstocked. No mystery, suspense, western, religious, military, adventure, fantasy, romance. Published *Joel in Tananar*, by Robert M. Walton (juvenile); *Contemporary Insanities*, by Charles Brashers (short fiction). Publishes fiction by a previously unpublished writer "every 2-3 years."

How to Contact: Accepts unsolicited mss. Submit outline/synopsis and 1-2 sample chapters. SASE (IRCs). Agented fiction 5%. Reports in 2 weeks on queries; 2 months on mss. Simultaneous submissions OK.

Terms: Pays in royalties. Sends galleys to author. "Unfortunately, it may be 2 years" before publication after acceptance. Writer's guidelines for SASE. Book catalog for 6×9 SAE.

Advice: "Publishing less fiction than in the past. Demonstrate a following by documenting publication in literary magazines, general magazines or anthologies."

PUCKERBRUSH PRESS, (I,II), 76 Main St., Orono ME 04473. (207)581-3832. Publisher/Editor: Constance Hunting. Estab. 1979. One-person operation on part-time basis. Publishes paperback originals. Books: laser printing; perfect-bound; sometimes illustrations; average print order: 1,000. Averages 3 total titles each year. Sometimes comments on rejected ms. *If detailed comment, $500.*

- The publisher has been concentrating on poetry lately, but may consider fiction. See the listing for *Puckerbrush Review* in this book.

Needs: Contemporary, experimental, literary. Published new writers within the last year.

How to Contact: Accepts unsolicited mss. Submit complete ms with cover letter. SASE (IRCs). Reports in 2 weeks on queries; 2 months on mss.

Terms: Pays royalties of 10%; 10 author's copies. Sends galleys to author. Publishes ms usually 1 year after acceptance. Writer's guidelines for #10 SAE and 1 first-class stamp. "I have a book list and flyers."

‡*PYX PRESS, (III, IV)**, P.O. Box 620, Orem UT 84059-0620. Editor-in-Chief: C. Darren Butler. Fiction Editors: Julie Thomas, Patricia Hatch. Estab. 1990. Publishes hardcover and paperback originals and reprints. Books: offset or xerography printing; binding varies from saddle-stitched to hand-sewn; average print order: 100-2,500; first novel order: 200-1,000. Plans 0-2 first novels this year. Averages 5-12 total titles, 2-5 fiction titles each year. Sometimes comments on rejected ms.

- See *Magic Realism* and *A Theatre of Blood* listings in the Literary/Small Circulation section of this book.

Needs: Experimental, fantasy (magic realism, glib fantasy, folktales, literary fantasy, fables, fairy tales, exaggerated realism), horror (dark fantasy), literary, religious/inspirational (religious fantasy), science fiction (soft/sociological) short story collections. Plans to publish *A Theatre of Blood*, limited edition dark fantasy anthology and a fiction anthology by and about lawyers/law to include literary fantasy and humor. "We have expanded our operation from publishing two little magazines to include three chapbooks series, one serial anthology *A Theatre of Blood*, and 2-6 book projects per year." Chapbook series includes "North-American Magic Realism," "Strike Through the Mask" and "Avatar."

How to Contact: Accepts unsolicited mss. Query first with 2 paragraph bio, list of credits and first 3 pages of ms. SASE (IRCs) for reply. Reports in 1 month on queries; 6-12 months on mss.

Terms: Pays royalties of 8% minimum; 15% maximum (after we have broken even on the project). Provides 20 author's copies. *Subsidy publishes 10%.* Sends galleys to author. Publishes ms 2-18 months after acceptance. Writer's guidelines for #10 SAE and 1 first-class stamp or IRC. Book catalog for #10 SAE and 1 first-class stamp.

Advice: "Most authors who have placed book-length or chapbook collections with us have previously appeared in *Magic Realism* magazine. 95% of all books/chapbooks are by invitation."

*Q.E.D. PRESS, (I), 155 Cypress St., Ft. Bragg CA 95437. (707)964-9520. Senior Editor: John Fremont. Estab. 1985. "Small press publisher subsidiary of mid-size production house." Publishes hardcover and paperback originals. Books: acid-free recycled 60 lb. paper; offset or Cameron Belt printing; perfect or Smyth-sewn binding; average print order: 3,000; first novel print order: 1,000. Plans 1 first novel this year. Averages 10 total titles, 2-3 fiction titles each year.
  • The publisher received a 1993 American Book Award for the editing of *Paris Connections: African American Artists in Paris*.
Needs: Experimental, literary, mystery/suspense, translations. "Our needs are minimal, but we'll jump on something we think is hot. No formula anything." Recently published *The Long Reach*, by Susan Davis; *The Haole Substitute*, by Walt Novak; *The Man Who Owned the Hogs*, by Leonard Dugger; *Four Lives*, by Herman Pepper.
How to Contact: Accepts unsolicited mss. Submit outline/synopsis with 3 sample chapters. SASE (IRCs). Agented fiction 10%. Reports in 3 weeks on queries; 5 weeks on mss.
Terms: Pays royalties of 8-15%. *Subsidy publishes under another imprint.* Publishes ms 6 months-2 years after acceptance. Writer's guidelines not available. Book catalog free.

♣QUARRY PRESS, (I,II), Box 1061, Kingston, Ontario, K7L 4Y5 Canada. (613)548-8429. Managing Editor: Melanie Dugan. Estab. 1965. Small independent publisher with plans to expand. Publishes paperback originals. Books: Rolland tint paper; offset printing; perfect-bound; illustrations; average print order: 1,200; first novel print order: 1,200. Published new writers within the past year. Plans 1 first novel this year. Averages 20 total titles, 4 fiction titles each year. Sometimes comments on rejected mss.
Needs: Experimental, feminist, historical, literary, short story collections. Published *Ritual Slaughter*, by Sharon Drache; *Engaged Elsewhere*, edited by Kent Thompson (includes work by Mavis Gallant, Margaret Laurence, Dougles Glover, Ray Smitz, Keath Fraser and others); published fiction by previously unpublished writers within the last year.
How to Contact: Query first. SASE (IRCs) for query and ms. Reports in 4 months. Simultaneous submissions OK.
Terms: Pays royalties of 7-10%. Advance: negotiable. Provides 5-10 author's copies. Sends galleys to author. Publishes ms 6-8 months after acceptance. Book catalog free on request.
Advice: "Publishing more fiction than in the past. Encourages first novelists. Canadian authors only for New Canadian Novelists Series. If mailing from US, need SAE with IRCs (a must)."

‡♣RAGWEED PRESS INC./gynergy books, (IV), P.O. Box 2023, Charlottetown, Prince Edward Island C1A 7N7 Canada. (902)566-5750. Fax: (902)566-4473. Senior Editor: Lynn Henry. Estab. 1980. "Independent Canadian-owned press." Publishes paperback originals. Books: 60 lb. paper; perfect binding; average print order: 3,000. Averages 12 total titles, 3 fiction titles each year.
Needs: *Canadian-authored only.* Childrens/juvenile (adventure, girl-positive preschool/picture book), feminist, lesbian. Plans *Lesbian Parenting, Lesbian Sisters* anthology; writers submit to Anthology Editor; editor selects stories. "We do accept submissions to anthologies from US writers." Recently published *Dancing at the Club Holocaust*, by J.J. Steinfeld (short stories about Holocaust survivors); *Friends I Never Knew*, by Tanya Lester (feminist); *A House Not Her Own*, by Emily Nasrallah (translation). Published new writers within the last year.
How to Contact: Does not accept unsolicited mss. Query first. Include estimated word count, brief bio, list of publishing credits. SASE (IRCs) for reply. Reports in 16 weeks on queries. Simultaneous submissions OK.
Terms: Pays royalties of 10% minimum; offers negotiable advance. Provides 10 author's copies. Sends galleys to author. Publishes ms 12-18 months after acceptance. Writer's guidelines for #10 SAE and 1 first-class stamp. Book catalog for large SAE and 2 first-class stamps.
Advice: "Specialized market — lesbian novels especially. Be brief, give good outline, give resume."

*READ 'N RUN BOOKS (I), Subsidiary of Crumb Elbow Publishing, Box 294, Rhododendron OR 97049. (503)622-4798. Imprints are Elbow Books, Research Centrex, Wind Dancer Press, Silhouette Imprints, Tyee Press, Oregon Fever Books and Trillium Art Productions. Publisher: Michael P. Jones. Estab. 1978. Small independent publisher with three on staff. Publishes hardcover and paperback originals and reprints. Books: special order paper; offset printing; "usually a lot" of illustrations; average print order: varies. Published new writers within the last year. Plans 1 first novel this year. Averages 30 titles, 5 fiction titles each year. Sometimes comments on rejected ms; *$25-75 charge for critiques depending upon length.*

Needs: Adventure, contemporary, ethnic, experimental, fantasy, feminist, historical, horror, humor/satire, juvenile (animal, easy-to-read, fantasy, historical, sports, spy/adventure, contemporary), literary, mainstream, military/war, multicultural, preschool/picture book, psychic/supernatural/occult, regional, religious/inspirational, romance (contemporary, historical), science fiction, short story collections, spiritual, suspense/mystery, technical and professional translations, western, young adult/teen (easy-to-read, fantasy/science fiction, historical, problem novels, romance, sports, spy/adventure). Looking for fiction on "historical and wildlife" subjects. "Also, some creative short stories would be nice to see for a change. No pornography." Recently published *Umpqua Agriculture, 1851*, by Jesse Applegate; *Life on the Oregon*, by Alfred Setan; *Samuel Kimbrough Barlow: A Pioneer Road Builder of Oregon*, by Mary Barlow Wilkins. This year starting anthology to give writers a chance to express themselves about nature and the environment.
How to Contact: Accepts unsolicited ms. Query first. Submit outline/synopsis (*copies only*, no originals) and complete ms with cover letter. SASE (IRCs). Reports in 1 month on queries; 1-2 months on mss. Simultaneous submissions OK.
Terms: Provides 5+ author's copies (negotiated). Sends galleys to author. Publishes ms 10-12 months after acceptance. *Subsidy publishes two books or more/year*. Terms vary from book to book. Writer's guidelines for 45¢ postage. Book catalog for SASE or IRC and $2 postage.
Advice: Publishing "more hardcover fiction books based on real-life events. They are in demand by libraries. Submit everything you have—even artwork. Also, if you have ideas for layout, provide those also. If you have an illustrator that you're working with, be sure to get them in touch with us. Do not be pushy! We are very busy and deal with a lot of people, which means you and your needs are equal to everyone else's. Phone calls are fine, but we cannot return calls due to overwhelming volume. We are a great place for writers to get started if they have a professional working attitude and manner."

✷RED DEER COLLEGE PRESS, (II, IV), Box 5005, Red Deer, Alberta T4N 5H5 Canada. (403)342-3321. Managing Editor: Dennis Johnson. Estab. 1975. Publishes hardcover and paperback originals. Books: offset paper; offset printing; hardcover/perfect-bound; average print order: 1,000-4,000; first novel print order: 2,500. Averages 10-12 total titles, 2 fiction titles each year. Sometimes comments on rejected mss.
    • Red Deer College Press was the 1992 Alberta Publisher of the Year and has received honors and awards from the Alberta Book Publishers Association and the Canadian Children's Book Centre (designations for individual books).
Needs: Contemporary, experimental, literary, short story collections. No romance, sci-fi. Recently published *The Thirteenth Summer*, by José Luis Olaizola; *Don't Fence Me In*, by David Poulsen; *Prism Moon*, by Martina Bates (young adult novel).
How to Contact: *Canadian authors only*. Does not accept unsolicited mss. Query first or submit outline/synopsis and 2 sample chapters. SASE. Agented fiction 10%. Reports in 3 months on queries; 6 months on mss. Simultaneous submissions OK.
Terms: Pays royalties of 8-10%. Advance is negotiable. Sends galleys to author. Publishes ms 1 year after acceptance. Book catalog for 9×12 SASE (IRC).
Advice: "Final manuscripts must be submitted on Mac disk in MS Word. Absolutely *no* unsolicited mss. Query first."

✷REFERENCE PRESS, (IV), Box 70, Teeswater, Ontario N0G 2S0 Canada. (519)392-6634. Imprints are RP Large Print Books. Editor: Gordon Ripley. Estab. 1982. Small independent Canadian publisher of library reference material, computer software and large print books. Hardcover and paperback originals and hardcover reprints. Books: 70 lb. Zepher laid paper; offset printing; casebound, some perfect-bound; average print order: 600. Published new writers within the last year. Averages 10 total titles, 4 fiction titles each year. Always comments on rejected mss.
Needs: Sports. Published *Canadian Sports Stories* (anthology, fiction); *Dance Me Outside* and *Born Indian*, by W.P. Kinsella (large print).
Terms: Pays in royalties of 10%; 5 author's copies. Writer's guidelines and book catalog free. Accepts unsolicited mss. Accepts electronic submissions.

RIO GRANDE PRESS, (I), P.O. Box 71745, Las Vegas NV 89170. (702)894-4486. Imprints include *Se La Vie Writer's Journal*. Publisher: Rosalie Avara. Estab. 1989. "One-person operation on a half-time basis. Planning to continue story anthologies plus novelettes in 1994." Publishes paperback originals. Books: offset printing; saddle-stitched binding; average print order: 100. Plans 1-2 first novels next year. Averages 10 total titles, 2 fiction titles each year. Sometimes comments on rejected ms.

• Look for the *Se La Vie Writer's Journal* contest listing in this book. The publisher also sponsors a short-short story contest quarterly.

Needs: Adventure, contemporary, ethnic, family saga, fantasy, humor/satire, literary, mystery/suspense (amateur sleuth, private eye, romantic suspense), regional, short story collections. Looking for "general interest, slice of life stories; good, clean, wholesome stories about everyday people. No sex, no porn, no science fiction (although I may consider flights of fantasy, day dreams, etc.), no religious. Any subject within the 'wholesome' limits. No experimental styles, just good conventional plot, characters, dialogue." Recently published *The Story Shop* (short story anthology; 13 stories by individual authors). Published new writers within the last year. "Currently we are only accepting short stories for our story anthology. Limit: 1,500 words. Send up to two only; one will be selected."

How to Contact: Query first then submit short outline/synopsis. SASE (IRCs). Reports in 2 weeks on queries.

Terms: Pays 1 author's copy, depends on grant/award money (if contest is involved, up to $25.) "Short story collections and/or novelettes—individual arrangements with author, depending on ms—probably a contributor's copy plus publication and review in *Se La Vie Writer's Journal*." Sends galleys to author (once only). Publishes ms 4-6 months after acceptance. Writer's guidelines for #10 SAE and 2 first-class stamps. Book catalog for #10 SAE and 2 first-class stamps.

Advice: "I enjoy working with writers new to fiction, especially when I see that they have really worked hard on their craft, i.e., cutting out all unnecessary words, using action dialogue, interesting descriptive scenes, thought-out plots and well-rounded characters that are believable. Please read listing carefully noting what type and subject of fiction is desired. Don't send the entire ms (book) packed in a heavy (costly) book box. Please send me a short cover letter giving brief history of your writing experience or credits. If none, just say so. Or, send me a short synopsis. Would like to see more stories or novelettes with a Southwestern flavor; story collections centered around a central theme; novelettes that give a personal insight into age old problems of life."

RISING TIDE PRESS, (II), 5 Kivy St., Huntington Station NY 11746. (516)427-1289. Editor: Lee Boojamra. Estab. 1988. "Small, independent press, publishing lesbian fiction—novels only—no short stories." Publishes paperback trade originals. Books: 60 lb. vellum paper; web printing; perfect-bound; average print order: 5,000; first novel print order: 4,000-6,000. Plans 6 first novels this year. Averages 4-6 total titles. Comments on rejected ms.

• In 1993 *Return to Isis*, by Jean Stewart, published by Rising Tide Press, was nominated for a Lambda Literary Award in Science Fiction.

Needs: Lesbian adventure, contemporary, erotica, fantasy, feminist, romance, science fiction, suspense/mystery, western. Looking for romance and mystery. "Minimal heterosexual content." Recently published *Love Spell*, by Karen Williams; *Danger in High Places*, by Sharon Gilligan; *Shadows After Dark*, by Ouida Crozier. Developing a dark fantasy line.

How to Contact: Accepts unsolicited mss with SASE (IRCs). Reports in 1 week on queries; 2-3 months on mss.

Terms: Pays 10-15% royalties. "*We will assist writers who wish to self-publish for a nominal fee.*" Sends galleys to author. Publishes ms 6-18 months after acceptance. Writer's guidelines for #10 SAE and 1 first-class stamp.

‡*RIVERCROSS PUBLISHING, INC., (I, II), Subsidiary of Lantern Press, 127 E. 59th St., New York NY 10022. (212)421-1950. Fax: (212)644-0749. Editor-in-Chief: Josh Furman. Estab. 1945. "Small, independent publisher." Publishes hardcover and paperback originals. Books: book paper; offset printing. Sometimes comments on rejected ms.

Needs: Open. Recently published *Fools Gold*, by Charles Knickerbocker (novel); *The Consortium*, by David Stone (novel); *Uninvited Memories*, by Ina Smith (poetry). Published new writers within the last year.

How to Contact: Accepts unsolicited mss. Query first, submit outline/synopsis and sample chapters or complete ms with cover letter. SASE (IRCs) for reply. Reports in 3 weeks. Simultaneous submissions OK. Accepts electronic submissions.

Terms: Pays royalties of 40% maximum. *Subsidy publishes 50%.* Sends galleys to author. Publishes ms 6-12 months after acceptance. Writer's guidelines and book catalog free.

SAND RIVER PRESS, (I), 1319 14th St., Los Osos CA 93402. (805)543-3591. Editor: Bruce Miller. Estab. 1987. "Small press." Publishes paperback originals. Books: offset printing; b&w or color illustrations; average print order: 3,000; first novel print order: 2,000. Averages 2-3 total titles, 1 fiction title each year. Sometimes comments on rejected ms.

Needs: Childrens/juvenile, erotica, ethnic, multicultural (Native American), lesbian, literary, New Age/mystic/spiritual, regional (west). Publishes literary best anthology.
How to Contact: Accepts unsolicited mss. Submit outline/synopsis and 3 sample chapters. Include list of publishing credits. SASE (IRCs) for return of ms or a disposable copy of the ms. Reports in 3 weeks on queries; 6 weeks on mss. Simultaneous submissions OK.
Terms: Pays royalties of 8% minimum; 15% maximum. Average advance: $500-1,000. Provides 10 author's copies. Sends galleys to author. Publishes ms 1 year after acceptance. Book catalog for SASE.

SANDPIPER PRESS, (IV), Box 286, Brookings OR 97415. (503)469-5588. Owner: Marilyn Reed Riddle. Estab. 1979. One-person operation specializing in low-cost large-print 18 pt. books. Publishes paperback originals. Books: 70 lb. paper; saddle-stitched binding, perfect-bound; 84 pages maximum; leatherette cover; b&w sketches or photos; average print order 2,000; no novels. Averages 1 title every 2 years. Occasionally critiques or comments on rejected ms.
Needs: From Native American "Indian" writers only, *true* visions and prophesies; from general public writers, unusual quotations, sayings.
How to Contact: Does not accept unsolicited mss. Query first or submit outline/synopsis. SASE (IRCs). Reports in 1 month on queries; 1 month on mss. Simultaneous submissions OK.
Terms: Pays 2 author's copies and $10 Native American. Publisher buys true story and owns copyright. Author may buy any number of copies at 40% discount and postage. Book catalog for #10 SAE and 1 first-class stamp.
Advice: Send SASE for more information.

THE SAVANT GARDE WORKSHOP, (I, II, IV), a privately-owned affiliate of The Savant Garde Institute, Ltd., P.O. Box 1650, Sag Harbor NY 11963. (516)725-1414. Publisher: Vilna Jorgen II. Estab. 1953. "Midsize multiple-media publisher." Publishes hardcover and paperback originals and reprints. Averages 8 total titles. Sometimes comments on rejected ms.
• Be sure to look at this publisher's guidelines first. Works could best be described as avant-garde/post modern, experimental.
Needs: Contemporary, futuristic, humanist, literary, philosophical. "We are open to the best, whatever it is." No "mediocrity or pot boilers." Recently published *01 or a Machine Called SKEETS*, by Artemis Smith (avant-garde); *the children of THE CHILDREN OF . . .*, by D.L. Hiatt; *TREE: Spirit/Deer*, by Jim Meirose; *Bottomfeeder*, by Mark Spitzer. Series include "On-Demand Desktop Collectors' Editions," "Artists' Limited Editions," "Monographs of The Savant Garde Institute."
How to Contact: Query first with SASE (IRCs). Agented fiction 25%. Reports in 1 week on queries; 2 months on mss. Accepts electronic submissions, MS-DOS only.
Terms: Average advance: $500, provides author's copies, honorarium (depends on grant/award money). Terms set by individual arrangement with author depending on the book and previous professional experience. Sends galleys to author. Publishes ms 18 months after acceptance. Writer's guidelines free.
Advice: "Most of the time we recommend authors to literary agents who can get better deals for them with other publishers, since we are looking for extremely rare offerings. We are not interested in the usual commercial submissions. Convince us you are a real artist, not a hacker." Would like to see more "thinking for the 21st Century of Nobel Prize calibre. We're expanding into multimedia CD-ROM co-publishing and seek multitalented authors who can produce and perform their own multimedia work for CD-ROM release, primarily for the academic library market, later also for bookstores."

SEAL PRESS, (IV), 3131 Western Ave., Seattle WA 98121. (206)283-7844. President: Faith Conlon. Estab. 1976. Publishes hardcover and paperback originals. Books: acid-free paper; offset printing; perfect or cloth binding; average print order: 6,500. Averages 15 total titles, 2 fiction titles each year. Sometimes critiques rejected ms "very briefly."

Stay informed! Keep up with changes in the market by using the latest edition of Novel & Short Story Writer's Market. If this is 1995 or later, buy a new edition at your favorite bookstore or order directly from Writer's Digest Books.

Needs: Ethnic, feminist, lesbian, literary, mystery, young adult, anthologies. "We publish women only. Work must be feminist, non-racist, non-homophobic." Recently published *Disappearing Moon Cafe*, by Sky Lee (literary novel); *No Forwarding Address*, by Elisabeth Bowers (mystery novel); *Black Women's Health Book*, edited by Evelyn C. White.

How to Contact: Query first. SASE (IRCs). Reports in 1-2 months. Accepts "readable" computer printouts.

Terms: "Standard publishing practices; do not wish to disclose specifics." Sends galleys to author. Book catalog for SAE and 65¢ postage.

SECOND CHANCE PRESS AND THE PERMANENT PRESS, (II), Noyac Rd., Sag Harbor NY 11963. (516)725-1101. Publishers: Judith and Martin Shepard. Estab. 1977. Mid-size, independent publisher. Publishes hardcover originals and reprints. Books: hardcover; average print order: 1,500-2,000; first novel print order: 1,500-2,000. Published new writers within the last year. Plans 11 first novels this year. Averages 12 total titles; all fiction, each year.

● See the interview with Publisher Judith Shepard in the 1993 *Novel & Short Story Writer's Market*.

Needs: Contemporary, humor/satire, literary, supsense/mystery. "I like novels that have a unique point of view and have a high quality of writing." No gothic, romance, horror, science fiction, pulp. Recently published *Beyond Deserving*, by Sandra Scofield; *The Affair at Honey Hill*, by Berry Fleming (literary/historical); *Zulus*, by Percival Everett (literary/futuristic).

How to Contact: Query first. Submit outline and no more than 2 chapters. SASE (IRCs). Agented fiction 15%. Reports in 6 weeks on queries; 3 months on mss.

Terms: Pays royalties of 10-15%. Advance: $1,000. Sends galleys to author. Book catalog for $3.

Advice: "We are looking for good books, be they tenth novels or first novels, it makes little difference. The fiction is more important than the track record."

‡SENIOR PRESS, (I, IV), P.O. Box 21362, Hilton Head Island SC 29925. (803)681-2785. Editor: Miriam Bush. Estab. 1993. "This is a new small press interested in novels written by persons 50 years of age and older who have never had a book published. One-person, part-time staff." Publishes paperback originals. Books: 50 lb. white paper; offset printing; perfect binding; average print order: 2,000; first novel print order: 2,000. Plans 1-3 first novels this year. Always comments on rejected ms.

Needs: Adventure, family saga, historical, humor/satire, literary, mainstream/contemporary, mystery/suspense, regional, romance, thriller/espionage.

How to Contact: Accepts unsolicited mss. Query first or submit outline/synopsis and 2 sample chapters. Include estimated word count, bio (1 page), Social Security number and list of publishing credits. SASE (IRCs) for reply, or send disposable copy of the ms. Reports in 2-3 weeks on queries; 1-2 months on mss.

Terms: Pays royalties of 10%. Provides author's copies (depends on press run). Sends galleys to author. Publishes ms 10-12 months after acceptance. Writer's guidelines free.

Advice: "Let's face it. The big publishing companies are not interested in writers up in years, if they happen to be unknowns. We hope to serve the burgeoning senior population by creating a market for creative fiction works done by persons 50 and over. We want to start with those now laboring who have never had a book published. Especially seeking contemporary or historical novels that bespeak the maturity, depth of experience and knowledge possessed by seniors."

‡SERENDIPITY SYSTEMS, (I, II, IV), P.O. Box 140, San Simeon CA 93452. (805)927-5259. Imprints include Books-on-Disks™ and Bookware™. Publisher: John Galuszka. Estab. 1985. "Electronic publishing for IBM-PC compatible systems." Publishes "Electronic editions originals and reprints." Books on disk. Averages 36 total titles, 15 fiction titles each year (either publish or distribute). Often comments on rejected ms.

Needs: On disk only: adventure, children's/juvenile, erotica, ethnic/multicultural, experimental, family saga, feminist, gay, historical, horror, humor/satire, lesbian, literary, mainstream/contemporary, military/war, mystery/suspense, regional, science fiction, short story collections, thriller/espionage, translations, western, young adult/teen. "I would love to see works of interactive fiction." No romance, religion, occult. Recently published *A Maine Yankee at Big Sur*, by J. Peter (contemporary novel); *Ranger's Peril*, by A. Johnson (western novel); *Indians Scattered on Dawn's Highway*, by W.C. Leadbeater (sf/fantasy). Published new writers within the last year.

How to Contact: Submit complete ms with cover letter. *Disk required.* If files not in ASCII form, then list word processor used. Send SASE (or IRCs) for reply, return of ms or send disposable copy of ms. Reports in 2 weeks on queries; 1 month on mss.

Terms: Pays royalties of 25%. "We distribute the works of self-published authors and have a cooperative program for authors who don't have the skills to electronically self-publish. We also distribute shareware electronic editions." Publishes ms 1 month after acceptance. Writer's guidelines for 6×9 SAE and 2 first-class stamps. Book catalogs for $1 (on IBM-PC 360K disk).
Advice: "A number of new tools have recently become available, Hypertext publishing programs DART and ORPHEUS, for example, and we look forward to selling works which can take advantage of the features of these and other programs. Would like to see: more works of serious literature—novels, short stories, plays, etc. Would like to not see: right wing adventure fantasies from 'Tom Clancy wannabes.'"

SEVEN BUFFALOES PRESS, (II), Box 249, Big Timber MT 59011. Editor/Publisher: Art Cuelho. Estab. 1975. Publishes paperback originals. Averages 4-5 total titles each year.
• The Seven Buffaloes Press also publishes a number of magazines including *Azorean Express*, *Black Jack*, *Hill and Holler* and *Valley Grapevine*.
Needs: Contemporary, short story collections, "rural, American Hobo, Okies, Native American, Southern Appalachia, Arkansas and the Ozarks. Wants farm- and ranch-based stories." Published *Rig Nine*, by William Rintoul (collection of oilfield short stories).
How to Contact: Query first with SASE (IRCs). Reports in 1 week on queries; 2 weeks on mss.
Terms: Pays royalties of 10% minimum; 15% on second edition or in author's copies (10% of edition). No advance. Writer's guidelines and book catalog for SASE.
Advice: "There's too much influence from TV and Hollywood, media writing I call it. We need to get back to the people, to those who built and are still building this nation with sweat, blood and brains. More people are into it for the money, instead of for the good writing that is still to be cranked out by isolated writers. Remember, I was a writer for 10 years before I became a publisher."

HAROLD SHAW PUBLISHERS, (II), Box 567, 388 Gundersen Dr., Wheaton IL 60189. (708)665-6700. Director of Editorial Services: Ramona Cramer Tucker. Estab. 1968. "Small, independent religious publisher with expanding fiction line." Publishes paperback originals and reprints. Books: 35 lb. Mando Supreme paper; sheet-fed printing; perfect-bound; average print order: 5,000. Plans 1 novel per year in Northcote Books (our literary/academic fiction subsidiary). Averages 30 total titles, 1-2 fiction titles each year. Sometimes critiques rejected mss.
Needs: Literary, religious/inspirational. Looking for religious literary novels or young adult fiction (religious). No short stories, romances, children's fiction. Recently published *Stars Over East L.A.*, by Marian Flandnick Bray (novel); *The Sioux Society*, by Jeffrey Asher Nestib; *The Northcote Anthology of Short Stories*. Published new writers within the last year. Also publishes under OMF imprint: books published in conjunction with Overseas Missionary Fellowship.
How to Contact: Accepts unsolicited mss. Query first. Submit outline/synopsis and 2-3 sample chapters. SASE (IRCs). Reports in 2 weeks on queries; 2-4 weeks on mss. No simultaneous submissions.
Terms: Pays royalties of 10%. Provides 10 author's copies. Sends pages to author. Publishes ms 12-18 months after acceptance. Free writer's guidelines. Book catalog for 9×12 SAE and $1.25 postage.
Advice: "Character and plot development are important to us. We look for quality writing in word and in thought. 'Sappiness' and 'pop-writing' don't go over well at all with our editorial department."

THE SMITH (III), 69 Joralemon St., Brooklyn NY 11201. Editor: Harry Smith. Estab. 1964. Books: 70 lb. vellum paper for offset and 80 lb. vellum for letterpress printing; perfect binding; often uses illustrations; average print order: 1,000; first novel print order: 1,000. Plans 2 fiction titles this year.
• The Poor Richard Award was presented to publisher Harry Smith in Spring 1993 for his "three decades of independent literary publishing activities."
Needs: *Extremely* limited book publishing market—currently doing only 4-6 books annually, and these are of a literary nature, usually fiction or poetry. Recently published *The Cleveland Indian*, by Luke Salisbury (novel); *Ha, Ha! La Solution Imaginaire*, by Stephen Dwoskin (fiction/photography).
Advice: "We find most synopses are stupid. Our list is our only guide and our motto is: Anything goes as long as it's good. Remember: Although we maintain a large backlist, we currently publish 3 to 5 books per year. And SASE, please!"

SOHO PRESS, (I), 853 Broadway, New York NY 10003. (212)260-1900. Publisher: Juris Jurjevics. Publishes hardcover originals and trade paperback reprints. Averages 20 titles/year.
Needs: Adventure, ethnic, historical, literary, mainstream, mystery/espionage, suspense. "We do novels that are the very best of their kind." Recently published *The Curious Eat Themselves*, by John Straley; *The Liar*, by Stephen Fry; *The Queen & I*, by Sue Townsend. Published new writers within the

last year. Also publishes the Hera series (serious historical fiction with strong female leads.)

How to Contact: Submit query or complete ms with SASE (IRCs). Reports in 1 month on queries; 6 weeks on mss. Simultaneous submissions OK.

Terms: Pays royalties of 10-15% on retail price. For trade paperbacks pays 7½% royalties on first 10,000 copies; 10% after. Offers advance. Book catalog for $1 plus SASE (IRCs).

Advice: Greatest challenge is "introducing brand new, untested writers. We do not care if they are agented or not. Half the books we publish come directly from authors. We look for strong writing skills and compelling plots."

SOUTHERN METHODIST UNIVERSITY PRESS, (I), P.O. Box 415, Dallas TX 75275. (214)768-1433. Senior Editor: Kathryn M. Lang. Estab. 1936. "Small university press publishing in areas of film/theater, Southwest life and letters, religion/medical ethics and contemporary fiction." Publishes hardcover and paperback originals and reprints. Books: acid-free paper; perfect-bound; some illustrations; average print order 2,000. Plans 2 first novels this year. Averages 10-12 total titles; 3-4 fiction titles each year. Sometimes comments on rejected ms.

Needs: Contemporary, ethnic, literary, regional, short story collections. "We are booked for the next year or two; we always are willing to look at 'serious' or 'literary' fiction." No "mass market, science fiction, formula, thriller, romance." Recently published *The Names of the Lost*, by Liza Wieland (novel); *Things We Lost, Gave Away, Bought High and Sold Low*, by Deboray Navas (collection); *Careless Weeds*, edited by Tom Pilkington (collection of novellas). Published new writers within the last year.

How to Contact: Accepts unsolicited mss. Query first. Submit outline/synopsis and 3 sample chapters. SASE (IRCs). Reports in 3 weeks on queries; 3 months on mss. No simultaneous submissions.

Terms: Pays royalties of 10% of net, negotiable advance, 10 author's copies. Publishes ms 1 year after acceptance. Book catalog free.

Advice: "We view encouraging first time authors as part of the mission of a university press. Send query describing the project and your own background." Looks for "quality fiction from new or established writers."

SPACE AND TIME, (I, IV), (4-B), 138 W. 70th St., New York NY 10023-4432. Book Editor: Jani Anderson. Estab. 1966 – book line 1984. Two-person operation on part-time basis. Publishes paperback originals. Books: 60 lb. white recycled paper; offset printing; perfect-bound; illustrations on cover; average print order: 1,000; first novel print order: 1,000. Averages 1 fiction title each year. Often critiques or comments on rejected ms.

Needs: Fantasy, horror, mystery/suspense, science fiction. Wants to see "cross-genre material, such as horror-western, science fiction-mystery, occult-spy adventure, etc." Does not want "anything *without* some element of fantasy or science fiction (or at least the 'feel' of same)." Recently published *The Steel Eye*, by Chet Gottfried; *The Spy Who Drank Blood*, by Gordon Linzer; *The Gift*, by Scott Edelman (gay-horror).

How to Contact: *No unsolicited mss.* Query first or submit outline/synopsis and 3 sample chapters. Reports in 2 months on queries; 3-6 months on mss. Simultaneous submissions OK. "Prefer around 50,000 words."

Terms: Pays royalties of 10% based on cover price and print run, within 60 days of publication (additional royalties, if going back to press). Also pays author's copies. Sends galleys to author. Writer's guidelines for #10 SAE and 1 first-class stamp (IRC). Book catalog free on request.

SPECTRUM PRESS, (I), Box 109, 3023 N. Clark St., Chicago IL 60657. (312)281-1419. Editor D.P. Agin. Estab. 1991. "Small independent electronic publisher." Publishes computer disks only. Published new writers within the last year. Plans 5 first novels this year. Averages 30 total titles, 25 fiction titles each year. Sometimes comments on rejected ms.

Needs: Contemporary, erotica, experimental, feminist, gay, lesbian, literary, mainstream, short story collections, translations. "Quality lesbian fiction of all kinds, feminist writing, literary novels." No juvenile or young adult. Recently published *Shock Wave*, by Cathy Khadmy (novel); *The Best of Tomorrow*, (anthology); *Charly's Game*, by Bren Fleming (lesbian novel). "We now have four lines: Spectrum Classics (classic literature and nonfiction); Contemporary Fiction and Poetry; Spectrum Obelisk Library (erotica); Artemis Books (lesbian/feminist fiction and nonfiction).

How to Contact: Accepts unsolicited mss. Query first. Submit outline/synopsis and sample chapters or complete ms with cover letter. Reports in 2 weeks on queries; 1 month on mss. Simultaneous submissions OK. Accepts electronic submissions on disk only. Prefers submissions on IBM/MS-DOS computer disk.

Terms: Pays royalties of 10-15%. Sends disk to author. Publishes within 2 months after acceptance. Writer's guidelines available. Book catalog free.
Advice: "We are interested in new voices and new attitudes. We prefer disk submissions in ASCII code or WordPerfect 5.1 format. Contact us first for other formats."

THE SPEECH BIN, INC., (IV), 1965 25th Ave., Vero Beach FL 32960. (407)770-0007. Fax: (407)770-0006. Senior Editor: Jan J. Binney. Estab. 1984. Small independent publisher and major national and international distributor of books and material for speech-language pathologists, audiologists, special educators and caregivers. Publishes hardcover and paperback originals. Averages 15-20 total titles/year. "No fiction at present time, but we are very interested in publishing fiction relevant to our specialties."
Needs: "We are most interested in seeing fiction, including books for children, dealing with individuals experiencing communication disorders, other handicaps, and their families and caregivers, particularly their parents, or family members dealing with individuals who have strokes, physical disability, hearing loss, Alzheimer's and so forth."
How to Contact: Accepts unsolicited mss. Query first. SASE (IRCs). Agented fiction 10%. Reports in 4-6 weeks on queries; 1-3 months on mss. Simultaneous submissions OK, but only if notified by author.
Terms: Pays royalties of 8%. Sends galleys to author. Writer's guidelines for #10 SASE. Book catalog for 9×12 SAE with 3 first-class stamps.
Advice: "We are most interested in publishing fiction about individuals who have speech, hearing and other handicaps."

SPINSTERS INK, (IV), (formerly Spinsters Book Co.), (IV), P.O. Box 300170, Minneapolis MN 55403. Managing Editor: Kelly Kager. Estab. 1978. Moderate size women's publishing company growing steadily. Publishes paperback originals and reprints. Books: 55 lb. acid-free natural paper; photo offset printing; perfect-bound; illustrations when appropriate; average print order: 5,000. Plans 3 first novels this year. Averages 6 total titles, 3-5 fiction titles each year. Occasionally critiques rejected ms.
● Spinsters Ink published *The Two-Bit Tango*, by Elizabeth Pincus, which received a Lambda Award and *Vital Ties*, by Karen Kringle, a finalist for the ALA Gay and Lesbian Book Awards.
Needs: Feminist, lesbian. Wants "full-length quality fiction—thoroughly revised novels which display deep characterization, theme and style. We *only* consider books by women. No books by men, or books with sexist, racist or ageist content." Recently published *Final Rest*, by Mary Morell (mystery); *The Solitary Twist*, by Elizabeth Pincus (mystery); *As You Desire*, by Madeline Moore (fiction). Published new writers within the last year. Publishes anthologies. Writers may submit directly. Series include: "Coming of Age Series" and "Forgotten Women's Series."
How to Contact: Query or submit outline/synopsis and 2-5 sample chapters not to exceed 50 pages with SASE (IRCs). Reports in 1 month on queries; 2 months on mss. Simultaneous submissions discouraged. Disk submissions OK (DOS or Macintosh format—MS Word 4.0). Prefers hard copy with disk submission.
Terms: Pays royalties of 7-10%, plus 25 author's copies; unlimited extra copies at 45% discount. Free book catalog.
Advice: "In the past, lesbian fiction has been largely 'escape fiction' with sex and romance as the only required ingredients; however, we encourage more complex work that treats the lesbian lifestyle with the honesty it deserves."

THE SPIRIT THAT MOVES US PRESS, (II), P. O. Box 820-N, Jackson Heights NY 11372-0820. (718)426-8788. Editor/Publisher: Morty Sklar. Estab. 1974. Small independent literary publisher. Publishes hardcover and paperback originals. "We do, for the most part, simultaneous clothbound and trade paperbacks for the same title." Books: 60 lb. natural acid-free paper; mostly photo-offset, some letterpress; cloth and perfect binding; illustrations; average print order: 3,000; first novel print order: 3,000. Plans 1 first novel this year. Averages 2 fiction titles, mostly multi-author. Sometimes comments on rejected mss.
● The editor tells us that in 1983 he published the first collection in English in the US of Jaroslav Seifert, who won the Nobel Prize for literature a year later. Morty Sklar also received the CCLM Editor's Grant Award for excellence and vision (Coordinating Council of Literary Magazines) in 1985. See the listing for his magazine, *The Spirit That Moves Us*, in this book.
Needs: Literary. "Our choice of 'literary' does not exclude almost any other category—as long as the writing communicates on an emotional level, and is involved with people more than things. Nothing sensational or academic." Will publish anthology *Phoenix: Stories Poems and Essays from Former Drug*

INSIDER VIEWPOINT

Publisher Envisions a Brave New Publishing World

"I predict a revolution in literary publishing," says Daniel Agin, editor and publisher of Spectrum Press. "Ten to fifteen years from now there'll be hundreds of little electronic publishers like us. It'll change the whole character of publishing. The industry will no longer be dependent on the big New York houses."

Agin may be at the lead in his predicted revolution. One of only a few small electronic publishers—those that publish books on floppy disk—he says he is the only one specializing in contemporary fiction.

While most electronic publishers concentrate on nonfiction, reference and classic fiction, Agin looks for "quality literary fiction, poetry and criticism. Our real interest is literary and avant garde work—and we are very interested in strong voices against political and social injustice."

D.P. Agin

Agin's main goal is to make these works as accessible as possible. A writer, retired academic and computer enthusiast, he created a software program that would allow his disks to be used on almost any computer. Along the way, he also started to create disks that could be read easily by speech synthesizers and font enlarger machines used by visually-impaired and blind people.

"I wanted to create a small revolution by giving blind people access to contemporary literature. For the blind there's been no access at all to this type of fiction. What they get from other publishers are textbooks and classic fiction. They can get mass market fiction on audio, but have little access to literary work," Agin says.

The publisher says disk publishing is also a boon to writers in that costs are low, making electronic publishers less dependent on the bottom line and, therefore, more willing to take risks on new writers and work not considered mainstream. Agin manufactures his disks to order, on demand, so there are no warehouse or printing costs.

This has enabled him to publish many more writers than he would as a traditional press. In fact, he boasts 116 titles on his list and the press has only been in operation since 1991. Writers are paid in royalties and retain all print media rights, while Spectrum contracts generally ask for electronic rights for 10 years.

Although he wants to make available the work of many new writers, Agin says, he must reject a lot of what he receives. Quality is still the key, he says, whether your work will appear in print or on screen.

—Robin Gee

Addicts; look for announcements or send SASE for time. Published *Free Parking*, edited by Morty Sklar (collection of previously unpublished stories and poems) and *Editor's Choice: Fiction, Poetry & Art from the U.S. Small Press*, biennally, edited by Morty Sklar (work nominated by other publishers). Published new writers within the last year. Publishes Great American First Novel (new series; send SASE for guidelines).

How to Contact: Accepts unsolicited mss. Query letter only first "unless he/she sees an announcement that calls for manuscripts and gives a deadline." Should include estimated word count, bio and whether or not ms is a simultaneous submission. SASE (IRCs) for reply or return of ms. Reports on mss "if rejected, soon; if under consideration, from 1-3 months."

Terms: Pays royalties of 10% net, $1,000 advance for first novel, and authors copies, also honorarium, depends on grant/award money. Sends galleys to author. Publishes up to 1 year after acceptance. Plans and time-frames for #10 SAE and 1 first-class stamp or IRC "but the guidelines are only for certain books, like novels. We don't use general guidelines." Catalog for 6×9 SAE and 2 first-class stamps.

Advice: "Our plans include the Great American First Novel Series which will publish a novel from the manuscripts that come to us by an open submission policy (our regular policy). Offers $1,000 award against royalties for the winner of first novel search through an open call for mss, plus a public reading. We also have made our *Editor's Choice* series a biennial (work selected from nominations by other editors, from work they published in their books and magazines). We are interested in work that is not only well written, but that gets the reader involved on an emotional level. In other words, no matter how skilled the writing is, or how interesting or exciting the story, if we don't care about the people in it, we won't consider it. Also, we are open to a great variety of styles, so just be yourself and don't try to second-guess the editor. You may have our 15th Anniversary collection, *Free Parking*, for $5.50 as a sample book."

*STARBOOKS PRESS, Subsidiary of Woldt Corp., P.O. Box 2737, Sarasota FL 34230-2737. (813)957-1281. President/Publisher: Patrick J. Powers. Estab. 1978. "Small press specializing in mature adult fiction and nonfiction, including mainly titles of gay orientation." Publishes paperback originals. Averages 10-12 total titles, 3 anthologies each year. Comments on rejected ms.

• Woldt Corp. also distributes books by the Florida Literary Foundation Press listed in this book.

Needs: Gay fiction and nonfiction. Recently published *Boys of Spring, Boy Toy* and *Heartthrob*, by John Patrick; *The Boy on the Bicycle*, by Thom Nickels.

How to Contact: Accepts unsolicited mss. Submit outline/synopsis and sample chapters. SASE (IRCs). Reports in 1 month on queries; 6 weeks on mss. Simultaneous submissions OK.

Terms: Provides 5-25 contributor's copies on short stories or direct payment depending on author's publishing credits. Individual arrangement with author depending on the book. *Will consider subsidy publishing; offers co-op program.* Sends galleys to author. Publishes ms 6-8 months after acceptance. Writers guidelines for SASE. Book catalog free.

STONE BRIDGE PRESS, (IV), P.O. Box 8208, Berkeley CA 94707. (510)524-8732. Fax: (510)524-8711. Publisher: Peter Goodman. Estab. 1989. "Small press focusing on books about Japan in English (business, language, culture, literature)." Publishes paperback originals and reprints. Books: 60-70 lb. offset paper; web and sheet paper; perfect-bound; some illustrations; average print order: 3,000; first novel print order: 2,000-2,500. Averages 6 total titles, 2 fiction titles, each year. Sometimes comments on rejected ms.

• Stone Bridge Press received a PEN West Literary Award for Translation for *Still Life*, by Junzo Shono, translated by Wayne P. Lammers.

Needs: Japan-themed. If not translation, interested in the expatriate experience—all categories welcome: contemporary, erotica, ethnic, experimental, literary, science fiction, short story collections, translations (from Japanese). "Primarily looking at material relating to Japan. Mostly translations, but we'd like to see samples of work dealing with the expatriate experience. Also Asian- and Japanese-American. Recently published *Wind and Stone*, by Masaaki Tachihara; *Still Life and Other Stories*, by Junzo Shono; *One Hot Summer in Kyoto*, by John Haylock.

How to Contact: Accepts unsolicited mss. Query first. Submit outline/synopsis and 3 sample chapters. SASE (IRCs). Agented fiction 25%. Reports in 1 month on queries; 3-4 months on mss. Simultaneous submissions OK.

Terms: Pays royalties, offers negotiable advance. Publishes ms 18-24 months after acceptance. Book catalog for 2 first-class stamps.
Advice: "As we focus on Japan-related material there is no point in approaching us unless you are very familiar with Japan. We'd especially like to see submissions dealing with the expatriate experience and fantasy and science fiction on Japanese themes as well, but with a decided literary tone, not mass market. Please, no commercial fiction."

SUNSTONE PRESS, (IV), Box 2321, Santa Fe NM 87504-2321. (505)988-4418. Contact: James C. Smith, Jr. Estab. 1971. Midsize publisher. Publishes paperback originals. Average first novel print order: 2,000. Plans 2 first novels this year. Averages 16 total titles, 2-3 fiction titles, each year.
Needs: Western. "We have a Southwestern theme emphasis. Sometimes buys juvenile mss with illustrations." No science fiction, romance or occult. Published *Apache: The Long Ride Home*, by Grant Gall (Indian/Western); *Border Patrol*, by Cmdr. Alvin E. Moore; *The Last Narrow Gauge Train Robbery*, by Robert K. Swisher, Jr. Published new writers within the last year.
How to Contact: Accepts unsolicited mss. Query first or submit outline/synopsis and 2 sample chapters with SASE (IRCs). Reports in 2 weeks. Simultaneous submissions OK. Publishes ms 9-12 months after acceptance.
Terms: Pays royalties, 10% maximum, and 10 author's copies.

✸TANAGER PRESS, (II), 145 Troy St., Mississauga, Ontario L5G 1S8 Canada. (905)891-2502. Editorial contact persons: L. Hill, N. Ledwidge. Fiction Editor: J. Neveleff. Estab. 1977. Small publisher and mid-size distributor. Publishes hardcover originals and reprints and paperback originals. Books: H/3/pb; average print order: 3,000; first novel print order: 2,000-2,500. Plans 1 first novel this year. Averages 2 total titles, 1 fiction title.
Needs: Historical (general), humor/satire, mainstream/contemporary, mystery/suspense, religious/inspirational.
How to Contact: Does not accept unsolicited mss. Submit outline/synopsis and 1 sample chapter. Should include 50-word bio. SASE (IRCs). Reports in 3-6 weeks on queries. Simultaneous submissions OK.
Terms: Pays royalties of 10% minimum; offers negotiable advance. Book catalog free.

TEXTILE BRIDGE PRESS, (II), Subsidiary of Moody Street Irregulars, Inc., Box 157, Clarence Center NY 14032. (716)741-3393. Imprints include The Jack Kerouac Living Writers Reading Series. President/Editor: Joy Walsh. Fiction Editor: Marion Perry. Estab. 1978. "We publish a magazine on and about the work of Jack Kerouac. We also publish book length manuscripts in the spirit of Kerouac when available." Publishes paperback originals. Books: bond paper; offset printing; saddle or perfect binding; average print order: 300-500; first novel print order: 500. Plans 1 first novel this year. Averages 5 total titles each year, 2 fiction titles each year. Sometimes comments on rejected ms; charges for critiques.
● The Moody Street Irregulars also publish a newsletter dedicated to Jack Kerouac and the Beat writers.
Needs: Experimental, literary, short story collections. No romance, gothic. Published *Big Ben Hood*, by Emmanual Freed (literary); *Links of the Chain*, by William Harnock (short story collection); and *Walk With Me*, by Dorothy Smith (literary). Published new writers within the last year.
How to Contact: Accepts unsolicited mss. Submit complete ms with cover letter. SASE (IRCs). Agented fiction 1%. Reports in 1 week on queries; 1 month on mss. Simultaneous submissions OK.
Terms: Pays in author's copies "if run 300, 30 copies; if 500, 50 copies." Sends galleys to author. Publishes ms 1 year after acceptance. Writers guidelines not available. Book catalog free, if available.

‡THIRD SIDE PRESS, INC., (II), 2250 W. Farragut, Chicago IL 60625-1802. (312)271-3029. Fax: (312)271-0459. Publisher: Midge Stocker. Estab. 1991. "Small press, feminist." Publishes paperback originals. Books: 50 lb. recycled, acid-free paper; offset-wet or sheet printing; perfect binding; average print order: 3,000; first novel print order: 3,000. Averages 6 total titles, 3 fiction titles each year. Sometimes comments on rejected ms.
● Third Side Press Inc., published *Hawkings*, by Karen Lee Osborne, an ALA Gay & Lesbian Literature Award finalist and *Cancer as a Women's Issue* which won first prize from Chicago Women in Publishing for Women's Issues, in 1992.
Needs: Lesbian: erotica (lesbian only), feminist, historical, literary, mainstream/contemporary, mystery/suspense (amateur sleuth). No "collections of stories; horror; homophobic" material. Recently published *On Lill Street*, by Lynn Kanter (first novel); *Timber City Masks*, by Karen York (mystery);

After Shocks, by Jess Wells (first novel). Series include Royce Madison mysteries; Women/Cancer/ Fear/Power series. Published new writers within the last year.

How to Contact: Query first. Include bio (1-2 paragraphs) and synopsis. Send SASE (IRCs) for reply, return of ms or send a disposable copy of ms. Reports in 2-3 weeks on queries; 3-6 months on mss. Simultaneous submissions OK.

Terms: Pays royalties (varies). Provides 10 author's copies. Publishes ms 6-18 months after acceptance. Writer's guidelines for #10 SAE and 2 first-class stamps or IRCs. Book catalog for #10 SAE and 2 first-class stamps or IRCs.

Advice: "Look at our other books to see how yours might relate to them."

THIRD WORLD PRESS, P.O. Box 19730, Chicago IL 60619. (312)651-0700. Publisher: Haki Madhubuti. Editor: Bukari Kitwana. Estab. 1967. Black owned and operated independent publisher of fiction and nonfiction books about the Black experience throughout the Diaspora. Publishes paperback originals. Plans 1 first novel this year, as well as short story collections. Averages 10 total titles, 3 fiction titles each year. Average first novel print order 15,000 copies.

Needs: Ethnic, historical, juvenile (animal, contemporary, easy-to-read, fantasy, historical), preschool/ picture book, short story collections, and young adult/teen (easy-to-read/teen, folktales, historical). "We primarily publish nonfiction, but will consider fiction by and about Blacks."

How to Contact: Accepts unsolicited mss October-May each year. Query or submit outline/synopsis and 1 sample chapter with SASE (IRCs). Reports in 6 weeks on queries; 5 months on mss. Simultaneous submissions OK. Accepts computer printout submissions.

Terms: Individual arrangement with author depending on the book, etc.

✸THISTLEDOWN PRESS, (II, IV), 633 Main St., Saskatoon, Saskatchewan S7H 0J8 Canada. (306)244- 1722. Editor-in-Chief: Patrick O'Rourke. Estab. 1975. Publishes paperback originals. Books: Quality stock paper; offset printing; perfect-bound; occasional illustrations; average print order 1,500-2,000; first novel print order: 1,000-1,500. Publishes 12 titles/year, 6 or 7 fiction.

• A story included in the press' *The Blue Jean Collection* received a Vicky Metcalf Award and many books published by Thistledown have been selected as "Our Choice" by the Canadian Children's Book Centre.

Needs: Literary, experimental, short story collections, novels. Recently published *Yuletide Blues*, by R.P. MacIntyre (young adult novel); *The Women on the Bridge*, by Mel Dogg (short stories); *Night in the Yungas*, by Stephen Henighan (short stories). Also publishes The Mayer Mystery Series (mystery novels for young adults) and The New Leaf Series (first books for poetry and fiction).

How to Contact: "We *only* want to see Canadian-authored submissions. We will *not* consider multiple submissions." No unsolicited mss. Query first with SASE (IRCs). Photocopied submissions OK. Reports in 2 months on queries.

Advice: "We are primarily looking for quality writing that is original and innovative in its perspective and/or use of language. Thistledown would like to receive queries first before submission – perhaps with novel outline, some indication of previous publications, periodicals your work has appeared in. *We publish Canadian authors only.* We are continuing to publish more fiction and are looking for new fiction writers to add to our list. New Leaf Editions line is first books of poetry or fiction by emerging Western Canadian authors. Familiarize yourself with some of our books before submitting a query or manuscript to the press."

THREE CONTINENTS PRESS (II, IV), P.O. Box 38009, Colorado Springs CO 80937-8009. Fiction Editor: Donald Herdeck. Estab. 1973. Small independent publisher with expanding list. Publishes hardcover and paperback originals and reprints. Books: library binding; illustrations; average print order: 1,000-1,500; first novel print order: 1,000. Averages 15 total titles, 6-8 fiction titles each year. Average first novel print order: 1,000 copies. Occasionally critiques ("a few sentences") rejected mss.

Needs: "We publish original fiction only by writers from Africa, the Caribbean, the Middle East, Asia and the Pacific. No fiction by writers from North America or Western Europe."

How to Contact: Query with outline/synopsis and sample pages with SAE and IRCs. State "origins (non-Western), education and previous publications." Reports in 1 month on queries; 2 months on mss. Simultaneous submissions OK.

Terms: "Send enquiry letter first and ms only if so requested by us. We are not a subsidy publisher, but do a few specialized titles a year with grants. In those cases we accept institutional subventions. Foundation or institution receives 20-30 copies of book and at times royalty on first printing. We pay royalties twice yearly (against advance) as a percentage of net paid receipts." Royalties of 5% minimum; 10% maximum. Offers negotiable advance, $300 average. Provides 10 author's copies. Sends galleys to author. Free book catalog available.

THRESHOLD BOOKS, RD 4, Box 600, Dusty Ridge Rd., Putney VT 05346. (802)254-8300. Director: Edmund Helminski. Estab. 1981. Small independent publisher with plans for gradual expansion. Publishes paperback originals. Books: 60 lb. natural paper; offset litho printing; sew-wrap binding; average print order: 2,500. Averages 2-3 total titles each year. Occasionally critiques rejected ms.
Needs: Spiritual literature and translations of sacred texts. Recently published *Awakened Dreams*, by Ahmet Hilmi, translated by Camille Helminski and Refik Algan.
How to Contact: Accepts unsolicited mss. Query first, submit outline/synopsis and sample chapters or complete ms with SASE (IRCs). Reports in 2 months. Simultaneous submissions OK. Publishes ms an average of 18 months after acceptance.
Terms: Pays in royalties of 7% of gross. Sometimes sends galleys to author. Book catalog free on request.
Advice: "We are still small and publishing little fiction." Publishing "less fiction, more paperbacks due to our particular area of concentration and our size."

TIMES EAGLE BOOKS, (IV), Box 2441, Berkeley CA 94702. Fiction Editor: Mark Hurst. Estab. 1971. "Small operation on part-time basis." Specialized publisher limited to contributors from West Coast region. First novel print order: 2,500. Plans 2 first novels this year. Averages 2 titles each year, all fiction.
Needs: Contemporary. "Graphic descriptions of teenage life by West Coast youth, such as Bret Easton Ellis's *Less than Zero*." Published *Equator: The Story and the Letters*, by V.O. Blum (erotic/philosophical novel).
How to Contact: Does not accept or return unsolicited mss. Query first in one paragraph. Typically reports in 3 weeks.
Terms: Pays in royalties of 10%.

THE TRANSLATION CENTER, (II), 412 Dodge Hall, Columbia University, New York NY 10027. (212)854-2305. Editors: Frank MacShane, Lori Carlson. Estab. 1972. Publishes hardcover and paperback originals. Books: perfect bound; high-quality paper. Averages 3-4 total titles/year.
Needs: Translations.
How to Contact: Query first for upcoming anthologies. Recently published *Translation*, Vol. 28, "Israel Feature Issue"; *Running Wild: China's New Writers* (contemporary Chinese story collection).
Terms: Pays in 2 translator's copies.

TUDOR PUBLISHERS, INC., (II), P.O. Box 38366, Greensboro NC 27438. (919)282-5907. Editor: Pam Cox. Estab. 1986. Small independent press. Publishes hardcover and paperback originals. Book: offset; Smyth-sewn hardcover/trade paperback; occasional illustrations; average print order: 3,000; first novel print order: 1,000-2,000. Plans 1 first novel this year. Averages 3-5 total titles, 1-2 fiction titles each year. Sometimes comments on rejected ms.
Needs: Literary, mystery/suspense, thriller (adult and young adult), regional (Southeast), young adult/teen (10-18 years). "Especially needs suspense. No romance, western." Published *The Mean Lean Weightlifting Queen*, by Mark Emerson (young adult novel); *Just Plane Murder*, by Dicey Thomas (mystery); published new writers within the last year.
How to Contact: Accepts unsolicited mss. "Outline and query first, please." Submit outline/synopsis and 3 sample chapters. SASE (IRCs). Reports in 2 weeks on queries; 6 weeks on mss.
Terms: Pays royalties of 10%. Sends galleys to author. Publishes ms 12-18 months after acceptance. Book catalog for # 10 SASE or IRC and one first-class stamp.
Advice: "Tell us of any publishing done previously. Send a clear summary or outline of the book with a cover letter and SASE. Interested in suspense in both adult and young adult; also literary fiction of high quality. Send only your best work. No romance, science fiction, western; no multigenerational sagas unless of extremely high quality. Prefer work by previously-published author."

✸TURNSTONE PRESS, (II), 607-100 Arthur St., Winnipeg, Manitoba R3B 1H3 Canada. (204)947-1555. Managing Editor: Jamie Hutchison. Estab. 1976. Books: Offset paper; perfect-bound; average first novel print order: 1,500. Published new writers within the last year. Averages 8 total titles/year. Occasionally critiques rejected ms.

Needs: Experimental and literary. "We will be doing only 2-3 fiction titles a year. Interested in new work exploring new narrative/fiction forms. We publish some anthologies (e.g., *Made in Manitoba*, edited by Wayne Tefs). Stories are nominated." Published *Raised by the River*, by Jake MacDonald; *Some Great Thing*, by Lawrence Hill; *Touch the Dragon*, by Karen Connelly.

How to Contact: *Canadian authors only.* Send SASE or SAE and IRCs. Reports in 1 month on queries; 2-4 months on mss.

Terms: Pays royalties of 10%; 10 author's copies. Book catalog free on request.

Advice: "Like most Canadian literary presses, we depend heavily on government grants which are not available for books by non-Canadians. Do some homework before submitting work to make sure your subject matter/genre/writing style falls within the publishers area of interest. Specializes in experimental literary, and prairie writing."

‡TURTLE POINT PRESS, (II), Turtle Point Rd., Tuxedo Park NY 10987. (914)351-5650. President: J.D. Rabinowitz. Estab. 1990. "Small press publishing mostly lost literary fiction in quality paperback editions. Beginning in 1994 doing contemporary fiction as well." Publishes paperback originals and reprints. Books: recycled 60 lb. stock paper; sewn binding; occasional illustrations; average print order: 1,500; first novel print order 800-1,500. Plans 2 first novels this year. 4-5 fiction titles each year. Sometimes comments on rejected ms.

Needs: Literary, short story collections, translations. "Literary fiction, *tranlations* particularly from French, Spanish and Italian." Recently published *The Toys of Princes*, by Ghislain de Diesbach (Richard Howard, translator) (short stories); *Clovis*, by Michael Ferrier (social-satire fiction); *The Diary of a Forty-Niner*, edited by Jackson/Carfield (journal). Submit outline/synopsis and sample chapters. Include estimated word count, short bio, list of publishing credits. Send SASE (IRCs) for reply, return of ms or send a disposable copy of ms. Reports in 1 month.

Terms: Pays royalty (varies), negotiable advance or honorarium. Publishes ms 4-12 months after acceptance. Book catalogs are free.

Advice: "We are publishers of lost fiction with a keen interest in doing contemporary writing and contemporary translation."

ULTRAMARINE PUBLISHING CO., INC., (III), Box 303, Hastings-on-the-Hudson NY 10706. (914)478-2522. Publisher: Christopher P. Stephens. Estab. 1973. Small publisher. "We have 150 titles in print. We also distribute for authors where a major publisher has dropped a title." Encourages new writers. Averages 15 total titles, 12 fiction titles each year. Buys 90% agented fiction. Occasionally critiques rejected ms.

Needs: Experimental, fantasy, mainstream, science fiction, short story collections. No romance, westerns, mysteries.

How to Contact: Prefers agented ms. Does not accept unsolicited mss. Submit outline/synopsis and 2 sample chapters with SASE (IRCs). Reports in 6 weeks. Simultaneous submissions OK.

Terms: Pays royalties of 10% minimum; advance is negotiable. Publishes ms an average of 8 months after acceptance. Free book catalog.

*UNIVERSITY EDITIONS, (I, II), 59 Oak Lane, Spring Valley, Huntington WV 25704. Imprint of Aegina Press. Managing Editor: Ira Herman. Estab. 1983. Independent publisher presently expanding. Publishes hardcover and paperback originals and reprints. Books: 50 lb. library-weight paper; litho offset printing; most are perfect-bound; illustrations; average print order: 500-1,000; first novel print order: 500-1,000. Plans 10 first novels this year. "We strongly encourage new writers." Averages 25 total titles, approximately 15 fiction titles each year. Often critiques rejected ms.

● See also the listing for Aegina Press in this section.

Needs: Adventure, contemporary, ethnic, experimental, fantasy, feminist, historical, romance (gothic), horror, humor/satire, juvenile (all types), literary, mainstream, mystery/suspense (private eye, romantic suspense, young adult), regional, science fiction (hard science, soft sociological), short story collections, translations, war. "Historical, literary and regional fiction are our main areas of emphasis." Recently published *Vendetta*, by Jim Dunn (novel); *Journey Into Mystery*, by Richard Lazarus (short story collection); *Valhalla's Child*, by Arthur K. Pirkle (novel).

How to Contact: Accepts unsolicited mss. "We depend upon manuscripts that arrive unsolicited." Query or submit outline/synopsis and 3 or more sample chapters or complete ms. "We prefer to see entire manuscripts; we will consider queries and partials as well." SASE (IRCs). Reports in 1 week on queries; 1 month on mss. Simultaneous submissions OK.

THE UNIVERSITY OF ARKANSAS PRESS, (I), Fayetteville AR 72701. (501)575-3246. Director: Miller Williams. Acquisitions Editor: Scot Danforth. Estab. 1980. Small university press. Publishes hardcover and paperback originals. Average print order 750 cloth and 2,000 paper copies. Averages 25 total titles, 2 short fiction titles (rarely a novel), each year.

Needs: Literary, mainstream, novels, short story collections, translations. Publishes anthologies or special editions. Stories are usually selected by the editor. Published *Writing for Love and Money*, by Katherin Perutz (novel); *A New Geography of Poets*, edited by Edward Field, Gerald Locklin and Charles Stetler (poetry); *Plato at Scratch Daniel's and Other Stories*, by Edward Falco (short stories).

How to Contact: Accepts unsolicited mss. Query first with SASE (IRCs). Reports in 2 weeks. Simultaneous submissions OK.

Terms: Pays royalties of 10%; 10 author's copies. Publishes ms an average of 1 year after acceptance. Writer's guidelines and book catalog for 9 × 12 SASE.

Advice: "We are looking for fiction written with energy, clarity and economy. Apart from this, we have no predisposition concerning style or subject matter. The University of Arkansas Press does not respond to queries or proposals not accompanied by SASE."

‡UNIVERSITY OF MISSOURI PRESS, (II), 2910 LeMone Blvd., Columbia MO 65201. (314)882-7641. Fax: (314)884-4498. Fiction Editor: Clair Willcox. Estab. 1958. "University press." Publishes hardcover originals (short story collections only). Averages 50 total titles, 4 short story collections each year. Sometimes comments on rejected ms.

Needs: Short story collections. No children's fiction. Recently published *Thief of Lives*, by Kit Reed (short stories); *Small Caucasian Woman*, by Elaine Fowler Palencia (short stories); *From Hunger*, by Gerald Shapiro (short stories). Published new writers within the last year.

How to Contact: Query first. Include estimated word count. "Bio/publishing credits optional." SASE (IRCs) for reply. Simultaneous submissions OK.

Terms: Pays in royalties. Sends galleys to author. Book catalogs are free.

VANDAMERE PRESS, (II), AB Associates, P.O. Box 5243, Arlington VA 22205. Editor: Jerry Frank. Estab. press 1984; firm 1976. "Small press, independent publisher of quality hard and soft cover books." Publishes hardcover and paperback originals. Published new writers within the last year. Averages 6+ total titles, 1+ fiction title each year. Sometimes comments on rejected ms.

Needs: Adventure, erotica, humor/satire, military/war. No childrens/juvenile/young adult. Recently published *The War That Never Was*, by Michael Palmer (novel); *FDR's Splendid Deception*, by Hugh Gallagher (biography).

How to Contact: Accepts unsolicited mss. Submit outline/synopsis and 3-4 sample chapters or complete ms with cover letter. Include bio (1-2 pages), list of publishing credits. Send SASE (IRCs) for reply, return of ms or send a disposable copy of the ms. Reporting time varies with work load. Simultaneous submissions OK.

Terms: Pays royalties; negotiable small advance. Sends galleys to author. Publishes ms 3 months-2 years after acceptance.

‡❀VÉHICULE PRESS (IV), Box 125, Place du Parc Station, Montreal, Quebec H2W 2M9 Canada. Imprint: Signal Editions for poetry. Publisher/Editor: Simon Dardick. Estab. 1973. Small publisher of scholarly, literary and cultural books. Publishes hardcover and paperback originals. Books: good quality paper; offset printing; perfect and cloth binding; illustrations; average print order: 1,000-3,000. Averages 13 total titles each year.

Needs: Feminist, literary, regional, short story collections, translations—"*by Canadian residents only.*" No romance or formula writing. "We do not accept novels at this point."
How to Contact: Query first or send sample chapters. SASE or SAE and IRC ("no US stamps, please"). Reports in 2 weeks on queries; 2 months on mss. Attention: Linda Leith, Fiction Editor.
Terms: Pays in royalties of 10% minimum; 12% maximum. "Depends on press run and sales." Sends galleys to author. "Translators of fiction can receive Canada Council funding, which publisher applies for." Book catalog for 9×12 SASE.
Advice: "Quality in almost any style is acceptable. We believe in the editing process."

‡**VISTA PUBLICATIONS, (II),** P.O. Box 661447, 107 Westward Dr., Miami Springs FL 33166. Owner: Helen Brose. Estab. 1988. One-person operation. Publishes paperback originals. Books: bond paper; offset printing; perfect binding; average print order: 1,000-1,200; first novel print order: 1,000. Averages 2 total titles, 1-2 fiction titles each year. Sometimes comments on rejected ms.
Needs: Adventure, ethnic/multicultural, historical, mystery/suspense, regional (Guatemala and Central America), romance, short story collections. "We publish books about Guatemala and/or Latin America in English or Spanish." Recently published *El Salvador de Buques*, by Rodrigo Rey Rosa (novel).
How to Contact: Accepts unsolicited mss. Query first. Include bio, list of publishing credits. SASE (IRCs) for reply. Agented fiction 30%. Reports in 1 month on queries; 3 months on mss. Simultaneous submissions OK. Accepts electronic submissions.
Terms: Pays royalties of 10% minimum; 15% maximum. Sends galleys to author. Publishes ms 6-12 months after acceptance. Writer's guidelines free. Book catalogs free.
Advice: "We publish fiction and nonfiction in English and/or Spanish which relate to Guatemala or the Central America area. Each book is judged on its own merit; category is not important."

W.W. PUBLICATIONS, (IV), Subsidiary of A.T.S., Box 373, Highland MI 48357-0373. (813)585-0985. Also publishes *Minas Tirith Evening Star*. Editor: Philip Helms. Estab. 1967. One-man operation on part-time basis. Publishes paperback originals and reprints. Books: typing paper; offset printing; staple-bound; black ink illustrations; average print order: 500+; first novel print order: 500. Averages 1 title (fiction) each year. Occasionally critiques rejected ms.
● *Minas Tirith Evening Star* is also listed in this book. The publisher is an arm of the American Tolkien Society.
Needs: Fantasy, science fiction, and young adult/teen (fantasy/science fiction). "Specializes in Tolkien-related or middle-earth fiction." Recently published *The Adventures of Fungo Hafurse*, Philip W. Helms; *The New Hobbit*, by Philip W. Helms and David L. Dettman.
How to Contact: Accepts unsolicited mss. Submit complete ms with SASE (IRCs). Reports in 1 month. Simultaneous submissions OK.
Terms: Individual arrangement with author depending on book, etc.; provides 5 author's copies. Free book catalog.
Advice: "We are publishing more fiction and more paperbacks. The author/editor relationship: a friend and helper."

WHITE PINE PRESS, (I), 10 Village Square, Fredonia NY 14063. (716)672-5743. Fax: (716)672-5743. Director: Dennis Maloney. Fiction Editor: Elaine La Mattina. Estab. 1973. Independent literary publisher. Publishes paperback originals and reprints. Books: 60 lb. natural paper; offset; perfect binding; average print order: 2,000-3,000; first novel print order: 2,000. Averages 8-10 total titles, 6-7 fiction titles each year.
Needs: Ethnic/multicultural, literary, short story collections. Looking for "strong novels." No romance, science fiction. Plans anthology of Caribbean stories. Editors select stories. Recently published *Crossing Wyoming*, by David Romtvedt (novel); *Herman*, by Lars Saabye Christensen (novel); *An Occasion of Sin*, by John Montague; *Myths and Voices* (Canadian short fiction). Publishes series of international fiction.
How to Contact: Accepts unsolicited mss. Query letter with outline/synopsis and 2 sample chapters. Should include estimated word count and list of publishing credits. SASE (IRCs) for reply or return of ms. Agented fiction 10%. Reports in 2 weeks on queries; 3 months on mss. Simultaneous submissions OK.
Terms: Pays royalties of 5% minimum; 10% maximum. Offers negotiable advance. Pays in author's copies; payment depends on grant/award money. Sends galleys to author. Publishes 1-2 years after acceptance. Book catalog free for #10 SASE.

WILLOWISP PRESS, INC., (II), Division of Pages, 801 94th Ave. N., St. Petersburg FL 33702-2426. (813)578-7600. Imprints include Worthington Press, Hamburger Press, Riverbank Press. Address material to Acquisitions Editor. Estab. 1984. Publishes paperback originals for children. Published new writers within the last year. Sometimes critiques rejected mss.
Needs: "Children's fiction and nonfiction, K-middle school." Adventure, contemporary and romance, for grades 5-8; preschool/picture book. No "violence, sex; romance must be very lightly treated." Recently published *Sister vs. Sister*, by Carol Perry; *No Time to Cry*, by Lurlene McDaniel; *Earthquake!*, by Alida E. Young.
How to Contact: Accepts unsolicited mss. Query (except picture books) with outline/synopsis and 2 sample chapters. Must send SASE (IRCs). Reporting time on queries varies; 2 months on mss. Simultaneous submissions OK. "Prefer hard copy for original submissions; prefer disk for publication."
Terms: Pay "varies." Publishes ms 6-12 months after acceptance. Writer's guidelines for #10 SAE and 1 first-class stamp. Book catalog for 9 × 12 SAE with $1.25 postage.
Advice: "We publish what *kids* want to read, so tell your story in a straightforward way with 'kid-like' language that doesn't convey an adult tone or sentence structure. When possible and natural, consider incorporating multicultural themes and characters."

‡WOMAN IN THE MOON PUBLICATIONS, (I,IV), P.O. Box 2087, Cupertino CA 95015-2087. (408)253-3329. Publisher: Dr. SDiane A. Bogus. Estab. 1979. "We are a small press with a primary publishing agenda for poetry, New Age and reference books of no more than 1,000 words quarterly. We accept short story manuscripts." Averages 2-4 total titles each year. Comments on rejected mss.
Needs: Contemporary, ethnic, fantasy, gay, lesbian, psychic/supernatural/occult, prisoner's stories, short story collections.
How to Contact: Accepts unsolicited mss between January 1-April 30 only up to 100 mss. Query first or submit outline/synopsis and sample chapters. Query by letter, phone or fax. SASE (IRCs) for query. Acknowledges in 1 week; reports during or at end of season. Simultaneous submissions OK.
Terms: *$8 reading fee required*. Pays in author's copies (half of press run). Pays $25 plus 2 copies for short stories in quarterly newsletters. Publishes ms within 2 years after acceptance. Writer's guidelines for #10 SAE and 1 first-class stamp. Book catalog for 6 × 9 SAE and 98¢ postage.
Advice: "To the short story writer, write us a real life lesbian gay set of stories. Tell us how life is for a Black person in an enlightened world. Create a possibility, an ideal that humanity can live toward. Write a set of stories that will free, redeem and instruct humanity. The trends in fiction by women have to do with the heroine as physical and capable and not necessarily defended by or romantically linked to a male." Sponsors fiction and nonfiction prose contest in the name of Audre Lorde. Awards two $250 prizes. Contest runs from September 1 to November 30. Winners announced in February.

✽WOMEN'S PRESS, (I, II, IV), Suite 233, 517 College St., Toronto, Ontario M6G 4A2 Canada. (416)921-2425. Estab. 1972. Publishes paperback originals. Books: web coat paper; web printing; perfect-bound; average print order: 2,000; first novel print order: 1,500. Plans 2 first novels this year. Averages 8 total titles each year. Sometimes "briefly" critiques rejected ms.
Needs: Contemporary, feminist, lesbian, juvenile, adolescent (contemporary, fantasy, historical), literary, preschool/picture book, short story collections, mysteries, women's and young adult/teen (problem novels). Nothing sexist, pornographic, racist. Recently published *S.P. Likes A.D.*, by Catherine Brett; *Catherine, Catherine*, by Ingrid MacDonald; *Harriet's Daughter*, by Marlene Nourbese Philip; *The Shrunken Brain*, by Jane Tapsubei Creider. Published new writers within the last year.
How to Contact: Submit complete ms with SAE and "Canadian stamps or a check. Our mandate is to publish Canadian women or landed immigrants." Reports in 3 months. Simultaneous submissions OK.
Terms: Pays in royalties of 10% maximum; small advance. Sends galleys to author. Free book catalog.
Advice: "We publish feminist, lesbian and adolescent novels, anthologies of short stories and single-author story collections. We encourage women of all races and ethnicities to submit work and we have a particular interest in publishing writers of color."

WOODLEY MEMORIAL PRESS, (IV), English Dept., Washburn University, Topeka KS 66621. (913)231-1010, ext. 1448. Editor: Robert N. Lawson. Estab. 1980. "Woodley Memorial Press is a small press which publishes book-length poetry and fiction collections by Kansas writers only; by 'Kansas writers' we mean writers who reside in Kansas or have a Kansas connection." Publishes paperback originals. Averages 2 titles each year. Sometimes comments on rejected ms.
● The most recent contest sponsored by Woodley Memorial Press was for a short story collec-

tion, but deadline has passed. Check for next short story collection contest. Work must be by a Kansas resident only.

Needs: Contemporary, experimental, literary, mainstream, short story collection. "We do not want to see genre fiction, juvenile, or young adult." Recently published three novellas: *Little Fugue*, by Laura McGhee; *She Wants to Know*, by Donn Irving; *Ballad of Spring River*, by Charles Cagle.

How to Contact: *Charges $5 reading fee.* Accepts unsolicited mss. Send complete ms. SASE (IRCs). Reports in 2 weeks on queries; 2 months on mss.

Terms: "Terms are individually arranged with author after acceptance of manuscript." Publishes ms one year after acceptance. Writer's guidelines for #10 SAE and 1 first-class stamp.

Advice: "We only publish one work of fiction a year, on average, and definitely want it to be by a Kansas author. We are more likely to do a collection of short stories by a single author."

YITH PRESS, (I, IV), 1051 Wellington Rd., Lawrence KS 66049. (913)843-4341. Subsidiary: *Eldritch Tales Magazine.* Editor/Publisher: Crispin Burnham. Estab. 1984. One-man operation on part-time basis. Publishes paperback originals and reprints. Books: offset printing; perfect binding; illustrations; average print order: 500-1,000. Averages 1-2 titles each year. Average first novel print order: 500-1,000 (depending on pre-publication orders). Occasionally critiques rejected ms.

Needs: Fantasy and horror. Accepts short stories for collections only. Novel needs include "anything in the supernatural horror category." No "mad slasher or sword and sorcery."

How to Contact: Accepts unsolicited mss. Submit complete ms with SASE (IRCs). Reports in 2 months. Simultaneous submissions OK. Prefers letter-quality. Disk submissions OK with MacIntosh II system.

Terms: Individual arrangement with author depending on the book. Sends galleys to author. Pays in royalties of 25% minimum; 35% maximum.

Advice: "Be original, don't try to be the next Lovecraft or Stephen King. Currently, I plan to publish one or two books/year, along with *Eldritch Tales*. The author/editor relationship should be give and take on both sides. I will try *not* to rewrite the author's work. If I feel that it needs some changes then I'll suggest them to the author. We are currently on hold with the book line as we are trying to get *Eldritch Tales* out on a quarterly schedule. Any potential submitter should send a card to inquire as to status."

ZEPHYR PRESS, (III), 13 Robinson St., Somerville MA 02145. Subsidiary of Aspect, Inc. Editorial Directors: Ed Hogan and Leora Zeitlin. Estab. 1980. Publishes hardcover and paperback originals. Books: acid-free paper; offset printing; Smyth-sewn binding; some illustrations; average print order: 1,500-2,000; first novel print order: 1,000-1,500. Averages 5 total titles, 1-2 fiction titles each year.

Needs: Contemporary, ethnic, experimental, feminist/lesbian, gay, historical, humor/satire, literary, mainstream, regional, short story collections, translations (French, Russian, Eastern European fiction). Published *Two Novels*, by Philip Whalen; *The St. Veronica Gig Stories*, by Jack Pulaski.

How to Contact: "We no longer read unsolicited mss. We read small press and literary magazines to find promising writers. We accept queries from agents, and from authors whose previous publications and professional credits (you must include a summary of these), evince work of exceptional talent and vision. Queries should include vita, list of publications, and up to 10 sample pages, photocopies only. If we are interested, we will request the full manuscript. Otherwise, we will make no response."

Terms: Pays royalties of approximately 12% of publisher's net for first edition. "There can be some flexibility of terms, based on mutual arrangements, if desired by author and publisher." Sends galleys to author. Book catalog for SASE (IRCs).

Advice: "Seek well qualified feedback from literary magazine editors or agents and/or professionally established writers before submitting manuscripts to publishers. We regard the author/editor relationship as one of close cooperation, from editing through promotion."

ZOLAND BOOKS, INC., (II), 384 Huron Ave., Cambridge MA 02138. (617)864-6252. Publisher: Roland Pease. Assistant Editor: Paul Karns. Marketing Director: Christine Alaimo. Estab. 1987. "We are a literary press, publishing poetry, fiction, photography, and other titles of literary interest." Publishes hardcover and paperback originals. Books: acid-free paper; sewn binding; some with illustrations; average print order: 2,000-5,000. Averages 10 total titles each year.

● For more on Zoland Books, see the interview with Publisher Roland Pease in the 1991 *Novel & Short Story Writer's Market.*

Needs: Contemporary, feminist, literary, short story collections. Recently published *Small Victories*, by Sallie Bingham (novel); *Whistling and Other Stories*, by Myra Goldberg; *An Untold Tale*, by Jonathan Strong (novel).

There are six **Writer's Digest School** courses to help you write better and sell more:

Novel Writing Workshop. A professional novelist helps you iron out your plot, develop your main characters, write the background for your novel, and complete the opening scene and a summary of your novel's complete story. You'll even identify potential publishers and write a query letter.

Nonfiction Book Workshop. You'll work with your mentor to create a book proposal that you can send directly to a publisher. You'll develop and refine your book idea, write a chapter-by-chapter outline of your subject, line up your sources of information, write sample chapters, and complete your query letter.

Writing to Sell Fiction. Learn the basics of writing/selling short stories: plotting, characterization, dialogue, theme, conflict, and other elements of a marketable short story. Course includes writing assignments and one complete short story.

Writing to Sell Nonfiction. Master the fundamentals of writing/selling nonfiction articles: finding article ideas, conducting interviews, writing effective query letters and attention-getting leads, targeting your articles to the right publication, and other important elements of a salable article. Course includes writing assignments and one complete article manuscript (and its revision).

Science Fiction and Fantasy Workshops. Explore the exciting world of science fiction and fantasy with one of our professional science fiction writers as your guide. Besides improving your general writing skills, you'll learn the special techniques of creating worlds, science and magic, shaping time and place. And how to get published in this world. Choose Short Story or Novel Writing.

Mystery Writing Workshops. With the personal attention, experience and advice from a professional, published mystery writer, you'll uncover the secrets of writing suspenseful, involving mysteries. In addition to learning the genre's special techniques like how to drop red herrings, when and where to plant critical clues and what to keep hidden from your reader, you'll continue to improve your general writing skills that will lay a critical foundation for your story. Choose Short Story or Novel Writing.

Mail this card today for **FREE** information!

How to Contact: Accepts unsolicited mss. Query first, then send complete ms with cover letter. SASE (IRCs). Reports in 4-6 weeks on queries; 3-6 months on mss.
Terms: Pays royalties of 5-8%. Average advance: $1,500; negotiable (also pays author's copies). Sends galleys to author. Publishes ms 1-2 years after acceptance. Book catalog for 6×9 SAE and 2 first-class stamps.

International small press

The following small presses from countries outside the U.S. and Canada will consider novels or short stories in English. Some of the countries represented here include Australia, England, India, Ireland, Italy, Malawi, New Zealand, Nigeria, Sweden, Germany and Zimbabwe. Many of these markets do not pay in cash, but may provide author copies. Always include a self-addressed envelope with International Reply Coupons to ensure a response or the return of your manuscript. International Reply Coupons are available at the main branch of your local post office. To save the cost of return postage on your manuscript, you may want to send a copy of your manuscript for the publisher to keep or throw away and enclose a return postcard with one IRC for a reply.

AFRICA CHRISTIAN PRESS, P.O. Box 30, Achimota, Ghana, West Africa. Fiction Editor: Mr. Raymond Mills-Tetteh. Averages 6 fiction titles/year. "We are a Christian publishing house specializing in Christian fiction works by Africans or expatriates with a long association with Africa." Length: 15,000 words minimum. Send: Cover letter, synopsis, brief summary, sample chapter/s and/or entire manuscript. Pays royalties. Mss should be "typewritten, double spaced, with generous margins." Send 2 copies and a SAE with IRCs for response/return. Write for catalog and/or writer's guidelines.

ANOWUO EDUCATIONAL PUBLICATIONS, P.O. Box 3918, 2R McCarthy Hill, Accra, Ghana. Fiction Editor: Samuel Asare Konadu. Average 5-10 fiction titles/year. "Publication development organization for Ghanaian, African and world literature: novels, workbooks, language development, etc." Length: 8-250 typed pages. Send brief summary and first and last chapter. Pays advance and royalties. Looks for cultural development, romance.

ASHTON SCHOLASTIC LTD., Private Bag 92801, Auckland, New Zealand. Fiction Editor: Penny Scown. Publishes 20-30 fiction titles annually. "Educational publishing with a focus on books for the teaching of language arts and children's literature for all ages from picture books to teen novels." Pays royalties. "Do not 'write down' to children—write the story you want to tell using the best language— i.e., most appropriate vocabulary, letting the story only dictate the length."

ATTIC PRESS, (IV), 4 Upper Mount St., Dublin, 2, Ireland. Contact: Editor. Averages 6-8 fiction titles/ year. "Attic Press is an independent, export-oriented, Irish-owned publishing house with a strong international profile. The press specializes in the publication of fiction and nonfiction books by and about women by Irish and international authors." Send cover letter, synopsis, brief summary, sample chapters. Pays advance on signing contract and royalties. "Please ensure that your book is by/about women; that it is properly laid out for reading—double-spaced, typewritten etc." Write for catalog.

BIBLIOTECA DI NOVA SF, FUTURO, GREAT WORKS OF SF, (IV), Perseo Libri srl, Box 1240, I-40100 Bologna, Italy. Fiction Editor: Ugo Malaguti. "Science fiction and fantasy; novels and/or collections of stories." Pays 7% royalties on cover price; advance: $800-1,000 on signing contract. Buys Italian book rights; other rights remain with author. "While preferring published writers, we also consider new writers."

‡CANONGATE PRESS, 14 Frederick St., Edinburgh EH2 2 HB Scotland, UK. Fiction Editor: Richard Ayles. Averages 1-4 fiction titles/year. "Cultural contribution rather than just hedonistic exuberance provides the flavor of novels published by Canongate in the past, but this criterion is not inflexible if the exuberance has, in our view, genuine quality." Length: 40,000 words minimum; 500,000 words maximum. Send cover letter, synopsis and 3 sample chapters. Pays advance and 10% royalty. Submitting writers should be sure ms "possesses literary merit and commercial potential." Write for information and guidelines.

CHRISTCHURCH PUBLISHERS LTD., 2 Caversham St., London SW3, 4AH UK. Fiction Editor: James Hughes. Averages 25 fiction titles/year. "Miscellaneous fiction, also poetry. More 'literary' style of fiction, but also thrillers, crime fiction etc." Length: 30,000 words minimum. Send a cover letter, synopsis, brief summary. "Preliminary letter and *brief* synopsis favored." Pays advance and royalties. "We have contacts and agents worldwide." Write for catalog.

‡EASTERN CARIBBEAN INSTITUTE (ECI), (IV), Box 1338, Frederiksted, Virgin Islands 00841. Editor/President: S.B. Jones-Hendrickson, PhD. Estab. 1982. Small press with plans to expand. Publishes hardcover originals and paperback originals. Regional. Needs for novels include Caribbean issues and settings. No religious. Length: 10,000 words minimum. Send cover letter with synopsis and 1 sample chapter. Reports in 1 week on queries; 1 month for mss. Write for catalog.

AIDAN ELLIS PUBLISHING, Cobb House, Nuffield, Henley-on-Thames, Oxon RG9 5RT England. Fiction Editor: Aidan Ellis. Averages 12 fiction titles/year. "Founded in 1971, with an annual turnover of around £250,000 we are a small publishing house publishing fiction and general trade books." Send a cover letter, synopsis, brief summary, sample chapter/s or entire manuscript. Pays advance on publication, royalties twice yearly. Write for catalog.

GMP PUBLISHER LTD., Box 247, London N17 9QR England. Editor: David Fernbach. Publishes 12-13 novels yearly and the occasional short story collection. "Principally publishing works of gay interest—both popular and literary." Pays royalties. Send synopsis and/or sample chapters first. "We're particularly interested in authors who use a word processor and can supply material on disk. This is particularly true with writers sending in work from abroad."

‡HANDSHAKE EDITIONS, Atelier A2, 83 rue de la Tombe Issoire, 75014 Paris France. Editor: Jim Haynes. Publishes 4 story collections or novels/year. "Only face-to-face submissions accepted. More interested in 'faction' and autobiographical writing." Pays in copies. Writers interested in submitting a manscript should "have lunch or dinner with me in Paris."

HEMKUNT, Publishers A-78 Naraina Industrial Area Ph.I, New Delhi India 110028. Managing Director: G.P. Singh. Export Directors: Deepinder Singh/Arvinder Singh. "We would be interested in novels, preferably by authors with a published work. Would like to have distribution rights for US, Canada and UK beside India." Send a cover letter, brief summary, 3 sample chapters (first, last and one other chapter). "Writer should have at least 1-2 published novels to his/her credit." Catalog on request.

KAWABATA PRESS, (II), Knill Cross House, Knill Cross, Millbrook, Torpoint, Cornwall PL10 1DX England. Fiction Editor: C. Webb. "Mostly poetry—but prose should be realistic, free of genre writing and clichés and above all original in ideas and content." Length: 200-4,000 words (for stories). "Don't forget return postage (IRCs)." Writers receive half of profits after print costs are covered. Write for guidelines and book list.

THE LITERATURE BUREAU, P.O. Box 8137 Causeway, Harare Zimbabwe. Fiction Editor: B.C. Chitsike. Averages 12 fiction titles/year. "All types of fiction from the old world novels to the modern ones with current issues. We publish these books in association with commercial publishers but we also publish in our own right." Length: 7,000-30,000 words. Send entire manuscript. Pays royalties. "Send the complete manuscript for assessment. If it is a good one it is either published by the Bureau or sponsored for publication. If it needs any correction, a full report will be sent to the author." Obtain guidelines by writing to the Bureau. "We have 'Hints to New Authors,' a pamphlet for aspiring authors. These can be obtained on request."

‡THE LUTTERWORTH PRESS, P.O. Box 60, Cambridge CB1 2NT England. Fiction Editor: Colin Lester. "Almost 200-year-old small press publishing wide range of adult nonfiction, religious and children's books. The only fiction we publish is for children: picture books (with text from 0-10,000 words), educational, young novels, story collections. Also nonfiction as well as religious children's books." Send synopsis and sample chapter. Pays advance plus royalty. "Send IRCs. English language is universal, i.e., mid-Atlantic English." Write for information and guidelines.

THE MALVERN PUBLISHING CO. LTD., 32 Old Street, Upton-Upon-Severn, Worcs. WR8 OHW England. Fiction Editor: Catherine Whiting. Publishes 12 stories/year. "Full length adult fiction — 60,000-80,000 words." Pays in royalties. "No science fiction or fantasy."

‡**MAROVERLAG**, Riedingerstrasse 24, D-86153, Augsburg West Germany. Editor: Benno Käsmayr. Publishes 4-6 novels or story collections/year. Publishes "exciting American authors in excellent translations; e.g. Charles Bukowski, Jack Kerouac, William Burroughs, Paul Bowles, Gerald Locklin, Keith Abbott, Raymond Federman and Gilbert Sorrentin." Send a cover letter, synopsis, brief summary and 2 sample chapters. Writers paid for published fiction. "Please include SAE and postage. Our books and catalogs can be ordered at every German bookstore. Most of them send to the US too."

‡**PEEPAL TREE BOOKS**, 17 King's Ave., Leeds LS6 1QS England. Fiction Editor: Jeremy Poynting. Averages 12-14 fiction titles/year. "Peepal Tree publishes primarily Caribbean and Black British fiction, though it has begun to expand into African and South Asian writing. We publish both novels and collections of short stories." Length: 25,000 words minimum; 100,000 words maximum. Send a cover letter, synopsis and 3 sample chapters. Pays 10% royalties, in general no advances. "We suggest that authors send for a copy of our catalog to get some sense of the range and parameters of what we do." Peepal Tree publishes an annual catalog and a quarterly newsletter available from the address above.

‡**DAVID PHILIP PUBLISHERS**, P.O. Box 23408, Claremont 7735, Cape Province South Africa. "Fiction with Southern African concern or focus. Progressive, often suitable for school or university prescription, literary, serious." Send synopsis and 1 sample chapter. Pays royalties. "Familiarize yourself with list of publisher to which you wish to submit work — don't work blindly." Write for guidelines.

‡**POLYGON**, 22 George Square, Edinburgh EH8 9LF UK. Fiction Editor: Marion Sinclair. Averages 10 fiction titles/year. "Contemporary, slightly 'off-beat' fiction." Send cover letter, synopsis and sample chapter. Must include SAE and IRCs. Pays advance plus royalties. "Request a catalogue initially to check whether your work fits into our list. Write to the publicity officer at Polygon and a catalogue will then be sent out."

PUBLISHERS GROUP SOUTH WEST (IRELAND), (IV), Allihies, Bantry, Country Cork IP2 91 Ireland. Executive Editor: Peter Haston. Averages 6-10 fiction titles/year. "Experimental fiction of all kinds, including audiobooks." Send synopsis and sample chapter, typed and posted registered airmail. Payment by agreement. Advice: "Contact publishers associations and research a publishing house that already produces work of the same kind. Determine which editor there has on his list the works most akin to yours. Do your research. Follow up." Send postcard of inquiry for catalog.

‡**RENDITIONS, (IV)**, Chinese University of Hong Kong. Editor: Dr. Eva Hung. Averages 2-3 fiction titles annually. "Academic specialist publisher. Will only consider English translations of Chinese fiction. Fiction published either in semiannual journal (*Renditions*) or in the Renditions Paperback series." For fiction over 5,000 words in translation, sample is required. Sample length: 1,000-2,000 words. Send sample chapter. Pays honorarium for publication in *Renditions*; royalties for paperback series. "Submit only works in our specialized area. One copy of translation accompanied by one copy of original Chinese text." Fax requests for information and guidelines to Mrs. Cecila Yip, (852)6035149.

‡**SERPENT'S TAIL**, 4 Blackstock Mews, London N4 2BT UK. Fiction Editor: Peter Ayrton. Averages 30 fiction titles/year. "We are an up-market literary house whose tastes are well out of the mainstream. We see our audience as young and urban-based. Translations, first novels and cultural studies are our forte." Length: 30,000 words minimum; 100,000 words maximum. Send cover letter; enclose IRCs or postage. Pays advance plus royalties. "Send query letter first, and only after you have looked at the books we publish. For us, writers need not give extra background to their work, its context, etc. regarding the fact that they are not British. We are a cosmopolitan bunch." Write office for catalog.

‡**SHIKSHA BHARATI**, 1590 Madarsa Rd, Kashmere Gate, Delhi-110 006 India. Fiction Editor: Mrs. Meera Johri. Averages 6 fiction titles/year. "Our publishing house specializes in children's literature, science and adventure for young readers." Length: 25,000 words minimum; 30,000 words maximum. Send cover letter and synopsis. Pays 10% royalty "with a reasonable advance." Ms should be in the following areas: children's fiction, popular science and education. Write for information and guidelines.

‡SINCLAIR-STEVENSON LTD., 718 Kendrick Mews, London SW7 3HG England. Fiction Editors: Penelope Hoarls, Christopher Sinclair-Stevenson, Caroline Upcher. Averages 30 fiction titles/year. "Trade hardbacks of quality fiction from new and established authors: Rose Tremain, Susan Hill, Matthew Kneel, Peter Ackroyd." Length: open. Send cover letter. Pays advance and royalties. Contact Sales Manager for catalog. No guidelines available.

‡TEMPLE PRESS, (IV), P.O. Box 227, Brighton, Sussex BN2 3GL England. Averages 3 fiction titles/year. "Radical press dealing in new writings. We specialize in avant-garde material unsuited to the major publishing houses and also occult and metaphysics." Length: 10,000-100,000 words. Send a cover letter, synopsis, 3 sample chapters or entire manuscript. Pays mix of royalty and advances. "Writers must be offering a new angle/vision. 80% of our writers are based overseas." When writing send 3 International Reply Coupons.

VIRAGO PRESS LIMITED, 20-23 Mandela St., London NWI OHQ England. Fiction Editors: Ruth Petrie, Lennie Goodings, Lynn Knight, Melanie Silgardo. Averages approximately 20 fiction titles/year. "Women's press—romance wanted. Anything top quality." Length: 60,000-120,000 words. Send cover letter with brief summary and 3 sample chapters. Pays advance and royalty. "Be original and interesting!"

Small press/'93-'94 changes

The following small presses appeared in the 1993 edition of *Novel & Short Story Writer's Market* but are not in the 1994 edition. Those presses whose editors did not respond to our request for an update are listed below without explanation. If an explanation was given, it is next to the listing.

Arrowood Books
Bamboo Ridge Press
Barn Owl Books (asked to be left out this year)
Black Tie Press
Blind Beggar Press
Bottom Dog Press (too many submissions)
British American Publishing, Ltd. (asked to be left out this year)
Burning Books (unable to locate)
Jonathan Cape (asked to be deleted)
Capra Press (no unsolicited fiction)
Chelsea Green Publishing Co. (no fiction)
Cheops Books (out of business)
Cliffhanger Press (asked to be deleted)
Clockwatch Review Press (lost funding)
Creative Arts Book Co.
Dayspring Press, Inc. (com

plaints)
The Dragonsbreath Press (asked to be left out this year)
Evergreen Publications (suspended operations)
Fifth House Publishers
1st Amendment Publishers (asked to be left out this year)
Haypenny Press (suspended operations)
Infinite Savant Publishing
J&P Books
Kar-Ben Copies, Inc. (inappropriate submissions)
Lollipop Power Books
Los Hombres Press (asked to be deleted)
McKnight Books
Manic D Press
Marron Publishers, Inc. (asked to be left out this year)
Nuage Editions
Ommation Press
Owl Creek Press

Papyrus Publishers (asked to be left out this year)
Paycock Press (asked to be left out this year)
Pippin Press
Polestar Book Publishers (asked to be deleted)
Shoestring Press
Slough Press
Soleil Press (asked to be left out this year)
Starburst Publishers (asked to be left out this year)
Station Hill Press
Stemmer House Publishers, Inc.
University of Idaho Press (no fiction)
Virago Press Limited
Wild East Publishing Co-Operative Ltd.
Woodsong Graphics Inc. (asked to be left out this year)

International small press/'93-'94 changes

Bellew Publishing Company Ltd.
Jonathan Cape (asked to be

deleted)
Karnak House
Obobo Books

Sheba Feminist Press
The Vanitas Press
Virago Press Limited

Commercial Book Publishers

With close to 125 listings, the Commercial Book Publisher section is one of the smaller sections in this book. Yet, it is in this section that you'll find the big publishers — Avon Books, Bantam Doubleday Dell, Harcourt Brace & Co., Harlequin, Alfred A. Knopf, Little, Brown and Company . . . the list goes on and on. Here is where you will find the publishers of blockbuster fiction, big-name authors and billion-dollar sales figures.

As we reported last year, the word in commercial book publishing continues to be caution, but things are beginning to look up. The buyout, merger and takeover frenzy of the past decade has passed and it appears publishers are starting to turn their attention to other things besides worrying about the bottom line.

For writers, breaking into the commercial publishing market remains a difficult, but not impossible task. Each year a lucky few new writers make it into a big publishing house and even into what could be called the publishing stratosphere as did new novelist Nancy Taylor Rosenberg. Her first book, *Mitigating Circumstances*, a legal thriller, was published by NAL/Penguin USA in hardcover and then paperback, garnering an impressive movie deal at the same time. It only happens to a few, but it happens.

Types of commercial publishers

The publishers in this section publish books "for the trade." That is, unlike textbook, technical or scholarly publishers, trade publishers publish books to be sold to the general consumer through bookstores, chain stores or other retail outlets. Within the trade book field, however, there are a number of different types of books.

The easiest way to categorize books is by their physical appearance and the way they are marketed. Hardcover books are the more expensive editions of a book, sold through bookstores and carrying a price tag of around $20 and up. Trade paperbacks are soft-bound books, also sold mostly in bookstores, but they carry a more modest price tag of usually around $10 to $20. Today a lot of fiction is published in this form because it means a lower financial risk than hardcover.

Mass market paperbacks are another animal altogether. These are the smaller "pocket-size" books available at bookstores, grocery stores, drug stores, chain retail outlets, etc. Much genre or category fiction is published in this format. This area of the publishing industry is very open to the work of talented new writers who write in specific genres such as science fiction, romance and mystery.

At one time publishers could be easily identified and grouped by the type of books they do. Today, however, the line between hardcover and paperback books is blurred. Many publishers known for publishing hardcover books also publish trade paperbacks and have paperback imprints. This enables them to offer established authors (and a very few lucky newcomers) hard-soft deals in which their books come out in both versions. Thanks to the mergers of the past decade, too, the same company may own several hardcover and paperback subsidiaries and imprints, even though their editorial focuses may remain separate.

Choosing a commercial publisher

In addition to checking the bookstores and libraries for books by publishers that interest you, you may want to refer to the Category Index located near the back of the book to find publishers divided by specific subject categories. The subjects listed in the Index are general. Read the individual listings to find which subcategories interest a publisher. For example, you will find several publishers who publish romance listed under that heading in the Category Index, but read the listings to find which type of romance is considered — gothic, contemporary, Regency or futuristic. See How to Get the Most out of This Book for more on how to refine your list of potential markets.

The Roman numeral ranking codes appearing after the names of the publishers will also help you in selecting a publisher. These codes are especially important in this section, because many of the publishing houses listed here require writers to submit through an agent. A numeral **III** identifies these and also those that mostly publish established authors, while a numeral **I** points to listings most open to new writers. See the end of this introduction for a complete list of ranking codes.

In the listings

As with other sections in this book, we identify new listings with a double-dagger symbol (‡). In this section, many of these are not new publishers, but instead are established publishers who decided to list this year in the hope of finding promising new writers.

We've also added a maple leaf symbol (✹) this year to identify the Canadian publishers. North American commercial publishers are grouped together and are followed by a group of publishers from around the world. Remember, self-addressed envelopes for replies from countries other than your own should include International Reply Coupons rather than stamps.

Book packagers, companies who produce books for publishers, are identified by a box symbol (■). Most book packagers pay writers a flat fee rather than royalties and buy all rights. Writers may not even get credit for the books they do for packagers, but they are very open to working with new writers.

You may also see an asterisk (*) at the start of a listing. This lets you know a press sometimes funds the publishing of its books through a subsidy arrangement. By subsidy, we mean any arrangement in which the writer is expected to pay all or part of the cost of producing, distributing and marketing his book. Approach subsidy publishers with caution. Find out exactly how many books they plan to produce and what paper and binding will be used. Check with a printer to find out how much those books would cost to be printed. If the subsidy amount is more, ask what specific marketing and distribution will be done for the additional money. As with any business arrangement, feel free to ask any questions about the arrangement that concern you.

We're continuing to include editorial comments this year, set off by a bullet symbol (●) within the listing. This is where we can tell you of any honors or awards received by publishers or their books. We include information about any special requirements or circumstances that will help you learn even more about the publisher's needs and policies.

A note about agents

The Business of Fiction Writing, earlier in this book, outlines how to prepare work to submit directly to a publisher. Many publishers are willing to look at unsolicited submissions, but most feel having an agent is to the writer's best advantage. In this section more than any other, you'll find a number of publishers who prefer submissions from agents.

Because the commercial fiction field has become so competitive, and publishers have so little time, more and more are relying on agents. For publishers, agents act as "first readers," wading through the deluge of submissions from writers to find the very best. For writers, a good agent can be a foot in the door—someone willing to do the necessary work to put your manuscript in the right editor's hands.

Because it is almost as hard to find a good agent as it is to find a publisher, many writers see agents as just one more roadblock to publication. Yet those who have agents say they are invaluable. Not only can a good agent help you make your work more marketable, an agent acts as your business manager and adviser, keeping your interests up front during contract negotiations.

Still, finding an agent can be very difficult for a new writer. Those already published in magazines or other periodicals have a better chance than someone with no publishing credits. Although many agents will read queries, packages and manuscripts from unpublished authors without introduction, referrals from other clients can be a big help. If you don't know any published authors, you may want to try to meet an agent at a conference before approaching one with your manuscript. Some agents even set aside time at conferences to meet new writers.

For listings of agents and more information on how to approach and deal with them, see the 1994 *Guide to Literary Agents and Art/Photo Reps*, published by Writer's Digest Books. The book separates nonfee- and fee-charging agents. While many agents do not charge any fees up front, others charge writers up to $100 to cover the costs of using outside readers. Be wary of those who charge large sums of money for reading a manuscript. Reading fees do not guarantee representation. Think of an agent as a potential business partner and feel free to ask tough questions about his or her credentials, experience and business practices.

For more . . .

For more information on publishing trends and news about the commercial fiction industry, see the Commercial Fiction Trend Report in the Writing Techniques part of this book. Also check issues of *Publishers Weekly* for publishing industry trade news in the U.S. and around the world or *Quill & Quire* for book publishing news in the Canadian book industry.

The ranking system we've used for listings in this section is as follows:

I **Publisher encourages beginning or unpublished writers to submit work for consideration and publishes new writers frequently.**

II **Publisher accepts work by established writers and by new writers of exceptional talent.**

III **Publisher does not encourage beginning writers; publishes mostly writers with extensive previous publication credits or agented writers and very few new writers.**

IV **Special-interest or regional publisher, open only to writers on certain topics or from certain geographical areas.**

ACADEMY CHICAGO PUBLISHERS, (I), 213 W. Institute Place, Chicago IL 60610. (312)751-7302. Senior Editor: Anita Miller. Estab. 1975. Midsize independent publisher. Publishes hardcover and paperback originals and paperback reprints.
Needs: Biography, history, feminist, academic and anthologies. Only the most unusual mysteries, no private-eyes or thrillers. No explicit sex or violence. Serious fiction, not romance/adventure. "We will consider historical fiction that is well researched. No science fiction/fantasy, no religious/inspirational, no how-to, no cookbooks. In general, we are very conscious of women's roles. We publish very few

children's books." Recently published *Threshold of Fire*, by Hella Haasse; *Celibacy of Felix Greenspan*, by Lionel Abrahams; *Murder in Miniature*, by Leo Bruce.

How to Contact: Accepts unsolicited mss. Query and submit first three chapters, double spaced, with SASE (IRCs). No simultaneous submissions. "Manuscripts without envelopes will be discarded. *Mailers* are a *must*."

Terms: Pays 5-10% on net in royalties; no advance. Sends galleys to author.

Advice: "At the moment we are swamped with manuscripts and anything under consideration can be under consideration for months."

ACE SCIENCE FICTION, Berkley Publishing Group, 200 Madison Ave., New York NY 10016. (212)951-8800. Estab. 1977. Publishes paperback originals and reprints. See Berkley Ace Science Fiction.

ALGONQUIN BOOKS OF CHAPEL HILL, 708 Broadway, New York NY 10003. Prefers not to share information.

ARCADE PUBLISHING, (III), Distributed by Little, Brown & Co., 141 Fifth Ave., New York NY 10010. (212)475-2633. Fax: (212)353-8148. President, Editor-in-Chief: Richard Seaver. Fiction Editors: Richard Seaver, Jeannette Seaver, Cal Barksdale, Tim Bent. Estab. 1988. Independent publisher. Publishes hardcover originals and paperback reprints. Books: 50-55 lb. paper; Cameron Web press printing; notch, perfect-bound; illustrations; average print order: 10,000; first novel print order: 3,000-5,000. Averages 40 total titles, 12 fiction titles each year. Does not comment on rejected ms.

Needs: Children's/juvenile (animal, easy-to-read, preschool/picture book), literary, mainstream/contemporary, translations. No romance, science fiction, young adult. Published *Texas Summer*, by Terry Southern (literary); *Fields of Glory*, by Jean Rouaud (translation); *The Great Indian Novel*, by Shashi Tharoor (literary). Published new writers within the last year.

How to Contact: No unsolicited mss; unsolicited mss will be returned (SASE, IRCs). Submit through an agent only. Agented fiction 100%. Reports in 2 weeks on queries; 3 months on mss.

Terms: Pays negotiable advances and royalties. 10 author's copies. Writer's guidelines and book catalog free.

ARCHWAY PAPERBACKS/MINSTREL BOOKS, 1230 Avenue of the Americas, New York NY 10020. (212)698-7268. Editorial Director: Patricia MacDonald. Published by Pocket Books. Imprints: Minstrel Books (ages 7-11); and Archway (ages 11 and up). Publishes paperback originals and reprints.

Needs: Young adult: mystery, suspense/adventure, thrillers. Young readers (80 pages and up): adventure, animals, family, fantasy, friends, mystery, school, etc. No picture books. Recently published *Fear Street: Sunburn*, by R.L. Stine; and *Aliens Ate My Homework*, by Bruce Corille. Published new writers this year.

How to Contact: Submit query first with outline; SASE (IRCs) "mandatory. If SASE not attached, query letter will not be answered."

ATHENEUM BOOKS FOR CHILDREN, (II), Imprint of the Macmillan Children's Book Group, 866 Third Ave., New York NY 10022. (212)702-7894. Vice President/Editorial Director: Jonathan J. Lanman. Fiction Editor: Marcia Marshall (especially science fiction/fantasy). Second largest imprint of large publisher/corporation. Publishes hardcover originals. Books: Illustrations for picture books, some illustrated short novels; average print order: 6,000-7,500; first novel print order: 5,000. Averages 60 total titles, 30 middle grade and YA fiction titles each year. Very rarely critiques rejected mss.

● Books published by Atheneum Books for Children have received the Newbury Medal (*Shiloh*, by Phyllis Reynolds Naylor) and the Christopher Award (*The Gold Coin*, by Alma Flor Ada, illustrated by Neal Waldman). At press time we learned that Macmillan Inc., including its Children's Book Group, was sold to Paramount Communications. This could affect the publisher's policies so watch *Publishers Weekly* and other trade journals for details.

Market categories: (I) Open to new writers; (II) Open to both new and established writers; (III) Interested mostly in established writers; (IV) Open to writers whose work is specialized.

Needs: Juvenile (adventure, animal, contemporary, fantasy, historical, sports), preschool/picture book, young adult/teen (fantasy/science fiction, historical, mystery, problem novels, sports, spy/adventure). No "paperback romance type" fiction. Published books include *Albert's Alphabet*, by Lesle Tryon (3-6, picture book); *Downriver*, by Will Hobbs (3-6, picture book); *Shiloh*, by Phyllis Reynolds Naylor (8-12, middle grade novel); *Keep Laughing*, by Cynthia Grant (8-12 middle grade novel).
How to Contact: Accepts unsolicited mss "if novel length; we want outline and 3 sample chapters." SASE (IRCs). Agented fiction 40%. Reports in 4-6 weeks on queries; 8-10 weeks on mss. Simultaneous submissions OK "if we are so informed and author is unpublished."
Terms: Pays in royalties of 10%. Average advance: $3,000 "along with advance and royalties, authors standardly receive ten free copies of their book and can purchase more at a special discount." Sends galleys to author. Writer's guidelines for #10 SAE and 1 first-class stamp. Book catalog for 9 × 12 SAE and 6 first-class stamps.
Advice: "We publish all hardcover originals, occasionally an American edition of a British publication. Our fiction needs have not varied in terms of quantity—of the 60-70 titles we do each year, 30 are fiction in different age levels. We are less interested in specific topics or subject matter than in overall quality of craftsmanship. First, know your market thoroughly. We publish only children's books, so caring for and *respecting* children is of utmost importance. Also, fad topics are dangerous, as are works you haven't polished to the best of your ability. (Why should we choose a 'jewel in the rough' when we can get a manuscript a professional has polished to be ready for publication.) The juvenile market is not one in which a writer can 'practice' to become an adult writer. In general, be professional. We appreciate the writers who take the time to find out what type of books we publish by visiting the libraries and reading the books. Neatness is a pleasure, too."

AVALON BOOKS, (I, II, IV), 401 Lafayette St., New York NY 10003. (212)598-0222. Vice President/ Publisher: Marcia Markland. Imprint of Thomas Bouregy Company, Inc. Publishes hardcover originals. Average print order for all books (including first novels): 2,100. Averages 60 titles/year.
Needs: "Avalon Books publishes wholesome romances, mysteries and westerns that are sold to libraries throughout the country. Intended for family reading, our books are read by adults as well as teenagers, and their characters are all adults. There is no graphic sex in any of our novels; kisses and embraces are as far as our characters go. Currently, we publish five books a month: two romances, one mystery romance, one career romance and one western. All the romances are contemporary; all the westerns are historical." Recently published *Mountain Love Song*, by Georgette Livingston (career romance); *Bachelor for Rent*, by Karen Morrell (career romance); *Night Run*, by Alice Sharpe (mystery); *Valley of the Lawless*, by Lee Martin (western). Books range in length from a minimum of 40,000 words to a maximum of 50,000 words.
How to Contact: Submit the first three chapters. "We'll contact you if we're interested." Publishes many first novels. Enclose ms-size SASE (IRCs). Reports in about 3 months. "Send SASE for a copy of our tip sheet."
Terms: The first half of the advance is paid upon signing of the contract; the second within 30 days after publication. Usually publishes within 6 to 8 months.

AVON BOOKS, (II), The Hearst Corporation, 1350 Avenue of the Americas, New York NY 10019. (212)261-6800. Imprints include Avon, Camelot and Flare. Editor-in-Chief Avon Books: Robert Mecoy. Estab. 1941. Large paperback publisher. Publishes paperback originals and reprints. Averages 300 titles a year.
Needs: Fantasy, historical romance, mainstream, science fiction, medical thrillers, intrigue, war, western and young adult/teen. No poetry, short story collections, religious, limited literary or esoteric nonfiction. Published *Butterfly*, by Kathryn Harvey; *So Worthy My Love*, by Kathleen Woodiwiss.
How to Contact: Query letters only. SASE (IRCs) to insure response.
Terms: Vary. Sponsors Flare Novel competition.

BAEN BOOKS, (II), P.O. Box 1403, Riverdale NY 10471. (212)548-3100. Baen Science Fiction, Baen Fantasy. Publisher and Editor: Jim Baen. Executive Editor: Toni Weisskopf. Consulting Editor: Josepha Sherman. Estab. 1983. Independent publisher; books are distributed by Simon & Schuster. Publishes hardcover and paperback originals and paperback reprints. Plans 6-10 first novels this year. Averages 60 fiction titles each year. Occasionally critiques rejected mss.
Needs: Fantasy and science fiction. Interested in science fiction novels (generally "hard" science fiction) and fantasy novels "that are not rewrites of last year's bestsellers." Recently published *The City Who Fought*, by Anne McCaffrey and S.M. Stirling (science fiction); *When The Bough Breaks*, by

Mercedes Lackey and Holly Lisle (fantasy); and *Brother to Dragons*, by Charles Sheffield (science fiction). Published new writers within the last year.
How to Contact: Accepts unsolicited mss. Submit ms or outline/synopsis and 3 consecutive sample chapters with SASE (IRCs). Reports in 2-3 weeks on partials; 4-8 weeks on mss. Will consider simultaneous submissions, "but grudgingly and not as seriously as exclusives."
Terms: Pays in royalties; offers advance. Sends galleys to author. Writer's guidelines for SASE.
Advice: "Keep an eye and a firm hand on the overall story you are telling. Style is important but less important than plot. We like to maintain long-term relationships with authors."

BAKER BOOK HOUSE, (II), P.O. Box 6287, Grand Rapids MI 49516. (616)676-9185. Assistant to Director of Publications: Jane Dekker. Estab. 1939. "Midsize Evangelical publisher." Publishes hardcover and paperback originals. Books: web offset print; average print order: 5,000-10,000; first novel print order: 5,000. Averages 130 total titles. Sometimes comments on rejected ms.
Needs: "We are mainly seeking Christian fiction of two genres: Contemporary women's fiction and mystery." No fiction that is not written from a Christian perspective or of a genre not specified.
How to Contact: Does not accept unsolicited mss. Submit outline/synopsis and sample chapters. SASE. Agented fiction 100% (so far). Reports in 3-4 weeks on queries. Simultaneous submissions OK.
Terms: Pays royalties of 14% (of net). Sometimes offers advance. Sends galleys to author. Publishes ms 1 year after acceptance. Writer's guidelines for #10 SAE and 1 first-class stamp (IRCs). Book catalog for 9½×12½ SAE and 3 first-class stamps.
Advice: "I would suggest that authors interested in writing contemporary women's fiction write us for more information regarding this genre."

BALLANTINE BOOKS, 201 E. 50th St., New York NY 10022. Subsidiary of Random House. Vice Pres. and Senior Editor: Pamela D. Strickler. Publishes originals (general fiction, mass-market, trade paperback and hardcover). Averages over 120 total titles each year.
Needs: Major historical fiction, women's mainstream and general fiction. Manuscripts can be submitted unsolicited to Pamela D. Strickler. Recently published *Leading the Way*, by Al Santol; *The Iron Men*, by Leonard Scott; and *Texas Sunrise*, by Fern Michaels. Published new writers this year.
How to Contact: Submit query letter or brief synopsis and first 100 pages of ms. SASE (IRCs) required. Reports in 2 months on queries; 4-5 months on mss.
Terms: Pays in royalties and advance.

BANTAM BOOKS, (II), Division of Bantam Doubleday Dell Publishing Group, Inc., 1540 Broadway, New York NY 10036. (212)354-6500. Imprints include Skylark, New Age, Loveswept, Spectra, Crime Line, Domain, Fanfare. Estab. 1945. Complete publishing: hard-cover, trade, mass market. Number of titles: Planned 400 for 1993.
Needs: Contemporary, literary, adventure, mystery, spy, historical, western, war, family saga, glitz, gothic, romance, feminist, gay/lesbian, ethnic, psychic/supernatural, religious/inspirational, science fiction, fantasy, horror, humor/satire. Recently published *Venus Envy*, by Rita Mae Brown; *Deception*, by Amanda Quick; *Missing Joseph*, by Elizabeth George.
How to Contact: Submit through agent. No unsolicited material accepted. Simultaneous submissions OK. Reports on queries as soon as possible.
Terms: Individually negotiated; offers advance.

‡BANTAM DOUBLEDAY DELL BOOKS FOR YOUNG READERS DIVISION, (III), Bantam Doubleday Dell Publishing Group, Inc., 1540 Broadway, New York NY 10036. (212)354-6500. Imprints include Delacort Hardcover, Doubleday Picture Books; Paperback line: Dell Yearling, Laurel-Leaf, Skylark, Star Fire, Little Rooster, Sweet Dreams, Sweet Valley High. President: Georg Richiter. Editor-in-Chief to the Young Readers Division: Beverly Horowitz. Estab. 1945. Complete publishing: hardcover, trade, mass market.
● The Young Readers Division offers two contests, the Delacorte Press Annual Prize for a First Young Adult Novel and the Marguerite DeAngeli Prize. Both are listed in the Contests and Awards section.
Needs: Children's/juvenile, young adult/teen. Recently published *Baby*, by Patricia MacLachlan; *Whatever Happened to Janie*, by Caroline Cooney; *Nate the Great and the Pillowcase*, by Marjorie Sharmat.

How to Contact: Does not accept unsolicited mss. Submit through agent. Agented fiction 100%. Reports on queries "as soon as possible." Simultaneous submissions OK.
Terms: Individually negotiated; offers advance.

BANTAM SPECTRA BOOKS, (II, IV), Subsidiary of Bantam Doubleday Dell Publishing Group, Inc., 1540 Broadway, New York NY 10036. (212)354-6500. Vice-President and Publisher: Lou Aronica. Senior Editors: Tom Dupree and Jennifer Hershey. Editor: Janna Silverstein. Estab. 1985. Large science fiction, fantasy and speculative fiction line. Publishes hardcover originals, paperback originals and trade paperbacks. Averages 60 total titles each year, all fiction.
Needs: Fantasy, literary, science fiction. Needs include novels that attempt to broaden the traditional range of science fiction and fantasy. Strong emphasis on characterization. Especially well written traditional science fiction and fantasy will be considered. No fiction that doesn't have at least some element of speculation or the fantastic.
How to Contact: Query first with 3 chapters and a short (no more than 3 pages double-spaced) synopsis. SASE (IRCs). Agented fiction 90%. Reports in 6-8 weeks on queries.
Terms: Pays in royalties; negotiable advance. Sends galleys to author.

THE BERKLEY PUBLISHING GROUP, (III), Subsidiary of G.P. Putnam's Sons, 200 Madison Ave., New York NY 10016. (212)951-8800. Imprints are Berkley, Jove, Diamond, Ace Science Fiction, Pacer. Editor-in-Chief: Leslie Gelbman. Fiction Editors: Natalee Rosenstein, Judith Stern, John Talbot, Melinda Metz, Susan Allison, Ginger Buchanan, Carrie Feron, Gary Goldstein and Hillary Cige. Nonfiction: Elizabeth Beier and Hillary Cige. Large commercial category line. Publishes paperback originals, trade paperbacks and hardcover and paperback reprints. Books: Paperbound printing; perfect binding; average print order: "depends on position in list." Plans approx. 10 first novels this year. Averages 1,180 total titles, 1,000 fiction titles each year. Sometimes critiques rejected mss.
Needs: Fantasy, mainstream, mystery/suspense, psychic/supernatural/occult, romance (contemporary, historical), science fiction, war.
How to Contact: Accepts no unsolicited mss. Submit through agent only. Agented fiction 98%. Reports in 6-8 weeks on mss. Simultaneous submissions OK.
Terms: Pays royalties of 4-10%. Provides 25 author's copies. Writer's guidelines and book catalog not available.
Advice: "Aspiring novelists should keep abreast of the current trends in publishing by reading *The New York Times* Bestseller Lists, trade magazines for their desired genre and *Publishers Weekly*."

BERKLEY/ACE SCIENCE FICTION, (II), Berkley Publishing Group, 200 Madison Ave., New York NY 10016. (212)951-8800. Editor-in-Chief: Susan Allison. Estab. 1948. Publishes paperback originals and reprints and 6-10 hardcovers per year. Number of titles: 8/month. Buys 85-95% agented fiction.
Needs: Science fiction and fantasy. No other genre accepted. No short stories. Published *The Cat Who Walks Through Walls*, by Robert Heinlein; *Neuromancer*, by William Gibson.
How to Contact: Submit outline/synopsis and 3 sample chapters with SASE (IRCs). No simultaneous submissions. Reports in 2 months minimum on mss. "Queries answered immediately if SASE enclosed." Publishes ms an average of 18 months after acceptance.
Terms: Standard for the field. Sends galleys to author.
Advice: "Good science fiction and fantasy are almost always written by people who have read and loved a lot of it. We are looking for knowledgeable science or magic, as well as sympathetic characters with recognizable motivation. We are looking for solid, well-plotted science fiction: good action adventure, well-researched hard science with good characterization and books that emphasize characterization without sacrificing plot. In fantasy we are looking for all types of work, from high fantasy to sword and sorcery." Submit fantasy and science fiction to Susan Allison, Ginjer Buchanan and Laura Anne Gilman.

✝ *The double dagger before a listing indicates that the listing is new in this edition. New markets are often the most receptive to submissions by new writers.*

JOHN F. BLAIR, PUBLISHER, (II, IV), 1406 Plaza Dr., Winston-Salem NC 27103. (919)768-1374. President: Carolyn Sakowski. Editor: Stephen Kirk. Estab. 1954. Small independent publisher. Publishes hardcover and paperback originals. Books: Acid-free paper; offset printing; illustrations; average print order: 2,500-5,000. Number of titles: 8 in 1992, 12 in 1993. "Among our 10-12 books, we do one novel a year." Occasionally comments on rejected mss.
  • For more on John F. Blair see the interview with Stephen Kirk in the 1993 *Writer's Market*.
Needs: Contemporary, literary and regional. Generally prefers regional material dealing with southeastern U.S. No confessions or erotica. "We do not limit our consideration of manuscripts to those representing specific genres or styles. Our primary concern is that anything we publish be of high literary quality." Published works include *Blackbeard's Cup and Stories of the Outer Banks*, by Charles Harry Whedbee (folklore); and *The Legend of Nance Dude*, by Maurice Stanley (novel). Encourages new writers.
How to Contact: Query or submit with SASE (IRCs). Simultaneous submissions OK. Reports in 1 month. Publishes ms 1-2 years after acceptance. Free book catalog.
Terms: Negotiable.
Advice: "We are primarily interested in serious adult novels of high literary quality. Most of our titles have a tie-in with North Carolina or the southeastern United States. Please enclose a cover letter and outline with the manuscript. We prefer to review queries before we are sent complete manuscripts. Queries should include an approximate word count."

BOOKCRAFT, INC., (I), 1848 W. 2300 South, Salt Lake City UT 84119. (801)972-6180. Editorial Manager: Cory H. Maxwell. Publishes hardcover originals. Books: 60 lb. stock paper; sheet-fed and web press; average print order: 5,000-7,000; 3,000 for reprints. "We are always open for creative, fresh ideas."
  • Books published by Bookcraft have received several awards from the Association of Mormon Letters.
Needs: Contemporary, family saga, historical, mystery/suspense (private eye, romantic suspense, young adult), romance (gothic), religious/inspirational, thriller/espionage and western (traditional frontier, young adult). Published *Cottonwood Summer*, by Jean Liebenthal; *Dominions of the Gadiantons*, by Robert Marcum; *The Work and the Glory: Like a Fire is Burning*, by Gerald N. Lund. Published new writers within the last year.
How to Contact: Query, submit outline/synopsis and sample chapters, or submit complete ms with SASE (IRCs). Reports in 2 months.
Terms: Pays royalties; no advance. Sends galleys to author. Free book catalog and writer's guidelines.
Advice: "Our principal market is the membership of The Church of Jesus Christ of Latter-Day Saints (Mormons) and manuscripts should relate to the background, doctrines or practices of that church. The tone should be fresh, positive and motivational, but not preachy. We do not publish anti-Mormon works. We publish both fiction and nonfiction, and publish in hardcover and softcover."

BOOKS IN MOTION, (I), Suite #501, 9212 E. Montgomery, Spokane WA 99206. (509)922-1646. President: Gary Challender. Estab. 1980. "Audiobook company, national marketer. Publishes novels, novellas and short stories in audiobook form *only*." Plans 12 first novels this year. Averages 70 total titles, 65 fiction titles each year.
  • Books in Motion is known for its audio westerns. The publisher has received favorable reviews from *Library Journal*, *Kliatt Magazine* and *Audio-File* magazine.
Needs: Recently published *The Mystery of the Shot Tower*, by Marion Lillie (novella)(mystery); *The Golden Bullet*, by M & M Lehman (western); and *To A Promise True*, by Barbara Francis (sequel)(historical drama). Published new writers within the last year.
How to Contact: Accepts unsolicted mss. Submit outline/synopsis and 4 sample chapters. SASE (IRCs) for ms. Reports within 3 weeks to 3 months. Simultaneous submissions OK.
Terms: Pays royalties of 10%. "We pay royalties every 6 months. Royalties that are received are based on the gross sales that any given title generates during the 6-month interval. Authors must be patient since it usually takes a minimum of one year before new titles will have significant sales." Publishes ms 6-12 months after acceptance. Book catalog free on request.
Advice: "We prefer light cuss words and sex scenes, or none at all. We want novels with a strong plot. The fewer the characters, the better it will work on tape. Six-tape audiobooks sell and rent better than any other size in the unabridged format. One hour of tape is equal to 40 pages of double-spaced, 12 pitch, normal margin, typed pages."

THOMAS BOUREGY & COMPANY, INC., 401 Lafayette St., New York NY 10003. Small category line. See Avalon Books.

BOYDS MILLS PRESS, (II), Subsidiary of Highlights for Children, 815 Church St., Honesdale PA 18431. (717)253-1164. Manuscript Coordinator: Beth Troop. Estab. 1990. "Independent publisher of quality books for children of all ages." Publishes hardcover. Books: Coated paper; offset printing; case binding; 4-color illustrations; average print order varies. Plans 4 fiction titles (novels).
   • Boyd Mills Press is the publishing arm of *Highlights for Children*. See listings for the related magazine, a contest and a conference in this book.
Needs: Juvenile, young adult (adventure, animal, contemporary, ethnic, historical, sports). Recently published *Grandfather's Day*, by Ingrid Tomey; *My Sister Annie*, by Bill Dodds; *Annie's Choice*, by Clara Gillow Clark.
How to Contact: Accepts unsolicited mss. Send complete ms with cover letter. Reports in 1 month. Simultaneous submissions OK.
Terms: Pays standard rates. Sends pre-publication galleys to author. Time between acceptance and publication depends on "what season it is scheduled for." Writer's guidelines for #10 SAE and 1 first-class stamp (IRCs).
Advice: "We're interested in young adult novels of real literary quality as well as middle grade fiction that's imaginative with fresh ideas. Getting into the mode of thinking like a child is important."

BRADBURY PRESS, INC., (I, II), Affiliate of Macmillan, Inc., 866 Third Ave., New York NY 10022. (212)702-9809. Vice President and Editorial Director: Barbara Lalicki. Publishes juvenile hardcover originals. Books: Excellent quality paper printing and binding; full-color or black-and-white illustrations—depends on what the book needs. Seldom comments on rejected mss.
Needs: Juvenile and young adult: adventure, contemporary, science fiction. Published *Woodsong*, by Gary Paulsen; *Windcatcher*, by Avi; and *Cricket and the Crackerbox Kid*, by Alane Ferguson.
How to Contact: Query first on novels. Send complete picture book ms with SASE (IRCs). Specify simultaneous submissions. Reports in 3 months on mss.
Terms: Pays royalty based on retail price. Advance negotiable.

BRANDEN PUBLISHING CO., (I, II), Subsidiary of Branden Press, Box 843, 17 Station St., Brookline Village MA 02147. Imprint: I.P.L. Estab. 1967. Publishes hardcover and paperback originals and reprints. Books: 55-60 lb. acid-free paper; case- or perfect-bound; illustrations; average print order: 5,000. Plans 5 first novels this year. Averages 15 total titles, 5 fiction titles each year.
Needs: Adventure, contemporary, ethnic, historical, literary, mainstream, military/war, mystery/suspense, short story collections and translations. Looking for "contemporary, fast pace, modern society." No porno, experimental or horror. Published *Payola!*, by Gerry Cagle; *Miss Emily Martine*, by Lynn Thorsen; *Tales of Suicide*, by Luigi Pirandello; and *The Saving Rain*, by Elsie Webber.
How to Contact: Does not accept unsolicited mss. Query *only* with SASE (IRCs). Reports in 1 week on queries.
Terms: Pays royalties of 5-10% minimum. Advance negotiable. Provides 10 author's copies. Sends galleys to author. Publishes ms "several months" after acceptance.
Advice: "Publishing more fiction because of demand. *Do not make phone inquiries.* Do not oversubmit; single submissions only; do not procrastinate if contract is offered."

*GEORGE BRAZILLER, INC., (III), 60 Madison Ave., New York NY 10010. (212)889-0909. President: George Braziller. Manuscript submissions: Adrienne Baxter. Estab. 1955. Publishes hardcover originals and paperback reprints. Books: Cloth binding; illustrations sometimes; average print order: 4,000. Average first novel print order: 3,000. Buys 10% agented fiction. Averages 25 total titles, 6 fiction titles each year. Occasionally critiques rejected mss.

 The asterisk indicates a publisher who sometimes offers subsidy arrangements. Authors are asked to subsidize part of the cost of book production. See the introduction for more information.

Needs: Art, feminist, literary, short story collections and translations. Recently published *The Laws*, by Connie Palmen (literary); *There Is No Borges*, by Gerhard Köpf (literary); *The African in Me*, by Howard Gordon (African-American/literary).

How to Contact: Query first with SASE. Reports in 2 weeks on queries. Publishes ms an average of 1 year after acceptance.

Terms: *Some subsidy publishing.* Negotiates advance. Must return advance if book is not completed or is not acceptable. Sends galleys to author. Free book catalog on request with oversized SASE (IRCs).

Advice: "Only send work which, in your eyes, is *completely* finished—in other words, don't send it until you are 100% certain that you've submitted the best manuscript you can."

*BRIDGE PUBLISHING, INC., (II, IV), 2500 Hamilton Blvd., South Plainfield NJ 07080. (908)754-0745. Editor: Catherine J. Barrier. Estab. 1981. Midsize independent publisher of Christian literature. Publishes hardback and paperback originals and reprints. Averages 25 total titles/year.

Needs: "We want quality, literary Christian fiction, written in styles such as those of Frederick Buechner, John Cheever, and John Updike. *No* 'genre fiction' (romance, biblical novels, gothics, sci-fi, etc.). We want well-written fiction that shows believable characters struggling to 'work out their salvations' in believable situations, books that exhibit real human drama and stylistic craftsmanship."

How to Contact: Accepts complete unsolicited mss (with cover letter), but prefers proposals (including cover letter, detailed outline of the book's chapters—a synopsis of the plot and the first 3-4 chapters). SASE (IRCs) required if materials are to be returned. Reports in 2-3 months. Simultaneous submissions OK.

Terms: *Offers self/cooperative publishing services.* Writer's guidelines for #10 SAE and 1 first-class stamp. Book catalog for $2.95.

Advice: "While we have not generally accepted fiction much in the recent past, we are now open to consider manuscripts of exceptional merit. Authors must already have material published and/or other books published by reputable publishers. The work must be written from a biblical Christian world-view, but does not necessarily need to be explicitly religious in nature. Only mss that have already been completed will be considered."

BROADMAN & HOLMAN PUBLISHERS, (II), (formerly Broadman Press), 127 9th Ave. N., Nashville TN 37234. (615)251-2000. Editorial Director: Michael S. Hyatt. Religious publisher associated with the Southern Baptist Convention. Publishes hardcover and paperback originals. Books: Offset paper stock; offset printing; perfect or Smythe sewn binding; illustrations possible; average print order depends on forecast. Average number of titles: 3/year.

Needs: Christian living, religious/inspirational, humor/satire, juvenile, and young adult. Will accept no other genre. Published: *Recovery of the Lost Sword*, L.L. Chaikin; *Mary of Magdala*, by Anne C. Williman; *Journey to Amanah: The Beginning*, by Colleen K. Snyder.

How to Contact: Query, but decision is not made until ms is reviewed. No simultaneous submissions. Reports in 2 months on queries and mss.

Terms: Pays 10% in royalties. Sends galleys to author if requested.

Advice: "We publish very few fiction works, but we encourage first novelists. We encourage a close working relationship with the author to develop the best possible product."

CAMELOT BOOKS, (II), Imprint of Avon Books, (Division of the Hearst Corporation), 1350 Avenue of the Americas, New York NY 10019. (212)261-6816. Editorial Director: Ellen E. Krieger. Estab. 1961. Publishes paperback originals and reprints for middle-grade juvenile list. Books: 6-10 line drawings in a few of the younger books. No color.

Needs: Juvenile (fantasy—"very selective," contemporary—"selective"). Looking for "contemporary, humorous books about real kids in real-life situations." No "science fiction, animal stories, picture books." Published *Haunting in Williamsburg*, by Lou Kassem; *The Return of the Plant that Ate Dirty Socks*, by Nancy McArthur; and *The Secret of the Indian*, by Lynne Reid Banks.

How to Contact: Accepts unsolicited mss. Submit complete ms with cover letter (preferred) or outline/synopsis and 3 sample chapters. Agented fiction 75%. Reports in 3-4 weeks on queries; 6-10 weeks on mss. Simultaneous submissions OK.

Terms: Royalties and advance negotiable. Sends galleys to author. Writer's guidelines for #10 SAE and 1 first-class stamp (IRCs). Book catalog for 9×11 SAE and 98¢ postage.

CARROLL & GRAF PUBLISHERS, INC., (III), 260 Fifth Ave., New York NY 10001. (212)889-8772. Editor: Kent Carroll. Estab. 1983. Publishes hardcover and paperback originals and paperback reprints. Plans 5 first novels this year. Averages 120 total titles, 75 fiction titles each year. Average first novel print order 7,500 copies. Occasionally critiques rejected mss.
Needs: Contemporary, erotica, fantasy, science fiction, literary, mainstream and mystery/suspense. No romance.
How to Contact: Does not accept unsolicited mss. Query first or submit outline/synopsis and sample chapters. SASE (IRCs). Reports in 2 weeks.
Terms: Pays in royalties of 6% minimum; 15% maximum; advance negotiable. Sends galleys to author. Free book catalog on request.

CHRONICLE BOOKS, (I), 275 Fifth St., San Francisco CA 94103. (415)777-7240. Fiction Editor: Jay Schaefer. Estab. 1966. "Full-line publisher of 150 books per year." Publishes hardcover and paperback originals. Averages 150 total titles, 10 fiction this year. Sometimes comments on rejected ms.
Needs: Open. Looking for novellas, collections and novels. No romances, science fiction or any genre fiction: no category fiction. Publishes anthologies. Published *Griffin & Sabine*, by Bantok; *Parallel Life and Other Stories*, by Beeman; *New Orleans Stories*, edited by Miller.
How to Contact: Accepts unsolicited mss. Submit complete ms with cover letter. "No queries, please." Send SASE (IRCs) for reply, return of ms or send a disposable copy of the ms. Agented fiction 50%. No simultaneous submissions.
Terms: Standard rates. Sends galleys to author. Publishes ms 9-12 months after acceptance. No writer's guidelines available.

CITADEL PRESS, (II), Carol Publishing Group, 120 Enterprise Ave., Secaucus NJ 07094. (201)866-4199. Editor: Allan J. Wilson. Estab. 1942. Publishes hardcover and paperback originals and paperback reprints. Averages 65 total titles, 4-7 fiction titles each year. Occasionally critiques rejected mss.
Needs: No religious, romantic or detective. Published *The Rain Maiden*, by Jill M. Phillips and *Human Oddities*, by Martin Monestiere.
How to Contact: Accepts unsolicited mss. Query first with SASE (IRCs). Reports in 6 weeks on queries; 2 months on mss. Simultaneous submissions OK.
Terms: Pays in royalties of 10% minimum; 15% maximum; 12-25 author's copies. Advance is more for agented ms; depends on grant/award money.

■CLOVERDALE PRESS INC., (II), 109 W. 17th St., New York NY 10011. (212)727-3370. Editorial Director: Jane Thornton. Estab. 1980. Book packager.
● For more on Cloverdale see the interview with the editors in the 1990 *Novel & Short Story Writer's Market*.
Needs: "Needs vary greatly and frequently, depending on publishers' requirements." Currently producing *Sweet Dreams*, YA romances, YA fiction, and adult nonfiction and how-to.
How to Contact: Does *not* accept unsolicited mss. Write for guidelines. Include SASE (IRCs).

DAVID C. COOK PUBLISHING COMPANY, 850 N. Grove, Elgin IL 60120. (708)741-2400. Imprints: Chariot Books, Life Journey Books. Executive Editor: Catherine L. Davis. Estab. 1875. Publishes hardcover and paperback originals. Number of fiction titles: 35-40 juvenile, 4-6 adult. Encourages new writers.
Needs: Religious/inspirational, juvenile, young adult and adult; sports, animal, spy/adventure, historical, Biblical, fantasy/science fiction, picture book and easy-to-read. Published *With Wings as Eagles*, by Elaine Schulte; *Mystery of the Laughing Cat*, by Elspeth Campbell Murphy; *Mystery Rider at Thunder Ridge*, by David Gillett. Published new writers within the last year.

Listings marked with a solid box are book packagers. See the introduction for more information.

How to Contact: All unsolicited mss are returned unopened. Query with SASE. Simultaneous submissions OK. Accepts computer printout submissions. Reports in 3 months.

Terms: Royalties vary ("depending on whether it is trade, mass market or cloth" and whether picture book or novel). Offers advance. Writer's guidelines with SASE.

Advice: "Chariot Books publishes books for toddlers through teens which help children better understand their relationship with God, and/or the message of God's book, the Bible. Interested in seeing contemporary novels (*not* Harlequin-type) adventure, romance, suspense with Christian perspective."

CROSSWAY BOOKS, (II, IV), Division of Good News Publishers, 1300 Crescent, Wheaton IL 60187. Editorial Director: Leonard G. Goss. Estab. 1938. Midsize independent religious publisher with plans to expand. Publishes paperback originals. Average print order 5,000-10,000 copies. Averages 50 total titles, 20-25 fiction titles each year.

Needs: Contemporary, adventure, literary, religious/inspirational, science fiction and young adult (fantasy/science fiction). "All fiction published by Crossway Books must be written from the perspective of evangelical Christianity. It must understand and view the world through Christian principle. For example, our books *Taliesin* and *Merlin* take place in a pre-Christian era, but Christian themes (e.g., sin, forgiveness, sacrifice, redemption) are present. We are *eager* to discover and nurture Christian novelists." No sentimental, didactic, "inspirational" religious fiction; heavy-handed allegorical or derivative (of C.S. Lewis or J.R.R. Tolkien) fantasy. Recently published *Glastonbury*, by Donna Fletcher Crow; *Prophet*, by Frank E. Peretti; *Day of the East Wind*, by Julia Shuken.

How to Contact: Does not accept unsolicited mss. Send query with synopsis and sample chapters only. Reports in 4-6 months on queries. Publishes ms 1-2 years after acceptance.

Terms: Pays in royalties and negotiates advance. Book catalog for 9×12 SAE and $1.25.

Advice: "We feel called to publish fiction in the following categories: Supernatural fiction, fantasy/science fiction, Christian realism, historical fiction, mystery fiction, intrigue, western fiction and children's fiction. All fiction should include explicit Christian content, artfully woven into the plot, and must be consistent with our statements of vision, purpose and commitment. Crossway can successfully publish and market *quality* Christian novelists. Also read John Gardner's *On Moral Fiction*. The market for fantasy/science fiction continues to expand (and genre fiction in general). There are more attempts lately at Christian science fiction and fantasy, though they generally fail from didacticism or from being overly derivative. We have a western adult and youth series, a mystery series."

THE CROWN PUBLISHING GROUP, (II), 201 E. 50th St., New York NY 10022. (212)572-6190. Imprints include Crown, Harmony Books, Orion Books, Clarkson N. Potter, Inc. Executive Vice Pres., Editor-in-Chief: Betty A. Prashker. Executive Editor, Crown: James O'Shea Wade. Editorial Director, Harmony Books: Peter Guzzardi. President and Publisher, Clarkson N. Potter: Michelle Sidrane. Executive Editor: Lauren Shakely. Editorial Director, Orion Books: James O'Shea Wade. Executive Managing Editor: Laurie Stark. Estab. 1936. Large independent publisher of fiction and nonfiction. Publishes hardcover and paperback originals and reprints. Books: 50 lb. paper; offset printing; hardcover binding; sometimes illustrations; average print order: 15,000. Plans 4 first novels this year. Averages 250 total titles, 20 fiction titles each year. Average first novel print order: 15,000 copies. Occasionally critiques rejected mss.

Needs: Adventure, contemporary, historical, horror, humor/satire, literary, mainstream, science, war. Published *Plains of Passage*, by Jean Auel; *Dave Barry Talks Back*, by Dave Barry; *Russka*, by Edward Rutherfurd; *Zapp!*, by William Byam with Jeff Cox; and *Martha Stewart's Gardening*, by Martha Stewart.

How to Contact: Does not accept unsolicited mss. "Query letters only addressed to the Editorial Department. Complete mss are returned unread . . ." SASE (IRCs). Reports in 3-4 months.

Terms: Pays advance against royalty; terms vary and are negotiated per book.

DARK HORSE COMICS, INC., (II, IV), 10956 SE Main St., Milwaukee OR 97222. (503)652-8815. Contact: Submissions Editor. Estab. 1986. "Dark Horse publishes all kinds of comics material, and we try not to limit ourselves to any one genre or any one philosophy. Most of our comics are intended for readers 15-40, though we also publish material that is accessible to younger readers." Comic books: newsprint or glossy paper, each title 24-28 pages. Averages 10-30 total titles each year.

● Dark Horse Press recently signed an agreement with Turner Publishing to produce new comics books featuring characters by Tex Avery.

Needs: Comics: adventure, childrens/juvenile, fantasy (space fantasy, super hero, sword and sorcery), horror, humor/satire, mystery/suspense (private eye/hardboiled), psychic/supernatural, romance (contemporary), science fiction (hard science, soft/sociological), western (traditional). Proposals or scripts for comic books only. Plans anthology. Published comics by Andrew Vachss, Frank Miller, John Byrne, Chris Claremont, Clive Barker. Recently published short story comic anthologies: *Dark Horse Comics*, *Dark Horse Presents, Cheval Noir* and *Hard Looks*.

How to Contact: Does not accept unsolicited mss. Query letter first. Should include one-page bio, list of publishing credits. SASE (IRC) or disposable copy of ms. Reports in 1-2 months. Simultaneous submissions OK.

Terms: Pays $25-100/page and 5-25 author's copies. "We usually buy first and second rights, other rights on publication." Writer's guidelines free for #10 SASE and 1 first-class stamp (IRCs).

Advice: "Obtain copies of our Writer's Guidelines, Proposal Guidelines and Script Format Guidelines before making a submission." Looks for "originality, a sense of fun."

DAW BOOKS, INC., (I), 375 Hudson St., New York NY 10014. Publishers: Elizabeth R. Wollheim and Sheila E. Gilbert. Executive VP/Secretary-Treasurer: Elsie B. Wollheim. Submissions Editor: Peter Stampfel. Estab. 1971. Publishes paperback originals and hardcover originals. Books: Illustrations sometimes; average print and first novel order vary widely. May publish as many as 6 or more first novels a year. Averages 36 new titles plus 40 or more reissues, all fiction, each year. Occasionally critiques rejected mss.

• For more on DAW Books, see the interview with Sheila Gilbert in the 1990 *Novel & Short Story Writer's Market*.

Needs: Science fiction (hard science, soft sociological) and fantasy only. Recently published *Skybowl*, by Melanie Rawn (novel); *Winds of Fury*, by Mercedes Lackey (novel); *Foreigner*, by C.J. Cherryh; *His Conquering Sword*, by Kate Elliott. Publishes many original and reprint anthologies including *Sword & Sorceress* (edited by Marion Zimmer Bradley); *Cat Fantastic* (edited by Martin H. Greenberg); *Tales From the Twilight Zone* (edited by Carol Serling). "You may write to the editors (after looking at the anthology) for guidelines % DAW."

How to Contact: Submit complete ms with return postage and SASE (IRCs). Usually reports in 3-5 months on mss, but in special cases may take longer. "No agent required."

Terms: Pays an advance against royalties. Sends galleys to author (if there is time).

Advice: "We strongly encourage new writers. We are currently working with more than a dozen additional new authors whose first novels we plan to publish in 1993 and 1994. We like a close and friendly relationship with authors. We are publishing more fantasy than previously, but we are looking for more *serious* fantasy and especially need science fiction. To unpublished authors: Try to make an educated submission and don't give up; write for our guidelines."

DEL REY BOOKS, Subsidiary of Ballantine Books, 201 E. 50 St., New York NY 10022. (212)572-2677. Estab. 1977. Publishes hardcover originals and paperback originals and reprints. Plans 6-7 first novels this year. Publishes 60 titles each year, all fiction. Sometimes critiques rejected mss.

Needs: Fantasy and science fiction. Fantasy must have magic as an intrinsic element to the plot. No flying-saucer, Atlantis or occult novels. Recently published *The Chronicles of Pern*, by Anne McCaffrey (science fiction/hardcover original); *The Shining Ones*, by David Eddings (fantasy/hardcover original); and *Jack the Bodiless*, by Julian May (science fiction/paperback reprint).

How to Contact: Accepts unsolicited mss. Submit cover letter with complete manuscript or brief outline/synopsis and *first* 3 chapters. Prefers complete ms. Address science fiction to SF editor; fantasy to fantasy editor. Reports in 2 weeks on queries; 2-10 months on mss.

Terms: Pays in royalties; "advance is competitive." Sends pre-publication galleys to author. Writer's guidelines for #10 SAE and 1 first-class stamp (IRCs).

Advice: Has been publishing "more fiction and more hardcovers, because the market is there for them. Read a lot of science fiction and fantasy, such as works by Anne McCaffrey, David Eddings, Larry Niven, Arthur C. Clarke, Terry Brooks, Frederik Pohl, Barbara Hambly. When writing, pay particular attention to plotting (and a satisfactory conclusion) and characters (sympathetic and well-rounded)—because those are what readers look for."

DELACORTE/DELL BOOKS FOR YOUNG READERS/DOUBLEDAY, (II, III, IV), Division of Bantam Doubleday Dell Publishing Group, Inc., 1540 Broadway, New York NY 10036. See listing for Bantam Doubleday Dell Books for Young Readers.

DELL PUBLISHING, 1540 Broadway, New York NY 10036. (212)354-6500. Imprints include Delacorte Press, Delta, Dell, Laurel. Estab. 1922. Publishes hardcover and paperback originals and paperback reprints.

Needs: See below for individual imprint requirements.

How to Contact: Reports in 3 months. Simultaneous submissions OK. Please adhere strictly to the following procedures: 1. Send *only* a 4-page synopsis or outline with a cover letter stating previous work published or relevant experience. Enclose SASE (IRCs). 2. *Do not* send ms, sample chapters or artwork. 3. *Do not* register, certify or insure your letter. Dell is comprised of several imprints, each with its own editorial department. Please review carefully the following information and direct your submissions to the appropriate department. Your envelope must be marked: Attention: (One of the following names of imprints), Editorial Department—Proposal.

DELACORTE: Publishes in hardcover; looks for top-notch commercial fiction and nonfiction; 35 titles/year.

DELTA: Publishes trade paperbacks including original fiction and nonfiction; 20 titles/year.

DELL: Publishes mass-market and trade paperbacks; looks for family sagas, historical romances, sexy modern romances, adventure and suspense thrillers, mysteries, psychic/supernatural, horror, war novels, fiction and nonfiction. 200 titles/year.

DIAL PRESS: Publishes literary fiction and high-end nonfiction; 2 titles/year.

Terms: Pays 6-15% in royalties; offers advance. Sends galleys to author. Book catalog for 8½×11 SAE plus $1.30 postage (Attention: Customer Service).

Advice: "Don't get your hopes up. Query first only with 4-page synopsis plus SASE. Study the paperback racks in your local drugstore. We encourage first novelists. We also encourage all authors to seek agents."

DIAL BOOKS FOR YOUNG READERS, (II), Division of Penguin Books U.S.A. Inc., 375 Hudson St., New York NY 10014. (212)366-2000. Imprints include Pied Piper Books, Easy-to-Read Books. Editor-in-Chief/Pres./Publisher: Phyllis Fogelman. Estab. 1961. Trade children's book publisher, "looking for picture book mss and novels." Publishes hardcover originals. Plans 1 first novel this year. Averages 100 titles, mainly fiction. Occasionally critiques or comments on rejected ms.

Needs: Juvenile (1-9 yrs.) including: animal, fantasy, spy/adventure, contemporary and easy-to-read; young adult/teen (10-16 years) including: fantasy/science fiction, literary and commercial mystery and fiction. Recently published *Waiting for the Evening Star*, by Rosemary Wells and Susan Jeffers; *Soul Looks Back in Wonder*, by Tom Feelings, Maya Angelou, Langston Hughes and others; *Parents in the Pigpen and Pigs in the Tub*, by Steven Kellogg and Amy Ehrlich.

How to Contact: Accepts unsolicited mss. Submit outline/synopsis and 2-3 sample chapters or complete ms with cover letter. SASE (IRCs). Agented fiction 50%. Reports in 3-4 weeks on queries. Simultaneous brief submissions OK.

Terms: Pays advance against royalties. Writer's guidelines for #10 SAE and 1 first-class stamp. Book catalog for 9×12 SAE and $1.92 postage.

Advice: "We are publishing more fiction books than in the past, and we publish only hardcover originals, most of which are fiction. At this time we are particularly interested in both fiction and nonfiction for the middle grades, and innovative picture book manuscripts. We also are looking for easy-to-reads for first and second graders. Plays, collections of games and riddles, and counting and alphabet books are generally discouraged. Before submitting a manuscript to a publisher, it is a good idea to request a catalog to see what the publisher is currently publishing. As the 'Sweet Valley High' phenomenon has loosened its stranglehold on YA fiction, we are seeing more writers able to translate traditional values of literary excellence and contemporary innovation into the genre. Make your cover letters read like jacket flaps—short and compelling. Don't spend a lot of time apologizing for a lack of qualifications. In fact, don't mention them at all unless you have publishing credits, or your background is directly relevant to the story: 'I found this folktale during a return trip to the Tibetan village where I spent the first ten years of my life.' "

DOUBLEDAY, (III), a Division of Bantam Doubleday Dell Publishing Group, Inc., 1540 Broadway., New York NY 10036. (212)354-6500. Estab. 1897. Publishes hardcover and paperback originals and paperback reprints.

Needs: "Doubleday is not able to consider unsolicited queries, proposals or manuscripts unless submitted through a bona fide literary agent, except that we will consider fiction for Perfect Crime line, romance and western imprints."

How to Contact: Send copy of complete ms (60,000-80,000 words) to Perfect Crime Editor, Loveswept Editor or Western Editor as appropriate. Sufficient postage (IRCs) for return via fourth class mail must accompany ms. Reports in 2-6 months.

Terms: Pays in royalties; offers advance.

DOUBLEDAY CANADA LIMITED, 105 Bond St., Toronto, Ontario M5B 1Y3 Canada. No unsolicited submissions. Prefers not to share information.

EAKIN PRESS, (II, IV), Box 90159, Austin TX 78709-0159. (512)288-1771. Imprint: Nortex. Editor: Edwin M. Eakin. Estab. 1978. Publishes hardcover originals. Books: Old style (acid-free); offset printing; case binding; illustrations; average print order 2,000; first novel print order 5,000. Plans 2 first novels this year. Averages 80 total titles each year.
Needs: Juvenile. Specifically needs historical fiction for school market, juveniles set in Texas for Texas grade schoolers. Published *Wall Street Wives*, by Ande Ellen Winkler; *Jericho Day*, by Warren Murphy; and *Blood Red Sun*, by Stephen Mertz. Published new writers within the last year.
How to Contact: Accepts unsolicited mss. First send query or submit outline/synopsis and 2 sample chapters. SASE (IRCs). Agented fiction 5%. Simultaneous submissions OK. Reports in 3 months on queries.
Terms: Pays royalties; average advance: $1,000. Sends galleys to author. Publishes ms 1-1½ years after acceptance. Writers guidelines for #10 SAE and 1 first-class stamp. Book catalog for 75¢.
Advice: "Juvenile fiction only with strong Texas theme. We receive around 600 queries or unsolicited mss a year."

ECLIPSE BOOKS/ECLIPSE COMICS, (II, IV), P.O. Box 1099, Forestville CA 95436. (707)887-1521. Editor-in-Chief: Catherine Yronwode. Estab. 1978. Books: White or coated stock, up to 200 pages, every page illustrated. "Publishes 10-20 titles—comics and graphic novels each month."
● For more on Eclipse, see "Off the Beaten Path" in the 1991 *Novel & Short Story Writer's Market*. Eclipse, in conjunction with HarperCollins, publishes the Harper-Eclipse line of graphic novels featuring work by Doris Lessing, Dean Koontz and Jonathan Carroll.
Needs: Comics and graphic novels: adventure, condensed/excerpted novel, contemporary, ethnic, experimental, fantasy, feminist, gay, historical, horror, juvenile, lesbian, literary, mainstream, mystery/suspense, psychic/supernatural/occult, romance, science fiction, serialized novel, thriller/espionage, translations, westerns, young adult. "No religious, nationalistic, racist material." Receives "hundreds" of unsolicited fiction mss/year. Published *Tecumsed*, by Allan Eckert and Tim Truman; *Dread*, by Clive Barker and Dan Brereton; and *Playing the Game*, by Doris Lessing and Daniel Vallely.
How to Contact: Send a cover letter, proposal, sample of script for artist to draw from. Reports in 3 months. SASE (IRCs). Simultaneous and reprint submissions (especially adaptations of well-known prose fiction) OK. Sample copy for $3. Fiction guidelines for #10 SAE.
Terms: Pays $35-50/page (for a screenplay-type of comics script, not a page of prose); advance against royalties (royalties are about 8%, but must be shared with the artist). Also pays 2-5 contributor's copies and discount on extras.
Advice: Looks for "interesting, original stories with in-depth characterization."

PAUL S. ERIKSSON, PUBLISHER, (II), Suite 208, Battell-on-the-Otter, Middlebury VT 05753. (802)388-7303. Editor: Paul S. Eriksson. Estab. 1960. Publishes hardcover and paperback originals.
Needs: Mainstream. Published *The Headmaster's Papers*, by Richard A. Hawley and *Hand in Hand*, by Tauno Yliruusi.
How to Contact: Query first. Publishes ms an average of 6 months after acceptance.
Terms: Pays 10-15% in royalties; advance offered if necessary. Free book catalog.
Advice: "Our taste runs to serious fiction."

M. EVANS & CO., INC., (II), 216 E. 49th St., New York NY 10017. (212)688-2810. Westerns Editor: Patrick Lo Brutto. Publishes hardcover and trade paper fiction and nonfiction. Publishes 40-50 titles each year.
Needs: Western.
How to Contact: Accepts unsolicited mss. Query first with outline/synopsis and 3 sample chapters. SASE (IRCs). Agented fiction: 100%. Recently published *Gun Fight*, by Richard Matheson; *Warhawk*, by R.C. House; *Friends*, by Charles Hockenberry; *Buscadero*, by Bill Brooks. Reports on queries in 3-5 weeks. Simultaneous submissions OK.

● *A bullet introduces comments by the editor of* Novel & Short Story Writer's Market *indicating special information about the listing.*

Know Your Market for Commercial Success

If you wish to be successful in selling your manuscript to a commercial publisher, "know what market you are going for," says Barbara Dicks, executive editor at Fawcett and Ivy Books. "If you are writing a literary book, don't send it to us. Although we sometimes publish reprints of successful literary books, we are really looking for something with mass appeal."

A division of Random House/Ballantine, Fawcett publishes paperback reprints of such bestselling hardcover authors as Marge Piercy and John Updike. However, they also publish original paperbacks, primarily under the Ivy and Gold Medal imprints. The number of new writers Fawcett publishes each year varies, says Dicks, "but it's not more than half a dozen."

Given the difficulty of making a successful sale to Fawcett, which categories should new writers focus on? "Historical romances are a good entry point with us," says Dicks, "although they are much more difficult to write than people might imagine." She recommends writers do thorough research to ensure accuracy of settings and other period details.

Dicks also notes that romances in general have changed in many ways during the past several years. "There are all kinds of new and unusual elements being used, such as time travel. There is also more humor—they don't take themselves quite so seriously anymore. And the characters and stories tend to be more sophisticated now. The good stories are not just sexy; they also tug at the reader emotionally."

Since she estimates that 99 percent of Fawcett's acquisitions are agented, Dicks strongly suggests finding an agent. "Although we do take some unsolicited manuscripts, agented manuscripts are processed more quickly. A good agent can also give writers advice on how to make their manuscripts more acceptable to the publisher. They generally know what we're looking for."

As for trends in the commercial publishing industry, Dicks remembers a time when movie rights to a book "didn't mean anything. Now, a movie makes a very big impact on a book." Michael Crichton's *Jurassic Park*, for example, was a very important book for Fawcett's parent company, Ballantine, even before the movie was released. Since the movie's successful run and the ensuing publicity, says Dicks, "not only has that book been selling extremely well, but Crichton's entire backlist has been hot also." Commercial publishers are naturally eager to see this trend continue.

Dicks also sees continuing strength in the mystery category. "Mysteries are a tremendous resource for us," she says. She considers the proliferation of mystery bookstores to be a significant factor in the growth of the category. "Those stores have a big impact, because the people who work in them are frequently very knowledgeable about the genre. And if there is a series of mysteries that is successful, they very often keep the author's complete backlist in stock as well."

The most important advice for new writers to remember in developing their stories, according to Dicks, is to have a clear understanding of the category in which they are writing. "If you want to write a Regency romance, for example," she says, "make sure you know what it is, and stay within those boundaries."
—Jamie Harding

Terms: Pays in royalties and offers advance; amounts vary. Sends galleys to author. Publishes ms 6-12 months after acceptance.

FANTAGRAPHICS BOOKS, (II, IV), 7563 Lake City Way, Seattle WA 98115. (206)524-1967. Publisher: Gary Groth. Estab. 1976. Publishes comic books, comics series and graphic novels. Books: offset printing; saddle-stitched periodicals and smythe-sewn books; heavily illustrated. Publishes originals and reprints. Publishes 10 titles each month.
● For more on Fantagraphics see "Off the Beaten Path" in the 1991 *Novel & Short Story Writer's Market*.
Needs: Comic books and graphic novels (adventure, fantasy, horror, mystery, romance, science, social parodies). "We look for subject matter that is more or less the same as you would find in mainstream fiction." Published *Blood of Palomar*, by Gilbert Hernandez; *The Dragon Bellows Saga*, by Stan Sakai; *Death of Speedy*; *Housebound With Rick Geary*; *Little Nemo in Slumberland*.
How to Contact: Send a plot summary, pages of completed art (photocopies only) and character sketches. May send completed script if the author is willing to work with an artist of the publisher's choosing. Include cover letter and SASE (IRCs). Reports in 1 month.
Terms: Pays in royalties of 8% (but must be split with artist) and advance.

FARRAR, STRAUS & GIROUX, (III), 19 Union Square W., New York NY 10003. (212)741-6900. Imprints include Hill & Wang, The Noonday Press. Editor-in-Chief: Jonathan Galassi. Midsized, independent publisher of fiction, nonfiction, poetry. Publishes hardcover originals. Published new writers within the last year. Plans 2 first novels this year. Averages 100 total titles, 30 fiction titles each year.
Needs: Open. No genre material. Published *The Mambo Kings Play Songs of Love*, by Oscar Hijuelos; *My Son's Story*, by Nadine Gordimer; *The Burden of Proof*, by Scott Turow.
How to Contact: Does not accept unsolicited mss. Query first. "Vast majority of fiction is agented." Reports in 2 months. Simultaneous submissions OK.
Terms: Pays royalties (standard, subject to negotiation). Advance. Sends galleys to author. Publishes ms one year after acceptance. Writer's guidelines for #10 SAE and 1 first-class stamp.

FARRAR, STRAUS & GIROUX/CHILDREN'S BOOKS, (II), 19 Union Square W., New York NY 10003. Children's Books Publisher: Stephen Roxburgh. Editor-in-Chief: Margaret Ferguson. Number of titles: 40. Published new writers within the last year. Buys juvenile mss with illustrations. Buys 25% agented fiction.
Needs: Children's picture books, juvenile novels, nonfiction. Recently published *The Secret Room*, by Uri Shulevitz; *Demons and Shadows*, by Robert Westall; *Making Sense*, by Bruce Brooks.
How to Contact: Submit outline/synopsis and 3 sample chapters, summary of ms and any pertinent information about author, author's writing, etc. No simultaneous submissions. No unsolicited submissions during the month of August. Reports in 1 month on queries, 3 months on mss. Publishes ms 18 months to 2 years after acceptance.
Terms: Pays in royalties; offers advance. Book catalog with 6½×9½ SASE (IRCs).
Advice: "Study our list before sending something inappropriate. Publishing more titles—our list has expanded."

FAWCETT, (I, II, III), Division of Random House/Ballantine, 201 E. 50th St., New York NY 10022. (212)751-2600. Imprints include Ivy, Crest, Gold Medal, Columbine and Juniper. Executive Editor: Barbara Dicks. Editor-in-Chief: Leona Nevler. Estab. 1955. Major publisher of mass market and trade paperbacks. Publishes paperback originals and reprints. Prints 160 titles annually. Encourages new writers. "Always looking for *great* first novels."
● See the interview with Executive Editor Barbara Dicks in this section.

Needs: Historical, suspense, occult, adventure, mysteries, romance (regency). Published *The Omega Command*, by John Land; *Mid-town South*, by Christopher O'Brian; *The Incense Tree*, by Jacqueline La Tourette.
How to Contact: Query with SASE (IRCs). Send outline and sample chapters for adult mass market. If ms is requested, simultaneous submissions OK. Prefers letter-quality. Reports in 2-4 months.
Terms: Pays usual advance and royalties.
Advice: "Gold Medal list consists of 4 paperbacks per month—usually 3 are originals."

FLARE BOOKS, (II), Imprint of Avon Books, Div. of the Hearst Corp., 1350 Avenue of the Americas, New York NY 10019. (212)261-6816. Editorial Director: Ellen Krieger. Estab. 1981. Small, young adult line. Publishes paperback originals and reprints. Plans 2-3 first novels this year. Averages 24 titles, all fiction each year.
Needs: Young adult (easy-to-read [hi-lo], problem novels, romance, spy/adventure) "very selective." Looking for contemporary fiction. No historical, science fiction/fantasy, heavy problem novels. Recently published *Nothing But the Truth: A Documentary Novel*, by Avi; *Night Cries*, by Barbara Steiner; and *The Weirdo*, by Theodore Taylor.
How to Contact: Accepts unsolicited mss. Submit complete ms with cover letter (preferred) or outline/synopsis and 3 sample chapters. Agented fiction 75%. Reports in 3-4 weeks on queries; 6-10 weeks on mss. Simultaneous submissions OK.
Terms: Royalties and advance negotiable. Sends galleys to author. Writer's guidelines for #10 SAE and 1 first-class stamp (IRCs). Book catalog for 9×12 SAE with 98¢ postage. "We run a young adult novel competition each year."

FOUR WINDS PRESS, (II), Imprint of Macmillan Children's Book Group, 866 Third Ave., New York NY 10022. Editor-in-Chief: Virginia Duncan. Estab. 1966. A children's trade book imprint. Publishes hardcover originals. Books: 3 piece binding for older reading books, 1 piece binding for picture books. Books for children ages 3-12 usually illustrated; average print orders vary. Published new writers within the last year. Publishes 25 total titles each year. No longer publishing young adult fiction.
• At press time we learned that Macmillan Inc., including its Children's Book Group, was sold to Paramount Communications. This could affect the publisher's policies, so watch *Publishers Weekly* and other trade journals for details.
Needs: Picture book manuscripts for ages 2-4 and 5-8, middle grade novels for ages 8-12. Recently published *Masai and I*, by Virginia Kroll; *Augusta & Trab*, by Christopher deVinck.
How to Contact: Accepts unsolicited mss. SASE (IRCs) required. Reports in 8-12 weeks.
Terms: Pays royalties, negotiable advance and author's copies. Manuscript guidelines and portfolio guidelines are available on request with #10 SAE (IRCs) and 1 first-class stamp. "No calls, please."
Advice: "The majority of the fiction manuscripts accepted by Four Winds Press are picture book texts; we publish very little older fiction. Due to volume of submissions received, we cannot guarantee a quick response time or answer queries about manuscript status."

GARETH STEVENS, INC., (II, IV), 1555 N. River Center Dr., Milwaukee WI 53212. Not accepting mss at this time.

GESSLER PUBLISHING COMPANY, 55 W. 13th St., New York NY 10011. (212)627-0099. Editorial Contact Person: Seth C. Levin. Estab. 1932. "Publisher/distributor of foreign language educational materials (primary/secondary schools)." Publishes paperback originals and reprints, videos and software. Averages 75 total titles each year. Sometimes comments on rejected ms.
Needs: "Foreign language or English as a Second Language." Needs juvenile, literary, preschool/picture book, short story collections, translations. Published *Don Quixote de la Mancha, (cartoon version of classic, in Spanish); El Cid*, (prose and poetry version of the classic, in Spanish); and *Les Miserables* (simplified version of Victor Hugo classic, in French).
How to Contact: Query first, then send outline/synopsis and 2-3 sample chapters; complete ms with cover letter. Agented fiction 40%. Reports on queries in 1 month; on mss in 6 weeks. Simultaneous submissions OK.
Terms: Pay varies with each author and contract. Sends galleys to author. "Varies on time of submission and acceptance relating to our catalog publication date." Writer's guidelines not available. Book catalog free on request.
Advice: "We specialize in the foreign language market directed to teachers and schools. A book that would interest us has to be attractive to that market. A teacher would be most likely to create a book for us."

GLOBE FEARON, (II), (formerly Fearon/Janus/Quercus), Subsidiary of Simon & Schuster, Secondary Education Group, 240 Frisch Court, Paramus NJ 07652. (201)909-6206. Associate Publisher: Virginia Seeley. Estab. 1954. Publisher of multicultural, remedial and special education products. Publishes paperback originals and reprints. Books: 3 lb. book set paper; offset printing; perfect or saddle-wired binding; line art illustrations; average print order: 5,000.
Needs: "All materials are written to specification. It's a hard market to crack without some experience writing at low reading levels. Manuscripts for specific series of fiction are solicited from time to time, and unsolicited manuscripts are accepted occasionally." Published *A Question of Freedom*, by Lucy Jane Bledsoe (adventure novella—one of series of eight); *Just for Today*, by Tana Reiff (one novella of series of seven life-issues stories); and *The Everett Eyes*, by Bernard Jackson & Susie Quintanilla (one of 20 in a series of extra-short thrillers).
How to Contact: Submit outline/synopsis and sample chapters. SASE (IRCs). Reports in 3 months. Simultaneous submissions OK.
Terms: Authors usually receive a predetermined project fee. Book catalog for 9 × 12 SAE with 4 first-class stamps.

‡DAVID R. GODINE, PUBLISHER, INC., (I, II), 300 Massachusetts Ave., Boston MA 02115. (617)536-0761. Imprints: Nonpareil Books (trade paperbacks), Verba Mundi (literature, translation), Imago Mundi (photography). President: David R. Godine. Editorial Director: Mark Polizzotti. Juvenile ms submissions: Audrey Bryant. Estab. 1970. Books: acid free paper; sewn binding; illustrations; average print order: 4,000-5,000; first novel print order: 3,500-6,500. Small independent publisher (12-person staff). Publishes hardcover and paperback originals and reprints. Comments on rejected mss "only if of particular interest."
Needs: Literary, mystery, collecting, historical, food and wine and juvenile. Recently published *The Last Giants*, by Francois Place; *Sherlock in Love*, by Sena Jeter Naslund; and *The Book of Nights*, by Sylvie Germain.
How to Contact: Accepts unsolicited mss with self-addressed, stamped (IRCs) book envelope. Query with outline/synopsis. "We prefer query letters—include publishing history, complete outline of story and SASE. Do not call to follow up on submission." Simultaneous submissions OK.
Terms: Standard royalties; offers advance. Sends galleys to author. Free book catalog.
Advice: "Keep trying. Remember that every writer now published was rejected countless times at the beginning."

GROSSET & DUNLAP, INC., (III), A Division of the Putnam & Grosset Group, 11th Floor, 200 Madison Ave., New York NY 10016. (212)951-8700. Publisher/Vice President: Jane O'Connor. Editor-in-Chief: Craig Walker.
Needs: Juvenile, preschool/picture book.
How to Contact: Queries only. "Include such details as length and intended age group and any other information that you think will help us to understand the nature of your material. Be sure to enclose a stamped, self-addressed envelope (IRCs) for our reply. We can no longer review manuscripts that we have not asked to see, and they will be returned unread."

HARCOURT BRACE & CO., (III), (formerly Harcourt Brace Jovanovich), 1250 Sixth Ave., San Diego CA 92101. (619)699-6810. Fax: (619)699-6777. Imprints include Harcourt Brace Children's Books, Gulliver Books, Jane Yolen Books and Browndeer Press. Director: Louise Howton. Executive Editor of Gulliver Books: Elizabeth Van Doren. Senior Editors: Diane D'Andrade and Allyn Johnston. Editor: Karen Grove. Editorial Director of Browndeer Press: Linda Zuckerman. Publishes hardcover originals and paperback reprints. Averages 100 titles/year. Published new writers within the last year.
  • Books published by Harcourt Brace & Co. have received numerous awards including the Caldecott and Newbery honors and selections as the American Library Association's "Best Books for Young Adults." Recent changes at the publisher include a new simultaneous format—paperback and hardcover at the same time—and a new imprint, Browndeer Press, a small general list of books for children (all ages). The editorial director of this new line is Linda Zuckerman
Needs: Young adult fiction, nonfiction for all ages, picture books for very young children, historical, mystery. Recently published *Raven*, by Gerald McDermott; *Timothy of the Cay*, by Theodore Taylor; *Nuts to You*, by Lois Ehlert; *Time for Bed*, by Mem Fox.
How to Contact: Unsolicited mss currently accepted *only* by Harcourt Brace Children's Books and Browndeer Press. Send to "Manuscript Submissions, Harcourt Brace Children's Books." SASE (IRCs). For picture books, send complete ms; for novels, send outline/synopsis and 2-4 sample chap-

ters. No simultaneous submissions. No phone calls. Responds in 6-8 weeks.
Terms: Terms vary according to individual books; pays on royalty basis. Writers' guidelines for #10 SASE; catalog for 9 × 12 SASE.
Advice: "Read as much current fiction as you can; familiarize yourself with the type of fiction published by a particular house; interact with young people to obtain a realistic picture of their concerns, interests and speech patterns."

❦HARLEQUIN ENTERPRISES, LTD., (II, IV), 225 Duncan Mill Rd., Don Mills, Ontario M3B 3K9 Canada. (416)445-5860. Imprints include Harlequin Romances, Harlequin Presents, Harlequin American Romances, Superromances, Temptation, Intrigue and Regency, Silhouette, Worldwide Mysteries, Gold Eagle. Editorial Director Harlequin: Karin Stoecker; Silhouette: Isabel Swift; Gold Eagle: Randall Toye. Estab. 1949. Publishes paperback originals and reprints. Books: Newsprint paper; web printing; perfect-bound. Published new writers within the last year. Number of titles: Averages 700/year. Buys agented and unagented fiction.
Needs: Romance, glitz, heroic adventure, mystery/suspense (romantic suspense *only*). Will accept nothing that is not related to the desired categories.
How to Contact: Send query letter or send outline and first 50 pages (2 or 3 chapters) or submit through agent with SAE and IRC or SASE (Canadian). Absolutely no simultaneous submissions. Reports in 1 month on queries; 2 months on mss.
Terms: Offers royalties, advance. Must return advance if book is not completed or is unacceptable. Sends galleys to author. Guidelines available.
Advice: "The quickest route to success is to follow directions for submissions: Query first. We encourage first novelists. Before sending a manuscript, read as many current Harlequin titles as you can. It's very important to know the genre and the series most appropriate for your submission." Submissions for Harlequin Romance and Harlequin Presents should go to: Mills & Boon Limited Eton House, 18-24 Paradise Road, Richmond, Surrey TW9 1SR United Kingdom; Superromances: Marsha Zinberg, senior editor; Temptation: Birgit Davis-Todd, senior editor; Regencies: Maureen Stonehouse, editor. American Romances and Intrigue: Debra Matteucci, senior editor and editorial coordinator, Harlequin Books, 6th Floor, 300 E. 42 Street, New York, NY 10017. Silhouette submissions should also be sent to the New York office, attention Isabel Swift. Gold Eagle query letters should be addressed to Feroze Mohammed, senior editor, at the Canada address. "The relationship between the novelist and editor is regarded highly and treated with professionalism."

HARMONY BOOKS, (II), Subsidiary of Crown Publishers, 201 E. 50th St., New York NY 10022. (212)572-6121. Contact: General Editorial Department. Publishes hardcover and paperback originals.
Needs: Literary fiction. Also publishes serious nonfiction, history, biography, personal growth, media and music fields.
How to Contact: Accepts unsolicited mss. Query first with outline/synopsis and 2-3 sample chapters. SASE (IRCs). Agented fiction: 75%. Simultaneous submissions OK.
Terms: Pays royalties and advance; amounts negotiable. Sends galleys to authors.

‡HARPERCOLLINS CHILDREN'S BOOKS, (II), 10 E. 53rd St., New York NY 10022. (212)207-7044. Publisher: Marilyn Kriney. Editor-in-Chief: Joanne Cotler. Publisher, Michael Di Capua Books: Michael Di Capua. Editorial Director, Trophy Paperback: Jennifer Brown. Editorial Director, Laura Geringer Books: Laura Geringer. Publishes hardcover originals and paperback reprints.
Needs: Picture books, easy-to-read, middle-grade, teenage and young adult novels; fiction, fantasy, animal, sports, spy/adventure, historical, science fiction, problem novels and contemporary. Published Harper/Charlotte Zolotow Books: *Fell Back*, by M.E. Kerr (ages 12 and up); Harper: *My Daniel*, by Pam Conrad (ages 10 and up); Crowell: *Lucie Babbidge's House*, by Sylvia Cassedy (ages 9-12); Lippincott: *Yours Till Forever*, by David Gifaldi (ages 12 and up).
How to Contact: Query; submit complete ms; submit outline/synopsis and sample chapters; submit through agent. SASE (IRCs) for query, ms. Please identify simultaneous submissions. Reports in 2-3 months.

 The maple leaf symbol before a listing indicates a Canadian publisher.

Terms: Average 10% in royalties. Royalties on picture books shared with illustrators. Offers advance. Book catalog for self-addressed label.

Advice: "Write from your own experience and the child you once were. Read widely in the field of adult and children's literature. Realize that writing for children is a difficult challenge. Read other young adult novelists as well as adult novelists. Pay attention to styles, approaches, topics. Be willing to rewrite, perhaps many times. We have no rules for subject matter, length or vocabulary but look instead for ideas that are fresh and imaginative. Good writing that involves the reader in a story or subject that has appeal for young readers is also essential. One submission is considered by four imprints."

HARVEST HOUSE PUBLISHERS, (II, IV), 1075 Arrowsmith, Eugene OR 97402. (503)343-0123. Manuscript Coordinator: LaRae Weikert. Vice President of Editorial: Eileen L. Mason. Estab. 1974. Midsize independent publisher with plans to expand. Publishes hardcover and paperback originals and reprints. Books: 40 lb. ground wood paper; offset printing; perfect binding; average print order: 10,000; first novel print order: 10,000-15,000. Averages 80 total titles, 6 fiction titles each year.

Needs: Christian living, contemporary issues, family saga, humor, Christian preschool/picture books, mystery (romantic suspense, young adult), religious/inspirational and Christian romance (historical). Especially seeks inspirational, romance/historical and mystery. Recently published *The Hawk and the Jewel*, by Lori Wick; *Return to the Heartland*, by June Masters Bacher; *A Wolf Story*, by James Byron Huggins; and *Samson*, by Ellen Gunderson Traylor. New fiction series for youth: "Addie McCormick Adventures," by Leanne Lucas.

How to Contact: Accepts unsolicited mss. Query first or submit outline/synopsis and 2 sample chapters with SASE (IRCs). Reports on queries in 2-8 weeks; on mss in 6-8 weeks. Simultaneous submissions OK.

Terms: Pays in royalties of 14-18%; 10 author's copies. Sends galleys to author. Writer's guidelines for SASE. Book catalog for 8½×11 SASE.

‡HEARTFIRE ROMANCE, (I), 475 Park Ave. S., New York NY 10016. (212)889-2299. Executive Editor, Zebra Books: Ann La Farge. Executive Editor, Pinnacle Books: Paul Dinos. Senior Editor, Z-Fave Books: Elise Donner. Executive Editor, Kensington Books: Sarah Gallick. Publishes paperback originals and reprints. Publishes 48 fiction titles each year.

Needs: Historical, Regency and multicultural romance. Published *Blood Wings*, by Stephen Gresham; *Lovers' Masquerade*, by Robin St. Thomas; and *Last of the California Girls*, by Pamela Jekel. Ms length ranges from 125,000 to 150,000 words.

How to Contact: Submit short (no more than 3 page) synopsis and first several chapters. SASE (IRCs). Simultaneous submissions OK.

Terms: Pays royalties and negotiable advance. Writer's guidelines and book catalog for SASE.

Advice: "Target your market. Know what we want."

HERALD PRESS, (II), Division of Mennonite Publishing House, 616 Walnut Ave., Scottdale PA 15683. (412)887-8500. Imprints include Congregational Literature Division; Herald Press. Book Editor: S. David Garber. Fiction Editor: Michael A. King. Estab. 1908. "Church-related midsize publisher." Publishes paperback originals. Books: Recycled, acid-free Glatfelter thor paper; offset printing; adhesive binding; illustrations for children; average print order: 4,000; first novel print order: 3,500. Published new writers in the last year. Company publishes 30 titles/year. Number of fiction titles: 5/year. Sometimes critiques rejected mss.

Needs: Adventure, family saga, historical, juvenile (contemporary, historical, spy/adventure), literary, religious/inspirational, young adult/teen (historical, mystery, problem novels and spy/adventure). "Does not want to see fantasy, picture books." Recently published *Deborah*, by James R Shott; *Beyond This Darkness*, by Linn Creighton; *Andy*, by Mary Borntrager; *A Fruitful Vine*, by Carrie Bender.

How to Contact: Accepts unsolicited mss. Submit outline/synopsis and 2 sample chapters with SASE (IRCs). Agented fiction 2%. Reports in 1 month on queries, 2 months on mss. Accepts electronic submissions (only *with* paper copy).

Terms: Pays 10-12% in royalties; 12 free author's copies. Pays after first 3 months, then once/year. Sends galleys to author. Publishes ms 1 year after acceptance. Writer's guidelines free. Book catalog for 50¢.

Advice: "Need more stories with Christian faith integrated smoothly and not as a tacked-on element."

HOLIDAY HOUSE, INC., (I, II), 425 Madison, New York NY 10017. (212)688-0085. Editor-in-Chief: Margery Cuyler. Estab. 1935. Independent publisher. Children's books only. Books: high quality printing; occasionally reinforced binding; illustrations sometimes. Publishes hardcover originals and paperback reprints. Published new writers within the last year. Number of titles: Approximately 50 hardcovers and 15 paperbacks each year.
- *The Wright Brothers: How They Invented the Airplane* by Russell Freedman and published by Holiday House is a Newbery Honor Book.

Needs: Contemporary, Judaica and holiday, literary, adventure, humor and animal stories for young readers—preschool through middle grade. Recently published *The Battle for the Castle*, by Elizabeth Winthrop; *Twelve Days in August*, by Liza Ketchum Murrow. "We're not in a position to be too encouraging, as our list is tight, but we're always open to good 'family' novels and humor."

How to Contact: "We prefer query letters and three sample chapters for novels; complete manuscripts for shorter books and picture books." Simultaneous submissions OK as long as a cover letter mentions that other publishers are looking at the same material. Reports in 1 month on queries, 6-8 weeks on mss.

Terms: Advance and royalties are flexible, depending upon whether the book is illustrated.

Advice: "We have received an increasing number of manuscripts, but the quality has not improved vastly. This appears to be a decade in which publishers are interested in reviving the type of good, solid story that was popular in the '50s. Certainly there's a trend toward humor, family novels, novels with school settings, biographies and historical novels. Problem-type novels and romances seem to be on the wane. We are always open to well-written manuscripts, whether by a published or nonpublished author. Submit only one project at a time."

HENRY HOLT & COMPANY, (II), 6th Floor, 115 W. 18th St., New York NY 10011. (212)886-9200. Imprint includes Owl (paper). Publishes hardcover and paperback originals and reprints. Averages 50-60 total original titles, 20% of total is fiction each year.

Needs: Adventure, contemporary, feminist, historical, humor/satire, juvenile (5-9 years, including animal, easy-to-read, fantasy, historical, sports, spy/adventure and contemporary), literary, mainstream, suspense/mystery, translations and young adult/teen (10-18 years including easy-to-read, fantasy/science fiction, historical, problem novels, romance, sports and spy/adventure). Published *Fool's Progress*, by Edward Abbey; *Tracks*, by Louise Erdrich; *Trust*, by George V. Higgins; and *Frank Furbo*, by Wm. Wherton.

How to Contact: Accepts queries; no unsolicited mss. Agented fiction 95%.

Terms: Pays in royalties of 10% minimum; 15% maximum; advance. Sends galleys to author. Book catalog sent on request.

◼HORIZON PUBLISHERS & DIST., INC., (III, IV), Box 490, 50 S. 500 West, Bountiful UT 84011-0490. (801)295-9451. President: Duane S. Crowther. Estab. 1971. "Midsize independent publisher with in-house printing facilities, staff of 30+." Publishes hardcover and paperback originals and reprints. Books: 60 lb. offset paper; hardbound, perfect and saddle-stitch binding; illustrations; average print order: 3,000; first novel print order: 3,000. Plans 2 first novels this year. Averages 25-30 total titles; 1-3 fiction titles each year.

Needs: Adventure, historical, humor/satire, juvenile, literary, mainstream, military/war, religious/inspirational, romance (contemporary and historical), science fiction, spiritual and young adult/teen (romance and spy/adventure). "Religious titles are directed only to the LDS (Latter-day Saints) market. General titles are marketed nationwide." Looking for "good quality writing in salable subject areas. Will also consider well-written books on social problems and issues, (divorce, abortion, child abuse, suicide, capital punishment and homosexuality)." Published *The Couchman and the Bells*, by Ted C. Hindmarsh.

How to Contact: Accepts unsolicited mss. Query first. SASE (IRCs). Include Social Security number with submission. Reports in 2-4 weeks on queries; 10-12 weeks on mss. Simultaneous submissions OK if identified as such.

Terms: Pays royalties of 6% minimum; 12% maximum. Provides 10 author's copies. Sends page proofs to author. Publishes ms 3-9 months after acceptance. "We are not a subsidy publisher but we do job printing, book production for private authors and book packaging." Writer's guidelines for #10 SAE and 1 first-class stamp.

Advice: Encourages "only those first novelists who write very well, with saleable subjects. Please avoid the trite themes which are plaguing LDS fiction such as crossing the plains, conversion stories, and struggling courtships that always end in temple marriage. While these themes are important, they have been used so often that they are now frequently perceived as trite and are often ignored by those shopping for new books. In religious fiction we hope to see a process of moral, spiritual, or emotional growth presented. Some type of conflict is definitely essential for good plot development. Watch your vocabulary too—use appropriate words for the age group for which you are writing. We don't accept children's mss for elementary grades."

HOUGHTON MIFFLIN COMPANY, (III), 222 Berkeley St., Boston MA 02116-3764. (617)351-5000. Managing Editor: Christina Coffin. Subsidiary: Ticknor and Fields Inc. Publishes hardcover and paperback originals and paperback reprints. Averages 100 total titles, 50 fiction titles each year.
Needs: None at present. Published *The Translator*, by Ward Just.
How to Contact: Does not accept unsolicited mss. Buys virtually 100% agented fiction.

INTERLINK PUBLISHING GROUP, INC., (IV), 99 Seventh Ave., Brooklyn NY 11215. (718)797-4292. Imprints include: Interlink Books, Olive Branch Press and Crocodile Books USA. Contemporary fiction in translation published under Emerging Voices: New International Fiction. Publisher: Michel Moushabeck. Fiction Editor: Phyllis Bennis. Estab. 1987. "Midsize independent publisher." Publishes hardcover and paperback originals. Books: 55 lb. Warren Sebago Cream white paper; web offset printing; perfect binding; average print order: 5,000; first novel print order: 5,000. Plans 5-8 first novels this year. Averages 30 total titles, 5-8 fiction titles each year.
Needs: Needs adult fiction—relating to the Middle East, Africa or Latin America; translations accepted. Published *A Woman of Nazareth*, by Hala Deeb Jabbour; *The Children Who Sleep by the River*, by Debbie Taylor; *Prairies of Fever*, by Ibrahim/Nasrallah; and *The Silencer*, by Simon Louvish. Published new writers within the last year.
How to Contact: Does not accept unsolicited mss. Submit outline/synopsis only. SASE (IRCs). Reports in 2 weeks on queries.
Terms: Pays royalties of 5% minimum; 8% maximum. Sends galleys to author. Publishes ms 1-1½ years after acceptance.

JAMESON BOOKS, (I, II, IV), Jameson Books, Inc., The Frontier Library, 722 Columbus St., Ottawa IL 61350. (815)434-7905. Editor: Jameson G. Campaigne, Jr. Estab. 1986. Publishes hardcover and paperback originals and reprints. Books: free sheet paper; offset printing; average print order: 10,000; first novel print order: 5,000. Plans 6-8 novels this year. Averages 12-16 total titles, 4-8 fiction titles each year. Occasionally critiques or comments on rejected mss.
Needs: Very well-researched western (frontier pre-1850). No romance, science fiction, mystery, et al. Published *Wister Trace*, by Loren Estelman; *Buckskin Brigades*, by L. Ron Hubbard; *One-Eyed Dream*, by Terry Johnston.
How to Contact: Does not accepted unsolicited mss. Submit outline/synopsis and 3 consecutive sample chapters. SASE (IRCs). Agented fiction 50%. Reports in 2 weeks on queries; 2-5 months on mss. Simultaneous submissions OK.
Terms: Pays royalties of 5% minimum; 15% maximum. Average advance: $1,500. Sends galleys to author. Book catalog for 6×9 SASE.

ALFRED A. KNOPF, (II), 201 E. 50th St., New York NY 10022. Contact: The Editors. Estab. 1915. Publishes hardcover originals. Number of titles: 46 in 1993. Buys 75% agented fiction. Published 7 new writers in 1993.
Needs: Contemporary, literary, suspense and spy. No western, gothic, romance, erotica, religious or science fiction. Recently published *Mystery Ride*, by Robert Boswell; *The Night Manager*, by John Le Carre; *Lasher*, by Anne Rice. Published new writers within the last year.
How to Contact: Submit outline or synopsis with SASE (IRCs). Reports within 1 month on mss. Publishes ms an average of 1 year after acceptance.
Terms: Pays 10-15% in royalties; offers advance. Must return advance if book is not completed or is unacceptable.
Advice: Publishes book-length fiction of literary merit by known and unknown writers.

KNOPF BOOKS FOR YOUNG READERS, (II), 201 E. 50th St., New York NY 10022. Subsidiary of Random House, Inc. Editor-in-Chief: Janet Schulman. Publishes hardcover and paperback originals and reprints. New paperback imprint: Dragonfly Books (picture books). Averages 50 total titles, approximately 20 fiction titles each year.
Needs: "High-quality contemporary, humor, picture books, middle grade novels." Published *No Star Nights*, by Anna Smucker; *Mirandy and Brother Wind*, by Patricia McKissoch; *The Boy Who Lost His Face*, by Lewis Sachar.

How to Contact: Query with outline/synopsis and 2 sample chapters with SASE (IRCs). Simultaneous submissions OK. Reports in 6-8 weeks on mss.
Terms: Sends galleys to author.

LEISURE BOOKS, (II), Division of Dorchester Publishing Co., Inc., Suite 1008, 276 Fifth Ave., New York NY 10001. (212)725-8811. Address submissions to Kim Mattson, editorial assistant. Mass-market paperback publisher—originals and reprints. Books: Newsprint paper; offset printing; perfect-bound; average print order: variable; first novel print order: variable. Plans 25 first novels this year. Averages 150 total titles, 145 fiction titles each year. Comments on rejected ms "only if requested ms requires it."
• See the information on Leisure Books' new imprint, Love Spell, listed in this book. The publisher has become known for its time travel and futuristic romances.
Needs: Romance (historical), horror. Looking for "historical romance (115,000 words)." Recently published *A Fire In The Blood*, by Shirl Henke; *Fire In The Night*, by Madeline Baker.
How to Contact: Accepts unsolicited mss. Query first. SASE (IRCs). Agented fiction 70%. Reports in 1 month on queries; 2 months on mss. "All mss must be typed, double-spaced on one side and left unbound."
Terms: Offers negotiable advance. Payment depends "on category and track record of author." Sends galleys to author. Publishes ms within 2 years after acceptance. Romance guidelines and book catalog for #10 SASE.
Advice: Encourages first novelists "if they are talented and willing to take direction, *and* write the kind of category fiction we publish. Please include a brief synopsis if sample chapters are requested."

LERNER PUBLICATIONS COMPANY, (II), 241 1st Ave. N., Minneapolis MN 55401. Imprints include First Avenue Editions. Editor: Jennifer Martin. Estab. 1959. "Midsize independent *children's* publisher." Publishes hardcover originals and paperback reprints. Books: Offset printing; reinforced library binding; perfect binding; average print order: 5,000-7,500; first novel print order: 5,000. Averages 70 total titles, 1-2 fiction titles each year. Sometimes comments on rejected ms.
• Lerner Publication's joke book series was recommended by "Reading Rainbow" (associated with the popular television show of the same name). The publisher is currently working on developing a line of fiction with specific geographic interest.
Needs: Young adult: general, problem novels, sports, adventure, mystery (young adult). Looking for "well-written middle grade and young adult. No *adult fiction* or single short stories." Recently published *Ransom for a River Dolphin*, by Sarita Kendall.
How to Contact: Accepts unsolicited mss. Query first or submit outline/synopsis and 2 sample chapters. Reports in 1 month on queries; 2 months on mss. Simultaneous submissions OK.
Terms: Pays royalties. Offers advance. Provides author's copies. Sends galleys to author. Publishes ms 12-18 months after acceptance. Writer's guidelines for #10 SAE and 1 first-class stamp (IRCs). Book catalog for 9×12 SAE with $1.90 postage.
Advice: Would like to see "less gender and racial stereotyping; protagonists from many cultures."

LION PUBLISHING, (II), 20 Lincoln Ave., Elgin IL 60120. (708)741-4256. Editor: R.M. Bittner. Estab. 1984. "Christian book publisher publishing books for the *general* market." Publishes hardcover and paperback originals and paperback reprints. Books: Average print order 7,500; first novel print order 5,000. Plans 1-2 first novels this year. Averages 10 total titles, 2-3 fiction titles each year. Often comments on rejected ms.
• Lion Publishing's books *The Paradise War* and *The Silver Hand*, both by Stephen Lawhead, won the Critics' Choice Award by *Christianity Today* and Book of the Year from *Cornerstone* magazine. Another book, *Midnight Blue*, by Pauline Fisk received England's Smarties Award, the largest cash prize for children's literature.
Needs: Open. "Because we are a Christian publisher, all books should be written from a Christian perspective." Recently published *The Silver Hand*, by Stephen Lawhead (fantasy); *An Ordinary Exodus*, by Roger Bichelberger (literary); *Bury Her Sweetly*, by Linda Amey (mystery).
How to Contact: Accepts unsolicited mss. Submit first two chapters with a synopsis and cover letter. SASE (IRCs) *required*. Agented fiction 5%. Reports in 1-4 weeks on queries; 1-3 months on mss.
Terms: Pays negotiable royalties. Sends galleys to author. Publishes ms 18 months after acceptance. Writer's guidelines and book catalog free.
Advice: "We are interested in growing our line of women's suspense/mystery fiction. We are also open to additional titles in our fantasy line, but the ideas presented need to be fresh, informed by what's currently marketable—and not satisfied with work in the 'tradition' of J.R.R. Tolkien and C.S.

Lewis. Lion books are written by Christians, but Lion is a *general-market* house. Compare your work with similar books currently selling in your local bookstore. Too many Christian writers seem out of touch with current books and genres, as if Christian imaginative writing ended with Tolkien, Lewis, etc. Read widely and write for the world at large, not fellow churchgoers."

LITTLE, BROWN AND COMPANY CHILDREN'S BOOKS, (II), Trade Division; Children's Books, 34 Beacon St., Boston MA 02108. Editorial Department. Contact: John G. Keller, publisher; Maria Modugno, editor-in-chief. Books: 70 lb. paper; sheet-fed printing; illustrations. Sometimes buys juvenile mss with illustrations "if they are done by professional artist." Buys about 60% agented fiction each year.
   • *Maniac Magee*, by Jerry Spinelli and published by Little, Brown and Company Children's Books, received a Newbery Award in 1991.
Needs: Middle grade fiction and young adult. Recently published *Dear Mom, Get Me Out of Here!*, by Ellen Conford; *Take Care of My Girl*, by Patricia Hermes; *The Eyes of Kid Midas*, by Neal Shusterman. Published new writers within the last year.
How to Contact: Submit through agent only.
Terms: Pays on royalty basis. Sends galleys to author. Publishes ms 1-2 years after acceptance.
Advice: "We are looking for trade books with bookstore appeal. Young adult 'problem' novels are no longer in vogue, but there is now a dearth of good fiction for that age group. We are looking for young children's (ages 3-5) books and first chapter books. We encourage first novelists. New authors should be aware of what is currently being published. We recommend they spend time at the local library familiarizing themselves with new publications." Known for "humorous middle grade fiction with lots of kid appeal. Literary, multi-layered young adult fiction with distinctive characters and complex plots."

LITTLE, BROWN AND COMPANY, INC., (II, III), 1271 Avenue of the Americas, New York NY 10020 and 34 Beacon St., Boston MA 02108. (212)522-8700 and (617)227-0730. Imprints include Little, Brown; Back Bay; Bulfinch Press. Medium-size house. Publishes adult and juvenile hardcover and paperback originals. Averages 200-225 total adult titles/year. Number of fiction titles varies.
   • Children's submissions must be agented. See listing at Boston address. Include SASE (IRCs).
   See above.
Needs: Open. No science fiction. Recently published *Along Came a Spider*, by James Patterson; *The Black Ice*, by Michael Connelly; *The Pugilist at Rest: Stories*, by Thom Jones. Published new writers within the last year.
How to Contact: Does not accept unsolicited adult mss. Query editorial department first; "we accept submissions from authors who have published before, in book form, magazines, newspapers or journals. No submissions from unpublished writers." Reports in 4-6 months on queries. Simultaneous and photocopied submissions OK.
Terms: "We publish on a royalty basis, with advance."

LODESTAR BOOKS, (II), An affiliate of Dutton Children's Books; A division of Penguin Books USA, Inc., 375 Hudson St., New York NY 10014. (212)366-2627. Editorial Director: Virginia Buckley. Senior Editor: Rosemary Brosnan. Books: 50 or 55 lb. antique cream paper; offset printing; hardcover binding; illustrations sometimes; average print order: 5,000-6,500; first novel print order 5,000. Number of titles: Approximately 25 annually, 12-15 fiction titles annually. Buys 50% agented fiction.
   • Books published by Lodestar have won numerous awards including the American Library Association's "Notable Children's Books" and "Best Books for Young Adults," the New England Book Award for Children's Books and the Scott O'Dell Award for Historical Fiction.
Needs: Contemporary, family saga, humorous, sports, mystery, adventure, for middle-grade and young adult. Recently published *Crocodile Burning*, by Michael Williams (ages 12 up); *Sweet Notes, Sour Notes*, by Nancy Smiler Levinson (ages 7-10); *The Sabbath Garden*, by Patricia Baird Greene (ages 12 up). Published new writers within the last year.
How to Contact: Send query letter plus first three chapters. SASE (IRCs). Simultaneous submissions OK. Reports in 2-4 months. Publishes ms an average of 18 months after acceptance.
Terms: Pays 8-10% in royalties; offers negotiable advance. Sends galleys to author. Free book catalog.
Advice: "We are looking to add to our list more books about African-American, Hispanic, Native American, and Asian children, in particular. We encourage first novelists. Publishing fewer young adult novels. Although they are difficult to find and difficult to sell reprint rights, we are doing well with our multicultural fiction, especially novels on Hispanic and African-American themes."

LOUISIANA STATE UNIVERSITY PRESS, (II), P.O. Box 25053, Baton Rouge LA 70894-5053. (504)388-6618. Fax: (504)388-6461. Editor-in-Chief: Margaret Fisher Dalrymple. Fiction Editor: Martha Lacy Hall. Estab. 1935. University press—medium size. Publishes hardcover originals. Average print order: 1,500-2,500; first novel print order: 2,000. Averages 60-70 total titles, 4 fiction titles each year.
Needs: Contemporary, literary, mainstream, short story collections. No genre fiction and/or juvenile material. Published *Marquis at Bay*, by Albert Belisle Davis (novel); *The Burning Glass*, by Helen Norris (stories); and *The Stars of Constantinople*, by Ólafur Jóhann Sigurdsson (stories). Publishes fiction anthologies. Author should submit proposal listing contents.
How to Contact: Does not accept unsolicited mss. Query first. "We provide a questionnaire to authors of mss we take under consideration." Send SASE (IRC) for reply, return of ms or send disposable copy of ms. Reports in 2-3 months on queries and mss. Simultaneous submissions OK.
Terms: Pays in royalties, which vary. Sends pre-publication galleys to the author.

‡LOVE SPELL, (II), Division of Dorchester Publishing Co., Inc., Suite 1008, 276 Fifth Ave., New York NY 10001. (212)725-8811. Editorial Assistant: Kim Mattson. Mass market paperback publisher—originals and reprints. Books: newsprint paper; offset printing; perfect-bound; average print order: varies; first novel print order: varies. Plans 15 first novels this year. Comments "only if requested ms requires it."
• See also the listing in this book for Leisure Books.
Needs: Romance (futuristic time travel, historical). Looking for romances of 115,000 words. Recently published *A Time to Love Again*, by Flora Speer (time-travel romance); *Heart of the Wolf*, by Saranne Dawson (futuristic romance).
How to Contact: Accepts unsolicited mss. Query first. "All mss must be typed, double-spaced on one side and left unbound." SASE (or IRC) for return of ms. Agented fiction 70%. Reports in 1 month on queries; 2 months on mss.
Terms: Offers negotiable advance. "Payment depends on category and track record of author." Sends galleys to author. Publishes ms within 2 years after acceptance. Writer's guidelines for #10 SASE. Book catalogs for #10 SASE.
Advice: Encourages first novelists "if they are talented and willing to take direction, *and* write the kind of category fiction we publish. Please include a brief synopsis if sample chapters are requested."

LOVESWEPT, (I, II), Bantam Books, 1540 Broadway, New York NY 10036. (212)354-6500. Associate Publisher: Nita Taublib. Consulting Editors: Susann Brailey, Elizabeth Barrett. Senior Editors: Wendy McCurdy, Beth de Guzman. Imprint estab. 1982. Publishes paperback originals. Plans several first novels this year. Averages 72 total titles each year.
Needs: "Contemporary romance, highly sensual, believable primary characters, fresh and vibrant approaches to plot. No gothics, regencies or suspense."
How to Contact: Query with SASE (IRCs); no unsolicited mss or partial mss. "Query letters should be no more than two to three pages. Content should be a brief description of the plot and the two main characters."
Terms: Pays in royalties of 6%; negotiates advance.
Advice: "Read extensively in the genre. Rewrite, polish and edit your own work until it is the best it can be—before submitting."

■LUCAS/EVANS BOOKS, INC., (II), 1123 Broadway, New York NY 10010. (212)929-2583. Executive Director: Barbara Lucas. Projects Coordinator: Katherine Gleason. Editorial and Production Manager: Cassandra Conyers. Estab. 1984. "Book packager—specializes in children's books." Publishes hardcover and paperback originals. Averages 10-15 titles, preschool through young adult books fiction and nonfiction.
• *Sing for a Gentle Rain* won an IRA-CBC Young Adult Choice award and another book published by Lucas/Evans Books, *Breaking Barriers*, was a New York Public Library Young Adult selection in 1992.
Needs: "Looking for fiction and nonfiction series proposals and selected single juvenile books, preschool through high school. Recently published *Bees Dance and Whales Sing*, by Margery Facklam (Sierra Club); *Ghost Dog*, by Ellen Leroe (Hyperion); *They Had a Dream*, by Jules Archer (Viking); and *The Keepers*, by Ann Downer (Atheneum). Published new writers within the last year.
How to Contact: No unsolicited mss. Query first or submit outline/synopsis and 1 or 2 sample chapters. SASE (IRCs). Agented fiction 15 to 25%. Reports in 2 months on mss.
Terms: Pays royalties; variable advance. Also makes work-for-hire assignments.

MARGARET K. McELDERRY BOOKS, (I, II), Imprint of the Macmillan Children's Book Group, 866 3rd Ave., New York NY 10022. (212)702-7855. Publisher: Margaret K. McElderry. Publishes hardcover originals. Books: High quality paper; offset printing; cloth and three-piece bindings; illustrations; average print order: 15,000; first novel print order: 6,000. Published new writers within the last year. Number of titles: 25/year. Buys juvenile and young adult mss, agented or non-agented.

● Books published by Margaret K. McElderry Books have received numerous awards including the Newbery and the Caldecott Awards. At press time we learned that Macmillan Inc. was sold to Paramount Communications. Watch *Publishers Weekly* and other trade journals for details.

Needs: All categories (fiction and nonfiction) for juvenile and young adult: picture books, early chapter books, contemporary, literary, adventure, mystery and fantasy. "We will consider any category. Results depend on the quality of the imagination, the artwork and the writing." Recently published *The Boggart*, by Susan Cooper; *Switching Well*, by Peni R. Griffin; *Emmy*, by Connie Jordan Green.

Terms: Pays in royalties; offers advance.

Advice: "Imaginative writing of high quality is always in demand; also picture books that are original and unusual. Picture book manuscripts written in prose are totally acceptable. We are trying to publish more beginning chapter books—about 48 pages with text geared toward the 6-9 year old reader. Keep in mind that McElderry Books is a very small imprint which only publishes 12 or 13 books per season, so we are very selective about the books we will undertake for publication. Anyone hoping to become a children's book author should familiarize herself with the books (both good and bad) already on the market for children."

✸MACMILLAN CANADA, (II), A Division of Canada Publishing Corporation, 29 Birch Ave., Toronto, Ontario M4V 1E2 Canada. (416)963-8830. Senior Editor: Kristen Hansen. Estab. 1905. Publishes hardcover and trade paperback originals. Books: average print order: 4,000-5,000; first novel print order: 1,500. Averages 35 total titles, 5-6 fiction titles each year. Rarely comments on rejected mss.

Needs: Literary, mainstream and mystery/suspense. Published *Last Rights*, by David Laing Dawson; *Tall Lives*, by Bill Gaston; *Swimming Toward the Light*, by Joan Clark; *The Nest Egg*, by S.L. Sparling; and *The Jacamar Nest*, by David Parry and Patrick Withrow. Published new writers within the last year.

How to Contact: No longer accepts unsolicited mss. Agented material only. SASE (IRCs) for return of ms. Reports in 1-2 months on mss. Simultaneous submissions OK.

Terms: Pays royalties of 8% minimum; 15% maximum; advance negotiable. Provides 10 author's copies. Sends galleys to author. Book catalog for 9 × 12 SASE.

Advice: "Canadian material only."

MACMILLAN CHILDREN'S BOOKS, (II), Macmillan Publishing Co., 866 Third Ave., New York NY 10022. (212)702-4299. Imprint of Macmillan Publishing/Children's Book Group. Contact: Submissions Editor. Estab. 1919. Large children's trade list. Publishes hardcover originals.

● At press time we learned that Macmillan Inc., including its Children's Book Group, was sold to Paramount Communications. This could affect the publisher's policies, so watch *Publishers Weekly* and other trade journals for details.

Needs: Juvenile submissions. Not interested in series. "We generally are not interested in short stories as such, unless intended as the basis for a picture book. As the YA market is weak, only extremely distinctive and well-written YA novels will be considered (and must be preceded by a query letter)." Published *Weasel*, by Cyntha De Felice; *Dynamite Dinah*, by Claudia Mills; *Borgel*, by Daniel Pinkwater.

How to Contact: Accepts unsolicited mss or for novel send query letter with outline, sample chapter and SASE (IRCs). Response in 6-8 weeks. No simultaneous submissions.

Terms: Pays in royalties. Advance negotiable at time of contract. For catalog, send 9 × 12 envelope with 4 oz. postage.

MACMILLAN PUBLISHING CO, INC., 866 3rd Ave., New York NY 10022. Does not accept fiction mss.

Check the Category Indexes, located at the back of the book, for publishers interested in specific fiction subjects.

MODERN PUBLISHING, A Division of Unisystems, Inc., (II), 155 E. 55th St., New York NY 10022. (212)826-0850. Imprint: Honey Bear Books. Editorial Director: Kathy O'Hehir. Fiction Editor: Mandy Bond. Estab. 1973. "Mass-market juvenile publisher; list mainly consists of picture, coloring and activity, and novelty books for ages 2-8 and board books." Publishes hardcover and paperback originals, and Americanized hardcover and paperback reprints from foreign markets. Average print order: 50,000-100,000 of each title within a series. "85% of our list are first novels this year." Averages 100+ total titles each year. Sometimes comments on rejected mss.
Needs: Juvenile (5-9 yrs, including animal, easy-to-read, fantasy, historical, sports, spy/adventure and contemporary), preschool/picture book, young adult/teen (easy-to-read). Published new writers within the last year.
How to Contact: Accepts unsolicited mss. Submit complete ms. SASE (IRCs). Agented fiction 5%. Simultaneous submissions OK. Reports in 2 months.
Terms: Pays by work-for-hire or royalty arrangements. Advance negotiable. Publishes ms 7-12 months after acceptance.
Advice: "We publish picture storybooks, board books, coloring and activity books, bath books, shape books and any other new and original ideas for the children's publishing arena. We gear our books for the preschool through third-grade market and publish series of four to six books at a time. Presently we are looking for new material as we are expanding our list and would appreciate receiving any new submissions. We will consider manuscripts with accompanying artwork or by themselves, and submissions from illustrators who would like to work in the juvenile books publishing genre and can adapt their style to fit our needs. However, we will only consider those projects that are written and illustrated for series of four to six books. Manuscripts must be neatly typed and submitted either as a synopsis of the series and broken-down plot summaries of the books within the series, or full manuscripts for review with a SASE."

WILLIAM MORROW AND COMPANY, INC., (II), 1350 Avenue of the Americas, New York NY 10019. (212)261-6500. Imprints include Hearst Books, Hearst Marine Books, Mulberry Books, Tambourine Books, Beech Tree Books, Quill Trade Paperbacks, Perigord, Greenwillow Books, Lothrop, Lee & Shepard and Fielding Publications (travel books), and Morrow Junior Books. Estab. 1926. Approximately one fourth of books published are fiction.
Needs: "Morrow accepts only the highest quality submissions" in contemporary, literary, experimental, adventure, mystery/suspense, spy, historical, war, feminist, gay/lesbian, science fiction, horror, humor/satire and translations. Juvenile and young adult divisions are separate. Published *Gate of Rage*, by C.Y. Lee; *The Gold Bug Variations*, by Richard Powers; and *This Earth of Mankind*, by Pramoedya Ananta Toer. Published work by previously unpublished writers within the last year.
How to Contact: Submit through agent. All unsolicited mss are returned unopened. "We will accept queries, proposals or mss only when submitted through a literary agent." Simultaneous submissions OK. Reports in 2-3 months.
Terms: Pays in royalties; offers advance. Sends galleys to author. Free book catalog.
Advice: "The Morrow divisions of Morrow Junior Books, Greenwillow Books, Tambourine Books, Mulberry Books, Beech Tree Books, and Lothrop, Lee and Shepard handle juvenile books. We do five to ten first novels every year and about one-fourth of the titles are fiction. Having an agent helps to find a publisher."

MORROW JUNIOR BOOKS, (III), 1350 Avenue of the Americas, New York NY 10019. (212)261-6691. Editor-In-Chief: David L. Reuther. Plans 1 first novel this year. Averages 55 total titles each year.
Needs: Juvenile (5-9 years) including animal, easy-to-read, fantasy (little), spy/adventure (very little), preschool/picture book, young adult/teen (10-18 years) including historical, sports.
How to Contact: Does not accept unsolicited fiction mss.
Terms: Authors paid in royalties. Books published 12-18 months after acceptance. Book catalog free on request.
Advice: "Our list is very full at this time. No unsolicited manuscripts."

‡MULTNOMAH BOOKS, (II), Questar Publishers, Inc., P.O. Box 1720, Sisters OR 97759. (503)549-1144. Editorial Coordinator: Brenda Saltzer. Fiction Editor: Rodney L. Morris. Estab. 1987. Midsize independent publisher of evangelical fiction and nonfiction. Publishes paperback originals. Books: perfect binding; average print order: 12,000. Plans 3 first novels this year. Averages 35 total titles, 6-7 fiction titles each year.
• Multnomah Books has received several Medallion Book Awards from the Evangelical Christian Publishers Association.

Needs: Literary, religious/inspirational (general, children's religious, religious fantasy). Recently published *Once Upon a Cross*, by Thom Lemmons (historical); *A Promise Unbroken*, by Al Lacy (historical/romance); *Jordan's Crossing*, by Randall Arthur (religious/adventure). Publishes "Battles of Destiny" (Civil War series).

How to Contact: Does not accept unsolicited mss. Submit outline/synopsis and 2 sample chapters. Include 1-2 paragraph bio, list of publishing credits with submission. Send SASE (or IRC) for reply, return of ms or send a disposable copy of ms. Reports in 3-4 weeks on queries; 6-8 weeks on mss. Simultaneous submissions OK.

Terms: Pays royalties. Provides 100 author's copies. Sends galleys to author. Publishes ms 8-10 months after acceptance. Writer's guidelines for SASE.

THE MYSTERIOUS PRESS, (III), 1271 Ave. of the Americas, New York NY 10120. (212)522-7200. Crime and mystery fiction imprint for Warner Books. Editor-in-Chief: William Malloy. Editors: Sara Ann Freed and Amye Dyer. Estab. 1976. Publishes hardcover originals and paperback reprints. Books: Hardcover (some Smyth-sewn) and paperback binding; illustrations rarely. Average first novel print order 5,000 copies. Critiques "only those rejected writers we wish particularly to encourage."

Needs: Mystery/suspense. Recently published *Voodoo, Ltd.*, by Ross Thomas; *The Mexican Tree Duck*, by James Crumley; *Bootlegger's Daughter*, by Margaret Maron; published new writers within the last year.

How to Contact: Agented material only.

Terms: Pays in royalties of 10% minimum; offers negotiable advance. Sends galleys to author. Buys hard and softcover rights. Book catalog for SASE (IRCs).

Advice: "We have a strong belief in the everlasting interest in and strength of mystery fiction. Don't talk about writing, do it. Don't ride bandwagons, create them. Our philosophy about publishing first novels is the same as our philosophy about publishing: The cream rises to the top. We are looking for writers with whom we can have a long-term relationship. A good editor is an angel, assisting according to the writer's needs. My job is to see to it that the writer writes the best book he/she is capable of, *not* to have the writer write *my* book. Don't worry, publishing will catch up to you; the cycles continue as they always have. If your work is good, keep it circulating and begin the next one, and keep the faith. Get an agent."

NAL/DUTTON, (III), A division of Penguin USA, 375 Hudson St., New York NY 10014. (212)366-2000. Imprints include Dutton, Onyx, Signet, Topaz, Mentor, Signet Classic, Plume, Plume Fiction, DAW, Meridian, Roc. Contact: Michaela Hamilton, editor-in-chief, Signet and Onyx; Arnold Dolin, associate publisher, Dutton; Rachel Klayman, Plume; Christopher Schelling, executive editor, Roc. Estab. 1948. Publishes hardcover and paperback originals and paperback reprints.

● For more information, see the interview with Michaela Hamilton in the 1993 *Novel & Short Story Writer's Market*.

Needs: "All kinds of commercial and literary fiction, including mainstream, historical, Regency, New Age, western, thriller, science fiction, fantasy, gay. Full length novels and collections." Published *Needful Things*, by Stephen King; *Night Over Water*, by Ken Follett; *Against the Wind*, by J.F. Freedman. Published new writers within the last year.

How to Contact: Agented mss only. Queries accepted with SASE (IRCs). "State type of book and past publishing projects." Simultaneous submissions OK. Reports in 3 months.

Terms: Pays in royalties and author's copies; offers advance. Sends galleys to author. Book catalog for SASE.

Advice: "Write the complete manuscript and submit it to an agent or agents. We publish The Destroyer, The Trailsman, Battletech and other western and science fiction series—all by ongoing authors. Would be receptive to ideas for new series in commercial fiction."

NEW READERS PRESS, (IV), Publishing division of Laubach Literacy International, Box 131, Syracuse NY 13210. (315)422-9121. Directors of Acquisitions: Christina Jagger. Estab. 1959. Publishes paperback originals. Books: offset printing; paper binding; 6-12 illustrations per fiction book; average print order: 7,500; first novel print order: 5,000. Fiction titles may be published both in book form and as read-along audio tapes. Averages 30 total titles, 8-12 fiction titles each year.

Needs: High-interest, low-reading-level materials for adults with limited reading skills. Short novels of 12,000-15,000 words, written on 2nd-5th grade level. "Can be mystery, romance, adventure, science fiction, sports or humor. Characters are well-developed, situations realistic, and plot developments believable." Accepts short stories only in collections of 8-20 very short stories of same genre. Will accept collections of one-act plays that can be performed in a single class period (45-50 min.) with

settings than can be created within a classroom. Short stories and plays can be at 3rd-5th grade reading level. All material must be suitable for classroom use in public education, i.e., little violence and no explicit sex. "We will not accept anything at all for readers under 16 years of age." Published *The Orange Grove & Other Stories*, by Rosanne Keller; *The Kite Flyer & Other Stories* by Rosanne Keller.
How to Contact: Accepts unsolicited mss. Query first or submit outline/synopsis and 3 sample chapters. SASE (IRCs). Reports in 1 month on queries; 3 months on mss.
Terms: Pays royalties of 5% minimum, 7.5% maximum on gross sales. Average advance: $200. "We may offer authors a choice of a royalty or flat fee. The fee would vary depending on the type of work." Book catalog, authors' brochure and guidelines for short novels free.
Advice: "Many of our fiction authors are being published for the first time. It is necessary to have a sympathetic attitude toward adults with limited reading skills and an understanding of their life situation. Direct experience with them is helpful."

W.W. NORTON & COMPANY, INC., (II), 500 Fifth Ave., New York NY 10110. (212)354-5500. For unsolicited mss contact: Liz Malcolm. Estab. 1924. Midsize independent publisher of trade books and college textbooks. Publishes hardcover originals. Occasionally comments on rejected mss.
Needs: High-quality fiction (preferably literary). No occult, science fiction, religious, gothic, romances, experimental, confession, erotica, psychic/supernatural, fantasy, horror, juvenile or young adult. Published *The Unquiet Earth*, by Denise Giardina; *Natural History*, by Maureen Howard; and *White Butterfly*, by Walter Mosely
How to Contact: Submit outline/synopsis and first 50 pages. SASE (IRCs). Simultaneous submissions OK. Reports in 8-10 weeks. Packaging and postage must be enclosed to ensure safe return of materials.
Terms: Graduated royalty scale starting at 7½% or 10% of net invoice price, in addition to 15 author's copies; offers advance. Free book catalog.
Advice: "We will occasionally encourage writers of promise whom we do not immediately publish. We are principally interested in the literary quality of fiction manuscripts. A familiarity with our current list of titles will give you an idea of what we're looking for. Chances are, if your book is good and you have no agent you will eventually succeed; but the road to success will be easier and shorter if you have an agent backing the book. We encourage the submission of first novels."

PANTHEON BOOKS, (III), Subsidiary of Random House, 201 E. 50th St., New York NY 10022. (212)572-2404. Estab. 1942. "Small but well-established imprint of well-known large house." Publishes hardcover and trade paperback originals and trade paperback reprints. Averages 75 total titles, about one-third fiction, each year.
Needs: Quality fiction and nonfiction.
How to Contact: Query letter and sample material. SASE (IRCs). Attention: Editorial Department.

PELICAN PUBLISHING COMPANY, (IV), Box 3110, Gretna LA 70054. Editor: Nina Kooij. Estab. 1926. Publishes hardcover reprints and originals. Books: Hardcover and paperback binding; illustrations sometimes. Buys juvenile mss with illustrations. Comments on rejected mss "infrequently."
Needs: Juvenile fiction, especially with a regional and/or historical focus. Recently published *When the Great Canoes Came*, by Mary Louise Clifford; *A Bullet for Lincoln*, by Benjamin King; *Bluebonnet at Johnson Space Center*, by Mary Brooke Casad. Published new writers within the last year.
How to Contact: Prefers query. May submit outline/synopsis and 2 sample chapters with SASE (IRCs). No simultaneous submissions. "Not responsible if writer's only copy is sent." Reports in 1 month on queries; 3 months on mss. Publishes ms 12-18 months after acceptance.
Terms: Pays 10% in royalties; 10 contributor's copies; advance considered. Sends galleys to author. Catalog of titles and writer's guidelines for SASE (IRCs).
Advice: "Research the market carefully. Order and look through publishing catalogs to see if your work is consistent with their lists. No more adult fiction, please. For ages 8-12, story must be planned in chapters that will fill at least 150 double-spaced ms pages. Topic should be historical and, preferably, linked to a particular region or culture."

PHILOMEL BOOKS, (II), The Putnam & Grosset Book Group, 200 Madison Ave., New York NY 10016. (212)951-8712. Editor-in-Chief: Paula Wiseman. Editorial Assistant: Laura Walsh. "A high-quality oriented imprint focused on stimulating picture books for children and young adult novels." Publishes hardcover originals and paperback reprints. Averages 50 total titles, 45 fiction titles/year. Sometimes comments on rejected ms.
  • Books published by Philomel have won numerous awards. Most recently *Seven Blind Mice*, by Ed Young, was a Caldecott Honor book in 1993.

Needs: Adventure, ethnic, family saga, fantasy, historical, juvenile (5-9 years), literary, preschool/picture book, regional, short story collections, translations, western (young adult), young adult/teen (10-18 years). Looking for "ethnic novels with a strong cultural voice but which speak universally." No "generic, mass-market oriented fiction." Recently published *Salamandastron*, by Brian Jacques; *Back to Before*, by Jan Slepian; *The Ancient One*, by T.A. Barron. Published new writers within the last year.

How to Contact: Accepts unsolicited mss. Query first or submit outline/synopsis and 3 sample chapters. SASE (IRCs). Agented fiction 40%. Reports in 6-8 weeks on queries; 6-10 weeks on mss. Simultaneous submissions OK.

Terms: Pays royalties, negotiable advance and author's copies. Sends galleys to author. Publishes ms anywhere from 1-3 years after acceptance. Writer's guidelines for #10 SAE and 1 first-class stamp (IRCs). Book catalog for 9×12 SASE.

Advice: "We are not a mass-market publisher and do not publish short stories independently. In addition, we do just a few novels a year."

POCKET BOOKS, (II), Division of Simon & Schuster, 1230 Avenue of the Americas, New York NY 10020. (212)698-7000. Imprints include Washington Square Press and Star Trek. Executive Vice President/Editorial Director: William Grose. Publishes paperback and hardcover originals and reprints. Averages 300 titles each year. Buys 90% agented fiction. Sometimes critiques rejected mss.

Needs: Contemporary, literary, adventure, spy, historical, western, gothic, romance, military/war, mainstream, suspense/mystery, feminist, ethnic, erotica, psychic/supernatural, fantasy, horror and humor/satire. Recently published *Waiting to Exhale*, by Terry McMillan; *The Way Things Ought To Be*, by Rush Limbaugh (hardcover); *Perfect*, by Judith McNaught (hardcover); *The Red Horseman*, by Stephen Coonts (hardcover); published new writers within the last year.

How to Contact: Query with SASE (IRCs). No unsolicited mss. Reports in 6 months on queries only. Publishes ms 12-18 months after acceptance.

Terms: Pays in royalties and offers advance. Sends galleys to author. Writer must return advance if book is not completed or is not acceptable. Free book catalog.

‡CLARKSON N. POTTER, INC., 201 E. 50th St., New York NY 10022. (212)572-6162. Distributed by Crown Publishers, Inc. Editorial Director: Lauren Shakely.

Needs: Illustrated fiction, biography, style and gardening. Published *Black Water: The Book of Fantastic Literature*, by Alberto Manguel.

How to Contact: Submissions through agent only.

Terms: Pays 6-12% in royalties on hardcover; 6-7½% in royalties on paperback; offers $5,000 up in advance.

PRESIDIO PRESS (IV), 505B San Marin Dr., Novato CA 94945. (415)898-1081. Editors: Dale Wilson (ext. 125), Joan Griffin (ext. 126) and Robert Tate (ext. 127). Estab. 1976. Small independent general trade—specialist in military. Publishes hardcover originals. Books: 20 lb regular paper, average print order: 5,000. Publishes an average of two works of fiction per list under its Lyford Books imprint. Averages 26 total titles each year. Critiques or comments on rejected ms.

Needs: Historical with military background, war. Also mystery/suspense (police procedural, private eye), western (traditional, frontier saga, adult), thriller/espionage. Recently published *Hard Road to Gettysburg*, by Ted Jones; *Scatterpath*, by Maralys Wills; and *Falcons*, by Ray Rosenbaum. Regularly publishes new writers.

How to Contact: Accepts unsolicited mss. Query first or submit 3 sample chapters. SASE (IRCs). Reports in 2 weeks on queries; 2 months on mss. Simultaneous submissions OK.

Terms: Pays in royalties of 15% of net minimum; advance: $1,000 average. Sends edited manuscripts and page proofs to author. Book catalog and guidelines free on request. Send 9×12 SASE with $1.30 postage.

Advice: "Think twice before entering any highly competitive genre; don't imitate; do your best. Have faith in your writing and don't let the market disappoint or discourage you."

‡G.P. PUTNAM'S SONS, (III), The Putnam Publishing Group, 200 Madison Ave., New York NY 10016. (212)951-8400. Imprints include Perigee, Philomel, Platt and Munk, Coward McCann, Grosset and Dunlap Pacer. Publishes hardcover originals.

Needs: Published fiction by Stephen King, Lawrence Sanders, Alice Hoffman; published new writers within the last year.

How to Contact: Does not accept unsolicited mss. Query.

QUILL, (III), William Morrow & Co., Inc., 1350 Avenue of the Americas, New York NY 10019. (212)261-6500. Editor: Andy Dutter. "Trade paperback line of William Morrow & Co.—adult trade—midsize." Publishes paperback originals and reprints. Plans 1 first novel this year. Averages 50 total titles, 1 fiction title each year.
Needs: Experimental, feminist, gay, humor/satire, lesbian, literary, mainstream/contemporary. Published new writers within the last year.
How to Contact: Does not accept unsolicited mss. Strongly suggests submitting outline/synopsis and 1 sample chapter through an agent. Include one-paragraph bio, list of publishing credits. SASE (IRCs) for a reply to query or send a disposable copy of the ms. Agented fiction 99.5%. Reports in 2 months. Simultaneous submissions OK.
Terms: Standard rates. Sends galleys to author. Publishes ms 1 year after acceptance.
Advice: "Our parent company, William Morrow, publishes fiction in hardcover and sells the rights to other, larger paperback imprints and houses. We have done fiction in the past and do the occasional paperback original, but for the most part we do nonfiction. Write, rewrite, and rewrite again. Then find an agent. Never be afraid to throw out a year's worth of work and start again—that's the sign of a writer on the way to becoming an author. No matter what the genre, write clearly and cut the fat. Look at what the masters of the genre do that others don't and learn from that."

RANDOM HOUSE, INC., 201 E. 50th St., New York NY 10022. (212)751-2600. Imprints include Pantheon Books, Panache Press at Random House, Vintage Books, Times Books, Villard Books and Knopf. Contact: Adult Trade Division. Publishes hardcover and paperback originals. Encourages new writers. Rarely comments on rejected mss.
Needs: Adventure, contemporary, historical, literary, mainstream, short story collections, mystery/suspense. "We publish fiction of the highest standards." Authors include James Michener, Robert Ludlum, Mary Gordon.
How to Contact: Query with SASE (IRCs). Simultaneous submissions OK. Reports in 4-6 weeks on queries, 2 months on mss.
Terms: Payment as per standard minimum book contracts. Free writer's guidelines.
Advice: "Please try to get an agent because of the large volume of manuscripts received, agented work is looked at first."

RESOURCE PUBLICATIONS, INC., (I, IV), Suite 290, 160 E. Virginia St., San Jose CA 95112. (408)286-8505. Book Editor: Kenneth Guentert. Estab. 1973. "Independent book and magazine publisher focusing on imaginative resources for professionals in ministry, education and counseling." Publishes paperback originals. Averages 12-14 total titles, 2-3 fiction titles each year.
Needs: Story collections for storytellers, "not short stories in the usual literary sense." Published *Jesus on the Mend: Healing Stories for Ordinary People,* by Andre Papineau; and *The Magic Stone: Stories for Your Faith Journey,* by James Henderschedt. Occasionally publishes book-length stories that meet some need (*The Cure: The Hero's Journey with Cancer*). No novels in the literary sense.
How to Contact: Query first or submit outline/synopsis and 1 sample chapter with SASE (IRCs). Reports in 2 weeks on queries; 6 weeks on mss. No simultaneous submissions. Accepts disk submissions compatible with CP/M, IBM system. Prefers hard copy with disk submissions.
Terms: Pays in royalties of 8% minimum, 10% maximum; 10 author's copies. "We require first-time authors purchase a small portion of the press-run, but we do not subsidy publish under the Resource Publications imprint. However, our graphics department will help author's self-publish for a fee."

‡ST. MARTIN'S PRESS, 175 Fifth Ave., New York NY 10010. (212)674-5151. Imprint: Thomas Dunne. Chairman and CEO: Thomas J. McCormack. President: Roy Gainsburg. Publishes hardcover and paperback reprints and originals.
Needs: Contemporary, literary, experimental, adventure, mystery/suspense, spy, historical, war, gothic, romance, confession, feminist, gay, lesbian, ethnic, erotica, psychic/supernatural, religious/inspirational, science fiction, fantasy, horror and humor/satire. No plays, children's literature or short fiction. Published *The Silence of the Lambs,* by Thomas Harris; *The Shell Seekers* and *September* by Rosamunde Pilcher.

Read the Business of Fiction Writing section to learn the correct way to prepare and submit a manuscript.

How to Contact: Query or submit complete ms with SASE (IRCs). Simultaneous submissions OK (if declared as such). Reports in 2-3 weeks on queries, 4-6 weeks on mss.
Terms: Pays standard advance and royalties.

‡ST. PAUL BOOKS AND MEDIA, (I), Subsidiary of Daughters of St. Paul, 50 St. Paul's Ave., Jamaica Plain, Boston MA 02130. (617)522-8911. Children's Editor: Sister Anne Joan, fsp. Estab. 1934. Roman Catholic publishing house. Publishes hardcover and paperback originals. Averages 20 total titles, 5 fiction titles each year.
Needs: Juvenile (animal, easy-to-read, fantasy, historical, religion, contemporary), preschool/picture book. All fiction must communicate high moral and family values. "Our fiction needs are entirely in the area of children's literature. We are looking for bedtime stories, historical and contemporary novels for children. Would like to see characters who manifest faith and trust in God." Does not want "characters whose lifestyles are not in conformity with Catholic teachings."
How to Contact: Does not accept unsolicited mss. Query first. SASE. Reports in 2 weeks.
Terms: Pays royalties of 8% minimum; 12% maximum. Provides negotiable number of author's copies. Publishes ms approx 2 or 3 years after acceptance. Writer's guidelines for #10 SAE and 1 first-class stamp (IRCs).
Advice: "There is a dearth of juvenile fiction appropriate for Catholics and other Christians."

CHARLES SCRIBNER'S SONS, 866 3rd Ave., New York NY 10022. Overstocked. Prefers not to share information.

CHARLES SCRIBNER'S SONS, BOOKS FOR YOUNG READERS, Division of Macmillan Publishing Co., 866 Third Ave., New York NY 10022. (212)702-7885. Editorial Director: Clare Costello. Publishes hardcover originals. Averages 20-25 total titles, 8-13 fiction titles each year.
Needs: Juvenile (animal, easy-to-read, fantasy, historical, picture book, sports, spy/adventure, contemporary, ethnic and science fiction) and young adult (fantasy/science fiction, romance, historical, problem novels, sports and spy/adventure). Recently published *The Legend of Lightning Larry*, by Aaron Shepard (illustrated by Toni Goffe) (picture book); *Letters from a Slave Girl*, by Mary E. Lyons (fiction). *Note: Macmillan Inc. recently sold to Paramount Communications.*
How to Contact: Submit complete ms with SASE (IRCs). Simultaneous submissions OK. Reports in 8-10 weeks on mss.
Terms: Free book catalog on request. Sends galleys to author.

SIERRA CLUB BOOKS, 100 Bush St., San Francisco CA 94104. (415)291-1617. Fax: (415)291-1602. Senior Editor: Jim Cohee. Estab. 1892. Midsize independent publisher. Publishes hardcover and paperback originals and paperback reprints. Averages 20-25 titles, 1-2 fiction titles each year.
Needs: Contemporary (conservation, environment).
How to Contact: Submit complete ms. Simultaneous submissions OK. Reports in 6 weeks on queries.
Terms: Pays in royalties. Book catalog for SASE (IRCs).
Advice: "Only rarely do we publish fiction. We will consider novels on their quality and on the basis of their relevance to our organization's environmentalist aims."

SILHOUETTE BOOKS, (II, IV), 6th Floor, 300 E. 42nd St., New York NY 10017. (212)682-6080. Imprints include Silhouette Romance, Silhouette Special Edition, Silhouette Desire, Silhouette Intimate Moments, Silhouette Shadows, Harlequin Historicals; also Silhouette Christmas Stories, Silhouette Summer Sizzlers, Harlequin Historical Christmas Stories. Editorial Director: Isabel Swift. Senior Editor & Editorial Coordinator (SIM, SS): Leslie J. Wainger. Seniors Editors: (SE) Tara Hughes Gavin, (SD) Lucia Macro, (SR) Anne Canadeo. Editor: Melissa Senate, Gail Chasan. Historicals: Senior Editor: Tracy Farrell. Estab. 1979. Publishes paperback originals. Buys agented and unagented adult romances. Number of titles: 316/year. Occasionally comments on rejected mss.
  ● Books published by Silhouette Books have received numerous awards including Romance Writers of America's Rita Award, awards from *Romantic Times* and best selling awards from Walden and B. Dalton bookstores.
Needs: Contemporary romances, historical romances. Published *Emmett*, by Diana Palmer (SR); *Hazards of the Heart*, by Dixie Browning (SD); *Falling for Rachel*, by Nora Roberts (SE); *Between Roc and a Hard Place*, by Heather Graham Pozzassere (IM); *Garters and Spurs*, by Deloras Scott, *Imminent Thunder*, by Rachel Lee (SS). Published 10-20 new writers within the last year.

How to Contact: Submit query letter with brief synopsis and SASE (IRCs). No unsolicited or simultaneous submissions. Publishes ms 9-24 months after acceptance.

Terms: Pays in royalties; offers advance (negotiated on an individual basis). Must return advance if book is not completed or is unacceptable.

Advice: "You are competing with writers that love the genre and know what our readers want—because many of them started as readers. Please note that the fact that our novels are fun to read doesn't make them easy to write. Storytelling ability, clean compelling writing and love of the genre are necessary."

SIMON & SCHUSTER, 1230 Avenue of the Americas, New York NY 10020. (212)698-7000. Imprints include Pocket Books, Poseidon Press.

Needs: General adult fiction, mostly commercial fiction.

How to Contact: Agented material 100%.

STANDARD PUBLISHING, (II, IV), 8121 Hamilton Ave., Cincinnati OH 45231. (513)931-4050. Director: Mark Plunkett. Estab. 1866. Independent religious publisher. Publishes paperback originals and reprints. Books: offset printing; paper binding; b&w line art; average print order: 7,500; first novel print order: 5,000-7,500. Rarely buys juvenile mss with illustrations. Occasionally comments on rejected mss.

● Standard publishes *The Lookout, R-A-D-A-R* and *Seek* listed in the Commercial Periodicals section.

Needs: Religious/inspirational and easy-to-read. "We do not accept adult fiction at this time; some fiction for very young children accepted. Should have some relation to moral values or Biblical concepts and principles." Katie Hooper Series, by Jane Sorenson; Julie McGregor Series, by Kristi Holl. Published *A Change of Heart* and *A Tangled Webb*, by Kristi Holl; *Jaws of Terror*, by Dayle Courtney.

How to Contact: Query or submit outline/synopsis and 2-3 sample chapters with SASE (IRCs). Reports in 1 month on queries, 3 months on mss. Publishes ms 1-2 years after acceptance.

Terms: Pays varied royalties and by outright purchase; offers varied advance. Sends galleys to author. Writer's guidelines and catalog with SASE.

Advice: Publishes fiction with "strong moral and ethical implications." First novels "should be appropriate, fitting into new or existing series. We're dealing more with issues."

‡STARLOG GROUP, (II), Subsidiary of Starlog Communications International, Inc., 475 Park Ave. S., New York NY 10016. (212)689-2380. Fax: (212)889-7933. Associate Publisher: Milburn Smith. "Commercial, category magazine publisher." Publishes paperback originals (magazines containing 1 complete novel). Books: 6 × 10; paper binding. Averages 12 fiction titles each year.

● Starlog Group has just launched two bimonthly romance magazines, *Moonlight* for contemporary romance and *Rhapsody* for historicals. Each includes a complete romance novel each issue.

Needs: Romance (contemporary—send to *Moonlight* magazine, historical—send to *Rhapsody* magazine). Length: 75,000 words.

How to Contact: Does not accept unsolicited mss. Submit outline/synopsis and 3 sample chapters (first 2, plus an important love scene). Include estimated word count. SASE (or IRC) for reply, for return of ms. Accepts electronic submissions. "If accepted we will need both hard copy and disk."

Terms: Pays $1,500 for first-time author; more depending on credits. Buys magazine rights only. Writer's guidelines for #10 SASE and 1 first-class stamp or IRC.

Advice: "We're looking for romance novels (either historical, contemporary, futuristic or time-travel)—powerful stories of romantic relationships, the kind of love that changes a woman's life forever. The essential elements are: one man, one woman, an overwhelming attraction and a believable obstacle that keeps the plot boiling until the final moment when love triumphs. Plots should be revealed in dramatic scenes of tension and conflict. Historicals should be set between 1600 and 1900, but a really good story would make us consider an earlier period. Contemporary heroines should be American and most of the action set in the USA, but international heroes are fine. The heroine can be sexually experienced—but she's never met anyone like the hero! Subjects can range from glitzy to intrigue to office to homey—but remember, we're looking for contemporary *romances* centering on a relationship, not mainstream contemporary *novels* centering on a woman's emotional or psychological dilemma."

STODDART, 34 Lesmill Rd., Toronto, Ontario M3B 2T6 Canada. No American authors. Prefers not to share information.

TAB BOOK CLUB (TEEN AGE BOOK CLUB), (II), Scholastic Inc., 555 Broadway, New York NY 10012. (212)343-6100. Editor: Greg Holch.
Needs: "TAB Book Club publishes novels for young teenagers in seventh through ninth grades. We do not publish short stories, problem novels or standard teenage romances. A book has to be unique, different, and of high literary quality." Published new writers within the last year.
How to Contact: "Due to the extremely large number of submissions, we will not be looking at new manuscripts this year."
Advice: "The books we are publishing now are literary works that we hope will become the classics of the future. They are novels that reveal the hearts and souls of their authors."

THORNDIKE PRESS, (IV), Division of Macmillan, Inc., Box 159, Thorndike ME 04986. (800)223-6121. Contact: Nivette Jackaway. Estab. 1979. Midsize publisher of hardcover and paperback large print *reprints*. Books: alkaline paper; offset printing; Smythe-sewn library binding; average print order: 4,000. Publishes 300 total titles each year.
Needs: *No fiction that has not been previously published. Note: Macmillan Inc. recently sold to Paramount Communications.* Published *The Kitchen God's Wife*, by Amy Tan; *Hideaway*, by Dean R. Koontz.
How to Contact: Does not accept unsolicited mss. Query.
Terms: Pays 10% in royalties.
Advice: "We do not accept unpublished works. With the exception of our new Young Adult Series (Teen Scene), our audience is comprised, primarily, of seniors."

‡TICKNOR & FIELDS, (I, II), Affiliate of Houghton Mifflin, 215 Park Ave. S., New York NY 10003. (212)420-5800. Estab. 1979. Publishes hardcover originals.
Needs: Open to all categories, but selective list of only 30 titles a year. Published *Closing Arguments*, by Frederich Busch; *Forms of Shelter*, by Angela Davis-Gardner; *Afghanistan*, by Alex Ullmann; *Mister Touch*, by Malcolm Bosse.
How to Contact: Query letters only; no unsolicited mss accepted. No simultaneous submissions (unless very special). Reports in 2 months.
Terms: Pays standard royalties. Offers advance depending on the book.

TOR BOOKS, (II), 175 Fifth Ave., New York NY 10010. (212)388-0100. Editor-in-Chief: Robert Gleason. Estab. 1980. Publishes hardcover and paperback originals, plus some paperback reprints. Books: 5 point Dombook paper; offset printing; Bursel and perfect binding; few illustrations. Averages 200 total titles, mostly fiction, each year. Some nonfiction titles.
Needs: Fantasy, mainstream, science fiction, suspense and westerns. Published *Xenocide*, by Orson Scott Card; *Midnight Sun*, by Ramsey Campbell; *The Nemesis Mission*, by Dean Ing; and *The Dragon Reborn*, by Robert Jordan.
How to Contact: Agented mss preferred. Buys 90% agented fiction. No simultaneous submissions. Address manuscripts to "Editorial," *not* to the Managing Editor's office.
Terms: Pays in royalties and advance. Writer must return advance if book is not completed or is unacceptable. Sends galleys to author. Free book catalog on request.

TRILLIUM PRESS, (I, II), First Avenue, Unionville NY 10988. (914)726-4444. Vice President: Thomas Holland. Fiction Editor: William Neumann. Estab. 1978. Independent educational publisher. Publishes hardcover and paperback originals and paperback reprints. Plans 40 first novels this year. Averages 150 total titles, 70 fiction titles each year.
Needs: Young adult/teen (10-18 years), fantasy/science fiction, historical, problem novels, romance (ya), sports and mystery/adventure, middle school/young adult (10-18) series. Published the following young adult series: Mystery & Adventure (including historical novels); Growing Up Right (values, relationships, adult development); science fiction. Also published *The Journal of Jenny September*, by Isaacsen-Bright; *The T-206 Honus Wagner Caper*, by Janet Amann; *A Matter of Choice*, by H. Henry Williams. Published new writers within the last year.
How to Contact: Accepts unsolicited mss. SASE. Reports in 3 months on mss.
Terms: Negotiated "as appropriate." Sends galleys to author. Writer's guidelines for #10 SAE and 1 first-class stamp (IRCs). Book catalog for 9 × 12 SAE and 3 first-class stamps.

TROLL ASSOCIATES, (II), Watermill Press, 100 Corporate Dr., Mahwah NJ 07430. (201)529-4000. Editorial Contact Person: M. Frances. Estab. 1968. Midsize independent publisher. Publishes hardcover originals, paperback originals and reprints. Averages 100-300 total titles each year.

Needs: Adventure, historical, juvenile (5-9 yrs. including: animal, easy-to-read, fantasy), preschool/picture book, young adult/teen (10-18 years) including: easy-to-read, fantasy/science fiction, historical, romance (ya), sports, spy/adventure. Published new writers within the last year.
How to Contact: Accepts and returns unsolicited mss. Query first. SASE (IRCs). Submit outline/synopsis and sample chapters. Reports in 2-3 weeks on queries.
Terms: Pays royalties. Sometimes sends galleys to author. Publishes ms 6-18 months after acceptance.

TSR, INC., Box 756, Lake Geneva WI 53147. (414)248-3625. Imprints include the Dragonlance® series, Forgotten Realms® series, Dungeons & Dragons® Books, Dark Sun Books, TSR® Books, Ravenloft® Books. Executive Editor: Brian Thomsen. Estab. 1974. "We publish original paperback and hardcover novels and 'shared world' books." TSR publishes games as well, including the Dungeons & Dragons® role-playing game. Books: standard paperbacks; offset printing; perfect binding; b&w (usually) illustrations; average first novel print order: 75,000. Averages 20-30 fiction titles each year.
• TSR also publishes the magazine *Amazing Stories* and *Dragon* listed in this book.
Needs: "We most often publish character-oriented fantasy and science fiction; all horror must be suitable for line of Ravenloft® Books. We work with authors who can deal in a serious fashion with the genres we concentrate on and can be creative within the confines of our work-for-hire contracts." Recently published *The Legacy*, by R.A. Salvatore; *The Valorian*, by Mary H. Herbert; and *Before the Mask*, by Michael and Teri Williams.
How to Contact: "Because most of our books are strongly tied to our game products, we expect our writers to be very familiar with those products."
Terms: Pays royalties of 4% of cover price. Offers advances. "Commissioned works, with the exception of our TSR® Books line, are written as work-for-hire, with TSR, Inc., holding all copyrights."
Advice: "With the huge success of our Dragonlance® series and Forgotten Realms® books, we expect to be working even more closely with TSR-owned fantasy worlds. Be familiar with our line and query us regarding a proposal."

TYNDALE HOUSE PUBLISHERS, (II, IV), P.O. Box 80, 351 Executive Drive, Wheaton IL 60189. (708)668-8300. Vice President of Editorial: Ron Beers. Acquisition Director: Ken Petersen. Estab. 1960. Privately owned religious press. Publishes hardcover and mass paperback originals and paperback reprints. Plans 1 first novel this year. Averages 100 total titles, 20 fiction titles each year. Average first novel print order: 5,000-15,000 copies.
• *Tourmaline*, by Jon Henderson and published by Tyndale House, received a Campus Life Book Award in 1993.
Needs: Religious/inspirational. Recently published *A Voice in the Wind*, by Francine Rivers (historical romance); *The Eleventh Hour*, by Michael Phillips; *Gate of His Enemies*, by Gil Morris. Series include "Grace Livingston Hill," "Appomattax Saga" and "Reno Western" series.
How to Contact: Does not accept unsolicited mss. Queries only. Reports in 6-10 weeks. Publishes ms an average of 1-2 years after acceptance.
Terms: Pays in royalties of 10% minimum; negotiable advance. Writer's guidelines and book catalog for 9 × 12 SAE and $2.40 for postage (IRCs).
Advice: "We are a religious publishing house, looking for spiritual themes and content within established genres."

✱*VESTA PUBLICATIONS, LTD, (II), Box 1641, Cornwall, Ontario K6H 5V6 Canada. (613)932-2135. Editor: Stephen Gill. Estab. 1974. Midsize publisher with plans to expand. Publishes hardcover and paperback originals. Books: bond paper; offset printing; paperback and sewn hardcover binding; illustrations; average print order: 1,200; first novel print order: 1,000. Plans 7 first novels this year. Averages 18 total titles, 5 fiction titles each year. *Negotiable charge for critiquing rejected mss.*
Needs: Adventure, contemporary, ethnic, experimental, faction, fantasy, feminist, historical, juvenile, literary, mainstream, psychic/supernatural/occult, regional, religious/inspirational, romance, science fiction, short story collections, mystery/suspense, translations, war and young adult/teen. Published *Sodom in Her Heart*, by Donna Nevling (religious); *The Blessings of a Bird*, by Stephen Gill (juvenile); and *Whistle Stop and Other Stories*, by Ordrach.
How to Contact: Accepts unsolicited mss. Submit 2-3 sample chapters with SASE or SAE and IRC. Reports in 1 month. Simultaneous submissions OK. Disk submissions OK with CPM/Kaypro 2 system.
Terms: Pays in royalties of 10% minimum. Sends galleys to author. *"For first novel we usually ask authors from outside of Canada to pay half of our printing cost."* Free book catalog.

VILLARD BOOKS, (II, III), Random House, Inc., 201 E. 50th St., New York NY 10022. (212)572-2720. Editor-in-Chief: Peter Gethers. Fiction Editors: Diane Reverand, Stephanie Long, Emily Bestler. Estab. 1983. Imprint specializes in commercial fiction and nonfiction. Publishes hardcover and trade paperback originals. Plans 2 first novels this year. Averages 40-45 total titles, approx. 10 fiction titles each year. Sometimes critiques rejected mss.
Needs: Strong commercial fiction and nonfiction. Adventure, contemporary, historical, horror, humor/satire, literary, mainstream, romance (contemporary and historical), mystery/suspense. Special interest in mystery, thriller, and literary novels. Published *How to Make an American Quilt*, by Whitney Otto (bestseller); *Domestic Pleasure*, by Beth Eutcheon; *First Hubby*, by Roy Blount. Published new writers within the last year.
How to Contact: Does not accept unsolicited mss. Submit outline/synopsis and 1-2 sample chapters to a specific editor. Agented fiction: 95%. Reports in 2-3 weeks. Simultaneous submissions OK.
Terms: "Depends upon contract negotiated." Sends galleys to author. Writer's guidelines for 8½ × 11 SAE with 1 first-class stamp (IRCs). Book catalog free on request.
Advice: "Most fiction published in hardcover."

WALKER AND COMPANY, (I), 720 5th Ave., New York NY 10019. Editors: Michael Seidman (mystery), Jacqueline Johnson (western), Emily Easton (young adult), Mary Kennan Herbert (trade nonfiction). Midsize independent publisher with plans to expand. Publishes hardcover and trade paperback. Average first novel print order: 2,000-3,000. Number of titles: 120/year. Published many new writers within the last year. Occasionally comments on rejected mss.
• Books published by Walker and Company have received numerous awards including the Spur Award (for westerns) and nominations for the Shamus Awards for Best First Private Eye Novel and Best Novel.
Needs: Nonfiction, sophisticated, quality mystery (cozy, amateur sleuth, private eye, police procedural), traditional western and children's and young adult nonfiction. Recently published *By Evil Means*, by Sandra West Prowell; *The Man Who Was Taller Than God*, by Harold Adams; *Clear-Cut Murder*, by Lee Wallingford.
How to Contact: Submit outline and chapters as preliminary. Query letter should include "a concise description of the story line, including its outcome, word length of story, writing experience, publishing credits, particular expertise on this subject and in this genre. Common mistakes: Sounding unprofessional (i.e. too chatty, too braggardly). Forgetting SASE." Buys 50% agented fiction. Notify if multiple or simultaneous submissions. Reports in 3-5 months. Publishes ms an average of 1 year after acceptance.
Terms: Negotiable (usually advance against royalty). Must return advance if book is not completed or is unacceptable.
Advice: "As for mysteries, we are open to all types, including suspense novels and offbeat, cross genre books that maintain a 'play fair' puzzle. We are always looking for well-written western novels and thrillers that are offbeat and strong on characterization. Character development is most important in all Walker fiction. We expect the author to be expert in the categories, to know the background and foundations of the genre. To realize that just because some subgenre is hot it doesn't mean that that is the area to mine—after all, if everyone is doing female p.i.s, doesn't it make more sense to do something that isn't crowded, something that might serve to balance a list, rather than make it top heavy? Finally, don't tell us why your book is going to be a success; instead, show me that you can write and write well. It is your writing, and not your hype that interests us."

WASHINGTON SQUARE PRESS, (III), Subsidiary of Pocket Books/Simon & Schuster, 1230 Avenue of the Americas, New York NY 10020. Senior Fiction Editor: Jane Rosenman. Estab. 1962. Quality imprint of mass-market publisher. Publishes very few paperback originals, mostly reprints. Averages 15 titles, mostly fiction, each year.
Needs: Literary, high quality novels; serious nonfiction, journalistic nonfiction. Published *Pizza Face*, by Ken Siman; *Trouble the Water*, by Melvin Dixon; and *The World Around Midnight*, by Patricia Browning Griffith (all novels).
How to Contact: Query first. Agented fiction nearly all. Simultaneous submissions OK. "We cannot promise an individual response to unsolicited mss."

‡■**DANIEL WEISS ASSOCIATES, INC., (II)**, 33 W. 17th St., New York NY 10011. Editor-in-Chief: Elise Howard. Estab. 1987. "Packager of 75 titles a year including juvenile and adult fiction as well as nonfiction titles. We package for a range of publishers within their specifications." Publishes hardcover

and paperback originals. All titles by first-time writers are commissioned for established series. Averages 120 total titles, 100 fiction titles each year. Sometimes critiques rejected mss.
Needs: Juvenile (animal, contemporary, easy-to-read, historical, sports, spy/adventure), mainstream, preschool/picture book, young adult (easy-to-read, fantasy/science fiction, historical, problem novels, romance, sports, spy/adventure). "We cannot acquire single-title manuscripts that are not part of a series the author is proposing or submitted specifically according to our guidelines for an established series." Published *Sweet Valley High*, by Francine Pascal (young adult series); *Hollywood Daughters*, by Joan Lowery Nixon (young adult historical trilogy); *Pets, Inc.*, by Jennifer Armstrong (elementary fiction series).
How to Contact: Accepts unsolicited mss. Query first with synopsis/outline and 2 sample chapters. SASE (IRCs). Agented fiction 75%. Reports in 2 months. Simultaneous submissions OK.
Terms: Pays flat fee plus royalty. Advance is negotiable. Sends galleys to author. Publishes ms 1 year after acceptance. Writer's guidelines for #10 SAE and 1 first-class stamp.
Advice: "We are always happy to work with and encourage first time novelists. Being packagers, we often create and outline books by committee. This system is quite beneficial to writers who may be less experienced. Usually we are contacted by the agent rather than writer directly. Occasionally, however, we do work with writers who send in unsolicited material. I think that a professionally presented manuscript is of great importance."

WESTERN PUBLISHING COMPANY, INC., 850 3rd Ave., New York NY 10022. (212)753-8500. Imprint: Golden Books. Juvenile Editors-in-Chief: Marilyn Salomon. Estab. 1907. High-volume mass market and trade publisher. Publishes hardcover and paperback originals. Number of titles: Averages 160/year. Buys 20-30% agented fiction.
Needs: Juvenile: Adventure, mystery, humor, sports, animal, easy-to-read picture books, and "a few" nonfiction titles. Published *Little Critter's Bedtime Story*, by Mercer Mayer; *Cyndy Szekeres' Mother Goose Rhymes*; and *Spaghetti Manners*, by Stephanie Calmenson, illustrated by Lisa MaCue Karsten.
How to Contact: Unsolicited mss are returned unread. Publishes ms an average of 1 year after acceptance.
Terms: Pays by outright purchase or royalty.
Advice: "Read our books to see what we do. Call for appointment if you do illustrations, to show your work. Do not send illustrations. Illustrations are not necessary; if your book is what we are looking for, we can use one of our artists."

ALBERT WHITMAN & COMPANY, (I), 6340 Oakton St., Morton Grove IL 60053. (708)581-0033. Assistant Editor: Christy Grant. Associate Editor: Judith Mathews. Senior Editor: Abby Levine. Editor-in-Chief: Kathleen Tucker. Estab. 1919. Small independent juvenile publisher. Publishes hardcover originals and paperback reprints. Books: paper varies; printing varies; library binding; most books illustrated; average print order: 7,500. Average 30 total titles/year. Number of fiction titles varies.
Needs: Juvenile (2-12 years including easy-to-read, fantasy, historical, adventure, contemporary, mysteries, picture-book stories). Primarily interested in picture book manuscripts and nonfiction for ages 2-8. Published *All About Asthma*, by William Ostrow and Vivian Ostrow; *You Push, I Ride*, by Abby Levine; *How the Ox Star Fell from Heaven*, by Lily Toy Hong; published new writers within the last year.
How to Contact: Accepts unsolicited mss. Submit complete ms, if not possible—3 sample chapters and outline; complete ms for picture books. "Queries don't seem to work for us." SASE (IRCs). "Half or more fiction is not agented." Reports in 3 weeks on outline; 2 months average on mss. Simultaneous submissions OK. ("We prefer to be told.")
Terms: Payment varies. Royalties, advance; number of author's copies varies. Some flat fees. Sends galleys to author. Writer's guidelines for SASE. Book catalog for 9×12 SAE and $1.21 postage.
Advice: "Writers need only to send a manuscript; artwork does not need to be included. If we decide to buy the story, *we* will find an artist. Though it's *okay* to send a whole package, it's not necessary."

Successful marketing requires the proper tools. Make sure you have the latest edition of Novel & Short Story Writer's Market. *If you're still using this book and it's 1995 or later, buy the new edition at your favorite bookstore or order directly from* Writer's Digest Books.

*WINSTON-DEREK PUBLISHERS, (II), Box 90883, Nashville TN 37209. (615)321-0535, 329-1319. Senior Editor: Marjorie Staton. Estab. 1978. Midsize publisher. Publishes hardcover and paperback originals and reprints. Books: 60 lb. old Warren style paper; litho press; perfect and/or sewn binding; illustrations sometimes; average print order: 3,000-5,000 copies; first novel print order: 2,000 copies. Plans 10 first novels this year. Averages 55-65 total titles, 20 fiction titles each year; "90% of material is from freelance writers; each year we add 15 more titles."
Needs: Historical, juvenile (historical), religious/inspirational, and young adult (easy-to-read, historical, romance) and programmed reading material for middle and high school students. "Must be 65,000 words or less. Novels strong with human interest. Characters overcoming a weakness or working through a difficulty. Prefer plots related to a historical event but not necessary. No science fiction, explicit eroticism, minorities in conflict without working out a solution to the problem. Downplay on religious ideal and values." Published *The Train that Never Ran*, by George K. Bowers; *An Irregular Moon*, by Sara King; and *Lucy Lola's Come Next Year*, by Earnie Danat. Published new writers within the last year.
How to Contact: Submit outline/synopsis and 3-4 sample chapters with SASE (IRCs). Simultaneous submissions OK. Reports in 4-6 weeks on queries; 6-8 weeks on mss. Must query first. Do not send complete ms.
Terms: Pays in royalties of 10% minimum, 15% maximum; negotiates advance. *Offers some subsidy arrangements.* Book catalog on request for $1 postage.
Advice: "We need highly plotted fiction relative to African-American and other ethnic minorities. The public is reading contemplative literature. Authors should strive for originality and a clear writing style, depicting universal themes which portray character building and are beneficial to mankind. Consider the historical novel; there is always room for one more."

★WORLDWIDE LIBRARY, (II), Division of Harlequin Books, 225 Duncan Mill Rd., Don Mills, Ontario M3B 3K9 Canada. (416)445-5860. Imprints are Worldwide Library Mystery; Gold Eagle Books. Senior Editor: Feroze Mohammed. Estab. 1979. Large commercial category line. Publishes paperback originals and reprints. Published new writers within the last year. Averages 60 titles, all fiction, each year. Sometimes critiques rejected ms. "Mystery program is largely reprint; no originals please."
Needs: "We are looking for action-adventure series; future fiction." Recently published *Hatchet, Code Zero, Time Raider, Cade, Nomad, Warkeep 2030; Jake Strait; Earthblood; Omega.*
How to Contact: Query first or submit outline/synopsis/series concept or overview and sample chapters. SAE. U.S. stamps do not work in Canada; use International Reply Coupons or money order. Agented fiction 95%. Reports in 10 weeks on queries. Simultaneous submissions OK.
Terms: Advance and sometimes royalties; copyright buyout. Publishes ms 1-2 years after acceptance.
Advice: "Publishing fiction in very selective areas. As a genre publisher we are always on the lookout for innovative series ideas, especially in the men's adventure area."

‡ZEBRA BOOKS, (II), 475 Park Ave. S., New York NY 10016. (212)889-2299. Contact: Editorial Director. Estab. 1975. Publishes hardcover reprints and paperback originals. Averages 400 total titles/year.
Needs: Contemporary, adventure, English-style mysteries, historical, war, gothic, saga, romance, true crime, nonfiction, women's, erotica, thrillers and horror. No science fiction. Published *Missing Beauty*, by Teresa Carpenter; *Kiss of the Night Wind*, by Janelle Taylor; *Stardust*, by Nan Ryan; and *Wolf Time*, by Joe Gores.
How to Contact: Query or submit complete ms or outline/synopsis and sample chapters with SASE (IRCs). Simultaneous submissions OK. Address women's mss to Carin Cohen Ritter and male adventure mss to Editorial Director. Reports in 3-5 months.
Terms: Pays royalties and advances. Free book catalog.
Advice: "Put aside your literary ideals and be commercial. We like big contemporary women's fiction, glitzy career novels, high-tech espionage and horror. Work fast and on assignment. Keep your cover letter simple and to the point. Too many times, 'cutesy' letters about category or content turn us off some fine mss. We are more involved with family and historical sagas. But please do research. We buy many unsolicited manuscripts, but we're slow readers. Have patience."

ZONDERVAN, (III, IV), 5300 Patterson SE, Grand Rapids MI 49530. (616)698-6900. Contact: Manuscript Submissions. Large evangelical Christian publishing house. Publishes hardcover and paperback originals and reprints, though fiction is generally in paper only. Published new writers in the last year. Averages 150 total titles, 5-10 fiction titles each year. Average first novel: 5,000 copies.

Needs: Adult fiction, (mainstream, biblical, historical, adventure, sci-fi, fantasy, mystery), "Inklings-style" fiction of high literary quality and juvenile fiction (primarily mystery/adventure novels for 8-12-year-olds). Christian relevance necessary in all cases. Will *not* consider collections of short stories or inspirational romances. Recently published *McKinney High, 1946*, by Ken Gire.

How to Contact: Accepts unsolicited mss. Write for writer's guidelines first. Include #10 SASE (IRCs). Query or submit outline/synopsis and 2 sample chapters. Reports in 4-6 weeks on queries; 3-4 months on mss.

Terms: "Standard contract provides for a percentage of the net price received by publisher for each copy sold, usually 14-17% of net."

Advice: "Almost no unsolicited fiction is published. Send plot outline and one or two sample chapters. Most editors will *not* read entire mss. Your proposal and opening chapter will make or break you."

International commercial publishers

The following commercial publishers, all located outside the United States and Canada, also accept work from fiction writers. The majority are from England, a few are from India and one each is from Scotland and Ghana. As with other publishers, obtain catalogs and writer's guidelines from those that interest you to determine the types of fiction published and how well your work might fit alongside other offerings.

Remember to use self-addressed envelopes (SAEs) with International Reply Coupons (IRCs) in all correspondence with publishers outside your own country. IRCs may be purchased at the main branch of your local post office. In general, send IRCs in amounts roughly equivalent to return postage. When submitting work to international publishers, you may want to send a disposable copy of your manuscript and only one IRC along with a self-addressed postcard for a reply. This saves you the cost of having work returned.

MARION BOYARS PUBLISHERS INC., 237 E. 39th St., New York NY 10016. Editorial Office: 24 Lacy Road, London SW15 1NL England. Fiction Editor: Marion Boyars. Publishes 15 novels or story collections/year. "A lot of American fiction. Authors include Ken Kesey, Eudora Welty, Stephen Koch, Samuel Charters, Page Edwards, Viatia Spiegelman, Kenneth Gangemi, Tim O'Brien, Julian Green. British and Irish fiction. Translations from the French, German, Turkish, Arabic, Italian, Spanish." Send cover letter and entire manuscript "always with sufficient return postage by check." Pays advance against royalties. "Most fiction working *well* in one country does well in another. We usually have world rights, i.e. world English plus translation rights." Enclose return postage by check, minimum $3, for catalog.

‡CONSTABLE AND COMPANY, (IV), 3 The Lanchesters, 162 Fulham Palace Rd., London W6 9ER England. Fiction Editor: Robin Baird-Smith. Averages 40 fiction titles/year. Publishes "literary fiction and crime fiction (mysteries)." Length: 30,000 words minimum; 150,000 words maximum. Send brief summary and 3 sample chapters. Pays advance and royalties. Write to publishers for catalog.

ROBERT HALE LIMITED (II), Clerkenwell House, 45/47 Clerkenwell Green, London EC1R 0HT England. Publishes hardcover and trade paperback originals and hardcover reprints. Historical, mainstream and western. Length: 40,000-150,000 words. Send cover letter, synopsis or brief summary and 2 sample chapters.

HAMISH HAMILTON LTD., (IV), 27 Wrights Lane, London W8 5TZ England. Fiction Editors: Andrew Franklin, Kate Jones and Alexandra Pringle. General trade hardback and paperback publisher of quality fiction—literary plus some crime and thrillers. Advance on delivery of accepted book or on accepted commission. Send first chapter with synopsis before submitting whole manuscript. SAE essential.

HARPERCOLLINS PUBLISHERS (NEW ZEALAND) LIMITED, (IV), P.O. Box 1, Auckland New Zealand. Publisher: Paul Bradwell. Averages 20-24 fiction titles/year (15-20 nonfiction). Teen fiction: 12 years plus: Tui imprint; Junior fiction: 8-11 years: Tui Junior imprint. Tui Turbo imprint, 6-10 years and slow readers. Length: Tui: 30-40,000 words; Tui Junior: 15-17,000 words. Tui Turbo: 2-3,000 words and line drawings. Full ms preferred. Pays royalties. "It helps if the author and story have New Zealand connections/content. Write and ask for guidelines."

HEADLINE BOOK PUBLISHING LTD., 79 Great Titchfield St., London W1P 7FN England. Editorial Director (Fiction): Jane Morpeth. Averages approximately 400 titles/year. Mainstream publisher of popular fiction and nonfiction in hardcover and mass-market paperback. Length: 120,000-200,000 words. "Study UK publishers' catalogs to see what is published in both the USA and the UK. Read the UK trade press: *The Bookseller* and *Publishing News* to get a feel for our market. *The Writers' & Artists' Yearbook* is useful." Pays advance against royalties. "Send a synopsis/5 consecutive chapters and *curriculum vitae* first, and return postage." Catalog available.

JULIA MACRAE BOOKS, Random House, 20 Vauxhall Bridge Road, London SW1V 2SA England. Editors: Julia MacRae, Delia Huddy, Anne Tothill. Children's books: Board books, picture books, fiction for juniors and teenagers, nonfiction. Adult titles: biography, history, music, religion. Send cover letter and entire manuscript. Writers are paid by royalties. Julia MacRae Books is an imprint of Random House.

MILLS & BOON, (IV), Eton House, 18-24 Paradise Road, Richmond, Surrey TW9 1SR England. Publishes 250 fiction titles/year. Modern romantic fiction, historical romances and medical romances. "We are happy to see the whole manuscript or 3 sample chapters and synopsis."

MY WEEKLY STORY LIBRARY, (IV), D.C. Thomson and Co., Ltd., 22 Meadowside, Dundee DD19QJ, Scotland. Fiction Editor: Mrs. D. Hunter. Publishes 48, 35,000-word romantic novels/year. "Cheap paperback story library with full-colour cover. Material should not be violent, controversial or sexually explicit." Length: 35,000-45,000 words. Writers are paid on acceptance. "Send the opening 3 chapters and a synopsis. Avoid too many colloquialisms/Americanisms. Stories can be set anywhere but local colour not too "local" as to be alien." Both contemporary and historical novels considered. Guidelines available on request.

PETER OWEN PUBLISHERS, 73 Kenway Rd., London SW5 ORE England. Fiction Editor: Jill Foulston. Averages 25 fiction titles/year. "Independent publishing house now 42 years old. Publish fiction from around the world, from Russia to Japan. Publishers of Shusaku Endo, Paul and Jane Bowles, Hermann Hesse, Octavio Paz, Colette etc." Send cover letter, synopsis, brief summary. Please include SASE (or IRCs). Pays advance and standard royalty. "Be concise. Always include SASE and/or international reply coupon. Do not send inappropriate material. Best to work through agent. Writers can obtain copy of our catalogue by SASE, and/or interntional reply coupon. No guidelines but it would help greatly if author was familiar with the list."

PICADOR, (IV), Pan MacMillan Ltd., 18-21 Cavaye Place, London SW10 9PG England. Publishing Director: Peter Straus. Publishes hardbound and paperback titles. "Picador is a literary imprint specializing in the best international fiction and nonfiction in recent years. Its authors include G. Garcia Marquez, Umberto Eco, Bruce Chatwin, Clive James, Julian Barnes, Graham Swift, Ian McEwan, Toni Morrison, Tom Wolfe." Length: 50,000-150,000 words. Send cover letter, synopsis, brief summary and 2 sample chapters. For catalog, send large addressed envelope and IRCs.

POPULAR PUBLICATIONS, (IV), P.O. Box 5592, Limbe, Malawi. Fiction Editor: Joseph-Claude Simwaka. Averages between 3-5 titles/year. "Popular Publications is probably the biggest publisher of Malawian fiction in the country. In order to boost and promote Malawian literary writers (creative works) the publishing house launched the Malawian Writers Series in 1974 for fiction, short story collections and poetry. We also publish children's books on fiction." Length: 5,000-125,000 words. Send cover letter and entire manuscript. We pay 10% royalties by 31st December every year. "Submit a typewritten manuscript, double-spaced on A4 paper. It is also advisable for the writer to submit two copies of the same manuscript, one for us and the other for the Government Censorship Board. Writer too, should keep a triplicate copy." Write for catalog or guidelines.

QUARTET BOOKS LIMITED, (IV), 27 Goodge Street, London W1P1FD England. Chief Editor: Stephen Pickles. Publishes 50 novels/year. "Middle East fiction, European classics in translation, musical biography, original novels." Payment is: advance—half on signature, half on delivery or publication. "Send brief synopsis and sample chapters. *No* romantic fiction, historical fiction, crime, science fiction or thrillers."

‡REED PUBLISHING (NZ) LTD., (IV), Private Bag, Birkenhead, Auckland 10, New Zealand. Fiction Editor: Ian Watt. Averages 5 or 6 fiction titles/year. "Reed Publishing NZ has three divisions: Reed Books (trade publishing); Heinemann Education; and Octopus Books (mass-market paperbacks and children's books). We publish literary fiction, mass-market fiction and children's books, with a strong bias towards writing by New Zealanders or about New Zealand and the Pacific." Length: 40,000 words minimum. Send a cover letter with synopsis and 3 sample chapters. SASE (SAE and IRCs). "Authors are paid a royalty. Advances are negotiable. It is unlikely that we would accept fiction not written by a New Zealander or Pacific Islander or without some content that relates to New Zealand." Catalog available on request.

‡SINCLAIR-STEVENSON, (II), Reed Consumer Books Ltd., Michelin House, 81 Fulham Road, London SW3 6RB England. Fiction Editors: Penelope Hoare, Christopher Sinclair-Stevenson. Averages 30 fiction titles/year. "Trade hardbacks of quality fiction from new and established authors: Jane Gordam, Rose Tremain, Susan Hill, William Boyd, Peter Ackroyd." Length: open. Send a cover letter. Pays advance and royalties. Contact sales manager for catalog. No guidelines available.

*TOUCHSTONE PUBLISHING, PVT. LIMITED, (IV), (formerly Harsha Book Agency), T.D. East Sannidhi Road, P.O. Box 3549, Kochi-682 035, Kerala, India. Managing and Editorial Director: C. I. Oommen. Publishers of fiction for children and educational books for pre-school and primary school children. Accepts unsolicited mss, simultaneous and photocopied submissions and computer printouts. Reports in 2 months. Pays in royalties of 10% maximum.

‡THE WOMEN'S PRESS, (IV), 34 Great Sutton St., London EC1V 0DX England. Publishes approx. 50 titles/year. "Women's fiction, written by women. Centered on women. Theme can be anything— all themes may be women's concern—but we look for political/feminist awareness, originality, wit, fiction of ideas. Includes genre fiction, science fiction, crime, and teenage list *Livewire*." Writers receive royalty, including advance. Writers should ask themselves, "Is this a manuscript which would interest a feminist/political press?

Commercial publishers/'93-'94 changes

The following commercial publishers appeared in the 1993 edition of *Novel & Short Story Writer's Market* but do not appear in the 1994 edition. Those listings that did not respond to our request for an update are listed without further explanation below. There are several reasons why a publisher did not return an update—they could be overstocked, no longer taking taking fiction or have been recently sold—or they may have responded too late for taking fiction or have been recently sold—or they may have responded too late for inclusion. If a reason for the omission is known, it is included next to the publisher's name.

Contemporary Books (out of business)
Delacorte/Dell Books for Young Readers/Doubleday (see listing for Bantam/Doubleday/Dell Books for Young Readers)

Dell Yearling (see Bantam Doubleday Dell)
Gareth Stevens, Inc. (no unsolicited mss)
Gibbs Smith (no longer publishing fiction)
Joy Street Books (see listing for

Little, Brown and Co.)
Poseidon Press (out of business)
Warner Books (asked to be deleted)
Windsong Books (asked to be deleted)

International commercial publishers/'93-'94 changes
The Blackstaff Press
Hodder & Stoughton Publishers
Weidenfeld and Nicolson Ltd. (asked to be deleted)

Contests and Awards

In addition to honors and quite often cash awards, contests and awards programs offer writers the opportunity to be judged on the basis of quality alone without the outside factors that sometimes influence publishing decisions. New writers who win contests may be published for the first time, while more experienced writers may gain public recognition of an entire body of work.

There are contests for almost every type of fiction writing. Some focus on form, such as the Long Fiction Contest, for stories up to 14,000 words. Others feature writing on particular themes or topics including the Japanophile Short Story Contest, the Stephen Leacock Medal for Humor and the Maggie Award. Still others are prestigious prizes or awards for work that must be nominated such as National Endowment for the Arts Fellowship and Pulitzer Prize in Fiction. Chances are no matter what type of fiction you write, there is a contest or award program that may interest you.

Selecting and submitting to a contest

Use the same care in submitting to contests as you would sending your manuscript to a publication or book publisher. Deadlines are very important and where possible we've included this information. At times contest deadlines were only approximate at our press deadline, so be sure to write or call for complete information and additional rules.

Follow the rules to the letter. If, for instance, contest rules require you to put your name on a cover sheet only, you will be disqualified if you ignore this and put your name on every page. Find out how many copies to send. If you don't send the correct amount, by the time you are contacted to send more it may be past the submission deadline.

As with publishers, of course, your submission must be clean, neatly typed and professionally presented. Do not cost yourself points by sending a manuscript no one cares to handle or read.

One note of caution: Beware of contests that charge entry fees that are disproportionate to the amount of the prize. Contests offering a $10 prize, but charging $7 in entry fees, are a waste of your time and money.

If you are interested in a contest or award that requires your publisher to nominate your work, it's acceptable to make your interest known. Be sure to leave them plenty of time, however, to make the nomination deadline.

The Roman numeral coding we use to rank listings in this section is different than that used in previous sections. The following is our ranking system:

    I Contest for unpublished fiction, usually open to both new and experienced writers.

    II Contest for published (usually including self-published) fiction, which may be entered by the author.

    III Contest for fiction, which must be nominated by an editor, publisher or other nominating body.

    IV Contest limited to residents of a certain region, of a certain age or to writing on certain themes or subjects.

EDWARD ABBEY AWARD, (II, IV), *Earth Journal* (formerly *Buzzworm*), Suite 206, 2305 Canyon Blvd., Boulder CO 80302. (303)442-1969. Assistant Editor: Deborah Houy. "To honor novel-length fiction written in the spirit of Edward Abbey." Awarded to best published (or accepted for publication) novel in the previous year on environmental themes. Annual competition for novels. Award: $2,000 and an excerpt published in the July/August issue of *Earth Journal*. Judges: Editors of *Earth Journal*. Deadline: March 1.

AIM MAGAZINE SHORT STORY CONTEST, (I), P.O. Box 20554, Chicago IL 60620. (312)874-6184. Contact: Ruth Apilado and Mark Boone, publisher and fiction editor. Estab. 1984. Contest offered annually if money available. "To encourage and reward good writing in the short story form. The contest is particularly for new writers." Award: $100 plus publication in fall issue. "Judged by *Aim*'s editorial staff." Sample copy for $3.50. Contest rules for SASE. Unpublished submissions. "We're looking for compelling, well-written stories with lasting social significance."

ALABAMA STATE COUNCIL ON THE ARTS INDIVIDUAL ARTIST FELLOWSHIP, (II, IV), #1 Dexter Ave., Montgomery AL 36130. (205)242-4076. Contact: Randy Shoults. "To provide assistance to an individual artist." Semiannual awards: $5,000 and $10,000 grants awarded in even-numbered years ('94-'96). Competition receives approximately 30 submissions annually. Judges: Independent peer panel. Entry forms or rules for SASE. Deadline: May 1. Two-year Alabama residency required.

ALASKA STATE COUNCIL ON THE ARTS LITERARY ARTS FELLOWSHIPS, (I, IV), Alaska State Council on the Arts, Suite 1E, 411 W. 4th Ave., Anchorage AK 99501-2343. (907)279-1558. Contact: Christine D'Arcy. "Open-ended grant award, non-matching, to enable creative writers to advance their careers as they see it." Biennial. Award: $5,000. Judges: Peer panel review. Deadline: October 1. **Alaskan writers only!**

THE NELSON ALGREN AWARD FOR SHORT FICTION, (I), *Chicago Tribune*, 435 N. Michigan Ave., Chicago IL 60611. (312)222-4540. Annual award to recognize an outstanding, unpublished short story, minimum 2,500 words, maximum 10,000 words. Awards: $5,000 first prize; three runners-up receive $1,000 awards. Publication of four winning stories in the *Chicago Tribune*. No entry fee. "All entries must be from 'the Heartland,' typed, double spaced and accompanied by SASE." A brochure bearing the rules of the contest will be sent to writers who inquire in writing. Deadline: Entries are accepted only from November 30-February 1.

AMBERGRIS ANNUAL FICTION AWARD, (I), *Ambergris* Magazine, Dept. N, P.O. Box 29919, Cincinnati OH 45229. Editor: Mark Kissling. Award "to recognize and reward excellence in short fiction." Annual competition for short stories. Award: $100 and nomination to *The Pushcart Prize*. Competition receives more than 1,000 mss/year. Judges: Editorial staff. Guidelines for #10 SASE. Unpublished submissions. "We give special but not exclusive consideration to works by Ohio writers or about the Midwest in general. Winner is chosen from all works submitted during the year. We prefer works under 5,000 words. Writers should review the results of previous contests. Current issue is $5.95 and sample copies are $3.95. See listing in Literary and Small Circulation Magazines for more details."

AMELIA MAGAZINE AWARDS, (I), 329 "E" St., Bakersfield CA 93304. (805)323-4064. Contact: Frederick A. Raborg, Jr., editor. The Reed Smith Fiction Prize; The Willie Lee Martin Short Story Award; The Cassie Wade Short Fiction Award; The Patrick T. T. Bradshaw Fiction Award; and four annual genre awards in science fiction, romance, western and fantasy/horror. Estab. 1984. Annual. "To publish the finest fiction possible and reward the writer; to allow good writers to earn some money in small press publication. *Amelia* strives to fill that gap between major circulation magazines and quality university journals." Unpublished submissions. Length: The Reed Smith—3,000 words maximum; The Willie Lee Martin—3,500-5,000 words; The Cassie Wade—4,500 words maximum; The Patrick T. T. Bradshaw—10,000 words; the genre awards—science fiction, 5,000 words; romance, 3,000 words; western, 5,000 words; fantasy/horror, 5,000 words. Award: "Each prize consists of $200 plus publication and two copies of issue containing winner's work." The Reed Smith Fiction Prize offers two additional awards when quality merits of $100 and $50, and publication; Bradshaw Book Award: $250 plus serialization in 4 issues of *Amelia*, 2 copies. Deadlines: The Reed Smith Prize—September 1; The Willie Lee Martin—March 1; The Cassie Wade—June 1; The Patrick T. T. Bradshaw—February 15; *Amelia* fantasy/horror—February 1; *Amelia* western—April 1; *Amelia* romance—October 1; *Amelia* science fiction—December 15. Entry fee: $5. Bradshaw Award fee: $15. Contest rules for SASE. Looking for "high quality work equal to finest fiction being published today."

DISCOVER TODAY'S MOST
NOTEWORTHY
FICTION

Subscribe to *Story*, the most widely circulated literary magazine published in America.

Winner of the distinguished National Magazine Award for Fiction, *Story* contains no poetry, no essays or reviews. Just good fiction that touches the reader long after the final page is turned...fiction that will enlighten and inspire you as a writer.

Each quarterly issue brings you a wide selection of richly textured short stories, many from yet-to-be-discovered writers. Enjoy them for the sheer pleasure of a good read—and study them to see what today's literaries are looking for in a short story.

Be on hand for the next issue of *Story*, the award-winning magazine that sets the standards for literary excellence.

illustration by R.O. Blechman

Introductory Subscription Invitation

☐ I accept! Please enter my one-year subscription and send me the next four quarterly issues for just $19. I save 20% off the single copy price!

☐ Payment enclosed. *Thank you!*   ☐ Please bill me.

☐ Charge my ☐ Visa ☐ MC

Card Number _____Exp_____

Signature_____

Name _____

Address _____Apt._____

City _____

State _____ Zip _____

STORY

*Outside U.S. add $7 (includes GST in Canada) and remit in U.S. funds.

MY 100% RISK-FREE GUARANTEE: If I'm ever dissatisfied with *Story* for any reason, I may cancel and receive a full refund for all unmailed issues.

JPNS5

"...firmly committed to discovering and showcasing the best new voices in American fiction."

—Richard Currey

Since 1931, *Story* has helped some of the finest writers of this century break into print. William Saroyan, Erskine Caldwell, Truman Capote, J.D. Salinger, Norman Mailer—to name just a few.

Today *Story* is still taking chances, publishing cutting edge stories other magazines are often too timid to touch, and introducing fresh new writing talent like Abraham Rodriguez, Jr., A.M. Homes and Susan Power.

Subscribe to *Story* today—and begin enjoying the extraordinary literary magazine that commits itself to the up-and-coming.

National Magazine Award for Fiction

NO POSTAGE
NECESSARY
IF MAILED
IN THE
UNITED STATES

BUSINESS REPLY MAIL

FIRST CLASS MAIL   PERMIT NO. 156   HARLAN, IOWA

POSTAGE WILL BE PAID BY ADDRESSEE

STORY

P O BOX 5068
HARLAN IA 51593-2568

THE AMERICAN WAY FAUX FAULKNER CONTEST, (I), *American Way Magazine, Faulkner Newsletter of Yoknapatawpha Press* and University of Mississippi, P.O. Box 248, Oxford MS 38655. (601)234-0909. "To honor William Faulkner by imitating his style, themes and subject matter in a short parody." Annual competition for a 500-word (2-pages) parody. Award: 2 round-trip tickets to Memphis, plus 2 round-trip tickets anywhere in the world that American Airlines flies. Competition receives approx. 750-1,000 submissions. Judges: Willie Morris, Barry Hannah, Wallace Stegner (judges rotate every year or so—well-known authors). Guidelines for SASE. Deadline: February 1. Previously unpublished submissions. "*American Way* (in-flight courtesy magazine of American Airlines) runs an ad for their Faux Faulkner Contest in every other issue. Winner will be notified in May—announcement made August 1, at Faulkner's home in Oxford MS. Contestants grant publication rights and the right to release entries to other media—to the sponsors."

SHERWOOD ANDERSON SHORT FICTION PRIZE, (I), *Mid-American Review*, Dept. of English, Bowling Green State University, Bowling Green OH 43403. (419)372-2725. Contact: Ellen Behrens, fiction editor. Award frequency is subject to availability of funds. "To encourage the writer of quality short fiction." No entry fee. No deadline. Unpublished material. "Winners are selected from stories published by the magazine, so submission for publication is the first step."

♣THE ANNUAL/ATLANTIC WRITING COMPETITIONS, (I, IV), Writers' Federation of Nova Scotia, Suite 901, 1809 Barrington St., Halifax, Nova Scotia B3J 3K8 Canada. (902)423-8116. Executive Director: Jane Buss. "To recognize and encourage unpublished writers in the region of Atlantic Canada. (Competition only open to residents of Nova Scotia, Newfoundland, Prince Edward Island and New Brunswick, the four Atlantic Provinces.)" Annual competition for short stories, novels, poetry, nonfiction, children's writing, drama, magazine feature/essay. Award: Various cash awards. Competition receives approximately 10-12 submissions for novels; 75 for poetry; 75 for children's; 75 for short stories; 10 for nonfiction. Judges: Professional writers, librarians, booksellers. Entry fee $15/entry. Guidelines for SASE. Unpublished submissions.

***ANTIETAM REVIEW* LITERARY AWARD, (I, IV),** *Antietam Review*, 7 W. Franklin St., Hagerstown MD 21740. (301)791-3132. Executive Editor: Susanne Kass. Annual award to encourage and give recognition to excellence in short fiction. Open to writers from Maryland, Pennsylvania, Virginia, West Virginia, Washington DC and Delaware. "We consider only previously unpublished work. We read manuscripts between September 1 and February 1." Award: $100 plus $100 for the story; the story is printed as lead in the magazine. "We consider all fiction mss sent to *Antietam Review* as entries for the prize. We look for well-crafted, serious literary prose fiction under 5,000 words." Award dependent on funding situation. Send #10 SASE for guidelines.

♣ANVIL PRESS 3-DAY NOVEL WRITING CONTEST, (I), Anvil Press, Box 1575, Station A, Vancouver, British Columbia V6C 2P7 Canada. (604)876-8710. Contact: Editor. Contest to write the best novel in 3 days, held every Labor Day weekend. Annual for unpublished novels. "Prize is publication." Receives approximately 500 entries for each award. Judges: Anvil Press editorial board. Entry fee $15. Guidelines for SASE or SAE and IRC. Deadline: Friday before Labor Day weekend. "Entrants must register with Anvil Press. Winner is announced October 31."

ARIZONA AUTHORS' ASSOCIATION NATIONAL LITERARY CONTEST, (I), Suite 117, 3509 E. Shea Blvd., Phoenix AZ 85028. (602)942-4240. Contact: Gerry Benninger. Estab. 1981. Annual award "to encourage AAA members and all other writers in the country to write regularly for competition and publication." Award: "Cash prizes totalling $1,000 for winners and honorable mentions in short stories, essays and poetry. Winning entries are published in the *Arizona Literary Magazine*." Entry fee: $6 for poetry, $8 for essays and short stories. Contest rules for SASE. Deadline: July 29. Unpublished submissions. Looking for "strong concept; good, effective writing, with emphasis on the subject/story."

 The maple leaf symbol before a listing indicates a Canadian contest.

ARIZONA COMMISSION ON THE ARTS CREATIVE WRITING FELLOWSHIPS, (I, IV), 417 W. Roosevelt St., Phoenix AZ 85003. (602)255-5882. Literature Director: Tonda Gorton. Fellowships awarded in alternate years to fiction writers and poets. Award: $5,000-7,500. Judges: Out-of-state writers/ editors. Next deadline for fiction writers: September 9, 1995. Arizona resident poets and writers over 18 years of age only.

ARTIST TRUST ARTIST FELLOWSHIPS; GAP GRANTS, (I, II, IV), Artist Trust, #415, 1402 Third Ave., Seattle WA 98101-2118. (206)467-8734. Awards Coordinator: Gabrielle Dean. Awards to "offer direct support to individual artists in all disciplines in Washington state: The Fellowship Program and the GAP (Grants for Artist Projects) Program. Our goal is to offer financial support for an artist's creative process, therefore grants are made to generative, rather than interpretive, artists." Annual fellowships and biannual grants for short stories, novels and story collections. Awards: $5,000 fellowship; up to $1,000 GAP. Competition receives approx. 200-300 submissions. Judges: Fellowship—Peer panel of 3 professional artists and arts professionals in each discipline; GAP—Interdisciplinary peer panel of 6-8 artists and arts professionals. Guidelines for SASE. Deadlines: Fellowship—winter; ; GAP—spring and fall. Limited to Washington state artists only. Students not eligible.

ASF TRANSLATION PRIZE, (II, IV), American-Scandinavian Foundation, 725 Park Ave., New York NY 10021. (212)879-9779. Contact: Publishing office. Estab. 1980. Annual award "to encourage the translation and publication of the best of contemporary Scandinavian poetry and fiction and to make it available to a wider American audience." Competition includes submissions of poetry, drama, literary prose and fiction translations. Award: $2,000, a bronze medallion and publication in *Scandinavian Review*. Competition rules and entry forms available with SASE. Deadline: June 1. Submissions must have been previously published in the original Scandinavian language. No previously translated material. Original authors should have been born within past 200 years.

‡THE ISAAC ASIMOV AWARD, (I, IV), International Association for the Fantastic in the Arts and *Asimov*'s magazine, Isaac Asimov Award, USF 3177, 4204 E. Fowler, Tampa FL 33620-3177. (813)974-6792. Awards Coordinator: Rick Wilber. "The award honors the legacy of one of science fiction's most distinguished authors through an award aimed at undergraduate writers." Annual award for short stories. Award: $500 and consideration for publication in *Asimov's*. Judges: *Asimov*'s editors. No entry fee. Guidelines available for SASE (IRCs). Deadline: November 15. Unpublished submissions. Full-time college undergraduates only.

✸ASTED/GRAND PRIX DE LITTERATURE JEUNESSE DU QUEBEC-ALVINE-BELISLE, (III, IV), Association pour l'avancement des sciences et des techniques de la documentation, 1030 rue Cherrier, Bureau 505, Montréal, Québec H2L 1H7 Canada. (514)521-9561. President: Johanne Petel. "Prize granted for the best work in youth literature edited in French in the Quebec Province. Authors and editors can participate in the contest." Annual competition for fiction and nonfiction for children and young adults. Award: $500. Deadline: June 1. Contest entry limited to editors of books published during the preceding year. French translations of other languages are not accepted.

THE ATHENAEUM LITERARY AWARD, (II, IV), The Athenaeum of Philadelphia, 219 S. 6th St., Philadelphia PA 19106. Contact: Literary Award Committee. Annual award to recognize and encourage outstanding literary achievement in Philadelphia and its vicinity. Award: A bronze medal bearing the name of the award, the seal of the Athenaeum, the title of the book, the name of the author and the year. Judged by committee appointed by Board of Directors. Deadline: December. Submissions must have been published during the preceding year. Nominations shall be made in writing to the Literary Award Committee by the author, the publisher or a member of the Athenaeum, accompanied by a copy of the book. The Athenaeum Literary Award is granted for a work of general literature, not exclusively for fiction. Juvenile fiction is not included. .

AWP AWARD SERIES IN THE NOVEL AND SHORT FICTION, (I), The Associated Writing Programs, c/o Old Dominion University, Norfolk VA 23529-0079. Annual award. The AWP Award Series was established in cooperation with several university presses in order to publish and make fine fiction available to a wide audience. Awards: $1,500 honorarium and publication with a university press. In addition, AWP tries to place mss of finalists with participating presses. Judges: Distinguished writers in each genre. Entry fee $15 nonmembers, $10 AWP members. Contest/award rules for SASE. Mss must be postmarked between January 1-February 29. Only book-length mss in the novel and short story collections are eligible. Manuscripts previously published in their entirety, including self-publishing, are not eligible. No mss returned.

AWP INTRO JOURNALS PROJECT, (I, IV), Old Dominion University, Norfolk VA 23529-0079. (804)683-3840. Contact: Charles Fort. "This is a prize for students in AWP member university creative writing programs only. Authors are nominated by the head of the creative writing department. Each school may send 2 nominated short stories." Annual competition for short stories. Award: $50 plus publication in participating journal. 1993 journals included *New England Review, Puerto del Sol, Indiana Review, Quarterly West, Mid-American Review, Willow Springs* and *Hayden's Ferry Review*. Judges: AWP. Deadline: December 18. Unpublished submissions.

MILDRED L. BATCHELDER AWARD, (II), Association for Library Service to Children/American Library Association, 50 E. Huron St., Chicago IL 60611. (312)944-6780. To encourage international exchange of quality children's books by recognizing US publishers of such books in translation. Annual competition for translations. Award: Citation. Judge: Mildred L. Batchelder award committee. Guidelines for SASE. Deadline: December. Books should be US trade publications for which children, up to and including age 14, are potential audience.

GEORGE BENNETT FELLOWSHIP, (I), Phillips Exeter Academy, Exeter NH 03833. (603)772-4311. Coordinator, Selection Committee: Charles Pratt. "To provide time and freedom from monetary concerns to a person contemplating or pursuing a career as a professional writer." Annual award of writing residency. Award: A stipend ($5,000 at present), plus room and board for academic year. Competition receives approximately 130 submissions. Judges are a committee of the English department. Entry fee $5. SASE for application form and guidelines. Deadline: December 1.

BEST FIRST MALICE DOMESTIC NOVEL, (I, IV), Thomas Dunne Books, St. Martin's Press, 175 Fifth Ave., New York NY 10010. "To publish a writer's first 'malice domestic novel.' " Annual competition for novels. Award: Publication by St. Martin's Press in the US. Advance: $10,000 (and standard royalties). Judges are selected by sponsors. Guidelines for SASE. Deadline: November 1. Unpublished submissions. "Open to any professional or nonprofessional writer who has never published a malice domestic novel and who is not under contract with a publisher to publish one. Malice domestic is a traditional mystery novel that is not hardboiled; emphasis is on the solution rather than the details of the crime. Suspects and victims know one another. In marginal cases, judges will decide whether entry qualifies."

‡BEST FIRST NEW MYSTERY AWARD, (I, IV), *New Mystery Magazine*, Suite 2001, 175 Fifth Ave., New York NY 10010. (212)353-1582. Awards coordinator: Linda Wong. Award to "find the best new mystery, crime or suspense writer, and promote high standards in the short story form." Annual award for short stories. Award: publication in *New Mystery Magazine*. Competition receives approximately 800 submissions. Judges: editorial panel of veteran mystery writers. No entry fee. No guidelines available. Deadline: July 4. Unpublished submissions. Word length: 1,000-5,000 words.

BEST FIRST PRIVATE EYE NOVEL CONTEST, (I, IV), Private Eye Writers of America, Thomas Dunne Books, St. Martin's Press, 175 Fifth Ave., New York NY 10010. Annual award. To publish a writer's first "private eye" novel. Award: Publication of novel by St. Martin's Press. Advance: $10,000 against royalties (standard contract). Judges are selected by sponsors. Guidelines for SASE. Deadline: August 1. Unpublished submissions. "Open to any professional or nonprofessional writer who has never published a 'private eye' novel and who is not under contract with a publisher for the publication of a 'private eye' novel. As used in the rules, private eye novel means: a novel in which the main character is an independent investigator who is not a member of any law enforcement or government agency."

‡BEST OF SOFT SCIENCE FICTION CONTEST, (II, IV), Soft SF Writers Assoc., 1277 Joan Dr., Merritt Island FL 32952. (407)454-2424. Contest Director: Lela E. Buis. Award to "encourage the publication of science fiction styles in which values, emotional content and artistic effect are emphasized rather than plot and deterministic science. Adult issues are encouraged, but gratuitous violence and graphic sex are not the emotional impacts we want." Annual award for short stories. Awards: $100 (1st prize), $50 (2nd prize), $25 (3rd prize). Received 100 entries in 1993 (first year of contest). Judges: members of the Soft SF Writers Association. No entry fee. Guidelines for SASE. Entries accepted October 1 through December 15. Entries must have been submitted for publication or published between January 1 and December 15. Word length: 7,000 words. Story must have elements of science fiction, though cross-genre stories are acceptable. Judging criteria: emotional impact, artistic style, clarity, originality, characterization, theme weight, imagery, sensuality; violence or sex added for shock value are discouraged. Format: Send disposable manuscript in standard format. Securely attach name and address.

IRMA S. AND JAMES H. BLACK CHILDREN'S BOOK AWARD, (II), Bank Street College, 610 W. 112th St., New York NY 10025. (212)875-4452, ext. 587. Children's Librarian: Linda Greengrass. Annual award "to honor the young children's book published in the preceding year judged the most outstanding in text as well as in art. Book must be published the year preceding the May award." Award: Press luncheon at Harvard Club, a scroll and seals by Maurice Sendak for attaching to award book's run. No entry fee. Deadline: January 15. "Write to address above. Usually publishers submit books they want considered, but individuals can too. No entries are returned."

‡JAMES TAIT BLACK MEMORIAL PRIZES, (III, IV), Department of English Literature, University of Edinburgh, Edinburgh EH8 9JX Scotland. Contact: Professor C.I.E. Donaldson. "Two prizes are awarded: one for the best work of fiction, one for the best biography or work of that nature, published during the calendar year." Annual competition for short stories, novels and story collections. Award: £1,500 each. Competition receives approx. 200 submissions. Judge: Professor C.I.E. Donaldson, Chairman, Dept. of English Literature. Guidelines for SASE or SAE and IRC. Deadline: November 30. Previously published submissions. "Eligible works are those written in English, originating with a British publisher, and first published in Britain in the year of the award. Works should be submitted by publishers."

THE BLACK WARRIOR REVIEW LITERARY AWARD, (II, III), P.O. Box 2936, Tuscaloosa AL 35486. (205)348-4518. Editor: Leigh Ann Sackrider. "Award is to recognize the best fiction published in *BWR* in a volume year. Only fiction accepted for publication is considered for the award." Competition is for short stories and novel chapters. Award: $500. Competition receives approximately 3,000 submissions. Prize awarded by an outside judge.

BOARDMAN TASKER PRIZE, (III, IV), 14 Pine Lodge, Dairyground Rd., Bramhall, Stockport, Cheshire SK7 2HS United Kingdom. Contact: Mrs. D. Boardman. "To reward a book which has made an outstanding contribution to mountain literature. A memorial to Peter Boardman and Joe Tasker, who disappeared on Everest in 1982." Award: £2,000. Competition receives approx. 15 submissions. Judges: A panel of 3 judges elected by trustees. Guidelines for SASE or SAE and IRC. Deadline: August 1. Limited to works published or distributed in the UK for the first time between November 1 and October 31. Publisher's entry only. "May be fiction, nonfiction, poetry or drama. Not an anthology. The prize is not primarily for fiction though that is not excluded. Subject must be concerned with mountain environment. Previous winners have been books on expeditions, climbing experiences; a biography of a mountaineer; novels."

BOSTON GLOBE-HORN BOOK AWARDS, (II), *Boston Globe* Newspaper, *Horn Book Magazine*, 14 Beacon St., Boston MA 02108. Annual award. "To honor most outstanding children's fiction or poetry, picture and nonfiction books published within the US." Award: $500 first prize in each category; silver plate for the 2 honor books in each category. No entry fee. Entry forms or rules for SASE. Deadline: May 15. Previously published material from July 1-June 30 of previous year.

‡BOSTON REVIEW SHORT STORY CONTEST, (II), *Boston Review*, 33 Harrison Ave., Boston MA 02111. Annual award for short stories. Guidelines for 1994 contest were not set at press time. Send SASE for details.

BRANDEIS UNIVERSITY CREATIVE ARTS AWARDS, (III), Brandeis University, Irving Enclave, Commission Office, Waltham MA 02254-9110. (617)736-3021 or 736-3010. Special Assistants to the President: Mary R. Anderson and Suzanne Yates. Annual awards: the Poses Medal to an established artist in celebration of a lifetime of achievement; three Brandeis Awards to artists whose careers hold promise of future distinction. Awards made by internal selection only and may not be applied for.

BRAZOS BOOKSTORE (HOUSTON) AWARD (SINGLE SHORT STORY), (II, IV), The Texas Institute of Letters, P.O. Box 9032, Wichita Falls TX 76308. (817)689-4123. Awards Coordinator: James Hoggard. Award to "honor the writer of the best short story published for the first time during the calendar year before the award is given." Annual competition for short stories. Award: $500. Competition receives approx. 40-50 submissions. Judges: Panel selected by TIL Council. Guidelines for SASE.

Deadline: January 4. Previously published submissions. Entries must have appeared in print between January 1 and December 31 of the year prior to the award. "Award available to writers who, at some time, have lived in Texas at least two years consecutively or whose work has a significant Texas theme. Entries must be sent directly to the three judges. Their names and addresses are available from the TIL office. Include SASE."

BREVILOQUENCE, (I, IV), *Writer's NW*, 24450 NW Hansen Rd., Hillsboro OR 97124. (503)621-3911. Contact: L. Stovall. "To create—with 99 words or less—a story with all the important elements of the form. Only open to writers in the Northwest—Oregon, Washington, Alaska, Idaho, Montana and British Columbia." Annual competition for short stories. Award: Books—usually reference. Judges: Editors of newspaper. Entry fee $1. Deadline: May 1. Unpublished submissions.

BUMBERSHOOT WRITTEN WORKS COMPETITION, (I), Seattle's Arts Festival, P.O. Box 9750, Seattle WA 98109-0750. (206)622-5123. Editor: Judith Roche. Annual award for short stories. Awards: 18 awards of $250 for poetry or literary prose. Winners published in Bumbershoot arts magazine, *Ergo!* and read at Bumbershoot Festival. Judges are professional writers/publishers. Entry forms or rules for SASE. Deadline: Mid-February.

✹BURNABY WRITERS' SOCIETY ANNUAL COMPETITION, (I, IV), 6450 Gilpin St., Burnaby, British Columbia V5G 2J3 Canada. (604)435-6500. Annual competition to encourage creative writing in British Columbia. "Category varies from year to year." Award: $200, $100 and $50 (Canadian) prizes. Receives 400-600 entries for each award. Judge: "independent recognized professional in the field." Entry fee $5. Contest requirements for SASE. Deadline: May 31. Open to British Columbia authors only.

BUSH ARTIST FELLOWSHIPS, (I, IV), The Bush Foundation, E-900 First Nat'l Bank Building, 332 Minnesota St., St. Paul MN 55101. (612)227-5222. Contact: Sally Dixon, Program Director. "To provide artists of exemplary talent time to work in their chosen art forms." Annual grant. Award: Stipend maximum of $26,000 for 12-18 months, plus a production and travel allowance of $7,000. Competition receives approximately 550 submissions. Judges are writers, critics and editors from outside Minnesota, South Dakota, North Dakota or Wisconsin. Applicants must be at least 25 years old, and Minnesota, South Dakota, North Dakota or Western Wisconsin residents. Students not eligible.

BYLINE **MAGAZINE LITERARY AWARDS, (I, IV),** P.O. Box 130596, Edmond OK 73013. (405)348-5591. Executive editor/publisher: Marcia Preston. "To encourage our subscribers in striving for high quality writing." Annual awards for short stories and poetry. Award: $250 in each category. Judges are published writers not on the *Byline* staff. Entry fee $5 for stories; $3 for poems. Postmark deadline: December 1. "Entries should be unpublished and not have won money in any previous contest. Winners announced in February issue and published in March issue with photo and short bio. Open to subscribers only."

CALIFORNIA WRITERS' CLUB CONTEST, (I), California Writers' Club, 2214 Derby St., Berkeley CA 94705. (510)841-1217. Cash awards "to encourage writing." Prizes are cash. Competition receives varying number of submissions. Judges: Professional writers, members of California Writers' Club. Entry fee to be determined. For the contest rules, write to the Secretary. Deadline is mid-April. Next conference will be July 1995. Unpublished submissions. "Open to all."

CALIFORNIA WRITERS' ROUNDTABLE ANNUAL WRITING CONTESTS, (I), The Los Angeles Chapter, Women's National Book Association, Suite 807, 11684 Ventura Blvd., Studio City CA 91604-2652. Contact: Lou Carter Keay. Annual competition for short stories. Award: $150 first prize; $75 second prize; $25 third prize. Entry fee $5 to nonmembers of Women's National Book Association. Guidelines for SASE. Deadline: September 30. Previously unpublished submissions. 3,000 word limit. "Manuscripts must be typed, on standard paper, 8½x11 inches. Margins of one inch on all sides. The title of short story must appear on each page, all pages numbered. Send 3 copies of the short story. Include a small envelope with a card containing the author's name, address and phone number, along with the title of short story. Do not put the name of author on the manuscript itself. If you wish one copy of your manuscript returned, include a SASE."

JOHN W. CAMPBELL MEMORIAL AWARD FOR THE BEST SCIENCE-FICTION NOVEL OF THE YEAR; THEODORE STURGEON MEMORIAL AWARD FOR THE BEST SF SHORT FICTION, (II, III), Center for the Study of Science Fiction, English Dept., University of Kansas, Lawrence KS 66045. (913)864-

3380. Professor and Director: James Gunn. "To honor the best novel and short science fiction of the year." Annual competition for short stories and novels. Award: Certificate. "Winners' names are engraved on a trophy." Competition receives approx. 50-100 submissions. Judges: 2 separate juries. Deadline: May 1. For previously published submissions. "Ordinarily publishers should submit work, but authors have done so when publishers would not. Send for list of jurors."

❦CANADA COUNCIL AWARDS, (III, IV), Canada Council, P.O. Box 1047, Ottawa, Ontario K1P 5V8 Canada. (613)598-4365. The Canada Council sponsors the following awards, for which no applications are accepted. *Canada-Australia Literary Prize*: 1 prize of $3,000, awarded in alternate years to an Australian or Canadian writer for the author's complete work; *Canada-French Community of Belgium Literary Prize*: 1 prize of $3,500, awarded in alternate years to a Canadian or Belgian writer on the basis of the complete works of the writer; *Canada-Switzerland Literary Prize*: 1 prize of $2,500, awarded in alternate years to a Canadian or Swiss writer for a work published in French during the preceding 8 years.

❦CANADA COUNCIL GOVERNOR GENERAL'S LITERARY AWARDS, (III, IV), Canada Council, P.O. Box 1047, Ottawa, Ontario K1P 5V8 Canada. (613)598-4376. Contact: Writing and Publishing Section. "Awards of $10,000 each are given annually to the best English-language and best French-language Canadian work in each of seven categories: children's literature (text) and children's literature (illustration), drama, fiction, poetry, nonfiction and translation." All literary works published by Canadians between October 1 and September 30 the following year are considered. Canadian authors, illustrators and translators only. Books must be submitted by publishers and accompanied by a Publisher's Submissions Form, available from the Writing and Publishing Section.

❦CANADIAN AUTHOR STUDENT'S CREATIVE WRITING CONTEST, (I, IV), Suite 500, 275 Slater St., Ottawa, Ontario K1P 5H9 Canada. (613)233-2846. Fax: (613)235-8237. Contact: Gordon Symons. "To encourage writing among secondary school students." Annual competition for short stories. Award: $100 plus $100 to the nominating teacher; $500 to pay for undergraduate education to a worthy student enrolled at a college. Receives 100-120 submissions. Judges: Magazine editors. "Entry form in Winter and Spring issues of *Canadian Author*." Deadline: March. Unpublished submissions. Length: 2,500 words. Writer must be nominated by teacher.

❦CANADIAN AUTHORS ASSOCIATION LITERARY AWARDS (FICTION), (II, IV), Canadian Authors Association, Suite 500, 275 Slater St., Ottawa, Ontario K1P 5H9 Canada. (613)233-2846. Fax: (613)235-8237. President: Jeffrey Holmes. Annual award "to honor writing that achieves literary excellence without sacrificing popular appeal." For novels published during the previous calendar year. Award: $5,000 plus silver medal. No entry fee. Entry forms or rules for SASE. Deadline: December 15. Restricted to full-length English language novels. Author must be Canadian or Canadian landed immigrant. CAA also sponsors the Air Canada Award, literary awards as above in poetry, nonfiction and drama, and the Vicky Metcalf Awards for children's literature.

CAPRICORN BOOK AWARD—FICTION, (I), The Writer's Voice, 5 W. 63rd St., New York NY 10023. (212)875-4124. Annual competition for novels or story collections. Award: $1,000, plus featured reading. Entry fee $15. Deadline: December 31. Previously unpublished. Submit 100-200 double-spaced pages.

RAYMOND CARVER SHORT STORY CONTEST, (I, IV), Dept. of English, Humboldt State University, Arcata CA 95521-4957. Contact: Coordinator. Annual award for previously unpublished short stories. First prize: $500 and publication in *Toyon*. Second Prize: $250. Entry fee $7.50/story. SASE for rules. Deadline: November 1. For authors living in United States only. Send 2 copies of story; author's name, address, phone number and title of story on separate cover page only. Story must be no more than 25 pages. Title must appear on first page. For notification of receipt of ms, include self-addressed stamped postcard. For Winners List include SASE.

WILLA CATHER FICTION PRIZE, (I, IV), Helicon Nine Editions, 9000 W. 64th Terrace, Merriam KS 66202. (913)722-2999. Contact: Gloria Vando Hickock. Annual competition for novels, story collections and novellas. Award: $1,000. Winners chosen by nationally recognized writers. Entry fee $15. Guidelines for SASE. Deadline December 1. Unpublished submissions. Open to all writers residing in the US and its territories. Mss will not be returned.

‡CCL STUDENT WRITING CONTEST (I, IV), Conference on Christianity and Literature. Dept. of English, West Georgia College, Carrollton GA 30118. (404)836-6512. Contact: Robert Lance Snyder. Annual award. "To recognize excellence in undergraduate writing." Unpublished submissions. Award: $75, $50 and $25 awarded in book certificates. Deadline: February 15. Looking for "excellence in artistic achievement and reflection of writer's Christian premises." Contest open to all regularly enrolled undergraduate students. Entries will not be returned. Winners will be announced in summer issue of *Christianity and Literature*.

THE *CHELSEA* AWARDS, (I), P.O. Box 5880, Grand Central Station, New York NY 10163. *Mail entries to*: Richard Foerster, Associate Editor, P.O. Box 1040, York Beach ME 03910. Annual competition for short stories. Prize: $500 and publication in *Chelsea* (all entries are considered for publication). Judges: The editors. Entry fee: $10 (for which entrants also receive a subscription). Guidelines for SASE. Deadline: June 15. Unpublished submissions. Manuscripts may not exceed 30 typed pages or about 7,500 words. The stories must not be under consideration elsewhere or scheduled for book publication within 6 months of the competition deadline.

‡CHICAGO FOUNDATION FOR LITERATURE AWARD, (III, IV), Friends of Literature, P.O. Box 31486, Chicago IL 60631-0486. (312)792-2756. Contact: James W. Conklin, President. Mission statement: To aid and encourage meritorious work by American writers of fiction and nonfiction . . . novels, short stories, poetry, drama and other forms of literature, by means of prizes, awards, scholarships and other methods determined by the Foundation. Annual award for short stories, novels and story collections. Award: $500 each for fiction and nonfiction; $250 for poetry. Competition receives approximately 50 entries for each award. Judges: Friends of Literature Board of Directors. No entry fee. Guidelines available for SASE. Deadline: January 15, 1995. Previously published submissions. Writers must be either native to the Chicago area or have lived there some time in their lives. Works must be submitted by a recognized publisher.

CHILD STUDY CHILDREN'S BOOK AWARD, (III, IV), Child Study Children's Book Committee at Bank St. College, 610 W. 112th St., New York NY 10025. Contact: Anita Wilkes Dore, Committee Chair. Annual award. "To honor a book for children or young people which deals realistically with problems in their world. It may concern social, individual and ethical problems." Only books sent by publishers for review are considered. No personal submissions. Books must have been published within current calendar year. Award: Certificate and cash prize.

THE CHILDREN'S BOOK AWARD, (II), Federation of Children's Book Groups, 30 Senneleys Park Rd., Northfield, Birmingham B31 1AL England. Award "to promote the publication of good quality books for children." Annual award for short stories, novels, story collections and translations. Award: "Portfolio of children's writing and drawings and a magnificent trophy of silver and oak." Judges: Thousands of children from all over the United Kingdom. Guidelines for SASE or SAE and IRC. Deadline: December 31. Published and previously unpublished submissions (first publication in UK). "The book should be suitable for children."

THE CHRISTOPHER AWARD, (II), The Christophers, 12 E. 48th St., New York NY 10017. (212)759-4050. Contact: Ms. Peggy Flanagan, awards coordinator. Annual award "to encourage creative people to continue to produce works which affirm the highest values of the human spirit in adult and children's books." Published submissions only. Award: Bronze medallion. "Award judged by a grassroots panel and a final panel of experts. Juvenile works are 'children tested.' " Examples of books awarded: *Dear Mr. Henshaw*, by Beverly Cleary (ages 8-10); *Sarah, Plain and Tall*, by Patricia MacLachlan (ages 10-12).

CINTAS FELLOWSHIP, (I, II, IV), Cintas Foundation/Arts International Program of I.I.E., 809 U.N. Plaza, New York NY 10017. (212)984-5370. Contact: Vanessa Palmer. "To foster and encourage the professional development and recognition of talented Cuban creative artists. *Not* intended for furtherance of academic or professional study, nor for research or writings of a scholarly nature." Annual competition for authors of short stories, novels, story collections and poetry. 5-12 awards of $10,000 each. Fellowship receives approx. 40 literature applicants/year. Judges: Selection committee. Guidelines for SASE. Deadline: March 1. Previously published or unpublished submissions. Limited to artists of Cuban lineage *only*. "Awards are given to artists in the following fields: visual arts, literature, music composition and architecture."

✿**CITY OF REGINA WRITING AWARD, (I, IV),** City of Regina Arts Commission, Saskatchewan Writers Guild, P.O. Box 3986, Regina, Saskatchewan S4P 3R9 Canada. (306)757-6310. "To enable a writer to work for 3 months on a specific writing project; to reward merit in writing." Annual competition for short stories, novels and story collections. Award: $4,000. Competition receives approx. 21 submissions. Judges: Selection committee of SWG. Guidelines for SASE. Deadline is mid-March. Unpublished submissions. "Grant available only to residents of Regina for previous year."

COMMONWEALTH CLUB OF CALIFORNIA, (II, IV), California Book Awards, 595 Market St., San Francisco CA 94105. (415)597-6700. Contact: Annie Hayflick, Member services Manager. Main contest established in 1931. Annual. "To encourage California writers and honor literary merit." Awards: Gold and silver medals. Judges: Jury of literary experts. For books published during the year preceding the particular contest. Three copies of book and a completed entry form required. "Write or phone asking for the forms. Either an author or publisher may enter a book. We usually receive over 300 entries."

CONNECTICUT COMMISSION ON THE ARTS ARTIST GRANTS, (I, II, IV), 227 Lawrence St., Hartford CT 06106. (203)566-4770. Program Manager: Linda Dente. "To support the creation of new work by a creative artist *living in Connecticut.*" Biennial competition for the creation or completion of new works in literature, i.e. short stories, novels, story collections, poetry and playwriting. Award: $5,000. Judges: Peer professionals (writers, editors). Guidelines available in August. Deadline: January 1996. Writers may send either previously published or unpublished submissions—up to 10 pages of material. Connecticut residents only.

‡**COUNCIL FOR WISCONSIN WRITERS ANNUAL WRITING CONTEST (II, IV),** Box 55322, Madison WI 53705. President: Russell King. "To recognize excellence in Wisconsin writing published during the year in 12 categories." Annual competition for short stories and novels. Award: $500 for 9 categories, $1,000 for 2 categories, $1,500 for 1 category. Competition receives between 5 and 80 entries, depending on category. Judges: qualified judges from other states. Entry fee $15/for nonmembers only. Guidelines for SASE (IRCs). Previously published submissions. Wisconsin residents only. Official entry form (available in November) required. Deadline: mid-January.

CRIME WRITERS' ASSOCIATION AWARDS, (III, IV), Box 172, Tring Herts HP23 5LP England. Six awards. Annual awards for crime novels. Deadline: October 1. Published submissions in UK in current year. Book must be nominated by UK publishers.

THE CRITIC **BIANNUAL SHORT STORY CONTEST, (I),** *The CRITIC* magazine, Thomas More Association, 6th Floor, 205 W. Monroe, Chicago IL 60606-5097. (312)609-8880. "To foster original fiction (short story) writing by new or established writers." Biannual competition for short stories. Award: $1,000. Competition receives approx. 250-300 submissions. Judges: Editorial staff of the Thomas More Association. Guidelines for SASE. Limit one submission. Next contest tentatively set for 1994. Deadline September 1 or 15, 1994. Previously unpublished. "No regional restrictions or word-length requirements, but 3,500 to 4,000 words is considered appropriate. Entrants should be aware that *The CRITIC* is a Catholic, cultural and literary magazine."

THE *CRUCIBLE* POETRY AND FICTION COMPETITION, (I), *Crucible*, Barton College, College Station, Wilson NC 27893. Annual competition for short stories. Award: $150 (1st prize); $100 (2nd prize) and publication in *Crucible*. Judges: The editors. Guidelines for SASE. Deadline April. Unpublished submissions. Fiction should be 8,000 words or less.

DALY CITY POETRY AND SHORT STORY CONTEST, (I), Daly City History, Arts and Science Commission, % Serramonte Library, 40 Wembley Dr., Daly City CA 94015. (415)991-8025. Contest coordinator: Ruth Hoppin. "To encourage poets and writers and to recognize and reward excellence." Annual competition for short stories. Awards: $35, $20, $10 and $5. Competition receives 50 submissions. Judges are usually teachers of creative writing. Entry fee: $2/story. Guidelines for SASE. Deadline January 2. Unpublished submissions. Length: 3,000 words maximum. "No profanity."

MARGUERITE DE ANGELI PRIZE, (I), Doubleday Books for Young Readers, 666 Fifth Ave., New York NY 10103. "To encourage the writing of fiction that examines the diversity of the American experience in the same spirit as the works of Marguerite de Angeli." Open to US and Canadian writers. Annual competition for first novels for middle-grade readers (ages 7-10). Award: One Doubleday hardcover and Dell paperback book contract, with $1,500 cash prize and $3,500 advance against royalties. Judges: Editors of Doubleday Books for Young Readers. Guidelines for SASE (IRCs). Deadline: Submissions must be postmarked between April 1 and June 30. Previously unpublished (middle-grade) fiction.

DEEP SOUTH WRITERS CONFERENCE ANNUAL COMPETITION, (I), DSWC Inc., English Dept., University of Southwestern Louisiana, P.O. Box 44691, Lafayette LA 70504. (318)231-6908. Contact: Carl Wooton, director. Annual awards "to encourage aspiring, unpublished writers." Awards: Certificates and cash plus possible publication of shorter works. Contest rules for SASE and addition to mailing list. Deadline: July 15. Unpublished submissions.

DELACORTE PRESS ANNUAL PRIZE FOR A FIRST YOUNG ADULT NOVEL (I), Delacorte Press, Department BFYR, 1540 Broadway, New York NY 10036. (212)354-6500. Estab. 1983. Annual award "to encourage the writing of contemporary young adult fiction." Award: Contract for publication of book; $1,500 cash prize and a $6,000 advance against royalties. Judges are the editors of Delacorte Press Books for Young Readers. Contest rules for SASE. Unpublished submissions; fiction with a contemporary setting that will be suitable for ages 12-18. Deadline: December 31 (no submissions accepted prior to Labor Day). Writers may be previously published, but cannot have published a young adult novel before.

DELAWARE STATE ARTS COUNCIL, (I, IV), 820 N. French St., Wilmington DE 19801. (302)577-3540. Coordinator: Barbara R. King. "To help further careers of emerging and established professional artists." Annual awards for Delaware residents only. Awards: $5,000 for established professionals; $2,000 for emerging professionals. Judges are out-of-state professionals in each division. Entry forms or rules for SASE. Deadline: March 1.

●*DREAMS & VISIONS*: BEST SHORT STORY OF THE YEAR, (I, IV), Skysong Press, RR1, Washago, Ontario L0K 2B0 Canada. Contact: Steve Stanton. The "competition serves the dual purpose of rewarding literary excellence among the authors published in *Dreams & Visions*, and of providing feedback from subscribers as to the type of literature they prefer." Annual award for short stories. Award: $100. "Only the 21 stories published in *Dreams & Visions* each year are eligible for the award." Judges: Subscribers to *Dreams & Visions*. Guidelines for SASE. Unpublished submissions. Sample copy $3.95.

EATON LITERARY ASSOCIATES' LITERARY AWARDS PROGRAM, (I), Eaton Literary Associates, P.O. Box 49795, Sarasota FL 34230. (813)366-6589. Vice President: Richard Lawrence. Biannual award for short stories and novels. Award: $2,500 for best book-length ms, $500 for best short story. Competition receives approximately 2,000 submissions annually. Judges are 2 staff members in conjunction with an independent agency. Entry forms or rules for SASE. Deadline: March 31 for short stories; August 31 for book-length mss.

EYSTER PRIZES, (II), *The New Delta Review*, LSU/Dept. of English, Baton Rouge LA 70803. (504)388-5922. Editors: Randi Gray, Nicola Mason, Catherine Williamson. "To honor author and teacher Warren Eyster, who served as advisor to *New Delta Review* predecessors *Manchac* and *Delta*." Semiannual awards for best short story and best poem in each issue. Award: $50 and 2 free copies of publication. Competition receives approximately 400 submissions/issue. Judges are published authors. Deadlines: September 1 for fall, February 15 for spring.

ROBERT L. FISH MEMORIAL AWARD, (II, IV), Mystery Writers of America, Inc., 6th Floor, 17 E. 47th St., New York NY 10017. Estab. 1984. Annual award "to encourage new writers in the mystery/detective/suspense short story — and, subsequently, larger work in the genre." Award: $500 and plaque. Judges: The MWA committee for best short story of the year in the mystery genre. Deadline: December 1. Previously published submissions published the year prior to the award. Looking for "a story with a crime that is central to the plot that is well written and distinctive."

DOROTHY CANFIELD FISHER AWARD, (III), Vermont PTA, % Southwest Regional Library, Pierpoint Avenue, Rutland VT 05701. (802)828-3261. Contact: Grace Greene, chairperson. Estab. 1957. Annual award. "To encourage Vermont schoolchildren to become enthusiastic and discriminating readers and to honor the memory of one of Vermont's most distinguished and beloved literary figures." Award: Illuminated scroll. Publishers send the committee review copies of books to consider. Only books of the current publishing year can be considered for next year's award. Master list of titles is drawn up in March each year. Children vote each year in the spring and the award is given before the school year ends. Submissions must be "written by living American authors, be suitable for children in grades 4-8, and have literary merit. Can be nonfiction also."

FLORIDA STATE WRITING COMPETITION, (I), Florida Freelance Writers Association, Maple Ridge Rd., North Sandwich NH 03259. (603)284-6367. "To offer additional opportunities for writers to earn income from their stories." Annual competition for short stories and novels. Award: Varies from $50-150. Competition receives approx. 300 short stories; 125 novels. Judges: Authors, editors and teachers. Entry fee from $5-15. Guidelines for SASE. Deadline: March 15. Unpublished submissions. Categories include literary, science fiction/fantasy, genre and novel chapter. Length: 7,500 words maximum. "Guidelines are revised each year and subject to change. New guidelines are available in fall of each year."

✸FOUNDATION FOR THE ADVANCEMENT OF CANADIAN LETTERS AUTHOR'S AWARDS, (II, IV), In conjunction with Periodical Marketers of Canada (PMC), Suite 503, 2 Berkeley St., Toronto, Ontario M5A 2W3 Canada. (416)363-8779. Award Coordinators: Ray Argyle, Janette Hatcher. "To recognize outstanding Canadian writing and design." Annual award for short stories, novels. Previous competition judged by an independent panel. Deadline: July 15. "Must be published in a Canadian 'mass market' publication."

FRIENDS OF AMERICAN WRITERS AWARDS, (III, IV), #1602, 5555 N. Sheridan Rd., Chicago IL 60640. Contact: President. "To encourage high standards and to promote literary ideals among American writers." Annual award for prose writing. Awards: $1,200 (1st prize) and $750 (2nd prize). Judges: a committee of 14. Deadline: December 31. Manuscripts must have been published during current year. Limited to midwestern authors who have previously published no more than 3 books; or to authors of books set in the midwest and have not published more than 3 books previously. Two copies of the book are to be submitted to awards chairman by the publisher of the book. Young Peoples' books awards judged by committee of 9. Awards: $700 (1st prize); $400 (2nd prize). Same limitations.

GEORGIA COUNCIL FOR THE ARTS INDIVIDUAL ARTIST GRANTS, (I, IV), Suite 115, 530 Means St. NW, Atlanta GA 30318. (404)651-7920. Contact: Ann Davis. Annual award for "artist's option for creation of new work." Award: $5,000 maximum. Competition receives approximately 125 submissions. Judges: Professional advisory panel. Guidelines for SASE (IRCs). Deadline April 1. "Support material must be current within past two years; application must be for new work. Artist must be resident of Georgia for at least one year prior to application date."

‡GLIMMER TRAIN STORIES ANNUAL NW SHORT-STORY AWARD FOR NEW WRITERS, (I), Glimmer Train Press, Inc., #1205, 812 S.W. Washington St., Portland OR 97205. Annual competition for short stories. Winner receives $1,200, publication in Fall *Glimmer Train Stories* and 20 copies of that issue. First/second runners up will receive $500/$300 respectively and honorable mention in Fall issue. Judges: Editors of *GTS*. Entry fee $10. Guidelines for SASE. Submissions must be postmarked between February 1 and March 31. Unpublished submissions. "Open to any writer whose fiction has not appeared in a nationally distributed publication. In addition to reading fee, include cover letter with your name, address, phone and the words 'NW Short-Story Award for New Writers.' No more than 2 stories per entry, sent in the same envelope. We cannot acknowledge receipt or provide status of any particular ms." All applicants receive the Fall issue.

GOLD MEDALLION BOOK AWARDS, (III, IV), Evangelical Christian Publishers Association, Suite 101, 3225 S. Hardy Dr., Tempe AZ 85282. (602)966-3998. Executive Director of ECPA: Doug Ross. Annual award to "encourage excellence in evangelical Christian book publishing in 21 categories." Judges: "At least eight judges for each category chosen from among the ranks of evangelical leaders and book-review editors." Entry fee $100 for ECPA member publishers; $250 for non-member publishers. Deadline: December 1. For books published the previous year: Publishers submit entries.

THE WILLIAM GOYEN PRIZE FOR FICTION, (I), *TriQuarterly Magazine*, 2020 Ridge Ave., Evanston IL 60208-4302. (708)491-7614. "To award outstanding fiction; to bring recognition to newer/lesser-known writers." Biennial award for novels. Award: $3,000 and publication by TriQuarterly Books/Northwestern University Press. Competition receives approx. 350 submissions. Entry fee $15, includes 1-year subscription; $5 for current subscribers. Guidelines for SASE. Postmark deadline: June 1-3.

Award is biennial, held in 1995, 1997, etc. "Mss should be 150-400 pages in length, double-spaced. Original works in English and translations into English are eligible. Enclose SASE for return of your manuscript and our reply. Entry fee subject to change."

GREAT LAKES COLLEGES ASSOCIATION NEW WRITERS AWARDS, (III), Great Lakes Colleges Association, Wabash College, Crawfordsville IN 47933. Director: Marc Hudson. Annual award "to recognize new young writers; promote and encourage interest in good literature." For first books published "during the year preceding each year's February 28 deadline for entry, or the following spring." Award: "Invited tour of up to 12 Great Lakes Colleges (usually 7 or 8) with honoraria and expenses paid." Award judged by critics and writers in residence at Great Lakes Colleges Association colleges and universities. Entry form or rules for SASE. "Entries in fiction (there is also a poetry section) must be first novels or first volumes of short stories already published, and must be submitted (four copies) *by publishers only* —but this may include privately published books. Only one entry per publisher in each genre."

GREAT PLAINS STORYTELLING & POETRY READING CONTEST, (I,II), P.O. Box 438, Walnut IA 51577. (712)784-3001. Director: Robert Everhart. Estab. 1976. Annual award "to provide an outlet for writers to present not only their works, but also to provide a large audience for their presentation *live* by the writer. Attendance at the event, which takes place annually in Avoca, Iowa, is *required*." Award: 1st prize $75; 2nd prize $50; 3rd prize $25; 4th prize $15; and 5th prize $10. Entry fee: $5. Entry forms or rules for SASE. Deadline is day of contest, which takes place over Labor Day Weekend. Previously published or unpublished submissions.

THE GREENSBORO REVIEW LITERARY AWARDS, (I), Dept. of English, UNC-Greensboro, Greensboro NC 27412. (919)334-5459. Editor: Jim Clark. Annual award. Award: $250. Contest rules for SASE. Deadline: September 15. Unpublished submissions.

‡GUARDIAN CHILDREN'S FICTION AWARD, (II, IV), The Guardian, 119 Farringdon Rd., London EC1R 3ER England. Contact: Joanna Carey, children's books editor. "To recognize an outstanding work of children's fiction—and gain publicity for the field of children's books." Annual competition for fiction. Award: £1000. Competition receives approx. 100 submissions. Judges: 4 eminent children's writers plus children's books editor of the *Guardian*. Deadline: December 31. "British or Commonwealth authors only; published in UK; no picture books. Awarded every March for book published in previous year."

HACKNEY LITERARY AWARDS, (I), Box A-3, Birmingham Southern College, Birmingham AL 35254. (205)226-4921. Contact: Special Events Office. Annual award for previously unpublished short stories, poetry and novels. Rules/entry form for SASE. Novel submissions must be postmarked on or before September 30. Short stories and poetry submissions must be postmarked on or before December 31.

HAMMETT PRIZE (NORTH AMERICAN), (II, IV), International Association of Crime Writers, North American Branch, JAF Box 1500, New York NY 10116. (212)757-3915. Award to promote "excellence in the field of crime writing as reflected in a book published in the English language in the US and/ or Canada." Annual competition for novels or nonfiction. Award: trophy. Competition receives approx. 150 submissions. Judges: Nominations committee made up of IACW members screens titles and selects 3-5 nominated books. These go to three outside judges, who choose the winner. Guidelines for SASE. Deadline: December 1. Previously published submissions. Published entries must have appeared in print between January 1 and December 31 (of contest year). "Writers must be US or Canadian citizens or permanent residents working in the field of crime writing (either fiction or nonfiction). No word-length requirement."

BAXTER HATHAWAY PRIZE, (I), *Epoch Magazine*, 251 Goldwin Smith, Cornell University, Ithaca NY 14853-3201. (607)255-3385. Contact: Michael Koch. Award "to honor the memory of Baxter Hathaway, founder of *Epoch*, and to encourage new poets and fiction writers." Biennial award for a novella or long poem, depending on the year (1995, novella; 1997, long poem). Award: $1,000 and publication in *Epoch*. Competition receives 400+ submissions. Judge: A distinguished outsider. Guidelines for SASE. Sample copies with past winners for $4 each. Unpublished submissions. "Limited to writers who have published not more than one book of fiction or poetry (chapbooks excluded)."

‡THE HEARTLAND PRIZES, (II), *The Chicago Tribune*, 435 N. Michigan Ave., Chicago IL 60611-4041. "The Heartland Prizes are for nonfiction and the novel. To honor a novel and a book of nonfiction embodying the spirit of the nation's Heartland." Annual competition for novels. Award: $5,000. Previously published submissions from August 1-July 31 of the previous year. Send SASE for information. Winners are notified in August.

DRUE HEINZ LITERATURE PRIZE, (II), University of Pittsburgh Press, 127 N. Bellefield Ave., Pittsburgh PA 15260. (412)624-4111. Annual award "to support the writer of short fiction at a time when the economics of commercial publishing make it more and more difficult for the serious literary artist working in the short story and novella to find publication." Award: $7,500 and publication by the University of Pittsburgh Press. Request complete rules of the competition before submitting a manuscript. Submissions will be received only during the months of July and August. Deadline: August 31. Manuscripts must be unpublished in book form. The award is open to writers who have published a book-length collection of fiction or a minimum of three short stories or novellas in commercial magazines or literary journals of national distribution.

HEMINGWAY DAYS SHORT STORY COMPETITION, (I), Hemingway Days Festival, P.O. Box 4045, Key West FL 33041. (305)294-4440. "To honor Nobel laureate Ernest Hemingway, who was often pursued during his lifetime by young writers hoping to learn the secrets of his success." Annual competition for short stories. Awards: $1000 — 1st; $500 — 2nd; $500 — 3rd. Competition receives approx. 900 submissions. Judges: Panel lead by Lorian Hemingway, granddaughter of Ernest Hemingway and novelist based out of Seattle, WA. Entry fee $10/story. Deadline: July 1. "Open to anyone so long as the work is unpublished. No longer than 2,500 words." Send SASE for guidelines.

ERNEST HEMINGWAY FOUNDATION AWARD, (II), PEN American Center, 568 Broadway, New York NY 10012. Contact: John Morrone, coordinator of programs. Annual award "to give beginning writers recognition and encouragement and to stimulate interest in first novels among publishers and readers." Award: $7,500. Novels or short story collections must have been published during calendar year under consideration. Entry form or rules for SASE. Deadline: December 31. "The Ernest Hemingway Foundation Award is given to an American author of the best first-published book-length work of fiction published by an established publishing house in the US each calendar year."

THE O. HENRY AWARDS, (III), Doubleday, 1540 Broadway, New York NY 10036. Associate Editor: Arabella Meyer. Annual award "to honor the memory of O. Henry with a sampling of outstanding short stories and to make these stories better known to the public." These awards are published by Doubleday in hardcover and by Anchor Books in paperback every spring. Previously published submissions. "All selections are made by the editor of the volume, William Abrahams. No stories may be submitted."

HIGHLIGHTS FOR CHILDREN, (I, IV), 803 Church St., Honesdale PA 18431. Editor: Kent L. Brown, Jr. "To honor quality stories (previously unpublished) for young readers." Three $1,000 awards. Stories: up to 500 words for beginning readers (to age 8) and 900 words for more advanced readers (ages 9 to 12). No minimum word length. No entry form necessary. To be submitted between January 1 and February 28 to "Fiction Contest" at address above. "No violence, crime or derogatory humor." Nonwinning entries returned in June if SASE is included with ms. "This year's category is action/adventure stories for children." Send SASE for information.

THE ALFRED HODDER FELLOWSHIP, (II), The Council of the Humanities, Princeton University, 122 E. Pyne, Princeton NJ 08544. Executive Director: Carol Rigolot. "This fellowship is awarded for the pursuit of independent work in the humanities. The recipient is usually a writer or scholar in the early stages of his or her career, a person 'with more than ordinary learning' and with 'much more than ordinary intellectual and literary gifts.' " Traditionally, the Hodder Fellow has been a humanist outside

---

Market categories: (I) Unpublished entries; (II) Published entries nominated by the author; (III) Entries nominated by the editor, publisher or nominating body; (IV) Specialized entries.

of academia. Candidates for the Ph.D. are not eligible. Award: $40,000. The Hodder Fellow spends an academic year in residence at Princeton working independently. Judges: Princeton Committee on Humanistic Studies. Deadline: November 15. Applicants must submit a résumé, a sample of previous work (10 page maximum, not returnable), and a project proposal of 2 to 3 pages. Letters of recommendation are not required.

THEODORE CHRISTIAN HOEPFNER AWARD, (I), *Southern Humanities Review*, 9088 Haley Center, Auburn University AL 36849. Contact: Dan R. Latimer or R.T. Smith, co-editors. Annual. "To award the authors of the best essay, the best short story and the best poem published in *SHR* each year." Award: $100 for the best short story. Judges: Editorial staff. Unpublished submissions to the magazine only. Only published work in the current volume (4 issues) will be judged.

HONOLULU MAGAZINE/PARKER PEN COMPANY FICTION CONTEST, (I, IV), *Honolulu* Magazine, 36 Merchant St., Honolulu HI 96813. (808)524-7400. Editor: John Heckathorn. "We do not accept fiction except during our annual contest, at which time we welcome it." Annual award for short stories. Award: $1,000 and publication in the April issue of *Honolulu* Magazine. Competition receives approximately 400 submissions. Judges: Panel of well-known Hawaii-based writers. Rules for SASE. Deadline: early December. "Stories must have a Hawaii theme, setting and/or characters. Author should enclose name and address in separate small envelope. Do not put name on story."

HOUSEWIFE WRITER'S FORUM SHORT STORY CONTEST, (I), Housewife-Writer's Forum, P.O. Box 780, Lyman WY 82937. (307)786-4513. "To give new fiction writers a chance to have their work recognized." Annual contest for short stories. Awards: $30, $20, $10. Competition receives approx. 75 submissions. Judges: Fiction Editor Bob Haynie and Editor Diane Wolverton. Entry fee: $4. Guidelines for SASE. Unpublished submissions. Any genre except risqué; 2,000 words maximum.

L. RON HUBBARD'S WRITERS OF THE FUTURE CONTEST, (I, IV), P.O. Box 1630, Los Angeles CA 90078. Contest Administrator: Rachel Denk. Estab. 1984. Quarterly. "To find, reward and publicize new speculative fiction writers, so that they may more easily attain professional writing careers." Competition open to new and amateur writers of short stories or novelettes of science fiction or fantasy. Awards: 1st prize, $1,000; 2nd prize, $750; 3rd prize, $500. Annual grand prize $4,000. SASE for contest rules. Deadline: September 30. Unpublished submissions.

THE 'HUGO' AWARD (Science Fiction Achievement Award), (III, IV), The World Science Fiction Convention, c/o Howard DeVore, 4705 Weddel St., Dearborn Heights MI 48125. Temporary; address changes each year. "To recognize the best writing in various categories related to science fiction and fantasy." Award: Metal spaceship 15 inches high. "Winning the award almost always results in reprints of the original material and increased payment. Winning a 'Hugo' in the novel category frequently results in additional payment of $10,000-20,000 from future publishers." The award is voted on by ballot by the members of the World Science Fiction Convention from previously published material of professional publications. Writers may not nominate their own work.

‡ILLINOIS ARTS COUNCIL ARTISTS FELLOWSHIPS, (I, IV), Illinois Arts Council, #10-500, James R. Thompson Center, 100 W. Randolph, Chicago IL 60601. (312)814-4990. Contact: Richard Gage. Award "to enable Illinois artists of exceptional talent to pursue their artistic goals." Annual award for short stories, novels, story collections and creative nonfiction (essays, memoirs) completed within four years prior to the deadline. Awards: $500, $5,000 and $10,000. Competition receives approximately 165 prose submissions and 120 poetry submissions. Judges: non-Illinois writers/editors of exceptional talent. Deadline: September 1. Recipients must have been Illinois residents for at least 1 year prior to deadline. Prose applicants limited to 30 pages; poetry limited to 15 pages.

ILLINOIS STATE UNIVERSITY NATIONAL FICTION COMPETITION, (I), Illinois State University/Fiction Collective Two, English Dept., Illinois State University, Normal IL 61761. (309)438-3025. Curtis White, series editor. Annual award for novels, novellas and story collections. Award: Publication. Competition receives approximately 150 submissions each year. Judges different each year. Entry fee $10. Deadline: November 15. Entry forms or rules for SASE.

INTERNATIONAL JANUSZ KORCZAK LITERARY COMPETITION, (II, IV), Joseph H. and Belle R. Braun Center for Holocaust Studies Anti-Defamation League of B'nai B'rith, 823 United Nations Plaza, New York NY 10017. (212)490-2525. Contact: Dr. Dennis B. Klein, director. For published novels, novellas, translations, short story collections. "Books for or about children which best reflect the humanitarianism and leadership of Janusz Korczak, a Jewish and Polish physician, educator and author." Inquire for deadline.

INTERNATIONAL READING ASSOCIATION CHILDREN'S BOOK AWARDS, (II), Sponsored by IRA, P.O. Box 8139, 800 Barksdale Rd., Newark DE 19714-8139. (302)731-1600. Annual award to encourage an author who shows unusual promise in the field of children's books. Two awards will be given for a first or second book in two categories: one for literature for older children, 10-16 years old; one for literature for younger children, 4-10 years old. Award: $1,000 stipend. No entry fee. Contest/award rules and awards flyer available from IRA. Deadline: December 1. Submissions must have been published during the calendar year prior to the year in which the award is given. Send 10 copies of book to Mary Dupuis, 3203 Buffalo Run Rd., Bellefonte PA 16823.

‡INTERNATIONAL WRITERS CONTEST (I), Foster City Arts and Culture Committee, 650 Shell Blvd., Foster City CA 94404. (415)345-5731. Contact: Contest chairman. Annual. "To foster and encourage aspiring writers." Unpublished submissions. Award: 1st prize in each of five categories $250. The five categories are Best Fiction, Best Poem, Best Mystery Story, Best Story for Children and Best Science Fiction. Deadline: October 1. Winner will be notified by October 31. English language entries only. Entry fee: $10. Contest rules for SASE.

IOWA SCHOOL OF LETTERS AWARD FOR SHORT FICTION, THE JOHN SIMMONS SHORT FICTION AWARD, (I), Iowa Writers' Workshop, 436 English-Philosophy Building, The University of Iowa, Iowa City IA 52242. Annual awards for short story collections. To encourage writers of short fiction. Two awards of $1,000 each, plus publication of winning collections by University of Iowa Press the following fall. Entries must be at least 150 pages, typewritten, and submitted between August 1 and September 30. Stamped, self-addressed return packaging must accompany manuscript. Rules for SASE. Iowa Writer's Workshop does initial screening of entries; finalists (about 6) sent to outside judge for final selection. "A different well-known writer is chosen each year as judge. Any writer who has not previously published a volume of prose fiction is eligible to enter the competition for these prizes. Revised manuscripts which have been previously entered may be resubmitted."

IOWA WOMAN CONTEST, INTERNATIONAL WRITING CONTEST, (I, IV), P.O. Box 2938, Waterloo IA 50704. Annual award for short fiction, poetry and essays. Awards first place of $300; second place $150, in each category. Judges: anonymous, women writers who have published work in the category. Entry fee: (Subscriber) – $8 for one story, essay or up to 3 poems; (Non-subscriber) – $10 for one story, essay, or up to 3 poems. Guidelines available for SASE. Deadline: December 31. Previously unpublished submissions *only*. Entries may not be simultaneously under consideration elsewhere in *any* form. Limited to women writers, with a 6,500 word limit on fiction and essays. "Submit typed or computer printed manuscripts with a cover sheet listing category, title, name, address and phone number. A single cover sheet per category is sufficient. Identify actual entry by title only. Do not identify author on the manuscript. Manuscripts cannot be returned; do not send SASE for return."

JAPANOPHILE SHORT STORY CONTEST, (I, IV), *Japanophile*, P.O. Box 223, Okemos MI 48864. (517)669-2109. Contact: Earl R. Snodgrass, editor. Estab. 1974. Annual award "to encourage quality writing on Japan-America understanding." Award: $100 plus possible publication. Entry fee: $5. Send $4 for sample copy of magazine. Contest rules for SASE. Deadline: December 31. Prefers unpublished submissions. Stories should involve Japanese and non-Japanese characters.

JESSE JONES AWARD FOR FICTION (BOOK), (II, IV), The Texas Institute of Letters, P.O. Box 9032, Wichita Falls TX 76308. (817)689-4123. Awards Coordinator: James Hoggard. "To honor the writer of the best novel or collection of short fiction published during the calendar year before the award is given." Annual award for novels or story collections. Award: $6,000. Competition receives approx. 30-40 entries per year. Judges: Panel selected by TIL Council. Guidelines for SASE. Deadline: January 4. Previously published fiction, which must have appeared in print between January 1 and December 31 of the prior year. "Award available to writers who, at some time, have lived in Texas at least two years consecutively or whose work has a significant Texas theme."

KANSAS QUARTERLY/KANSAS ARTS COMMISSION AWARDS, (I), *Kansas Quarterly*, 122 Denison Hall, Dept. of English, Kansas State University, Manhattan KS 66506-0703. Contact: Editors. Annual awards "to reward and recognize the best fiction published in *Kansas Quarterly* during the year from authors anywhere in the US or abroad. Anyone who submits unpublished material which is then accepted for publication becomes eligible for the awards." Award: Recognition and monetary sums of $250, $200, $100, $50. "Ours are not 'contests'; they are monetary awards and recognition given by persons of national literary stature." Fiction judges recently have included David Bradley, James B. Hall, Gordon Weaver and Mary Morris. No deadline; material simply may be submitted for consideration at any time. Include SASE.

ROBERT F. KENNEDY BOOK AWARDS, (II, IV), 1206 30th St. NW, Washington DC 20007. (202)333-1880. Endowed by Arthur Schlesinger, Jr., from proceeds of his biography, *Robert Kennedy and His Times*. Annual. "To award the author of a book which most faithfully and forcefully reflects Robert Kennedy's purposes." For books published during the calendar year. Award: $2,500 cash prize awarded in the spring. Deadline: January 4. Looking for "a work of literary merit in fact or fiction that shows compassion for the poor or powerless or those suffering from injustice." Four copies of each book submitted should be sent, along with a $25 entry fee.

KENTUCKY ARTS COUNCIL, KENTUCKY ARTISTS FELLOWSHIPS, (I, IV), 31 Fountain Place, Frankfort KY 40601. (502)564-3757. "To encourage and assist the professional development of Kentucky artists." Writing fellowships offered every other year in fiction, poetry, playwriting. Award: $5,000. Competition received approximately "211 submissions in 1992 in all writing categories." Judges are out-of-state panelists (writers, editors, playwrights, etc.) of distinction. Open only to Kentucky residents (minimum one year). Entry forms available for *Kentucky residents*." Deadline: September 15.

KILLER FROG CONTEST, (I, II, IV), *Scavenger's Newsletter*, 519 Ellinwood, Osage City KS 66523. (913)528-3538. Contact: Janet Fox. Competition "to see who can write the funniest/most overdone horror story, or poem, or produce the most outrageous artwork on a horror theme." Annual award for short stories, poems and art. Award: $25 for each of 4 categories and "coveted froggie statuette." Winners also receive complimentary copies of *The Killer Frog* Anthology. Judge: Editor of *Scavenger*, Janet Fox. Guidelines available for SASE. Submissions must be postmarked between April 1 and July 1. Published or previously unpublished submissions. Limited to horror/humor. Length: up to 4,000 words.

❦LE PRIX MOLSON DE L'ACADÉMIE DES LETTRES DU QUÉBEC, (II, IV), Union des écrivaines et écrivains québécois, 3492 Rue Laval, Montréal, Québec H2X 3C8 Canada. (514)849-8540. Annual prize for a novel in French by a writer from Québec or another province in Canada. Award: $5,000 (Canadian). Judges: 5 persons, members of the Académie des Lettres du Québec. Guidelines for SASE. Deadline: June 10. Five copies of the work must be submitted. Write for guidelines and entry forms (in French).

❦STEPHEN LEACOCK MEDAL FOR HUMOUR, (II, IV), Stephen Leacock Associates, P.O. Box 854, Orillia, Ontario L3V 6K8 Canada. (705)325-6546. Award "to encourage writing of humour by Canadians." Annual competition for short stories, novels and story collections. Award: Stephen Leacock (silver) medal for humour and Manulife Bank of Canada cash award of $5,000 (Canadian). Receives 25-40 entries. Five judges selected across Canada. Entry fee $25 (Canadian). Guidelines for SASE. Deadline: December 30. Submissions should have been published in the previous year. Open to Canadian citizens or landed immigrants only.

❦LES GRANDS PRIX DU *JOURNAL DE MONTRÉAL, (II, IV)*, Union des écrivaines et écrivains Québécois, 3492 Rue Laval, Montréal, Québec H2X 3C8 Canada. (514)849-8540. "To support the development of the literature of Québec and assure the public recognition of its authors." Three annual awards, one each for prose, poetry and theater. Award: $12,000 each (Canadian). Judges: 5 judges, nominated by the *Journal de Montréal*. Deadline: June 10. For books published within the 12 months preceding June 1. Writers must have published at least 3 books of literary creation including the one already submitted and must submit 6 copies of the work to be considered. Write for rules and entry form (in French).

***LETRAS DE ORO* SPANISH LITERARY PRIZES, (I, IV)**, The Graduate School of International Studies, University of Miami, P.O. Box 248123, Coral Gables FL 33124. (305)284-3266. Director: Joaquin-Roy. "The *Letras de Oro* Spanish Literary Prizes were created in order to reward creative excellence in the Spanish language and to promote Spanish literary production in this country. *Letras de Oro* also serves to recognize the importance of Hispanic culture in the United States." Annual award for novels, story collections, drama, essays and poetry. The prizes are $2,500 cash. Deadline: October 12.

LITERATURE AND BELIEF WRITING CONTEST, (I, IV), Center for the Study of Christian Values in Literature, 3076-E JKHB, Brigham Young University, Provo UT 84602. (801)378-3073. Director: Jay Fox. Award to "encourage affirmative literature in the Judeo-Christian tradition." Annual competition for short stories. Award $150 (1st place); $100 (2nd place). Competition receives 200-300 entries. Judges: BYU faculty. Guidelines for SASE. Deadline: May 15. Unpublished submissions, up to 30 pages. All winning entries are considered for publication in the annual journal *Literature and Belief.*

LOFT-MCKNIGHT WRITERS AWARDS, (I, IV), The Loft, Pratt Community Center, 66 Malcolm Ave. SE, Minneapolis MN 55414. (612)379-8999. Program Coordinator: David Cline. "To give Minnesota writers of demonstrated ability an opportunity to work for a concentrated period of time on their writing." Annual award for creative prose. 5 awards of $7,500; 2 awards of distinction of $10,500. Competition receives approximately 275 submissions/year. Judges are from out-of-state. Entry forms or rules for SASE. "Applicants must be Minnesota residents and must send for and observe guidelines."

‡LONG FICTION CONTEST, (I), White Eagle Coffee Store Press, P.O. Box 383, Fox River Grove IL 60021-0383. (708)639-9200. Contact: Publisher. To promote and support the long fiction form. Annual award for short stories. Winning story published as chapbook plus $200, 25 contributor's copies; 40 additional copies sent to book publishers/agents and 10 press kits. Entry fee: $10. SASE (IRCs) for results. Deadline: December 15. Accepts previously unpublished, but previous publication of small parts with acknowledgements is okay. Simultaneous submissions okay. No limits on style or subject matter. Length: 8,000-14,000 words (30-50 pages double spaced) single story; may have multiparts or be a self-contained novel segment. Send cover with title, name, address, phone; second title page with title only. Submissions are not returned; they are recycled.

‡*LOS ANGELES TIMES* BOOK PRIZES (III), *L.A. Times*, Times Mirror Square, Los Angeles CA 90053. Contact: Jack Miles, director. Annual award. "To recognize finest books published each year." For books published between August 1 and July 31. Award: $1,000 cash prize. Entry is by nomination. Juries appointed by the *Times*. No entry fee.

LOUISIANA LITERARY AWARD, (II, IV), Louisiana Library Association (LLA), P.O. Box 3058, Baton Rouge LA 70821. (504)342-4928. Contact: Chair, Louisiana Literary Award Committee. Annual award "to promote interest in books related to Louisiana and to encourage their production." Submissions must have been published during the calendar year prior to presentation of the award. (The award is presented in March or April.) Award: Bronze medallion and $250. No entry fee. Books must be published by December 31 to be eligible. "All Louisiana-related books which committee members can locate are considered, whether submitted or not. Interested parties may correspond with the committee chair at the address above. All books considered *must* be on subject(s) related to Louisiana or be written by a Louisiana author. Each year, there may be a fiction *and/or* nonfiction award. Most often, however, there is only one award recipient."

THE JOHN H. MCGINNIS MEMORIAL AWARD, (I), *Southwest Review*, Box 374, 307 Fondren Library West, Southern Methodist University, Dallas TX 75275. (214)768-1037. Contact: Elizabeth Mills, senior editor. Annual awards (fiction and nonfiction). Stories or essays must have been published in the *Southwest Review* prior to the announcement of the award. Awards: $1,000. Pieces are not submitted directly for the award, but simply for publication in the magazine.

THE ENID MCLEOD LITERARY PRIZE, (II, IV), Franco-British Society, Room 623, Linen Hall, 162-168 Regent St., London W1R 5TB England. Executive Secretary: Mrs. Marian Clarke. "To recognize the work of the author published in the UK which in the opinion of the judges has contributed most to Franco-British understanding." Annual competition for short stories, novels and story collections. Award: Cheque and copy of Enid McLeod's memoirs. Competition receives approx. 6-12 submissions. Judges: The Marquis of Lansdowne (FBS President), Martyn Goff and Professor Douglas Johnson. Guidelines for SASE. Deadline: December 31. Previously published submissions. "Writers, or their publishers, may submit 4 copies to the London Office. No nominations are necessary."

MAGGIE AWARD, (I, IV), Georgia Romance Writers, Inc., P.O. Box 142, Acworth GA 30101. (404)974-6678. Contact: Marian Oaks. "To encourage and instruct unpublished writers in the romance genre." Annual competition for novels. Award: Silver pendant (1st place), certificates (2nd-4th). 4

categories—short contemporary romance, long contemporary romance, historical romance, mainstream. Judges: Published romance authors. Entry fee $25. Guidelines for SASE. Deadline is on or about June 1 (deadline not yet final). Unpublished submissions. Writers must be members of Romance Writers of America. Entries consist of 3 chapters plus synopsis.

❦MANITOBA ARTS COUNCIL SUPPORT TO INDIVIDUAL ARTISTS, (II, IV), Manitoba Arts Council, 525-93 Lombard Ave., Winnipeg, Manitoba R3B 3B1 Canada. (204)945-2237. Grants "to encourage and support Manitoba writers." Five awards: Major Arts Grant ($25,000 Canadian) for writers of national or international reputation. Writers Grants "A" ($10,000 Canadian) for writers who have published a book or had a full-length script produced. Writers Grants "B" for writers who have published. Writers Grants "C" for unpublished writers, research and travel. Deadlines: April 15 and September 15. Open only to Manitoba writers.

WALTER RUMSEY MARVIN GRANT, (I, IV), Ohioana Library Association, Room 1105, 65 S. Front St., Columbus OH 43215. (614)466-3831. Contact: Linda Hengst. "To encourage young unpublished writers (under age 30)." Biennial competition for short stories. Award: $1,000. Guidelines for SASE. Deadline: January 31, 1996. Open to unpublished authors born in Ohio or who have lived in Ohio for a minimum of five years. Must be under 30 years of age. Up to six pieces of prose may be submitted; maximum 60 pages, minimum 10 pages.

‡MASTERS LITERARY AWARD, (I), Center Press, P.O. Box 16452, Encino CA 91416-6452. "One yearly Grand Prize of $1,500, and four quarterly awards in either 1) fiction; 2) poetry and song lyrics; 3) nonfiction." Judges: Three anonymous literary professionals. Entry fee: $10. Awards are given on March 15, June 15, September 15 and December 15. Any submission received prior to an award date is eligible for the subsequent award. Submissions accepted throughout the year. Fiction and nonfiction must be no more than 10 pages; poetry no more than 150 lines. All entries must be in the English language. #10 SASE (IRCs) required for guidelines.

❦THE VICKY METCALF BODY OF WORK AWARD, (II, IV), Canadian Authors Association, Suite 500, 275 Slater St., Ottawa, Ontario K1P 5H9 Canada. (613)233-2846. President: Jeffrey Holmes. Annual award. "The prize is given solely to stimulate writing for children, written by Canadians, for a *number* of strictly children's books—fiction, nonfiction or even picture books. No set formula." To be considered, a writer must have published at least 4 books. Award: $10,000 for a body of work inspirational to Canadian youth. Deadline: December 31. No entry fee. "Nominations may be made by any individual or association by letter *in triplicate* listing the published works of the nominee and providing biographical information. The books are usually considered in regard to their inspirational value for children. Entry forms or rules for SASE."

❦VICKY METCALF SHORT STORY AWARD, (II, IV), Canadian Authors Association, Suite 500, 275 Slater St., Ottawa, Ontario K1P 5H9 Canada. (613)233-2846. Fax: (613)235-8237. President: Jeffrey Holmes. "To encourage Canadian writing for children (open only to Canadian citizens)." Submissions must have been published during previous calendar year in Canadian children's magazine or anthology. Award: $3,000 (Canadian). Award of $1,000 to editor of winning story if published in a Canadian journal or anthology. No entry fee. Entry forms or rules for #10 SASE. Deadline: December 15. Looking for "stories with originality, literary quality for ages 7-17."

MICHIGAN CREATIVE ARTIST GRANT (I, II, IV), Arts Foundation of Michigan, Suite 2164, 645 Griswold, Detroit MI 48226. (313)964-2244. Annual competition for short stories, novels, story collections, translations, poetry, body of work. Award: up to $7,000. Competition receives approx. 300 submissions. Judges: Board of Trustees and Advisors. Guidelines for SASE. Query for deadline. Previously published submissions but can be for work-in-progress. Michigan residents only.

MICHIGAN GENERAL GRANTS, (IV), Arts Foundation of Michigan, Suite 2164, 645 Griswold, Detroit MI 48226. (313)964-2244. "To support writers while creating new work." Deadlines change each year; inquire. Award: cash, amount varies. Competition receives approx. 50 submissions. Judges: Board of Trustees and Advisors. Guidelines available for SASE. Michigan residents only.

MIDLAND AUTHORS' AWARD, (II, IV), Society of Midland Authors, % Phyllis Ford-Choyke, 29 E. Division St., Chicago IL 60611. (312)337-1482. "To honor outstanding books published during the previous year by Midwestern authors." Award: Monetary sum and plaque. Competition receives approximately 30-50 book submissions. Judges are usually members of Society of Midland Authors. Entry forms or rules for SASE. Authors must be residents of Illinois, Indiana, Iowa, Kansas, Michigan, Minnesota, Missouri, Nebraska, Ohio, South Dakota, North Dakota or Wisconsin. Send for entry form.

MILITARY LIFESTYLE SHORT STORY CONTEST, (I, IV), Suite 710, 4800 Montgomery Lane, Bethesda MD 20814-5341. "To publish the work of previously unpublished writers; to encourage our readers to send us short stories about a lifestyle they know very well." Annual competition for short stories. Cash prizes. "Also, all winners are published in the July/August issue of *Military Lifestyle*." Competition receives 400 submissions. Judges: Editorial staff of *Military Lifestyle*. Guidelines for SASE (IRCs). Deadline: March 31. Unpublished submissions. "Theme of contest changes annually. Contact magazine for details and contest rules."

THE MILNER AWARD, (III, IV), Friends of the Atlanta-Fulton Public Library, 1 Margaret Mitchell Square, Atlanta GA 30303. (404)730-1710. Priscilla Glass, Milner chair. Award to a living American author of children's books. Annual competition for authors of children's books. Award: $1,000 honorarium and specially commissioned glass sculpture by Hans Frabel. Judges: Children of Atlanta vote during children's book week. Prior winners not eligible. Children vote at will—no list from which to select. Winner must be able to appear personally in Atlanta to receive the award at a formal program.

‡MIND BOOK OF THE YEAR—THE ALLEN LANE AWARD, (II, IV), MIND, 22 Harley St., London W1N 2ED England. Contact: Ms. A. Brackx. "To award a prize to the work of fiction or nonfiction which outstandingly furthers public understanding of the causes, experience or treatment of mental health problems." Annual competition for novels and works of nonfiction. Award: £1,000. Competition receives approx. 50-100 submissions. Judges: A panel drawn from MIND's Council of Management. Deadline: December. Previously published submissions. Author's nomination is accepted. All books must be published in English in the UK.

MINNESOTA STATE ARTS BOARD/ARTISTS ASSISTANCE FELLOWSHIP, (I, II, IV), 432 Summit Ave., St. Paul MN 55102-2624. (612)297-2603. Artist Assistance Program Associate: Karen Mueller. "To provide support and recognition to Minnesota's outstanding literary artists." Annual award for fiction writers, creative nonfiction writers and poets. Award: Up to $6,000. Competition receives approx. 150 submissions/year. Deadline: October. Previously published or unpublished submissions. Send request or call the above number for application guidelines. *Minnesota residents only.*

MINNESOTA VOICES PROJECT, (IV), New Rivers Press, #910, 420 N. Fifth St., Minneapolis MN 55401. Contact: C.W. Truesdale, editor/publisher. Annual award "to foster and encourage new and emerging regional writers of short fiction, novellas, personal essays and poetry." Requires entry form. Awards: $500 to each author published in the series plus "a generous royalty agreement if book goes into second printing." No entry fee. Send request with SASE for guidelines in October. Deadline: April 1. Restricted to new and emerging writers from Minnesota, Wisconsin, North and South Dakota and Iowa.

MISSISSIPPI ARTS COMMISSION ARTIST FELLOWSHIP GRANT, (I, IV), Suite 207, 239 N. Lamar St., Jackson MS 39201. (601)359-6030. Contact: Program Administrator. "To support the creation of new work and recognize the contributions made by aritsts of exceptional talent to Mississippi's culture. Awards are based on mastery of artistic discipline and originality of prior art work; and evidence that new work of significant value and originality be produced during the grant period." Award granted every 2 years on a rotating basis. Award for writers of short stories, novels and story collections. Grant: $5,000. Judges: Peer panel. Guidelines for SASE. "The next available grants for creative writing, including fiction, nonfiction and poetry will be in 1995-96." Deadline: March 1. Applicants must be Mississippi residents. The Mississippi Arts Commission's Art in Education Program contains a creative writing component. For more information, contact the AIE Coordinator. The Mississippi Touring Arts program offers writers the opportunity to give readings and workshops. For more information, contact the Program Administrator.

MISSOURI WRITERS' BIENNIAL, (I, IV), Missouri Arts Council, Suite 105, 111 N. Seventh St., St. Louis MO 63101-2188. (314)340-6845. Award to support and promote Missouri writers. Every 2 year competition for short stories, essays and poetry. Award: $5,000 each to up to 5 writers. Competition receives approx. 600 submissions. Judges: Panel of national judges. Guidelines for SASE. Deadline:

"approx." July 30. Unpublished submissions. "Writers must have lived in Missouri for at least 2 years immediately preceding submission. Writers *must* request complete written guidelines."

MONTANA ARTS COUNCIL FIRST BOOK AWARD, (IV), Room 252, 316 N. Park Ave., Helena MT 59620. (406)444-6430. Director of Artist Services-Programs: Martha Sprague. Biennial award for publication of a book of poetry or fiction—the best work in Montana. Submissions may be short stories, novellas, story collections or poetry. Award: Publication. Competition receives about 35 submissions/ year. Judges are professional writers. Entry forms or rules for SASE. Deadline is early April (1995). Restricted to residents of Montana; not open to degree-seeking students.

MONTANA ARTS COUNCIL INDIVIDUAL ARTIST FELLOWSHIP, (IV), Room 252, 316 N. Park Ave., Helena MT 59620. (406)444-6430. Director of Artist Services-Programs: Martha Sprague. Annual award of $2,000. Competition receives about 80-100 submissions/year. Panelists are professional artists. Contest requirements available for SASE. Deadline: Spring. Restricted to residents of Montana; not open to degree-seeking students.

‡**MPE CHILDREN'S BOOK AWARD, (I)**, Multicultural Publishers Exchange and the Highsmith Press, P.O. Box 9869, Madison WI 53715. (608)244-5633. Annual award for children's books. Award: $2,000 plus publication. Competition receives approximately 30-100 submissions. Judge: MPE member committee. No entry fee. Guidelines available for SASE (IRCs). Deadline: March 30. Unpublished submissions.

‡**MYTHOPOEIC FANTASY AWARD (III)**, The Mythopoeic Society, Box 6707, Altadena CA 91003. Chair, awards committee: David Bratman. Annual award for novels. "A statue of a lion is given to the author; magazines and publishers are notified, plus we announce the award in our publications." Judges: members of the Mythopoeic Society who volunteer for the selection committee. Guidelines for SASE. Deadline: February. Fantasy novels only. "Books are nominated by Society members. If an author has published his/her work during the previous year, and is a member of the Society, he/she can nominate his/her own work." Two categories: adult and children's literature.

NATIONAL BOOK COUNCIL/BANJO AWARDS, (III, IV), National Book Council, Suite 3, 21 Drummond Place, Carlton, Victoria 3053 Australia. "For a book of highest literary merit which makes an outstanding contribution to Australian literature." Annual competition for creative writing. Award: $15,000 each for a work of fiction and nonfiction. Competition receives approx. 100-140 submissions. Judges: 4 judges chosen by the National Book Council. Entry fee $30. Guidelines for SASE. Deadline: March 20. Previously published submissions. For works "written by Australian citizens or permanent residents and first published in Australia during the qualifying period." Books must be nominated by the publisher.

NATIONAL ENDOWMENT FOR THE ARTS CREATIVE WRITING FELLOWSHIP, (I), Literature Program, Room 722, Pennsylvania Ave. NW, Washington DC 20506. (202)682-5451. "The mission of the NEA is to foster the excellence, diversity and vitality of the arts in the United States, and to help broaden the availability and appreciation of such excellence, diversity and vitality." The purpose of the fellowship is to enable creative writers "to set aside time for writing, research or travel and generally to advance their careers." Competition open to fiction writers who have published a novel or novella, a collection of stories or at least 5 stories in 2 or more magazines since January 1. Annual award: $20,000. All mss are judged anonymously. Application and guidelines available upon request. Deadline: May 27.

‡**NATIONAL FOUNDATION FOR ADVANCEMENT IN THE ARTS, ARTS RECOGNITION AND TALENT SEARCH (ARTS), (I, IV)**, 3915 Biscayne Blvd., Miami FL 33137. (305)573-0490. President: William H. Banchs. "To encourage 17- and 18-year-old writers and put them in touch with institutions which offer scholarships." Annual award for short stories, novels, "fiction, essay, poetry, scriptwriting." Awards: $3,000, $1,500, $500, and $100. Judges: Nationally selected panel. Entry fee $25 before June 1, $35 until October 1. Guidelines for SASE. 17- and 18-year-old writers only.

NATIONAL WRITERS ASSOCIATION ANNUAL NOVEL WRITING CONTEST, (I), National Writers Association, Suite 424, 1450 S. Havana, Aurora CO 80012. (303)751-7844. Contact: Sandy Whelchel, director. Annual award to "recognize and reward outstanding ability and to increase the opportunity for publication." Award: $500 first prize; $300 second prize; $100 third prize. Award judged by successful writers. Charges $25 entry fee. Contest rules and entry forms available with SASE. Opens December 1. Deadline: April 1. Unpublished submissions, any genre or category. Length: 20,000-100,000 words.

NATIONAL WRITERS ASSOCIATION ANNUAL SHORT STORY CONTEST, (I), National Writers Association, Suite 424, 1450 S. Havana, Aurora CO 80012. (303)751-7844. Contact: Sandy Whelchel, Executive Director. Annual award to encourage and recognize writing by freelancers in the short story field. Award: $200 first prize; $100 second prize; $50 third prize. Opens April 1. Charges $10 entry fee. Write for entry form and rule sheet. All entries must be postmarked by July 1. Unpublished submissions. Length: No more than 5,000 words.

THE NATIONAL WRITTEN & ILLUSTRATED BY . . . AWARDS CONTEST FOR STUDENTS, (I, IV), Landmark Editions, Inc., P.O. Box 4469, Kansas City MO 64127. (816)241-4919. Contact: Nan Thatch. "Contest initiated to encourage students to write and illustrate original books and to inspire them to become published authors and illustrators." Annual competition. "Each student whose book is selected for publication will be offered a complete publishing contract. To insure that students benefit from the proceeds, royalties from the sale of their books will be placed in an individual trust fund, set up for each student by his or her parents or legal guardians, at a bank of their choice. Funds may be withdrawn when a student becomes of age, or withdrawn earlier (either in whole or in part) for educational purposes or in case of proof of specific needs due to unusual hardship. Reports of book sales and royalties will be sent to the student and the parents or guardians annually." Winners also receive an all-expense-paid trip to Kansas City to oversee final reproduction phases of their books. Books by students may be entered in one of three age categories: A—6 to 9 years old; B—10 to 13 years old; C—14 to 19 years old. Each book submitted must be both written and illustrated by the same student. "Any books that are written by one student and illustrated by another will be automatically disqualified." Book entries must be submitted by a teacher or librarian. Entry fee: $1. For rules and guidelines, send a #10 SAE with 58¢ postage. Deadline: May 1 of each year.

NEBULA® AWARDS, (III, IV), Science Fiction and Fantasy Writers of America, Inc., #1B, 5 Winding Brook Dr., Guilderland NY 12084. (518)869-5361. Executive Secretary: Peter Dennis Pautz. Annual awards for previously published short stories, novels, novellas, novelettes. Science fiction/fantasy only. "No submissions; nominees upon recommendation of members only." Deadline: December 31. "Works are nominated throughout the year by active members of the SFWA."

NEGATIVE CAPABILITY SHORT FICTION COMPETITION, (I, IV), *Negative Capability*, 62 Ridgelawn Dr. E., Mobile AL 36608. (205)343-6163. Contact: Sue Walker. "To promote and publish excellent fiction and to promote the ideals of human rights and dignity." Annual award for short stories. Award: $1,000 best story. Judge: Leon Driskell. Reading fee $10, "includes copy of journal publishing the award." Guidelines for SASE. Deadline: December 15. Length: 1,500-4,500 words.

THE NENE AWARD, (II), Hawaii Association of School Libraries and the Hawaii Library Association Children and Youth Section, % Jan Yap, chairperson, 2716 Woodlawn Dr., Honolulu HI 96822. (808)988-7208. Chairperson changes every year. Annual award "to help the children of Hawaii become acquainted with the best contemporary writers of fiction for children; to become aware of the qualities that make a good book; to choose the best rather than the mediocre; and to honor an author whose book has been enjoyed by the children of Hawaii." Award: Koa plaque. Judged by the children of Hawaii. No entry fee. A reading list of 48-52 books is compiled by the Selection Committee and submitted to children in schools across the state. Review copies may be sent for consideration to the Selection Committee.

NEUSTADT INTERNATIONAL PRIZE FOR LITERATURE, (III), *World Literature Today*, 110 Monnet Hall, University of Oklahoma, Norman OK 73019-0375. Contact: Dr. Djelal Kadir, director. Biennial award to recognize distinguished and continuing achievement in fiction, poetry or drama. Awards: $40,000, an eagle feather cast in silver, an award certificate and a special issue of *WLT* devoted to the laureate. "We are looking for outstanding accomplishment in world literature. The Neustadt Prize is not open to application. Nominations are made only by members of the international jury, which changes for each award. Jury meetings are held in March of even-numbered years. Unsolicited manuscripts, whether published or unpublished, cannot be considered."

THE *NEW ERA* WRITING, ART, PHOTOGRAPHY AND MUSIC CONTEST, (I, IV), *New Era Magazine* (LDS Church), 50 E. North Temple, Salt Lake City UT 84150. (801)240-2951. Managing Editor: Richard M. Romney. "To encourage young Mormon writers and artists." Annual competition for short stories. Award: partial scholarship to Brigham Young University or Ricks College or cash awards. Competition receives approx. 300 submissions. Judges: *New Era* editors. Guidelines for SASE. Deadline: December 31. Unpublished submissions. Contest open only to 12-23-year-old members of the Church of Jesus Christ of Latter-Day Saints.

NEW HAMPSHIRE STATE COUNCIL ON THE ARTS INDIVIDUAL ARTIST FELLOWSHIP, (I, II, IV), 40 N. Main St., Concord NH 03301-4974. (603)271-2789. Artist Services Coordinator: Audrey V. Sylvester. Fellowship "for career development to professional artists who are legal/permanent residents of the state of New Hampshire." Annual award: Up to $3,000. Competition receives 150 entries for 15 awards in all disciplines. Judges: 7 panels of in-state and out-of-state experts (music, theater, dance, literature, film, etc.). Guidelines for SASE. Deadline: July 1. Submissions may be either previously published or unpublished. Applicants must be over 18 years of age; not enrolled as fulltime students; permanent, legal residents of New Hampshire 1 year prior to application. Application form required.

NEW LETTERS LITERARY AWARD, (I), *New Letters*, UMKC, 5100 Rockhill, Kansas City MO 64110. (816)235-1168. Administrative Assistant: Glenda McCrary. Award to "discover and reward good writing." Annual competition for short stories. Award: $750. Competition receives 500 entries/year. Entry fee $10. Guidelines for SASE. Deadline: May 15. Submissions must be unpublished. Length requirement: 5,000 words or less.

NEW VOICES IN POETRY AND PROSE SPRING AND FALL COMPETITION, (I), *New Voices in Poetry and Prose Magazine*, P.O. Box 52196, Shreveport LA 71135. (318)797-8243. Publisher: Cheryl White. "To recognize and publish a previously unpublished work of outstanding short fiction." Biannual award for short stories. Award: $75 (first place) and publication in *New Voices*. Competition receives approx. 50 submissions. Judges: Panel. Entry fee $10/short story. Guidelines for SASE. Deadlines: April 30 and September 30. Unpublished submissions. "All writers welcome. There is no line limit, but as a general rule, works under 5,000 words are preferred."

NEW WRITING AWARD, (I), *New Writing Magazine*, P.O. Box 1812, Amherst NY 14226-7812. "We wish to reward *new* writing. Looking for originality in form and content." New and beginning writers encouraged. Annual open competition for prose (novel excerpt, scripts, short story, essay, humor, other) and poetry. Deadline: December 31. Award: Varies, but hope it to be $1,000. Additional awards for finalists. Possible publication. Judges: Panel of editors. Entry fee $10, $5 for each additional. Guidelines for SASE. No application form required—simply send submission with reading fee, SASE for manuscript return or notification, and 3×5 card for each entry, including: story name, author and address.

NEW YORK FOUNDATION FOR THE ARTS FELLOWSHIP, (I, II, IV), New York Foundation for the Arts, 14th Floor, 155 Avenue of Americas, New York NY 10013. Contact: Penelope Dannenberg. Biennial competition for short stories and novels. Approximately 15 awards of $7,000 each. Competition receives approx. 600 submissions. Judges: Fiction writers. Call for guidelines or send SASE. Next deadline in 1995. Previously published or unpublished submissions. Applicants must be over 18; must have lived in New York state at least 2 years immediately prior to application deadline; and may not be currently enrolled in any degree program.

NEW YORK STATE EDITH WHARTON CITATION OF MERIT (State Author), (III, IV), NYS Writers Institute, Humanities 355, University at Albany/SUNY, Albany NY 12222. (518)442-5620. Contact: Thomas Smith, associate director. Awarded biennially to honor a New York State fiction writer for a lifetime of works of distinction. Fiction writers living in New York State are nominated by an advisory panel. Recipients receive an honorarium of $10,000 and must give two public readings a year.

JOHN NEWBERY AWARD, (III, IV), American Library Association (ALA) Awards and Citations Program, Association for Library Service to Children, 50 E. Huron St., Chicago IL 60611. Executive Director: S. Roman. Annual award. Only books for children published during the preceding year are eligible. Award: Medal. Entry restricted to US citizens-residents.

CHARLES H. AND N. MILDRED NILON EXCELLENCE IN MINORITY FICTION AWARD, (I, IV), University of Colorado at Boulder and the Fiction Collective Two, English Dept. Publications Center, Campus Box 494, University of Colorado, Boulder CO 80309-0494. "We recognize excellence in new minority fiction." Annual competition for novels, story collections and novellas. Award: $1,000 cash prize; joint publications of mss by CU-Boulder and Fiction Collective Two. Competition receives approx. 60 submissions. Judges: Well-known minority writers. Guidelines for SASE. Deadline: November 30. Unpublished submissions. "Only specific recognized US racial and ethnic minorities are eligible. The definitions are in the submission guidelines. The ms must be book length (a minimum of 250 pages)."

THE NOMA AWARD FOR PUBLISHING IN AFRICA, (III, IV), % Hans Zell Associates, P.O. Box 56, Oxford OX1 2SJ England. Sponsored by Kodansha Ltd. Administered by *The African Book Publishing Record.* Award "to encourage publications of works by African writers and scholars in Africa, instead of abroad as is still too often the case at present." Annual competition for a new book in any of these categories: Scholarly or academic; books for children; literature and creative writing, including fiction, drama and poetry. Award: $5,000. Competition receives approx. 100 submissions. Judges: A committee of African scholars and book experts and representatives of the international book community. Chairman: Professor Abiola Irele. Guidelines for SASE. Previously published submissions. Submissions are through publishers only.

NORDMANNS-FORBUNDET TRANSLATION GRANT, (II, IV), Nordmann-Forbundet, Rädhusgt 23B, N-0158 Oslo 1 Norway. Fax: (02)425163. Contact: Dina Tolfsby, information officer. Annual award for translation of Norwegian poetry or fiction, preferably contemporary. Award: Maximum NOK 15,000. Competition receives approx. 10 submissions. Judges: A committee of three members. Deadline: March 1. "The grants are awarded to foreign publishing houses that want to publish Norwegian literature in translation." Payment is made at the time of publication.

NORTH CAROLINA ARTS COUNCIL FELLOWSHIP, (IV), 221 E. Lane St., Raleigh NC 27611. (919)733-2111. Literature Director: Deborah McGill. Grants program "to encourage the continued achievements of North Carolina's fiction writers and poets." Annual award: Up to $8,000 each for 4 writers. Council receives approximately 200 submissions. Judges are a panel of editors and published writers from outside the state. Writers must be over 18 years old, not currently enrolled in degree-granting program, and must have been a resident of North Carolina for 1 full year prior to applying. Writers may apply in either poetry or fiction. Deadline: February 1.

NORTH CAROLINA ARTS COUNCIL SCHOLARSHIPS, (IV), 221 E. Lane St., Raleigh NC 27611. (919)733-2111. Literature Director: Deborah McGill. "To provide North Carolina writers of fiction, poetry, and literary nonfiction with opportunities for research or enrichment. Available on six-weeks' notice throughout the year." Award up to $500 (with $1,500 budgeted for the category). "To be eligible writers must have lived in the state for at least a year and must have published a stipulated amount of work in his/her genre. Self-published or vanity-press published work is ineligible." Call Council for details.

THE FLANNERY O'CONNOR AWARD FOR SHORT FICTION, (I), The University of Georgia Press, 330 Research Dr., Athens GA 30602. (706)369-6130. Contact: Award coordinator. Annual award "to recognize outstanding collections of short fiction. Published and unpublished authors are welcome." Award: $1,000 and publication by the University of Georgia Press. Deadline: June 1-July 31. "Manuscripts cannot be accepted at any other time." Entry fee: $10. Contest rules for SASE. Ms will not be returned.

FRANK O'CONNOR FICTION AWARD, (I), *descant,* Dept. of English, Texas Christian University, Fort Worth TX 76129. (817)921-7240. Contact: Betsy Colquitt, Harry Opperman, Steve Sherwood or Stan Trachbenberg, Editors. Estab. 1979 with *descant;* earlier awarded through *Quartet.* Annual award to honor achievement in short fiction. Submissions must be published in the magazine during its current volume. Award: $500 prize. No entry fee. "About 12 to 15 stories are published annually in *descant.* Winning story is selected from this group."

THE SCOTT O'DELL AWARD FOR HISTORICAL FICTION, (II, IV), Scott O'Dell (personal donation). Contact: Mrs. Zena Sutherland, professor, 1418 E. 57th St., Chicago IL 60637. Annual award "to encourage the writing of good historical fiction about the New World (Canada, South and Central

America, and the United States) for children and young people." Award: $5,000. Rules for SASE. Deadline: December 31. For books published during the year preceding the year in which the award is given. To be written in English by a U.S. citizen and published in the U.S. Looking for "accuracy in historical details, and all the standard literary criteria for excellence: style, setting, characterization, etc."

OHIOANA AWARD FOR CHILDREN'S LITERATURE, ALICE WOOD MEMORIAL, (IV), Ohioana Library Association, Room 1105, 65 S. Front St., Columbus OH 43215. (614)466-3831. Director: Linda Hengst. Competition "to honor an individual whose body of work has made, and continues to make, a significant contribution to literature for children or young adults." Annual award for body of work. Amount of award varies (approx. $500-700). Guidelines for SASE. Deadline: December 31 prior to year award is given. "Open to authors born in Ohio or who have lived in Ohio for a minimum of five years."

OHIOANA BOOK AWARDS, (II, IV), Ohioana Library Association, Room 1105, 65 S. Front St., Columbus OH 43215. Contact: Linda R. Hengst, director. Annual awards granted (only if the judges believe a book of sufficiently high quality has been submitted) to bring recognition to outstanding books by Ohioans or about Ohio. Criteria: Books written or edited by a native Ohioan or resident of the state for at least 5 years; two copies of the book MUST be received by the Ohioana Library by December 31 prior to the year the award is given; literary quality of the book must be outstanding. Awards: Certificate and glass sculpture (up to 6 awards given annually). Each spring a jury considers all books received since the previous jury. Award judged by a jury selected from librarians, book reviewers, writers and other knowledgeable people. No entry forms are needed, but they are available. "We will be glad to answer letters asking specific questions."

✴THE OKANAGAN SHORT FICTION AWARD, (I, IV), *Canadian Author*, Suite 500, 275 Slater St., Ottawa, Ontario K1P 5H9 Canada. Contact: Veronica Ross, fiction editor. Award offered 4 times a year. To present good fiction "in which the writing surpasses all else" to an appreciative literary readership, and in turn help Canadian writers retain an interest in good fiction. Award: $125 to each author whose story is accepted for publication. Entries are invited in each issue of the quarterly *CA*. Sample copy $5.50. "Our award regulations stipulate that writers must be Canadian, stories must not have been previously published and be under 3,000 words. Mss should be typed double-spaced on 8½×11 bond. SASE with Canadian postage or mss will not be returned. Looking for superior writing ability, stories with good plot, movement, dialogue and characterization. A selection of winning stories has been anthologized as *Pure Fiction: The Okanagan Award Winners*, and is essential reading for prospective contributors."

OMMATION PRESS BOOK AWARD, (I, II), Ommation Press, 5548 N. Sawyer, Chicago IL 60625. (312)539-5745. Annual competition for short stories, novels, story collections and poetry. Award: Book publication, 100 copies of book. Competition receives approx. 60 submissions. Judge: Effie Mihopoulos (editor). Entry fee $15, includes copy of former award-winning book. Guidelines for SASE. Deadline: December 30. Either previously published or unpublished submissions. Submit no more than 50 pages.

OREGON INDIVIDUAL ARTIST FELLOWSHIP, (I, IV), Oregon Arts Commission, 550 Airport Rd. SE, Salem OR 97310. (503)387-3625. Assistant Director: Vincent Dunn. "Award enables professional artists to undertake projects to assist their professional development." Biennial competition for short stories, novels, poetry and story collections. Award: $3,000. (Please note: ten $3,000 awards are spread over 5 disciplines—literature, music/opera, media arts, dance and theatre awarded in even-numbered years.) Competition receives approx. 140 entries/year. Judges: Professional advisors from outside the state. Guidelines and application for SASE. Deadline: September 1. Competition limited to Oregon residents.

Stay informed! Keep up with changes in the market by using the latest edition of Novel & Short Story Writer's Market. *If this is 1995 or later, buy a new edition at your favorite bookstore or order directly from Writer's Digest Books.*

PACIFIC NORTHWEST WRITERS CONFERENCE LITERARY AWARD, (I), Suite 804, 2033 Sixth Ave., Seattle WA 98121-2526. (206)443-3807. Annual competition for short stories and novels (adult and juvenile). Also for nonfiction articles and books, poetry and screenplays/scripts. First prize each category is $300. Entry fee $20 for members, $30 for nonmembers. Guidelines for 3 ounce postage. Deadline: Mid-April. Previously unpublished submissions.

DOBIE PAISANO FELLOWSHIPS, (IV), Office of Graduate Studies, University of Texas at Austin, Austin TX 78712. (512)471-7213. Coordinator: Audrey N. Slate. Annual fellowships for creative writing (includes short stories, novels and story collections). Award: 6 months residence at ranch; $7,200 stipend. Competition receives approx. 100 submissions. Judges: faculty of University of Texas and members of Texas Institute of Letters. Entry fee: $10. Application and guidelines on request. "Open to writers with a Texas connection—native Texans, people living in Texas now or writers whose work focuses on Texas and Southwest." Deadline is the third week in January.

‡KENNETH PATCHEN COMPETITION, (I, II), Pig Iron Press, P.O. Box 237, Youngstown OH 44501. (216)747-6932. Contact: Jim Villani. Awards works of fiction and poetry in alternating years. Award: publication; $100; 50 copies. Judge with national visibility selected annually. Entry fee: $10. Guidelines available for SASE (IRCs). Reading period: December 1 to October 31. Award for fiction: 1994, 1996, 1998; fiction award for novel or short story collection, either form eligible. Previous publication of individual stories, poems or parts of novel OK. Submit acknowledgement list with entry. Ms should not exceed 500 typed pages.

PEARL SHORT STORY CONTEST, (I), *Pearl* Magazine, 3030 E. Second St., Long Beach CA 90803. (310)434-4523. Contact: Marilyn Johnson, editor. Award to "provide a larger forum and help widen publishing opportunities for fiction writers in the small press; and to help support the continuing publication of *Pearl*." Annual competition for short stories. Award: $50, publication in *Pearl* and 10 copies. Competition receives approx. 100 submissions. Judges: Editors of *Pearl* (Marilyn Johnson, Joan Jobe Smith, Barbara Hauk). Entry fee $5 per story. Guidelines for SASE. Deadline: December 1-March 1. Unpublished submissions. Length: 4,000 words maximum. Include a brief biographical note and SASE for reply or return of manuscript. Accepts simultaneous submissions, but asks to be notified if story is accepted elsewhere. All submissions are considered for publication in *Pearl*. "Although we are open to all types of fiction, we look most favorably upon coherent, well-crafted narratives, containing interesting, believable characters and meaningful situations."

JUDITH SIEGEL PEARSON AWARD, (I, IV), Wayne State University, Detroit MI 48202. Contact: Chair, English Dept. Competition "to honor writing about women." Annual award. Short stories up to 20 pages considered every third year (poetry and drama/nonfiction in alternate years). Award: Up to $400. Competition receives up to 100 submissions/year. Submissions are internally screened; then a noted writer does final reading. Entry forms for SASE.

PEGASUS PRIZE, (III), Mobil Corporation, (Room 3C916), 3225 Gallows Rd., Fairfax VA 22037-0001. (703)846-2375. Director: Michael Morgan. To recognize distinguished works from literature not normally translated into English. Award for novels. "Prize is given on a country-by-country basis and does not involve submissions unless requested by national juries."

PEN/BOOK-OF-THE-MONTH CLUB TRANSLATION PRIZE, (II, IV), PEN American Center, 568 Broadway, New York NY 10012. (212)334-1660. Awards Coordinator: John Morrone. Award "to recognize the art of the literary translator." Annual competition for translations. Award: $3,000. Deadline: December 31. Previously published submissions within the calendar year. "Translators may be of any nationality, but book must have been published in the US and must be a book-length literary translation." Books may be submitted by publishers, agents or translators. No application form. Send three copies. "Early submissions are strongly recommended."

THE PEN/FAULKNER AWARD FOR FICTION, (II, III, IV), c/o The Folger Shakespeare Library, 201 E. Capitol St. SE, Washington DC 20003. (202)544-7077. Attention: Janice Delaney, PEN/Faulkner Foundation Executive Director. Annual award. "To award the most distinguished book-length work of fiction published by an American writer." Award: $15,000 for winner; $5,000 for nominees. Judges: Three writers chosen by the Trustees of the Award. Deadline: December 31. Published submissions only. Writers and publishers submit four copies of eligible titles published the current year. No juvenile. Authors must be American citizens.

PENNSYLVANIA COUNCIL ON THE ARTS, FELLOWSHIP PROGRAM, (I, IV), 216 Finance Bldg., Harrisburg PA 17120. (717)787-6883. Annual awards to provide fellowships for writers of adult fiction and poetry. Award: Up to $5,000. Competition receives approx. 175 submissions for 12 to 15 awards/year. Six judges: Three poetry, three fiction, different each year. Guidelines mailed upon request. Deadline: August 1. Applicants must be Pennsylvania residents.

✸PENNY DREADFUL ANNUAL SHORT STORY CONTEST, (I), *sub-TERRAIN Magazine*, P.O. Box 1575, Station A, Vancouver, British Columbia V6C 2P7 Canada. (604)876-8710. Contact: Brian Kaufman. "To inspire writers to get down to it and struggle with a form that is condensed and difficult. To encourage clean, powerful writing." Annual award for short stories. Prize: $100 and publication. Runners-up also receive publication. Competition receives about 300 submissions. Judges: An editorial collective. Entry fee $10 (includes 4-issue subscription). Guidelines for SASE, or SAE and IRC, in November. "Contest kicks off in November." Deadline: April 15. Unpublished submissions. Length: 1,000 words maximum. "We are looking for work that is trying to do something unique/new in form or content. Radical as opposed to the standard short story format. Experiment, take risks."

JAMES D. PHELAN AWARD, (I, IV), The San Francisco Foundation, Suite 910, 685 Market St., San Francisco CA 94105. Contact: Awards Program Coordinator. Annual award "to author of an unpublished work-in-progress of fiction (novel or short story), nonfictional prose, poetry or drama." Award: $2,000 and certificate. Rules and entry forms available after November 1 for SASE. Deadline: January 15. Unpublished submissions. Applicant must have been born in the state of California and be 20-35 years old.

***PLAYBOY* COLLEGE FICTION CONTEST, (I, IV)**, *Playboy* Magazine, 680 North Lake Shore Dr., Chicago IL 60611. (312)751-8000. Fiction Editor: Alice K. Turner. Award "to foster young writing talent." Annual competition for short stories. Award: $3,000 plus publication in the magazine. Judges: Staff. Guidelines available for SASE. Deadline: January 1. Submissions should be unpublished. No age limit; college affiliation required. Stories should be 25 pages or fewer. "Manuscripts are not returned. Results of the contest will be sent via SASE."

EDGAR ALLAN POE AWARDS, (II, IV), Mystery Writers of America, Inc., 6th Floor, 17 E. 47th St., New York NY 10017. Executive Director: Priscilla Ridgway. Annual awards to enhance the prestige of the mystery. For mystery works published or produced during the calendar year. Award: Ceramic bust of Poe. Awards for best mystery novel, best first novel by an American author, best softcover original novel, best short story, best critical/biographical work, best fact crime, best young adult, best juvenile novel, best screenplay, best television feature and best episode in a series. Contact above address for specifics. Deadline: December 1.

THE RENATO POGGIOLI TRANSLATION AWARD, (I, IV), PEN American Center, 568 Broadway, New York NY 10012. (212)334-1660. Awards Coordinator: John Morrone. Award "to encourage beginning and promising translator who is working on a book-length translation from Italian to English." Annual competition for translations. Award: $3,000. Competition receives approx. 25 submissions. Judges: A panel of three translators. Guidelines for SASE. Deadline: January 15. Unpublished submissions. "Letters of application should be accompanied by a curriculum vitae, including Italian studies and samples of translation-in-progress."

KATHERINE ANNE PORTER PRIZE FOR FICTION, (I), *Nimrod*, Arts and Humanities Council of Tulsa, 2210 S. Main St., Tulsa OK 74114. (918)584-3333. Editor: Francine Ringold. "To award promising young writers and to increase the quality of manuscripts submitted to *Nimrod*." Annual award for short stories. Award: $1,000 first prize, $500 second prize plus publication, two contributors copies and $5/page up to $25 total. Receives approx. 700 entries/year. Judge varies each year. Past judges: Ron Carlson, Rosellen Brown, Alison Lurie, Gordon Lish, George Garrett, Toby Olson, John Leonard and Gladys Swan. Entry fee: $10. Guidelines for #10 SASE. Deadline for submissions: April 18. Previously unpublished manuscripts. Length: 7,500 words maximum. "Must be typed, double-spaced. Our contest is judged anonymously, so we ask that writers take their names off of their manuscripts (need 2 copies total). Include a cover sheet containing your name, full address, phone and the title of your work. Include a SASE for notification of the results. We encourage writers to read *Nimrod* before submission to discern whether or not their work is compatible with the style of our journal. Back awards issues are $4.50 (book rate postage included), current issue is $6.90."

PRAIRIE SCHOONER **THE LAWRENCE FOUNDATION AWARD, (I)**, 201 Andrews Hall, University of Nebraska, Lincoln NE 68588-0334. (402)472-1812. Contact: Hilda Raz, editor. Annual award "given to the author of the best short story published in *Prairie Schooner* during the preceding year." Award: $500. "Only short fiction published in *Prairie Schooner* is eligible for consideration."

❦PRISM INTERNATIONAL SHORT FICTION CONTEST, (I), *Prism International*, Dept. of Creative Writing, University of British Columbia, E455-1866 Main Mall, Vancouver, British Columbia V6T 1Z1 Canada. (604)822-2514. Contact: Publicity Manager. Award: $2,000 first prize and five $200 consolation prizes. Entry fee $15 plus $5 reading fee for each story (includes a 1 year subscription). SASE or SAE and IRC for rules/entry forms.

PULITZER PRIZE IN FICTION, (III, IV), Graduate School of Journalism, 702 Journalism Bldg., Columbia University, New York NY 10027. Annual award for distinguished fiction *first* published in America in book form during the year by an American author, preferably dealing with American life. Award: $3,000. Deadline: Books published between January 1 and June 30 must be submitted by July 1. Books published between July 1 and December 31 must be submitted by November 1; books published between November 1 and December 31 must be submitted in galleys or page proofs by November 1. Submit 4 copies of the book, entry form, biography and photo of author and $20 handling fee. Open to American authors.

PURE BRED DOGS/AMERICAN KENNEL GAZETTE, (I, IV), 51 Madison Ave., New York NY 10010. (212)696-8333. Executive Editor: Beth Adelman. Annual contest for short stories under 2,000 words. Award: Prizes of $500, $250 and $150 for top three entries. Top entry published in magazine. Judge: Panel. Contest requirements available for SASE. "The *Gazette* sponsors an annual fiction contest for short short stories on some subject relating to pure-bred dogs. Fiction for our magazine needs a slant toward the serious fancier with real insight into the human/dog bond and breed-specific pure-bred behavior."

PUSHCART PRIZE, (III), Pushcart Press, P.O. Box 380, Wainscott NY 11975. (516)324-9300. Contact: Bill Henderson, editor. Annual award "to publish and recognize the best of small press literary work." Previously published submissions, short stories, poetry or essays on any subject. Must have been published during the current calendar year. Award: Publication in *Pushcart Prize: Best of the Small Presses*. Deadline: December 1. Nomination by small press publishers/editors only.

SIR WALTER RALEIGH AWARD, (II, IV), North Carolina Literary and Historical Association, 109 E. Jones St., Raleigh NC 27601-2807. (919)733-7305. Secretary-Treasurer: Jeffrey J. Crow. "To promote among the people of North Carolina an interest in their own literature." Annual award for novels. Award: Statue of Sir Walter Raleigh. Judges: University English and history professors. Guidelines for SASE. Book must be an original work published during the twelve months ending June 30 of the year for which the award is given. Writer must be a legal or physical resident of North Carolina for the three years preceding the close of the contest period. Authors or publishers may submit 3 copies of their book to the above address.

‡❦THE REGINA BOOK AWARD, (II, IV), The Saskatchewan Writers Guild, P.O. Box 3986, Regina, Saskatchewan S4P 3R9 Canada. Award "to recognize the vitality of the literary community in Regina." Annual awards for fiction (short stories, novels, novellas), children's (stories, poems), drama, nonfiction and poetry. Award: $1,000 and commemorative certificates for the writer and publisher and a sticker for display on the award-winning book. Entry fee: $15 (per title). Submissions must be received between June 1 and August 1. Published submissions. "Books may have been published anywhere in the world, but authors must have been residents of Regina in 3 of the last 5 years. Eligible books, with the exception of children's, must be written in English, at least 48 pages long, have an ISBN number and be professionally printed and bound. No anthologies will be accepted, but collected works by a single author are eligible. Work may be submitted (three copies) by writers or publishers.

‡REGINA MEDAL AWARD (III), Catholic Library Association, St. Joseph Central High School Library, 22 Maplewood Ave., Pittsfield MA 01201. Contact: Jean R. Bostley, SSJ Chair, CLA Awards Committee. Annual award. To honor a continued distinguished contribution to children's literature. Award: Silver medal. Award given during Easter week. Selection by a special committee; nominees are suggested by the Catholic Library Association Membership.

RHODE ISLAND STATE COUNCIL ON THE ARTS, (I, IV), Individual Artist's Fellowship in Literature, Suite 103, 95 Cedar St., Providence RI 02903-1062. (401)277-3880. Fellowship Program Director: Dawn Dunley Roch. Annual fellowship. Award: $5,000. Competition receives approximately 50 submissions. In-state panel makes recommendations to an out-of-state judge, who recommends finalist to the council. Entry forms for SASE. Deadline: April 1. Artists must be Rhode Island residents and not undergraduate or graduate students. "Program guidelines may change. Prospective applicants should contact RISCA prior to deadline."

HAROLD U. RIBALOW PRIZE, (II, IV), *Hadassah Magazine*, 50 W. 58th St., New York NY 10019. (212)333-59456. Contact: Alan M. Tigay, Executive Editor. Estab. 1983. Annual award "for a book of fiction on a Jewish theme. Harold U. Ribalow was a noted writer and editor who devoted his time to the discovery and encouragement of young Jewish writers." Book should have been published the year preceding the award. Award: $1,000 and excerpt of book in *Hadassah Magazine*. Deadline is April of the year following publication.

THE MARY ROBERTS RINEHART FUND, (III), George Mason University, 4400 University Dr., Fairfax VA 22030. (703)993-1185. Roger Lathbury, director. Biennial award for short stories, novels, novellas and story collections by unpublished writers (that is, writers ineligible to apply for NEA grants). Award: Two grants whose amount varies depending upon income the fund generates. Competition receives approx. 75-100 submissions annually. Rules for SASE. Next fiction deadline: November 30, 1995. Writers must be nominated by a sponsoring writer, writing teacher, editor or agent.

‡*RIVER CITY* WRITING AWARDS IN FICTION, (I), *River City*, Dept. of English/Memphis State U., Memphis TN 38152. (901)678-8888. Awards Coordinator: Sharon Bryan. "Annual award to reward the best short stories." Award: $2,000 first prize; $500 second; $300 third. Competition receives approximately 280 submissions. Judge: To be announced. Entry fee $9; waived for subscribers to *River City*. Guidelines available for SASE. Deadline: December 6. Unpublished fiction. Open to all writers. Word length: 7,500 maximum.

SUMMERFIELD G. ROBERTS AWARD, (I, II, IV), The Sons of the Republic of Texas, Suite 222, 5942 Abrams Rd., Dallas TX 75231. Executive Secretary: Maydee J. Scurlock. "Given for the best book or manuscript of biography, essay, fiction, nonfiction, novel, poetry or short story that describes or represents the Republic of Texas, 1836-1846." Annual award of $2,500. Deadline: January 15. "The manuscripts must be written or published during the calendar year for which the award is given. Entries are to be submitted in quintuplicate and will not be returned."

ROBERTS WRITING AWARDS, (I), H. G. Roberts Foundation, P.O. Box 1868, Pittsburg KS 66762. (316)231-2998. Awards Coordinator: Stephen E. Meats. "To reward and recognize exceptional fiction writers with money and publication." Annual competition for short stories. Award: $500 (first place); $200 (second place); $100 (third place); publication for prize winners and honorable mention receipts. Competition receives approx. 600 submissions. Judge: Established fiction writer, different each year. Entry fee $6/story. Guidelines and entry form for SASE. Deadline: September 15. Previously unpublished submissions. "Open to any type of fiction, up to 15 typed pages."

‡ROMANTIC NOVELISTS' ASSOCIATION ROMANTIC NOVEL OF THE YEAR AWARD, (II, IV), 35 Ruddles Way, Windsor, Berks SL4 5SF England. Tel: 0753/867100. Contact: Major Award Organiser, Romantic Novelists' Association. "To publish good romantic fiction and therefore raise the prestige of the genre." Annual competition for novels. Award: under consideration. Competition receives approx. 150 submissions. Submissions period: September 1-December 1. For novels "published in the U.K. A modern or historical romantic novel. Three copies of each entry are required. They may be hardback or paperback. Only novels written in English and published in the U.K. during the previous 12 months (1 December-30 November) are eligible. Authors must be domiciled in U.K. or temporarily living abroad whilst in possession of British passport."

SAN JOSE STUDIES BEST STORY AWARD, (I), Bill Casey Memorial Fund, 1 Washington Square, San José CA 95192-0090. Contact: D. Mesher. Winning author receives a year's complimentary subscription to journal, which prints notice of award, and is also considered for the Bill Casey Memorial Award of $100 for the best contribution in each year's volume of *San José Studies* in essay, fiction or poetry.

CARL SANDBURG AWARDS, (I, IV), Friends of the Chicago Public Library, Harold Washington Library Center, 400 S. State St., Chicago IL 60605. (312)747-4907. Annual. To honor excellence in Chicago or Chicago area authors (including 6 counties). Books published between May 31 and June 1 (the following year). $1,000 honorarium for fiction, nonfiction, poetry and children's literature. Medal awarded also. Deadline: August 1. All entries become the property of the Friends.

‡✲SASKATCHEWAN BOOK AWARDS, (II, IV), Saskatchewan Publishers Group, Saskatchewan Library Association, Saskatchewan Writers Guild, P.O. Box 3986, Regina, Saskatchewan S4P 3R9 Canada. (306)757-6310. Award "to celebrate the achievements of Saskatchewan publishers and writers and to increase promotion and marketing of Saskatchewan writing and publishing and to recognize the diversity of Saskatchewan writing and publishing." Saskatchewan Book Awards consist of three categories: Saskatchewan Book of the Year Award (sponsored by Regina News/Midwest News), the Saskatchewan Publisher's Prize, and the Saskatchewan Book Award. Annual awards for fiction (short stories, novels, novellas), children's (stories, poems), drama, nonfiction and poetry. Award: $1,000, a commemorative certificate and specially designed sticker to be displayed on the book for each category. No entry fee. Submissions must be received between June 1 and August 1. Published submissions.

SASSY FICTION CONTEST, (I, IV), *Sassy*, 7th Floor, 230 Park Ave., New York NY 10169. (212)551-9500. Competition "to recognize promise in fiction writers aged 13-19 and to encourage teenagers to write." Annual award for short stories. Award: Scholarship. Competition receives approximately 5,000 submissions. Judges: Christina Kelly, Virginia O'Brien, Jane Pratt. No entry fee. Guidelines available for SASE. Information in June issue of magazine; winners published in December issue. Unpublished fiction. Only for writers aged 13-19.

‡THE SCHOLASTIC WRITING AWARDS, (I, IV), 730 Broadway, New York NY 10003. (212)505-3566. Program Coordinator: Lori Maccione. To provide opportunity for recognition of young writers. Annual award for short stories and other categories. Award: Cash awards and grants. Competition receives 25,000 submissions/year. Judges vary each year. Deadline: mid-January. Unpublished submissions. Contest limited to junior high and senior high students; grades 7-12. Entry blank must be signed by teacher. "Program is run through school and is only open to students in grades 7 through 12, regularly and currently enrolled in public and non-public schools in the United States and its territories, U.S.-sponsored schools abroad or any schools in Canada."

SCIENCE FICTION WRITERS OF EARTH (SFWoE) SHORT STORY CONTEST, (I, IV), Science Fiction Writers of Earth, P.O. Box 121293, Fort Worth TX 76121. (817)451-8674. SFWoE Administrator: Gilbert Gordon Reis. Purpose "to promote the art of science fiction/fantasy short story writing." Annual award for short stories. Award: $100 (1st prize); $50 (2nd prize); $25 (3rd prize). Competition receives approx. 75 submissions/year. Judge: Author Edward Bryant. Entry fee: $5 for 1st entry; $2 for additional entries. Guidelines for SASE. Deadline: October 30. Submissions must be unpublished. Stories should be science fiction or fantasy, 2,000-7,500 words. "Although many of our past winners are now published authors, there is still room for improvement. The odds are good for a well-written story."

‡SCRIBBLES SHORT STORY CONTEST, (I), Scribes, P.O. Box 1392, Ronald WA 98940. Contact: Judith R. Paul. Award "to promote new writers of fiction and poetry." Award granted when money is available. Award for short stories and poetry. Award: $10 and publication (1st prize); $5 and publication (2nd prize). Competition receives approx. 10-20 entries. Judges: Published authors. Entry fee $10. Guidelines available for SASE. Deadline: March 31. Previously unpublished submissions. "All genre's but *no pornography*. Short stories—2,500 word maximum, no minimum; poetry—24 lines maximum, no minimum. *Scribbles* is published annually."

SE LA VIE WRITER'S JOURNAL CONTEST, (I, IV), Rio Grande Press, P.O. Box 71745, Las Vegas NV 89170. (702)894-4486. Contact: Rosalie Avara, editor. Competition offered quarterly for short stories. Award: Publication in the *Se La Vie Writer's Journal* plus up to $10 and contributor's copy. Judge: Editor. Entry fee $4 for each or $7 for two. Guidelines for SASE. Deadlines: March 31, June 30, September 30, December 31. Unpublished submissions. Themes: slice-of-life, mystery, adventure, social. Length: 500 words maximum.

THE SEATON AWARDS, (I, IV), *Kansas Quarterly*, Kansas State University KS 66506-0703. Annual awards to reward and recognize the best fiction published in *KQ* during the year from authors native to or resident in Kansas. Submissions must be previously unpublished. Anyone who submits unpublished material which is then accepted for publication becomes eligible for the awards. Award: Recognition and monetary sums of $250, $150, $100 and $50. No deadline. Material simply may be submitted for consideration at any time with SASE. "Ours are not contests. We give monetary awards and recognition to Kansas writers of national literary stature."

SEVENTEEN MAGAZINE FICTION CONTEST, (I, IV), *Seventeen Magazine*, 850 Third Ave., New York NY 10022. Contact: Joe Bargmann. To honor best short fiction by a young writer. Rules are found in the November issue. Contest for 13-21 year olds. Deadline: April 30. Submissions judged by a panel of outside readers and *Seventeen's* editors. Cash awarded to winners. First-place story considered for publication.

✸SHORT GRAIN CONTEST, (I), Box 1154, Regina, Saskatchewan S4P 3B4 Canada. Contact: Geoffrey Ursell. Annual competition for postcard stories and prose poems. Awards: $250 (1st prize), $150 (2nd prize) and $100 (third prize) in each category. "All winners and Honourable Mentions will also receive regular payment for publication in *Grain*." Competition receives approximately 600 submissions. Judges: Canadian writers with national and international reputations. Entry fee $19.95 for 2 entries in one category (includes one-year subscription); each additional entry in the same category $5. Guidelines for SASE or SAE and IRC. Deadline: April 30. Unpublished submissions. Contest entries must be either an original postcard story (a work of narrative fiction written in 500 words or less) or a prose poem (a lyric poem written as a prose paragraph or paragraphs in 500 words or less).

SIDE SHOW ANNUAL SHORT STORY CONTEST, (I), Somersault Press, P.O. Box 1428, El Cerrito CA 94530-1428. (510)215-2207. Editor: Shelley Anderson. "To attract quality writers for our 300-odd page paperback fiction annual." Awards: 1st: $30; 2nd: $25; 3rd: $20; $5/printed page paid to all accepted writers (on publication). Judges: The editors of *Side Show*. Entry fee $10 (includes subscription). Leaflet available. Sample copy for $10 plus $2 postage. Deadline: June 30. Multiple submissions encouraged (only one entry fee required for each writer). All mss with SASE critiqued. "A story from *Side Show* was selected for inclusion in *Pushcart Prize XVIII: Best of the Small Presses*."

CHARLIE MAY SIMON BOOK AWARD, (III, IV), Arkansas Department of Education, Elementary School Council, State Education Building, Capitol Mall, Division of School Improvement, Room 402-B, Little Rock AR 72201. (501)682-4371. Contact: James A. Hester, Secretary/Treasurer, Arkansas Elementary School Council. Annual award "to encourage reading by children of Arkansas, to promote book discussions of books read, and to bring before children of Arkansas examples of quality children's literature they would not normally read or would have heard read." Award: Medallion (1st prize); trophy (1st runner-up). No entry fee. Previously published submissions. "The committee doesn't accept requests from authors. They will look at booklists of books produced during the previous year and check recommendations from the following sources: *Booklist, Bulletin of the Center for Children's Books, Children's Catalog, Elementary School Library Collection, Hornbook, Library of Congress Children's Books, School Library Journal*."

✸SMITH BOOKS/BOOKS IN CANADA NOVEL AWARD, (III, IV), Books in Canada, #603, 130 Spadina Ave., Toronto, Ontario M5V 2L4 Canada. (416)601-9880. Contact: Paul Stuewe, editor. Annual award "to promote and recognize Canadian writing." Award: $5,000. No entry fee. Submissions are made by publishers. Contest is restricted to published first novels in English, intended for adults, written by Canadian citizens or residents.

SNAKE NATION PRESS ANNUAL SUMMER CONTEST, (I), 110-#2 W. Force St., Valdosta GA 31601. (912)249-8334. Contact: Roberta George. "Because we pay only in contributor's copy, this contest allows us to give some financial compensation." Annual award for short stories. Awards: $300, $200, $100. Competition receives approx. 500 submissions. Judge: Independent ("it varies"). Entry fee $5 (includes contest issue). Guidelines for SASE. Deadline: March 1 (for annual summer issue). Unpublished submissions only. Length: 5,000 words maximum.

KAY SNOW CONTEST, (I, IV), Willamette Writers, Suite 5-A, 9045 SW Barbur Blvd., Portland OR 97219. (503)452-1592. Contact: Contest Coordinator. Award "to create a showcase for writers of all fields of literature." Annual competition for short stories; also poetry (structured and nonstructured), nonfiction, juvenile and student writers. Award: $200 1st prize in each category, 2nd and 3rd prizes, honorable mentions. Competition receives approx. 500-1,000 submissions. Judges: Nationally recognized writers and teachers. Entry fee $20, nonmembers; $15, members; $10, students. Guidelines for

#10 SASE. Deadline: October 1 postmark. Unpublished submissions. Maximum 5 double-spaced pages or up to 3 poems per entry fee with maximum 5 double-spaced pages. Prize winners will be honored at the December monthly Willamette writers meeting. Press releases will be sent to local and national media announcing the winners, and excerpts from winning entries will run in the January newsletter.

SOCIETY OF CHILDREN'S BOOK WRITERS AND ILLUSTRATORS GOLDEN KITE AWARDS (II, IV), Society of Children's Book Writers and Illustrators, Suite 106, 22736 Vanowen St., West Hills CA 91307. (818)888-8760. Contact: Sue Alexander, chairperson. Annual award. "To recognize outstanding works of fiction, nonfiction and picture illustration for children by members of the Society of Children's Book Writers and published in the award year." Published submissions should be submitted from January to December of publication year. Deadline entry: December 15. Rules for SASE. Award: Statuette and plaque. Looking for quality material for children. Individual "must be member of the SCBWI to submit books."

SOCIETY OF CHILDREN'S BOOK WRITERS AND ILLUSTRATORS WORK-IN-PROGRESS GRANTS, (I, IV), Suite 106, 22736 Vanowen St., West Hills CA 91307. (818)888-8760. Contact: SCBWI. Annual grant for contemporary novel for young people; also nonfiction research grant and grant for work whose author has never been published. Award: 1st-$1,000, 2nd-$500 (work-in-progress); 1st-$1,000, 2nd-$400 (Judy Blume/SCBWI contemporary novel grant). Competition receives approx. 80 submissions. Judges: Members of children's book field—editors, authors, etc. Guidelines for SASE. Deadline: February 1-May 1. Unpublished submissions. Applicants must be SCBWI members.

‡*SONORA REVIEW* FICTION CONTEST, (I), Dept. of English, University of Arizona, Tucson AZ 85721. (602)621-1836. Contact: Editor-in-Chief. Annual award "to encourage and support quality short fiction, poetry and creative nonfiction." Awards prizes plus publication in *Sonora*. Contest rules for SASE (IRCs). Unpublished submissions. "We accept manuscripts all year."

‡SOUTH CAROLINA ARTS COMMISSION AND *THE POST AND COURIER* NEWSPAPER (CHARLESTON, SC) SOUTH CAROLINA FICTION PROJECT, (I, IV), 1800 Gervais St., Columbia SC 29201. (803)734-8696. Steve Lewis, director, Literary Arts Program. The purpose of the award is "to get money to fiction writers and to get their work published and read." Annual award for short stories. Award: $500 and publication in *The Post and Courier*. Competition receives between 300 and 400 submissions for 12 awards (up to 12 stories chosen). Judges are a panel of professional writers and Book Editor/Features writer for *The Post and Courier*. Entry forms or rules for SASE. Deadline: May 1. *South Carolina residents only.*

‡SOUTH CAROLINA ARTS COMMISSION LITERATURE FELLOWSHIPS AND LITERATURE GRANTS, (I, IV), 1800 Gervais St., Columbia SC 29201. (803)734-8696. Steve Lewis, director, Literary Arts Program. "The purpose of the fellowships is to give a cash award to two deserving writers (one in poetry, one in creative prose) whose works are of the highest caliber." Award: $7,500 fellowship. Matching grants up to $7,500. Competition receives approximately 40 submissions/fellowship. Judges are out-of-state panel of professional writers and editors for fellowships, and panels and SCAC staff for grants. Entry forms or rules for SASE. Fellowship deadline September 15. Grants deadline January 15. *South Carolina residents only.*

SOUTH DAKOTA ARTS COUNCIL, ARTIST FELLOWSHIP, (I, II, IV), Suite 204, 230 S. Phillips Ave., Sioux Falls SD 57102-0720. (605)339-6646. Award "to assist artists with career development. Grant can be used for supplies or to set aside time to work, but cannot be used for academic research or formal study toward a degree." Annual competition for writers. Award: Artist Career Development grant, $1,000; Artist Fellowship, $5,000. Competition receives approx. 80 submissions. "Grants are awarded on artists' work and *not* on financial need." Judges: Panels of in-state and out-of-state experts in each discipline. Guidelines for SASE. Deadline: February 1. Previously published or unpublished submissions. Fellowships are open only to residents of South Dakota.

SOUTHERN ARTS LITERATURE PRIZE, (II, IV), 13 St. Clement St., Winchester, Hampshire S023 9DQ England. Award "to recognize good works by authors (known or unknown) in the southern region (of the U.K.)." Annual competition run on a three-year cycle alternating fiction, poetry and nonfiction. Award £1,000 (plus winner commissions piece of work; value to £600). Competition receives approx. 20-30 submissions. Judges: 3 people (involved in literature or authors themselves), different each year.

Guidelines for SASE. Southern arts region covers Hampshire, Berkshire, Wiltshire, Oxfordshire, Buckinghamshire, Isle of Wight and East Dorset. Write for information.

THE SOUTHERN REVIEW/LOUISIANA STATE UNIVERSITY ANNUAL SHORT FICTION AWARD, (II), *The Southern Review*, 43 Allen Hall, Louisiana State University, Baton Rouge LA 70803. (504)388-5108. Contact: Editors, *The Southern Review*. Annual award "to encourage publication of good fiction." For a first collection of short stories by an American writer appearing during calendar year. Award: $500 to author. Possible campus reading. Deadline: A month after close of each calendar year. The book of short stories must be released by a US publisher. Two copies to be submitted by publisher or author. Looking for "style, sense of craft, plot, in-depth characters."

‡SPIRIT OF ARTS PRESS SHORT STORY CONTEST, (I), Spirit of Arts Press, % 7871 Ravencrest Court, Cincinnati OH 45255. Contact: Tom Arbino. Award "to encourage creative (non-mass market) fiction that is truly art and not a product." Annual award for short stories. Award: winner percentage of take and publication. All selected published in anthology. Judge: Tom Arbino, editor/publisher. Entry fee $7.50 ($6.50/story if submitting more than one). Deadline: April 30. Unpublished submissions. Length: 3,000 words maximum.

WALLACE E. STEGNER FELLOWSHIP, (I, IV), Creative Writing Program, Stanford University, Stanford CA 94305-2087. (415)723-2637. Contact: Gay Pierce, program coordinator. Annual award. Four two-year fellowships in fiction ($11,500 stipend plus required tuition of $4,500 annually). Entry fee $20. Deadline: January 2. For unpublished or previously published fiction writers. Residency required.

‡THE JOAN G. SUGARMAN CHILDREN'S BOOK AWARD, (II, IV), Washington Independent Writers Legal and Educational Fund, Inc., 220 Woodward Bldg., 733 15th St. NW, Washington D.C. 20005 (202)347-4973. The Joan G. Sugarman Children's Book Award was established in 1987 to recognize excellence in children's literature. Biennial competition for "children's literature, both fiction and nonfiction, geared for children ages 15 and under." Award: $1,000. Competition receives approximately 100 submissions. Judges are selected by the WIW Legal and Educational Fund, Inc. They have included librarians, professors of children's literature and children's bookstore owners. Guidelines for SASE. For the 1994-1995 award, the expected deadline is the end of January 1996. Previously published submissions from 1994 and 1995 for the next award. The authors must reside in Washington DC, Maryland or Virginia. There is no word-length requirement.

✷SWG LITERARY AWARDS, (I, IV), Saskatchewan Writers Guild, Box 3986, Regina, Saskatchewan S4P 3R9 Canada. (306)757-6310. Awards "to recognize excellence in work by Saskatchewan writers." Annual competition for short stories, poetry, nonfiction and children's literature. Also a long manuscript category that rotates through poetry, nonfiction, drama and fiction. Awards: Manuscript awards (3) are $1,000; 3 awards of $150 in each of the short categories. Judges: Writers from outside the Province. Entry fee: $15 (one ms allowed); $4 for other categories (multiple submissions allowed). Guidelines for SASE. Deadline changes; write for guidelines. Unpublished submissions. Available only to Saskatchewan citizens.

TEXAS-WIDE WRITERS CONTEST, (I, IV), Byliners, P.O. Box 6218, Corpus Christi TX 78413. Contact: Contest Chairman. "Contest to fund a scholarship in journalism or creative writing." Annual contest for adult and children's short stories, novels and poems. Award: Novels—1st $100, 2nd $75, 3rd $50; short stories—1st $75, 2nd $50, 3rd $25. Competition receives approximately 50 novel, 125 short story and 62 children's story submissions. Judges: Varies each year. Entry fee $5/story, $10/novel. Guidelines available for SASE. Deadline is March 1 (date remains same each year). Unpublished submissions. Limited to Texas residents and winter Texans. Length: Children's story limit 2,000 words; short story limit 3,000 words; novel 3 page synopsis plus chapter one. "Contest also has nostalgia, article and nonfiction book categories."

THURBER HOUSE RESIDENCIES, (II), The Thurber House, 77 Jefferson Ave., Columbus OH 43215. (614)464-1032. Literary Director: Michael J. Rosen. "Four writers/year are chosen as writers-in-residence, one for each quarter." Award for writers of novels and story collections. $5,000 stipend and housing for a quarter in the furnished third-floor apartment of James Thurber's boyhood home. Judges: Advisory panel. To apply send letter of interest and curriculum vitae. Deadline: December 15. "The James Thurber Writer-in-Residence will teach a class in the Creative Writing Program at the Ohio State University in either fiction or poetry, and will offer one public reading and a short workshop for writers in the community. Significant time outside of teaching is reserved for the writer's own work in progress. Candidates should have published at least one book with a major publisher, in any area of fiction, nonfiction or poetry, and should possess some experience in teaching."

TOWSON STATE UNIVERSITY PRIZE FOR LITERATURE, (II, IV), Towson State University Foundation, Towson State University, Towson MD 21204. (410)830-2128. Contact: Annette Chappell, Dean, College of Liberal Arts. Annual award for novels or short story collections, previously published. Award: $1,000. Requirements: Writer must not be over 40; must be a Maryland resident. SASE for rules/entry forms. Deadline: May 15.

TRANSLATORS ASSOCIATION AWARDS, (III, IV), 84 Drayton Gardens, London SW10 9SB England. Scott Moncrieff Prize for best translation into English of 20th century French work; Schlegel-Tieck Prize for translations from German; John Florio Prize for translations from Italian into English; Bernard Shaw Prize for translations from Swedish. Award: Scott Moncrieff Prize: £1,500; Schlegel-Tieck Prize: £2,000; John Florio Prize (biannual): £900; Bernard Shaw Prize (every 3 years): £ 1,000. Judges: 3 translators. Deadline: December 31. Previously published submissions. Awards for translations published in UK during year of award. UK publishers submit books for consideration.

TRI-STATE FAIR LITERARY AWARDS, (I), % Marianne McNeil, Suite 16, 7003 Amarillo Blvd. E., Amarillo TX 79107. (806)379-5032. Annual competition for short stories and poetry. Award: small cash awards, Best of Show Awards. Judges: Different each year. Entry fee $7 prose, $5 poetry. Guidelines for SASE. Deadline: August 1. Unpublished submissions. Length: 3,500 words maximum. "Categories may change a bit from year to year. Guidelines required. Open. Entries are displayed at Literary Booth at Tri-State Fair during fair week."

‡MARK TWAIN AWARD, (III, IV), Missouri Association of School Librarians, 5552 S. Kingshighway, St. Louis MO 63109-3258. Estab. 1970. Annual award to introduce children to the best of current literature for children and to stimulate reading. Award: A bronze bust of Mark Twain, created by Barbara Shanklin, a Missouri sculptor. A committee selects pre-list of the books nominated for the award; statewide reader/selectors review and rate the books, and then children throughout the state vote to choose a winner from the final list. Books must be published two years prior to nomination for the award list. Publishers may send books they wish to nominate for the list to the committee members. 1) Books should be of interest to children in grades 4 through 8; 2) written by an author living in the U.S.; 3) of literary value which may enrich children's personal lives.

‡UPC SCIENCE FICTION AWARD, (I, IV), Universitat Politècnica de Catalunya Board of Trustees, Diagonal 649, 08028 Barcelona, Spain. (93)401 43 63. "The award is based on the desire for integral education at UPC. The literary genre of science fiction is undoubtedly the most suitable for a university such as UPC, since it unifies the concepts of science and literature." Annual award for short stories; 1,000,000 pesetas (about 10,000 U.S. $). Judges: professors of the university and science fiction writers. Deadline: August 30th. Previously unpublished entries. Length: 75-110 pages, double-spaced, 30 lines/page, 70 characters/line. Submissions may be made in Spanish, English, Catalan or French. The author must sign his work with a pseudonym and enclose a sealed envelope with full name, a personal ID number, address and phone. The pseudonym at title of work must appear on the envelope. Write for more details.

UTAH ORIGINAL WRITING COMPETITION, (I, IV), Utah Arts Council, 617 E. South Temple, Salt Lake City UT 84102. (801)533-5895. Literary Arts Coordinator: G. Barnes. Annual competition for poetry, essays, nonfiction books, short stories, novels and story collections. Awards: Vary; last year between $200-1,000. Competition receives 700 entries. Judges: "Published and award-winning judges from across America." Guidelines available, no SASE necessary. Deadline: Mid-June or later. Submissions should be unpublished. Limited to Utah residents. "Some limitation on word-length. See guidelines for details."

VERMONT COUNCIL ON THE ARTS FELLOWSHIP, (I, II, IV), Vermont Council on the Arts, 136 State St., Montpelier VT 05602. (802)828-3291. Contact: Cornelia Carey, Grants Officer. "To support creative development." Annual competition for short stories, novels, story collections, playwrighting and translations. Award: $3,500. The VCA awards approximately 8 Fellowships annually. There is no predetermined number of Fellowships by discipline. Judges: A peer panel makes recommendations to the VCA Board of Trustees. Guidelines for SASE after December 1. Previously published and unpublished submissions. Applicants must be legal residents of Vermont and must have lived in Vermont at least 1 year prior to date of application. Word length: 10-15 pages poetry, 10-20 pages fiction. Applicants may include a synopsis or summary of longer works in addition to submitted excerpts. Applicants must be 18 or older, may not be enrolled as fulltime students, and must have submitted all reports on past council grants. Grant money may not be used for foreign travel, tuition applied to academic programs, or purchase of permanent equipment. *Manuscripts should be unsigned and should indicate completion date.* Manuscripts must be sent with completed application. Call for application and additional information.

‡**VICTORIAN FELLOWSHIP OF AUSTRALIAN WRITERS ANNUAL NATIONAL LITERARY AWARDS,** **(I, II, IV),** 1/317 Barkers Rd., Kew (Melbourne) Victoria 3101 Australia. Contact: J.S. Hamilton, president, Victorian FAW. Sponsors 20 awards for Australian writers, both published and unpublished. Annual competitions for poetry, short stories, novels, nonfiction books and story collections. Awards vary: Largest award is $1,200. Competition receives over 200 entries for books, at least 100 for manuscripts. Judges: Writers and critics appointed by the organizer. Guidelines for SASE. Deadline: December 31. Published or previously unpublished submissions, depending on award. Awards offered to Australians (including those living overseas) or residents of Australia. Send for guidelines, but only from October each year.

VOGELSTEIN FOUNDATION GRANTS, (II), The Ludwig Vogelstein Foundation, Inc., P.O. Box 4924, Brooklyn NY 11240-4924. Executive Director: Frances Pishny. "A small foundation awarding grants to individuals in the arts and humanities. Criteria are merit and need. No student aid given." Send SASE for complete information after January 31.

WALDEN FELLOWSHIP, (I, IV), Coordinated by The Northwest Writing Institute, Lewis & Clark College, Campus Box 100, Portland OR 97219. (503)768-7745. Award "to give Oregon writers of fiction, poetry and creative nonfiction the opportunity to pursue their work at a quiet, beautiful farm in Southern Oregon." Annual competition for all types of writing. Award: 3-6 week residencies. Competition receives approx. 30 submissions. Judges: Committee judges selected by the sponsor. Guidelines for SASE. Deadline end of November. Oregon writers only. Word length: Maximum 30 pages prose, 8-10 poems.

EDWARD LEWIS WALLANT MEMORIAL BOOK AWARD, (II, IV), 3 Brighton Rd., West Hartford CT 06117. Sponsored by Dr. and Mrs. Irving Waltman. Contact: Mrs. Irving Waltman. Annual award. Memorial to Edward Lewis Wallant, which offers incentive and encouragement to beginning writers, for books published the year before the award is conferred in the spring. Award: $350 plus award certificate. Books may be submitted for consideration to Dr. Sanford Pinsker, Department of English, Franklin & Marshall College, P.O. Box 3003, Lancaster PA 17604-3003. "Looking for creative work of fiction by an American which has significance for the American Jew. The novel (or collection of short stories) should preferably bear a kinship to the writing of Wallant. The award will seek out the writer who has not yet achieved literary prominence."

WASHINGTON PRIZE FOR FICTION, (I), 1301 S. Scott St., Arlington VA 22204. (703)920-3771. Director: Larry Kaltman. Awards: $3,000 (1st prize), $2,000 (2nd prize), $1,000 (3rd prize). The judges are the English Department chairpersons of three Washington-area universities. The submission may be a novel, several novellas or a collection of short stories. There are no restrictions as to setting or theme. Contestants may reside anywhere. Length: 65,000 words minimum, previously unpublished. Entry fee: $25. Deadline: November 30 annually.

‡**WATTIE BOOK AWARD, (III, IV),** Wattie Industries/Ltd., Book Publishers Association of New Zealand (BPANZ), Box 386, Auckland, New Zealand. Contact: Tony Hawkins, Convenor, Wattie Committee. "To recognize excellence in writing and publishing books by New Zealanders. This is not a category award. Fiction/nonfiction/children's etc. are all included." Award: 1st: NZ$20,000; 2nd: NZ$10,000; 3rd: NZ$5,000. Competition receives approx. 80-90 submissions. Judges: Panel of 3 selected annually by the BPANZ—1 writer, 1 book trade person and 1 other. Entry fee NZ$75. Guidelines for SASE. Deadline: April 5. "Writer must be New Zealander or resident of New Zealand and its former Pacific territories. Must be submitted by publisher. Full details available from BPANZ."

WELLSPRING **SHORT FICTION CONTEST,** *Wellspring Magazine,* 770 Tonkawa Rd., Long Lake MN 55356. (612)471-9259. Award "to select well-crafted short fiction with interesting story lines." Biannual competition for short stories. Awards: $100, $75, $25 and publication. Competition receives approximately 40 submissions. Judges: writers and readers. Entry fee $10. Guidelines for SASE (IRCs). Deadlines July 1, January 1. Unpublished submissions. Word length: 2,000 words maximum.

♣WESTERN CANADIAN MAGAZINE AWARDS, (II, IV), 3898 Hillcrest Ave., North Vancouver, British Columbia V7R 4B6 Canada. (604)984-7525. "To honour and encourage editorial excellence." Annual competition for short stories (fiction articles in magazines). Award: $500. Entry fee: $18-24 (depending on circulation of magazine). Deadline: January. Previously published submissions (between January and December). "Must be Canadian or have earned immigrant status or be a full-time Canadian resident, and the fiction article must have appeared in a publication (magazine) that has its main editorial offices located in the 4 Western provinces, the Yukon or Northwest territories."

WESTERN HERITAGE AWARDS, (II, IV), National Cowboy Hall of Fame, 1700 NE 63rd St., Oklahoma City OK 73111. (405)478-2250. Contact: Dana Sullivant, public relations director. Annual award "to honor outstanding quality in fiction, nonfiction and art literature." Submissions are to have been published during the previous calendar year. Award: The Wrangler, a replica of a C.M. Russell Bronze. No entry fee. Entry forms and rules available October 1 for SASE. Deadline: December 31. Looking for "stories that best capture the spirit of the West."

WESTERN STATES BOOK AWARDS, (III, IV), Western States Arts Federation, 236 Montezuma, Santa Fe NM 87501. (505)988-1166. Literature Coordinator: Robert Sheldon. Annual award "to recognize writers living in the West; encouragement of effective production and marketing of quality books published in the West; increase of sales and critical attention." For unpublished manuscripts submitted by publisher. Award: $5,000 for authors; $5,000 for publishers. Contest rules for SASE. Write for information on deadline.

WHITING WRITERS' AWARDS, (III), Mrs. Giles Whiting Foundation, Room 3500, 30 Rockefeller Place, New York NY 10112. Director: Dr. Gerald Freund. Annual award for writers of fiction, poetry, nonfiction and plays with an emphasis on emerging writers. Award: $30,000 (10 awards). Writers are submitted by appointed nominators and chosen for awards by an appointed selection committee. Direct applications and informal nominations not accepted by the foundation.

LAURA INGALLS WILDER AWARD, (III), American Library Association/Association for Library Service to Children, 50 E. Huron St., Chicago IL 60611. Executive Director: S. Roman. Award offered every 3 years; next year 1995. "To honor a significant body of work for children, for illustration, fiction or nonfiction." Award: Bronze medal.

LAURENCE L. WINSHIP BOOK AWARD, (III, IV), *The Boston Globe*, P.O. Box 2378, Boston MA 02107-2378. (617)929-2649. Contact: Marianne Callahan, public affairs department. Annual award "to honor *The Globe*'s late editor who did much to encourage young talented New England authors." Award: $2,000. Contest rules for SASE. Deadline: June 30. Previously published submissions from July 1 to June 30 each year. Book must have some relation to New England—author, theme, plot or locale. To be submitted by publishers.

WISCONSIN INSTITUTE FOR CREATIVE WRITING FELLOWSHIP, (I, II, IV), University of Wisconsin—Creative Writing, English Department, Madison WI 53705. Director: Ron Wallace. Competition "to provide time, space and an intellectual community for writers working on first books." Annual award for short stories, novels and story collections. Award: $20,000/9-month appointment. Competition receives approximately 400 submissions. Judges: English Department faculty. Required guidelines available for SASE; write to Ron Kuka. Deadline is month of February. Published or unpublished submissions. Applicants must have received an M.F.A. or comparable graduate degree in creative writing. Limit one story up to 30 pages in length. Two letters of recommendation required.

‡PAUL A. WITTY SHORT STORY AWARD, (II), International Reading Association, P.O. Box 8139, 800 Barksdale Rd., Newark DE 19714-8139. (302)731-1600. Annual award "given to the author of an original short story published for the first time in the prior year in a periodical for children." Award: $1,000. Judges: International Reading Association committees. For guidelines write to: Barbara D. Stoodt, 5011 Manning Drive, Greensboro NC 27410. Deadline: December 1. Published submissions.

WRITER'S DIGEST ANNUAL WRITING COMPETITION (Short Story Division), (I), *Writer's Digest,* 1507 Dana Ave., Cincinnati OH 45207. (513)531-2690. Contact: Contest Director. Grand Prize is an expenses paid trip to New York City with arrangements to meet editors/agents in writer's field. Other awards include cash, reference books, plaques and certificates of recognition. Names of grand prize winner and top 100 winners are announced in the October issue of *Writer's Digest.* Top two entries published in booklet ($4.50). Send SASE to *WD* Writing Competition for rules and entry form, or see January-May issues of *Writer's Digest.* Deadline: May 31. Entry fee: $5. All entries must be original, unpublished and not previously submitted to a *Writer's Digest* contest. Length: 2,000 words maximum, one entry only. No acknowledgment will be made of receipt of mss nor will mss be returned.

✷**WRITERS GUILD OF ALBERTA LITERARY AWARD, (II, IV),** Writers Guild of Alberta, 10523-100 Avenue, Edmonton, Alberta T5J 0A8 Canada. (403)426-5892. Executive Director: Miki Andrejevic. "To recognize, reward and foster writing excellence." Annual competition for novels and story collections. Award: $500, plus leather-bound copy of winning work. Short story competition receives 5-10 submissions; novel competition receives about 20; children's literature category up to 40. Judges: 3 published writers. Guidelines for SASE. Deadline: December 31. Previously published submissions (between January and December). Open to Alberta authors, resident for previous 18 months. Entries must be book-length and published within the current year.

WRITERS' JOURNAL ANNUAL FICTION CONTEST, (I), 27 Empire Dr., St. Paul MN 55103. (612)225-1306. Publisher/Managing Editor: Valerie Hockert. Annual award for short stories. Award: 1st place: $100; 2nd place: $50; 3rd place: $25. Also gives honorable mentions. Competition receives approximately 500 submissions/year. Judges are Valerie Hockert, Steven Petsch and others. Entry fee $5 each. Maximum of 3 entries/person. Entry forms or rules for SASE. Maximum length is 3,000 words. Two copies of each entry are required—one *without* name or address of writer.

‡**WRITERS' OPEN FORUM SUMMER WRITING CONTEST, (I),** *Writers' Open Forum,* P.O. Box 516, Tracyton WA 98393. Editorial Director: Sandra E. Haven. Annual award "to encourage strong writing skills for short story writers." Awards: $50 (1st place); $25 (2nd place); $10 (3rd place). Competition receives approximately 150 entries. Judges: *Writers' Open Forum* staff. No entry fee for subscribers; $5 entry fee for nonsubscribers. Guidelines available for SASE (IRCs). Deadline: July 31. Previously unpublished submissions. "Length, theme and other requirements vary for each contest. Send for guidelines available three months prior to deadline. Entries judged on creativity, technique, mechanics and appeal."

‡**WRITERS' OPEN FORUM WINTER WRITING CONTEST, (I),** *Writers' Open Forum,* P.O. Box 516, Tracyton WA 98393. Editorial Director: Sandra E. Haven. Annual award "to encourage strong writing skills for short story writers." Awards: $50 (1st place); $25 (2nd place); $10 (3rd place). Competition receives approximately 150 entries. Judges: *Writers' Open Forum* staff. No entry fee for subscribers; $5 entry fee for nonsubscribers. Guidelines available for SASE (IRCs). Deadline: January 31. Previously unpublished submissions. "Length, theme and other requirements vary for each contest. Send for guidelines available three months prior to deadline. Entries are judged on creativity, technique, mechanics and appeal."

THE WRITERS' WORKSHOP INTERNATIONAL FICTION CONTEST, (I), The Writers' Workshop, P.O. Box 696, Asheville NC 28802. (704)254-8111. Executive Director: Karen Tager. Annual awards for fiction. Awards: $500 and submission to *The Paris Review* (1st prize); $250 (2nd prize), $100 (3rd prize). Winners also receive one year's membership to The Writers' Workshop. Competition receives approximately 350 submissions. Past judges have been E.L. Doctorow, Reynolds Price, Peter Matthiessen and Nikki Giovanni. Entry fee $15/$12 members. Guidelines for SASE. Deadline: Varies. Unpublished submissions. Length: 30 typed, double-spaced pages/story. Multiple submissions accepted.

‡**WRITING COMPETITION FOR WRITERS OVER 50, (I, IV),** Yachats Literary Festival, 124 NE California, Yachats OR 97498. (503)547-3271. Director: Frena Bloomfield. "For writers over 50." Annual competition for various categories. Award: $250 per category plus attendance at the Yachats Literary Festival. Judges: Panel of writers, academics and editors. Guidelines for SASE. Previously unpublished submissions. Contest closes end of April.

WYOMING ARTS COUNCIL LITERARY FELLOWSHIPS, (I, IV), Wyoming Arts Council, 2320 Capitol Ave., Cheyenne WY 82002. (307)777-7742. Contact: Literature consultant. Annual awards to "honor the most outstanding new work of Wyoming writers—fiction, nonfiction, drama, poetry." Award: 4

awards of $2,500 each. Competition receives approx. 70-90 submissions. Judges: Panel of three writers selected each year from outside Wyoming. Guidelines for SASE. Deadline: June 15. Applicants "must be Wyoming resident for one year prior to application deadline. Must not be a full-time student." No genre exclusions; combined genres acceptable. 25 pages double-spaced maximum; 10 pages maximum for poetry. Winners may not apply for 4 years after receiving fellowships.

YOUNG READER'S CHOICE AWARD, (III), Pacific Northwest Library Association, Graduate School of Library and Information Sciences, 133 Suzzallo Lib., FM-30, University of Washington, Seattle WA 98195. (206)543-1897. Contact: Carol A. Doll. Annual award "to promote reading as an enjoyable activity and to provide children an opportunity to endorse a book they consider an excellent story." Award: Silver medal. Judges: Children's librarians and teachers nominate; children in grades 4-8 vote for their favorite book on the list. Guidelines for SASE. Deadline: February 1. Previously published submissions. Writers must be nominated by children's librarians and teachers.

Contests and awards/'93-'94 changes

The following contests, grants and awards appeared in the 1993 edition of *Novel & Short Story Writer's Market* but do not appear in the 1994 edition. Those contests, grants and awards that did not respond to our request for an update appear below without further explanation. If a reason was given, it is included next to the listing name.

Jane Addams Children's Book Award
Alberta New Fiction Competition
The Alberta Writing for Young People Competition
Allegheny Review Awards
American Academy and Institute of Arts and Letters Literary Awards (asked to be deleted)
Analecta College Fiction
Emily Clark Balch Awards
The F.G. Bressani Prize
Bunting Institute Fellowship
Canadian Library Association Book of the Year for Children Award
Conseil de la vie Francaise en Amerique/Prix Champlain
John Dos Passos Prize
Epiphany Short Fiction Contest (no longer awarded)
Fantastic Four Short Story Writing Contests
Florida Arts Council/Literature Fellowships
Miles Franklin Literary Award
Joseph Henry Jackson Award
Japan-United States Friendship Commission Prize for the Translation of Japanese Literature

The Janet Heidinger Kafka Prize
Jack Kerouac Literary Prize
Aga Khan Prize (asked to be deleted)
Lawrence Fellowship (temporarily suspended)
The Leading Edge Contest
The Marten Bequest Award
Maryland State Arts Council Individual Artists Awards
Michigan Arts Awards (asked to be deleted)
Milkweed Editions National Fiction Prize
The Missouri Review Editors' Prize Contest
Jenny Moore Writer-in-Washington
National Book Foundation Inc.
National Jewish Book Awards
North Carolina Arts Council
Ohio Arts Council Aid to Individual Artists Fellowship
Open Voice Awards
Palm Council Philippine-American Short Story Contest
William Peden Prize in Fiction

Quarterly West Novella Competition
Rocky Mountain Women's Institute Associateship
Romance Writers of America Golden Heart and the Rita Awards
Sacramento Public Library Focus on Writers Contest
Short and Sweet Contest
Short Story Science Fiction/Fantasy Competition
Spur Award Contest
Stand Magazine Short Story Competition
Sugar Mill Press Contests (complaints)
Tennessee Arts Commission
John Train Humor Prize (asked to be deleted)
Translation Center Awards
Harold D. Vursell Memorial Award (asked to be deleted)
William Allen White Children's Book Award
Wisconsin Arts Board Individual Artist Program
World's Best Short Short Story

Resources

Resources

Conferences and Workshops

Welcome to Conferences and Workshops, the fastest growing section in this book. Why are conferences so popular? Writers and conference directors alike tell us it's because writing can be such a lonely business otherwise—that at conferences writers have the opportunity to meet (and commiserate) with fellow writers, as well as meet and network with publishers, editors and agents. Conferences and workshops provide some of the best opportunities for writers to make publishing contacts and pick up valuable information on the business, as well as the craft, of writing.

The bulk of the listings in this section are for conferences. Most conferences last from one day to one week and offer a combination of workshop-type writing sessions, panel discussions, and a variety of guest speakers. Topics may include all aspects of writing from fiction to poetry to scriptwriting or they may focus on a specific area such as those sponsored by the Society of Children's Book Writers and Illustrators, which cater to the interests of those who write for children.

Workshops, however, tend to run longer—usually one to two weeks. Designed to operate like writing classes, most require writers to be prepared to work on and discuss their work-in-progress while attending. The draw of workshops is they provide writers the opportunity for an intensive critique of their work, often by professional writing teachers and established writers.

Each of the listings here includes information on the specific focus of an event as well as planned panels, guest speakers and workshop topics. It is important to note, however, some conference directors were still in the planning stages for 1994 when we contacted them. If it was not possible to include 1994 dates, fees or topics, we have provided information from 1993 so you can get an idea of what to expect. For the most current information, it's best to send a self-addressed, stamped envelope to the director in question about three months before the date(s) listed.

New this year

Many writers try to make it to at least one conference a year, but cost and location count as much as subject matter or other considerations when determining which conference to attend. There are conferences in almost every state and province and even some in Europe open to North Americans.

To make it easier for you to find a conference close to home—or to find one in an exotic locale to fit into your vacation plans—this year we've divided this section into geographic regions. The conferences appear in alphabetical order under the appropriate regional heading.

Note that conferences appear under the regional heading according to where they will be held, which is sometimes different than the address given as the place to register or send for information. For example, The Summer in France Writing Workshops are held in Paris and are listed under the International heading, although writers are instructed to write to Plainview, Texas, for information.

The regions are as follows:

Northeast: Connecticut, Massachusetts, Maine, New Hampshire, New York, Rhode Island, Vermont

Midatlantic: Washington DC, Delaware, Maryland, New Jersey, Pennsylvania

Midsouth: North Carolina, South Carolina, Tennessee, Virginia, West Virginia

Southeast: Alabama, Arkansas, Florida, Georgia, Louisiana, Mississippi, Puerto Rico

Midwest: Illinois, Indiana, Kentucky, Michigan, Ohio

North Central: Iowa, Minnesota, Nebraska, North Dakota, South Dakota, Wisconsin

South Central: Colorado, Kansas, Missouri, New Mexico, Oklahoma, Texas

West: Arizona, California, Hawaii, Nevada, Utah

Northwest: Alaska, Idaho, Montana, Oregon, Washington, Wyoming

Canada

International

Learning and networking

Besides learning from workshop leaders and panelists in formal sessions, writers at conferences also benefit from conversations with other attendees. Writers on all levels enjoy sharing insights. Often, a conversation over lunch can reveal a new market for your work or let you know which editors are most receptive to the work of new writers. You can find out about recent editorial changes and about specific agents. A casual chat could lead to a new contact or resource in your area.

Many editors and agents make visiting conferences a part of their regular search for new writers. A cover letter or query that starts with "I met you at the National Writers Association Conference," or "I found your talk on your company's new romance line at the Cape Cod Writers Conference most interesting . . . " may give you a small leg up on the competition.

While a few writers have been successful in selling their manuscript at a conference, the availability of editors and agents does not usually mean these folks will have the time there to read your novel or six best short stories (unless, of course, you've scheduled an individual meeting with them ahead of time). While editors and agents are glad to meet writers and discuss work in general terms, usually they don't have the time (or energy) to give an extensive critique during a conference. In other words, use the conference as a way to make a first, brief contact.

Selecting a conference

Besides the obvious considerations of time, place and cost, choose your conference based on your writing goals. If, for example, your goal is to improve the quality of your writing, it will be more helpful to you to choose a hands-on craft workshop rather than a conference offering a series of panels on marketing and promotion. If, on the other hand, you are a science fiction novelist who would like to meet your fans, try one of the many science fiction conferences or "cons" held throughout the country and the world.

Look for panelists and workshop instructors whose work you admire and who seem to be writing in your general area. Check for specific panels or discussions of topics relevant to what you are writing now. Think about the size—would you feel more comfortable with a small workshop of eight people or a large group of 100 or more attendees?

If your funds are limited, start by looking for conferences close to home, but you may want to explore those that offer contests with cash prizes—and a chance to recoup your expenses. A few conferences and workshops also offer scholarships, but the competition is stiff and writers interested in these should find out the requirements early. Finally, students may want to look for conferences and workshops that offer college credit. You will find these options included in the listings here. Again, send a self-addressed envelope for the most current details.

The science fiction field in particular offers hundreds of conventions each year for writers, illustrators and fans. To find additional listings for these, see *Locus* (P.O. Box 13305, Oakland CA 94661) or the *Science Fiction Convention Register* (Box 3343, Fairfax VA 22038). For more information on conferences and even more conferences from which to choose, check the May issue of *Writer's Digest. The Guide to Writers Conferences* (Shaw Associates, publishers, Suite 1406, 625 Biltmore Way, Coral Gables FL 33134) is another helpful resource.

Northeast (CT, MA, ME, NH, NY, RI, VT)

‡BENNINGTON SUMMER WRITING WORKSHOPS, Bennington College, Bennington VT 05201. (802)442-5401, ext. 320. Assistant Director: Priscilla Hodgkins. Estab. 1977. Workshop held July. Next workshop: July 3-July 30. Holds two 2-week sessions or one 4-week session. Average attendance: approximately 90 each session. Fiction, nonfiction and poetry. "Located on 550-acre Bennington College campus in the foothills of the Green Mountains. Participants stay in college housing and eat in Commons dining hall. There is a lake nearby and many trails to walk, hike or bike." Publishing panels focused on Magazine Publishing and Book Publishing. In addition two editors (one in each session) are in residence for three days and meet with students individually. Featured guest readers in 1993 included John Irving, Donald Hall, Jane Kenyon, Frank Bidart, Louis Simpson, Jamaica Kincaid, Stephen Sandy, Ed Ochester, Nicholas Delbanco.
Costs: Fees in 1993: $815 tuition; $455 board for two weeks.
Accommodations: "Our participants are invited to live on campus. It is part of the experience of the workshop—to live in a community of writers." Cost of campus room and board for two weeks in 1993 was $455.
Additional Information: "We ask applicants to submit writing sample as part of the application process. They are encouraged to write while they are here. Finished pieces and/or works-in-progress are critiqued within the workshops." Brochures/guidelines available beginning in February, no SASE required.

BREAD LOAF WRITERS' CONFERENCE, Middlebury College, Middlebury VT 05753. (802)388-3711 ext. 5286. Administrative Coordinator: Carol Knauss. Estab. 1926. Annual. Conference held in late August. Conference duration: 12 days. Average attendance: 230. For fiction, nonfiction and poetry. Held at the summer campus in Ripton Vermont (belongs to Middlebury College).
Costs: $1,450 (includes room/board) (1993).
Accommodations: Accommodations are at Ripton. Onsite accommodations $500 (1993).

CAPE COD WRITERS CENTER, INC., % Cape Cod Conservatory, Route 132, West Barnstable MA 02668. (508)775-4811. Executive Director: Marion Vuillenmier. Estab. 1963. Annual. Conference held: August 15-20. Conference duration: one week. Average attendance: 125. For fiction, nonfiction, poetry, juvenile writing and mystery/suspense. Held at Craigville Conference Center, a campus arrangement on shore of Cape's south side. Guest speakers and panelists for 1992 were Nancy Thayer, novelist; Chad Hoffman, Hollywood producer; Judson Hale, editor *Yankee* magazine; agent Alison Picard; editor Dana Isaacson of Pocket Books.
Costs: $80 registration and $50 per course; housing and meals separate, paid to the Conference Center.
Accommodations: Information on overnight accommodations made available. On-site accommodations at Craigville Conference Center plus 3 meals, approx. $70/day.
Additional Information: Conference brochures/guidelines are available for SASE.

CAPE LITERARY ARTS WORKSHOP, sponsored by Cape Cod Writers Center, Inc., % Cape Cod Conservatory, Route 132, West Barnstable MA 02668. (508)775-4811. Executive Director: Marion Vuillenmier. Estab. 1985. Annual. Workshops held in 5 sessions, simultaneously. Workshop duration: 6 days. Average attendance: limit to 10/workshop. Concentrations include mystery/suspense, scriptwriting, children's book writing and illustration. August workshop held at Parish House South Congregational Church in Centerville (Cape Cod)."
Costs: $75 registration; $335 tuition.
Accommodations: Information on overnight accommodations is made available. Accommodations are made at nearby bed and breakfast establishments.
Additional Information: Brochures are available for SASE.

EASTERN WRITERS' CONFERENCE, English Dept., Salem State College, Salem MA 01970. (508)741-6330. Conference Director: Rod Kessler. Estab. 1977. Annual. Conference held over a weekend in late June. Average attendance: 60. Conference to "provide a sense of community and support for area poets and fiction writers. We try to present speakers and programs of interest, changing our format from time to time. Conference-goers usually have an opportunity to read to an audience or have manuscripts professionally critiqued. We tend to draw regionally." Previous speakers have included Nancy Muirs, Susannah Kaysen, Ivan Gold.
Costs: "Under $100."
Accommodations: Information on overnight accommodations is made available.
Additional Information: "Optional ms critiques are available for an additional fee." Conference brochures/guidelines available for SASE.

‡**FEMINIST WOMEN'S WRITING WORKSHOPS, INC.**, P.O. Box 6583, Ithaca NY 14851. Directors: Mary Beth O'Connor and Margo Gumosky. Estab. 1975. Workshop held every summer. Workshop duration: 8 days. Average attendance: 20 women writers. "Workshops are a women-centered community for writers of all levels and genres. Workshops are held on the campuses of Hobart/William Smith Colleges in Geneva, NY. Geneva is approximately mid-way between Rochester and Syracuse. Each writer has a private room and 3 meals daily. College facilities such as pool, tennis courts and weight room are available. Reading held in auditorium." FWWW invites all interests. Past speakers include Kwelismith, poet, performance artist, vocalist from Washington, DC; Nancy Bereano, publisher of Firebrand Books, Ithaca, NY.
Costs: $450 for tuition, room, board.
Accommodations: Shuttle service from airports available for a small fee.
Additional Information: "Writers may submit manuscripts up to 10 pages for critique." Brochures/guidelines available for SASE.

HOFSTRA UNIVERSITY SUMMER WRITERS' CONFERENCE, 110 Hofstra University, UCCE, 205 Davison Hall, Hempstead NY 11550. (516)463-5016. Director, Liberal Arts: Lewis Shena. Estab. 1972. Annual (Every summer starting week after July 4). Conference to be held July 11 to July 22. Average attendance: 50. Conference offers workshops in fiction, nonfiction, poetry, juvenile fiction, stage/screenwriting and one other genre such as detective fiction or science fiction. Site is the university campus, a suburban setting, 25 miles from NYC. Guest speakers are not yet known. "We have had the likes of Oscar Hijuelos, Clive Barnes, Hilma and Meg Wolitzer, Budd Schulberg and Cynthia Ozick."
Costs: Non-credit (no meals, no room): approximately $600 for 3 workshops. Credit: Approximately $800/workshop (2 credits).
Accommodations: Free bus operates between Hempstead Train Station and campus for those commuting from NYC. Dormitory rooms are available for approximately $275. Those who request area hotels will receive a list. Hotels are approximately $75 and above/night.
Additional Information: "All workshops include critiquing. Each participant is given one-on-one time of ½ hour with workshop leader. Only credit students must submit manuscripts when registering. We submit work to the *Paris Review* when appropriate."

‡**THE INTERNATIONAL FILM WORKSHOPS**, 2 Central St., Rockport ME 04856. (207)236-8581. Director: David Lyman. Estab. 1973. Workshops held weekly throughout each summer. Summer workshop series begins June 8. Workshops last one and two weeks. 8-week "in residence" program also available. Average attendance: Maximum of 16/workshop. Conference promotes screenwriting, feature film scripts, television documentaries, TV episodes, novels, short stories and nonfiction writing. "The workshop is located in old Town Hall in the small harbor village of Rockport, Maine—facilities

include library, gallery, theater, darkrooms, studios, feature film production center, accommodations for 150, dining room. Themes planned for next workshops include the feature film script, the TV doc script, writing drama, the mystery writer, the scene writing workshop, comedy writing, writing horror, the first novel. Faculty include Christopher Keane, Stanley Ralph Ross, Janet Roach.

Costs: Course tuition, one week: $500. Meals and accommodations: $350-650.

Accommodations: Discount airline ticket, airport van service. "Our lodging department can make appointments on campus ($250-500/week).

Additional Information: "Writing samples or a professional resumé must accompany application. Scripts must be submitted 3 weeks prior to the first day of class. Critiques are written and verbal." Workshop brochures/guidelines are available. "But no SASE—it's too big!"

MANHATTANVILLE COLLEGE WRITERS' WEEK, 2900 Purchase St., Purchase NY 10577. (914)694-3425. Dean of Adult and Special Programs: Ruth Dowd, R.S.C.J. Estab. 1982. Annual. Conference held June 27 to July 1. Average attendance: 80. "The Conference is designed not only for writers but for teachers of writing. Each workshop is attended by a Master teacher who works with the writers/ teachers in the afternoon to help them to translate their writing skills for classroom use. Workshops include children's literature, journal writing, creative nonfiction, personal essay, poetry, fiction. Manhanttanville is a suburban campus 30 miles from New York City. The campus centers around Reid Castle, the administration building, the former home of Whitelaw Reid. Workshops are conducted in Reid Castle. We usually feature a major author as guest lecturer during the Conference. Past speakers have included such authors as Toni Morrison, Mary Gordon, Gail Godwin, Elizabeth Janeway."

Costs: Conference cost was $596 in 1993 which included 2 graduate credits plus $40 fee.

Accommodations: Students may rent rooms in the college residence halls. More luxurious accommodations are available at neighboring hotels. In the summer of 1993 the cost of renting a room in the residence halls was: $22 per night (single); $17 per night (double).

Additional Information: Conference brochures/guidelines are available for SASE.

ROBERT QUACKENBUSH'S CHILDREN'S BOOK WRITING & ILLUSTRATING WORKSHOPS, 460 E. 79th St., New York NY 10021. (212)744-3822. Instructor: Robert Quackenbush. Estab. 1982. Annual. Workshop held the second week in July. Average attendance: limited to 10. Workshops to promote writing and illustrating books for children. Held at the Manhattan studio of Robert Quackenbush, author and illustrator of over 150 books for young readers. "Focus is generally on picture books. All classes led by Robert Quackenbush."

Costs: $650 tuition covers all costs of the workshop, but does not include housing and meals. A $100 nonrefundable deposit is required with the $550 balance due one month prior to attendance.

Accommodations: A list of recommended hotels and restaurants is sent upon receipt of deposit.

Additional Information: Class is for beginners and professionals. Work submission required. Critiques during workshop. Conference brochures/guidelines are available for SASE.

ROMANCE WRITERS OF AMERICA NATIONAL CONFERENCE, Suite 315, 13700 Veteran Memorial Dr., Houston TX 77014. (713)440-6885. Office Supervisor: Linda Fisher. Estab. 1981. Annual. Conference held from July 27 to July 31. Average attendance: 1,200. "Popular fiction, emphasis on all forms of romance and women's fiction. Held at Marriott Marquis Hotel in New York City. Our conference always focuses on selling romantic fiction with special workshops from publishers telling attendees how, specifically to sell to their houses." Past keynote and special speakers have included Sandra Canfield and Sandra Brown.

Market conditions are constantly changing! If you're still using this book and it is 1995 or later, buy the newest edition of Novel & Short Story Writer's Market at your favorite bookstore or order directly from Writer's Digest Books.

Costs: Fee for 1992 was $260 and included a reception, four meals plus two continental breakfasts. Room rates are separate.
Accommodations: Special conference rates are available.
Additional Information: Annual RITA awards are presented for romance authors. Annual Golden Heart awards are present for unpublished writers. Entry is restricted to RWA members. Conference brochures/guidelines are available for SASE.

‡**ROMANCE WRITERS OF AMERICA/NEW YORK CITY CHAPTER/FROM DREAM TO REALITY,** Bowling Green Station, P.O. Box 1719, New York NY 10274-1133. (718)441-5214. President, RWA/ NYC: Maria C. Ferrer. Estab. 1986. Annual. Workshop held February 25-27, 1994. Duration of conference: 3 days. Average attendence: 80. For those interested in writing and selling a romance novel. The conference is held at the Skyline Hotel on 50th Street in New York City. "The 1994 conference will include writing basics, the business of writing, editors panel, one-on-one conference sessions with published authors, handling your writing income. Speakers will include leading romance authors and professional editors from major romance publishing houses."
Costs: "For 1994, the 3-day program is *less than* $100 (not including meals and accommodations). The hotel rate is $90 for 1-3 people in a room per night with free parking."
Additional Information: "Our Love and Laughter contest is opened to all unpublished writers. Fee is $10. Deadline: January. Winner is announced at the workshop. Grand prize is $50 and a critique by an editor." Brochure/guidelines for SASE. "For 1994 workshop, there will be a welcoming reception with guest speaker on Friday evening. Saturday will be the all-day writers' workshop. Saturday evening plans are in the works for dinner and an off-Broadway show. Sunday there will be a special finance brunch or a visit to a bookstore."

S.U.N.Y. COLLEGE WRITING ARTS FESTIVALS, State University of New York at Oswego, Oswego NY 13126. (315)341-2602. Director of the Program in Writing Arts: Lewis Turco. Estab. 1968. Annual. Conference held October and April. Conference duration: 4 days, Monday-Thursday. Average attendance: 40-60. For fiction, poetry, drama writing. Conference held at the Student Union facilities. Past themes have included gay and lesbian writing, Afro-American writing.
Costs: All sessions free and open to public.
Accommodations: Attendees must make their own arrangements for board and accommodations. May be given information through the Office of Continuing Education at Swetmen Hall, State University College, Oswego NY 13126.
Additional Information: Information poster available for SASE.

SCBWI CONFERENCE IN CHILDREN'S LITERATURE, NYC, P.O. Box 20233, Park West Finance Station, New York NY 10025-1511. Chairman: Kimberly Colen. Estab. 1975. Annual. Conference held "usually" 1st (or 2nd) Saturday in November. Average attendance: 350-400. Conference is to promote writing for children: Picture books, fiction, nonfiction, middle grade and young adult. "The past 3 years it has been at 3 different schools. Most recently it was held at Bank Street College."
Costs: $55, members; $60 nonmembers; $5 additional on day of conference.
Accommodations: No accommodations available. Write for information; hotel names will be supplied.
Additional Information: Conference brochures/guidelines are available for SASE.

SCBWI/HOFSTRA CHILDREN'S LITERATURE CONFERENCE, Hofstra University, University College of Continuing Education, 205 Davison Hall, Hempstead NY 11550. (516)463-5016. Co-organizers: Connie C. Epstein, Adrienne Betz, Lewis Shena. Estab. 1985. Annual. Conference to be held April 23. Average attendance: 160. Conference to encourage good writing for children. "Purpose is to bring together various professional groups—writers, illustrators, librarians, teachers—who are interested in writing for children. Each year we organize program around a theme. Last year it was Style and Substance, and this year it will be A Tenth Anniversary Celebration." The conference takes place at the Student Center Building of Hofstra University, located in Hempstead, Long Island. "We have two general sessions and five or six break-out groups that we hold in rooms in the Center or nearby classrooms. Lunch is provided." This year's conference will feature Ed Young and Sara Miller as general speakers and offer special-interest groups in nonfiction (James C. Giblin), picture books (Jean Marzollo), fiction (Jan Marmo), short stories (Donald Gallo), poetry (Bernice Cullman), submission procedures (Barbara Kouts).
Cost: $50 (previous year) for SCBWI members; $55 for nonmembers. Lunch included.

STATE OF MAINE WRITERS' CONFERENCE, P.O. Box 296, Ocean Park ME 04063. (207)934-5034 June-August; (413)596-6734 September-May. Chairman: Richard F. Burns. Estab. 1941. Annual. Conference held in August. Conference duration: 4 days. Average attendance: 70-75. "We try to present a balanced as well as eclectic conference. There is quite a bit of time and attention given to poetry but we also have children's literature, mystery writing, travel, novels/fiction and lots of items and issues of interest to writers such as speakers who are: publishers, editors, illustrators and the like. Our concentration is, by intention, a general view of writing to publish. We are located in Ocean Park, a small seashore village 14 miles south of Portland. Ours is a summer assembly center with many buildings from the Victorian Age. The conference meets in Porter Hall, one of the assembly buildings which is listed on the National Register of Historic Places. Within recent years our guest list has included Lewis Turco, Bob Anderson, David McCord, Dorothy Clarke Wilson, Dennis LeDoux, Will Anderson, Christopher Keane and many others. We usually have about 10 guest presenters a year." **Costs:** $70 (1993) includes the conference banquet. There is a reduced fee, $30, for students ages 21 and under. The fee does not include housing or meals which must be arranged separately by the conferees.
Accommodations: An accommodations list is available. "We are in a summer resort area and motels, guest houses and restaurants abound."
Additional Information: "We have a contest announcement which comes out in January-March and has about 17 contests on various genres. The prizes, all modest, are awarded at the end of the conference and only to those who are registered." Program guide comes out in April-June.

‡STONECOAST WRITERS' CONFERENCE, Summer Session Office, University of Southern Maine, 96 Falmouth St., Portland ME 04103. (207)280-4076. Contact: Barbara Hope, Director. Estab. 1977. Annual. Conference held from late July to early August. Conference duration: 10 days. Average attendance: over 100. "Stonecoast is a teaching conference emphasizing short fiction, the novel, creative nonfiction, poetry, genre writing and children's. The conference is held in Portland, a resort city by the sea. Activities are held at the University of Southern Maine campus." Guest speakers at the next conference include Carolyn Chute, Joyce Johnson, Gerald Stern, Robley Wilson.
Costs: $395 (tuition only).
Accommodations: Attendees must make their own transporation arrangements. Dormitory accommodations (including private bath) available for $70/week.
Additional Information: Activities include "daily workshops—work is submitted prior to conference." Also offers 2 scholarships for participants. Brochures available for SASE.

UNIVERSITY OF MASSACHUSETTS LOWELL WRITING PROGRAM, One University Ave., Lowell MA 01854. (508)934-2405. Program Coordinator: John Hurtado. Estab. 1989. Annual. Conference held July to mid-August. Conference duration: 6 weeks. Average attendance: 250 in 15 courses. Conference includes "credit courses in expository writing, fiction, poetry, playwriting, journalism, arts reporting, desktop publishing, writing children's literature and screenwriting in addition to free readings by nationally-known, award-winning, local writers. Courses are held at the University's Mogan Cultural Center, a renovated Millgirl Boardinghouse within the Lowell National Park and in various classrooms on both the North and South campuses."
Costs: In 1993, $300 per 3 credit undergraduate course, plus a $25 registration fee per session.
Accommodations: Dormitory accommodations available on campus include board option.
Additional Information: Brochures available. "Audit option available at full tuition (pass/fail not available due to nature of courses and requirements)."

VASSAR COLLEGE INSTITUTE OF PUBLISHING AND WRITING: CHILDREN'S BOOKS IN THE MARKETPLACE, Vassar College, Box 300, Poughkeepsie NY 12601. (914)437-5903. Associate Director of College Relations: Maryann Bruno. Estab. 1983. Annual. Conference held in second week of June

or July. Conference duration: 1 week. Average attendance: 40. Writing and publishing children's literature. "The conference is held at Vassar College, a 1,000-acre campus located in the mid-Hudson valley. The campus is self-contained, with residence halls, dining facilities, and classroom and meeting facilities. Vassar is located 90 miles north of New York City, and is accessible by car, train and air. Participants have use of Vassar's athletic facilities, including swimming, squash, tennis and jogging. Vassar is known for the beauty of its campus." The panel theme for 1993 was "Making It." In 1993 guest speakers included Barry Moser, Nancy Willard, Rafe Martin, Margery Facklam, Jean Marzollo, M.J. Auch, Emily Arnold McCully, and others.
Costs: $700, includes full tuition, room and three meals a day.
Accommodations: There are special conference attendee accommodations on campus in a residence hall.
Additional Information: Writers may submit a 10-page sample of their writing for critique, which occurs during the week of the conference. Conference brochures/guidelines are available for SASE.

WELLS WRITERS' WORKSHOPS, 69 Broadway, Concord NH 03301. (603)225-9162. Director: Vic Levine. Estab. 1988. Held: 2 times/year in Wells, Maine. Conferences held from May 15 to May 20; September 11 to September 16. Maximum attendance: 5. "Workshop concentrates on short and long fiction, especially the novel. Focus is on the rational structuring of a story, using Aristotelian and scriptwriting insights. Throughout, the workshop balances direct instruction with the actual plotting and writing of the basic scenes of a novel or short story." Conference located in a "large, airy and light house overlooking the ocean with ample individual space for writers and group conferences. While the purposes of the workshop is to teach the process of plotting as it applies across the board—to all kinds of fiction, including novels, short stories, movies—it strives to meet the specific needs of participants, especially through individual conferences with the instructor."
Costs: "The cost of $750 covers tuition, room and board. Registration cost is $50 (nonrefundable). Payment may be in two or three installments."
Accommodations: Workshop supplies transportation from/to Portland International Airport—or other places, by arrangement. Workshop supplies accommodations.
Additional Information: Conference brochures/guidelines available for SASE. "Workshop has a scholarship fund which can, as it has in the past, defray part of the total expense of $750."

WESLEYAN WRITERS CONFERENCE, Wesleyan University, Middletown CT 06459. (203)343-3938. Director: Anne Greene. Estab. 1956. Annual. 1993 Conference held from June 26 to July 1. Average attendance: 100. For novel, short story, poetry, nonfiction, literary journalism. The conference is held on the campus of Wesleyan University, in the hills overlooking the Connecticut River. Meals and lodging are provided on campus. Readings of new fiction. Guest lectures on a range of topics including the art of memoir.
Costs: In 1993, tuition $415; meals $165; room $90.
Accommodations: "Participants can fly to Hartford or take Amtrak to Meriden, CT. We are happy to help participants make travel arrangements." Overnight participants stay on campus.
Additional Information: Ms critiques are available as part of the program but are not required. "We sponsor several scholarship competitions and award teaching fellowships. Application info is in conference brochure." Brochures/guidelines are available for SASE.

‡WESTCHESTER WRITERS' CONFERENCE, 16 Lawrence Dr., N. White Plains NY 10603. (914)682-1574. Conference Director: Sarah White. Estab. 1985. Annual. Conference held April 11. Average attendance: 200. Conference includes fiction, journalism, poetry, writing for children, enhancing creativity, writers and computers; writers' rights. Conference held on private college campus. Panels include: fictional characters; the young adult market; the short story.
Costs: $75 includes all workshops and luncheon.
Additional Information: Conference brochures/guidelines are available for SASE.

THE WRITERS' CENTER AT CHAUTAUQUA, P.O. Box 408, Chautauqua NY 14722. (716)357-2445 or (717)872-8337. Director: Mary Jean Irion. Estab. 1987. Annual. Workshops held late June to August "are offered in combination with a vacation at historic Chautauqua Institution, a large cultural resort in wester New York for families and singles." Average attendance 12. "Workshops are 2 hours, Monday-Friday; average attendance is 12." Past guest speakers and panelists: Susan Rowan Masters taught the young writers section; Joan Millman and Stanley W. Lindberg taught the short story sessions; Zena Collier taught the novel session.

Costs: In 1992 $50/week. Meals, housing, gate ticket (about $135 per week), parking ($20) are in addition.
Accommodations: Information is available; but no special rates have been offered.
Additional Information: Each leader specifies the kind of workshop offered. Most accept submissions in advance; information is made available in March on request. Conference brochures/guidelines are available for SASE.

WRITERS ON WRITING AT BARNARD, 3009 Broadway, New York NY 10027-6598. (212)854-7489. Director: Ann Birstein. Estab. 1988. Annual. Conference held in June. Conference duration: 1 month. Average attendance: 10-12/workshop. Includes 2 fiction workshops, 2 poetry workshops, 1 writing for children, 1 workshop for biography/memoir, 1 nonfiction. Held at "Barnard College, beautifully appointed lounge, comfortable classrooms, lovely rooms for readings and receptions." Past guest speakers have included Gwendolyn Brooks in honor of her 75th birthday; Virginia Barber, agent, Jill Bialosky, W.W. Norton editor, Michael Anderson, *New York Times Book Review* editor and others.
Costs: $950 non-credit, $1,050 credit (workshop fee only). Reduced fee for 2 workshops.
Accommodations: Campus housing is available. Information about hotels and parking garages will be sent to inquirers. Dorm rooms are approx. $100/week.
Additional Information: Conference brochures/guidelines are available on request.

‡**WRITING WITH YOUR WHOLE SELF**, P.O. Box 1310, Boston MA 02117. (617)266-1613. Director: Marcia Yudkin. Estab. 1991. Workshop held approximately 5 times/year. Workshop held on one Saturday in April, June, September, November, February. Average attendance 15. "Creativity workshop for fiction writers and others. Based on latest discoveries about the creative process, participants learn to access their unconscious wisdom, find their own voice, utilize kinesthetic, visual and auditory methods of writing, and bypass longstanding blocks and obstacles. Held at a hotel in central Boston."
Costs: $99.
Accommodations: List of area hotels and bed & breakfasts provided.
Additional Information: "Audiotapes of seminar information also available."

Midatlantic (DC, DE, MD, NJ, PA)

HIGHLIGHTS FOUNDATION WRITERS WORKSHOP AT CHAUTAUQUA, Dept. NM, 711 Court St., Honesdale PA 18431. (717)253-1192. Conference Director: Jan Keen. Estab. 1985. Annual. Workshop held July 16 to July 23. Average attendance: 100. "Writer workshops geared toward beginner, intermediate, advanced levels. Small group workshops, one-to-one interaction between faculty and participants plus panel sessions, lectures and large group meetings. Workshop site is the picturesque community of Chautauqua, New York." Classes offered include Children's Interests, Writing Dialogue, Outline for the Novel, Conflict and Developing Plot. Past faculty has included Eve Bunting, Pam Conrad, James Cross Giblin, Walter Dean Myers, Laurence Pringle.
Accommodations: "We coordinate ground transportation to and from airports, trains and bus stations in the Erie, PA and Jamestown/Buffalo, NY area. We also coordinate accommodations for conference attendees."
Additional Information: "We offer the opportunity for attendees to submit a manuscript for review at the conference." Workshop brochures/guidelines are available for SASE.

LIGONIER VALLEY WRITERS CONFERENCE, RR4, Box 8, Ligonier PA 15658. (412)238-6397 or (412)238-5749. Director: Tina Thoburn. Estab. 1986. Annual. Conference held from July 8 to 10. Average attendance: 100. Conference concentrates on fiction, nonfiction, poetry, writing for children, play and script writing. The conference is centered in a scenic small town with classrooms in the town hall and several nearby inns, hotels and restaurants. Included are a picnic and brunch featuring faculty readings and a noon garden luncheon. This year's conference may include more on marketing with a literary agent and/or an editor on the faculty or available to offer one-on-one critiques of pre-submitted work. David McCullough has been a keynote speaker.
Accommodations: All registrants are provided with a list of motels, inns and bed and breakfasts. Last year's special rates began at $65 per night.
Additional Information: "Work to be critiqued must be submitted by June 1." Participants are invited to submit work to our literary journal—*Loyalhanna*. Brochures/guidelines available for SASE after March 1.

‡**MID-ATLANTIC MYSTERY BOOK FAIR & CONVENTION,** Detecto Mysterioso Books at Society Hill Playhouse, 507 South 8th St., Philadelphia PA 19147. Contact: Deen Kogan, chairperson. Estab. 1991. Annual. Convention held in early November. Average attendance: 350-400. Focus is on mystery, suspense, thriller, true crime novels. "An examination of the genre from many points of view." The convention is held at the Holiday Inn-Independence Mall, located in the historic area of Philadelphia. Speakers at 1993 convention included Lawrence Block, Jeremiah Healy, Neil Albert, Joan Hess, Martha Grimes, Gillian Roberts, William Caunitz.
Costs: $40 registration fee.
Accommodations: Attendees must make their own transportation arrangements. Special room rate of $79/room available at convention hotel.
Additional Information: "The Bookroom is a focal point of the convention. Twenty-five specialty dealers are expected to exhibit and collectables range from hot-off-the-press bestsellers to 1930's pulp; from fine editions to reading copies."

‡**PENNWRITERS CONFERENCE,** RR2, Box 241, Middlebury Center PA 16935. Conference Coordinator: C.J. Houghtaling. Estab. 1988. Annual. Conference held third Saturday in May. Average attendance: 150. Conference to promote fiction, nonfiction, screenwriting and more. Agents and editors are present as guests/speakers as well as writers. Site: Holiday Inn, Grantville PA.
Additional Information: Sponsors contest: Categories: 1st chapter of novel, 10 page limit; short story, 3,000 word limit; nonfiction article, 1,500 word limit. Conference brochures/guidelines are available for SASE.

‡**TRENTON STATE COLLEGE WRITERS' CONFERENCE,** English Dept., Trenton State College, Hillwood Lakes CN 4700, Trenton NJ 08650-4700. (609)771-3254. Director: Jean Hollander. Estab. 1980. Annual. Conference held every spring. Conference duration: 9 a.m. to 10:30 p.m. Average attendance: 600-1,000. "Conference concentrates on fiction (the largest number of participants), poetry, children's literature, play and screenwriting, magazine and newspaper journalism, overcoming writer's block, nonfiction books. Conference is held at the student center at the college in two auditoriums and workshop rooms; also Kendall Theatre on campus." We focus on various genres: romance, detective, mystery, TV writing, etc. Last year's topics included "How to Get Happily Published," "How to Get an Agent" and "Earning a Living as a Writer." The conference usually presents twenty or so authors, plus two featured speakers, who have included Arthur Miller, Saul Bellow, Toni Morrison, Joyce Carol Oates, Erica Jong, etc. in the past.
Costs: General registration $45, plus $5 for each workshop. Lower rates for students.
Additional Information: Brochures/guidelines available.

‡**WASHINGTON INDEPENDENT WRITERS (WIW) SPRING WRITERS CONFERENCE,** #220, 733 15th St. NW, Washington DC 20005. (202)347-4973. Executive Director: Isolde Chapin. Estab. 1980. Annual. Conference held in May. Conference duration: one Saturday. Average attendance: approximately 350. "Gives participants a chance to hear from and talk with dozens of experts on book and magazine publishing as well as on the craft, tools and business of writing." In 1993, the keynote speaker was Erica Jong.
Costs: $85 members; $110 nonmembers; $150 membership and conference.
Additional Information: Brochures/guidelines available for SASE in mid-March.

WRITING BY THE SEA, 1511 New York Ave., Cape May NJ 08204. (609)884-7117, ext. 15. CMI Managing Director: Natalie Newton. Estab. 1990. Annual. Conference held November 7 to 11. Conference duration: 5 days. Average attendance: 70. Conference offers "about 10 seminars on fiction and nonfiction writing in a retreat atmosphere at the Virginia Hotel." Conference held at "the Cape May Institute, an adult continuing education, nonprofit organization located in Victorian Cape May. Our modern facilities include a comfortable lecture hall and world class b&w photographic darkrooms. The Institute is noted for its support of the arts and hosts annual music and theater performances." Guest speakers have included Robert Brown (writer, editor), Frank Green (writing coach), Jurgen Wolff (screenwriter), Patricia Hagan (author).
Costs: $295 for 5 days or $125/day—conference fee only.
Accommodations: For 1993, we had the entire Virginia Hotel, a luxuriously refurbished Victorian Inn from November 7-11. Cost was $65 (single) or $75 (double occupancy) per night.
Additional Information: Conference brochures/guidelines are available for SASE.

‡YOUNG WRITERS AT PENN CONFERENCE, Suite 100, 3440 Market St., Philadelphia PA 19104-3335. (215)898-6763. Coordinator: Greg Frost. Estab. 1987. Annual. Conference held in March. Average attendance: 225. "The purpose is to offer 2-hour seminars on all aspects of writing for high school students who wish to pursue careers as writers, poets, journalists, playwrights. The conference takes place on the University of Pennsylvania campus." Previous speakers included Robb Armstrong, creator of the syndicated cartoon strip *JumpStart*, and *Philadelphia Inquirer* book reviewer Carlin Romano.
Costs: $60 includes lunch on campus.
Additional Information: "Some workshop instructors—notably in poetry and fiction—require submission of work prior to the conference, and that work is discussed in the workshop. The conference is offered to students in 9th through 12th grade. They can have a brochure sent to them by calling the program number. Discovery also runs various writing programs on weekends during the school year, as well as one-to-four week intensive writing courses in the summer. The nature and quantities of these vary from year to year."

Midsouth (NC, SC, TN, VA, WV)

APPALACHIAN WRITERS CONFERENCE, Box 6935, Radford University, Radford VA 24142-6935. (703)831-5269; 639-0812. AWA President: Dr. R. Parks Lanier, Jr. Estab. 1980. Annual. Conference held from July 8 to July 10. Average attendance: 60. "Fiction, nonfiction, poetry, drama, story telling and grants writing are some of the topics discussed at each AWA Conference. Writers have some form of identification with the Appalachian region, either as the place from which they come, the place in which they live or the place about which they write." Radford University is located just off I-81 on the banks of the historic New River, 40 miles Southwest of Roanoke in Radford, Virginia. Participants may stay "in a newly renovated air-conditioned dormitory at very reasonable rates, cool, quiet, comfortable." The AWA is now regularly inviting editors to speak. Guest speakers. "Most of the AWA members are themselves authors with a national reputation."
Costs: AWA annual dues are $10. Meals in university cafeteria cost $5 or less.
Accommodations: Rooms are less than $50 for two nights, single occupancy.
Additional Information: There are contests for fiction, poetry, nonfiction and younger writers. AWA members are judges. Conference brochures/guidelines available for SASE.

BLUE RIDGE WRITERS CONFERENCE, 1942 Avon Rd., Roanoke VA 24015. President: Liz Jones. Estab. 1984. Annual. One-day conference held in October ("usually first Saturday, but this may change depending upon availability of speakers."). Average attendance: 150. Conference "to make available an opportunity for networking and exchange of ideas between writers, both aspiring and professional. Also, to enhance the status of writers and writing and to bring this artistic endeavor to the same level of public recognition, appreciation and pride in performance that is already enjoyed by music, the theater, dance and the fine arts." Site: Roanoke College, Salem, VA. Special bookstore features publications of speakers and books on writing. "Plans are incomplete for 1994, Keynote for 1993 was Ellen Gilchrist."
Costs: $50; $25 for fulltime students. Includes luncheon and reception.
Additional Information: Brochures available for SASE.

‡THE CHARLESTON WRITERS' CONFERENCE, Lightsey Conference Center, College of Charleston, Charleston SC 29424. (803)953-5822. Conference Coordinator: Judy Sawyer. Estab. 1991. Annual. Conference held in March. Conference duration: 3½ days. Average attendance: 125. "Conference concentrates on fiction, poetry and nonfiction. The conference is held at conference center on urban campus in historic setting." Themes are different each year and varied within confines of each conference. 1993 speakers included Robin Hemley, Lois Rosenthal, Marian Young and Joy Williams.
Costs: Under $100. Includes receptions and breaks.
Accommodations: Special rates available at hotels within walking distance.
Additional Information: "Critiques are available for an extra fee—not a requirement." Those making inquiries are placed on mailing list.

CHRISTOPHER NEWPORT UNIVERSITY WRITERS' CONFERENCE, 50 Shoe Lane, Newport News VA 23606-2998. (804)594-7158. Coordinator: Doris Gwaltney. Estab. 1981. Annual. Conference held April 1-2. Average attendance: 100. "Our workshop is for both published and unpublished writers in all genres. It provides a network for area writers, connecting them with markets, literary agents, editors

We've just made getting your words published a little easier

Getting Published: **What Every Writer Needs to Know**

Writer's DIGEST

Subscribe to WRITER'S DIGEST now, and get this invaluable guide, *Getting Published: What Every Writer Needs to Know*, FREE with your paid subscription.

SPECIAL FREE GIFT OFFER!

INSIDE: How to write irresistible query letters and prepare polished manuscripts. How to give an editor nothing to do—except buy your work. Where to find ideas. And the "test" every editor gives...14 questions you can use to evaluate your freelancing savvy.

Use the card below to start your subscription today!

Subscription Savings Card

☐ Yes! I want professional advice on how to write publishable material and sell it to the best-paying markets. Start my 1-year (12 issues) subscription to WRITER'S DIGEST for just $18.97...**a 46% savings off the newsstand price.**

Name_____

Address_____

City _____

State _____Zip _____

☐ Payment enclosed. Send my FREE gift right away!
☐ Bill me, and send my free gift upon payment.
Charge my ☐ Visa   ☐ MasterCard

Card #_____Exp. _____

Signature _____

Guarantee: If you aren't completely satisfied with your subscription at any time, simply cancel and receive a full refund on all unmailed issues due you.
Outside the U.S. add $7 (includes GST) and remit in U.S. funds. Newsstand rate $35.40.

JPNS5

No other source offers so much information and instruction...

on writing...

WRITER'S DIGEST is packed with advice from the experts that can make you a better writer. Whatever your challenge...from generating plot ideas to overcoming writer's block. Whatever your specialty...from writing poetry to children's stories.

and selling what you write!

Learn the secrets of top-dollar freelancers. How to slant your writing for multiple sales and negotiate contracts with editors and publishers. How to make and keep contacts that help your career. Find out what markets are hot for your work right now, how much they're paying, and how to get in touch with the right people.

Subscribe today and save 46% off the newsstand price!

and printers." The conference is held on the campus of Christopher Newport University in Newport News, Va. "We have a good food service, a bookstore, adequate meeting rooms and total access for the handicapped." Workshop presenters: Susan Hankla, Poetry; W.B. Taylor, nonfiction; and other literary experts.

Costs: $65, includes wine-and-cheese reception on Friday evening in "Celebration of the Arts," coffee and pastries and lunch on Saturday.

Accommodations: Adequate parking available. "Our staff could help with arrangements for overnight accommodations."

Additional Information: "We have a literary contest in four areas: poetry, fiction, nonfiction and juvenile fiction. Each entry is critiqued by a judge who is a published writer in the field." Conference brochures/guidelines available for SASE.

DUKE UNIVERSITY WRITERS' WORKSHOP, The Bishop's House, Durham NC 27708. (919)684-3255. Director: Marilyn Hartman. Estab. 1978. Annual. Workshop held June 19-24. Average attendance: 50. To promote "creative writing: beginning, intermediate and advanced fiction; short story; scriptwriting; children's writing; mystery; poetry; creative nonfiction." Workshop held at "Duke University campus classrooms and meeting facilities. Gothic architecture, rolling green hills. Nationally recognized for its beauty and academic excellence, Duke sponsors this workshop annually for creative writers of various genres." Theme is creative writing ("that's our only song!").

Costs: $345 for conference (most meals not included).

Accommodations: Hotel rooms available near campus.

Additional Information: Critiques available. "Works-in-progress requested 3 weeks before workshop. Each participant gets *private* consult plus small-group in-class critiques." Brochures/guidelines are available. "No 'big' names, no mammoth lectures; simply *excellent*, concentrated instruction plus time to work. No glitz. Hard work. Great results."

FRANCIS MARION WRITERS' CONFERENCE, Francis Marion University, Florence SC 29501. (803)661-1500. Director: David Starkey. Estab. 1982. Conference held annually in June. Conference duration: 3 days. Average attendance: 40-50. Conference for "fiction, poetry, nonfiction and drama." Held in classrooms/college auditorium at Francis Marion University.

Costs: $85.

Accommodations: Information on overnight accommodations made available through directors.

Additional Information: Some workshops for fiction writers are included. Sponsors a chapbook competition for participants. Brochures or guidelines available for SASE.

HIGHLAND SUMMER CONFERENCE, Box 6935, Radford University, Radford VA 24142. (703)831-5366. Chair, Appalachian Studies Program: Dr. Grace Toney Edwards. Estab. 1978. Annual. Conference held in mid-June. Conference duration: 12 days. Average attendance: 25. "The HSC features one (two weeks) or two (one week each) guest leaders each year. As a rule, our leaders are well known writers who have connections, either thematic, or personal, or both, to the Appalachian region. The genre(s) of emphasis depends upon the workshop leader(s). In the past we have had as our leaders Bill Brown, poet, author, teacher and Wilma Dykemen, novelist, journalist, social critic, author of *Tall Woman* among others. The Highland Summer Conference is held at Radford University, a school of about 9,000 students. Radford is in the Blue Ridge Mountain of southwest Virginia about 45 miles west of Roanoke, VA."

Costs: "The cost is based on current Radford tuition for 3 credit hours plus an additional conference fee. On-campus meals and housing are available at additional cost. In 1993 conference tuition was $306 for undergraduates, $321 for graduate student."

Accommodations: We do not have special rate arrangements with local hotels. We do offer accommodations on the Radford University Campus in a recently refurbished residence hall. (In 1992 cost was $15.25-25 per night.)

Additional Information: "Conference leaders do typically critique work done during the two-week conference, but do not ask to have any writing submitted prior to the conference beginning." Conference brochures/guidelines are available for SASE.

NATIONAL LEAGUE OF AMERICAN PEN WOMEN CONFERENCE, P.O. Box 1707, Midlothian VA 23112. (804)744-6503. Conference Director: Rosemary Dietrich. Estab. 1983. Conference held every two years. Conference duration: One day. Average attendance: 50-100. "For fiction, nonfiction, travel, regional, writing for children. Conference is usually held in a Richmond, Virginia hotel with banquet

facilities. The day includes continental breakfast, lunch, book sales, autographing with well-known, published speakers."
Costs: $55 fee includes lunch, continental breakfast; $15 contest entry; $10 critique of contest entry.
Accommodations: Special rates for overnight stay the night before conference.
Additional Information: Critiques available. Sponsors contest: fiction or nonfiction, 1,500 word maximum, fee charged. Judges are professional writers in NLAPW. Conference brochures/guidelines are available for SASE.

‡**NORTH CAROLINA WRITERS' NETWORK FALL CONFERENCE**, P.O. Box 954, Carrboro NC 27510. (919)967-9540. Executive Director: Marsha Warren. Estab. 1985. Annual. "Conference will be held in Charlotte, NC, in October or November." Average attendance: 350. "The conference is a weekend full of workshops, panels, readings and discussion groups. We try to have *all* genres represented. In the past we have had novelists, poets, journalists, editors, children's writers, YA writers, storytellers, puppetry, screenwriters, etc. We take the conference to a different location in North Carolina each year in order to best serve our entire state. We hold the conference at a conference center with hotel rooms available."
Costs: "Conference cost is approximately $95 and includes three to four meals."
Accommodations: "Special conference hotel rates are obtained, but the individual makes his/her own reservations. If requested, we will help the individual find a roommate."
Additional Information: Conference brochures/guidelines are available for 2 first-class stamps.

SCBWI/MID-ATLANTIC, P.O. Box 1707, Midlothian VA 23112. (804)744-6503. Regional Advisor: T.R. Hollingsworth. Estab. 1984. Annual. Conference held in the fall. Conference duration: one day. Average attendance: 100. Writing for children. Usually held at a conference center of a well-knwon hotel chain. Past themes have been "Marketing," fiction workshops for writers and "How-to" for illustrators. Past guest speakers have included Connie Epstein, Jim Giblin, Norm Bomor, editors and writers.
Costs: $55 members, $60 non-members, includes continental breakfast and lunch.
Accommodations: Special conference rate on-site.
Additional Information: Sponsors writer's contest, illustrator's display and critique of contest entries. Entry requirements: Paid registration; 1,500 word ms, typed, double-spaced; limited to one manuscript per person. Conference brochures/guidelines are available for SASE.

‡**SHENANDOAH VALLEY WRITERS GUILD**, P.O. Box 47, Middletown VA 22645. (703)869-1120. Faculty Liaison: Felicia Cogan, assoc. professor at Lord Fairfax Community College. Estab. 1978. Conferences/workshops held in May and November. Duration: November, 1 day; May, 1 day. Average attendance: 50. Conferences to promote fiction, poetry, writing for children and articles. Both conferences held at Lord Fairfax Community College.
Costs: Fees are $10 for November conference; $25 for May conference.
Accommodations: No information given.
Additional Information: Workshops for fiction writers include critiques and may require writers to submit for critique prior to the conference/workshop. Conference brochures/guidelines are available for SASE.

THE WRITERS' WORKSHOP, P.O. Box 696, Asheville NC 28802. (800)627-0142. Executive Director: Karen Tager. Estab. 1984. Held 4 times/year. Conference duration: varies from 1 day to 20 weeks. Average attendance: 10. "All areas, for adults and children. We do not offer workshops dealing with romance or religion, however." Sites are throughout the South, especially North Carolina. Guest speaker was John Le Carré in 1992; in 1993 Writer's retreat was in the Florida Keys with Peter Matthiessen in March; writers retreat was in Nice, France with D.M. Thomas October 28-31.
Costs: Vary. Financial assistance available to low-income writers. Information on overnight accommodations is made available.

Southeast (AL, AR, FL, GA, LA, MS, PR [Puerto Rico])

ALABAMA WRITERS' CONCLAVE, 3225 Burning Tree Dr., Birmingham AL 35226. President: Ann Moon Rabb. Estab. 1923. Annual. Conference held August 3 to August 5. Average attendance: 85-120. Conference to promote "all phases" of writing. Held at the Ramsay Conference Center (University of

Montevallo). "We attempt to contain all workshops under this roof. Some functions take place at other campus buildings."
Costs: In 1993 fees for 3 days were $35 for members; $45 for nonmembers. Lower rates for one- or two-day attendence.
Accommodations: Accommodations available on campus (charged separately).
Additional Information: "We have had a works-in-progress group with members helping members." Sponsors a contest. Conference brochures/guidelines available for SASE. Membership dues are $15. Membership information from Harriette Dawkins, 117 Hanover Rd., Homewood AL 35209.

ARKANSAS WRITERS' CONFERENCE, 1115 Gillette Dr., Little Rock AR 72207. (501)225-0166. Director: Clovita Rice. Estab. 1944. Annual. Conference held: June. Average attendence: 225. "We have a variety of subjects related to writing—we have some general sessions, some more specific, but try to vary each year's subjects."
Costs: Registration: $10; luncheon: $11; banquet: $13.
Accommodations: "We meet at a Holiday Inn—rooms available at reasonable rate." Holiday has a bus to bring anyone from airport. Rooms average $56/single.
Additional Information: "We have 36 contest categories. Some are open only to Arkansans, most are open to all writers. Our judges are not announced before conference, but are qualified, many out of state." Conference brochures are available for SASE after February 1. "We have had 226 attending from 12 states—over 2,200 contest entries from 43 states and New Zealand. We have a get acquainted party at my home on Thursday evening for early arrivers."

FLORIDA CHRISTIAN WRITERS CONFERENCE, 2600 Park Ave., Titusville FL 32780. (407)269-6702. Conference Director: Billie Wilson. Estab. 1988. Annual. Conference is held in late January. Conference duration: 5 days. Average attendance: 150. To promote "all areas of writing." Conference held at Park Avenue Retreat Center, a conference complex at a large church near Kennedy Space Center. Len and Sandra LeSourd were scheduled to speak at next conference. Editors will represent over 30 publications and publishing houses.
Costs: Tuition $360, included tuition, room and board (double occupancy).
Accommodations: "We provide shuttle from the airport and from the hotel to retreat center. We make reservations at major hotel chain."
Additional Information: Critiques available. "Each writer may submit 3 works for critique. We have specialists in every area of writing to critique. We also provide line by line, written critique for a $30 fee." Conference brochures/guidelines are available for SASE.

FLORIDA STATE WRITERS CONFERENCE, % CNW, Maple Ridge Rd., North Sandwich NH 03259. (603)284-6367. Executive Director: Dana K. Cassell. Estab. 1983. Annual. Conference held in May. Conference duration: 3 days. Average attendance 300. Four Tracks: fiction, nonfiction, general interest, specialty. Held at a hotel. (1993: Altamonte Hilton, Orlando). Guest speakers and panelists include published book authors, full-time freelance writers, agents, and editors.
Costs: Several packages with or without meals, single-day, 2-day, complete package, member/ nonmember, early-bird specials. Range: $30-300.
Accommodations: Special hotel rate on-site.
Additional Information: Critiques available for small extra fee depending upon length of material. Sponsors a contest. Judges: editors, authors, college professors. Conference brochures/guidelines are available for 9 × 12 SASE and 52¢ postage after February 1.

‡FLORIDA SUNCOAST WRITERS' CONFERENCE, University of South Florida—St. Petersburg Campus, 140 7th Ave. South, St. Petersburg FL 33701. (813)974-1711. Associate Director: Steve Rubin. Estab. 1970. Annual. 3-day conference held in late January/early February. Average attendance: 400. Conference "to provide a 'hands-on' experience for both would-be writers and professional writers. We offer workshops and seminars in poetry, short story, novel, science fiction, detective, travel writing, nonfiction, drama, TV scripts, photojournalism and juvenile." The conference is held on "the picturesque university campus fronting on the bay of St. Petersburg, Fl. We do not focus on any one particular aspect of the writing profession; we have panels with agents and editors every year."

Costs: $95, early registration.
Accommodations: "Special rates are available at area motels. All information is contained in our brochure."
Additional Information: "Participants may submit work for critiquing. Extra fee charged for this service." Conference brochures/guidelines available for SASE.

HEMINGWAY DAYS WRITER'S WORKSHOP AND CONFERENCE, P.O. Box 4045, Key West FL 33041. (305)294-4440. Director of Workshop: Dr. James Plath. Festival Director: Michael Whalton. Estab. 1988. Annual. Conference/workshop held July 19 to July 21. Average attendance: 90. "The Hemingway Days Writer's Workshop and Conference focuses on fiction, poetry, stage and screenwriting, with one session per day concentrating on the craft as it relates to Ernest Hemingway and his work. Sessions are held in the Caribbean Spa Grand Cayman Room at the Pier House Resort, which has excellent audio visual facilities and seats 100." All sessions on day one deal with fiction writing; day two—poetry writing; day three—screen and playwriting.
Costs: $75. Guaranteed admission on a space-available basis includes admission to all sessions, workshop t-shirt and complementary snacks each day.
Accommodations: "As the time draws nearer, Hemingway Days packages will be available through Ocean Key House, Pier House, Southernmost Motel and Holiday Inn LaConcha. Last year the cost for 3 nights ranged from $60/2 in room per night plus tax; $160/3 in room per night suite, plus tax."
Additional Information: Brochures/guidelines are available for SASE. "The conference/workshop is unique in its daily emphasis on a different genre, but since it celebrates Hemingway the writer, the workshop will also uniquely include scholarly/critical sessions dealing with Hemingway's work."

KEY WEST LITERARY SEMINAR, 419 Petronia St., Key West FL 33040. (305)293-9291. Executive Director: Monica Haskell. Estab. 1983. Annual. Conference held second week in January. Conference duration: 3-5 days. Average attendance: 450. "Each year a different topic of literary interest is examined. Writers, scholars, editors, publishers, critics, and the public meet for panel discussions and dialogue. The agenda also includes readings, performances, question and answer sessions, book sales, a writers' workshop, social receptions, and a literary walking tour of Key West. The sessions are held at various locations in Key West, Florida, including the San Carlos Institute, 516 Duval Street and the Key West Art and Historical Society's East Martello Museum. Theme for 1994 is *Biography and Autobiography*; theme for 1995 is *Journalism*. Past speakers include William Goldman, Elmore Leonard, Jan Morris, Octavio Paz, Russell Banks, Mary Higgins Clark, James Merrill, John Wideman.
Costs: Seminar $275 and workshop $200 plus tax.
Accommodations: Catalogs detailing the seminar schedule, guest speakers, registration, accommodations and local interest items are available for SASE. Special room rates are available at participating hotels, motels, guest houses and inns. Room rates usually begin around $100.
Additional Information: Manuscript critique is an optional component of the writers' workshop. No more than 10 typewritten, double spaced pages may be submitted with workshop registration. Brochures are available for SASE.

‡MOONLIGHT AND MAGNOLIAS WRITER'S CONFERENCE, 4128 Manson Ave., Smyrna GA 30082. (404)432-4860. President-Georgia Romance Writers: Sandra Chastain. Estab. 1982. Annual. Conference held 2nd weekend in October. Average attendance: 275. "Conference concentrates on writing of women's fiction with emphasis on romance. The conference site is the Doubletree Hotel located just off I-285, the perimeter highway which circles Atlanta. There is limo service to Atlanta International Airport." Themes include Hands-on Learning for the Beginner, Crossing Genres, Promotion Networking, Self-Help for the Published. Past speakers include approximately 10 editors from major publishing houses and 3-5 agents, along with published writers who make up 25-30% of attendees.
Costs: Hotel $65/day single or double, conference—non GRW members $110 (1992) includes continental breakfast, lunch and banquet.
Additional Information: Maggie Awards are presented to unpublished writers. Synopsis and first 3 chapters must be submitted in early June. Please check with president for new dates. Published writers judge first round: Editors in category judge finals. Brochures/guidelines available for SASE in spring. The Maggie Award for published writers is an award limited to members of Region III Romance Writers of America. Published writers in Region III must submit 1 copy of each book from August to Sept. for consideration.

OZARK CREATIVE WRITERS, INC., 6817 Gingerbread Lane, Little Rock AR 72204. (501)565-8889. Director (Pres. of Board): Peggy Vining. Estab. 1973. Annual. Conference always held 2nd weekend in October. Conference duration: 2½ days. Average attendance: 135-140. "All types of writing. Main speaker for workshop in morning sessions—usually a novelist. Satellite speakers—afternoon—various types. Have included Songwriting Seminar last two years. Eureka Springs is a small resort town in the foothills of the beautiful Ozarks. Conference site is the convention center. Very nice for a small group setting. Reserve early prior to Sept. 1 to insure place." Guest speaker in 1992 was Cherry Weiner, an agent from Manasplain, NJ.
Costs: $25, prior to Sept. 1st; $35 afterwards. Rooms are approx. $59/night and meals (2 banquets) $12 and 13.
Accommodations: Chamber of Commerce will send list; 50 rooms are blocked off for OCW prior to Sept. 1st. Accommodations vary at hotels. Many campsites also available.
Additional Information: We have approximately 20 various categories of writing contests. Selling writers are our judges. Entry fee is $25 full participation. Brochures are available for SASE after May 1. "The 1993 conference was a 'Reunion Conference' of 20 years."

‡SEA OATS WRITER'S CONFERENCE, P.O. Box 16101, Mobile AL 36616. (205)343-8235. President: Bob Henry; Chairman: Donna Kyle. Annual. Conference held April 20. "Conference concentrates on fiction. The emphasis of the conference is to prepare writers for publication by inviting publishers and agents who will critique our work. Each writer is invited to submit a synopsis for that purpose. Fairhope campus of Faulkner State Community College is the location. Weather permitting, attendees may be seated on the lawn outside the hall under a canopy of ancient Live Oak trees. Fairhope, by the way, is a haven for writers and artists."
Costs: Fees are kept low, usually under $50.
Accommodations: Fairhope is a 45-minute drive from the Mobile Municipal Airport. Special arrangements for transportation are made for speakers only. Most hotels are within 20 minutes of the conference site. Prices average $35/night.
Additional Information: Brochures/guidelines available for SASE. "We encourage new writers to submit a synopsis only for the critique session. However, the first two chapters of the manuscript may be requested by a publisher or agent so be prepared."

SOUTHEASTERN WRITERS ASSOCIATION ANNUAL WORKSHOP, 4021 Gladesworth Lane, Decatur GA 30035. (404)288-2064. Director: Nancy Knight. Estab. 1976. Annual. Conference held from June 19 to June 25. Average attendance: 75. "For poetry, short story, mass market fiction, novel, playwriting, children's literature, nonfiction, inspiration. The conference is held at Epworth-by-the-Sea on St. Simon's Island, GA. The immaculate grounds are expansive and inspirational for writers. Several historical buildings are located on the site. Housing is reasonable and includes all meals."
Costs: $200 nonmembers, $170 members, $150 seniors.
Accommodations: 1992 rates—all on-site/handicap accessible, $234-274 (double), $319-391 (single), includes *all* meals including banquet.
Additional Information: Three mss may be submitted for critique and private consultation. Sponsors a contest. All categories of mss are judged for contests by the instructor. Conference attendance is the requirement. Conference brochures/guidelines are available for SASE. "We stress interaction between students and staff. Teachers are housed in the same area and available to students at almost any time. We are a hands on kind of workshop—students are assigned work to be completed during free time which is usually read in class."

SOUTHEASTERN WRITERS CONFERENCE, Rt. 1, Box 102, Cuthbert GA 31740. (912)679-5445. Advertising Director: Pat Laye. Estab. 1975. Annual. Conference held June 19 to June 26. Conference duration: 1 week. Average attendence: 80 (Limited to 100 participants). Concentration is on fiction, poetry and juvenile—plus nonfiction and playwriting." Site is "St. Simons Island, GA. Conference held at Epworth-by-the-Sea Conference Center—tropical setting, beaches. Each year we offer market advice, agent updates. All our instructors are professional writers presently selling in New York."
Costs: $200. Meals and lodging are separate. Senior citizen discount.
Accommodations: Air and bus attendees will be picked up at their arrival point and returned there. Information on overnight accommodations is made available. "On-site-facilities at a remarkably low cost. Facilities are motel style of excellent quality. Other hotels are available on the island."
Additional Information: Three manuscripts of 1 chapter each are allowed in three different categories. Sponsors a contest, many cash prizes. Brochures are available for SASE.

WRITE FOR SUCCESS WORKSHOP: CHILDREN'S BOOKS, 3748 Harbor Heights Dr., Largo FL 34644. (813)581-2484. Speaker/Coordinator: Theo Carroll. Estab. 1988. Held irregularly. Conference duration: 1 day. Average attendance: 110. Concentration is writing for children. Site is the Belleview Mido Resort Hotel. Large conference rooms. Promoted as the largest occupied wooden structure in the world; a Victorian landmark built in 1896 in Clearwater, Florida."
Costs: $85 includes breakfast, lunch and materials. Limo available from Tampa airport. Information on overnight accommodations made available and special conference attendee accommodations are made.
Additional Information: Brochures for latest seminar are available for SASE.

‡**WRITING TODAY—BIRMINGHAM-SOUTHERN COLLEGE**, Box A-3, Birmingham AL 35254. (205)226-4921. Contact: Martha Andrews, Director of Special Events. Estab. 1978. Annual. Conference held April 8 and 9. Average attendance: 400-500. "This is a two day conference with approximately 18 workshops, lectures and readings. We try to offer workshops in short fiction, novels, poetry, children's literature, magazine writing, and general information of concern to aspiring writers such as publishing, agents, markets and research. The conference is sponsored by Birmingham-Southern College and is held on the campus in classrooms and lecture halls." The 1993 conference emphasized poetry and featured Pulitzer Prize winning poet Donald Justice. Novelists Ric Patterson and Lauren Hemingway presented workshops. The 1994 conference speakers will include Gwendolyn Brooks, Howell Raines, Charles Gaines.
Costs: $75 for both days. This includes lunches, reception and morning coffee and rolls.
Accommodations: Attendees must arrange own transporation. Local hotels and motels offer special rates, but participants make their own reservations.
Additional Information: "We usually offer a critique for interested writers. We have had poetry and short fiction critiques. There is an additional charge for these critiques." Sponsors the Hackney Literary Awards for poetry, short fiction and novels. Brochures available for SASE.

Midwest (IL, IN, KY, MI, OH)

ANTIOCH WRITERS' WORKSHOP, P.O. Box 494, Yellow Springs OH 45387. Director: Susan Carpenter. Estab. 1984. Annual. Average attendance: 80. Workshop concentration: poetry, nonfiction and fiction. Workshop located on Antioch College campus in the Village of Yellow Springs. Speakers planned for next workshop include John Jakes, Joe David Bellamy, Ralph Keyes and Stanley Plumly.
Costs: Tuition is $450—lower for local and repeat—plus meals.
Accommodations: "We pick up free at airport." Accommodations made at dorms and area hotels. Cost is $16-20/night (for dorms).
Additional Information: Offers free critique sessions. Conference brochures/guidelines are available for SASE.

AUTUMN AUTHORS' AFFAIR, 1507 Burnham Ave., Calumet City IL 60409. (708)862-9797. President: Nancy McCann. Estab. 1983. Annual. Conference held in late October. Begins with Friday night dinner and ends with Sunday brunch. Average attendance: 300. "Focused on romance, contemporary and historical, but also features poetry, short story, mystery, young adult, childrens, screenplay writing and journalism." Site: Hyatt Regency, Lisle. Panels planned include "everything from the basics, to getting started, to how to handle the business aspects of your writing. Out of 25 workshops, 23 focus on 'fiction' writing."
Costs: 1993 cost was $100, which included Friday night buffet, Saturday continental breakfast, Saturday night dessert buffet and luncheon and Sunday brunch. Saturday only package available for $65.
Accommodations: Information on overnight accommodations is made available with a "special" room rate for those attending conference.
Additional Information: Brochures/guidelines available for SASE.

CHRISTIAN WRITERS CONFERENCE, 177 E. Crystal Lake Ave., Lake Mary FL 32746. (407)324-5465. Fax: (407)324-0209. Conference Director: Dottie McBroom. Estab. 1948. Annual. Conference in Wheaton, Illinois on June 2-5, 1994 will feature Stephen Strang and Robert Walker as speakers. Average attendance: 150. For fiction, writing for children, nonfiction. Held at Wheaton College. Themes: Writing for broadcast media. In 1992 guest speakers were Len and Sandy LeSourd.

Costs: $335/single or $305/double for tuition, meals and room.
Accommodations: United Airlines conference rates available. Accommodations are dorms at Wheaton College. Onsite accommodations are included in cost.
Additional Information: Sponsors a contest: 1. Must register for entire conference; 2. Editors on staff judge the entries. Conference brochures/guidelines are available for SASE. Also holds a conference for advanced and beginning writers in February in Florida.

‡CLARION SCIENCE FICTION & FANTASY WRITING WORKSHOP, Lyman Briggs School, E−28 Holmes Hall, Michigan State University, East Lansing MI 48825-1107. (517)353-7196. Administrative Assistant: Mary Sheridan. Estab. 1967. Workshop held annually for six weeks in the summer. Average attendance: 17-20. "Workshop concentrates on science fiction and fantasy writing. The workshop is held at Michigan State University and is sponsored by Lyman Briggs School, a residential program linking the sciences and humanities. Participants are housed in single rooms in a graduate residence hall adjoining the workshop site. Facilities are handicapped accessible." Guest writers in residence during the summer of 1993 included Tim Powers, Joe Haldeman, Karen Flowler, Eleanor Arnason, Kate Wilhelm and Damon Knight.
Costs: Fees for the 1993 Clarion workshop were $803 for both Michigan residents and non-residents. Students will be enrolled as Life-Long Education students and will receive four undergraduate semester credits and a transcript from MSU.
Accommodations: Rates for a single room and meals in a graduate residence hall on the MSU campus are being negotiated.
Additional Information: Admission to the workshop is based on submission of a writing sample of two complete short stories between 10 and 25 pages long and a completed application form with a $25 application fee. A $100 fee is required upon acceptance. Brochures/guidelines available for SASE.

‡CLEVELAND HEIGHTS/UNIVERSITY HEIGHTS WRITERS MINI CONFERENCE, #110, 34200 Ridge Rd., Willoughby OH 44094. (216)943-3047. Coordinator: Lea Leever Oldham. Estab. 1992. Annual. Conference held November 19. Average attendance: 75. "Fiction, nonfiction, science fiction, poetry, children's, etc." Held at Wiley Middle School, University Heights, in classrooms. Wheelchair accessible. East of Cleveland off 271. Panels include "no theme, just published authors sharing their secrets."
Costs: $25.
Additional Information: Conference brochures/guidelines are available for SASE.

EASTERN KENTUCKY UNIVERSITY CREATIVE WRITING CONFERENCE, Eastern Kentucky University, Richmond KY 40475. (606)622-5861. Conference Director: Dorothy Sutton. Estab. 1962. Annual. Conference held June 13-17 (usually 3rd week in June). Average attendance: 12-15. Conference to promote poetry, fiction and creative nonfiction, including lectures, workshops, private conferences and peer group manuscript evaluation. The conference is held on the campus of Eastern Kentucky University "in the rolling hills of Eastern Kentucky, between the horse farms of the Bluegrass and the scenic mountains of the Appalachian chain." Three distinguished visiting writers will teach at the conference. Past speakers have included Donald Justice, Richard Marius, Gregory Orr, David Citino. Also helping with workshops will be EKU faculty Harry Brown, Hal Blythe, Charlie Sweet.
Costs: $55 for undergraduates ($153 if out-of-state); $79 for graduates ($224 if out-of-state). Cost includes 1 hour of credit in creative writing and is subject to change (please check brochure for changes). Auditors welcome at same price. Dining in the cafeteria is approximately $6-8/day.
Accommodations: Air-conditioned dormitory rooms are available for $32 (double) or $46 (single) per week. "Linens furnished. Bring your own blankets, pillow and telephone."
Additional Information: "Participants are asked to submit manuscript by May 15 to be approved before June 1." For conference brochure, send SASE to English Department (attn: Creative Writing Conference).

CHARLENE FARIS SEMINARS FOR BEGINNERS, 9524 Guilford Dr. #A, Indianapolis IN 46240. (317)848-2634. Director: Charlene Faris. Estab. 1985. Held 2 or 3 times/year in various locations in spring and fall. Conference duration: 2 days. Average attendence: 10. Concentration on all areas of publishing and writing. Locations have included Phoenix, Chicago and Los Angeles.
Costs: $125, tuition only.
Accommodations: "Can assist attendees with information on overnite accommodations."
Additional Information: Guidelines available for SASE.

GREEN RIVER NOVELS-IN-PROGRESS WORKSHOP, 11906 Locust Rd., Louisville KY 40243. (502)245-4902. Director: Mary E. O'Dell. Estab. 1991. Annual. Conference held in early January. Conference duration: 1 week. Average attendance: 35. "For novels; mainstream and genres handled by individual instructors. Short fiction collections, essay collections, and a few nonfiction welcome. Each novelist instructor works with a small group (5-7 people) for five days; then agents/editors are there for panels and appointments on the weekend." Site is The University of Louisville's Shelby Campus, suburban setting, graduate dorm housing (private rooms available w/shared bath for each 2 rooms). Meetings and classes held in nearby classroom building. Grounds available for walking, etc. Lovely setting, restaurants and shopping available nearby. Participants carpool to restaurants, etc." This year we are covering mystery, romance, thriller, fantasy/horror, sf, mainstream/literary. Guest speakers are Steve Womack (mainstream and mystery); Gary Raisor (fantasy/horror); Karen Field (mainstream and romance); Bob Mayer (thriller); Kathryn Hammer (nonfiction).
Costs: Tuition—$250, housing $17 per night private, $12 shared. Does not include meals.
Accommodations: "We do meet participants' planes and see that participants without cars have transportation to meals, etc. If participants would rather stay in hotel, we will make that information available."
Additional Information: Participants send 60 pages/3 chapters upon application; these pages are turned over to participants' novelists, from whom each participant receives critique by a novelist and, during Workshop Week, a private conference with same. Conference brochures/guidelines are available for SASE.

‡IMAGINATION, Cleveland State University, Cleveland OH 44115. (216)687-4522. Contact: Neal Chandler. Estab. 1991. Annual. Conference will be held from July 16-21, 1994. Average attendance: 60. "Conference concentrates on fiction, poetry and writing for children. Held at Mather Mansion, a restored 19th Century Euclid Blvd. Mansion on the campus of Cleveland State University." 1993 themes included Writing Beyond Realism, Business of Writing and Writing for Children. For more information send SASE for brochure.

‡KENSTON WRITERS MINI CONFERENCE, #110, 34200 Ridge Rd., Willoughby OH 44094. (216)943-3047. Coordinator: Lea Leever Oldham. Estab. 1993. Annual. Conference held October 8. "Fiction, nonfiction, science fiction, poetry, children's, etc." Held at Kenston High School, Chagrin Falls, Ohio, southeast of Cleveland off 422. Panels include "no theme, just published authors sharing their secrets."
Costs: $25.
Additional Information: Conference brochures/guidelines are available for SASE.

‡LAKELAND WRITERS MINI CONFERENCE, #110, 34200 Ridge Rd., Willoughby OH 44094. (216)943-3047. Coordinator: Lea Leever Oldham Estab. 1992. Annual. Conference held March 26. Average attendance: 100. "Fiction, nonfiction, science fiction, poetry, childrens." Held at "Lakeland Community College Mentor, Ohio. Classrooms, wheelchair accessible—right off I-90, east of Cleveland." Panels include "no theme, just published authors sharing their secrets."
Costs: $25.
Additional Information: Offers critiques for manuscripts which must be submitted at least 2 weeks in advance. Conference brochures/guidelines are available for SASE.

MIDLAND WRITERS CONFERENCE, Grace A. Dow Memorial Library, 1710 W. St. Andrews, Midland MI 48640. (517)835-7151. Conference Co-Chairs: Eileen Finzel, Margaret Allen. Estab. 1980. Annual. Conference held June 11. Average attendance: 100. "The Conference is composed of a well-known keynote speaker and then, six workshops on a variety of subjects ranging from poetry, children's writing, freelancing, agents, etc. The attendees are both published and unpublished authors. The Conference is held at the Grace A. Dow Memorial Library in the auditorium and conference rooms. Keynoters in the past have included Andrew Greeley, Kurt Vonnegut, David Halberstam."
Costs: Adult - $45 before May 15, after May 15 the fee is $55; student, senior citizen and handicapped - $35 before May 15, after May 15 the fee is $45. A box lunch is available for $7.
Accommodations: A list of area hotels is available.
Additional Information: Conference brochures/guidelines are available for SASE.

MIDWEST WRITERS' CONFERENCE, 6000 Frank Ave. NW, Canton OH 44720 (216)499-9600. Conference Coordinator: Debbie Ruhe. Estab. 1968. Annual. Conference held in early October. Conference duration: 2 days. Average attendance: 250. "The conference provides an atmosphere in which aspiring writers can meet with and learn from experienced and established writers through

lectures, workshops, competitive contest, personal interviews and informal group discussions. The areas of concentration include fiction, nonfiction, juvenile literature and poetry. The Midwest Writers' Conference is held on Kent State University Stark Campus in Canton, Ohio. This two-day conference is held in Main Hall, a four-story building and wheel chair accessible." Past topics have included "Dialogue With Edward Albee," "Lifting Them Up To Our Windows: Writing For Kids," "The Business of Writing," "Finding The Poem," "The Gentle Art of Interviewing," "A Story Is A Journey," "Public And Private Grants For The Creative Writer," "Why You Never Had A Column In The Can," "Non-Fiction In A Nutshell," "Write The Perfect Book Proposal." 1993 Presenters included: Tricia Springstubb: Author, Lecturer; Sheree Bykofsky: President, Sheree Bykofsky Associates, Inc., Literary Agency; Richard Hague: Teacher, Author, Lecturer; Linda Rome: Editor, *Ohio Writer*; Columnist, CN Service; Robert Pope: Professor of English, The University of Akron; Robert Fox: Literature Coordinator, The Ohio Arts Council; Stuart Warner: Deputy Managing Editor, *Beacon Journal*; Katina Jones: Writer, Lecturer; Deborah Adams: Vice President of Jeff Herman Literary Agency.
Costs: $65 includes Friday workshops, keynote address, Saturday workshops, box luncheon and manuscript entry fee (limited to two submissions); $40 for contest only (includes two manuscripts).
Accommodations: Arrangements are made with the Parke Hotel. The Parke Hotel is nearest Kent Stark, and offers a special reduced rate for conference attendees. Conferees must make their own reservations 3 weeks before the conference to be guaranteed this special conference rate.
Additional Information: Each manuscript entered in the contest will receive a critique. If the manuscript is selected for final judging, it will receive an additional critique from the final judge. Conference attendees are not required to submit manuscripts to the writing contest. Manuscript deadline is early August. For contest: A maximum of 1 entry for each category is permitted. Entries must be typed on 8½ × 11 paper, double-spaced. A separate page must accompany each entry bearing the author's name, address, phone, category and title of the work. Entries are not to exceed 3,000 words in length. Work must be original, unpublished and not a winner in any contest at the time of entry. Conference brochures and guidelines are available for SASE.

MIDWEST WRITERS WORKSHOP, Dept. of Journalism, Ball State University, Muncie IN 47306. (317)285-8200. Co-Director: Earl L. Conn. Estab. 1974. Annual. Workshop to be held July 27-30. Average attendance: 100. For fiction, nonfiction, poetry. Conference held at Hotel Roberts in downtown Muncie.
Costs: In 1993, cost was $160 including opening reception, hospitality room and closing banquet.
Accommodations: Special hotel rates offered.
Additional Information: Critiques available. $25 for individual critiquing. Conference brochures/guidelines are available for SASE.

MISSISSIPPI VALLEY WRITERS CONFERENCE, Augustana College, Rock Island IL 61201. (309)762-8985. Conference Founder/Director: David R. Collins. Estab. 1973. Annual. Conference held June 5 to June 10. Average attendance: 80. "Conference for all areas of writing for publication." Conference held at Augustana College, a liberal arts school along the Mississippi River. 1994 guest speakers include Evelyn Witter, Mel Boring, Max Collins, Kim Bush, H.E. Francis, Karl Largent, Roald Tweet, Rich Johnson.
Costs: $25 for registration; $40 for 1 workshop; $75 for two; plus $30 for each additional workshops; $20 to audit.
Accommodations: On-campus facitilites available. Accommodations are available at Westerlin Hall on the Augustana College campus. Cost for 6 nights is $85; cost for 15 meals is $75.
Additional Information: Conferees may submit manuscripts to workshop leaders for personal conferences during the week. Cash awards are given at the end of the conference week by workshop leaders based on manuscripts submitted. Conference brochures/guidelines are available for SASE. "Conference is open to the beginner as well as the polished professional—all are welcome."

OAKLAND UNIVERSITY WRITERS' CONFERENCE, 265 SFH, Rochester MI 48309-4401. (313)370-3120. Program Director: Nadine Jakobowski. Estab. 1961. Annual. Conference held from October 15 to October 16. Average attendance: 400. "All areas; all purposes." Held at Oakland University Oakland Center: meetings rooms, dining area; O'Dowd Hall: lecture rooms; Meadow Brook Hall (on campus) evening reception. "Each annual conference covers all aspects and types of writing in 40 concurrent workshops on Saturday. Major writers from various genres are speakers the Saturday conference luncheon program. Individual critiques and hands-on writing workshops are conducted Friday. Areas: Poetry, articles, fiction, short stories, playwriting, nonfiction, young adult, children's literature. Guest speaker in 1993: Tom KaKonis, author of crime novels.

Costs: 1993: Conference registration: $55; luncheon, $8.50; individual manuscript, $43; writing workshop, $33; writing ms audit, $23; poetry critiquing, $42.
Accommodations: List is available.
Additional Information: Conference brochure/guidelines available for SASE.

‡OF DARK & STORMY NIGHTS, Mystery Writers of America—Midwest Chapter, %200 S. Garden Ave., Roselle IL 60172. (708)980-9535. Workshop Director: Marilyn Nelson. Estab. 1982. Annual. Workshop held June. Workshop duration: 1 day. Average attendance: 150. Dedicated to "writing *mystery* fiction and crime related nonfiction. Workshops and panels presented on techniques of mystery writing from ideas to revision, marketing, investigative techniques and more by published writers, law enforcement experts and publishing professionals. 1993 luncheon speaker was John Lutz." Site is Holiday Inn, Rolling Meadows IL.
Costs: $80 for MWA members; $90 for non-members; $30 for manuscript critique.
Accommodations: Easily accessible by car or train (from Chicago). Holiday Inn, Rolling Meadows $65 per night + tax; free airport bus and previously arranged rides from train.
Additional Information: "We accept manuscript critiques (first 25 pages maximum) for $30 cost. Writers meet with critiquer during one of the sessions for one-on-one discussion." Brochures available for SASE after March 30.

‡SCBWI/MIDWEST WRITER'S CONFERENCE, 532 W. Jewel, Kirkwood MO 63122. (314)965-4274. Contact: Vicki B. Erwin, Midwest Coordinator, or Ellen Howard, Michigan Regional Advisor, 2011 Waite Ave., Kalamazoo MI 49008. Estab. 1987. Held every two years. Next conference scheduled for June 10 to June 12, 1994. Average attendance: 200. Focus on writing and illustrating for children. "The 1994 conference will be held at the Novi Hilton in the Detroit area." The hotel has its own restaurants and recreation facilities, with golf, tennis and racquetball available nearby. "In 1992 there were workshops, panels and plenary sessions addressing such subjects as 'How to Build and Sustain Your Career as a Children's Book Writer,' 'Picture Books,' and 'What's Telling Your Story?' Featured speakers were James Cross Giblin, agent Kendra Marcus, Nancy Carlson, editor Regina Hayes, art director Jim Simondet, publisher George Nicholson, Marion Dane Bauer."
Costs: Fees for 1992 were $175 for SCBWI members, $195 for nonmembers (included all sessions, 2 banquets and 1 luncheon).
Accommodations: Attendees must make their own transporation arrangements. Rooms available at Novi Hilton for special rate of $62/night single or double.
Additional Information: "Both portfolio and manuscript critiques will be available. Information about this will be sent with registration confirmation." Brochures available for SASE.

THUNDER BAY LITERARY CONFERENCE, 211 N. First, Alpena MI 49707. (517)356-6188. Assistant Director: Judi Stillion. Estab. 1990. Annual. Two-day conference held in September or October. Average attendance: 100-150. "Our current area of concentration is Michigan writers. One objective is to heighten awareness and understanding of the heritage and current status of literature in the state." The conference is held at the Alpena Civic Center.
Costs: $25 (nonrefundable) $6.50 luncheon, $10 breakfast (1993).
Accommodations: Information on overnight accommodations is made available. Special rates are available at the Fletcher Motel for those who specify the conference.
Additional Information: Sponsors contest for adult short fiction and poetry. Michigan residents only. A panel of University of Michigan faculty will judge entries. Write for more information. Conference brochures/guidelines available for SASE.

‡TRI C WEST WRITERS CONFERENCE, #110, 34200 Ridge Rd., Willoughby OH 44094. (216)943-3047. Coordinator: Lea Leever Oldham. Estab. 1993. Annual. Conference held June 18. "Fiction, nonfiction, poetry, science fiction, mystery, children's, copyright and tax information, etc." Held at Cuyahoga Community College, Western Campus, Parma, OH. Wheelchair accessible. Use classrooms. Southwest of Cleveland, take I-77. Panels include "no theme, just published authors and experts sharing their expertise."
Costs: $44 includes lunch.
Additional Information: Conference brochures/guidelines are available for SASE.

‡WESTERN RESERVE WRITERS & FREELANCE CONFERENCE, #110, 34200 Ridge Rd., Willoughby OH 44094. (216)943-3047. Coordinator: Lea Leever Oldham. Estab. 1984. Annual. Conference held Sept. 10. Average attendance: 150. "Fiction, nonfiction, inspirational, children's, poetry, humor, scifi,

copyright and tax information, etc." Held at Lakeland Community College, Mentor, OH. Classrooms wheelchair accessible. Accessible from I-90, east of Cleveland. Panels include "no themes, simply published authors and other experts sharing their secrets."
Costs: $44 includes lunch.
Additional Information: Offers critiques for ms submitted at least 2 weeks in advance. Conference brochures/guidelines are available for SASE.

North Central (IA, MN, NE, ND, SD, WI)

‡GREAT LAKES WRITER'S WORKSHOP, Alverno College, 3401 S. 39 St., P.O. Box 343922, Milwaukee WI 53234-3922. (414)382-6176. Contact: Debra Pass, Director, Telesis Institute. Estab. 1985. Annual. Workshop held during second week in July (Friday through Thursday). Average attendance: 250. "Workshop focuses on a variety of subjects including fiction, writing for magazines, freelance writing, writing for children, poetry, marketing, etc. The workshop is held in Milwaukee, Wisconsin at Alverno College."
Costs: In 1993, cost was $99 for entire workshop. "Individual classes are priced as posted in the brochure."
Accommodations: Attendees must make their own travel arrangements. Accommodations are available on campus; rooms are in residence halls and are not air-conditioned. Cost in 1993 was $22 for single, $17 per person for double. There are also hotels in the surrounding area. Call (414)382-6040 for information regarding overnight accommodations.
Additional Information: "Some workshop instructors may provide critiques, but this changes depending upon the workshop and speaker. This would be indicated in the workshop brochure." Brochures available for SASE.

GREEN LAKE CHRISTIAN WRITERS CONFERENCE, American Baptist Assembly, Green Lake WI 54941-9589. (800)558-8898. Estab. 1948. Annual. Conference held in mid-July for 1 week. Average attendance: 80. "The mission of the conference is to provide a setting and appropriate resource persons so Christian writers can further develop their writing skills—whether a beginner or seasoned writer. Held annually at the American Baptist Assembly which is a 1,000-acre conference center on Green Lake. The center offers lodging and meals as well as wide range of recreational opportunities. The Assembly is the national training center for American Baptist Churches. The conference is ecumenical." Conference speakers have included Gianfranco Pagnucci, Susan Pagnucci, Lenore Coberly, Jeri McCormick, Kristen Ingram, Jan White, Jeanne Donovan and Sally Stuart.
Costs: Tuition is $80/person.
Accommodations: "We can provide ground transportation from Appleton and Oshkosh, Wisconsin airports; the Columbus, WI Amtrak station and Ripon, WI Greyhound Bus Stop—there is a charge and advance reservation is required." On-site facilities available. Costs: Rooms range (double occupancy) from $21 to $34/night; meals $18.75/day. Campground available as well as cottages, cabins and homes.
Additional Information: "Personal critique sessions with leaders may be scheduled. Major seminars include group critique. No advance submissions." Conference brochures/guidelines are available for SASE."Once a person has attended the writers conference they may return during specified fall, winter and spring weeks at a special low cost of $10/night—no instruction."

IOWA SUMMER WRITING FESTIVAL, 116 International Center, University of Iowa, Iowa City IA 52242. (319)335-2534. Director: Peggy Houston. Assistant Director: Karen Burgus Schootman. Estab. 1987. Annual. Festival held June 12 to July 27. Workshops are one week, two weeks or a weekend. Average attendance: limited to 12/class—over 1,000 participants throughout the summer. "We offer courses in most areas of writing: novel, fiction, essay, poetry, playwriting, screenwriting, freelance, nonfiction, writing for children, memoirs, women's writing and science fiction." Site is the University of Iowa campus. Guest speakers are undetermined at this time. Last year's guest readers were Robert Olen Butler, Ethan Canin, Clark Blaise, Robert Waller, Gordon Mennenga, Gerald Stern, Kathleen Peirce.
Costs: $315, one-week workshop; $630, two-week workshop; $150, weekend workshop (1993 rates). Discounts available for early registration. Housing and meals are separate.
Accommodations: Shuttle service from the Cedar Rapids airport to the university is available for a reasonable fee. "We offer participants a choice of accommodations: Dormitory, $23/night; Iowa House, $43/night; Holiday Inn, $55/night (rates subject to changes)."

Additional Information: Brochure/guidelines are available.

LAKEWOOD COMMUNITY COLLEGE WRITERS' SEMINAR, 3401 Century Ave,, White Bear Lake MN 55110. (612)779-3259. Director Continuing Education: Pat Lockyear. Estab. 1990. Held quarterly in fall, winter and spring. Workshop duration: 1 day. Average attendance: 30-50. "Workshops concentrate on either fiction or writing for children. Held on campus in college conference room with tables for individuals." Peter Davidson was a guest speaker in 1993.
Costs: $55.
Additional Information: Brochures/guidelines available for SASE.

‡SCBWI/MINNESOTA CHAPTER WORKSHOP, 4042 24th Ave. S., Minneapolis MN 55406. (612)724-2097. Co-Advisor: Carol Marron. Conference held 1 day in spring. Average Attendance: 100. Features authors and/or editors.
Costs: Around $65.
Accommodations: No accommodations available. Write for information. Hotel names will be supplied.
Additional Information: Workshop brochure available for SASE. "In the past we have featured author Jane Yolen; editor Susan Pearson of Lothrop, Lee, & Shephard Books; and Patricia Lee Gauch of Philomel Books. Our 1993 featured editor was Jane Snyder of Candlewick Press."

SCBWI/WISCONSIN FALL RETREAT, 26 Lancaster Ct., Madison WI 53719-1433. (608)271-0433. Regional Advisor: Sheri Cooper Sinykin. Estab. 1991. Annual. Conference held in late September or early October in Madison. Average attendance: 60. Writing for children. In 1993 (and odd years) held at Siena Center in Racine, in even years, if available, held at St. Benedict's Center in Madison. Speakers in 1993 were Lois Lowry, editor Elizabeth Isele, illustrator Beth Peck.
Costs: In 1993 cost was $175 for SCBWI members ($195 non-members), includes room, board, program and book.
Accommodations: We try to have volunteers assist with airport transportation. Overnights are on-site and included. On-site housing runs about $25/night.
Additional Information: Critiques were offered in 1993 for an extra fee of $25. Conference brochures/guidelines are available in June for SASE.

SINIPEE WRITERS' WORKSHOP, P.O. Box 902, Dubuque IA 52004-0902. (319)556-0366. Director: John Tigges. Estab. 1985. Annual conference held in April. Average attendance: 50-75. To promote "primarily fiction although we do include a poet and a nonfiction writer on each program. The two mentioned areas are treated in such a way that fiction writers can learn new ways to expand their abilities and writing techniques." The workshop is held on the campus of Clarke College in Dubuque. "This campus holds a unique atmosphere and everyone seems to love the relaxed and restful mood it inspires. This in turn carries over to the workshop and friendships are made that last in addition to learning and experiencing what other writers have gone through to attain success in their chosen field." 1994 guest speakers will include Jodi Jill, literary agent; Janet Pack, nonfiction author; Rebecca Christian, playwright plus a poet and a romance novelist, to be announced.
Costs: $60 early registration/$65 at the door. Includes all handouts, necessary materials for the workshop, coffee/snack break, lunch, drinks and snacks at autograph party following workshop.
Accommodations: Information is available for out-of-town participants, concerning motels etc. even though the workshop is one day long.
Additional Information: Sponsors fiction and poetry contests: limit 1,500 words (fiction), 40 lines (poetry). 1st prize in both categories: $75 plus publication in an area newspaper or magazine; 2nd prize in both categories: $35; 3rd prize in both categories: $10. Written critique service available for contest entries, $15 extra.

SPLIT ROCK ARTS PROGRAM, University of Minnesota, 306 Wesbrook Hall, 77 Pleasant St. SE, Minneapolis MN 55455. (612)624-6800. Estab. 1982. Annual. Workshops held in July and August. Over 45 one-week intensive residential workshops held. "The Split Rock Arts Program, now in its tenth season, is offered through the University of Minnesota on its Duluth campus. Over 45 one-week intensive residential workshops in writing, visual arts, fine crafts and the process of creativity are held for six weeks in July and August. This unique arts community provides a nurturing environment in a beautiful setting overlooking Lake Superior and the cool summer port city of Duluth. Courses, which can be taken for credit, are offered in long and short fiction, nonfiction, poetry and children's literature." Instructors in 1993 included Paulette Bates Alden, Christina Baldwin, David Bradley,

Michael Dennis Browne, Lucille Clifton, Carolyn Forché, Phebe Hanson, Alexs Pate, Madelon Sprengnether, Robert Hill Whiteman, Jane Yolen, Sharon Doubiago.
Costs: $330, tuition (may vary with options). Moderately priced housing available for additional cost.
Accommodations: Campus apartments available.
Additional Information: A limited number of scholarships are available based on qualification and need. Call for catalog.

UNIVERSITY OF WISCONSIN AT MADISON SCHOOL OF THE ARTS AT RHINELANDER, 726 Lowell Hall, 610 Langdon St., Madison WI 53703. Administrative Coordinator: Kathy Berigan. Estab. 1964. Annual. Conference held from July 25-29. Average attendance: 300. Courses offered in writing, visual arts, drama, photography, music, folk arts, folk dancing. Conference held in junior high school in the city of Rhinelander in northern Wisconsin (James Williams Junior High School).
Costs: Tuition only—ranges from $100-215. Some courses require materials or lab fee.
Accommodations: Information on overnight accommodations (cabins, motels, camping) made available.
Additional Information: Ms critique workshop available. Request to be put on mailing list.

‡THE WRITE TOUCH VI, P. O. Box 92277, Milwaukee WI 53202. Conference Coordinator: Peggy Hoffman. Estab. 1988. Annual. Conference held in May. Conference duration: 2 days. Average attendance: 100. "For romance writing (fiction). Site changes annually; in 1993 Write Touch was held at the Olympia Village Conference Center and Resort in Oconomowoc, Wisconsin (just 30 minutes west of Milwaukee). "Our conferences always focus on writing the romance novel; in 1993, however, we offered an advanced look at romantic suspense, with panels on criminology and law enforcement techniques. Other seminars include contemporary and historical romance genres, writing the series or multiple-character novels." Sheryl Woods, who writes for Silhouette Books and Dell Paperbacks (both romance and mystery) was featured speaker in 1993. Guest editors included Leslie Wainger from Silhouette.
Costs: Approximately $75/attendee.
Additional Information: Brochures/guidelines available for SASE.

WRITER'S SEMINAR/ANOKA-RAMSEY COMMUNITY COLLEGE, 11200 Mississippi Blvd. NW, Coon Rapids MN 55345. (612)422-3301. Director, Center for Business & Industry: Rosie Mortenson. Estab. 1987. Annual. Conference held in fall. Conference duration: 1 day. Average attendance: 30. "Goal is how to get published! Conference held in a seminar room in the College Development Center which is separate from the rest of the college."
Costs: In 1993 cost was $59.

South Central (CO, KS, MO, NM, OK, TX)

AUSTIN WRITERS' LEAGUE FALL AND SPRING WORKSHOPS, E-2, 1501 W. Fifth, Austin TX 78703. (512)499-8914. Executive Director: Angela Smith. Estab. 1982. Held each fall and spring (March, April, May, September, October, November). Workshop duration: 2 days; Saturdays, Sundays. Average attendance: at least 14 workshops in each series, each drawing from 15 to 150. To promote "all genres, fiction and nonfiction, poetry, writing for children, screenwriting, playwriting, legal and tax information for writers, also writing workshops for children and youth." Workshop held at "St. Edward's University—classroom space and auditoriums. Located at 3001 S. Congress, Austin, Texas 78704." Workshop topics include: Finding and working with agents and publishers; writing and publishing short fiction; dialogue; characterization; voice of the fiction writer; basic and advanced fiction writing; book marketing and promotion; business of writing; also workshops for genres. "Spring '94 series now being planned. Past speakers have included Dwight Swain, Natalie Goldberg, David Lindsey, D.F. Mills, Shelby Hearon, Gabriele Rico, C. Michael Curtis, Sterling Lord."
Costs: Each three-hour workshop is $35-45 (members); $25 more for nonmembers. Six-hour labs are $75 (members); $25 more for nonmembers.
Accommodations: Austin Writers' League will provide assistance with transportation arrangements on request. List of hotels is available for SASE. Special rates given at some hotels for workshop participants.
Additional Information: Critique sessions offered. Individual presenters determine critique requirements. Those requirements are then made available through Austin Writers' League office and in workshop promotion. Contests and awards programs are offered separately from workshops.

Workshop brochures/guidelines are available on request. "In addition to regular series of workshops, Austin Writers' League sponsors ongoing informal classes in writing, plus weekend seminars and retreats throughout the year."

CRAFT OF WRITING, UTD Box 830688, CN 1.1, Richardson TX 75083. (214)690-2204. Director: Janet Harris. Estab. 1983. Annual. Conference held September (check for exact dates). Average attendance: 150. "To provide information to accomplished and aspiring writers on how to write and how to get published. All genres are included. Areas of writing covered include characterization and dialogue to working with an agent." Workshops in 1993 included a panel of editors and agents (both national and local), "Your First Steps Toward an Agent," "Great Aunt Agata is Dead: Elements of the Mystery," "The ABC's of Writing Commercial Novels," "Writing a Non-Fiction Proposal," and "The Future of Women's Fiction."
Costs: $175; includes 2 lunches and a banquet.
Accommodations: A block of rooms is held at the Richardson Hilton for $49/night. Call (214)644-4000 for reservations.
Additional Information: Critiques available. "There are no requirements. Participants may have manuscripts critiqued by members of the Greater Dallas Writers Association. Two manuscript critique sessions are scheduled. A manuscript contest is held prior to the conference. The deadline for submissions is July. Judges are specialists in the areas they are critiquing. There are nine categories with several cash prizes. Conference brochures/guidelines are available. Twenty-eight workshops are scheduled on a wide range of topics. Presenters include nationally known authors, agents, editors and publishers."

‡FICTION FROM THE HEARTLAND CONFERENCE, P.O. Box 32186, Kansas City MO 64111. Conference Coordinator: Carla Bracale. Estab. 1987. Annual. Conference held February. Conference duration: 2-3 days. Average attendance: 200. Conference concentrates on fiction with main focus on romance and mystery. The conference is held at the Allis Plaza Hotel in Kansas City, MO." Barbara Bretton was the keynote speaker in 1993.
Costs: $60 includes banquet luncheon on Saturday.
Accommodations: The Allis Plaza Hotel offers special conference rates.
Additional Information: Conference Brochures/guidelines available for SASE.

FORT CONCHO MUSEUM PRESS LITERARY FESTIVAL, 213 East Ave. D, San Angelo TX 76903. (915)657-4441. Contact: Cora Pugmire. Estab. 1988. Annual. Conference held the first weekend in August. Average attendance: 450. "The purposes of the festival are to showcase writers—from beginners to professionals—of Texas and the southwest through public readings, book displays and informal gatherings; to offer help for writers through writing workshops and informal gatherings with other writers, editors and publishers; and, generally, to support and encourage the literary arts in Texas and the Southwest." Location: A 22-building, 40-acre historic site. The festival is held in the oldest, fully restored building (1865). Several of the other buildings are also used for workshops. Free tours are offered to all participants. "Current festival plans include no special topic, but we will have at least one fiction workshop. Guest speakers will be published Texas writers and publishers/editors of Texas journals of books."
Costs: All events except the banquet are free. Banquet fee is between $8-12.
Accommodations: Transportation arrangements are made on an informal basis only. ("That is, people who need a ride can always find one.") Special accommodations are made at our motel; a list of other area motels and hotels is available.
Additional Information: Current contests are "literary performance" contests. Of those who read from their works during the festival, one poet and one prose writer receive an award. Conference brochures/guidelines are available for SASE.

‡GOLDEN TRIANGLE WRITERS GUILD, 4245 Calder, Beaumont TX 77705. (409)898-4894. Contact: Becky Blanchard, administrative assistant. Estab. 1984. Annual. Conference held during third weekend in October. Attendance limited to 350. Held at the Holiday Inn on Walden Road in Beaumont, Texas.

Costs: In 1993 cost was $185 for members, $205 for nonmembers before October 1; after October 1 it was $205 for members, $225 for nonmembers. Cost covers conference only; room not included.
Accommodations: Special conference rates available at Holiday Inn (Beaumont).
Additional Information: Sponsors a contest. Attendance required. Preliminary judging done by published authors in each specific genre. Final judging done by editors and/or agents specializing in each specific area.

MAPLE WOODS COMMUNITY COLLEGE WRITER'S CONFERENCE, 2601 NE Barry Rd., Kansas City MO 64156. (816)734-4878. Coordinator Continuing Education: Pattie Smith. Estab. 1983. Annual. Conference held in early October. Conference duration: 1 day. Average attendance: 100-125. Concentration varies from year to year. Conference site is at an area hotel.
Costs: $40 in past years for registration, lunch and entrance to conference.
Accommodations: Check for current costs.

NATIONAL WRITERS ASSOCIATION, (formerly National Writers Club Writer's Conference), Suite 424, 1450 S. Havana, Aurora CO 80012. (303)751-7844. Executive Director: Sandy Whelchel. Estab. 1950's. Annual. Conference held in June. Conference duration: 3 days. Average attendance: 200-300. General writing and marketing. Hotel with conference facilities in suburban Denver. Theme "Write Today, Sell Tomorrow."
Costs: Approx. $250, will include meals.
Accommodations: Shuttle service from Stapleton International Airport will be available. Currently working on group air rates. Special hotel rates for attendees. On-site facilities at hotel.
Additional Information: Awards for previous contests will be presented at the conference. Conference brochures/guidelines are available for SASE.

‡NOVELISTS, INC. ANNUAL NATIONAL CONFERENCE, P.O. Box 1166, Mission KS 66222. Estab. 1990. Annual. Held in October. Conference duration: 4 days. Average attendance: 100. Designed "for multi-published writers of popular fiction." Conference is held at a hotel; contact for specific location. Panels for 1993 focused on business and creative aspects of writing fiction. William Brohaugh, editorial director of Writer's Digest Books, and Nora Rawlinson, editor-in-chief of Publishers Weekly, spoke at 1993 conference.
Costs: $225; includes several meals and receptions.
Accommodations: Contact for assistance with transportation arrangements. Special room rates are available at the host hotel.
Additional Information: Brochures available for SASE. "Conference is open only to members of Novelists, Inc. To qualify for membership, you must have published 2 book-length works of fiction, at least one of which must have been published in the last 5 years."

OKLAHOMA FALL ARTS INSTITUTES, P.O. Box 18154, Oklahoma City OK 73154. (405)842-0890. Contact: Associate Director of Programs. Estab. 1983. Annual. Conference held in late October. Conference duration: 4 days. Average attendance 100. "This year we had: "Writing and the Art of Teaching Writing" (William Stafford); "Children's Writing" (Crescent Dragonwagon); "Poetry" (Alicia Ostriker)." Held at "Quartz Mountain Arts and Conference Center, an Oklahoma state lodge located in Southwest Oklahoma at the edge of Lake Altus/Lugert in the Quartz Mountains. Workshop participants are housed either in the lodge itself (in hotel-room accommodations) or in cabins or duplexes with kitchens. Classes are held in special pavilions built expressly for the Arts Institute. Pavilions offer a view of the lake and mountains. Each year the Institute, as part of its 'Origins Oklahoma' humanities project, focuses on the cultural contributions of a different ethnic or cultural group within the state. 1991 focused on Native Americans, 1992 on African-Americans, and 1993 on Russian influences to our culture." No featured panelists. Classes are taught by nationally recognized writers.
Costs: $450, which includes double-occupancy lodging, meals, tuition and application fee.
Accommodations: The Oklahoma Arts Institute leases all facilities at Quartz Mountain Arts and Conference Center for the exclusive use of the Fall Arts Institutes participants. Lodging is included in workshop cost.
Additional Information: Critique is usually done in class. Writers will need to bring completed works with them. 1993 Course Catalog is available. Scholarships are available for a limited number of local community artists. However, the Institutes are open to anyone.

PROFESSIONALISM IN WRITING SCHOOL, Suite 701, 4308 S. Peoria, Tulsa OK 74105. (918)PIW-5588. Coordinator: Norma Jean Lutz. Estab. 1983. Annual. Conference held from March 25 to March 26. Average attendance: 180. "A conference for Christians who write. Many areas are covered. From editing, to picture books, to play writing, to poetry, to fiction. Always a strong emphasis on fiction." Held in a large spacious church in Tulsa, OK. 1994 theme: "Walk in wisdom . . . redeeming the time," Colossians 4:5. Keynote speaker, Pulitzer Prize Nominee, Clifton Lemoure Taulbert. Publishing houses represented: Scripture Press, Tyndale House, Guideposts, Lillenas Drama, Salvation Army, and Parents of Teenagers Magazine.
Costs: $145 advance $165 at door. (Includes Friday and Saturday lunches, banquet, packet, freebies, door prizes, all workshops for 2 days. Partials are available).
Accommodations: Shuttle from airport to selected hotel. Rides available from hotel to site at church. Nearby hotel offering PIW conferees special rates.
Additional Information: "We have a critique service. $10 per submissions." Sponsors a contest: 4 categories w/cash prizes; $10 entry fee each. Conference brochures/guidelines are available for SASE. "This is in conjunction with the Tulsa Christian Writers Club, in existence since 1977. Anyone can be an 'at large' member of TCW and receive monthly newletter for $10/yr."

ROCKY MT. FICTION WRITERS COLORADO GOLD, P.O. Box 260244, Denver CO 80226-0244. (303)791-3941. Conference Co-chair (1994): Vickie Ferguson. Estab. 1983. Annual. Conference held in September. Conference duration: 3 days. Average attendance: 150. For novel length fiction. The conference will be held at the Sheraton Denver West in their conference facility. Themes included general novel length fiction, genre fiction, contemporary romance, mystery, sf/f, mainstream, history with possible horror and techno-thriller in 1993. Guest speakers and panelists have included Terry Brooks, Dorothy Cannell, Phoebe Conn, Patricia Gardner Evans, Constance O'Day Flannery and Michael Palmer; 5 editors and 2 agents unknown at this time.
Costs: In 1993, cost was $130 (includes conference, reception, banquet). Editor workshop $20 additional.
Accommodations: Information on overnight accommodations made available of area hotels. The conference will be at the Sheraton Hotel. Conference rates available.
Additional Information: Editor conducted workshops are limited to 10 participants for critique with auditing available. First 10 pages to be brought alone. Workshops in science fiction, mainstream, mystery, historical, contemporary romance. Sponsors a contest. For 30-page mss and 10-page synopsis; 5 categories mentioned above. First rounds are done by qualified members, published and nonpublished, with editors doing the final ranking; 2 copies need to be submitted without author's name. $20 entry only, $30 entry and (one) critique. Guidelines available for SASE.

SANTA FE WRITERS' CONFERENCE, 826 Camino de Monte Rey, Santa Fe NM 87501. (505)982-9301. Seminar Coordinator: Julie Shigekuni. Estab. 1984. Annual. Conference held in August. Conference duration: 5 days. Maximum attendance: 60. Concentrations are fiction and poetry. Held at Plaza Resolana, a Ghost Ranch Study and Conference Center in downtown Santa Fe. Lodging, double and single rooms; dining room, cafeteria, meeting rooms.
Costs: $630 (1993 costs); lodging and food included.
Accommodations: On-site accommodations at Plaza Resolana.
Additional Information: Workshops for fiction and poetry. Submit 10 pages with $30 reading fee. Brochures are available for SASE.

SCBWI/DRURY COLLEGE WRITING FOR CHILDREN WORKSHOP, 900 N. Benton, Springfield MO 65802. (417)865-8731. Directors: Lynn Doke or Sandy Asher. Estab. 1986. Annual. One-day workshop held in October. Average attendance: 45. Workshop to promote writing and illustrating fiction and nonfiction for young readers, held at Drury College. Panels planned for 1993 included Writing and Illustrating Picture Books, Marketing Your Work, and Writing for Middle Grade and Young Adult Readers. Faculty includes an editor from a major publishing house (i.e. Bantam, Scholastic) and invited authors. 1993 guest speakers include Barbara Sealing (author of *How to Write a Children's Book and Get it Published*) and Paula Morrow (editor, *Ladybug*).
Costs: $50, includes continental breakfast and luncheon. Discount for SCBWI members and early registrants.
Accommodations: Hotel information is made available.
Additional Information: Faculty will meet with individuals to discuss manuscripts and/or illustrations, $25 fee. Workshop brochures/guidelines are available for SASE.

SCBWI/ROCKY MOUNTAIN CHAPTER FALL/WINTER WORKSHOPS, 8600 Firethorn Dr., Loveland CO 80538. (303)669-3755. Regional Advisor: Vivian Dubrovin. Annual. Fall Conference held 3rd Saturday of September; Winter Workshop held in February; Illustrators Workshop held in May. All last 1 day. Average attendance: 100-175. Fall conference features authors, editors and agents for children's work (picture book—YA). Winter workshop features headline authors. Also 3-day retreat in July, attendance 50-75. "Emphasis on small-group workshops on characterization, plotting, second level of writing, publishing etc." Illustrators workshop features illustrators of children's books and workshops on writing/illustrating and technical aspects particular to children's books. Conferences rotate between college facilities, hotels and other meeting spaces. Brochures available approximately 3-4 weeks prior to event.
Costs: Generally around $50/day, less for SCBWI members. Lunch and snacks plus handouts included. 3-day retreat around $200.

SCBWI/ROCKY MOUNTAIN CHAPTER SUMMER RETREAT, 1712 Morning Dr., Loveland CO 80538. (303)667-2793. RMC/SCBW President: Ellen Javernick. Estab. 1981. Annual. Conference held from July 29-31. Average attendance 50-60. Writing for children. Held at a retreat center near mountains outside of Colorado Springs, Colorado.
Costs: $180-200 (approximately).
Accommodations: On site double rooms (some singles available) single beds; accommodations included in price.
Additional Information: Critiques by speakers will be available at additional cost. Conference brochures/guidelines are available for SASE (after May 1994).

‡SOUTHWEST WRITERS WORKSHOP CONFERENCE, Suite A, 1338 Wyoming NE, Albuquerque NM 87112-5000. (505)293-0303. Fax: (505)237-2665. Office Manager: Suzanne Spletzer. Estab. 1983. Annual. Conference held in September. Average attendance: 500-600. "Conference concentrates on all areas of writing." Workshops and speakers include writers and editors of all genres for all levels from beginners to advanced. 1993 theme was "Building on the Basics." Keynote speaker was Lawrence Block. Featured speaker: Daniel Stern.
Costs: $225 includes 2 luncheons, banquets, snack, 2 continental breakfasts, and desserts.
Accommodations: Usually have official airline and discount rates. Special conference rates are available at hotel. A list of other area hotels and motels is available.
Additional Information: Sponsors a contest judged by editors and agents from New York, Los Angeles, etc. from major publishing houses. Sixteen categories. Deadline: June 1 every year. Entry fee is $20. Brochures/guidelines available for SASE. "An appointment (15 minute one-on-one) may be set up with editor or agent of your choice on a first registered/first served basis."

STEAMBOAT SPRINGS WRITERS GROUP, P.O. Box 774284, Steamboat Springs CO 80477. (303)879-9008. Chairperson: Harriet Freiberger. Estab. 1982. Annual. Conference held in summer. Conference duration: 1 day. Average attendance: 40. "Our conference emphasizes instruction within the seminar format. Novices and polished professionals benefit from the individual attention and the camaraderie which can be established within small groups. A pleasurable and memorable learning experience is guaranteed by the relaxed and friendly atmosphere of the old train depot." Steamboat Arts Council sponsors the group at the restored Train Depot.
Costs: $40 for members; $50 for nonmembers. Fee covers all conference activities, including lunch. Lodging available at Steamboat Resorts; 10% discount for participants."

MARK TWAIN WRITERS CONFERENCE, Suite A, 921 Center, Hannibal MO 63401. (800)747-0738. Contact: Cyndi Allison. Estab. 1984. Annual. Conference held in June. Conference duration: 5 days. Average attendance: 100. "Concentration in fiction and nonfiction with specialization in humor, children's writing, Mark Twain, poetry, etc." Site is the "Hannibal-LaGrange College campus. Excellent classroom and dining facilities near Mark Twain museum and other historical sites."
Costs: $395, includes meal, lodging, all program fees, trips to Mark Twain sites and pick up at area airport.
Accommodations: Free pickup at Quincy, IL airport and Amtrak station. Accommodations made available in college residence hall.
Additional Information: Fiction or nonfiction critiques limited to two articles or short stories, or one book chapter with book outline. Brochures are available by calling or writing.

WRITERS WORKSHOP IN SCIENCE FICTION, English Department/University of Kansas, Lawrence KS 66045. (913)864-3380. Professor: James Gunn. Estab. 1985. Annual. Conference held for two weeks in mid to late July. Average attendance: 8-10. Conference for writing and marketing science fiction. "Housing is provided and classes meet in university housing on the University of Kansas campus. Workshop sessions operate informally in an lounge." 1993 guest speaker: Frederik Pohl, SF writer and former editor and agent.

Costs: Tuition: $400. Housing and meals are additional.

Accommodations: Several airport shuttle services offer reasonable transportation from the Kansas City International Airport to Lawrence. In 1993 students were housed in a student dormitory at $11/day single, $16/day double.

Additional Information: "Admission to the workshop is by submission of an acceptable story. Two additional stories should be submitted by the end of June. These three stories are copied and distributed to other participants for critiquing and are the basis for the first week of the workshop; one story is rewritten for the second week." Brochures/guidelines are available for SASE. "The Writers Workshop in Science Fiction is intended for writers who have just started to sell their work or need that extra bit of understanding or skill to become a published writer."

West (AZ, CA, HI, NV, UT)

ARIZONA CHRISTIAN WRITERS CONFERENCE, P.O. Box 5168, Phoenix AZ 85010. (602)838-4919. Director: Reg Forder. Estab. 1981. Annual. Conference held November 11 to November 13. Average attendance: 200. To promote all forms of Christian writing. Conference held in new Holiday Inn Hotel near airport in Phoenix. Panels planned for next conference include "Writing as a Ministry." Representatives from several publishing houses: Tyndale; Harvest House; Regal Books; *Christian Parenting Today Magazine*, are scheduled to speak at next conference.

Costs: Approximately $100 plus meals and accommodation.

Accommodations: Special price in our host hotel (Holiday Inn) $47 per night for 1 or 2 persons.

Additional Information: Conference brochures/guidelines are available for SASE. "This annual conference is held in Phoenix always on the 2nd weekend in November."

BAY AREA WRITERS WORKSHOP, P.O. Box 620327, Woodside CA 94062. (415)851-4568. Co-Directors: Laura Jason, Joyce Jenkins. Estab. 1988. Annual. Offers 4-5 separate weekend intensive workshops and a biennial 1-day conference, "Literary Publishing Day." Average attendance for 1-day conference: 250; each weekend workshop: 15. Workshops are offered in short story, novel and poetry, "both with a strong literary bent and a master class format." Sites: San Francisco, Berkeley and South Bay. "Literary Publishing & Resources" features agents and editors from large and small presses. Workshop leaders for the last three years included Robert Hass, Li-Young Lee, Wanda Coleman, Olga Broumas, Larry Heinemann, Robert Olmstead, Carolyn Forché, Jessica Hagedorn, Jack Gilbert, Joy Williams, David Shields and Clarence Major."

Costs: $250/weekend workshop plus $15 application fee. Ten scholarships are available for writers based on the quality of the application manuscript. Cost for Literary Publishing & Resources: $50.

Additional Information: Weekend workshops include 15 hours of in-class time. No individual consultations. Brochures are available for SASE.

BE THE WRITER YOU WANT TO BE MANUSCRIPT CLINIC, 23350 Sereno Ct., Villa 30, Cupertino CA 95014. (415)691-0300. Contact: Louise Purwin Zobel. Estab. 1969. Workshop held irregularly—usually semiannually at several locations. Workshop duration: 1-2 days. Average attendance: 20-30. "This manuscript clinic enables writers of any type of material to turn in their work-in-progress—at any stage of development—to receive help with structure and style, as well as marketing advice." It is held on about 40 campuses at different times, including University of California and other university and college campuses throughout the west.

Costs: Usually $45-65/day, "depending on campus."

Additional Information: Brochures/guidelines available for SASE.

I'VE ALWAYS WANTED TO WRITE BUT . . ., 23350 Sereno Ct., Villa 30, Cupertino CA 95014. (415)691-0300. Contact: Louise Purwin Zobel. Estab. 1969. Workshop held irregularly, several times a year at different locations. Workshop duration: 1-2 days. Average attendance: 30-50. Workshop "encourages real beginners to get started on a lifelong dream. Focuses on the basics of writing."

Workshops held at about 40 college and university campuses in the west, including University of California.
Costs: Usually $45-65/day "depending on college or university."
Additional Information: Brochures/guidelines available for SASE.

‡JACK LONDON WRITERS' CONFERENCE, 1500 Ralston Ave., Belmont CA 94403. (415)508-3708. Head, Department of English College of Notre Dame: Dr. Marc Wolterbeck. Estab. 1988. Annual. Conference held in mid-March from 8:30-4:30. Average attendance: 200. "Bestselling authors lecture on fiction and nonfiction. Individual appointments are made with 10 published members of the California Writers Club for poetry, children's, self publishing, getting started, fiction-novel, short story, journalism. The College of Notre Dame is a four year liberal arts school set in the suburbs of San Francisco." Panels planned for the next conference include Gus Lee, Herbert Crowder, Muriel James and others.
Costs: $25 students, $55 adults.
Additional Information: "On a first come first serve basis, private 15 minute consultations—one on one—with published member of the California Writers Club." Sponsors a contest judged by the California Writers Club (requirements in brochure). Students can win a $2,000 scholarship to the college of Notre Dame. Brochures/guidelines available for SASE. The Jack London Conference has had over 80 professional writers speak and 800 participants. It's sponsored by the California Writers' Club and The College of Notre Dame, English Dept.

MENDOCINO COAST WRITERS CONFERENCE, 1211 Del Mar Dr., Fort Bragg CA 95437. (707)961-1001. Director: Marlis Manley Broadhead. Estab. 1990. Annual. Conference held in June. Conference duration: 3 days. Average attendance: 70-80. "Inclusive—poetry, long and short fiction, science fiction, mystery, food, travel, personal histories, screenplay, publishing and marketing, writing for children, self-publishing, etc." Workshops and editing sessions. Dean's Scholarship Award. Held at "College of the Redwoods at the south edge of Fort Bragg, CA, a small mill town/tourist and retirees center. The tiny campus overlooks the Pacific and is 8 miles north of Mendocino Village, a preserved Victorian town. Over 25 movies and TV shows have been filmed in this area."
Costs: $70, for Friday night through Sunday noon (sessions, readings, etc.) $10 extra/writing workshop (1993).
Accommodations: Information on overnight accommodations made available. Local rooms go from $42 to $125 (elegant B&Bs)."
Additional Information: Conference brochures/guidelines are available for SASE. "The purpose of this conference is to study and celebrate writing in a supportive atmosphere. In the past, we've gotten high marks from attendees and presentors alike on the substance and atmosphere of the conferences."

MOUNT HERMON CHRISTIAN WRITERS CONFERENCE, P.O. Box 413, Mount Hermon CA 95041. (408)335-4466. Fax: (408)335-9218. Director of Public Affairs David R. Talbott. Estab. 1970. Annual. Conference held Friday-Tuesday over Palm Sunday weekend (March 25-29). Average attendance: 175. "We are a broad-ranging conference for all areas of Christian writing, including fiction, children's, poetry, nonfiction, magazines, books, educational curriculum and radio and TV script writing. This is a working, how-to conference, with many workshops within the conference involving on-site writing assignments. The conference is sponsored by and held at the 440-acre Mount Hermon Christian Conference Center near San Jose, California, in the heart of the coastal redwoods. Registrants stay in hotel-style accommodations, and full board is provided as part of conference fees. Meals are taken family style, with faculty joining registrants. The faculty/student ratio is about 1:6 or 7. The bulk of our faculty are editors and publisher representatives from major Christian publishing houses nationwide."
Costs: Registration fees include tuition, conference sessions, resource notebook, refreshment breaks, room and board and vary from $485 economy to $590 deluxe, double occupancy.
Accommodations: Airport shuttles are available from the San Jose International Airport. Housing is not required of registrants, but about 95% of our registrants use Mount Hermon's own housing facilities (hotel style double-occupancy rooms). Meals with the conference are required, and are included in all fees.
Additional Information: Registrants may submit work for critique (2 works) in advance of the conference, then have personal interviews with critiquers during the conference. No advance work is required, however. Conference brochures/guidelines are available for SASE. "The residential nature of our conference makes this a unique setting for one-on-one interaction with faculty/staff. There is also a decided inspirational flavor to the conference, and general sessions with well-known speakers are a highlight."

‡NAPA VALLEY WRITERS' CONFERENCE, Napa Valley College, 2277 Napa-Vallejo Hwy., Napa CA 94558. (707)253-3070. Program Director: John Leggett. Managing Director: Sherri Hallgren. Estab. 1980. Annual. Conference held first week of August. Average attendance: 70-80. Conference to promote literary fiction and poetry. "No real work in genres and an emphasis on craft rather than marketing." Also promotes new poetry. "Emphasis is on generating new poems, though there is also a critique of already finished work." Workshops are held on the campus of Napa Valley College, in the heart of the famed wine growing region of California. Evenings feature readings hosted by valley wineries. "We have visiting agents and publishers on panels. Each faculty writer gives a craft talk and a public reading."
Costs: $450. Scholarships available.
Accommodations: Attendees are mailed a list of Napa Valley motels, many of which offer a package rate. "We also offer some community housing (guest rooms or spare sofas in the homes of Napa residents) for a charge of $20 for the week."
Additional Information: "We require a qualifying manuscript of 10 pages of fiction or 5 pages of poetry as well as a letter describing applicant's background as a writer. In workshops we critique a 25-page ms of fiction." Conference brochures/guidelines are available for SASE.

PASADENA WRITERS' FORUM, P.C.C. Community Education Dept., 1570 E. Colorado Blvd., Pasadena CA 91106-2003. (818)585-7602. Coordinator: Meredith Brucker. Estab. 1954. Annual. Conference held in March. Conference duration: 1 day (Saturday). Average attendance: 225. "For the novice as well as the professional writer in any field of interest: fiction or nonfiction, including scripts, childrens, humor, poetry." Conference held on the campus of Pasadena City College. A panel discussion by agents, editors or authors is featured at the end of the day.
Costs: $75, including box lunch and coffee hour.
Additional Information: Brochure upon request, no SASE necessary. "Pasadena City College also offers an eight-week class 'Writing For Publication' periodically."

PIMA WRITERS' WORKSHOP, 2202 W. Anklam Rd., Tucson AZ 85709. (602)884-6974. Director: Peg Files. Estab. 1988. Annual. Conference held in May. Conference duration 3 days. Average attendance 150. "For anyone interested in writing—beginning or experienced writer. The workshop offers sessions on writing short stories, novels, nonfiction articles and books, children's and juvenile stories, poetry and screenplays." Sessions are held in the new Center for the Arts on Pima Community College's West Campus. Past speakers include Brian Garfield, Barbara Kingsolver, Mark Harris, Michael Collins, Nancy Mairs, Larry McMurtry, Lawrence Lieberman and Ron Powers. 1993 workshop featured John Weston, Ron Powers, Allen Woodman and Nancy Mairs, among others.
Costs: $60. (Or participants may attend for college credit, in which case fees are $62 for Arizona residents and $283 for out-of-state residents). Meals and accommodations not included.
Accommodations: Information on local accommodations is made available, and special workshop rates are available at a specified motel close to the workshop site. The 1993 workshop motel's rate was $47/night, single or double.
Additional Information: Participants may have up to 20 pages critiqued by the author of their choice. Manuscripts must be submitted 2 weeks before the workshop. Conference brochure/guidelines available for SASE. "The workshop atmosphere is casual, friendly, and supportive, and guest authors are very accessible. Readings, films and panel discussions are offered as well as talks and manuscript sessions."

SAN DIEGO STATE UNIVERSITY WRITERS CONFERENCE, SDSU-Aztec Center, San Diego CA 92182-0723. (619)594-2517. Assistant to Director of Extension: Erin Alcaraz. Estab. 1984. Annual. Conference held on 3rd weekend in January. Conference duration: 2 days. Average attendance: Approx. 350. "This conference is held on the San Diego State University campus at the Aztec Center. The Aztec Center is conveniently located near parking. The meeting rooms are spacious and comfortable. All sessions meet in the same general area. Each year the SDSU Writers Conference offers a variety of workshops for the beginner and the advanced writer. This conference allows the individual writer to choose which workshop best suits his/her needs. In addition, read and critique and office hours are provided so attendees may meet with speakers, editors and agents in small, personal groups to discuss specific questions. A wine-and-cheese reception is offered Saturday immediately following the workshops where attendees may socialize with the faculty in a relaxed atmosphere. Keynote speaker is to be determined."

Costs: Not to exceed $190. This includes all conference workshops and office hours, coffee and pastries in the morning, lunch and wine-and-cheese reception Saturday evening.
Accommodations: The Howard Johnson offers conference attendees a reduced rate, $45/night. Attendees must say they are with the SDSU Writers Conference.
Additional Information: A critique session will be offered. To receive a brochure, call or send a postcard with address to: SDSU Writers Conference, College of Extended Studies, San Diego State University, San Diego CA 92182. No SASE required.

SCBWI/LOS ANGELES/WRITERS CONFERENCE IN CHILDREN'S LITERATURE, P.O. Box 66296, Mar Vista Station, Los Angeles CA 90066. (818)347-2849. Executive Director: Lin Oliver. Estab. 1972. Annual. Conference held in August. Conference duration 4 days. Average attendance: 350. Writing for children. Site: Doubletree Inn in the Marina Del Rey area (at the beach) in Los Angeles. Theme: "The Business of Writing."
Costs: $225 (does not include hotel room).
Accommodations: Information on overnight accommodations made available. Conference rates at the hotel about $100/night.
Additional Information: Ms critiques are available. Conference brochures/guidelines are available (after June 1993) for SASE.

‡SCBWI/NORCAL CHAPTER RETREAT AT ASILOMAR, 1316 Rebecca Dr., Suisun CA 94585-3603. (707)426-6776. Contact: Bobi Martin, Regional Advisor. Estab. 1984. Annual. Conference held during last weekend in February. Attendance limited to 65. "The retreat is designed to refresh and encourage writers and illustrators for children. Speakers have been published writers, illustrators and editors. Writing techniques are taught, understanding marketing, plotting, pacing, etc. Topics vary year to year. The retreat is held at the Asilomar conference grounds in Monterey. There is time for walking on the beach or strolling through the woods. Rooms have private baths, two double beds, fireplace and small patio. Meals are served semi-cafeteria style, the group eats together. Vegetarian meals are available. Focus for 1994 was picture books and middle grade novels. Gloria and Ted Rand and Ivy Ruckman were scheduled to speak at 1994 conference.
Costs: $160 for SCBWI members; $185 for nonmembers. Includes room, meals and retreat. Attendees must make their own transportation arrangements. "All accommodations are on-site and are included in the cost. All rooms are double occupancy. rooms are disabled accessible. Those insisting on a private room may stay off grounds."
Additional Information: "Attendess may sign up for critique group when registering. Groups limited to 7 or less. Work is brought to the conference." Scholarship available. "Applicants write a letter explaining their financial need and describing how attending the retreat will help further their career. All applications kept fully confidential." Brochures available for SASE. "Registration begins in October of previous year and fills quickly but a waiting list is always formed and late applicants frequently do get in."

‡SCBWI/SOUTHERN CALIFORNIA SCBWI WRITERS' DAY, 11943 Montana, Los Angeles CA 90049. (310)820-5601. Contact: Judy or Stephanie, Regional Advisors. Annual. Conference held April 17. Average attendance: 80-100. Conference to promote writing and marketing of children's books. Held on private school grounds. Themes for 1994 are picture books, fiction, multicultural education, poetry.
Costs: $60-70 (discount for early registration). "Bring your own lunch or eat nearby."
Additional Information: Sponsors contests for picture books, middle grade and young adult fiction, nonfiction, poetry. Contests open to attendees only. Submit up to 10 pages plus synopsis. Brochures available for SASE. "This one-day conference is popular and growing. A good place to network with other children's book writers, both published and unpublished."

SOCIETY OF SOUTHWESTERN AUTHORS WRITERS' CONFERENCE, P.O. Box 30355, Tucson AZ 85751-0355. (602)795-0571. Conference Chair: Evelyn Lee. Estab. 1972. Annual. Conference held in January. Average attendance: 150-250. Conference "covers a spectrum of practical topics for writers. Each year varies, but there is a minimum of 12 different classes during the day, plus the keynote speaker." Conference held at Hotel Park Tucson.
Costs: $40 general ($50 walk-in); $30 students ($40 walk-in).
Additional Information: Conference brochures/guidelines are available for SASE.

‡SQUAW VALLEY COMMUNITY OF WRITERS, P.O. Box 2352, Olympic Valley CA 96146. (916)583-5200. Programs Director: Brett Hall Jones. Estab. 1969. Annual. Conference held in July and August. Each program is one week. Average attendance approximately 120. "Squaw Valley Workshops include four separate one-week programs—Art of the Wild, Poetry, Fiction and Screenwriting. Each concentrates on its particular discipline except the Art of the Wild which includes poetry, fiction and nonfiction about nature, the environment and the ecological crisis. The workshops are conducted in the Olympic House, a large ski lodge built for the 1960 Winter Olympics. The environment includes pine trees, alpine lakes, rivers and streams; the elevation is 6200 feet, and we have cool mornings and sunny, warm afternoons."
Costs: Tuition is $550 for the week. Scholarships are available.
Accommodations: "We have vans which will pick up participants at the Reno airport and at the Truckee Bus and train stations. The Community of Writers rents large ski houses in the Valley to house the attendees. This fosters the community atmosphere which makes our experience unique, as well as allowing us to keep the weekly rate reasonable: $160 multi, 220 double and 320 single."
Additional Information: Acceptance is based on submitted work. Each participant's manuscript is critiqued in depth during the week of the workshop. A written critique is not available for each work submitted. Brochures/guidelines available.

UCLA EXTENSION WRITERS' PROGRAM, 10995 Le Conte Ave., Los Angeles CA 90024. (310)825-9415 or (800)388-UCLA. Program Manager: Meryl Ginsberg. Estab. 1891. Courses held ongoingly, 4 quarters/year. New course line-up 4 times/year, with special intensive courses in summer. Program duration varies 12-week, 10-week, 6-week, 4-day and 2-day courses. Average attendence: 12-25 per class. "We cover fiction, nonfiction, poetry, playwriting, writing for young people, and we have the largest, most comprehensive screenwriting curriculum in the country, with special 4-day intensive courses every summer for people coming from out of town. Classes are held primarily on the UCLA campus in regular classrooms and conference rooms. We also hold classes in outlying areas around the city: Santa Monica, the San Fernando Valley, Pasadena." Guest speakers "are too numerous to mention. Ongoing series such as Playwrights on Playwriting have featured Larry Gelbart, Terrence McNalley and Screenwriters on Screenwriting has featured Tom Schulman, Joe Eszterhas, Ray Bradbury. New speakers lined up every quarter."
Costs: Vary from $65-395. Intensive 4-day couses in summer cost $285.
Accommodations: Students make own arrangements. We can provide assistance in locating local accommodations.
Additional Information: "Some advanced-level classes have manuscript submittal requirements; instructions are always detailed in the quarterly UCLA Extension course catalog. The Writers' Program publishes an annual literary journal. Work can be submitted by current and former Writers' Program students. An annual fiction prize, The James Kirkwood Prize in Creative Writing, has been established and is given annually to one fiction writer who was published that year in *WEST/WORD*, our literary journal. The $500 prize is judged by a New York literary agent and the contest's sponsors."

WRITE YOUR LIFE STORY FOR PAY, 23350 Sereno Ct., Villa 30, Cupertino CA 95014. (415)691-0300. Contact: Louise Purwin Zobel. Estab. 1969. Workshop held irregularly, usually semiannually at several locations. Workshop duration: 1-2 days. Average attendance: 30-50. "Because every adult has a story worth telling, this conference helps participants to write fiction and nonfiction in books and short forms, using their own life stories as a base." This workshop is held on about 40 campuses at different times, inluding University of California and other university and college campuses in the west.
Costs: Usually $45-65/day, "depending on campus."
Additional Information: Brochures/guidelines available for SASE.

WRITERS CONNECTION SELLING TO HOLLYWOOD, Suite 103, 275 Saratoga Ave., Santa Clara CA 95050. (408)554-2090. Directors: Steve and Meera Lester. Estab. 1988. Annual. Conference held second week in August in L.A. area. Conference duration: 3 days. Average attendance: 200. "Conference targets scriptwriters and fiction writers, whose short stories, books, or plays have strong cinematic potential, and who want to make valuable contracts in the film industry. Full conference registrants receive a private consultation with the film industry producer or professional of his/her choice who make up the faculty. Panels, workshops, and 'Ask a Pro' discussion groups include agents, professional film and TV scriptwriters, and independent as well as studio and TV and feature film producers.

Costs: In 1993: full conference by July, $470 members, $495 nonmembers, after July 10 $495, $520 (included meals). Partial registration available.
Accommodations: Discount with designated conference airline. "We make hotel reservations—get a special rate. $100/night (in L.A.) private room; $50/shared room."
Additional Information: "This is the premiere screenwriting conference of its kind in the country, unique in its offering of an industry-wide perspective from pros working in all echelons of the film industry. Great for making contacts." Conference brochure/guidelines available for SASE.

Northwest (AK, ID, MT, OR, WA, WY)

ARTS AT MENUCHA, P.O. Box 4958, Portland OR 97208. (503)234-6827. Board Member: Connie Cheifetz. Estab. 1966. Annual. Conference held August 7 to August 20. Conference duration: Each class lasts 1 week. Average attendance: 60 overall (6-10 per class). Conference held at a "residential private estate with dorm rooms, most with private bath. 100-acre wooded grounds overlooking the Columbia River. A beautiful, relaxing place with pool, tennis, volleyball and walking trails. Meals provided (family-style). 1993 saw us offering fiction and poetry workshops. Also we offer visual arts class."
Costs: '93 Rates $450/1 week; $800/2 weeks; includes room and board.
Accommodations: "We will pick folks up from Portland Airport, bus or train depot." Everyone, including instructors, stays at "Menucha" overnight Sun.-Sat. a.m.
Additional Information: Conference brochures/guidelines are available (no SASE needed).

‡**CLARION WEST WRITERS' WORKSHOP,** Suite 350, 340 15th Ave. E., Seattle WA 98112. (206)322-9083. Contact: Admissions Department. Estab. 1983. Annual. Workshop held June 20-July 30. Workshop duration: 6 weeks. Average attendance: 20. "Conference to prepare students for professional careers in science fiction and fantasy writing. Held at Seattle Central Community College on Seattle's Capitol Hill. An urban site close to restaurants and cafes, not too far from downtown." 1993 instructors included Pat Murphy, Connie Willis, Lucius Shepard, Geoff Ryman, Greg Bear, Alice Turner and others.
Costs: Workshop: $1095 ($100 discount if application received by March 1). Dormitory housing: $750, meals not included.
Accommodations: "We will be happy to pick students up at Seattle-Tacoma airport on their arrival. Air transportation to Seattle is up to to them." Students are strongly encouraged to stay on-site, in dormitory housing at Seattle University. Cost: $750, meals not included, for 6-week stay.
Additional Information: "This is a critique-based workshop. Students are encouraged to write a story a week; the critique of student material produced at the workshop forms the principle activity of the workshop. Students and instructors critique mss as a group." Conference guidelines available for SASE. "Scholarships are available, based on financial need. Students must submit 20-30 pages of ms to qualify for admission. Dormitory and classrooms are handicapped accessible."

‡**COLUMBIA GORGE WRITER'S CONFERENCE,** 2470 Lichens Dr., Hood River OR 97031. (503)386-3112. Contact: Lana Fox. Annual. Conference held in April. Conference duration: 1 day. Average attendance: 20-25. "We try to have a fiction writer, a nonfiction writer, a children's book author and/ or an agent. This changes every year."
Additional Information: "In the past our workshop has been co-sponsored by SCBWI-NW (Society of Children's Book Writers and Illustrators-Northwest)."

‡**FREEFALL WRITING WORKSHOPS,** 12708 2nd NW, Seattle WA 98177. (206)368-8054. Contact: Dr. Barbara Turner-Vesselago. Estab. 1985. Workshops held approximately 9 times a year. Workshops are scheduled for February, March, April, May, last week of June, last 2 weeks of August, and November. Workshop duration: 1 week. Average attendance: 8 minimum-12 maximum. "Freefall writing workshops are intended for beginning writers, blocked writers, and writers who feel their work needs to be re-energized. They emphasize an approach to writing designed to stimulate creativity at the same time as it guides the writer to a fuller awareness of narrative voice, point of view, scene-making and scructure. These workshops are held at a variety of sites: November and March workshops are held at a resort on the LaPush Reservation on the Olympic Peninsula; the January workshop is held in Wales, UK, in a Victorian mansion on the River Wye; February workshop is at Abundare River Ranch, near Bandera Texas; the May workshop was recently held on the top of a mountain on Saltspring Island in the gulf between Victoria and Vancouver BC; and the summer workshops are

held in cottages at Golden Lake, in Ontario, Canada. Hiking, and ocean, river or lake activities are always available. In April of 1994, I will be giving a workshop at the seaside near Melbourne, Australia."
Cost: $445, including lodging. "At all except the Texas and Wales workshops, participants make their own breakfast and lunch, and contribute to one dinner."
Accommodations: "Carpooling is arranged for anyone who requires it. Onsite accommodations are always available, and the cost is included in the fee. Only the Texas workshop is more expensive than $450 — all meals are catered, and the accommodation is very luxurious there. Thus the total for that workshop fee is $850."
Additional Information: "Everything that is written each day (during the 4-5 hour writing period) is submitted to be read, commented upon by the workshop leader and (potentially) discussed the next day in the morning seminar. No prior submissions are required." Brochures available for SASE.

‡**HAYSTACK WRITING PROGRAM**, PSU School of Extended Studies, P.O. Box 1491, Portland OR 97207. (503)725-8500. Contact: Maggie Herrington. Estab. 1968. Annual. Program runs from last week of June through first week of August. Workshop duration varies; one-week and weekend workshops are available throughout the six-week program. Average attendance: 10-15/workshop; total program: 325. "The program features a broad range of writing courses for writers at all skill levels. Classes are held in the local school at Cannon Beach, Oregon." Past instructors have included William Stafford, Ursula K. LeGuin, Craig Lesley, Molly Gloss, Mark Medoff, Tom Spanbauer.
Costs: Approximately $285-315/course. Does not include room and board.
Accommodations: Attendees must make their own transportation arrangements. Various accommodations available including: B&B, motel, hotel, private rooms, camping, etc. A list of specific accommodations is provided.
Additional Information: Work is critiqued in classes. Free brochure available. University credit (graduate or undergraduate) is available.

PACIFIC NORTHWEST WRITERS SUMMER CONFERENCE, #804, 2033 6th Ave., Seattle WA 98121. (206)443-3807. Contact: Shirley Bishop. Estab. 1955. Annual. Conference held the last weekend in July. Average attendance: 600. Conference focuses on "fiction, nonfiction, poetry, film, drama, self-publishing, the creative process, critiques, core groups, advice from pros and networking." Site is Holiday Inn, Everett WA. "Editors and agents come from both coasts. They bring lore from the world of publishing. The PNWC provides opportunities for writers to get to know editors and agents. The literary contest provides feedback from professionals and possible fame for the winners." The 1993 guest speaker was Stewart Stern, screenwriter and author.
Costs: $90-110/day. Meals and lodging are available at hotel.
Accommodations: Buses take attendees to a salmon barbeque on Puget Sound. Lodging is available at conference rates.
Additional Information: On-site critiques are available in small groups. Literary contest in these categories: adult article/essay, adult genre novel, adult mainstream novel, adult short story, juvenile article or short story, juvenile novel, nonfiction book, picture books for children, playwriting and poetry. Send SASE for guidelines.

PACIFIC NORTHWEST WRITERS WINTER CONFERENCE, #804, 2033 6th Ave., Seattle WA 98121. (206)443-3807. Contact: Shirley Bishop. Estab. 1981. Annual. Weekend conference held in February. Average attendance: 200. "The conference is mostly hands-on workshops: novel, short story, nonfiction, film, poetry, article, children's, getting started, keeping going." Site is the Embassy Suites, Bellevue, WA. "The winter conference is a good place to get started. Or a good place to recharge your batteries if your writing is stalled. If you're new in town, it's a good place to meet other writers." The 1993 guest speaker was Susan Stanley, author of *Maternity Ward*.
Costs: $85-95/day. Two days for $145-165. Lunch is included in registration.
Accommodations: Lodging is available at the hotel or at surrounding motels.

PORT TOWNSEND WRITERS' CONFERENCE, Centrum, Box 1158, Port Townsend WA 98368. (206)385-3102. Director: Carol Jane Bangs. Estab. 1974. Annual. Conference held July 7-17. Average attendance: 180. Conference to promote poetry, fiction, creative nonfiction, writing for children. The conference is held at a 700-acre state park on the strait of Juan de Fuca. "The site is a Victorian-era military fort with miles of beaches, wooded trails and recreation facilities. The park is within the limits of Port Townsend, a historic seaport and arts community, approximately 80 miles northwest of Seattle, on the Olympic Peninsula." Panels include "Writing About Nature," "Journal Writing," "Literary

Translation." There will be 5-10 guest speakers in addition to 10 fulltime faculty.

Costs: $350 approx. tuition and $200 approx. room and board.

Accommodations: City bus transports ferry passengers to site. "Modest room and board facilities on site." Also list of hotels/motels/inns/bed & breakfasts/private rentals available.

Additional Information: "Admission to workshops is selective, based on manuscript submissions." Brochures/guidelines available for SASE. "The conference focus is on the craft of writing and the writing life, not on marketing."

‡WILLAMETTE WRITERS CONFERENCE, Suite 5-A, 9045 SW Barbur, Portland OR 97219. (503)452-1592. Contact: Conference Director. Estab. 1968. Annual. Conference held August 13-14. Average attendance: 220. "Willamette Writers is open to all writers, and we plan our conference accordingly. We offer workshops on all aspects of fiction, nonfiction, marketing, the creative process, etc. Also we invite top notch inspirational speakers for keynote addresses. Most often the conference is held on a local college campus which offers a scholarly atmosphere and allows us to keep conference prices down." 1993 theme was "Within Each Writer." "We always include at least one agent or editor panel and offer a variety of topics of interest to fiction writers." 1993 panelists included author Nadine Epel, author of *Writers Dreaming*, legendary teacher R.V. Cassill, romance writers Susan Crose and Nancy Bush, mystery writer Gabrielle Kraft, p.r. guru Michael Levine and numerous agents and editors.

Costs: 1993 cost for full conference including meals was $185.

Accomodations: If necessary, these can be made on an individual basis. Some years special rates are available.

Additional Information: "In 1993 we had an open critique session where anyone could read." Conference brochures/guidelines are available for SASE.

‡THE WRITE MAGIC, 1140 Waverly St., Eugene OR 97401-5235. (503)485-0583 (evenings). Conference Chair: Ann Simas. Estab. 1990. Annual. Conference held in May. Conference duration: 2 days. Average attendance: 150. "Conference concentrates on fiction with specific emphasis on topics. For instance, 1992, 'If the Crime Fits, Write it!'; 1993, 'Time Travel, Fantasy, Paranormal and Things That Go Bump in the Night.' Also in 1993: 'P is for Peril, Passion and a Piece of Paranormal,' with emphasis on sensuality and the supernatural. We provide writing basics along with the specifics, editor appointments and other fun events. All workshops are taped and available for purchase. Bookfair and authors' booksigning held in conjunction. Conference workshops and meals are held in the Eugene Hilton in downtown Eugene. Hotel offers a discount room rate to attendees. Facilities are modern, clean and convenient to downtown area (walking distance to just about everywhere, including river walk)." Past guest speakers include a panel of law enforcement personnel, psychics, award winning authors Sherryl Woods, Eileen Dreyer, Earl Emerson; Anne Stuart scheduled for 1994.

Costs: Early registration, $135; late registration, $150; at the door, $175. Includes Saturday continental breakfast, lunch and banquet, Sunday continental breakfast and lunch.

Accommodations: Major airlines such as United, America West, Alaska Airlines fly into Eugene, as well as Amtrak. We are on the I-5 corridor. There is transportation from the airport via the Hilton van. Special arrangements can be made for transportation from air/train in advance. All attendees from out of town/state get hotel information.

Additional Information: Our contest is called Dark Shadows. Entry is $15/entry for RWA member; $20 for non-RWA members: query letter, prologue/first chapter, and synopsis, to total not more than 32 pages. Postmark deadline is February 15. Judge is Leslie Wainger of Silhouette Books on top 5 finalists. Awards. Brochures/guidelines available for #10 SASE. Conference flyer will also be available for a #10 SASE after January 15. Tapes available from 1992 and 1993 conference; for list and prices, send #10 SASE: 1140 Waverly Street, Eugene, OR 97401-5235; mark RWA Tapes.

‡WRITE ON THE SOUND WRITERS' CONFERENCE, 700 Main St., Edmonds WA 98020. (206)771-0228. Arts Coordinator: Christine Sidwell. Estab. 1986. Annual. Conference held in October. Conference duration: 2 days. Average attendance: 150. "We try to offer something in all writing disciplines. Large sessions are held in the Plaza Room of the Edmonds Library (also City council Chambers—holds 165). Classes are held in the Frances Anderson Center next door (it is the Edmonds Parks and Rec. Building—an old elementary school)." 1993 conference featured a keynote address by Ann Rule.
Costs: $35 includes tuition and continental breakfast. Box lunches available at additional cost.
Additional Information: Brochures available for SASE.

‡YACHATS LITERARY FESTIVAL, 124 NE California, Yachats OR 97498. (503)547-3271. Contact: Frena Bloomfield, Director. Estab. 1993. Annual. Conference will be held September 5 to 10. Topics include "all classifications" of writing. Conference activities are "held at various sites in the extraordinarily beautiful setting of ancient forest, agate beaches, spectacular rocky promontaries of the Oregon Coast." Themes planned for 1994 include fantasy and science fiction, short story, life story, writing over 50 and children's. Ursula K. LeGuin is among the speakers scheduled for the 1994 conference.
Costs: In 1993, $250 for the week plus meal plan of $50 (optional). Accommodations extra.
Accommodations: Conference organizers will assist with transporation arrangements "if asked." Accommodation information available with brochure request.
Additional Information: Sponsors a contest "for writers over 50, previously unpublished in major media, judged by a panel of writers, academics and editors. Contest closes April 20." Brochures available for SASE.

YELLOW BAY WRITERS' WORKSHOP, Center for Continuing Education, University of Montana, Missoula MT 59812. (406)243-6486. Program Manager: Judy Jones. Estab. 1988. Annual. Conference held from mid to late August. Average attendance: 50-60. Includes four workshops: 2 fiction; 1 poetry; 1 creative nonfiction/personal essay. Conference "held at the University of Montana's Flathead Lake Biological Station, a research station with informal educational facilities and rustic cabin living. Located in northwestern Montana on Flathead Lake, the largest natural freshwater lake west of the Mississippi River. All faculty are requested to present a craft lecture—usually also have an editor leading a panel discussion." 1993 faculty included Elizabeth Cox, Ian Frazier, Patricia Goedicke, Ron Hansen and editors: C. Michael Curtis (senior editor of *The Atlantic*) and Leonard W. Robinson (former managing editor of *Esquire*).
Costs: In 1993, $725 for all workshops, lodging (single occupancy) and meals; $695 with double occupancy; $425 for commuters.
Accommodations: Shuttle is available from Missoula to Yellow Bay for those flying to Montana. Cost of shuttle is $40 (1993).
Additional Information: Brochures/guidelines are available for SASE.

Canada

CANADIAN AUTHORS ASSOCIATION CONFERENCE, Suite 500, 275 Slater St., Ottawa, Ontario K1P 5H9 Canada. (613)233-2846. Fax: (613)235-8237. President: Jeffrey Holmes. Estab. 1921. Annual conference held June 23-28. Average attendance: 150. To promote "all genres—varies from year to year." University dormitory—beautiful campus. On city bus line route. 1994 conference is to be held at the Conference Centre of the campus of the University of Waterloo, Ontario."
Costs: Approx. $160 (Canadian); accommodation and meals extra, except for keynote breakfast and awards banquet. Special early-bird discounts.
Accommodations: Special accommodations available on request.
Additional Information: Conference brochures/registration forms are available for SAE and IRC.

SAGE HILL WRITING EXPERIENCE, Box 1731, Saskatoon, Saskatchewan S7K 3S1 Canada. Executive Director: Steven Smith. Annual. Workshops held in August. Workshop duration 7-14 days. Attendance: limited to 36-40. "Sage Hill Writing Experience offers a special working and learning opportunity to writers at different stages of development. Top quality instruction, low instructor-student ratio and the beautiful Sage Hill setting offer conditions ideal for the pursuit of excellence in the arts of fiction, poetry and playwriting." The Sage Hill location features "individual accommodation, in-room writing area, lounges, meeting rooms, home-style cooking, gymnasium,

bowling alley, swimming pool and walking woods and vistas in several directions." Six classes are held: Introduction to Creative Writing, Fiction & Poetry; Fiction Workshop, Poetry Workshop, Intermediate; Poetry Colloquium, Advanced; Fiction Colloquium, Advanced; Playwriting Lab. 1993 faculty included Judith Krause, David Margoshes, Edna Alford, Frank Moher, Tim Lilburn, Ven Begamudré.
Costs: $475 (Canadian) includes instruction, accommodation, meals and all facilities.
Accommodations: Bus service from Saskatoon to Prudhomme departs at 5:25 pm daily. Pre-arranged auto transportation also available. On-site individual accommodations located 75 kilometers outside Saskatoon.
Additional Information: For Introduction to Creative Writing: A five-page sample of your writing or a statement of your interest in creative writing; list of courses taken required. For intermediate and colloquium classes: A resume of your writing career and a 10-page sample of your work plus 5 pages of published work required. Guidelines are available for SASE. Scholarships and bursaries are available.

THE VANCOUVER INTERNATIONAL WRITERS FESTIVAL, 1243 Cartwright St., Vancouver, British Columbia V6H 4B7 Canada. (604)681-6330. Estab. 1988. Annual. Held during the 3rd week of October. Average attendance: 7,000. "This is a festival for readers and writers. The program of events is diverse and includes readings, panel discussions, seminars. Lots of opportunities to interact with the writers who attend." Held on Granville Island—in the heart of Vancouver. Three professional theaters are used as well as space in the Community Centre. "We try to avoid specific themes. Programming takes place between February and June each year and is by invitation."
Costs: Tickets are $8 and $12 (Canadian); some special events are a little more.
Accommodations: Local tourist info can be provided when necessary and requested.
Additional Information: Brochures/guidelines are available for SASE. "A reminder—this is a festival, a celebration, not a conference or workshop."

‡**WEST WORD SUMMER SCHOOL/WRITING RETREAT FOR WOMEN**, #210, 640 W. Broadway, Vancouver British Columbia V5Z 1G4 Canada. (604) 872-8014. Coordinator: Gloria Greenfield. Estab. 1985. Annual. Workshop usually held 2nd & 3rd weeks in August. Average attendance: 24. "We usually offer 3 genres: fiction, poetry and creative documentary. There are classes each weekday morning—one to one critique in the afternoon by instructor, guest readings. Purpose is to hone the writer's craft and to give and accept critiquing of the writer's work. Very intensive process. For the past 3 years, has been held at a small college with each participant having a room of her own in which to write as well as a staff office where work in progress can be photocopied as well as a reference library and willing ears to any problems. Location is easy to get to but away from an urban setting."
Costs: Fees include accommodation, meals, classes.
Additional Information: "Work must be submitted in advance and a selections process is followed, trying to reflect diversity in ethnicity, age, region, etc. but writer must show some promise in her work."

International

‡**THE AEGEAN CENTER FOR THE FINE ARTS WORKSHOPS**, Paros 84400, Cyclades, Greece. (30)284-23287. Director: John A. Pack. Held 2 times/year. Workshop held April 1, July 3-16, July 24-August 6, and September 1. Workshop duration: Spring—13 weeks; Summer sessions: 2 sessions, each 2 weeks; Fall—14 weeks. Average attendance: 15. "Creative writing in all its aspects." Spring workshop held at the Aegean Center "in a neoclassical 16th century townhouse in the village of Parikia with a gallery/lecture hall, well-equipped darkroom, modest library, rooms for studio space and classrooms." Location is on Paros, an island about 100 miles southeast of Athens. Fall workshop held in Italy starting in Pistoia in 16th century Villa Rospigliosi and includes travel to Pisa, Lucca, Prato, Siena, Florence and Rome in Italy as well as Athens and, finally, Paros.
Costs: There is a $35 application fee. For Spring workshop, tuition was $4,000 in 1993, transportation and board not included. Summer sessions $800 tuition; see below for tuition plus housing. For Fall workshop, tuition was $5,500 in 1993, transportation and some board not included (check for details). Some scholarships available.
Accommodations: Information on overnight accommodations is available and special workshop attendee accommodations are made. In Paros, accommodations (single occupancy apartment) on-site; other accommodations in hotels (double occupancy). For summer, "the optional housing arranged by the center will be at the lovely Aegean Village apartments in a garden setting five minute's walk from

the center. The double occupancy apartments have two separate bedrooms. All rooms have small equipped kitchen areas and private bathroom. If you want the center to arrange housing, we must have a 50% nonrefundable down payment no later than May 5, 1994. The costs of the two-week program, including housing, are as follows: $1400 for a double occupancy apartment, or $1725 for a single occupancy studio apartment."
Additional Information: College credit is available. Workshop brochures/guidelines are available for SASE.

‡**ART WORKSHOP INTERNATIONAL,** 463 West St. 1028H, New York NY 10014. (212)691-1159. Contact: Bea Kreloff, Co-director. Estab. 1977. Annual. Workshop to be held in summer. Workshop lasts 1 month. Average attendance: 20-25. Held in Assisi, Italy hotel; room, board and tuition. Instructional program plus independent program for professional writers and artists. Panels planned for next workshop include Creative Writing Workshop with instructor, novelist and editor Lucy Rosenthal.
Costs: Fee of $2,790 (in 1993). Includes room, board and tuition. Attendees must make their own travel arrangements.
Additional Information: For independent programs submission of written work and curriculum vita is required. Workshop brochures/guidelines are available for SASE. Writing workshop is combined with an art workshop. Please send for brochure for details on additional workshops.

‡**THE ARVON FOUNDATION LTD. WORKSHOPS,** Totleigh Barton Sheepwash, Beaworthy, Devon EX21 5NS United Kingdom. 040-923-338. National Director: David Pease. Estab. 1968 (workshops). Workshops held April through November at three centers. Workshops last 4½ days. Average attendence: 16/workshop. Workshops cover all types of fiction writing. "Totleigh Barton in Devon was the first Arvon centre. Next came Lumb Bank (Hebden Bridge, West Yorkshire HX7 6DF) and this year, 7 courses at Moniack Mhor (Moniack, Kirkhill, Inverness IV 5 7PQ)." Totleigh Barton is a thatched manor house. Lumb Bank is an 18th century mill owner's home and Moniack Mhor is a traditional croft house. All are in peaceful, rural settings. In the three houses there are living rooms, reading rooms, rooms for private study, dining rooms and well equipped kitchens.
Costs: In 1993 course fee was £220 which included food, tuition and accommodation. For those in need, a limited number of grants and bursaries are available from the Arvon Foundation.
Accommodations: There is sleeping accommodation for up to sixteen course members, but only limited single room accommodation (there are eight bedrooms at Lumb Bank, twelve bedrooms at Moniack Mhor and nine bedrooms at Totleigh Barton). The adjacent barns at Lumb Bank and Totleigh Barton have been converted into workshop/studio space and there are writing huts in the garden.
Additional Information: Sometimes writers are required to submit work. Check for details. Workshop brochure/guidelines available for SASE.

‡**COUNCIL OF ADULT EDUCATION (CAE) SUMMER WRITING FESTIVAL,** 256 Flinders St., Melbourne 3000 Australia. (61)33520611. Contact: Marian Letcher. Conference held January. Duration of conference: 1 week. Average attendance: 200. Workshop is "across the genres." Located at the CAE Conference Centre in the central business district of Melbourne.
Costs: Tuition only is approximately $100 or $20 for 2 hour session (Australian funds).
Accommodations: Write for more information.

‡**EDINBURGH UNIVERSITY CENTRE FOR CONTINUING EDEUCATION CREATIVE WRITING WORKSHOPS,** 11 Buccleuch Place, Edinburgh Scotland EH8 9LW. (31)650-4400. Administrative Director of International Summer Schools: Bridget M. Stevens. Estab. 1990. Introductory course held July 9-15; short story course held July 16-22; playwriting course held July 23-29. Average attendance: 12. Courses cover "basic techniques of creative writing, the short story and playwriting. The University of Edinburgh Centre for continuing education occupies traditional 18th century premises near the

---

✝ *The double dagger before a listing indicates that the listing is new in this edition. New markets are often the most receptive to submissions by new writers.*

George Square Campus. Located nearby are libraries, banks, recreational facilities and the university faculty club which workshop participants are invited to use."
Costs: In 1993 cost was £170 per one-week course (tuition only).
Accommodations: Information on overnight accommodations is available. Accommodations include student dormitories, self-catering apartment and local homes.
Additional Information: Participants are encouraged to submit work in advance, but this is not obligatory. Conference brochures/guidelines available for SASE.

‡**FICTION WRITING RETREAT IN ACAPULCO**, 3584 Kirkwood Place, Boulder CO 80304. (303)444-0086. Conference Director: Barbara Steiner. Estab. 1991. Annual. Conference held in November. Conference duration: 1 week. Average attendance: 10. Conference concentrates on "advanced fiction technique/any market. Oceanfront accommodations on private estate of Mexican artist Nora Beteta. Rooms in villa have bath (private) but usually dual occupancy. Swimming in pool or ocean/bay. Classes held on large porches with ocean breeze and views."
Costs: $495 for 1 week includes room, meals, classes.
Accommodations: Airfare separate. Travel agent books flights for groups from Denver. Will book from anyplace in US.
Additional Information: "Writers submit one short fiction piece in advance of workshop. Classes include writing, lecture and assignments." Brochures/guidelines available for SASE.

‡**PARIS WRITERS' WORKSHOP/WICE**, 20, Bd du Montparnasse, Paris, France 75015. (33-1)45.66.75.50. Fax: (33-1)40.65.96.53. Director: Carol Allen. Estab. 1987. Annual. Conference held from June 26 to July 1. Average attendance: 40-50. "Conference concentrates on fiction (2 sections), nonfiction and poetry. Visiting lecturers speak on screenwriting, travel writing, marketing, etc. WICE, a nonprofit educational and cultural institute, is located in the heart of Paris on the Bd. du Montparnasse, the stomping grounds of such famous American writers as Ernest Hemingway, Henry Miller, George Sand and F. Scott Fitzgerald. The site consists of 3 classrooms, a resource center/library, computer room and private terrace."
Costs: $380 – tuition only; $300 – student tuition (full-time/university ID); $630 – tuition for two workshops (fiction and poetry or nonfiction).
Additional Information: "Students submit 2 copies of complete ms or work-in-progress. One copy is sent in advance to writer in residence. Each student has a one-on-one consultation with writer in residence concerning ms that was submitted." Sponsors a short story contest in conjunction with *Paris-Transcontinental*. Requirements: up to 3,000 words; unpublished ms editorial staff of *Paris Transcontinental* judges. Brochures/guidelines available for SASE. "Workshop attracts mostly expatriate Americans and other English language students from all over Europe. Some students come from the US, Canada or South America."

PLOUGHSHARES INTERNATIONAL FICTION WRITING SEMINAR, Emerson College, European & Los Angeles Programs, 100 Beacon St., Boston MA 02116. (617)578-8567. Contact person: Hank Zappala. Estab. 1990. Annual. Conference/workshop held in summer. Conference duration: 2 weeks. Average attendance: 25. "Castle Well is not a classroom, but a community of practicing writers who breathe, think, discuss and debate fiction with their peers and a group of professional authors." Castle Well is a Renaissance Castle. Located in the Village of Well on the river Maas in southeastern Holland. Co-Directors are James Carroll and Robie Macauley.
Costs: In 1993, cost was $1,750 plus transportation. Tuition includes room and board, special events, workshops and excursions.
Accommodations: On-site accommodations.
Additional Information: Sample work required – 1 short story or short segment of a longer work, no more than 15 pages. Brochures/guidelines available for SASE. "Seminar members may earn four credits toward graduate or undergraduate degrees."

‡**WOMEN'S WILDERNESS CANOE TRIPS WRITING RETREAT**, P.O. Box 9109, Santa Fe NM 87504. (505)984-2268. Owner and Guide: Beverly Antaeus. Estab. 1985. Annual. Conference held in November. Conference duration: 8 days. Average attendance: 20. Writing retreat with Sharon Olds. "All genres welcome as the means to bring forth something truer and newer than ever before." Held "on the beach, Sea of Cortez, Baja California, Mexico. Living under sun and moon; tents and palapas available for sleeping."

Costs: For 1993 cost was $1,045; land costs, tuition and food included in fee.
Accommodations: All transportation details are provided upon enrollment. "We live outdoors throughout the workshop—all rendezvous and departure details provided in full."
Additional Information: Brochures/guidelines available upon request.

‡THE WRITERS' SUMMER SCHOOL, SWANWICK, The Red House, Mardens Hill, Crowborough East Sussex TN6 1XN England. Secretary: Philippa Boland. Estab. 1949. Annual. Conference held August 13-19. Average attendance: 300 plus. "Conference concentrates on all fields of writing." In 1993 panelists' topics included: The Novel, Poetry, Writing for Children, Journalism, ALCS and CLA. Speakers in 1993 included Robert Birmingham, Eric Chappell, Gerald Cole, Ursula A. Fanthorpe, Liz Hodgkinson, Peter Zing, David Neal and Stephanie Nettell.
Costs: £167 inclusive.
Accommodations: Buses from main line station to conference centre provided.
Additional Information: "Members who are tutoring courses will accept mss prior to the conference. The Writer's Summer School is a nonprofit-making organization and any surplus generated is used solely to further its educational purposes."

Conferences and workshops/changes '93-'94

The following conferences and workshops appeared in the 1993 edition of *Novel & Short Story Writer's Market* but do not appear in the 1994 edition. Those conferences and workshops that did not respond to our request for an update appear below without further explanation. If a reason for the omission is available, it is included next to the listing name. There are several reasons why a conference or workshop may not appear—it may not be an annual event, for example, or it may no longer be held.

Alabama Writers' Conclave
Annual Writers Institute
Baltimore Science Fiction Society Writer's Workshop
Blue Ridge Writers Conference
Children's Book Publishing: An Intensive Writing & Editing Workshop
Copyright Workshop
Cumberland Valley Writers Workshop
Cuyahoga Writers' Conference
Deep South Writers Conference
Desert Writers Workshop/Canyonlands Field Institute
Fairview Summit Writers Sanctuary Workshops
The Festival of the Written Arts
Festival of the Written Arts Writers-in-Residence Program
Florida First Coast Writers' Festival
Florida Romance Writers' Fun-in-the-Sun Conference
Heart of America Writers' Conference
IWWG Early Spring in California Conference
IWWG Meet the Agents and

Editors: The Big Apple Workshops
IWWG Midwestern Conference
IWWG New Jersey Conference
IWWG Summer Conference
IWWG Write Your Own Story Conference
LDS Writers' Workshop
Maritime Writers' Workshop
Median-Wayne Writers Conference
National Women's Music Festival Writers Conference
Ohio Writers' Holiday
OWFI Annual Conference
Prairie State College Writers Conference
Rice University Writers' Conference
Ropewalk Writers' Retreat
San Diego County Christian Writers' Guild
SCBWI/North Central Texas Chapter Annual Conference
Seattle Pacific University Christian Writers Conference
Sewanee Writers' Conference
Shooting Star Writers Conference

Southern California Writers Conference/San Diego
Southwest Christian Writers Association
Southwest Florida Writers' Conference
Summer in France Writing Workshops
Texas Writers Association Fall, Spring and Summer Workshops (asked to be deleted)
Ty Newydd Writer's Centre
University of Kentucky Women Writers Conference
University of Massachusetts Lowell Writing Program
University of Wisconsin at Madison Writers Institute
Wildacres Writers Workshop
Write to Sell Writer's Conference
The Writer's Edge Workshop
Writers Tour of Greece
The Writers' Workshop
Writing by the Sea
Writing for Publication (Pittsburgh PA)
Writing for Publication (Villanova PA)
Writing Workshop

Retreats and Colonies

If you are looking for a quiet place to start or complete your novel or short story collection, a retreat or writers' colony may offer you just what you need. Often located in tranquil settings, these are places for writers to find solitude and concentrated time to focus solely on their writing. Unlike conferences or workshop settings, communal meals may be the only scheduled activities. Also, a writer's stay at a retreat or colony is typically anywhere from one to twelve weeks (sometimes longer), while time spent at a conference or workshop is generally anywhere from one day to two weeks (perhaps a month at most).

Like conferences and workshops, however, retreats and colonies span a wide range. Some, such as The Blue Mountain Center offer residencies for established writers, while others, such as the Dorset Colony House for Writers is open to writers on all levels. Other programs are restricted to writers from certain areas or who write on certain subjects such as the Camargo Foundation retreat for a writer working on a project relating to French culture or the Weymouth Center retreats for North Carolina writers or those working on projects relating to North Carolina. And you'll find retreats and colonies located in Pahoa, Hawaii; Tel-Aviv, Israel; Cape Cod, Massachusetts and Banff, Alberta. Accommodations vary from a restored antebellum home in Mississippi to a castle in Scotland to wood-frame cottages on an island off the coast of Washington state.

Despite different focuses and/or locations, all retreats and colonies have one thing in common: They are places where writers may work undisturbed, usually in very nature-oriented and secluded settings. A retreat or colony serves as a place for rejuvenation; a writer can find new ideas, rework old ones or put the finishing touches to works-in-progress.

Arrangements at retreats and colonies differ dramatically so it may help to determine your own work habits before you begin searching through these pages. While some retreats house writers in one main building, others provide separate cottages. In both cases, residents are generally given private work space, although they usually must bring along their own typewriters or personal computers. Some colonies offer communal, family-style meals at set times, some prepare meals for each resident individually and still others require residents to prepare meals themselves. If you tend to work straight through meals now, you might want to consider a retreat or colony that offers the last option.

A related consideration for most folks is cost. Again, the types of arrangements vary. A good number of residencies are available at no cost or only a minimal daily cost, sometimes including the cost of meals, sometimes not. The Ragdale Foundation charges a mere $10 a day and offers scholarships, for example, and Weymouth Center charges no fees, although donations are accepted. Other residencies, such as those through the Ucross Foundation, are "awards," resulting from competitive applications. Finally, for those residencies that are fairly expensive, scholarships or fee waivers are often available.

In general, residencies at retreats and colonies are competitive because only a handful of spots are available at each place. Writers must often apply at least six months in advance for the time period they desire. While some locations are open year-round, others are available only during certain seasons. Planning to go during the "off-season" may lessen your competition. Also, most places will want to see a writing sample with your application, so be prepared to show your best work—whether you are a beginning writer or an established one. In addition, it will help to have an idea of the project you'll work on while in residence, since some places request this information with their applications as well.

Each listing in this section provides information about the type of writers the retreat or colony accepts; the location, accommodations and meal plan available; the costs; and, finally, the application process. As with markets and conferences and workshops, changes in policies may be made after this edition has gone to press. Send a self-addressed, stamped envelope to the places that interest you to receive the most up-to-date details.

For other listings of retreats and colonies, you may want to see *The Guide to Writers Conferences* (Shaw Associates, publishers, Suite 1406, 625 Biltmore Way, Coral Gables FL 33134), which not only provides information about conferences, workshops and seminars but also residencies, retreats and organizations. An exceptional resource is *Havens for Creatives*, available from ACTS Institute, Inc. (P.O. Box 10153, Kansas City MO 64111), which features almost 400 retreats, colonies, art programs and creative vacation opportunities for writers, artists, photographers and other creative types. Their directory also includes a bibliography of works written about art and writing colonies and a selection of creative work written during residencies.

EDWARD F. ALBEE FOUNDATION (THE BARN), 14 Harrison St., New York NY 10013. (212)226-2020. Foundation Secretary: David Briggs. For writers (fiction, nonfiction, playwrights, etc.) and visual artists (painters, sculptors, etc.). " 'The Barn' is located in Montauk, NY." Available for 1 month residencies from June-September. Provisions for the writer include private rooms. Accommodates 4 writers at one time. Residencies supported by the Edward F. Albee Foundation Fellowship.
Costs: No cost, but residents are responsible for their food, travel and supplies.
To Apply: Write or call for information and applications (accepted January 1 to April 1). Brochures or guidelines are available for SASE (IRCs).

ATLANTIC CENTER FOR THE ARTS, 1414 Art Center Ave., New Smyrna Beach FL 32168. (904)427-6975. Program Director: Suzanne Fetscher. Estab. 1980. "Residencies at Atlantic Center are open to all who meet selection requirements. Master Artists, who are selected in consultation with the Advisory Council, set the structure of the residency, determine what will be accomplished and set criteria for selection of Associates. Associates, who are typically artists at mid-career, are selected by Master Artists through portfolio review (in this case, examples of writing, résumés, etc.). Atlantic Center is located on 67-acres of hammockland on Turnbull Bay, a tidal estuary in New Smyrna Beach, Florida. Buildings include the administration building, workshop, fieldhouse, 3 Master Artists' cottages and 28 units of Associate housing. All buildings are air-conditioned and connected by raised wooden walkways. Associate units have private bath, desk and refrigerator. Writers often meet in fieldhouse, which has copy machine, kitchen, bath, typewriters, tables and chairs." The Center usually offers 6 residencies each year, usually three weeks in length. Residencies occur throughout the year, but may not always offer opportunities to writers. Accommodates up to 28 Associates (including all disciplines).
Costs: $600, including private room/bath; $200, tuition only and Associates provide their own accommodations and transportation. Depending on the many factors involved, costs for the 3-week residency may vary from $900 to $1,500. Scholarships are available in selected disciplines for some residencies.
To Apply: Application requirements are different for each residency. Send for information or call toll free 1-800-393-6975. Application deadlines are generally 4-5 months before start of a residency; notification usually occurs 3-4 weeks after application deadline. Brochure/guidelines available for SASE (IRCs). Some college credit available.

BELLAGIO STUDY AND CONFERENCE CENTER, Rockefeller Foundation, 1133 Avenue of the Americas, New York NY 10036. (212)852-8431. Manager: Susan Garfield. Estab. 1960. "Scholars and artists from any country and in any discipline are invited to apply. Successful applicants will be individuals of achievement with significant publications, exhibitions or shows to their credit. Bellagio Study and Conference Center, also known as Villa Serbelloni, occupies a wooded promontory . . . Includes main house and seven other buildings. Set in the foothills of the Italian Alps." Residencies are approximately 4 weeks long. Offered February through mid-December. Each scholar and artist is provided with a private room and bath and with a study in which to work. IBM and Apple PCs and printers available. Accommodates 130 residents. Quarterly deadlines: March 1, June 1, September 1, December 1.
Costs: "The Center does not provide financial assistance to scholars in residence nor does it ordinarily contribute to travel expenses. Once at the center, all scholars and spouses are guests of the foundation."

To Apply: Send for application. Application must include form, half-page abstract describing purpose of project, detailed project description, brief curriculum vitae, one sample of published work, reviews. Brochure/guidelines available. Do not send SASE.

THE BLUE MOUNTAIN CENTER, Blue Mountain Lake, New York NY 12812. (518)352-7391. Director: Harriet Barlow. Residencies for established writers. "Provides a peaceful environment where residents may work free from distractions and demands of normal daily life." Residencies awarded for 1 month between June and October. For provisions, costs, other information, send SASE (IRCs) for brochure. **To Apply:** Application deadline: February 1.

CAMARGO FOUNDATION, 64 Main St., P.O. Box 32, East Haddam CT 06423. Administrative Assistant: Jane M. Viggiani. Estab. 1971. For one artist, one writer, one musician; and graduate students and scholars working on projects relating to French culture. There are facilities for 12 grantees each semester. "Grantees are given a furnished apartment, rent free, on an estate on the Mediterranean about twenty miles east of Marseilles. Families may accompany grantee, but must remain the entire period of the grant." Grant period is from early September to mid-December or from mid-January to May 31. Minimum residency is three months. "A workroom is available and computer facilities, though it is suggested that writers bring their own equipment; space and scheduling may be tight." **Costs:** None. There is no stipend. **To Apply:** "There is no fee. Write to Administrative Assistant giving name and address to request application materials. Packet will be mailed upon request. All materials requested must be received in this office by March 1 of the year previous to the one for which application is being made. Applicant will be notified of selection decisions by April 15 of that year."

‡CENTRUM ARTIST-IN-RESIDENCE, P.O. Box 1158, Port Townsend WA 98368. (206)385-3102. Program Coordinator: Sarah Muirhead. Estab. 1978. Open to writers, visual artists, composers, performers. "Artists stay in private 2-3 bedroom cottages on the grounds of Fort Worden State Park, a former military fort. Located on Admiralty Inlet with beaches, woods, trails, turn-of-the century buildings." Month-long residencies, September-May. Stipend of $75 per week. Accommodates approximately 4/month. There is handicapped access. **Costs:** $10 application fee. **To Apply:** Call or send SASE (IRCs) for brochure.

THE CLEARING, P.O. Box 65, Ellison Bay WI 54210. (414)854-4088. Resident Manager: Louise or Don Buchholz. Estab. 1935. Open to "any adult 18 to 81 (and we'll relax the 81 requirement)." Located in "historic native log and stone buildings on 128-acres of native forest on the shore of Green Bay. Hiking trails, beach, swimming, enjoyable countryside for bicycling. Housed in twin bedded, private bath facility. Meals served family style. Classroom is large hall in wooded setting. Clearing open mid-May to mid-October for week-long sessions beginning Sunday night with supper, ending Saturday morning with breakfast—usually 2 or 3 writing weeks per year." Provisions for the writer include options of sharing a twin bedroom or 6-bed dorm, meals furnished, workspace in bedroom, living room, school building or quiet nooks on the grounds. Accommodates 20-24 writers. **Costs:** $435-480/person per week includes board, room and tuition. (No Thursday night supper.) Scholarships are available. Brochure/guidelines available.

‡COTTAGES AT HEDGEBROOK, 2197 E. Millman Rd., Langley WA 98260. (206)321-4786. Director: Linda Haverfield. Estab. 1988. For "women writers, published or not, of all ages and from all cultural backgrounds." Located on "30-acres on Whidbey Island one hour north of Seattle, WA. Six individual cottages, a bathhouse for showers and a farmhouse where dinner is served. The cottages are wood frame, wood heat, electricity, no TV or phone." Applicants request a stay of 1 week to 3 months (may attend only once). Two application periods a year January 10-June 14; July 1-December 10. "Writers must provide their writing equipment. Very good writing space and relaxing space in each cottage; sleeping loft, down comforters. Lunch delivered, small kitchen facility—dinner in the farmhouse." Accommodates 6 writers. **Costs:** No charge for food or housing. Writers provide extras. Meals are nutritious, diet conscious. There is a travel scholarship fund. **To Apply:** Deadlines are October 1 and April 1. Application form—5 copies needed for committee review. Approximately 25 writers are invited each of 2 sessions a year. Limited facility for a differently-abled person; wheelchair accessible. Brochure/guidelines available for SASE (IRCs).

CUMMINGTON COMMUNITY OF THE ARTS, R.R. 1, Box 145, Cummington MA 01026. (413)634-2172. Contact: Rick Reiken. Estab. 1923. Open to all artists. "Land is rural; 110 acres of rolling hills in Berkshires, western Massachusetts. Buildings vary from large old-style homes to individual cabins. Private." Offered April to November for 2 weeks to 3 months. Provisions for the writer include private room/studio (one room total), meals included. Accommodates up to 20 writers. Workshop space also available.
Costs: $650, all inclusive. Send $20 with application. Brochure/guidelines available for SASE (IRCs).

CURRY HILL PLANTATION WRITER'S RETREAT, 404 Cresmont Ave., Hattiesburg MS 39401. (601)264-7034. Director: Elizabeth Bowne. Estab. 1977. Open to all fiction and nonfiction writing, except poetry and technical writing. This workshop is held at an antebellum home, located on 400-acres of land. It is limited to only eight guests who live in, all of whom receive individual help with their writing, plus a 3-hour workshop each evening when the group meets together. The location is six miles east of Bainbridge, Georgia. Offered March 20-26. "The date of the retreat is different every year but always in the spring—March/April." Provisions for the writer include room and board. Accommodates 8 writers.
Costs: $400 for the week; includes room and board and individual help, one hour per guest each day.
To Apply: Interested persons should apply *early* January. Brochure/guidelines available for SASE (IRCs).

DJERASSI RESIDENT ARTISTS PROGRAM, (formerly Djerassi Foundation), 2325 Bear Gulch Rd., Woodside CA 94062-4405. Executive Director: Charles Amirkhanian. "The Djerassi Program appoints approximately 30 artists a year to spend 1 to 2 months working on independent or collaborative projects in a setting of unusual beauty and privacy. The facility is located on a former cattle ranch 1 hour south of San Francisco in the Santa Cruz mountains facing the Pacific Ocean. We are seeking applications at two levels. One is the level of great promise: artists who have a record of solid achievement but are not yet very well known, for whom appointments as resident artists might make a difference. The other is the level of national or international distinction: artists with established reputations, for whom a change of scene might offer refreshment and inspiration." Provisions for the writer include living/studio accommodations with balcony or garden access, as well as meals. Accommodates 12 artists of various disciplines at one time. Open April 1-October 31.
Costs: "The Djerassi Program award is strictly a residential grant." All accommodations are provided at no cost.
To Apply: Send SASE (IRCs) to: Djerassi Resident Artists Program at above address and request application packet. Deadline for 1995 season is February 15, 1994.

‡DORLAND MOUNTAIN ARTS COLONY, P.O. Box #6, Temecula CA 92593. (909)676-5039. Fellows' Liaison: Karen Parrott. Estab. 1978. Open to visual artists, composers, writers, playwrights, theater artists. Provides uninterrupted time in a natural environment. The colony is located on a 300-acre nature preserve. No electricity, rustic single wall constructed cabins; large oak grove; 2 ponds; trails. Available for 2-week to 2-month residencies year round. Provisions for the writer include private cabins with living and work space. Manual (older) typewriters provided. Responsible for own meals. There are a total of 6 cabins.
Costs: $150/month or $5 a day for shorter stays.
To Apply: Application deadlines: March 1 and September 1. $50 nonrefundable processing fee upon acceptance. Brochure/guidelines available for SASE (IRCs).

DORSET COLONY HOUSE FOR WRITERS, Box 519, Dorset VT 05251. (802)867-2223. Director: John Nassivera. Estab. 1980. Colony is open to all writers. Facility and grounds include large 19th century house in New England village setting; national historic landmark house and village. Available 2 months in spring and 2 months in fall. Accommodates 8 writers.
Costs: $75/week; meals not included; fully functional kitchen in house and restaurants easy walk away.
To Apply: No fees to apply; send inquiry anytime. Brochures are available for SASE (IRCs).

Stay informed! Keep up with changes in the market by using the latest edition of Novel & Short Story Writer's Market. *If this is 1995 or later, buy a new edition at your favorite bookstore or order directly from Writer's Digest Books.*

FINE ARTS WORK CENTER IN PROVINCETOWN, P.O. Box 565, Provincetown MA 02657. (508)487-9960. Contact: Writing Coordinator. Estab. 1968. Open to emerging writers and visual artists. "Located on the grounds of the former Days Lumberyard complex, the facility has offered studio space to artists and writers since 1914. Renovated coal bins provide artist studios; several houses and a refurbished Victorian Barn offer apartments for writers. The complex encircles the Stanley Kunitz Common Room where fellows and visiting artists offer readings to the public." A seven-month residency offered from October 1 to May 1 each year. "Each writer is awarded his/her own apartment with kitchen and bath. All apartments are furnished and equipped with kitchen supplies. A monthly stipend of $375 is also provided." Accommodates 10 writers (four fiction, four poets).
Costs: No fees other than application fee ($20).
To Apply: Application deadline: February 1. Writing sample: Send 1 or 2 short stories. If novel, excerpt including opening section and synopsis. Limit: 40 pages. Send up to 20 pages of poetry. Send six copies. Check guidelines for details. Brochure/guidelines available for SASE (IRCs).

THE TYRONE GUTHRIE CENTRE AT ANNAGHMAKERRIG, Newbliss, County Monaghan, Ireland. Tel: 047-54003. Resident Director: Bernard Loughlin. Estab. 1981. Open to writers, painters, sculptors, composers, directors, artists. There are "11 work rooms in house, generally with private bathroom. Also 5 new houses which are self-contained. 400-acres, large lake and gardens. Sitting room, library, kitchen, dining room." Closed for 2-week period at Christmas only. Provisions for the writer include private room and meals. Accommodates 16 writers and other artists.
Costs: IR £1,000-£1,350, depending on season, per month in Big House, all meals included. IR £150/week for self-contained houses—also have to pay food, heating, electricity and outgoings.
To Apply: Write for application form. Considered at bimonthly board meeting. Brochure/guidelines available for SASE (IRCs).

THE HAMBIDGE CENTER, P.O. Box 339, Rabun Gap GA 30568. Estab. 1934. Open to artists from all fields. Includes "600 acres of wooded, rural property serenely set in north Georgia mountains; traversed by streams and waterfalls." 2-week to 2-month stays from May to October, with limited winter residencies also. Provisions for writers include private cottages and studios. Accommodates 7 artists.
Costs: $125/week with dinner provided Monday-Friday. Some scholarships available (very limited and reviewed individually).
To Apply: Deadline for first round reviews is February 28. Application fee is $20. Application form mailed upon request. Brochure/guidelines available for SASE (IRCs).

‡HAWTHORNDEN CASTLE, Lasswade, Midlothian, Scotland EH181E9. 031-440-2180. Contact: Administrator. Estab. 1982. "For dramatists, novelists, poets or other creative writers who have published one piece of work." Located in a "remotely situated castle amid wild romantic scenery, a 30-minute bus ride to Edinburgh." Offers 8 four-week sessions from February to July and September to December. Provisions for the writer include: study bedrooms; daytime silence rule; communal breakfast and evening meal. Accommodates 5 writers.
Costs: Residence is free.
To Apply: "Application form is available from Administrator. September 15 deadline for following year."

KALANI HONUA, RR2, Box 4500, Pahoa HI 96778. (808)965-7828. Director: Michael Fleck. Estab. 1980. Open to all education interests. "Kalani Honua, the 'harmony of heaven and earth,' provides an environment where the spirit of aloha flourishes. Located on 20 secluded acres bordered by lush jungle and rugged coastline forged by ancient lava flows, Kalani Honua offers an authentic experience of rural Hawaii. The surrounding area, including sacred sites and state and national parks, is rich with the island's history and magic." Available year-round, although greatest availability is May and June and September, October, November, December. Provisions for the writer include "comfortable, private room and workspace. 3 meals offered/day, beautiful coastal surroundings and recreation facilities (pool, sauna, jacuzzi, tennis, volleyball, biking) near beaches and Volcanoes National Park. (Qualifying writers receive stipend to help with costs.)" Accommodates usually 1-5 as artists-in-residence.
Costs: $26-85/night depending on choice of lodging (varying from private room with shared bath to private cottage with private bath) and depending on stipend amount. Meals are approximately $24/day or may be self-provided in kitchen. Scholarships available. Professional career documentation and assurance the residency will be successfully completed.
To Apply: Application fee $10. Brochure/guidelines available for SASE (IRCs). College credit may be arranged through University of Hawaii.

LEIGHTON ARTIST COLONY, THE BANFF CENTRE, Box 1020 Station 22, Banff, Alberta T0L 0C0 Canada. (403)762-6180. Registrar: Susan Adams. Estab. 1984. "The Leighton Artist Colony provides time and space for professional artists to produce new work. The colony is situated in a pine grove on the side of a mountain and consists of eight specially designed studios set apart from one another. Available for one week to three month residencies. Apply at anytime. Juries are held three times a year. Space is limited and artists are encouraged to apply at least six months in advance of start date. Provisions include private room, studio and choice of meal plan. Accommodates 3 professional artists at one time.
Costs: Approximately $72-81/day (Canadian). Financial subsidy for those who demonstrate need is offered in the form of a discount. Maximum discount for Canadians $36/day; for others $25/day.
To Apply: Send completed application form, résumé, press releases, reviews and a selection of published work or manuscripts in progress. Brochures or guidelines available for free.

THE MACDOWELL COLONY, 100 High St., Peterborough NH 03458. (603)924-3886 or (212)966-4860. Admissions Coordinator: Pat Dodge. Estab. 1907. Open to writers, composers, visual artists, film/video artists, interdisciplinary artists and architects. Includes "main building, library, 3 residence halls and 31 individual studios on over 400 mostly wooded acres, one mile from center of small town in southern New Hampshire." Available up to 8 weeks year-round. Provisions for the writer include meals, private sleeping room, individual secluded studio. Accommodates variable number of writers, averaging 14 at a time.
Costs: Artists are asked to contribute toward the cost of their residency according to their financial resources.
To Apply: Application forms available. Application deadline: January 15 for summer; April 15 for fall/winter, September 15 for winter/spring. Writing sample required. For novel, send a chapter or section. For short stories, send 2-3. Send 6 copies. Brochure/guidelines available for SASE. (IRCs).

MILLAY COLONY FOR THE ARTS, Steepletop, P.O. Box 3, Austerlitz NY 12017-0003. (518)392-3103. Executive Director: Ann-Ellen Lesser. Assistant Director: Gail Giles. Estab. 1973. Open to professional writers, composers, visual artists. Includes "600-acres—mostly wooded, fields, old farm. Two buildings house artists—separate studios (14×20) and bedrooms." Available year round. Accommodates 5 people at a time for one month residencies.
Costs: No fees.
To Apply: Requires sample of work and 1 professional reference. Application deadlines: February 1 for June-September; May 1 for October-January; September 1 for February-May. Brochure/guidelines available for SASE (IRCs).

‡N.A.L.L. ASSOCIATION, 232 Blvd. de Lattre, 06140 Vence France. (33)93 58 13 26. Contact: NALL, founder. Estab. 1993. "The N.A.L.L. is open to artists of all vocations—painters, sculptors, writers, playwrights, musicians—regardless of race, religion or age. There are 9 houses available on 8 acres of grounds between Saint Paul and Vence." Available in "minimal seasonal three-month terms. Yearly sabbatical programs are also available." Provisions for the artist include housing only; meals not included. Accommodates 10 writers at a time.
Costs: Range from 1,500-6,000 FF/month, depending on type of accommodation and season.
To Apply: "The artist is to send a curriculum vitae of accomplishments and future projects."

‡OREGON WRITERS COLONY, P.O. Box 15200, Portland OR 97215. (503)771-0428. Contact: Marlene Howard, property manager. Estab. 1986. The Oregon Writers Colony is open to members only ($20 annual dues). The colony is located in a large log house containing 4 bedrooms and 2 baths. Available from September through May only. Accommodates a maximum of 4 writers.
Costs: $350/week; during second week of month, $100/week.
To Apply: Brochure/guidelines available for SASE (IRCs).

PALENVILLE INTERARTS COLONY, P.O. Box 59, Palenville NY 12463. (518)678-3332. Contact: Admissions Director. "Artists residencies for professional and emerging literary artists." Located at base of Catskill Mountains on a 120-acre wooded estate. Main house has 8 rooms, kitchen and dining hall. Cabins for studios and living space. Trails, fields, dance studio, theater. Available June-September. Accommodates up to 12-15 writers or other artists.

Costs: Write for details.
To Apply: Application fee: $10. Writing samples required. Applications are considered on a competition basis; judges are a panel of 8 distinguished artists. Deadline: April 1. Brochure/guidelines available for SASE (IRCs).

‡**PENDLE HILL**, Box G, 338 Plush Mill Rd., Wallingford PA 19086-6099. (800)742-3150. Information Services Associate: Mary Helgesen. Estab. 1930. "Grounded in the social and spiritual values of the Religious Society of Friends (Quakers), Pendle Hill welcomes people of all faiths who seek a time of spiritual renewal through reading, writing, study, solitude, or time in community. It is an adult interfaith center for study and contemplation, set on 25 acres of beautiful trees and gardens 12 miles southwest of Philadelphia. Its 16 buildings include a conference center, crafts studio, library, book store, meeting room, dining room, classrooms and dormitories." The Resident Study Program offers three 10-week terms between October and June. "People may also come to 'sojourn' or come for a short stay for a self-directed retreat. Sojourning is an ideal way to come and have time for writing." The Extension Program offers weekend conferences on topics of interest to writers. The conference center is also available for groups wishing to rent it for their own program. Provisions for the writer include private room, meals, a library, crafts studio and bookstore. Accommodates 30 in Resident Study program; 12 sojourners; 30 conferees. The cost of sojourning is $53.50 per day; $49.50 per day after one week. Conferences range from $160 for a weekend to $325 for one week in the summer. The cost of the Resident Study Program is $3,600 per term; $10,500 for three. All rates include room and board. Please call for rental rates. Scholarships and financial aid available for Resident Study Program.
To Apply: Call 1-800-742-3150, or write for application packet. Applications for Resident Study Program are accepted throughout the year. Those interested in sojourning or conferences may call the registrar at the toll-free number to make arrangements.

RAGDALE FOUNDATION, 1260 N. Green Bay Rd., Lake Forest IL 60045. (708)234-1063. Director: Michael Wilkerson. Estab. 1976. For qualified writers, artists and composers. Ragdale, located 30 miles north of Chicago near Lake Michigan, is "the grounds of acclaimed Chicago architect Howard Van Doren Shaw's historic family home." Accommodations include the Ragdale House, the Barnhouse and the new Friends Studio. Available in 2-week to 2-month sessions year-round, except for the last 2 weeks in early summer and 2 weeks in December. Provisions for the writer include room; linens, laundered by Ragdale and meals. "Breakfast and lunch supplies are stocked in communal kitchens, enabling residents to work throughout the day uninterrupted by scheduled meals. The evening meal is the only exception: wholesome, well-prepared dinners are served six nights a week. The Ragdale House and Barnhouse both contain informal libraries, and the property overlooks a large nature preserve." Accommodates 12.
Costs: $10/day. Scholarships based on financial need are available. "Fee waiver application and decision process is separate from artistic admission process."
To Apply: "Residents are chosen by a selection committee composed of professionals in their artistic discipline. Applicants are required to submit an application, project description, slides or a writing sample and three references." Application fee: $20. Deadlines: September 15 for January-April, January 15 for May-August and April 15 for September-December. Brochure/guidelines available for SASE (IRCs).

‡✽**SASKATCHEWAN WRITERS'/ARTISTS' COLONIES**, Box 3986, Regina, Saskatchewan S4P 3R9 Canada. (306)757-6310. Program Director: Paul Wilson. Estab. 1979. For all writers and artists, "although priority is given to Saskatchewan residents." St. Peter's College is "a Benedictine Abbey in a serene location just outside the village of Muenster. Emma Lake is located in a forest region approximately 25 miles north of Prince Albert." An 8-week summer colony and year-round individual retreats are held at St. Peter's. A 2-week colony is held in August at Emma Lake. St. Peter's provides private rooms and "home-grown meals" served in the college facility. Residents at Emma Lake "are housed in separate cabins or in single rooms in a one-story unit. The dining room and lounge are located in a central building." The 8-week summer colony at St. Peter's accommodates 8 people a week, "but applicants may request as much time as they need." The individual retreats accommodate no more than 3 at one time.
Costs: $100 (Canadian)/week, includes meals and accommodation.
To Apply: Applications should be typewritten and include a check for length of stay as well as 10 ms pages or slides of artwork, a brief résumé, a project description and 2 references. Deadline for 8-week summer colony: April 15. Deadline for individual retreats: 1 month before preferred date of attendance. Brochure/guidelines available for SASE (IRCs).

‡SELU WRITERS RETREAT, Box 6935, Radford University, Radford VA 24142-6935. (703)831-5269 or (703)639-0812. Estab. 1992. "Offers unstructured time in congenial, quiet campus setting. Writers stay in a newly-renovated air-conditioned dormitory with private baths. Radford University is located off I-81 on the banks of the historic New River, 40 miles southwest of Roanoke." Available July 3-10. Accommodates 12 writers at a time.
Costs: Private room, $180; meal plan, $75.
To Apply: "Writers should apply 6 months in advance. Include a brief bio."

THE SYVENNA FOUNDATION WRITERS-IN-RESIDENCE, Route 1, Box 193, Linden TX 75563. (903)835-8252. Associate Director: Barbara Carroll. Estab. 1987; first resident in 1989. For beginning and intermediate women writers, all genres. "Two private cottages in rural, wooded area of Northeast Texas, 6½ miles from nearest town. Cottages are within walking distance of main house and administrative offices. Cottages are self-sufficient and equipped with all modern conveniences." Available in four 2- or 3-month terms, January through November. Provisions for the writer include rent- and utilities-free private cottage with workspace. "Residents are responsible for their own meals, laundry and other personal needs. Pick-up truck available once a week for residents without their own transportation." Accommodates 2 at one time (1/cottage).
Costs: "No charge for application or residency. Monthly stipend provided to help offset living expenses."
To Apply: Send SASE (IRCs) to Syvenna Foundation for application materials. Deadlines: April 1 for September-November; August 1 for January-March; October 1 for April-May; and December 1 for June-August.

UCROSS FOUNDATION, 2836 U.S. Hwy. 14-16 East, Clearmont WY 82835. (307)737-2291. Executive Director: Elizabeth Guheen. Estab. 1982. For "artists of *all* disciplines. We are in a rural setting of Wyoming, in a town with a very small population. The facilities are part of a renovated ranch." Available for 2 weeks to 2 months. "Each artist is provided a private studio, private bedroom, common living area and meals. We have the potential of accommodating 4 writers at one time."
Costs: Ucross Foundation awards residencies.
To Apply: Residents are selected through biannual competition, judged by a 3-member committee. Deadlines: March 1 for August-December; October 1 for February-June. Brochure/guidelines available for SASE (IRCs).

‡VALLECITOS RETREAT, Box 226, Vallecitos NM 87581. (505)582-4226. Contact: Gina Covina, Co-director. Estab. 1990. For "writers, visual artists, composers—also open to people in any field whose day-to-day lives do not allow time or opportunity for creative expression." The retreat is housed in a "2-story adobe farmhouse, with 4 large bright studio rooms, shared kitchen, bathrooms, meeting room and library. The house is surrounded by pastures, fruit trees and gardens. The grounds are bordered by Rio Vallecitos and national forest land, with many trails." Available year-round, for periods of one week to 2 months. Provisions for the writer include private room with large work table, well-stocked library and use of kitchen. Accommodates 4 writers at a time.
Costs: For 1993, $185 weekly; $460 monthly. (The 1994 rates will be higher). "At this time the only scholarships available are for poets for one-month residencies January-March, 1994. We are working on fundraising now to provide scholarships for 1994—criteria not yet set."
To Apply: "For fee-paying residencies, simply make a reservation (usually booked 2 months in advance, sometimes more)." Brochure/guidelines available for SASE (IRCs).

VERMONT STUDIO CENTER, P.O. Box 613NW, Johnson VT 05656. (802)635-2727. Fax: (802)635-2730. Estab. 1984. "The Vermont Studio Center now offers six 2-week Writing Studio Sessions in fiction, nonfiction and poetry during February, March and April. These are limited to 12 writers and feature individual conferences and readings by prominent visiting and staff writers. We invite serious writers to participate in workshops, readings and private conferences focusing on the craft of writing. Independent Writers' Retreats are also available year-round for 2-12 weeks for those wishing more solitude. Room/private studio and excellent meals are included in all our programs. Generous work-exchange Fellowships are available."
Costs: All-inclusive fees are $1,200 per 2-week Writing Studio Session and $1,300 per 4-week Writing Residency ($750 for 2 weeks). Financial assistance up to 50% is available based on documented need and several full fellowships are available for Writing Studio Sessions. Write for application.

VILLA MONTALVO ARTIST RESIDENCY PROGRAM, P.O. Box 158, Saratoga CA 95071. Artist Residency Program Manager: Lori A. Wood. Estab. 1942. For "writers, visual artists, musicians and composers. Villa Montalvo is a 1912 Mediterranean-style villa on 176 acres. There are extensive formal gardens and miles of redwood trails. Residencies are from 1-3 months, year-round. Each writer is given a private apartment with kitchen. Apartments for writers have either 2 rooms or a unique balcony or veranda. All apartments are fully-stocked (dishes, linens, etc.), except for food. Artists provide their own food." Accommodates 3 writers (5 artists in total).

Costs: "There are no costs for residency. We require a $100 security deposit, which is returned at end of residency. There are 4 fellowships available each year. These are awarded on the basis of merit to the 4 most highly-rated applicants. One of these must be a writer, and one a woman artist or writer."

To Apply: Application form, résumé, statement of proposed project, 3 professional recommendations, $20 application fee. Brochure/guidelines available for SASE (IRCs).

VIRGINIA CENTER FOR THE CREATIVE ARTS, Mt. San Angelo, Box VCCA, Sweet Briar VA 24595. (804)946-7236. Director: William Smart. Estab. 1971. For writers, visual artists and composers. "Located in a rural setting, within sight of the Blue Ridge Mountains. 450-acre estate, with a herd of Holsteins. Fellows live in a 10-year-old residence; there are 22 bedrooms, dining room, living rooms, library, laundry room, etc. Studios are located some 5 minutes away by foot. There are a few other small buildings, outdoor swimming pool and year-round swimming available across the road at Sweet Briar College." Available year-round for residencies from 2 weeks to 3 months. Provisions for the writer include private bedroom, private soundproof studio and all meals. Accommodates 13 writers.

Costs: "The standard fee is $20/day, which includes everything." Scholarships are available.

To Apply: $15 application fee. Write or call for application form. Deadlines: January 15, May 15, September 15. Brochure/guidelines available for SASE (IRCs).

‡WEYMOUTH CENTER, P.O. Box 939, Southern Pines NC 28388. (919)692-6261. Committee Chair of Writers-in-Residence: Sam Ragan. Estab. 1979. Primarily for North Carolina writers or writers who are connected in some way to North Carolina. "Located in the Georgian manor home of the late Katherine and James Boyd. There are 7 bedrooms, 2 kitchens, 2 libraries and various other rooms (25 in all). The Gardens and grounds are open to the public. The house sits on 24 acres and it is near Weymouth Woods Nature Preserve." Available for 2-week sessions year-round, except first weekend in December. Provisions for the writer include private room and workspace. Kitchen facilities available; writers must provide their own meals. Accommodates 7 writers at a time.

Cotsts: "There is no fee, although donations are accepted to help benefit the house and grounds."

To Apply: Send name, request, brief bio and SASE to Writers-in-Residence Program, P.O. Box 939, Southern Pines NC 28388. Brochures/guidelines available for SASE (IRCs).

THE WOODSTOCK GUILD'S BYRDCLIFFE ARTIST RESIDENCY PROGRAM, 34 Tinker St., Woodstock NY 12498. (914)679-2079. Executive Director: Sondra Howell. Estab. 1902. For writers, playwrights and visual artists. "The historic 600-acre Byrdcliffe Arts Colony is in Woodstock, one and a half miles from the village center. The residency program takes place in the Villetta Inn and Annex and includes a large community living room and common kitchen." Available for four one-month periods starting in June. Provisions for writer include a private room and studio space. "Meals are not provided; residents share a large fully equipped communal kitchen." Accommodates 10 writers.

Costs: $400-500 per month. Fee reductions available for writers staying for more than one period. Financial aid is available. "Potential residents are asked to include a list of savings and holdings, a list of income from the last two years (photocopied tax forms), and a projection of income and expenses for the current year."

To Apply: Submit application with $5 handling fee. Literary artists must submit no more than 12 pages of poetry, one chapter or story-length prose piece, professional résumé, reviews of articles (if available) and 2 references. Residents are selected by a committee of professionals in the arts. Brochure and application available for SASE (IRCs).

HELENE WURLITZER FOUNDATION OF NEW MEXICO, Box 545, Taos NM 87571. (505)758-2413. President: Henry A. Sauerwein, Jr. Estab. 1953. "No restrictions. 12 separate houses, studios." Available April 1-September 30 annually. Provisions for the writer include single house/studio dwelling.

Costs: No charge. (Must supply own food.)

To Apply: Write to the Foundation.

‡YADDO, Box 395, Saratoga Springs NY 12866-0395. Contact: Admissions Committee. Estab. 1926. "Those qualified for invitations to Yaddo are highly qualified writers, visual artists, composers, choreographers, performance artists and film and video artists who have already published, exhibited or performed works of high artistic merit and now have other projects under way. Artists who are able to collaborate are encouraged to apply. Sometimes, but not customarily, the novice may be given admittance to Yaddo, if the advisory committee feels candidate shows promise." Includes mansion, garage, three smaller houses and several studios. Site includes four small lakes, a rose garden, woodland. Two seasons: large season is mid-May-Labor Day; small season is October-May (stays from 2 weeks to 2 months; average stay is 5 weeks). Accommodates 35 writers in large season.
Costs: Voluntary payment of $20/day encouraged. "No artist who is deemed qualified for residency will be denied admission because of inability to contribute."
To Apply: Filing fee is $20 (checks to Corporation of Yaddo). Applications are considered by the Advisory Committee and invitations are issued by April (Deadline: January 15) and September (Deadline: August 1).

Retreats and colonies/changes '93-'94

The following retreats and colonies appeared in the 1993 edition of *Novel & Short Story Writer's Market* but do not appear in the 1994 edition. Those that did not respond to our request for an update appear below without further explanation. If a reason for the omission is available, it is included next to the listing name. There are several reasons why a retreat or colony may not appear—it may not have room for fiction writers this year or it may no longer be open.

Act I Creativity Center
Chateau de Lesvault

Organizations and Resources

When you write, you write alone. It's just you and the typewriter or computer screen. Yet the writing life does not need to be a lonely one. Joining a writing group or organization can be an important step in your writing career. By meeting other writers, discussing your common problems and sharing ideas, you can enrich your writing and increase your understanding of this sometimes difficult, but rewarding life.

The variety of writers' organizations seems endless—encompassing every type of writing and writer—from small, informal groups that gather at a local coffee house twice a month to critique each other's work to regional groups that hold annual conferences to share technique and marketing tips. National organizations and unions fight for writers' rights and higher wages for freelancers, and international groups monitor the treatment of writers around the world.

We're pleased this year to include listings for several very active writers' organizations. In this section you will find state-, province- and region-based groups such as the North Carolina Writers Network, the Society of Midland Authors and the Federation of British Columbia Writers. You'll also find national organizations including the National Writers Association (formerly the National Writers Club) and the Canadian Authors Association. The Romance Writers of America, Mystery Writers of America and the Small Press Writers and Artists Organization are examples of groups devoted to a particular type of writing. Whatever your needs or goals, you're likely to find a group listed here to interest you.

A few organizations helpful to writers are not clubs or groups and they do not fit neatly into any one category. We've included a few of these here, too, as "resources." These are gathering places or helpful services available to writers. The Writer's Center in Bethesda, Maryland, and the Writer's Helpline are two examples of those featured here.

Selecting a writers' organization

To help you make an informed decision, we've provided information on the scope, membership and goals of the organizations listed on these pages. We asked groups to outline the types of memberships available and the benefits members can expect. Most groups will provide additional information for a self-addressed, stamped envelope and you may be able to get a sample copy of their newsletter for a modest fee.

Keep in mind joining a writers' organization is a two-way street. When you join an organization, you become a part of it and, in addition to membership fees, most groups need and want your help. If you want to get involved, opportunities can include everything from chairing a committee to writing for the newsletter to helping set up an annual conference. The level of your involvement is up to you and almost all organizations welcome contributions of time and effort.

The group you select to join depends on a number of factors. As a first step, you must determine what you want from membership in a writers' organization. Then send away for more information on the groups that seem to fit your needs. Start, however, by asking yourself:

● Would I like to meet writers in my city? Am I more interested in making contacts with other writers across the country or around the world?

● Am I interested in a group that will critique my work and give me feedback on my work-in-progress?

- Do I want marketing information and tips on dealing with editors?
- Would I like to meet other writers who write the same type of work I do or am I interested in meeting writers from a variety of fields?
- How much time can I devote to meetings and are regular meetings important to me?
- How much can I afford to pay in dues?
- Would I like to get involved in running the group, working on the group's newsletters, planning a conference?
- Am I interested in a group devoted to writers' rights and treatment or would I rather concentrate on the business of writing?

For more information

Because they do not usually have the resources or inclination to promote themselves widely, finding a local writers' group is usually a word-of-mouth process. If you think you'd like to join a local writer's group and do not know of any in your area, check notices at your library or contact a local college English department. You might also try contacting a group based in your state, province or region listed here for information on smaller groups in your area.

For more information on writers' organizations, check *The Writer's Essential Desk Reference* (Writer's Digest Books, 1507 Dana Ave., Cincinnati OH 45207). Other directories listing organizations for writers include the *Literary Market Place* and *International Literary Market Place* (R.R. Bowker, 121 Chanlon Rd., New Providence NJ 07974). The National Writers Association also maintains a list of writers' organizations.

ARIZONA AUTHORS ASSOCIATION, Suite 117, 3509 E. Shea Blvd., Phoenix AZ 85028. (602)942-4240. President: Gerry Benninger. Estab. 1978. Number of Members: 500. Type of Memberships: Professional, writers with published work; associate, writers working toward publication; affiliate, professionals in the publishing industry. "Primarily an Arizona organization but open to writers nationally." Benefits include bimonthly newsletter, discount rates on seminars, workshops and newsletter ads, discounts on writing books, discounts at bookstores, copy shops, critique groups and networking events. "Sponsors workshops on a variety of topics of interest to writers (e.g. publishing, marketing, structure, genres)." Publishes *Authors Newsletter*, bimonthly ($25/yr.). Dues: Professional and associate, $40/year; affiliate: $45/year; student: $25/year. Holds monthly critique group, quarterly networking events and annual literary contest. Send SASE (IRCs) for information.

ASSOCIATED WRITING PROGRAMS, Old Dominion University, Norfolk VA 23529-0079. (804)683-3839. Publications Editor: D.W. Fenza. Estab. 1967. Number of Members: 1,300 (individual members). Types of Membership: Institutional (universities); graduate students; *Chronicle* subscribers. Open to any person interested in writing; most members are students or faculty of university writing programs (worldwide). Benefits include information on creative writing programs; grants and awards to writers; a job placement service for writers in academe and beyond. AWP holds an Annual Conference in a different US city every spring; also conducts an annual Award Series in poetry, short story collections, novel and creative nonfiction, in which winner receives $1,500 honorarium and publication by a participating press. AWP acts as agent for finalists in Award Series and tries to place their manuscript with publishers throughout the year. Manuscripts accepted January 1-February 28 only. SASE (IRCs) for guidelines. Publishes *AWP Chronicle* 6 times/year; 3 times/academic semester. Available to members for free. Nonmembers may order a subscription $18/yr. Also publishes the *AWP Official Guide to Writing Programs* which lists about 330 creative writing programs in universities across the country and in Canada. *Guide* is updated every 2 years; cost is $15.95 plus $3 for library rate shipping or $4 for 1st class. Dues: $45 for individual membership and an additional $37 for our placement service. AWP keeps dossiers on file and sends them to school or organization of person's request. You must be a member to be a part of the placement service. Holds two meetings per year for the Board of Directors. Send SASE for information.

AUSTIN WRITERS' LEAGUE RESOURCE CENTER, Austin Writers' League, E-2, 1501 W. 5th, Austin TX 78703. (512)499-8914. Executive Director: Angela Smith. Estab. 1981. Number of Members: 1,600. Types of Memberships: Regular, student/senior citizen, organization, corporate. Monthly meetings and use of resource center/library is open to the public. "Membership includes both aspiring and professional writers, all ages and all ethnic groups." Job bank is also open to the public. Public also has access to technical assistance. Partial and full scholarships offered for some programs. Of 1,600 members, 800 reside in Austin. Remaining 800 live all over the US and in other countries. Benefits include monthly newsletter, monthly meetings, study groups, resource center/library-checkout privileges, discounts on workshops, seminars, classes, job bank, access to insurance information, discounts on books and tapes, participation in awards programs, technical/marketing assistance, copyright forms and information, access to computers and printers. Center has 4 rooms plus 2 offices and storage area. Public space includes reception and job bank area; conference/classroom; library/computer room; and copy/mail room. Library includes 800 titles. Two computers and printers are available for member use. Sponsors fall and spring workshops, weekend seminars, informal classes, sponsorships for special events such as readings, production of original plays, media conferences, creative writing programs for children and youth; Violet Crown Book Awards, newsletter writing awards, Young Texas Writers awards contests for various anthologies. Publishes *Austin Writer* (monthly newsletter), membership/subscription: $40, $35-students, senior citizens. Monthly meetings. Study groups set their own regular meeting schedules. Send SASE (IRCs) for information.

THE AUTHORS GUILD, 330 W. 42nd St., New York NY 10036. (212)563-5904. Executive Director: Robin Davis Miller. Estab. 1921. Number of Members: 6,500. Membership dues based on income scale from writing. Open to published authors or those with firm contract offers. "The Authors Guild is a national society of professional authors." Benefits through "collective power and voice," achieving many direct economic benefits from improvement of contracts and royalty statement to the protection of authors' First Amendment rights. Other benefits: Contract advice, surveys and reports and assistance, group insurance available. Publishes the *Authors Guild Bulletin*, containing information on matters of interest to writers. Also publishes *Your Book Contract*, a 35-page pamphlet analyzing publishing contracts and *The Authors Guild Recommended Trade Book Contract and Guide*. Dues: $90 for first year; then dues are based on income scale from $90-500, depending on writing income. Send SASE for information.

CALIFORNIA WRITERS' CLUB, 2214 Derby St., Berkeley CA 94705. (510)841-1217. Estab. 1909. Number of Members: 900. Type of Memberships: Associate and active. Open to: "All published writers and those deemed able to publish within five years." Benefits include speakers—authors, editors, agents, anyone connected with writing—heard at monthly meetings, marketing information, workshops, camaraderie of fellow writers. Sponsors workshops, conferences, awards programs/contests. Publishes a monthly newsletter at state level, monthly newsletter at branch level. Available to members only. Dues: $35/year. Meets monthly. Send SASE for information.

✸CANADIAN AUTHORS ASSOCIATION, #500, 275 Slater St., Ottawa, Ontario K1P 5H9 Canada. (613)233-2846. Fax: (613)235-8237. President: Jeffrey Holmes. Estab. 1921. Number of Members: 800. Type of Memberships: Member (voting); Associate (non-voting). "Member must have minimum sales to commercial publications. Associates need not have published yet." National scope (Canada) with 17 regional branches. Benefits include networking, marketing advice, legal advice, several publications, annual conference, awards programs. Sponsors workshops, conferences, awards programs/contests. Publishes *Canadian Author*, quarterly $15 (Canadian)/year; $20 (Canadian) for foreign and *National Newsline* (to members only). Dues: $107 (Canadian). "Each branch meets monthly." Send SASE for information.

FAIRBANKS ARTS ASSOCIATION, P.O. Box 72786, Fairbanks AK 99707-2786. (907)456-6485. Contact: Al Geist, editor of *Fairbanks Arts*. Estab. 1966. Members: 400. "Membership is open to anyone interested in supporting Fairbanks' arts and cultural community." Scope: Regional (interior Alaska) although a number of members are scattered throughout Alaska and the lower 48 states. Benefits include reduced fees for technical and professional workshops; assistance in all of art (or technique, great writing, resumes, etc.); invitations to all association events (including gallery openings, political forums, workshops, etc.); group medical insurance (including studio insurance); discount on all items purchased through gallery store; subscription to *Fairbanks Arts*. Sponsors several art-related events. "We publish *Fairbanks Arts*, a bimonthly magazine that is also sent to 100+ subscribers and sold in local retail outlets throughout interior Alaska." Subscriptions are $15/year. Membership $25/year (includes magazine, etc.). Board of Directors meets 1st Thursday every month, plus monthly visual, literary and community arts meetings. Send SASE for information.

✸FEDERATION OF BRITISH COLUMBIA WRITERS, MPO Box 2206, Vancouver, British Columbia V6B 3W2 Canada. Manager: Corey Van't Haaff. Estab. 1982. Number of Members: 650. Types of Membership: regular and subsidized for those with limited income. "Open to established and emerging writers in any genre, provincial-wide." Benefits include newsletter, liaison with funding bodies, publications, workshops, readings, literary contest, various retail and educational discounts. Sponsors readings and workshops. Publishes a newsletter 4 times/year, included in membership. Dues: $50 Canadian (regional) regular; $25 limited income. Send SASE for information.

HORROR WRITERS OF AMERICA, 5336 Reef Way, Oxnard CA 93035. (805)985-2320. Executive Secretary: V. Aalko. Write for more information.

INTERNATIONAL ASSOCIATION OF CRIME WRITERS (NORTH AMERICAN BRANCH), JAF Box 1500, New York NY 10116. (212)757-3915. Executive Director: Mary A. Frisque. Estab. 1987. Number of Members: 225. Open to: "Published authors of crime fiction, nonfiction, screenplays and professionals in the mystery field (agents, editors, booksellers). Our branch covers the US and Canada, there are other branches world-wide." Benefits include information about crime-writing world-wide and publishing opportunities in other countries. "We sponsor annual members' receptions during the Edgar awards week in New York and in the spring and in the fall we host a reception at the Bouchercon. We also have occasional receptions for visiting authors/publishers. We give an annual award, the North American Hammett Prize, for the best work (fiction or nonfiction) of literary excellence in the crime writing field. We publish a quarterly newsletter, *Border Patrol*, available to members only." Dues: $50 year. Send SASE (IRCs) for information.

‡JUST BUFFALO LITERARY CENTER, INC., 493 Franklin St., Buffalo NY 14202-1109. (716)881-3211. Executive Director: Deborah Ott. "Just Buffalo is a community-based literary center that recognizes the contemporary writer as a cultural bridge among peoples and supports the development, the study, and the appreciation of contemporary writing in its cultural and ethnic diversity, through performance, instruction and promotion. Just Buffalo seeks to amplify voices not always heard in the mainstream, and brings contemporary literature to people of all ages, ethnic, educational and economic backgrounds to help them appreciate the lives, experiences and communicative arts of others. Just Buffalo's programs include: readings, lectures, performances, residencies and workshops by prominent and emerging writers; a Writers-in-Education component in the Buffalo schools, whose purpose is to enrich the lives of children through language arts; Spoken Arts Radio, a bi-weekly literary arts broadcast, and interdisciplinary Programs in music and poetry with writers, composers and musicians of African American and Latin American descent." Send SASE (IRCs) for information.

MYSTERY WRITERS OF AMERICA (MWA), 6th Floor, 17 E. 47th St., New York NY 10017. Executive Director: Priscilla Ridgway. Estab. 1945. Number of Members: 2,500. Type of memberships: Active members (professional, published writers of fiction or nonfiction crime/mystery/suspense); Associate members (professionals in allied fields, i.e. editor, publisher, writer, critic, news reporter, publicist, librarian, bookseller, etc.); Corresponding members (writers qualified for active membership who live outside the US). Unpublished writers, students and mystery fans may petition for Affiliate member status. Benefits include promotion and protection of writers' rights and interests, including counsel and advice on contracts, MWA courses and workshops, a national office with an extensive library, an annual conference featuring the Edgar Allan Poe Awards, the *MWA Mystery Writer's Handbook*, the *MWA Anthology*, a national newsletter, regional conferences, meetings and newsletters. Newsletter, *The Third Degree*, is published 10 times/year for members. Annual dues: $65 for US members; $32.50 for Corresponding members.

THE NATIONAL LEAGUE OF AMERICAN PEN WOMEN, INC., Headquarters: Pen Arts Building, 1300 17th St. NW, Washington DC 20036. (202)785-1997. Contact: National President. Estab. 1897. Number of Members: 5,000. Type of Memberships: Three classifications: Arts, letters, music composition. Open to: Professional women. "Professional to us means our membership is only open to women who sell their art, writings or music compositions. We have 200 branches in the continental US, Hawaii and the Republic of Panama. Some branches have as many as 100 members, some as few as 10 or 12. It is necessary to have 5 members to form a new branch." Benefits include marketing advice, use of a facility, critiques and competitions. Our facility is national headquarters which has a few rooms available for Pen Women visiting the D.C. area, and for Board members in session 3 times a year. Branch and State Association competitions, as well as biennial convention competitions. Offers a research library of books and histories of our organization only. Sponsors awards biennially to Pen Women in each classification: Art, letters, music and $1,000 award biennially to nonPen Women in each classification for women over 35 years of age who wish to pursue special work in her field. *The Pen Woman* is our membership magazine, published 6 times a year, free to members, $7 a year for nonmember subscribers. Dues: $25/year for national organization, from $5-10/year for branch membership and from $1-5 for state association dues. Branches hold regular meeting each month, September through May except in northern states which meet usually March through September (for travel convenience). Send SASE for information.

NATIONAL WRITERS ASSOCIATION, (formerly National Writers Club), Suite 424, 1450 S. Havana, Aurora CO 80012. (303)751-7844. Executive Director: Sandy Whelchel. Estab. 1937. Number of Members: 4,000. Types of Memberships: Regular membership for those without published credits; professional membership for those with published credits. Open to: Any interested writer. National/International plus we have 16 chapters in various states. Benefits include critiques, marketing advice, editing, literary agency, complaint service, chapbook publishing service, research reports on various aspects of writing, 4 contests, National Writers Press—self-publishing operation, computer bulletin board service, regular newsletter with updates on marketing, bimonthly magazine on writing related subjects, discounts on supplies, magazines and some services. Sponsors periodic conferences and workshops: short story contest opens April, closes July 1; novel contest opens December, closes April 28. Publishes *Flash Market News* (monthly publication for professional members only); *NWC Newsletter* (monthly publication for members only); *Authorship Magazine* (bimonthly publication available by subscription $18 to nonmembers). Dues: $50 regular; $60 professional. For professional membership requirement is equivalent of 3 articles or stories in a national or regional magazine; a book published by a royalty publisher, a play, TV script, or movie produced. An initial $15 set up fee is required for first time members. Send SASE (IRCs) for information. Chapters hold meetings on a monthly basis.

NEW HAMPSHIRE WRITERS AND PUBLISHERS PROJECT, P.O. Box 150, Portsmouth NH 03802-0150. (603)436-6331. Executive Director: Barbara Tsairis. Estab. 1988. Number of Members: 395. Type of Memberships: Senior/student; individual; business; institutional. Open to anyone interested in the literary arts—writers (fiction, nonfiction, journalists, poets, scriptwriters, etc.), teachers, librarians, publishers and *readers*. Statewide scope. Benefits include a bimonthly publication featuring articles about NH writers and publishers; leads for writers, new books listings; and NH literary news. Also—use of resource library and discounts on workshops, readings, conferences. Dues: $25 for individuals; $15 for seniors, students; $50 for businesses; $35 for libraries and other institutions. Send SASE for information.

‡NORTH CAROLINA WRITERS' NETWORK, P.O. Box 954, Carrboro NC 27510. (919)967-9540. Executive Director: Marsha Warren. Estab. 1985. Number of Members: 1,600. Open to: All writers, all levels of skill and friends of literature. Membership is approximately 1,400 in North Carolina and 200 in 28 other states. Benefits include bimonthly newsletter, reduced rates for fall conference, workshops, etc., use of critiquing service, use of library and resource center, press release and publicity service, information database(s). Sponsors annual Fall Conference, Creative Journalism Competition, statewide workshops, Writers & Readers Series, Randall Jarrell Poetry Prize, Poetry Chapbook Competition, Thomas Wolfe Fiction Prize, Fiction Competition, One-Act Play Competition. Publishes *The Network News*, 24-pages, bimonthly. Subscription included in dues. Dues: $25/year, $15/year (students to age 23, seniors 65+ and disabled). Meetings held annually in spring; again at fall conference. Send SASE for information.

OZARKS WRITERS LEAGUE, P.O. Box 1433, Branson MO 65616. (417)334-6016. Board Member: Debbie Redford. Estab. 1983. Number of Members: 250. Open to: Anyone interested in writing, photography and art. Regional Scope: Missouri, Arkansas, Oklahoma, Kansas—"Greater Ozarks" area. Benefits include mutual inspiration and support; information exchange. Sponsors quarterly seminars/workshops, two annual writing competitions, one annual photography competition, special conferences. Publishes quarterly newsletter, the *Owls Hoot*, available to nonmembers for limited receipt. Dues: $10/year. Meets quarterly—February, May, August, November. Send SASE for information.

PHILADELPHIA WRITERS ORGANIZATION, P.O. Box 42497, Philadelphia PA 19101. (215)649-8918. Administrative Coordinator: Jane Brooks. Estab. 1981. Number of members: 250. Types of membership: full (voting), associate, student. Open to any writer, published or unpublished. Scope is tri-state area—Pennsylvania, Delaware, New Jersey, but mostly Philadelphia area. Benefits include medical insurance (for full members only), monthly meetings with guest panelists, Spring workshop (full day) plus Editors Marketplace. Publishes a monthly newsletter for members only. Dues: $50 (full and associate); $25-student. Proof of publication required for full members (minimum of 2,000 words). Meets monthly throughout year except July and August. Send SASE for information.

‡ROMANCE WRITERS OF AMERICA (RWA), Suite 315, 13700 Veterans Memorial, Houston TX 77014. (713)440-6885. Office Supervisor: Linda Fisher. Estab. 1981. Number of members: over 6,500. Type of Memberships: General and associate. Open to: "Any person actively pursuing a writing career in the romance field." Membership is international. Benefits include annual conference, contests and awards, magazine, forums with publishing representatives, network for published authors, group insurance, regional newsletters and more. Dues: $55/new members; $45/renewal fee. Send SASE (IRCs) for information.

SCIENCE FICTION AND FANTASY WORKSHOP, 1193 South 1900 East, Salt Lake City UT 84108. (801)582-2090. Director/Editor: Kathleen D. Woodbury. Estab. 1980. Number of members: 400. Types of membership: "Active" is listed in the membership roster and so is accessible to all other members; "inactive" is not listed in the roster. Open to "anyone, anywhere. Our scope is international although over 96% of our members are in the US." Benefits include "several different critique groups: short stories, novels, articles, screenplays, poetry, etc. We also offer services such as copyediting, working out the numbers in planet building (give us the kind of planet you want and we'll tell you how far it is from the sun, etc.—or tell us what kind of sun you have and we'll tell you what your planet is like), brainstorming story, fragments or cultures or aliens, a clearing house for information on groups who write/critique science fiction and fantasy in your area, etc. We sponsored a writing contest at a science fiction convention last year and plan to do so this year." Publishes *SF and Fantasy Workshop* (monthly); non-members subscribe for $10/year; samples are $1 and trial subscription: $6/6 issues. "We are starting publication on a quarterly basis that will contain outlines, synopses, proposals that authors submitted or used for novels that sold. The purpose is to show new and aspiring novelists what successful outlines, etc. look like, and to provide authors (with books coming out) advance publicity. Authors may contact Kathleen about publication. Cost is $2.50/issue or $9/4 issues. We also publish a fiction booklet on an irregular basis. It contains one short story and three critiques by professional writers. Cost to anyone is $5/5 issues or $8/10 issues." Dues: Members pay a one-time fee of $5 (to cover the cost of the roster and the new-member information packet) and the annual $10 subscription fee. To renew membership, members simply renew their subscriptions. "Our organization is strictly by mail." Send SASE (IRCs) for information.

SCIENCE FICTION AND FANTASY WRITERS OF AMERICA, INC., 5 Winding Brook Dr. #1B, Guilderland NY 12084. (518)869-5361. Executive Secretary: Peter Dennis Pautz. Estab. 1965. Number of Members: 1,200. Type of Memberships: Active, associate, affiliate, institutional, estate. Open to: "Professional writers, editors, anthologists, artists in the science fiction/fantasy genres and allied professional individuals and institutions. Our membership is international; we currently have members throughout Europe, Australia, Central and South America, Canada and some in Asia." We produce a variety of journals for our members, annual membership directory and provide a grievance committee, publicity committee, circulating book plan and access to TEIGIT medical/life/disability insurance. We award the SFWA Nebula Awards each year for outstanding achievement in the genre at novel, novella, novelet and short story lengths." Quarterly *SFWA Bulletin* to members; nonmembers may subscribe at $15/4 issues within US/Canada; $18.50 overseas. Bimonthly *SFWA Forum* for active members only. Annual *SFWA Membership Directory* for members; available to professional organizations for $60. Active membership requires professional sale in the US of at least 3 short stories or 1 full-length book. Affiliate or associate membership requires at least 1 professional sale in the US or other professional sale in the US or other professional involvement in the field. Dues are pro-rated quarterly; info available upon request. Business meetings are held during Annual Nebula Awards weekend and usually during the annual World SF Convention. Send SASE (IRCs) for information.

SCIENCE FICTION WRITERS OF EARTH, P.O. Box 121293, Fort Worth TX 76121. (817)451-8674. Administrator: Gilbert Gordon Reis. Estab. 1980. Number of Members: 64-100. Open to: Unpublished writers of science fiction and fantasy short stories. "We have a few writers in Europe, Canada and

Australia, but the majority are from the US. Writers compete in our annual contest. This allows the writer to find out where he/she stands in writing ability. Winners often receive requests for their story from publishers. Many winners have told us that they believe that placing in the top ten of our contest gives them recognition and has assisted in getting their first story published." Dues: One must submit a science fiction or fantasy short story to our annual contest to be a member. Cost is $5 for membership and first story. $2 for each additional ms. The nominating committee meets several times a year to select the top ten stories of the annual contest. Author Edward Bryant selects the winners from the top ten stories. Information about the organization is available for SASE (IRCs).

SMALL PRESS WRITERS AND ARTISTS ORGANIZATION (SPWAO), 309 N. Humphrey Circle, Shawano WI 54166. (715)524-2750. SPWAO President: Mike Olson. Estab. 1977. Number of members: 300-400. Open to all members (anyone who paid dues for current year). Scope is international. "A service organization dedicated to the promotion of excellence in the small press fields of science fiction, fantasy and horror." Benefits include market news, critiquing services (art, poetry, fiction), grievance arbitration, reviews, nonfiction articles and essays, editor-mentor program, info-swap/collaboration service, etc. "We've added two new benefits for members: publisher's clearance, and newsletters on tape for the blind or visually impaired." Facilities include SPWAO library/archives. Sponsors awards and contests; have held conventions in conjunction with known cons—NECON, BUBONICON. Publishes *SPWAO Newsletter* (monthly), 3 most recent issues available to nonmembers for $4 postage; *Showcase* (yearly or as funding allows), $8.95; *Alpha Gallery* (funding allows) $7.50. Dues: US: $17.50 initial, $15 renew; 2 year new member option $28.50; *rebate available new members joining under current year plan after May 1*; Canadian: $20 new, $17.50 renew; International: $20 new and renew. Send SASE (IRCs) for information.

SOCIETY OF MIDLAND AUTHORS, % Ford-Choyke, 29 E. Division St., Chicago IL 60610. (312)337-1482. President: Phyllis Ford-Choyke. Estab. 1915. Number of Members: 180. Type of memberships: Regular, published authors and performed playwrights; Associate, librarians, editors, etc., others involved in publishing. Open to: Residents or natives of 12 midland states: Illinois, Iowa, Indiana, Michigan, Wisconsin, Nebraska, S. Dakota, N. Dakota, Ohio, Kansas, Missouri and Minnesota. Benefits include newsletter, listing in directory. Sponsors annual awards in 7 categories, with upwards of $300 prizes. Awards dinner in May at 410 Club (Wrigley Bldg.), Chicago. Publishes newsletter several times/year. Dues: $25/year. Holds "5 program meetings/year, open to public at 410 Club, Chicago, featuring writers, editors, etc. on bookwriting subjects, setlling, etc." Brochures are available for SASE.

WASHINGTON CHRISTIAN WRITERS FELLOWSHIP, P.O. Box 11337, Bainbridge Island WA 98110. (206)842-9103. Director: Elaine Wright Colvin. Estab. 1982. Number of Members: 300. Open to: All writers. Scope is state-wide. Benefits include meetings, speakers, how-to critiques, private consultation. Sponsors a monthly seminar first Saturday each month 9:30 am-2 pm. Publishes a bimonthly newsletter, *W.I.N.* Dues: $20. Meetings $3 (members), $6 (non members). Meets monthly—first Saturday. Brochures are available for SASE.

WASHINGTON INDEPENDENT WRITERS, #220, 733 15th St. NW, Washington DC 20005. (202)347-4973. Executive Director: Isolde Chapin. Estab. 1975. Number of Members: 2,500. Type of Memberships: Full, associate, senior, student, dual. Open to any writer or person who has an interest in writing. Regional scope. Benefits include group health insurance, grievance committee, job bank, social events, workshops, small groups, networking, etc. Sponsors monthly workshops, spring conference. Publishes *The Independent Writer* newsletter, published 11 times/year. Newsletter subscription $35/year, must live outside metropolitan area. Dues: $75/year full and associate members; $45 senior and student members; $120 dual members (2 writers living at the same address). Holds monthly workshops and small group meetings. Send SASE for information.

WESTERN WRITERS OF AMERICA, Office of the Secretary-Treasurer, 416 Bedford, El Paso TX 79922. (915)532-3222. Secretary-Treasurer: Nancy Hamilton. Estab. 1953. Number of Members: 528. Type of Membership: Active, Associate, Patron. Open to: Professional, published writers who have multiple publications of fiction or nonfiction (usually at least three) about the West. Associate membership open to those with one book, a lesser number of short stories or publications or participation in the field such as editors, agents, reviewers, librarians, television producers, directors (dealing with the West). Patron memberships open to corporations, organizations and individuals with an interest in the West. Scope is international. Benefits: "By way of publications and conventions, members are kept abreast of developments in the field of Western literature and the publishing field, marketing requirements, income tax problems, copyright law, research facilities and techniques, and new publications. At conventions members have the opportunity for one-on-one conferences with editor, publishers and agents." Sponsors an annual four-day conference during fourth week of June featuring panels, lectures and seminars on publishing, writing and research. Includes the Spur Awards to honor authors of the best Western literature of the previous year. Publishes a newsletter six times/year for members. Also publishes *The Roundup* (reviews of Western fiction and works by Western writers) available to nonmembers for $30. Publishes membership directory. Dues; $60 for active membership, $60 for associate membership, $100 for patron. For information on Spur Awards, send SASE.

THE WRITERS ALLIANCE, 12 Skylark Lane, Stony Brook NY 11790. Executive Director: Kiel Stuart. Estab. 1979. Number of Members: 125. Open to all writers: Professional, aspiring, those who have to write business memos or brochures; those interested in desktop publishing. National scope. Benefits: Members can run one classified or display ad in each issue of membership newsletter, *Keystrokes*; which also provides software and hardware reviews, how-to articles, market information and general support. Sponsors local writer's workshops. Publishes *Keystrokes*, quarterly, $15/year (payable to Exec. Dir. Kiel Stuart) covers both the cost of membership and newsletter. Local writer's critique group meets every two weeks. Send SASE for information.

THE WRITER'S CENTER, 4508 Walsh St., Bethesda MD 20815. (301)654-8664. Director: Jane Fox. Estab. 1977. Number of Members: 2,200. Open to: Anyone interested in writing. Scope is regional DC, Maryland, Virginia, West Virginia, Pennsylvania. Benefits include newsletter, discounts in bookstore, workshops, public events, subscriptions to *Poet Lore*, use of equipment and library. Center offers workshops, reading series, research library, equipment, newsletter and limited workspace. Sponsors workshops, conferences, award for narrative poem. Publishes *Carousel*, bimonthly. Nonmembers can pick it up at the Center. Dues: $30/year. Fees vary with service, see publications. Brochures are available for SASE.

✷WRITERS' FEDERATION OF NEW BRUNSWICK, 103 Church St., P.O. Box 37, Station A, Fredericton, New Brunswick E3B 4Y2 Canada. Project Coordinator: Anna Mae Snider. Estab. 1983. Number of Members: 210. Membership is open to anyone interested in writing. "This a provincial organization. Benefits include promotion of members' works through newsletter announcements and readings and launchings held at fall festival and annual general meeting, participation in a Writers-in-Schools Program, manuscript reading service, workshops held at fall and spring events. The WFNB sponsors a fall festival and an annual general meeting which features workshops, readings and book launchings." There is also an annual literary competition, open to residents of New Brunswick only, which has prizes of $200, $100 and $30 in four categories: Fiction, nonfiction, children's literature and poetry and $400 prize for the best manuscript of poems (48 pgs.) Publishes a quarterly newsletter. Dues: $15/year. Board of Directors meets approximately 5 times a year. Annual General Meeting is held in April of each year. Send SASE for information.

✷WRITERS' FEDERATION OF NOVA SCOTIA, Suite 901, 1809 Barrington St., Halifax, Nova Scotia B3J 3K8 Canada. Executive Director: Jane Buss. Estab. 1976. Number of Members: 500. Type of Memberships: General membership, student membership, Nova Scotia Writers' Council membership (professional), Honorary Life Membership. Open to: Anyone who writes, and is a resident or native of Nova Scotia. Provincial scope, with a few members living elsewhere in the country or the world. Benefits include advocacy of all kinds for writers, plus such regular programs as workshops and regular publications, including directories and a newsletter. Sponsors workshops, two annual conferences (one for general membership, the other for the professional wing), two book awards, one annual competition for unpublished manuscripts in seven categories; a writers in the schools program, a manuscript reading service, reduced photocopying and typing rates, a typing referral service. Publishes *Eastword*, 6 issues annually, available by subscription for $30 (Canadian) to nonmembers. Dues: $30/year (Canadian). Holds an annual general meeting, an annual meeting of the Nova Scotia Writers' Council, several board meetings annually. Send 5×7 SASE for information.

✷WRITERS GUILD OF ALBERTA, WordWorks Building, 10523-100 Avenue, Edmonton, Alberta T5J 0A8 Canada. (403)426-5892. Executive Director: Miki Andrejevic. Estab. 1980. Number of Members: 700. Membership open to current and past residents of Alberta. Regional (provincial) scope. Benefits include discounts on programs offered; manuscript evaluation service available; bimonthly newsletter; contacts; use of photocopier at discount; info on workshops, retreats, readings, etc. Sponsors workshops 2 times/year, retreats 3 times/year, annual conference, annual book awards program (Alberta

DON'T TAKE ANY CHANCES GETTING YOUR MANUSCRIPT PUBLISHED!

Stop! Before you send off that manuscript, are you sure it will reach the right buyer, at the right address? Is the publisher still looking for the type of fiction you're submitting? You worked so hard getting it right, why take a chance? Be sure! Check it out in the most current edition of *Novel and Short Story Writer's Market!*

You work hard... and you deserve the best opportunity to get published. The only way to do that is to make your submission as accurate as possible. And *1995 Novel & Short Story Writer's Market* can help ensure that accuracy. With constant changes in the industry it's difficult to keep up with who the buyers are, what they're looking for, where and how to submit your work, and what they're paying; not to mention finding all the new publishers who are looking for your work. You'll be sure to have the latest information at your fingertips by ordering the 1995 edition of *Novel & Short Story Writer's Market* **now**.

When you use the order card below, you'll also receive our price guarantee — you'll get the 1995 edition at the same low price as the 1994 edition — just $19.95 (plus postage).

So, don't take any chances when submitting your work! Order today and we'll send you the *1995 Novel & Short Story Writer's Market* as soon as it's available — February 1995!

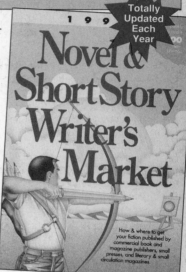

See other side for more books to help you get published!

To order, drop this postpaid card in the mail.

30-DAY MONEY BACK GUARANTEE

OFFER EXPIRES DECEMBER 31, 1995!

☐ **YES!** I want the most current edition of *Novel & Short Story Writer's Market.*. Please send me the 1995 edition at the 1994 price -- $19.95.* (NOTE: *The 1995 Edition* will be ready for shipment in February 1995.) #10405

Also send me the following books NOW,

_____ (#10366) *20 Master Plots (And How to Build Them)*, $16.95*

_____ (#10393) *Writing the Blockbuster Novel*, $17.95*

_____ (#10373) *Private Eyes*, $15.95*

_____ (#10374) *Police Procedural*, $16.95*

_____ (#10318) *Cause of Death* $15.95*

_____ (#10319) *Scene of Crime* $15.95*

_____ (#10176) *Armed & Dangerous*, $14.95*

_____ (#10177) *Deadly Doses*, $16.95*

*Plus postage & handling: $3.00 for one book, $1.00 for each additional book. Ohio residents add 5.5% sales tax.

☐ Please send me a FREE catalog of your books for writers.

Visa/MasterCard Orders Call Toll-Free 1-800-289-0963

☐ Payment enclosed (Slip this card and payment into an envelope)

☐ Please charge my:

☐ Visa   ☐ MasterCard   Exp._____

Acct # _____

Signature _____

Name _____

Address _____

City _____

State _____ Zip _____

6543

MORE BOOKS TO HELP YOU GET PUBLISHED!

20 Master Plots (And How to Build Them), *by Ronald B. Tobias* — By analyzing twenty plots that recur through all fiction — no matter what the genre — you'll learn what makes a successful plot and how to integrate those components into your own work.
236 pages/$16.95, hardcover

Writing the Blockbuster Novel, *by Albert Zuckerman* — Here successful agent Zuckerman explains what the essential elements are — memorable characters, exotic settings, big scenes and clashing conflicts — and shows how to put them to work in your own books.
224 pages/$17.95, hardcover

The HOWDUNIT Series

Get your facts straight when "killing off" your fictional characters. You'll hook your reader and weave a credible story with these authentic details.

Scene of the Crime: A Writer's Guide to Crime-Scene Investigations, *by Anne Wingate, Ph.D.*
240 pages/$15.95, paperback

Cause of Death: A Writer's Guide to Death, Murder & Forensic Medicine, *by Keith D. Wilson, M.D.*
240 pages/$15.95, paperback

Armed & Dangerous: A Writer's Guide to Weapons, *by Michael Newton*
186 pages/$14.95, paperback

Deadly Doses: A Writer's Guide to Poisons, *by Serita Deborah Stevens with Ann Klarner*
298 pages/$16.95, paperback

Private Eyes: A Writer's Guide to Private Investigations, *by Hal Blythe, Charlie Sweet & John Landreth*
208 pages/$15.95, paperback

Police Procedural: A Writer's Guide to the Police and How They Work, *by Russell Bintliff*
272 pages/$16.95, paperback

Use coupon on the other side to order these books today!

writers only). Publishes *WestWord* 6 times/year; available for $55/year (Canadian) to nonmembers. Dues: $55/year for regular membership; $20/year senior/students/limited income; $100/year donating membership—charitable receipt issued (Canadian funds). Organized monthly meetings. Send SASE for information.

WRITER'S HELPLINE, Craigville Press, P.O. Box 86, Centerville MA 02632. Proprietor: Marion Vuilleumier. Estab. 1991. Writers' Helpline number is 1-900-988-1838 ext. 549. Cost is $2/minute. Must be 18 years or older. "For the latest market needs and writing tips dial the Writer's Helpline on your Touchtone phone—available 24 hrs., 7 days, messages changed as new information is received from agents, editors, publishers, etc. Messages are brief, so for the price of a long distance phone call, the latest news is available."

WRITERS INFORMATION NETWORK, P.O. Box 11337, Bainbridge Island WA 98110. (206)842-9103. Director: Elaine Wright Colvin. Estab. 1980. Number of Members: 1,000. Open to: All interested in writing for religious publications/publishers. Scope is national and several foreign countries. Benefits include bimonthly newsletter, market news, advocacy/grievance procedures, professional advice, writers conferences, press cards, author referral, free consultation. Sponsors workshops, conferences throughout the country each year—mailing list and advertised in *W.I.N.* newsletter. Bimonthly newsletter: $20 US; $30 foreign/year. Dues: $20 US (newsletter subscription included). Holds monthly meetings in Seattle, WA. Brochures are available for SASE (IRCs).

THE WRITERS ROOM, INC., 5th Floor, 153 Waverly Place, New York NY 10014. (212)807-9519. Executive Director: Renata Miller. Estab. 1978. Number of Members: 150. Open to: Any writer who shows a serious commitment to writing. "We serve a diverse population of writers, but most of our residents live in or around the NYC area. We encourage writers from around the country (and world!) to apply for residency if they plan to visit NYC for a while." Benefits include 24-hour access to the facility. "We provide desk space, storage areas for computers, typewriters, etc., a kitchen where coffee and tea are always available, bathrooms, a library and lounge. We also offer in-house workshops on topics of practical importance to writers and monthly readings of work-in-progress." Dues: $165 per quarter/year. Send SASE for application and background information.

THE WRITERS' WORKSHOP, P.O. Box 696, Asheville NC 28802. (800)627-0142. Executive Director: Karen Tager. Estab. 1984. Number of Members: 1,250. Type of Memberships: Student/low income $15; family/organization $40; individual $25; friend $50. Open to all writers. Scope is national. Benefits include discounts on workshops, quarterly newsletter, admission to Annual Celebration every summer, critiquing services through the mail. Center offers reading room, assistance with editing your work, contacts with NY writers and agents. Publishes a newsletter. Available to nonmembers. Published 4 times/year. $15 low income; $25 other. Dues: $15 low income/student, $25 individual (includes newsletter). Meets several times a year. Annual meeting is in July. Brochures are available for SASE.

Organizations and resources/changes '93-'94

The following organizations and resources appeared in the 1993 edition of *Novel & Short Story Writer's Market* but do not appear in the 1994 edition. Those that did not respond to our request for an update appear below without further explanation. There are several reasons why an organization may not appear—its membership may be too full or the group may have disbanded.

The Nebraska Writers Guild
Western Writers of America
Writers Connection

Publications of Interest to Fiction Writers

This section features listings for magazines and newsletters that focus on writing or the publishing industry. While many of these are not markets for fiction, they do offer articles, marketing advice or other information valuable to the fiction writer. Several magazines in this section offer actual market listings while others feature reviews of books in the field and news on the industry.

The timeliness factor is a primary reason most writers read periodicals. Changes in publishing happen very quickly and magazines can help you keep up with the latest news. Some magazines listed here, including *Writer's Digest* and the *Canadian Writer's Journal* cover the entire field of writing, while others such as *The Mystery Review* and *Regency Plume* focus on a particular type of writing. We've also added publications which focus on a particular segment of the publishing industry, including *Small Magazine Review* and *The Small Press Book Review*.

You will also find information on other publications for writers in the introductions to the sections in this book. Many of the literary and commercial magazines for writers listed in the markets sections are also helpful. Keep an eye on the newsstand and the library shelves for others and let us know if you've found a publication particularly useful.

‡AFRAID: The Newsletter for Horror Professionals, #4, 857 N. Oxford Ave., Los Angeles CA 90029. Editor: Mike Baker. Monthly. "A monthly newsletter (20 pages) for horror writers. Regular columns by pros like Gary Brandner, Brian Hodge and others, plus industry news, in-depth interviews, reviews and guest contributors." Lists fiction markets. Reviews novels and short story collections. Send review copies to the above address. Sample copies available; single copy price is $3. Subscriptions: one year, $25; two years, $40; outside US add $10.

‡AWARDS FOR WRITERS, #104, P.C. Box 4437, Ithaca NY 14851. Editor: Tilman Gates. Published 6 times/year. "A newsletter listing contests, grants and fellowships for writers that are offered by universities, publishers, small presses, literary journals and other organizations. Also features unique publishing opportunities." Lists fiction markets (contest/award fellowships); sometimes lists other unique fiction opportunities. Sample copies available; single copy price is $3. Subscription: $14.

AWP CHRONICLE, Associated Writing Programs, Old Dominion University, Norfolk VA 23529. (804)683-3839. Editor: D.W. Fenza. 6 times/year. Essays on contemporary literature and articles on the teaching of creative writing only. Does *not* publish fiction. Lists fiction markets (back pages for "Submit"). Sample copies available; single copy price $3.50. Subscription: $18/year; $25/year overseas.

CANADIAN CHILDREN'S LITERATURE/LITTÉRATURE CANADIENNE POUR LA JEUNESSE, Department of English, University of Guelph, Guelph, Ontario N1G 2W1 Canada. (519)824-4120, ext. 3189. Editors: Mary Rubio and Daniel Chouinard. Bimonthly. "In-depth criticism of English and French Canadian literature for young people. Scholarly articles and reviews are supplemented by illustrations, photographs, and interviews with authors of children's books. The main themes and genres of children's literature are covered in special issues." Reviews novels and short story collections. Send review copies to the editors. Sample copies available; single copy price is $8 (Canadian) plus $2 postage. Subscriptions: $25 (Canadian), plus $8 for non-Canadian addresses.

CANADIAN WRITER'S JOURNAL, Box 6618, Depot 1, Victoria, British Columbia V8P 5N7 Canada. (604)477-8807. Editor: Gordon M. Smart. Quarterly. "Mainly short how-to and motivational articles related to all types of writing and of interest to both new and established writers. Sponsors annual short fiction contest." Lists markets for fiction. Sample copies available for $4 ($C for Canadian orders, $US for US orders). Subscription price: $15/year; $25/2 years ($C for Canadian orders, $US for US orders).

CAROUSEL, The Writer's Center, 4508 Walsh St., Bethesda MD 20815. (301)654-8664. Editors: Allan Lefcowitz and Jeff Minerd. Bimonthly. *"Carousel* is the newsletter for The Writer's Center. We publish book reviews and articles about writing and the writing scene." Lists fiction markets. Reviews novels and short story collections. Sample copies available. Subscriptions: $30 Writer's Center Membership.

CHILDREN'S BOOK INSIDER, P.O. Box 2290, Evergreen CO 80439. Editor: Laura Backes. Monthly. "Publication is devoted solely to children's book writers and illustrators. 'At Presstime' section gives current market information each month for fiction, nonfiction and illustration submissions to publishers. Other articles include information on the publishing contract and how to negotiate, how to write a cover letter, how to assemble a strong portfolio, writing and illustration tips, and interviews with published authors and illustrators. Each issue contains articles geared toward both the beginner and the more experienced author and illustrator." Sample copies for SASE (no charge). Single copy price: $2.75. Subscription price: $33/year (US); $38/year (Canadian).

‡CROW QUARTERLY REVIEW, 147 Vera Marie Lane, Box 170, Rollinsville CO 80474. (303)258-3851. Editor: Kevin McCarthy. Quarterly. "A new review of *unpublished* work—sent to writers, editors, agents and producers. Serves to bridge the gap between the professions with writer's Crow Bar columns; writer's, editor's, agent's, producer's POV columns, Good Words column, profiles of various professionals and feature articles and classified ads. Send SASE (IRCs) for more info." Critiques and reviews novels and short story collections. Send review copies to Kevin McCarthy. Sample copies available; single copy price is $5. Subscriptions: $20/year; $35/2 years; $45/3 years.

‡FACTSHEET FIVE, P.O. Box 170099, San Francisco CA 94117-0099. Editor: R. Seth Friedman. Bimonthly. "The definitive guide to the 'zine revolution. *Factsheet Five* reviews over 1,000 small press publications each issue. Send in your independent magazine for review." Sample copy: $6. Subscriptions: $20 for individuals and $40 for institutions.

FAIRBANKS ARTS, P.O. Box 72786, Fairbanks AK 99707. (907)456-6485. Editor: Heather Robertson. Bimonthly. *"Fairbanks Arts,* a publication of the Fairbanks Arts Association, is designed to promote excellence in Alaskan contemporary and traditional arts. Publishes fiction (2,000 words)." Sample copies available; single copy price is $2.75. Subscriptions: $15/year.

GILA QUEEN'S GUIDE TO MARKETS, P.O. Box 97, Newton NJ 07860-0097. Editor: Kathy Ptacek. "Includes *complete* guidelines for fiction (different genres), poetry, nonfiction, greeting cards, etc. Also includes 'theme section' each month—science fiction/fantasy/horror, mystery/suspense, romance, western, comics, Canadian, regional, outdoor/sports, etc., and 'mini-markets.' Regular departments include new address listings, dead/suspended markets, moving editors, anthologies, markets to be wary of, publishing news, etc. Every issue contains updates (of stuff listed in previous issues), new markets, conferences, contests. Publishes articles on writing topics, self-promotion, reviews of software and books of interest to writers, etc." Sample copy: $5. Subscriptions: $28/year (US); $32/year (Canada); $45/year (overseas). Writer's guidelines available for SASE (IRCs). Yearly Index of Markets available for $3 plus SASE. Dead Market Listings (1988—present; updated monthly) available for $4.

‡GOTHIC JOURNAL, 19210 Forest Rd. N., Forest Lake MN 55025-9766. (612)464-1119. Fax: (612)464-1331. Editor: Kristi Lyn Glass. Bimonthly. *"Gothic Journal* is a news and review publication for readers, writers and publishers of romantic suspense, romantic mysteries, and supernatural, gothic, and woman-in-jeopardy romance novels. It contains articles, reviews, letters, author profiles, market news, book lists and more." Lists fiction markets. Reviews novels and short story collections. Sample copies available for $3 plus $1 postage and handling. Subscriptions: $18/year (6 issues); $24/year (Canada); $30/year (foreign).

LAMBDA BOOK REPORT, 1625 Connecticut Ave. NW, Washington DC 20009-1013. (202)462-7924. Editor: Jim Marks. Bimonthly. "This review journal of contemporary gay and lesbian literature appeals to both readers and writers. Fiction queries published regularly." Lists fiction markets. Reviews novels and short story collections. Send review copies to Attn: Book Review Editor. Single copy price is $3.95/ US. Subscriptions: $19.95/year (US); international rate: $31.95 (US $).

LOCUS, The Newspaper of the Science Fiction Field, P.O. Box 13305, Oakland CA 94661. Editor: Charles N. Brown. Monthly. "Professional newsletter of science fiction, fantasy and horror; has news, interviews of authors, book reviews, column on electronic publishing, forthcoming books listings, monthly books-received listings, etc." Occasionally lists markets for fiction. Reviews novels or short story collections. Sample copies available. Single copy price: $3.95. Subscription price: $38/year, (2nd class mail) for US, $43 (US)/year, (2nd class) for Canada; $43 (US)/year (2nd class) for overseas.

‡**THE MYSTERY REVIEW, A Quarterly Publication for Mystery & Suspense Readers**, P.O. Box 233, Colborne, Ontario K0K 1S0 Canada. (613)475-4440. Editor: Barbara Davey. Quarterly. "Book reviews, information on new releases, interviews with authors and other people involved in mystery, 'real life' mysteries, out-of-print mysteries, mystery/suspense films, kids corner, word games and puzzles with a mystery theme." Reviews mystery/suspense novels and short story collections. Send review copies to editor. Single copy price is $5.95 CDN in Canada/$5.95 US in the United States. Subscriptions: $21.50 CDN (includes GST) in Canada; $20 US in the US and $25 US elsewhere.

NEW WRITER'S MAGAZINE, P.O. Box 5976, Sarasota FL 34277. (813)953-7903. Editor: George J. Haborak. Bimonthly. *"New Writer's Magazine* is a publication for aspiring writers. It features 'how-to' articles, news and interviews with published and recently published authors. Will use fiction that has a tie-in with the world of the writer." Lists markets for fiction. Reviews novels and short story collections. Send review copies to editor. Sample copies available; single copy price is $3. Subscriptions: $14/year; $25/two years. Canadian $20 (US funds). International $30/year (US funds).

‡**THE NIGHTMARE EXPRESS**, 11 W. Winona St., St. Paul MN 55107. (612)227-6958. Editor: Donald L. Miller. Bimonthly. *"The Nightmare Express* was established in 1986 as a vehicle for horror writers (both published/unpublished). Its purpose is to give market information, ideas, how-to information to help the author further advance his or her career." Recent articles included "One Way to Write Your Novel," "Cover Letters and Their Friends." Articles include "Dark Windows," "NightTime Selections," etc. Lists markets for horror (6-12 markets) each issue. Reviews novels or short story collections. Sample copies available. Single copy price; $1.50 U.S.; subscription price: $10/year plus *Terror Time Again*; $8 renewals; foreign orders add $4. Please remit in U.S. funds.

‡**THE NOOK NEWS CONFERENCES & KLATCHES BULLETIN**, Suite 181, 38114 Third St., Willoughby OH 44094. (216)953-9292. Editor: Eugene Ortiz. Quarterly. *"The Nook News Conferences & Klatches Bulletin* is a spin-off from *The Writer's Nook News* column of the same name. It is published for those writers looking for upcoming workshops, conferences, and other in-person events such as local regularly-scheduled writers groups (klatches)." Single copy price: $5. Subscription price: one year, $18; two years, $32 (add 50% if outside U.S. or Canada).

‡**THE NOOK NEWS CONTESTS & AWARDS BULLETIN**, Suite 181, 38114 Third St., Willoughby OH 44094. (216)953-9292. Editor: Eugene Ortiz. Quarterly. *"The Nook News Contests & Awards Bulletin* is a spin-off of *The Writer's Nook News* column of the same name. It is widely recognized that writing competitions help incite writers to continue writing, gives them a deadline to shoot for, and sometimes the added bonus of a free critique, not to mention monetary return and of course publication. *NNCAB* lists complete information and contacts for these competitions." Lists markets for fiction. Single copy price: $5. Subscription price: one year, $18; two years, $32 (add 50% if outside U.S. or Canada).

‡**THE NOOK NEWS MARKET BULLETIN**, Suite 181, 38114 Third St., Willoughby OH 44094. (216)953-9292. Editor: Eugene Ortiz. Quarterly. *"The Nook News Market Bulletin* is a spin-off of *The Writer's Nook News* column of the same name. It lists up-to-date market information and contacts for writers of fiction, nonfiction and poetry." Lists markets for fiction. Single copy price: $5. Subscription price: one year, $18; two years, $32 (add 50% if outside U.S. or Canada).

‡**THE NOOK NEWS REVIEW OF WRITER'S PUBLICATIONS**, Suite 181, 38114 Third St., Willoughby Oh 44094. (216)953-9292. Editor: Eugene Ortiz. *"NNRWP* reviews books and magazines, newsletters, etc., useful to freelance writers." Single copy price: $5. Subscription price: one year, $18; two years, $32 (add 50% if outside U.S. or Canada). Now accepting freelance submissions. 400 word maximum. Pays 6¢ per word on acceptance for First North American serial rights.

POETS & WRITERS, 72 Spring St., New York NY 10012. Covers all types of writing. Bimonthly. "Keeps writers in touch with the news they need. Reports on grants and awards, including deadlines for applications; publishes manuscript requests from editors and publishers; covers topics such as book contracts, taxes, writers' colonies and publishing trends; features essays by and interviews with poets and fiction writers. Lists markets for fiction. Sample copies available; single copy price is $3.95. Subscriptions: $18/year; $32/2 years; $46/3 years.

‡THE REGENCY PLUME, 711 D. St. NW, Ardmore OK 73401. Editor: Marilyn Clay. Bimonthly. "The newsletter focus is on providing accurate historical facts relating to the Regency period: customs, clothes, entertainment, the wars, historical figures, etc. I stay in touch with New York editors who acquire Regency romance novels. Current market info appears regularly in newsletter—see Bits & Scraps." "Previews" current releases; send copies to editor. Sample copy available for $3; single copy price is $3, $4 outside States. Subscriptions: $10/year for 6 issues; $14 outside US. ("Check must be drawn on a US bank. Postal money order okay.") Back issues available. Send SASE (IRCs) for subscription information or article guidelines.

SCAVENGER'S NEWSLETTER, 519 Ellinwood, Osage City KS 66523. (913)528-3538. Editor: Janet Fox. Monthly. "A market newsletter for SF/fantasy/horror/mystery writers with an interest in the small press. Articles about SF/fantasy/horror/mystery writing/marketing." Lists markets for fiction. Sample copies available. Single copy price: $2. Subscription price: $14/year, $7/6 months. Canada: $17, $8.50; overseas $23, $11.50 (US funds only).

SCIENCE FICTION CHRONICLE, P.O. Box 022730, Brooklyn NY 11202-0056. (718)643-9011. Editor: Andrew Porter. Monthly. "Monthly newsmagazine for professional writers, editors, readers of SF, fantasy, horror." Lists markets for fiction "updated every 4 months." Reviews novels and short story collections. Send review copies to SFC and to D'Ammassa, 323 Dodge St. E., Providence RI 02914. Sample copies available with 9×12 SAE with $1.21 postage; single copy price is $2.75 (US) or £3 (UK). Subscriptions: $30 bulk, $36 first class US and Canada; $41 overseas.

SCIENCE FICTION CONVENTION REGISTER, Box 3343, Fairfax VA 22038. (703)273-3297. Editor: Erwin S. Strauss. 3 issues/year. "Directory of over 500 upcoming science fiction and related conventions." Sample copies available; single copy price is $4. Subscriptions: $10/year.

‡SMALL MAGAZINE REVIEW, P.O. Box 100, Paradise CA 95967. (916)877-6110. Editor: Len Fulton. Monthly. "Reviews, articles, interviews about small magazines worldwide." Lists fiction markets. Sample copies available; single copy price is $2. Subscriptions: $20/year.

THE SMALL PRESS BOOK REVIEW, P.O. Box 176, Southport CT 06490. (203)268-4878. Editor: Henry Berry. Quarterly. "Brief reviews of all sorts of books from small presses/independent publishers." Addresses of publishers are given in reviews. Reviews novels and short story collections. Send review copies to editor. Sample copies available for $4; single copy price is $5. Subscriptions: $28/year, six-issue subscription.

SMALL PRESS REVIEW, P.O. Box 100, Paradise CA 95967. (916)877-6110. Editor: Len Fulton. Monthly. "Publishes news and reviews about small publishers, books." Lists markets for fiction and poetry. Reviews novels, short story and poetry collections. Sample copies available. Subscription price: $23/year.

‡A VIEW FROM THE LOFT, 66 Malcolm Ave. SE, Minneapolis MN 55414. (612)379-8999. Editor: Ellen Hawley. Monthly. "Publishes articles on writing and list of markets for fiction, poetry and creative nonfiction." Sample copies available; single copy price is $4 US. Subscriptions: $35 in Twin Cities metro area; $20 elsewhere in US; $18 low income student. (Subscription available only as part of Loft membership; rates are membership rates.)

‡WORDWEAVERS, 2112 Arbor Dr., Shrewsbury MA 01545. (508)842-1593. Editor: Jean White. Quarterly. "WordWeavers is an information and service organization for freelance writers. Our quarterly newsletter offers in-depth market, contest and industry news. Articles provide encouragement, information, motivation. Our networking concept is designed to bring writers together through the sharing of experiences, knowledge and goals." Lists fiction markets. Reviews novels and short story collections. Send review copies to Jean White, Editor. Sample copies available; single copy price is $3 in US funds. Subscriptions: $12 US; $15 Canada; Overseas $18. (Check and money orders in US funds.)

THE WRITER, 120 Boylston St., Boston MA 02116-4615. Editor: Sylvia K. Burack. Monthly. Lists markets for fiction (March and October issues have special fiction lists annually. July lists book publishers). Single copy price: $2.25. Subscription price: $27/year, $50/2 years. Special introductory offer: 5 issues $10. Canadian and foreign at additional $8 (US) per year. Also publishes *The Writer's Handbook*, an annual directory of magazine and book publisher listings.

WRITERS CONNECTION, Suite 103, 275 Saratoga Ave., Santa Clara CA 95050. (408)554-2090. Editor: Jan Stiles. Monthly. "How-to articles for writers, editors and self-publishers. Topics cover all types of writing, from fiction to technical writing. Columns include markets, contests and writing events and conferences for fiction, nonfiction and occasionally poetry." Lists markets for fiction. Sample copies available. Single copy price: $5. Subscription included with membership. For information, call (408)554-2090. "We do not publish fiction or poetry."

WRITER'S DIGEST, 1507 Dana Ave., Cincinnati OH 45207. (513)531-2222. Editor: Bruce Woods. Monthly. "*Writer's Digest* is a magazine of techniques and markets. We *inspire* the writer to write, *instruct* him or her on how to improve that work, and *direct* it toward appropriate markets." Lists markets for fiction, nonfiction, poetry. Single copy price: $2.75. Subscription price: $21.

‡WRITER'S DIGEST BOOKS—MARKET BOOKS, 1507 Dana Ave., Cincinnati OH 45207. (513)531-2222. Annual. In addition to *Novel & Short Story Writer's Market*, Writer's Digest Books also publishes *Writer's Market*, *Poet's Market*, *Children's Writer's and Illustrator's Market* and the *Guide to Literary Agents and Art/Photo Reps*. All include articles and listings of interest to writers. All are available at bookstores, libraries or through the publisher. (Request catalog.)

WRITER'S GUIDELINES, HC77 Box 608, Pittsburg MO 65724. Fax: (417)993-5544. Editor: Susan Salaki. Bimonthly. "Fiction writers are welcome to submit material for our Roundtable Discussions, a section devoted to the grassroots approach to getting your work published. Our magazine also assists writers in obtaining guidelines from over 200 different magazine and book editors through our Guidelines Service. We also offer a Adopt-A-Writer program whereby the managing editor of WGM 'adopts' up to 10 writers and works with each writer on a one-on-one basis for six months." Lists markets for fiction. Reviews novels and short story collections of subscribers. Send SASE (IRCs) for guidelines. Single copy price: $4. Subscription price: $18; Canada, $26; Overseas, $36.

WRITERS' JOURNAL, (Minnesota Ink section), 27 Empire Dr., St. Paul MN 55103. (612)225-1306. Managing Editor: Valerie Hockert. Bimonthly. "Provides a creative outlet for writers of fiction." Sample copies available. Single copy price: $3.25; $4 (Canadian). Subscription price: $14.97; $18.97 Canada.

WRITERS NEWS, P.O. Box 4, Nairn 1V12 4HU Scotland. "Practical advice for established and aspiring writers. How-to articles, news, markets and competitions." Lists markets for fiction. Free trial issue available. Subscriptions: £33.90 (UK), £43.90 (Europe/Eire), £48.90 (elsewhere) on direct debit or credit card; or £38.90 (UK), £48.90 (Europe/Eire), £53.90 (elsewhere) if paying cash.

‡THE WRITER'S NOOK NEWS, Suite 181, 38114 Third St., Willoughby OH 44094. (216)953-9292. Editor: Eugene Ortiz. Quarterly. "*The Writer's Nook News* is a national quarterly publication dedicated to giving freelance writers specific information for their immediate practical use in getting published and staying published. It contains news; writing tips; books; reviews; legislative/tax updates; conference, contest, and market listings; and various other topics." Lists markets for fiction. Single copy price: $5. Subscription price: $18/year; 2 years/$32 (add 50% if outside U.S. or Canada).

WRITER'S YEARBOOK, 1507 Dana Ave., Cincinnati OH 45207. (513)531-2222. Editor: Bruce Woods. Annual. "An annual collection of the best writing *about* writing, with a survey of the year's 100 top markets for freelancers." Single copy price: $3.95.

THE WRITING SELF, P.O. Box 245, Lenox Hill Station, New York NY 10021. Editor: Scot Nourok. Quarterly. "*The Writing Self* is devoted to the act of writing. The goal of this publication is to create a network and support for creative writers, i.e., poets, novelists, short story writers, as well as playwrights and journalists. We publish personal essays that describe what it is like to be a writer. Each issue includes an interview, book review, contest, a particular column: Inner Voices, Short Shorts, The Workshop Beat, Short Fiction." Sometimes lists markets for fiction. Reviews novels, short story collections and books on writing. Send review copies to editor. Sample copies available; single copy price is $2.50. Subscriptions: $9.95 (US), $14.95 in Canada and $21.95 overseas.

Publications of interest to fiction writers/ changes '93-'94

The following publications appeared in the 1993 edition of *Novel & Short Story Writer's Market* but do not appear in the 1994 edition. Those that did not respond to our request for an update appear below without further explanation. If a reason for the omission is available, it is included next to the listing name.

Feminist Bookstore News
The Fiction Writer (ceased
   publication)

New Writer's Magazine
Ohio Writer

Quantum—Science Fiction and
   Fantasy Review
Rising Star

Glossary

Advance. Payment by a publisher to an author prior to the publication of a book, to be deducted from the author's future royalties.

All rights. The rights contracted to a publisher permitting a manuscript's use anywhere and in any form, including movie and book-club sales, without additional payment to the writer.

Anthology. A collection of selected writings by various authors.

Auction. Publishers sometimes bid against each other for the acquisition of a manuscript that has excellent sales prospects.

Backlist. A publisher's books not published during the current season but still in print.

Belles lettres. A term used to describe fine or literary writing more to entertain than to inform or instruct.

Book producer/packager. An organization that may develop a book for a publisher based upon the publisher's idea or may plan all elements of a book, from its initial concept to writing and marketing strategies, and then sell the package to a book publisher and/or movie producer.

Category fiction. See Genre.

Chapbook. A booklet of 15-30 pages of fiction or poetry.

Cliffhanger. Fictional event in which the reader is left in suspense at the end of a chapter or episode, so that interest in the story's outcome will be sustained.

Clip. Sample, usually from newspaper or magazine, of a writer's published work.

Cloak-and-dagger. A melodramatic, romantic type of fiction dealing with espionage and intrigue.

Commercial. Publishers whose concern is salability, profit and success with a large readership.

Contemporary. Material dealing with popular current trends, themes or topics.

Contributor's copy. Copy of an issue of a magazine or published book sent to an author whose work is included.

Copublishing. An arrangement in which the author and publisher share costs and profits.

Copyediting. Editing a manuscript for writing style, grammar, punctuation and factual accuracy.

Copyright. The legal right to exclusive publication, sale or distribution of a literary work.

Cover letter. A brief letter sent with a complete manuscript submitted to an editor.

"Cozy" (or "teacup") mystery. Mystery usually set in a small British town, in a bygone era, featuring a somewhat genteel, intellectual protagonist.

Cyberpunk. Type of science fiction, usually concerned with computer networks and human-computer combinations, involving young, sophisticated protagonists.

Division. An unincorporated branch of a company (e.g. Viking Penguin, a division of Penguin USA).

Experimental fiction. Fiction that is innovative in subject matter and style; avant-garde, non-formulaic, usually literary material.

Exposition. The portion of the storyline, usually the beginning, where background information about character and setting is related.

Fair use. A provision in the copyright law that says short passages from copyrighted material may be used without infringing on the owner's rights.

Fanzine. A noncommercial, small-circulation magazine usually dealing with fantasy, horror or science-fiction literature and art.

First North American serial rights. The right to publish material in a periodical before it appears in book form, for the first time, in the United States or Canada.

Formula. A fixed and conventional method of plot development, which varies little from one book to another in a particular genre.

Frontier novel. Novel that has all the basic elements of a traditional western but is based upon the frontier history of "unwestern" places like Florida or East Tennessee.

Galleys. The first typeset version of a manuscript that has not yet been divided into pages.

Genre. A formulaic type of fiction such as romance, western or horror.

Gothic. A genre in which the central character is usually a beautiful young woman and the setting an old mansion or castle, involving a handsome hero and real danger, either natural or supernatural.

Graphic novel. An adaptation of a novel into a long comic strip or heavily illustrated story of 40 pages or more, produced in paperback.

Hard-boiled detective novel. Mystery novel featuring a private eye or police detective as the protagonist; usually involves a murder. The emphasis is on the details of the crime.

Honorarium. A small, token payment for published work.

Horror. A genre stressing fear, death and other aspects of the macabre.

Imprint. Name applied to a publisher's specific line (e.g. Owl, an imprint of Henry Holt).

Interactive fiction. Fiction in book or computer-software format where the reader determines the path the story will take by choosing from several alternatives at the end of each chapter or episode.

International Reply Coupon (IRC). A form purchased at a post office and enclosed with a letter or manuscript to a international publisher, to cover return postage costs.

Juvenile. Fiction intended for children 2-12.

Libel. Written or printed words that defame, malign or damagingly misrepresent a living person.

Literary. The general category of serious, non-formulaic, intelligent fiction, sometimes experimental, that most frequently appears in little magazines.

Literary agent. A person who acts for an author in finding a publisher or arranging contract terms on a literary project.

Mainstream. Traditionally written fiction on subjects or trends that transcend experimental or genre fiction categories.

Malice domestic novel. A traditional mystery novel that is not hard-boiled; emphasis is on the solution. Suspects and victims know one another.

Manuscript. The author's unpublished copy of a work, usually typewritten, used as the basis for typesetting.

Mass market paperback. Softcover book on a popular subject, usually around 4×7, directed to a general audience and sold in drugstores and groceries as well as in bookstores.

Ms(s). Abbreviation for manuscript(s).

Multiple submission. Submission of more than one short story at a time to the same editor. Do not make a multiple submission unless requested.

Narration. The account of events in a story's plot as related by the speaker or the voice of the author.

Narrator. The person who tells the story, either someone involved in the action or the voice of the writer.

New Age. A term including categories such as astrology, psychic phenomena, spiritual healing, UFOs, mysticism and other aspects of the occult.

Nom de plume. French for "pen name"; a pseudonym.

Novella (also novelette). A short novel or long story, approximately 7,000-15,000 words.

#10 envelope. 4×9½ envelope, used for queries and other business letters.

Novels of the West. Novels that have elements of the western but contain more complex characters and subjects such as fur trading, cattle raising and coal mining.

Offprint. Copy of a story taken from a magazine before it is bound.

One-time rights. Permission to publish a story in periodical or book form one time only.

Outline. A summary of a book's contents, often in the form of chapter headings with a few sentences outlining the action of the story under each one; sometimes part of a book proposal.

Over the transom. Slang for the path of an unsolicited manuscript into the slush pile.

Page rate. A fixed rate paid to an author per published page of fiction.

Payment on acceptance. Payment from the magazine or publishing house as soon as the decision to print a manuscript is made.

Payment on publication. Payment from the publisher after a manuscript is printed.

Pen name. A pseudonym used to conceal a writer's real name.

Periodical. A magazine or journal published at regular intervals.

Plot. The carefully devised series of events through which the characters progress in a work of fiction.

Proofreading. Close reading and correction of a manuscript's typographical errors.

Proofs. A typeset version of a manuscript used for correcting errors and making changes, often a photocopy of the galleys.

Proposal. An offer to write a specific work, usually consisting of an outline of the work and one or two completed chapters.

Prose poem. Short piece of prose with the language and expression of poetry.

Protagonist. The principal or leading character in a literary work.

Public domain. Material that either was never copyrighted or whose copyright term has expired.

Pulp magazine. A periodical printed on inexpensive paper, usually containing lurid, sensational stories or articles.

Purple prose. Ornate writing using exaggerated and excessive literary devices.

Query. A letter written to an editor to elicit interest in a story the writer wants to submit.

Reader. A person hired by a publisher to read unsolicited manuscripts.

Reading fee. An arbitrary amount of money charged by some agents and publishers to read a submitted manuscript.

Regency romance. A genre romance, usually set in England between 1811-1820.

Remainders. Leftover copies of an out-of-print book, sold by the publisher at a reduced price.

Reporting time. The number of weeks or months it takes an editor to report back on an author's query or manuscript.

Reprint rights. Permission to print an already published work whose rights have been sold to another magazine or book publisher.

Roman à clef. French "novel with a key." A novel that represents actual living or historical characters and events in fictionalized form.

Romance. The genre relating accounts of passionate love and fictional heroic achievements.

Royalties. A percentage of the retail price paid to an author for each copy of the book that is sold.

SASE. Self-addressed stamped envelope.

Science fiction. Genre in which scientific facts and hypotheses form the basis of actions and events.

Second serial rights. Permission for the reprinting of a work in another periodical after its first publication in book or magazine form.

Self-publishing. In this arrangement, the author keeps all income derived from the book, but he pays for its manufacturing, production and marketing.

Sequel. A literary work that continues the narrative of a previous, related story or novel.

Serial rights. The rights given by an author to a publisher to print a piece in one or more periodicals.

Serialized novel. A book-length work of fiction published in sequential issues of a periodical.

Setting. The environment and time period during which the action of a story takes place.

Short short story. A condensed piece of fiction, usually under 700 words.

Simultaneous submission. The practice of sending copies of the same manuscript to several editors or publishers at the same time. Some people refuse to consider such submissions.

Slant. A story's particular approach or style, designed to appeal to the readers of a specific magazine.

Slice of life. A presentation of characters in a seemingly mundane situation which offers the reader a flash of illumination about the characters or their situation.

Slush pile. A stack of unsolicited manuscripts in the editorial offices of a publisher.

Speculation (or Spec). An editor's agreement to look at an author's manuscript with no promise to purchase.

Splatterpunk. Type of horror fiction known for its very violent and graphic content.

Subsidiary. An incorporated branch of a company or conglomerate (e.g. Alfred Knopf, Inc., a subsidiary of Random House, Inc.).

Subsidiary rights. All rights other than book publishing rights included in a book contract, such as paperback, book-club and movie rights.

Subsidy publisher. A book publisher who charges the author for the cost of typesetting, printing and promoting a book. Also Vanity publisher.

Suspense. A genre of fiction where the plot's primary function is to build a feeling of anticipation and fear in the reader over its possible outcome.

Synopsis. A brief summary of a story, novel or play. As part of a book proposal, it is a comprehensive summary condensed in a page or page and a half.

Tabloid. Publication printed on paper about half the size of a regular newspaper page (e.g. *The National Enquirer*).

Tearsheet. Page from a magazine containing a published story.

Theme. The dominant or central idea in a literary work; its message, moral or main thread.

Trade paperback. A softbound volume, usually around 5 × 8, published and designed for the general public, available mainly in bookstores.

Unsolicited manuscript. A story or novel manuscript that an editor did not specifically ask to see.

Vanity publisher. See Subsidy publisher.

Viewpoint. The position or attitude of the first- or third-person narrator or multiple narrators, which determines how a story's action is seen and evaluated.

Western. Genre with a setting in the West, usually between 1860-1890, with a formula plot about cowboys or other aspects of frontier life.

Whodunit. Genre dealing with murder, suspense and the detection of criminals.

Work-for-hire. Work that another party commissions you to do, generally for a flat fee. The creator does not own the copyright and therefore can not sell any rights.

Young adult. The general classification of books written for readers 12-18.

Category Index

The Category Index is a good place to begin searching for a market for your fiction. Below is an alphabetical list of subjects of particular interest to editors listed in *Novel & Short Story Writer's Market*. The index is divided into four sections: literary and small circulation magazines; commercial periodicals; small press and commercial publishers.

Some of the markets listed in the book do not appear in the Category Index, because they have not indicated specific subject preferences. Most of these said they accept "all categories." Listings that were very specific also do not appear here. An example of this might be a magazine accepting "fiction about fly fishing only."

If you'd like to market your hard-boiled mystery novel to a major publishing house, for example, check the Commercial Publishers subhead under Mystery. There you will find a list of those publishers interested in the subject along with the page numbers on which their listings appear. Then read the listings *carefully* to find the mystery publishers best suited to your work.

Literary and Small Circulation Magazines

Adventure Abyss Magazine 81; Advocate, The 82; Aguilar Expression, The 83; Amateur Writers Journal 85; Amelia 86; Angst 88; Animal Trails 89; Ansuda Magazine 89; Anterior Fiction Quarterly 90; Arnazella 94; Array 94; Art's Garbage Gazzette 96; Atalantik 97; Atlantean Press Review, The 98; Belletrist Review, The 101; Black Jack 105; Blue Water Review, The 109; Blueline 109; Bohemian Chronicle 110; Chrysalis 120; Cochran's Corner 122; Columbus Literary Gazette, The 124; Compenions 125; Crime Club 131; Dagger of the Mind 132; Dan River Anthology 133; Dogwood Tales Magazine 138; Downstate Story 138; Dream International/Quarterly 139; Elf: Eclectic Literary Forum 142; Escapist, The 144; Explosive Decompression 146; Fighting Woman News 149; Fugue 153; Galaxy Class 154; Ghost Town 156; Gotta Write Network Litmag 158; Grasslands Review 159; Green Mountains Review 160; Green's Magazine 161; Hawaii Pacific Review 164; Hob-Nob 168; Hyperbole 172; Iconoclast, The 173; Infinity Limited 174; Inkslinger, The 174; Innisfree 175; Journal of Regional Criticism 181; Just A Moment 181; Kokopelli Notes 185; Kumquat Meringue 186; Lactuca 186; Leading Edge, The 188; Legend 189; Lines In The Sand 191; Llamas Magazine 194; Longneck, The 194; MacGuffin, The 197; Medley of Pens 201; Meme-Shot Magazine 201; Merlyn's Pen 202; Milwaukee Undergraduate Review, The 204; Mixed Media 207; Monocacy Valley Review, The 208; Monthly Independent Tribune Times Journal Post Gazette News Chronicle Bulletin, The 208; Mostly Maine 209; Mystic Fiction 211; Nahant Bay 212; Negative Capability 214; New Methods 216; New Press Literary Quarterly, The 217; New Voices in Poetry and Prose 218; Nimrod 219; No Idea Magazine 219; Noisy Concept 220; Northwoods Journal 223; Oak, The 225; Olympia Review, The 227; Oxalis 231; Palo Alto Review 233; Paper Bag, The 234; Perceptions (Montana) 238; Pirate Writings 241; Portable Wall, The 244; Post, The 245; Potpourri 246; Queen's Quarterly 253; Rag Mag 254; Rajah 254; Re Arts & Letters 255; Reach Magazine 256; Renegade 258; Renovated Lighthouse Publications 258; Rock Falls Review 261; S.L.U.G.fest, Ltd. 263; San Gabriel Valley Magazine 264; San Miguel Writer 264; Scifant 265; Scream of the Buddha 266; Sensations Magazine 267; Shift Magazine 269; Short Stuff Magazine for Grown-ups 270; Slate and Style 273; SPSM&H 283; Tall Tales & Short Stories 289; Thema 293; Tickled By Thunder 295; Timberlines 295; Tucumcari Literary Review 298; VeriTales 302; Villager, The 303; Vincent Brothers Review, The 303; Vintage Northwest 304; Virginia Quarterly Review 304; Wagons of Steel Magazine 305; Westview 307; Whisper 308; Wisconsin Restaurateur, The 312; Words of Wisdom 313; Writers' Open Forum 315

Children's/Juvenile Acorn, The 81; Advocate, The 82; Animal Trails 89; Art's Garbage Gazzette 96; Atalantik 97; Bohemian Chronicle 110; Brilliant Star 112; Cochran's Corner 122; Columbus Literary Gazette, The 124; Hob-Nob 168; Hopscotch: The Magazine for Girls 170; Hunted News, The 172; Inkslinger, The 174; Lines In The Sand 191; Majestic Books 199; Medley of Pens 201; Otterwise 229; Reach Magazine 256; Shattered Wig Review 269; Stone Soup 285; Two-Ton Santa 299; Wisconsin Restaurateur, The 312; Writers' Open Forum 315; Young Judaean 317; Young Voices Magazine 318

Comic/Graphic Novels Corona 127; Fat Tuesday 147; Processed World 249; Rag Mag 254; Sign of the Times 271; Wagons of Steel Magazine 305; Yellow Silk 317

Experimental

view, The 262; Round Table, The 263; S.L.U.G.fest, Ltd. 263; Salmon Magazine 263; Salt Lick Press 264; San Miguel Writer 264; Sanskrit 265; Scifant 265; Scream of the Buddha 266; Seattle Review, The 266; Semiotext(e) 267; Sequoia 268; Shattered Wig Review 269; Shift Magazine 269; Shockbox 269; Short Fiction By Women 270; Sidewalks 271; Sign of the Times 271; Silver Web, The 272; Single Scene, The 272; Skylark 273; Slipstream 274; Snake Nation Review 275; South Dakota Review 276; Southern California Anthology 277; Spectrum (Massachusetts) 279; Spit: A Journal of the Arts 281; SPSM&H 283; Story 285; Struggle 286; Sub-Terrain 287; Sycamore Review 288; Tamaqua 290; Tampa Review 290; Temporary Culture 291; Theatre ov the Night 292; Thema 293; This Magazine 294; Thrust 295; Tributary 296; Turnstile 298; 2 AM Magazine 299; Two-Ton Santa 299; Underpass 300; Urbanite, The 301; Urbanus/Raizirr 302; VeriTales 302; Videomania 303; Vincent Brothers Review, The 303; Wagons of Steel Magazine 305; West 305; West Coast Line 307; Westview 307; Whetstone 308; Widener Review 309; Willow Review 310; Wisconsin Academy Review 311; Wisconsin Review 312; Wolfridgereview 312; WonderDisk 312; Worm 314; Writing For Our Lives 315; Xavier Review 316; Xib 316; Xtreme 317; Yellow Silk 317; Zero Hour 318; Zoiks! 318; Zyzzyva 319

Fantasy Aberations 80; Abyss Magazine 81; Advocate, The 82; Alabama Literary Review 84; Alternate Hilarities 85; Amateur Writers Journal 85; Amelia 86; Ansuda Magazine 89; Argonaut 93; Arnazella 94; Art:Mag 95; Art's Garbage Gazzette 96; Bahlasti Paper 99; Ball Magazine 100; Bardic Runes 100; Black Hammock Review, The 104; Blis Magazine 107; Blue Ryder 108; Bradley's Fantasy Magazine, Marion Zimmer 111; Bravo Mundo Nuevo 112; Clifton Magazine 121; Columbus Literary Gazette, The 124; Companion in Zeor, A 125; Compenions 125; Compost Newsletter 126; Corona 127; Crazyquilt 129; Crime Club 131; Dagger of the Mind 132; Dan River Anthology 133; Dark Regions 134; Daughters of Nyx 134; Dead of Night™ Magazine 135; Deathrealm 136; Deuterium 137; Dream International/Quarterly 139; Dreams & Nightmares 139; Dreams & Visions 139; Elf: Eclectic Literary Forum 142; Escapist, The 144; Explosive Decompression 146; Eyes 146; Fighting Woman News 149; Figment Magazine 150; Fish Drum Magazine 151; Fugue 153; Gaslight 155; Glimpses Magazine 157; Golden Isis Magazine 157; Gotta Write Network Litmag 158; Grasslands Review 159; Green Egg/How About Magic? 160; Green's Magazine 161; Haunts 164; Hawaii Pacific Review 164; Hayden's Ferry Review 165; Heart Attack Magazine 165; Heaven Bone 166; His Garden Magazine 168; Hob-Nob 168; Hobson's Choice 169; Hor-Tasy 171; Hyperbole 172; Immanent Face Magazine 173; Infinity Limited 174; Inkslinger, The 174; Innisfree 175; Journal of Regional Criticism 181; Just A Moment 181; Kennesaw Review 183; Language Bridges Quarterly 187; Leading Edge, The 188; Legend 189; Lines In The Sand 191; Lite 192; Longneck, The 194; Lost Creek Letters 195; Lost Worlds 196; MacGuffin, The 197; Magic Changes 198; Magic Realism 199; Medley of Pens 201; Meme-Shot Magazine 201; Merlyn's Pen 202; Midnight Zoo 204; Milwaukee Undergraduate Review, The 204; Minas Tirith Evening-Star 205; Mind in Motion 205; Mississippi Review 207; Mixed Media 207; Mobius 208; Mostly Maine 209; Mystic Fiction 211; Mythic Circle, The 211; Nahant Bay 212; Nassau Review 212; Negative Capability 214; New Laurel Review 215; New Press Literary Quarterly, The 217; New Voices in Poetry and Prose 218; Next Phase 219; Night Owl's Newsletter 219; No Idea Magazine 219; Nocturnal Lyric, The 220; Noisy Concept 220; Northwoods Journal 223; Nuclear Fiction 224; Office Number One 225; Offworld 226; Old Hickory Review 226; Once Upon A World 227; Oxalis 231; Pablo Lennis 232; Palo Alto Review 233; Paper Bag, The 234; Paper Radio 234; Perceptions (Montana) 238; Pirate Writings 241; Pléiades Magazine/Philae 242; Poetic Space 243; Poetry Forum Short Stories 243; Poetry Motel 243; Poskisnolt Press 244; Potpourri 246; Primavera 247; Processed World 249; Puck! 250; Pulphouse 251; Quanta 252; Quarry 252; Queen's Quarterly 253; Rag Mag 254; Rajah 254; Random Realities 254; Redcat Magazine 257; Rejects 258; Renegade 258; Renovated Lighthouse Publications 258; Riverside Quarterly 261; Rock Falls Review 261; Rockford Review, The 262; Salmon Magazine 263; San Miguel Writer 264; Scifant 265; Seattle Review, The 266; Semiotext(e) 267; Sensations Magazine 267; Shadow Sword 268; Sidetrekked 271; Single Scene, The 272; Skylark 273; Slate and Style 273; Snake Nation Review 275; Southern Humanities Review 278; Spellbound 280; SPSM&H 283; Square One 283; Strange Days 285; Tails of Wonder 288; Tales of the Heart 289; Tall Tales & Short Stories 289; Tampa Review 290; Theatre ov the Night 292; Thin Ice 293; This Magazine 294; Tickled By Thunder 295; Tomorrow 296; Tributary 296; Twisted 299; 2 AM Magazine 299; Unreality 301; Urbanite, The 301; VeriTales 302; Videomania 303; Vintage Northwest 304; Wagons of Steel Magazine 305; Whisper 308; WonderDisk 312; Writers' Open Forum 315; Wyrd 316; Xib 316; Yellow Silk 317

Feminist ACM, (Another Chicago Magazine) 81; Adrift 82; Advocate, The 82; Alabama Literary Review 84; Amelia 86; American Voice, The 88; Americas Review, The 88; Antietam Review 90; Apalachee Quarterly 92; Arizona Unconservative, The 94; Arnazella 94; Art:Mag 95; Bahlasti Paper 99; Bakunin 99; Ball Magazine 100; Big Rain 103; Broomstick 113; Brownbag Press 113; Callaloo 114; Calyx 115; Changing Men 118; Clifton Magazine 121; Collages and Bricolages 123; Columbus Literary Gazette, The 124; Communities: Journal of Cooperation 124; Compenions 125;

Compost Newsletter 126; Corona 127; Creative Woman, The 130; Crucible 131; Daughters of Nyx 134; Daughters of Sarah 135; Earth's Daughters 140; Elf: Eclectic Literary Forum 142; Emrys Journal 142; Event 144; Farmer's Market, The 146; Feminist Studies 148; Fighting Woman News 149; Fireweed 150; Frontiers 153; Fuel Magazine 153; Graffiti Off The Asylum Walls 158; Gypsy 162; Hayden's Ferry Review 165; Herspectives 167; Home Planet News 170; Hyphen Magazine 172; Illinois Review, The 173; Inkslinger, The 174; Iowa Woman 176; Iris (VA) 177; Kennesaw Review 183; Kenyon Review, The 184; Kestrel 185; Kumquat Meringue 186; Left Bank 188; Little Magazine, The 193; Lizard's Eyelid Magazine 194; Long Story, The 194; Longneck, The 194; Lost Creek Letters 195; Medley of Pens 201; Midland Review 203; Milwaukee Undergraduate Review, The 204; Minnesota Review, The 206; Mixed Media 207; Mobius 208; Mostly Maine 209; Muse Portfolio 210; Mystic Fiction 211; Nahant Bay 212; NCASA Journal 213; Negative Capability 214; Noisy Concept 220; North Dakota Quarterly 221; Northwest Review 223; Obsidian II: Black Literature in Review 225; Olympia Review, The 227; Onionhead 228; Orange Coast Review 228; Oxalis 231; Oxford Magazine 231; Oxygen 232; Pacific Coast Journal 232; Painted Bride Quarterly 233; Palo Alto Review 233; Paper Bag, The 234; Pennsylvania Review 238; Perceptions (Montana) 238; Phoebe (New York) 239; Pinehurst Journal, The 241; Poetic Space 243; Poetry Forum Short Stories 243; Poetry Motel 243; Portable Wall, The 244; Poskisnolt Press 244; Primavera 247; Psychotrain 250; Puck! 250; Rag Mag 254; Rajah 254; Re Arts & Letters 255; Red Cedar Review 256; Red Dancefloor 256; Renegade 258; River Styx 260; RiverSedge 260; Riverwind 261; Room of One's Own 262; Salmon Magazine 263; Salt Lick Press 264; San Miguel Writer 264; Sanskrit 265; Seattle Review, The 266; Semiotext(e) 267; Shattered Wig Review 269; Shift Magazine 269; Short Fiction By Women 270; Side Show 270; Sing Heavenly Muse! 272; Sinister Wisdom 273; Skylark 273; Snake Nation Review 275; Southern California Anthology 277; Southern Exposure 277; Southern Humanities Review 278; Spit: A Journal of the Arts 281; SPSM&H 283; Struggle 286; Studio One 286; Tall Tales & Short Stories 289; Tamaqua 290; 13th Moon 294; This Magazine 294; Two-Ton Santa 299; Unforgettable Fire, The 300; Urbanus/Raizirr 302; VeriTales 302; Videomania 303; Vincent Brothers Review, The 303; Virginia Quarterly Review 304; West 305; West Coast Line 307; Willow Review 310; Wisconsin Restaurateur, The 312; Words of Wisdom 313; Writing For Our Lives 315; Xib 316; Yellow Silk 317; Zero Hour 318; Zuzu's Petals Quarterly 319

Gay ACM, (Another Chicago Magazine) 81; Adrift 82; Amelia 86; Apalachee Quarterly 92; Arizona Unconservative, The 94; Arnazella 94; Art:Mag 95; As If 96; Bahlasti Paper 99; Bakunin 99; Ball Magazine 100; bare wire 101; Big Rain 103; Black Fire 103; Bohemian Chronicle 110; Brave New Tick, (the) 111; Brownbag Press 113; Changing Men 118; Columbus Literary Gazette, The 124; Compost Newsletter 126; Crazyquilt 129; Creative Woman, The 130; Crucible 131; Deuterium 137; Duckabush Journal, The 140; Evergreen Chronicles, The 144; Feminist Studies 148; Fish Drum Magazine 151; Gay Chicago Magazine 155; Hayden's Ferry Review 165; Home Planet News 170; Hunted News, The 172; Hyphen Magazine 172; Illinois Review, The 173; Inkslinger, The 174; Iris (GA) 177; Kennesaw Review 183; Kenyon Review, The 184; Kumquat Meringue 186; Left Bank 188; Libido 189; Longneck, The 194; Milwaukee Undergraduate Review, The 204; Minnesota Review, The 206; Mixed Media 207; Mobius 208; Mostly Maine 209; Nahant Bay 212; National Gay & Lesbian Reader, The 212; NCASA Journal 213; Northeast Arts Magazine 221; Onionhead 228; Orange Coast Review 228; Oxalis 231; Oxford Magazine 231; Painted Bride Quarterly 233; PBW 236; Pendragon 237; Pennsylvania Review 238; Perceptions (Ohio) 239; Phoebe (New York) 239; Pinehurst Journal, The 241; Poetic Space 243; Poetry Motel 243; Poskisnolt Press 244; Primavera 247; Psychotrain 250; Puck! 250; Puckerbrush Review 251; RFD 259; River Styx 260; Salmon Magazine 263; Salt Lick Press 264; San Miguel Writer 264; Sanskrit 265; Seattle Review, The 266; Semiotext(e) 267; Sensations Magazine 267; Shattered Wig Review 269; Shift Magazine 269; Short Fiction By Women 270; Side Show 270; Sign of the Times 271; Snake Nation Review 275; Southern Exposure 277; Spit: A Journal of the Arts 281; SPSM&H 283; Tall Tales & Short Stories 289; Tamaqua 290; This Magazine 294; Two-Ton Santa 299; Unforgettable Fire, The 300; Urbanus/Raizirr 302; VeriTales 302; West 305; West Coast Line 307; White Review, The James 308; Wilde Oaks 310; Worm 314; Xib 316; Yellow Silk 317; Zero Hour 318; Zuzu's Petals Quarterly 319

Historical Advocate, The 82; Alabama Literary Review 84; Amelia 86; Anterior Fiction Quarterly 90; Appalachian Heritage 92; Ararat Quarterly 93; Archae 93; Arnazella 94; Array 94; Art:Mag 95; Art's Garbage Gazzette 96; Atalantik 97; Blue Ryder 108; Callaloo 114; Caribbean Writer, The 116; Chrysalis 120; Cochran's Corner 122; Columbus Literary Gazette, The 124; Compenions 125; Concho River Review 126; Crazyquilt 129; Creative Woman, The 130; Crime Club 131; Dan River Anthology 133; Daughters of Sarah 135; Deuterium 137; Downstate Story 138; Dream International/Quarterly 139; Elf: Eclectic Literary Forum 142; Fugue 153; Gettysburg Review, The 156; Gotta Write Network Litmag 158; Hayden's Ferry Review 165; Home Planet News 170; Housewife-Writer's Forum 171; Hyperbole 172; Hyphen Magazine 172; Infinity Limited 174; Inkslinger, The 174; Iowa Woman 176; Journal of Regional Criticism 181; Just A Moment 181; Kenyon Review, The 184; Kokopelli Notes 185; Lamplight, The 186; Language Bridges Quarterly 187; Legend 189;

Linington Lineup 191; Lite 192; Llamas Magazine 194; Longneck, The 194; MacGuffin, The 197; Medley of Pens 201; Merlyn's Pen 202; Midland Review 203; Milwaukee Undergraduate Review, The 204; Mind Matters Review 205; Minnesota Review, The 206; Mobius 208; Monocacy Valley Review, The 208; Mostly Maine 209; Mountain Laurel, The 210; Muse Portfolio 210; Mystic Fiction 211; Nahant Bay 212; Nassau Review 212; Negative Capability 214; New Methods 216; New Voices in Poetry and Prose 218; Nomos 220; North Dakota Quarterly 221; Northeast Arts Magazine 221; Oak, The 225; Olympia Review, The 227; Oxalis 231; Pacific Coast Journal 232; Palo Alto Review 233; Pendragon 237; Pinehurst Journal, The 241; Pipe Smoker's Ephemeris, The 241; Poetry Forum Short Stories 243; Portable Wall, The 244; Potpourri 246; Prophetic Voices 249; Puck! 250; Queen's Quarterly 253; Rajah 254; Re Arts & Letters 255; Renegade 258; Renovated Lighthouse Publications 258; RiverSedge 260; Riverwind 261; Rock Falls Review 261; S.L.U.G.fest, Ltd. 263; San Miguel Writer 264; Scifant 265; Seattle Review, The 266; Sensations Magazine 267; Shift Magazine 269; Short Stuff Magazine for Grown-ups 270; Southern California Anthology 277; Spectrum (Massachusetts) 279; Spit: A Journal of the Arts 281; SPSM&H 283; Struggle 286; Tall Tales & Short Stories 289; Tampa Review 290; Timberlines 295; Tucumcari Literary Review 298; VeriTales 302; Villager, The 303; Vincent Brothers Review, The 303; Vintage Northwest 304; West 305; Westview 307; Willow Review 310; Wisconsin Academy Review 311; Words of Wisdom 313; Worm 314; Writers' Open Forum 315; Xavier Review 316; Xib 316

Horror Aberations 80; Abyss Magazine 81; Aguilar Expression, The 83; Alternate Hilarities 85; Angst 88; Ansuda Magazine 89; Art:Mag 95; Art's Garbage Gazzette 96; Bahlasti Paper 99; Belletrist Review, The 101; Black Lace (FL) 106; Bloodreams 108; Blue Ryder 108; Cat's Ear 117; Cemetary Plot 117; Clifton Magazine 121; Cochran's Corner 122; Columbus Literary Gazette, The 124; Compenions 125; D.C. 132; Dagger of the Mind 132; Dan River Anthology 133; Dark Regions 134; Dark Tome 134; Dead of Night™ Magazine 135; Deathrealm 136; Downstate Story 138; Dream International/Quarterly 139; Dreams & Nightmares 139; Eldritch Tales 142; Eyes 146; Fugue 153; Gaslight 155; Glimpses Magazine 157; Graffiti Off The Asylum Walls 158; Grasslands Review 159; Grue Magazine 161; Haunts 164; Heart Attack Magazine 165; Heliocentric Net 166; Hor-Tasy 171; Hyperbole 172; Journal of Regional Criticism 181; Just A Moment 181; Kennesaw Review 183; Lines In The Sand 191; Lite 192; Lizard's Eyelid Magazine 194; Longneck, The 194; Lost Worlds 196; Medley of Pens 201; Meme-Shot Magazine 201; Merlyn's Pen 202; Midnight Zoo 204; Milwaukee Undergraduate Review, The 204; Mixed Media 207; Mobius 208; Mystic Fiction 211; Nahant Bay 212; New Voices in Poetry and Prose 218; No Idea Magazine 219; Nocturnal Lyric, The 220; Noisy Concept 220; Nuclear Fiction 224; Office Number One 225; Oxalis 231; Paper Bag, The 234; Pinehurst Journal, The 241; Pléiades Magazine/Philae 242; Puck! 250; Pulphouse 251; Rajah 254; Random Realities 254; Redcat Magazine 257; Rejects 258; Renegade 258; Riverwind 261; S.L.U.G.fest, Ltd. 263; Salmon Magazine 263; Scifant 265; Seattle Review, The 266; Sensations Magazine 267; Silver Web, The 272; Snake Nation Review 275; SPSM&H 283; Square One 283; Strange Days 285; Tall Tales & Short Stories 289; Terminal Fright 291; Terror Time Again 291; Theater Of Blood, A 292; Theatre ov the Night 292; Thin Ice 293; Tomorrow 296; Twisted 299; 2 AM Magazine 299; Two-Ton Santa 299; Unreality 301; Urbanite, The 301; Urbanus/Raizirr 302; Videomania 303; Virgin Meat 304; Wagons of Steel Magazine 305; Wicked Mystic 309; WonderDisk 312; Wyrd 316; Xib 316

Humor/Satire Aberations 80; Advocate, The 82; Alabama Literary Review 84; Alternate Hilarities 85; Amateur Writers Journal 85; Amelia 86; Anterior Fiction Quarterly 90; Ararat Quarterly 93; Archae 93; Arnazella 94; Array 94; Art:Mag 95; Art's Garbage Gazzette 96; Atalantik 97; Atrocity 98; Azorean Express, The 98; Baby Sue 99; Bad Haircut 99; Bahlasti Paper 99; Ball Magazine 100; bare wire 101; Belletrist Review, The 101; Big Rain 103; Black Hammock Review, The 104; Black Jack 105; Black River Review 106; Blis Magazine 107; Blood & Aphorisms 108; Blue Ryder 108; Blue Water Review, The 109; Blueline 109; Bohemian Chronicle 110; Brownbag Press 113; Bukowski and Serial Killers 114; Callaloo 114; Caribbean Writer, The 116; Cat's Ear 117; Cemetary Plot 117; Chaminade Literary Review 117; Changing Men 118; Clockwatch Review 122; Cochran's Corner 122; Collages and Bricolages 123; Columbus Literary Gazette, The 124; Companion in Zeor, A 125; Compenions 125; Compost Newsletter 126; Concho River Review 126; Corona 127; Crazyquilt 129; Cream City Review, The 130; Creative Woman, The 130; Crime Club 131; D.C. 132; Dan River Anthology 133; DIS 138; Downstate Story 138; Dream International/Quarterly 139; Dreams & Nightmares 139; Dreams & Visions 139; Duckabush Journal, The 140; Eidos 141; 1812 141; Elf: Eclectic Literary Forum 142; Escapist, The 144; Event 144; Explorations '94 145; Farmer's Market, The 146; Fat Tuesday 147; Fathers, Brothers, Sons 148; Fiction 149; Friction 153; Fugue 153; Gettysburg Review, The 156; Golden Isis Magazine 157; Gotta Write Network Litmag 158; Graffiti Off The Asylum Walls 158; Grasslands Review 159; Green Mountains Review 160; Green's Magazine 161; Gulf Coast 162; Hawaii Pacific Review 164; Hawaii Review 164; Hayden's Ferry Review 165; Heart Attack Magazine 165; Heartlands Today, The 165; High Plains Literary Review 167; Hill and Holler 168; Hob-Nob 168; Hopewell Review, The 170; Housewife-

Writer's Forum 171; Hunted News, The 172; Hyperbole 172; Hyphen Magazine 172; Iconoclast, The 173; Infinity Limited 174; Inkslinger, The 174; International Quarterly 175; Journal of Polymorphous Perversity 180; Journal of Regional Criticism 181; Just A Moment 181; Kennesaw Review 183; Kenyon Review, The 184; Kumquat Meringue 186; Lamplight, The 186; Language Bridges Quarterly 187; Leading Edge, The 188; Left Bank 188; Life Enrichment 190; Light Quarterly 190; Lines In The Sand 191; Lite 192; Little Magazine, The 193; Lizard's Eyelid Magazine 194; Llamas Magazine 194; Longneck, The 194; Lost Creek Letters 195; MacGuffin, The 197; Magic Mountain, The 198; Mark 200; Maryland Review, The 200; Medley of Pens 201; Meme-Shot Magazine 201; Merlyn's Pen 202; Milwaukee Undergraduate Review, The 204; Mimsy Musing 204; Mind in Motion 205; Mississippi Review 207; Mixed Media 207; Mobius 208; Monocacy Valley Review, The 208; Monthly Independent Tribune Times Journal Post Gazette News Chronicle Bulletin, The 208; Mostly Maine 209; Mountain Laurel, The 210; Mystic Fiction 211; Nahant Bay 212; NCASA Journal 213; Nebraska Review, The 213; New Delta Review 214; New Letters Magazine 216; New Press Literary Quarterly, The 217; new renaissance, the 217; New Voices in Poetry and Prose 218; New Writing 218; Night Owl's Newsletter 219; No Idea Magazine 219; Nocturnal Lyric, The 220; Noisy Concept 220; Nomos 220; North Dakota Quarterly 221; Oak, The 225; Office Number One 225; Olympia Review, The 227; Onionhead 228; Orange Coast Review 228; Other Voices 228; Owen Wister Review 230; Oxalis 231; Oxford Magazine 231; Pacific Coast Journal 232; Palo Alto Review 233; Pearl 236; Pegasus Review, The 237; Pennsylvania Review 238; Perceptions (Ohio) 239; Phoebe (New York) 239; Pinehurst Journal, The 241; Pipe Smoker's Ephemeris, The 241; Poetic Space 243; Poetry Motel 243; Portable Wall, The 244; Portland Review 244; Poskisnolt Press 244; Potato Eyes 245; Potpourri 246; Primavera 247; Processed World 249; Psychotrain 250; Puck! 250; Queen's Quarterly 253; Rajah 254; Reach Magazine 256; Red Cedar Review 256; Renegade 258; River Styx 260; Riverwind 261; Rock Falls Review 261; Rocket Literary Quarterly 262; Rockford Review, The 262; S.L.U.G.fest, Ltd. 263; San Gabriel Valley Magazine 264; San Jose Studies 264; San Miguel Writer 264; Sanskrit 265; Scifant 265; Seattle Review, The 266; Secret Alameda, The 266; Sensations Magazine 267; Shattered Wig Review 269; Shift Magazine 269; Shockbox 269; Short Stuff Magazine for Grown-ups 270; Side Show 270; Sidewalks 271; Silver Web, The 272; Single Scene, The 272; Skylark 273; Slate and Style 273; Slipstream 274; Snake Nation Review 275; Snake River Reflections 275; South Carolina Review 276; Southern California Anthology 277; Southern Exposure 277; Southern Humanities Review 278; Spit: A Journal of the Arts 281; Spoofing! 281; SPSM&H 283; Story 285; Strange Days 285; Struggle 286; Studio One 286; Sub-Terrain 287; Sycamore Review 288; Tales of the Heart 289; Tall Tales & Short Stories 289; Tamaqua 290; Tampa Review 290; Thema 293; Thin Ice 293; Tickled By Thunder 295; Timberlines 295; Touchstone Literary Journal 296; Tributary 296; Tucumcari Literary Review 298; Turnstile 298; 2 AM Magazine 299; Two-Ton Santa 299; Unforgettable Fire, The 300; Urbanite, The 301; Urbanus/Raizirr 302; VeriTales 302; Videomania 303; Villager, The 303; Vincent Brothers Review, The 303; Vintage Northwest 304; Virginia Quarterly Review 304; Wagons of Steel Magazine 305; Wascana Review 305; West 305; Westview 307; Whisper 308; William and Mary Review, The 310; Willow Review 310; Wisconsin Academy Review 311; Wisconsin Restaurateur, The 312; Wolfridgereview 312; Words of Wisdom 313; Writers' Open Forum 315; Writing For Our Lives 315; Wyrd 316; Xib 316; Yellow Silk 317; Zero Hour 318; Zoiks! 318; Zuzu's Petals Quarterly 319

Lesbian ACM, (Another Chicago Magazine) 81; Adrift 82; Amelia 86; Apalachee Quarterly 92; Arizona Unconservative, The 94; Arnazella 94; Art:Mag 95; Bahlasti Paper 99; Bakunin 99; Ball Magazine 100; bare wire 101; Big Rain 103; Black Lace (CA) 105; Brownbag Press 113; Changing Men 118; Columbus Literary Gazette, The 124; Common Lives/Lesbian Lives 124; Compost Newsletter 126; Creative Woman, The 130; Crucible 131; Daughters of Nyx 134; Evergreen Chronicles, The 144; Feminist Studies 148; Fish Drum Magazine 151; Frontiers 153; Gay Chicago Magazine 155; Herspectives 167; Home Planet News 170; Hunted News, The 172; Hyphen Magazine 172; Illinois Review, The 173; Inkslinger, The 174; Iris (VA) 177; Kenyon Review, The 184; Kumquat Meringue 186; Left Bank 188; Libido 189; Longneck, The 194; Milwaukee Undergraduate Review, The 204; Minnesota Review, The 206; Mixed Media 207; Mobius 208; Mostly Maine 209; Nahant Bay 212; National Gay & Lesbian Reader, The 212; Onionhead 228; Orange Coast Review 228; Oxalis 231; Oxford Magazine 231; Painted Bride Quarterly 233; PBW 236; Pendragon 237; Pennsylvania Review 238; Perceptions (Ohio) 239; Phoebe (New York) 239; Pinehurst Journal, The 241; Poetic Space 243; Poetry Motel 243; Poskisnolt Press 244; Primavera 247; Psychotrain 250; Puck! 250; Rajah 254; River Styx 260; Room of One's Own 262; Salmon Magazine 263; Salt Lick Press 264; San Miguel Writer 264; Sanskrit 265; Seattle Review, The 266; Sensations Magazine 267; Shattered Wig Review 269; Shift Magazine 269; Short Fiction By Women 270; Side Show 270; Sign of the Times 271; Sinister Wisdom 273; Snake Nation Review 275; Southern Exposure 277; Spit: A Journal of the Arts 281; SPSM&H 283; Tall Tales & Short Stories 289; This Magazine 294; Two-Ton Santa 299; Unforgettable Fire, The 300; Urbanus/Raizirr 302; VeriTales 302; Videomania

303; West 305; Wilde Oaks 310; Worm 314; Writing For Our Lives 315; Xib 316; Yellow Silk 317; Zuzu's Petals Quarterly 319

Literary ACM, (Another Chicago Magazine) 81; Adrift 82; Advocate, The 82; Alabama Fiction Review 83; Alabama Literary Review 84; Alaska Quarterly Review 84; Alpha Beat Press 84; Ambergris 85; Amelia 86; American Fiction 87; American Literary Review 87; American Short Fiction 87; American Voice, The 88; Americas Review, The 88; Ansuda Magazine 89; Antaeus 89; Anterior Fiction Quarterly 90; Antietam Review 90; Antigonish Review, The 91; Antioch Review 91; Apalachee Quarterly 92; Appalachian Heritage 92; Ararat Quarterly 93; Archae 93; Arizona Unconservative, The 94; Arnazella 94; Array 94; Artemis 95; Artful Dodge 95; Art:Mag 95; Art's Garbage Gazzette 96; Asylum Annual 97; Atalantik 97; Atlantean Press Review, The 98; Azorean Express, The 98; Bahlasti Paper 99; Bakunin 99; Ball Magazine 100; Bamboo Ridge 100; bare wire 101; Belletrist Review, The 101; Bellingham Review, The 102; Bellowing Ark 102; Beloit Fiction Journal 102; Big Rain 103; Black Hammock Review, The 104; Black Ice 105; Black Jack 105; Black Mountain Review 106; Black River Review 106; Black Warrior Review 107; Blis Magazine 107; Blood & Aphorisms 108; Blue Ryder 108; Blue Water Review, The 109; Blueline 109; Bohemian Chronicle 110; Boulevard 111; Brownbag Press 113; Bukowski and Serial Killers 114; Byline 114; Callaloo 114; Calliope 115; Capilano Review, The 115; Caribbean Writer, The 116; Carolina Quarterly 116; Carousel Literary Arts Magazine 116; Cat's Ear 117; Chaminade Literary Review 117; Changing Men 118; Chariton Review, The 118; Chattahoochee Review, The 118; Chelsea 119; Chicago Review 119; Chrysalis 120; Cimarron Review 121; Clifton Magazine 121; Clockwatch Review 122; Collages and Bricolages 123; Colorado Review 123; Columbus Literary Gazette, The 124; Compenions 125; Concho River Review 126; Confrontation 126; Cornfield Review 127; Corona 127; Cottonwood 129; Crazyhorse 129; Crazyquilt 129; Cream City Review, The 130; Creative Woman, The 130; Crime Club 131; Crucible 131; Dalhousie Review, The 133; Dan River Anthology 133; Dandelion Magazine 133; Daughters of Nyx 134; Denver Quarterly 137; Descant (Ontario) 137; Descant (Texas) 137; Downstate Story 138; Dream International/Quarterly 139; Dreams & Visions 139; Duckabush Journal, The 140; Eagle's Flight 140; 1812 141; Elf: Eclectic Literary Forum 142; Emrys Journal 142; Epiphany 143; Epoch Magazine 143; Escapist, The 144; Event 144; Explorer Magazine 145; Farmer's Market, The 146; Fat Tuesday 147; Fathers, Brothers, Sons 148; Fiction 149; Fiction International 149; Fiddlehead, The 149; Fine Madness 150; Fish Drum Magazine 151; Flipside 151; Florida Review, The 151; Folio: A Literary Journal 152; Friction 153; Fuel Magazine 153; Fugue 153; Gaia 154; Georgetown Review 155; Georgia Review, The 156; Gettysburg Review, The 156; Glimmer Train Stories 157; Gotta Write Network Litmag 158; Grain 159; Grand Street 159; Grasslands Review 159; Green Mountains Review 160; Green's Magazine 161; Greensboro Review 161; Gulf Coast 162; Gulf Stream Magazine 162; Gypsy 162; Habersham Review 163; Hawaii Pacific Review 164; Hawaii Review 164; Hayden's Ferry Review 165; Heartlands Today, The 165; High Plains Literary Review 167; Hill and Holler 168; Hob-Nob 168; Home Planet News 170; Hopewell Review, The 170; Housewife-Writer's Forum 171; Hunted News, The 172; Hyperbole 172; Hyphen Magazine 172; Iconoclast, The 173; Illinois Review, The 173; Immanent Face Magazine 173; Indiana Review 174; Infinity Limited 174; Inkslinger, The 174; Innisfree 175; Interim 175; International Quarterly 175; Iowa Woman 176; Iris (VA) 177; Journal, The (Ohio) 180; Journal of Regional Criticism 181; Just A Moment 181; Kaleidoscope 182; Kalliope 182; Karamu 183; Kennesaw Review 183; Kenyon Review, The 184; Kestrel 185; Kumquat Meringue 186; Lactuca 186; Lamplight, The 186; Language Bridges Quarterly 187; Laurel Review, The 187; Ledge Poetry and Fiction Magazine, The 188; Left Bank 188; Life Enrichment 190; Light Quarterly 190; Limestone: A Literary Journal 190; Linden Lane Magazine 191; Lines In The Sand 191; Linington Lineup 191; Lite 192; Literary Review, The 192; Little Magazine, The 193; Long Story, The 194; Longneck, The 194; Loonfeather 195; Lost and Found Times 195; Lost Creek Letters 195; Louisiana Literature 196; MacGuffin, The 197; Madison Review, The 198; Magic Changes 198; Magic Realism 199; Manoa 200; Mark 200; Maryland Review, The 200; Medley of Pens 201; Men As We Are 202; Merlyn's Pen 202; Metropolitan 202; Michigan Quarterly Review 203; Mid-American Review 203; Midland Review 203; Milwaukee Undergraduate Review, The 204; Mind in Motion 205; Mind Matters Review 205; Minnesota Review, The 206; Minus 7 Magazine 206; Mississippi Review 207; Mississippi Valley Review 207; Missouri Review, The 207; Mixed Media 207; Mobius 208; Monocacy Valley Review, The 208; Moody Street Review, The 209; Mostly Maine 209; Muse Portfolio 210; Mystic Fiction 211; Nahant Bay 212; Nassau Review 212; NCASA Journal 213; Nebo 213; Nebraska Review, The 213; Negative Capability 214; New Delta Review 214; New England Review 215; New Laurel Review 215; New Letters Magazine 216; New Orleans Review 216; New Press Literary Quarterly, The 217; new renaissance, the 217; New Virginia Review 217; New Voices in Poetry and Prose 218; New Writing 218; Night Owl's Newsletter 219; Noisy Concept 220; North American Review, The 221; North Dakota Quarterly 221; Northeast Arts Magazine 221; Northwest Review 223; Northwoods Journal 223; Now & Then 224; Oasis 225; Office Number One 225; Ohio Review, The 226; Old Hickory Review 226; Old Red Kimono, The 227; Olympia

Stream Magazine 162; Habersham Review 163; Hawaii Pacific Review 164; Hawaii Review 164; Hayden's Ferry Review 165; Heartlands Today, The 165; High Plains Literary Review 167; Hill and Holler 168; Hob-Nob 168; Home Planet News 170; Hopewell Review, The 170; Housewife-Writer's Forum 171; Hunted News, The 172; Hyperbole 172; Hyphen Magazine 172; Iconoclast, The 173; Illinois Review, The 173; Immanent Face Magazine 173; Indiana Review 174; Infinity Limited 174; Inkslinger, The 174; Innisfree 175; International Quarterly 175; Iris (VA) 177; Journal, The (Pennsylvania) 180; Journal of Regional Criticism 181; Just A Moment 181; Karamu 183; Kennesaw Review 183; Kentucky Writing 184; Kenyon Review, The 184; Kestrel 185; Kumquat Meringue 186; Lactuca 186; Laurel Review, The 187; Left Bank 188; Life Enrichment 190; Limestone: A Literary Journal 190; Linden Lane Magazine 190; Lines In The Sand 191; Long Story, The 194; Longneck, The 194; Lost and Found Times 195; Lost Creek Letters 195; Louisiana Literature 196; MacGuffin, The 197; Manoa 200; Mark 200; Maryland Review, The 200; Medley of Pens 201; Men As We Are 202; Merlyn's Pen 202; Metropolitan 202; Milwaukee Undergraduate Review, The 204; Mimsy Musing 204; Minus 7 Magazine 206; Mississippi Review 207; Mississippi Valley Review 207; Missouri Review, The 207; Mixed Media 207; Mobius 208; Monocacy Valley Review, The 208; Moody Street Review, The 209; Mostly Maine 209; Muse Portfolio 210; Mystic Fiction 211; Nahant Bay 212; Nassau Review 212; NCASA Journal 213; Nebo 213; Nebraska Review, The 213; Negative Capability 214; New Delta Review 214; New Laurel Review 215; New Letters Magazine 216; New Methods 216; New Orleans Review 216; New Press Literary Quarterly, The 217; New Virginia Review 217; New Voices in Poetry and Prose 218; New Writing 218; Noisy Concept 220; North Atlantic Review 221; North Dakota Quarterly 221; Northwest Review 223; Northwoods Journal 223; Oak, The 225; Oasis 225; Ohio Review, The 226; Old Hickory Review 226; Olympia Review, The 227; Onionhead 228; Orange Coast Review 228; Other Voices 228; Oxalis 231; Oxygen 232; Painted Bride Quarterly 233; Palo Alto Review 233; Paper Bag, The 234; Partisan Review 235; Pearl 236; Pendragon 237; Pennsylvania English 238; Perceptions (Montana) 238; Phoebe (Virginia) 240; Pikestaff Forum, The 240; Pinehurst Journal, The 241; Poetic Space 243; Poetry Forum Short Stories 243; Poetry Motel 243; Pointed Circle, The 243; Portable Wall, The 244; Portland Review 244; Poskisnolt Press 244; Potato Eyes 245; Potpourri 246; Prairie Fire 246; Prairie Journal of Canadian Literature, The 247; Primavera 247; Prism International 248; Processed World 249; Puerto Del Sol 251; Quarterly West 252; Queen's Quarterly 253; Rag Mag 254; Rajah 254; Re Arts & Letters 255; Reach Magazine 256; Redneck Review of Literature, The 257; Renegade 258; Renovated Lighthouse Publications 258; River Styx 260; RiverSedge 260; Riverwind 261; Rock Falls Review 261; Round Table, The 263; S.L.U.G.fest, Ltd. 263; Salmon Magazine 263; Salt Lick Press 264; San Gabriel Valley Magazine 264; Sanskrit 265; Santa Monica Review 265; Seattle Review, The 266; Sensations Magazine 267; Sewanee Review, The 268; Shattered Wig Review 269; Shift Magazine 269; Short Fiction By Women 270; Short Stuff Magazine for Grown-ups 270; Side Show 270; Sidewalks 271; Single Scene, The 272; Skylark 273; Slate and Style 273; Slipstream 274; Snake Nation Review 275; Soundings East 276; South Carolina Review 276; South Dakota Review 276; Southern California Anthology 277; Southern Exposure 277; Southern Review, The 278; Spectrum (Massachusetts) 279; Spirit That Moves Us, The 280; Spit: A Journal of the Arts 281; SPSM&H 283; Square One 283; Story 285; Stroker Magazine 286; Struggle 286; Studio One 286; Sycamore Review 288; Tall Tales & Short Stories 289; Tamaqua 290; Tampa Review 290; Texas Review, The 292; Thema 293; This Magazine 294; Tickled By Thunder 295; Timberlines 295; Touchstone Literary Journal 296; Triquarterly 298; Tucumcari Literary Review 298; Turnstile 298; Two-Ton Santa 299; Underpass 300; Unmuzzled Ox 301; Urbanus/Raizirr 302; VeriTales 302; Videomania 303; Vincent Brothers Review, The 303; West 305; West Branch 306; Westview 307; Whetstone 308; Whisper 308; Widener Review 309; William and Mary Review, The 310; Willow Review 310; Wind Magazine 311; Wisconsin Academy Review 311; Wisconsin Restaurateur, The 312; Wolfridgereview 312; Words of Wisdom 313; Worm 314; Writers' Forum 314; Writers' Open Forum 315; Writing on the Wall, The 316; Xavier Review 316; Xtreme 317; Zyzzyva 319

Mystery/Suspense Acorn, The 81; Advocate, The 82; Aguilar Expression, The 83; Amateur Writers Journal 85; Amelia 86; Angst 88; Ansuda Magazine 89; Anterior Fiction Quarterly 90; Arnazella 94; Array 94; Art:Mag 95; Art's Garbage Gazzette 96; Atalantik 97; Atlantean Press Review, The 98; Belletrist Review, The 101; Blue Water Review, The 109; Bohemian Chronicle 110; Cemetary Plot 117; Chrysalis 120; Cochran's Corner 122; Columbus Literary Gazette, The 124; Compenions 125; Crazyquilt 129; Crime Club 131; Dagger of the Mind 132; Dan River Anthology 133; Dead of Night™ Magazine 135; Deuterium 137; Dogwood Tales Magazine 138; Downstate Story 138; Dream International/Quarterly 139; Eagle's Flight 140; Elf: Eclectic Literary Forum 142; Escapist, The 144; Fighting Woman News 149; Fugue 153; Gaslight 155; Glimpses Magazine 157; Grasslands Review 159; Green's Magazine 161; Hardboiled 163; Heart Attack Magazine 165; Hob-Nob 168; Housewife-Writer's Forum 171; Hyperbole 172; Infinity Limited 174; Inkslinger, The 174; Innisfree 175; Just A Moment 181; Lamplight, The 186; Lines In The Sand 191; Linington Lineup 191; Lite

216; New Voices in Poetry and Prose 218; NeWest Review 218; Northwoods Journal 223; Now & Then 224; Oak, The 225; Olympia Review, The 227; Onionhead 228; Oxalis 231; Palo Alto Review 233; Partisan Review 235; Pendragon 237; Pennsylvania Review 238; Phoebe (Virginia) 240; Poetic Space 243; Pointed Circle, The 243; Portable Wall, The 244; Portland Review 244; Potato Eyes 245; Prairie Journal of Canadian Literature, The 247; Puck! 250; Rag Mag 254; Rajah 254; Raven Chronicles, The 255; Re Arts & Letters 255; Reach Magazine 256; Red Cedar Review 256; Renovated Lighthouse Publications 258; RiverSedge 260; Riverwind 261; Rock Falls Review 261; Rockford Review, The 262; S.L.U.G.fest, Ltd. 263; Salmon Magazine 263; San Jose Studies 264; San Miguel Writer 264; Sanskrit 265; Seattle Review, The 266; Sensations Magazine 267; Shattered Wig Review 269; Shift Magazine 269; Short Stuff Magazine for Grown-ups 270; Sidewalks 271; Skylark 273; Snake Nation Review 275; Snake River Reflections 275; South Dakota Review 276; Southern California Anthology 277; Southern Exposure 277; Southern Humanities Review 278; Spit: A Journal of the Arts 281; Spoofing! 281; SPSM&H 283; Struggle 286; Studio One 286; Sycamore Review 288; Tall Tales & Short Stories 289; Tamaqua 290; Thema 293; This Magazine 294; Timberlines 295; Tucumcari Literary Review 298; Turnstile 298; Valley Grapevine 302; VeriTales 302; Vincent Brothers Review, The 303; Washington Review 305; West 305; Widener Review 309; Willow Review 310; Wisconsin Academy Review 311; Wisconsin Restaurateur, The 312; Words of Wisdom 313; Writers' Forum 314; Writers' Open Forum 315; Xavier Review 316; Xib 316; Zuzu's Petals Quarterly 319; Zyzzyva 319

Religious/Inspirational Acorn, The 81; Amateur Writers Journal 85; Ararat Quarterly 93; Art's Garbage Gazzette 96; Being 101; Beloit Fiction Journal 102; Chaminade Literary Review 117; Cochran's Corner 122; Crime Club 131; Daughters of Sarah 135; Dreams & Visions 139; Escapist, The 144; Explorer Magazine 145; Heaven Bone 166; Hob-Nob 168; Inkslinger, The 174; Journal of Regional Criticism 181; Language Bridges Quarterly 187; Life Enrichment 190; Living Water Magazine 193; Medley of Pens 201; Milwaukee Undergraduate Review, The 204; Miraculous Medal, The 207; New Press Literary Quarterly, The 217; New Voices in Poetry and Prose 218; Now & Then 224; Oxygen 232; Pegasus Review, The 237; Perceptions (Montana) 238; Poetry Forum Short Stories 243; Puck! 250; Queen of All Hearts 253; Reach Magazine 256; Renegade 258; Riverwind 261; Rock Falls Review 261; S.L.U.G.fest, Ltd. 263; Skylark 273; Starlight 284; Tickled By Thunder 295; Two-Ton Santa 299; VeriTales 302; Xavier Review 316; Young Judaean 317

Romance Acorn, The 81; Advocate, The 82; Aguilar Expression, The 83; Amateur Writers Journal 85; Anterior Fiction Quarterly 90; Array 94; Art's Garbage Gazzette 96; As If 96; Atalantik 97; Black Hammock Review, The 104; Bohemian Chronicle 110; Cochran's Corner 122; Compenions 125; Dan River Anthology 133; Deuterium 137; Dogwood Tales Magazine 138; Downstate Story 138; Dream International/Quarterly 139; Eagle's Flight 140; Explorer Magazine 145; Eyes 146; Fugue 153; Galaxy Class 154; Gay Chicago Magazine 155; Gotta Write Network Litmag 158; Hayden's Ferry Review 165; Heart Attack Magazine 165; Hob-Nob 168; Housewife-Writer's Forum 171; Infinity Limited 174; Inkslinger, The 174; Journal of Regional Criticism 181; Just A Moment 181; Lamplight, The 186; Medley of Pens 201; Merlyn's Pen 202; Milwaukee Undergraduate Review, The 204; Mixed Media 207; Mostly Maine 209; Muse Portfolio 210; Negative Capability 214; New Voices in Poetry and Prose 218; Northwoods Journal 223; Oak, The 225; Oxalis 231; Palo Alto Review 233; Peoplenet 238; Poetry Forum Short Stories 243; Poskisnolt Press 244; Post, The 245; Potpourri 246; PSI 250; Reach Magazine 256; Renegade 258; Rock Falls Review 261; San Miguel Writer 264; Scifant 265; Sensations Magazine 267; Short Stuff Magazine for Grownups 270; Skylark 273; SPSM&H 283; Tails of Wonder 288; Tall Tales & Short Stories 289; 2 AM Magazine 299; VeriTales 302; Villager, The 303; Virginia Quarterly Review 304; Wolfridgereview 312; Writers' Open Forum 315

Science Fiction Aberations 80; Abyss Magazine 81; Acorn, The 81; Advocate, The 82; Alabama Literary Review 84; Alternate Hilarities 85; Amateur Writers Journal 85; Amelia 86; Argonaut 93; Array 94; Art:Mag 95; Art's Garbage Gazzette 96; Atalantik 97; Atlantean Press Review, The 98; Bahlasti Paper 99; Ball Magazine 100; Black Hammock Review, The 104; Blis Magazine 107; Blue Ryder 108; Blue Water Review, The 109; Bohemian Chronicle 110; Bravo Mundo Nuevo 112; Callaloo 114; Cat's Ear 117; Chrysalis 120; Clifton Magazine 121; Cochran's Corner 122; Columbus Literary Gazette, The 124; Communities: Journal of Cooperation 124; Companion in Zeor, A 125; Compenions 125; Compost Newsletter 126; Cosmic Landscapes 127; Cottonwood 129; Crazyquilt 129; Crime Club 131; Dagger of the Mind 132; Dan River Anthology 133; Dark Regions 134; Daughters of Nyx 134; Dead of Night™ Magazine 135; Deathrealm 136; Deuterium 137; Downstate Story 138; Dream International/Quarterly 139; Dreams & Nightmares 139; Dreams & Visions 139; Elf: Eclectic Literary Forum 142; Escapist, The 144; Explorer Magazine 145; Explosive Decompression 146; Fighting Woman News 149; Figment Magazine 150; Fish Drum Magazine 151; Fugue 153; Gaia 154; Galaxy Class 154; Gaslight 155; Glimpses Magazine 157; Gotta Write Network Litmag 158; Grasslands Review 159; Green's Magazine 161; Hawaii Pacific Review 164; Hayden's

Ferry Review 165; Heart Attack Magazine 165; Hob-Nob 168; Hobson's Choice 169; Home Planet News 170; Hyperbole 172; Hyphen Magazine 172; Iconoclast, The 173; Immanent Face Magazine 173; Infinity Limited 174; Inkslinger, The 174; Innisfree 175; Journal of Regional Criticism 181; Just A Moment 181; Leading Edge, The 188; Lines In The Sand 191; Lite 192; Lost Creek Letters 195; Lost Worlds 196; MacGuffin, The 197; Magic Changes 198; Magic Mountain, The 198; Mark 200; Medley of Pens 201; Meme-Shot Magazine 201; Merlyn's Pen 202; Midnight Zoo 204; Milwaukee Undergraduate Review, The 204; Mind in Motion 205; Mobius 208; Mostly Maine 209; Mystic Fiction 211; Nahant Bay 212; Negative Capability 214; New Voices in Poetry and Prose 218; Nimrod 219; No Idea Magazine 219; Nocturnal Lyric, The 220; Noisy Concept 220; Nomos 220; Northwoods Journal 223; Nuclear Fiction 224; Offworld 226; Olympia Review, The 227; Once Upon A World 227; Other Worlds 229; Oxalis 231; Pablo Lennis 232; Pacific Coast Journal 232; Palo Alto Review 233; Paper Radio 234; Perceptions (Montana) 238; Perceptions (Ohio) 239; Pirate Writings 241; Poetry Forum Short Stories 243; Poetry Motel 243; Portable Wall, The 244; Potpourri 246; Primavera 247; Processed World 249; Puck! 250; Pulphouse 251; Quanta 252; Queen's Quarterly 253; Random Realities 254; Re Arts & Letters 255; Rejects 258; Renegade 258; Renovated Lighthouse Publications 258; Riverside Quarterly 261; Rock Falls Review 261; Rocket Literary Quarterly 262; Rockford Review, The 262; Salmon Magazine 263; San Miguel Writer 264; Scifant 265; Scream of the Buddha 266; Seattle Review, The 266; Semiotext(e) 267; Sensations Magazine 267; Sidetrekked 271; Silver Web, The 272; Skylark 273; Snake Nation Review 275; SPSM&H 283; Square One 283; Strange Days 285; Struggle 286; Tails of Wonder 288; Tales of the Heart 289; Tall Tales & Short Stories 289; Temporary Culture 291; Thema 293; Tickled By Thunder 295; Tomorrow 296; Tributary 296; 2 AM Magazine 299; Urbanite, The 301; Urbanus/Raizirr 302; VeriTales 302; Videomania 303; Vincent Brothers Review, The 303; Westview 307; Whisper 308; Wisconsin Restaurateur, The 312; WonderDisk 312; Worm 314; Writers' Open Forum 315; Wyrd 316; Xib 316; Yellow Silk 317

Senior Citizen/Retirement Advocate, The 82; Amelia 86; Dan River Anthology 133; Fathers, Brothers, Sons 148; Hayden's Ferry Review 165; Hob-Nob 168; Inkslinger, The 174; Just A Moment 181; Life Enrichment 190; Lines In The Sand 191; Medley of Pens 201; Muse Portfolio 210; Negative Capability 214; Oxalis 231; Pléiades Magazine/Philae 242; Poetry Forum Short Stories 243; Portable Wall, The 244; Poskisnolt Press 244; Rock Falls Review 261; Salmon Magazine 263; San Miguel Writer 264; Snake Nation Review 275; Spit: A Journal of the Arts 281; SPSM&H 283; Struggle 286; Tall Tales & Short Stories 289; Timberlines 295; Tucumcari Literary Review 298; Two-Ton Santa 299; VeriTales 302; Vincent Brothers Review, The 303; Vintage Northwest 304; Writers' Open Forum 315; Xib 316

Serialized/Excerpted Novel Agni 83; Alabama Fiction Review 83; Alabama Literary Review 84; Antaeus 89; Art:Mag 95; Art's Garbage Gazzette 96; Bahlasti Paper 99; Bakunin 99; Ball Magazine 100; Bellowing Ark 102; Black Hammock Review, The 104; Black Jack 105; Bohemian Chronicle 110; Callaloo 114; Columbus Literary Gazette, The 124; Compost Newsletter 126; Crazyquilt 129; Crime Club 131; Farmer's Market, The 146; Fat Tuesday 147; Gettysburg Review, The 156; Green Mountains Review 160; Gypsy 162; Hob-Nob 168; Hunted News, The 172; Hyperbole 172; Hyphen Magazine 172; Immanent Face Magazine 173; Inkslinger, The 174; Lost Worlds 196; Madison Review, The; Mid-American Review 203; Mystery Notebook 210; Nassau Review 212; NCASA Journal 213; New Press Literary Quarterly, The 217; New Virginia Review 217; Now & Then 224; Orange Coast Review 228; Other Voices 228; Phoebe (Virginia) 240; Pikestaff Forum, The 240; Pléiades Magazine/Philae 242; Poetic Space 243; Prairie Journal of Canadian Literature, The 247; Puerto Del Sol 251; Quarry 252; Rajah 254; Reach Magazine 256; River City 260; River Styx 260; Salmon Magazine 263; San Miguel Writer 264; Scifant 265; Seattle Review, The 266; Shift Magazine 269; Short Fiction By Women 270; Skylark 273; South Dakota Review 276; Southern California Anthology 277; Tales of the Heart 289; Vincent Brothers Review, The 303; Virginia Quarterly Review 304; Widener Review 309; Writing on the Wall, The 316; Xavier Review 316

Short Story Collections Ararat Quarterly 93; Painted Bride Quarterly 233

Sports Advocate, The 82; Aethlon 82; Amelia 86; Anterior Fiction Quarterly 90; Art's Garbage Gazzette 96; Atlantean Press Review, The 98; Beloit Fiction Journal 102; Blue Water Review, The 109; Changing Men 118; Chrysalis 120; Elf: Eclectic Literary Forum 142; Fugue 153; Hob-Nob 168; Iconoclast, The 173; Inkslinger, The 174; Just A Moment 181; Magic Changes 198; Medley of Pens 201; Milwaukee Undergraduate Review, The 204; Mostly Maine 209; New Press Literary Quarterly, The 217; Northwoods Journal 223; Now & Then 224; Oxalis 231; Portable Wall, The 244; Reach Magazine 256; Riverwind 261; Rock Falls Review 261; Skylark 273; Spitball 281; Tall Tales & Short Stories 289; Thema 293; VeriTales 302; Writers' Open Forum 315

Translations ACM, (Another Chicago Magazine) 81; Adrift 82; Agni 83; Alabama Fiction Review 83; Alabama Literary Review 84; Alaska Quarterly Review 84; Amelia 86; Antaeus 89; Antigonish Review, The 91; Antioch Review 91; Apalachee Quarterly 92; Ararat Quarterly 93; Archae 93; Arnazella 94; Artful Dodge 95; Art:Mag 95; Art's Garbage Gazzette 96; Asylum Annual 97; Atalantik 97; Atlantean Press Review, The 98; Bad Haircut 99; Bakunin 99; Ball Magazine 100; Big

Rain 103; Black Hammock Review, The 104; Black Ice 104; Brownbag Press 113; Callaloo 114; Chaminade Literary Review 117; Chariton Review, The 118; Chelsea 119; Cicada 120; Colorado Review 123; Compenions 125; Confrontation 126; Cream City Review, The 130; Descant (Ontario) 137; Dream International/Quarterly 139; 1812 141; Escapist, The 144; Fiction 149; Fighting Woman News 149; Fine Madness 150; Folio: A Literary Journal 152; Grand Street 159; Green Mountains Review 160; Gulf Coast 162; Gypsy 162; Hawaii Pacific Review 164; Hawaii Review 164; Hopewell Review, The 170; Hunted News, The 172; Hyperbole 172; Hyphen Magazine 172; Immanent Face Magazine 173; Infinity Limited 174; Inkslinger, The 174; International Quarterly 175; Jewish Currents Magazine 179; Kenyon Review, The 184; Kestrel 185; Language Bridges Quarterly 187; MacGuffin, The 197; Manoa 200; Medley of Pens 201; Men As We Are 202; Mid-American Review 203; Midland Review 203; Mississippi Review 207; Moody Street Review, The 209; Nahant Bay 212; NCASA Journal 213; Negative Capability 214; New Delta Review 214; New Laurel Review 215; New Letters Magazine 216; New Orleans Review 216; New Press Literary Quarterly, The 217; new renaissance, the 217; New Writing 218. Nimrod 219; Northwest Review 223; Olympia Review, The 227; Orange Coast Review 228; Owen Wister Review 230; Oxford Magazine 231; Oxygen 232; Painted Bride Quarterly 233; Palo Alto Review 233; Partisan Review 235; Pennsylvania Review 238; Phoebe (New York) 239; Phoebe (Virginia) 240; Poetic Space 243; Portable Wall, The 244; Porter International, Bern 244; Prism International 248; Psychotrain 250; Puck! 250; Puerto Del Sol 251; Quarry 252; Quarterly West 252; Rajah 254; Renegade 258; River Styx 260; RiverSedge 260; Riverwind 261; Salmon Magazine 263; San Miguel Writer 264; Sanskrit 265; Seattle Review, The 266; Semiotext(e) 267; Shift Magazine 269; Short Fiction By Women 270; Silverfish Review 272; South Dakota Review 276; Spit: A Journal of the Arts 281; SPSM&H 283; Story 285; Struggle 286; Sycamore Review 288; Tales of the Heart 289; Tampa Review 290; Thrust 295; Touchstone Literary Journal 296; Translation 296; Triquarterly 298; Unmuzzled Ox 301; Vincent Brothers Review, The 303; Virginia Quarterly Review 304; Webster Review 305; West 305; West Branch 306; Wind Magazine 311; Writing For Our Lives 315; Xavier Review 316; Xib 316; Yellow Silk 317; Zero Hour 318; Zoiks! 318

Western Advocate, The 82; Amelia 86; Art's Garbage Gazzette 96; Atlantean Press Review, The 98; Azorean Express, The 98; Black Jack 105; Columbus Literary Gazette, The 124; Compenions 125; Concho River Review 126; Dan River Anthology 133; Downstate Story 138; Elf: Eclectic Literary Forum 142; Fugue 153; Ghost Town 156; Grasslands Review 159; Hob-Nob 168; Inkslinger, The 174; Innisfree 175; Just A Moment 181; Lines In The Sand 191; Medley of Pens 201; Merlyn's Pen 202; Milwaukee Undergraduate Review, The 204; Mostly Maine 209; Mystic Fiction 211; Northwoods Journal 223; Oxalis 231; Palo Alto Review 233; Paper Bag, The 234; Pléiades Magazine/Philae 242; Poskisnolt Press 244; Post, The 245; Potpourri 246; PSI 250; Renegade 258; Riverwind 261; Rock Falls Review 261; San Gabriel Valley Magazine 264; Seattle Review, The 266; Sensations Magazine 267; Short Stuff Magazine for Grown-ups 270; Skylark 273; SPSM&H 283; Tall Tales & Short Stories 289; Thema 293; Tickled By Thunder 295; Tucumcari Literary Review 298; Valley Grapevine 302; VeriTales 302; Vincent Brothers Review, The 303; Vintage Northwest 304; Western Tales 307; Westview 307; Wisconsin Restaurateur, The 312; Wolfridgereview 312; Words of Wisdom 313; Writers' Open Forum 315

Young Adult/Teen Acorn, The 81; Advocate, The 82; Amateur Writers Journal 85; Animal Trails 89; Art's Garbage Gazzette 96; Brilliant Star 112; Cemetary Plot 117; Claremont Review, The 121; Cochran's Corner 122; Columbus Literary Gazette, The 124; Dream International/Quarterly 139; Ghost Town 156; Hob-Nob 168; Inkslinger, The 174; Language Bridges Quarterly 187; Lines In The Sand 191; Medley of Pens 201; Merlyn's Pen 202; Mimsy Musing 204; Muse Portfolio 210; Noisy Concept 220; Poetry Forum Short Stories 243; Poskisnolt Press 244; Reach Magazine 256; Shattered Wig Review 269; Struggle 286; Tall Tales & Short Stories 289; Timberlines 295; Wisconsin Restaurateur, The 312; Writers' Open Forum 315

Commercial Periodicals

Adventure Art Times 338; Bowbender 342; Bowhunter Magazine 343; Boys' Life 343; Buffalo Spree Magazine 344; Bugle 344; Career Focus; College Preview; Direct Aim; Journey; Visions 346; Clubhouse 349; Companion of St. Francis and St. Anthony, The 350; Cosmopolitan Magazine 351; Dialogue 353; Fifty Something Magazine 356; Florida Wildlife 357; Gallery Magazine 358; Gold And Treasure Hunter 360; Grit 362; International Bowhunter 368; Lethbridge Magazine 371; New Hampshire Life 378; Pockets 383; Ranger Rick Magazine 387; Road King Magazine 388

Childrens/Juvenile Associate Reformed Presbyterian, The 339; Bugle 344; Calliope 344; Chickadee 347; Child Life 348; Children's Digest 348; Children's Playmate 348; Clubhouse 349; Cobblestone 349; Creative Kids 352; Cricket Magazine 352; Crusader Magazine 352; Discoveries 353; Faces 355; Faith 'n Stuff 356; Friend Magazine, The 358; GUIDE Magazine 362; Highlights for Children

376; New Hampshire Life 378; New Yorker, The 379; Northeast 379; Other Side, The 382; Oui Magazine 382; Pockets 383; Portland Magazine 384; Redbook 387; St. Anthony Messenger 388; St. Joseph's Messenger and Advocate of the Blind 389; Sassy Magazine 389; Singles Almanac 393; Street News 395; Tikkun 398; Virtue 400

Military/War Military Lifestyle 376

Mystery/Suspense bePuzzled 341; Boys' Life 343; Buffalo Spree Magazine 344; Career Focus; College Preview; Direct Aim; Journey; Visions 346; Cosmopolitan Magazine 351; Dialogue 353; Gallery Magazine 358; Gold And Treasure Hunter 360; Grit 362; Hitchcock Mystery Magazine, Alfred 364; New Mystery 378; Other Side, The 382; Oui Magazine 382; Pockets 383; Queen's Mystery Magazine, Ellery 385; Ranger Rick Magazine 387; Road King Magazine 388; Singles Almanac 393; Street News 395; Woman's World Magazine 401

Psychic/Supernatural/Occult Iniquities 367; Singles Almanac 393

Regional Aloha 334; Boston Review 342; Buzz 344; Dialogue 353; First 357; Lady's Circle 370; Lethbridge Magazine 371; New Hampshire Life 378; Northeast 379; Northwest Journal 380; Rhode Islander Magazine, The 388; Sassy Magazine 389; Singles Almanac 393; Street News 395; TWN 400; Washingtonian, The 401; Wy'East Historical Journal 403; Yankee Magazine 403

Religious/Inspirational Associate Reformed Presbyterian, The 339; Baltimore Jewish Times 340; Bread 343; Campus Life Magazine 345; Canadian Messenger 346; Christian Single 349; Clubhouse 349; Companion of St. Francis and St. Anthony, The 350; Cornerstone Magazine 350; Crusader Magazine 352; Detroit Jewish News 352; Discoveries 353; Evangel 354; Faith 'n Stuff 356; Family, The 356; Freeway 357; Friend Magazine, The 358; Gem, The 359; Grit 362; GUIDE Magazine 362; Hi-Call 363; High Adventure 364; Home Times 365; Indian Life Magazine 367; Inside 368; Junior Trails 369; Lady's Circle 370; Liguorian 371; Live 372; Lookout, The 373; Lutheran Journal, The 373; Magazine for Christian Youth! 373; Mature Living 374; Mature Years 375; Messenger of the Sacred Heart 375; Metro Singles Lifestyles 375; My Friend 377; New Era Magazine 378; Noah's Ark 379; On the Line 381; Other Side, The 382; Pockets 383; Purpose 385; R-a-d-a-r 386; Reform Judaism 388; St. Anthony Messenger 388; St. Joseph's Messenger and Advocate of the Blind 389; Seek 391; Shining Star 392; Shofar 392; Singles Almanac 393; Standard 394; Story Friends 394; Straight 395; Student Leadership Journal 395; Teen Power 397; Teens Today 397; Touch 399; Virtue 400; Vista 400; With Magazine 401; Wonder Time 402; Young Salvationist/Young Soldier 404

Romance Baby Connection News Journal, The 340; Career Focus; College Preview; Direct Aim; Journey; Visions 346; Cosmopolitan Magazine 351; Fifty Something Magazine 356; Good Housekeeping 361; Grit 362; Metro Singles Lifestyles 375; St. Anthony Messenger 388; St. Joseph's Messenger and Advocate of the Blind 389; Singles Almanac 393; Virtue 400; Woman's World Magazine 401

Science Fiction Aboriginal Science Fiction 333; AMAZING® Stories 334; Analog Science Fiction & Fact 335; Art Times 338; Asimov's Science Fiction 338; Boys' Life 343; Career Focus; College Preview; Direct Aim; Journey; Visions 346; Expanse® Magazine 355; Grit 362; Iniquities 367; Juggler's World 369; Magazine of Fantasy and Science Fiction 374; New Hampshire Life 378; Omni 380; Playboy Magazine 383; Ranger Rick Magazine 387; Singles Almanac 393

Senior Citizen/Retirement Arizona Coast 338; Dialogue 353; Fifty Something Magazine 356; Gold And Treasure Hunter 360; Grand Times 361; Lady's Circle 370; Mature Living 374; Mature Years 375; Montana Senior Citizens News 376; New Hampshire Life 378; St. Anthony Messenger 388; St. Joseph's Messenger and Advocate of the Blind 389; Street News 395; Vista 400

Serialized/Excerpted Novel Analog Science Fiction & Fact 335; Arizona Coast 338; Bomb Magazine 342; Campus Life Magazine 345; Capper's 346; New Hampshire Life 378; Singles Almanac 393; Street News 395

Sports American Citizen Italian Press, The 335; Appalachia Journal 338; Balloon Life 340; Beckett Baseball Card Monthly 341; Bike Report 341; Black Belt 342; Bowbender 342; Bowhunter Magazine 343; Boys' Life 343; Career Focus; College Preview; Direct Aim; Journey; Visions 346; Florida Wildlife 357; Golf Journal 360; International Bowhunter 368; Outlaw Biker 383; Playboy Magazine 383; Prime Time Sports and Fitness 384; Ranger Rick Magazine 387; Street News 395; Thrasher 398

Translations American Citizen Italian Press, The 335; Boston Review 342; India Currents 366; Inside 368; New Hampshire Life 378; Street News 395; Tikkun 398

Western Arizona Coast 338; Boys' Life 343; Bugle 344; Fifty Something Magazine 356; Grit 362; L'Amour Western Magazine, Louis 371; Montana Senior Citizens News 376; Playboy Magazine 383; Road King Magazine 388

Young Adult/Teen American Newspaper Carrier, The 335; Associate Reformed Presbyterian, The 339; Beckett Baseball Card Monthly 341; Boys' Life 343; Bread 343; Campus Life Magazine 345; Career Focus; College Preview; Direct Aim; Journey; Visions 346; Clubhouse 349; Creative Kids 352; Freeway 357; GUIDE Magazine 362; Hi-Call 363; High Adventure 364; Indian Life Magazine

367; Magazine for Christian Youth! 373; New Era Magazine 378; Noah's Ark 379; On the Line 381; Sassy Magazine 389; Seventeen 391; Straight 395; Street News 395; Teen Magazine 397; Teen Power 397; Teens Today 397; Thrasher 398; With Magazine 401; Young Salvationist/Young Soldier 404

Small Press

Adventure Aegina Press, Inc. 413; Ariadne Press 415; Arjuna Library Press 415; Atlantean Press, The 416; Authors Unlimited 417; Black Heron Press 418; Bryans & Bryans 419; Cave Books 423; Dan River Press 428; Dare to Dream Books 429; E.M. Press, Inc. 430; Earth-Love Publishing House 430; Fasa Corporation 431; Gryphon Publications 433; Jesperson Press Ltd. 438; Jordan Enterprizes Publishing Company 438; Mey-House Books 444; Mid-List Press 444; Our Child Press 449; Pando Publications 450; Paper Bag Press, The 450; Read 'n Run Books 455; Senior Press 459; Serendipity Systems 459; Soho Press 460; University Editions 468; Vandamere Press 469; Vista Publications 470

Childrens/Juvenile Advocacy Press 412; Annick Press Ltd. 414; Arjuna Library Press 415; Atlantean Press, The 416; Black Moss Press 418; Borealis Press 419; Carolina Wren Press 422; Colonial Press 425; Coteau Books 426; Creative with Words Publications 427; Cross-Cultural Communications 427; Crystal River Press 428; E.M. Press, Inc. 430; Homestead Publishing 436; Jesperson Press Ltd. 438; Jordan Enterprizes Publishing Company 438; Kruza Kaleidoscopix, Inc. 439; Lee & Low Books 440; Lester Publishing Limited 440; Long Publishing Co., Hendrick 441; Mayhaven Publishing 443; Milkweed Editions 444; Misty Hill Press 445; Orca Book Publishers Ltd. 447; Our Child Press 449; Overlook Press, The 449; Pando Publications 450; Permeable Press 451; Prairie Publishing Company, The 453; Read 'n Run Books 455; Sand River Press 457; Serendipity Systems 459; Third World Press 466; University Editions 468; Willowisp Press, Inc. 471; Women's Press 471

Erotica Arjuna Library Press 415; Asylum Arts 416; Creative Arts Book Co. 426; Guyasuta Publisher 434; HMS Press 436; Mid-List Press 444; Paper Bag Press, The 450; Permeable Press 451; Press Gang Publishers 453; Sand River Press 457; Serendipity Systems 459; Vandamere Press 469

Ethnic/Multicultural Alaska Native Language Center 413; Arte Publico Press 416; Authors Unlimited 417; Bilingual Press/Editorial Bilingüe 417; BkMk Press 418; Carolina Wren Press 422; China Books 424; Coffee House Press 425; Council for Indian Education 426; Cross-Cultural Communications 427; Eighth Mt. Press, The 431; Feminist Press at the City University of New York, The 431; Griffon House Publications 433; Guernica Editions 434; Helicon Nine Editions 435; HerBooks 435; Heritage Press 435; Island House 437; Jordan Enterprizes Publishing Company 438; Kitchen Table: Women of Color Press 439; Lincoln Springs Press 441; Loonfeather Press 442; Mage Publishers 443; Mayhaven Publishing 443; Mey-House Books 444; Mid-List Press 444; Paper Bag Press, The 450; Path Press, Inc. 451; Pocahontas Press, Inc. 452; Press Gang Publishers 453; Read 'n Run Books 455; Sand River Press 457; Sandpiper Press 458; Seal Press 458; Serendipity Systems 459; Seven Buffaloes Press 460; Soho Press 460; Southern Methodist University Press 461; Stone Bridge Press 464; Third World Press 466; Three Continents Press 466; University Editions 468; Vista Publications 470; White Pine Press 470; Woman in the Moon Publications 471; Zephyr Press 472

Experimental Aegina Press, Inc. 413; Anvil Press 414; Applezaba Press 415; Arjuna Library Press 415; Asylum Arts 416; BkMk Press 418; Black Heron Press 418; Cacanadadada 421; Carolina Wren Press 422; Carpenter Press 423; Coffee House Press 425; Cross-Cultural Communications 427; Dan River Press 428; Griffon House Publications 433; Gryphon Publications 433; Heaven Bone Press 434; Helicon Nine Editions 435; Hermes House Press 436; Independence Publishers of Georgia Inc. 436; Island House 437; Jordan Enterprizes Publishing Company 438; Lincoln Springs Press 441; Mid-List Press 444; New Directions 446; New Rivers Press 446; Paper Bag Press, The 450; Permeable Press 451; Pikestaff Publications, Inc. 451; Pineapple Press 452; Puckerbrush Press 454; Pyx Press 454; Q.E.D. Press 455; Quarry Press 455; Read 'n Run Books 455; Red Deer College Press 456; Serendipity Systems 459; Textile Bridge Press 465; Thistledown Press 466; Turnstone Press 467; Ultramarine Publishing Co., Inc. 468; University Editions 468; Zephyr Press 472

Family Saga E.M. Press, Inc. 430; Mayhaven Publishing 443; Mid-List Press 444; Savant Garde Workshop, The 458; Senior Press 459; Serendipity Systems 459

Fantasy Aegina Press, Inc. 413; Applezaba Press 415; Ariadne Press 415; Arjuna Library Press 415; Authors Unlimited 417; Carpenter Press 423; Dan River Press 428; Dare to Dream Books 429; E.M. Press, Inc. 430; Jesperson Press Ltd. 438; Jordan Enterprizes Publishing Company 438; Mayhaven Publishing 443; Mid-List Press 444; Our Child Press 449; Overlook Press, The 449; Paper Bag Press, The 450; Press of Macdonald and Reinecke, The 454; Pyx Press 454; Read 'n Run Books 455; Savant Garde Workshop, The 458; Serendipity Systems 459; Space and Time 461;

Ultramarine Publishing Co., Inc. 468; University Editions 468; W.W. Publications 470; Woman in the Moon Publications 471; Yith Press 472

Feminist Applezaba Press 415; Ariadne Press 415; Authors Unlimited 417; Calyx Books 422; Carolina Wren Press 422; Cleis Press 424; Coach House Press 424; Creative Arts Book Co. 426; Eighth Mt. Press, The 431; Feminist Press at the City University of New York, The 431; Firebrand Books 432; HerBooks 435; Hermes House Press 436; Kitchen Table: Women of Color Press 439; Lincoln Springs Press 441; Mid-List Press 444; Mother Courage Press 445; New Victoria Publishers 447; Outrider Press 449; Papier-Mache Press 450; Permeable Press 451; Post-Apollo Press, The 453; Press Gang Publishers 453; Quarry Press 455; Ragweed Press Inc./gynergy books 455; Read 'n Run Books 455; Savant Garde Workshop, The 458; Seal Press 458; Serendipity Systems 459; Spectrum Press 461; Spinsters Ink 462; Third Side Press, Inc. 465; University Editions 468; Véhicule Press 469; Women's Press 471; Zephyr Press 472; Zoland Books, Inc. 472

Gay Alyson Publications, Inc. 413; Applezaba Press 415; Authors Unlimited 417; Carolina Wren Press 422; Coach House Press 424; Feminist Press at the City University of New York, The 431; Fire Island Press 432; Gay Sunshine Press and Leyland Publications 432; Lavender Press 439; Mid-List Press 444; Permeable Press 451; Serendipity Systems 459; Starbooks Press 464; Woman in the Moon Publications 471; Zephyr Press 472

Glitz Authors Unlimited 417

Historical Aegina Press, Inc. 413; Ariadne Press 415; Atlantean Press, The 416; Authors Unlimited 417; BkMk Press 418; Bryans & Bryans 419; Clear Light Publishers 424; Colonial Press 425; Creative Arts Book Co. 426; Dan River Press 428; Goose Lane Editions 433; HerBooks 435; HMS Press 436; Independence Publishers of Georgia Inc. 436; Jordan Enterprizes Publishing Company 438; Kruza Kaleidoscopix, Inc. 439; Lester Publishing Limited 440; Lincoln Springs Press 441; Long Publishing Co., Hendrick 441; Mayhaven Publishing 443; Mid-List Press 444; Pando Publications 450; Paper Bag Press, The 450; Path Press, Inc. 451; Permeable Press 451; Pineapple Press 452; Pocahontas Press, Inc. 452; Press of Macdonald and Reinecke, The 454; Quarry Press 455; Read 'n Run Books 455; Senior Press 459; Serendipity Systems 459; Soho Press 460; Southern Methodist University Press 461; Tanager Press 465; Third World Press 466; University Editions 468; Vista Publications 470; Zephyr Press 472

Horror Aegina Press, Inc. 413; Arjuna Library Press 415; Authors Unlimited 417; Bryans & Bryans 419; Dan River Press 428; E.M. Press, Inc. 430; Gryphon Publications 433; Mid-List Press 444; Paper Bag Press, The 450; Read 'n Run Books 455; Serendipity Systems 459; Space and Time 461; University Editions 468

Humor/Satire Applezaba Press 415; Ariadne Press 415; Authors Unlimited 417; Beil, Publisher, Inc., Frederic C. 417; Black Heron Press 418; Black Moss Press 418; Bryans & Bryans 419; Catbird Press 423; Clear Light Publishers 424; Coffee House Press 425; Confluence Press Inc. 425; Creative with Words Publications 427; Cross-Cultural Communications 427; Dan River Press 428; Dare to Dream Books 429; E.M. Press, Inc. 430; HMS Press 436; Homestead Publishing 436; Independence Publishers of Georgia Inc. 436; Jesperson Press Ltd. 438; Lester Publishing Limited 440; Mid-List Press 444; Nightshade Press 447; Paper Bag Press, The 450; Press Gang Publishers 453; Press of Macdonald and Reinecke, The 454; Read 'n Run Books 455; Senior Press 459; Serendipity Systems 459; Tanager Press 465; University Editions 468; Vandamere Press 469; Zephyr Press 472

Lesbian Alyson Publications, Inc. 413; Applezaba Press 415; Arjuna Library Press 415; Authors Unlimited 417; Calyx Books 422; Carolina Wren Press 422; Cleis Press 424; Coach House Press 424; Eighth Mt. Press, The 431; Feminist Press at the City University of New York, The 431; Fire Island Press 432; Firebrand Books 432; HerBooks 435; Kitchen Table: Women of Color Press 439; Lavender Press 439; Madwoman Press 443; Mid-List Press 444; Mother Courage Press 445; Naiad Press, Inc., The 445; New Victoria Publishers 447; Outrider Press 449; Permeable Press 451; Post-Apollo Press, The 453; Press Gang Publishers 453; Ragweed Press Inc./gynergy books 455; Rising Tide Press 457; Sand River Press 457; Seal Press 458; Serendipity Systems 459; Spectrum Press 461; Spinsters Ink 462; Third Side Press, Inc. 465; Woman in the Moon Publications 471; Women's Press 471; Zephyr Press 472

Literary Aegina Press, Inc. 413; Another Chicago Press 414; Anvil Press 414; Applezaba Press 415; Ariadne Press 415; Asylum Arts 416; Atlantean Press, The 416; Authors Unlimited 417; Beil, Publisher, Inc., Frederic C. 417; Bilingual Press/Editorial Bilingüe 417; Black Heron Press 418; Books for All Times, Inc. 419; Borealis Press 419; Bryans & Bryans 419; Cacanadadada 421; Cadmus Editions 421; Cane Hill Press 422; Carolina Wren Press 422; Carpenter Press 423; Catbird Press 423; Coffee House Press 425; Confluence Press Inc. 425; Creative Arts Book Co. 426; Cross-Cultural Communications 427; Dan River Press 428; Daniel and Company, Publishers, John 429; E.M. Press, Inc. 430; Ecco Press, The 430; Faber and Faber, Inc. 431; Feminist Press at the City University of New York, The 431; Florida Literary Foundation Press 432; Four Walls Eight Windows 432; Goose Lane Editions 433; Graywolf Press 433; Griffon House Publications 433; Guernica Editions 434; Heaven Bone Press 434; Helicon Nine Editions 435; Hermes House Press 436; HMS

Romance Aegina Press, Inc. 413; Arjuna Library Press 415; Authors Unlimited 417; Bryans & Bryans 419; Dare to Dream Books 429; E.M. Press, Inc. 430; Jordan Enterprizes Publishing Company 438; Marie's Books 443; Mayhaven Publishing 443; Read 'n Run Books 455; Senior Press 459; University Editions 468; Vista Publications 470

Science Fiction Aegina Press, Inc. 413; Aegina Press, Inc. 413; Arjuna Library Press 415; Authors Unlimited 417; Black Heron Press 418; Dan River Press 428; Fasa Corporation 431; Feminist Press at the City University of New York, The 431; Gryphon Publications 433; Heaven Bone Press 434; Jordan Enterprizes Publishing Company 438; Mayhaven Publishing 443; Mey-House Books 444; Mid-List Press 444; Overlook Press, The 449; Permeable Press 451; Press Gang Publishers 453; Pyx Press 454; Read 'n Run Books 455; Savant Garde Workshop, The 458; Serendipity Systems 459; Space and Time 461; Ultramarine Publishing Co., Inc. 468; University Editions 468; W.W. Publications 470

Short Story Collections Aegina Press, Inc. 413; Anvil Press 414; Applezaba Press 415; Asylum Arts 416; Atlantean Press, The 416; Beil, Publisher, Inc., Frederic C. 417; Bilingual Press/Editorial Bilingüe 417; BkMk Press 418; Books for All Times, Inc. 419; Calyx Books 422; Cane Hill Press 422; Carolina Wren Press 422; Coffee House Press 425; Colonial Press 425; Confluence Press Inc. 425; Coteau Books 426; Council for Indian Education 426; Dan River Press 428; Daniel and Company, Publishers, John 429; Ecco Press, The 430; Eighth Mt. Press, The 431; Goose Lane Editions 433; Graywolf Press 433; Gryphon Publications 433; Guyasuta Publisher 434; Helicon Nine Editions 435; Hermes House Press 436; Homestead Publishing 436; Independence Publishers of Georgia Inc. 436; Ironwood Press, Inc. 437; Island House 437; Kitchen Table: Women of Color Press 439; Les éditions de L'instant même 440; Lester Publishing Limited 440; Lincoln Springs Press 441; Mid-List Press 444; New Rivers Press 446; Outrider Press 449; Papier-Mache Press 450; Path Press, Inc. 451; Peachtree Publishers, Ltd. 451; Permeable Press 451; Post-Apollo Press, The 453; Press Gang Publishers 453; Press of Macdonald and Reinecke, The 454; Quarry Press 455; Read 'n Run Books 455; Red Deer College Press 456; Rio Grande Press 456; Seal Press 458; Serendipity Systems 459; Seven Buffaloes Press 460; Southern Methodist University Press 461; Spectrum Press 461; Textile Bridge Press 465; Third World Press 466; Thistledown Press 466; Three Continents Press 466; Turtle Point Press 468; Ultramarine Publishing Co., Inc. 468; University Editions 468; University of Arkansas Press, The 469; University of Missouri Press 469; Véhicule Press 469; Vista Publications 470; White Pine Press 470; Woman in the Moon Publications 471; Women's Press 471; Zephyr Press 472; Zoland Books, Inc. 472

Sports Authors Unlimited 417; Path Press, Inc. 451; Pocahontas Press, Inc. 452; Reference Press 456

Thriller/Espionage Aegina Press, Inc. 413; Atlantean Press, The 416; Authors Unlimited 417; E.M. Press, Inc. 430; Gryphon Publications 433; Independence Publishers of Georgia Inc. 436; Mayhaven Publishing 443; Mid-List Press 444; Overlook Press, The 449; Permeable Press 451; Savant Garde Workshop, The 458; Senior Press 459; Serendipity Systems 459; Tudor Publishers, Inc. 467

Translations Applezaba Press 415; Asylum Arts 416; Atlantean Press, The 416; Beil, Publisher, Inc., Frederic C. 417; Bilingual Press/Editorial Bilingüe 417; BkMk Press 418; Calyx Books 422; Carolina Wren Press 422; Catbird Press 423; Cleis Press 424; Creative Arts Book Co. 426; Cross-Cultural Communications 427; Feminist Press at the City University of New York, The 431; Griffon House Publications 433; Helicon Nine Editions 435; Hermes House Press 436; Independence Publishers of Georgia Inc. 436; Italica Press 438; Les éditions de L'instant même 440; Mayhaven Publishing 443; Mercury House 444; Milkweed Editions 444; New Rivers Press 446; Overlook Press, The 449; Pocahontas Press, Inc. 452; Post-Apollo Press, The 453; Q.E.D. Press 455; Read 'n Run Books 455; Serendipity Systems 459; Stone Bridge Press 464; Three Continents Press 466; Translation Center, The 467; Turtle Point Press 468; University Editions 468; University of Arkansas Press, The 469; Véhicule Press 469; Women's Press 471; Zephyr Press 472; Zoland Books, Inc. 472

Western Atlantean Press, The 416; Authors Unlimited 417; Clear Light Publishers 424; Coteau Books 426; Creative Arts Book Co. 426; Dan River Press 428; Dare to Dream Books 429; Homestead Publishing 436; Mid-List Press 444; Pocahontas Press, Inc. 452; Read 'n Run Books 455; Serendipity Systems 459; Sunstone Press 465

Young Adult/Teen Arjuna Library Press 415; Bethel Publishing 417; Borealis Press 419; Colonial Press 425; Cross-Cultural Communications 427; Crystal River Press 428; Dare to Dream Books 429; Davenport Publishers, May 429; Homestead Publishing 436; Jordan Enterprizes Publishing Company 438; Lester Publishing Limited 440; Long Publishing Co., Hendrick 441; Mayhaven Publishing 443; Orca Book Publishers Ltd. 447; Our Child Press 449; Pando Publications 450; Pocahontas Press, Inc. 452; Read 'n Run Books 455; Seal Press 458; Serendipity Systems 459; Shaw Publishers, Harold 460; Shaw Publishers, Harold 460; Third World Press 466; Tudor Publishers, Inc. 467; W.W. Publications 470; Women's Press 471

Commercial Publishers

Adventure Bantam Books 482; Books in Motion 484; Bouregy & Company, Inc., Thomas 485; Branden Publishing Co. 485; Crown Publishing Group, The 488; Dell Publishing 489; Fawcett 493; Harlequin Enterprises, Ltd. 496; Herald Press 497; Holiday House, Inc. 498; Holt & Company, Henry 498; Horizon Publishers and Dist., Inc. 498; Morrow and Company, Inc., William 504; New Readers Press 505; Philomel Books 506; Pocket Books 507; Random House, Inc. 508; St. Martin's Press 508; Vesta Publications, Ltd 512; Villard Books 513; Worldwide Library 515; Zebra Books 515

Childrens/Juvenile Arcade Publishing 480; Atheneum Books for Children 480; Bantam Doubleday Dell Books for Young Readers Division 482; Boyds Mills Press 485; Bradbury Press, Inc. 485; Broadman & Holman Publishers 486; Camelot Books 486; Delacorte/Dell Books for Young Readers/Doubleday 489; Dial Books for Young Readers 490; Eakin Press 491; Farrar, Straus & Giroux/Children's Books 493; Four Winds Press 494; Gareth Stevens, Inc. 494; Gessler Publishing Company 494; Godine, Publisher, Inc., David R. 495; Grosset & Dunlap, Inc. 495; Harcourt Brace & Co. 495; HarperCollins Children's Books 496; Herald Press 497; Holiday House, Inc. 498; Holt & Company, Henry 498; Horizon Publishers and Dist., Inc. 498; Knopf Books for Young Readers 499; Little, Brown and Company Children's Books 501; Lodestar Books 501; Lucas/Evans Books Inc. 502; McElderry Books, Margaret K. 503; Macmillan Children's Books 503; Modern Publishing 504; Morrow Junior Books 504; Pelican Publishing Company 506; Philomel Books 506; St. Paul Books and Media 509; Scribner's Sons Books for Young Readers, Charles 509; Standard Publishing 510; Troll Associates 511; Vesta Publications, Ltd 512; Weiss Associates, Inc., Daniel 513; Western Publishing Company, Inc. 514; Whitman & Company, Albert 514; Winston-Derek Publishers 515

Comic/Graphic Novels Dark Horse Comics, Inc. 488; Fantagraphics Books 493

Erotica Carroll & Graf Publishers, Inc. 487; Pocket Books 507; St. Martin's Press 508; Zebra Books 515; Bantam Books 482; Branden Publishing Co. 485; Interlink Publishing Group, Inc. 499; Philomel Books 506; Pocket Books 507; St. Martin's Press 508; Vesta Publications, Ltd 512

Experimental Morrow and Company, Inc., William 504; Quill 507; St. Martin's Press 508; Vesta Publications, Ltd 512

Family Saga Bantam Books 482; Bookcraft, Inc. 484; Dell Publishing 489; Harvest House Publishers 497; Herald Press 497; Philomel Books 506

Fantasy Avon Books 481; Baen Books 482; Bantam Books 482; Bantam Spectra Books 483; Berkley Publishing Group, The 483; Berkley/Ace Science Fiction 483; Carroll & Graf Publishers, Inc. 487; Daw Books, Inc. 489; Del Rey Books 489; Delacorte/Dell Books for Young Readers/Doubleday 489; NAL/Dutton 505; Philomel Books 506; Pocket Books 507; St. Martin's Press 508; Tor Books 511; TSR, Inc. 512; Vesta Publications, Ltd 512

Feminist Academy Chicago Publishers 479; Ballantine Books 482; Bantam Books 482; Braziller, Inc., George 485; Holt & Company, Henry 498; Morrow and Company, Inc., William 504; Pocket Books 507; Quill 507; St. Martin's Press 508; Vesta Publications, Ltd 512

Gay Bantam Books 482; Morrow and Company, Inc., William 504; NAL/Dutton 505; Quill 507; St. Martin's Press 508

Glitz Bantam Books 482; Harlequin Enterprises, Ltd. 496

Historical Academy Chicago Publishers 479; Avon Books 481; Ballantine Books 482; Bantam Books 482; Bookcraft, Inc. 484; Branden Publishing Co. 485; Crown Publishing Group, The 488; Dell Publishing 489; Fawcett 493; Godine, Publisher, Inc., David R. 495; Harvest House Publishers 497; Herald Press 497; Holt & Company, Henry 498; Horizon Publishers and Dist., Inc. 498; Morrow and Company, Inc., William 504; NAL/Dutton 505; Philomel Books 506; Pocket Books 507; Presidio Press 507; Random House, Inc. 508; St. Martin's Press 508; Vesta Publications, Ltd 512; Villard Books 513; Winston-Derek Publishers 515; Zebra Books 515

Horror Avon Books 481; Bantam Books 482; Crown Publishing Group, The 488; Dell Publishing 489; Leisure Books 500; Morrow and Company, Inc., William 504; Pocket Books 507; St. Martin's Press 508; TSR, Inc. 512; Villard Books 513; Walker and Company 513; Zebra Books 515

Humor/Satire Bantam Books 482; Books in Motion 484; Broadman & Holman Publishers 486; Crown Publishing Group, The 488; Harvest House Publishers 497; Holt & Company, Henry 498; Horizon Publishers and Dist., Inc. 498; Morrow and Company, Inc., William 504; New Readers Press 505; Pocket Books 507; Potter, Inc., Clarkson N. 507; Quill 507; St. Martin's Press 508; Vesta Publications, Ltd 512; Villard Books 513

Lesbian Morrow and Company, Inc., William 504; Quill 507; St. Martin's Press 508

Literary Arcade Publishing 480; Bantam Spectra Books 483; Blair, Publisher, John F. 484; Branden Publishing Co. 485; Braziller, Inc., George 485; Carroll & Graf Publishers, Inc. 487; Crown Publishing Group, The 488; Gessler Publishing Company 494; Godine, Publisher, Inc., David R. 495;

Harmony Books 496; Herald Press 497; Holt & Company, Henry 498; Horizon Publishers and Dist., Inc. 498; Knopf, Alfred A. 499; Louisiana State University Press 502; Macmillan Canada 503; Morrow and Company, Inc., William 504; Norton & Company, Inc., W.W. 506; Philomel Books 506; Pocket Books 507; Quill 507; Random House, Inc. 508; St. Martin's Press 508; Vesta Publications, Ltd 512; Villard Books 513; Washington Square Press 513

Mainstream/Contemporary Arcade Publishing 480; Avon Books 481; Ballantine Books 482; Berkley Publishing Group, The 483; Blair, Publisher, John F. 484; Bookcraft, Inc. 484; Branden Publishing Co. 485; Carroll & Graf Publishers, Inc. 487; Crown Publishing Group, The 488; Dell Publishing 489; Eriksson, Publisher, Paul S. 491; Harvest House Publishers 497; Holt & Company, Henry 498; Horizon Publishers and Dist., Inc. 498; Knopf, Alfred A. 499; Louisiana State University Press 502; Macmillan Canada 503; Morrow and Company, Inc., William 504; NAL/Dutton 505; Pocket Books 507; Quill 507; Random House, Inc. 508; St. Martin's Press 508; Tor Books 511; Vesta Publications, Ltd 512; Villard Books 513; Zebra Books 515

Military/War Avon Books 481; Bantam Books 482; Berkley Publishing Group, The 483; Branden Publishing Co. 485; Crown Publishing Group, The 488; Dell Publishing 489; Horizon Publishers and Dist., Inc. 498; Morrow and Company, Inc., William 504; Pocket Books 507; Presidio Press 507; St. Martin's Press 508; Vesta Publications, Ltd 512; Zebra Books 515

Mystery/Suspense Avalon Books 481; Bantam Books 482; Berkley Publishing Group, The 483; Bookcraft, Inc. 484; Books in Motion 484; Branden Publishing Co. 485; Carroll & Graf Publishers, Inc. 487; Dell Publishing 489; Doubleday 490; Fawcett 493; Godine, Publisher, Inc., David R. 495; Harlequin Enterprises, Ltd. 496; Harvest House Publishers 497; Holt & Company, Henry 498; Knopf, Alfred A. 499; Macmillan Canada 503; Morrow and Company, Inc., William 504; Mysterious Press, The 505; New Readers Press 505; Philomel Books 506; Pocket Books 507; Presidio Press 507; Random House, Inc. 508; St. Martin's Press 508; Tor Books 511; Vesta Publications, Ltd 512; Villard Books 513; Walker and Company 513; Zebra Books 515

New Age/Mystic/Spiritual NAL/Dutton 505

Psychic/Supernatural/Occult Avon Books 481; Bantam Books 482; Berkley Publishing Group, The 483; Dell Publishing 489; Fawcett 493; Pocket Books 507; St. Martin's Press 508; Vesta Publications, Ltd 512

Regional Blair, Publisher, John F. 484; Philomel Books 506; Vesta Publications, Ltd 512

Religious/Inspirational Baker Book House 482; Bantam Books 482; Bookcraft, Inc. 484; Bridge Publishing, Inc. 486; Broadman & Holman Publishers 486; Cook Publishing Company, David C. 487; Crossway Books 488; Harvest House Publishers 497; Herald Press 497; Holiday House, Inc. 498; Horizon Publishers and Dist., Inc. 498; Lion Publishing 500; Multnomah Books 504; Resource Publications, Inc. 508; St. Martin's Press 508; St. Paul Books and Media 509; Tyndale House Publishers 512; Vesta Publications, Ltd 512; Winston-Derek Publishers 515; Zondervan 515

Romance Avalon Books 481; Bantam Books 482; Berkley Publishing Group, The 483; Bookcraft, Inc. 484; Bouregy & Company, Inc., Thomas 485; Dell Publishing 489; Doubleday 490; Fawcett 493; Harlequin Enterprises, Ltd. 496; Harvest House Publishers 497; Heartfire Romance 497; Horizon Publishers and Dist., Inc. 498; Leisure Books 500; Love Spell 502; Loveswept 502; NAL/Dutton 505; New Readers Press 505; Pocket Books 507; St. Martin's Press 508; Silhouette Books 509; Starlog Group 510; Vesta Publications, Ltd 512; Villard Books 513; Zebra Books 515

Science Fiction Avon Books 481; Baen Books 481; Bantam Books 482; Bantam Spectra Books 483; Berkley Publishing Group, The 483; Berkley/Ace Science Fiction 483; Carroll & Graf Publishers, Inc. 487; Crown Publishing Group, The 488; Daw Books, Inc. 489; Del Rey Books 489; Horizon Publishers and Dist., Inc. 498; Morrow and Company, Inc., William 504; NAL/Dutton 505; New Readers Press 505; St. Martin's Press 508; Tor Books 511; TSR, Inc. 512; Vesta Publications, Ltd 512

Short Story Collections Branden Publishing Co. 485; Braziller, Inc., George 485; Gessler Publishing Company 494; Louisiana State University Press 502; Philomel Books 506; Random House, Inc. 508; Resource Publications, Inc. 508; Vesta Publications, Ltd 512

Sports New Readers Press 505

Thriller/Espionage Bookcraft, Inc. 484; Morrow and Company, Inc., William 504; NAL/Dutton 505; Presidio Press 507; St. Martin's Press 508; Zebra Books 515

Translations Arcade Publishing 480; Branden Publishing Co. 485; Braziller, Inc., George 485; Gessler Publishing Company 494; Holt & Company, Henry 498; Interlink Publishing Group, Inc. 499; Morrow and Company, Inc., William 504; Philomel Books 506; Vesta Publications, Ltd 512

Western Avalon Books 481; Avon Books 481; Bookcraft, Inc. 484; Bouregy & Company, Inc., Thomas 485; Doubleday 490; Evans & Co., Inc., M. 491; Jameson Books 499; NAL/Dutton 505; Philomel Books 506; Pocket Books 507; Presidio Press 507; Tor Books 511; Walker and Company 513

Young Adult/Teen Archway Paperbacks/Minstrel Books 480; Atheneum Books for Children 480; Avon Books 481; Bantam Doubleday Dell Books for Young Readers Division 482; Bookcraft, Inc. 484; Boyds Mills Press 485; Bradbury Press, Inc. 485; Broadman & Holman Publishers 486;

Cloverdale Press Inc. 487; Crossway Books 488; Delacorte/Dell Books for Young Readers/Double-day 489; Flare Books 494; Harcourt Brace & Co. 495; HarperCollins Children's Books 496; Herald Press 497; Holiday House, Inc. 498; Holt & Company, Henry 498; Horizon Publishers and Dist., Inc. 498; Lerner Publications Company 500; Little, Brown and Company Children's Books 501; Lodestar Books 501; Lucas/Evans Books Inc. 502; McElderry Books, Margaret K. 503; Modern Publishing 504; Morrow Junior Books 504; Philomel Books 506; Scribner's Sons Books for Young Readers, Charles 509; Tab Book Club 511; Trillium Press 511; Troll Associates 511; Vesta Publications, Ltd 512; Weiss Associates, Inc., Daniel 513; Winston-Derek Publishers 515

Markets Index

Can't find a listing? Check pages 329-330 for Literary and Small Circulation Magazines/ '93-'94 Changes, pages 407-408 for Commercial Periodicals/'93-'94 Changes, page 476 for Small Presses, page 518 for Commercial Publishers/'93-'94 Changes, page 556 for Contests/'93-'94 Changes, page 598 for Conferences and Workshops, page 608 for Retreats and Colonies/'93-'94 Changes or page 617 for Organizations/'93-'94 Changes.